Collins

Collins
French
Dictionary

HarperCollins Publishers
Westerhill Road
Bishopbriggs
Glasgow
G64 2QT
Great Britain

This edition 2012

Reprint 10 9 8 7 6 5 4 3 2 1 0

© HarperCollins Publishers 2012

ISBN 978-0-00-791703-7

Collins® is a registered trademark of
HarperCollins Publishers Limited

www.collinslanguage.com

A catalogue record for this book is
available from the British Library

Typeset by Wordcraft, Glasgow

Printed and bound in Great Britain by
Clays Ltd, St Ives plc

Acknowledgements
We would like to thank those
authors and publishers who kindly
gave permission for copyright
material to be used in the Collins
Word Web. We would also like to thank
Times Newspapers Ltd for providing
valuable data.

MANAGING EDITOR
Gaëlle Amiot-Cadey

CONTRIBUTORS
Jean-François Allain
Cécile Aubinière-Robb
Sabine Citron
Wendy Lee
Catherine Love
Rose Rociola

EDITORIAL COORDINATION
Susie Beattie

SERIES EDITOR
Rob Scriven

BASED ON THE COLLINS FRENCH GEM
Pierre-Henri Cousin
Renée Birks
Elizabeth Campbell
Hélène Lewis
Claude Nimmo
Philippe Patry
Lorna Knight

TABLE DES MATIÈRES   CONTENTS

LES MARQUES DÉPOSÉES

Les termes qui constituent à notre connaissance une marque déposée ont été désignés comme tels. La présence ou l'absence de cette désignation ne peut toutefois être considérée comme ayant valeur juridique.

NOTE ON TRADEMARKS

Words which we have reason to believe constitute trademarks have been designated as such. However, neither the presence nor the absence of such designation should be regarded as affecting the legal status of any trademark.

William Collins' dream of knowledge for all began with the publication of his first book in 1819. A self-educated mill worker, he not only enriched millions of lives, but also founded a flourishing publishing house. Today, staying true to this spirit, Collins books are packed with inspiration, innovation, and practical expertise. They place you at the centre of a world of possibility and give you exactly what you need to explore it.

Language is the key to this exploration, and at the heart of Collins Dictionaries is language as it is really used. New words, phrases, and meanings spring up every day, and all of them are captured and analysed by the Collins Word Web. Constantly updated, and with over 2.5 billion entries, this living language resource is unique to our dictionaries.

Words are tools for life. And a Collins Dictionary makes them work for you.

Collins. Do more

INTRODUCTION

Nous sommes très heureux que vous ayez choisi ce dictionnaire et espérons que vous aimerez l'utiliser et que vous en tirerez profit au lycée, à la maison, en vacances ou au travail.

INTRODUCTION

We are delighted that you have decided to buy this dictionary and hope you will enjoy and benefit from using it at school, at home, on holiday or at work.

ABRÉVIATIONS

ABBREVIATIONS

abréviation	*ab(b)r*	abbreviation
adjectif, locution adjectivale	*adj*	adjective, adjectival phrase
administration	*Admin*	administration
adverbe, locution adverbiale	*adv*	adverb, adverbial phrase
agriculture	*Agr*	agriculture
anatomie	*Anat*	anatomy
architecture	*Archit*	architecture
article défini	*art déf*	definite article
article indéfini	*art indéf*	indefinite article
automobile	*Aut(o)*	the motor car and motoring
aviation, voyages aériens	*Aviat*	flying, air travel
biologie	*Bio(l)*	biology
botanique	*Bot*	botany
anglais britannique	*BRIT*	British English
chimie	*Chem*	chemistry
commerce, finance, banque	*Comm*	commerce, finance, banking
informatique	*Comput*	computing
conjonction	*conj*	conjunction
construction	*Constr*	building
nom utilisé comme adjectif	*cpd*	compound element
cuisine	*Culin*	cookery
article défini	*def art*	definite article
déterminant: article; adjectif démonstratif ou indéfini *etc*	*dét*	determiner: article, demonstrative *etc*
économie	*Écon, Econ*	economics
électricité, électronique	*Élec, Elec*	electricity, electronics
en particulier	*esp*	especially
exclamation, interjection	*excl*	exclamation, interjection
féminin	*f*	feminine
langue familière (! emploi vulgaire)	*fam(!)*	colloquial usage (! particularly offensive)
emploi figuré	*fig*	figurative use
(verbe anglais) dont la particule est inséparable	*fus*	(phrasal verb) where the particle is inseparable
généralement	*gén, gen*	generally
géographie, géologie	*Géo, Geo*	geography, geology
géométrie	*Géom, Geom*	geometry
langue familière (! emploi vulgaire)	*inf(!)*	colloquial usage (! particularly offensive)
infinitif	*infin*	infinitive
informatique	*Inform*	computing
invariable	*inv*	invariable
irrégulier	*irreg*	irregular
domaine juridique	*Jur*	law

ABRÉVIATIONS

ABBREVIATIONS

grammaire, linguistique	Ling	grammar, linguistics
masculin	m	masculine
mathématiques, algèbre	Math	mathematics, calculus
médecine	Méd, Med	medical term, medicine
masculin ou féminin	m/f	masculine or feminine
domaine militaire, armée	Mil	military matters
musique	Mus	music
nom	n	noun
navigation, nautisme	Navig, Naut	sailing, navigation
nom ou adjectif numéral	num	numeral noun or adjective
	o.s.	oneself
péjoratif	péj, pej	derogatory, pejorative
photographie	Phot(o)	photography
physiologie	Physiol	physiology
pluriel	pl	plural
politique	Pol	politics
participe passé	pp	past participle
préposition	prép, prep	preposition
pronom	pron	pronoun
psychologie, psychiatrie	Psych	psychology, psychiatry
temps du passé	pt	past tense
quelque chose	qch	
quelqu'un	qn	
religion, domaine ecclésiastique	Rel	religion
	sb	somebody
enseignement, système scolaire et universitaire	Scol	schooling, schools and universities
singulier	sg	singular
	sth	something
subjonctif	sub	subjunctive
sujet (grammatical)	su(b)j	(grammatical) subject
superlatif	superl	superlative
techniques, technologie	Tech	technical term, technology
télécommunications	Tél, Tel	telecommunications
télévision	TV	television
typographie	Typ(o)	typography, printing
anglais des USA	US	American English
verbe (auxiliare)	vb (aux)	(auxiliary) verb
verbe intransitif	vi	intransitive verb
verbe transitif	vt	transitive verb
zoologie	Zool	zoology
marque déposée	®	registered trademark
indique une équivalence culturelle	≈	introduces a cultural equivalent

TRANCRIPTION PHONÉTIQUE

CONSONNES

NB. **p, b, t, d, k, g** sont suivis d'une aspiration en anglais.

CONSONANTS

NB. **p, b, t, d, k, g** are not aspirated in French.

poupée	p	puppy
bombe	b	baby
tente thermal	t	tent
dinde	d	daddy
coq qui képi	k	cork kiss chord
gage bague	g	gag guess
sale ce nation	s	so rice kiss
zéro rose	z	cousin buzz
tache chat	ʃ	sheep sugar
gilet juge	ʒ	pleasure beige
	tʃ	church
	dʒ	judge general
fer phare	f	farm raffle
verveine	v	very revel
	θ	thin maths
	ð	that other
lent salle	l	little ball
rare rentrer	ʀ	
	r	rat rare
maman femme	m	mummy comb
non bonne	n	no ran
agneau vigne	ɲ	
	ŋ	singing bank
	h	hat rehearse
yeux paille pied	j	yet
nouer oui	w	wall wail
huile lui	ɥ	
	x	loch

DIVERS

pour l'anglais: le r final se prononce en liaison devant une voyelle

pour l'anglais: précède la syllabe accentuée

MISCELLANEOUS

r — in English transcription: final r can be pronounced before a vowel

' — in French wordlist: no liaison before aspirate h

En règle générale, la prononciation est donnée entre crochets après chaque entrée. Toutefois, du côté anglais-français et dans le cas des expressions composées de deux ou plusieurs mots non réunis par un trait d'union et faisant l'objet d'une entrée séparée, la prononciation doit être cherchée sous chacun des mots constitutifs de l'expression en question.

PHONETIC TRANCRIPTION

VOYELLES		VOWELS
NB. La mise en équivalence de certains sons n'indique qu'une ressemblance approximative.		NB. The pairing of some vowel sounds only indicates approximate equivalence.
ici vie lyrique	i i:	heel bead
	ɪ	hit pity
jouer été	e	
lait jouet merci	ɛ	set tent
plat amour	a æ	bat apple
bas pâte	ɑ ɑ:	after car calm
	ʌ	fun cousin
le premier	ə	over above
beurre peur	œ	
peu deux	ø ə:	urgent fern work
or homme	ɔ	wash pot
mot eau gauche	o ɔ:	born cork
genou roue	u	full hook
	u:	boom shoe
rue urne	y	

DIPHTONGUES		DIPHTHONGS
	ɪə	beer tier
	ɛə	tear fair there
	eɪ	date plaice day
	aɪ	life buy cry
	au	owl foul now
	əu	low no
	ɔɪ	boil boy oily
	uə	poor tour

NASALES		NASAL VOWELS
matin plein	ɛ̃	
brun	œ̃	
sang an dans	ɑ̃	
non pont	ɔ̃	

In general, we give the pronunciation of each entry in square brackets after the word in question. However, on the English-French side, where the entry is composed of two or more unhyphenated words, each of which is given elsewhere in this dictionary, you will find the pronunciation of each word in its alphabetical position.

FRENCH VERB TABLES

1 Present participle 2 Past participle 3 Present 4 Imperfect 5 Future
6 Conditional 7 Present subjunctive

acquérir 1 acquérant 2 acquis
3 acquiers, acquérons,
acquièrent 4 acquérais
5 acquerrai 7 acquière

ALLER 1 allant 2 allé 3 vais, vas, va,
allons, allez, vont 4 allais 5 irai
6 irais 7 aille

asseoir 1 asseyant 2 assis 3 assieds,
asseyons, asseyez, asseyent
4 asseyais 5 assiérai 7 asseye

atteindre 1 atteignant 2 atteint
3 atteins, atteignons
4 atteignais 7 atteigne

AVOIR 1 ayant 2 eu 3 ai, as, a,
avons, avez, ont 4 avais 5 aurai
6 aurais 7 aie, aies, ait, ayons,
ayez, aient

battre 1 battant 2 battu 3 bats, bat,
battons 4 battais 7 batte

boire 1 buvant 2 bu 3 bois, buvons,
boivent 4 buvais 7 boive

bouillir 1 bouillant 2 bouilli 3 bous,
bouillons 4 bouillais 7 bouille

conclure 1 concluant 2 conclu
3 conclus, concluons
4 concluais 7 conclue

conduire 1 conduisant 2 conduit
3 conduis, conduisons
4 conduisais 7 conduise

connaître 1 connaissant 2 connu
3 connais, connaît, connaissons
4 connaissais 7 connaisse

coudre 1 cousant 2 cousu 3 couds,
cousons, cousez, cousent
4 cousais 7 couse

courir 1 courant 2 couru 3 cours,
courons 4 courais 5 courrai
7 coure

couvrir 1 couvrant 2 couvert
3 couvre, couvrons 4 couvrais
7 couvre

craindre 1 craignant 2 craint
3 crains, craignons 4 craignais
7 craigne

croire 1 croyant 2 cru 3 crois,
croyons, croient 4 croyais
7 croie

croître 1 croissant 2 crû, crue, crus,
crues 3 croîs, croissons
4 croissais 7 croisse

cueillir 1 cueillant 2 cueilli
3 cueille, cueillons 4 cueillais
5 cueillerai 7 cueille

devoir 1 devant 2 dû, due, dus,
dues 3 dois, devons, doivent
4 devais 5 devrai 7 doive

dire 1 disant 2 dit 3 dis, disons,
dites, disent 4 disais 7 dise

dormir 1 dormant 2 dormi 3 dors,
dormons 4 dormais 7 dorme

écrire 1 écrivant 2 écrit 3 écris,
écrivons 4 écrivais 7 écrive

ÊTRE 1 étant 2 été 3 suis, es, est,
sommes, êtes, sont 4 étais
5 serai 6 serais 7 sois, sois, soit,
soyons, soyez, soient

FAIRE 1 faisant 2 fait 3 fais, fais,
fait, faisons, faites, font
4 faisais 5 ferai 6 ferais 7 fasse

falloir 2 fallu 3 faut 4 fallait
5 faudra 7 faille

FINIR 1 finissant 2 fini 3 finis,
finis, finit, finissons, finissez,
finissent 4 finissais 5 finirai
6 finirais 7 finisse

fuir 1 fuyant 2 fui 3 fuis, fuyons,
fuient 4 fuyais 7 fuie

joindre 1 joignant 2 joint 3 joins,
joignons 4 joignais 7 joigne

lire 1 lisant 2 lu 3 lis, lisons 4 lisais
7 lise

luire 1 luisant 2 lui 3 luis, luisons

4 luisais 7 luise

maudire 1 maudissant 2 maudit
3 maudis, maudissons
4 maudissait 7 maudisse

mentir 1 mentant 2 menti 3 mens,
mentons 4 mentais 7 mente

mettre 1 mettant 2 mis 3 mets,
mettons 4 mettais 7 mette

mourir 1 mourant 2 mort 3 meurs,
mourons, meurent 4 mourais
5 mourrai 7 meure

naître 1 naissant 2 né 3 nais, naît,
naissons 4 naissais 7 naisse

offrir 1 offrant 2 offert 3 offre,
offrons 4 offrais 7 offre

PARLER 1 parlant 2 parlé 3 parle,
parles, parle, parlons, parlez,
parlent 4 parlais, parlais,
parlait, parlions, parliez,
parlaient 5 parlerai, parleras,
parlera, parlerons, parlerez,
parleront 6 parlerais, parlerais,
parlerait, parlerions, parleriez,
parleraient 7 parle, parles,
parle, parlions, parliez, parlent
impératif parle! parlons! parlez!

partir 1 partant 2 parti 3 pars,
partons 4 partais 7 parte

plaire 1 plaisant 2 plu 3 plais, plaît,
plaisons 4 plaisais 7 plaise

pleuvoir 1 pleuvant 2 plu 3 pleut,
pleuvent 4 pleuvait 5 pleuvra
7 pleuve

pourvoir 1 pourvoyant 2 pourvu
3 pourvois, pourvoyons,
pourvoient 4 pourvoyais
7 pourvoie

pouvoir 1 pouvant 2 pu 3 peux,
peut, pouvons, peuvent 4
pouvais 5 pourrai 7 puisse

prendre 1 prenant 2 pris 3 prends,
prenons, prennent 4 prenais
7 prenne

prévoir like voir 5 prévoirai

RECEVOIR 1 recevant 2 reçu
3 reçois, reçois, reçoit, recevons,
recevez, rerçoivent 4 recevais

5 recevrai 6 recevrais 7 reçoive

RENDRE 1 rendant 2 rendu
3 rends, rends, rend, rendons,
rendez, rendent 4 rendais
5 rendrai 6 rendrais 7 rende

résoudre 1 résolvant 2 résolu
3 résous, résout, résolvons
4 résolvais 7 résolve

rire 1 riant 2 ri 3 ris, rions 4 riais
7 rie

savoir 1 sachant 2 su 3 sais,
savons, savent 4 savais 5 saurai
7 sache *impératif* sache! sachons!
sachez!

servir 1 servant 2 servi 3 sers,
servons 4 servais 7 serve

sortir 1 sortant 2 sorti 3 sors,
sortons 4 sortais 7 sorte

souffrir 1 souffrant 2 souffert
3 souffre, souffrons 4 souffrais
7 souffre

suffire 1 suffisant 2 suffi 3 suffis,
suffisons 4 suffisais 7 suffise

suivre 1 suivant 2 suivi 3 suis,
suivons 4 suivais 7 suive

taire 1 taisant 2 tu 3 tais, taisons
4 taisais 7 taise

tenir 1 tenant 2 tenu 3 tiens,
tenons, tiennent 4 tenais
5 tiendrai 7 tienne

vaincre 1 vainquant 2 vaincu
3 vaincs, vainc, vainquons
4 vainquais 7 vainque

valoir 1 valant 2 valu 3 vaux, vaut,
valons 4 valais 5 vaudrai 7 vaille

venir 1 venant 2 venu 3 viens,
venons, viennent 4 venais
5 viendrai 7 vienne

vivre 1 vivant 2 vécu 3 vis, vivons
4 vivais 7 vive

voir 1 voyant 2 vu 3 vois, voyons,
voient 4 voyais 5 verrai 7 voie

vouloir 1 voulant 2 voulu 3 veux,
veut, voulons, veulent 4 voulais
5 voudrai 7 veuille; *impératif*
veuillez!

VERBES IRRÉGULIERS ANGLAIS

PRÉSENT	PASSÉ	PARTICIPE	PRÉSENT	PASSÉ	PARTICIPE
arise	arose	arisen	fight	fought	fought
awake	awoke	awoken	find	found	found
be	was, were	been	flee	fled	fled
(am, is,			fling	flung	flung
are; being)			fly	flew	flown
bear	bore	born(e)	forbid	forbad(e)	forbidden
beat	beat	beaten	forecast	forecast	forecast
become	became	become	forget	forgot	forgotten
begin	began	begun	forgive	forgave	forgiven
bend	bent	bent	forsake	forsook	forsaken
bet	bet,	bet,	freeze	froze	frozen
	betted	betted	get	got	got,
bid (at auction,	bid	bid			(US) gotten
cards)			give	gave	given
bid (say)	bade	bidden	go (goes)	went	gone
bind	bound	bound	grind	ground	ground
bite	bit	bitten	grow	grew	grown
bleed	bled	bled	hang	hung	hung
blow	blew	blown	hang (execute)	hanged	hanged
break	broke	broken	have	had	had
breed	bred	bred	hear	heard	heard
bring	brought	brought	hide	hid	hidden
build	built	built	hit	hit	hit
burn	burnt,	burnt,	hold	held	held
	burned	burned	hurt	hurt	hurt
burst	burst	burst	keep	kept	kept
buy	bought	bought	kneel	knelt,	knelt,
can	could	(been able)		kneeled	kneeled
cast	cast	cast	know	knew	known
catch	caught	caught	lay	laid	laid
choose	chose	chosen	lead	led	led
cling	clung	clung	lean	leant,	leant,
come	came	come		leaned	leaned
cost	cost	cost	leap	leapt,	leapt,
cost (work	costed	costed		leaped	leaped
out price of)			learn	learnt,	learnt,
creep	crept	crept		learned	learned
cut	cut	cut	leave	left	left
deal	dealt	dealt	lend	lent	lent
dig	dug	dug	let	let	let
do (does)	did	done	lie (lying)	lay	lain
draw	drew	drawn	light	lit,	lit,
dream	dreamed,	dreamed,		lighted	lighted
	dreamt	dreamt	lose	lost	lost
drink	drank	drunk	make	made	made
drive	drove	driven	may	might	–
dwell	dwelt	dwelt	mean	meant	meant
eat	ate	eaten	meet	met	met
fall	fell	fallen	mistake	mistook	mistaken
feed	fed	fed	mow	mowed	mown,
feel	felt	felt			mowed

xii

PRÉSENT	PASSÉ	PARTICIPE	PRÉSENT	PASSÉ	PARTICIPE
must	(had to)	(had to)	spend	spent	spent
pay	paid	paid	spill	spilt,	spilt,
put	put	put		spilled	spilled
quit	quit,	quit,	spin	spun	spun
	quitted	quitted	spit	spat	spat
read	read	read	spoil	spoiled,	spoiled,
rid	rid	rid		spoilt	spoilt
ride	rode	ridden	spread	spread	spread
ring	rang	rung	spring	sprang	sprung
rise	rose	risen	stand	stood	stood
run	ran	run	steal	stole	stolen
saw	sawed	sawed,	stick	stuck	stuck
		sawn	sting	stung	stung
say	said	said	stink	stank	stunk
see	saw	seen	stride	strode	stridden
seek	sought	sought	strike	struck	struck
sell	sold	sold	strive	strove	striven
send	sent	sent	swear	swore	sworn
set	set	set	sweep	swept	swept
sew	sewed	sewn	swell	swelled	swollen,
shake	shook	shaken			swelled
shear	sheared	shorn,	swim	swam	swum
		sheared	swing	swung	swung
shed	shed	shed	take	took	taken
shine	shone	shone	teach	taught	taught
shoot	shot	shot	tear	tore	torn
show	showed	shown	tell	told	told
shrink	shrank	shrunk	think	thought	thought
shut	shut	shut	throw	threw	thrown
sing	sang	sung	thrust	thrust	thrust
sink	sank	sunk	tread	trod	trodden
sit	sat	sat	wake	woke,	woken,
slay	slew	slain		waked	waked
sleep	slept	slept	wear	wore	worn
slide	slid	slid	weave	wove	woven
sling	slung	slung	weave (wind)	weaved	weaved
slit	slit	slit	wed	wedded,	wedded,
smell	smelt,	smelt,		wed	wed
	smelled	smelled	weep	wept	wept
sow	sowed	sown,	win	won	won
		sowed	wind	wound	wound
speak	spoke	spoken	wring	wrung	wrung
speed	sped,	sped,	write	wrote	written
	speeded	speeded			
spell	spelt,	spelt,			
	spelled	spelled			

LES NOMBRES

un (une)	1	one
deux	2	two
trois	3	three
quatre	4	four
cinq	5	five
six	6	six
sept	7	seven
huit	8	eight
neuf	9	nine
dix	10	ten
onze	11	eleven
douze	12	twelve
treize	13	thirteen
quatorze	14	fourteen
quinze	15	fifteen
seize	16	sixteen
dix-sept	17	seventeen
dix-huit	18	eighteen
dix-neuf	19	nineteen
vingt	20	twenty
vingt et un (une)	21	twenty-one
vingt-deux	22	twenty-two
trente	30	thirty
quarante	40	forty
cinquante	50	fifty
soixante	60	sixty
soixante-dix	70	seventy
soixante-et-onze	71	seventy-one
soixante-douze	72	seventy
quatre-vingts	80	eighty
quatre-vingt-un (-une)	81	eighty-one
quatre-vingt-dix	90	ninety
cent	100	a hundred, one hundred
cent un (une)	101	a hundred and one
deux cents	200	two hundred
deux cent un (une)	201	two hundred and one
quatre cents	400	four hundred
mille	1000	a thousand
cinq mille	5000	five thousand
un million	1000000	a million

NUMBERS

LES NOMBRES

premier (première), 1er (1ère)
deuxième, 2e or 2ème
troisième, 3e or 3ème
quatrième, 4e or 4ème
cinquième, 5e or 5ème
sixième, 6e or 6ème
septième
huitième
neuvième
dixième
onzième
douzième
treizième
quartorzième
quinzième
seizième
dix-septième
dix-huitième
dix-neuvième
vingtième
vingt-et-unième
vingt-deuxième
trentième
centième
cent-unième
millième

LES FRACTIONS ETC

un demi
un tiers
un quart
un cinquième
zéro virgule cinq, 0,5
trois virgule quatre, 3,4
dix pour cent
cent pour cent

EXEMPLES

elle habite au septième (étage)
il habite au sept
au chapitre/à la page sept
il est arrivé (le) septième

NUMBERS

first, 1st
second, 2nd
third, 3rd
fourth, 4th
fifth, 5th
sixth, 6th
seventh
eighth
ninth
tenth
eleventh
twelfth
thirteenth
fourteenth
fifteenth
sixteenth
seventeenth
eighteenth
nineteenth
twentieth
twenty-first
twenty-second
thirtieth
hundredth
hundred-and-first
thousandth

FRACTIONS ETC

a half
a third
a quarter
a fifth
(nought) point five, 0.5
three point four, 3.4
ten per cent
a hundred per cent

EXAMPLES

she lives on the 7th floor
he lives at number 7
chapter/page 7
he came in 7th

L'HEURE	THE TIME
quelle heure est-il?	*what time is it?*
il est ...	*it's* ou *it is ...*
minuit	midnight, twelve p.m.
une heure (du matin)	one o'clock (in the morning), one (a.m.)
une heure cinq	five past one
une heure dix	ten past one
une heure et quart	a quarter past one, one fifteen
une heure vingt-cinq	twenty-five past one, one twenty-five
une heure et demie, une heure trente	half-past one, one thirty
deux heures moins vingt-cinq, une heure trente-cinq	twenty-five to two, one thirty-five
deux heures moins vingt, une heure quarante	twenty to two, one forty
deux heures moins le quart, une heure quarante-cinq	a quarter to two, one forty-five
deux heures moins dix, une heure cinquante	ten to two, one fifty
midi	twelve o'clock, midday, noon
deux heures (de l'après-midi), quatorze heures	two o'clock (in the afternoon), two (p.m.)
sept heures (du soir), dix-sept heures	seven o'clock (in the evening), seven (p.m.)
à quelle heure?	*(at) what time?*
à minuit	at midnight
à sept heures	at seven o'clock
dans vingt minutes	in twenty minutes
il y a un quart d'heure	fifteen minutes ago

FRANÇAIS | ANGLAIS
FRENCH | ENGLISH

7 (*caractérisation, manière*): **l'homme aux yeux bleus** the man with the blue eyes; **à leur grande surprise** much to their surprise; **à ce qu'il prétend** according to him, from what he says; **à la russe** the Russian way; **à nous deux nous n'avons pas su le faire** we couldn't do it, even between the two of us
8 (*but, destination*): **tasse à café** coffee cup; **maison à vendre** house for sale; **je n'ai rien à lire** I don't have anything to read; **à bien réfléchir ...** thinking about it ..., on reflection ...
9 (*rapport, évaluation, distribution*): **100 km/unités à l'heure** 100 km/units per *ou* an hour; **payé au mois/à l'heure** paid monthly/by the hour; **cinq à six** five to six; **ils sont arrivés à quatre** four of them arrived

a

a [a] *vb voir* **avoir**

🔵 **MOT-CLÉ**

à [a] (*à* + *le* = **au**, *à* + *les* = **aux**) *prép* **1** (*endroit, situation*) at, in; **être à Paris/au Portugal** to be in Paris/Portugal; **être à la maison/à l'école** to be at home/at school; **à la campagne** in the country; **c'est à 10 km/à 20 minutes (d'ici)** it's 10 km/20 minutes away
2 (*direction*) to; **aller à Paris/au Portugal** to go to Paris/Portugal; **aller à la maison/à l'école** to go home/to school; **à la campagne** to the country
3 (*temps*): **à 3 heures/minuit** at 3 o'clock/midnight; **au printemps/mois de juin** in the spring/the month of June; **à Noël/Pâques** at Christmas/Easter; **à demain/lundi!** see you tomorrow/on Monday!
4 (*attribution, appartenance*) to; **le livre est à Paul/à lui/à nous** this book is Paul's/his/ours; **un ami à moi** a friend of mine; **donner qch à qn** to give sth to sb
5 (*moyen*) with; **se chauffer au gaz** to have gas heating; **à bicyclette** on a *ou* by bicycle; **à pied** on foot; **à la main/machine** by hand/machine
6 (*provenance*) from; **boire à la bouteille** to drink from the bottle

abaisser [abese] *vt* to lower, bring down; (*manette*) to pull down; **s'abaisser** *vi* to go down; (*fig*) to demean o.s.
abandon [abɑ̃dɔ̃] *nm* abandoning; giving up; withdrawal; **être à l'~** to be in a state of neglect; **laisser à l'~** to abandon
abandonner [abɑ̃dɔne] *vt* (*personne*) to abandon; (*projet, activité*) to abandon, give up; (*Sport*) to retire *ou* withdraw from; (*céder*) to surrender; **s'~ à** (*paresse, plaisirs*) to give o.s. up to
abat-jour [abaʒuʀ] *nm inv* lampshade
abats [aba] *nmpl* (*de bœuf, porc*) offal *sg*; (*de volaille*) giblets
abattement [abatmɑ̃] *nm*: **abattement fiscal** ≈ tax allowance
abattoir [abatwaʀ] *nm* slaughterhouse
abattre [abatʀ] *vt* (*arbre*) to cut down, fell; (*mur, maison*) to pull down; (*avion, personne*) to shoot down; (*animal*) to shoot, kill; (*fig*) to wear out, tire out; to demoralize; **s'abattre** *vi* to crash down; **ne pas se laisser ~** to keep one's spirits up, not to let things get one down; **s'~ sur** to beat down on; (*fig*) to rain down on; **~ du travail** *ou* **de la besogne** to get through a lot of work
abbaye [abei] *nf* abbey
abbé [abe] *nm* priest; (*d'une abbaye*) abbot
abcès [apsɛ] *nm* abscess
abdiquer [abdike] *vi* to abdicate
abdominaux [abdɔmino] *nmpl*: **faire des ~** to do sit-ups
abeille [abɛj] *nf* bee
aberrant, e [abeʀɑ̃, ɑ̃t] *adj* absurd
aberration [abeʀasjɔ̃] *nf* aberration
abîme [abim] *nm* abyss, gulf
abîmer [abime] *vt* to spoil, damage; **s'abîmer** *vi* to get spoilt *ou* damaged
aboiement [abwamɑ̃] *nm* bark, barking
abolir [abɔliʀ] *vt* to abolish
abominable [abɔminabl] *adj* abominable

abondance [abɔ̃dɑ̃s] *nf* abundance
abondant, e [abɔ̃dɑ̃, ɑ̃t] *adj* plentiful, abundant, copious; **abonder** *vi* to abound, be plentiful; **abonder dans le sens de qn** to concur with sb
abonné, e [abɔne] *nm/f* subscriber; season ticket holder
abonnement [abɔnmɑ̃] *nm* subscription; (*transports, concerts*) season ticket
abonner [abɔne] *vt*: **s'~ à** to subscribe to, take out a subscription to
abord [abɔʀ] *nm*: **au premier ~** at first sight, initially; **abords** *nmpl* (*environs*) surroundings; **d'~** first
abordable [abɔʀdabl] *adj* (*prix*) reasonable; (*personne*) approachable
aborder [abɔʀde] *vi* to land ▷ *vt* (*sujet, difficulté*) to tackle; (*personne*) to approach; (*rivage etc*) to reach
aboutir [abutiʀ] *vi* (*négociations etc*) to succeed; **~ à** to end up at; **n'~ à rien** to come to nothing
aboyer [abwaje] *vi* to bark
abréger [abʀeʒe] *vt* to shorten
abreuver [abʀœve]: **s'abreuver** *vi* to drink; **abreuvoir** *nm* watering place
abréviation [abʀevjasjɔ̃] *nf* abbreviation
abri [abʀi] *nm* shelter; **être à l'~** to be under cover; **se mettre à l'~** to shelter; **à l'~ de** (*vent, soleil*) sheltered from; (*danger*) safe from
abricot [abʀiko] *nm* apricot
abriter [abʀite] *vt* to shelter; **s'abriter** *vt* to shelter, take cover
abrupt, e [abʀypt] *adj* sheer, steep; (*ton*) abrupt
abruti, e [abʀyti] *adj* stunned, dazed ▷ *nm/f* (*fam*) idiot, moron; **~ de travail** overworked
absence [apsɑ̃s] *nf* absence; (*Méd*) blackout; **avoir des ~s** to have mental blanks
absent, e [apsɑ̃, ɑ̃t] *adj* absent ▷ *nm/f* absentee; **absenter: s'absenter** *vi* to take time off work; (*sortir*) to leave, go out
absolu, e [apsɔly] *adj* absolute; **absolument** *adv* absolutely
absorbant, e [apsɔʀbɑ̃, ɑ̃t] *adj* absorbent
absorber [apsɔʀbe] *vt* to absorb; (*gén Méd: manger, boire*) to take
abstenir [apstəniʀ] *vb*: **s'~ de qch/de faire** to refrain from sth/from doing
abstrait, e [apstʀɛ, ɛt] *adj* abstract
absurde [apsyʀd] *adj* absurd
abus [aby] *nm* abuse; **~ de confiance** breach of trust; **il y a de l'~!** (*fam*) that's a bit much!; **abuser** *vi* to go too far, overstep the mark; **abuser de** (*duper*) to take advantage of; **s'abuser** *vi* (*se méprendre*) to be mistaken; **abusif, -ive** *adj* exorbitant; (*punition*) excessive
académie [akademi] *nf* academy; (*Scol:*

circonscription) ≈ regional education authority

acajou [akaʒu] *nm* mahogany
acariâtre [akaʀjɑtʀ] *adj* cantankerous
accablant, e [akablɑ̃, ɑ̃t] *adj* (*chaleur*) oppressive; (*témoignage, preuve*) overwhelming
accabler [akable] *vt* to overwhelm, overcome; **~ qn d'injures** to heap ou shower abuse on sb; **~ qn de travail** to overwork sb
accalmie [akalmi] *nf* lull
accaparer [akapaʀe] *vt* to monopolize; (*suj: travail etc*) to take up (all) the time ou attention of
accéder [aksede]: **~ à** *vt* (*lieu*) to reach; (*accorder: requête*) to grant, accede to
accélérateur [akseleʀatœʀ] *nm* accelerator
accélérer [akseleʀe] *vt* to speed up ▷ *vi* to accelerate
accent [aksɑ̃] *nm* accent; (*Phonétique, fig*) stress; **mettre l'~ sur** (*fig*) to stress; **~ aigu/grave/circonflexe** acute/grave/circumflex accent; **accentuer** *vt* (*Ling*) to accent; (*fig*) to accentuate, emphasize; **s'accentuer** *vi* to become more marked ou pronounced
acceptation [akseptasjɔ̃] *nf* acceptance
accepter [aksɛpte] *vt* to accept; **~ de faire** to agree to do; **acceptez-vous les cartes de crédit?** do you take credit cards?
accès [aksɛ] *nm* (*à un lieu*) access; (*Méd: de toux*) fit; (*: de fièvre*) bout; **d'~ facile** easily accessible; **facile d'~** easy to get to; **accès de colère** fit of anger; **accessible** *adj* accessible; (*livre, sujet*) **accessible à qn** within the reach of sb
accessoire [akseswaʀ] *adj* secondary; incidental ▷ *nm* accessory; (*Théâtre*) prop
accident [aksidɑ̃] *nm* accident; **par ~** by chance; **j'ai eu un ~** I've had an accident; **accident de la route** road accident; **accidenté, e** *adj* damaged; injured; (*relief, terrain*) uneven; hilly; **accidentel, le** *adj* accidental
acclamer [aklame] *vt* to cheer, acclaim
acclimater [aklimate]: **s'acclimater** *vi* (*personne*) to adapt (o.s.)

accolade [akɔlad] *nf* (*amicale*) embrace; (*signe*) brace

accommoder [akɔmɔde] *vt* (*Culin*) to prepare; **s'accommoder de** *vt* to put up with; (*se contenter de*) to make do with

accompagnateur, -trice [akɔ̃paɲatœʀ, tʀis] *nm/f* (*Mus*) accompanist; (*de voyage: guide*) guide; (*de voyage organisé*) courier

accompagner [akɔ̃paɲe] *vt* to accompany, be *ou* go *ou* come with; (*Mus*) to accompany

accompli, e [akɔ̃pli] *adj* accomplished; *voir aussi* **fait**

accomplir [akɔ̃pliʀ] *vt* (*tâche, projet*) to carry out; (*souhait*) to fulfil; **s'accomplir** *vi* to be fulfilled

accord [akɔʀ] *nm* agreement; (*entre des styles, tons etc*) harmony; (*Mus*) chord; **d'~!** OK!; **se mettre d'~** to come to an agreement; **être d'~ (pour faire qch)** to agree (to do sth)

accordéon [akɔʀdeɔ̃] *nm* (*Mus*) accordion

accorder [akɔʀde] *vt* (*faveur, délai*) to grant; (*harmoniser*) to match; (*Mus*) to tune; (*valeur, importance*) attach

accoster [akɔste] *vt* (*Navig*) to draw alongside ▷ *vi* to berth

accouchement [akuʃmɑ̃] *nm* delivery, (child)birth; labour

accoucher [akuʃe] *vi* to give birth, have a baby; **~ d'un garçon** to give birth to a boy

accouder [akude]: **s'accouder** *vi*: **s'~ à/ contre/sur** to rest one's elbows on/against/ on; **accoudoir** *nm* armrest

accoupler [akuple] *vt* to couple; (*pour la reproduction*) to mate; **s'accoupler** *vt* to mate

accourir [akuʀiʀ] *vi* to rush *ou* run up

accoutumance [akutymɑ̃s] *nf* (*gén*) adaptation; (*Méd*) addiction

accoutumé, e [akutyme] *adj* (*habituel*) customary, usual

accoutumer [akutyme] *vt*: **s'~ à** to get accustomed *ou* used to

accroc [akʀo] *nm* (*déchirure*) tear; (*fig*) hitch, snag

accrochage [akʀɔʃaʒ] *nm* (*Auto*) collision; (*dispute*) clash, brush

accrocher [akʀɔʃe] *vt* (*fig*) to catch, attract; **s'accrocher** (*se disputer*) to have a clash *ou* brush; **~ qch à** (*suspendre*) to hang sth (up) on; (*attacher: remorque*) to hitch sth (up) to; **~ qch (à)** (*déchirer*) to catch sth (on); **il a accroché ma voiture** he bumped into my car; **s'~ à** (*rester pris à*) to catch on; (*agripper, fig*) to hang on *ou* cling to

accroissement [akʀwasmɑ̃] *nm* increase

accroître [akʀwatʀ]: **s'accroître** *vi* to increase

accroupir [akʀupiʀ]: **s'accroupir** *vi* to squat, crouch (down)

accru, e [akʀy] *pp de* **accroître**

accueil [akœj] *nm* welcome; **comité d'~** reception committee; **accueillir** *vt* to welcome; (*aller chercher*) to meet, collect

accumuler [akymyle] *vt* to accumulate, amass; **s'accumuler** *vi* to accumulate; to pile up

accusation [akyzasjɔ̃] *nf* (*gén*) accusation; (*Jur*) charge; (*partie*): **l'~** the prosecution

accusé, e [akyze] *nm/f* accused; defendant; **accusé de réception** acknowledgement of receipt

accuser [akyze] *vt* to accuse; (*fig*) to emphasize, bring out; to show; **~ qn de** to accuse sb of; (*Jur*) to charge sb with; **~ réception de** to acknowledge receipt of

acéré, e [aseʀe] *adj* sharp

acharné, e [aʃaʀne] *adj* (*efforts*) relentless; (*lutte, adversaire*) fierce, bitter

acharner [aʃaʀne] *vb*: **s'~ contre** to set o.s. against; (*suj: malchance*) to dog; **s'~ à faire** to try doggedly to do; (*persister*) to persist in doing; **s'~ sur qn** to hound sb

achat [aʃa] *nm* purchase; **faire des ~s** to do some shopping; **faire l'~ de qch** to purchase sth

acheter [aʃ(ə)te] *vt* to buy, purchase; (*soudoyer*) to buy; **~ qch à** (*marchand*) to buy *ou* purchase sth from; (*ami etc: offrir*) to buy sth for; **où est-ce que je peux ~ des cartes postales?** where can I buy (some) postcards?; **acheteur, -euse** *nm/f* buyer; shopper; (*Comm*) buyer

achever [aʃ(ə)ve] *vt* to complete, finish; (*blessé*) to finish off; **s'achever** *vi* to end

acide [asid] *adj* sour, sharp; (*Chimie*) acid(ic) ▷ *nm* (*Chimie*) acid; **acidulé, e** *adj* slightly acid; **bonbons acidulés** acid drops

acier [asje] *nm* steel; **aciérie** *nf* steelworks *sg*

acné [akne] *nf* acne

acompte [akɔ̃t] *nm* deposit

à-côté [akote] *nm* side-issue; (*argent*) extra

à-coup [aku] *nm*: **par ~s** by fits and starts

acoustique [akustik] *nf* (*d'une salle*) acoustics *pl*

acquéreur [akeʀœʀ] *nm* buyer, purchaser

acquérir [akeʀiʀ] *vt* to acquire

acquis, e [aki, iz] *pp de* **acquérir** ▷ *nm* (accumulated) experience; **son aide nous est ~e** we can count on her help

acquitter [akite] *vt* (*Jur*) to acquit; (*facture*) to pay, settle; **s'acquitter de** *vt* (*devoir*) to discharge; (*promesse*) to fulfil

âcre [ɑkʀ] *adj* acrid, pungent

acrobate [akʀɔbat] *nm/f* acrobat; **acrobatie** *nf* acrobatics *sg*

acte [akt] *nm* act, action; (*Théâtre*) act; **prendre ~ de** to note, take note of; **faire ~ de candidature** to apply; **faire ~ de présence** to put in an appearance; **acte de naissance**

birth certificate

acteur [aktœʀ] *nm* actor

actif, -ive [aktif, iv] *adj* active ▷ *nm* (*Comm*) assets *pl*; (*fig*): **avoir à son ~** to have to one's credit; **population active** working population

action [aksjɔ̃] *nf* (*gén*) action; (*Comm*) share; **une bonne ~** a good deed; **actionnaire** *nm/f* shareholder; **actionner** *vt* (*mécanisme*) to activate; (*machine*) to operate

activer [aktive] *vt* to speed up; **s'activer** *vi* to bustle about; to hurry up

activité [aktivite] *nf* activity; **en ~** (*volcan*) active; (*fonctionnaire*) in active life

actrice [aktʀis] *nf* actress

actualité [aktɥalite] *nf* (*d'un problème*) topicality; (*événements*): **l'~** current events; **actualités** *nfpl* (*Cinéma*, TV) the news; **d'~** topical

actuel, le [aktɥɛl] *adj* (*présent*) present; (*d'actualité*) topical; **à l'heure ~le** at the present time; **actuellement** *adv* at present, at the present time

▌ Attention à ne pas traduire *actuellement* par *actually*.

acuponcture [akypɔ̃ktyʀ] *nf* acupuncture

adaptateur [adaptatœʀ] *nm* (*Élec*) adapter

adapter [adapte] *vt* to adapt; **s'adapter (à)** (*suj: personne*) to adapt (to); **~ qch à** (*approprier*) to adapt sth to (fit); **~ qch sur/dans/à** (*fixer*) to fit sth on/into/to

addition [adisjɔ̃] *nf* addition; (*au café*) bill; **l'~, s'il vous plaît** could I have the bill, please?; **additionner** *vt* to add (up)

adepte [adɛpt] *nm/f* follower

adéquat, e [adekwa(t), at] *adj* appropriate, suitable

adhérent, e [aderɑ̃, ɑ̃t] *nm/f* member

adhérer [adere]: **~ à** *vt* (*coller*) to adhere *ou* stick to; (*se rallier à*) to join; **adhésif, -ive** *adj* adhesive, sticky; **ruban adhésif** sticky *ou* adhesive tape

adieu, x [adjø] *excl* goodbye ▷ *nm* farewell

adjectif [adʒɛktif] *nm* adjective

adjoint, e [adʒwɛ̃, wɛ̃t] *nm/f* assistant; **adjoint au maire** deputy mayor; **directeur adjoint** assistant manager

admettre [admɛtʀ] *vt* (*laisser entrer*) to admit; (*candidat: Scol*) to pass; (*tolérer*) to allow, accept; (*reconnaître*) to admit, acknowledge

administrateur, -trice [administʀatœʀ, tʀis] *nm/f* (*Comm*) director; (*Admin*) administrator

administration [administʀasjɔ̃] *nf* administration; **l'A~** ≈ the Civil Service

administrer [administʀe] *vt* (*firme*) to manage, run; (*biens, remède, sacrement etc*) to administer

admirable [admiʀabl] *adj* admirable,

wonderful

admirateur, -trice [admiʀatœʀ, tʀis] *nm/f* admirer

admiration [admiʀasjɔ̃] *nf* admiration

admirer [admiʀe] *vt* to admire

admis, e [admi, iz] *pp de* **admettre**

admissible [admisibl] *adj* (*candidat*) eligible; (*comportement*) admissible, acceptable

ADN *sigle m* (= *acide désoxyribonucléique*) DNA

adolescence [adɔlesɑ̃s] *nf* adolescence

adolescent, e [adɔlesɑ̃, ɑ̃t] *nm/f* adolescent, teenager

adopter [adɔpte] *vt* to adopt; **adoptif, -ive** *adj* (*parents*) adoptive; (*fils, patrie*) adopted

adorable [adɔʀabl] *adj* delightful, adorable

adorer [adɔʀe] *vt* to adore; (*Rel*) to worship

adosser [adose] *vt*: **~ qch à** *ou* **contre** to stand sth against; **s'adosser à/contre** to lean with one's back against

adoucir [adusiʀ] *vt* (*goût, température*) to make milder; (*avec du sucre*) to sweeten; (*peau, voix*) to soften; (*caractère*) to mellow

adresse [adʀɛs] *nf* (*domicile*) address; (*dextérité*) skill, dexterity; **~ électronique** email address

adresser [adʀese] *vt* (*lettre: expédier*) to send; (: *écrire l'adresse sur*) to address; (*injure, compliments*) to address; **s'adresser à** (*parler à*) to speak to, address; (*s'informer auprès de*) to go and see; (: *bureau*) to inquire at; (*suj: livre, conseil*) to be aimed at; **~ la parole à** to speak to, address

adroit, e [adʀwa, wat] *adj* skilful, skilled

ADSL *sigle m* (= *asymmetrical digital subscriber line*) ADSL, broadband

adulte [adylt] *nm/f* adult, grown-up ▷ *adj* (*chien, arbre*) fully-grown, mature; (*attitude*) adult, grown-up

adverbe [advɛʀb] *nm* adverb

adversaire [advɛʀsɛʀ] *nm/f* (*Sport, gén*) opponent, adversary

aération [aeʀasjɔ̃] *nf* airing; (*circulation de l'air*) ventilation

aérer [aeʀe] *vt* to air; (*fig*) to lighten

aérien, ne [aeʀjɛ̃, jɛn] *adj* (*Aviat*) air *cpd*, aerial; (*câble, métro*) overhead; (*fig*) light; **compagnie ~ne** airline

aéro... [aeʀo] *préfixe*: **aérobic** *nm* aerobics *sg*; **aérogare** *nf* airport (buildings); (*en ville*) air terminal; **aéroglisseur** *nm* hovercraft; **aérophagie** *nf* (*Méd*) wind, aerophagia (*Méd*); **aéroport** *nm* airport; **aérosol** *nm* aerosol

affaiblir [afebliʀ]: **s'affaiblir** *vi* to weaken

affaire [afɛʀ] *nf* (*problème, question*) matter; (*criminelle, judiciaire*) case; (*scandaleuse etc*) affair; (*entreprise*) business; (*marché, transaction*) deal; business *no pl*; (*occasion intéressante*) bargain; **affaires** *nfpl* (*intérêts publics et privés*) affairs; (*activité commerciale*) business sg; (effets personnels) things, belongings; **ce sont mes ~s** (cela me concerne) that's my business; **occupe-toi de tes ~s!** mind your own business!; **ça fera l'~** that will do (nicely); **se tirer d'~** to sort it ou things out for o.s.; **avoir ~ à** (être en contact) to be dealing with; **les A~s étrangères** Foreign Affairs; **affairer: s'affairer** vi to busy o.s., bustle about

affamé, e [afame] adj starving

affecter [afɛkte] vt to affect; **~ qch à** to allocate ou allot sth to; **~ qn à** to appoint sb to; (diplomate) to post sb to

affectif, -ive [afɛktif, iv] adj emotional

affection [afɛksjɔ̃] nf affection; (mal) ailment; **affectionner** vt to be fond of; **affectueux, -euse** adj affectionate

affichage [afiʃaʒ] nm billposting; (électronique) display; **"~ interdit"** "stick no bills"; **affichage à cristaux liquides** liquid crystal display, LCD

affiche [afiʃ] nf poster; (officielle) notice; (Théâtre) bill; **être à l'~** to be on

afficher [afiʃe] vt (affiche) to put up; (réunion) to put up a notice about; (électroniquement) to display; (fig) to exhibit, display; **"défense d'~"** "no bill posters"; **s'afficher** vr (péj) to flaunt o.s.; (électroniquement) to be displayed

affilée [afile]: **d'~** adv at a stretch

affirmatif, -ive [afiʀmatif, iv] adj affirmative

affirmer [afiʀme] vt to assert

affligé, e [afliʒe] adj distressed, grieved; **~ de** (maladie, tare) afflicted with

affliger [afliʒe] vt (peiner) to distress, grieve

affluence [aflyãs] nf crowds pl; **heures d'~** rush hours; **jours d'~** busiest days

affluent [aflyã] nm tributary

affolement [afɔlmã] nm panic

affoler [afɔle] vt to throw into a panic; **s'affoler** vi to panic

affranchir [afʀãʃiʀ] vt to put a stamp ou stamps on; (à la machine) to frank (BRIT), meter (US); (fig) to free, liberate; **affranchissement** nm postage

affreux, -euse [afʀø, øz] adj dreadful, awful

affront [afʀɔ̃] nm affront; **affrontement** nm clash, confrontation

affronter [afʀɔ̃te] vt to confront, face

affût [afy] nm: **à l'~ (de)** (gibier) lying in wait (for); (fig) on the look-out (for)

Afghanistan [afganistã] nm: **l'~** Afghanistan

afin [afɛ̃]: **~ que** conj so that, in order that; **~ de faire** in order to do, so as to do

africain, e [afʀikɛ̃, ɛn] adj African ▷ nm/f: **A~, e** African

Afrique [afʀik] nf: **l'~** Africa; **l'Afrique du Nord/Sud** North/South Africa

agacer [agase] vt to irritate

âge [aʒ] nm age; **quel ~ as-tu?** how old are you?; **prendre de l'~** to be getting on (in years); **le troisième ~** (période) retirement; (personnes âgées) senior citizens; **âgé, e** adj old, elderly; **âgé de 10 ans** 10 years old

agence [aʒãs] nf agency, office; (succursale) branch; **agence de voyages** travel agency; **agence immobilière** estate (BRIT) ou real estate (US) agent's (office)

agenda [aʒɛ̃da] nm diary; **~ électronique** PDA
Attention à ne pas traduire **agenda** par le mot anglais **agenda**.

agenouiller [aʒ(ə)nuje]: **s'agenouiller** vi to kneel (down)

agent, e [aʒã, ãt] nm/f (aussi: **~(e) de police**) policeman(policewoman); (Admin) official, officer; **agent immobilier** estate agent (BRIT), realtor (US)

agglomération [aglɔmeʀasjɔ̃] nf town; built-up area; **l'~ parisienne** the urban area of Paris

aggraver [agʀave]: **s'aggraver** vi to worsen

agile [aʒil] adj agile, nimble

agir [aʒiʀ] vi to act; **il s'agit de** (ça traite de) it is about; (il est important de) it's a matter ou question of; **il s'agit de faire** we (ou you etc) must do; **de quoi s'agit-il?** what is it about?

agitation [aʒitasjɔ̃] nf (hustle and) bustle; (trouble) agitation, excitement; (politique) unrest, agitation

agité, e [aʒite] adj fidgety, restless; (troublé) agitated, perturbed; (mer) rough

agiter [aʒite] vt (bouteille, chiffon) to shake; (bras, mains) to wave; (préoccuper, exciter) to perturb

agneau, x [aɲo] nm lamb

agonie [agɔni] nf mortal agony, death pangs pl; (fig) death throes pl

agrafe [agʀaf] nf (de vêtement) hook, fastener; (de bureau) staple; **agrafer** vt to fasten; to staple; **agrafeuse** nf stapler

agrandir [agʀãdiʀ] vt to enlarge; **s'agrandir** vi (ville, famille) to grow, expand; (trou, écart) to get bigger; **agrandissement** nm (Photo) enlargement

agréable [agʀeabl] adj pleasant, nice

agréé, e [agʀee] adj: **concessionnaire ~** registered dealer

agréer [agʀee] vt (requête) to accept; **~ à** to please, suit; **veuillez ~, Monsieur/Madame, mes salutations distinguées** (personne nommée) yours sincerely; (personne non nommée) yours faithfully

agrégation [agʀegasjɔ̃] nf highest teaching diploma in France; **agrégé, e** nm/f holder of the agrégation

agrément [agʀemã] nm (accord) consent, approval; (attraits) charm, attractiveness; (plaisir) pleasure

agresser [agʀese] vt to attack; **agresseur** nm aggressor, attacker; (Pol, Mil) aggressor; **agressif, -ive** adj aggressive

agricole [agʀikɔl] adj agricultural; **agriculteur** nm farmer; **agriculture** nf agriculture, farming

agripper [agʀipe] vt to grab, clutch; **s'agripper à** to cling (on) to, clutch, grip

agro-alimentaire [agʀoalimãtɛʀ] nm farm-produce industry

agrumes [agʀym] nmpl citrus fruit(s)

aguets [agɛ] nmpl: **être aux ~** to be on the look out

ai [ɛ] vb voir **avoir**

aide [ɛd] nm/f assistant; carer ▷ nf assistance, help; (secours financier) aid; **à l'~ de** (avec) with the help ou aid of; **appeler (qn) à l'~** to call for help (from sb); **à l'~!** help!; **aide judiciaire** legal aid; **aide ménagère** ≈ home help (BRIT) ou helper (US); **aide-mémoire** nm inv memoranda pages pl; (key facts) handbook; **aide-soignant, e** nm/f auxiliary nurse

aider [ede] vt to help; **~ à qch** to help (towards) sth; **~ qn à faire qch** to help sb to do sth; **pouvez-vous m'~?** can you help me?; **s'aider de** (se servir de) to use, make use of

aïe [aj] excl ouch!

aie etc [ɛ] vb voir **avoir**

aigle [ɛgl] nm eagle

aigre [ɛgʀ] adj sour, sharp; (fig) sharp, cutting; **aigre-doux, -ce** adj (sauce) sweet and sour; **aigreur** nf sourness; sharpness; **aigreurs d'estomac** heartburn sg

aigu, ë [egy] adj (objet, douleur) sharp; (son, voix) high-pitched, shrill; (note) high(-pitched)

aiguille [egɥij] nf needle; (de montre) hand; **aiguille à tricoter** knitting needle

aiguiser [egize] vt to sharpen; (fig) to stimulate; (: sens) to excite

ail [aj] nm garlic

aile [ɛl] nf wing; **aileron** nm (de requin) fin; **ailier** nm winger

aille etc [aj] vb voir **aller**

ailleurs [ajœʀ] adv elsewhere, somewhere else; **partout/nulle part ~** everywhere/nowhere else; **d'~** (du reste) moreover, besides; **par ~** (d'autre part) moreover, furthermore

aimable [ɛmabl] adj kind, nice

aimant [ɛmã] nm magnet

aimer [eme] vt to love; (d'amitié, affection, par goût) to like; (souhait): **j'aimerais ...** I would like ...; **j'aime faire du ski** I like skiing; **je t'aime** I love you; **bien ~ qn/qch** to like sb/sth; **j'aime mieux Paul (que Pierre)** I prefer Paul (to Pierre); **j'aimerais mieux faire** I'd much rather do

aine [ɛn] nf groin

aîné, e [ene] adj elder, older; (le plus âgé) eldest, oldest ▷ nm/f oldest child ou one, oldest boy

ou son/girl ou daughter

ainsi [ɛ̃si] adv (de cette façon) like this, in this way, thus; (ce faisant) thus ▷ conj thus, so; **~ que** (comme) (just) as; (et aussi) as well as; **pour ~ dire** so to speak; **et ~ de suite** and so on

air [ɛʀ] nm air; (mélodie) tune; (expression) look, air; **prendre l'~** to get some (fresh) air; **avoir l'~** (sembler) to look, appear; **il a l'~ triste/malade** he looks sad/ill; **avoir l'~ de** to look like; **il a l'~ de dormir** he looks as if he's sleeping; **en l'~** (promesses) empty

airbag [ɛʀbag] nm airbag

aisance [ɛzãs] nf ease; (richesse) affluence

aise [ɛz] nf comfort; **être à l'~** ou **à son ~** to be comfortable; (pas embarrassé) to be at ease; (financièrement) to be comfortably off; **se mettre à l'~** to make o.s. comfortable; **être mal à l'~** to be uncomfortable; (gêné) to be ill at ease; **en faire à son ~** to do as one likes; **aisé, e** adj easy; (assez riche) well-to-do, well-off

aisselle [ɛsɛl] nf armpit

ait [ɛ] vb voir **avoir**

ajonc [aʒɔ̃] nm gorse no pl

ajourner [aʒuʀne] vt (réunion) to adjourn; (décision) to defer, postpone

ajouter [aʒute] vt to add

alarme [alaʀm] nf alarm; **donner l'~** to give ou raise the alarm; **alarmer** vt to alarm; **s'alarmer** vi to become alarmed

Albanie [albani] nf: **l'~** Albania

album [albɔm] nm album

alcool [alkɔl] nm: **l'~** alcohol; **un ~** a spirit, a brandy; **bière sans ~** non-alcoholic ou alcohol-free beer; **alcool à brûler** methylated spirits (BRIT), wood alcohol (US); **alcool à 90°** surgical spirit; **alcoolique** adj, nm/f alcoholic; **alcoolisé, e** adj alcoholic; **une boisson non alcoolisée** a soft drink; **alcoolisme** nm alcoholism; **alco(o)test®** nm Breathalyser®; (test) breath-test

aléatoire [aleatwaʀ] adj uncertain; (Inform) random

alentour [alãtuʀ] adv around, round about; **alentours** nmpl (environs) surroundings; **aux ~s de** in the vicinity ou neighbourhood of, round about; (temps) round about

alerte [alɛʀt] adj agile, nimble; brisk, lively ▷ nf alert; warning; **alerte à la bombe** bomb scare; **alerter** vt to alert

algèbre [alʒɛbʀ] nf algebra

Alger [alʒe] n Algiers

Algérie [alʒeʀi] nf: **l'~** Algeria; **algérien, ne** adj Algerian ▷ nm/f: **Algérien, ne** Algerian

algue [alg] nf (gén) seaweed no pl; (Bot) alga

alibi [alibi] nm alibi

aligner [aliɲe] vt to align, line up; (idées, chiffres) to string together; (adapter): **~ qch sur** to bring sth into alignment with; **s'aligner**

(*soldats etc*) to line up; **s'~ sur** (*Pol*) to align o.s. on

aliment [alimɑ̃] *nm* food; **alimentation** *nf* (*commerce*) food trade; (*magasin*) grocery store; (*régime*) diet; (*en eau etc, de moteur*) supplying; (*Inform*) feed; **alimenter** *vt* to feed; (*Tech*): **alimenter (en)** to supply (with); to feed (with); (*fig*) to sustain, keep going

allaiter [alete] *vt* to (breast-)feed, nurse; (*suj: animal*) to suckle

allécher [aleʃe] *vt*: **~ qn** to make sb's mouth water; to tempt *ou* entice sb

allée [ale] *nf* (*de jardin*) path; (*en ville*) avenue, drive; **~s et venues** comings and goings

allégé, e [aleʒe] *adj* (*yaourt etc*) low-fat

alléger [aleʒe] *vt* (*voiture*) to make lighter; (*chargement*) to lighten; (*souffrance*) to alleviate, soothe

Allemagne [almaɲ] *nf*: **l'~** Germany; **allemand, e** *adj* German ▷ *nm/f*: **Allemand, e** German ▷ *nm* (*Ling*) German

aller [ale] *nm* (*trajet*) outward journey; (*billet: aussi*: **~ simple**) single (*BRIT*) *ou* one-way (*US*) ticket; **~ (et) retour** return (ticket) (*BRIT*), round-trip ticket (*US*) ▷ *vi* (*gén*) to go; **~ à** (*convenir*) to suit; (*suj: forme, pointure etc*) to fit; **~ (bien) avec** (*couleurs, style etc*) to go (well) with; **je vais y ~/me fâcher** I'm going to go/to get angry; **~ chercher qn** to go and get *ou* fetch (*BRIT*) sb; **~ voir** to go and see, go to see; **allez!** come on!; **allons!** come now!; **comment allez-vous?** how are you?; **comment ça va?** how are you?; (*affaires etc*) how are things?; **il va bien/mal** he's well/not well, he's fine/ill; **ça va bien/mal** (*affaires etc*) it's going well/not going well; **~ mieux** to be better; **s'en ~** (*partir*) to be off, go, leave; (*disparaître*) to go away

allergie [alɛrʒi] *nf* allergy

allergique [alɛrʒik] *adj*: **~ à** allergic to; **je suis ~ à la pénicilline** I'm allergic to penicillin

alliance [aljɑ̃s] *nf* (*Mil, Pol*) alliance; (*bague*) wedding ring

allier [alje] *vt* (*Pol, gén*) to ally; (*fig*) to combine; **s'allier** to become allies; to combine

allô [alo] *excl* hullo, hallo

allocation [alɔkasjɔ̃] *nf* allowance; **allocation (de) chômage** unemployment benefit; **allocations familiales** ≈ child benefit

allonger [alɔ̃ʒe] *vt* to lengthen, make longer; (*étendre: bras, jambe*) to stretch (out); **s'allonger** *vi* to get longer; (*se coucher*) to lie down, stretch out; **~ le pas** to hasten one's step(s)

allumage [alymaʒ] *nm* (*Auto*) ignition

allume-cigare [alymsigar] *nm inv* cigar lighter

allumer [alyme] *vt* (*lampe, phare, radio*) to put *ou* switch on; (*pièce*) to put *ou* switch

the light(s) on in; (*feu*) to light; **s'allumer** *vi* (*lumière, lampe*) to come *ou* go on; **je n'arrive pas à ~ le chauffage** I can't turn the heating on

allumette [alymɛt] *nf* match

allure [alyr] *nf* (*vitesse*) speed, pace; (*démarche*) walk; (*aspect, air*) look; **avoir de l'~** to have style; **à toute ~** at top speed

allusion [a(l)lyzjɔ̃] *nf* allusion; (*sous-entendu*) hint; **faire ~ à** to allude *ou* refer to; to hint at

○ **MOT-CLÉ**

alors [alɔr] *adv* **1** (*à ce moment-là*) then, at that time; **il habitait alors à Paris** he lived in Paris at that time

2 (*par conséquent*) then; **tu as fini? alors je m'en vais** have you finished? I'm going then; **et alors?** so what?

▷ *conj*: **alors que 1** (*au moment où*) when, as; **il est arrivé alors que je partais** he arrived as I was leaving

2 (*tandis que*) whereas, while; **alors que son frère travaillait dur, lui se reposait** while his brother was working hard, HE would rest

3 (*bien que*) even though; **il a été puni alors qu'il n'a rien fait** he was punished, even though he had done nothing

alourdir [alurdir] *vt* to weigh down, make heavy

Alpes [alp] *nfpl*: **les ~** the Alps

alphabet [alfabɛ] *nm* alphabet; (*livre*) ABC (book)

alpinisme [alpinism] *nm* mountaineering, climbing

Alsace [alzas] *nf* Alsace; **alsacien, ne** *adj* Alsatian ▷ *nm/f*: **Alsacien, ne** Alsatian

altermondialisme [altɛrmɔ̃djalism] *nm* anti-globalism; **altermondialiste** *adj, nm/f* anti-globalist

alternatif, -ive [altɛrnatif, iv] *adj* alternating; **alternative** *nf* (*choix*) alternative; **alterner** *vi* to alternate

altitude [altityd] *nf* altitude, height

alto [alto] *nm* (*instrument*) viola

aluminium [alyminjɔm] *nm* aluminium (*BRIT*), aluminum (*US*)

amabilité [amabilite] *nf* kindness

amaigrissant, e [amegrisɑ̃, ɑ̃t] *adj* (*régime*) slimming

amande [amɑ̃d] *nf* (*de l'amandier*) almond; **amandier** *nm* almond (tree)

amant [amɑ̃] *nm* lover

amas [ama] *nm* heap, pile; **amasser** *vt* to amass

amateur [amatœr] *nm* amateur; **en ~** (*péj*) amateurishly; **amateur de musique/sport** music/sport lover

ambassade [ɑ̃basad] nf embassy; **l'~ de France** the French Embassy; **ambassadeur, -drice** nm/f ambassador(-dress)

ambiance [ɑ̃bjɑ̃s] nf atmosphere; **il y a de l'~** there's a great atmosphere

ambigu, ë [ɑ̃bigy] adj ambiguous

ambitieux, -euse [ɑ̃bisjø, jøz] adj ambitious

ambition [ɑ̃bisjɔ̃] nf ambition

ambulance [ɑ̃bylɑ̃s] nf ambulance; **appelez une ~!** call an ambulance!; **ambulancier, -ière** nm/f ambulance man(-woman) (BRIT), paramedic (US)

âme [ɑm] nf soul; **âme sœur** kindred spirit

amélioration [ameljɔrasjɔ̃] nf improvement

améliorer [ameljɔre] vt to improve; **s'améliorer** vi to improve, get better

aménager [amenaʒe] vt (agencer, transformer) to fit out; to lay out; (: quartier, territoire) to develop; (installer) to fix up, put in; **ferme aménagée** converted farmhouse

amende [amɑ̃d] nf fine; **faire ~ honorable** to make amends

amener [am(ə)ne] vt to bring; (causer) to bring about; **s'amener** vi to show up (fam), turn up; **~ qn à faire qch** to lead sb to do sth

amer, amère [amɛr] adj bitter

américain, e [amerikɛ̃, ɛn] adj American ▷ nm/f: **A~, e** American

Amérique [amerik] nf: **l'~** America; **Amérique centrale/latine** Central/Latin America; **l'Amérique du Nord/Sud** North/South America

amertume [amɛrtym] nf bitterness

ameublement [amœbləmɑ̃] nm furnishing; (meubles) furniture

ami, e [ami] nm/f friend; (amant/maîtresse) boyfriend/girlfriend ▷ adj: **pays/groupe ~** friendly country/group; **petit ~/petite ~e** boyfriend/girlfriend

amiable [amjabl]: **à l'~** adv (Jur) out of court; (gén) amicably

amiante [amjɑ̃t] nm asbestos

amical, e, -aux [amikal, o] adj friendly; **amicalement** adv in a friendly way; (dans une lettre) (with) best wishes

amincir [amɛ̃sir] vt: **~ qn** to make sb thinner ou slimmer; (suj: vêtement) to make sb look slimmer

amincissant, e [amɛ̃sisɑ̃, ɑ̃t] adj: **régime ~** (slimming) diet; **crème ~e** slimming cream

amiral, -aux [amiral, o] nm admiral

amitié [amitje] nf friendship; **prendre en ~ to** befriend; **faire** ou **présenter ses ~s à qn** to send sb one's best wishes; **"~s"** (dans une lettre) "(with) best wishes"

amonceler [amɔ̃s(ə)le] vt to pile ou heap up; **s'amonceler** vi to pile ou heap up; (fig) to accumulate

amont [amɔ̃]: **en ~** adv upstream

amorce [amɔrs] nf (sur un hameçon) bait; (explosif) cap; primer; priming; (fig: début) beginning(s), start

amortir [amɔrtir] vt (atténuer: choc) to absorb, cushion; (bruit, douleur) to deaden; (Comm: dette) to pay off; **~ un achat** to make a purchase pay for itself; **amortisseur** nm shock absorber

amour [amur] nm love; **faire l'~** to make love; **amoureux, -euse** adj (regard, tempérament) amorous; (vie, problèmes) love cpd; (personne): **être amoureux (de qn)** to be in love (with sb); **tomber amoureux (de qn)** to fall in love (with sb) ▷ nmpl courting couple(s); **amour-propre** nm self-esteem, pride

ampère [ɑ̃pɛr] nm amp(ere)

amphithéâtre [ɑ̃fiteatr] nm amphitheatre; (d'université) lecture hall ou theatre

ample [ɑ̃pl] adj (vêtement) roomy, ample; (gestes, mouvement) broad; (ressources) ample; **amplement** adv: **c'est amplement suffisant** that's more than enough; **ampleur** nf (de dégâts, problème) extent

amplificateur [ɑ̃plifikatœr] nm amplifier

amplifier [ɑ̃plifje] vt (fig) to expand, increase

ampoule [ɑ̃pul] nf (électrique) bulb; (de médicament) phial; (aux mains, pieds) blister

amusant, e [amyzɑ̃, ɑ̃t] adj (divertissant, spirituel) entertaining, amusing; (comique) funny, amusing

amuse-gueule [amyzgœl] nm inv appetizer, snack

amusement [amyzmɑ̃] nm (divertissement) amusement; (jeu etc) pastime, diversion

amuser [amyze] vt (divertir) to entertain, amuse; (égayer, faire rire) to amuse; **s'amuser** vi (jouer) to play; (se divertir) to enjoy o.s., have fun; (fig) to mess around

amygdale [amidal] nf tonsil

an [ɑ̃] nm year; **avoir quinze ans** to be fifteen (years old); **le jour de l'an, le premier de l'an, le nouvel an** New Year's Day

analphabète [analfabɛt] nm/f illiterate

analyse [analiz] nf analysis; (Méd) test; **analyser** vt to analyse; to test

ananas [anana(s)] nm pineapple

anatomie [anatɔmi] nf anatomy

ancêtre [ɑ̃sɛtr] nm/f ancestor

anchois [ɑ̃ʃwa] nm anchovy

ancien, ne [ɑ̃sjɛ̃, jɛn] adj old; (de jadis, de l'antiquité) ancient; (précédent, ex-) former, old; (par l'expérience) senior ▷ nm/f (dans une tribu) elder; **ancienneté** nf (Admin) (length of) service; (privilèges obtenus) seniority

ancre [ɑ̃kr] nf anchor; **jeter/lever l'~** to cast/weigh anchor; **ancrer** vt (Constr: câble etc) to anchor; (fig) to fix firmly

Andorre [ɑ̃dɔr] nf Andorra

andouille [ɑ̃duj] nf (Culin) sausage made of

chitterlings; (*fam*) clot, nit

âne [ɑn] *nm* donkey, ass; (*péj*) dunce

anéantir [aneɑ̃tiʀ] *vt* to annihilate, wipe out; (*fig*) to obliterate, destroy

anémie [anemi] *nf* anaemia; **anémique** *adj* anaemic

anesthésie [anɛstezi] *nf* anaesthesia; **faire une ~ locale/générale à qn** to give sb a local/general anaesthetic

ange [ɑ̃ʒ] *nm* angel; **être aux ~s** to be over the moon

angine [ɑ̃ʒin] *nf* throat infection; **angine de poitrine** angina

anglais, e [ɑ̃glɛ, ɛz] *adj* English ▷ *nm/f*: **A~, e** Englishman(-woman) ▷ *nm* (*Ling*) English; **les A~** the English; **filer à l'~e** to take French leave

angle [ɑ̃gl] *nm* angle; (*coin*) corner; **angle droit** right angle

Angleterre [ɑ̃glətɛʀ] *nf*: **l'~** England

anglo... [ɑ̃glɔ] *préfixe* Anglo-, anglo(-); **anglophone** *adj* English-speaking

angoisse [ɑ̃gwas] *nf* anguish, distress; **angoissé, e** *adj* (*personne*) distressed

anguille [ɑ̃gij] *nf* eel

animal, e, -aux [animal, o] *adj, nm* animal

animateur, -trice [animatœʀ, tʀis] *nm/f* (*de télévision*) host; (*de groupe*) leader, organizer

animation [animasjɔ̃] *nf* (*voir animé*) busyness, liveliness; (*Cinéma: technique*) animation

animé, e [anime] *adj* (*lieu*) busy, lively; (*conversation, réunion*) lively, animated

animer [anime] *vt* (*ville, soirée*) to liven up; (*mener*) to lead

anis [ani(s)] *nm* (*Culin*) aniseed; (*Bot*) anise

ankyloser [ɑ̃kiloze]: **s'ankyloser** *vi* to get stiff

anneau, x [ano] *nm* (*de rideau, bague*) ring; (*de chaîne*) link

année [ane] *nf* year

annexe [anɛks] *adj* (*problème*) related; (*document*) appended; (*salle*) adjoining ▷ *nf* (*bâtiment*) annex(e); (*jointe à une lettre*) enclosure

anniversaire [anivɛʀsɛʀ] *nm* birthday; (*d'un événement, bâtiment*) anniversary

annonce [anɔ̃s] *nf* announcement; (*signe, indice*) sign; (*aussi*: **~ publicitaire**) advertisement; **les petites ~s** the classified advertisements, the small ads

annoncer [anɔ̃se] *vt* to announce; (*être le signe de*) to herald; **s'~ bien/difficile** to look promising/difficult

annuaire [anɥɛʀ] *nm* yearbook, annual; **annuaire téléphonique** (telephone) directory, phone book

annuel, le [anɥɛl] *adj* annual, yearly

annulation [anylasjɔ̃] *nf* cancellation

annuler [anyle] *vt* (*rendez-vous, voyage*) to cancel, call off; (*jugement*) to quash (BRIT), repeal (US); (*Math, Physique*) to cancel out; **je voudrais ~ ma réservation** I'd like to cancel my reservation

anonymat [anɔnima] *nm* anonymity; **garder l'~** to remain anonymous

anonyme [anɔnim] *adj* anonymous; (*fig*) impersonal

anorak [anɔʀak] *nm* anorak

anorexie [anɔʀɛksi] *nf* anorexia

anormal, e, -aux [anɔʀmal, o] *adj* abnormal

ANPE *sigle f* (= *Agence nationale pour l'emploi*) national employment agency

antarctique [ɑ̃taʀktik] *adj* Antarctic ▷ *nm*: **l'A~** the Antarctic

antenne [ɑ̃tɛn] *nf* (*de radio*) aerial; (*d'insecte*) antenna, feeler; (*poste avancé*) outpost; (*petite succursale*) sub-branch; **passer à l'~** to go on the air; **antenne parabolique** satellite dish

antérieur, e [ɑ̃teʀjœʀ] *adj* (*d'avant*) previous, earlier; (*de devant*) front

anti... [ɑ̃ti] *préfixe* anti...; **antialcoolique** *adj* anti-alcohol; **antibiotique** *nm* antibiotic; **antibrouillard** *adj*: **phare antibrouillard** fog lamp (BRIT) *ou* light (US)

anticipation [ɑ̃tisipasjɔ̃] *nf*: **livre/film d'~** science fiction book/film

anticipé, e [ɑ̃tisipe] *adj*: **avec mes remerciements ~s** thanking you in advance *ou* anticipation

anticiper [ɑ̃tisipe] *vt* (*événement, coup*) to anticipate, foresee

anti...: anticorps *nm* antibody; **antidote** *nm* antidote; **antigel** *nm* antifreeze; **antihistaminique** *nm* antihistamine

antillais, e [ɑ̃tijɛ, ɛz] *adj* West Indian, Caribbean ▷ *nm/f*: **A~, e** West Indian, Caribbean

Antilles [ɑ̃tij] *nfpl*: **les ~** the West Indies; **les Grandes/Petites ~** the Greater/Lesser Antilles

antilope [ɑ̃tilɔp] *nf* antelope

anti...: antimite(s) *adj, nm*: **(produit) antimite(s)** mothproofer; moth repellent; **antimondialisation** *nf* anti-globalization; **antipathique** *adj* unpleasant, disagreeable; **antipelliculaire** *adj* anti-dandruff

antiquaire [ɑ̃tikɛʀ] *nm/f* antique dealer

antique [ɑ̃tik] *adj* antique; (*très vieux*) ancient, antiquated; **antiquité** *nf* (*objet*) antique; **l'Antiquité** Antiquity; **magasin d'antiquités** antique shop

anti...: antirabique *adj* rabies *cpd*; **antirouille** *adj inv* anti-rust *cpd*; **antisémite** *adj* anti-Semitic; **antiseptique** *adj, nm* antiseptic

antivirus [ɑ̃ti'viʀys] *nm* (*Inform*) antivirus; **antivol** *adj, nm*: **(dispositif) antivol** anti-theft device

anxieux, -euse [ɑ̃ksjø, jøz] *adj* anxious,

worried

AOC sigle f (= appellation d'origine contrôlée) label guaranteeing the quality of wine

août [u(t)] nm August

apaiser [apeze] vt (colère, douleur) to soothe; (personne) to calm (down), pacify; **s'apaiser** vi (tempête, bruit) to die down, subside; (personne) to calm down

apercevoir [apɛʀsəvwaʀ] vt to see; **s'apercevoir de** vt to notice; **s'~ que** to notice that

aperçu [apɛʀsy] nm (vue d'ensemble) general survey

apéritif [apeʀitif] nm (boisson) aperitif; (réunion) drinks pl

à-peu-près [apøpʀɛ] (péj) nm inv vague approximation

apeuré, e [apœʀe] adj frightened, scared

aphte [aft] nm mouth ulcer

apitoyer [apitwaje] vt to move to pity; **s'apitoyer (sur)** to feel pity (for)

aplatir [aplatiʀ] vt to flatten; **s'aplatir** vi to become flatter; (écrasé) to be flattened

aplomb [aplɔ̃] nm (équilibre) balance, equilibrium; (fig) self-assurance; nerve; **d'~** steady

apostrophe [apɔstʀɔf] nf (signe) apostrophe

apparaître [apaʀɛtʀ] vi to appear

appareil [apaʀɛj] nm (outil, machine) piece of apparatus, device; (électrique, ménager) appliance; (avion) (aero)plane, aircraft inv; (téléphonique) phone; (dentier) brace (BRIT), braces (US); **"qui est à l'~?"** "who's speaking?"; **dans le plus simple ~** in one's birthday suit; **appareil(-photo)** camera; **appareiller** vi (Navig) to cast off, get under way ▷ vt (assortir) to match up

apparemment [apaʀamã] adv apparently

apparence [apaʀɑ̃s] nf appearance; **en ~** apparently

apparent, e [apaʀã, ɑ̃t] adj visible; (évident) obvious; (superficiel) apparent

apparenté, e [apaʀɑ̃te] adj: **~ à** related to; (fig) similar to

apparition [apaʀisjɔ̃] nf appearance; (surnaturelle) apparition

appartement [apaʀtəmã] nm flat (BRIT), apartment (US)

appartenir [apaʀtəniʀ]: **~ à** vt to belong to; **il lui appartient de** it is his duty to

apparu, e [apaʀy] pp de **apparaître**

appât [apɑ] nm (Pêche) bait; (fig) lure, bait

appel [apɛl] nm call; (nominal) roll call; (: Scol) register; (Mil: recrutement) call-up; **faire ~ à** (invoquer) to appeal to; (avoir recours à) to call on; (nécessiter) to call for, require; **faire ou interjeter ~** (Jur) to appeal; **faire l'~** to call the roll; (Scol) to call the register; **sans ~** (fig) final, irrevocable; **faire un ~ de phares** to flash one's headlights; **appel d'offres** (Comm) invitation to tender; **appel (téléphonique)** (tele)phone call

appelé [ap(ə)le] nm (Mil) conscript

appeler [ap(ə)le] vt to call; (faire venir: médecin etc) to call, send for; **s'appeler** vi: **elle s'appelle Gabrielle** her name is Gabrielle, she's called Gabrielle; **comment vous appelez-vous?** what's your name?; **comment ça s'appelle?** what is it called?; **être appelé à** (fig) to be destined to

appendicite [apɑ̃disit] nf appendicitis

appesantir [apəzɑ̃tiʀ]: **s'appesantir** vi to grow heavier; **s'~ sur** (fig) to dwell on

appétissant, e [apetisɑ̃, ɑ̃t] adj appetizing, mouth-watering

appétit [apeti] nm appetite; **bon ~!** enjoy your meal!

applaudir [aplodiʀ] vt to applaud ▷ vi to applaud, clap; **applaudissements** nmpl applause sg, clapping sg

application [aplikasjɔ̃] nf application

appliquer [aplike] vt to apply; (loi) to enforce; **s'appliquer** vi (élève etc) to apply o.s.; **s'~ à** to apply to

appoint [apwɛ̃] nm (extra) contribution ou help; **avoir/faire l'~** to have/give the right change ou money; **chauffage d'~** extra heating

apporter [apɔʀte] vt to bring

appréciable [apʀesjabl] adj appreciable

apprécier [apʀesje] vt to appreciate; (évaluer) to estimate, assess

appréhender [apʀeɑ̃de] vt (craindre) to dread; (arrêter) to apprehend

apprendre [apʀɑ̃dʀ] vt to learn; (événement, résultats) to learn of, hear of; **~ qch à qn** (informer) to tell sb (of) sth; (enseigner) to teach sb sth; **~ à faire qch** to learn to do sth; **~ à qn à faire qch** to teach sb to do sth; **apprenti, e** nm/f apprentice; **apprentissage** nm learning; (Comm, Scol: période) apprenticeship

apprêter [apʀete] vt: **s'~ à faire qch** to get ready to do sth

appris, e [apʀi, iz] pp de **apprendre**

apprivoiser [apʀivwaze] vt to tame

approbation [apʀɔbasjɔ̃] nf approval

approcher [apʀɔʃe] vi to approach, come near ▷ vt to approach; (rapprocher): **~ qch (de qch)** to bring ou put sth near (to sth); **s'approcher de** to approach, go ou come near to; **~ de** (lieu, but) to draw near to; (quantité, moment) to approach

approfondir [apʀɔfɔ̃diʀ] vt to deepen; (question) to go further into

approprié, e [apʀɔpʀije] adj: **~ (à)** appropriate (to), suited to

approprier [apʀɔpʀije]: **s'approprier** vt to appropriate, take over; **s'~ en** to stock up with

a

approuver [apʀuve] vt to agree with; (trouver louable) to approve of

approvisionner [apʀɔvizjɔne] vt to supply; (compte bancaire) to pay funds into; **s'approvisionner en** to stock up with

approximatif, -ive [apʀɔksimatif, iv] adj approximate, rough; (termes) vague

appt abr = **appartement**

appui [apɥi] nm support; **prendre ~ sur** to lean on; (objet) to rest on; **l'~ de la fenêtre** the windowsill, the window ledge

appuyer [apɥije] vt (poser): **~ qch sur/contre** to lean ou rest sth on/against; (soutenir: personne, demande) to support, back (up) ▷ vi: **~ sur** (bouton) to press, push; (mot, détail) to stress, emphasize; **~ sur le frein** to brake, to apply the brakes; **s'appuyer sur** to lean on; (fig: compter sur) to rely on

après [apʀɛ] prép after ▷ adv afterwards; **2 heures ~** 2 hours later; **~ qu'il est** ou **soit parti** after he left; **~ avoir fait** after having done; **d'~** (selon) according to; **~ coup** after the event, afterwards; **~ tout** (au fond) after all; **et (puis) ~?** so what?; **après-demain** adv the day after tomorrow; **après-midi** nm ou nf inv afternoon; **après-rasage** nm inv aftershave; **après-shampooing** nm inv conditioner; **après-ski** nm inv snow boot

après-soleil [apʀɛsɔlej] adj inv after-sun cpd ▷ nm after-sun cream ou lotion

apte [apt] adj capable; **~ à qch/faire qch** capable of sth/doing sth; **~ (au service)** (Mil) fit (for service)

aquarelle [akwaʀɛl] nf watercolour

aquarium [akwaʀjɔm] nm aquarium

arabe [aʀab] adj Arabic; (désert, cheval) Arabian; (nation, peuple) Arab ▷ nm/f: **A~** Arab ▷ nm (Ling) Arabic

Arabie [aʀabi] nf: **l'~ (Saoudite)** Saudi Arabia

arachide [aʀaʃid] nf (plante) groundnut (plant); (graine) peanut, groundnut

araignée [aʀeɲe] nf spider

arbitraire [aʀbitʀɛʀ] adj arbitrary

arbitre [aʀbitʀ] nm (Sport) referee; (: Tennis, Cricket) umpire; (fig) arbiter, judge; (Jur) arbitrator; **arbitrer** vt to referee; to umpire; to arbitrate

arbre [aʀbʀ] nm tree; (Tech) shaft

arbuste [aʀbyst] nm small shrub

arc [aʀk] nm (arme) bow; (Géom) arc; (Archit) arch; **en ~ de cercle** semi-circular

arcade [aʀkad] nf arch(way); **arcades** nfpl (série) arcade sg, arches

arc-en-ciel [aʀkɑ̃sjɛl] nm rainbow

arche [aʀʃ] nf arch; **arche de Noé** Noah's Ark

archéologie [aʀkeɔlɔʒi] nf arch(a)eology; **archéologue** nm/f arch(a)eologist

archet [aʀʃɛ] nm bow

archipel [aʀʃipɛl] nm archipelago

architecte [aʀʃitɛkt] nm architect

architecture [aʀʃitɛktyʀ] nf architecture

archives [aʀʃiv] nfpl (collection) archives

arctique [aʀktik] adj Arctic ▷ nm: **l'A~** the Arctic

ardent, e [aʀdɑ̃, ɑ̃t] adj (soleil) blazing; (amour) ardent, passionate; (prière) fervent

ardoise [aʀdwaz] nf slate

ardu, e [aʀdy] adj (travail) arduous; (problème) difficult

arène [aʀɛn] nf arena; **arènes** nfpl (amphithéâtre) bull-ring sg

arête [aʀɛt] nf (de poisson) bone; (d'une montagne) ridge

argent [aʀʒɑ̃] nm (métal) silver; (monnaie) money; **argent de poche** pocket money; **argent liquide** ready money, (ready) cash; **argenterie** nf silverware

argentin, e [aʀʒɑ̃tɛ̃, in] adj Argentinian ▷ nm/f: **A~, e** Argentinian

Argentine [aʀʒɑ̃tin] nf: **l'~** Argentina

argentique [aʀʒɑ̃tik] adj (appareil-photo) film cpd

argile [aʀʒil] nf clay

argot [aʀgo] nm slang; **argotique** adj slang cpd; (très familier) slangy

argument [aʀgymɑ̃] nm argument

argumenter [aʀgymɑ̃te] vi to argue

aride [aʀid] adj arid

aristocratie [aʀistɔkʀasi] nf aristocracy; **aristocratique** adj aristocratic

arithmétique [aʀitmetik] adj arithmetic(al) ▷ nf arithmetic

arme [aʀm] nf weapon; **armes** nfpl (armement) weapons, arms; (blason) (coat of) arms; **~s de destruction massive** weapons of mass destruction; **arme à feu** firearm

armée [aʀme] nf army; **armée de l'air** Air Force; **armée de terre** Army

armer [aʀme] vt to arm; (arme à feu) to cock; (appareil-photo) to wind on; **~ qch de** to reinforce sth with; **s'armer de** to arm o.s. with

armistice [aʀmistis] nm armistice; **l'A~** ≈ Remembrance (BRIT) ou Veterans (US) Day

armoire [aʀmwaʀ] nf (tall) cupboard; (penderie) wardrobe (BRIT), closet (US)

armure [aʀmyʀ] nf armour no pl, suit of armour; **armurier** nm gunsmith

arnaque [aʀnak] (fam) nf swindling; **c'est de l'~** it's a rip-off; **arnaquer** (fam) vt to swindle

arobase [aʀobaz] nf (symbole) at symbol; **"paul ~ société point fr"** "paul at société dot fr"

aromates [aʀɔmat] nmpl seasoning sg, herbs (and spices)

aromathérapie [aʀɔmateʀapi] nf aromatherapy

aromatisé, e [aʀɔmatize] adj flavoured

arôme [aʀom] nm aroma

arracher [aʀaʃe] vt to pull out; (page etc) to tear off, tear out; (légumes, herbe) to pull up; (bras etc) to tear off; **s'arracher** vt (article recherché) to fight over; **~ qch à qn** to snatch sth from sb; (fig) to wring sth out of sb

arrangement [aʀɑ̃ʒmɑ̃] nm agreement, arrangement

arranger [aʀɑ̃ʒe] vt (gén) to arrange; (réparer) to fix, put right; (régler: différend) to settle, sort out; (convenir à) to suit, be convenient for; **cela m'arrange** that suits me (fine); **s'arranger** vi (se mettre d'accord) to come to an agreement; **je vais m'~** I'll manage; **ça va s'~** it'll sort itself out

arrestation [aʀɛstasjɔ̃] nf arrest

arrêt [aʀɛ] nm stopping; (de bus etc) stop; (Jur) judgment, decision; **à l'~** stationary; **tomber en ~ devant** to stop short in front of; **sans ~** (sans interruption) non-stop; (très fréquemment) continually; **arrêt de travail** stoppage (of work)

arrêter [aʀete] vt to stop; (chauffage etc) to turn off, switch off; (fixer: date etc) to appoint, decide on; (criminel, suspect) to arrest; **s'arrêter** vi to stop; **~ de faire** to stop doing; **arrêtez-vous ici/au coin, s'il vous plaît** could you stop here/at the corner, please?

arrhes [aʀ] nfpl deposit sg

arrière [aʀjɛʀ] nm back; (Sport) fullback ▷ adj inv: **siège/roue ~** back ou rear seat/wheel; **à l'~** behind, at the back; **en ~** behind; (regarder) back, behind; (tomber, aller) backwards; **arrière-goût** nm aftertaste; **arrière-grand-mère** nf great-grandmother; **arrière-grand-père** nm great-grandfather; **arrière-pays** nm inv hinterland; **arrière-pensée** nf ulterior motive; mental reservation; **arrière-plan** nm background; **à l'arrière-plan** in the background; **arrière-saison** nf late autumn

arrimer [aʀime] vt to secure; (cargaison) to stow

arrivage [aʀivaʒ] nm consignment

arrivée [aʀive] nf arrival; (ligne d'arrivée) finish

arriver [aʀive] vi to arrive; (survenir) to happen, occur; **il arrive à Paris à 8h** he gets to ou arrives in Paris at 8; **à quelle heure arrive le train de Lyon?** what time does the train from Lyons get in?; **~ à** (atteindre) to reach; **~ à faire qch** to succeed in doing sth; **en ~ à** (finir par) to come to; **il arrive que** it happens that; **il lui arrive de faire** he sometimes does

arrobase [aʀɔbaz] nf (Inform) @, 'at' sign

arrogance [aʀɔgɑ̃s] nf arrogance

arrogant, e [aʀɔgɑ̃, ɑ̃t] adj arrogant

arrondissement [aʀɔ̃dismɑ̃] nm (Admin) ≈ district

arroser [aʀoze] vt to water; (victoire) to celebrate (over a drink); (Culin) to baste; **arrosoir** nm watering can

arsenal, -aux [aʀsənal, o] nm (Navig) naval dockyard; (Mil) arsenal; (fig) gear, paraphernalia

art [aʀ] nm art

artère [aʀtɛʀ] nf (Anat) artery; (rue) main road

arthrite [aʀtʀit] nf arthritis

artichaut [aʀtiʃo] nm artichoke

article [aʀtikl] nm article; (Comm) item, article; **à l'~ de la mort** at the point of death

articulation [aʀtikylasjɔ̃] nf articulation; (Anat) joint

articuler [aʀtikyle] vt to articulate

artificiel, le [aʀtifisjɛl] adj artificial

artisan [aʀtizɑ̃] nm artisan, (self-employed) craftsman; **artisanal, e, -aux** adj of ou made by craftsmen; (péj) cottage industry cpd; **de fabrication artisanale** home-made; **artisanat** nm arts and crafts pl

artiste [aʀtist] nm/f artist; (de variétés) entertainer; (musicien etc) performer; **artistique** adj artistic

as¹ [a] vb voir **avoir**

as² [ɑs] nm ace

ascenseur [asɑ̃sœʀ] nm lift (BRIT), elevator (US)

ascension [asɑ̃sjɔ̃] nf ascent; (de montagne) climb; **l'A~** (Rel) the Ascension

● **ASCENSION**
●
● The **fête de l'Ascension** is a public holiday
● in France. It always falls on a Thursday,
● usually in May. Many French people take
● the following Friday off work too and enjoy
● a long weekend.

asiatique [azjatik] adj Asiatic, Asian ▷ nm/f: **A~** Asian

Asie [azi] nf: **l'~** Asia

asile [azil] nm (refuge) refuge, sanctuary; (Pol): **droit d'~** (political) asylum

aspect [aspɛ] nm appearance, look; (fig) aspect, side; **à l'~ de** at the sight of

asperge [aspɛʀʒ] nf asparagus no pl

asperger [aspɛʀʒe] vt to spray, sprinkle

asphalte [asfalt] nm asphalt

asphyxier [asfiksje] vt to suffocate, asphyxiate; (fig) to stifle

aspirateur [aspiʀatœʀ] nm vacuum cleaner; **passer l'~** to vacuum

aspirer [aspiʀe] vt (air) to inhale; (liquide) to suck (up); (suj: appareil) to suck up; **~ à** to aspire to

aspirine [aspiʀin] nf aspirin

assagir [asaʒiʀ]: **s'assagir** vi to quieten down, settle down

assaisonnement [asɛzɔnmɑ̃] nm seasoning

assaisonner [asɛzɔne] vt to season

assassin [asasɛ̃] nm murderer; assassin;

assassiner vt to murder; (esp Pol) to assassinate

assaut [aso] nm assault, attack; **prendre d'~** to storm, assault; **donner l'~ à** to attack

assécher [aseʃe] vt to drain

assemblage [asɑ̃blaʒ] nm (action) assembling; (de couleurs, choses) collection

assemblée [asɑ̃ble] nf (réunion) meeting; (assistance) gathering; (Pol) assembly; **l'A~ nationale** the National Assembly (the lower house of the French Parliament)

assembler [asɑ̃ble] vt (joindre, monter) to assemble, put together; (amasser) to gather (together), collect (together); **s'assembler** vi to gather

asseoir [aswaʀ] vt (malade, bébé) to sit up; (personne debout) to sit down; (autorité, réputation) to establish; **s'asseoir** vi to sit (o.s.) down

assez [ase] adv (suffisamment) enough, sufficiently; (passablement) rather, quite, fairly; **~ de pain/livres** enough ou sufficient bread/ books; **vous en avez ~?** have you got enough?; **j'en ai ~!** I've had enough!

assidu, e [asidy] adj (appliqué) assiduous, painstaking; (ponctuel) regular

assied etc [asje] vb voir **asseoir**

assiérai etc [asjeʀe] vb voir **asseoir**

assiette [asjɛt] nf plate; (contenu) plate(ful); **il n'est pas dans son ~** he's not feeling quite himself; **assiette à dessert** dessert plate; **assiette anglaise** assorted cold meats; **assiette creuse** (soup) dish, soup plate; **assiette plate** (dinner) plate

assimiler [asimile] vt to assimilate, absorb; (comparer): **~ qch/qn à** to liken ou compare sth/sb to; **s'assimiler** vr (s'intégrer) to be assimilated, assimilate

assis, e [asi, iz] pp de **asseoir** ▷ adj sitting (down), seated

assistance [asistɑ̃s] nf (public) audience; (aide) assistance; **enfant de l'A~ publique** child in care

assistant, e [asistɑ̃, ɑ̃t] nm/f assistant; (d'université) probationary lecturer; **assistant(e) social(e)** social worker

assisté, e [asiste] adj (Auto) power assisted; **~ par ordinateur** computer-assisted; **direction ~e** power steering

assister [asiste] vt (aider) to assist; **~ à** (scène, événement) to witness; (conférence, séminaire) to attend, be at; (spectacle, match) to be at, see

association [asɔsjasjɔ̃] nf association

associé, e [asɔsje] nm/f associate; (Comm) partner

associer [asɔsje] vt to associate; **s'associer** vi to join together; **s'~ à qn pour faire** to join (forces) with sb to do; **s'~ à** (couleurs, qualités) to be combined with; (opinions, joie de qn) to

share in; **~ qn à** (profits) to give sb a share of; (affaire) to make sb a partner in; (joie, triomphe) to include sb in; **~ qch à** (allier à) to combine sth with

assoiffé, e [aswafe] adj thirsty

assommer [asɔme] vt (étourdir, abrutir) to knock out, stun

Assomption [asɔ̃psjɔ̃] nf: **l'~** the Assumption

assorti, e [asɔʀti] adj matched, matching; (varié) assorted; **~ à** matching; **assortiment** nm assortment, selection

assortir [asɔʀtiʀ] vt to match; **~ qch à** to match sth with; **~ qch de** to accompany sth with

assouplir [asupliʀ] vt to make supple; (fig) to relax; **assouplissant** nm (fabric) softener

assumer [asyme] vt (fonction, emploi) to assume, take on

assurance [asyʀɑ̃s] nf (certitude) assurance; (confiance en soi) (self-)confidence; (contrat) insurance (policy); (secteur commercial) insurance; **assurance au tiers** third-party insurance; **assurance maladie** health insurance; **assurance tous risques** (Auto) comprehensive insurance; **assurances sociales** ≈ National Insurance (BRIT), ≈ Social Security (US); **assurance-vie** nf life assurance ou insurance

assuré, e [asyʀe] adj (certain: réussite, échec) certain, sure; (air) assured; (pas) steady ▷ nm/f insured (person); **assurément** adv assuredly, most certainly

assurer [asyʀe] vt (Finance) to insure; (victoire etc) to ensure; (frontières, pouvoir) to make secure; (service) to provide, operate; **s'assurer (contre)** (Comm) to insure o.s. (against); **s'~ de/que** (vérifier) to make sure of/that; **s'~ (de)** (aide de qn) to secure; **~ à qn que** to assure sb that; **~ qn de** to assure sb of

asthmatique [asmatik] adj, nm/f asthmatic

asthme [asm] nm asthma

asticot [astiko] nm maggot

astre [astʀ] nm star

astrologie [astʀɔlɔʒi] nf astrology

astronaute [astʀonot] nm/f astronaut

astronomie [astʀɔnɔmi] nf astronomy

astuce [astys] nf shrewdness, astuteness; (truc) trick, clever way; **astucieux, -euse** adj clever

atelier [atəlje] nm workshop; (de peintre) studio

athée [ate] adj atheistic ▷ nm/f atheist

Athènes [atɛn] n Athens

athlète [atlɛt] nm/f (Sport) athlete; **athlétisme** nm athletics sg

atlantique [atlɑ̃tik] adj Atlantic ▷ nm: **l'(océan) A~** the Atlantic (Ocean)

atlas [atlɑs] nm atlas

atmosphère [atmɔsfɛʀ] nf atmosphere

atome [atom] nm atom; **atomique** adj atomic, nuclear

atomiseur [atɔmizœʀ] nm atomizer

atout [atu] nm trump; (fig) asset

atroce [atʀɔs] adj atrocious

attachant, e [ataʃɑ̃, ɑ̃t] adj engaging, lovable, likeable

attache [ataʃ] nf clip, fastener; (fig) tie

attacher [ataʃe] vt to tie up; (étiquette) to attach, tie on; (ceinture) to fasten ▷ vi (poêle, riz) to stick; **s'attacher à** (par affection) to become attached to; **~ qch à** to tie ou attach sth to

attaque [atak] nf attack; (cérébrale) stroke; (d'épilepsie) fit

attaquer [atake] vt to attack ▷ vi to attack; **s'attaquer à** vt (personne) to attack; (problème) to tackle; **~ qn en justice** to bring an action against sb, sue sb

attarder [ataʀde]: **s'attarder** vi to linger

atteindre [atɛ̃dʀ] vt to reach; (blesser) to hit; (émouvoir) to affect; **atteint, e** adj (Méd): **être atteint de** to be suffering from; **atteinte** nf: **hors d'atteinte** out of reach; **porter atteinte à** to strike a blow at

attendant [atɑ̃dɑ̃] adv: **en ~** meanwhile, in the meantime

attendre [atɑ̃dʀ] vt (gén) to wait for; (être destiné ou réservé à) to await, be in store for ▷ vi to wait; **s'attendre à (ce que)** to expect (that); **attendez-moi, s'il vous plaît** wait for me, please; **~ un enfant** to be expecting a baby; **~ de faire/d'être** to wait until one does/is; **attendez qu'il vienne** wait until he comes; **~ qch de** to expect sth of

Attention à ne pas traduire *attendre* par *to attend*.

attendrir [atɑ̃dʀiʀ] vt to move (to pity); (viande) to tenderize

attendu, e [atɑ̃dy] adj (visiteur) expected; (événement) long-awaited; **~ que** considering that, since

attentat [atɑ̃ta] nm assassination attempt; **attentat à la pudeur** indecent assault no pl; **attentat suicide** suicide bombing

attente [atɑ̃t] nf wait; (espérance) expectation

attenter [atɑ̃te]: **~ à** vt (liberté) to violate; **~ à la vie de qn** to make an attempt on sb's life

attentif, -ive [atɑ̃tif, iv] adj (auditeur) attentive; (examen) careful; **~ à** careful to

attention [atɑ̃sjɔ̃] nf attention; (prévenance) attention, thoughtfulness no pl; **à l'~ de** for the attention of; **faire ~ (à)** to be careful (of); **faire ~ (à ce) que** to be ou make sure that; **~!** careful!, watch out!; **~ à la voiture!** watch out for that car!; **attentionné, e** adj thoughtful, considerate

atténuer [atenɥe] vt (douleur) to alleviate, ease; (couleurs) to soften; **s'atténuer** vi to ease; (violence etc) to abate

atterrir [ateʀiʀ] vi to land; **atterrissage** nm landing

attestation [atɛstasjɔ̃] nf certificate

attirant, e [atiʀɑ̃, ɑ̃t] adj attractive, appealing

attirer [atiʀe] vt to attract; (appâter) to lure, entice; **~ qn dans un coin/vers soi** to draw sb into a corner/towards one; **~ l'attention de qn** to attract sb's attention; **~ l'attention de qn sur** to draw sb's attention to; **s'~ des ennuis** to bring trouble upon o.s., get into trouble

attitude [atityd] nf attitude; (position du corps) bearing

attraction [atʀaksjɔ̃] nf (gén) attraction; (de cabaret, cirque) number

attrait [atʀɛ] nm appeal, attraction

attraper [atʀape] vt (gén) to catch; (habitude, amende) to get, pick up; (fam: duper) to con; **se faire ~** (fam) to be told off

attrayant, e [atʀɛjɑ̃, ɑ̃t] adj attractive

attribuer [atʀibɥe] vt (prix) to award; (rôle, tâche) to allocate, assign; (imputer): **~ qch à** to attribute sth to; **s'attribuer** vt (s'approprier) to claim for o.s.

attrister [atʀiste] vt to sadden

attroupement [atʀupmɑ̃] nm crowd

attrouper [atʀupe]: **s'attrouper** vi to gather

au [o] prép + dét = **à +le**

aubaine [obɛn] nf godsend

aube [ob] nf dawn, daybreak; **à l'~** at dawn ou daybreak

aubépine [obepin] nf hawthorn

auberge [obɛʀʒ] nf inn; **auberge de jeunesse** youth hostel

aubergine [obɛʀʒin] nf aubergine

aucun, e [okœ̃, yn] dét no, tournure négative +any; (positif) any ▷ pron none, tournure négative +any; any(one); **sans ~ doute** without any doubt; **plus qu'~ autre** more than any other; **il le fera mieux qu'~ de nous** he'll do it better than any of us; **~ des deux** neither of the two; **~ d'entre eux** none of them

audace [odas] nf daring, boldness; (péj) audacity; **audacieux, -euse** adj daring, bold

au-delà [od(ə)la] adv beyond ▷ nm: **l'~** the hereafter; **~ de** beyond

au-dessous [odsu] adv underneath; below;

~ de under(neath), below; (*limite, somme etc*) below, under; (*dignité, condition*) below
au-dessus [odsy] *adv* above; **~ de** above
au-devant [od(ə)vã]: **~ de** *prép*: **aller ~ de** (*personne, danger*) to go (out) and meet; (*souhaits de qn*) to anticipate
audience [odjãs] *nf* audience; (*Jur: séance*) hearing
audiovisuel, le [odjovizɥel] *adj* audiovisual
audition [odisjõ] *nf* (*ouïe, écoute*) hearing; (*Jur: de témoins*) examination; (*Mus, Théâtre: épreuve*) audition
auditoire [oditwaʀ] *nm* audience
augmentation [ɔgmãtasjõ] *nf* increase; **augmentation (de salaire)** rise (in salary) (*BRIT*), (pay) raise (*US*)
augmenter [ɔgmãte] *vt* (*gén*) to increase; (*salaire, prix*) to increase, raise, put up; (*employé*) to increase the salary of ▷ *vi* to increase
augure [ogyʀ] *nm*: **de bon/mauvais ~** of good/ill omen
aujourd'hui [oʒuʀdɥi] *adv* today
aumône [omon] *nf inv* alms *sg*; **aumônier** *nm* chaplain
auparavant [opaʀavã] *adv* before(hand)
auprès [opʀe]: **~ de** *prép* next to, close to; (*recourir, s'adresser*) to; (*en comparaison de*) compared with
auquel [okel] *prép + pron* = **à + lequel**
aurai *etc* [ɔʀe] *vb voir* **avoir**
aurons *etc* [ɔʀõ] *vb voir* **avoir**
aurore [ɔʀɔʀ] *nf* dawn, daybreak
ausculter [ɔskylte] *vt* to sound (the chest of)
aussi [osi] *adv* (*également*) also, too; (*de comparaison*) as ▷ *conj* therefore, consequently; **~ fort que** as strong as; **moi ~** me too
aussitôt [osito] *adv* straight away, immediately; **~ que** as soon as
austère [ostɛʀ] *adj* austere
austral, e [ɔstʀal] *adj* southern
Australie [ɔstʀali] *nf*: **l'~** Australia; **australien, ne** *adj* Australian ▷ *nm/f*: **Australien, ne** Australian
autant [otã] *adv* (*intensité*) so much; **je ne savais pas que tu la détestais ~** I didn't know you hated her so much; (*comparatif*): **~ (que)** as much (as); (*nombre*) as many (as); **~ (de)** so much (*ou* many); as much (*ou* many); **~ partir** we (*ou* you *etc*) may as well leave; **~ dire que ...** one might as well say that ...; **pour ~** for all that; **d'~ plus/mieux (que)** all the more/the better (since)
autel [otɛl] *nm* altar
auteur [otœʀ] *nm* author
authentique [otãtik] *adj* authentic, genuine
auto [oto] *nf* car
auto...: **autobiographie** *nf* autobiography;

autobronzant *nm* self-tanning cream (*or* lotion *etc*); **autobus** *nm* bus; **autocar** *nm* coach
autochtone [otɔktɔn] *nm/f* native
auto...: **autocollant, e** *adj* self-adhesive; (*enveloppe*) self-seal ▷ *nm* sticker; **autocuiseur** *nm* pressure cooker; **autodéfense** *nf* self-defence; **autodidacte** *nm/f* self-taught person; **auto-école** *nf* driving school; **autographe** *nm* autograph
automate [ɔtɔmat] *nm* (*machine*) (automatic) machine
automatique [ɔtɔmatik] *adj* automatic ▷ *nm*: **l'~** direct dialling
automne [ɔtɔn] *nm* autumn (*BRIT*), fall (*US*)
automobile [ɔtɔmɔbil] *adj* motor *cpd*, car *cpd* ▷ *nf* (motor) car; **automobiliste** *nm/f* motorist
autonome [ɔtɔnɔm] *adj* autonomous; **autonomie** *nf* autonomy; (*Pol*) self-government, autonomy
autopsie [ɔtɔpsi] *nf* post-mortem (examination), autopsy
autoradio [otoʀadjo] *nm* car radio
autorisation [ɔtɔʀizasjõ] *nf* permission, authorization; (*papiers*) permit
autorisé, e [ɔtɔʀize] *adj* (*opinion, sources*) authoritative
autoriser [ɔtɔʀize] *vt* to give permission for, authorize; (*fig*) to allow (of)
autoritaire [ɔtɔʀitɛʀ] *adj* authoritarian
autorité [ɔtɔʀite] *nf* authority; **faire ~** to be authoritative; **les ~s** the authorities
autoroute [otoʀut] *nf* motorway (*BRIT*), highway (*US*); **~ de l'information** (*Inform*) information superhighway

⬤ **AUTOROUTE**

- Motorways in France, indicated by blue
- road signs with the letter A followed by a
- number, are toll roads. The speed limit is
- 130 km/h (110 km/h when it is raining). At
- the tollgate, the lanes marked 'réservé' and
- with an orange 't' are reserved for people
- who subscribe to 'télépéage', an electronic
- payment system.

auto-stop [otostɔp] *nm*: **faire de l'~** to hitch-hike; **prendre qn en ~** to give sb a lift; **auto-stoppeur, -euse** *nm/f* hitch-hiker
autour [otuʀ] *adv* around; **~ de** around; **tout ~** all around

⬤ **MOT-CLÉ**

autre [otʀ] *adj* **1** (*différent*) other, different; **je préférerais un autre verre** I'd prefer another *ou* a different glass

2 (*supplémentaire*) other; **je voudrais un autre verre d'eau** I'd like another glass of water **3**: **autre chose** something else; **autre part** somewhere else; **d'autre part** on the other hand
▷ *pron*: **un autre** another (one); **nous/vous autres** us/you; **d'autres** others; **l'autre** the other (one); **les autres** the others; (*autrui*) others; **l'un et l'autre** both of them; **se détester l'un l'autre/les uns les autres** to hate each other *ou* one another; **d'une semaine à l'autre** from one week to the next; (*incessamment*) any week now; **entre autres** (*personnes*) among others; (*choses*) among other things

autrefois [otʀəfwa] *adv* in the past
autrement [otʀəmɑ̃] *adv* differently; (*d'une manière différente*) in another way; (*sinon*) otherwise; **~ dit** in other words
Autriche [otʀiʃ] *nf*: **l'~** Austria; **autrichien, ne** *adj* Austrian ▷ *nm/f*: **Autrichien, ne** Austrian
autruche [otʀyʃ] *nf* ostrich
aux [o] *prép +dét* = **à +les**
auxiliaire [ɔksiljɛʀ] *adj, nm/f* auxiliary
auxquelles [okɛl] *prép +pron* = **à +lesquelles**
auxquels [okɛl] *prép +pron* = **à +lesquels**
avalanche [avalɑ̃ʃ] *nf* avalanche
avaler [avale] *vt* to swallow
avance [avɑ̃s] *nf* (*de troupes etc*) advance; progress; (*d'argent*) advance; (*sur un concurrent*) lead; **avances** *nfpl* (*amoureuses*) advances; **(être) en ~** (to be) early; (*sur un programme*) (to be) ahead of schedule; **à l'~, d'~** in advance
avancé, e [avɑ̃se] *adj* advanced; (*travail*) well on, well under way
avancement [avɑ̃smɑ̃] *nm* (*professionnel*) promotion
avancer [avɑ̃se] *vi* to move forward, advance; (*projet, travail*) to make progress; (*montre, réveil*) to be fast; to gain ▷ *vt* to move forward, advance; (*argent*) to advance; (*montre, pendule*) to put forward; **s'avancer** *vi* to move forward, advance; (*fig*) to commit o.s.
avant [avɑ̃] *prép, adv* before ▷ *adj inv*: **siège/roue ~** front seat/wheel ▷ *nm* (*d'un véhicule, bâtiment*) front; (*Sport: joueur*) forward; **~ qu'il (ne) parte** before he goes *ou* leaves; **~ de partir** before leaving; **~ tout** (*surtout*) above all; **à l'~** (*dans un véhicule*) in (the) front; **en ~** (*se pencher, tomber*) forward(s); **partir en ~** to go on ahead; **en ~ de** in front of
avantage [avɑ̃taʒ] *nm* advantage; **avantages sociaux** fringe benefits; **avantager** *vt* (*favoriser*) to favour; (*embellir*) to flatter; **avantageux, -euse** *adj* (*prix*) attractive
avant...: **avant-bras** *nm inv* forearm; **avant-coureur** *adj inv*: **signe avant-coureur** advance indication *ou* sign; **avant-dernier, -ière** *adj, nm/f* next to last, last but one; **avant-goût** *nm* foretaste; **avant-hier** *adv* the day before yesterday; **avant-première** *nf* (*de film*) preview; **avant-veille** *nf*: **l'avant-veille** two days before

avare [avaʀ] *adj* miserly, avaricious ▷ *nm/f* miser; **~ de** (*compliments etc*) sparing of
avec [avɛk] *prép* with; (*à l'égard de*) to(wards), with; **et ~ ça?** (*dans magasin*) anything else?
avenir [avniʀ] *nm* future; **à l'~** in future; **politicien/métier d'~** politician/job with prospects *ou* a future
aventure [avɑ̃tyʀ] *nf* adventure; (*amoureuse*) affair; **aventureux, -euse** *adj* adventurous, venturesome; (*projet*) risky, chancy
avenue [avny] *nf* avenue
avérer [aveʀe]: **s'avérer** *vb +attrib* to prove (to be)
averse [avɛʀs] *nf* shower
averti, e [avɛʀti] *adj* (well-)informed
avertir [avɛʀtiʀ] *vt*: **~ qn (de qch/que)** to warn sb (of sth/that); (*renseigner*) to inform sb (of sth/that); **avertissement** *nm* warning; **avertisseur** *nm* horn, siren
aveu, x [avø] *nm* confession
aveugle [avœgl] *adj* blind ▷ *nm/f* blind man/woman
aviation [avjasjɔ̃] *nf* aviation; (*sport*) flying; (*Mil*) air force
avide [avid] *adj* eager; (*péj*) greedy, grasping
avion [avjɔ̃] *nm* (*aero*)plane (BRIT), (air)plane (US); **aller (quelque part) en ~** to go (somewhere) by plane, fly (somewhere); **par ~** by airmail; **avion à réaction** jet (plane)
aviron [aviʀɔ̃] *nm* oar; (*sport*): **l'~** rowing
avis [avi] *nm* opinion; (*notification*) notice; **à mon ~** in my opinion; **changer d'~** to change one's mind; **jusqu'à nouvel ~** until further notice
aviser [avize] *vt* (*informer*): **~ qn de/que** to advise *ou* inform sb of/that ▷ *vi* to think about things, assess the situation; **nous ~ons sur place** we'll work something out once we're there; **s'~ de qch/que** to become suddenly aware of sth/that; **s'~ de faire** to take it into one's head to do
avocat, e [avɔka, at] *nm/f* (*Jur*) barrister (BRIT), lawyer ▷ *nm* (*Culin*) avocado (pear); **~ de la défense** counsel for the defence; **avocat général** assistant public prosecutor
avoine [avwan] *nf* oats *pl*

🅞 **MOT-CLÉ**

avoir [avwaʀ] *nm* assets *pl*, resources *pl*; (*Comm*) credit
▷ *vt* **1** (*posséder*) to have; **elle a 2 enfants/une belle maison** she has (got) 2 children/a lovely

b

house; **il a les yeux bleus** he has (got) blue eyes; **vous avez du sel?** do you have any salt?; **avoir du courage/de la patience** to be brave/patient

2 (*âge, dimensions*) to be; **il a 3 ans** he is 3 (years old); **le mur a 3 mètres de haut** the wall is 3 metres high; *voir aussi* **faim**; **peur** *etc*

3 (*fam: duper*) to do, have; **on vous a eu!** (*dupé*) you've been done *ou* had!; (*fait une plaisanterie*) we *ou* they had you there

4: **en avoir après** *ou* **contre qn** to have a grudge against sb; **en avoir assez** to be fed up; **j'en ai pour une demi-heure** it'll take me half an hour

5 (*obtenir, attraper*) to get; **j'ai réussi à avoir mon train** I managed to get *ou* catch my train; **j'ai réussi à avoir le renseignement qu'il me fallait** I managed to get (hold of) the information I needed

6 (*éprouver*): **avoir de la peine** to be *ou* feel sad
▷ *vb aux* **1** to have; **avoir mangé/dormi** to have eaten/slept

2 (*avoir +à +infinitif*): **avoir à faire qch** to have to do sth; **vous n'avez qu'à lui demander** you only have to ask him
▷ *vb impers* **1**: **il y a** (+ *singulier*) there is; (+ *pluriel*) there are; **il y avait du café/des gâteaux** there was coffee/there were cakes; **qu'y-a-t-il?, qu'est-ce qu'il y a?** what's the matter?, what is it?; **il doit y avoir une explication** there must be an explanation; **il n'y a qu'à ...** we (*ou* you *etc*) will just have to ...; **il ne peut y en avoir qu'un** there can only be one

2 (*temporel*): **il y a 10 ans** 10 years ago; **il y a 10 ans/longtemps que je le sais** I've known it for 10 years/a long time; **il y a 10 ans qu'il est arrivé** it's 10 years since he arrived

avortement [avɔʀtəmɑ̃] *nm* abortion
avouer [avwe] *vt* (*crime, défaut*) to confess (to); **~ avoir fait/que** to admit *ou* confess to having done/that
avril [avʀil] *nm* April
axe [aks] *nm* axis; (*de roue etc*) axle; (*fig*) main line; **axe routier** main road, trunk road (*BRIT*), highway (*US*)
ayons *etc* [ɛjɔ̃] *vb voir* **avoir**

bâbord [babɔʀ] *nm*: **à ~** to port, on the port side
baby-foot [babifut] *nm* table football
bac [bak] *abr m* = **baccalauréat** ▷ *nm* (*récipient*) tub
baccalauréat [bakalɔʀea] *nm* high school diploma
bâcler [bakle] *vt* to botch (up)
baffe [baf] (*fam*) *nf* slap, clout
bafouiller [bafuje] *vi, vt* to stammer
bagage [bagaʒ] *nm* piece of luggage; (*connaissances*) background, knowledge; **nos ~s ne sont pas arrivés** our luggage hasn't arrived; **bagage à main** piece of hand-luggage
bagarre [bagaʀ] *nf* fight, brawl; **bagarrer: se bagarrer** *vi* to have a fight *ou* scuffle, fight
bagnole [baɲɔl] (*fam*) *nf* car
bague [bag] *nf* ring; **bague de fiançailles** engagement ring
baguette [bagɛt] *nf* stick; (*cuisine chinoise*) chopstick; (*de chef d'orchestre*) baton; (*pain*) stick of (French) bread; **baguette magique** magic wand
baie [bɛ] *nf* (*Géo*) bay; (*fruit*) berry; **baie (vitrée)** picture window
baignade [bɛɲad] *nf* bathing; **"~ interdite"** "no bathing"
baigner [beɲe] *vt* (*bébé*) to bath; **se baigner** *vi* to have a swim, go swimming *ou* bathing;

baignoire nf bath(tub)

bail [baj, bo] (pl **baux**) nm lease

bâiller [baje] vi to yawn; (être ouvert) to gape

bain [bɛ̃] nm bath; **prendre un ~** to have a bath; **se mettre dans le ~** (fig) to get into it ou things; **bain de bouche** mouthwash; **bain moussant** bubble bath; **bain de soleil: prendre un bain de soleil** to sunbathe; **bain-marie** nm: **faire chauffer au bain-marie** (boîte etc) to immerse in boiling water

baiser [beze] nm kiss ▷ vt (main, front) to kiss; (fam!) to screw (!)

baisse [bɛs] nf fall, drop; **être en ~** to be falling, be declining

baisser [bese] vt to lower; (radio, chauffage) to turn down ▷ vi to fall, drop, go down; (vue, santé) to fail, dwindle; **se baisser** vi to bend down

bal [bal] nm dance; (grande soirée) ball; **bal costumé** fancy-dress ball

balade [balad] (fam) nf (à pied) walk, stroll; (en voiture) drive; **balader** (fam): **se balader** vi to go for a walk ou stroll; to go for a drive; **baladeur** nm personal stereo, Walkman®

balai [balɛ] nm broom, brush

balance [balɑ̃s] nf scales pl; (signe): **la B~** Libra; **balance commerciale** balance of trade

balancer [balɑ̃se] vt to swing; (fam: lancer) to fling, chuck; (: jeter) to chuck out; **se balancer** vi to swing, rock; **se ~ de** (fam) not to care about; **balançoire** nf swing; (sur pivot) seesaw

balayer [baleje] vt (feuilles etc) to sweep up, brush up; (pièce) to sweep; (objections) to sweep aside; (suj: radar) to scan; **balayeur, -euse** nm/f roadsweeper

balbutier [balbysje] vi, vt to stammer

balcon [balkɔ̃] nm balcony; (Théâtre) dress circle; **avez-vous une chambre avec ~?** do you have a room with a balcony?

Bâle [bal] n Basle, Basel

Baléares [baleaʀ] nfpl: **les ~** the Balearic Islands, the Balearics

baleine [balɛn] nf whale

balise [baliz] nf (Navig) beacon; (marker) buoy; (Aviat) runway light, beacon; (Auto, Ski) sign, marker; **baliser** vt to mark out (with lights etc)

balle [bal] nf (de fusil) bullet; (de sport) ball; (fam: franc) franc

ballerine [bal(ə)ʀin] nf (danseuse) ballet dancer; (chaussure) ballet shoe

ballet [balɛ] nm ballet

ballon [balɔ̃] nm (de sport) ball; (jouet, Aviat) balloon; **ballon de football** football

balnéaire [balneɛʀ] adj seaside cpd; **station ~** seaside resort

balustrade [balystʀad] nf railings pl, handrail

bambin [bɑ̃bɛ̃] nm little child

bambou [bɑ̃bu] nm bamboo

banal, e [banal] adj banal, commonplace; (péj) trite; **banalité** nf banality

banane [banan] nf banana; (sac) waist-bag, bum-bag

banc [bɑ̃] nm seat, bench; (de poissons) shoal; **banc d'essai** (fig) testing ground

bancaire [bɑ̃kɛʀ] adj banking; (chèque, carte) bank cpd

bancal, e [bɑ̃kal] adj wobbly

bandage [bɑ̃daʒ] nm bandage

bande [bɑ̃d] nf (de tissu etc) strip; (Méd) bandage; (motif) stripe; (magnétique etc) tape; (groupe) band; (: péj) bunch; **faire ~ à part** to keep to o.s.; **bande dessinée** comic strip; **bande sonore** sound track

bande-annonce [bɑ̃danɔ̃s] nf trailer

bandeau, x [bɑ̃do] nm headband; (sur les yeux) blindfold

bander [bɑ̃de] vt (blessure) to bandage; **~ les yeux à qn** to blindfold sb

bandit [bɑ̃di] nm bandit

bandoulière [bɑ̃duljɛʀ] nf: **en ~** (slung ou worn) across the shoulder

Bangladesh [bɑ̃gladeʃ] nm: **le ~** Bangladesh

banlieue [bɑ̃ljø] nf suburbs pl; **lignes/quartiers de ~** suburban lines/areas; **trains de ~** commuter trains

bannir [baniʀ] vt to banish

banque [bɑ̃k] nf bank; (activités) banking; **banque de données** data bank

banquet [bɑ̃kɛ] nm dinner; (d'apparat) banquet

banquette [bɑ̃kɛt] nf seat

banquier [bɑ̃kje] nm banker

banquise [bɑ̃kiz] nf ice field

baptême [batɛm] nm christening; baptism; **baptême de l'air** first flight

baptiser [batize] vt to baptize, christen

bar [baʀ] nm bar

baraque [baʀak] nf shed; (fam) house; (dans une fête foraine) stall, booth; **baraqué, e** (fam) adj well-built, hefty

barbare [baʀbaʀ] adj barbaric

barbe [baʀb] nf beard; **la ~!** (fam) damn it!; **quelle ~!** (fam) what a drag ou bore!; **à la ~ de qn** under sb's nose; **barbe à papa** candy-floss (BRIT), cotton candy (US)

barbelé [baʀbəle] adj, nm: **(fil de fer) ~** barbed wire no pl

barbiturique [baʀbityʀik] nm barbiturate

barbouiller [baʀbuje] vt to daub; **avoir l'estomac barbouillé** to feel queasy

barbu, e [baʀby] adj bearded

barder [baʀde] (fam) vi: **ça va ~** sparks will fly, things are going to get hot

barème [baʀɛm] nm (Scol) scale; (table de référence) table

baril [baʀi(l)] nm barrel; (poudre) keg

bariolé, e [baʀjɔle] adj gaudily-coloured

baromètre [baʀɔmɛtʀ] nm barometer
baron, ne [baʀɔ̃] nm/f baron(ess)
baroque [baʀɔk] adj (Art) baroque; (fig) weird
barque [baʀk] nf small boat
barquette [baʀkɛt] nf (pour repas) tray; (pour fruits) punnet
barrage [baʀaʒ] nm dam; (sur route) roadblock, barricade
barre [baʀ] nf bar; (Navig) helm; (écrite) line, stroke
barreau, x [baʀo] nm bar; (Jur): **le ~** the Bar
barrer [baʀe] vt (route etc) to block; (mot) to cross out; (chèque) to cross (BRIT); (Navig) to steer; **se barrer** (fam) ▷ vi to clear off
barrette [baʀɛt] nf (pour cheveux) (hair) slide (BRIT) ou clip (US)
barricader [baʀikade]: **se barricader** vi to barricade o.s.
barrière [baʀjɛʀ] nf fence; (obstacle) barrier; (porte) gate
barrique [baʀik] nf barrel, cask
bar-tabac [baʀtaba] nm bar (which sells tobacco and stamps)
bas, basse [bɑ, bɑs] adj low ▷ nm bottom, lower part; (vêtement) stocking ▷ adv low; (parler) softly; **au ~ mot** at the lowest estimate; **en ~** down below; (d'une liste, d'un mur etc) at/to the bottom; (dans une maison) downstairs; **en ~ de** at the bottom of; **un enfant en ~ âge** a young child; **à ~ ...!** down with ...!
bas-côté [bɑkote] nm (de route) verge (BRIT), shoulder (US)
basculer [baskyle] vi to fall over, topple (over); (benne) to tip up ▷ vt (contenu) to tip out; (benne) to tip up
base [bɑz] nf base; (Pol) rank and file; (fondement, principe) basis; **de ~** basic; **à ~ de café** etc coffee etc -based; **base de données** database; **baser** vt to base; **se baser sur** vt (preuves) to base one's argument on
bas-fond [bɑfɔ̃] nm (Navig) shallow; **bas-fonds** nmpl (fig) dregs
basilic [bazilik] nm (Culin) basil
basket [baskɛt] nm trainer (BRIT), sneaker (US); (aussi: **~-ball**) basketball
basque [bask] adj Basque ▷ nm/f: **B~** Basque; **le Pays Basque** the Basque Country
basse [bɑs] adj voir **bas** ▷ nf (Mus) bass; **basse-cour** nf farmyard
bassin [basɛ̃] nm (pièce d'eau) pond, pool; (de fontaine,: Géo) basin; (Anat) pelvis; (portuaire) dock
bassine [basin] nf (ustensile) basin; (contenu) bowl(ful)
basson [basɔ̃] nm bassoon
bat [ba] vb voir **battre**
bataille [bataj] nf (Mil) battle; (rixe) fight; **elle avait les cheveux en ~** her hair was a mess

bateau, x [bato] nm boat, ship; **bateau-mouche** nm passenger pleasure boat (on the Seine)
bâti, e [bɑti] adj: **bien ~** well-built; **terrain ~** piece of land that has been built on
bâtiment [bɑtimɑ̃] nm building; (Navig) ship, vessel; (industrie) building trade
bâtir [bɑtiʀ] vt to build
bâtisse [bɑtis] nf building
bâton [bɑtɔ̃] nm stick; **parler à ~s rompus** to chat about this and that
bats [ba] vb voir **battre**
battement [batmɑ̃] nm (de cœur) beat; (intervalle) interval; **10 minutes de ~** 10 minutes to spare
batterie [batʀi] nf (Mil, Élec) battery; (Mus) drums pl, drum kit; **batterie de cuisine** pots and pans pl, kitchen utensils pl
batteur [batœʀ] nm (Mus) drummer; (appareil) whisk
battre [batʀ] vt to beat; (blé) to thresh; (passer au peigne fin) to scour; (cartes) to shuffle ▷ vi (cœur) to beat; (volets etc) to bang, rattle; **se battre** vi to fight; **~ la mesure** to beat time; **~ son plein** to be at its height, be going full swing; **~ des mains** to clap one's hands
baume [bom] nm balm
bavard, e [bavaʀ, aʀd] adj (very) talkative; gossipy; **bavarder** vi to chatter; (commérer) to gossip; (divulguer un secret) to blab
baver [bave] vi to dribble; (chien) to slobber; **en ~** (fam) to have a hard time (of it)
bavoir [bavwaʀ] nm bib
bavure [bavyʀ] nf smudge; (fig) hitch; (policière etc) blunder
bazar [bazaʀ] nm general store; (fam) jumble; **bazarder** (fam) vt to chuck out
BCBG sigle adj (= bon chic bon genre) preppy, smart and trendy
BD sigle f = **bande dessinée**
bd abr = **boulevard**
béant, e [beɑ̃, ɑ̃t] adj gaping
beau, bel, belle [bo, bɛl] (mpl **~x**) adj beautiful, lovely; (homme) handsome; (femme) beautiful ▷ adv: **il fait ~** the weather's fine ▷ nm: **faire le ~** (chien) to sit up and beg; **un ~ jour** one (fine) day; **de plus belle** more than ever, even more; **on a ~ essayer** however hard we try; **bel et bien** well and truly; **le plus ~ c'est que ...** the best of it is that ...

MOT-CLÉ

beaucoup [boku] adv **1** a lot; **il boit beaucoup** he drinks a lot; **il ne boit pas beaucoup** he doesn't drink much ou a lot
2 (suivi de plus, trop etc) much, a lot; **il est beaucoup plus grand** he is much ou a lot taller; **c'est beaucoup plus cher** it's a lot ou

much more expensive; **il a beaucoup plus de temps que moi** he has much *ou* a lot more time than me; **il y a beaucoup plus de touristes ici** there are a lot *ou* many more tourists here; **beaucoup trop vite** much too fast; **il fume beaucoup trop** he smokes far too much

3: **beaucoup de** (*nombre*) many, a lot of; (*quantité*) a lot of; **beaucoup d'étudiants/de touristes** a lot of *ou* many students/tourists; **beaucoup de courage** a lot of courage; **il n'a pas beaucoup d'argent** he hasn't got much *ou* at lot of money

4: **de beaucoup** by far

beau...: **beau-fils** *nm* son-in-law; (*remariage*) stepson; **beau-frère** *nm* brother-in-law; **beau-père** *nm* father-in-law; (*remariage*) stepfather
beauté [bote] *nf* beauty; **de toute ~** beautiful; **finir qch en ~** to complete sth brilliantly
beaux-arts [bozar] *nmpl* fine arts
beaux-parents [boparã] *nmpl* wife's/husband's family, in-laws
bébé [bebe] *nm* baby
bec [bɛk] *nm* beak, bill; (*de théière*) spout; (*de casserole*) lip; (*fam*) mouth; **bec de gaz** (street) gaslamp
bêche [bɛʃ] *nf* spade; **bêcher** *vt* to dig
bedaine [bədɛn] *nf* paunch
bedonnant, e [bədɔnã, ãt] *adj* potbellied
bée [be] *adj*: **bouche ~** gaping
bégayer [begeje] *vt, vi* to stammer
beige [bɛʒ] *adj* beige
beignet [bɛɲe] *nm* fritter
bel [bɛl] *adj voir* **beau**
bêler [bele] *vi* to bleat
belette [bəlɛt] *nf* weasel
belge [bɛlʒ] *adj* Belgian ▷ *nm/f*: **B~** Belgian
Belgique [bɛlʒik] *nf*: **la ~** Belgium
bélier [belje] *nm* ram; (*signe*): **le B~** Aries
belle [bɛl] *adj voir* **beau** ▷ *nf* (*Sport*): **la ~** the decider; **belle-fille** *nf* daughter-in-law; (*remariage*) stepdaughter; **belle-mère** *nf* mother-in-law; stepmother; **belle-sœur** *nf* sister-in-law
belvédère [bɛlvedɛr] *nm* panoramic viewpoint (*or small building there*)
bémol [bemɔl] *nm* (*Mus*) flat
bénédiction [benediksjɔ̃] *nf* blessing
bénéfice [benefis] *nm* (*Comm*) profit; (*avantage*) benefit; **bénéficier**: **bénéficier de** *vt* to enjoy; (*situation*) to benefit by *ou* from; **bénéfique** *adj* beneficial
Benelux [benelyks] *nm*: **le ~** Benelux, the Benelux countries
bénévole [benevɔl] *adj* voluntary, unpaid
bénin, -igne [benɛ̃, iɲ] *adj* minor, mild; (*tumeur*) benign
bénir [benir] *vt* to bless; **bénit, e** *adj*

consecrated; **eau bénite** holy water
benne [bɛn] *nf* skip; (*de téléphérique*) (cable) car; **benne à ordures** (*amovible*) skip
béquille [bekij] *nf* crutch; (*de bicyclette*) stand
berceau, x [bɛrso] *nm* cradle, crib
bercer [bɛrse] *vt* to rock, cradle; (*suj: musique etc*) to lull; **~ qn de** (*promesses etc*) to delude sb with; **berceuse** *nf* lullaby
béret [berɛ] *nm* (*aussi*: **~ basque**) beret
berge [bɛrʒ] *nf* bank
berger, -ère [bɛrʒe, ɛr] *nm/f* shepherd(-ess); **berger allemand** alsatian (*brit*), German shepherd
Berlin [bɛrlɛ̃] *n* Berlin
Bermudes [bɛrmyd] *nfpl*: **les (îles) ~** Bermuda
Berne [bɛrn(ə)] *n* Bern
berner [bɛrne] *vt* to fool
besogne [bəzɔɲ] *nf* work *no pl*, job
besoin [bəzwɛ̃] *nm* need; **avoir ~ de qch/ faire qch** to need sth/to do sth; **au ~** if need be; **le ~** (*pauvreté*) need, want; **être dans le ~** to be in need *ou* want; **faire ses ~s** to relieve o.s.
bestiole [bɛstjɔl] *nf* (tiny) creature
bétail [betaj] *nm* livestock, cattle *pl*
bête [bɛt] *nf* animal; (*bestiole*) insect, creature ▷ *adj* stupid, silly; **il cherche la petite ~** he's being pernickety *ou* over fussy; **bête noire** pet hate; **bête sauvage** wild beast *ou* animal
bêtise [betiz] *nf* stupidity; (*action*) stupid thing (to say *ou* do)
béton [betɔ̃] *nm* concrete; **(en) ~** (*alibi, argument*) cast iron; **béton armé** reinforced concrete
betterave [bɛtrav] *nf* beetroot (*brit*), beet (*us*); **betterave sucrière** sugar beet
Beur [bœr] *nm/f* person of North African origin living in France
beurre [bœr] *nm* butter; **beurrer** *vt* to butter; **beurrier** *nm* butter dish
biais [bjɛ] *nm* (*moyen*) device, expedient; (*aspect*) angle; **en ~, de ~** (*obliquement*) at an angle; **par le ~ de** by means of
bibelot [biblo] *nm* trinket, curio
biberon [bibrɔ̃] *nm* (feeding) bottle; **nourrir au ~** to bottle-feed
bible [bibl] *nf* bible
biblio... [bibl] *préfixe*: **bibliobus** *nm* mobile library van; **bibliothécaire** *nm/f* librarian; **bibliothèque** *nf* library; (*meuble*) bookcase
bic® [bik] *nm* Biro®
bicarbonate [bikarbɔnat] *nm*: **~ (de soude)** bicarbonate of soda
biceps [bisɛps] *nm* biceps
biche [biʃ] *nf* doe
bicolore [bikɔlɔr] *adj* two-coloured
bicoque [bikɔk] (*péj*) *nf* shack
bicyclette [bisiklɛt] *nf* bicycle

bidet [bidɛ] *nm* bidet
bidon [bidɔ̃] *nm* can ▷ *adj inv* (*fam*) phoney
bidonville [bidɔ̃vil] *nm* shanty town
bidule [bidyl] (*fam*) *nm* thingumajig

⊙ **MOT-CLÉ**

bien [bjɛ̃] *nm* **1** (*avantage, profit*): **faire du bien à qn** to do sb good; **dire du bien de** to speak well of; **c'est pour son bien** it's for his own good
2 (*possession, patrimoine*) possession, property; **son bien le plus précieux** his most treasured possession; **avoir du bien** to have property; **biens (de consommation** *etc*) (consumer *etc*) goods
3 (*moral*): **le bien** good; **distinguer le bien du mal** to tell good from evil
▷ *adv* **1** (*de façon satisfaisante*) well; **elle travaille/mange bien** she works/eats well; **croyant bien faire, je/il ...** thinking I/he was doing the right thing, I/he ...; **tiens-toi bien!** (*assieds-toi correctement*) sit up straight!; (*debout*) stand up straight!; (*sois sage*) behave yourself!; (*prépare-toi*) wait for it!; **c'est bien fait!** it serves him (*ou* her *etc*) right!
2 (*valeur intensive*) quite; **bien jeune** quite young; **bien assez** quite enough; **bien mieux** (very) much better; **j'espère bien y aller** I do hope to go; **je veux bien le faire** (*concession*) I'm quite willing to do it; **il faut bien le faire** it has to be done; **Paul est bien venu, n'est-ce pas?** Paul did come, didn't he?; **où peut-il bien être passé?** where can he have got to?
3 (*beaucoup*): **bien du temps/des gens** quite a time/a number of people
4 (*au moins*) at least; **cela fait bien deux ans que je ne l'ai pas vu** I haven't seen him for at least *ou* a good two years
▷ *adj inv* **1** (*en bonne forme, à l'aise*): **je me sens bien** I feel fine; **je ne me sens pas bien** I don't feel well; **on est bien dans ce fauteuil** this chair is very comfortable
2 (*joli, beau*) good-looking; **tu es bien dans cette robe** you look good in that dress
3 (*satisfaisant*) good; **elle est bien, cette maison/secrétaire** it's a good house/she's a good secretary; **c'est bien?** is that *ou* it O.K.?; **c'est très bien (comme ça)** it's fine (like that)
4 (*moralement*) right; (: *personne*) good, nice; (*respectable*) respectable; **ce n'est pas bien de ...** it's not right to ...; **elle est bien, cette femme** she's a nice woman, she's a good sort; **des gens bien** respectable people
5 (*en bons termes*): **être bien avec qn** to be on good terms with sb
▷ *préfixe*: **bien-aimé, e** *adj, nm/f* beloved; **bien-être** *nm* well-being; **bienfaisance** *nf* charity; **bienfait** *nm* act of generosity, benefaction;

(*de la science etc*) benefit; **bienfaiteur, -trice** *nm/f* benefactor/benefactress; **bien-fondé** *nm* soundness; **bien que** *conj* (al)though; **bien sûr** *adv* certainly

bientôt [bjɛ̃to] *adv* soon; **à ~** see you soon
bienveillant, e [bjɛ̃vejɑ̃, ɑ̃t] *adj* kindly
bienvenu, e [bjɛ̃vəny] *adj* welcome; **bienvenue** *nf*: **souhaiter la bienvenue à** to welcome; **bienvenue à** welcome to
bière [bjɛʀ] *nf* (*boisson*) beer; (*cercueil*) bier; **bière blonde** lager; **bière brune** brown ale (*BRIT*), dark beer (*US*); **bière (à la) pression** draught beer
bifteck [biftɛk] *nm* steak
bigorneau, x [bigɔʀno] *nm* winkle
bigoudi [bigudi] *nm* curler
bijou, x [biʒu] *nm* jewel; **bijouterie** *nf* jeweller's (shop); **bijoutier, -ière** *nm/f* jeweller
bikini [bikini] *nm* bikini
bilan [bilɑ̃] *nm* (*fig*) (net) outcome; (: *de victimes*) toll; (*Comm*) balance sheet(s); **un ~ de santé** a (medical) checkup; **faire le ~ de** to assess, review; **déposer son ~** to file a bankruptcy statement
bile [bil] *nf* bile; **se faire de la ~** (*fam*) to worry o.s. sick
bilieux, -euse [biljø, øz] *adj* bilious; (*fig: colérique*) testy
bilingue [bilɛ̃g] *adj* bilingual
billard [bijaʀ] *nm* (*jeu*) billiards *sg*; (*table*) billiard table
bille [bij] *nf* (*gén*) ball; (*du jeu de billes*) marble
billet [bijɛ] *nm* (*aussi*: **~ de banque**) (bank)note; (*de cinéma, de bus etc*) ticket; (*courte lettre*) note; **billet électronique** e-ticket; **billetterie** *nf* ticket office; (*distributeur*) ticket machine; (*Banque*) cash dispenser
billion [biljɔ̃] *nm* billion (*BRIT*), trillion (*US*)
bimensuel, le [bimɑ̃sɥɛl] *adj* bimonthly
bio [bjɔ] *adj inv* organic
bio... [bjɔ] *préfixe* bio...; **biochimie** *nf* biochemistry; **biographie** *nf* biography; **biologie** *nf* biology; **biologique** *adj* biological; (*produits, aliments*) organic; **biométrie** *nf* biometrics; **biotechnologie** *nf* biotechnology; **bioterrorisme** *nm* bioterrorism
Birmanie [biʀmani] *nf* Burma
bis [bis] *adv*: **12 ~ 12a** *ou* A ▷ *excl, nm* encore
biscotte [biskɔt] *nf* toasted bread (*sold in packets*)
biscuit [biskɥi] *nm* biscuit (*BRIT*), cookie (*US*)
bise [biz] *nf* (*fam: baiser*) kiss; (*vent*) North wind; **grosses ~s (de)** (*sur lettre*) love and kisses (from)
bisexuel, le [bisɛksɥɛl] *adj* bisexual
bisou [bizu] (*fam*) *nm* kiss
bissextile [bisɛkstil] *adj*: **année ~** leap year

bistro(t) [bistʀo] nm bistro, café
bitume [bitym] nm asphalt
bizarre [bizaʀ] adj strange, odd
blague [blag] nf (propos) joke; (farce) trick;
 sans ~! no kidding!; **blaguer** vi to joke
blaireau, x [blɛʀo] nm (Zool) badger; (brosse)
 shaving brush
blâme [blɑm] nm blame; (sanction) reprimand;
 blâmer vt to blame
blanc, blanche [blɑ̃, blɑ̃ʃ] adj white;
 (non imprimé) blank ▷ nm/f white, white
 man(-woman) ▷ nm (couleur) white; (espace
 non écrit) blank; (aussi: **~ d'œuf**) (egg-)white;
 (aussi: **~ de poulet**) breast, white meat; (aussi:
 vin ~) white wine; **~ cassé** off-white; **chèque
 en ~** blank cheque; **à ~** (chauffer) white-hot;
 (tirer, charger) with blanks; **blanche** nf (Mus)
 minim (BRIT), half-note (US); **blancheur** nf
 whiteness
blanchir [blɑ̃ʃiʀ] vt (gén) to whiten; (linge) to
 launder; (Culin) to blanch; (fig: disculper) to
 clear ▷ vi (cheveux) to go white; **blanchisserie**
 nf laundry
blason [blazɔ̃] nm coat of arms
blasphème [blasfɛm] nm blasphemy
blazer [blazɛʀ] nm blazer
blé [ble] nm wheat; **blé noir** buckwheat
bled [blɛd] (péj) nm hole
blême [blɛm] adj pale
blessé, e [blese] adj injured ▷ nm/f injured
 person, casualty
blesser [blese] vt to injure; (délibérément) to
 wound; (offenser) to hurt; **se blesser** to injure
 o.s.; **se ~ au pied** to injure one's foot; **blessure**
 nf (accidentelle) injury; (intentionnelle) wound
bleu, e [blø] adj blue; (bifteck) very rare ▷ nm
 (couleur) blue; (contusion) bruise; (vêtement:
 aussi: **~s**) overalls pl; (fromage) blue cheese;
 bleu marine navy blue; **bleuet** nm cornflower
bloc [blɔk] nm (de pierre etc) block; (de papier
 à lettres) pad; (ensemble) group, block; **serré
 à ~** tightened right down; **en ~** as a whole;
 bloc opératoire operating ou theatre block;
 blocage nm (des prix) freezing; (Psych) hang-
 up; **bloc-notes** nm note pad
blog, blogue [blɔɡ] nm blog; **bloguer** vi to
 blog
blond, e [blɔ̃, blɔ̃d] adj fair, blond; (sable, blés)
 golden
bloquer [blɔke] vt (passage) to block; (pièce
 mobile) to jam; (crédits, compte) to freeze
blottir [blɔtiʀ]: **se blottir** vi to huddle up
blouse [bluz] nf overall
blouson [bluzɔ̃] nm blouson jacket; **blouson
 noir** (fig) ≈ rocker
bluff [blœf] nm bluff
bobine [bɔbin] nf reel; (Élec) coil
bobo [bobo] abr m/f = bourgeois bohème (fam)
 boho

bocal, -aux [bɔkal, o] nm jar
bock [bɔk] nm glass of beer
bœuf [bœf] nm ox; (Culin) beef
bof [bɔf] (fam) excl don't care!; (pas terrible)
 nothing special
bohémien, ne [bɔemjɛ̃, -ɛn] nm/f gipsy
boire [bwaʀ] vt to drink; (s'imprégner de) to
 soak up; **~ un coup** (fam) to have a drink
bois [bwa] nm wood; **de ~, en ~** wooden;
 boisé, e adj woody, wooded
boisson [bwasɔ̃] nf drink
boîte [bwat] nf box; (fam: entreprise) firm;
 aliments en ~ canned ou tinned (BRIT) foods;
 boîte à gants glove compartment; **boîte à
 ordures** dustbin (BRIT), trashcan (US); **boîte
 aux lettres** letter box; **boîte d'allumettes**
 box of matches; (vide) matchbox; **boîte de
 conserves** can ou tin (BRIT) of food; **boîte
 (de nuit)** night club; **boîte de vitesses** gear
 box; **boîte postale** PO Box; **boîte vocale** (Tél)
 voice mail
boiter [bwate] vi to limp; (fig: raisonnement)
 to be shaky
boîtier [bwatje] nm case
boive etc [bwav] vb voir **boire**
bol [bɔl] nm bowl; **un ~ d'air** a breath of fresh
 air; **j'en ai ras le ~** (fam) I'm fed up with this;
 avoir du ~ (fam) to be lucky
bombarder [bɔ̃baʀde] vt to bomb; **~ qn de**
 (cailloux, lettres) to bombard sb with
bombe [bɔ̃b] nf bomb; (atomiseur) (aerosol)
 spray

⊙ MOT-CLÉ

bon, bonne [bɔ̃, bɔn] adj **1** (agréable,
 satisfaisant) good; **un bon repas/restaurant**
 a good meal/restaurant; **être bon en maths**
 to be good at maths (BRIT) ou math (US)
 2 (charitable): **être bon (envers)** to be good
 (to)
 3 (correct) right; **le bon numéro/moment** the
 right number/moment
 4 (souhaits): **bon anniversaire!** happy
 birthday!; **bon voyage!** have a good trip!;
 bonne chance! good luck!; **bonne année!**
 happy New Year!; **bonne nuit!** good night!
 5 (approprié, apte): **bon à/pour** fit to/for; **à
 quoi bon?** what's the use?
 6: **bon enfant** adj inv accommodating, easy-
 going; **bonne femme** (péj) woman; **de bonne
 heure** early; **bon marché** adj inv, adv cheap;
 bon mot witticism; **bon sens** common sense;
 bon vivant jovial chap; **bonnes œuvres**
 charitable works, charities
 ▷ nm **1** (billet) voucher; (aussi: **bon cadeau**) gift
 voucher; **bon d'essence** petrol coupon; **bon
 du Trésor** Treasury bond
 2: **avoir du bon** to have its good points; **pour**

de bon for good
▷ *adv* : **il fait bon** it's *ou* the weather is fine; **sentir bon** to smell good; **tenir bon** to stand firm
▷ *excl* good!; **ah bon?** really?; **bon, je reste** right then, I'll stay; *voir aussi* **bonne**

bonbon [bɔ̃bɔ̃] *nm* (boiled) sweet
bond [bɔ̃] *nm* leap; **faire un ~** to leap in the air
bondé, e [bɔ̃de] *adj* packed (full)
bondir [bɔ̃diʀ] *vi* to leap
bonheur [bɔnœʀ] *nm* happiness; **porter ~ (à qn)** to bring (sb) luck; **au petit ~** haphazardly; **par ~** fortunately
bonhomme [bɔnɔm] (*pl* **bonshommes**) *nm* fellow; **bonhomme de neige** snowman
bonjour [bɔ̃ʒuʀ] *excl, nm* hello; (*selon l'heure*) good morning/afternoon; **c'est simple comme ~!** it's easy as pie!
bonne [bɔn] *adj voir* **bon** ▷ *nf* (*domestique*) maid
bonnet [bɔnɛ] *nm* hat; (*de soutien-gorge*) cup; **bonnet de bain** bathing cap
bonsoir [bɔ̃swaʀ] *excl* good evening
bonté [bɔ̃te] *nf* kindness *no pl*
bonus [bɔnys] *nm* no-claims bonus; (*de DVD*) extras *pl*
bord [bɔʀ] *nm* (*de table, verre, falaise*) edge; (*de rivière, lac*) bank; (*de route*) side; **(monter) à ~** (to go) on board; **jeter par-dessus ~** to throw overboard; **le commandant de/les hommes du ~** the ship's master/crew; **au ~ de la mer** at the seaside; **au ~ de la route** at the roadside; **être au ~ des larmes** to be on the verge of tears
bordeaux [bɔʀdo] *nm* Bordeaux (wine) ▷ *adj inv* maroon
bordel [bɔʀdɛl] *nm* brothel; (*fam!*) bloody mess (*!*)
border [bɔʀde] *vt* (*être le long de*) to line; (*qn dans son lit*) to tuck up; (*garnir*): **~ qch de** to edge sth with
bordure [bɔʀdyʀ] *nf* border; **en ~ de** on the edge of
borne [bɔʀn] *nf* boundary stone; (*aussi*: **~ kilométrique**) kilometre-marker, ≈ milestone; **bornes** *nfpl* (*fig*) limits; **dépasser les ~s** to go too far
borné, e [bɔʀne] *adj* (*personne*) narrow-minded
borner [bɔʀne] *vt* : **se ~ à faire** (*se contenter de*) to content o.s. with doing; (*se limiter à*) to limit o.s. to doing
bosniaque [bɔsnjak] *adj* Bosnian ▷ *nm/f* : **B~** Bosnian
Bosnie-Herzégovine [bɔsniɛʀzegɔvin] *nf* Bosnia-Herzegovina
bosquet [bɔskɛ] *nm* grove
bosse [bɔs] *nf* (*de terrain etc*) bump; (*enflure*)

lump; (*du bossu, du chameau*) hump; **avoir la ~ des maths** *etc* (*fam*) to have a gift for maths *etc*; **il a roulé sa ~** (*fam*) he's been around
bosser [bɔse] (*fam*) *vi* (*travailler*) to work; (*travailler dur*) to slave (away)
bossu, e [bɔsy] *nm/f* hunchback
botanique [bɔtanik] *nf* botany ▷ *adj* botanic(al)
botte [bɔt] *nf* (*soulier*) (high) boot; (*gerbe*): **~ de paille** bundle of straw; **botte de radis/d'asperges** bunch of radishes/asparagus; **bottes de caoutchouc** wellington boots
bottin [bɔtɛ̃] *nm* directory
bottine [bɔtin] *nf* ankle boot
bouc [buk] *nm* goat; (*barbe*) goatee; **bouc émissaire** scapegoat
boucan [bukɑ̃] (*fam*) *nm* din, racket
bouche [buʃ] *nf* mouth; **faire du ~ à ~ à qn** to give sb the kiss of life *ou* mouth-to-mouth resuscitation (BRIT); **rester ~ bée** to stand open-mouthed; **bouche d'égout** manhole; **bouche d'incendie** fire hydrant; **bouche de métro** métro entrance
bouché, e [buʃe] *adj* (*flacon etc*) stoppered; (*temps, ciel*) overcast; (*péj fam: personne*) thick (*fam*); **c'est un secteur ~** there's no future in that area; **avoir le nez ~** to have a blocked(-up) nose; **l'évier est ~** the sink's blocked
bouchée [buʃe] *nf* mouthful; **bouchées à la reine** chicken vol-au-vents
boucher, -ère [buʃe] *nm/f* butcher ▷ *vt* (*trou*) to fill up; (*obstruer*) to block (up); **se boucher** *vi* (*tuyau etc*) to block up, get blocked up; **j'ai le nez bouché** my nose is blocked; **se ~ le nez** to hold one's nose; **boucherie** *nf* butcher's (shop); (*fig*) slaughter
bouchon [buʃɔ̃] *nm* stopper; (*de tube*) top; (*en liège*) cork; (*fig: embouteillage*) holdup; (*Pêche*) float
boucle [bukl] *nf* (*forme, figure*) loop; (*objet*) buckle; **boucle (de cheveux)** curl; **boucle d'oreille** earring
bouclé, e [bukle] *adj* (*cheveux*) curly
boucler [bukle] *vt* (*fermer: ceinture etc*) to fasten; (*terminer*) to finish off; (*fam: enfermer*) to shut away; (*quartier*) to seal off ▷ *vi* to curl
bouder [bude] *vi* to sulk ▷ *vt* to stay away from
boudin [budɛ̃] *nm* : **~ (noir)** black pudding; **boudin blanc** white pudding
boue [bu] *nf* mud
bouée [bwe] *nf* buoy; **bouée (de sauvetage)** lifebuoy
boueux, -euse [bwø, øz] *adj* muddy
bouffe [buf] (*fam*) *nf* grub (*fam*), food
bouffée [bufe] *nf* (*de cigarette*) puff; **une ~ d'air pur** a breath of fresh air; **bouffée de chaleur** hot flush (BRIT) *ou* flash (US)
bouffer [bufe] (*fam*) *vi* to eat

bouffi, e [bufi] *adj* swollen

bouger [buʒe] *vi* to move; *(dent etc)* to be loose; *(s'activer)* to get moving ▷ *vt* to move; **les prix/les couleurs n'ont pas bougé** prices/colours haven't changed

bougie [buʒi] *nf* candle; *(Auto)* spark(ing) plug

bouillabaisse [bujabɛs] *nf* type of fish soup

bouillant, e [bujɑ̃, ɑ̃t] *adj (qui bout)* boiling; *(très chaud)* boiling (hot)

bouillie [buji] *nf (de bébé)* cereal; **en ~** *(fig)* crushed

bouillir [bujiR] *vi, vt* to boil; **~ d'impatience** to seethe with impatience

bouilloire [bujwaR] *nf* kettle

bouillon [bujɔ̃] *nm (Culin)* stock *no pl*; **bouillonner** *vi* to bubble; *(fig: idées)* to bubble up

bouillotte [bujɔt] *nf* hot-water bottle

boulanger, -ère [bulɑ̃ʒe, ɛR] *nm/f* baker; **boulangerie** *nf* bakery

boule [bul] *nf (gén)* ball; *(de pétanque)* bowl; **boule de neige** snowball

boulette [bulɛt] *nf (de viande)* meatball

boulevard [bulvaR] *nm* boulevard

bouleversement [bulvɛRsəmɑ̃] *nm* upheaval

bouleverser [bulvɛRse] *vt (émouvoir)* to overwhelm; *(causer du chagrin)* to distress; *(pays, vie)* to disrupt; *(papiers, objets)* to turn upside down

boulimie [bulimi] *nf* bulimia

boulimique [bulimik] *adj* bulimic

boulon [bulɔ̃] *nm* bolt

boulot, te [bulo, ɔt] *adj* plump, tubby ▷ *nm (fam: travail)* work

boum [bum] *nm* bang ▷ *nf (fam)* party

bouquet [bukɛ] *nm (de fleurs)* bunch (of flowers), bouquet; *(de persil etc)* bunch; **c'est le ~!** *(fam)* that takes the biscuit!

bouquin [bukɛ̃] *(fam) nm* book; **bouquiner** *(fam) vi* to read

bourdon [buRdɔ̃] *nm* bumblebee

bourg [buR] *nm* small market town

bourgeois, e [buRʒwa, waz] *(péj) adj* ≈ (upper) middle class; **bourgeoisie** *nf* ≈ upper middle classes *pl*

bourgeon [buRʒɔ̃] *nm* bud

Bourgogne [buRgɔɲ] *nf*: **la ~** Burgundy ▷ *nm*: **bourgogne** burgundy (wine)

bourguignon, ne [buRgiɲɔ̃, ɔn] *adj* of *ou* from Burgundy, Burgundian

bourrasque [buRask] *nf* squall

bourratif, -ive [buRatif, iv] *(fam) adj* filling, stodgy *(pej)*

bourré, e [buRe] *adj (fam: ivre)* plastered, tanked up (BRIT); *(rempli)*: **~ de** crammed full of

bourrer [buRe] *vt (pipe)* to fill; *(poêle)* to pack; *(valise)* to cram (full)

bourru, e [buRy] *adj* surly, gruff

bourse [buRs] *nf (subvention)* grant; *(porte-monnaie)* purse; **la B~** the Stock Exchange

bous [bu] *vb voir* **bouillir**

bousculade [buskylad] *nf (hâte)* rush; *(cohue)* crush; **bousculer** *vt (heurter)* to knock into; *(fig)* to push, rush

boussole [busɔl] *nf* compass

bout [bu] *vb voir* **bouillir** ▷ *nm* bit; *(d'un bâton etc)* tip; *(d'une ficelle, table, rue, période)* end; **au ~ de** at the end of, after; **pousser qn à ~** to push sb to the limit; **venir à ~ de** to manage to finish; **à ~ portant** (at) point-blank (range)

bouteille [butɛj] *nf* bottle; *(de gaz butane)* cylinder

boutique [butik] *nf* shop

bouton [butɔ̃] *nm* button; *(sur la peau)* spot; *(Bot)* bud; **boutonner** *vt* to button up; **boutonnière** *nf* buttonhole; **bouton-pression** *nm* press stud

bovin, e [bɔvɛ̃, in] *adj* bovine; **bovins** *nmpl* cattle *pl*

bowling [buliŋ] *nm* (tenpin) bowling; *(salle)* bowling alley

boxe [bɔks] *nf* boxing

BP *abr* = **boîte postale**

bracelet [bRaslɛ] *nm* bracelet

braconnier [bRakɔnje] *nm* poacher

brader [bRade] *vt* to sell off; **braderie** *nf* cut-price shop/stall

braguette [bRagɛt] *nf* fly *ou* flies *pl* (BRIT), zipper (US)

braise [bRɛz] *nf* embers *pl*

brancard [bRɑ̃kaR] *nm (civière)* stretcher; **brancardier** *nm* stretcher-bearer

branche [bRɑ̃ʃ] *nf* branch

branché, e [bRɑ̃ʃe] *(fam) adj* trendy

brancher [bRɑ̃ʃe] *vt* to connect (up); *(en mettant la prise)* to plug in

brandir [bRɑ̃diR] *vt* to brandish

braquer [bRake] *vi (Auto)* to turn (the wheel) ▷ *vt (revolver etc)*: **~ qch sur** to aim sth at, point sth at; *(mettre en colère)*: **~ qn** to put sb's back up

bras [bRɑ] *nm* arm; **~ dessus, ~ dessous** arm in arm; **se retrouver avec qch sur les ~** *(fam)* to be landed with sth; **bras droit** *(fig)* right hand man

brassard [bRasaR] *nm* armband

brasse [bRas] *nf (nage)* breast-stroke; **brasse papillon** butterfly (stroke)

brassée [bRase] *nf* armful

brasser [bRase] *vt* to mix; **~ l'argent/les affaires** to handle a lot of money/business

brasserie [bRasRi] *nf (restaurant)* café-restaurant; *(usine)* brewery

brave [bRav] *adj (courageux)* brave; *(bon, gentil)* good, kind

braver [bRave] *vt* to defy

bravo [bRavo] *excl* bravo ▷ *nm* cheer

bravoure [bʀavuʀ] nf bravery

break [bʀɛk] nm (Auto) estate car

brebis [bʀəbi] nf ewe; **brebis galeuse** black sheep

bredouiller [bʀəduje] vi, vt to mumble, stammer

bref, brève [bʀɛf, ɛv] adj short, brief ▷ adv in short; **d'un ton ~** sharply, curtly; **en ~** in short, in brief

Brésil [bʀezil] nm Brazil

Bretagne [bʀətaɲ] nf Brittany

bretelle [bʀətɛl] nf (de vêtement, de sac) strap; (d'autoroute) slip road (BRIT), entrance/exit ramp (US); **bretelles** nfpl (pour pantalon) braces (BRIT), suspenders (US)

breton, ne [bʀətɔ̃, ɔn] adj Breton ▷ nm/f: **B~, ne** Breton

brève [bʀɛv] adj voir **bref**

brevet [bʀəvɛ] nm diploma, certificate; **brevet des collèges** exam taken at the age of 15; **brevet (d'invention)** patent; **breveté, e** adj patented

bricolage [bʀikɔlaʒ] nm: **le ~** do-it-yourself

bricoler [bʀikɔle] vi (petits travaux) to do DIY jobs; (passe-temps) to potter about ▷ vt (réparer) to fix up; **bricoleur, -euse** nm/f handyman(-woman), DIY enthusiast

bridge [bʀidʒ] nm (Cartes) bridge

brièvement [bʀijɛvmɑ̃] adv briefly

brigade [bʀigad] nf (Police) squad; (Mil) brigade; **brigadier** nm sergeant

brillamment [bʀijamɑ̃] adv brilliantly

brillant, e [bʀijɑ̃, ɑ̃t] adj (remarquable) bright; (luisant) shiny, shining

briller [bʀije] vi to shine

brin [bʀɛ̃] nm (de laine, ficelle etc) strand; (fig): **un ~ de** a bit of

brindille [bʀɛ̃dij] nf twig

brioche [bʀijɔʃ] nf brioche (bun); (fam: ventre) paunch

brique [bʀik] nf brick; (de lait) carton

briquet [bʀikɛ] nm (cigarette) lighter

brise [bʀiz] nf breeze

briser [bʀize] vt to break; **se briser** vi to break

britannique [bʀitanik] adj British ▷ nm/f: **B~** British person, Briton; **les B~s** the British

brocante [bʀɔkɑ̃t] nf junk, second-hand goods pl; **brocanteur, -euse** nm/f junkshop owner; junk dealer

broche [bʀɔʃ] nf brooch; (Culin) spit; (Méd) pin; **à la ~** spit-roasted

broché, e [bʀɔʃe] adj (livre) paper-backed

brochet [bʀɔʃɛ] nm pike inv

brochette [bʀɔʃɛt] nf (ustensile) skewer; (plat) kebab

brochure [bʀɔʃyʀ] nf pamphlet, brochure, booklet

broder [bʀɔde] vt to embroider ▷ vi: **~ (sur les faits ou une histoire)** to embroider the facts;

broderie nf embroidery

bronches [bʀɔ̃ʃ] nfpl bronchial tubes; **bronchite** nf bronchitis

bronze [bʀɔ̃z] nm bronze

bronzer [bʀɔ̃ze] vi to get a tan; **se bronzer** to sunbathe

brosse [bʀɔs] nf brush; **coiffé en ~** with a crewcut; **brosse à cheveux** hairbrush; **brosse à dents** toothbrush; **brosse à habits** clothesbrush; **brosser** vt (nettoyer) to brush; (fig: tableau etc) to paint; **se brosser les dents** to brush one's teeth

brouette [bʀuɛt] nf wheelbarrow

brouillard [bʀujaʀ] nm fog

brouiller [bʀuje] vt (œufs, message) to scramble; (idées) to mix up; (rendre trouble) to cloud; (désunir: amis) to set at odds; **se brouiller** vi (vue) to cloud over; (gens): **se ~ (avec)** to fall out (with)

brouillon, ne [bʀujɔ̃, ɔn] adj (sans soin) untidy; (qui manque d'organisation) disorganized ▷ nm draft; **(papier) ~** rough paper

broussailles [bʀusaj] nfpl undergrowth sg; **broussailleux, -euse** adj bushy

brousse [bʀus] nf: **la ~** the bush

brouter [bʀute] vi to graze

brugnon [bʀyɲɔ̃] nm (Bot) nectarine

bruiner [bʀɥine] vb impers: **il bruine** it's drizzling, there's a drizzle

bruit [bʀɥi] nm: **un ~** a noise, a sound; (fig: rumeur) a rumour; **le ~** noise; **sans ~** without a sound, noiselessly; **bruit de fond** background noise

brûlant, e [bʀylɑ̃, ɑ̃t] adj burning; (liquide) boiling (hot)

brûlé, e [bʀyle] adj (fig: démasqué) blown ▷ nm: **odeur de ~** smell of burning

brûler [bʀyle] vt to burn; (suj: eau bouillante) to scald; (consommer: électricité, essence) to use; (feu rouge, signal) to go through ▷ vi to burn; (jeu): **tu brûles!** you're getting hot!; **se brûler** to burn o.s.; (s'ébouillanter) to scald o.s.

brûlure [bʀylyʀ] nf (lésion) burn; **brûlures d'estomac** heartburn sg

brume [bʀym] nf mist

brun, e [bʀœ̃, bʀyn] adj (gén, bière) brown; (cheveux, tabac) dark; **elle est ~e** she's got dark hair

brunch [bʀœntʃ] nm brunch

brushing [bʀœʃiŋ] nm blow-dry

brusque [bʀysk] adj abrupt

brut, e [bʀyt] adj (minerai, soie) raw; (diamant) rough; (Comm) gross; **(pétrole) ~** crude (oil)

brutal, e, -aux [bʀytal, o] adj brutal

Bruxelles [bʀysɛl] n Brussels

bruyamment [bʀɥijamɑ̃] adv noisily

bruyant, e [bʀɥijɑ̃, ɑ̃t] adj noisy

bruyère [bʀyjɛʀ] nf heather

BTS sigle m (= brevet de technicien supérieur) vocational training certificate taken at the end of a higher education course

bu, e [by] pp de **boire**

buccal, e, -aux [bykal, o] adj: **par voie ~e** orally

bûche [byʃ] nf log; **prendre une ~** (fig) to come a cropper; **bûche de Noël** Yule log

bûcher [byʃe] nm (funéraire) pyre; (supplice) stake ▷ vi (fam) to swot (BRIT), slave (away) ▷ vt (fam) to swot up (BRIT), slave away at

budget [bydʒɛ] nm budget

buée [bɥe] nf (sur une vitre) mist

buffet [byfɛ] nm (meuble) sideboard; (de réception) buffet; **buffet (de gare)** (station) buffet, snack bar

buis [bɥi] nm box tree; (bois) box(wood)

buisson [bɥisɔ̃] nm bush

bulbe [bylb] nm (Bot, Anat) bulb

Bulgarie [bylgaʀi] nf Bulgaria

bulle [byl] nf bubble

bulletin [byltɛ̃] nm (communiqué, journal) bulletin; (Scol) report; **bulletin d'informations** news bulletin; **bulletin (de vote)** ballot paper; **bulletin météorologique** weather report

bureau, x [byʀo] nm (meuble) desk; (pièce, service) office; **bureau de change** (foreign) exchange office ou bureau; **bureau de poste** post office; **bureau de tabac** tobacconist's (shop); **bureaucratie** [byʀokʀasi] nf bureaucracy

bus¹ [by] vb voir **boire**

bus² [bys] nm bus; **à quelle heure part le ~?** what time does the bus leave?

buste [byst] nm (torse) chest; (seins) bust

but¹ [by] vb voir **boire**

but² [by(t)] nm (cible) target; (fig) goal, aim; (Football etc) goal; **de ~ en blanc** point-blank; **avoir pour ~ de faire** to aim to do; **dans le ~ de** with the intention of

butane [bytan] nm (camping) butane; (usage domestique) Calor gas®

butiner [bytine] vi (abeilles) to gather nectar

buvais etc [byvɛ] vb voir **boire**

buvard [byvaʀ] nm blotter

buvette [byvɛt] nf bar

C

c' [s] dét voir **ce**

ça [sa] pron (pour désigner) this; (: plus loin) that; (comme sujet indéfini) it; **ça m'étonne que ...** it surprises me that ...; **comment ça va?** how are you?; **ça va?** (d'accord?) O.K.?, all right?; **où ça?** where's that?; **pourquoi ça?** why's that?; **qui ça?** who's that?; **ça alors!** well really!; **ça fait 10 ans (que)** it's 10 years (since); **c'est ça** that's right; **ça y est** that's it

cabane [kaban] nf hut, cabin

cabaret [kabaʀɛ] nm night club

cabillaud [kabijo] nm cod inv

cabine [kabin] nf (de bateau) cabin; (de piscine etc) cubicle; (de camion, train) cab; (d'avion) cockpit; **cabine d'essayage** fitting room; **cabine (téléphonique)** call ou (tele)phone box

cabinet [kabinɛ] nm (petite pièce) closet; (de médecin) surgery (BRIT), office (US); (de notaire etc) office; (: clientèle) practice; (Pol) Cabinet; **cabinets** nmpl (w.-c.) toilet sg; **cabinet de toilette** toilet

câble [kabl] nm cable; **le ~** (TV) cable television, cablevision (US)

cacahuète [kakaɥɛt] nf peanut

cacao [kakao] nm cocoa

cache [kaʃ] nm mask, card (for masking)

cache-cache [kaʃkaʃ] nm: **jouer à ~** to play hide-and-seek

cachemire [kaʃmiʀ] nm cashmere

cacher [kaʃe] vt to hide, conceal; **se cacher** vi (volontairement) to hide; (être caché) to be hidden ou concealed; **~ qch à qn** to hide ou conceal sth from sb

cachet [kaʃe] nm (comprimé) tablet; (de la poste) postmark; (rétribution) fee; (fig) style, character

cachette [kaʃet] nf hiding place; **en ~** on the sly, secretly

cactus [kaktys] nm cactus

cadavre [kadavʀ] nm corpse, (dead) body

caddie® [kadi] nm (supermarket) trolley (BRIT), (grocery) cart (US)

cadeau, x [kado] nm present, gift; **faire un ~ à qn** to give sb a present ou gift; **faire ~ de qch à qn** to make a present of sth to sb, give sb sth as a present

cadenas [kadna] nm padlock

cadet, te [kade, ɛt] adj younger; (le plus jeune) youngest ▷ nm/f youngest child ou one

cadran [kadʀã] nm dial; **cadran solaire** sundial

cadre [kadʀ] nm frame; (environnement) surroundings pl ▷ nm/f (Admin) managerial employee, executive; **dans le ~ de** (fig) within the framework ou context of

cafard [kafaʀ] nm cockroach; **avoir le ~** (fam) to be down in the dumps

café [kafe] nm coffee; (bistro) café ▷ adj inv coffee(-coloured); **café au lait** white coffee; **café noir** black coffee; **café tabac** tobacconist's or newsagent's serving coffee and spirits; **cafetière** nf (pot) coffee-pot

cage [kaʒ] nf cage; **cage (d'escalier)** stairwell; **cage thoracique** rib cage

cageot [kaʒo] nm crate

cagoule [kagul] nf (passe-montagne) balaclava

cahier [kaje] nm notebook; **cahier de brouillon** jotter (BRIT), rough notebook; **cahier d'exercices** exercise book

caille [kaj] nf quail

caillou, x [kaju] nm (little) stone; **caillouteux, -euse** adj (route) stony

Caire [kɛʀ] nm: **le ~** Cairo

caisse [kɛs] nf box; (tiroir où l'on met la recette) till; (où l'on paye) cash desk (BRIT), check-out; (de banque) cashier's desk; **caisse d'épargne** savings bank; **caisse de retraite** pension fund; **caisse enregistreuse** cash register; **caissier, -ière** nm/f cashier

cake [kɛk] nm fruit cake

calandre [kalɑ̃dʀ] nf radiator grill

calcaire [kalkɛʀ] nm limestone ▷ adj (eau) hard; (Géo) limestone cpd

calcul [kalkyl] nm calculation; **le ~** (Scol) arithmetic; **calcul (biliaire)** (gall)stone; **calculatrice** nf calculator; **calculer** vt to calculate, work out; **calculette** nf pocket calculator

cale [kal] nf (de bateau) hold; (en bois) wedge

calé, e [kale] (fam) adj clever, bright

caleçon [kalsɔ̃] nm (d'homme) boxer shorts; (de femme) leggings

calendrier [kalɑ̃dʀije] nm calendar; (fig) timetable

calepin [kalpɛ̃] nm notebook

caler [kale] vt to wedge ▷ vi (moteur, véhicule) to stall

calibre [kalibʀ] nm calibre

câlin, e [kalɛ̃, in] adj cuddly, cuddlesome; (regard, voix) tender

calmant [kalmɑ̃] nm tranquillizer, sedative; (pour la douleur) painkiller

calme [kalm] adj calm, quiet ▷ nm calm(ness), quietness; **sans perdre son ~** without losing one's cool (inf) ou composure; **calmer** vt to calm (down); (douleur, inquiétude) to ease, soothe; **se calmer** vi to calm down

calorie [kalɔʀi] nf calorie

camarade [kamaʀad] nm/f friend, pal; (Pol) comrade

Cambodge [kɑ̃bɔdʒ] nm: **le ~** Cambodia

cambriolage [kɑ̃bʀijɔlaʒ] nm burglary; **cambrioler** vt to burgle (BRIT), burglarize (US); **cambrioleur, -euse** nm/f burglar

camelote [kamlɔt] (fam) nf rubbish, trash, junk

caméra [kameʀa] nf (Cinéma, TV) camera; (d'amateur) cine-camera

Cameroun [kamʀun] nm: **le ~** Cameroon

caméscope® [kameskɔp] nm camcorder®

camion [kamjɔ̃] nm lorry (BRIT), truck; **camion de dépannage** breakdown (BRIT) ou tow (US) truck; **camionnette** nf (small) van; **camionneur** nm (chauffeur) lorry (BRIT) ou truck driver; (entrepreneur) haulage contractor (BRIT), trucker (US)

camomille [kamɔmij] nf camomile; (boisson) camomile tea

camp [kɑ̃] nm camp; (fig) side

campagnard, e [kɑ̃paɲaʀ, aʀd] adj country cpd

campagne [kɑ̃paɲ] nf country, countryside; (Mil, Pol, Comm) campaign; **à la ~** in the country

camper [kɑ̃pe] vi to camp ▷ vt to sketch; **se ~ devant** to plant o.s. in front of; **campeur, -euse** nm/f camper

camping [kɑ̃piŋ] nm camping; **faire du ~** to go camping; **(terrain de) camping** campsite, camping site; **camping-car** nm camper, motorhome (US); **camping-gaz®** nm inv camp(ing) stove

Canada [kanada] nm: **le ~** Canada; **canadien, ne** adj Canadian ▷ nm/f: **Canadien, ne** Canadian; **canadienne** nf (veste) fur-lined jacket

canal, -aux [kanal, o] nm canal; (naturel, TV) channel; **canalisation** nf (tuyau) pipe

canapé [kanape] *nm* settee, sofa

canard [kanaʀ] *nm* duck; (*fam: journal*) rag

cancer [kɑ̃sɛʀ] *nm* cancer; (*signe*): **le C~** Cancer

cancre [kɑ̃kʀ] *nm* dunce

candidat, e [kɑ̃dida, at] *nm/f* candidate; (*à un poste*) applicant, candidate; **candidature** *nf* (*Pol*) candidature; (*à poste*) application; **poser sa candidature à un poste** to apply for a job

cane [kan] *nf* (female) duck

canette [kanɛt] *nf* (*de bière*) (flip-top) bottle

canevas [kanvɑ] *nm* (*Couture*) canvas

caniche [kaniʃ] *nm* poodle

canicule [kanikyl] *nf* scorching heat

canif [kanif] *nm* penknife, pocket knife

canne [kan] *nf* (walking) stick; **canne à pêche** fishing rod; **canne à sucre** sugar cane

cannelle [kanɛl] *nf* cinnamon

canoë [kanɔe] *nm* canoe; (*sport*) canoeing; **canoë (kayak)** kayak

canot [kano] *nm* ding(h)y; **canot de sauvetage** lifeboat; **canot pneumatique** inflatable ding(h)y

cantatrice [kɑ̃tatʀis] *nf* (opera) singer

cantine [kɑ̃tin] *nf* canteen

canton [kɑ̃tɔ̃] *nm* *district consisting of several communes*; (*en Suisse*) canton

caoutchouc [kautʃu] *nm* rubber; **caoutchouc mousse** foam rubber

cap [kap] *nm* (*Géo*) cape; (*promontoire*) headland; (*fig: tournant*) watershed; (*Navig*): **changer de ~** to change course; **mettre le ~ sur** to head *ou* steer for

CAP *sigle m* (= *Certificat d'aptitude professionnelle*) *vocational training certificate taken at secondary school*

capable [kapabl] *adj* able, capable; **~ de qch/faire** capable of sth/doing

capacité [kapasite] *nf* (*compétence*) ability; (*Jur, contenance*) capacity

cape [kap] *nf* cape, cloak; **rire sous ~** to laugh up one's sleeve

CAPES [kapɛs] *sigle m* (= *Certificat d'aptitude pédagogique à l'enseignement secondaire*) *teaching diploma*

capitaine [kapitɛn] *nm* captain

capital, e, -aux [kapital, o] *adj* (*œuvre*) major; (*question, rôle*) fundamental ▷ *nm* capital; (*fig*) stock; **d'une importance ~e** of capital importance; **capitaux** *nmpl* (*fonds*) capital *sg*; **capital (social)** authorized capital; **capitale** *nf* (*ville*) capital; (*lettre*) capital (letter); **capitalisme** *nm* capitalism; **capitaliste** *adj, nm/f* capitalist

caporal, -aux [kapɔʀal, o] *nm* lance corporal

capot [kapo] *nm* (*Auto*) bonnet (BRIT), hood (US)

câpre [kɑpʀ] *nf* caper

caprice [kapʀis] *nm* whim, caprice; **faire des ~s** to make a fuss; **capricieux, -euse** *adj* (*fantasque*) capricious, whimsical; (*enfant*) awkward

Capricorne [kapʀikɔʀn] *nm*: **le ~** Capricorn

capsule [kapsyl] *nf* (*de bouteille*) cap; (*Bot etc, spatiale*) capsule

capter [kapte] *vt* (*ondes radio*) to pick up; (*fig*) to win, capture

captivant, e [kaptivɑ̃, ɑ̃t] *adj* captivating

capturer [kaptyʀe] *vt* to capture

capuche [kapyʃ] *nf* hood

capuchon [kapyʃɔ̃] *nm* hood; (*de stylo*) cap, top

car [kaʀ] *nm* coach ▷ *conj* because, for

carabine [kaʀabin] *nf* rifle

caractère [kaʀaktɛʀ] *nm* (*gén*) character; **avoir bon/mauvais ~** to be good-/ill-natured; **en ~s gras** in bold type; **en petits ~s** in small print; **~s d'imprimerie** (block) capitals

caractériser [kaʀakteʀize] *vt* to be characteristic of; **se ~ par** to be characterized *ou* distinguished by

caractéristique [kaʀakteʀistik] *adj, nf* characteristic

carafe [kaʀaf] *nf* (*pour eau, vin ordinaire*) carafe

caraïbe [kaʀaib] *adj* Caribbean ▷ *n*: **les C~s** the Caribbean (Islands)

carambolage [kaʀɑ̃bɔlaʒ] *nm* multiple crash, pileup

caramel [kaʀamɛl] *nm* (*bonbon*) caramel, toffee; (*substance*) caramel

caravane [kaʀavan] *nf* caravan; **caravaning** *nm* caravanning

carbone [kaʀbɔn] *nm* carbon; (*double*) carbon (copy)

carbonique [kaʀbɔnik] *adj*: **gaz ~** carbon dioxide; **neige ~** dry ice

carbonisé, e [kaʀbɔnize] *adj* charred

carburant [kaʀbyʀɑ̃] *nm* (motor) fuel

carburateur [kaʀbyʀatœʀ] *nm* carburettor

cardiaque [kaʀdjak] *adj* cardiac, heart *cpd* ▷ *nm/f* heart patient; **être ~** to have heart trouble

cardigan [kaʀdigɑ̃] *nm* cardigan

cardiologue [kaʀdjɔlɔg] *nm/f* cardiologist, heart specialist

carême [kaʀɛm] *nm*: **le C~** Lent

carence [kaʀɑ̃s] *nf* (*manque*) deficiency

caresse [kaʀɛs] *nf* caress

caresser [kaʀese] *vt* to caress; (*animal*) to stroke

cargaison [kaʀgɛzɔ̃] *nf* cargo, freight

cargo [kaʀgo] *nm* cargo boat, freighter

caricature [kaʀikatyʀ] *nf* caricature

carie [kaʀi] *nf*: **la ~ (dentaire)** tooth decay; **une ~** a bad tooth

carnaval [kaʀnaval] *nm* carnival

carnet [kaʀnɛ] *nm* (*calepin*) notebook; (*de*

tickets, timbres etc) book; **carnet de chèques**
cheque book
carotte [kaʀɔt] nf carrot
carré, e [kaʀe] adj square; (fig: franc)
straightforward ▷ nm (Math) square; **mètre/
kilomètre ~** square metre/kilometre
carreau, x [kaʀo] nm (par terre) (floor) tile;
(au mur) (wall) tile; (de fenêtre) (window)
pane; (motif) check, square; (Cartes: couleur)
diamonds pl; **tissu à ~x** checked fabric
carrefour [kaʀfuʀ] nm crossroads sg
carrelage [kaʀlaʒ] nm (sol) (tiled) floor
carrelet [kaʀlɛ] nm (poisson) plaice
carrément [kaʀemɑ̃] adv (franchement)
straight out, bluntly; (sans hésiter) straight;
(intensif) completely; **c'est ~ impossible** it's
completely impossible
carrière [kaʀjɛʀ] nf (métier) career; (de roches)
quarry; **militaire de ~** professional soldier
carrosserie [kaʀɔsʀi] nf body, coachwork no
pl
carrure [kaʀyʀ] nf build; (fig) stature, calibre
cartable [kaʀtabl] nm satchel, (school)bag
carte [kaʀt] nf (de géographie) map; (marine,
du ciel) chart; (d'abonnement, à jouer) card; (au
restaurant) menu; (aussi: **~ de visite**) (visiting)
card; **pouvez-vous me l'indiquer sur la ~?**
can you show me (it) on the map?; **à la ~** (au
restaurant) à la carte; **est-ce qu'on peut voir
la ~?** can we see the menu?; **donner ~ blanche
à qn** to give sb a free rein; **carte bancaire** cash
card; **Carte Bleue®** debit card; **carte à puce**
smart card; **carte de crédit** credit card; **carte
de fidélité** loyalty card; **carte d'identité**
identity card; **carte de séjour** residence
permit; **carte grise** (Auto) ≈ (car) registration
book, logbook; **carte memoire** (d'appareil-
photo numérique) memory card; **carte postale**
postcard; **carte routière** road map
carter [kaʀtɛʀ] nm sump
carton [kaʀtɔ̃] nm (matériau) cardboard;
(boîte) (cardboard) box; **faire un ~** (fam) to
score a hit; **carton (à dessin)** portfolio
cartouche [kaʀtuʃ] nf cartridge; (de
cigarettes) carton
cas [kɑ] nm case; **ne faire aucun ~ de** to take
no notice of; **en aucun ~** on no account; **au ~
où** in case; **en ~ de** in case of, in the event of;
en ~ de besoin if need be; **en tout ~** in any
case, at any rate
cascade [kaskad] nf waterfall, cascade
case [kɑz] nf (hutte) hut; (compartiment)
compartment; (sur un formulaire, de mots croisés
etc) box
caser [kɑze] (fam) vt (placer) to put (away);
(loger) to put up; **se caser** vi (se marier) to
settle down; (trouver un emploi) to find a
(steady) job
caserne [kazɛʀn] nf barracks pl

casier [kazje] nm (pour courrier) pigeonhole;
(compartiment) compartment; (à clef) locker;
casier judiciaire police record
casino [kazino] nm casino
casque [kask] nm helmet; (chez le coiffeur)
(hair-)drier; (pour audition) (head-)phones pl,
headset
casquette [kaskɛt] nf cap
casse...: **casse-croûte** nm inv snack; **casse-
noix** nm inv nutcrackers pl; **casse-pieds**
(fam) adj inv: **il est casse-pieds** he's a pain in
the neck
casser [kase] vt to break; (Jur) to quash; **se
casser** vi to break; **~ les pieds à qn** (fam:
irriter) to get on sb's nerves; **se ~ la tête** (fam)
to go to a lot of trouble
casserole [kasʀɔl] nf saucepan
casse-tête [kastɛt] nm inv (difficultés)
headache (fig)
cassette [kasɛt] nf (bande magnétique)
cassette; (coffret) casket
cassis [kasis] nm blackcurrant
cassoulet [kasulɛ] nm bean and sausage
hot-pot
catalogue [katalɔg] nm catalogue
catalytique [katalitik] adj: **pot ~** catalytic
convertor
catastrophe [katastʀɔf] nf catastrophe,
disaster
catéchisme [kateʃism] nm catechism
catégorie [kategɔʀi] nf category;
catégorique adj categorical
cathédrale [katedʀal] nf cathedral
catholique [katɔlik] adj, nm/f (Roman)
Catholic; **pas très ~** a bit shady ou fishy
cauchemar [koʃmaʀ] nm nightmare
cause [koz] nf cause; (Jur) lawsuit, case; **à ~ de**
because of, owing to; **pour ~ de** on account
of; **(et) pour ~** and for (a very) good reason;
être en ~ (intérêts) to be at stake; **remettre
en ~** to challenge; **causer** vt to cause ▷ vi to
chat, talk
caution [kosjɔ̃] nf guarantee, security; (Jur)
bail (bond); (fig) backing, support; **libéré sous
~** released on bail
cavalier, -ière [kavalje, jɛʀ] adj (désinvolte)
offhand ▷ nm/f rider; (au bal) partner ▷ nm
(Échecs) knight
cave [kav] nf cellar
CD sigle m (= compact disc) CD
CD-ROM [sedeʀɔm] sigle m CD-ROM

⊙ **MOT-CLÉ**

ce, cette [sə, sɛt] (devant nm **cet** + voyelle ou h
aspiré; pl **ces**) dét (proximité) this; these pl; (non-
proximité) that; those pl; **cette maison(-ci/là)**
this/that house; **cette nuit** (qui vient) tonight;
(passée) last night

▷ *pron* 1: **c'est** it's *ou* it is; **c'est un peintre** he's *ou* he is a painter; **ce sont des peintres** they're *ou* they are painters; **c'est le facteur** *etc* (à la porte) it's the postman; **c'est toi qui lui a parlé** it was you who spoke to him; **qui est-ce?** who is it?; (en désignant) who is he/she?; **qu'est-ce?** what is it?

2: **ce qui, ce que: ce qui me plaît, c'est sa franchise** what I like about him *ou* her is his *ou* her frankness; **il est bête, ce qui me chagrine** he's stupid, which saddens me; **tout ce qui bouge** everything that *ou* which moves; **tout ce que je sais** all I know; **ce dont j'ai parlé** what I talked about; **ce que c'est grand!** it's so big!; *voir aussi* **-ci; est-ce que; n'est-ce pas; c'est-à-dire**

ceci [səsi] *pron* this

céder [sede] *vt* (donner) to give up ▷ *vi* (chaise, barrage) to give way; (personne) to give in; **~ à** to yield to, give in to

CEDEX [sedɛks] *sigle m* (= courrier d'entreprise à distribution exceptionnelle) postal service for bulk users

cédille [sedij] *nf* cedilla

ceinture [sɛ̃tyʀ] *nf* belt; (taille) waist; **ceinture de sécurité** safety *ou* seat belt

cela [s(ə)la] *pron* that; (comme sujet indéfini) it; **~ m'étonne que ...** it surprises me that ...; **quand/où ~?** when/where (was that)?

célèbre [selɛbʀ] *adj* famous; **célébrer** *vt* to celebrate

céleri [selʀi] *nm*: **~(-rave)** celeriac; **céleri en branche** celery

célibataire [selibatɛʀ] *adj* single, unmarried ▷ *nm* bachelor ▷ *nf* unmarried woman

celle, celles [sɛl] *pron voir* **celui**

cellule [selyl] *nf* (gén) cell; **~ souche** stem cell

cellulite [selylit] *nf* cellulite

MOT-CLÉ

celui, celle [səlɥi, sɛl] (*mpl* **ceux**, *fpl* **celles**) *pron* 1: **celui-ci/là, celle-ci/là** this one/that one; **ceux-ci, celles-ci** these (ones); **ceux-là, celles-là** those (ones)

2: **celui qui bouge** the one which *ou* that moves; (personne) the one who moves; **celui que je vois** the one (which *ou* that) I see; (personne) the one (whom) I see; **celui dont je parle** the one I'm talking about; **celui de mon frère** my brother's; **celui du salon/du dessous** the one in (*ou* from) the lounge/below

3: (valeur indéfinie): **celui qui veut** whoever wants

cendre [sɑ̃dʀ] *nf* ash; **cendres** *nfpl* (d'un défunt) ashes; **sous la ~** (Culin) in (the) embers;

cendrier [sɑ̃dʀije] *nm* ashtray

censé, e [sɑ̃se] *adj*: **être ~ faire** to be supposed to do

censeur [sɑ̃sœʀ] *nm* (Scol) deputy-head (BRIT), vice-principal (US)

censure [sɑ̃syʀ] *nf* censorship; **censurer** *vt* (Cinéma, Presse) to censor; (Pol) to censure

cent [sɑ̃] *num* a hundred, one hundred ▷ *nm* (US, Canada etc) cent; (partie de l'euro) cent; **centaine** *nf*: **une centaine (de)** about a hundred, a hundred or so; **des centaines (de)** hundreds (of); **centenaire** *adj* hundred-year-old ▷ *nm* (anniversaire) centenary; (monnaie) cent; **centième** *num* hundredth; **centigrade** *nm* centigrade; **centilitre** *nm* centilitre; **centime** *nm* centime; **centime d'euro** *nm* euro cent; **centimètre** *nm* centimetre; (ruban) tape measure, measuring tape

central, e, -aux [sɑ̃tʀal, o] *adj* central ▷ *nm*: **~ (téléphonique)** (telephone) exchange; **centrale** *nf* power station; **centrale électrique/nucléaire** power/nuclear power station

centre [sɑ̃tʀ] *nm* centre; **centre commercial/sportif/culturel** shopping/sports/arts centre; **centre d'appels** call centre; **centre-ville** *nm* town centre, downtown (area) (US)

cèpe [sɛp] *nm* (edible) boletus

cependant [s(ə)pɑ̃dɑ̃] *adv* however

céramique [seʀamik] *nf* ceramics *sg*

cercle [sɛʀkl] *nm* circle; **cercle vicieux** vicious circle

cercueil [sɛʀkœj] *nm* coffin

céréale [seʀeal] *nf* cereal

cérémonie [seʀemɔni] *nf* ceremony; **sans ~** (inviter, manger) informally

cerf [sɛʀ] *nm* stag

cerf-volant [sɛʀvɔlɑ̃] *nm* kite

cerise [s(ə)ʀiz] *nf* cherry; **cerisier** *nm* cherry (tree)

cerner [sɛʀne] *vt* (Mil etc) to surround; (fig: problème) to delimit, define

certain, e [sɛʀtɛ̃, ɛn] *adj* certain ▷ *dét* certain; **d'un ~ âge** past one's prime, not so young; **un ~ temps** (quite) some time; **un ~ Georges** someone called Georges; **~s** *pron* some; **certainement** *adv* (probablement) most probably *ou* likely; (bien sûr) certainly, of course

certes [sɛʀt] *adv* (sans doute) admittedly; (bien sûr) of course

certificat [sɛʀtifika] *nm* certificate

certifier [sɛʀtifje] *vt*: **~ qch à qn** to assure sb of sth; **copie certifiée conforme** certified copy of the original

certitude [sɛʀtityd] *nf* certainty

cerveau, x [sɛʀvo] *nm* brain

cervelas [sɛʀvəla] *nm* saveloy

cervelle [sɛʀvɛl] *nf* (Anat) brain; (Culin) brains

ces [se] *dét voir* **ce**
CES *sigle m* (= *collège d'enseignement secondaire*) ≈ (junior) secondary school (BRIT)
cesse [sɛs]: **sans ~** *adv* (*tout le temps*) continually, constantly; (*sans interruption*) continuously; **il n'a eu de ~ que** he did not rest until; **cesser** *vt* to stop ▷ *vi* to stop, cease; **cesser de faire** to stop doing; **cessez-le-feu** *nm inv* ceasefire
c'est-à-dire [sɛtadiʀ] *adv* that is (to say)
cet, cette [sɛt] *dét voir* **ce**
ceux [sø] *pron voir* **celui**
chacun, e [ʃakœ̃, yn] *pron* each; (*indéfini*) everyone, everybody
chagrin [ʃagʀɛ̃] *nm* grief, sorrow; **avoir du ~** to be grieved
chahut [ʃay] *nm* uproar; **chahuter** *vt* to rag, bait ▷ *vi* to make an uproar
chaîne [ʃɛn] *nf* chain; (*Radio, TV*: *stations*) channel; **travail à la ~** production line work; **réactions en ~** chain reaction *sg*; **chaîne de montagnes** mountain range; **chaîne (hi-fi)** hi-fi system
chair [ʃɛʀ] *nf* flesh; **avoir la ~ de poule** to have goosepimples *ou* gooseflesh; **bien en ~** plump, well-padded; **en ~ et en os** in the flesh; **~ à saucisse** sausage meat
chaise [ʃɛz] *nf* chair; **chaise longue** deckchair
châle [ʃɑl] *nm* shawl
chaleur [ʃalœʀ] *nf* heat; (*fig: accueil*) warmth; **chaleureux, -euse** *adj* warm
chamailler [ʃamaje]: **se chamailler** *vi* to squabble, bicker
chambre [ʃɑ̃bʀ] *nf* bedroom; (*Pol, Comm*) chamber; **faire ~ à part** to sleep in separate rooms; **je voudrais une ~ pour deux personnes** I'd like a double room; **chambre à air** (*de pneu*) (inner) tube; **chambre à coucher** bedroom; **chambre à un lit/à deux lits** (*à l'hôtel*) single-/twin-bedded room; **chambre d'amis** spare *ou* guest room; **chambre d'hôte** ≈ bed and breakfast; **chambre meublée** bedsit(ter) (BRIT), furnished room; **chambre noire** (*Photo*) darkroom
chameau, x [ʃamo] *nm* camel
chamois [ʃamwa] *nm* chamois
champ [ʃɑ̃] *nm* field; **champ de bataille** battlefield; **champ de courses** racecourse
champagne [ʃɑ̃paɲ] *nm* champagne
champignon [ʃɑ̃piɲɔ̃] *nm* mushroom; (*terme générique*) fungus; **champignon de Paris** *ou* **de couche** button mushroom
champion, ne [ʃɑ̃pjɔ̃, jɔn] *adj, nm/f* champion; **championnat** *nm* championship
chance [ʃɑ̃s] *nf*: **la ~** luck; **chances** *nfpl* (*probabilités*) chances; **avoir de la ~** to be lucky; **il a des ~s de réussir** he's got a good chance of passing; **bonne ~!** good luck!
change [ʃɑ̃ʒ] *nm* (*devises*) exchange

changement [ʃɑ̃ʒmɑ̃] *nm* change; **changement de vitesses** gears *pl*
changer [ʃɑ̃ʒe] *vt* (*modifier*) to change, alter; (*remplacer, Comm*) to change ▷ *vi* to change, alter; **se changer** *vi* to change (o.s.); **~ de** (*remplacer: adresse, nom, voiture etc*) to change one's; (*échanger: place, train etc*) to change; **~ d'avis** to change one's mind; **~ de vitesse** to change gear; **il faut ~ à Lyon** you *ou* we *etc* have to change in Lyons; **où est-ce que je peux ~ de l'argent?** where can I change some money?
chanson [ʃɑ̃sɔ̃] *nf* song
chant [ʃɑ̃] *nm* song; (*art vocal*) singing; (*d'église*) hymn
chantage [ʃɑ̃taʒ] *nm* blackmail; **faire du ~** to use blackmail
chanter [ʃɑ̃te] *vt, vi* to sing; **si cela lui chante** (*fam*) if he feels like it; **chanteur, -euse** *nm/f* singer
chantier [ʃɑ̃tje] *nm* (building) site; (*sur une route*) roadworks *pl*; **mettre en ~** to put in hand; **chantier naval** shipyard
chantilly [ʃɑ̃tiji] *nf voir* **crème**
chantonner [ʃɑ̃tɔne] *vi, vt* to sing to oneself, hum
chapeau, x [ʃapo] *nm* hat; **~!** well done!
chapelle [ʃapɛl] *nf* chapel
chapitre [ʃapitʀ] *nm* chapter
chaque [ʃak] *dét* each, every; (*indéfini*) every
char [ʃaʀ] *nm* (*Mil*): **~ (d'assaut)** tank; **~ à voile** sand yacht
charbon [ʃaʀbɔ̃] *nm* coal; **charbon de bois** charcoal
charcuterie [ʃaʀkytʀi] *nf* (*magasin*) pork butcher's shop and delicatessen; (*produits*) cooked pork meats *pl*; **charcutier, -ière** *nm/f* pork butcher
chardon [ʃaʀdɔ̃] *nm* thistle
charge [ʃaʀʒ] *nf* (*fardeau*) load, burden; (*Élec, Mil, Jur*) charge; (*rôle, mission*) responsibility; **charges** *nfpl* (*du loyer*) service charges; **à la ~ de** (*dépendant de*) dependent upon; (*aux frais de*) chargeable to; **prendre en ~** to take charge of; (*suj: véhicule*) to take on; (*dépenses*) to take care of; **charges sociales** social security contributions
chargement [ʃaʀʒəmɑ̃] *nm* (*objets*) load
charger [ʃaʀʒe] *vt* (*voiture, fusil, caméra*) to load; (*batterie*) to charge ▷ *vi* (*Mil etc*) to charge; **se ~ de** to see to, take care of
chariot [ʃaʀjo] *nm* trolley; (*charrette*) waggon
charité [ʃaʀite] *nf* charity; **faire la ~ à** to give (something) to
charmant, e [ʃaʀmɑ̃, ɑ̃t] *adj* charming
charme [ʃaʀm] *nm* charm; **charmer** *vt* to charm
charpente [ʃaʀpɑ̃t] *nf* frame(work); **charpentier** *nm* carpenter

charrette [ʃaʀɛt] nf cart

charter [ʃaʀtɛʀ] nm (vol) charter flight

chasse [ʃas] nf hunting; (au fusil) shooting; (poursuite) chase; (aussi: ~ **d'eau**) flush; **prendre en ~** to give chase to; **tirer la ~ (d'eau)** to flush the toilet, pull the chain; **~ à courre** hunting; **chasse-neige** nm inv snowplough (BRIT), snowplow (US); **chasser** vt to hunt; (expulser) to chase away ou out, drive away ou out; **chasseur, -euse** nm/f hunter ▷ nm (avion) fighter

chat¹ [ʃa] nm cat

chat² [tʃat] nm (Internet) chat room

châtaigne [ʃatɛɲ] nf chestnut

châtain [ʃatɛ̃] adj inv (cheveux) chestnut (brown); (personne) chestnut-haired

château, x [ʃato] nm (forteresse) castle; (résidence royale) palace; (manoir) mansion; **château d'eau** water tower; **château fort** stronghold, fortified castle

châtiment [ʃatimɑ̃] nm punishment

chaton [ʃatɔ̃] nm (Zool) kitten

chatouiller [ʃatuje] vt to tickle; **chatouilleux, -euse** adj ticklish

chatte [ʃat] nf (she-)cat

chatter [tʃate] vi (Internet) to chat

chaud, e [ʃo, ʃod] adj (gén) warm; (très chaud) hot; **il fait ~** it's warm; it's hot; **avoir ~** to be warm; to be hot; **ça me tient ~** it keeps me warm; **rester au ~** to stay in the warm

chaudière [ʃodjɛʀ] nf boiler

chauffage [ʃofaʒ] nm heating; **chauffage central** central heating

chauffe-eau [ʃofo] nm inv water-heater

chauffer [ʃofe] vt to heat ▷ vi to heat up, warm up; (trop chauffer: moteur) to overheat; **se chauffer** vi (au soleil) to warm o.s.

chauffeur [ʃofœʀ] nm driver; (privé) chauffeur

chaumière [ʃomjɛʀ] nf (thatched) cottage

chaussée [ʃose] nf road(way)

chausser [ʃose] vt (bottes, skis) to put on; (enfant) to put shoes on; **~ du 38/42** to take size 38/42

chaussette [ʃosɛt] nf sock

chausson [ʃosɔ̃] nm slipper; (de bébé) bootee; **chausson (aux pommes)** (apple) turnover

chaussure [ʃosyʀ] nf shoe; **chaussures basses** flat shoes; **chaussures montantes** ankle boots; **chaussures de ski** ski boots

chauve [ʃov] adj bald; **chauve-souris** nf bat

chauvin, e [ʃovɛ̃, in] adj chauvinistic

chaux [ʃo] nf lime; **blanchi à la ~** whitewashed

chef [ʃɛf] nm head, leader; (de cuisine) chef; **commandant en ~** commander-in-chief; **chef d'accusation** charge; **chef d'entreprise** company head; **chef d'État** head of state; **chef de famille** head of the family; **chef de**

file (de parti etc) leader; **chef de gare** station master; **chef d'orchestre** conductor; **chef-d'œuvre** nm masterpiece; **chef-lieu** nm county town

chemin [ʃ(ə)mɛ̃] nm path; (itinéraire, direction, trajet) way; **en ~** on the way; **chemin de fer** railway (BRIT), railroad (US)

cheminée [ʃ(ə)mine] nf chimney; (à l'intérieur) chimney piece, fireplace; (de bateau) funnel

chemise [ʃ(ə)miz] nf shirt; (dossier) folder; **chemise de nuit** nightdress

chemisier [ʃ(ə)mizje] nm blouse

chêne [ʃɛn] nm oak (tree); (bois) oak

chenil [ʃ(ə)nil] nm kennels pl

chenille [ʃ(ə)nij] nf (Zool) caterpillar

chèque [ʃɛk] nm cheque (BRIT), check (US); **est-ce que je peux payer par ~?** can I pay by cheque?; **chèque sans provision** bad cheque; **chèque de voyage** traveller's cheque; **chéquier** [ʃekje] nm cheque book

cher, -ère [ʃɛʀ] adj (aimé) dear; (coûteux) expensive, dear ▷ adv: **ça coûte ~** it's expensive

chercher [ʃɛʀʃe] vt to look for; (gloire etc) to seek; **aller ~** to go for, go and fetch; **~ à faire** to try to do; **chercheur, -euse** nm/f researcher, research worker

chéri, e [ʃeʀi] adj beloved, dear; **(mon) ~** darling

cheval, -aux [ʃ(ə)val, o] nm horse; (Auto): **~ (vapeur)** horsepower no pl; **faire du ~** to ride; **à ~** on horseback; **à ~ sur** astride; (fig) overlapping; **cheval de course** racehorse

chevalier [ʃ(ə)valje] nm knight

chevalière [ʃ(ə)valjɛʀ] nf signet ring

chevaux [ʃevo] nmpl de **cheval**

chevet [ʃ(ə)vɛ] nm: **au ~ de qn** at sb's bedside; **lampe de chevet** bedside lamp

cheveu, x [ʃ(ə)vø] nm hair; **cheveux** nmpl (chevelure) hair sg; **avoir les ~x courts** to have short hair

cheville [ʃ(ə)vij] nf (Anat) ankle; (de bois) peg; (pour une vis) plug

chèvre [ʃɛvʀ] nf (she-)goat

chèvrefeuille [ʃɛvʀəfœj] nm honeysuckle

chevreuil [ʃəvʀœj] nm roe deer inv; (Culin) venison

⊙ **MOT-CLÉ**

chez [ʃe] prép **1** (à la demeure de) at; (: direction) to; **chez qn** at/to sb's house ou place; **je suis chez moi** I'm at home; **je rentre chez moi** I'm going home; **allons chez Nathalie** let's go to Nathalie's
2 (+profession) at; (: direction) to; **chez le boulanger/dentiste** at ou to the baker's/dentist's

3 (*dans le caractère, l'œuvre de*) in; **chez ce poète** in this poet's work; **c'est ce que je préfère chez lui** that's what I like best about him

chic [ʃik] *adj inv* chic, smart; (*fam: généreux*) nice, decent ▷ *nm* stylishness; **~ (alors)!** (*fam*) great!; **avoir le ~ de** to have the knack of

chicorée [ʃikɔʀe] *nf* (*café*) chicory; (*salade*) endive

chien [ʃjɛ̃] *nm* dog; **chien d'aveugle** guide dog; **chien de garde** guard dog

chienne [ʃjɛn] *nf* dog, bitch

chiffon [ʃifɔ̃] *nm* (piece of) rag; **chiffonner** *vt* to crumple; (*fam: tracasser*) to concern

chiffre [ʃifʀ] *nm* (*représentant un nombre*) figure, numeral; (*montant, total*) total, sum; **en ~s ronds** in round figures; **chiffre d'affaires** turnover; **chiffrer** *vt* (*dépense*) to put a figure to, assess; (*message*) to (en)code, cipher; **se chiffrer à** to add up to, amount to

chignon [ʃiɲɔ̃] *nm* chignon, bun

Chili [ʃili] *nm*: **le ~** Chile; **chilien, ne** *adj* Chilean ▷ *nm/f*: **Chilien, ne** Chilean

chimie [ʃimi] *nf* chemistry; **chimiothérapie** [ʃimjɔteʀapi] *nf* chemotherapy; **chimique** *adj* chemical; **produits chimiques** chemicals

chimpanzé [ʃɛ̃pɑ̃ze] *nm* chimpanzee

Chine [ʃin] *nf*: **la ~** China; **chinois, e** *adj* Chinese ▷ *nm/f*: **Chinois, e** Chinese ▷ *nm* (*Ling*) Chinese

chiot [ʃjo] *nm* pup(py)

chips [ʃips] *nfpl* crisps (BRIT), (potato) chips (US)

chirurgie [ʃiʀyʀʒi] *nf* surgery; **chirurgie esthétique** plastic surgery; **chirurgien, ne** *nm/f* surgeon

chlore [klɔʀ] *nm* chlorine

choc [ʃɔk] *nm* (*heurt*) impact, shock; (*collision*) crash; (*moral*) shock; (*affrontement*) clash

chocolat [ʃɔkɔla] *nm* chocolate; **chocolat au lait** milk chocolate

chœur [kœʀ] *nm* (*chorale*) choir; (*Opéra, Théâtre*) chorus; **en ~** in chorus

choisir [ʃwaziʀ] *vt* to choose, select

choix [ʃwa] *nm* choice, selection; **avoir le ~** to have the choice; **premier ~** (*Comm*) class one; **de ~** choice, selected; **au ~** as you wish

chômage [ʃomaʒ] *nm* unemployment; **mettre au ~** to make redundant, put out of work; **être au ~** to be unemployed *ou* out of work; **chômeur, -euse** *nm/f* unemployed person

choquer [ʃɔke] *vt* (*offenser*) to shock; (*deuil*) to shake

chorale [kɔʀal] *nf* choir

chose [ʃoz] *nf* thing; **c'est peu de ~** it's nothing (really)

chou, x [ʃu] *nm* cabbage; **mon petit ~** (my) sweetheart; **chou à la crème** choux

bun; **chou de Bruxelles** Brussels sprout; **choucroute** *nf* sauerkraut

chouette [ʃwɛt] *nf* owl ▷ *adj* (*fam*) great, smashing

chou-fleur [ʃuflœʀ] *nm* cauliflower

chrétien, ne [kʀetjɛ̃, jɛn] *adj, nm/f* Christian

Christ [kʀist] *nm*: **le ~** Christ; **christianisme** *nm* Christianity

chronique [kʀɔnik] *adj* chronic ▷ *nf* (*de journal*) column, page; (*historique*) chronicle; (*Radio, TV*): **la ~ sportive** the sports review

chronologique [kʀɔnɔlɔʒik] *adj* chronological

chronomètre [kʀɔnɔmɛtʀ] *nm* stopwatch; **chronométrer** *vt* to time

chrysanthème [kʀizɑ̃tɛm] *nm* chrysanthemum

⬤ **CHRYSANTHÈME**
⬤
⬤ Chrysanthemums are strongly associated
⬤ with funerals in France, and therefore
⬤ should not be given as gifts.

chuchotement [ʃyʃɔtmɑ̃] *nm* whisper

chuchoter [ʃyʃɔte] *vt, vi* to whisper

chut [ʃyt] *excl* sh!

chute [ʃyt] *nf* fall; (*déchet*) scrap; **faire une ~ (de 10 m)** to fall (10 m); **chute (d'eau)** waterfall; **chute libre** free fall; **chutes de pluie/neige** rainfall/snowfall

Chypre [ʃipʀ] *nm/f* Cyprus

-ci [si] *adv voir* **par** ▷ *dét*: **ce garçon~** this boy; **ces femmes~** these women

cible [sibl] *nf* target

ciboulette [sibulet] *nf* (small) chive

cicatrice [sikatʀis] *nf* scar; **cicatriser** *vt* to heal

ci-contre [sikɔ̃tʀ] *adv* opposite

ci-dessous [sidəsu] *adv* below

ci-dessus [sidəsy] *adv* above

cidre [sidʀ] *nm* cider

Cie *abr* (= *compagnie*) Co.

ciel [sjɛl] *nm* sky; (*Rel*) heaven

cieux [sjø] *nmpl de* **ciel**

cigale [sigal] *nf* cicada

cigare [sigaʀ] *nm* cigar

cigarette [sigaʀɛt] *nf* cigarette

ci-inclus, e [siɛ̃kly, yz] *adj, adv* enclosed

ci-joint, e [siʒwɛ̃, ɛ̃t] *adj, adv* enclosed

cil [sil] *nm* (eye)lash

cime [sim] *nf* top; (*montagne*) peak

ciment [simɑ̃] *nm* cement

cimetière [simtjɛʀ] *nm* cemetery; (*d'église*) churchyard

cinéaste [sineast] *nm/f* film-maker

cinéma [sinema] *nm* cinema

cinq [sɛ̃k] *num* five; **cinquantaine** *nf*: **une cinquantaine (de)** about fifty; **avoir la**

cinquantaine (*âge*) to be around fifty;
cinquante *num* fifty; **cinquantenaire** *adj*,
nm/f fifty-year-old; **cinquième** *num* fifth ▷ *nf*
(*Scol*) year 8 (*BRIT*), seventh grade (*US*)
cintre [sɛ̃tʀ] *nm* coat-hanger
cintré, e [sɛ̃tʀe] *adj* (*chemise*) fitted
cirage [siʀaʒ] *nm* (shoe) polish
circonflexe [siʀkɔ̃flɛks] *adj*: **accent ~**
circumflex accent
circonstance [siʀkɔ̃stɑ̃s] *nf* circumstance;
(*occasion*) occasion; **circonstances**
atténuantes mitigating circumstances
circuit [siʀkɥi] *nm* (*Élec, Tech*) circuit; (*trajet*)
tour, (round) trip
circulaire [siʀkylɛʀ] *adj*, *nf* circular
circulation [siʀkylasjɔ̃] *nf* circulation; (*Auto*):
la ~ (the) traffic
circuler [siʀkyle] *vi* (*sang, devises*) to circulate;
(*véhicules*) to drive (along); (*passants*) to walk
along; (*train, bus*) to run; **faire ~** (*nouvelle*) to
spread (about), circulate; (*badauds*) to move on
cire [siʀ] *nf* wax; **ciré** *nm* oilskin; **cirer** *vt* to
wax, polish
cirque [siʀk] *nm* circus; (*fig*) chaos, bedlam;
quel ~! what a carry-on!
ciseau, x [sizo] *nm*: **~ (à bois)** chisel; **ciseaux**
nmpl (*paire de ciseaux*) (pair of) scissors
citadin, e [sitadɛ̃, in] *nm/f* city dweller
citation [sitasjɔ̃] *nf* (*d'auteur*) quotation; (*Jur*)
summons *sg*
cité [site] *nf* town; (*plus grande*) city; **cité**
universitaire students' residences *pl*
citer [site] *vt* (*un auteur*) to quote (from);
(*nommer*) to name; (*Jur*) to summon
citoyen, ne [sitwajɛ̃, jɛn] *nm/f* citizen
citron [sitʀɔ̃] *nm* lemon; **citron pressé** (fresh)
lemon juice; **citron vert** lime; **citronnade** *nf*
still lemonade
citrouille [sitʀuj] *nf* pumpkin
civet [sivɛ] *nm*: **~ de lapin** rabbit stew
civière [sivjɛʀ] *nf* stretcher
civil, e [sivil] *adj* (*mariage, poli*) civil; (*non
militaire*) civilian; **en ~** in civilian clothes; **dans
le ~** in civilian life
civilisation [sivilizasjɔ̃] *nf* civilization
clair, e [klɛʀ] *adj* light; (*pièce*) light, bright; (*eau,
son, fig*) clear ▷ *adv*: **voir ~** to see clearly; **tirer
qch au ~** to clear sth up, clarify sth; **mettre
au ~** (*notes etc*) to tidy up ▷ *nm*: **~ de lune**
moonlight; **clairement** *adv* clearly
clairière [klɛʀjɛʀ] *nf* clearing
clandestin, e [klɑ̃dɛstɛ̃, in] *adj* clandestine,
secret; (*mouvement*) underground; (*travailleur,
immigration*) illegal; **passager ~** stowaway
claque [klak] *nf* (*gifle*) slap; **claquer** *vi* (*porte*)
to bang, slam; (*fam: mourir*) to snuff it ▷ *vt*
(*porte*) to slam, bang; (*doigts*) to snap; (*fam:
dépenser*) to blow; **il claquait des dents** his
teeth were chattering; **être claqué** (*fam*) to

be dead tired; **se claquer un muscle** to pull *ou*
strain a muscle; **claquettes** *nfpl* tap-dancing
sg; (*chaussures*) flip-flops
clarinette [klaʀinɛt] *nf* clarinet
classe [klɑs] *nf* class; (*Scol: local*) class(room);
(*: leçon, élèves*) class; **aller en ~** to go to school;
classement *nm* (*rang: Scol*) place; (*: Sport*)
placing; (*liste: Scol*) class list (in order of merit);
(*: Sport*) placings *pl*
classer [klɑse] *vt* (*idées, livres*) to classify;
(*papiers*) to file; (*candidat, concurrent*) to grade;
(*Jur: affaire*) to close; **se ~ premier/dernier**
to come first/last; (*Sport*) to finish first/last;
classeur *nm* (*cahier*) file
classique [klɑsik] *adj* classical; (*sobre: coupe
etc*) classic(al); (*habituel*) standard, classic
clavecin [klav(ə)sɛ̃] *nm* harpsichord
clavicule [klavikyl] *nf* collarbone
clavier [klavje] *nm* keyboard
clé [kle] *nf* key; (*Mus*) clef; (*de mécanicien*)
spanner (*BRIT*), wrench (*US*); **prix ~s en
main** (*d'une voiture*) on-the-road price; **clé de
contact** ignition key; **clé USB** USB key
clef [kle] *nf* = **clé**
clergé [klɛʀʒe] *nm* clergy
cliché [kliʃe] *nm* (*fig*) cliché; (*négatif*) negative;
(*photo*) print
client, e [klijɑ̃, klijɑ̃t] *nm/f* (*acheteur*)
customer, client; (*d'hôtel*) guest, patron; (*du
docteur*) patient; (*de l'avocat*) client; **clientèle**
nf (*du magasin*) customers *pl*, clientèle; (*du
docteur, de l'avocat*) practice
cligner [kliɲe] *vi*: **~ des yeux** to blink (one's
eyes); **~ de l'œil** to wink; **clignotant** *nm*
(*Auto*) indicator; **clignoter** *vi* (*étoiles etc*) to
twinkle; (*lumière*) to flicker
climat [klima] *nm* climate
climatisation [klimatizasjɔ̃] *nf* air
conditioning; **climatisé, e** *adj* air-conditioned
clin d'œil [klɛ̃dœj] *nm* wink; **en un clin d'œil**
in a flash
clinique [klinik] *nf* private hospital
clip [klip] *nm* (*boucle d'oreille*) clip-on; **(vidéo)
~** (pop) video
cliquer [klike] *vt* to click; **~ sur** to click on
clochard, e [klɔʃaʀ, aʀd] *nm/f* tramp
cloche [klɔʃ] *nf* (*d'église*) bell; (*fam*) clot;
clocher *nm* church tower; (*en pointe*) steeple
▷ *vi* (*fam*) to be *ou* go wrong; **de clocher** (*péj*)
parochial
cloison [klwazɔ̃] *nf* partition (wall)
clonage [klɔnaʒ] *nm* cloning
cloner [klone] *vt* to clone
cloque [klɔk] *nf* blister
clore [klɔʀ] *vt* to close
clôture [klotyʀ] *nf* closure; (*barrière*) enclosure
clou [klu] *nm* nail; **clous** *nmpl* (*passage clouté*)
pedestrian crossing; **pneus à ~s** studded
tyres; **le ~ du spectacle** the highlight of the

show; **clou de girofle** clove

clown [klun] nm clown

club [klœb] nm club

CNRS sigle m (= Centre nationale de la recherche scientifique) ≈ SERC (BRIT), ≈ NSF (US)

coaguler [kɔagyle] vt, vi (aussi: **se ~**: sang) to coagulate

cobaye [kɔbaj] nm guinea-pig

coca [kɔka] nm Coke®

cocaïne [kɔkain] nf cocaine

coccinelle [kɔksinɛl] nf ladybird (BRIT), ladybug (US)

cocher [kɔʃe] vt to tick off

cochon, ne [kɔʃɔ̃, ɔn] nm pig ▷ adj (fam) dirty, smutty; **cochon d'Inde** guinea pig; **cochonnerie** (fam) nf (saleté) filth; (marchandise) rubbish, trash

cocktail [kɔktɛl] nm cocktail; (réception) cocktail party

cocorico [kɔkɔʀiko] excl, nm cock-a-doodle-do

cocotte [kɔkɔt] nf (en fonte) casserole; **ma ~** (fam) sweetie (pie); **cocotte (minute)®** pressure cooker

code [kɔd] nm code ▷ adj: **phares ~s** dipped lights; **se mettre en ~(s)** to dip one's (head)lights; **code à barres** bar code; **code civil** Common Law; **code de la route** highway code; **code pénal** penal code; **code postal** (numéro) post (BRIT) ou zip (US) code

cœur [kœʀ] nm heart; (Cartes: couleur) hearts pl; (: carte) heart; **avoir bon ~** to be kind-hearted; **avoir mal au ~** to feel sick; **par ~** by heart; **de bon ~** willingly; **cela lui tient à ~** that's (very) close to his heart

coffre [kɔfʀ] nm (meuble) chest; (d'auto) boot (BRIT), trunk (US); **coffre-fort** nm safe; **coffret** nm casket

cognac [kɔɲak] nm brandy, cognac

cogner [kɔɲe] vi to knock; **se ~ contre** to knock ou bump into; **se ~ la tête** to bang one's head

cohérent, e [kɔeʀɑ̃, ɑ̃t] adj coherent, consistent

coiffé, e [kwafe] adj: **bien/mal ~** with tidy/untidy hair; **~ d'un chapeau** wearing a hat

coiffer [kwafe] vt (fig: surmonter) to cover, top; **se coiffer** vi to do one's hair; **~ qn** to do sb's hair; **coiffeur, -euse** nm/f hairdresser; **coiffeuse** nf (table) dressing table; **coiffure** nf (cheveux) hairstyle, hairdo; (art): **la coiffure** hairdressing

coin [kwɛ̃] nm corner; (pour coincer) wedge; **l'épicerie du ~** the local grocer; **dans le ~** (aux alentours) in the area, around about; (habiter) locally; **je ne suis pas du ~** I'm not from here; **au ~ du feu** by the fireside; **regard en ~** sideways glance

coincé, e [kwɛ̃se] adj stuck, jammed; (fig:

inhibé) inhibited, hung up (fam)

coïncidence [kɔɛ̃sidɑ̃s] nf coincidence

coing [kwɛ̃] nm quince

col [kɔl] nm (de chemise) collar; (encolure, cou) neck; (de montagne) pass; **col de l'utérus** cervix; **col roulé** polo-neck

colère [kɔlɛʀ] nf anger; **une ~** a fit of anger; **(se mettre) en ~ (contre qn)** (to get) angry (with sb); **coléreux, -euse, colérique** adj quick-tempered, irascible

colin [kɔlɛ̃] nm hake

colique [kɔlik] nf diarrhoea

colis [kɔli] nm parcel

collaborer [kɔ(l)labɔʀe] vi to collaborate; **~ à** to collaborate on; (revue) to contribute to

collant, e [kɔlɑ̃, ɑ̃t] adj sticky; (robe etc) clinging, skintight; (péj) clinging ▷ nm (bas) tights pl; (de danseur) leotard

colle [kɔl] nf glue; (à papiers peints) (wallpaper) paste; (fam: devinette) teaser, riddle; (Scol: fam) detention

collecte [kɔlɛkt] nf collection; **collectif, -ive** adj collective; (visite, billet) group cpd

collection [kɔlɛksjɔ̃] nf collection; (Édition) series; **collectionner** vt to collect; **collectionneur, -euse** nm/f collector

collectivité [kɔlɛktivite] nf group; **collectivités locales** (Admin) local authorities

collège [kɔlɛʒ] nm (école) (secondary) school; (assemblée) body; **collégien** nm schoolboy

collègue [kɔ(l)lɛg] nm/f colleague

coller [kɔle] vt (papier, timbre) to stick (on); (affiche) to stick up; (enveloppe) to stick down; (morceaux) to stick ou glue together; (Comput) to paste; (fam: mettre, fourrer) to stick, shove; (Scol: fam) to keep in ▷ vi (être collant) to be sticky; (adhérer) to stick; **~ à** to stick to; **être collé à un examen** (fam) to fail an exam

collier [kɔlje] nm (bijou) necklace; (de chien, Tech) collar

colline [kɔlin] nf hill

collision [kɔlizjɔ̃] nf collision, crash; **entrer en ~ (avec)** to collide (with)

collyre [kɔliʀ] nm eye drops

colombe [kɔlɔ̃b] nf dove

Colombie [kɔlɔ̃bi] nf: **la ~** Colombia

colonie [kɔlɔni] nf colony; **colonie (de vacances)** holiday camp (for children)

colonne [kɔlɔn] nf column; **se mettre en ~ par deux** to get into twos; **colonne (vertébrale)** spine, spinal column

colorant [kɔlɔʀɑ̃] nm colouring

colorer [kɔlɔʀe] vt to colour

colorier [kɔlɔʀje] vt to colour (in)

coloris [kɔlɔʀi] nm colour, shade

colza [kɔlza] nm rape(seed)

coma [kɔma] nm coma; **être dans le ~** to be in a coma

combat [kɔ̃ba] nm fight, fighting no pl;

combat de boxe boxing match; **combattant** nm: **ancien combattant** war veteran;
combattre vt to fight; (épidémie, ignorance) to combat, fight against

combien [kɔ̃bjɛ̃] adv (quantité) how much; (nombre) how many; **~ de** (quantité) how much; (nombre) how many; **~ de temps** how long; **~ ça coûte/pèse?** how much does it cost/weigh?; **on est le ~ aujourd'hui?** (fam) what's the date today?

combinaison [kɔ̃binɛzɔ̃] nf combination; (astuce) scheme; (de femme) slip; (de plongée) wetsuit; (bleu de travail) boiler suit (BRIT), coveralls pl (US)

combiné [kɔ̃bine] nm (aussi: **~ téléphonique**) receiver

comble [kɔ̃bl] adj (salle) packed (full) ▷ nm (du bonheur, plaisir) height; **combles** nmpl (Constr) attic sg, loft sg; **c'est le ~!** that beats everything!

combler [kɔ̃ble] vt (trou) to fill in; (besoin, lacune) to fill; (déficit) to make good; (satisfaire) to fulfil

comédie [kɔmedi] nf comedy; (fig) playacting no pl; **faire la ~** (fam) to make a fuss; **comédie musicale** musical; **comédien, ne** nm/f actor(-tress)

comestible [kɔmɛstibl] adj edible

comique [kɔmik] adj (drôle) comical; (Théâtre) comic ▷ nm (artiste) comic, comedian

commandant [kɔmɑ̃dɑ̃] nm (gén) commander, commandant; (Navig, Aviat) captain

commande [kɔmɑ̃d] nf (Comm) order; **commandes** nfpl (Aviat etc) controls; **sur ~** to order; **commander** vt (Comm) to order; (diriger, ordonner) to command; **commander à qn de faire** to command ou order sb to do; **je peux commander, s'il vous plaît?** can I order, please?

〇 MOT-CLÉ

comme [kɔm] prép 1 (comparaison) like; **tout comme son père** just like his father; **fort comme un bœuf** as strong as an ox; **joli comme tout** ever so pretty
2 (manière) like; **faites-le comme ça** do it like this, do it this way; **comme ci, comme ça** so-so, middling; **comme il faut** (correctement) properly
3 (en tant que) as a; **donner comme prix** to give as a prize; **travailler comme secrétaire** to work as a secretary
▷ conj 1 (ainsi que) as; **elle écrit comme elle parle** she writes as she talks; **comme si** as if
2 (au moment où, alors que) as; **il est parti comme j'arrivais** he left as I arrived
3 (parce que, puisque) as; **comme il était en**

retard, il ... as he was late, he ...
▷ adv: **comme il est fort/c'est bon!** he's so strong/it's so good!

commencement [kɔmɑ̃smɑ̃] nm beginning, start

commencer [kɔmɑ̃se] vt, vi to begin, start; **~ à** ou **de faire** to begin ou start doing

comment [kɔmɑ̃] adv how; **~?** (que dites-vous) pardon?; **et ~!** and how!

commentaire [kɔmɑ̃tɛʀ] nm (remarque) comment, remark; (exposé) commentary

commerçant, e [kɔmɛʀsɑ̃, ɑ̃t] nm/f shopkeeper, trader

commerce [kɔmɛʀs] nm (activité) trade, commerce; (boutique) business; **~ électronique** e-commerce; **~ équitable** fair trade; **commercial, e, -aux** adj commercial, trading; (péj) commercial; **les commerciaux** the sales people; **commercialiser** vt to market

commissaire [kɔmisɛʀ] nm (de police) ≈ (police) superintendent; **commissaire aux comptes** (Admin) auditor; **commissariat** nm police station

commission [kɔmisjɔ̃] nf (comité, pourcentage) commission; (message) message; (course) errand; **commissions** nfpl (achats) shopping sg

commode [kɔmɔd] adj (pratique) convenient, handy; (facile) easy; (personne): **pas ~** awkward (to deal with) ▷ nf chest of drawers

commun, e [kɔmœ̃, yn] adj common; (pièce) communal, shared; (effort) joint; **ça sort du ~** it's out of the ordinary; **le ~ des mortels** the common run of people; **en ~** (faire) jointly; **mettre en ~** to pool, share; **communs** nmpl (bâtiments) outbuildings; **d'un ~ accord** by mutual agreement

communauté [kɔmynote] nf community

commune [kɔmyn] nf (Admin) commune, ≈ district; (: urbaine) ≈ borough

communication [kɔmynikasjɔ̃] nf communication

communier [kɔmynje] vi (Rel) to receive communion

communion [kɔmynjɔ̃] nf communion

communiquer [kɔmynike] vt (nouvelle, dossier) to pass on, convey; (peur etc) to communicate ▷ vi to communicate; **se communiquer à** (se propager) to spread to

communisme [kɔmynism] nm communism; **communiste** adj, nm/f communist

commutateur [kɔmytatœʀ] nm (Élec) (change-over) switch, commutator

compact, e [kɔ̃pakt] adj (dense) dense; (appareil) compact

compagne [kɔ̃paɲ] nf companion

compagnie [kɔ̃paɲi] nf (firme, Mil) company;

tenir **~ à qn** to keep sb company; **fausser ~ à qn** to give sb the slip, slip *ou* sneak away from sb; **compagnie aérienne** airline (company)
compagnon [kɔ̃paɲɔ̃] *nm* companion
comparable [kɔ̃paʀabl] *adj:* **~ (à)** comparable (to)
comparaison [kɔ̃paʀɛzɔ̃] *nf* comparison
comparer [kɔ̃paʀe] *vt* to compare; **~ qch/qn à** *ou* **et** (*pour choisir*) to compare sth/sb with *ou* and; (*pour établir une similitude*) to compare sth/sb to
compartiment [kɔ̃paʀtimɑ̃] *nm* compartment; **un ~ non-fumeurs** a non-smoking compartment (BRIT) *ou* car (US)
compas [kɔ̃pɑ] *nm* (*Géom*) (pair of) compasses *pl;* (*Navig*) compass
compatible [kɔ̃patibl] *adj* compatible
compatriote [kɔ̃patʀijɔt] *nm/f* compatriot
compensation [kɔ̃pɑ̃sasjɔ̃] *nf* compensation
compenser [kɔ̃pɑ̃se] *vt* to compensate for, make up for
compétence [kɔ̃petɑ̃s] *nf* competence
compétent, e [kɔ̃petɑ̃, ɑ̃t] *adj* (*apte*) competent, capable
compétition [kɔ̃petisjɔ̃] *nf* (*gén*) competition; (*Sport: épreuve*) event; **la ~ automobile** motor racing
complément [kɔ̃plemɑ̃] *nm* complement; (*reste*) remainder; **complément d'information** (*Admin*) supplementary *ou* further information; **complémentaire** *adj* complementary; (*additionnel*) supplementary
complet, -ète [kɔ̃plɛ, ɛt] *adj* complete; (*plein: hôtel etc*) full ▷ *nm* (*aussi:* **~-veston**) suit; **pain complet** wholemeal bread; **complètement** *adv* completely; **compléter** *vt* (*porter à la quantité voulue*) to complete; (*augmenter: connaissances, études*) to complement, supplement; (: *garde-robe*) to add to
complexe [kɔ̃plɛks] *adj, nm* complex; **complexe hospitalier/industriel** hospital/industrial complex; **complexé, e** *adj* mixed-up, hung-up
complication [kɔ̃plikasjɔ̃] *nf* complexity, intricacy; (*difficulté, ennui*) complication; **complications** *nfpl* (*Méd*) complications
complice [kɔ̃plis] *nm* accomplice
compliment [kɔ̃plimɑ̃] *nm* (*louange*) compliment; **compliments** *nmpl* (*félicitations*) congratulations
compliqué, e [kɔ̃plike] *adj* complicated, complex; (*personne*) complicated
comportement [kɔ̃pɔʀtəmɑ̃] *nm* behaviour
comporter [kɔ̃pɔʀte] *vt* (*consister en*) to consist of, comprise; (*inclure*) to have; **se comporter** *vi* to behave
composer [kɔ̃poze] *vt* (*musique, texte*) to compose; (*mélange, équipe*) to make up; (*numéro*) to dial; (*constituer*) to make up, form

▷ *vi* (*transiger*) to come to terms; **se composer de** to be composed of, be made up of; **compositeur, -trice** *nm/f* (*Mus*) composer; **composition** *nf* composition; (*Scol*) test
composter [kɔ̃pɔste] *vt* (*billet*) to punch

● **COMPOSTER**
●
● In France you have to punch your ticket on
● the platform to validate it before getting
● onto the train.

compote [kɔ̃pɔt] *nf* stewed fruit *no pl;* **compote de pommes** stewed apples
compréhensible [kɔ̃pʀeɑ̃sibl] *adj* comprehensible; (*attitude*) understandable
compréhensif, -ive [kɔ̃pʀeɑ̃sif, iv] *adj* understanding

Attention à ne pas traduire *compréhensif* par *comprehensive*.

comprendre [kɔ̃pʀɑ̃dʀ] *vt* to understand; (*se composer de*) to comprise, consist of
compresse [kɔ̃pʀɛs] *nf* compress
comprimé [kɔ̃pʀime] *nm* tablet
compris, e [kɔ̃pʀi, iz] *pp de* **comprendre** ▷ *adj* (*inclus*) included; **~ entre** (*situé*) contained between; **l'électricité ~e/non ~e, y/non ~ l'électricité** including/excluding electricity; **100 euros tout ~** 100 euros all inclusive *ou* all-in
comptabilité [kɔ̃tabilite] *nf* (*activité*) accounting, accountancy; (*comptes*) accounts *pl*, books *pl;* (*service*) accounts office
comptable [kɔ̃tabl] *nm/f* accountant
comptant [kɔ̃tɑ̃] *adv:* **payer ~** to pay cash; **acheter ~** to buy for cash
compte [kɔ̃t] *nm* count; (*total, montant*) count, (right) number; (*bancaire, facture*) account; **comptes** *nmpl* (*Finance*) accounts, books; (*fig*) explanation *sg;* **en fin de ~** all things considered; **s'en tirer à bon ~** to get off lightly; **pour le ~ de** on behalf of; **pour son propre ~** for one's own benefit; **régler un ~** (*s'acquitter de qch*) to settle an account; (*se venger*) to get one's own back; **rendre des ~s à qn** (*fig*) to be answerable to sb; **tenir ~ de** to take account of; **travailler à son ~** to work for oneself; **rendre ~ (à qn) de qch** to give (sb) an account of sth; *voir aussi* **rendre**; **compte à rebours** countdown; **compte courant** current account; **compte rendu** account, report; (*de film, livre*) review; **compte-gouttes** *nm inv* dropper
compter [kɔ̃te] *vt* to count; (*facturer*) to charge for; (*avoir à son actif, comporter*) to have; (*prévoir*) to allow, reckon; (*penser, espérer*): **~ réussir** to expect to succeed ▷ *vi* to count; (*être économe*) to economize; (*figurer*): **~ parmi** to be *ou* rank among; **~ sur** to count (up)on; **~**

avec qch/qn to reckon with *ou* take account of sth/sb; **sans ~ que** besides which

compteur [kɔ̃tœʀ] *nm* meter; **compteur de vitesse** speedometer

comptine [kɔ̃tin] *nf* nursery rhyme

comptoir [kɔ̃twaʀ] *nm* (*de magasin*) counter; (*bar*) bar

con, ne [kɔ̃, kɔn] (*fam!*) *adj* damned *ou* bloody (*BRIT*) stupid (!)

concentrer [kɔ̃sɑ̃tʀe] *vt* to concentrate; **se concentrer** *vi* to concentrate

concerner [kɔ̃sɛʀne] *vt* to concern; **en ce qui me concerne** as far as I am concerned

concert [kɔ̃sɛʀ] *nm* concert; **de ~** (*décider*) unanimously

concessionnaire [kɔ̃sesjɔnɛʀ] *nm/f* agent, dealer

concevoir [kɔ̃s(ə)vwaʀ] *vt* (*idée, projet*) to conceive (of); (*comprendre*) to understand; (*enfant*) to conceive; **bien/mal conçu** well-/badly-designed

concierge [kɔ̃sjɛʀʒ] *nm/f* caretaker

concis, e [kɔ̃si, iz] *adj* concise

conclure [kɔ̃klyʀ] *vt* to conclude; **conclusion** *nf* conclusion

conçois *etc* [kɔ̃swa] *vb voir* **concevoir**

concombre [kɔ̃kɔ̃bʀ] *nm* cucumber

concours [kɔ̃kuʀ] *nm* competition; (*Scol*) competitive examination; (*assistance*) aid, help; **concours de circonstances** combination of circumstances; **concours hippique** horse show

concret, -ète [kɔ̃kʀɛ, ɛt] *adj* concrete

conçu, e [kɔ̃sy] *pp de* **concevoir**

concubinage [kɔ̃kybinaʒ] *nm* (*Jur*) cohabitation

concurrence [kɔ̃kyʀɑ̃s] *nf* competition; **faire ~ à** to be in competition with; **jusqu'à ~ de** up to

concurrent, e [kɔ̃kyʀɑ̃, ɑ̃t] *nm/f* (*Sport, Écon etc*) competitor; (*Scol*) candidate

condamner [kɔ̃dane] *vt* (*blâmer*) to condemn; (*Jur*) to sentence; (*porte, ouverture*) to fill in, block up; **~ qn à 2 ans de prison** to sentence sb to 2 years' imprisonment

condensation [kɔ̃dɑ̃sasjɔ̃] *nf* condensation

condition [kɔ̃disjɔ̃] *nf* condition; **conditions** *nfpl* (*tarif, prix*) terms; (*circonstances*) conditions; **sans ~s** unconditionally; **à ~ de** *ou* **que** provided that; **conditionnel, le** *nm* conditional (tense)

conditionnement [kɔ̃disjɔnmɑ̃] *nm* (*emballage*) packaging

condoléances [kɔ̃dɔleɑ̃s] *nfpl* condolences

conducteur, -trice [kɔ̃dyktœʀ, tʀis] *nm/f* driver ▷ *nm* (*Élec etc*) conductor

conduire [kɔ̃dyiʀ] *vt* to drive; (*délégation, troupeau*) to lead; **se conduire** *vi* to behave; **~ à** to lead to; **~ qn quelque part** to take sb

somewhere; **to drive sb somewhere**

conduite [kɔ̃dyit] *nf* (*comportement*) behaviour; (*d'eau, de gaz*) pipe; **sous la ~ de** led by

confection [kɔ̃fɛksjɔ̃] *nf* (*fabrication*) making; (*Couture*): **la ~** the clothing industry

conférence [kɔ̃feʀɑ̃s] *nf* conference; (*exposé*) lecture; **conférence de presse** press conference

confesser [kɔ̃fese] *vt* to confess; **confession** *nf* confession; (*culte: catholique etc*) denomination

confetti [kɔ̃feti] *nm* confetti *no pl*

confiance [kɔ̃fjɑ̃s] *nf* (*en l'honnêteté de qn*) confidence, trust; (*en la valeur de qch*) faith; **avoir ~ en** to have confidence *ou* faith in, trust; **faire ~ à qn** to trust sb; **mettre qn en ~** to win sb's trust; **confiance en soi** self-confidence

confiant, e [kɔ̃fjɑ̃, jɑ̃t] *adj* confident; trusting

confidence [kɔ̃fidɑ̃s] *nf* confidence; **confidentiel, le** *adj* confidential

confier [kɔ̃fje] *vt*: **~ à qn** (*objet, travail*) to entrust to sb; (*secret, pensée*) to confide to sb; **se ~ à qn** to confide in sb

confirmation [kɔ̃fiʀmasjɔ̃] *nf* confirmation

confirmer [kɔ̃fiʀme] *vt* to confirm

confiserie [kɔ̃fizʀi] *nf* (*magasin*) confectioner's *ou* sweet shop; **confiseries** *nfpl* (*bonbons*) confectionery *sg*

confisquer [kɔ̃fiske] *vt* to confiscate

confit, e [kɔ̃fi, it] *adj*: **fruits ~s** crystallized fruits; **confit d'oie** *nm* conserve of goose

confiture [kɔ̃fityʀ] *nf* jam

conflit [kɔ̃fli] *nm* conflict

confondre [kɔ̃fɔ̃dʀ] *vt* (*jumeaux, faits*) to confuse, mix up; (*témoin, menteur*) to confound; **se confondre** *vi* to merge; **se ~ en excuses** to apologize profusely

conforme [kɔ̃fɔʀm] *adj*: **~ à** (*loi, règle*) in accordance with; **conformément** *adv*: **conformément à** in accordance with; **conformer** *vt*: **se conformer à** to conform to

confort [kɔ̃fɔʀ] *nm* comfort; **tout ~** (*Comm*) with all modern conveniences; **confortable** *adj* comfortable

confronter [kɔ̃fʀɔ̃te] *vt* to confront

confus, e [kɔ̃fy, yz] *adj* (*vague*) confused; (*embarrassé*) embarrassed; **confusion** *nf* (*voir confus*) confusion; embarrassment; (*voir confondre*) confusion, mixing up

congé [kɔ̃ʒe] *nm* (*vacances*) holiday; **en ~** on holiday; **semaine/jour de ~** week/day off; **prendre ~ de qn** to take one's leave of sb; **donner son ~ à** to give in one's notice to; **congé de maladie** sick leave; **congé de maternité** maternity leave; **congés payés** paid holiday

congédier [kɔ̃ʒedje] *vt* to dismiss

congélateur [kɔ̃ʒelatœʀ] *nm* freezer

congeler [kɔ̃ʒ(ə)le] vt to freeze; **les produits congelés** frozen foods

congestion [kɔ̃ʒɛstjɔ̃] nf congestion

Congo [kɔ̃o] nm: **le ~** Congo, the Democratic Republic of the Congo

congrès [kɔ̃gʀɛ] nm congress

conifère [kɔnifɛʀ] nm conifer

conjoint, e [kɔ̃ʒwɛ̃, wɛ̃t] adj joint ▷ nm/f spouse

conjonctivite [kɔ̃ʒɔ̃ktivit] nf conjunctivitis

conjoncture [kɔ̃ʒɔ̃ktyʀ] nf circumstances pl; **la ~ actuelle** the present (economic) situation

conjugaison [kɔ̃ʒygɛzɔ̃] nf (Ling) conjugation

connaissance [kɔnɛsɑ̃s] nf (savoir) knowledge no pl; (personne connue) acquaintance; **être sans ~** to be unconscious; **perdre/reprendre ~** to lose/regain consciousness; **à ma/sa ~** to (the best of) my/his knowledge; **faire la ~ de qn** to meet sb

connaisseur, -euse [kɔnɛsœʀ, øz] nm/f connoisseur

connaître [kɔnɛtʀ] vt to know; (éprouver) to experience; (avoir: succès) to have, enjoy; **~ de nom/vue** to know by name/sight; **ils se sont connus à Genève** they (first) met in Geneva; **s'y ~ en qch** to know a lot about sth

connecter [kɔnɛkte] vt to connect; **se ~ à Internet** to log onto the Internet

connerie [kɔnʀi] (fam!) nf stupid thing (to do/say)

connexion [kɔnɛksjɔ̃] nf connection

connu, e [kɔny] adj (célèbre) well-known

conquérir [kɔ̃keʀiʀ] vt to conquer; **conquête** nf conquest

consacrer [kɔ̃sakʀe] vt (employer) to devote, dedicate; (Rel) to consecrate; **se ~ à qch** to dedicate ou devote o.s. to sth

conscience [kɔ̃sjɑ̃s] nf conscience; **avoir/prendre ~ de** to be/become aware of; **perdre ~** to lose consciousness; **avoir bonne/mauvaise ~** to have a clear/guilty conscience; **consciencieux, -euse** adj conscientious; **conscient, e** adj conscious

consécutif, -ive [kɔ̃sekytif, iv] adj consecutive; **~ à** following upon

conseil [kɔ̃sɛj] nm (avis) piece of advice; (assemblée) council; **des ~s** advice; **prendre ~ (auprès de qn)** to take advice (from sb); **conseil d'administration** board (of directors); **conseil des ministres** ≈ the Cabinet; **conseil municipal** town council

conseiller, -ère [kɔ̃seje, ɛʀ] nm/f adviser ▷ vt (personne) to advise; (méthode, action) to recommend, advise; **~ à qn de** to advise sb to; **pouvez-vous me ~ un bon restaurant?** can you suggest a good restaurant?

consentement [kɔ̃sɑ̃tmɑ̃] nm consent

consentir [kɔ̃sɑ̃tiʀ] vt to agree, consent

conséquence [kɔ̃sekɑ̃s] nf consequence;

en ~ (donc) consequently; (de façon appropriée) accordingly; **conséquent, e** adj logical, rational; (fam: important) substantial; **par conséquent** consequently

conservateur, -trice [kɔ̃sɛʀvatœʀ, tʀis] nm/f (Pol) conservative; (de musée) curator ▷ nm (pour aliments) preservative

conservatoire [kɔ̃sɛʀvatwaʀ] nm academy

conserve [kɔ̃sɛʀv] nf (gén pl) canned ou tinned (BRIT) food; **en ~** canned, tinned (BRIT)

conserver [kɔ̃sɛʀve] vt (faculté) to retain, keep; (amis, livres) to keep; (préserver, Culin) to preserve

considérable [kɔ̃sideʀabl] adj considerable, significant, extensive

considération [kɔ̃sideʀasjɔ̃] nf consideration; (estime) esteem

considérer [kɔ̃sideʀe] vt to consider; **~ qch comme** to regard sth as

consigne [kɔ̃siɲ] nf (de gare) left luggage (office) (BRIT), checkroom (US); (ordre, instruction) instructions pl; **consigne automatique** left-luggage locker

consister [kɔ̃siste] vi: **~ en/à faire** to consist of/in doing

consoler [kɔ̃sɔle] vt to console

consommateur, -trice [kɔ̃sɔmatœʀ, tʀis] nm/f (Écon) consumer; (dans un café) customer

consommation [kɔ̃sɔmasjɔ̃] nf (boisson) drink; (Écon) consumption; **de ~** (biens, sociétés) consumer cpd

consommer [kɔ̃sɔme] vt (suj: personne) to eat ou drink, consume; (: voiture, machine) to use, consume; (mariage) to consummate ▷ vi (dans un café) to (have a) drink

consonne [kɔ̃sɔn] nf consonant

constamment [kɔ̃stamɑ̃] adv constantly

constant, e [kɔ̃stɑ̃, ɑ̃t] adj constant; (personne) steadfast

constat [kɔ̃sta] nm (de police, d'accident) report; **~ (à l')amiable** jointly-agreed statement for insurance purposes; **~ d'échec** acknowledgement of failure

constatation [kɔ̃statasjɔ̃] nf (observation) (observed) fact, observation

constater [kɔ̃state] vt (remarquer) to note; (Admin, Jur: attester) to certify

consterner [kɔ̃stɛʀne] vt to dismay

constipé, e [kɔ̃stipe] adj constipated

constitué, e [kɔ̃stitɥe] adj: **~ de** made up ou composed of

constituer [kɔ̃stitɥe] vt (équipe) to set up; (dossier, collection) to put together; (suj: éléments: composer) to make up, constitute; (représenter, être) to constitute; **se ~ prisonnier** to give o.s. up

constructeur, -trice [kɔ̃stʀyktœʀ, tʀis] nm/f manufacturer, builder

constructif, -ive [kɔ̃stʀyktif, iv] adj

constructive

construction [kɔ̃stʀyksjɔ̃] *nf* construction, building

construire [kɔ̃stʀɥiʀ] *vt* to build, construct

consul [kɔ̃syl] *nm* consul; **consulat** *nm* consulate

consultant [kɔ̃syltɑ̃] *adj, nm* consultant

consultation [kɔ̃syltasjɔ̃] *nf* consultation; **heures de ~** (*Méd*) surgery (BRIT) *ou* office (US) hours

consulter [kɔ̃sylte] *vt* to consult ▷ *vi* (*médecin*) to hold surgery (BRIT), be in (the office) (US)

contact [kɔ̃takt] *nm* contact; **au ~ de** (*air, peau*) on contact with; (*gens*) through contact with; **mettre/couper le ~** (*Auto*) to switch on/off the ignition; **entrer en** *ou* **prendre ~ avec** to get in touch *ou* contact with; **contacter** *vt* to contact, get in touch with

contagieux, -euse [kɔ̃taʒjø, jøz] *adj* infectious; (*par le contact*) contagious

contaminer [kɔ̃tamine] *vt* to contaminate

conte [kɔ̃t] *nm* tale; **conte de fées** fairy tale

contempler [kɔ̃tɑ̃ple] *vt* to contemplate, gaze at

contemporain, e [kɔ̃tɑ̃pɔʀɛ̃, ɛn] *adj, nm/f* contemporary

contenir [kɔ̃t(ə)niʀ] *vt* to contain; (*avoir une capacité de*) to hold

content, e [kɔ̃tɑ̃, ɑ̃t] *adj* pleased, glad; **~ de** pleased with; **contenter** *vt* to satisfy, please; **se contenter de** to content o.s. with

contenu [kɔ̃t(ə)ny] *nm* (*d'un récipient*) contents *pl*; (*d'un texte*) content

conter [kɔ̃te] *vt* to recount, relate

conteste [kɔ̃tɛst]: **sans ~** *adv* unquestionably, indisputably; **contester** *vt* to question ▷ *vi* (*Pol, gén*) rebel (against established authority)

contexte [kɔ̃tɛkst] *nm* context

continent [kɔ̃tinɑ̃] *nm* continent

continu, e [kɔ̃tiny] *adj* continuous; **faire la journée ~e** to work without taking a full lunch break; **(courant) continu** direct current, DC

continuel, le [kɔ̃tinɥɛl] *adj* (*qui se répète*) constant, continual; (*continu*) continuous

continuer [kɔ̃tinɥe] *vt* (*travail, voyage etc*) to continue (with), carry on (with), go on (with); (*prolonger: alignement, rue*) to continue ▷ *vi* (*vie, bruit*) to continue, go on; **~ à** *ou* **de faire** to go on *ou* continue doing

contourner [kɔ̃tuʀne] *vt* to go round; (*difficulté*) to get round

contraceptif, -ive [kɔ̃tʀasɛptif, iv] *adj, nm* contraceptive; **contraception** *nf* contraception

contracté, e [kɔ̃tʀakte] *adj* tense

contracter [kɔ̃tʀakte] *vt* (*muscle etc*) to tense, contract; (*maladie, dette*) to contract; (*assurance*) to take out; **se contracter** *vi*

(*muscles*) to contract

contractuel, le [kɔ̃tʀaktɥɛl] *nm/f* (*agent*) traffic warden

contradiction [kɔ̃tʀadiksjɔ̃] *nf* contradiction; **contradictoire** *adj* contradictory, conflicting

contraignant, e [kɔ̃tʀɛɲɑ̃, ɑ̃t] *adj* restricting

contraindre [kɔ̃tʀɛ̃dʀ] *vt*: **~ qn à faire** to compel sb to do; **contrainte** *nf* constraint

contraire [kɔ̃tʀɛʀ] *adj, nm* opposite; **~ à** contrary to; **au ~** on the contrary

contrarier [kɔ̃tʀaʀje] *vt* (*personne: irriter*) to annoy; (*fig: projets*) to thwart, frustrate; **contrariété** *nf* annoyance

contraste [kɔ̃tʀast] *nm* contrast

contrat [kɔ̃tʀa] *nm* contract

contravention [kɔ̃tʀavɑ̃sjɔ̃] *nf* parking ticket

contre [kɔ̃tʀ] *prép* against; (*en échange*) (in exchange) for; **par ~** on the other hand

contrebande [kɔ̃tʀəbɑ̃d] *nf* (*trafic*) contraband, smuggling; (*marchandise*) contraband, smuggled goods *pl*; **faire la ~ de** to smuggle

contrebas [kɔ̃tʀəbɑ]: **en ~** *adv* (down) below

contrebasse [kɔ̃tʀəbas] *nf* (double) bass

contre...: **contrecoup** *nm* repercussions *pl*; **contredire** *vt* (*personne*) to contradict; (*faits*) to refute

contrefaçon [kɔ̃tʀəfasɔ̃] *nf* forgery

contre...: **contre-indication** (*pl* **contre-indications**) *nf* (*Méd*) contra-indication; **"contre-indication en cas d'eczéma"** "should not be used by people with eczema"; **contre-indiqué, e** *adj* (*Méd*) contraindicated; (*déconseillé*) unadvisable, ill-advised

contremaître [kɔ̃tʀəmɛtʀ] *nm* foreman

contre-plaqué [kɔ̃tʀəplake] *nm* plywood

contresens [kɔ̃tʀəsɑ̃s] *nm* (*erreur*) misinterpretation; (*de traduction*) mistranslation; **à ~** the wrong way

contretemps [kɔ̃tʀətɑ̃] *nm* hitch; **à ~** (*fig*) at an inopportune moment

contribuer [kɔ̃tʀibɥe]: **~ à** *vt* to contribute towards; **contribution** *nf* contribution; **mettre à contribution** to call upon; **contributions directes/indirectes** direct/indirect taxation

contrôle [kɔ̃tʀol] *nm* checking *no pl*, check; (*des prix*) monitoring, control; (*test*) test, examination; **perdre le ~ de** (*véhicule*) to lose control of; **contrôle continu** (*Scol*) continuous assessment; **contrôle d'identité** identity check

contrôler [kɔ̃tʀole] *vt* (*vérifier*) to check; (*surveiller: opérations*) to supervise; (: *prix*) to monitor, control; (*maîtriser, Comm: firme*) to control; **contrôleur, -euse** *nm/f* (*de train*) (ticket) inspector; (*de bus*) (bus) conductor(-tress)

controversé, e [kɔ̃trɔvɛrse] adj (personnage, question) controversial

contusion [kɔ̃tyzjɔ̃] nf bruise, contusion

convaincre [kɔ̃vɛ̃kr] vt: **~ qn (de qch)** to convince sb (of sth); **~ qn (de faire)** to persuade sb (to do)

convalescence [kɔ̃valesɑ̃s] nf convalescence

convenable [kɔ̃vnabl] adj suitable; (assez bon, respectable) decent

convenir [kɔ̃vnir] vi to be suitable; **~ à** to suit; **~ de** (bien-fondé de qch) to admit (to), acknowledge; (date, somme etc) to agree upon; **~ que** (admettre) to admit that; **~ de faire** to agree to do

convention [kɔ̃vɑ̃sjɔ̃] nf convention; **conventions** nfpl (convenances) convention sg; **convention collective** (Écon) collective agreement; **conventionné, e** adj (Admin) applying charges laid down by the state

convenu, e [kɔ̃vny] pp de **convenir** ▷ adj agreed

conversation [kɔ̃vɛrsasjɔ̃] nf conversation

convertir [kɔ̃vɛrtir] vt: **~ qn (à)** to convert sb (to); **se convertir (à)** to be converted (to); **~ qch en** to convert sth into

conviction [kɔ̃viksjɔ̃] nf conviction

convienne etc [kɔ̃vjɛn] vb voir **convenir**

convivial, e, -aux [kɔ̃vivjal, jo] adj (Inform) user-friendly

convocation [kɔ̃vɔkasjɔ̃] nf (document) notification to attend; (: Jur) summons sg

convoquer [kɔ̃vɔke] vt (assemblée) to convene; (subordonné) to summon; (candidat) to ask to attend

coopération [kɔɔperasjɔ̃] nf co-operation; (Admin): **la C~** ≈ Voluntary Service Overseas (BRIT), ≈ Peace Corps (US)

coopérer [kɔɔpere] vi: **~ (à)** to co-operate (in)

coordonné, e [kɔɔrdɔne] adj coordinated; **coordonnées** nfpl (adresse etc) address and telephone number

coordonner [kɔɔrdɔne] vt to coordinate

copain [kɔpɛ̃] (fam) nm mate, pal; (petit ami) boyfriend

copie [kɔpi] nf copy; (Scol) script, paper; **copier** vt, vi to copy; **copier coller** (Comput) copy and paste; **copier sur** to copy from; **copieur** nm (photo)copier

copieux, -euse [kɔpjø, jøz] adj copious

copine [kɔpin] (fam) nf mate, pal; (petite amie) girlfriend

coq [kɔk] nm cock, rooster

coque [kɔk] nf (de noix, mollusque) shell; (de bateau) hull; **à la ~** (Culin) (soft-)boiled

coquelicot [kɔkliko] nm poppy

coqueluche [kɔklyʃ] nf whooping-cough

coquet, te [kɔkɛ, ɛt] adj appearance-conscious; (logement) smart, charming

coquetier [kɔk(ə)tje] nm egg-cup

coquillage [kɔkijaʒ] nm (mollusque) shellfish inv; (coquille) shell

coquille [kɔkij] nf shell; (Typo) misprint; **coquille St Jacques** scallop

coquin, e [kɔkɛ̃, in] adj mischievous, roguish; (polisson) naughty

cor [kɔr] nm (Mus) horn; (Méd): **~ (au pied)** corn

corail, -aux [kɔraj, o] nm coral no pl

Coran [kɔrɑ̃] nm: **le ~** the Koran

corbeau, x [kɔrbo] nm crow

corbeille [kɔrbɛj] nf basket; **corbeille à papier** waste paper basket ou bin

corde [kɔrd] nf rope; (de violon, raquette) string; **usé jusqu'à la ~** threadbare; **corde à linge** washing ou clothes line; **corde à sauter** skipping rope; **cordes vocales** vocal cords; **cordée** nf (d'alpinistes) rope, roped party

cordialement [kɔrdjalmɑ̃] adv (formule épistolaire) (kind) regards

cordon [kɔrdɔ̃] nm cord, string; **cordon de police** police cordon; **cordon ombilical** umbilical cord

cordonnerie [kɔrdɔnri] nf shoe repairer's (shop); **cordonnier** nm shoe repairer

Corée [kɔre] nf: **la ~ du Sud/du Nord** South/North Korea

coriace [kɔrjas] adj tough

corne [kɔrn] nf horn; (de cerf) antler

cornée [kɔrne] nf cornea

corneille [kɔrnɛj] nf crow

cornemuse [kɔrnəmyz] nf bagpipes pl

cornet [kɔrnɛ] nm (paper) cone; (de glace) cornet, cone

corniche [kɔrniʃ] nf (route) coast road

cornichon [kɔrniʃɔ̃] nm gherkin

Cornouailles [kɔrnwaj] nf Cornwall

corporel, le [kɔrpɔrɛl] adj bodily; (punition) corporal

corps [kɔr] nm body; **à ~ perdu** headlong; **prendre ~** to take shape; **corps électoral** the electorate; **corps enseignant** the teaching profession

correct, e [kɔrɛkt] adj correct; (fam: acceptable: salaire, hôtel) reasonable, decent; **correcteur, -trice** nm/f (Scol) examiner; **correction** nf (voir corriger) correction; (voir correct) correctness; (coups) thrashing

correspondance [kɔrɛspɔ̃dɑ̃s] nf correspondence; (de train, d'avion) connection; **cours par ~** correspondence course; **vente par ~** mail-order business

correspondant, e [kɔrɛspɔ̃dɑ̃, ɑ̃t] nm/f correspondent; (Tél) person phoning (ou being phoned)

correspondre [kɔrɛspɔ̃dr] vi to correspond, tally; **~ à** to correspond to; **~ avec qn** to correspond with sb

corrida [kɔʀida] *nf* bullfight

corridor [kɔʀidɔʀ] *nm* corridor

corrigé [kɔʀiʒe] *nm* (*Scol: d'exercice*) correct version

corriger [kɔʀiʒe] *vt* (*devoir*) to correct; (*punir*) to thrash; **~ qn de** (*défaut*) to cure sb of

corrompre [kɔʀɔ̃pʀ] *vt* to corrupt; (*acheter: témoin etc*) to bribe

corruption [kɔʀypsjɔ̃] *nf* corruption; (*de témoins*) bribery

corse [kɔʀs] *adj, nm/f* Corsican ▷ *nf*: **la C~** Corsica

corsé, e [kɔʀse] *adj* (*café*) full-flavoured; (*sauce*) spicy; (*problème*) tough

cortège [kɔʀtɛʒ] *nm* procession

cortisone [kɔʀtizɔn] *nf* cortisone

corvée [kɔʀve] *nf* chore, drudgery *no pl*

cosmétique [kɔsmetik] *nm* beauty care product

cosmopolite [kɔsmɔpɔlit] *adj* cosmopolitan

costaud, e [kɔsto, od] (*fam*) *adj* strong, sturdy

costume [kɔstym] *nm* (*d'homme*) suit; (*de théâtre*) costume; **costumé, e** *adj* dressed up; **bal costumé** fancy dress ball

cote [kɔt] *nf* (*en Bourse*) quotation; **cote d'alerte** danger *ou* flood level; **cote de popularité** (popularity) rating

côte [kot] *nf* (*rivage*) coast(line); (*pente*) hill; (*Anat*) rib; (*d'un tricot, tissu*) rib, ribbing *no pl*; **~ à ~** side by side; **la Côte (d'Azur)** the (French) Riviera

côté [kote] *nm* (*gén*) side; (*direction*) way, direction; **de chaque ~ (de)** on each side (of); **de tous les ~s** from all directions; **de quel ~ est-il parti?** which way did he go?; **de ce/de l'autre ~** this/the other way; **du ~ de** (*provenance*) from; (*direction*) towards; (*proximité*) near; **de ~** (*regarder*) sideways; **mettre qch de ~** to put sth aside; **mettre de l'argent de ~** to save some money; **à ~** (right) nearby; (*voisins*) next door; **à ~ de** beside, next to; (*en comparaison*) compared to; **être aux ~s de** to be by the side of

Côte d'Ivoire [kotdivwaʀ] *nf*: **la Côte d'Ivoire** Côte d'Ivoire, the Ivory Coast

côtelette [kotlɛt] *nf* chop

côtier, -ière [kotje, jɛʀ] *adj* coastal

cotisation [kɔtizasjɔ̃] *nf* subscription, dues *pl*; (*pour une pension*) contributions *pl*

cotiser [kɔtize] *vi*: **~ (à)** to pay contributions (to); **se cotiser** *vi* to club together

coton [kɔtɔ̃] *nm* cotton; **coton hydrophile** cotton wool (BRIT), absorbent cotton (US); **Coton-tige®** *nm* cotton bud

cou [ku] *nm* neck

couchant [kuʃɑ̃] *adj*: **soleil ~** setting sun

couche [kuʃ] *nf* layer; (*de peinture, vernis*) coat; (*de bébé*) nappy (BRIT), diaper (US); **couches**

sociales social levels *ou* strata

couché, e [kuʃe] *adj* lying down; (*au lit*) in bed

coucher [kuʃe] *vt* (*personne*) to put to bed; (: *loger*) to put up; (*objet*) to lay on its side ▷ *vi* to sleep; **~ avec qn** to sleep with sb; **se coucher** *vi* (*pour dormir*) to go to bed; (*pour se reposer*) to lie down; (*soleil*) to set; **coucher de soleil** sunset

couchette [kuʃɛt] *nf* couchette; (*pour voyageur, sur bateau*) berth

coucou [kuku] *nm* cuckoo

coude [kud] *nm* (*Anat*) elbow; (*de tuyau, de la route*) bend; **~ à ~** shoulder to shoulder, side by side

coudre [kudʀ] *vt* (*bouton*) to sew on ▷ *vi* to sew

couette [kwɛt] *nf* duvet, quilt; **couettes** *nfpl* (*cheveux*) bunches

couffin [kufɛ̃] *nm* Moses basket

couler [kule] *vi* to flow, run; (*fuir: stylo, récipient*) to leak; (*nez*) to run; (*sombrer: bateau*) to sink ▷ *vt* (*cloche, sculpture*) to cast; (*bateau*) to sink; (*faire échouer: personne*) to bring down

couleur [kulœʀ] *nf* colour (BRIT), color (US); (*Cartes*) suit; **film/télévision en ~s** colo(u)r film/television; **de ~** (*homme, femme: vieilli*) colo(u)red

couleuvre [kulœvʀ] *nf* grass snake

coulisses [kulis] *nfpl* (*Théâtre*) wings; (*fig*): **dans les ~** behind the scenes

couloir [kulwaʀ] *nm* corridor, passage; (*d'avion*) aisle; (*de bus*) gangway; **~ aérien/de navigation** air/shipping lane

coup [ku] *nm* (*heurt, choc*) knock; (*affectif*) blow, shock; (*agressif*) blow; (*avec arme à feu*) shot; (*de l'horloge*) stroke; (*tennis, golf*) stroke; (*boxe*) blow; (*fam: fois*) time; **donner un ~ de balai** to give the floor a sweep; **boire un ~** (*fam*) to have a drink; **être dans le ~** (*impliqué*) to be in on it; (*à la page*) to be hip *ou* trendy; **du ~ ...** as a result; **d'un seul ~** (*subitement*) suddenly; (*à la fois*) at one go; **du premier ~** first time; **du même ~** at the same time; **à tous les ~s** (*fam*) every time; **tenir le ~** to hold out; **après ~** afterwards; **à ~ sûr** definitely, without fail; **~ sur ~** in quick succession; **sur le ~** outright; **sous le ~ de** (*surprise etc*) under the influence of; **coup de chance** stroke of luck; **coup de coude** nudge (with the elbow); **coup de couteau** stab (of a knife); **coup d'envoi** kick-off; **coup d'essai** first attempt; **coup d'État** coup; **coup de feu** shot; **coup de filet** (*Police*) haul; **coup de foudre** (*fig*) love at first sight; **coup de frein** (sharp) braking *no pl*; **coup de grâce** coup de grâce, death blow; **coup de main**: **donner un coup de main à qn** to give sb a (helping) hand; **coup d'œil** glance; **coup de pied** kick; **coup de poing** punch; **coup de soleil** sunburn *no pl*; **coup de sonnette** ring of the bell; **coup de téléphone** phone call; **coup de tête** (fig) (sudden) impulse; **coup de théâtre** (fig) dramatic turn of events; **coup de tonnerre** clap of thunder; **coup de vent** gust of wind; **en coup de vent** (rapidement) in a tearing hurry; **coup franc** free kick

coupable [kupabl] adj guilty ▷ nm/f (gén) culprit; (Jur) guilty party

coupe [kup] nf (verre) goblet; (à fruits) dish; (Sport) cup; (de cheveux, de vêtement) cut; (graphique, plan) (cross) section

couper [kupe] vt to cut; (retrancher) to cut (out); (route, courant) to cut off; (appétit) to take away; (vin à table) to dilute ▷ vi to cut; (prendre un raccourci) to take a short-cut; **se couper** vi (se blesser) to cut o.s.; **~ la parole à qn** to cut sb short; **nous avons été coupés** we've been cut off

couple [kupl] nm couple

couplet [kuplɛ] nm verse

coupole [kupɔl] nf dome

coupon [kupɔ̃] nm (ticket) coupon; (reste de tissu) remnant

coupure [kupyʀ] nf cut; (billet de banque) note; (de journal) cutting; **coupure de courant** power cut

cour [kuʀ] nf (de ferme, jardin) (court)yard; (d'immeuble) back yard; (Jur, royale) court; **faire la ~ à qn** to court sb; **cour d'assises** court of assizes; **cour de récréation** playground

courage [kuʀaʒ] nm courage, bravery; **courageux, -euse** adj brave, courageous

couramment [kuʀamɑ̃] adv commonly; (parler) fluently

courant, e [kuʀɑ̃, ɑ̃t] adj (fréquent) common; (Comm, gén: normal) standard; (en cours) current ▷ nm current; (fig) movement; (: d'opinion) trend; **être au ~ (de)** (fait, nouvelle) to know (about); **mettre qn au ~ (de)** to tell sb (about); (nouveau travail etc) to teach sb the basics (of); **se tenir au ~ (de)** (techniques etc) to keep o.s. up-to-date (on); **dans le ~ de** (pendant) in the course of; **le 10 ~** (Comm) the 10th inst.; **courant d'air** draught; **courant électrique** (electric) current, power

courbature [kuʀbatyʀ] nf ache

courbe [kuʀb] adj curved ▷ nf curve

coureur, -euse [kuʀœʀ, øz] nm/f (Sport) runner (ou driver); (péj) womanizer; manhunter

courge [kuʀʒ] nf (Culin) marrow; **courgette** nf courgette (BRIT), zucchini (US)

courir [kuʀiʀ] vi to run ▷ vt (Sport: épreuve) to compete in; (risque) to run; (danger) to face; **~ les magasins** to go round the shops; **le bruit court que** the rumour is going round that

couronne [kuʀɔn] nf crown; (de fleurs) wreath, circlet

courons etc [kuʀɔ̃] vb voir **courir**

courriel [kuʀjɛl] nm e-mail

courrier [kuʀje] nm mail, post; (lettres à écrire) letters pl; **est-ce que j'ai du ~?** are there any letters for me?; **courrier électronique** e-mail

> Attention à ne pas traduire **courrier** par le mot anglais **courier**.

courroie [kuʀwa] nf strap; (Tech) belt

courrons etc [kuʀɔ̃] vb voir **courir**

cours [kuʀ] nm (leçon) class; (: particulier) lesson; (série de leçons, cheminement) course; (écoulement) flow; (Comm: de devises) rate; (: de denrées) price; **donner libre ~ à** to give free expression to; **avoir ~** (Scol) to have a class ou lecture; **en ~** (année) current; (travaux) in progress; **en ~ de route** on the way; **au ~ de** in the course of, during; **le ~ de change** the exchange rate; **cours d'eau** waterway; **cours du soir** night school

course [kuʀs] nf running; (Sport: épreuve) race; (d'un taxi) journey, trip; (commission) errand; **courses** nfpl (achats) shopping sg; **faire des ~s** to do some shopping

court, e [kuʀ, kuʀt(ə)] adj short ▷ adv short ▷ nm: **~ (de tennis)** (tennis) court; **à ~ de** short of; **prendre qn de ~** to catch sb unawares; **court-circuit** nm short-circuit

courtoisie [kuʀtwazi] nf courtesy

couru, e [kuʀy] pp de **courir**

cousais etc [kuze] vb voir **coudre**

couscous [kuskus] nm couscous

cousin, e [kuzɛ̃, in] nm/f cousin

coussin [kusɛ̃] nm cushion

cousu, e [kuzy] pp de **coudre**

coût [ku] nm cost; **le ~ de la vie** the cost of living

couteau, x [kuto] nm knife

coûter [kute] vt, vi to cost; **combien ça coûte?** how much is it?, what does it cost?; **ça coûte trop cher** it's too expensive; **coûte que coûte** at all costs; **coûteux, -euse** adj costly, expensive

coutume [kutym] nf custom

couture [kutyʀ] nf sewing; (profession) dressmaking; (points) seam; **couturier** nm fashion designer; **couturière** nf dressmaker

couvent [kuvɑ̃] nm (de sœurs) convent; (de frères) monastery

couver [kuve] vt to hatch; (maladie) to be coming down with ▷ vi (feu) to smoulder; (révolte) to be brewing

couvercle [kuvɛʀkl] nm lid; (de bombe aérosol etc, qui se visse) cap, top

couvert, e [kuvɛʀ, ɛʀt] pp de **couvrir** ▷ adj (ciel) overcast ▷ nm place setting; (place à table) place; **couverts** nmpl (ustensiles) cutlery sg; **~ de** covered with ou in; **mettre le ~** to lay the table

couverture [kuvɛʀtyʀ] nf blanket; (de livre, assurance, fig) cover; (presse) coverage

couvre-lit [kuvʀəli] nm bedspread

couvrir [kuvʀiʀ] vt to cover; **se couvrir** vi (s'habiller) to cover up; (se coiffer) to put on one's hat; (ciel) to cloud over

cow-boy [kɔbɔj] nm cowboy

crabe [kʀɑb] nm crab

cracher [kʀaʃe] vi, vt to spit

crachin [kʀaʃɛ̃] nm drizzle

craie [kʀɛ] nf chalk

craindre [kʀɛ̃dʀ] vt to fear, be afraid of; (être sensible à: chaleur, froid) to be easily damaged by

crainte [kʀɛ̃t] nf fear; **de ~ de/que** for fear of/that; **craintif, -ive** adj timid

crampe [kʀɑ̃p] nf cramp; **j'ai une ~ à la jambe** I've got cramp in my leg

cramponner [kʀɑ̃pɔne] vb: **se ~ (à)** to hang ou cling on (to)

cran [kʀɑ̃] nm (entaille) notch; (de courroie) hole; (fam: courage) guts pl

crâne [kʀɑn] nm skull

crapaud [kʀapo] nm toad

craquement [kʀakmɑ̃] nm crack, snap; (du plancher) creak, creaking no pl

craquer [kʀake] vi (bois, plancher) to creak; (fil, branche) to snap; (couture) to come apart; (fig: accusé) to break down; (: fam) to crack up ▷ vt (allumette) to strike; **j'ai craqué** (fam) I couldn't resist it

crasse [kʀas] nf grime, filth; **crasseux, -euse** adj grimy, filthy

cravache [kʀavaʃ] nf (riding) crop

cravate [kʀavat] nf tie

crawl [kʀol] nm crawl; **dos ~é** backstroke

crayon [kʀɛjɔ̃] nm pencil; **crayon à bille** ball-point pen; **crayon de couleur** crayon, colouring pencil; **crayon-feutre** (pl **crayons-feutres**) nm felt(-tip) pen

création [kʀeasjɔ̃] nf creation

crèche [kʀɛʃ] nf (de Noël) crib; (garderie) crèche, day nursery

crédit [kʀedi] nm (gén) credit; **crédits** nmpl (fonds) funds; **payer/acheter à ~** to pay/buy on credit ou on easy terms; **faire ~ à qn** to give sb credit; **créditer** vt: **créditer un compte (de)** to credit an account (with)

créer [kʀee] vt to create

crémaillère [kʀemajɛʀ] nf: **pendre la ~** to have a house-warming party

crème [kʀɛm] nf cream; (entremets) cream dessert ▷ adj inv cream(-coloured); **un (café) ~** ≈ a white coffee; **crème anglaise** (egg) custard; **crème Chantilly** whipped cream; **crème à raser** shaving cream; **crème solaire** suntan lotion

créneau, x [kʀeno] nm (de fortification) crenel(le); (dans marché) gap, niche; (Auto): **faire un ~** to reverse into a parking space (between two cars alongside the kerb)

crêpe [kʀɛp] nf (galette) pancake ▷ nm (tissu) crêpe; **crêperie** nf pancake shop ou restaurant

crépuscule [kʀepyskyl] nm twilight, dusk

cresson [kʀesɔ̃] nm watercress

creuser [kʀøze] vt (trou, tunnel) to dig; (sol) to dig a hole in; (fig) to go (deeply) into; **ça creuse** that gives you a real appetite; **se ~ la cervelle** (fam) to rack one's brains

creux, -euse [kʀø, kʀøz] adj hollow ▷ nm hollow; **heures creuses** slack periods; (électricité, téléphone) off-peak periods; **avoir un ~** (fam) to be hungry

crevaison [kʀəvɛzɔ̃] nf puncture

crevé, e [kʀəve] (fam) adj (fatigué) shattered (BRIT), exhausted

crever [kʀəve] vt (ballon) to burst ▷ vi (pneu) to burst; (automobiliste) to have a puncture (BRIT) ou a flat (tire) (US); (fam) to die

crevette [kʀəvɛt] nf: **~ (rose)** prawn; **crevette grise** shrimp

cri [kʀi] nm cry, shout; (d'animal: spécifique) cry, call; **c'est le dernier ~** (fig) it's the latest fashion

criard, e [kʀijaʀ, kʀijaʀd] adj (couleur) garish, loud; (voix) yelling

cric [kʀik] nm (Auto) jack

crier [kʀije] vi (pour appeler) to shout, cry (out); (de douleur etc) to scream, yell ▷ vt (injure) to shout (out), yell (out)

crime [kʀim] nm crime; (meurtre) murder; **criminel, le** nm/f criminal; (assassin) murderer

crin [kʀɛ̃] nm (de cheval) hair no pl

crinière [kʀinjɛʀ] nf mane

crique [kʀik] nf creek, inlet

criquet [kʀike] nm grasshopper

crise [kʀiz] nf crisis; (Méd) attack; (: d'épilepsie) fit; **piquer une ~ de nerfs** to go hysterical; **crise cardiaque** heart attack; **crise de foie: avoir une crise de foie** to have really bad indigestion

cristal, -aux [kʀistal, o] nm crystal

critère [kʀitɛʀ] nm criterion

critiquable [kʀitikabl] adj open to criticism

critique [kʀitik] adj critical ▷ nm/f (de théâtre, musique) critic ▷ nf criticism; (Théâtre etc: article) review

critiquer [kʀitike] vt (dénigrer) to criticize; (évaluer) to assess, examine (critically)

croate [kʀɔat] adj Croatian ▷ nm/f: **C~** Croat, Croatian

Croatie [kʀɔasi] nf: **la ~** Croatia

crochet [kʀɔʃe] nm hook; (détour) detour; (Tricot: aiguille) crochet hook; (: technique) crochet; **vivre aux ~s de qn** to live ou sponge off sb

crocodile [kʀɔkɔdil] nm crocodile

croire [kʀwaʀ] vt to believe; **se ~ fort** to think one is strong; **~ que** to believe ou think that; **~ à, ~ en** to believe in

croisade [kʀwazad] nf crusade

croisement [kʀwazmɑ̃] *nm* (*carrefour*) crossroads *sg*; (*Bio*) crossing; (: *résultat*) crossbreed

croiser [kʀwaze] *vt* (*personne, voiture*) to pass; (*route*) to cross, cut across; (*Bio*) to cross; **se croiser** *vi* (*personnes, véhicules*) to pass each other; (*routes, lettres*) to cross; (*regards*) to meet; **~ les jambes/bras** to cross one's legs/fold one's arms

croisière [kʀwazjɛʀ] *nf* cruise

croissance [kʀwasɑ̃s] *nf* growth

croissant [kʀwasɑ̃] *nm* (*à manger*) croissant; (*motif*) crescent

croître [kʀwatʀ] *vi* to grow

croix [kʀwa] *nf* cross; **la Croix Rouge** the Red Cross

croque-monsieur [kʀɔkməsjø] *nm inv* toasted ham and cheese sandwich

croquer [kʀɔke] *vt* (*manger*) to crunch; (: *fruit*) to munch; (*dessiner*) to sketch; **chocolat à croquer** plain dessert chocolate

croquis [kʀɔki] *nm* sketch

crotte [kʀɔt] *nf* droppings *pl*; **crottin** *nm* dung, manure; (*fromage*) (small round) cheese (*made of goat's milk*)

croustillant, e [kʀustijɑ̃, ɑ̃t] *adj* crisp

croûte [kʀut] *nf* crust; (*du fromage*) rind; (*Méd*) scab; **en ~** (*Culin*) in pastry

croûton [kʀutɔ̃] *nm* (*Culin*) crouton; (*bout du pain*) crust, heel

croyant, e [kʀwajɑ̃, ɑ̃t] *nm/f* believer

CRS *sigle fpl* (= *Compagnies républicaines de sécurité*) state security police force ▷ *sigle m* member of the CRS

cru, e [kʀy] *pp de* **croire** ▷ *adj* (*non cuit*) raw; (*lumière, couleur*) harsh; (*paroles*) crude ▷ *nm* (*vignoble*) vineyard; (*vin*) wine; **un grand ~** a great vintage; **jambon ~** Parma ham

crû [kʀy] *pp de* **croître**

cruauté [kʀyote] *nf* cruelty

cruche [kʀyʃ] *nf* pitcher, jug

crucifix [kʀysifi] *nm* crucifix

crudités [kʀydite] *nfpl* (*Culin*) selection of raw vegetables

crue [kʀy] *nf* (*inondation*) flood

cruel, le [kʀyɛl] *adj* cruel

crus *etc* [kʀy] *vb voir* **croire**; **croître**

crûs *etc* [kʀy] *vb voir* **croître**

crustacés [kʀystase] *nmpl* shellfish

Cuba [kyba] *nf* Cuba; **cubain, e** *adj* Cuban ▷ *nm/f*: **Cubain, e** Cuban

cube [kyb] *nm* cube; (*jouet*) brick; **mètre ~** cubic metre; **2 au ~** 2 cubed

cueillette [kœjɛt] *nf* picking; (*quantité*) crop, harvest

cueillir [kœjiʀ] *vt* (*fruits, fleurs*) to pick, gather; (*fig*) to catch

cuiller [kɥijɛʀ], **cuillère** [kɥijɛʀ] *nf* spoon; **cuiller à café** coffee spoon; (*Culin*)

≈ teaspoonful; **cuiller à soupe** soup-spoon; (*Culin*) ≈ tablespoonful; **cuillerée** *nf* spoonful

cuir [kɥiʀ] *nm* leather; **cuir chevelu** scalp

cuire [kɥiʀ] *vt* (*aliments*) to cook; (*au four*) to bake ▷ *vi* to cook; **bien cuit** (*viande*) well done; **trop cuit** overdone

cuisine [kɥizin] *nf* (*pièce*) kitchen; (*art culinaire*) cookery, cooking; (*nourriture*) cooking, food; **faire la ~** to cook; **cuisiné, e** *adj*: **plat cuisiné** ready-made meal *ou* dish; **cuisiner** *vt* to cook; (*fam*) to grill ▷ *vi* to cook; **cuisinier, -ière** *nm/f* cook; **cuisinière** *nf* (*poêle*) cooker

cuisse [kɥis] *nf* thigh; (*Culin*) leg

cuisson [kɥisɔ̃] *nf* cooking

cuit, e [kɥi, kɥit] *pp de* **cuire**

cuivre [kɥivʀ] *nm* copper; **les cuivres** (*Mus*) the brass

cul [ky] (*fam!*) *nm* arse (!)

culminant, e [kylminɑ̃, ɑ̃t] *adj*: **point ~** highest point

culot [kylo] (*fam*) *nm* (*effronterie*) cheek

culotte [kylɔt] *nf* (*de femme*) knickers *pl* (BRIT), panties *pl*

culte [kylt] *nm* (*religion*) religion; (*hommage, vénération*) worship; (*protestant*) service

cultivateur, -trice [kyltivatœʀ, tʀis] *nm/f* farmer

cultivé, e [kyltive] *adj* (*personne*) cultured, cultivated

cultiver [kyltive] *vt* to cultivate; (*légumes*) to grow, cultivate

culture [kyltyʀ] *nf* cultivation; (*connaissances etc*) culture; **les ~s intensives** intensive farming; **culture physique** physical training; **culturel, le** *adj* cultural

cumin [kymɛ̃] *nm* cumin

cure [kyʀ] *nf* (*Méd*) course of treatment; **cure d'amaigrissement** slimming (BRIT) *ou* weight-loss (US) course; **cure de repos** rest cure

curé [kyʀe] *nm* parish priest

cure-dent [kyʀdɑ̃] *nm* toothpick

curieux, -euse [kyʀjø, jøz] *adj* (*indiscret*) curious, inquisitive; (*étrange*) strange, curious ▷ *nmpl* (*badauds*) onlookers; **curiosité** *nf* curiosity; (*site*) unusual feature

curriculum vitae [kyʀikylɔmvite] *nm inv* curriculum vitae

cutané, e [kytane] *adj* skin

cuve [kyv] *nf* vat; (*à mazout etc*) tank

cuvée [kyve] *nf* vintage

cuvette [kyvɛt] *nf* (*récipient*) bowl, basin; (*Géo*) basin

CV *sigle m* (*Auto*) = **cheval vapeur**; (*Comm*) = **curriculum vitae**

cybercafé [sibɛʀkafe] *nm* Internet café

cyberespace [sibɛʀɛspas] *nm* cyberspace

cybernaute [sibɛʀnot] *nm/f* Internet user

cyclable [siklabl] *adj*: **piste ~** cycle track

cycle [sikl] *nm* cycle; **cyclisme** *nm* cycling; **cycliste** *nm/f* cyclist ▷ *adj* cycle *cpd*; **coureur cycliste** racing cyclist

cyclomoteur [siklomɔtœʀ] *nm* moped

cyclone [siklon] *nm* hurricane

cygne [siɲ] *nm* swan

cylindre [silɛ̃dʀ] *nm* cylinder; **cylindrée** *nf* (*Auto*) (cubic) capacity; **une (voiture de) grosse cylindrée** a big-engined car

cymbale [sɛ̃bal] *nf* cymbal

cynique [sinik] *adj* cynical

cystite [sistit] *nf* cystitis

d' [d] *prép voir* **de**

dactylo [daktilo] *nf* (*aussi:* **~graphe**) typist; (*aussi:* **~graphie**) typing

dada [dada] *nm* hobby-horse

daim [dɛ̃] *nm* (fallow) deer *inv*; (*cuir suédé*) suede

daltonien, ne [daltɔnjɛ̃, jɛn] *adj* colour-blind

dame [dam] *nf* lady; (*Cartes, Échecs*) queen; **dames** *nfpl* (*jeu*) draughts *sg* (BRIT), checkers *sg* (US)

Danemark [danmaʀk] *nm* Denmark

danger [dɑ̃ʒe] *nm* danger; **être en ~** (*personne*) to be in danger; **mettre en ~** (*personne*) to put in danger; (*projet, carrière*) to jeopardize; **dangereux, -euse** *adj* dangerous

danois, e [danwa, waz] *adj* Danish ▷ *nm/f*: **D~, e** Dane ▷ *nm* (*Ling*) Danish

 MOT-CLÉ

dans [dɑ̃] *prép* **1** (*position*) in; (*à l'intérieur de*) inside; **c'est dans le tiroir/le salon** it's in the drawer/lounge; **dans la boîte** in *ou* inside the box; **je l'ai lu dans le journal** I read it in the newspaper; **marcher dans la ville** to walk about the town

2 (*direction*) into; **elle a couru dans le salon** she ran into the lounge; **monter dans une voiture/le bus** to get into a car/on to the bus

3 (*provenance*) out of, from; **je l'ai pris dans**

le tiroir/salon I took it out of *ou* from the drawer/lounge; **boire dans un verre** to drink out of *ou* from a glass
4 (*temps*) in; **dans 2 mois** in 2 months, in 2 months' time
5 (*approximation*) about; **dans les 20 euros** about 20 euros

danse [dɑ̃s] *nf*: **la ~** dancing; **une ~** a dance; **la ~ classique** ballet; **danser** *vi, vt* to dance; **danseur, -euse** *nm/f* ballet dancer; (*au bal etc*) dancer; (: *cavalier*) partner
date [dat] *nf* date; **de longue ~** longstanding; **date de naissance** date of birth; **date limite** deadline; **dater** *vt, vi* to date; **dater de** to date from; **à dater de** (as) from
datte [dat] *nf* date
dauphin [dofɛ̃] *nm* (*Zool*) dolphin
davantage [davɑ̃taʒ] *adv* more; (*plus longtemps*) longer; **~ de** more

 MOT-CLÉ

de, d' [də] (*de +le* = **du**, *de +les* = **des**) *prép*
1 (*appartenance*) of; **le toit de la maison** the roof of the house; **la voiture d'Ann/de mes parents** Ann's/my parents' car
2 (*provenance*) from; **il vient de Londres** he comes from London; **elle est sortie du cinéma** she came out of the cinema
3 (*caractérisation, mesure*): **un mur de brique/bureau d'acajou** a brick wall/mahogany desk; **un billet de 50 euros** a 50 euro note; **une pièce de 2 m de large** *ou* **large de 2 m** a room 2m wide, a 2m-wide room; **un bébé de 10 mois** a 10-month-old baby; **12 mois de crédit/travail** 12 months' credit/work; **être payé 20 euros de l'heure** to be paid 20 euros an *ou* per hour; **augmenter de 10 euros** to increase by 10 euros; **de 14 à 18** from 14 to 18
4 (*moyen*) with; **je l'ai fait de mes propres mains** I did it with my own two hands
5 (*cause*): **mourir de faim** to die of hunger; **rouge de colère** red with fury
6 (*devant infinitif*) to; **il m'a dit de rester** he told me to stay
▷ *dét* **1** (*phrases affirmatives*) some (*souvent omis*); **du vin, de l'eau, des pommes** (some) wine, (some) water, (some) apples; **des enfants sont venus** some children came; **pendant des mois** for months
2 (*phrases interrogatives et négatives*) any; **a-t-il du vin?** has he got any wine?; **il n'a pas de pommes/d'enfants** he hasn't (got) any apples/children, he has no apples/children

dé [de] *nm* (*à jouer*) die *ou* dice; (*aussi*: **dé à coudre**) thimble
déballer [debale] *vt* to unpack

débarcadère [debaʁkadɛʁ] *nm* wharf
débardeur [debaʁdœʁ] *nm* (*maillot*) tank top
débarquer [debaʁke] *vt* to unload, land ▷ *vi* to disembark; (*fig: fam*) to turn up
débarras [debaʁɑ] *nm* (*pièce*) lumber room; (*placard*) junk cupboard; **bon ~!** good riddance!; **débarrasser** *vt* to clear; **se débarrasser de** *vt* to get rid of; **débarrasser qn de** (*vêtements, paquets*) to relieve sb of; **débarrasser (la table)** to clear the table
débat [deba] *nm* discussion, debate; **débattre** *vt* to discuss, debate; **se débattre** *vi* to struggle
débit [debi] *nm* (*d'un liquide, fleuve*) flow; (*d'un magasin*) turnover (of goods); (*élocution*) delivery; (*bancaire*) debit; **débit de boissons** drinking establishment; **débit de tabac** tobacconist's
déblayer [debleje] *vt* to clear
débloquer [debloke] *vt* (*prix, crédits*) to free
déboîter [debwate] *vt* (*Auto*) to pull out; **se ~ le genou** *etc* to dislocate one's knee *etc*
débordé, e [debɔʁde] *adj*: **être ~ (de)** (*travail, demandes*) to be snowed under (with)
déborder [debɔʁde] *vi* to overflow; (*lait etc*) to boil over; **~ (de) qch** (*dépasser*) to extend beyond sth; **~ de** (*joie, zèle*) to be brimming over with *ou* bursting with
débouché [debuʃe] *nm* (*pour vendre*) outlet; (*perspective d'emploi*) opening
déboucher [debuʃe] *vt* (*évier, tuyau etc*) to unblock; (*bouteille*) to uncork ▷ *vi*: **~ de** to emerge from; **~ sur** (*études*) to lead on to
debout [d(ə)bu] *adv*: **être ~** (*personne*) to be standing, stand; (: *levé, éveillé*) to be up; **se mettre ~** to stand up; **se tenir ~** to stand; **~!** stand up!; (*du lit*) get up!; **cette histoire ne tient pas ~** this story doesn't hold water
déboutonner [debutɔne] *vt* to undo, unbutton
débraillé, e [debʁaje] *adj* slovenly, untidy
débrancher [debʁɑ̃ʃe] *vt* to disconnect; (*appareil électrique*) to unplug
débrayage [debʁɛjaʒ] *nm* (*Auto*) clutch; **débrayer** *vi* (*Auto*) to declutch; (*cesser le travail*) to stop work
débris [debʁi] *nmpl* fragments; **des ~ de verre** bits of glass
débrouillard, e [debʁujaʁ, aʁd] (*fam*) *adj* smart, resourceful
débrouiller [debʁuje] *vt* to disentangle, untangle; **se débrouiller** *vi* to manage; **débrouillez-vous** you'll have to sort things out yourself
début [deby] *nm* beginning, start; **débuts** *nmpl* (*de carrière*) début *sg*; **~ juin** in early June; **débutant, e** *nm/f* beginner, novice; **débuter** *vi* to begin, start; (*faire ses débuts*) to start out
décaféiné, e [dekafeine] *adj* decaffeinated

décalage [dekalaʒ] nm gap; **décalage horaire** time difference

décaler [dekale] vt to shift

décapotable [dekapɔtabl] adj convertible

décapsuleur [dekapsylœʀ] nm bottle-opener

décédé, e [desede] adj deceased

décéder [desede] vi to die

décembre [desɑ̃bʀ] nm December

décennie [deseni] nf decade

décent, e [desɑ̃, ɑ̃t] adj decent

déception [desɛpsjɔ̃] nf disappointment

décès [desɛ] nm death

décevoir [des(ə)vwaʀ] vt to disappoint

décharge [deʃaʀʒ] nf (dépôt d'ordures) rubbish tip ou dump; (électrique) electrical discharge; **décharger** vt (marchandise, véhicule) to unload; (tirer) to discharge; **décharger qn de** (responsabilité) to relieve sb of, release sb from

déchausser [deʃose] vt (skis) to take off; **se déchausser** vi to take off one's shoes; (dent) to come ou work loose

déchet [deʃɛ] nm (reste) scrap; **déchets** nmpl (ordures) refuse sg, rubbish sg; **~s nucléaires** nuclear waste

déchiffrer [deʃifʀe] vt to decipher

déchirant, e [deʃiʀɑ̃, ɑ̃t] adj heart-rending

déchirement [deʃiʀmɑ̃] nm (chagrin) wrench, heartbreak; (gén pl: conflit) rift, split

déchirer [deʃiʀe] vt to tear; (en morceaux) to tear up; (arracher) to tear out; (fig: conflit) to tear (apart); **se déchirer** vi to tear, rip; **se ~ un muscle** to tear a muscle

déchirure [deʃiʀyʀ] nf (accroc) tear, rip; **déchirure musculaire** torn muscle

décidé, e [deside] adj (personne, air) determined; **c'est ~** it's decided; **décidément** adv really

décider [deside] vt: **~ qch** to decide on sth; **~ de faire/que** to decide to do/that; **~ qn (à faire qch)** to persuade sb (to do sth); **se décider (à faire)** to decide (to do), make up one's mind (to do); **se ~ pour** to decide on ou in favour of

décimal, e, -aux [desimal, o] adj decimal

décimètre [desimɛtʀ] nm decimetre

décisif, -ive [desizif, iv] adj decisive

décision [desizjɔ̃] nf decision

déclaration [deklaʀasjɔ̃] nf declaration; (discours: Pol etc) statement; **déclaration d'impôts** ou **de revenus** ≈ tax return; **déclaration de vol: faire une déclaration de vol** to report a theft

déclarer [deklaʀe] vt to declare; (décès, naissance) to register; **se déclarer** vi (feu) to break out

déclencher [deklɑ̃ʃe] vt (mécanisme etc) to release; (sonnerie) to set off; (attaque, grève) to launch; (provoquer) to trigger off; **se**

déclencher vi (sonnerie) to go off

décliner [dekline] vi to decline ▷ vt (invitation) to decline; (nom, adresse) to state

décoiffer [dekwafe] vt: **~ qn** to mess up sb's hair; **je suis toute décoiffée** my hair is in a real mess

déçois etc [deswa] vb voir **décevoir**

décollage [dekɔlaʒ] nm (Aviat) takeoff

décoller [dekɔle] vt to unstick ▷ vi (avion) to take off; **se décoller** vi to come unstuck

décolleté, e [dekɔlte] adj low-cut ▷ nm low neck(line); (plongeant) cleavage

décolorer [dekɔlɔʀe]: **se décolorer** vi to fade; **se faire ~ les cheveux** to have one's hair bleached

décommander [dekɔmɑ̃de] vt to cancel; **se décommander** vi to cry off

déconcerter [dekɔ̃sɛʀte] vt to disconcert, confound

décongeler [dekɔ̃ʒ(ə)le] vt to thaw

déconner [dekɔne] (fam) vi to talk rubbish

déconseiller [dekɔ̃seje] vt: **~ qch (à qn)** to advise (sb) against sth; **c'est déconseillé** it's not recommended

décontracté, e [dekɔ̃tʀakte] adj relaxed, laid-back (fam)

décontracter [dekɔ̃tʀakte]: **se décontracter** vi to relax

décor [dekɔʀ] nm décor; (paysage) scenery; **décorateur** nm (interior) decorator; **décoration** nf decoration; **décorer** vt to decorate

décortiquer [dekɔʀtike] vt to shell; (fig: texte) to dissect

découdre [dekudʀ]: **se découdre** vi to come unstitched

découper [dekupe] vt (papier, tissu etc) to cut up; (viande) to carve; (article) to cut out

décourager [dekuʀaʒe] vt to discourage; **se décourager** vi to lose heart, become discouraged

décousu, e [dekuzy] adj unstitched; (fig) disjointed, disconnected

découvert, e [dekuvɛʀ, ɛʀt] adj (tête) bare, uncovered; (lieu) open, exposed ▷ nm (bancaire) overdraft; **découverte** nf discovery; **faire la découverte de** to discover

découvrir [dekuvʀiʀ] vt to discover; (enlever ce qui couvre) to uncover; (dévoiler) to reveal; **se découvrir** vi (chapeau) to take off one's hat; (vêtement) to take something off; (ciel) to clear

décrire [dekʀiʀ] vt to describe

décrocher [dekʀɔʃe] vt (détacher) to take down; (téléphone) to take off the hook; (: pour répondre) to lift the receiver; (fam: contrat etc) to get, land ▷ vi (fam: abandonner) to drop out; (: cesser d'écouter) to switch off

déçu, e [desy] pp de **décevoir**

dédaigner [dedeɲe] vt to despise, scorn;

(*négliger*) to disregard, spurn; **dédaigneux, -euse** *adj* scornful, disdainful; **dédain** *nm* scorn, disdain

dedans [dədã] *adv* inside; (*pas en plein air*) indoors, inside ▷ *nm* inside; **au ~** inside

dédicacer [dedikase] *vt*: **~ (à qn)** to sign (for sb), autograph (for sb)

dédier [dedje] *vt*: **~ à** to dedicate to

dédommagement [dedɔmaʒmã] *nm* compensation

dédommager [dedɔmaʒe] *vt*: **~ qn (de)** to compensate sb (for)

dédouaner [dedwane] *vt* to clear through customs

déduire [dedɥiʀ] *vt*: **~ qch (de)** (*ôter*) to deduct sth (from); (*conclure*) to deduce *ou* infer sth (from)

défaillance [defajãs] *nf* (*syncope*) blackout; (*fatigue*) (sudden) weakness *no pl*; (*technique*) fault, failure; **défaillance cardiaque** heart failure

défaire [defɛʀ] *vt* to undo; (*installation*) to take down, dismantle; **se défaire** *vi* to come undone; **se ~ de** to get rid of

défait, e [defɛ, ɛt] *adj* (*visage*) haggard, ravaged; **défaite** *nf* defeat

défaut [defo] *nm* (*moral*) fault, failing, defect; (*tissus*) fault, flaw; (*manque, carence*): **~ de** shortage of; **prendre qn en ~** to catch sb out; **faire ~** (*manquer*) to be lacking; **à ~ de** for lack *ou* want of

défavorable [defavɔʀabl] *adj* unfavourable (BRIT), unfavorable (US)

défavoriser [defavɔʀize] *vt* to put at a disadvantage

défectueux, -euse [defɛktɥø, øz] *adj* faulty, defective

défendre [defãdʀ] *vt* to defend; (*interdire*) to forbid; **se défendre** *vi* to defend o.s.; **~ à qn qch/de faire** to forbid sb sth/to do; **il se défend** (*fam*: *se débrouille*) he can hold his own; **se ~ de/contre** (*se protéger*) to protect o.s. from/against; **se ~ de** (*se garder de*) to refrain from

défense [defãs] *nf* defence; (*d'éléphant etc*) tusk; **ministre de la ~** Minister of Defence (BRIT), Defence Secretary (US); **"~ de fumer"** "no smoking"

défi [defi] *nm* challenge; **lancer un ~ à qn** to challenge sb; **sur un ton de ~** defiantly

déficit [defisit] *nm* (Comm) deficit

défier [defje] *vt* (*provoquer*) to challenge; (*mort, autorité*) to defy; **~ qn de faire qch** to challenge *ou* defy sb to do sth

défigurer [defigyʀe] *vt* to disfigure

défilé [defile] *nm* (Géo) (narrow) gorge *ou* pass; (*soldats*) parade; (*manifestants*) procession, march

défiler [defile] *vi* (*troupes*) to march past; (*sportifs*) to parade; (*manifestants*) to march; (*visiteurs*) to pour, stream; **faire ~ un document** (Comput) to scroll a document; **se défiler** *vi*: **il s'est défilé** (*fam*) he wriggled out of it

définir [definiʀ] *vt* to define

définitif, -ive [definitif, iv] *adj* (*final*) final, definitive; (*pour longtemps*) permanent, definitive; (*refus*) definite; **définitive** *nf*: **en définitive** eventually; (*somme toute*) in fact; **définitivement** *adv* (*partir, s'installer*) for good

déformer [defɔʀme] *vt* to put out of shape; (*pensée, fait*) to distort; **se déformer** *vi* to lose its shape

défouler [defule]: **se défouler** *vi* to unwind, let off steam

défunt, e [defœ̃, œ̃t] *adj* (*mort*) late *before n* ▷ *nm/f* deceased

dégagé, e [degaʒe] *adj* (*route, ciel*) clear; **sur un ton ~** casually

dégager [degaʒe] *vt* (*exhaler*) to give off; (*délivrer*) to free, extricate; (*désencombrer*) to clear; (*isoler: idée, aspect*) to bring out; **~ qn de** (*engagement, parole etc*) to release *ou* free sb from; **se dégager** *vi* (*passage, ciel*) to clear

dégâts [dega] *nmpl* damage *sg*; **faire des ~** to cause damage

dégel [deʒɛl] *nm* thaw; **dégeler** *vt* to thaw (out)

dégivrer [deʒivʀe] *vt* (*frigo*) to defrost; (*vitres*) to de-ice

dégonflé, e [degɔ̃fle] *adj* (*pneu*) flat

dégonfler [degɔ̃fle] *vt* (*pneu, ballon*) to let down, deflate; **se dégonfler** *vi* (*fam*) to chicken out

dégouliner [deguline] *vi* to trickle, drip

dégourdi, e [deguʀdi] *adj* smart, resourceful

dégourdir [deguʀdiʀ] *vt*: **se ~ les jambes** to stretch one's legs (*fig*)

dégoût [degu] *nm* disgust, distaste; **dégoûtant, e** *adj* disgusting; **dégoûté, e** *adj* disgusted; **dégoûté de** sick of; **dégoûter** *vt* to disgust; **dégoûter qn de qch** to put sb off sth

dégrader [degʀade] *vt* (Mil: *officier*) to degrade; (*abîmer*) to damage, deface; **se dégrader** *vi* (*relations, situation*) to deteriorate

degré [dəgʀe] *nm* degree

dégressif, -ive [degʀesif, iv] *adj* on a decreasing scale

dégringoler [degʀɛ̃gɔle] *vi* to tumble (down)

déguisement [degizmã] *nm* (*pour s'amuser*) fancy dress

déguiser [degize]: **se déguiser (en)** *vi* (*se costumer*) to dress up (as); (*pour tromper*) to disguise o.s. (as)

dégustation [degystasjɔ̃] *nf* (*de fromages etc*) sampling; **~ de vins** wine-tasting session

déguster [degyste] vt (vins) to taste; (fromages etc) to sample; (savourer) to enjoy, savour

dehors [dəɔʀ] adv outside; (en plein air) outdoors ▷ nm outside ▷ nmpl (apparences) appearances; **mettre** ou **jeter ~** (expulser) to throw out; **au ~** outside; **au ~ de** outside; **en ~ de** (hormis) apart from

déjà [deʒa] adv already; (auparavant) before, already

déjeuner [deʒœne] vi to (have) lunch; (le matin) to have breakfast ▷ nm lunch

delà [dəla] adv: **en ~ (de), au ~ (de)** beyond

délacer [delase] vt (chaussures) to undo

délai [delɛ] nm (attente) waiting period; (sursis) extension (of time); (temps accordé) time limit; **sans ~** without delay; **dans les ~s** within the time limit

délaisser [delese] vt to abandon, desert

délasser [delɑse] vt to relax; **se délasser** vi to relax

délavé, e [delave] adj faded

délayer [deleje] vt (Culin) to mix (with water etc); (peinture) to thin down

delco(r) [dɛlko] nm (Auto) distributor

délégué, e [delege] nm/f representative

déléguer [delege] vt to delegate

délibéré, e [delibeʀe] adj (conscient) deliberate

délicat, e [delika, at] adj delicate; (plein de tact) tactful; (attention) thoughtful; **délicatement** adv delicately; (avec douceur) gently

délice [delis] nm delight

délicieux, -euse [delisjø, jøz] adj (au goût) delicious; (sensation) delightful

délimiter [delimite] vt (terrain) to delimit, demarcate

délinquant, e [delɛ̃kɑ̃, -ɑ̃t] adj, nm/f delinquent

délirer [deliʀe] vi to be delirious; **tu délires!** (fam) you're crazy!

délit [deli] nm (criminal) offence

délivrer [delivʀe] vt (prisonnier) to (set) free, release; (passeport) to issue

deltaplane(r) [dɛltaplan] nm hang-glider

déluge [delyʒ] nm (pluie) downpour; (biblique) Flood

demain [d(ə)mɛ̃] adv tomorrow; **~ matin/soir** tomorrow morning/evening

demande [d(ə)mɑ̃d] nf (requête) request; (revendication) demand; (d'emploi) application; (Écon): **la ~** demand; **"~s d'emploi"** (annonces) "situations wanted"

demandé, e [d(ə)mɑ̃de] adj (article etc): **très ~** (very) much in demand

demander [d(ə)mɑ̃de] vt to ask for; (chemin, heure etc) to ask; (nécessiter) to require, demand; **~ qch à qn** to ask sb for sth; **~ un service à qn** to ask sb a favour; **~ à qn de faire qch** to ask sb to do sth; **je ne demande pas mieux que de ...** I'll be only too pleased to ...; **se ~ si/pourquoi** etc to wonder whether/why etc; **demandeur, -euse** nm/f: **demandeur d'emploi** job-seeker; **demandeur d'asile** asylum-seeker

démangeaison [demɑ̃ʒɛzɔ̃] nf itching; **avoir des ~s** to be itching

démanger [demɑ̃ʒe] vi to itch

démaquillant [demakijɑ̃] nm make-up remover

démaquiller [demakije] vt: **se démaquiller** to remove one's make-up

démarche [demaʀʃ] nf (allure) gait, walk; (intervention) step; (fig: intellectuelle) thought processes pl; **faire les ~s nécessaires (pour obtenir qch)** to take the necessary steps (to obtain sth)

démarrage [demaʀaʒ] nm start

démarrer [demaʀe] vi (conducteur) to start (up); (véhicule) to move off; (travaux) to get moving; **démarreur** nm (Auto) starter

démêlant [demɛlɑ̃] nm conditioner

démêler [demele] vt to untangle; **démêlés** nmpl problems

déménagement [demenaʒmɑ̃] nm move; **camion de déménagement** removal van

déménager [demenaʒe] vt (meubles) to (re)move ▷ vi to move (house); **déménageur** nm removal man

démerder [demɛʀde] (fam): **se démerder** vi to sort things out for o.s.

démettre [demɛtʀ] vt: **~ qn de** (fonction, poste) to dismiss sb from; **se ~ l'épaule** etc to dislocate one's shoulder etc

demeurer [d(ə)mœʀe] vi (habiter) to live; (rester) to remain

demi, e [dəmi] adj half ▷ nm (bière) ≈ half-pint (0,25 litres) ▷ préfixe: **~...** half-, semi..., demi-; **trois heures/bouteilles et ~es** three and a half hours/bottles, three hours/bottles and a half; **il est 2 heures et ~e/midi et ~** it's half past 2/half past 12; **à ~** half-; **à la ~e** (heure) on the half-hour; **demi-douzaine** nf half-dozen, half a dozen; **demi-finale** nf semifinal; **demi-frère** nm half-brother; **demi-heure** nf half-hour, half an hour; **demi-journée** nf half-day, half a day; **demi-litre** nm half-litre, half a litre; **demi-livre** nf half-pound, half a pound; **demi-pension** nf (à l'hôtel) half-board; **demi-pensionnaire** nm/f: **être demi-pensionnaire** to take school lunches

démis, e [demi, iz] adj (épaule etc) dislocated

demi-sœur [dəmisœʀ] nf half-sister

démission [demisjɔ̃] nf resignation; **donner sa ~** to give ou hand in one's notice; **démissionner** vi to resign

demi-tarif [dəmitaʀif] nm half-price;

voyager à ~ to travel half-fare
demi-tour [dəmituʀ] *nm* about-turn; **faire ~**
to turn (and go) back
démocratie [demɔkʀasi] *nf* democracy;
démocratique *adj* democratic
démodé, e [demɔde] *adj* old-fashioned
demoiselle [d(ə)mwazɛl] *nf* (*jeune fille*) young
lady; (*célibataire*) single lady, maiden lady;
demoiselle d'honneur bridesmaid
démolir [demɔliʀ] *vt* to demolish
démon [demɔ̃] *nm* (*enfant turbulent*) devil,
demon; **le D~** the Devil
démonstration [demɔ̃stʀasjɔ̃] *nf*
demonstration
démonter [demɔ̃te] *vt* (*machine etc*) to take
down, dismantle; **se démonter** (*meuble*) to be
dismantled, be taken to pieces; (*personne*) to
lose countenance
démontrer [demɔ̃tʀe] *vt* to demonstrate
démouler [demule] *vt* to turn out
démuni, e [demyni] *adj* (*sans argent*)
impoverished; **~ de** without
dénicher [deniʃe] (*fam*) *vt* (*objet*) to unearth;
(*restaurant etc*) to discover
dénier [denje] *vt* to deny
dénivellation [denivelasjɔ̃] *nf* (*pente*) slope
dénombrer [denɔ̃bʀe] *vt* to count
dénomination [denɔminasjɔ̃] *nf*
designation, appellation
dénoncer [denɔ̃se] *vt* to denounce; **se
dénoncer** to give o.s. up, come forward
dénouement [denumɑ̃] *nm* outcome
dénouer [denwe] *vt* to unknot, undo
denrée [dɑ̃ʀe] *nf*: **denrées alimentaires**
foodstuffs
dense [dɑ̃s] *adj* dense; **densité** *nf* density
dent [dɑ̃] *nf* tooth; **dent de lait/de sagesse**
milk/wisdom tooth; **dentaire** *adj* dental;
cabinet dentaire dental surgery (BRIT),
dentist's office (US)
dentelle [dɑ̃tɛl] *nf* lace *no pl*
dentier [dɑ̃tje] *nm* denture
dentifrice [dɑ̃tifʀis] *nm* toothpaste
dentiste [dɑ̃tist] *nm/f* dentist
dentition [dɑ̃tisjɔ̃] *nf* teeth
dénué, e [denɥe] *adj*: **~ de** devoid of
déodorant [deɔdʀɑ̃] *nm* deodorant
déontologie [deɔ̃tɔlɔʒi] *nf* code of practice
dépannage [depanaʒ] *nm*: **service de ~**
(*Auto*) breakdown service
dépanner [depane] *vt* (*voiture, télévision*)
to fix, repair; (*fig*) to bail out, help out;
dépanneuse *nf* breakdown lorry (BRIT), tow
truck (US)
dépareillé, e [depaʀeje] *adj* (*collection,
service*) incomplete; (*objet*) odd
départ [depaʀ] *nm* departure; (*Sport*) start; **au
~** at the start; **la veille de son ~** the day before
he leaves/left

département [depaʀtəmɑ̃] *nm* department

● **DÉPARTEMENT**
●
● France is divided into 96 administrative
● units called **départements**. These local
● government divisions are headed by a state-
● appointed 'préfet', and administered by an
● elected 'Conseil général'. **Départements**
● are usually named after prominent
● geographical features such as rivers or
● mountain ranges.

dépassé, e [depase] *adj* superseded,
outmoded; **il est complètement ~** he's
completely out of his depth, he can't cope
dépasser [depase] *vt* (*véhicule, concurrent*) to
overtake; (*endroit*) to pass, go past; (*somme,
limite*) to exceed; (*fig: en beauté etc*) to surpass,
outshine ▷ *vi* (*jupon etc*) to show; **se dépasser**
to excel o.s.
dépaysé, e [depeize] *adj* disoriented
dépaysement [depeizmɑ̃] *nm* (*changement*)
change of scenery
dépêcher [depeʃe]: **se dépêcher** *vi* to hurry
dépendance [depɑ̃dɑ̃s] *nf* dependence;
(*bâtiment*) outbuilding
dépendre [depɑ̃dʀ]: **~ de** *vt* to depend on;
(*financièrement etc*) to be dependent on; **ça
dépend** it depends
dépens [depɑ̃] *nmpl*: **aux ~ de** at the expense
of
dépense [depɑ̃s] *nf* spending *no pl*, expense,
expenditure *no pl*; **dépenser** *vt* to spend;
(*énergie*) to expend, use up; **se dépenser** *vi* to
exert o.s.
dépeupler [depœple]: **se dépeupler** *vi* to
become depopulated
dépilatoire [depilatwaʀ] *adj*: **crème ~** hair-
removing *ou* depilatory cream
dépister [depiste] *vt* to detect; (*voleur*) to
track down
dépit [depi] *nm* vexation, frustration; **en ~ de**
in spite of; **en ~ du bon sens** contrary to all
good sense; **dépité, e** *adj* vexed, frustrated
déplacé, e [deplase] *adj* (*propos*) out of place,
uncalled-for
déplacement [deplasmɑ̃] *nm* (*voyage*) trip,
travelling *no pl*; **en ~** away
déplacer [deplase] *vt* (*table, voiture*) to move,
shift; **se déplacer** *vi* to move; (*voyager*) to
travel; **se ~ une vertèbre** to slip a disc
déplaire [deplɛʀ] *vt*: **ça me déplaît** I don't
like this, I dislike this; **se déplaire** *vi* to be
unhappy; **déplaisant, e** *adj* disagreeable
dépliant [deplijɑ̃] *nm* leaflet
déplier [deplije] *vt* to unfold
déposer [depoze] *vt* (*gén: mettre, poser*) to
lay *ou* put down; (*à la banque, à la consigne*) to

deposit; (*passager*) to drop (off), set down; (*roi*) to depose; (*plainte*) to lodge; (*marque*) to register; **se déposer** *vi* to settle; **dépositaire** *nm/f* (*Comm*) agent; **déposition** *nf* statement

dépôt [depo] *nm* (*à la banque, sédiment*) deposit; (*entrepôt*) warehouse, store

dépourvu, e [depuʀvy] *adj*: ~ **de** lacking in, without; **prendre qn au** ~ to catch sb unprepared

dépression [depʀesjɔ̃] *nf* depression; **dépression (nerveuse)** (nervous) breakdown

déprimant, e [depʀimɑ̃, ɑ̃t] *adj* depressing

déprimer [depʀime] *vi* to be/get depressed

O **MOT-CLÉ**

depuis [dəpɥi] *prép* **1** (*point de départ dans le temps*) since; **il habite Paris depuis 1983/l'an dernier** he has been living in Paris since 1983/ last year; **depuis quand?** since when?; **depuis quand le connaissez-vous?** how long have you known him?
2 (*temps écoulé*) for; **il habite Paris depuis 5 ans** he has been living in Paris for 5 years; **je le connais depuis 3 ans** I've known him for 3 years
3 (*lieu*): **il a plu depuis Metz** it's been raining since Metz; **elle a téléphoné depuis Valence** she rang from Valence
4 (*quantité, rang*) from; **depuis les plus petits jusqu'aux plus grands** from the youngest to the oldest
▷ *adv* (*temps*) since (then); **je ne lui ai pas parlé depuis** I haven't spoken to him since (then); **depuis que** *conj* (ever) since; **depuis qu'il m'a dit ça** (ever) since he said that to me

député, e [depyte] *nm/f* (*Pol*) ≈ Member of Parliament (*BRIT*), ≈ Member of Congress (*US*)

dérangement [deʀɑ̃ʒmɑ̃] *nm* (*gêne*) trouble; (*gastrique etc*) disorder; **en** ~ (*téléphone, machine*) out of order

déranger [deʀɑ̃ʒe] *vt* (*personne*) to trouble, bother; (*projets*) to disrupt, upset; (*objets, vêtements*) to disarrange; **se déranger** *vi*: **surtout ne vous dérangez pas pour moi** please don't put yourself out on my account; **est-ce que cela vous dérange si ...?** do you mind if ...?

déraper [deʀape] *vi* (*voiture*) to skid; (*personne, semelles*) to slip

dérégler [deʀegle] *vt* (*mécanisme*) to put out of order; (*estomac*) to upset

dérisoire [deʀizwaʀ] *adj* derisory

dérive [deʀiv] *nf*: **aller à la** ~ (*Navig, fig*) to drift

dérivé, e [deʀive] *nm* (*Tech*) by-product

dermatologue [dɛʀmatɔlɔg] *nm/f* dermatologist

dernier, -ière [dɛʀnje, jɛʀ] *adj* last; (*le plus récent*) latest, last; **lundi/le mois** ~ last Monday/month; **c'est le** ~ **cri** it's the very latest thing; **en** ~ last; **ce** ~ the latter; **dernièrement** *adv* recently

dérogation [deʀɔgasjɔ̃] *nf* (special) dispensation

dérouiller [deʀuje] *vt*: **se** ~ **les jambes** to stretch one's legs (*fig*)

déroulement [deʀulmɑ̃] *nm* (*d'une opération etc*) progress

dérouler [deʀule] *vt* (*ficelle*) to unwind; **se dérouler** *vi* (*avoir lieu*) to take place; (*se passer*) to go (off); **tout s'est déroulé comme prévu** everything went as planned

dérouter [deʀute] *vt* (*avion, train*) to reroute, divert; (*étonner*) to disconcert, throw (out)

derrière [dɛʀjɛʀ] *adv, prép* behind ▷ *nm* (*d'une maison*) back; (*postérieur*) behind, bottom; **les pattes de** ~ the back *ou* hind legs; **par** ~ from behind; (*fig*) behind one's back

des [de] *dét voir* **de** ▷ *prép* +*dét* = **de** +**les**

dès [dɛ] *prép* from; ~ **que** as soon as; ~ **son retour** as soon as he was (*ou* is) back

désaccord [dezakɔʀ] *nm* disagreement

désagréable [dezagʀeabl] *adj* unpleasant

désagrément [dezagʀemɑ̃] *nm* annoyance, trouble *no pl*

désaltérer [dezaltere] *vt*: **se désaltérer** to quench one's thirst

désapprobateur, -trice [dezapʀɔbatœʀ, tʀis] *adj* disapproving

désapprouver [dezapʀuve] *vt* to disapprove of

désarmant, e [dezaʀmɑ̃, ɑ̃t] *adj* disarming

désastre [dezastʀ] *nm* disaster; **désastreux, -euse** *adj* disastrous

désavantage [dezavɑ̃taʒ] *nm* disadvantage; **désavantager** *vt* to put at a disadvantage

descendre [desɑ̃dʀ] *vt* (*escalier, montagne*) to go (*ou* come) down; (*valise, paquet*) to take *ou* get down; (*étagère etc*) to lower; (*fam: abattre*) to shoot down ▷ *vi* to go (*ou* come) down; (*passager: s'arrêter*) to get out, alight; ~ **à pied/ en voiture** to walk/drive down; ~ **de** (*famille*) to be descended from; ~ **du train** to get out of *ou* get off the train; ~ **de cheval** to dismount; ~ **d'un arbre** to climb down from a tree; ~ **à l'hôtel** to stay at a hotel

descente [desɑ̃t] *nf* descent, going down; (*chemin*) way down; (*Ski*) downhill (race); **au milieu de la** ~ halfway down; **descente de lit** bedside rug; **descente (de police)** (police) raid

description [dɛskʀipsjɔ̃] *nf* description

déséquilibre [dezekilibʀ] *nm* (*position*): **en** ~ unsteady; (*fig: des forces, du budget*) imbalance

désert, e [dezɛʀ, ɛʀt] *adj* deserted ▷ *nm* desert; **désertique** *adj* desert *cpd*

désespéré, e [dezɛspere] *adj* desperate

désespérer [dezɛspeʀe] *vi*: ~ **(de)** to despair (of); **désespoir** *nm* despair; **en désespoir de cause** in desperation

déshabiller [dezabije] *vt* to undress; **se déshabiller** *vi* to undress (o.s.)

déshydraté, e [dezidʀate] *adj* dehydrated

désigner [dezine] *vt* (*montrer*) to point out, indicate; (*dénommer*) to denote; (*candidat etc*) to name

désinfectant, e [dezɛ̃fɛktɑ̃, ɑ̃t] *adj, nm* disinfectant

désinfecter [dezɛ̃fɛkte] *vt* to disinfect

désintéressé, e [dezɛ̃teʀese] *adj* disinterested, unselfish

désintéresser [dezɛ̃teʀese] *vt*: **se ~ (de)** to lose interest (in)

désintoxication [dezɛ̃tɔksikasjɔ̃] *nf*: **faire une cure de ~** to undergo treatment for alcoholism (*ou* drug addiction)

désinvolte [dezɛ̃vɔlt] *adj* casual, off-hand

désir [deziʀ] *nm* wish; (*sensuel*) desire; **désirer** *vt* to want, wish for; (*sexuellement*) to desire; **je désire ...** (*formule de politesse*) I would like ...

désister [deziste]: **se désister** *vi* to stand down, withdraw

désobéir [dezɔbeiʀ] *vi*: ~ **(à qn/qch)** to disobey (sb/sth); **désobéissant, e** *adj* disobedient

désodorisant [dezɔdɔʀizɑ̃] *nm* air freshener, deodorizer

désolé, e [dezɔle] *adj* (*paysage*) desolate; **je suis ~** I'm sorry

désordonné, e [dezɔʀdɔne] *adj* untidy

désordre [dezɔʀdʀ] *nm* disorder(liness), untidiness; (*anarchie*) disorder; **en ~** in a mess, untidy

désormais [dezɔʀmɛ] *adv* from now on

desquelles [dekɛl] *prép +pron* = **de +lesquelles**

desquels [dekɛl] *prép +pron* = **de +lesquels**

dessécher [deseʃe]: **se dessécher** *vi* to dry out

desserrer [deseʀe] *vt* to loosen; (*frein*) to release

dessert [desɛʀ] *nm* dessert, pudding

desservir [desɛʀviʀ] *vt* (*ville, quartier*) to serve; (*débarrasser*): ~ **(la table)** to clear the table

dessin [desɛ̃] *nm* (*œuvre, art*) drawing; (*motif*) pattern, design; **dessin animé** cartoon (film); **dessin humoristique** cartoon; **dessinateur, -trice** *nm/f* drawer; (*de bandes dessinées*) cartoonist; (*industriel*) draughtsman(-woman) (BRIT), draftsman(-woman) (US); **dessiner** *vt* to draw; (*concevoir*) to design; **se dessiner** *vi* (*forme*) to be outlined; (*fig: solution*) to emerge

dessous [d(ə)su] *adv* underneath, beneath ▷ *nm* underside ▷ *nmpl* (*sous-vêtements*) underwear *sg*; **en ~, par ~** underneath; **au-~**

(de) below; (*peu digne de*) beneath; **avoir le ~** to get the worst of it; **les voisins du ~** the downstairs neighbours; **dessous-de-plat** *nm inv* tablemat

dessus [d(ə)sy] *adv* on top; (*collé, écrit*) on it ▷ *nm* top; **en ~** above; **par ~** *adv* over it ▷ *prép* over; **au-~ (de)** above; **les voisins de ~** the upstairs neighbours; **avoir le ~** to get the upper hand; **sens ~ dessous** upside down; **dessus-de-lit** *nm inv* bedspread

destin [dɛstɛ̃] *nm* fate; (*avenir*) destiny

destinataire [dɛstinatɛʀ] *nm/f* (*Postes*) addressee; (*d'un colis*) consignee

destination [dɛstinasjɔ̃] *nf* (*lieu*) destination; (*usage*) purpose; **à ~ de** bound for, travelling to

destiner [dɛstine] *vt*: ~ **qch à qn** (*envisager de donner*) to intend sb to have sth; (*adresser*) to intend sth for sb; **être destiné à** (*usage*) to be meant for; **se ~ à l'enseignement** to intend to become a teacher

détachant [detaʃɑ̃] *nm* stain remover

détacher [detaʃe] *vt* (*enlever*) to detach, remove; (*délier*) to untie; (*Admin*): ~ **qn (auprès de** *ou* **à)** to post sb (to); **se détacher** *vi* (*se séparer*) to come off; (: *page*) to come out; (*se défaire*) to come undone; **se ~ sur** to stand out against; **se ~ de** (*se désintéresser*) to grow away from

détail [detaj] *nm* detail; (*Comm*): **le ~** retail; **en ~** in detail; **au ~** (*Comm*) retail; **détaillant** *nm* retailer; **détaillé, e** *adj* (*plan, explications*) detailed; (*facture*) itemized; **détailler** *vt* (*expliquer*) to explain in detail

détecter [detɛkte] *vt* to detect

détective [detɛktiv] *nm*: **détective (privé)** private detective

déteindre [detɛ̃dʀ] *vi* (*au lavage*) to run, lose its colour; ~ **sur** (*vêtement*) to run into; (*fig*) to rub off on

détendre [detɑ̃dʀ] *vt* (*corps, esprit*) to relax; **se détendre** *vi* (*ressort*) to lose its tension; (*personne*) to relax

détenir [det(ə)niʀ] *vt* (*record, pouvoir, secret*) to hold; (*prisonnier*) to detain, hold

détente [detɑ̃t] *nf* relaxation

détention [detɑ̃sjɔ̃] *nf* (*d'armes*) possession; (*captivité*) detention; **détention préventive** custody

détenu, e [det(ə)ny] *nm/f* prisoner

détergent [detɛʀʒɑ̃] *nm* detergent

détériorer [deteʀjɔʀe] *vt* to damage; **se détériorer** *vi* to deteriorate

déterminé, e [detɛʀmine] *adj* (*résolu*) determined; (*précis*) specific, definite

déterminer [detɛʀmine] *vt* (*fixer*) to determine; ~ **qn à faire qch** to decide sb to do sth; **se ~ à faire qch** to make up one's mind to do sth

détester [detɛste] *vt* to hate, detest

détour [detuʀ] *nm* detour; (*tournant*) bend, curve; **ça vaut le ~** it's worth the trip; **sans ~** (*fig*) plainly

détourné, e [detuʀne] *adj* (*moyen*) roundabout

détourner [detuʀne] *vt* to divert; (*par la force*) to hijack; (*yeux, tête*) to turn away; (*de l'argent*) to embezzle; **se détourner** *vi* to turn away

détraquer [detʀake] *vt* to put out of order; (*estomac*) to upset; **se détraquer** *vi* (*machine*) to go wrong

détriment [detʀimɑ̃] *nm*: **au ~ de** to the detriment of

détroit [detʀwa] *nm* strait

détruire [detʀɥiʀ] *vt* to destroy

dette [dɛt] *nf* debt

DEUG *sigle m* (= *diplôme d'études universitaires générales*) *diploma taken after 2 years at university*

deuil [dœj] *nm* (*perte*) bereavement; (*période*) mourning; **être en ~** to be in mourning

deux [dø] *num* two; **tous les ~** both; **ses ~ mains** both his hands, his two hands; **~ fois** twice; **deuxième** *num* second; **deuxièmement** *adv* secondly; **deux-pièces** *nm inv* (*tailleur*) two-piece suit; (*de bain*) two-piece (swimsuit); (*appartement*) two-roomed flat (BRIT) *ou* apartment (US); **deux-points** *nm inv* colon *sg*; **deux-roues** *nm inv* two-wheeled vehicle

devais [dəvɛ] *vb voir* **devoir**

dévaluation [devaluasjɔ̃] *nf* devaluation

devancer [d(ə)vɑ̃se] *vt* (*coureur, rival*) to get ahead of; (*arriver*) to arrive before; (*prévenir: questions, désirs*) to anticipate

devant [d(ə)vɑ̃] *adv* in front; (*à distance: en avant*) ahead ▷ *prép* in front of; (*en avant*) ahead of; (*avec mouvement: passer*) past; (*en présence de*) in front of; (*étant donné*) in view of ▷ *nm* front; **prendre les ~s** to make the first move; **les pattes de ~** the front legs, the forelegs; **par ~** (*boutonner*) at the front; (*entrer*) the front way; **aller au-~ de qn** to go out to meet sb; **aller au-~ de** (*désirs de qn*) to anticipate

devanture [d(ə)vɑ̃tyʀ] *nf* (*étalage*) display; (*vitrine*) (shop) window

développement [dev(ə)lɔpmɑ̃] *nm* development; **pays en voie de ~** developing countries

développer [dev(ə)lɔpe] *vt* to develop; **se développer** *vi* to develop

devenir [dəv(ə)niʀ] *vb +attrib* to become; **que sont-ils devenus?** what has become of them?

devez [dəve] *vb voir* **devoir**

déviation [devjasjɔ̃] *nf* (*Auto*) diversion (BRIT), detour (US)

devienne *etc* [dəvjɛn] *vb voir* **devenir**

deviner [d(ə)vine] *vt* to guess; (*apercevoir*) to distinguish; **devinette** *nf* riddle

devis [d(ə)vi] *nm* estimate, quotation

devise [dəviz] *nf* (*formule*) motto, watchword; **devises** *nfpl* (*argent*) currency *sg*

dévisser [devise] *vt* to unscrew, undo; **se dévisser** *vi* to come unscrewed

devoir [d(ə)vwaʀ] *nm* duty; (*Scol*) homework *no pl*; (: *en classe*) exercise ▷ *vt* (*argent, respect*): **~ qch (à qn)** to owe (sb) sth; (+*infin: obligation*): **il doit le faire** he has to do it, he must do it; (: *intention*): **le nouveau centre commercial doit ouvrir en mai** the new shopping centre is due to open in May; (: *probabilité*): **il doit être tard** it must be late; (: *fatalité*): **cela devait arriver** it was bound to happen; **combien est-ce que je vous dois?** how much do I owe you?

dévorer [devɔʀe] *vt* to devour

dévoué, e [devwe] *adj* devoted

dévouer [devwe]: **se dévouer** *vi* (*se sacrifier*): **se ~ (pour)** to sacrifice o.s. (for); (*se consacrer*): **se ~ à** to devote *ou* dedicate o.s. to

devrai [dəvʀe] *vb voir* **devoir**

dézipper [dezipe] *vt* to unzip

diabète [djabɛt] *nm* diabetes *sg*; **diabétique** *nm/f* diabetic

diable [djɑbl] *nm* devil

diabolo [djabɔlo] *nm* (*boisson*) lemonade with fruit cordial

diagnostic [djagnɔstik] *nm* diagnosis *sg*; **diagnostiquer** *vt* to diagnose

diagonal, e, -aux [djagɔnal, o] *adj* diagonal; **diagonale** *nf* diagonal; **en diagonale** diagonally

diagramme [djagʀam] *nm* chart, graph

dialecte [djalɛkt] *nm* dialect

dialogue [djalɔg] *nm* dialogue

diamant [djamɑ̃] *nm* diamond

diamètre [djamɛtʀ] *nm* diameter

diapositive [djapozitiv] *nf* transparency, slide

diarrhée [djaʀe] *nf* diarrhoea

dictateur [diktatœʀ] *nm* dictator; **dictature** *nf* dictatorship

dictée [dikte] *nf* dictation

dicter [dikte] *vt* to dictate

dictionnaire [diksjɔnɛʀ] *nm* dictionary

dièse [djɛz] *nm* sharp

diesel [djezɛl] *nm* diesel ▷ *adj inv* diesel

diète [djɛt] *nf* (*jeûne*) starvation diet; (*régime*) diet; **diététique** *adj*: **magasin diététique** health food shop (BRIT) *ou* store (US)

dieu, x [djø] *nm* god; **D~** God; **mon D~!** good heavens!

différemment [difeʀamɑ̃] *adv* differently

différence [difeʀɑ̃s] *nf* difference; **à la ~ de** unlike; **différencier** *vt* to differentiate

différent, e [difeʀɑ̃, ɑ̃t] *adj* (*dissemblable*) different; **~ de** different from; (*divers*) different, various

différer [difeʀe] vt to postpone, put off ▷ vi: ~ **(de)** to differ (from)

difficile [difisil] adj difficult; (exigeant) hard to please; **difficilement** adv with difficulty

difficulté [difikylte] nf difficulty; **en** ~ (bateau, alpiniste) in difficulties

diffuser [difyze] vt (chaleur) to diffuse; (émission, musique) to broadcast; (nouvelle) to circulate; (Comm) to distribute

digérer [diʒeʀe] vt to digest; (fam: accepter) to stomach, put up with; **digestif** nm (after-dinner) liqueur; **digestion** nf digestion

digne [diɲ] adj dignified; ~ **de** worthy of; ~ **de foi** trustworthy; **dignité** nf dignity

digue [dig] nf dike, dyke

dilemme [dilɛm] nm dilemma

diligence [diliʒɑ̃s] nf stagecoach

diluer [dilɥe] vt to dilute

dimanche [dimɑ̃ʃ] nm Sunday

dimension [dimɑ̃sjɔ̃] nf (grandeur) size; (dimensions) dimensions

diminuer [diminɥe] vt to reduce, decrease; (ardeur etc) to lessen; (dénigrer) to belittle ▷ vi to decrease, diminish; **diminutif** nm (surnom) pet name

dinde [dɛ̃d] nf turkey

dindon [dɛ̃dɔ̃] nm turkey

dîner [dine] nm dinner ▷ vi to have dinner

dingue [dɛ̃g] (fam) adj crazy

dinosaure [dinozɔʀ] nm dinosaur

diplomate [diplɔmat] adj diplomatic ▷ nm diplomat; (fig) diplomatist; **diplomatie** nf diplomacy

diplôme [diplom] nm diploma; **avoir des** ~**s** to have qualifications; **diplômé, e** adj qualified

dire [diʀ] nm: **au** ~ **de** according to ▷ vt to say; (secret, mensonge, heure) to tell; ~ **qch à qn** to tell sb sth; ~ **à qn qu'il fasse** ou **de faire** to tell sb to do; **on dit que** they say that; **ceci** ou **cela dit** that being said; **si cela lui dit** (plaire) if he fancies it; **que dites-vous de** (penser) what do you think of; **on dirait que** it looks (ou sounds etc) as if; **dis/dites (donc)!** I say!; **se** ~ **(à soi-même)** to say to o.s.; **se** ~ **malade** (se prétendre) to claim one is ill; **ça ne se dit pas** (impoli) you shouldn't say that; (pas en usage) you don't say that

direct, e [diʀɛkt] adj direct ▷ nm (TV): **en** ~ live; **directement** adv directly

directeur, -trice [diʀɛktœʀ, tʀis] nm/f (d'entreprise) director; (de service) manager(-eress); (d'école) head(teacher) (BRIT), principal (US)

direction [diʀɛksjɔ̃] nf (sens) direction; (d'entreprise) management; (Auto) steering; **"toutes** ~**s"** "all routes"

dirent [diʀ] vb voir **dire**

dirigeant, e [diʀiʒɑ̃, ɑ̃t] adj (classe) ruling

▷ nm/f (d'un parti etc) leader

diriger [diʀiʒe] vt (entreprise) to manage, run; (véhicule) to steer; (orchestre) to conduct; (recherches, travaux) to supervise; ~ **sur** (arme) to point ou level ou aim at; ~ **son regard sur** to look in the direction of; **se diriger** vi (s'orienter) to find one's way; **se** ~ **vers** ou **sur** to make ou head for

dis [di] vb voir **dire**

discerner [disɛʀne] vt to discern, make out

discipline [disiplin] nf discipline; **discipliner** vt to discipline

discontinu, e [diskɔ̃tiny] adj intermittent

discontinuer [diskɔ̃tinɥe] vi: **sans** ~ without stopping, without a break

discothèque [diskɔtɛk] nf (boîte de nuit) disco(thèque)

discours [diskuʀ] nm speech

discret, -ète [diskʀɛ, ɛt] adj discreet; (parfum, maquillage) unobtrusive; **discrétion** nf discretion; **à discrétion** as much as one wants

discrimination [diskʀiminasjɔ̃] nf discrimination; **sans** ~ indiscriminately

discussion [diskysjɔ̃] nf discussion

discutable [diskytabl] adj debatable

discuter [diskyte] vt (débattre) to discuss; (contester) to question, dispute ▷ vi to talk; (protester) to argue; ~ **de** to discuss

dise [diz] vb voir **dire**

disjoncteur [disʒɔ̃ktœʀ] nm (Élec) circuit breaker

disloquer [dislɔke]: **se disloquer** vi (parti, empire) to break up; (meuble) to come apart; (épaule) to be dislocated

disons [dizɔ̃] vb voir **dire**

disparaître [dispaʀɛtʀ] vi to disappear; (se perdre: traditions etc) to die out; **faire** ~ (tache) to remove; (douleur) to get rid of

disparition [dispaʀisjɔ̃] nf disappearance; **espèce en voie de** ~ endangered species

disparu, e [dispaʀy] nm/f missing person ▷ adj: **être porté** ~ to be reported missing

dispensaire [dispɑ̃sɛʀ] nm community clinic

dispenser [dispɑ̃se] vt: ~ **qn de** to exempt sb from

disperser [dispɛʀse] vt to scatter; **se disperser** vi to break up

disponible [dispɔnibl(ə)] adj available

disposé, e [dispoze] adj: **bien/mal** ~ (humeur) in a good/bad mood; ~ **à** (prêt à) willing ou prepared to

disposer [dispoze] vt to arrange ▷ vi: **vous pouvez** ~ you may leave; ~ **de** to have (at one's disposal); **se** ~ **à faire** to prepare to do, be about to do

dispositif [dispozitif] nm device; (fig) system, plan of action

disposition [dispozisjɔ̃] nf (arrangement) arrangement, layout; (humeur) mood;

d

prendre ses ~s to make arrangements; **avoir des ~s pour la musique** *etc* to have a special aptitude for music *etc*; **à la ~ de qn** at sb's disposal; **je suis à votre ~** I am at your service

disproportionné, e [dispRopoRsjone] *adj* disproportionate, out of all proportion

dispute [dispyt] *nf* quarrel, argument; **disputer** *vt* (*match*) to fight; (*combat*) to fight; **se disputer** *vi* to quarrel

disqualifier [diskalifje] *vt* to disqualify

disque [disk] *nm* (*Mus*) record; (*forme, pièce*) disc; (*Sport*) discus; **disque compact** compact disc; **disque dur** hard disk; **disquette** *nf* floppy disk, diskette

dissertation [disɛRtasjɔ̃] *nf* (*Scol*) essay

dissimuler [disimyle] *vt* to conceal

dissipé, e [disipe] *adj* (*élève*) undisciplined, unruly

dissolvant [disɔlvɑ̃] *nm* nail polish remover

dissuader [disɥade] *vt*: **~ qn de faire** to dissuade sb from doing

distance [distɑ̃s] *nf* distance; (*fig: écart*) gap; **à ~** at *ou* from a distance; **distancer** *vt* to outdistance

distant, e [distɑ̃, ɑ̃t] *adj* (*réservé*) distant; **~ de** (*lieu*) far away from

distillerie [distilRi] *nf* distillery

distinct, e [distɛ̃(kt), ɛ̃kt] *adj* distinct; **distinctement** *adv* distinctly, clearly; **distinctif, -ive** *adj* distinctive

distingué, e [distɛ̃ge] *adj* distinguished

distinguer [distɛ̃ge] *vt* to distinguish; **se ~ de** to be distinguished by

distraction [distRaksjɔ̃] *nf* (*inattention*) absent-mindedness; (*passe-temps*) distraction, entertainment

distraire [distRɛR] *vt* (*divertir*) to entertain, divert; (*déranger*) to distract; **se distraire** *vi* to amuse *ou* enjoy o.s.; **distrait, e** *adj* absent-minded

distrayant, e [distRɛjɑ̃, ɑ̃t] *adj* entertaining

distribuer [distRibɥe] *vt* to distribute, hand out; (*Cartes*) to deal (out); (*courrier*) to deliver; **distributeur** *nm* (*Comm*) distributor; **distributeur (automatique)** (vending) machine; **distributeur de billets** (cash) dispenser

dit, e [di, dit] *pp de* **dire** ▷ *adj* (*fixé*): **le jour ~** the arranged day; (*surnommé*): **X, ~ Pierrot** X, known as Pierrot

dites [dit] *vb voir* **dire**

divan [divɑ̃] *nm* divan

divers, e [divɛR, ɛRs] *adj* (*varié*) diverse, varied; (*différent*) different, various; **~es personnes** various *ou* several people

diversité [divɛRsite] *nf* (*variété*) diversity

divertir [divɛRtiR]: **se divertir** *vi* to amuse *ou* enjoy o.s.; **divertissement** *nm* distraction, entertainment

diviser [divize] *vt* to divide; **division** *nf* division

divorce [divɔRs] *nm* divorce; **divorcé, e** *nm/f* divorcee; **divorcer** *vi* to get a divorce, get divorced; **divorcer de** *ou* **d'avec qn** to divorce sb

divulguer [divylge] *vt* to disclose

dix [dis] *num* ten; **dix-huit** *num* eighteen; **dix-huitième** *num* eighteenth; **dixième** *num* tenth; **dix-neuf** *num* nineteen; **dix-neuvième** *num* nineteenth; **dix-sept** *num* seventeen; **dix-septième** *num* seventeenth

dizaine [dizɛn] *nf*: **une ~ (de)** about ten, ten or so

do [do] *nm* (*note*) C; (*en chantant la gamme*) do(h)

docile [dɔsil] *adj* docile

dock [dɔk] *nm* dock; **docker** *nm* docker

docteur [dɔktœR] *nm* doctor; **doctorat** *nm* doctorate

doctrine [dɔktRin] *nf* doctrine

document [dɔkymɑ̃] *nm* document; **documentaire** *adj, nm* documentary; **documentation** *nf* documentation, literature; **documenter** *vt*: **se documenter (sur)** to gather information (on)

dodo [dodo] *nm* (*langage enfantin*): **aller faire ~** to go to beddy-byes

dogue [dɔg] *nm* mastiff

doigt [dwa] *nm* finger; **à deux ~s de** within an inch of; **un ~ de lait/whiskey** a drop of milk/whisky; **doigt de pied** toe

doit *etc* [dwa] *vb voir* **devoir**

dollar [dɔlaR] *nm* dollar

domaine [dɔmɛn] *nm* estate, property; (*fig*) domain, field

domestique [dɔmɛstik] *adj* domestic ▷ *nm/f* servant, domestic

domicile [dɔmisil] *nm* home, place of residence; **à ~** at home; **livrer à ~** to deliver; **domicilié, e** *adj*: **"domicilié à ..."** "address ..."

dominant, e [dɔminɑ̃, ɑ̃t] *adj* (*opinion*) predominant

dominer [dɔmine] *vt* to dominate; (*sujet*) to master; (*surpasser*) to outclass, surpass; (*surplomber*) to tower above, dominate ▷ *vi* to be in the dominant position; **se dominer** *vi* to control o.s.

domino [dɔmino] *nm* domino; **dominos** *nmpl* (*jeu*) dominoes *sg*

dommage [dɔmaʒ] *nm*: **~s** (*dégâts*) damage *no pl*; **c'est ~!** what a shame!; **c'est ~ que** it's a shame *ou* pity that

dompter [dɔ̃(p)te] *vt* to tame; **dompteur, -euse** *nm/f* trainer

DOM-ROM [dɔmRɔm] *sigle m* (= *départements et régions d'outre-mer*) French overseas departments and regions

don [dɔ̃] *nm* gift; (*charité*) donation; **avoir des ~s pour** to have a gift *ou* talent for; **elle a le ~**

de m'énerver she's got a knack of getting on my nerves

donc [dɔ̃k] conj therefore, so; (après une digression) so, then

donné, e [dɔne] adj (convenu: lieu, heure) given; (pas cher: fam): **c'est ~** it's a gift; **étant ~ que ...** given that ...; **données** nfpl data

donner [dɔne] vt to give; (vieux habits etc) to give away; (spectacle) to put on; **~ qch à qn** to give sb sth, give sth to sb; **~ sur** (suj: fenêtre, chambre) to look (out) onto; **ça donne soif/faim** it makes you (feel) thirsty/hungry; **se ~ à fond** to give one's all; **se ~ du mal** to take (great) trouble; **s'en ~ à cœur joie** (fam) to have a great time

⊙ **MOT-CLÉ**

dont [dɔ̃] pron relatif **1** (appartenance: objets) whose, of which; (appartenance: êtres animés) whose; **la maison dont le toit est rouge** the house the roof of which is red, the house whose roof is red; **l'homme dont je connais la sœur** the man whose sister I know
2 (parmi lesquel(le)s): **2 livres, dont l'un est ...** 2 books, one of which is ...; **il y avait plusieurs personnes, dont Gabrielle** there were several people, among them Gabrielle; **10 blessés, dont 2 grièvement** 10 injured, 2 of them seriously
3 (complément d'adjectif, de verbe): **le fils dont il est si fier** the son he's so proud of; **le pays dont il est originaire** the country he's from; **la façon dont il l'a fait** the way he did it; **ce dont je parle** what I'm talking about

dopage [dɔpaʒ] nm (Sport) drug use; (de cheval) doping

doré, e [dɔʀe] adj golden; (avec dorure) gilt, gilded

dorénavant [dɔʀenavɑ̃] adv henceforth

dorer [dɔʀe] vt to gild; **(faire) ~** (Culin) to brown

dorloter [dɔʀlɔte] vt to pamper

dormir [dɔʀmiʀ] vi to sleep; (être endormi) to be asleep

dortoir [dɔʀtwaʀ] nm dormitory

dos [do] nm back; (de livre) spine; **"voir au ~"** "see over"; **de ~** from the back

dosage [dozaʒ] nm mixture

dose [doz] nf dose; **doser** vt to measure out; **il faut savoir doser ses efforts** you have to be able to pace yourself

dossier [dosje] nm (documents) file; (de chaise) back; (Presse) feature; (Comput) folder; **un ~ scolaire** a school report

douane [dwan] nf customs pl; **douanier, -ière** adj customs cpd ▷ nm customs officer

double [dubl] adj, adv double ▷ nm (2 fois plus):

le ~ (de) twice as much (ou many) (as); (autre exemplaire) duplicate, copy; (sosie) double; (Tennis) doubles sg; **en ~ (exemplaire)** in duplicate; **faire ~ emploi** to be redundant; **double-cliquer** vi (Inform) to double-click

doubler [duble] vt (multiplier par 2) to double; (vêtement) to line; (dépasser) to overtake, pass; (film) to dub; (acteur) to stand in for ▷ vi to double

doublure [dublyʀ] nf lining; (Cinéma) stand-in

douce [dus] adj voir **doux**; **douceâtre** adj sickly sweet; **doucement** adv gently; (lentement) slowly; **douceur** nf softness; (de quelqu'un) gentleness; (de climat) mildness

douche [duʃ] nf shower; **prendre une ~** to have ou take a shower; **doucher: se doucher** vi to have ou take a shower

doué, e [dwe] adj gifted, talented; **être ~ pour** to have a gift for

douille [duj] nf (Élec) socket

douillet, te [dujɛ, ɛt] adj cosy; (péj: à la douleur) soft

douleur [dulœʀ] nf pain; (chagrin) grief, distress; **douloureux, -euse** adj painful

doute [dut] nm doubt; **sans ~** no doubt; (probablement) probably; **sans aucun ~** without a doubt; **douter** vt to doubt; **douter de** (sincérité de qn) to have (one's) doubts about; (réussite) to be doubtful of; **douter que** to doubt if ou whether; **se douter de qch/que** to suspect sth/that; **je m'en doutais** I suspected as much; **douteux, -euse** adj (incertain) doubtful; (péj) dubious-looking

Douvres [duvʀ] n Dover

doux, douce [du, dus] adj soft; (sucré) sweet; (peu fort: moutarde, clément: climat) mild; (pas brusque) gentle

douzaine [duzɛn] nf (12) dozen; (environ 12): **une ~ (de)** a dozen or so

douze [duz] num twelve; **douzième** num twelfth

dragée [draʒe] nf sugared almond

draguer [drage] vt (rivière) to dredge; (fam) to try to pick up

dramatique [dramatik] adj dramatic; (tragique) tragic ▷ nf (TV) (television) drama

drame [dram] nm drama

drap [dra] nm (de lit) sheet; (tissu) woollen fabric

drapeau, x [drapo] nm flag

drap-housse [draus] nm fitted sheet

dresser [drese] vt (mettre vertical, monter) to put up, erect; (liste) to draw up; (animal) to train; **se dresser** vi (obstacle) to stand; (personne) to draw o.s. up; **~ qn contre qn** to set sb against sb; **~ l'oreille** to prick up one's ears

drogue [drɔg] nf drug; **la ~** drugs pl; **drogué, e** nm/f drug addict; **droguer** vt (victime) to drug; **se droguer** vi (aux stupéfiants) to take drugs; (péj: de médicaments) to dose o.s. up; **droguerie** nf hardware shop; **droguiste** nm keeper/owner of a hardware shop

droit, e [dʀwa, dʀwat] adj (non courbe) straight; (vertical) upright, straight; (fig: loyal) upright, straight(forward); (opposé à gauche) right, right-hand ▷ adv straight ▷ nm (prérogative) right; (taxe) duty, tax; (: d'inscription) fee; (Jur): **le ~** law; **avoir le ~ de** to be allowed to; **avoir ~ à** to be entitled to; **être dans son ~** to be within one's rights; **à ~e** on the right; (direction) (to the) right; **droits d'auteur** royalties; **droits d'inscription** enrolment fee; **droite** nf (Pol): **la droite** the right (wing); **droitier, -ière** adj right-handed

drôle [dʀol] adj funny; **une ~ d'idée** a funny idea

dromadaire [dʀɔmadɛʀ] nm dromedary

du [dy] dét voir **de** ▷ prép +dét = **de + le**

dû, due [dy] vb voir **devoir** ▷ adj (somme) owing, owed; (causé par): **dû à** due to ▷ nm due

dune [dyn] nf dune

duplex [dyplɛks] nm (appartement) split-level apartment, duplex

duquel [dykɛl] prép +pron = **de +lequel**

dur, e [dyʀ] adj (pierre, siège, travail, problème) hard; (voix, climat) harsh; (sévère) hard, harsh; (cruel) hard(-hearted); (porte, col) stiff; (viande) tough ▷ adv hard ▷ nm (fam: meneur) tough nut; **~ d'oreille** hard of hearing

durant [dyʀɑ̃] prép (au cours de) during; (pendant) for; **des mois ~** for months

durcir [dyʀsiʀ] vt, vi to harden; **se durcir** vi to harden

durée [dyʀe] nf length; (d'une pile etc) life; **de courte ~** (séjour) short

durement [dyʀmɑ̃] adv harshly

durer [dyʀe] vi to last

dureté [dyʀte] nf hardness; harshness; stiffness; toughness

durit(r) [dyʀit] nf (car radiator) hose

duvet [dyvɛ] nm down; (sac de couchage) down-filled sleeping bag

DVD sigle m (= digital versatile disc) DVD

dynamique [dinamik] adj dynamic; **dynamisme** nm dynamism

dynamo [dinamo] nf dynamo

dyslexie [dislɛksi] nf dyslexia, word-blindness

eau, x [o] nf water; **eaux** nfpl (Méd) waters; **prendre l'~** to leak, let in water; **tomber à l'~** (fig) to fall through; **eau de Cologne** eau de Cologne; **eau courante** running water; **eau de javel** bleach; **eau de toilette** toilet water; **eau douce** fresh water; **eau gazeuse** sparkling (mineral) water; **eau minérale** mineral water; **eau plate** still water; **eau salée** salt water; **eau-de-vie** nf brandy

ébène [ebɛn] nf ebony; **ébéniste** nm cabinetmaker

éblouir [ebluiʀ] vt to dazzle

éboueur [ebwœʀ] nm dustman (BRIT), garbageman (US)

ébouillanter [ebujɑ̃te] vt to scald; (Culin) to blanch

éboulement [ebulmɑ̃] nm rock fall

ébranler [ebʀɑ̃le] vt to shake; (affaiblir) to weaken; **s'ébranler** vi (partir) to move off

ébullition [ebylisjɔ̃] nf boiling point; **en ~** boiling

écaille [ekɑj] nf (de poisson) scale; (matière) tortoiseshell; **écailler** vt (poisson) to scale; **s'écailler** vi to flake ou peel (off)

écart [ekaʀ] nm gap; **à l'~** out of the way; **à l'~ de** away from; **faire un ~** (voiture) to swerve

écarté, e [ekaʀte] adj (lieu) out-of-the-way, remote; (ouvert): **les jambes ~es** legs apart; **les bras ~s** arms outstretched

écarter [ekaʀte] vt (séparer) to move apart,

separate; (*éloigner*) to push back, move away; (*ouvrir: bras, jambes*) to spread, open; (: *rideau*) to draw (back); (*éliminer: candidat, possibilité*) to dismiss; **s'écarter** *vi* to part; (*s'éloigner*) to move away; **s'~ de** to wander from

échafaudage [eʃafodaʒ] *nm* scaffolding

échalote [eʃalɔt] *nf* shallot

échange [eʃɑ̃ʒ] *nm* exchange; **en ~ de** in exchange *ou* return for; **échanger** *vt*: **échanger qch (contre)** to exchange sth (for)

échantillon [eʃɑ̃tijɔ̃] *nm* sample

échapper [eʃape]: **~ à** *vt* (*gardien*) to escape (from); (*punition, péril*) to escape; **s'échapper** *vi* to escape; **~ à qn** (*détail, sens*) to escape sb; (*objet qu'on tient*) to slip out of sb's hands; **laisser ~** (*cri etc*) to let out; **l'~ belle** to have a narrow escape

écharde [eʃaʁd] *nf* splinter (of wood)

écharpe [eʃaʁp] *nf* scarf; **avoir le bras en ~** to have one's arm in a sling

échauffer [eʃofe] *vt* (*moteur*) to overheat; **s'échauffer** *vi* (*Sport*) to warm up; (*dans la discussion*) to become heated

échéance [eʃeɑ̃s] *nf* (*d'un paiement: date*) settlement date; (*fig*) deadline; **à brève ~** in the short term; **à longue ~** in the long run

échéant [eʃeɑ̃]: **le cas ~** *adv* if the case arises

échec [eʃɛk] *nm* failure; (*Échecs*): **~ et mat/au roi** checkmate/check; **échecs** *nmpl* (*jeu*) chess *sg*; **tenir en ~** to hold in check

échelle [eʃɛl] *nf* ladder; (*fig, d'une carte*) scale

échelon [eʃ(ə)lɔ̃] *nm* (*d'échelle*) rung; (*Admin*) grade; **échelonner** *vt* to space out

échiquier [eʃikje] *nm* chessboard

écho [eko] *nm* echo; **échographie** *nf*: **passer une échographie** to have a scan

échouer [eʃwe] *vi* to fail; **s'échouer** *vi* to run aground

éclabousser [eklabuse] *vt* to splash

éclair [eklɛʁ] *nm* (*d'orage*) flash of lightning, lightning *no pl*; (*gâteau*) éclair

éclairage [eklɛʁaʒ] *nm* lighting

éclaircie [eklɛʁsi] *nf* bright interval

éclaircir [eklɛʁsiʁ] *vt* to lighten; (*fig: mystère*) to clear up; (: *point*) to clarify; **s'éclaircir** *vi* (*ciel*) to clear; **s'~ la voix** to clear one's throat; **éclaircissement** *nm* (*sur un point*) clarification

éclairer [eklere] *vt* (*lieu*) to light (up); (*personne: avec une lampe etc*) to light the way for; (*fig: problème*) to shed light on ▷ *vi*: **~ mal/bien** to give a poor/good light; **s'~ à la bougie** to use candlelight

éclat [ekla] *nm* (*de bombe, de verre*) fragment; (*du soleil, d'une couleur etc*) brightness, brilliance; (*d'une cérémonie*) splendour; (*scandale*): **faire un ~** to cause a commotion; **éclats de voix** shouts; **éclat de rire** roar of laughter

éclatant, e [eklatɑ̃, ɑ̃t] *adj* brilliant

éclater [eklate] *vi* (*pneu*) to burst; (*bombe*) to explode; (*guerre*) to break out; (*groupe, parti*) to break up; **~ en sanglots/de rire** to burst out sobbing/laughing

écluse [eklyz] *nf* lock

écœurant, e [ekœʁɑ̃, ɑ̃t] *adj* (*gâteau etc*) sickly; (*fig*) sickening

écœurer [ekœʁe] *vt*: **~ qn** (*nourriture*) to make sb feel sick; (*conduite, personne*) to disgust sb

école [ekɔl] *nf* school; **aller à l'~** to go to school; **école maternelle** nursery school; **école primaire** primary (BRIT) *ou* grade (US) school; **école secondaire** secondary (BRIT) *ou* high (US) school; **écolier, -ière** *nm/f* schoolboy(-girl)

écologie [ekɔlɔʒi] *nf* ecology; **écologique** *adj* environment-friendly; **écologiste** *nm/f* ecologist

économe [ekɔnɔm] *adj* thrifty ▷ *nm/f* (*de lycée etc*) bursar (BRIT), treasurer (US)

économie [ekɔnɔmi] *nf* economy; (*gain: d'argent, de temps etc*) saving; (*science*) economics *sg*; **économies** *nfpl* (*pécule*) savings; **économique** *adj* (*avantageux*) economical; (*Écon*) economic; **économiser** *vt, vi* to save

écorce [ekɔʁs] *nf* bark; (*de fruit*) peel

écorcher [ekɔʁʃe] *vt*: **s'~ le genou/la main** to graze one's knee/one's hand; **écorchure** *nf* graze

écossais, e [ekɔsɛ, ɛz] *adj* Scottish ▷ *nm/f*: **É~, e** Scot

Écosse [ekɔs] *nf*: **l'~** Scotland

écouter [ekute] *vt* to listen to; **s'écouter** (*malade*) to be a bit of a hypochondriac; **si je m'écoutais** if I followed my instincts; **écouteur** *nm* (*Tél*) receiver; **écouteurs** *nmpl* (*casque*) headphones *pl*, headset

écran [ekʁɑ̃] *nm* screen; **petit ~** television; **~ total** sunblock

écrasant, e [ekʁazɑ̃, ɑ̃t] *adj* overwhelming

écraser [ekʁaze] *vt* to crush; (*piéton*) to run over; **s'écraser** *vi* to crash; **s'~ contre** to crash into

écrémé, e [ekʁeme] *adj* (*lait*) skimmed

écrevisse [ekʁəvis] *nf* crayfish *inv*

écrire [ekʁiʁ] *vt* to write; **s'écrire** to write to each other; **ça s'écrit comment?** how is it spelt?; **écrit** *nm* (*examen*) written paper; **par écrit** in writing

écriteau, x [ekʁito] *nm* notice, sign

écriture [ekʁityʁ] *nf* writing; **écritures** *nfpl* (*Comm*) accounts, books; **l'É~ (sainte), les É~s** the Scriptures

écrivain [ekʁivɛ̃] *nm* writer

écrou [ekʁu] *nm* nut

écrouler [ekʁule]: **s'écrouler** *vi* to collapse

écru, e [ekʁy] *adj* (*couleur*) off-white, écru

écume [ekym] nf foam

écureuil [ekyʀœj] nm squirrel

écurie [ekyʀi] nf stable

eczéma [ɛgzema] nm eczema

EDF sigle f (= Électricité de France) national electricity company

Édimbourg [edɛ̃buʀ] n Edinburgh

éditer [edite] vt (publier) to publish; (annoter) to edit; **éditeur, -trice** nm/f publisher; **édition** nf edition; (industrie du livre) publishing

édredon [edʀədɔ̃] nm eiderdown

éducateur, -trice [edykatœʀ, tʀis] nm/f teacher; (en école spécialisée) instructor

éducatif, -ive [edykatif, iv] adj educational

éducation [edykasjɔ̃] nf education; (familiale) upbringing; (manières) (good) manners pl; **éducation physique** physical education

éduquer [edyke] vt to educate; (élever) to bring up

effacer [efase] vt to erase, rub out; **s'effacer** vi (inscription etc) to wear off; (pour laisser passer) to step aside

effarant, e [efaʀɑ̃, ɑ̃t] adj alarming

effectif, -ive [efɛktif, iv] adj real ▷ nm (Scol) (pupil) numbers pl; (entreprise) staff, workforce; **effectivement** adv (réellement) actually, really; (en effet) indeed

effectuer [efɛktɥe] vt (opération) to carry out; (trajet) to make

effervescent, e [efɛʀvesɑ̃, ɑ̃t] adj effervescent

effet [efɛ] nm effect; (impression) impression; **effets** nmpl (vêtements etc) things; **faire ~** (médicament) to take effect; **faire de l'~** (impressionner) to make an impression; **faire bon/mauvais ~ sur qn** to make a good/bad impression on sb; **en ~** indeed; **effet de serre** greenhouse effect

efficace [efikas] adj (personne) efficient; (action, médicament) effective; **efficacité** nf efficiency; effectiveness

effondrer [efɔ̃dʀe]: **s'effondrer** vi to collapse

efforcer [efɔʀse]: **s'efforcer de** vt: **s'~ de faire** to try hard to do

effort [efɔʀ] nm effort

effrayant, e [efʀɛjɑ̃, ɑ̃t] adj frightening

effrayer [efʀeje] vt to frighten, scare; **s'~ (de)** to be frightened ou scared (by)

effréné, e [efʀene] adj wild

effronté, e [efʀɔ̃te] adj cheeky

effroyable [efʀwajabl] adj horrifying, appalling

égal, e, -aux [egal, o] adj equal; (constant: vitesse) steady ▷ nm/f equal; **être ~ à** (prix, nombre) to be equal to; **ça lui est ~** it's all the same to him, he doesn't mind; **sans ~** matchless, unequalled; **d'~ à ~** as equals; **également** adv equally; (aussi) too, as well;

égaler vt to equal; **égaliser** vt (sol, salaires) to level (out); (chances) to equalize ▷ vi (Sport) to equalize; **égalité** nf equality; **être à égalité** to be level

égard [egaʀ] nm: **~s** mpl consideration sg; **à cet ~** in this respect; **par ~ pour** out of consideration for; **à l'~ de** towards

égarer [egaʀe] vt to mislay; **s'égarer** vi to get lost, lose one's way; (objet) to go astray

églefin [egləfɛ̃] nm haddock

église [egliz] nf church; **aller à l'~** to go to church

égoïsme [egɔism] nm selfishness; **égoïste** adj selfish

égout [egu] nm sewer

égoutter [egute] vi to drip; **s'égoutter** vi to drip; **égouttoir** nm draining board; (mobile) draining rack

égratignure [egʀatiɲyʀ] nf scratch

Égypte [eʒipt] nf: **l'~** Egypt; **égyptien, ne** adj Egyptian ▷ nm/f: **Égyptien, ne** Egyptian

eh [e] excl hey!; **eh bien!** well!

élaborer [elabɔʀe] vt to elaborate; (projet, stratégie) to work out; (rapport) to draft

élan [elɑ̃] nm (Zool) elk, moose; (Sport) run up; (fig: de tendresse etc) surge; **prendre de l'~** to gather speed

élancer [elɑ̃se]: **s'élancer** vi to dash, hurl o.s.

élargir [elaʀʒiʀ] vt to widen; **s'élargir** vi to widen; (vêtement) to stretch

élastique [elastik] adj elastic ▷ nm (de bureau) rubber band; (pour la couture) elastic no pl

élection [elɛksjɔ̃] nf election

électricien, ne [elɛktʀisjɛ̃, jɛn] nm/f electrician

électricité [elɛktʀisite] nf electricity; **allumer/éteindre l'~** to put on/off the light

électrique [elɛktʀik] adj electric(al)

électrocuter [elɛktʀɔkyte] vt to electrocute

électroménager [elɛktʀɔmenaʒe] adj, nm: **appareils ~s, l'~** domestic (electrical) appliances

électronique [elɛktʀɔnik] adj electronic ▷ nf electronics sg

élégance [elegɑ̃s] nf elegance

élégant, e [elegɑ̃, ɑ̃t] adj elegant

élément [elemɑ̃] nm element; (pièce) component, part; **élémentaire** adj elementary

éléphant [elefɑ̃] nm elephant

élevage [el(ə)vaʒ] nm breeding; (de bovins) cattle rearing; **truite d'~** farmed trout

élevé, e [el(ə)ve] adj high; **bien/mal ~** well-/ill-mannered

élève [elɛv] nm/f pupil

élever [el(ə)ve] vt (enfant) to bring up, raise; (animaux) to breed; (hausser: taux, niveau) to raise; (édifier: monument) to put up, erect; **s'élever** vi (avion) to go up; (niveau, *température*) to rise; **s'~ à** (*suj: frais, dégâts*) to amount to, add up to; **s'~ contre qch** to rise up against sth; **~ la voix** to raise one's voice; **éleveur, -euse** *nm/f* breeder

éliminatoire [eliminatwaʀ] *nf* (*Sport*) heat

éliminer [elimine] *vt* to eliminate

élire [eliʀ] *vt* to elect

elle [ɛl] *pron* (*sujet*) she; (: *chose*) it; (*complément*) her; it; **~s** (*sujet*) they; (*complément*) them; **~-même** herself; itself; **~s-mêmes** themselves; *voir aussi* **il**

éloigné, e [elwaɲe] *adj* distant, far-off; (*parent*) distant

éloigner [elwaɲe] *vt* (*échéance*) to put off, postpone; (*soupçons, danger*) to ward off; (*objet*): **~ qch (de)** to move *ou* take sth away (from); (*personne*): **~ qn (de)** to take sb away *ou* remove sb (from); **s'éloigner (de)** (*personne*) to go away (from); (*véhicule*) to move away (from); (*affectivement*) to grow away (from)

élu, e [ely] *pp de* **élire** ▷ *nm/f* (*Pol*) elected representative

Élysée [elize] *nm*: **(le palais de) l'~** the Élysee Palace (*the French president's residence*)

émail, -aux [emaj, o] *nm* enamel

e-mail [imɛl] *nm* e-mail; **envoyer qch par ~** to e-mail sth

émanciper [emãsipe]: **s'émanciper** *vi* (*fig*) to become emancipated *ou* liberated

emballage [ãbalaʒ] *nm* (*papier*) wrapping; (*boîte*) packaging

emballer [ãbale] *vt* to wrap (up); (*dans un carton*) to pack (up); (*fig: fam*) to thrill (to bits); **s'emballer** *vi* (*moteur*) to race; (*cheval*) to bolt; (*fig: personne*) to get carried away

embarcadère [ãbaʀkadɛʀ] *nm* wharf, pier

embarquement [ãbaʀkəmã] *nm* (*de passagers*) boarding; (*de marchandises*) loading

embarquer [ãbaʀke] *vt* (*personne*) to embark; (*marchandise*) to load; (*fam*) to cart off ▷ *vi* (*passager*) to board; **s'embarquer** *vi* to board; **s'~ dans** (*affaire, aventure*) to embark upon

embarras [ãbaʀa] *nm* (*gêne*) embarrassment; **mettre qn dans l'~** to put sb in an awkward position; **vous n'avez que l'~ du choix** the only problem is choosing

embarrassant, e [ãbaʀasã, ãt] *adj* embarrassing

embarrasser [ãbaʀase] *vt* (*encombrer*) to clutter (up); (*gêner*) to hinder, hamper; **~ qn** to put sb in an awkward position; **s'~ de** to burden o.s. with

embaucher [ãboʃe] *vt* to take on, hire

embêter [ãbete] *vt* to bother; **s'embêter** *vi* (*s'ennuyer*) to be bored

emblée [ãble]: **d'~** *adv* straightaway

embouchure [ãbuʃyʀ] *nf* (*Géo*) mouth

embourber [ãbuʀbe]: **s'embourber** *vi* to get stuck in the mud

embouteillage [ãbutɛjaʒ] *nm* traffic jam

embranchement [ãbʀãʃmã] *nm* (*routier*) junction

embrasser [ãbʀase] *vt* to kiss; (*sujet, période*) to embrace, encompass

embrayage [ãbʀɛjaʒ] *nm* clutch

embrouiller [ãbʀuje] *vt* to muddle up; (*fils*) to tangle (up); **s'embrouiller** *vi* (*personne*) to get in a muddle

embruns [ãbʀœ̃] *nmpl* sea spray *sg*

embué, e [ãbɥe] *adj* misted up

émeraude [em(ə)ʀod] *nf* emerald

émerger [emɛʀʒe] *vi* to emerge; (*faire saillie, aussi fig*) to stand out

émeri [em(ə)ʀi] *nm*: **toile** *ou* **papier ~** emery paper

émerveiller [emɛʀveje] *vt* to fill with wonder; **s'émerveiller de** to marvel at

émettre [emɛtʀ] *vt* (*son, lumière*) to give out, emit; (*message etc: Radio*) to transmit; (*billet, timbre, emprunt*) to issue; (*hypothèse, avis*) to voice, put forward ▷ *vi* to broadcast

émeus *etc* [emø] *vb voir* **émouvoir**

émeute [emøt] *nf* riot

émigrer [emigʀe] *vi* to emigrate

émincer [emɛ̃se] *vt* to cut into thin slices

émission [emisjɔ̃] *nf* (*Radio, TV*) programme, broadcast; (*d'un message*) transmission; (*de timbre*) issue

emmêler [ãmele] *vt* to tangle (up); (*fig*) to muddle up; **s'emmêler** *vi* to get in a tangle

emménager [ãmenaʒe] *vi* to move in; **~ dans** to move into

emmener [ãm(ə)ne] *vt* to take (with one); (*comme otage, capture*) to take away; **~ qn au cinéma** to take sb to the cinema

emmerder [ãmɛʀde] (*fam!*) *vt* to bug, bother; **s'emmerder** *vi* to be bored stiff

émoticone [emɔticon] *nm* smiley

émotif, -ive [emɔtif, iv] *adj* emotional

émotion [emɔsjɔ̃] *nf* emotion

émouvoir [emuvwaʀ] *vt* to move; **s'émouvoir** *vi* to be moved; (*s'indigner*) to be roused

empaqueter [ãpakte] *vt* to parcel up

emparer [ãpaʀe]: **s'emparer de** *vt* (*objet*) to seize, grab; (*comme otage, MIL*) to seize; (*suj: peur etc*) to take hold of

empêchement [ãpɛʃmã] *nm* (*unexpected*) obstacle, hitch

empêcher [ãpeʃe] *vt* to prevent; **~ qn de faire** to prevent *ou* stop sb (from) doing; **il n'empêche que** nevertheless; **il n'a pas pu s'~ de rire** he couldn't help laughing

empereur [ãpʀœʀ] *nm* emperor

empiffrer [ãpifʀe]: **s'~** (*fam*) *vi* to stuff o.s.

empiler [ãpile] *vt* to pile (up)

empire [ãpiʀ] *nm* empire; (*fig*) influence

empirer [ãpiʀe] *vi* to worsen, deteriorate

emplacement [ɑ̃plasmɑ̃] nm site
emploi [ɑ̃plwa] nm (utilisation) use; (Comm, Écon) employment; (poste) job, situation; **mode d'~** directions for use; **emploi du temps** timetable, schedule
employé, e [ɑ̃plwaje] nm/f employee; **employé de bureau** office employee ou clerk
employer [ɑ̃plwaje] vt to use; (ouvrier, main-d'œuvre) to employ; **s'~ à faire** to apply ou devote o.s. to doing; **employeur, -euse** nm/f employer
empoigner [ɑ̃pwaɲe] vt to grab
empoisonner [ɑ̃pwazɔne] vt to poison; (empester: air, pièce) to stink out; (fam): **~ qn** to drive sb mad
emporter [ɑ̃pɔrte] vt to take (with one); (en dérobant ou enlevant, emmener: blessés, voyageurs) to take away; (entraîner) to carry away; **s'emporter** vi (de colère) to lose one's temper; **l'~ (sur)** to get the upper hand (of); **plats à ~** take-away meals
empreinte [ɑ̃prɛ̃t] nf: **~ (de pas)** footprint; **empreintes (digitales)** fingerprints
empressé, e [ɑ̃prese] adj attentive
empresser [ɑ̃prese]: **s'empresser** vi: **s'~ auprès de qn** to surround sb with attentions; **s'~ de faire** (se hâter) to hasten to do
emprisonner [ɑ̃prizɔne] vt to imprison
emprunt [ɑ̃prœ̃] nm loan
emprunter [ɑ̃prœ̃te] vt to borrow; (itinéraire) to take, follow
ému, e [emy] pp de **émouvoir** ▷ adj (gratitude) touched; (compassion) moved

 MOT-CLÉ

en [ɑ̃] prép **1** (endroit, pays) in; (direction) to; **habiter en France/ville** to live in France/town; **aller en France/ville** to go to France/town
2 (moment, temps) in; **en été/juin** in summer/June; **en 3 jours** in 3 days
3 (moyen) by; **en avion/taxi** by plane/taxi
4 (composition) made of; **c'est en verre** it's (made of) glass; **un collier en argent** a silver necklace
5 (description, état): **une femme (habillée) en rouge** a woman (dressed) in red; **peindre qch en rouge** to paint sth red; **en T/étoile** T/star-shaped; **en chemise/chaussettes** in one's shirt-sleeves/socks; **en soldat** as a soldier; **cassé en plusieurs morceaux** broken into several pieces; **en réparation** being repaired, under repair; **en vacances** on holiday; **en deuil** in mourning; **le même en plus grand** the same but ou only bigger
6 (avec gérondif) while, on, by; **en dormant** while sleeping, as one sleeps; **en sortant** on going out, as he etc went out; **sortir en**

courant to run out
7 (comme) as; **je te parle en ami** I'm talking to you as a friend
▷ pron **1** (indéfini): **j'en ai/veux** I have/want some; **en as-tu?** have you got any?; **je n'en veux pas** I don't want any; **j'en ai 2** I've got 2; **combien y en a-t-il?** how many (of them) are there?; **j'en ai assez** I've got enough (of it ou them); (j'en ai marre) I've had enough
2 (provenance) from there; **j'en viens** I've come from there
3 (cause): **il en est malade/perd le sommeil** he is ill/can't sleep because of it
4 (complément de nom, d'adjectif, de verbe): **j'en connais les dangers** I know its ou the dangers; **j'en suis fier** I am proud of it ou him ou her ou them; **j'en ai besoin** I need it ou them

encadrer [ɑ̃kɑdre] vt (tableau, image) to frame; (fig: entourer) to surround; (personnel, soldats etc) to train
encaisser [ɑ̃kese] vt (chèque) to cash; (argent) to collect; (fam: coup, défaite) to take
en-cas [ɑ̃kɑ] nm snack
enceinte [ɑ̃sɛ̃t] adj f: **~ (de 6 mois)** (6 months) pregnant ▷ nf (mur) wall; (espace) enclosure; **enceinte (acoustique)** (loud)speaker
encens [ɑ̃sɑ̃] nm incense
enchaîner [ɑ̃ʃene] vt to chain up; (mouvements, séquences) to link (together) ▷ vi to carry on
enchanté, e [ɑ̃ʃɑ̃te] adj (ravi) delighted; (magique) enchanted; **~ (de faire votre connaissance)** pleased to meet you
enchère [ɑ̃ʃɛr] nf bid; **mettre/vendre aux ~s** to put up for (sale by)/sell by auction
enclencher [ɑ̃klɑ̃ʃe] vt (mécanisme) to engage; **s'enclencher** vi to engage
encombrant, e [ɑ̃kɔ̃brɑ̃, ɑ̃t] adj cumbersome, bulky
encombrement [ɑ̃kɔ̃brəmɑ̃] nm: **être pris dans un ~** to be stuck in a traffic jam
encombrer [ɑ̃kɔ̃bre] vt to clutter (up); (gêner) to hamper; **s'~ de** (bagages etc) to load ou burden o.s. with

 MOT-CLÉ

encore [ɑ̃kɔr] adv **1** (continuation) still; **il y travaille encore** he's still working on it; **pas encore** not yet
2 (de nouveau) again; **j'irai encore demain** I'll go again tomorrow; **encore une fois** (once) again; **(et puis) quoi encore?** what next?
3 (en plus) more; **encore un peu de viande?** a little more meat?; **encore deux jours** two more days
4 (intensif) even, still; **encore plus fort/mieux** even louder/better, louder/better still

5 (*restriction*) even so *ou* then, only; **encore pourrais-je le faire si ...** even so, I might be able to do it if ...; **si encore** if only

encourager [ãkuʀaʒe] *vt* to encourage; **~ qn à faire qch** to encourage sb to do sth
encourir [ãkuʀiʀ] *vt* to incur
encre [ãkʀ] *nf* ink; **encre de Chine** Indian ink
encyclopédie [ãsiklɔpedi] *nf* encyclopaedia
endetter [ãdete]: **s'endetter** *vi* to get into debt
endive [ãdiv] *nf* chicory *no pl*
endormi, e [ãdɔrmi] *adj* asleep
endormir [ãdɔrmiʀ] *vt* to put to sleep; (*suj: chaleur etc*) to send to sleep; (*Méd: dent, nerf*) to anaesthetize; (*fig: soupçons*) to allay; **s'endormir** *vi* to fall asleep, go to sleep
endroit [ãdʀwa] *nm* place; (*opposé à l'envers*) right side; **à l'~** (*vêtement*) the right way out; (*objet posé*) the right way round
endurance [ãdyʀãs] *nf* endurance
endurant, e [ãdyʀã, ãt] *adj* tough, hardy
endurcir [ãdyʀsiʀ]: **s'endurcir** *vi* (*physiquement*) to become tougher; (*moralement*) to become hardened
endurer [ãdyʀe] *vt* to endure, bear
énergétique [enɛʀʒetik] *adj* (*aliment*) energy-giving
énergie [enɛʀʒi] *nf* (*Physique*) energy; (*Tech*) power; (*morale*) vigour, spirit; **énergique** *adj* energetic, vigorous; (*mesures*) drastic, stringent
énervant, e [enɛʀvã, ãt] *adj* irritating, annoying
énerver [enɛʀve] *vt* to irritate, annoy; **s'énerver** *vi* to get excited, get worked up
enfance [ãfãs] *nf* childhood
enfant [ãfã] *nm/f* child; **enfantin, e** *adj* (*puéril*) childlike; (*langage, jeu etc*) children's *cpd*
enfer [ãfɛʀ] *nm* hell
enfermer [ãfɛʀme] *vt* to shut up; (*à clef, interner*) to lock up; **s'enfermer** to shut o.s. away
enfiler [ãfile] *vt* (*vêtement*) to slip on, slip into; (*perles*) to string; (*aiguille*) to thread
enfin [ãfɛ̃] *adv* at last; (*en énumérant*) lastly; (*toutefois*) still; (*pour conclure*) in a word; (*somme toute*) after all
enflammer [ãflame]: **s'enflammer** *vi* to catch fire; (*Méd*) to become inflamed
enflé, e [ãfle] *adj* swollen
enfler [ãfle] *vi* to swell (up)
enfoncer [ãfɔ̃se] *vt* (*clou*) to drive in; (*faire pénétrer*): **~ qch dans** to push (*ou* drive) sth into; (*forcer: porte*) to break open; **s'enfoncer** *vi* to sink; **s'~ dans** to sink into; (*forêt, ville*) to disappear into
enfouir [ãfwiʀ] *vt* (*dans le sol*) to bury; (*dans un tiroir etc*) to tuck away

enfuir [ãfɥiʀ]: **s'enfuir** *vi* to run away *ou* off
engagement [ãgaʒmã] *nm* commitment; **sans ~** without obligation
engager [ãgaʒe] *vt* (*embaucher*) to take on; (: *artiste*) to engage; (*commencer*) to start; (*lier*) to bind, commit; (*impliquer*) to involve; (*investir*) to invest, lay out; (*inciter*) to urge; (*introduire: clé*) to insert; **s'engager** *vi* (*promettre*) to commit o.s.; (*Mil*) to enlist; (*débuter: conversation etc*) to start (up); **s'~ à faire** to undertake to do; **s'~ dans** (*rue, passage*) to turn into; (*fig: affaire, discussion*) to enter into, embark on
engelures [ãʒlyʀ] *nfpl* chilblains
engin [ãʒɛ̃] *nm* machine; (*outil*) instrument; (*Auto*) vehicle; (*Aviat*) aircraft *inv*
Attention à ne pas traduire *engin* par le mot anglais *engine*.
engloutir [ãglutiʀ] *vt* to swallow up
engouement [ãgumã] *nm* (sudden) passion
engouffrer [ãgufʀe] *vt* to swallow up, devour; **s'engouffrer dans** to rush into
engourdir [ãguʀdiʀ] *vt* to numb; (*fig*) to dull, blunt; **s'engourdir** *vi* to go numb
engrais [ãgʀɛ] *nm* manure; **engrais chimique** chemical fertilizer
engraisser [ãgʀese] *vt* to fatten (up)
engrenage [ãgʀənaʒ] *nm* gears *pl*, gearing; (*fig*) chain
engueuler [ãgœle] (*fam*) *vt* to bawl at
enhardir [ãaʀdiʀ]: **s'enhardir** *vi* to grow bolder
énigme [enigm] *nf* riddle
enivrer [ãnivʀe] *vt*: **s'~** to get drunk
enjamber [ãʒãbe] *vt* to stride over
enjeu, x [ãʒø] *nm* stakes *pl*
enjoué, e [ãʒwe] *adj* playful
enlaidir [ãlediʀ] *vt* to make ugly ▷ *vi* to become ugly
enlèvement [ãlɛvmã] *nm* (*rapt*) abduction, kidnapping
enlever [ãl(ə)ve] *vt* (*ôter: gén*) to remove; (: *vêtement, lunettes*) to take off; (*emporter: ordures etc*) to take away; (*kidnapper*) to abduct, kidnap; (*obtenir: prix, contrat*) to win; (*prendre*): **~ qch à qn** to take sth (away) from sb
enliser [ãlize]: **s'enliser** *vi* to sink, get stuck
enneigé, e [ãneʒe] *adj* (*route, maison*) snowed-up; (*paysage*) snowy
ennemi, e [ɛnmi] *adj* hostile; (*Mil*) enemy *cpd* ▷ *nm/f* enemy
ennui [ãnɥi] *nm* (*lassitude*) boredom; (*difficulté*) trouble *no pl*; **avoir des ~s** to have problems; **ennuyer** *vt* to bother; (*lasser*) to bore; **s'ennuyer** *vi* to be bored; **si cela ne vous ennuie pas** if it's no trouble (to you); **ennuyeux, -euse** *adj* boring, tedious; (*embêtant*) annoying
énorme [enɔʀm] *adj* enormous, huge;

énormément *adv* enormously;
énormément de neige/gens an enormous
amount of snow/number of people
enquête [ɑ̃kɛt] *nf* (*de journaliste, de police*)
investigation; (*judiciaire, administrative*)
inquiry; (*sondage d'opinion*) survey; **enquêter**
vi: **enquêter (sur)** to investigate
enragé, e [ɑ̃ʀaʒe] *adj* (*Méd*) rabid, with rabies;
(*fig*) fanatical
enrageant, e [ɑ̃ʀaʒɑ̃, ɑ̃t] *adj* infuriating
enrager [ɑ̃ʀaʒe] *vi* to be in a rage
enregistrement [ɑ̃ʀ(ə)ʒistʀəmɑ̃] *nm*
recording; **enregistrement des bagages**
baggage check-in
enregistrer [ɑ̃ʀ(ə)ʒistʀe] *vt* (*Mus etc*) to
record; (*fig: mémoriser*) to make a mental note
of; (*bagages: à l'aéroport*) to check in
enrhumer [ɑ̃ʀyme] *vt:* **s'~, être enrhumé** to
catch a cold
enrichir [ɑ̃ʀiʃiʀ] *vt* to make rich(er); (*fig*) to
enrich; **s'enrichir** *vi* to get rich(er)
enrouer [ɑ̃ʀwe]: **s'enrouer** *vi* to go hoarse
enrouler [ɑ̃ʀule] *vt* (*fil, corde*) to wind (up); **s'~
(autour de qch)** to wind (around) sth
enseignant, e [ɑ̃sɛɲɑ̃, ɑ̃t] *nm/f* teacher
enseignement [ɑ̃sɛɲ(ə)mɑ̃] *nm* teaching;
(*Admin*) education
enseigner [ɑ̃seɲe] *vt, vi* to teach; **~ qch à qn**
to teach sb sth
ensemble [ɑ̃sɑ̃bl] *adv* together ▷ *nm*
(*groupement*) set; (*vêtements*) outfit; (*totalité*):
l'~ du/de la the whole *ou* entire; (*unité,
harmonie*) unity; **impression/idée d'~** overall
ou general impression/idea; **dans l'~** (*en gros*)
on the whole
ensoleillé, e [ɑ̃sɔleje] *adj* sunny
ensuite [ɑ̃sɥit] *adv* then, next; (*plus tard*)
afterwards, later
entamer [ɑ̃tame] *vt* (*pain, bouteille*) to start;
(*hostilités, pourparlers*) to open
entasser [ɑ̃tase] *vt* (*empiler*) to pile up, heap
up; **s'entasser** *vi* (*s'amonceler*) to pile up; **s'~
dans** (*personnes*) to cram into
entendre [ɑ̃tɑ̃dʀ] *vt* to hear; (*comprendre*) to
understand; (*vouloir dire*) to mean; **s'entendre**
vi (*sympathiser*) to get on; (*se mettre d'accord*)
to agree; **j'ai entendu dire que** I've heard (it
said) that; **~ parler de** to hear of
entendu, e [ɑ̃tɑ̃dy] *adj* (*réglé*) agreed; (*au
courant: air*) knowing; **(c'est) ~** all right,
agreed; **bien ~** of course
entente [ɑ̃tɑ̃t] *nf* understanding; (*accord,
traité*) agreement; **à double ~** (*sens*) with a
double meaning
enterrement [ɑ̃tɛʀmɑ̃] *nm* (*cérémonie*)
funeral, burial
enterrer [ɑ̃teʀe] *vt* to bury
entêtant, e [ɑ̃tɛtɑ̃, ɑ̃t] *adj* heady
en-tête [ɑ̃tɛt] *nm* heading; **papier à ~** headed

notepaper
entêté, e [ɑ̃tete] *adj* stubborn
entêter [ɑ̃tete]: **s'entêter** *vi:* **s'~ (à faire)** to
persist (in doing)
enthousiasme [ɑ̃tuzjasm] *nm* enthusiasm;
enthousiasmer *vt* to fill with enthusiasm;
s'enthousiasmer (pour qch) to get
enthusiastic (about sth); **enthousiaste** *adj*
enthusiastic
entier, -ère [ɑ̃tje, jɛʀ] *adj* whole; (*total:
satisfaction etc*) complete; (*fig: caractère*)
unbending ▷ *nm* (*Math*) whole; **en ~** totally;
lait ~ full-cream milk; **entièrement** *adv*
entirely, wholly
entonnoir [ɑ̃tɔnwaʀ] *nm* funnel
entorse [ɑ̃tɔʀs] *nf* (*Méd*) sprain; (*fig*): **~ au
règlement** infringement of the rule
entourage [ɑ̃tuʀaʒ] *nm* circle; (*famille*) circle
of family/friends; (*ce qui enclôt*) surround
entourer [ɑ̃tuʀe] *vt* to surround; (*apporter son
soutien à*) to rally round; **~ de** to surround with;
s'~ de to surround o.s. with
entracte [ɑ̃tʀakt] *nm* interval
entraide [ɑ̃tʀɛd] *nf* mutual aid
entrain [ɑ̃tʀɛ̃] *nm* spirit; **avec/sans ~**
spiritedly/half-heartedly
entraînement [ɑ̃tʀɛnmɑ̃] *nm* training
entraîner [ɑ̃tʀene] *vt* (*charrier*) to carry ou
drag along; (*Tech*) to drive; (*emmener: personne*)
to take (off); (*influencer*) to lead; (*Sport*) to train;
(*impliquer*) to entail; **s'entraîner** *vi* (*Sport*)
to train; **s'~ à qch/à faire** to train o.s. for
sth/to do; **~ qn à faire** (*inciter*) to lead sb to do;
entraîneur, -euse *nm/f* (*Sport*) coach, trainer
▷ *nm* (*Hippisme*) trainer
entre [ɑ̃tʀ] *prép* between; (*parmi*) among(st);
l'un d'~ eux/nous one of them/us; **ils se
battent ~ eux** they are fighting among(st)
themselves; **~ autres (choses)** among other
things; **entrecôte** *nf* entrecôte ou rib steak
entrée [ɑ̃tʀe] *nf* entrance; (*accès: au cinéma etc*)
admission; (*billet*) (admission) ticket; (*Culin*)
first course
entre...: **entrefilet** *nm* paragraph (*short
article*); **entremets** *nm* (cream) dessert
entrepôt [ɑ̃tʀəpo] *nm* warehouse
entreprendre [ɑ̃tʀəpʀɑ̃dʀ] *vt* (*se lancer dans*)
to undertake; (*commencer*) to begin ou start
(upon)
entrepreneur, -euse [ɑ̃tʀəpʀənœʀ, øz]
nm/f: **entrepreneur (en bâtiment)** (building)
contractor
entreprise [ɑ̃tʀəpʀiz] *nf* (*société*) firm,
concern; (*action*) undertaking, venture
entrer [ɑ̃tʀe] *vi* to go (ou come) in, enter ▷ *vt*
(*Inform*) to enter, input; **(faire) ~ qch dans** to
get sth into; **~ dans** (*gén*) to enter; (*pièce*) to go
(ou come) into, enter; (*club*) to join; (*heurter*)
to run into; **~ à l'hôpital** to go into hospital;

faire ~ (*visiteur*) to show in

entre-temps [ãtʀətã] *adv* meanwhile

entretenir [ãtʀət(ə)niʀ] *vt* to maintain; (*famille, maîtresse*) to support, keep; **~ qn (de)** to speak to sb (about)

entretien [ãtʀətjɛ̃] *nm* maintenance; (*discussion*) discussion, talk; (*pour un emploi*) interview

entrevoir [ãtʀəvwaʀ] *vt* (*à peine*) to make out; (*brièvement*) to catch a glimpse of

entrevue [ãtʀəvy] *nf* (*audience*) interview

entrouvert, e [ãtʀuvɛʀ, ɛʀt] *adj* half-open

énumérer [enymeʀe] *vt* to list

envahir [ãvaiʀ] *vt* to invade; (*suj: inquiétude, peur*) to come over; **envahissant, e** (*péj*) *adj* (*personne*) intrusive

enveloppe [ãv(ə)lɔp] *nf* (*de lettre*) envelope; (*crédits*) budget; **envelopper** *vt* to wrap; (*fig*) to envelop, shroud

enverrai etc [ãveʀe] *vb voir* **envoyer**

envers [ãvɛʀ] *prép* towards, to ▷ *nm* other side; (*d'une étoffe*) wrong side; **à l'~** (*verticalement*) upside down; (*pull*) back to front; (*chaussettes*) inside out

envie [ãvi] *nf* (*sentiment*) envy; (*souhait*) desire, wish; **avoir ~ de (faire)** to feel like (doing); (*plus fort*) to want (to do); **avoir ~ que** to wish that; **cette glace me fait ~** I fancy some of that ice cream; **envier** *vt* to envy; **envieux, -euse** *adj* envious

environ [ãviʀɔ̃] *adv*: **~ 3 h/2 km** (around) about 3 o'clock/2 km; *voir aussi* **environs**

environnant, e [ãviʀɔnã, ãt] *adj* surrounding

environnement [ãviʀɔnmã] *nm* environment

environs [ãviʀɔ̃] *nmpl* surroundings; **aux ~ de** (round) about

envisager [ãvizaʒe] *vt* to contemplate, envisage; **~ de faire** to consider doing

envoler [ãvɔle]: **s'envoler** *vi* (*oiseau*) to fly away *ou* off; (*avion*) to take off; (*papier, feuille*) to blow away; (*fig*) to vanish (into thin air)

envoyé, e [ãvwaje] *nm/f* (*Pol*) envoy; (*Presse*) correspondent; **envoyé spécial** special correspondent

envoyer [ãvwaje] *vt* to send; (*lancer*) to hurl, throw; **~ chercher** to send for; **~ promener qn** (*fam*) to send sb packing

épagneul, e [epaɲœl] *nm/f* spaniel

épais, se [epɛ, ɛs] *adj* thick; **épaisseur** *nf* thickness

épanouir [epanwiʀ]: **s'épanouir** *vi* (*fleur*) to bloom, open out; (*visage*) to light up; (*personne*) to blossom

épargne [epaʀɲ] *nf* saving

épargner [epaʀɲe] *vt* to save; (*ne pas tuer ou endommager*) to spare ▷ *vi* to save; **~ qch à qn** to spare sb sth

éparpiller [epaʀpije] *vt* to scatter; **s'éparpiller** *vi* to scatter; (*fig*) to dissipate one's efforts

épatant, e [epatã, ãt] (*fam*) *adj* super

épater [epate] (*fam*) *vt* (*étonner*) to amaze; (*impressionner*) to impress

épaule [epol] *nf* shoulder

épave [epav] *nf* wreck

épée [epe] *nf* sword

épeler [ep(ə)le] *vt* to spell

éperon [epʀɔ̃] *nm* spur

épervier [epɛʀvje] *nm* sparrowhawk

épi [epi] *nm* (*de blé, d'orge*) ear; (*de maïs*) cob

épice [epis] *nf* spice

épicé, e [epise] *adj* spicy

épicer [epise] *vt* to spice

épicerie [episʀi] *nf* grocer's shop; (*denrées*) groceries *pl*; **épicerie fine** delicatessen; **épicier, -ière** *nm/f* grocer

épidémie [epidemi] *nf* epidemic

épiderme [epidɛʀm] *nm* skin

épier [epje] *vt* to spy on, watch closely

épilepsie [epilɛpsi] *nf* epilepsy

épiler [epile] *vt* (*jambes*) to remove the hair from; (*sourcils*) to pluck

épinards [epinaʀ] *nmpl* spinach *sg*

épine [epin] *nf* thorn, prickle; (*d'oursin etc*) spine

épingle [epɛ̃gl] *nf* pin; **épingle de nourrice** *ou* **de sûreté** safety pin

épisode [epizɔd] *nm* episode; **film/roman à ~s** serial; **épisodique** *adj* occasional

épluche-légumes [eplyʃlegym] *nm inv* (potato) peeler

éplucher [eplyʃe] *vt* (*fruit, légumes*) to peel; (*fig*) to go over with a fine-tooth comb; **épluchures** *nfpl* peelings

éponge [epɔ̃ʒ] *nf* sponge; **éponger** *vt* (*liquide*) to mop up; (*surface*) to sponge; (*fig: déficit*) to soak up

époque [epɔk] *nf* (*de l'histoire*) age, era; (*de l'année, la vie*) time; **d'~** (*meuble*) period *cpd*

épouse [epuz] *nf* wife; **épouser** *vt* to marry

épousseter [epuste] *vt* to dust

épouvantable [epuvãtabl] *adj* appalling, dreadful

épouvantail [epuvãtaj] *nm* scarecrow

épouvante [epuvãt] *nf* terror; **film d'~** horror film; **épouvanter** *vt* to terrify

époux [epu] *nm* husband ▷ *nmpl* (married) couple

épreuve [epʀœv] *nf* (*d'examen*) test; (*malheur, difficulté*) trial, ordeal; (*Photo*) print; (*Typo*) proof; (*Sport*) event; **à toute ~** unfailing; **mettre à l'~** to put to the test

éprouver [epʀuve] *vt* (*tester*) to test; (*marquer, faire souffrir*) to afflict, distress; (*ressentir*) to experience

épuisé, e [epɥize] *adj* exhausted; (*livre*) out of

print; **épuisement** nm exhaustion

épuiser [epɥize] vt (fatiguer) to exhaust, wear ou tire out; (stock, sujet) to exhaust; **s'épuiser** vi to wear ou tire o.s. out, exhaust o.s.

épuisette [epɥizɛt] nf shrimping net

équateur [ekwatœʀ] nm equator; **(la république de) l'É~** Ecuador

équation [ekwasjɔ̃] nf equation

équerre [ekɛʀ] nf (à dessin) (set) square

équilibre [ekilibʀ] nm balance; **garder/ perdre l'~** to keep/lose one's balance; **être en ~** to be balanced; **équilibré, e** adj well-balanced; **équilibrer** vt to balance

équipage [ekipaʒ] nm crew

équipe [ekip] nf team; **travailler en ~** to work as a team

équipé, e [ekipe] adj: **bien/mal ~** well-/poorly-equipped

équipement [ekipmɑ̃] nm equipment

équiper [ekipe] vt to equip; **~ qn/qch de** to equip sb/sth with

équipier, -ière [ekipje, jɛʀ] nm/f team member

équitation [ekitasjɔ̃] nf (horse-)riding; **faire de l'~** to go riding

équivalent, e [ekivalɑ̃, ɑ̃t] adj, nm equivalent

équivaloir [ekivalwaʀ]: **~ à** vt to be equivalent to

érable [eʀabl] nm maple

érafler [eʀɑfle] vt to scratch; **éraflure** nf scratch

ère [ɛʀ] nf era; **en l'an 1050 de notre ~** in the year 1050 A.D.

érection [eʀɛksjɔ̃] nf erection

éroder [eʀɔde] vt to erode

érotique [eʀɔtik] adj erotic

errer [eʀe] vi to wander

erreur [eʀœʀ] nf mistake, error; **faire ~** to be mistaken; **par ~** by mistake

éruption [eʀypsjɔ̃] nf eruption; (Méd) rash

es [ɛ] vb voir **être**

ès [ɛs] prép: **licencié ès lettres/sciences** ≈ Bachelor of Arts/Science

ESB sigle f (= encéphalopathie spongiforme bovine) BSE

escabeau, x [ɛskabo] nm (tabouret) stool; (échelle) stepladder

escalade [ɛskalad] nf climbing no pl; (Pol etc) escalation; **escalader** vt to climb

escale [ɛskal] nf (Navig: durée) call; (endroit) port of call; (Aviat) stop(over); **faire ~ à** (Navig) to put in at; (Aviat) to stop over at; **vol sans ~** nonstop flight

escalier [ɛskalje] nm stairs pl; **dans l'~** ou **les ~s** on the stairs; **escalier mécanique** ou **roulant** escalator

escapade [ɛskapad] nf: **faire une ~** to go on a jaunt; (s'enfuir) to run away ou off

escargot [ɛskaʀgo] nm snail

escarpé, e [ɛskaʀpe] adj steep

esclavage [ɛsklavaʒ] nm slavery

esclave [ɛsklav] nm/f slave

escompte [ɛskɔ̃t] nm discount

escrime [ɛskʀim] nf fencing

escroc [ɛskʀo] nm swindler, conman; **escroquer** vt: **escroquer qch (à qn)** to swindle sth (out of sb); **escroquerie** nf swindle

espace [ɛspas] nm space; **espacer** vt to space out; **s'espacer** vi (visites etc) to become less frequent

espadon [ɛspadɔ̃] nm swordfish inv

espadrille [ɛspadʀij] nf rope-soled sandal

Espagne [ɛspaɲ] nf: **l'~** Spain; **espagnol, e** adj Spanish ▷ nm/f: **Espagnol, e** Spaniard ▷ nm (Ling) Spanish

espèce [ɛspɛs] nf (Bio, Bot, Zool) species inv; (gén: sorte) sort, kind, type; (péj): **~ de maladroit/de brute!** you clumsy oaf/you brute!; **espèces** nfpl (Comm) cash sg; **payer en ~** to pay (in) cash

espérance [ɛspeʀɑ̃s] nf hope; **espérance de vie** life expectancy

espérer [ɛspeʀe] vt to hope for; **j'espère (bien)** I hope so; **~ que/faire** to hope that/to do

espiègle [ɛspjɛgl] adj mischievous

espion, ne [ɛspjɔ̃, jɔn] nm/f spy; **espionnage** nm espionage, spying; **espionner** vt to spy (up)on

espoir [ɛspwaʀ] nm hope; **dans l'~ de/que** in the hope of/that; **reprendre ~** not to lose hope

esprit [ɛspʀi] nm (intellect) mind; (humour) wit; (mentalité, d'une loi etc, fantôme etc) spirit; **faire de l'~** to try to be witty; **reprendre ses ~s** to come to; **perdre l'~** to lose one's mind

esquimau, de, -x [ɛskimo, od] adj Eskimo ▷ nm/f: **E~, de** Eskimo ▷ nm: **E~®** ice lolly (BRIT), popsicle (US)

essai [ese] nm (tentative) attempt, try; (de produit) testing; (Rugby) try; (Littérature) essay; **à l'~** on a trial basis; **mettre à l'~** to put to the test

essaim [esɛ̃] nm swarm

essayer [eseje] vt to try; (vêtement, chaussures) to try (on); (méthode, voiture) to try (out) ▷ vi to try; **~ de faire** to try ou attempt to do

essence [esɑ̃s] nf (de voiture) petrol (BRIT), gas(oline) (US); (extrait de plante) essence; (espèce: d'arbre) species inv

essentiel, le [esɑ̃sjɛl] adj essential; **c'est l'~** (ce qui importe) that's the main thing; **l'~ de** the main part of

essieu, x [esjø] nm axle

essor [esɔʀ] nm (de l'économie etc) rapid expansion

essorer [esɔʀe] vt (en tordant) to wring (out);

(par la force centrifuge) to spin-dry; **essoreuse** nf spin-dryer

essouffler [esufle]: **s'essouffler** vi to get out of breath

essuie-glace [esɥiglas] nm inv windscreen (BRIT) ou windshield (US) wiper

essuyer [esɥije] vt to wipe; *(fig: échec)* to suffer; **s'essuyer** vi *(après le bain)* to dry o.s.; ~ **la vaisselle** to dry up

est' [ɛ] vb voir **être**

est² [ɛst] nm east ▷ adj inv east; *(région)* east(ern); **à l'~** in the east; *(direction)* to the east, east(wards); **à l'~ de** (to the) east of

est-ce que [ɛskə] adv: ~ **c'est cher/c'était bon?** is it expensive/was it good?; **quand est-ce qu'il part?** when does he leave?, when is he leaving?; voir aussi **que**

esthéticienne [ɛstetisjɛn] nf beautician

esthétique [ɛstetik] adj attractive

estimation [ɛstimasjɔ̃] nf valuation; *(chiffre)* estimate

estime [ɛstim] nf esteem, regard; **estimer** vt *(respecter)* to esteem; *(expertiser: bijou etc)* to value; *(évaluer: coût etc)* to assess, estimate; *(penser)*: **estimer que/être** to consider that/o.s. to be

estival, e, -aux [ɛstival, o] adj summer cpd

estivant, e [ɛstivɑ̃, ɑ̃t] nm/f (summer) holiday-maker

estomac [ɛstɔma] nm stomach

estragon [ɛstragɔ̃] nm tarragon

estuaire [ɛstɥɛʀ] nm estuary

et [e] conj and; **et lui?** what about him?; **et alors!** so what!

étable [etabl] nf cowshed

établi [etabli] nm (work)bench

établir [etabliʀ] vt *(papiers d'identité, facture)* to make out; *(liste, programme)* to draw up; *(entreprise)* to set up; *(réputation, usage, fait, culpabilité)* to establish; **s'établir** vi to be established; **s'~ (à son compte)** to set up in business; **s'~ à/près de** to settle in/near

établissement [etablismɑ̃] nm *(entreprise, institution)* establishment; **établissement scolaire** school, educational establishment

étage [etaʒ] nm *(d'immeuble)* storey, floor; **à l'~** upstairs; **au 2ème ~** on the 2nd (BRIT) ou 3rd (US) floor; **c'est à quel ~?** what floor is it on?

étagère [etaʒɛʀ] nf *(rayon)* shelf; *(meuble)* shelves pl

étai [etɛ] nm stay, prop

étain [etɛ̃] nm pewter no pl

étais etc [etɛ] vb voir **être**

étaler [etale] vt *(carte, nappe)* to spread (out); *(peinture)* to spread; *(échelonner: paiements, vacances)* to spread, stagger; *(marchandises)* to display; *(connaissances)* to parade; **s'étaler** vi *(liquide)* to spread out; *(fam)* to fall flat on one's face; **s'~ sur** *(suj: paiements etc)* to be spread out over

étalon [etalɔ̃] nm *(cheval)* stallion

étanche [etɑ̃ʃ] adj *(récipient)* watertight; *(montre, vêtement)* waterproof

étang [etɑ̃] nm pond

étant [etɑ̃] vb voir **être**; **donné**

étape [etap] nf stage; *(lieu d'arrivée)* stopping place; (: Cyclisme) staging point

état [eta] nm *(Pol, condition)* state; **en mauvais ~** in poor condition; **en ~ (de marche)** in (working) order; **remettre en ~** to repair; **hors d'~** out of order; **être en ~/hors d'~ de faire** to be in a/in no fit state to do; **être dans tous ses ~s** to be in a state; **faire ~ de** *(alléguer)* to put forward; **l'É~** the State; **état civil** civil status; **état des lieux** inventory of fixtures; **États-Unis** nmpl: **les États-Unis** the United States

etc. [ɛtsetera] adv etc

et c(a)etera [ɛtsetera] adv et cetera, and so on

été [ete] pp de **être** ▷ nm summer

éteindre [etɛ̃dʀ] vt *(lampe, lumière, radio)* to turn ou switch off; *(cigarette, feu)* to put out, extinguish; **s'éteindre** vi *(feu, lumière)* to go out; *(mourir)* to pass away; **éteint, e** adj *(fig)* lacklustre, dull; *(volcan)* extinct

étendre [etɑ̃dʀ] vt *(pâte, liquide)* to spread; *(carte etc)* to spread out; *(linge)* to hang up; *(bras, jambes)* to stretch out; *(fig: agrandir)* to extend; **s'étendre** vi *(augmenter, se propager)* to spread; *(terrain, forêt etc)* to stretch; *(s'allonger)* to stretch out; *(se coucher)* to lie down; *(fig: expliquer)* to elaborate

étendu, e [etɑ̃dy] adj extensive

éternel, le [etɛʀnɛl] adj eternal

éternité [etɛʀnite] nf eternity; **ça a duré une ~** it lasted for ages

éternuement [etɛʀnymɑ̃] nm sneeze

éternuer [etɛʀnɥe] vi to sneeze

êtes [ɛt(z)] vb voir **être**

Éthiopie [etjɔpi] nf: **l'~** Ethiopia

étiez [etje] vb voir **être**

étinceler [etɛ̃s(ə)le] vi to sparkle

étincelle [etɛ̃sɛl] nf spark

étiquette [etikɛt] nf label; *(protocole)*: **l'~** etiquette

étirer [etiʀe] **s'étirer** vi *(personne)* to stretch; *(convoi, route)*: **s'~ sur** to stretch out over

étoile [etwal] nf star; **à la belle ~** in the open; **étoile de mer** starfish; **étoile filante** shooting star; **étoilé, e** adj starry

étonnant, e [etɔnɑ̃, ɑ̃t] adj amazing

étonnement [etɔnmɑ̃] nm surprise, amazement

étonner [etɔne] vt to surprise, amaze; **s'étonner que/de** to be amazed that/at; **cela m'~ait (que)** *(j'en doute)* I'd be very surprised (if)

étouffer [etufe] vt to suffocate; (bruit) to muffle; (scandale) to hush up ▷ vi to suffocate; **s'étouffer** vi (en mangeant etc) to choke; **on étouffe** it's stifling

étourderie [etuʀdəʀi] nf (caractère) absent-mindedness no pl; (faute) thoughtless blunder

étourdi, e [etuʀdi] adj (distrait) scatterbrained, heedless

étourdir [etuʀdiʀ] vt (assommer) to stun, daze; (griser) to make dizzy ou giddy; **étourdissement** nm dizzy spell

étrange [etʀãʒ] adj strange

étranger, -ère [etʀãʒe, ɛʀ] adj foreign; (pas de la famille, non familier) strange ▷ nm/f foreigner; stranger ▷ nm: **à l'~** abroad

étrangler [etʀãɡle] vt to strangle; **s'étrangler** vi (en mangeant etc) to choke

⊙ MOT-CLÉ

être [ɛtʀ] nm being; **être humain** human being

▷ vb +attrib **1** (état, description) to be; **il est instituteur** he is ou he's a teacher; **vous êtes grand/intelligent/fatigué** you are ou you're tall/clever/tired

2 (+à: appartenir) to be; **le livre est à Paul** the book is Paul's ou belongs to Paul; **c'est à moi/eux** it is ou it's mine/theirs

3 (+de: provenance): **il est de Paris** he is from Paris; (: appartenance): **il est des nôtres** he is one of us

4 (date): **nous sommes le 10 janvier** it's the 10th of January (today)

▷ vi to be; **je ne serai pas ici demain** I won't be here tomorrow

▷ vb aux **1** to have; to be; **être arrivé/allé** to have arrived/gone; **il est parti** he has left, he has gone

2 (forme passive) to be; **être fait par** to be made by; **il a été promu** he has been promoted

3 (+à: obligation): **c'est à réparer** it needs repairing; **c'est à essayer** it should be tried; **il est à espérer que ...** it is ou it's to be hoped that ...

▷ vb impers **1**: **il est** +adjectif it is +adjective; **il est impossible de le faire** it's impossible to do it

2 (heure, date): **il est 10 heures** it is ou it's 10 o'clock

3 (emphatique): **c'est moi** it's me; **c'est à lui de le faire** it's up to him to do it

étrennes [etʀɛn] nfpl Christmas box sg

étrier [etʀije] nm stirrup

étroit, e [etʀwa, wat] adj narrow; (vêtement) tight; (fig: liens, collaboration) close; **à l'~** cramped; **~ d'esprit** narrow-minded

étude [etyd] nf studying; (ouvrage, rapport) study; (Scol: salle de travail) study room; **études** nfpl (Scol) studies; **être à l'~** (projet etc) to be under consideration; **faire des ~s (de droit/médecine)** to study (law/medicine)

étudiant, e [etydjã, jãt] nm/f student

étudier [etydje] vt, vi to study

étui [etɥi] nm case

eu, eue [y] pp de **avoir**

euh [ø] excl er

euro [øʀo] nm euro

Europe [øʀɔp] nf: **l'~** Europe; **européen, ne** adj European ▷ nm/f: **Européen, ne** European

eus etc [y] vb voir **avoir**

eux [ø] pron (sujet) they; (objet) them

évacuer [evakɥe] vt to evacuate

évader [evade]: **s'évader** vi to escape

évaluer [evalɥe] vt (expertiser) to appraise, evaluate; (juger approximativement) to estimate

évangile [evãʒil] nm gospel; **É~** Gospel

évanouir [evanwiʀ]: **s'évanouir** vi to faint; (disparaître) to vanish, disappear; **évanouissement** nm (syncope) fainting fit

évaporer [evapɔʀe]: **s'évaporer** vi to evaporate

évasion [evazjõ] nf escape

éveillé, e [eveje] adj awake; (vif) alert, sharp; **éveiller** vt to (a)waken; (soupçons etc) to arouse; **s'éveiller** vi to (a)waken; (fig) to be aroused

événement [evɛnmã] nm event

éventail [evãtaj] nm fan; (choix) range

éventualité [evãtɥalite] nf eventuality; possibility; **dans l'~ de** in the event of

éventuel, le [evãtɥɛl] adj possible

> Attention à ne pas traduire **éventuel** par **eventual**.

éventuellement adv possibly

> Attention à ne pas traduire **éventuellement** par **eventually**.

évêque [evɛk] nm bishop

évidemment [evidamã] adv (bien sûr) of course; (certainement) obviously

évidence [evidãs] nf obviousness; (fait) obvious fact; **de toute ~** quite obviously ou evidently; **être en ~** to be clearly visible; **mettre en ~** (fait) to highlight; **évident, e** adj obvious, evident; **ce n'est pas évident!** (fam) it's not that easy!

évier [evje] nm (kitchen) sink

éviter [evite] vt to avoid; **~ de faire** to avoid doing; **~ qch à qn** to spare sb sth

évoluer [evɔlɥe] vi (enfant, maladie) to develop; (situation, moralement) to evolve, develop; (aller et venir) to move about; **évolution** nf development, evolution

évoquer [evɔke] vt to call to mind, evoke; (mentionner) to mention

ex- [ɛks] préfixe ex-; **son ~mari** her ex-husband;

son ~ **femme** his ex-wife

exact, e [ɛgza(kt), ɛgzakt] adj exact; (correct) correct; (ponctuel) punctual; **l'heure ~e** the right ou exact time; **exactement** adv exactly

ex aequo [ɛgzeko] adj equally placed; **arriver ~** to finish neck and neck

exagéré, e [ɛgzaʒeRe] adj (prix etc) excessive

exagérer [ɛgzaʒeRe] vt to exaggerate ▷ vi to exaggerate; (abuser) to go too far

examen [ɛgzamɛ̃] nm examination; (Scol) exam, examination; **à l'~** under consideration; **examen médical** (medical) examination; (analyse) test

examinateur, -trice [ɛgzaminatœR, tRis] nm/f examiner

examiner [ɛgzamine] vt to examine

exaspérant, e [ɛgzaspeRɑ̃, ɑ̃t] adj exasperating

exaspérer [ɛgzaspeRe] vt to exasperate

exaucer [ɛgzose] vt (vœu) to grant

excéder [ɛksede] vt (dépasser) to exceed; (agacer) to exasperate

excellent, e [ɛkselɑ̃, ɑ̃t] adj excellent

excentrique [ɛksɑ̃tRik] adj eccentric

excepté, e [ɛksɛpte] adj, prép: **les élèves ~s, ~ les élèves** except for the pupils

exception [ɛksɛpsjɔ̃] nf exception; **à l'~ de** except for, with the exception of; **d'~** (mesure, loi) special, exceptional; **exceptionnel, le** adj exceptional; **exceptionnellement** adv exceptionally

excès [ɛksɛ] nm surplus ▷ nmpl excesses; **faire des ~** to overindulge; **excès de vitesse** speeding no pl; **excessif, -ive** adj excessive

excitant, e [ɛksitɑ̃, ɑ̃t] adj exciting ▷ nm stimulant; **excitation** nf (état) excitement

exciter [ɛksite] vt to excite; (suj: café etc) to stimulate; **s'exciter** vi to get excited

exclamer [ɛksklame]: **s'exclamer** vi to exclaim

exclure [ɛksklyR] vt (faire sortir) to expel; (ne pas compter) to exclude, leave out; (rendre impossible) to exclude, rule out; **il est exclu que** it's out of the question that ...; **il n'est pas exclu que ...** it's not impossible that ...; **exclusif, -ive** adj exclusive; **exclusion** nf exclusion; **à l'exclusion de** with the exclusion ou exception of; **exclusivité** nf (Comm) exclusive rights pl; **film passant en exclusivité à** film showing only at

excursion [ɛkskyRsjɔ̃] nf (en autocar) excursion, trip; (à pied) walk, hike

excuse [ɛkskyz] nf excuse; **excuses** nfpl (regret) apology sg, apologies; **excuser** vt to excuse; **s'excuser (de)** to apologize (for); **excusez-moi** I'm sorry; (pour attirer l'attention) excuse me

exécuter [ɛgzekyte] vt (tuer) to execute; (tâche etc) to execute, carry out; (Mus: jouer) to perform, execute; **s'exécuter** vi to comply

exemplaire [ɛgzɑ̃plɛR] nm copy

exemple [ɛgzɑ̃pl] nm example; **par ~** for instance, for example; **donner l'~** to set an example

exercer [ɛgzɛRse] vt (pratiquer) to exercise, practise; (influence, contrôle) to exert; (former) to exercise, train; **s'exercer** vi (sportif, musicien) to practise

exercice [ɛgzɛRsis] nm exercise

exhiber [ɛgzibe] vt (montrer: papiers, certificat) to present, produce; (péj) to display, flaunt; **s'exhiber** vi to parade; (suj: exhibitionniste) to expose o.s; **exhibitionniste** nm/f flasher

exigeant, e [ɛgziʒɑ̃, ɑ̃t] adj demanding; (péj) hard to please

exiger [ɛgziʒe] vt to demand, require

exil [ɛgzil] nm exile; **exiler** vt to exile; **s'exiler** vi to go into exile

existence [ɛgzistɑ̃s] nf existence

exister [ɛgziste] vi to exist; **il existe un/des** there is a/are (some)

exorbitant, e [ɛgzɔRbitɑ̃, ɑ̃t] adj exorbitant

exotique [ɛgzɔtik] adj exotic; **yaourt aux fruits ~s** tropical fruit yoghurt

expédier [ɛkspedje] vt (lettre, paquet) to send; (troupes) to dispatch; (fam: travail etc) to dispose of, dispatch; **expéditeur, -trice** nm/f sender; **expédition** nf sending; (scientifique, sportive, Mil) expedition

expérience [ɛkspeRjɑ̃s] nf (de la vie) experience; (scientifique) experiment

expérimenté, e [ɛkspeRimɑ̃te] adj experienced

expérimenter [ɛkspeRimɑ̃te] vt to test out, experiment with

expert, e [ɛkspɛR, ɛRt] adj, nm expert; **~ en objets d'art** art appraiser; **expert-comptable** nm ≈ chartered accountant (BRIT), ≈ certified public accountant (US)

expirer [ɛkspiRe] vi (prendre fin, mourir) to expire; (respirer) to breathe out

explication [ɛksplikasjɔ̃] nf explanation; (discussion) discussion; (dispute) argument

explicite [ɛksplisit] adj explicit

expliquer [ɛksplike] vt to explain; **s'expliquer** to explain (o.s.); **s'~ avec qn** (discuter) to explain o.s. to sb; **son erreur s'explique** one can understand his mistake

exploit [ɛksplwa] nm exploit, feat; **exploitant, e** nm/f: **exploitant (agricole)** farmer; **exploitation** nf exploitation; (d'une entreprise) running; **exploitation agricole** farming concern; **exploiter** vt (personne, don) to exploit; (entreprise, ferme) to run, operate; (mine) to exploit, work

explorer [ɛksploRe] vt to explore

exploser [ɛksploze] vi to explode, blow up; (engin explosif) to go off; (personne: de colère)

to flare up; **explosif, -ive** *adj, nm* explosive;
explosion *nf* explosion; (*de joie, colère*)
outburst

exportateur, -trice [ɛkspɔʀtatœʀ, tʀis] *adj*
export *cpd*, exporting ▷ *nm* exporter

exportation [ɛkspɔʀtasjɔ̃] *nf* (*action*)
exportation; (*produit*) export

exporter [ɛkspɔʀte] *vt* to export

exposant [ɛkspozɑ̃] *nm* exhibitor

exposé, e [ɛkspoze] *nm* talk ▷ *adj*: **~ au sud**
facing south

exposer [ɛkspoze] *vt* (*marchandise*) to display;
(*peinture*) to exhibit, show; (*parler de*) to explain,
set out; (*mettre en danger, orienter, Photo*) to
expose; **s'~ à** (*soleil, danger*) to expose o.s. to;
exposition *nf* (*manifestation*) exhibition;
(*Photo*) exposure

exprès¹ [ɛkspʀɛ] *adv* (*délibérément*) on
purpose; (*spécialement*) specially; **faire ~ de
faire qch** to do sth on purpose

exprès², -esse [ɛkspʀɛs] *adj inv* (*lettre, colis*)
express

express [ɛkspʀɛs] *adj, nm*: **(café) ~** espresso
(coffee); **(train) ~** fast train

expressif, -ive [ɛkspʀesif, iv] *adj* expressive

expression [ɛkspʀesjɔ̃] *nf* expression

exprimer [ɛkspʀime] *vt* (*sentiment, idée*) to
express; (*jus, liquide*) to press out; **s'exprimer**
vi (*personne*) to express o.s

expulser [ɛkspylse] *vt* to expel; (*locataire*) to
evict; (*Sport*) to send off

exquis, e [ɛkski, iz] *adj* exquisite

extasier [ɛkstɑzje]: **s'extasier sur** *vt* to go
into raptures over

exténuer [ɛkstenɥe] *vt* to exhaust

extérieur, e [ɛksteʀjœʀ] *adj* (*porte, mur
etc*) outer, outside; (*au dehors: escalier, w.-c.*)
outside; (*commerce*) foreign; (*influences*)
external; (*apparent: calme, gaieté etc*) surface
cpd ▷ *nm* (*d'une maison, d'un récipient etc*)
outside, exterior; (*apparence*) exterior; **à l'~**
outside; (*à l'étranger*) abroad

externat [ɛksteʀna] *nm* day school

externe [ɛksteʀn] *adj* external, outer ▷ *nm/f*
(*Méd*) non-resident medical student (BRIT),
extern (US); (*Scol*) day pupil

extincteur [ɛkstɛ̃ktœʀ] *nm* (fire)
extinguisher

extinction [ɛkstɛ̃ksjɔ̃] *nf*: **extinction de voix**
loss of voice

extra [ɛkstʀa] *adj inv* first-rate; (*fam*) fantastic
▷ *nm inv* extra help

extraire [ɛkstʀɛʀ] *vt* to extract; **~ qch de** to
extract sth from; **extrait** *nm* extract; **extrait
de naissance** birth certificate

extraordinaire [ɛkstʀaɔʀdinɛʀ] *adj*
extraordinary; (*Pol: mesures etc*) special

extravagant, e [ɛkstʀavagɑ̃, ɑ̃t] *adj*
extravagant

extraverti, e [ɛkstʀaveʀti] *adj* extrovert

extrême [ɛkstʀɛm] *adj, nm* extreme; **d'un
~ à l'autre** from one extreme to another;
extrêmement *adv* extremely; **Extrême-
Orient** *nm* Far East

extrémité [ɛkstʀemite] *nf* end; (*situation*)
straits *pl*, plight; (*geste désespéré*) extreme
action; **extrémités** *nfpl* (*pieds et mains*)
extremities

exubérant, e [ɛgzybeʀɑ̃, ɑ̃t] *adj* exuberant

F *abr* = **franc**; (*appartement*): **un F2/F3** a one-/two-bedroom flat (BRIT) *ou* apartment (US)

fa [fa] *nm inv* (Mus) F; (*en chantant la gamme*) fa

fabricant, e [fabʀikɑ̃, ɑ̃t] *nm/f* manufacturer

fabrication [fabʀikasjɔ̃] *nf* manufacture

fabrique [fabʀik] *nf* factory; **fabriquer** *vt* to make; (*industriellement*) to manufacture; (*fig*): **qu'est-ce qu'il fabrique?** (*fam*) what is he doing?

fac [fak] (*fam*) *abr f* (Scol) = **faculté**

façade [fasad] *nf* front, façade

face [fas] *nf* face; (*fig: aspect*) side ▷ *adj*: **le côté ~** heads; **en ~ de** opposite; (*fig*) in front of; **de ~** (*voir*) face on; **~ à** facing; (*fig*) faced with, in the face of; **faire ~ à** to face; **~ à ~** *adv* facing each other ▷ *nm inv* encounter

fâché, e [fɑʃe] *adj* angry; (*désolé*) sorry

fâcher [fɑʃe] *vt* to anger; **se fâcher (contre qn)** *vi* to get angry (with sb); **se ~ avec** (*se brouiller*) to fall out with

facile [fasil] *adj* easy; (*caractère*) easy-going; **facilement** *adv* easily; **facilité** *nf* easiness; (*disposition, don*) aptitude; **facilités** (*possibilités*) facilities; (Comm) terms; **faciliter** *vt* to make easier

façon [fasɔ̃] *nf* (*manière*) way; (*d'une robe etc*) making-up, cut; **façons** *nfpl* (*péj*) fuss *sg*; **de ~ à/à ce que** so as to/that; **de toute ~** anyway, in any case; **sans ~** (*accepter*) without fuss; **non merci, sans ~** no thanks, honestly

facteur, -trice [faktœʀ] *nm/f* postman(-woman) (BRIT), mailman(-woman) (US) ▷ *nm* (Math, *fig*: *élément*) factor

facture [faktyʀ] *nf* (*à payer: gén*) bill; (Comm) invoice

facultatif, -ive [fakyltatif, iv] *adj* optional

faculté [fakylte] *nf* (*intellectuelle, d'université*) faculty; (*pouvoir, possibilité*) power

fade [fad] *adj* insipid

faible [fɛbl] *adj* weak; (*voix, lumière, vent*) faint; (*rendement, revenu*) low ▷ *nm* (*pour quelqu'un*) weakness, soft spot; **faiblesse** *nf* weakness; **faiblir** *vi* to weaken; (*lumière*) to dim; (*vent*) to drop

faïence [fajɑ̃s] *nf* earthenware *no pl*

faillir [fajiʀ] *vi*: **j'ai failli tomber** I almost *ou* very nearly fell

faillite [fajit] *nf* bankruptcy; **faire ~** to go bankrupt

faim [fɛ̃] *nf* hunger; **avoir ~** to be hungry; **rester sur sa ~** (*aussi fig*) to be left wanting more

fainéant, e [fɛneɑ̃, ɑ̃t] *nm/f* idler, loafer

○ **MOT-CLÉ**

faire [fɛʀ] *vt* **1** (*fabriquer, être l'auteur de*) to make; **faire du vin/une offre/un film** to make wine/an offer/a film; **faire du bruit** to make a noise

2 (*effectuer: travail, opération*) to do; **que faites-vous?** (*quel métier etc*) what do you do?; (*quelle activité: au moment de la question*) what are you doing?; **faire la lessive** to do the washing

3 (*études*) to do; (*sport, musique*) to play; **faire du droit/du français** to do law/French; **faire du rugby/piano** to play rugby/the piano

4 (*simuler*): **faire le malade/l'innocent** to act the invalid/the innocent

5 (*transformer, avoir un effet sur*): **faire de qn un frustré/avocat** to make sb frustrated/a lawyer; **ça ne me fait rien** (*m'est égal*) I don't care *ou* mind; (*me laisse froid*) it has no effect on me; **ça ne fait rien** it doesn't matter; **faire que** (*impliquer*) to mean that

6 (*calculs, prix, mesures*): **2 et 2 font 4** 2 and 2 are *ou* make 4; **ça fait 10 m/15 euros** it's 10 m/15 euros; **je vous le fais 10 euros** I'll let you have it for 10 euros; **je fais du 40** I take a size 40

7 (*distance*): **faire du 50 (à l'heure)** to do 50 (km an hour); **nous avons fait 1000 km en 2 jours** we did *ou* covered 1000 km in 2 days; **faire l'Europe** to tour *ou* do Europe; **faire les magasins** to go shopping

8: **qu'a-t-il fait de sa valise?** what has he done with his case?

9: **ne faire que**: **il ne fait que critiquer** (*sans cesse*) all he (ever) does is criticize; (*seulement*)

he's only criticizing
10 (*dire*) to say; **"vraiment?" fit-il** "really?"
he said
11 (*maladie*) to have; **faire du diabète** to have
diabetes *sg*
▷ *vi* **1** (*agir, s'y prendre*) to act, do; **il faut
faire vite** we (*ou* you *etc*) must act quickly;
comment a-t-il fait pour? how did he
manage to?; **faites
comme chez vous** make yourself at home
2 (*paraître*) to look; **faire vieux/démodé** to
look old/old-fashioned; **ça fait bien** it looks
good
▷ *vb substitut* to do; **ne le casse pas comme je
l'ai fait** don't break it as I did; **je peux le voir?
— faites!** can I see it? — please do!
▷ *vb impers* **1**: **il fait beau** *etc* the weather is
fine *etc*; *voir aussi* **jour**; **froid** *etc*
2 (*temps écoulé, durée*): **ça fait 2 ans qu'il est
parti** it's 2 years since he left; **ça fait 2 ans
qu'il y est** he's been there for 2 years
▷ *vb semi-aux* **1**: **faire** (+*infinitif: action directe*)
to make; **faire tomber/bouger qch** to make
sth fall/move; **faire démarrer un moteur/
chauffer de l'eau** to start up an engine/heat
some water; **cela fait dormir** it makes you
sleep; **faire travailler les enfants** to make
the children work *ou* get the children to work;
il m'a fait traverser la rue he helped me to
cross the street
2 (*indirectement, par un intermédiaire*): **faire
réparer qch** to get *ou* have sth repaired;
faire punir les enfants to have the children
punished
se faire *vi* **1** (*être convenable*): **cela se fait
beaucoup/ne se fait pas** it's done a lot/not
done
2: **se faire** +*nom ou pron*: **se faire une jupe** to
make o.s. a skirt; **se faire des amis** to make
friends; **se faire du souci** to worry; **il ne s'en
fait pas** he doesn't worry
3: **se faire** +*adj* (*devenir*): **se faire vieux** to be
getting old; **se faire beau** to do o.s. up
4: **se faire à** (*s'habituer*) to get used to; **je
n'arrive pas à me faire à la nourriture/au
climat** I can't get used to the food/climate
5: **se faire** +*infinitif*: **se faire examiner la
vue/opérer** to have one's eyes tested/have an
operation; **se faire couper les cheveux** to get
one's hair cut; **il va se faire tuer/punir** he's
going to get himself killed/get punished; **il
s'est fait aider** he got somebody to help him;
il s'est fait aider par Simon he got Simon to
help him; **se faire faire un vêtement** to get a
garment made for o.s.
6 (*impersonnel*): **comment se fait-il/faisait-il
que?** how is it/was it that?

faire-part [fɛʀpaʀ] *nm inv* announcement (*of*

birth, marriage *etc*)
faisan, e [fəzɑ̃, an] *nm/f* pheasant
faisons [fəzɔ̃] *vb voir* **faire**
fait, e [fɛ, fɛt] *adj* (*mûr: fromage, melon*) ripe
▷ *nm* (*événement*) event, occurrence; (*réalité,
donnée*) fact; **être au ~ (de)** to be informed
(of); **au ~** (*à propos*) by the way; **en venir au
~** to get to the point; **du ~ de ceci/qu'il a
menti** because of *ou* on account of this/his
having lied; **de ce ~** for this reason; **en ~** in
fact; **prendre qn sur le ~** to catch sb in the act;
c'est bien ~ pour lui (*ou* **eux** *etc*) it serves him
(*ou* them *etc*) right; **fait divers** news item
faites [fɛt] *vb voir* **faire**
falaise [falɛz] *nf* cliff
falloir [falwaʀ] *vb impers*: **il faut qu'il parte/a
fallu qu'il parte** (*obligation*) he has to *ou*
must leave/had to leave; **il a fallu le faire**
it had to be done; **il faudrait qu'elle rentre**
she should come *ou* go back, she ought to
come *ou* go back; **il faut faire attention** you
have to be careful; **il me faudrait 100 euros**
I would need 100 euros; **il vous faut tourner
à gauche après l'église** you have to turn left
past the church; **nous avons ce qu'il (nous)
faut** we have what we need; **il ne fallait pas**
you shouldn't have (done); **comme il faut**
(*personne*) proper; (*agir*) properly; **s'en falloir**
vr: **il s'en est fallu de 100 euros/5 minutes**
we/they *etc* were 100 euros short/5 minutes
late (*ou* early); **il s'en faut de beaucoup qu'il
soit** he is far from being; **il s'en est fallu de
peu que cela n'arrive** it very nearly happened
famé, e [fame] *adj*: **mal ~** disreputable, of ill
repute
fameux, -euse [famø, øz] *adj* (*illustre*)
famous; (*bon: repas, plat etc*) first-rate, first-
class; (*valeur intensive*) real, downright
familial, e, -aux [familjal, jo] *adj* family *cpd*
familiarité [familjaʀite] *nf* familiarity
familier, -ère [familje, jɛʀ] *adj* (*connu*)
familiar; (*atmosphère*) informal, friendly; (*Ling*)
informal, colloquial ▷ *nm* regular (visitor)
famille [famij] *nf* family; **il a de la ~ à Paris** he
has relatives in Paris
famine [famin] *nf* famine
fanatique [fanatik] *adj* fanatical ▷ *nm/f*
fanatic
faner [fane]: **se faner** *vi* to fade
fanfare [fɑ̃faʀ] *nf* (*orchestre*) brass band;
(*musique*) fanfare
fantaisie [fɑ̃tezi] *nf* (*spontanéité*) fancy,
imagination; (*caprice*) whim ▷ *adj*: **bijou ~**
costume jewellery
fantasme [fɑ̃tasm] *nm* fantasy
fantastique [fɑ̃tastik] *adj* fantastic
fantôme [fɑ̃tom] *nm* ghost, phantom
faon [fɑ̃] *nm* fawn
FAQ *sigle f* (= *foire aux questions*) FAQ

farce [faʀs] nf (viande) stuffing; (blague) (practical) joke; (Théâtre) farce; **farcir** vt (viande) to stuff

farder [faʀde]: **se farder** vi to make (o.s.) up

farine [faʀin] nf flour

farouche [faʀuʃ] adj (timide) shy, timid

fart [faʀt] nm (ski) wax

fascination [fasinasjɔ̃] nf fascination

fasciner [fasine] vt to fascinate

fascisme [faʃism] nm fascism

fasse etc [fas] vb voir **faire**

fastidieux, -euse [fastidjø, jøz] adj tedious, tiresome

fatal, e [fatal] adj fatal; (inévitable) inevitable; **fatalité** nf (destin) fate; (coïncidence) fateful coincidence

fatidique [fatidik] adj fateful

fatigant, e [fatigɑ̃, ɑ̃t] adj tiring; (agaçant) tiresome

fatigue [fatig] nf tiredness, fatigue; **fatigué, e** adj tired; **fatiguer** vt to tire, make tired; (fig: agacer) to annoy ▷ vi (moteur) to labour, strain; **se fatiguer** to get tired

fauché, e [foʃe] (fam) adj broke

faucher [foʃe] vt (herbe) to cut; (champs, blés) to reap; (fig: véhicule) to mow down; (fam: voler) to pinch

faucon [fokɔ̃] nm falcon, hawk

faudra [fodʀa] vb voir **falloir**

faufiler [fofile]: **se faufiler** vi: **se ~ dans** to edge one's way into; **se ~ parmi/entre** to thread one's way among/between

faune [fon] nf (Zool) wildlife, fauna

fausse [fos] adj voir **faux**; **faussement** adv (accuser) wrongly, wrongfully; (croire) falsely

fausser [fose] vt (objet) to bend, buckle; (fig) to distort; **~ compagnie à qn** to give sb the slip

faut [fo] vb voir **falloir**

faute [fot] nf (erreur) mistake, error; (mauvaise action) misdemeanour; (Football etc) offence; (Tennis) fault; **c'est de sa/ma ~** it's his ou her/my fault; **être en ~** to be in the wrong; **~ de** (temps, argent) for ou through lack of; **sans ~** without fail; **faute de frappe** typing error; **faute professionnelle** professional misconduct no pl

fauteuil [fotœj] nm armchair; (au théâtre) seat; **fauteuil roulant** wheelchair

fautif, -ive [fotif, iv] adj (responsable) at fault, in the wrong; (incorrect) incorrect, inaccurate; **il se sentait ~** he felt guilty

fauve [fov] nm wildcat ▷ adj (couleur) fawn

faux¹ [fo] nf scythe

faux², fausse [fo, fos] adj (inexact) wrong; (voix) out of tune; (billet) fake, forged; (sournois, postiche) false ▷ adv (Mus) out of tune ▷ nm (copie) fake, forgery; **faire ~ bond à qn** to let sb down; **faire un ~ pas** to trip; (fig) to make a faux pas; **fausse alerte** false alarm; **fausse couche** miscarriage; **faux frais** nmpl extras, incidental expenses; **faux mouvement** awkward movement; **fausse note** wrong note; **faux témoignage** (délit) perjury; **faux-filet** nm sirloin

faveur [favœʀ] nf favour; **traitement de ~** preferential treatment; **en ~ de** in favour of

favorable [favɔʀabl] adj favourable

favori, te [favɔʀi, it] adj, nm/f favourite

favoriser [favɔʀize] vt to favour

fax [faks] nm fax

fécond, e [fekɔ̃, ɔ̃d] adj fertile; **féconder** vt to fertilize

féculent [fekylɑ̃] nm starchy food

fédéral, e, -aux [fedeʀal, o] adj federal

fée [fe] nf fairy

feignant, e [fɛɲɑ̃, ɑ̃t] nm/f = **fainéant, e**

feindre [fɛ̃dʀ] vt to feign; **~ de faire** to pretend to do

fêler [fele] vt to crack; **se fêler** to crack

félicitations [felisitasjɔ̃] nfpl congratulations

féliciter [felisite] vt: **~ qn (de)** to congratulate sb (on)

félin, e [felɛ̃, in] nm (big) cat

femelle [fəmɛl] adj, nf female

féminin, e [feminɛ̃, in] adj feminine; (sexe) female; (équipe, vêtements etc) women's ▷ nm (Ling) feminine; **féministe** adj feminist

femme [fam] nf woman; (épouse) wife; **femme au foyer** housewife; **femme de chambre** chambermaid; **femme de ménage** cleaning lady

fémur [femyʀ] nm femur, thighbone

fendre [fɑ̃dʀ] vt (couper en deux) to split; (fissurer) to crack; (traverser: foule, air) to cleave through; **se fendre** vi to crack

fenêtre [f(ə)nɛtʀ] nf window

fenouil [fənuj] nm fennel

fente [fɑ̃t] nf (fissure) crack; (de boîte à lettres etc) slit

fer [fɛʀ] nm iron; **fer à cheval** horseshoe; **fer à friser** curling tongs pl; **fer (à repasser)** iron; **fer forgé** wrought iron

ferai etc [fəʀe] vb voir **faire**

fer-blanc [fɛʀblɑ̃] nm tin(plate)

férié, e [feʀje] adj: **jour ~** public holiday

ferions etc [fəʀjɔ̃] vb voir **faire**

ferme [fɛʀm] adj firm ▷ adv (travailler etc) hard ▷ nf (exploitation) farm; (maison) farmhouse

fermé, e [fɛʀme] adj closed, shut; (gaz, eau etc) off; (fig: milieu) exclusive

fermenter [fɛʀmɑ̃te] vi to ferment

fermer [fɛʀme] vt to close, shut; (cesser l'exploitation de) to close down, shut down; (eau, électricité, robinet) to turn off; (aéroport, route) to close ▷ vi to close, shut; (magasin: definitivement) to close down, shut down; **~ à clef** to lock; **se fermer** vi to close, shut

fermeté [fɛrməte] nf firmness

fermeture [fɛrmətyr] nf closing; (dispositif) catch; **heures de ~** closing times; **fermeture éclair®** ou **à glissière** zip (fastener) (BRIT), zipper (US)

fermier [fɛrmje] nm farmer

féroce [feros] adj ferocious, fierce

ferons [fərõ] vb voir **faire**

ferrer [fere] vt (cheval) to shoe

ferroviaire [fɛrɔvjɛr] adj rail(way) cpd (BRIT), rail(road) cpd (US)

ferry(-boat) [fɛre(-bot)] nm ferry

fertile [fɛrtil] adj fertile; **~ en incidents** eventful, packed with incidents

fervent, e [fɛrvã, ãt] adj fervent

fesse [fɛs] nf buttock; **fessée** nf spanking

festin [fɛstɛ̃] nm feast

festival [fɛstival] nm festival

festivités [fɛstivite] nfpl festivities

fêtard, e [fetar, ard] (fam) nm/f high liver, merry-maker

fête [fɛt] nf (religieuse) feast; (publique) holiday; (réception) party; (kermesse) fête, fair; (du nom) feast day, name day; **faire la ~** to live it up; **faire ~ à qn** to give sb a warm welcome; **les ~s (de fin d'année)** the festive season; **la salle des ~s** the village hall; **la ~ des Mères/Pères** Mother's/Father's Day; **fête foraine** (fun) fair; **fêter** vt to celebrate; (personne) to have a celebration for

feu, x [fø] nm (gén) fire; (signal lumineux) light; (de cuisinière) ring; **feux** nmpl (Auto) (traffic) lights; **au ~!** (incendie) fire!; **à ~ doux/vif** over a slow/brisk heat; **à petit ~** (Culin) over a gentle heat; (fig) slowly; **faire ~** to fire; **ne pas faire long ~** not to last long; **prendre ~** to catch fire; **mettre le ~ à** to set fire to; **faire du ~** to make a fire; **avez-vous du ~?** (pour cigarette) have you (got) a light?; **feu arrière** rear light; **feu d'artifice** (spectacle) fireworks pl; **feu de joie** bonfire; **feu orange/rouge/vert** amber (BRIT) ou yellow (US)/red/green light; **feux de brouillard** fog lights ou lamps; **feux de croisement** dipped (BRIT) ou dimmed (US) headlights; **feux de position** sidelights; **feux de route** headlights

feuillage [fœjaʒ] nm foliage, leaves pl

feuille [fœj] nf (d'arbre) leaf; (de papier) sheet; **feuille de calcul** spreadsheet; **feuille d'impôts** tax form; **feuille de maladie** medical expenses claim form; **feuille de paie** pay slip

feuillet [fœjɛ] nm leaf

feuilleté, e [fœjte] adj: **pâte ~** flaky pastry

feuilleter [fœjte] vt (livre) to leaf through

feuilleton [fœjtõ] nm serial

feutre [føtr] nm felt; (chapeau) felt hat; (aussi: **stylo-~**) felt-tip pen; **feutré, e** adj (atmosphère) muffled

fève [fɛv] nf broad bean

février [fevrije] nm February

fiable [fjabl] adj reliable

fiançailles [fjãsɑj] nfpl engagement sg

fiancé, e [fjãse] nm/f fiancé(e) ▷ adj: **être ~ (à)** to be engaged (to)

fiancer [fjãse]: **se fiancer (avec)** vi to become engaged (to)

fibre [fibr] nf fibre; **fibre de verre** fibreglass, glass fibre

ficeler [fis(ə)le] vt to tie up

ficelle [fisɛl] nf string no pl; (morceau) piece ou length of string

fiche [fiʃ] nf (pour fichier) (index) card; (formulaire) form; (Élec) plug; **fiche de paye** pay slip

ficher [fiʃe] vt (dans un fichier) to file; (Police) to put on file; (fam: faire) to do; (: donner) to give; (: mettre) to stick ou shove; **fiche-(moi) le camp!** (fam) clear off!; **fiche-moi la paix!** (fam) leave me alone!; **se ficher de** (fam: rire de) to make fun of; (être indifférent à) not to care about

fichier [fiʃje] nm file; **~ joint** (Comput) attachment

fichu, e [fiʃy] pp de **ficher** (fam) ▷ adj (fam: fini, inutilisable) bust, done for; (: intensif) wretched, darned ▷ nm (foulard) (head)scarf; **mal ~** (fam) feeling lousy

fictif, -ive [fiktif, iv] adj fictitious

fiction [fiksjõ] nf fiction; (fait imaginé) invention

fidèle [fidɛl] adj faithful ▷ nm/f (Rel): **les ~s** (à l'église) the congregation sg; **fidélité** nf (d'un conjoint) fidelity, faithfulness; (d'un ami, client) loyalty

fier¹ [fje]: **se fier à** vt to trust

fier², fière [fjɛr] adj proud; **~ de** proud of; **fierté** nf pride

fièvre [fjɛvr] nf fever; **avoir de la ~/39 de ~** to have a high temperature/a temperature of 39°C; **fiévreux, -euse** adj feverish

figer [fiʒe]: **se figer** vi (huile) to congeal; (personne) to freeze

fignoler [fiɲɔle] (fam) vt to polish up

figue [fig] nf fig; **figuier** nm fig tree

figurant, e [figyrã, ãt] nm/f (Théâtre) walk-on; (Cinéma) extra

figure [figyr] nf (visage) face; (forme, personnage) figure; (illustration) picture, diagram

figuré, e [figyre] adj (sens) figurative

figurer [figyre] vi to appear ▷ vt to represent; **se figurer que** to imagine that

fil [fil] nm (brin, fig: d'une histoire) thread; (électrique) wire; (d'un couteau) edge; **au ~ des années** with the passing of the years; **au ~ de l'eau** with the stream ou current; **coup de ~** (fam) phone call; **donner/recevoir un coup de ~** to make/get ou receive a phone call; **fil de fer** wire; **fil de fer barbelé** barbed wire

file [fil] *nf* line; (*Auto*) lane; **en ~ indienne** in single file; **à la ~** (*d'affilée*) in succession; **file (d'attente)** queue (BRIT), line (US)

filer [file] *vt* (*tissu, toile*) to spin; (*prendre en filature*) to shadow, tail; (*fam: donner*): **~ qch à qn** to slip sb sth ▷ *vi* (*bas*) to run; (*aller vite*) to fly past; (*fam: partir*) to make *ou* be off; **~ doux** to toe the line

filet [file] *nm* net; (*Culin*) fillet; (*d'eau, de sang*) trickle; **filet (à provisions)** string bag

filiale [filjal] *nf* (*Comm*) subsidiary

filière [filjɛʀ] *nf* (*carrière*) path; **suivre la ~** (*dans sa carrière*) to work one's way up (through the hierarchy)

fille [fij] *nf* girl; (*opposé à fils*) daughter; **vieille ~** old maid; **fillette** *nf* (little) girl

filleul, e [fijœl] *nm/f* godchild, godson/daughter

film [film] *nm* (*pour photo*) (roll of) film; (*œuvre*) film, picture, movie

fils [fis] *nm* son; **fils à papa** daddy's boy

filtre [filtʀ] *nm* filter; **filtrer** *vt* to filter; (*fig: candidats, visiteurs*) to screen

fin¹ [fɛ̃] *nf* end; **fins** *nfpl* (*but*) ends; **prendre ~** to come to an end; **mettre ~ à** to put an end to; **à la ~** in the end, eventually; **en ~ de compte** in the end; **sans ~** endless; **~ juin** at the end of June; **fin prêt** quite ready

fin², e [fɛ̃, fin] *adj* (*papier, couche, fil*) thin; (*cheveux, visage*) fine; (*taille*) neat, slim; (*esprit, remarque*) subtle ▷ *adv* (*couper*) finely; **fines herbes** mixed herbs; **avoir la vue/l'ouïe fine** to have keen eyesight/hearing; **repas/vin fin** gourmet meal/fine wine

final, e [final, o] *adj* final ▷ *nm* (*Mus*) finale; **finale** *nf* final; **quarts de finale** quarter finals; **finalement** *adv* finally, in the end; (*après tout*) after all

finance [finãs]: **finances** *nfpl* (*situation*) finances; (*activités*) finance *sg*; **moyennant ~** for a fee; **financer** *vt* to finance; **financier, -ière** *adj* financial

finesse [finɛs] *nf* thinness; (*raffinement*) fineness; (*subtilité*) subtlety

fini, e [fini] *adj* finished; (*Math*) finite ▷ *nm* (*d'un objet manufacturé*) finish

finir [finiʀ] *vt* to finish ▷ *vi* to finish, end; **~ par faire** to end up *ou* finish up doing; **~ de faire** to finish doing; (*cesser*) to stop doing; **il finit par m'agacer** he's beginning to get on my nerves; **en ~ avec** to be *ou* have done with; **il va mal ~** he will come to a bad end

finition [finisjɔ̃] *nf* (*résultat*) finish

finlandais, e [fɛ̃lɑ̃dɛ, ɛz] *adj* Finnish ▷ *nm/f*: **F~, e** Finn

Finlande [fɛ̃lɑ̃d] *nf*: **la ~** Finland

finnois, e [finwa, waz] *adj* Finnish ▷ *nm* (*Ling*) Finnish

fioul [fjul] *nm* fuel oil

firme [fiʀm] *nf* firm

fis [fi] *vb voir* **faire**

fisc [fisk] *nm* tax authorities *pl*; **fiscal, e, -aux** *adj* tax *cpd*, fiscal; **fiscalité** *nf* tax system

fissure [fisyʀ] *nf* crack; **fissurer** *vt* to crack; **se fissurer** *vi* to crack

fit [fi] *vb voir* **faire**

fixation [fiksasjɔ̃] *nf* (*attache*) fastening; (*Psych*) fixation

fixe [fiks] *adj* fixed; (*emploi*) steady, regular ▷ *nm* (*salaire*) basic salary; (*téléphone*) landline; **à heure ~** at a set time; **menu à prix ~** set menu

fixé, e [fikse] *adj*: **être ~ (sur)** (*savoir à quoi s'en tenir*) to have made one's mind up (about)

fixer [fikse] *vt* (*attacher*): **~ qch (à/sur)** to fix *ou* fasten sth (to/onto); (*déterminer*) to fix, set; (*regarder*) to stare at; **se fixer** *vi* (*s'établir*) to settle down; **se ~ sur** (*suj: attention*) to focus on

flacon [flakɔ̃] *nm* bottle

flageolet [flaʒɔlɛ] *nm* (*Culin*) dwarf kidney bean

flagrant, e [flagʀɑ̃, ɑ̃t] *adj* flagrant, blatant; **en ~ délit** in the act

flair [flɛʀ] *nm* sense of smell; (*fig*) intuition; **flairer** *vt* (*humer*) to sniff (at); (*détecter*) to scent

flamand, e [flamɑ̃, ɑ̃d] *adj* Flemish ▷ *nm* (*Ling*) Flemish ▷ *nm/f*: **F~, e** Fleming

flamant [flamɑ̃] *nm* flamingo

flambant, e [flɑ̃bɑ̃, ɑ̃t] *adv*: **~ neuf** brand new

flambé, e [flɑ̃be] *adj* (*Culin*) flambé

flambée [flɑ̃be] *nf* blaze; (*fig: des prix*) explosion

flamber [flɑ̃be] *vi* to blaze (up)

flamboyer [flɑ̃bwaje] *vi* to blaze (up)

flamme [flam] *nf* flame; (*fig*) fire, fervour; **en ~s** on fire, ablaze

flan [flɑ̃] *nm* (*Culin*) custard tart *ou* pie

flanc [flɑ̃] *nm* side; (*Mil*) flank

flancher [flɑ̃ʃe] (*fam*) *vi* to fail, pack up

flanelle [flanɛl] *nf* flannel

flâner [flane] *vi* to stroll

flanquer [flɑ̃ke] *vt* to flank; (*fam: mettre*) to chuck, shove; (: *jeter*): **~ par terre/à la porte** to fling to the ground/chuck out

flaque [flak] *nf* (*d'eau*) puddle; (*d'huile, de sang etc*) pool

flash [flaʃ] (*pl* **-es**) *nm* (*Photo*) flash; **flash d'information** newsflash

flatter [flate] *vt* to flatter; **se ~ de qch** to pride o.s. on sth; **flatteur, -euse** *adj* flattering

flèche [flɛʃ] *nf* arrow; (*de clocher*) spire; **monter en ~** (*fig*) to soar, rocket; **partir en ~** to be off like a shot; **fléchette** *nf* dart

flétrir [fletʀiʀ]: **se flétrir** *vi* to wither

fleur [flœʀ] *nf* flower; (*d'un arbre*) blossom; **en ~** (*arbre*) in blossom; **à ~s** flowery

fleuri, e [flœʀi] *adj (jardin)* in flower *ou* bloom; *(tissu, papier)* flowery

fleurir [flœʀiʀ] *vi (rose)* to flower; *(arbre)* to blossom; *(fig)* to flourish ▷ *vt (tombe)* to put flowers on; *(chambre)* to decorate with flowers

fleuriste [flœʀist] *nm/f* florist

fleuve [flœv] *nm* river

flexible [flɛksibl] *adj* flexible

flic [flik] *(fam: péj) nm* cop

flipper [flipœʀ] *nm* pinball (machine)

flirter [flœʀte] *vi* to flirt

flocon [flɔkɔ̃] *nm* flake

flore [flɔʀ] *nf* flora

florissant, e [flɔʀisɑ̃, ɑ̃t] *adj (économie)* flourishing

flot [flo] *nm* flood, stream; **flots** *nmpl (de la mer)* waves; **être à ~** *(Navig)* to be afloat; **entrer à ~s** to stream *ou* pour in

flottant, e [flɔtɑ̃, ɑ̃t] *adj (vêtement)* loose

flotte [flɔt] *nf (Navig)* fleet; *(fam: eau)* water; (: *pluie)* rain

flotter [flɔte] *vi* to float; *(nuage, odeur)* to drift; *(drapeau)* to fly; *(vêtements)* to hang loose; *(fam: pleuvoir)* to rain; **faire ~** to float; **flotteur** *nm* float

flou, e [flu] *adj* fuzzy, blurred; *(fig)* woolly, vague

fluide [flɥid] *adj* fluid; *(circulation etc)* flowing freely ▷ *nm* fluid

fluor [flyɔʀ] *nm*: **dentifrice au ~** fluoride toothpaste

fluorescent, e [flyɔʀesɑ̃, ɑ̃t] *adj* fluorescent

flûte [flyt] *nf* flute; *(verre)* flute (glass); *(pain)* (thin) French stick; **~!** drat it!; **flûte traversière/à bec** flute/recorder

flux [fly] *nm* incoming tide; *(écoulement)* flow; **le ~ et le reflux** the ebb and flow

foc [fɔk] *nm* jib

foi [fwa] *nf* faith; **digne de ~** reliable; **être de bonne/mauvaise ~** to be sincere/insincere; **ma ~ ...** well ...

foie [fwa] *nm* liver; **crise de ~** stomach upset

foin [fwɛ̃] *nm* hay; **faire du ~** *(fig: fam)* to kick up a row

foire [fwaʀ] *nf* fair; *(fête foraine)* (fun) fair; **faire la ~** *(fig: fam)* to whoop it up; **~ aux questions** *(Internet)* FAQs; **foire (exposition)** trade fair

fois [fwa] *nf* time; **une/deux ~** once/twice; **2 ~ 2** 2 times 2; **une ~** *(passé)* once; *(futur)* sometime; **une ~ pour toutes** once and for all; **une ~ que** once; **des ~** *(parfois)* sometimes; **à la ~** *(ensemble)* at once

fol [fɔl] *adj voir* **fou**

folie [fɔli] *nf (d'une décision, d'un acte)* madness, folly; *(état)* madness, insanity; **la ~ des grandeurs** delusions of grandeur; **faire des ~s** *(en dépenses)* to be extravagant

folklorique [fɔlklɔʀik] *adj* folk *cpd*; *(fam)* weird

folle [fɔl] *adj, nf voir* **fou**; **follement** *adv (très)* madly, wildly

foncé, e [fɔ̃se] *adj* dark

foncer [fɔ̃se] *vi* to go darker; *(fam: aller vite)* to tear *ou* belt along; **~ sur** to charge at

fonction [fɔ̃ksjɔ̃] *nf* function; *(emploi, poste)* post, position; **fonctions** *nfpl (professionnelles)* duties; **voiture de ~** company car; **en ~ de** *(par rapport à)* according to; **faire ~ de** to serve as; **la ~ publique** the state *ou* civil (*BRIT*) service; **fonctionnaire** *nm/f* state employee, local authority employee; *(dans l'administration)* ≈ civil servant; **fonctionner** *vi* to work, function

fond [fɔ̃] *nm (d'un récipient, trou)* bottom; *(d'une salle, scène)* back; *(d'un tableau, décor)* background; *(opposé à la forme)* content; *(Sport)*: **le ~** long distance (running); **au ~ de** at the bottom of; at the back of; **à ~** *(connaître, soutenir)* thoroughly; *(appuyer, visser)* right down *ou* home; **à ~ (de train)** *(fam)* full tilt; **dans le ~, au ~** *(en somme)* basically, really; **de ~ en comble** from top to bottom; **fond de teint** foundation (cream); *voir aussi* **fonds**

fondamental, e, -aux [fɔ̃damɑ̃tal, o] *adj* fundamental

fondant, e [fɔ̃dɑ̃, ɑ̃t] *adj (neige)* melting; *(poire)* that melts in the mouth

fondation [fɔ̃dasjɔ̃] *nf* founding; *(établissement)* foundation; **fondations** *nfpl (d'une maison)* foundations

fondé, e [fɔ̃de] *adj (accusation etc)* well-founded; **être ~ à** to have grounds for *ou* good reason to

fondement [fɔ̃dmɑ̃] *nm*: **sans ~** *(rumeur etc)* groundless, unfounded

fonder [fɔ̃de] *vt* to found; *(fig)* to base; **se fonder sur** *(suj: personne)* to base o.s. on

fonderie [fɔ̃dʀi] *nf* smelting works *sg*

fondre [fɔ̃dʀ] *vt (aussi: **faire ~**)* to melt; *(dans l'eau)* to dissolve; *(fig: mélanger)* to merge, blend ▷ *vi (à la chaleur)* to melt; *(dans l'eau)* to dissolve; *(fig)* to melt away; *(se précipiter)*: **~ sur** to swoop down on; **~ en larmes** to burst into tears

fonds [fɔ̃] *nm (Comm)*: **~ (de commerce)** business ▷ *nmpl (argent)* funds

fondu, e [fɔ̃dy] *adj (beurre, neige)* melted; *(métal)* molten; **fondue** *nf (Culin)* fondue

font [fɔ̃] *vb voir* **faire**

fontaine [fɔ̃tɛn] *nf* fountain; *(source)* spring

fonte [fɔ̃t] *nf* melting; *(métal)* cast iron; **la ~ des neiges** the (spring) thaw

foot [fut] *(fam) nm* football

football [futbol] *nm* football, soccer; **footballeur** *nm* footballer

footing [futiŋ] *nm* jogging; **faire du ~** to go jogging

forain, e [fɔʀɛ̃, ɛn] *adj* fairground *cpd* ▷ *nm*

(*marchand*) stallholder; (*acteur*) fairground entertainer

forçat [fɔʀsa] nm convict

force [fɔʀs] nf strength; (*Physique, Mécanique*) force; **forces** nfpl (*physiques*) strength sg; (*Mil*) forces; **à ~ d'insister** by dint of insisting; as he (*ou I etc*) kept on insisting; **de ~** forcibly, by force; **dans la ~ de l'âge** in the prime of life; **les forces de l'ordre** the police no pl

forcé, e [fɔʀse] adj forced; **c'est ~** (*fam*) it's inevitable; **forcément** adv inevitably; **pas forcément** not necessarily

forcer [fɔʀse] vt to force; (*voix*) to strain ▷ vi (*Sport*) to overtax o.s.; **~ la dose** (*fam*) to overdo it; **se ~ (à faire)** to force o.s. (to do)

forestier, -ère [fɔʀɛstje, jɛʀ] adj forest cpd

forêt [fɔʀɛ] nf forest

forfait [fɔʀfɛ] nm (*Comm*) all-in deal ou price; **déclarer ~** to withdraw; **forfaitaire** adj inclusive

forge [fɔʀʒ] nf forge, smithy; **forgeron** nm (black)smith

formaliser [fɔʀmalize]: **se formaliser** vi: **se ~ (de)** to take offence (at)

formalité [fɔʀmalite] nf formality; **simple ~** mere formality

format [fɔʀma] nm size; **formater** vt (*disque*) to format

formation [fɔʀmasjɔ̃] nf (*développement*) forming; (*apprentissage*) training; **formation permanente** ou **continue** continuing education

forme [fɔʀm] nf (*gén*) form; (*d'un objet*) shape, form; **formes** nfpl (*bonnes manières*) proprieties; (*d'une femme*) figure sg; **en ~ de poire** pear-shaped, in the shape of a pear; **être en ~** (*Sport etc*) to be on form; **en bonne et due ~** in due form

formel, le [fɔʀmɛl] adj (*catégorique*) definite, positive; **formellement** adv (*absolument*) positively; **formellement interdit** strictly forbidden

former [fɔʀme] vt to form; (*éduquer*) to train; **se former** vi to form

formidable [fɔʀmidabl] adj tremendous

formulaire [fɔʀmylɛʀ] nm form

formule [fɔʀmyl] nf (*gén*) formula; (*expression*) phrase; **formule de politesse** polite phrase; (*en fin de lettre*) letter ending

fort, e [fɔʀ, fɔʀt] adj strong; (*intensité, rendement*) high, great; (*corpulent*) stout; (*doué*) good, able ▷ adv (*serrer, frapper*) hard; (*parler*) loud(ly); (*beaucoup*) greatly, very much; (*très*) very ▷ nm (*édifice*) fort; (*point fort*) strong point, forte; **forte tête** rebel; **forteresse** nf stronghold

fortifiant [fɔʀtifjɑ̃] nm tonic

fortune [fɔʀtyn] nf fortune; **faire ~** to make one's fortune; **de ~** makeshift; **fortuné, e** adj

wealthy

forum [fɔʀɔm] nm forum; **~ de discussion** (*Internet*) message board

fosse [fos] nf (*grand trou*) pit; (*tombe*) grave

fossé [fose] nm ditch; (*fig*) gulf, gap

fossette [fosɛt] nf dimple

fossile [fosil] nm fossil

fou (fol), folle [fu, fɔl] adj mad; (*déréglé etc*) wild, erratic; (*fam: extrême, très grand*) terrific, tremendous ▷ nm/f madman(-woman) ▷ nm (*du roi*) jester; **être fou de** to be mad ou crazy about; **avoir le fou rire** to have the giggles

foudre [fudʀ] nf: **la ~** lightning

foudroyant, e [fudʀwajɑ̃, ɑ̃t] adj (*progrès*) lightning cpd; (*succès*) stunning; (*maladie, poison*) violent

fouet [fwɛ] nm whip; (*Culin*) whisk; **de plein ~** (*se heurter*) head on; **fouetter** vt to whip; (*crème*) to whisk

fougère [fuʒɛʀ] nf fern

fougue [fug] nf ardour, spirit; **fougueux, -euse** adj fiery

fouille [fuj] nf search; **fouilles** nfpl (*archéologiques*) excavations; **fouiller** vt to search; (*creuser*) to dig ▷ vi to rummage; **fouillis** nm jumble, muddle

foulard [fular] nm scarf

foule [ful] nf crowd; **la ~** crowds pl; **une ~ de** masses of

foulée [fule] nf stride

fouler [fule] vt to press; (*sol*) to tread upon; **se ~ la cheville** to sprain one's ankle; **ne pas se ~** not to overexert o.s.; **il ne se foule pas** he doesn't put himself out; **foulure** nf sprain

four [fuʀ] nm oven; (*de potier*) kiln; (*Théâtre: échec*) flop

fourche [fuʀʃ] nf pitchfork

fourchette [fuʀʃɛt] nf fork; (*Statistique*) bracket, margin

fourgon [fuʀgɔ̃] nm van; (*Rail*) wag(g)on; **fourgonnette** nf (small) van

fourmi [fuʀmi] nf ant; **avoir des ~s dans les jambes/mains** to have pins and needles in one's legs/hands; **fourmilière** nf ant-hill; **fourmiller** vi to swarm

fourneau, x [fuʀno] nm stove

fourni, e [fuʀni] adj (*barbe, cheveux*) thick; (*magasin*): **bien ~ (en)** well stocked (with)

fournir [fuʀniʀ] vt to supply; (*preuve, exemple*) to provide, supply; (*effort*) to put in; **~ qch à qn** to supply sth to sb, supply ou provide sb with sth; **fournisseur, -euse** nm/f supplier; **fournisseur d'accès à Internet** (*Internet*) service provider, ISP; **fourniture** nf supply(ing); **fournitures scolaires** school stationery

fourrage [fuʀaʒ] nm fodder

fourré, e [fuʀe] adj (*bonbon etc*) filled; (*manteau etc*) fur-lined ▷ nm thicket

fourrer [fuʀe] (fam) vt to stick, shove; **se fourrer dans/sous** to get into/under
fourrière [fuʀjeʀ] nf pound
fourrure [fuʀyʀ] nf fur; (sur l'animal) coat
foutre [futʀ] (fam!) vt = **ficher**; **foutu, e** (fam!) adj = **fichu, e**
foyer [fwaje] nm (maison) home; (famille) family; (de cheminée) hearth; (de jeunes etc) (social) club; (résidence) hostel; (salon) foyer; **lunettes à double ~** bi-focals
fracassant, e [fʀakasɑ̃, ɑ̃t] adj (succès) thundering
fraction [fʀaksjɔ̃] nf fraction
fracture [fʀaktyʀ] nf fracture; **fracture du crâne** fractured skull; **fracturer** vt (coffre, serrure) to break open; (os, membre) to fracture; **se fracturer le crâne** to fracture one's skull
fragile [fʀaʒil] adj fragile, delicate; (fig) frail; **fragilité** nf fragility
fragment [fʀagmɑ̃] nm (d'un objet) fragment, piece
fraîche [fʀɛʃ] adj voir **frais**; **fraîcheur** nf coolness; (d'un aliment) freshness; **fraîchir** vi to get cooler; (vent) to freshen
frais, fraîche [fʀɛ, fʀɛʃ] adj fresh; (froid) cool ▷ adv (récemment) newly, fresh(ly) ▷ nm: **mettre au ~** to put in a cool place ▷ nmpl (gén) expenses; (Comm) costs; **il fait ~** it's cool; **servir ~** serve chilled; **prendre le ~** to take a breath of cool air; **faire des ~** to go to a lot of expense; **frais de scolarité** school fees (BRIT), tuition (US); **frais généraux** overheads
fraise [fʀɛz] nf strawberry; **fraise des bois** wild strawberry
framboise [fʀɑ̃bwaz] nf raspberry
franc, franche [fʀɑ̃, fʀɑ̃ʃ] adj (personne) frank, straightforward; (visage) open; (net: refus) clear; (: coupure) clean; (intensif) downright ▷ nm franc
français, e [fʀɑ̃sɛ, ɛz] adj French ▷ nm/f: **F~, e** Frenchman(-woman) ▷ nm (Ling) French
France [fʀɑ̃s] nf: **la ~** France; **~ 2, ~ 3** public-sector television channels

franche [fʀɑ̃ʃ] adj voir **franc**; **franchement** adv frankly; (nettement) definitely; (tout à fait: mauvais etc) downright
franchir [fʀɑ̃ʃiʀ] vt (obstacle) to clear, get over; (seuil, ligne, rivière) to cross; (distance) to cover
franchise [fʀɑ̃ʃiz] nf frankness; (douanière)

exemption; (Assurances) excess
franc-maçon [fʀɑ̃masɔ̃] nm freemason
franco [fʀɑ̃ko] adv (Comm): **~ (de port)** postage paid
francophone [fʀɑ̃kɔfɔn] adj French-speaking
franc-parler [fʀɑ̃paʀle] nm inv outspokenness; **avoir son ~** to speak one's mind
frange [fʀɑ̃ʒ] nf fringe
frangipane [fʀɑ̃ʒipan] nf almond paste
frappant, e [fʀapɑ̃, ɑ̃t] adj striking
frappé, e [fʀape] adj iced
frapper [fʀape] vt to hit, strike; (étonner) to strike; **~ dans ses mains** to clap one's hands; **frappé de stupeur** dumbfounded
fraternel, le [fʀatɛʀnɛl] adj brotherly, fraternal; **fraternité** nf brotherhood
fraude [fʀod] nf fraud; (Scol) cheating; **passer qch en ~** to smuggle sth in (ou out); **fraude fiscale** tax evasion
frayeur [fʀɛjœʀ] nf fright
fredonner [fʀədɔne] vt to hum
freezer [fʀizœʀ] nm freezing compartment
frein [fʀɛ̃] nm brake; **mettre un ~ à** (fig) to curb, check; **frein à main** handbrake; **freiner** vi to brake ▷ vt (progrès etc) to check
frêle [fʀɛl] adj frail, fragile
frelon [fʀəlɔ̃] nm hornet
frémir [fʀemiʀ] vi (de peur, d'horreur) to shudder; (de colère) to shake; (feuillage) to quiver
frêne [fʀɛn] nm ash
fréquemment [fʀekamɑ̃] adv frequently
fréquent, e [fʀekɑ̃, ɑ̃t] adj frequent
fréquentation [fʀekɑ̃tasjɔ̃] nf frequenting; **fréquentations** nfpl (relations) company sg; **avoir de mauvaises ~s** to be in with the wrong crowd, keep bad company
fréquenté, e [fʀekɑ̃te] adj: **très ~** (very) busy; **mal ~** patronized by disreputable elements
fréquenter [fʀekɑ̃te] vt (lieu) to frequent; (personne) to see; **se fréquenter** to see each other
frère [fʀɛʀ] nm brother
fresque [fʀɛsk] nf (Art) fresco
fret [fʀɛ(t)] nm freight
friand, e [fʀijɑ̃, fʀijɑ̃d] adj: **~ de** very fond of ▷ nm: **~ au fromage** cheese puff
friandise [fʀijɑ̃diz] nf sweet
fric [fʀik] (fam) nm cash, bread
friche [fʀiʃ]: **en ~** adj, adv (lying) fallow
friction [fʀiksjɔ̃] nf (massage) rub, rub-down; (Tech, fig) friction
frigidaire® [fʀiʒidɛʀ] nm refrigerator
frigo [fʀigo] (fam) nm fridge
frigorifique [fʀigɔʀifik] adj refrigerating
frileux, -euse [fʀilø, øz] adj sensitive to (the) cold

frimer [fʀime] (fam) vi to show off

fringale [fʀɛ̃gal] (fam) nf: **avoir la ~** to be ravenous

fringues [fʀɛ̃g] (fam) nfpl clothes

fripé, e [fʀipe] adj crumpled

frire [fʀiʀ] vt, vi: **faire ~** to fry

frisé, e [fʀize] adj (cheveux) curly; (personne) curly-haired

frisson [fʀisɔ̃] nm (de froid) shiver; (de peur) shudder; **frissonner** vi (de fièvre, froid) to shiver; (d'horreur) to shudder

frit, e [fʀi, fʀit] pp de **frire**; **frite** nf: **(pommes) frites** chips (BRIT), French fries; **friteuse** nf chip pan; **friteuse électrique** deep fat fryer; **friture** nf (huile) (deep) fat; (plat): **friture (de poissons)** fried fish

froid, e [fʀwa, fʀwad] adj, nm cold; **il fait ~** it's cold; **avoir/prendre ~** to be/catch cold; **être en ~ avec** to be on bad terms with; **froidement** adv (accueillir) coldly; (décider) coolly

froisser [fʀwase] vt to crumple (up), crease; (fig) to hurt, offend; **se froisser** vi to crumple, crease; (personne) to take offence; **se ~ un muscle** to strain a muscle

frôler [fʀole] vt to brush against; (suj: projectile) to skim past; (fig) to come very close to

fromage [fʀɔmaʒ] nm cheese; **fromage blanc** soft white cheese

froment [fʀɔmɑ̃] nm wheat

froncer [fʀɔ̃se] vt to gather; **~ les sourcils** to frown

front [fʀɔ̃] nm forehead, brow; (Mil) front; **de ~** (se heurter) head-on; (rouler) together (i.e. 2 or 3 abreast); (simultanément) at once; **faire ~ à** to face up to

frontalier, -ère [fʀɔ̃talje, jɛʀ] adj border cpd, frontier cpd; **(travailleurs) ~s** people who commute across the border

frontière [fʀɔ̃tjɛʀ] nf frontier, border

frotter [fʀɔte] vi to rub, scrape ▷ vt to rub; (pommes de terre, plancher) to scrub; **~ une allumette** to strike a match

fruit [fʀɥi] nm fruit gen no pl; **fruits de mer** seafood(s); **fruits secs** dried fruit sg; **fruité, e** adj fruity; **fruitier, -ère** adj: **arbre fruitier** fruit tree

frustrer [fʀystʀe] vt to frustrate

fuel(-oil) [fjul(ɔjl)] nm fuel oil; (domestique) heating oil

fugace [fygas] adj fleeting

fugitif, -ive [fyʒitif, iv] adj (fugace) fleeting ▷ nm/f fugitive

fugue [fyg] nf: **faire une ~** to run away, abscond

fuir [fɥiʀ] vt to flee from; (éviter) to shun ▷ vi to run away; (gaz, robinet) to leak

fuite [fɥit] nf flight; (écoulement, divulgation) leak; **être en ~** to be on the run; **mettre en ~** to put to flight

fulgurant, e [fylgyʀɑ̃, ɑ̃t] adj lightning cpd, dazzling

fumé, e [fyme] adj (Culin) smoked; (verre) tinted; **fumée** nf smoke

fumer [fyme] vi to smoke; (soupe) to steam ▷ vt to smoke

fûmes [fym] vb voir **être**

fumeur, -euse [fymœʀ, øz] nm/f smoker

fumier [fymje] nm manure

funérailles [fyneʀɑj] nfpl funeral sg

fur [fyʀ]: **au ~ et à mesure** adv as one goes along; **au ~ et à mesure que** as

furet [fyʀɛ] nm ferret

fureter [fyʀ(ə)te] (péj) vi to nose about

fureur [fyʀœʀ] nf fury; **être en ~** to be infuriated; **faire ~** to be all the rage

furie [fyʀi] nf fury; (femme) shrew, vixen; **en ~** (mer) raging; **furieux, -euse** adj furious

furoncle [fyʀɔ̃kl] nm boil

furtif, -ive [fyʀtif, iv] adj furtive

fus [fy] vb voir **être**

fusain [fyzɛ̃] nm (Art) charcoal

fuseau, x [fyzo] nm (pour filer) spindle; (pantalon) (ski) pants; **fuseau horaire** time zone

fusée [fyze] nf rocket

fusible [fyzibl] nm (Élec: fil) fuse wire; (: fiche) fuse

fusil [fyzi] nm (de guerre, à canon rayé) rifle, gun; (de chasse, à canon lisse) shotgun, gun; **fusillade** nf gunfire no pl, shooting no pl; **fusiller** vt to shoot; **fusiller qn du regard** to look daggers at sb

fusionner [fyzjone] vi to merge

fût [fy] vb voir **être** ▷ nm (tonneau) barrel, cask

futé, e [fyte] adj crafty; **Bison ~®** TV and radio traffic monitoring service

futile [fytil] adj futile; frivolous

futur, e [fytyʀ] adj, nm future

fuyard, e [fɥijaʀ, aʀd] nm/f runaway

Gabon [gabɔ̃] *nm*: **le ~** Gabon

gâcher [gɑʃe] *vt* (*gâter*) to spoil; (*gaspiller*) to waste; **gâchis** *nm* waste *no pl*

gaffe [gaf] *nf* blunder; **faire ~** (*fam*) to be careful

gage [gaʒ] *nm* (*dans un jeu*) forfeit; (*fig: de fidélité, d'amour*) token; **gages** *nmpl* (*salaire*) wages; **mettre en ~** to pawn

gagnant, e [gaɲɑ̃, ɑ̃t] *adj*: **billet/numéro ~** winning ticket/number ▷ *nm/f* winner

gagne-pain [gaɲpɛ̃] *nm inv* job

gagner [gaɲe] *vt* to win; (*somme d'argent, revenu*) to earn; (*aller vers, atteindre*) to reach; (*envahir: sommeil, peur*) to overcome; (: *mal*) to spread to ▷ *vi* to win; (*fig*) to gain; **~ du temps/de la place** to gain time/save space; **~ sa vie** to earn one's living

gai, e [ge] *adj* cheerful; (*un peu ivre*) merry; **gaiement** *adv* cheerfully; **gaieté** *nf* cheerfulness; **de gaieté de cœur** with a light heart

gain [gɛ̃] *nm* (*revenu*) earnings *pl*; (*bénéfice: gén pl*) profits *pl*

gala [gala] *nm* official reception; **de ~** (*soirée etc*) gala

galant, e [galɑ̃, ɑ̃t] *adj* (*courtois*) courteous, gentlemanly; (*entreprenant*) flirtatious, gallant; (*scène, rendez-vous*) romantic

galerie [galʀi] *nf* gallery; (*Théâtre*) circle; (*de voiture*) roof rack; (*fig: spectateurs*) audience; **galerie de peinture** (*private*) art gallery; **galerie marchande** shopping arcade

galet [galɛ] *nm* pebble

galette [galɛt] *nf* flat cake; **galette des Rois** *cake eaten on Twelfth Night*

● **GALETTE DES ROIS**
●
● A **galette des Rois** is a cake eaten on
● Twelfth Night containing a figurine. The
● person who finds it is the king (or queen)
● and gets a paper crown. They then choose
● someone else to be their queen (or king).

galipette [galipɛt] *nf* somersault

Galles [gal] *nfpl*: **le pays de ~** Wales; **gallois, e** *adj* Welsh ▷ *nm/f*: **Gallois, e** Welshman(-woman) ▷ *nm* (*Ling*) Welsh

galon [galɔ̃] *nm* (*Mil*) stripe; (*décoratif*) piece of braid

galop [galo] *nm* gallop; **galoper** *vi* to gallop

gambader [gɑ̃bade] *vi* (*animal, enfant*) to leap about

gamin, e [gamɛ̃, in] *nm/f* kid ▷ *adj* childish

gamme [gam] *nf* (*Mus*) scale; (*fig*) range

gang [gɑ̃g] *nm* (*de criminels*) gang

gant [gɑ̃] *nm* glove; **gant de toilette** face flannel (BRIT), face cloth

garage [gaʀaʒ] *nm* garage; **garagiste** *nm/f* garage owner; (*employé*) garage mechanic

garantie [gaʀɑ̃ti] *nf* guarantee; **(bon de) ~** guarantee *ou* warranty slip

garantir [gaʀɑ̃tiʀ] *vt* to guarantee; **~ à qn que** to assure sb that

garçon [gaʀsɔ̃] *nm* boy; (*célibataire*): **vieux ~** bachelor; **garçon (de café)** (*serveur*) waiter; **garçon de courses** messenger

garde [gaʀd(ə)] *nm* (*de prisonnier*) guard; (*de domaine etc*) warden; (*soldat, sentinelle*) guardsman ▷ *nf* (*soldats*) guard; **de ~** on duty; **monter la ~** to stand guard; **mettre en ~** to warn; **prendre ~ (à)** to be careful (of); **garde champêtre** *nm* rural policeman; **garde du corps** *nm* bodyguard; **garde à vue** *nf* (*Jur*) ≈ police custody; **garde-boue** *nm inv* mudguard; **garde-chasse** *nm* gamekeeper

garder [gaʀde] *vt* (*conserver*) to keep; (*surveiller: enfants*) to look after; (: *immeuble, lieu, prisonnier*) to guard; **se garder** *vi* (*aliment: se conserver*) to keep; **se ~ de faire** to be careful not to do; **~ le lit/la chambre** to stay in bed/indoors; **pêche/chasse gardée** private fishing/hunting (ground)

garderie [gaʀdəʀi] *nf* day nursery, crèche

garde-robe [gaʀdəʀɔb] *nf* wardrobe

gardien, ne [gaʀdjɛ̃, jɛn] *nm/f* (*garde*) guard; (*de prison*) warder; (*de domaine, réserve*) warden; (*de musée etc*) attendant; (*de phare, cimetière*) keeper; (*d'immeuble*) caretaker; (*fig*) guardian;

gardien de but goalkeeper; **gardien de la paix** policeman; **gardien de nuit** night watchman

gare¹ [gaʀ] nf station; **gare routière** bus station

gare² [gaʀ] excl: **~ à ...!** mind ...!; **~ à toi!** watch out!

garer [gaʀe] vt to park; **se garer** vi to park

garni, e [gaʀni] adj (plat) served with vegetables (and chips or rice etc)

garniture [gaʀnityʀ] nf (Culin) vegetables pl; **garniture de frein** brake lining

gars [ga] (fam) nm guy

Gascogne [gaskɔɲ] nf Gascony; **le golfe de ~** the Bay of Biscay

gas-oil [gazɔjl] nm diesel (oil)

gaspiller [gaspije] vt to waste

gastronome [gastʀɔnɔm] nm/f gourmet; **gastronomique** adj gastronomic

gâteau, x [gɑto] nm cake; **gâteau sec** biscuit

gâter [gɑte] vt to spoil; **se gâter** vi (dent, fruit) to go bad; (temps, situation) to change for the worse

gâteux, -euse [gɑtø, øz] adj senile

gauche [goʃ] adj left, left-hand; (maladroit) awkward, clumsy ▷ nf (Pol) left (wing); **le bras ~** the left arm; **le côté ~** the left-hand side; **à ~** on the left; (direction) (to the) left; **gaucher, -ère** adj left-handed; **gauchiste** nm/f leftist

gaufre [gofʀ] nf waffle

gaufrette [gofʀɛt] nf wafer

gaulois, e [golwa, waz] adj Gallic ▷ nm/f: **G~, e** Gaul

gaz [gaz] nm inv gas; **ça sent le ~** I can smell gas, there's a smell of gas

gaze [gaz] nf gauze

gazette [gazɛt] nf news sheet

gazeux, -euse [gazø, øz] adj (boisson) fizzy; (eau) sparkling

gazoduc [gazodyk] nm gas pipeline

gazon [gazɔ̃] nm (herbe) grass; (pelouse) lawn

geai [ʒɛ] nm jay

géant, e [ʒeɑ̃, ɑ̃t] adj gigantic; (Comm) giant-size ▷ nm/f giant

geindre [ʒɛ̃dʀ] vi to groan, moan

gel [ʒɛl] nm frost

gélatine [ʒelatin] nf gelatine

gelée [ʒ(ə)le] nf jelly; (gel) frost

geler [ʒ(ə)le] vt, vi to freeze; **il gèle** it's freezing

gélule [ʒelyl] nf (Méd) capsule

Gémeaux [ʒemo] nmpl: **les ~** Gemini

gémir [ʒemiʀ] vi to groan, moan

gênant, e [ʒenɑ̃, ɑ̃t] adj (irritant) annoying; (embarrassant) embarrassing

gencive [ʒɑ̃siv] nf gum

gendarme [ʒɑ̃daʀm] nm gendarme; **gendarmerie** nf military police force in countryside and small towns; their police station or barracks

gendre [ʒɑ̃dʀ] nm son-in-law

gêné, e [ʒene] adj embarrassed

gêner [ʒene] vt (incommoder) to bother; (encombrer) to be in the way; (embarrasser): **~ qn** to make sb feel ill-at-ease; **se gêner** to put o.s. out; **ne vous gênez pas!** don't mind me!

général, e, -aux [ʒeneral, o] adj, nm general; **en ~** usually, in general; **généralement** adv generally; **généraliser** vt, vi to generalize; **se généraliser** vi to become widespread; **généraliste** nm/f general practitioner, G.P.

génération [ʒenerasjɔ̃] nf generation

généreux, -euse [ʒenerø, øz] adj generous

générique [ʒenerik] nm (Cinéma) credits pl

générosité [ʒenerozite] nf generosity

genêt [ʒ(ə)nɛ] nm broom no pl (shrub)

génétique [ʒenetik] adj genetic

Genève [ʒ(ə)nɛv] n Geneva

génial, e, -aux [ʒenjal, jo] adj of genius; (fam: formidable) fantastic, brilliant

génie [ʒeni] nm genius; (Mil): **le ~** the Engineers pl; **génie civil** civil engineering

genièvre [ʒənjɛvʀ] nm juniper

génisse [ʒenis] nf heifer

génital, e, -aux [ʒenital, o] adj genital; **les parties ~es** the genitals

génoise [ʒenwaz] nf sponge cake

genou, x [ʒ(ə)nu] nm knee; **à ~x** on one's knees; **se mettre à ~x** to kneel down

genre [ʒɑ̃ʀ] nm kind, type, sort; (Ling) gender; **avoir bon ~** to look a nice sort; **avoir mauvais ~** to be coarse-looking; **ce n'est pas son ~** it's not like him

gens [ʒɑ̃] nmpl (f in some phrases) people pl

gentil, le [ʒɑ̃ti, ij] adj kind; (enfant: sage) good; (endroit etc) nice; **gentillesse** nf kindness; **gentiment** adv kindly

géographie [ʒeɔgrafi] nf geography

géologie [ʒeɔlɔʒi] nf geology

géomètre [ʒeɔmɛtʀ] nm/f (arpenteur) (land) surveyor

géométrie [ʒeɔmetʀi] nf geometry; **géométrique** adj geometric

géranium [ʒeʀanjɔm] nm geranium

gérant, e [ʒeʀɑ̃, ɑ̃t] nm/f manager(-eress); **gérant d'immeuble** (managing) agent

gerbe [ʒɛʀb] nf (de fleurs) spray; (de blé) sheaf

gercé, e [ʒɛʀse] adj chapped

gerçure [ʒɛʀsyʀ] nf crack

gérer [ʒeʀe] vt to manage

germain, e [ʒɛʀmɛ̃, ɛn] adj: **cousin ~** first cousin

germe [ʒɛʀm] nm germ; **germer** vi to sprout; (semence) to germinate

geste [ʒɛst] nm gesture

gestion [ʒɛstjɔ̃] nf management

Ghana [gana] nm: **le ~** Ghana

gibier [ʒibje] nm (animaux) game

gicler [ʒikle] vi to spurt, squirt

g

gifle [ʒifl] nf slap (in the face); **gifler** vt to slap (in the face)

gigantesque [ʒigɑ̃tɛsk] adj gigantic

gigot [ʒigo] nm leg (of mutton ou lamb)

gigoter [ʒigɔte] vi to wriggle (about)

gilet [ʒilɛ] nm waistcoat; (pull) cardigan; **gilet de sauvetage** life jacket

gin [dʒin] nm gin; **~-tonic** gin and tonic

gingembre [ʒɛ̃ʒɑ̃bʀ] nm ginger

girafe [ʒiʀaf] nf giraffe

giratoire [ʒiʀatwaʀ] adj: **sens ~** roundabout

girofle [ʒiʀɔfl] nf: **clou de ~** clove

girouette [ʒiʀwɛt] nf weather vane ou cock

gitan, e [ʒitɑ̃, an] nm/f gipsy

gîte [ʒit] nm (maison) home; (abri) shelter; **gîte (rural)** (country) holiday cottage (BRIT), gîte (self-catering accommodation in the country)

givre [ʒivʀ] nm (hoar) frost; **givré, e** adj covered in frost; (fam: fou) nuts; **orange givrée** orange sorbet (served in peel)

glace [glas] nf ice; (crème glacée) ice cream; (miroir) mirror; (de voiture) window

glacé, e [glase] adj (mains, vent, pluie) freezing; (lac) frozen; (boisson) iced

glacer [glase] vt to freeze; (gâteau) to ice; (fig): **~ qn** (intimider) to chill sb; (paralyser) to make sb's blood run cold

glacial, e [glasjal, jo] adj icy

glacier [glasje] nm (Géo) glacier; (marchand) ice-cream maker

glacière [glasjɛʀ] nf icebox

glaçon [glasɔ̃] nm icicle; (pour boisson) ice cube

glaïeul [glajœl] nm gladiolus

glaise [glɛz] nf clay

gland [glɑ̃] nm acorn; (décoration) tassel

glande [glɑ̃d] nf gland

glissade [glisad] nf (par jeu) slide; (chute) slip; **faire des ~s sur la glace** to slide on the ice

glissant, e [glisɑ̃, ɑ̃t] adj slippery

glissement [glismɑ̃] nm: **glissement de terrain** landslide

glisser [glise] vi (avancer) to glide ou slide along; (coulisser, tomber) to slide; (déraper) to slip; (être glissant) to be slippery ▷ vt to slip; **se glisser dans/entre** to slip into/between

global, e, -aux [glɔbal, o] adj overall

globe [glɔb] nm globe

globule [glɔbyl] nm (du sang): **~ blanc/rouge** white/red corpuscle

gloire [glwaʀ] nf glory

glousser [gluse] vi to cluck; (rire) to chuckle

glouton, ne [glutɔ̃, ɔn] adj gluttonous

gluant, e [glyɑ̃, ɑ̃t] adj sticky, gummy

glucose [glykoz] nm glucose

glycine [glisin] nf wisteria

GO sigle (= grandes ondes) LW

goal [gol] nm goalkeeper

gobelet [gɔblɛ] nm (en étain, verre, argent) tumbler; (d'enfant, de pique-nique) beaker; (à dés) cup

goéland [gɔelɑ̃] nm (sea)gull

goélette [gɔelɛt] nf schooner

goinfre [gwɛ̃fʀ] nm glutton

golf [gɔlf] nm golf; (terrain) golf course; **golf miniature** crazy (BRIT) ou miniature golf

golfe [gɔlf] nm gulf; (petit) bay

gomme [gɔm] nf (à effacer) rubber (BRIT), eraser; **gommer** vt to rub out (BRIT), erase

gonflé, e [gɔ̃fle] adj swollen; **il est ~** (fam: courageux) he's got some nerve; (impertinent) he's got a nerve

gonfler [gɔ̃fle] vt (pneu, ballon: en soufflant) to blow up; (: avec une pompe) to pump up; (nombre, importance) to inflate ▷ vi to swell (up); (Culin: pâte) to rise

gonzesse [gɔ̃zɛs] (fam) nf chick, bird (BRIT)

gorge [gɔʀʒ] nf (Anat) throat; (vallée) gorge; **gorgée** nf (petite) sip; (grande) gulp

gorille [gɔʀij] nm gorilla; (fam) bodyguard

gosse [gɔs] (fam) nm/f kid

goudron [gudʀɔ̃] nm tar; **goudronner** vt to tar(mac) (BRIT), asphalt (US)

gouffre [gufʀ] nm abyss, gulf

goulot [gulo] nm neck; **boire au ~** to drink from the bottle

goulu, e [guly] adj greedy

gourde [guʀd] nf (récipient) flask; (fam) (clumsy) clot ou oaf ▷ adj oafish

gourdin [guʀdɛ̃] nm club, bludgeon

gourmand, e [guʀmɑ̃, ɑ̃d] adj greedy; **gourmandise** nf greed; (bonbon) sweet

gousse [gus] nf: **gousse d'ail** clove of garlic

goût [gu] nm taste; **avoir bon ~** to taste good; **de bon ~** tasteful; **de mauvais ~** tasteless; **prendre ~ à** to develop a taste ou a liking for

goûter [gute] vt (essayer) to taste; (apprécier) to enjoy ▷ vi to have (afternoon) tea ▷ nm (afternoon) tea; **je peux ~?** can I have a taste?

goutte [gut] nf drop; (Méd) gout; (alcool) brandy; **tomber ~ à ~** to drip; **une ~ de whisky** a drop of whisky; **goutte-à-goutte** nm (Méd) drip

gouttière [gutjɛʀ] nf gutter

gouvernail [guvɛʀnaj] nm rudder; (barre) helm, tiller

gouvernement [guvɛʀnəmɑ̃] nm government

gouverner [guvɛʀne] vt to govern

grâce [gʀɑs] nf (charme, Rel) grace; (faveur) favour; (Jur) pardon; **faire ~ à qn de qch** to spare sb sth; **demander ~** to beg for mercy; **~ à** thanks to; **gracieux, -euse** adj graceful

grade [gʀad] nm rank; **monter en ~** to be promoted

gradin [gʀadɛ̃] nm tier; step; **gradins** nmpl (de stade) terracing sg

gradué, e [gʀadɥe] adj: **verre ~** measuring jug

graduel, le [gʀadɥɛl] adj gradual

graduer [gradye] vt (effort etc) to increase gradually; (règle, verre) to graduate

graffiti [grafiti] nmpl graffiti

grain [grɛ̃] nm (gén) grain; (Navig) squall; **grain de beauté** beauty spot; **grain de café** coffee bean; **grain de poivre** peppercorn

graine [grɛn] nf seed

graissage [grɛsaʒ] nm lubrication, greasing

graisse [grɛs] nf fat; (lubrifiant) grease; **graisser** vt to lubricate, grease; (tacher) to make greasy; **graisseux, -euse** adj greasy

grammaire [gra(m)mɛʀ] nf grammar

gramme [gram] nm gramme

grand, e [grɑ̃, grɑ̃d] adj (haut) tall; (gros, vaste, large) big, large; (long) long; (plus âgé) big; (adulte) grown-up; (important, brillant) great ▷ adv: **~ ouvert** wide open; **au ~ air** in the open (air); **les grands blessés** the severely injured; **grand ensemble** housing scheme; **grand magasin** department store; **grande personne** grown-up; **grande surface** hypermarket; **grandes écoles** prestigious schools at university level; **grandes lignes** (Rail) main lines; **grandes vacances** summer holidays (BRIT) ou vacation (US); **grand-chose** nm/f inv: **pas grand-chose** not much; **Grande-Bretagne** nf (Great) Britain; **grandeur** nf (dimension) size; **grandeur nature** life-size; **grandiose** adj imposing; **grandir** vi to grow ▷ vt: **grandir qn** (suj: vêtement, chaussure) to make sb look taller; **grand-mère** nf grandmother; **grand-peine**: **à grand-peine** adv with difficulty; **grand-père** nm grandfather; **grands-parents** nmpl grandparents

grange [grɑ̃ʒ] nf barn

granit [granit] nm granite

graphique [grafik] adj graphic ▷ nm graph

grappe [grap] nf cluster; **grappe de raisin** bunch of grapes

gras, se [grɑ, grɑs] adj (viande, soupe) fatty; (personne) fat; (surface, main) greasy; (plaisanterie) coarse; (Typo) bold ▷ nm (Culin) fat; **faire la ~se matinée** to have a lie-in (BRIT), sleep late (US); **grassement** adv: **grassement payé** handsomely paid

gratifiant, e [gratifjɑ̃, jɑ̃t] adj gratifying, rewarding

gratin [gratɛ̃] nm (plat) cheese-topped dish; (croûte) cheese topping; (fam: élite) upper crust; **gratiné, e** adj (Culin) au gratin

gratis [gratis] adv free

gratitude [gratityd] nf gratitude

gratte-ciel [gratsjɛl] nm inv skyscraper

gratter [grate] vt (avec un outil) to scrape; (enlever: avec un outil) to scrape off; (: avec un ongle) to scratch; (enlever avec un ongle) to scratch off ▷ vi (irriter) to be scratchy; (démanger) to itch; **se gratter** to scratch (o.s.)

gratuit, e [gratɥi, ɥit] adj (entrée, billet) free; (fig) gratuitous

grave [grav] adj (maladie, accident) serious, bad; (sujet, problème) serious, grave; (air) grave, solemn; (voix, son) deep, low-pitched; **gravement** adv seriously; (parler, regarder) gravely

graver [grave] vt (plaque, nom) to engrave; (CD, DVD) to burn

graveur [gravœr] nm engraver; **graveur de CD/DVD** CD/DVD writer

gravier [gravje] nm gravel no pl; **gravillons** nmpl loose chippings ou gravel sg

gravir [gravir] vt to climb (up)

gravité [gravite] nf (de maladie, d'accident) seriousness; (de sujet, problème) gravity

graviter [gravite] vi to revolve

gravure [gravyr] nf engraving; (reproduction) print

gré [gre] nm: **à son ~** to one's liking; **de bon ~** willingly; **contre le ~ de qn** against sb's will; **de son (plein) ~** of one's own free will; **bon ~ mal ~** like it or not; **de ~ ou de force** whether one likes it or not; **savoir ~ à qn de qch** to be grateful to sb for sth

grec, grecque [grɛk] adj Greek; (classique: vase etc) Grecian ▷ nm/f: **G~, Grecque** Greek ▷ nm (Ling) Greek

Grèce [grɛs] nf: **la ~** Greece

greffe [grɛf] nf (Bot, Méd: de tissu) graft; (Méd: d'organe) transplant; **greffer** vt (Bot, Méd: tissu) to graft; (Méd: organe) to transplant

grêle [grɛl] adj (very) thin ▷ nf hail; **grêler** vb impers: **il grêle** it's hailing; **grêlon** nm hailstone

grelot [grəlo] nm little bell

grelotter [grəlɔte] vi to shiver

grenade [grənad] nf (explosive) grenade; (Bot) pomegranate; **grenadine** nf grenadine

grenier [grənje] nm attic; (de ferme) loft

grenouille [grənuj] nf frog

grès [grɛ] nm sandstone; (poterie) stoneware

grève [grɛv] nf (d'ouvriers) strike; (plage) shore; **se mettre en/faire ~** to go on/be on strike; **grève de la faim** hunger strike; **grève sauvage** wildcat strike

gréviste [grevist] nm/f striker

grièvement [grijɛvmɑ̃] adv seriously

griffe [grif] nf claw; (de couturier) label; **griffer** vt to scratch

grignoter [griɲɔte] vt (personne) to nibble at; (souris) to gnaw at ▷ vi to nibble

gril [gril] nm steak ou grill pan; **faire cuire au ~** to grill; **grillade** nf (viande etc) grill

grillage [grijaʒ] nm (treillis) wire netting; (clôture) wire fencing

grille [grij] nf (clôture) wire fence; (portail) (metal) gate; (d'égout) (metal) grate; (fig) grid

grille-pain [grijpɛ̃] nm inv toaster

griller [gʀije] vt (pain) to toast; (viande) to grill; (fig: ampoule etc) to blow; **faire ~** to toast; to grill; (châtaignes) to roast; **~ un feu rouge** to jump the lights

grillon [gʀijɔ̃] nm cricket

grimace [gʀimas] nf grimace; (pour faire rire): **faire des ~s** to pull ou make faces

grimper [gʀɛ̃pe] vi, vt to climb

grincer [gʀɛ̃se] vi (objet métallique) to grate; (plancher, porte) to creak; **~ des dents** to grind one's teeth

grincheux, -euse [gʀɛ̃ʃø, øz] adj grumpy

grippe [gʀip] nf flu, influenza; **grippe aviaire** bird flu; **grippé, e** adj: **être grippé** to have flu

gris, e [gʀi, gʀiz] adj grey; (ivre) tipsy

grisaille [gʀizaj] nf greyness, dullness

griser [gʀize] vt to intoxicate

grive [gʀiv] nf thrush

Groenland [gʀɔɛnlɑ̃d] nm Greenland

grogner [gʀɔɲe] vi to growl; (fig) to grumble; **grognon, ne** adj grumpy

grommeler [gʀɔm(ə)le] vi to mutter to o.s.

gronder [gʀɔ̃de] vi to rumble; (fig: révolte) to be brewing ▷ vt to scold; **se faire ~** to get a telling-off

gros, se [gʀo, gʀos] adj big, large; (obèse) fat; (travaux, dégâts) extensive; (épais) thick; (rhume, averse) heavy ▷ adv: **risquer/gagner ~** to risk/win a lot ▷ nm/f fat man/woman ▷ nm (Comm): **le ~** the wholesale business; **le ~ de** the bulk of; **prix de gros** wholesale price; **par ~ temps/grosse mer** in rough weather/heavy seas; **en ~** roughly; (Comm) wholesale; **gros lot** jackpot; **gros mot** swearword; **gros plan** (Photo) close-up; **gros sel** cooking salt; **gros titre** headline; **grosse caisse** big drum

groseille [gʀozɛj] nf: **~ (rouge/blanche)** red/white currant; **groseille à maquereau** gooseberry

grosse [gʀos] adj voir **gros**; **grossesse** nf pregnancy; **grosseur** nf size; (tumeur) lump

grossier, -ière [gʀosje, jɛʀ] adj coarse; (insolent) rude; (dessin) rough; (travail) roughly done; (imitation, instrument) crude; (évident: erreur) gross; **grossièrement** adv (sommairement) roughly; (vulgairement) coarsely; **grossièreté** nf rudeness; (mot): **dire des grossièretés** to use coarse language

grossir [gʀosiʀ] vi (personne) to put on weight ▷ vt (exagérer) to exaggerate; (au microscope) to magnify; (suj: vêtement): **~ qn** to make sb look fatter

grossiste [gʀosist] nm/f wholesaler

grotesque [gʀɔtɛsk] adj (extravagant) grotesque; (ridicule) ludicrous

grotte [gʀɔt] nf cave

groupe [gʀup] nm group; **groupe de parole** support group; **groupe sanguin** blood group; **groupe scolaire** school complex; **grouper** vt to group; **se grouper** vi to gather

grue [gʀy] nf crane

GSM [ʒeɛsɛm] nm, adj GSM

guenon [gənɔ̃] nf female monkey

guépard [gepaʀ] nm cheetah

guêpe [gɛp] nf wasp

guère [gɛʀ] adv (avec adjectif, adverbe): **ne ... ~** hardly; (avec verbe: pas beaucoup): **ne ... ~** tournure négative +much; (pas souvent) hardly ever; (pas longtemps) tournure négative +(very) long; **il n'y a ~ que/de** there's hardly anybody (ou anything) but/hardly any; **ce n'est ~ difficile** it's hardly difficult; **nous n'avons ~ de temps** we have hardly any time

guérilla [geʀija] nf guerrilla warfare

guérillero [geʀijeʀo] nm guerrilla

guérir [geʀiʀ] vt (personne, maladie) to cure; (membre, plaie) to heal ▷ vi (malade, maladie) to be cured; (blessure) to heal; **guérison** nf (de maladie) curing; (de membre, plaie) healing; (de malade) recovery; **guérisseur, -euse** nm/f healer

guerre [gɛʀ] nf war; **en ~** at war; **faire la ~ à** to wage war against; **guerre civile/mondiale** civil/world war; **guerrier, -ière** adj warlike ▷ nm/f warrior

guet [gɛ] nm: **faire le ~** to be on the watch ou look-out; **guet-apens** [gɛtapɑ̃] nm ambush; **guetter** vt (épier) to watch (intently); (attendre) to watch (out) for; (hostilement) to be lying in wait for

gueule [gœl] nf (d'animal) mouth; (fam: figure) face; (: bouche) mouth; **ta ~!** (fam) shut up!; **avoir la ~ de bois** (fam) to have a hangover, be hung over; **gueuler** (fam) vi to bawl

gui [gi] nm mistletoe

guichet [giʃɛ] nm (de bureau, banque) counter; **les ~s** (à la gare, au théâtre) the ticket office sg

guide [gid] nm (personne) guide; (livre) guide (book) ▷ nf (éclaireuse) girl guide; **guider** vt to guide

guidon [gidɔ̃] nm handlebars pl

guignol [giɲɔl] nm ≈ Punch and Judy show; (fig) clown

guillemets [gijmɛ] nmpl: **entre ~** in inverted commas

guindé, e [gɛ̃de] adj (personne, air) stiff, starchy; (style) stilted

Guinée [gine] nf Guinea

guirlande [giʀlɑ̃d] nf (fleurs) garland; **guirlande de Noël** tinsel garland

guise [giz] nf: **à votre ~** as you wish ou please; **en ~ de** by way of

guitare [gitaʀ] nf guitar

Guyane [gɥijan] nf: **la ~ (française)** French Guiana

gym [ʒim] nf (exercices) gym; **gymnase** nm gym(nasium); **gymnaste** nm/f gymnast; **gymnastique** nf gymnastics sg; (au réveil etc)

keep-fit exercises *pl*
gynécologie [ʒinekɔlɔʒi] *nf* gynaecology;
  gynécologique *adj* gynaecological;
  gynécologue *nm/f* gynaecologist

habile [abil] *adj* skilful; (*malin*) clever; **habileté**
  [abilte] *nf* skill, skilfulness; cleverness
habillé, e [abije] *adj* dressed; (*chic*) dressy
habiller [abije] *vt* to dress; (*fournir en
  vêtements*) to clothe; (*couvrir*) to cover;
  s'habiller *vi* to dress (o.s.); (*se déguiser, mettre
  des vêtements chic*) to dress up
habit [abi] *nm* outfit; **habits** *nmpl* (*vêtements*)
  clothes; **habit (de soirée)** evening dress; (*pour
  homme*) tails *pl*
habitant, e [abitɑ̃, ɑ̃t] *nm/f* inhabitant; (*d'une
  maison*) occupant; **loger chez l'~** to stay with
  the locals
habitation [abitasjɔ̃] *nf* house; **habitations
  à loyer modéré** (block of) council flats
habiter [abite] *vt* to live in ▷ *vi*: **~ à/dans** to
  live in; **où habitez-vous?** where do you live?
habitude [abityd] *nf* habit; **avoir l'~ de qch**
  to be used to sth; **avoir l'~ de faire** to be in the
  habit of doing; (*expérience*) to be used to doing;
  d'~ usually; **comme d'~** as usual
habitué, e [abitɥe] *nm/f* (*de maison*) regular
  visitor; (*de café*) regular (customer)
habituel, le [abitɥɛl] *adj* usual
habituer [abitɥe] *vt*: **~ qn à** to get sb used to;
  s'habituer à to get used to
'hache ['aʃ] *nf* axe
'hacher ['aʃe] *vt* (*viande*) to mince; (*persil*)
  to chop; **'hachis** *nm* mince *no pl*; **hachis
  Parmentier** ≈ shepherd's pie

'haie ['ε] nf hedge; (Sport) hurdle

'haillons ['ajɔ̃] nmpl rags

'haine ['εn] nf hatred

'haïr ['aiʀ] vt to detest, hate

'hâlé, e ['ɑle] adj (sun)tanned, sunburnt

haleine [alεn] nf breath; **hors d'~** out of breath; **tenir en ~** (attention) to hold spellbound; (incertitude) to keep in suspense; **de longue ~** long-term

'haleter ['alte] vt to pant

'hall ['ol] nm hall

'halle ['al] nf (covered) market; **halles** nfpl (d'une grande ville) central food market sg

hallucination [alysinasjɔ̃] nf hallucination

'halte ['alt] nf stop, break; (endroit) stopping place ▷ excl stop!; **faire halte** to stop

haltère [altεʀ] nm dumbbell, barbell; **haltères** nmpl: **(poids et) ~s** (activité) weightlifting sg; **haltérophilie** nf weightlifting

'hamac ['amak] nm hammock

'hameau, x ['amo] nm hamlet

hameçon [amsɔ̃] nm (fish) hook

'hanche ['ɑ̃ʃ] nf hip

'handball ['ɑ̃dbal] nm handball

'handicapé, e ['ɑ̃dikape] adj disabled, handicapped ▷ nm/f handicapped person; **handicapé mental/physique** mentally/physically handicapped person; **'handicapé moteur** person with a movement disorder

'hangar ['ɑ̃gaʀ] nm shed; (Aviat) hangar

'hanneton ['ɑ̃tɔ̃] nm cockchafer

'hanter ['ɑ̃te] vt to haunt

'hantise ['ɑ̃tiz] nf obsessive fear

'harceler ['aʀsəle] vt to harass; **harceler qn de questions** to plague sb with questions

'hardi, e ['aʀdi] adj bold, daring

'hareng ['aʀɑ̃] nm herring; **hareng saur** kipper, smoked herring

'hargne ['aʀɲ] nf aggressiveness; **'hargneux, -euse** adj aggressive

'haricot ['aʀiko] nm bean; **'haricot blanc** haricot bean; **'haricot vert** green bean; **'haricot rouge** kidney bean

harmonica [aʀmɔnika] nm mouth organ

harmonie [aʀmɔni] nf harmony; **harmonieux, -euse** adj harmonious; (couleurs, couple) well-matched

'harpe ['aʀp] nf harp

'hasard ['azaʀ] nm: **le hasard** chance, fate; **un hasard** a coincidence; **au hasard** (aller) aimlessly; (choisir) at random; **par hasard** by chance; **à tout hasard** (en cas de besoin) just in case; (en espérant trouver ce qu'on cherche) on the off chance (BRIT)

'hâte ['ɑt] nf haste; **à la hâte** hurriedly, hastily; **en hâte** posthaste, with all possible speed; **avoir hâte de** to be eager ou anxious to; **'hâter** vt to hasten; **se hâter** vi to hurry;

'hâtif, -ive adj (travail) hurried; (décision, jugement) hasty

'hausse ['os] nf rise, increase; **être en hausse** to be going up; **'hausser** vt to raise; **hausser les épaules** to shrug (one's shoulders)

'haut, e ['o, 'ot] adj high; (grand) tall ▷ adv high ▷ nm top (part); **de 3 m de haut** 3 m high, 3 m in height; **des hauts et des bas** ups and downs; **en haut lieu** in high places; **à haute voix, (tout) haut** aloud, out loud; **du haut de** from the top of; **de haut en bas** from top to bottom; **plus haut** higher up, further up; (dans un texte) above; (parler) louder; **en haut** (être/aller) at/to the top; (dans une maison) upstairs; **en haut de** at the top of; **'haut débit** broadband

'hautain, e ['otɛ̃, εn] adj haughty

'hautbois ['obwɑ] nm oboe

'hauteur ['otœʀ] nf height; **à la hauteur de** (accident) near; (fig: tâche, situation) equal to; **à la hauteur** (fig) up to it

'haut-parleur nm (loud)speaker

Hawaï [awai] n: **les îles ~** Hawaii

'Haye ['ε] n: **la Haye** the Hague

hebdomadaire [εbdɔmadεʀ] adj, nm weekly

hébergement [ebεʀʒəmɑ̃] nm accommodation

héberger [ebεʀʒe] vt (touristes) to accommodate, lodge; (amis) to put up; (réfugiés) to take in

hébergeur [ebεʀʒœʀ] nm (Internet) host

hébreu, x [ebʀø] adj m, nm Hebrew

Hébrides [ebʀid] nf: **les ~** the Hebrides

hectare [εktaʀ] nm hectare

'hein ['ɛ̃] excl eh?

'hélas ['elɑs] excl alas! ▷ adv unfortunately

'héler ['ele] vt to hail

hélice [elis] nf propeller

hélicoptère [elikɔptεʀ] nm helicopter

helvétique [εlvetik] adj Swiss

hématome [ematom] nm nasty bruise

hémisphère [emisfεʀ] nm: **l'~ nord/sud** the northern/southern hemisphere

hémorragie [emɔʀaʒi] nf bleeding no pl, haemorrhage

hémorroïdes [emɔʀɔid] nfpl piles, haemorrhoids

'hennir ['eniʀ] vi to neigh, whinny

hépatite [epatit] nf hepatitis

herbe [εʀb] nf grass; (Culin, Méd) herb; **~s de Provence** mixed herbs; **en ~** unripe; (fig) budding; **herbicide** nm weed-killer; **herboriste** nm/f herbalist

héréditaire [eʀeditεʀ] adj hereditary

'hérisson ['eʀisɔ̃] nm hedgehog

héritage [eʀitaʒ] nm inheritance; (coutumes, système) heritage, legacy

hériter [eʀite] vi: **~ de qch (de qn)** to inherit sth (from sb); **héritier, -ière** nm/f heir(-ess)

hermétique [ɛʀmetik] *adj* airtight; watertight; (*fig: obscur*) abstruse; (: *impénétrable*) impenetrable

hermine [ɛʀmin] *nf* ermine

'hernie ['ɛʀni] *nf* hernia

héroïne [eʀɔin] *nf* heroine; (*drogue*) heroin

héroïque [eʀɔik] *adj* heroic

'héron ['eʀɔ̃] *nm* heron

'héros ['eʀo] *nm* hero

hésitant, e [ezitɑ̃, ɑ̃t] *adj* hesitant

hésitation [ezitasjɔ̃] *nf* hesitation

hésiter [ezite] *vi*: **~ (à faire)** to hesitate (to do)

hétérosexuel, le [eteʀɔsɛkɥɛl] *adj* heterosexual

'hêtre ['ɛtʀ] *nm* beech

heure [œʀ] *nf* hour; (*Scol*) period; (*moment*) time; **c'est l'~** it's time; **quelle ~ est-il?** what time is it?; **2 ~s (du matin)** 2 o'clock (in the morning); **être à l'~** to be on time; (*montre*) to be right; **mettre à l'~** to set right; **à une ~ avancée (de la nuit)** at a late hour (of the night); **de bonne ~** early; **à toute ~** at any time; **24 ~s sur 24** round the clock, 24 hours a day; **à l'~ qu'il est** at this time (of day); by now; **sur l'~** at once; **à quelle ~ ouvre le musée/ magasin?** what time does the museum/shop open?; **heures de bureau** office hours; **heure de pointe** rush hour; (*téléphone*) peak period; **heures supplémentaires** overtime *sg*

heureusement [œʀøzmɑ̃] *adv* (*par bonheur*) fortunately, luckily

heureux, -euse [œʀø, øz] *adj* happy; (*chanceux*) lucky, fortunate

'heurt ['œʀ] *nm* (*choc*) collision; (*conflit*) clash

'heurter ['œʀte] *vt* (*mur*) to strike, hit; (*personne*) to collide with

hexagone [ɛgzagɔn] *nm* hexagon; **l'H~** (*la France*) France (*because of its shape*)

hiberner [ibɛʀne] *vi* to hibernate

'hibou, x ['ibu] *nm* owl

'hideux, -euse ['idø, øz] *adj* hideous

hier [jɛʀ] *adv* yesterday; **~ matin/midi** yesterday morning/lunchtime; **~ soir** last night, yesterday evening; **toute la journée d'~** all day yesterday; **toute la matinée d'~** all yesterday morning

'hiérarchie ['jeʀaʀʃi] *nf* hierarchy

hindou, e [ɛ̃du] *adj* Hindu ▷ *nm/f*: **H~, e** Hindu

hippique [ipik] *adj* equestrian, horse *cpd*; **un club ~** a riding centre; **un concours ~** a horse show; **hippisme** *nm* (horse)riding

hippodrome [ipɔdʀom] *nm* racecourse

hippopotame [ipɔpɔtam] *nm* hippopotamus

hirondelle [iʀɔ̃dɛl] *nf* swallow

'hisser ['ise] *vt* to hoist, haul up

histoire [istwaʀ] *nf* (*science, événements*) history; (*anecdote, récit, mensonge*) story; (*affaire*) business *no pl*; **histoires** *nfpl* (*chichis*) fuss *no pl*; (*ennuis*) trouble *sg*; **historique** *adj* historical; (*important*) historic ▷ *nm*: **faire l'historique de** to give the background to

'hit-parade ['itpaʀad] *nm*: **le hit-parade** the charts

hiver [ivɛʀ] *nm* winter; **hivernal, e, -aux** *adj* winter *cpd*; (*glacial*) wintry; **hiverner** *vi* to winter

HLM *nm ou f* (= *habitation à loyer modéré*) council flat; **des ~** council housing

'hobby ['ɔbi] *nm* hobby

'hocher ['ɔʃe] *vt*: **hocher la tête** to nod; (*signe négatif ou dubitatif*) to shake one's head

'hockey ['ɔkɛ] *nm*: **hockey (sur glace/gazon)** (ice/field) hockey

'hold-up ['ɔldœp] *nm inv* hold-up

'hollandais, e ['ɔlɑ̃dɛ, ɛz] *adj* Dutch ▷ *nm* (*Ling*) Dutch ▷ *nm/f*: **Hollandais, e** Dutchman(-woman)

'Hollande ['ɔlɑ̃d] *nf*: **la Hollande** Holland

'homard ['ɔmaʀ] *nm* lobster

homéopathique [ɔmeɔpatik] *adj* homoeopathic

homicide [ɔmisid] *nm* murder; **homicide involontaire** manslaughter

hommage [ɔmaʒ] *nm* tribute; **rendre ~ à** to pay tribute to

homme [ɔm] *nm* man; **homme d'affaires** businessman; **homme d'État** statesman; **homme de main** hired man; **homme de paille** stooge; **l'homme de la rue** the man on the street

homo...: **homogène** *adj* homogeneous; **homologue** *nm/f* counterpart; **homologué, e** *adj* (*Sport*) ratified; (*tarif*) authorized; **homonyme** *nm* (*Ling*) homonym; (*d'une personne*) namesake; **homosexuel, le** *adj* homosexual

'Hong Kong ['ɔ̃gkɔ̃g] *n* Hong Kong

'Hongrie ['ɔ̃gʀi] *nf*: **la Hongrie** Hungary; **'hongrois, e** *adj* Hungarian ▷ *nm/f*: **Hongrois, e** Hungarian ▷ *nm* (*Ling*) Hungarian

honnête [ɔnɛt] *adj* (*intègre*) honest; (*juste, satisfaisant*) fair; **honnêtement** *adv* honestly; **honnêteté** *nf* honesty

honneur [ɔnœʀ] *nm* honour; (*mérite*) credit; **en l'~ de** in honour of; (*événement*) on the occasion of; **faire ~ à** (*engagements*) to honour; (*famille*) to be a credit to; (*fig: repas etc*) to do justice to

honorable [ɔnɔʀabl] *adj* worthy, honourable; (*suffisant*) decent

honoraire [ɔnɔʀɛʀ] *adj* honorary; **professeur ~** professor emeritus; **honoraires** *nmpl* fees

honorer [ɔnɔʀe] *vt* to honour; (*estimer*) to hold in high regard; (*faire honneur à*) to do credit to

'honte ['ɔ̃t] *nf* shame; **avoir honte de** to be ashamed of; **faire honte à qn** to make sb (feel) ashamed; **'honteux, -euse** *adj* ashamed; (*conduite, acte*) shameful, disgraceful

hôpital, -aux [ɔpital, o] *nm* hospital; **où est l'~ le plus proche?** where is the nearest hospital?

'hoquet [ɔkɛ] *nm*: **avoir le hoquet** to have (the) hiccoughs

horaire [ɔRER] *adj* hourly ▷ *nm* timetable, schedule; **horaires** *nmpl* (*d'employé*) hours; **horaire souple** flexitime

horizon [ɔRizɔ̃] *nm* horizon

horizontal, e, -aux [ɔRizɔ̃tal, o] *adj* horizontal

horloge [ɔRlɔʒ] *nf* clock; **l'~ parlante** the speaking clock; **horloger, -ère** *nm/f* watchmaker; clockmaker

'hormis ['ɔRmi] *prép* save

horoscope [ɔRɔskɔp] *nm* horoscope

horreur [ɔRœR] *nf* horror; **quelle ~!** how awful!; **avoir ~ de** to loathe *ou* detest; **horrible** *adj* horrible; **horrifier** *vt* to horrify

'hors ['ɔR] *prép*: **hors de** out of; **hors pair** outstanding; **hors de propos** inopportune; **être hors de soi** to be beside o.s.; **'hors d'usage** out of service; **'hors-bord** *nm inv* speedboat (*with outboard motor*); **'hors-d'œuvre** *nm inv* hors d'œuvre; **'hors-la-loi** *inv* outlaw; **'hors-service** *adj inv* out of order; **'hors-taxe** *adj* (*boutique, articles*) duty-free

hortensia [ɔRtɑ̃sja] *nm* hydrangea

hospice [ɔspis] *nm* (*de vieillards*) home

hospitalier, -ière [ɔspitalje, jɛR] *adj* (*accueillant*) hospitable; (*Méd: service, centre*) hospital *cpd*

hospitaliser [ɔspitalize] *vt* to take/send to hospital, hospitalize

hospitalité [ɔspitalite] *nf* hospitality

hostie [ɔsti] *nf* host (*Rel*)

hostile [ɔstil] *adj* hostile; **hostilité** *nf* hostility

hôte [ot] *nm* (*maître de maison*) host; (*invité*) guest

hôtel [otɛl] *nm* hotel; **aller à l'~** to stay in a hotel; **hôtel de ville** town hall; **hôtel (particulier)** (*private*) mansion; **hôtellerie** *nf* hotel business

● **HÔTELS**
●
● There are six categories of hotel in France,
● from zero ('non classé') to four stars and
● luxury four stars ('quatre étoiles luxe').
● Prices include VAT but not breakfast. In
● some towns, guests pay a small additional
● tourist tax, the 'taxe de séjour'.

hôtesse [otɛs] *nf* hostess; **hôtesse (de l'air)** stewardess, air hostess (*BRIT*)

'houblon ['ublɔ̃] *nm* (*Bot*) hop; (*pour la bière*) hops *pl*

'houille ['uj] *nf* coal; **'houille blanche** hydroelectric power

'houle ['ul] *nf* swell; **'houleux, -euse** *adj* stormy

'hourra ['uRa] *excl* hurrah!

'housse ['us] *nf* cover

'houx ['u] *nm* holly

'hublot ['yblo] *nm* porthole

'huche ['yʃ] *nf*: **huche à pain** bread bin

'huer ['ɥe] *vt* to boo

huile [ɥil] *nf* oil

huissier [ɥisje] *nm* usher; (*Jur*) ≈ bailiff

'huit ['ɥi(t)] *num* eight; **samedi en huit** a week on Saturday; **dans huit jours** in a week; **'huitaine** *nf*: **une huitaine (de jours)** a week or so; **'huitième** *num* eighth

huître [ɥitR] *nf* oyster

humain, e [ymɛ̃, ɛn] *adj* human; (*compatissant*) humane ▷ *nm* human (being); **humanitaire** *adj* humanitarian; **humanité** *nf* humanity

humble [œ̃bl] *adj* humble

'humer ['yme] *vt* (*plat*) to smell; (*parfum*) to inhale

humeur [ymœR] *nf* mood; **de bonne/ mauvaise ~** in a good/bad mood

humide [ymid] *adj* damp; (*main, yeux*) moist; (*climat, chaleur*) humid; (*saison, route*) wet

humilier [ymilje] *vt* to humiliate

humilité [ymilite] *nf* humility, humbleness

humoristique [ymɔRistik] *adj* humorous

humour [ymuR] *nm* humour; **avoir de l'~** to have a sense of humour; **humour noir** black humour

'huppé, e ['ype] (*fam*) *adj* posh

'hurlement ['yRləmɑ̃] *nm* howling *no pl*, howl, yelling *no pl*, yell

'hurler ['yRle] *vi* to howl, yell

'hutte ['yt] *nf* hut

hydratant, e [idRatɑ̃, ɑ̃t] *adj* (*crème*) moisturizing

hydraulique [idRolik] *adj* hydraulic

hydravion [idRavjɔ̃] *nm* seaplane

hydrogène [idRɔʒɛn] *nm* hydrogen

hydroglisseur [idRɔglisœR] *nm* hydroplane

hyène [jɛn] *nf* hyena

hygiène [iʒjɛn] *nf* hygiene

hygiénique [iʒenik] *adj* hygienic

hymne [imn] *nm* hymn

hyperlien [ipɛRljɛ̃] *nm* hyperlink

hypermarché [ipɛRmaRʃe] *nm* hypermarket

hypermétrope [ipɛRmetRɔp] *adj* long-sighted

hypertension [ipɛRtɑ̃sjɔ̃] *nf* high blood pressure

hypnose [ipnoz] *nf* hypnosis; **hypnotiser** *vt* to hypnotize

hypocrisie [ipɔkrizi] *nf* hypocrisy; **hypocrite** *adj* hypocritical

hypothèque [ipɔtɛk] *nf* mortgage
hypothèse [ipɔtɛz] *nf* hypothesis
hystérique [isteʀik] *adj* hysterical

iceberg [ajsbɛʀg] *nm* iceberg
ici [isi] *adv* here; **jusqu'~** as far as this; (*temps*)
so far; **d'~ demain** by tomorrow; **d'~ là** by
then, in the meantime; **d'~ peu** before long
icône [ikon] *nf* icon
idéal, e, -aux [ideal, o] *adj* ideal ▷ *nm* ideal;
idéaliste *adj* idealistic ▷ *nm/f* idealist
idée [ide] *nf* idea; **avoir dans l'~ que** to have
an idea that; **se faire des ~s** to imagine things,
get ideas into one's head; **avoir des ~s noires**
to have black *ou* dark thoughts; **idées reçues**
received wisdom *sg*
identifier [idɑ̃tifje] *vt* to identify; **s'identifier**
vi: **s'~ avec** *ou* **à qn/qch** (*héros etc*) to identify
with sb/sth
identique [idɑ̃tik] *adj*: **~ (à)** identical (to)
identité [idɑ̃tite] *nf* identity
idiot, e [idjo, idjɔt] *adj* idiotic ▷ *nm/f* idiot
idole [idɔl] *nf* idol
if [if] *nm* yew
ignoble [iɲɔbl] *adj* vile
ignorant, e [iɲɔʀɑ̃, ɑ̃t] *adj* ignorant; **~ de**
ignorant of, not aware of
ignorer [iɲɔʀe] *vt* not to know; (*personne*) to
ignore
il [il] *pron* he; (*animal, chose, en tournure
impersonnelle*) it; **il fait froid** it's cold; **Pierre
est-il arrivé?** has Pierre arrived?; **il a gagné** he
won; *voir* **avoir**
île [il] *nf* island; **l'île Maurice** Mauritius; **les**

îles anglo-normandes the Channel Islands; **les îles britanniques** the British Isles
illégal, e, -aux [i(l)legal, o] *adj* illegal
illimité, e [i(l)limite] *adj* unlimited
illisible [i(l)lizibl] *adj* illegible; (*roman*) unreadable
illogique [i(l)lɔʒik] *adj* illogical
illuminer [i(l)lymine] *vt* to light up; (*monument, rue: pour une fête*) to illuminate; (: *au moyen de projecteurs*) to floodlight
illusion [i(l)lyzjɔ̃] *nf* illusion; **se faire des ~s** to delude o.s.; **faire ~** to delude *ou* fool people
illustration [i(l)lystrasjɔ̃] *nf* illustration
illustré, e [i(l)lystre] *adj* illustrated ▷ *nm* comic
illustrer [i(l)lystre] *vt* to illustrate; **s'illustrer** to become famous, win fame
ils [il] *pron* they
image [imaʒ] *nf* (*gén*) picture; (*métaphore*) image; **image de marque** brand image; (*fig*) public image; **imagé, e** *adj* (*texte*) full of imagery; (*langage*) colourful
imaginaire [imaʒinɛr] *adj* imaginary
imagination [imaʒinasjɔ̃] *nf* imagination; **avoir de l'~** to be imaginative
imaginer [imaʒine] *vt* to imagine; (*inventer: expédient*) to devise, think up; **s'imaginer** *vt* (*se figurer: scène etc*) to imagine, picture; **s'~ que** to imagine that
imbécile [ɛ̃besil] *adj* idiotic ▷ *nm/f* idiot
imbu, e [ɛ̃by] *adj*: **~ de** full of
imitateur, -trice [imitatœr, tris] *nm/f* (*gén*) imitator; (*Music-Hall*) impersonator
imitation [imitasjɔ̃] *nf* imitation; (*de personnalité*) impersonation
imiter [imite] *vt* to imitate; (*contrefaire*) to forge; (*ressembler à*) to look like
immangeable [ɛ̃mɑ̃ʒabl] *adj* inedible
immatriculation [imatrikylasjɔ̃] *nf* registration

● **IMMATRICULATION**
●
● The last two numbers on vehicle licence
● plates show which 'département' of France
● the vehicle is registered in. For example, a
● car registered in Paris has the number 75 on
● its licence plates.

immatriculer [imatrikyle] *vt* to register; **faire/se faire ~** to register
immédiat, e [imedja, jat] *adj* immediate ▷ *nm*: **dans l'~** for the time being; **immédiatement** *adv* immediately
immense [i(m)mɑ̃s] *adj* immense
immerger [imɛrʒe] *vt* to immerse, submerge
immeuble [imœbl] *nm* building; (*à usage d'habitation*) block of flats
immigration [imigrasjɔ̃] *nf* immigration

immigré, e [imigre] *nm/f* immigrant
imminent, e [iminɑ̃, ɑ̃t] *adj* imminent
immobile [i(m)mɔbil] *adj* still, motionless
immobilier, -ière [imɔbilje, jɛr] *adj* property *cpd* ▷ *nm*: **l'~** the property business
immobiliser [imɔbilize] *vt* (*gén*) to immobilize; (*circulation, véhicule, affaires*) to bring to a standstill; **s'immobiliser** (*personne*) to stand still; (*machine, véhicule*) to come to a halt
immoral, e, -aux [i(m)mɔral, o] *adj* immoral
immortel, le [imɔrtɛl] *adj* immortal
immunisé, e [im(m)ynize] *adj*: **~ contre** immune to
immunité [imynite] *nf* immunity
impact [ɛ̃pakt] *nm* impact
impair, e [ɛ̃pɛr] *adj* odd ▷ *nm* faux pas, blunder
impardonnable [ɛ̃pardɔnabl] *adj* unpardonable, unforgivable
imparfait, e [ɛ̃parfɛ, ɛt] *adj* imperfect
impartial, e, -aux [ɛ̃parsjal, jo] *adj* impartial, unbiased
impasse [ɛ̃pɑs] *nf* dead end, cul-de-sac; (*fig*) deadlock
impassible [ɛ̃pasibl] *adj* impassive
impatience [ɛ̃pasjɑ̃s] *nf* impatience
impatient, e [ɛ̃pasjɑ̃, jɑ̃t] *adj* impatient; **impatienter: s'impatienter** *vi* to get impatient
impeccable [ɛ̃pekabl] *adj* (*parfait*) perfect; (*propre*) impeccable; (*fam*) smashing
impensable [ɛ̃pɑ̃sabl] *adj* (*événement hypothétique*) unthinkable; (*événement qui a eu lieu*) unbelievable
impératif, -ive [ɛ̃peratif, iv] *adj* imperative ▷ *nm* (*Ling*) imperative; **impératifs** *nmpl* (*exigences: d'une fonction, d'une charge*) requirements; (: *de la mode*) demands
impératrice [ɛ̃peratris] *nf* empress
imperceptible [ɛ̃pɛrsɛptibl] *adj* imperceptible
impérial, e, -aux [ɛ̃perjal, jo] *adj* imperial
impérieux, -euse [ɛ̃perjø, jøz] *adj* (*caractère, ton*) imperious; (*obligation, besoin*) pressing, urgent
impérissable [ɛ̃perisabl] *adj* undying
imperméable [ɛ̃pɛrmeabl] *adj* waterproof; (*fig*): **~ à** impervious to ▷ *nm* raincoat
impertinent, e [ɛ̃pɛrtinɑ̃, ɑ̃t] *adj* impertinent
impitoyable [ɛ̃pitwajabl] *adj* pitiless, merciless
implanter [ɛ̃plɑ̃te]: **s'implanter** *vi* to be set up
impliquer [ɛ̃plike] *vt* to imply; **~ qn (dans)** to implicate sb (in)
impoli, e [ɛ̃pɔli] *adj* impolite, rude

impopulaire [ɛ̃pɔpylɛʀ] *adj* unpopular
importance [ɛ̃pɔʀtɑ̃s] *nf* importance; (*de somme*) size; (*de retard, dégâts*) extent; **sans ~** unimportant
important, e [ɛ̃pɔʀtɑ̃, ɑ̃t] *adj* important; (*en quantité: somme, retard*) considerable, sizeable; (: *dégâts*) extensive; (*péj: airs, ton*) self-important ▷ *nm*: **l'~** the important thing
importateur, -trice [ɛ̃pɔʀtatœʀ, tʀis] *nm/f* importer
importation [ɛ̃pɔʀtasjɔ̃] *nf* importation; (*produit*) import
importer [ɛ̃pɔʀte] *vt* (*Comm*) to import; (*maladies, plantes*) to introduce ▷ *vi* (*être important*) to matter; **il importe qu'il fasse** it is important that he should do; **peu m'importe** (*je n'ai pas de préférence*) I don't mind; (*je m'en moque*) I don't care; **peu importe (que)** it doesn't matter (if); *voir aussi* **n'importe**
importun, e [ɛ̃pɔʀtœ̃, yn] *adj* irksome, importunate; (*arrivée, visite*) inopportune, ill-timed ▷ *nm* intruder; **importuner** *vt* to bother
imposant, e [ɛ̃pozɑ̃, ɑ̃t] *adj* imposing
imposer [ɛ̃poze] *vt* (*taxer*) to tax; **s'imposer** (*être nécessaire*) to be imperative; **~ qch à qn** to impose sth on sb; **en ~ à** to impress; **s'~ comme** to emerge as; **s'~ par** to win recognition through
impossible [ɛ̃pɔsibl] *adj* impossible; **il m'est ~ de le faire** it is impossible for me to do it, I can't possibly do it; **faire l'~** to do one's utmost
imposteur [ɛ̃pɔstœʀ] *nm* impostor
impôt [ɛ̃po] *nm* tax; **impôt foncier** land tax; **impôt sur le chiffre d'affaires** corporation (BRIT) *ou* corporate (US) tax; **impôt sur le revenu** income tax; **impôts locaux** rates, local taxes (US), ≈ council tax (BRIT)
impotent, e [ɛ̃pɔtɑ̃, ɑ̃t] *adj* disabled
impraticable [ɛ̃pʀatikabl] *adj* (*projet*) impracticable, unworkable; (*piste*) impassable
imprécis, e [ɛ̃pʀesi, iz] *adj* imprecise
imprégner [ɛ̃pʀeɲe] *vt* (*tissu*) to impregnate; (*lieu, air*) to fill; **s'imprégner de** (*fig*) to absorb
imprenable [ɛ̃pʀənabl] *adj* (*forteresse*) impregnable; **vue ~** unimpeded outlook
impression [ɛ̃pʀesjɔ̃] *nf* impression; (*d'un ouvrage, tissu*) printing; **faire bonne/ mauvaise ~** to make a good/bad impression; **impressionnant, e** *adj* (*imposant*) impressive; (*bouleversant*) upsetting; **impressionner** *vt* (*frapper*) to impress; (*bouleverser*) to upset
imprévisible [ɛ̃pʀeviziblbl] *adj* unforeseeable
imprévu, e [ɛ̃pʀevy] *adj* unforeseen, unexpected ▷ *nm* (*incident*) unexpected incident; **des vacances pleines d'~** holidays full of surprises; **en cas d'~** if anything unexpected happens; **sauf ~** unless anything

unexpected crops up
imprimante [ɛ̃pʀimɑ̃t] *nf* printer; **imprimante (à) laser** laser printer
imprimé [ɛ̃pʀime] *nm* (*formulaire*) printed form; (*Postes*) printed matter *no pl*; (*tissu*) printed fabric; **~ à fleur** floral print
imprimer [ɛ̃pʀime] *vt* to print; (*publier*) to publish; **imprimerie** *nf* printing; (*établissement*) printing works *sg*; **imprimeur** *nm* printer
impropre [ɛ̃pʀɔpʀ] *adj* inappropriate; **~ à** unfit for
improviser [ɛ̃pʀɔvize] *vt, vi* to improvise
improviste [ɛ̃pʀɔvist]: **à l'~** *adv* unexpectedly, without warning
imprudence [ɛ̃pʀydɑ̃s] *nf* (*d'une personne, d'une action*) carelessness *no pl*; (*d'une remarque*) imprudence *no pl*; **commettre une ~** to do something foolish
imprudent, e [ɛ̃pʀydɑ̃, ɑ̃t] *adj* (*conducteur, geste, action*) careless; (*remarque*) unwise, imprudent; (*projet*) foolhardy
impuissant, e [ɛ̃pɥisɑ̃, ɑ̃t] *adj* helpless; (*sans effet*) ineffectual; (*sexuellement*) impotent
impulsif, -ive [ɛ̃pylsif, iv] *adj* impulsive
impulsion [ɛ̃pylsjɔ̃] *nf* (*Élec, instinct*) impulse; (*élan, influence*) impetus
inabordable [inabɔʀdabl] *adj* (*cher*) prohibitive
inacceptable [inaksɛptabl] *adj* unacceptable
inaccessible [inaksesibl] *adj* inaccessible; **~ à** impervious to
inachevé, e [inaʃ(ə)ve] *adj* unfinished
inactif, -ive [inaktif, iv] *adj* inactive; (*remède*) ineffective; (*Bourse: marché*) slack
inadapté, e [inadapte] *adj* (*gén*): **~ à** not adapted to, unsuited to; (*Psych*) maladjusted
inadéquat, e [inadekwa(t), kwat] *adj* inadequate
inadmissible [inadmisibl] *adj* inadmissible
inadvertance [inadvɛʀtɑ̃s]: **par ~** *adv* inadvertently
inanimé, e [inanime] *adj* (*matière*) inanimate; (*évanoui*) unconscious; (*sans vie*) lifeless
inanition [inanisjɔ̃] *nf*: **tomber d'~** to faint with hunger (and exhaustion)
inaperçu, e [inapɛʀsy] *adj*: **passer ~** to go unnoticed
inapte [inapt] *adj*: **~ à** incapable of; (*Mil*) unfit for
inattendu, e [inatɑ̃dy] *adj* unexpected
inattentif, -ive [inatɑ̃tif, iv] *adj* inattentive; **~ à** (*dangers, détails*) heedless of; **inattention** *nf* lack of attention; **une faute** *ou* **une erreur d'inattention** a careless mistake
inaugurer [inogyʀe] *vt* (*monument*) to unveil; (*exposition, usine*) to open; (*fig*) to inaugurate
inavouable [inavwabl] *adj* shameful;

(*bénéfices*) undisclosable

incalculable [ɛ̃kalkylabl] *adj* incalculable

incapable [ɛ̃kapabl] *adj* incapable; **~ de faire** incapable of doing; (*empêché*) unable to do

incapacité [ɛ̃kapasite] *nf* (*incompétence*) incapability; (*impossibilité*) incapacity; **dans l'~ de faire** unable to do

incarcérer [ɛ̃kaʀseʀe] *vt* to incarcerate, imprison

incassable [ɛ̃kasabl] *adj* unbreakable

incendie [ɛ̃sɑ̃di] *nm* fire; **incendie criminel** arson *no pl*; **incendie de forêt** forest fire; **incendier** *vt* (*mettre le feu à*) to set fire to, set alight; (*brûler complètement*) to burn down

incertain, e [ɛ̃sɛʀtɛ̃, ɛn] *adj* uncertain; (*temps*) unsettled; (*imprécis: contours*) indistinct, blurred; **incertitude** *nf* uncertainty

incessamment [ɛ̃sesamɑ̃] *adv* very shortly

incident [ɛ̃sidɑ̃] *nm* incident; **incident de parcours** minor hitch *ou* setback; **incident technique** technical difficulties *pl*

incinérer [ɛ̃sineʀe] *vt* (*ordures*) to incinerate; (*mort*) to cremate

incisive [ɛ̃siziv] *nf* incisor

inciter [ɛ̃site] *vt*: **~ qn à (faire) qch** to encourage sb to do sth; (*à la révolte etc*) to incite sb to do sth

incivilité [ɛ̃sivilite] *nf* (*grossièreté*) incivility; **incivilités** *nfpl* antisocial behaviour *sg*

inclinable [ɛ̃klinabl] *adj*: **siège à dossier ~** reclining seat

inclination [ɛ̃klinasjɔ̃] *nf* (*penchant*) inclination

incliner [ɛ̃kline] *vt* (*pencher*) to tilt ▷ *vi*: **~ à qch/à faire** to incline towards sth/doing; **s'incliner** *vr* (*se pencher*) to bow; **s'~ devant** (*par respect*) to pay one's respects

inclure [ɛ̃klyʀ] *vt* to include; (*joindre à un envoi*) to enclose

inclus, e [ɛ̃kly, -yz] *pp de* **inclure** ▷ *adj* included; (*joint à un envoi*) enclosed ▷ *adv*: **est-ce que le service est ~?** is service included?; **jusqu'au 10 mars ~** until 10th March inclusive

incognito [ɛ̃kɔɲito] *adv* incognito ▷ *nm*: **garder l'~** to remain incognito

incohérent, e [ɛ̃kɔeʀɑ̃, ɑ̃t] *adj* (*comportement*) inconsistent; (*geste, langage, texte*) incoherent

incollable [ɛ̃kɔlabl] *adj* (*riz*) non-stick; **il est ~** (*fam*) he's got all the answers

incolore [ɛ̃kɔlɔʀ] *adj* colourless

incommoder [ɛ̃kɔmɔde] *vt* (*chaleur, odeur*): **~ qn** to bother sb

incomparable [ɛ̃kɔ̃paʀabl] *adj* incomparable

incompatible [ɛ̃kɔ̃patibl] *adj* incompatible

incompétent, e [ɛ̃kɔ̃petɑ̃, ɑ̃t] *adj* incompetent

incomplet, -ète [ɛ̃kɔ̃plɛ, ɛt] *adj* incomplete

incompréhensible [ɛ̃kɔ̃pʀeɑ̃sibl] *adj* incomprehensible

incompris, e [ɛ̃kɔ̃pʀi, iz] *adj* misunderstood

inconcevable [ɛ̃kɔ̃s(ə)vabl] *adj* inconceivable

inconfortable [ɛ̃kɔ̃fɔʀtabl(ə)] *adj* uncomfortable

incongru, e [ɛ̃kɔ̃gʀy] *adj* unseemly

inconnu, e [ɛ̃kɔny] *adj* unknown ▷ *nm/f* stranger ▷ *nm*: **l'~** the unknown; **inconnue** *nf* unknown factor

inconsciemment [ɛ̃kɔ̃sjamɑ̃] *adv* unconsciously

inconscient, e [ɛ̃kɔ̃sjɑ̃, jɑ̃t] *adj* unconscious; (*irréfléchi*) thoughtless, reckless; (*sentiment*) subconscious ▷ *nm* (*Psych*): **l'~** the unconscious; **~ de** unaware of

inconsidéré, e [ɛ̃kɔ̃sideʀe] *adj* ill-considered

inconsistant, e [ɛ̃kɔ̃sistɑ̃, ɑ̃t] *adj* (*fig*) flimsy, weak

inconsolable [ɛ̃kɔ̃sɔlabl] *adj* inconsolable

incontestable [ɛ̃kɔ̃tɛstabl] *adj* indisputable

incontinent, e [ɛ̃kɔ̃tinɑ̃, ɑ̃t] *adj* incontinent

incontournable [ɛ̃kɔ̃tuʀnabl] *adj* unavoidable

incontrôlable [ɛ̃kɔ̃tʀolabl] *adj* unverifiable; (*irrépressible*) uncontrollable

inconvénient [ɛ̃kɔ̃venjɑ̃] *nm* disadvantage, drawback; **si vous n'y voyez pas d'~** if you have no objections

incorporer [ɛ̃kɔʀpɔʀe] *vt*: **~ (à)** to mix in (with); **~ (dans)** (*paragraphe etc*) to incorporate (in); (*Mil: appeler*) to recruit (into); **il a très bien su s'~ à notre groupe** he was very easily incorporated into our group

incorrect, e [ɛ̃kɔʀɛkt] *adj* (*impropre, inconvenant*) improper; (*défectueux*) faulty; (*inexact*) incorrect; (*impoli*) impolite; (*déloyal*) underhand

incorrigible [ɛ̃kɔʀiʒibl] *adj* incorrigible

incrédule [ɛ̃kʀedyl] *adj* incredulous; (*Rel*) unbelieving

incroyable [ɛ̃kʀwajabl] *adj* incredible

incruster [ɛ̃kʀyste] *vt* (*Art*) to inlay; **s'incruster** *vi* (*invité*) to take root

inculpé, e [ɛ̃kylpe] *nm/f* accused

inculper [ɛ̃kylpe] *vt*: **~ (de)** to charge (with)

inculquer [ɛ̃kylke] *vt*: **~ qch à** to inculcate sth in *ou* instil sth into

Inde [ɛ̃d] *nf*: **l'~** India

indécent, e [ɛ̃desɑ̃, ɑ̃t] *adj* indecent

indécis, e [ɛ̃desi, iz] *adj* (*par nature*) indecisive; (*temporairement*) undecided

indéfendable [ɛ̃defɑ̃dabl] *adj* indefensible

indéfini, e [ɛ̃defini] *adj* (*imprécis, incertain*) undefined; (*illimité, Ling*) indefinite; **indéfiniment** *adv* indefinitely; **indéfinissable** *adj* indefinable

indélébile [ɛ̃delebil] *adj* indelible

indélicat, e [ɛ̃delika, at] adj tactless
indemne [ɛ̃dɛmn] adj unharmed;
  indemniser vt: **indemniser qn (de)** to
  compensate sb (for)
indemnité [ɛ̃dɛmnite] nf (dédommagement)
  compensation no pl; (allocation) allowance;
  indemnité de licenciement redundancy
  payment
indépendamment [ɛ̃depɑ̃damɑ̃] adv
  independently; **~ de** (abstraction faite de)
  irrespective of; (en plus de) over and above
indépendance [ɛ̃depɑ̃dɑ̃s] nf independence
indépendant, e [ɛ̃depɑ̃dɑ̃, ɑ̃t] adj
  independent; **~ de** independent of;
  travailleur ~ self-employed worker
indescriptible [ɛ̃dɛskriptibl] adj
  indescribable
indésirable [ɛ̃dezirabl] adj undesirable
indestructible [ɛ̃dɛstryktibl] adj
  indestructible
indéterminé, e [ɛ̃detɛrmine] adj (date, cause,
  nature) unspecified; (forme, longueur, quantité)
  indeterminate
index [ɛ̃dɛks] nm (doigt) index finger; (d'un livre
  etc) index; **mettre à l'~** to blacklist
indicateur [ɛ̃dikatœr] nm (Police) informer;
  (Tech) gauge, indicator ▷ adj: **panneau ~**
  signpost; **indicateur des chemins de fer**
  railway timetable; **indicateur de rues** street
  directory
indicatif, -ive [ɛ̃dikatif, iv] adj: **à titre ~** for
  (your) information ▷ nm (Ling) indicative;
  (Radio) theme ou signature tune; (Tél) dialling
  code (BRIT), area code (US); **quel est l'~ de ...**
  what's the code for ...?
indication [ɛ̃dikasjɔ̃] nf indication;
  (renseignement) information no pl; **indications**
  nfpl (directives) instructions
indice [ɛ̃dis] nm (marque, signe) indication,
  sign; (Police: lors d'une enquête) clue; (Jur:
  présomption) piece of evidence; (Science, Écon,
  Tech) index; **~ de protection** (sun protection)
  factor
indicible [ɛ̃disibl] adj inexpressible
indien, ne [ɛ̃djɛ̃, jɛn] adj Indian ▷ nm/f: **I~,
  ne** Indian
indifféremment [ɛ̃diferamɑ̃] adv (sans
  distinction) equally (well)
indifférence [ɛ̃diferɑ̃s] nf indifference
indifférent, e [ɛ̃diferɑ̃, ɑ̃t] adj (peu intéressé)
  indifferent; **ça m'est ~** it doesn't matter to me;
  elle m'est ~e I am indifferent to her
indigène [ɛ̃diʒɛn] adj native, indigenous; (des
  gens du pays) local ▷ nm/f native
indigeste [ɛ̃diʒɛst] adj indigestible
indigestion [ɛ̃diʒɛstjɔ̃] nf indigestion no pl;
  avoir une ~ to have indigestion
indigne [ɛ̃diɲ] adj unworthy
indigner [ɛ̃diɲe] vt: **s'~ de qch** to get annoyed

about sth; **s'~ contre qn** to get annoyed
  with sb
indiqué, e [ɛ̃dike] adj (date, lieu) agreed;
  (traitement) appropriate; (conseillé) advisable
indiquer [ɛ̃dike] vt (suj: pendule, aiguille) to
  show; (: étiquette, panneau) to show, indicate;
  (renseigner sur) to point out, tell; (déterminer:
  date, lieu) to give, state; (signaler, dénoter) to
  indicate, point to; **~ qch/qn à qn** (montrer du
  doigt) to point sth/sb out to sb; (faire connaître:
  médecin, restaurant) to tell sb of sth/sb;
  pourriez-vous m'~ les toilettes/l'heure?
  could you direct me to the toilets/tell me the
  time?
indiscipliné, e [ɛ̃disipline] adj undisciplined
indiscret, -ète [ɛ̃diskrɛ, ɛt] adj indiscreet
indiscutable [ɛ̃diskytabl] adj indisputable
indispensable [ɛ̃dispɑ̃sabl] adj
  indispensable, essential
indisposé, e [ɛ̃dispoze] adj indisposed
indistinct, e [ɛ̃distɛ̃(kt), ɛ̃kt] adj indistinct;
  indistinctement adv (voir, prononcer)
  indistinctly; (sans distinction) indiscriminately
individu [ɛ̃dividy] nm individual; **individuel,
  le** adj (gén) individual; (responsabilité, propriété,
  liberté) personal; **chambre individuelle** single
  room; **maison individuelle** detached house
indolore [ɛ̃dɔlɔr] adj painless
Indonésie [ɛ̃dɔnezi] nf Indonesia
indu, e [ɛ̃dy] adj: **à une heure ~e** at some
  ungodly hour
indulgent, e [ɛ̃dylʒɑ̃, ɑ̃t] adj (parent, regard)
  indulgent; (juge, examinateur) lenient
industrialisé, e [ɛ̃dystrijalize] adj
  industrialized
industrie [ɛ̃dystri] nf industry; **industriel, le**
  adj industrial ▷ nm industrialist
inébranlable [inebrɑ̃labl] adj (masse,
  colonne) solid; (personne, certitude, foi)
  unshakeable
inédit, e [inedi, it] adj (correspondance, livre)
  hitherto unpublished; (spectacle, moyen) novel,
  original; (film) unreleased
inefficace [inefikas] adj (remède, moyen)
  ineffective; (machine, employé) inefficient
inégal, e, -aux [inegal, o] adj unequal;
  (irrégulier) uneven; **inégalable** adj matchless;
  inégalé, e adj (record) unequalled; (beauté)
  unrivalled; **inégalité** nf inequality
inépuisable [inepɥizabl] adj inexhaustible
inerte [inɛrt] adj (immobile) lifeless; (sans
  réaction) passive
inespéré, e [inɛspere] adj unexpected,
  unhoped-for
inestimable [inɛstimabl] adj priceless; (fig:
  bienfait) invaluable
inévitable [inevitabl] adj unavoidable; (fatal,
  habituel) inevitable
inexact, e [inɛgza(kt), akt] adj inaccurate

inexcusable [inɛkskyzabl] *adj* unforgivable
inexplicable [inɛksplikabl] *adj* inexplicable
in extremis [inɛkstʀemis] *adv* at the last
minute ▷ *adj* last-minute
infaillible [ɛ̃fajibl] *adj* infallible
infarctus [ɛ̃faʀktys] *nm*: ~ **(du myocarde)**
coronary (thrombosis)
infatigable [ɛ̃fatigabl] *adj* tireless
infect, e [ɛ̃fɛkt] *adj* revolting; (*personne*)
obnoxious; (*temps*) foul
infecter [ɛ̃fɛkte] *vt* (*atmosphère, eau*) to
contaminate; (*Méd*) to infect; **s'infecter**
to become infected *ou* septic; **infection** *nf*
infection; (*puanteur*) stench
inférieur, e [ɛ̃feʀjœʀ] *adj* lower; (*en qualité,
intelligence*) inferior; ~ **à** (*somme, quantité*) less
ou smaller than; (*moins bon que*) inferior to
infernal, e, -aux [ɛ̃fɛʀnal, o] *adj*
(*insupportable: chaleur, rythme*) infernal; (:
enfant) horrid; (*satanique, effrayant*) diabolical
infidèle [ɛ̃fidɛl] *adj* unfaithful
infiltrer [ɛ̃filtʀe]: **s'infiltrer** *vr*: **s'~ dans** to
get into; (*liquide*) to seep through; (*fig: groupe,
ennemi*) to infiltrate
infime [ɛ̃fim] *adj* minute, tiny
infini, e [ɛ̃fini] *adj* infinite ▷ *nm* infinity; **à l'~**
endlessly; **infiniment** *adv* infinitely; **infinité**
nf: **une infinité de** an infinite number of
infinitif [ɛ̃finitif] *nm* infinitive
infirme [ɛ̃fiʀm] *adj* disabled ▷ *nm/f* disabled
person
infirmerie [ɛ̃fiʀməʀi] *nf* medical room
infirmier, -ière [ɛ̃fiʀmje] *nm/f* nurse;
infirmière chef sister
infirmité [ɛ̃fiʀmite] *nf* disability
inflammable [ɛ̃flamabl] *adj* (in)flammable
inflation [ɛ̃flasjɔ̃] *nf* inflation
influençable [ɛ̃flyɑ̃sabl] *adj* easily influenced
influence [ɛ̃flyɑ̃s] *nf* influence; **influencer** *vt*
to influence; **influent, e** *adj* influential
informaticien, ne [ɛ̃fɔʀmatisjɛ̃, jɛn] *nm/f*
computer scientist
information [ɛ̃fɔʀmasjɔ̃] *nf* (*renseignement*)
piece of information; (*Presse, TV: nouvelle*) item
of news; (*diffusion de renseignements, Inform*)
information; (*Jur*) inquiry, investigation;
informations *nfpl* (*TV*) news *sg*
informatique [ɛ̃fɔʀmatik] *nf* (*technique*)
data processing; (*science*) computer science
▷ *adj* computer *cpd*; **informatiser** *vt* to
computerize
informer [ɛ̃fɔʀme] *vt*: ~ **qn (de)** to inform sb
(of); **s'informer** *vr*: **s'~ (de/si)** to inquire *ou*
find out (about/whether); **s'~ sur** to inform
o.s. about
infos [ɛ̃fo] *nfpl*: **les** ~ the news *sg*
infraction [ɛ̃fʀaksjɔ̃] *nf* offence; ~ **à** violation
ou breach of; **être en** ~ to be in breach of the
law

infranchissable [ɛ̃fʀɑ̃ʃisabl] *adj* impassable;
(*fig*) insuperable
infrarouge [ɛ̃fʀaʀuʒ] *adj* infrared
infrastructure [ɛ̃fʀastʀyktyʀ] *nf* (*Aviat, Mil*)
ground installations *pl*; (*Écon: touristique etc*)
infrastructure
infuser [ɛ̃fyze] *vt, vi* (*thé*) to brew; (*tisane*) to
infuse; **infusion** *nf* (*tisane*) herb tea
ingénier [ɛ̃ʒenje]: **s'ingénier** *vi*: **s'~ à faire** to
strive to do
ingénierie [ɛ̃ʒeniʀi] *nf* engineering
ingénieur [ɛ̃ʒenjœʀ] *nm* engineer; **ingénieur
du son** sound engineer
ingénieux, -euse [ɛ̃ʒenjø, jøz] *adj* ingenious,
clever
ingrat, e [ɛ̃gʀa, at] *adj* (*personne*)
ungrateful; (*travail, sujet*) thankless; (*visage*)
unprepossessing
ingrédient [ɛ̃gʀedjɑ̃] *nm* ingredient
inhabité, e [inabite] *adj* uninhabited
inhabituel, le [inabitɥɛl] *adj* unusual
inhibition [inibisjɔ̃] *nf* inhibition
inhumain, e [inymɛ̃, ɛn] *adj* inhuman
inimaginable [inimaʒinabl] *adj*
unimaginable
ininterrompu, e [inɛ̃teʀɔ̃py] *adj* (*file, série*)
unbroken; (*flot, vacarme*) uninterrupted, non-
stop; (*effort*) unremitting, continuous; (*suite,
ligne*) unbroken
initial, e, -aux [inisjal, jo] *adj* initial;
initiales *nfpl* (*d'un nom, sigle etc*) initials
initiation [inisjasjɔ̃] *nf*: ~ **à** introduction to
initiative [inisjativ] *nf* initiative
initier [inisje] *vt*: ~ **qn à** to initiate sb into;
(*faire découvrir: art, jeu*) to introduce sb to
injecter [ɛ̃ʒekte] *vt* to inject; **injection** *nf*
injection; **à injection** (*Auto*) fuel injection *cpd*
injure [ɛ̃ʒyʀ] *nf* insult, abuse *no pl*; **injurier** *vt*
to insult, abuse; **injurieux, -euse** *adj* abusive,
insulting
injuste [ɛ̃ʒyst] *adj* unjust, unfair; **injustice**
nf injustice
inlassable [ɛ̃lasabl] *adj* tireless
inné, e [i(n)ne] *adj* innate, inborn
innocent, e [inɔsɑ̃, ɑ̃t] *adj* innocent;
innocenter *vt* to clear, prove innocent
innombrable [i(n)nɔ̃bʀabl] *adj* innumerable
innover [inɔve] *vi* to break new ground
inoccupé, e [inɔkype] *adj* unoccupied
inodore [inɔdɔʀ] *adj* (*gaz*) odourless; (*fleur*)
scentless
inoffensif, -ive [inɔfɑ̃sif, iv] *adj* harmless,
innocuous
inondation [inɔ̃dasjɔ̃] *nf* flood
inonder [inɔ̃de] *vt* to flood; ~ **de** to flood with
inopportun, e [inɔpɔʀtœ̃, yn] *adj* ill-timed,
untimely
inoubliable [inublijabl] *adj* unforgettable
inouï, e [inwi] *adj* unheard-of, extraordinary

inox [inɔks] *nm* stainless steel
inquiet, -ète [ɛ̃kjɛ, ɛ̃kjɛt] *adj* anxious;
inquiétant, e *adj* worrying, disturbing;
inquiéter *vt* to worry; **s'inquiéter** to worry;
s'inquiéter de to worry about; (*s'enquérir de*)
to inquire about; **inquiétude** *nf* anxiety
insaisissable [ɛ̃sezisabl] *adj* (*fugitif, ennemi*)
elusive; (*différence, nuance*) imperceptible
insalubre [ɛ̃salybʀ] *adj* insalubrious
insatisfait, e [ɛ̃satisfɛ, ɛt] *adj* (*non comblé*)
unsatisfied; (*mécontent*) dissatisfied
inscription [ɛ̃skʀipsjɔ̃] *nf* inscription;
(*immatriculation*) enrolment
inscrire [ɛ̃skʀiʀ] *vt* (*marquer: sur son calepin
etc*) to note *ou* write down; (: *sur un mur, une
affiche etc*) to write; (: *dans la pierre, le métal*) to
inscribe; (*mettre: sur une liste, un budget etc*) to
put down; **s'inscrire** (*pour une excursion etc*)
to put one's name down; **s'~ (à)** (*club, parti*)
to join; (*université*) to register *ou* enrol (at);
(*examen, concours*) to register (for); **~ qn à** (*club,
parti*) to enrol sb at
insecte [ɛ̃sɛkt] *nm* insect; **insecticide** *nm*
insecticide
insensé, e [ɛ̃sɑ̃se] *adj* mad
insensible [ɛ̃sɑ̃sibl] *adj* (*nerf, membre*) numb;
(*dur, indifférent*) insensitive
inséparable [ɛ̃sepaʀabl] *adj* inseparable
▷ *nm*: **~s** (*oiseaux*) lovebirds
insigne [ɛ̃siɲ] *nm* (*d'un parti, club*) badge;
(*d'une fonction*) insignia ▷ *adj* distinguished
insignifiant, e [ɛ̃siɲifjɑ̃, jɑ̃t] *adj*
insignificant; trivial
insinuer [ɛ̃sinɥe] *vt* to insinuate; **s'insinuer
dans** (*fig*) to worm one's way into
insipide [ɛ̃sipid] *adj* insipid
insister [ɛ̃siste] *vi* to insist; (*continuer à sonner*)
to keep on trying; **~ sur** (*détail, sujet*) to lay
stress on
insolation [ɛ̃sɔlasjɔ̃] *nf* (*Méd*) sunstroke *no pl*
insolent, e [ɛ̃sɔlɑ̃, ɑ̃t] *adj* insolent
insolite [ɛ̃sɔlit] *adj* strange, unusual
insomnie [ɛ̃sɔmni] *nf* insomnia *no pl*; **avoir
des ~s** to sleep badly, not be able to sleep
insouciant, e [ɛ̃susjɑ̃, jɑ̃t] *adj* carefree; **~ du
danger** heedless of (the) danger
insoupçonnable [ɛ̃supsɔnabl] *adj*
unsuspected; (*personne*) above suspicion
insoupçonné, e [ɛ̃supsɔne] *adj* unsuspected
insoutenable [ɛ̃sut(ə)nabl] *adj* (*argument*)
untenable; (*chaleur*) unbearable
inspecter [ɛ̃spɛkte] *vt* to inspect; **inspecteur,
-trice** *nm/f* inspector; **inspecteur
d'Académie** (regional) director of education;
inspecteur des finances ≈ tax inspector
(*BRIT*), ≈ Internal Revenue Service agent (*US*);
inspecteur (de police) (police) inspector;
inspection *nf* inspection
inspirer [ɛ̃spiʀe] *vt* (*gén*) to inspire ▷ *vi*

(*aspirer*) to breathe in; **s'inspirer** *vr*: **s'~ de** to
be inspired by
instable [ɛ̃stabl] *adj* unstable; (*meuble,
équilibre*) unsteady; (*temps*) unsettled
installation [ɛ̃stalasjɔ̃] *nf* (*mise en place*)
installation; **installations** *nfpl* (*de sport,
dans un camping*) facilities; **l'installation
électrique** wiring
installer [ɛ̃stale] *vt* (*loger, placer*) to put;
(*meuble, gaz, électricité*) to put in; (*rideau,
étagère, tente*) to put up; (*appartement*) to fit
out; **s'installer** (*s'établir: artisan, dentiste etc*)
to set o.s. up; (*se loger*) to settle; (*emménager*)
to settle in; (*sur un siège, à un emplacement*) to
settle (down); (*fig: maladie, grève*) to take a
firm hold
instance [ɛ̃stɑ̃s] *nf* (*Admin: autorité*) authority;
affaire en ~ matter pending; **être en ~ de
divorce** to be awaiting a divorce
instant [ɛ̃stɑ̃] *nm* moment, instant; **dans un
~** in a moment; **à l'~** this instant; **je l'ai vu à
l'~** I've just this minute seen him, I saw him a
moment ago; **pour l'~** for the moment, for the
time being
instantané, e [ɛ̃stɑ̃tane] *adj* (*lait, café*)
instant; (*explosion, mort*) instantaneous ▷ *nm*
snapshot
instar [ɛ̃staʀ]: **à l'~ de** *prép* following the
example of, like
instaurer [ɛ̃stɔʀe] *vt* to institute; (*couvre-
feu*) to impose; **s'instaurer** *vr* (*paix*) to be
established; (*doute*) to set in
instinct [ɛ̃stɛ̃] *nm* instinct; **instinctivement**
adv instinctively
instituer [ɛ̃stitɥe] *vt* to establish
institut [ɛ̃stity] *nm* institute; **institut de
beauté** beauty salon; **Institut universitaire
de technologie** ≈ polytechnic
instituteur, -trice [ɛ̃stitytœʀ, tʀis] *nm/f*
(primary school) teacher
institution [ɛ̃stitysjɔ̃] *nf* institution; (*collège*)
private school; **institutions** *nfpl* (*structures
politiques et sociales*) institutions
instructif, -ive [ɛ̃stʀyktif, iv] *adj* instructive
instruction [ɛ̃stʀyksjɔ̃] *nf* (*enseignement,
savoir*) education; (*Jur*) (preliminary)
investigation and hearing; **instructions**
nfpl (*ordres, mode d'emploi*) instructions;
instruction civique civics *sg*
instruire [ɛ̃stʀɥiʀ] *vt* (*élèves*) to teach;
(*recrues*) to train; (*Jur: affaire*) to conduct the
investigation for; **s'instruire** to educate o.s.;
instruit, e *adj* educated
instrument [ɛ̃stʀymɑ̃] *nm* instrument;
instrument à cordes/à vent stringed/
wind instrument; **instrument de mesure**
measuring instrument; **instrument de
musique** musical instrument; **instrument de
travail** (working) tool

insu [ɛ̃sy] *nm*: **à l'~ de qn** without sb knowing (it)

insuffisant, e [ɛ̃syfizɑ̃, ɑ̃t] *adj* (*en quantité*) insufficient; (*en qualité*) inadequate; (*sur une copie*) poor

insulaire [ɛ̃sylɛʀ] *adj* island *cpd*; (*attitude*) insular

insuline [ɛ̃sylin] *nf* insulin

insulte [ɛ̃sylt] *nf* insult; **insulter** *vt* to insult

insupportable [ɛ̃sypɔʀtabl] *adj* unbearable

insurmontable [ɛ̃syʀmɔ̃tabl] *adj* (*difficulté*) insuperable; (*aversion*) unconquerable

intact, e [ɛ̃takt] *adj* intact

intarissable [ɛ̃taʀisabl] *adj* inexhaustible

intégral, e, -aux [ɛ̃tegʀal, o] *adj* complete; **texte ~** unabridged version; **bronzage ~** all-over suntan; **intégralement** *adv* in full; **intégralité** *nf* whole; **dans son intégralité** in full; **intégrant, e** *adj*: **faire partie intégrante de** to be an integral part of

intègre [ɛ̃tegʀ] *adj* upright

intégrer [ɛ̃tegʀe]: **s'intégrer** *vr*: **s'~ à** *ou* **dans qch** to become integrated into sth; **bien s'~** to fit in

intégrisme [ɛ̃tegʀism] *nm* fundamentalism

intellectuel, le [ɛ̃telɛktɥel] *adj* intellectual ▷ *nm/f* intellectual; (*péj*) highbrow

intelligence [ɛ̃teliʒɑ̃s] *nf* intelligence; (*compréhension*): **l'~ de** the understanding of; (*complicité*): **regard d'~** glance of complicity; (*accord*): **vivre en bonne ~ avec qn** to be on good terms with sb

intelligent, e [ɛ̃teliʒɑ̃, ɑ̃t] *adj* intelligent

intelligible [ɛ̃teliʒibl] *adj* intelligible

intempéries [ɛ̃tɑ̃peʀi] *nfpl* bad weather *sg*

intenable [ɛ̃t(ə)nabl] *adj* (*chaleur*) unbearable

intendant, e [ɛ̃tɑ̃dɑ̃] *nm/f* (*Mil*) quartermaster; (*Scol*) bursar

intense [ɛ̃tɑ̃s] *adj* intense; **intensif, -ive** *adj* intensive; **un cours intensif** a crash course

intenter [ɛ̃tɑ̃te] *vt*: **~ un procès contre** *ou* **à** to start proceedings against

intention [ɛ̃tɑ̃sjɔ̃] *nf* intention; (*Jur*) intent; **avoir l'~ de faire** to intend to do; **à l'~ de** for; (*renseignement*) for the benefit of; (*film, ouvrage*) aimed at; **à cette ~** with this aim in view; **intentionné, e** *adj*: **bien intentionné** well-meaning *ou* -intentioned; **mal intentionné** ill-intentioned

interactif, -ive [ɛ̃teʀaktif, iv] *adj* (*Comput*) interactive

intercepter [ɛ̃teʀsepte] *vt* to intercept; (*lumière, chaleur*) to cut off

interchangeable [ɛ̃teʀʃɑ̃ʒabl] *adj* interchangeable

interdiction [ɛ̃teʀdiksjɔ̃] *nf* ban; **interdiction de fumer** no smoking

interdire [ɛ̃teʀdiʀ] *vt* to forbid; (*Admin*) to ban, prohibit; (: *journal, livre*) to ban; **~ à qn de faire** to forbid sb to do; (*suj: empêchement*) to prevent sb from doing

interdit, e [ɛ̃teʀdi, it] *pp de* **interdire** ▷ *adj* (*stupéfait*) taken aback; **film ~ aux moins de 18/12 ans** ≈ 18-/12A-rated film; **"stationnement ~"** "no parking"

intéressant, e [ɛ̃teʀesɑ̃, ɑ̃t] *adj* interesting; (*avantageux*) attractive

intéressé, e [ɛ̃teʀese] *adj* (*parties*) involved, concerned; (*amitié, motifs*) self-interested

intéresser [ɛ̃teʀese] *vt* (*captiver*) to interest; (*toucher*) to be of interest to; (*Admin: concerner*) to affect, concern; **s'intéresser** *vr*: **s'~ à** to be interested in

intérêt [ɛ̃teʀɛ] *nm* interest; (*égoïsme*) self-interest; **tu as ~ à accepter** it's in your interest to accept; **tu as ~ à te dépêcher** you'd better hurry

intérieur, e [ɛ̃teʀjœʀ] *adj* (*mur, escalier, poche*) inside; (*commerce, politique*) domestic; (*cour, calme, vie*) inner; (*navigation*) inland ▷ *nm*: **l'~** (*d'une maison, d'un récipient etc*) the inside; (*d'un pays, aussi: décor, mobilier*) the interior; **à l'~ (de)** inside; **ministère de l'I~e** ≈ Home Office (*BRIT*), ≈ Department of the Interior (*US*); **intérieurement** *adv* inwardly

intérim [ɛ̃teʀim] *nm* interim period; **faire de l'~** to temp; **assurer l'~ (de)** to deputize (for); **par ~** interim

intérimaire [ɛ̃teʀimɛʀ] *adj* (*directeur, ministre*) acting; (*secrétaire, personnel*) temporary ▷ *nm/f* (*secrétaire*) temporary secretary, temp (*BRIT*)

interlocuteur, -trice [ɛ̃teʀlɔkytœʀ, tʀis] *nm/f* speaker; **son ~** the person he was speaking to

intermédiaire [ɛ̃teʀmedjɛʀ] *adj* intermediate; (*solution*) temporary ▷ *nm/f* intermediary; (*Comm*) middleman; **sans ~** directly; **par l'~ de** through

interminable [ɛ̃teʀminabl] *adj* endless

intermittence [ɛ̃teʀmitɑ̃s] *nf*: **par ~** sporadically, intermittently

internat [ɛ̃teʀna] *nm* boarding school

international, e, -aux [ɛ̃teʀnasjɔnal, o] *adj, nm/f* international

internaute [ɛ̃teʀnot] *nm/f* Internet user

interne [ɛ̃teʀn] *adj* internal ▷ *nm/f* (*Scol*) boarder; (*Méd*) houseman

Internet [ɛ̃teʀnɛt] *nm*: **l'~** the Internet

interpeller [ɛ̃teʀpəle] *vt* (*appeler*) to call out to; (*apostropher*) to shout at; (*Police, Pol*) to question; (*concerner*) to concern

interphone [ɛ̃teʀfɔn] *nm* intercom; (*d'immeuble*) entry phone

interposer [ɛ̃teʀpoze] *vt*: **s'interposer** to intervene; **par personnes interposées** through a third party

interprète [ɛ̃teʀpʀɛt] *nm/f* interpreter; (*porte-*

parole) spokesperson; **pourriez-vous nous servir d' ~?** could you act as our interpreter?

interpréter [ɛ̃tɛʀpʀete] *vt* to interpret; *(jouer)* to play; *(chanter)* to sing

interrogatif, -ive [ɛ̃teʀɔgatif, iv] *adj (Ling)* interrogative

interrogation [ɛ̃teʀɔgasjɔ̃] *nf* question; *(action)* questioning; **~ écrite/orale** *(Scol)* written/oral test

interrogatoire [ɛ̃teʀɔgatwaʀ] *nm (Police)* questioning *no pl; (Jur, aussi fig)* cross-examination

interroger [ɛ̃teʀɔʒe] *vt* to question; *(Inform)* to consult; *(Scol)* to test

interrompre [ɛ̃teʀɔ̃pʀ] *vt (gén)* to interrupt; *(négociations)* to break off; *(match)* to stop; **s'interrompre** to break off; **interrupteur** *nm* switch; **interruption** *nf* interruption; *(pause)* break; **sans interruption** without stopping; **interruption (volontaire) de grossesse** termination (of pregnancy)

intersection [ɛ̃tɛʀseksjɔ̃] *nf* intersection

intervalle [ɛ̃tɛʀval] *nm (espace)* space; *(de temps)* interval; **dans l'~** in the meantime; **à deux jours d'~** two days apart

intervenir [ɛ̃tɛʀvəniʀ] *vi (gén)* to intervene; **~ auprès de qn** to intervene with sb; **intervention** *nf* intervention; *(discours)* speech; **intervention chirurgicale** *(Méd)* (surgical) operation

interview [ɛ̃tɛʀvju] *nf* interview

intestin [ɛ̃tɛstɛ̃] *nm* intestine

intime [ɛ̃tim] *adj* intimate; *(vie)* private; *(conviction)* inmost; *(dîner, cérémonie)* quiet ▷ *nm/f* close friend; **un journal ~** a diary

intimider [ɛ̃timide] *vt* to intimidate

intimité [ɛ̃timite] *nf:* **dans l'~** in private; *(sans formalités)* with only a few friends, quietly

intolérable [ɛ̃tɔleʀabl] *adj* intolerable

intox [ɛ̃tɔks] *(fam) nf* brainwashing

intoxication [ɛ̃tɔksikasjɔ̃] *nf:* **intoxication alimentaire** food poisoning

intoxiquer [ɛ̃tɔksike] *vt* to poison; *(fig)* to brainwash

intraitable [ɛ̃tʀɛtabl] *adj* inflexible, uncompromising

intransigeant, e [ɛ̃tʀɑ̃ziʒɑ̃, ɑ̃t] *adj* intransigent

intrépide [ɛ̃tʀepid] *adj* dauntless

intrigue [ɛ̃tʀig] *nf (scénario)* plot; **intriguer** *vt* to puzzle, intrigue

introduction [ɛ̃tʀɔdyksjɔ̃] *nf* introduction

introduire [ɛ̃tʀɔdɥiʀ] *vt* to introduce; *(visiteur)* to show in; *(aiguille, clef)*: **~ qch dans** to insert *ou* introduce sth into; **s'introduire** *vr (techniques, usages)* to be introduced; **s'~ (dans)** to get in(to); *(dans un groupe)* to get o.s. accepted (into)

introuvable [ɛ̃tʀuvabl] *adj* which cannot be found; *(Comm)* unobtainable

intrus, e [ɛ̃tʀy, yz] *nm/f* intruder

intuition [ɛ̃tɥisjɔ̃] *nf* intuition

inusable [inyzabl] *adj* hard-wearing

inutile [inytil] *adj* useless; *(superflu)* unnecessary; **inutilement** *adv* unnecessarily; **inutilisable** *adj* unusable

invalide [ɛ̃valid] *adj* disabled ▷ *nm:* **~ de guerre** disabled ex-serviceman

invariable [ɛ̃vaʀjabl] *adj* invariable

invasion [ɛ̃vazjɔ̃] *nf* invasion

inventaire [ɛ̃vɑ̃tɛʀ] *nm* inventory; *(Comm: liste)* stocklist; *(: opération)* stocktaking *no pl*

inventer [ɛ̃vɑ̃te] *vt* to invent; *(subterfuge)* to devise, invent; *(histoire, excuse)* to make up, invent; **inventeur** *nm* inventor; **inventif, -ive** *adj* inventive; **invention** *nf* invention

inverse [ɛ̃vɛʀs] *adj* opposite ▷ *nm:* **l'~** the opposite; **dans l'ordre ~** in the reverse order; **en sens ~** in *(ou* from) the opposite direction; **dans le sens ~ des aiguilles d'une montre** anticlockwise; **tu t'es trompé, c'est l'~** you've got it wrong, it's the other way round; **inversement** *adv* conversely; **inverser** *vt* to invert, reverse; *(Élec)* to reverse

investir [ɛ̃vɛstiʀ] *vt* to invest; **~ qn de** *(d'une fonction, d'un pouvoir)* to vest *ou* invest sb with; **s'investir** *vr:* **s'~ dans** *(Psych)* to put a lot into; **investissement** *nm* investment

invisible [ɛ̃vizibl] *adj* invisible

invitation [ɛ̃vitasjɔ̃] *nf* invitation

invité, e [ɛ̃vite] *nm/f* guest

inviter [ɛ̃vite] *vt* to invite; **~ qn à faire qch** to invite sb to do sth

invivable [ɛ̃vivabl] *adj* unbearable

involontaire [ɛ̃vɔlɔ̃tɛʀ] *adj (mouvement)* involuntary; *(insulte)* unintentional; *(complice)* unwitting

invoquer [ɛ̃vɔke] *vt (Dieu, muse)* to call upon, invoke; *(prétexte)* to put forward (as an excuse); *(loi, texte)* to refer to

invraisemblable [ɛ̃vʀɛsɑ̃blabl] *adj (fait, nouvelle)* unlikely, improbable; *(insolence, habit)* incredible

iode [jɔd] *nm* iodine

irai *etc* [iʀe] *vb voir* **aller**

Irak [iʀak] *nm* Iraq; **irakien, ne** *adj* Iraqi ▷ *nm/f:* **Irakien, ne** Iraqi

Iran [iʀɑ̃] *nm* Iran; **iranien, ne** *adj* Iranian ▷ *nm/f:* **Iranien, ne** Iranian

irions *etc* [iʀjɔ̃] *vb voir* **aller**

iris [iʀis] *nm* iris

irlandais, e [iʀlɑ̃dɛ, ɛz] *adj* Irish ▷ *nm/f:* **I~, e** Irishman(-woman)

Irlande [iʀlɑ̃d] *nf* Ireland; **la République d'~** the Irish Republic; **la mer d'~** the Irish Sea; **Irlande du Nord** Northern Ireland

ironie [iʀɔni] *nf* irony; **ironique** *adj* ironical; **ironiser** *vi* to be ironical

irons *etc* [iʀɔ̃] *vb voir* **aller**
irradier [iʀadje] *vt* to irradiate
irraisonné, e [iʀɛzɔne] *adj* irrational
irrationnel, le [iʀasjɔnɛl] *adj* irrational
irréalisable [iʀealizabl] *adj* unrealizable;
(*projet*) impracticable
irrécupérable [iʀekypeʀabl] *adj* beyond
repair; (*personne*) beyond redemption
irréel, le [iʀeɛl] *adj* unreal
irréfléchi, e [iʀefleʃi] *adj* thoughtless
irrégularité [iʀegylaʀite] *nf* irregularity; (*de
travail, d'effort, de qualité*) unevenness *no pl*
irrégulier, -ière [iʀegylje, jɛʀ] *adj* irregular;
(*travail, effort, qualité*) uneven; (*élève, athlète*)
erratic
irrémédiable [iʀemedjabl] *adj* irreparable
irremplaçable [iʀɑ̃plasabl] *adj* irreplaceable
irréparable [iʀepaʀabl] *adj* (*objet*) beyond
repair; (*dommage etc*) irreparable
irréprochable [iʀepʀɔʃabl] *adj*
irreproachable, beyond reproach; (*tenue*)
impeccable
irrésistible [iʀezistibl] *adj* irresistible; (*besoin,
désir, preuve, logique*) compelling; (*amusant*)
hilarious
irrésolu, e [iʀezɔly] *adj* (*personne*) irresolute;
(*problème*) unresolved
irrespectueux, -euse [iʀɛspɛktɥø, øz] *adj*
disrespectful
irresponsable [iʀɛspɔ̃sabl] *adj* irresponsible
irriguer [iʀige] *vt* to irrigate
irritable [iʀitabl] *adj* irritable
irriter [iʀite] *vt* to irritate
irruption [iʀypsjɔ̃] *nf*: **faire ~ (chez qn)** to
burst in (on sb)
Islam [islam] *nm*: **l'~** Islam; **islamique** *adj*
Islamic; **islamophobie** *nf* Islamophobia
Islande [islɑ̃d] *nf* Iceland
isolant, e [izɔlɑ̃, ɑ̃t] *adj* insulating;
(*insonorisant*) soundproofing
isolation [izɔlasjɔ̃] *nf* insulation; **~
acoustique** soundproofing
isolé, e [izɔle] *adj* isolated; (*contre le froid*)
insulated
isoler [izɔle] *vt* to isolate; (*prisonnier*) to put in
solitary confinement; (*ville*) to cut off, isolate;
(*contre le froid*) to insulate; **s'isoler** *vi* to isolate
o.s.
Israël [israɛl] *nm* Israel; **israélien, ne** *adj*
Israeli ▷ *nm/f*: **Israélien, ne** Israeli; **israélite**
adj Jewish ▷ *nm/f*: **Israélite** Jew (Jewess)
issu, e [isy] *adj*: **~ de** (*né de*) descended
from; (*résultant de*) stemming from; **issue**
nf (*ouverture, sortie*) exit; (*solution*) way out,
solution; (*dénouement*) outcome; **à l'issue de**
at the conclusion *ou* close of; **voie sans issue**
dead end; **issue de secours** emergency exit
Italie [itali] *nf* Italy; **italien, ne** *adj* Italian
▷ *nm/f*: **Italien, ne** Italian ▷ *nm* (*Ling*) Italian

italique [italik] *nm*: **en ~** in italics
itinéraire [itineʀɛʀ] *nm* itinerary, route;
itinéraire bis alternative route
IUT *sigle m* = **Institut universitaire de
technologie**
IVG *sigle f* (= *interruption volontaire de grossesse*)
abortion
ivoire [ivwaʀ] *nm* ivory
ivre [ivʀ] *adj* drunk; **~ de** (*colère, bonheur*) wild
with; **ivrogne** *nm/f* drunkard

J

j' [ʒ] *pron voir* **je**

jacinthe [ʒasɛ̃t] *nf* hyacinth

jadis [ʒadis] *adv* long ago

jaillir [ʒajiʀ] *vi (liquide)* to spurt out; *(cris, réponses)* to burst forth

jais [ʒɛ] *nm* jet; **(d'un noir) de ~** jet-black

jalousie [ʒaluzi] *nf* jealousy; *(store)* slatted blind

jaloux, -ouse [ʒalu, uz] *adj* jealous; **être ~ de** to be jealous of

jamaïquain, e [ʒamaikɛ̃, -ɛn] *adj* Jamaican ▷ *nm/f:* **J~, e** Jamaican

Jamaïque [ʒamaik] *nf:* **la ~** Jamaica

jamais [ʒamɛ] *adv* never; *(sans négation)* ever; **ne ... ~** never; **je ne suis ~ allé en Espagne** I've never been to Spain; **si ~ vous passez dans la région, venez nous voir** if you happen to be/if you're ever in this area, come and see us; **à ~** for ever

jambe [ʒɑ̃b] *nf* leg

jambon [ʒɑ̃bɔ̃] *nm* ham

jante [ʒɑ̃t] *nf (wheel)* rim

janvier [ʒɑ̃vje] *nm* January

Japon [ʒapɔ̃] *nm* Japan; **japonais, e** *adj* Japanese ▷ *nm/f:* **Japonais, e** Japanese ▷ *nm (Ling)* Japanese

jardin [ʒaʀdɛ̃] *nm* garden; **jardin d'enfants** nursery school; **jardinage** *nm* gardening; **jardiner** *vi* to do some gardening; **jardinier, -ière** *nm/f* gardener; **jardinière** *nf* planter; *(de fenêtre)* window box; **jardinière de légumes** *(Culin)* mixed vegetables

jargon [ʒaʀgɔ̃] *nm (baragouin)* gibberish; *(langue professionnelle)* jargon

jarret [ʒaʀɛ] *nm* back of knee; *(Culin)* knuckle, shin

jauge [ʒoʒ] *nf (instrument)* gauge; **jauge (de niveau) d'huile** *(Auto)* dipstick

jaune [ʒon] *adj, nm* yellow ▷ *adv (fam):* **rire ~** to laugh on the other side of one's face; **jaune d'œuf** *(egg)* yolk; **jaunir** *vi, vt* to turn yellow; **jaunisse** *nf* jaundice

Javel [ʒavɛl] *nf voir* **eau**

javelot [ʒavlo] *nm* javelin

je, j' [ʒə] *pron* I

jean [dʒin] *nm* jeans *pl*

Jésus-Christ [ʒezykʀi(st)] *n* Jesus Christ; **600 avant/après** *ou* **J.-C.** 600 B.C./A.D.

jet [ʒɛ] *nm (lancer: action)* throwing *no pl*; *(: résultat)* throw; *(jaillissement: d'eaux)* jet; *(: de sang)* spurt; **jet d'eau** spray

jetable [ʒ(ə)tabl] *adj* disposable

jetée [ʒəte] *nf* jetty; *(grande)* pier

jeter [ʒ(ə)te] *vt (gén)* to throw; *(se défaire de)* to throw away *ou* out; **~ qch à qn** to throw sth to sb; *(de façon agressive)* to throw sth at sb; **~ un coup d'œil (à)** to take a look (at); **~ un sort à qn** to cast a spell on sb; **se ~ sur qn** to rush at sb; **se ~ dans** *(suj: fleuve)* to flow into

jeton [ʒ(ə)tɔ̃] *nm (au jeu)* counter

jette *etc* [ʒɛt] *vb voir* **jeter**

jeu, x [ʒø] *nm (divertissement, Tech: d'une pièce)* play; *(Tennis: partie, Football etc: façon de jouer)* game; *(Théâtre etc)* acting; *(série d'objets, jouet)* set; *(Cartes)* hand; *(au casino):* **le ~** gambling; **remettre en ~** *(Football)* to throw in; **être en ~** *(fig)* to be at stake; **entrer/mettre en ~** *(fig)* to come/bring into play; **jeu de cartes** pack of cards; **jeu d'échecs** chess set; **jeu de hasard** game of chance; **jeu de mots** pun; **jeu de société** board game; **jeu télévisé** television quiz; **jeu vidéo** video game

jeudi [ʒødi] *nm* Thursday

jeun [ʒœ̃]: **à ~** *adv* on an empty stomach; **être à ~** to have eaten nothing; **rester à ~** not to eat anything

jeune [ʒœn] *adj* young; **jeunes** *nmpl:* **les ~s** young people; **jeune fille** girl; **jeune homme** young man; **jeunes gens** young people

jeûne [ʒøn] *nm* fast

jeunesse [ʒœnɛs] *nf* youth; *(aspect)* youthfulness

joaillier, -ière [ʒɔaje, -jɛʀ] *nm/f* jeweller

jogging [dʒɔgin] *nm* jogging; *(survêtement)* tracksuit; **faire du ~** to go jogging

joie [ʒwa] *nf* joy

joindre [ʒwɛ̃dʀ] *vt* to join; *(à une lettre):* **~ qch à** to enclose sth with; *(contacter)* to contact, get in touch with; **se ~ à qn** to join sb; **se ~ à**

qch to join in sth

joint, e [ʒwɛ̃, ɛ̃t] *adj*: **pièce ~e** (*de lettre*) enclosure; (*de mail*) attachment ▷ *nm* joint; (*ligne*) join; **joint de culasse** cylinder head gasket

joli, e [ʒɔli] *adj* pretty, attractive; **une ~e somme/situation** a tidy sum/a nice little job; **c'est du ~!** (*ironique*) that's very nice!; **c'est bien ~, mais ...** that's all very well but ...

jonc [ʒɔ̃] *nm* (*bul*) rush

jonction [ʒɔ̃ksjɔ̃] *nf* junction

jongleur, -euse [ʒɔ̃glœr, øz] *nm/f* juggler

jonquille [ʒɔ̃kij] *nf* daffodil

Jordanie [ʒɔrdani] *nf*: **la ~** Jordan

joue [ʒu] *nf* cheek

jouer [ʒwe] *vt* to play; (*somme d'argent, réputation*) to stake, wager; (*simuler: sentiment*) to affect, feign ▷ *vi* to play; (*Théâtre, Cinéma*) to act; (*au casino*) to gamble; (*bois, porte: se voiler*) to warp; (*clef, pièce: avoir du jeu*) to be loose; **~ sur** (*miser*) to gamble on; **~ de** (*Mus*) to play; **~ à** (*jeu, sport, roulette*) to play; **~ un tour à qn** to play a trick on sb; **~ serré** to play a close game; **~ la comédie** to put on an act; **à toi/nous de ~** it's your/our go *ou* turn; **bien joué!** well done!; **on joue Hamlet au théâtre X** Hamlet is on at the X theatre

jouet [ʒwe] *nm* toy; **être le ~ de** (*illusion etc*) to be the victim of

joueur, -euse [ʒwœr, øz] *nm/f* player; **être beau/mauvais ~** to be a good/bad loser

jouir [ʒwir] *vi* (*sexe: fam*) to come ▷ *vt*: **~ de** to enjoy

jour [ʒur] *nm* day; (*opposé à la nuit*) day, daytime; (*clarté*) daylight; (*fig: aspect*) light; (*ouverture*) gap; **de ~** (*crème, service*) day *cpd*; **travailler de ~** to work during the day; **voyager de ~** to travel by day; **au ~ le ~** from day to day; **de nos ~s** these days; **du ~ au lendemain** overnight; **il fait ~** it's daylight; **au grand ~** (*fig*) in the open; **mettre au ~** to disclose; **mettre à ~** to update; **donner le ~ à** to give birth to; **voir le ~** to be born; **le ~ J** D-day; **jour férié** public holiday; **jour ouvrable** working day

journal, -aux [ʒurnal, o] *nm* (*news*)paper; (*spécialisé*) journal; (*intime*) diary; **journal de bord** log; **journal parlé/télévisé** radio/television news *sg*

journalier, -ière [ʒurnalje, jɛr] *adj* daily; (*banal*) everyday

journalisme [ʒurnalism] *nm* journalism; **journaliste** *nm/f* journalist

journée [ʒurne] *nf* day; **faire la ~ continue** to work over lunch

joyau, x [ʒwajo] *nm* gem, jewel

joyeux, -euse [ʒwajø, øz] *adj* joyful, merry; **~ Noël!** merry Christmas!; **~ anniversaire!** happy birthday!

jubiler [ʒybile] *vi* to be jubilant, exult

judas [ʒyda] *nm* (*trou*) spy-hole

judiciaire [ʒydisjɛr] *adj* judicial

judicieux, -euse [ʒydisjø, jøz] *adj* judicious

judo [ʒydo] *nm* judo

juge [ʒyʒ] *nm* judge; **juge d'instruction** examining (BRIT) *ou* committing (US) magistrate; **juge de paix** justice of the peace

jugé [ʒyʒe] : **au ~** *adv* by guesswork

jugement [ʒyʒmɑ̃] *nm* judgment; (*Jur: au pénal*) sentence; (: *au civil*) decision

juger [ʒyʒe] *vt* to judge; (*estimer*) to consider; **~ qn/qch satisfaisant** to consider sb/sth (to be) satisfactory; **~ bon de faire** to see fit to do

juif, -ive [ʒɥif, ʒɥiv] *adj* Jewish ▷ *nm/f*: **J~, ive** Jew (Jewess)

juillet [ʒɥije] *nm* July

14 JUILLET

Le 14 juillet is a national holiday in France and commemorates the storming of the Bastille during the French Revolution. Throughout the country there are celebrations, which feature parades, music, dancing and firework displays. In Paris a military parade along the Champs-Élysées is attended by the President.

juin [ʒɥɛ̃] *nm* June

jumeau, -elle, x [ʒymo, ɛl] *adj, nm/f* twin

jumeler [ʒym(ə)le] *vt* to twin

jumelle [ʒymɛl] *adj, nf voir* **jumeau**; **jumelles** *nfpl* (*appareil*) binoculars

jument [ʒymɑ̃] *nf* mare

jungle [ʒɑ̃gl] *nf* jungle

jupe [ʒyp] *nf* skirt

jupon [ʒypɔ̃] *nm* waist slip

juré, e [ʒyre] *nm/f* juror ▷ *adj*: **ennemi ~** sworn enemy

jurer [ʒyre] *vt* (*obéissance etc*) to swear, vow ▷ *vi* (*dire des jurons*) to swear, curse; (*dissoner*): **~ (avec)** to clash (with); **~ de faire/que** to swear to do/that; **~ de qch** (*s'en porter garant*) to swear to sth

juridique [ʒyridik] *adj* legal

juron [ʒyrɔ̃] *nm* curse, swearword

jury [ʒyri] *nm* jury; (*Art, Sport*) panel of judges; (*Scol*) board of examiners

jus [ʒy] *nm* juice; (*de viande*) gravy, (meat) juice; **jus de fruit** fruit juice

jusque [ʒysk]: **jusqu'à** *prép* (*endroit*) as far as, (up) to; (*moment*) until, till; (*limite*) up to; **~ sur/dans** up to; (*y compris*) even on/in; **jusqu'à ce que** until; **jusqu'à présent** *ou* **maintenant** so far; **jusqu'où?** how far?

justaucorps [ʒystokɔr] *nm* leotard

juste [ʒyst] *adj* (*équitable*) just, fair; (*légitime*) just; (*exact*) right; (*pertinent*) apt; (*étroit*) tight;

(*insuffisant*) on the short side ▷ *adv* rightly,
correctly; (*chanter*) in tune; (*exactement,
seulement*) just; **~ assez/au-dessus** just
enough/above; **au ~** exactly; **le ~ milieu** the
happy medium; **c'était ~** it was a close thing;
pouvoir tout ~ faire to be only just able to
do; **justement** *adv* justly; (*précisément*) just,
precisely; **justesse** *nf* (*précision*) accuracy;
(*d'une remarque*) aptness; (*d'une opinion*)
soundness; **de justesse** only just
justice [ʒystis] *nf* (*équité*) fairness, justice;
(*Admin*) justice; **rendre ~ à qn** to do sb justice
justificatif, -ive [ʒystifikatif, iv] *adj*
(*document*) supporting; **pièce justificative**
written proof
justifier [ʒystifje] *vt* to justify; **~ de** to prove
juteux, -euse [ʒytø, øz] *adj* juicy
juvénile [ʒyvenil] *adj* youthful

K

K [ka] *nm* (*Inform*) K
kaki [kaki] *adj inv* khaki
kangourou [kɑ̃guʀu] *nm* kangaroo
karaté [karate] *nm* karate
kascher [kaʃɛʀ] *adj* kosher
kayak [kajak] *nm* canoe, kayak; **faire du ~** to
go canoeing
képi [kepi] *nm* kepi
kermesse [kɛʀmɛs] *nf* fair; (*fête de charité*)
bazaar, (charity) fête
kidnapper [kidnape] *vt* to kidnap
kilo [kilo] *nm* = **kilogramme**
kilo...: **kilogramme** *nm* kilogramme;
kilométrage *nm* number of kilometres
travelled, ≈ mileage; **kilomètre** *nm* kilometre;
kilométrique *adj* (*distance*) in kilometres
kinésithérapeute [kineziteʀapøt] *nm/f*
physiotherapist
kiosque [kjɔsk] *nm* kiosk, stall
kir [kiʀ] *nm* kir (*white wine with blackcurrant
liqueur*)
kit [kit] *nm* kit; **~ piéton** *ou* **mains libres**
hands-free kit; **en ~** in kit form
kiwi [kiwi] *nm* kiwi
klaxon [klaksɔn] *nm* horn; **klaxonner** *vi, vt* to
hoot (*BRIT*), honk (*US*)
km *abr* = **kilomètre**
km/h *abr* (= *kilomètres/heure*) ≈ mph
K.-O. (*fam*) *adj inv* shattered, knackered
Kosovo [kɔsɔvo] *nm* Kosovo

Koweit, Kuweit [kɔwɛt] *nm:* **le ~** Kuwait
k-way® [kawɛ] *nm* (lightweight nylon)
cagoule
kyste [kist] *nm* cyst

l' [l] *art déf voir* **le**
la [la] *art déf voir* **le** ▷ *nm* (*Mus*) A; (*en chantant la gamme*) la
là [la] *adv* there; (*ici*) here; (*dans le temps*) then; **elle n'est pas là** she isn't here; **c'est là que** this is where; **là où** where; **de là** (*fig*) hence; **par là** (*fig*) by that; *voir aussi* **-ci**; **ce**; **celui**; **là-bas** *adv* there
laboratoire [labɔʀatwaʀ] *nm* laboratory; **laboratoire de langues** language laboratory
laborieux, -euse [labɔʀjø, jøz] *adj* (*tâche*) laborious
labourer *vt* to plough
labyrinthe [labiʀɛ̃t] *nm* labyrinth, maze
lac [lak] *nm* lake
lacet [lasɛ] *nm* (*de chaussure*) lace; (*de route*) sharp bend; (*piège*) snare
lâche [lɑʃ] *adj* (*poltron*) cowardly; (*desserré*) loose, slack ▷ *nm/f* coward
lâcher [lɑʃe] *vt* to let go of; (*ce qui tombe, abandonner*) to drop; (*oiseau, animal: libérer*) to release, set free; (*fig: mot, remarque*) to let slip, come out with ▷ *vi* (*freins*) to fail; **~ les amarres** (*Navig*) to cast off (the moorings); **~ prise** to let go
lacrymogène [lakʀimɔʒɛn] *adj:* **gaz ~** teargas
lacune [lakyn] *nf* gap
là-dedans [ladədɑ̃] *adv* inside (there), in it; (*fig*) in that

là-dessous [ladsu] *adv* underneath, under there; (*fig*) behind that

là-dessus [ladsy] *adv* on there; (*fig: sur ces mots*) at that point; (: *à ce sujet*) about that

lagune [lagyn] *nf* lagoon

là-haut [lao] *adv* up there

laid, e [lɛ, lɛd] *adj* ugly; **laideur** *nf* ugliness *no pl*

lainage [lɛnaʒ] *nm* (*vêtement*) woollen garment; (*étoffe*) woollen material

laine [lɛn] *nf* wool

laïque [laik] *adj* lay, civil; (*Scol*) state *cpd* ▷ *nm/f* layman(-woman)

laisse [lɛs] *nf* (*de chien*) lead, leash; **tenir en ~** to keep on a lead *ou* leash

laisser [lese] *vt* to leave ▷ *vb aux:* **~ qn faire** to let sb do; **se ~ aller** to let o.s. go; **laisse-toi faire** let me (*ou* him *etc*) do it; **laisser-aller** *nm* carelessness, slovenliness; **laissez-passer** *nm inv* pass

lait [lɛ] *nm* milk; **frère/sœur de ~** foster brother/sister; **lait concentré/condensé** condensed/evaporated milk; **lait écrémé/entier** skimmed/full-cream (*BRIT*) *ou* whole milk; **laitage** *nm* dairy product; **laiterie** *nf* dairy; **laitier, -ière** *adj* dairy *cpd* ▷ *nm/f* milkman (dairywoman)

laiton [lɛtɔ̃] *nm* brass

laitue [lety] *nf* lettuce

lambeau, x [lɑ̃bo] *nm* scrap; **en ~x** in tatters, tattered

lame [lam] *nf* blade; (*vague*) wave; (*lamelle*) strip; **lame de fond** ground swell *no pl*; **lame de rasoir** razor blade; **lamelle** *nf* thin strip *ou* blade

lamentable [lamɑ̃tabl] *adj* appalling

lamenter [lamɑ̃te] *vb:* **se ~ (sur)** to moan (over)

lampadaire [lɑ̃padɛʀ] *nm* (*de salon*) standard lamp; (*dans la rue*) street lamp

lampe [lɑ̃p] *nf* lamp; (*Tech*) valve; **lampe à bronzer** sun lamp; **lampe à pétrole** oil lamp; **lampe de poche** torch (*BRIT*), flashlight (*US*); **lampe halogène** halogen lamp

lance [lɑ̃s] *nf* spear; **lance d'incendie** fire hose

lancée [lɑ̃se] *nf:* **être/continuer sur sa ~** to be under way/keep going

lancement [lɑ̃smɑ̃] *nm* launching

lance-pierres [lɑ̃spjɛʀ] *nm inv* catapult

lancer [lɑ̃se] *nm* (*Sport*) throwing *no pl*, throw ▷ *vt* to throw; (*émettre, projeter*) to throw out, send out; (*produit, fusée, bateau, artiste*) to launch; (*injure*) to hurl, fling; **se lancer** *vi* (*prendre de l'élan*) to build up speed; (*se précipiter*): **se ~ sur** *ou* **contre** to rush at; **se ~ dans** (*discussion*) to launch into; (*aventure*) to embark on; **~ qch à qn** to throw sth to sb; (*de façon agressive*) to throw sth at sb; **~ un cri** *ou* **un appel** to shout *ou* call out; **lancer du poids** putting the shot

landau [lɑ̃do] *nm* pram (*BRIT*), baby carriage (*US*)

lande [lɑ̃d] *nf* moor

langage [lɑ̃gaʒ] *nm* language

langouste [lɑ̃gust] *nf* crayfish *inv*; **langoustine** *nf* Dublin Bay prawn

langue [lɑ̃g] *nf* (*Anat, Culin*) tongue; (*Ling*) language; **tirer la ~ (à)** to stick out one's tongue (at); **de ~ française** French-speaking; **quelles ~s parlez-vous?** what languages do you speak?; **langue maternelle** native language, mother tongue; **langues vivantes** modern languages

langueur [lɑ̃gœʀ] *nf* languidness

languir [lɑ̃giʀ] *vi* to languish; (*conversation*) to flag; **faire ~ qn** to keep sb waiting

lanière [lanjɛʀ] *nf* (*de fouet*) lash; (*de sac, bretelle*) strap

lanterne [lɑ̃tɛʀn] *nf* (*portable*) lantern; (*électrique*) light, lamp; (*de voiture*) (side)light

laper [lape] *vt* to lap up

lapidaire [lapidɛʀ] *adj* (*fig*) terse

lapin [lapɛ̃] *nm* rabbit; (*peau*) rabbitskin; (*fourrure*) cony; **poser un ~ à qn** (*fam*) to stand sb up

Laponie [laponi] *nf* Lapland

laps [laps] *nm:* **~ de temps** space of time, time *no pl*

laque [lak] *nf* (*vernis*) lacquer; (*pour cheveux*) hair spray

laquelle [lakɛl] *pron voir* **lequel**

larcin [laʀsɛ̃] *nm* theft

lard [laʀ] *nm* (*bacon*) (streaky) bacon; (*graisse*) fat

lardon [laʀdɔ̃] *nm:* **~s** chopped bacon

large [laʀʒ] *adj* wide, broad; (*fig*) generous ▷ *adv:* **calculer/voir ~** to allow extra/think big ▷ *nm* (*largeur*): **5 m de ~** 5 m wide *ou* in width; (*mer*): **le ~** the open sea; **au ~ de** off; **large d'esprit** broad-minded; **largement** *adv* widely; (*de loin*) greatly; (*au moins*) easily; (*généreusement*) generously; **c'est largement suffisant** that's ample; **largesse** *nf* generosity; **largesses** *nfpl* (*dons*) liberalities; **largeur** *nf* (*qu'on mesure*) width; (*impression visuelle*) wideness, width; (*d'esprit*) broadness

larguer [laʀge] *vt* to drop; **~ les amarres** to cast off (the moorings)

larme [laʀm] *nf* tear; (*fam: goutte*) drop; **en ~s** in tears; **larmoyer** *vi* (*yeux*) to water; (*se plaindre*) to whimper

larvé, e [laʀve] *adj* (*fig*) latent

laryngite [laʀɛ̃ʒit] *nf* laryngitis

las, lasse [lɑ, lɑs] *adj* weary

laser [lazɛʀ] *nm:* (*rayon*) **~** laser (beam); **chaîne** *ou* **platine ~** laser disc (player); **disque ~** laser disc

lasse [lɑs] *adj voir* **las**

lasser [lɑse] *vt* to weary, tire; **se lasser de** *vt*

to grow weary ou tired of

latéral, e, -aux [lateral, o] *adj* side *cpd*, lateral

latin, e [latɛ̃, in] *adj* Latin ▷ *nm/f*: **L~, e** Latin ▷ *nm* (*Ling*) Latin

latitude [latityd] *nf* latitude

lauréat, e [lɔrea, at] *nm/f* winner

laurier [lɔrje] *nm* (*Bot*) laurel; **feuille de ~** (*Culin*) bay leaf

lavable [lavabl] *adj* washable

lavabo [lavabo] *nm* washbasin; **lavabos** *nmpl* (*toilettes*) toilet *sg*

lavage [lavaʒ] *nm* washing *no pl*, wash; **lavage de cerveau** brainwashing *no pl*

lavande [lavɑ̃d] *nf* lavender

lave [lav] *nf* lava *no pl*

lave-linge [lavlɛ̃ʒ] *nm inv* washing machine

laver [lave] *vt* to wash; (*tache*) to wash off; **se laver** *vi* to have a wash, wash; **se ~ les mains/dents** to wash one's hands/clean one's teeth; **~ la vaisselle/le linge** to wash the dishes/clothes; **~ qn de** (*accusation*) to clear sb of; **laverie** *nf*: **laverie (automatique)** launderette; **lavette** *nf* dish cloth; (*fam*) drip; **laveur, -euse** *nm/f* cleaner; **lave-vaisselle** *nm inv* dishwasher; **lavoir** *nm* wash house; (*évier*) sink

laxatif, -ive [laksatif, iv] *adj, nm* laxative

layette [lɛjɛt] *nf* baby clothes

 MOT-CLÉ

le [lə], **la**, **l'** (*pl* **les**) *art déf* **1** the; **le livre/la pomme/l'arbre** the book/the apple/the tree; **les étudiants** the students

2 (*noms abstraits*): **le courage/l'amour/la jeunesse** courage/love/youth

3 (*indiquant la possession*): **se casser la jambe** *etc* to break one's leg *etc*; **levez la main** put your hand up; **avoir les yeux gris/le nez rouge** to have grey eyes/a red nose

4 (*temps*): **le matin/soir** in the morning/evening; mornings/evenings; **le jeudi** *etc* (*d'habitude*) on Thursdays *etc*; (*ce jeudi-là etc*) on (the) Thursday

5 (*distribution, évaluation*) a, an; **10 euros le mètre/kilo** 10 euros a *ou* per metre/kilo; **le tiers/quart de** a third/quarter of

▷ *pron* **1** (*personne: mâle*) him; (: *femelle*) her; (: *pluriel*) them; **je le/la/les vois** I can see him/her/them

2 (*animal, chose: singulier*) it; (: *pluriel*) them; **je le** (*ou* **la**) **vois** I can see it; **je les vois** I can see them

3 (*remplaçant une phrase*): **je ne le savais pas** I didn't know (about it); **il était riche et ne l'est plus** he was once rich but no longer is

lécher [leʃe] *vt* to lick; (*laper: lait, eau*) to lick

ou lap up; **se ~ les doigts/lèvres** to lick one's fingers/lips; **lèche-vitrines** *nm*: **faire du lèche-vitrines** to go window-shopping

leçon [l(ə)sɔ̃] *nf* lesson; **faire la ~ à** (*fig*) to give a lecture to; **leçons de conduite** driving lessons; **leçons particulières** private lessons *ou* tuition *sg* (*BRIT*)

lecteur, -trice [lɛktœr, tris] *nm/f* reader; (*d'université*) foreign language assistant ▷ *nm* (*Tech*): **~ de cassettes/CD/DVD** cassette/CD/DVD player; **lecteur de disquette(s)** disk drive; **lecteur MP3** MP3 player

lecture [lɛktyr] *nf* reading

> Attention à ne pas traduire *lecture* par le mot anglais *lecture*.

ledit [lədi], **ladite** (*mpl* **lesdits**, *fpl* **lesdites**) *dét* the aforesaid

légal, e, -aux [legal, o] *adj* legal; **légaliser** *vt* to legalize; **légalité** *nf* law

légendaire [leʒɑ̃dɛr] *adj* legendary

légende [leʒɑ̃d] *nf* (*mythe*) legend; (*de carte, plan*) key; (*de dessin*) caption

léger, -ère [leʒe, ɛr] *adj* light; (*bruit, retard*) slight; (*personne: superficiel*) thoughtless; (: *volage*) free and easy; **à la légère** (*parler, agir*) rashly, thoughtlessly; **légèrement** *adv* (*s'habiller, bouger*) lightly; (*un peu*) slightly; **manger légèrement** to eat a light meal; **légèreté** *nf* lightness; (*d'une remarque*) flippancy

législatif, -ive [leʒislatif, iv] *adj* legislative; **législatives** *nfpl* general election *sg*

légitime [leʒitim] *adj* (*Jur*) lawful, legitimate; (*fig*) rightful, legitimate; **en état de ~ défense** in self-defence

legs [lɛg] *nm* legacy

léguer [lege] *vt*: **~ qch à qn** (*Jur*) to bequeath sth to sb

légume [legym] *nm* vegetable; **légumes secs** pulses; **légumes verts** green vegetables, greens

lendemain [lɑ̃dmɛ̃] *nm*: **le ~** the next *ou* following day; **le ~ matin/soir** the next *ou* following morning/evening; **le ~ de** the day after

lent, e [lɑ̃, lɑ̃t] *adj* slow; **lentement** *adv* slowly; **lenteur** *nf* slowness *no pl*

lentille [lɑ̃tij] *nf* (*Optique*) lens *sg*; (*Culin*) lentil; **lentilles de contact** contact lenses

léopard [leɔpar] *nm* leopard

lèpre [lɛpr] *nf* leprosy

 MOT-CLÉ

lequel, laquelle [ləkɛl, lakɛl] (*mpl* **lesquels**, *fpl* **lesquelles**) (*à + lequel = **auquel**, *de + lequel = **duquel** *etc*) *pron* **1** (*interrogatif*) which, which one; **lequel des deux?** which one?

2 (relatif: personne: sujet) who; (: objet, après préposition) whom; (: chose) which
▷ adj: **auquel cas** in which case

les [le] dét voir **le**
lesbienne [lɛsbjɛn] nf lesbian
léser [leze] vt to wrong
lésiner [lezine] vi: **ne pas ~ sur les moyens** (pour mariage etc) to push the boat out
lésion [lezjɔ̃] nf lesion, damage no pl
lessive [lesiv] nf (poudre) washing powder; (linge) washing no pl, wash; **lessiver** vt to wash; (fam: fatiguer) to tire out, exhaust
lest [lɛst] nm ballast
leste [lɛst] adj sprightly, nimble
lettre [lɛtr] nf letter; **lettres** nfpl (littérature) literature sg; (Scol) arts (subjects); **à la ~** literally; **en toutes ~s** in full; **lettre piégée** letter bomb
leucémie [løsemi] nf leukaemia

⊙ **MOT-CLÉ**

leur [lœr] adj possessif their; **leur maison** their house; **leurs amis** their friends
▷ pron **1** (objet indirect) (to) them; **je leur ai dit la vérité** I told them the truth; **je le leur ai donné** I gave it to them, I gave them it
2 (possessif): **le(la) leur, les leurs** theirs

levain [ləvɛ̃] nm leaven
levé, e [ləve] adj: **être ~** to be up; **levée** nf (Postes) collection
lever [l(ə)ve] vt (vitre, bras etc) to raise; (soulever de terre, supprimer: interdiction, siège) to lift; (impôts, armée) to levy ▷ vi to rise ▷ nm: **au ~** on getting up; **se lever** vi to get up; (soleil) to rise; (jour) to break; (brouillard) to lift; **ça va se ~** (temps) it's going to clear up; **lever de soleil** sunrise; **lever du jour** daybreak
levier [ləvje] nm lever
lèvre [lɛvr] nf lip
lévrier [levrije] nm greyhound
levure [l(ə)vyr] nf yeast; **levure chimique** baking powder
lexique [lɛksik] nm vocabulary; (glossaire) lexicon
lézard [lezar] nm lizard
lézarde [lezard] nf crack
liaison [ljezɔ̃] nf (rapport) connection; (transport) link; (amoureuse) affair; (Phonétique) liaison; **entrer/être en ~ avec** to get/be in contact with
liane [ljan] nf creeper
liasse [ljas] nf wad, bundle
Liban [libã] nm: **le ~** (the) Lebanon
libeller [libele] vt (chèque, mandat): **~ (au nom de)** to make out (to); (lettre) to word
libellule [libelyl] nf dragonfly

libéral, e, -aux [liberal, o] adj, nm/f liberal; **profession ~e** (liberal) profession
libérer [libere] vt (délivrer) to free, liberate; (relâcher: prisonnier) to discharge, release; (: d'inhibitions) to liberate; (gaz) to release; **se libérer** vi (de rendez-vous) to get out of previous engagements
liberté [libɛrte] nf freedom; (loisir) free time; **libertés** nfpl (privautés) liberties; **mettre/être en ~** to set/be free; **en ~ provisoire/surveillée/conditionnelle** on bail/probation/parole
libraire [librɛr] nm/f bookseller
librairie [libreri] nf bookshop

▮ Attention à ne pas traduire **librairie** par **library**.

libre [libr] adj free; (route, voie) clear; (place, salle) free; (ligne) not engaged; (Scol) non-state; **~ de qch/de faire** free from sth/to do; **la place est ~?** is this seat free?; **libre arbitre** free will; **libre-échange** nm free trade; **libre-service** nm self-service store
Libye [libi] nf: **la ~** Libya
licence [lisãs] nf (permis) permit; (diplôme) degree; (liberté) liberty; **licencié, e** nm/f (Scol): **licencié ès lettres/en droit** ≈ Bachelor of Arts/Law
licenciement [lisãsimã] nm redundancy
licencier [lisãsje] vt (débaucher) to make redundant, lay off; (renvoyer) to dismiss
licite [lisit] adj lawful
lie [li] nf dregs pl, sediment
lié, e [lje] adj: **très ~ avec** very friendly with ou close to
Liechtenstein [liʃtɛnʃtain] nm: **le ~** Liechtenstein
liège [ljɛʒ] nm cork
lien [ljɛ̃] nm (corde, fig: affectif) bond; (rapport) link, connection; **lien de parenté** family tie; **lien hypertexte** hyperlink
lier [lje] vt (attacher) to tie up; (joindre) to link up; (fig: unir, engager) to bind; **~ conversation (avec)** to strike up a conversation (with); **~ connaissance avec** to get to know
lierre [ljɛr] nm ivy
lieu, x [ljø] nm place; **lieux** nmpl (locaux) premises; (endroit: d'un accident etc) scene sg; **en ~ sûr** in a safe place; **en premier ~** in the first place; **en dernier ~** lastly; **avoir ~** to take place; **tenir ~ de** to serve as; **donner ~ à** to give rise to; **au ~ de** instead of; **arriver/être sur les ~x** to arrive at/be on the scene; **lieu commun** cliché; **lieu-dit** (pl **lieux-dits**) nm locality
lieutenant [ljøt(ə)nã] nm lieutenant
lièvre [ljɛvr] nm hare
ligament [ligamã] nm ligament
ligne [liɲ] nf (gén) line; (Transports: liaison) service; (: trajet) route; (silhouette) figure;

garder la ~ to keep one's figure; **entrer en ~ de compte** to come into it; **en ~** (*Inform*) online; **~ fixe** (*Tél*) land line (phone)
lignée [liɲe] *nf* line, lineage
ligoter [liɡɔte] *vt* to tie up
ligue [liɡ] *nf* league
lilas [lila] *nm* lilac
limace [limas] *nf* slug
limande [limɑ̃d] *nf* dab
lime [lim] *nf* file; **lime à ongles** nail file; **limer** *vt* to file
limitation [limitasjɔ̃] *nf*: **limitation de vitesse** speed limit
limite [limit] *nf* (*de terrain*) boundary; (*partie ou point extrême*) limit; **à la ~** (*au pire*) if the worst comes (*ou* came) to the worst; **vitesse/charge ~** maximum speed/load; **cas ~** borderline case; **date ~** deadline; **date ~ de vente/consommation** sell-by/best-before date; **limiter** *vt* (*restreindre*) to limit, restrict; (*délimiter*) to border; **limitrophe** *adj* border *cpd*
limoger [limɔʒe] *vt* to dismiss
limon [limɔ̃] *nm* silt
limonade [limɔnad] *nf* lemonade
lin [lɛ̃] *nm* (*tissu*) linen
linceul [lɛ̃sœl] *nm* shroud
linge [lɛ̃ʒ] *nm* (*serviettes etc*) linen; (*lessive*) washing; (*aussi*: **~ de corps**) underwear; **lingerie** *nf* lingerie, underwear
lingot [lɛ̃ɡo] *nm* ingot
linguistique [lɛ̃ɡɥistik] *adj* linguistic ▷ *nf* linguistics *sg*
lion, ne [ljɔ̃, ljɔn] *nm/f* lion (lioness); (*signe*): **le L~** Leo; **lionceau, x** *nm* lion cub
liqueur [likœr] *nf* liqueur
liquidation [likidasjɔ̃] *nf* (*vente*) sale
liquide [likid] *adj* liquid ▷ *nm* liquid; (*Comm*): **en ~** in ready money *ou* cash; **je n'ai pas de ~** I haven't got any cash; **liquider** *vt* to liquidate; (*Comm: articles*) to clear, sell off
lire [lir] *nf* (*monnaie*) lira ▷ *vt, vi* to read
lis [lis] *nm* = **lys**
Lisbonne [lizbɔn] *n* Lisbon
lisible [lizibl] *adj* legible
lisière [lizjɛr] *nf* (*de forêt*) edge
lisons [lizɔ̃] *vb voir* **lire**
lisse [lis] *adj* smooth
liste [list] *nf* list; **faire la ~ de** to list; **liste de mariage** wedding (present) list; **liste électorale** electoral roll; **listing** *nm* (*Inform*) printout
lit [li] *nm* bed; **petit ~, ~ à une place** single bed; **grand ~, ~ à deux places** double bed; **faire son ~** to make one's bed; **aller/se mettre au ~** to go to/get into bed; **lit de camp** campbed; **lit d'enfant** cot (*Brit*), crib (*US*)
literie [litri] *nf* bedding, bedclothes *pl*
litige [litiʒ] *nm* dispute

litre [litr] *nm* litre
littéraire [literɛr] *adj* literary ▷ *nm/f* arts student; **elle est très ~** she's very literary
littéral, e, -aux [literal, o] *adj* literal
littérature [literatyr] *nf* literature
littoral, -aux [litɔral, o] *nm* coast
livide [livid] *adj* livid, pallid
livraison [livrɛzɔ̃] *nf* delivery
livre [livr] *nm* book ▷ *nf* (*monnaie*) pound; (*poids*) half a kilo, ≈ pound; **livre de poche** paperback
livré, e [livre] *adj*: **~ à soi-même** left to o.s. *ou* one's own devices
livrer [livre] *vt* (*Comm*) to deliver; (*otage, coupable*) to hand over; (*secret, information*) to give away; **se livrer à** (*se confier*) to confide in; (*se rendre, s'abandonner*) to give o.s. up to; (*faire: pratiques, actes*) to indulge in; (*enquête*) to carry out
livret [livrɛ] *nm* booklet; (*d'opéra*) libretto; **livret de caisse d'épargne** (savings) bankbook; **livret de famille** (official) family record book; **livret scolaire** (school) report book
livreur, -euse [livrœr, øz] *nm/f* delivery boy *ou* man/girl *ou* woman
local, e, -aux [lɔkal] *adj* local ▷ *nm* (*salle*) premises *pl*; *voir aussi* **locaux**; **localité** *nf* locality
locataire [lɔkatɛr] *nm/f* tenant; (*de chambre*) lodger
location [lɔkasjɔ̃] *nf* (*par le locataire, le loueur*) renting; (*par le propriétaire*) renting out, letting; (*Théâtre*) booking office; **"~ de voitures"** "car rental"; **habiter en ~** to live in rented accommodation; **prendre une ~ (pour les vacances)** to rent a house *etc* (for the holidays)

Attention à ne pas traduire *location* par le mot anglais *location*.

locomotive [lɔkɔmɔtiv] *nf* locomotive, engine
locution [lɔkysjɔ̃] *nf* phrase
loge [lɔʒ] *nf* (*Théâtre: d'artiste*) dressing room; (: *de spectateurs*) box; (*de concierge, franc-maçon*) lodge
logement [lɔʒmɑ̃] *nm* accommodation *no pl* (*Brit*), accommodations *pl* (*US*); (*appartement*) flat (*Brit*), apartment (*US*); (*Pol, Admin*): **le ~** housing *no pl*
loger [lɔʒe] *vt* to accommodate ▷ *vi* to live; **être logé, nourri** to have board and lodging; **se loger** *vr*: **trouver à se ~** to find somewhere to live; **se ~ dans** (*suj: balle, flèche*) to lodge itself in; **logeur, -euse** *nm/f* landlord(-lady)
logiciel [lɔʒisjɛl] *nm* software
logique [lɔʒik] *adj* logical ▷ *nf* logic
logo [lɔɡo] *nm* logo
loi [lwa] *nf* law; **faire la ~** to lay down the law

loin [lwɛ̃] *adv* far; (*dans le temps: futur*) a long way off; (: *passé*) a long time ago; **plus ~** further; **~ de** far from; **c'est ~ d'ici?** is it far from here?; **au ~** far off; **de ~** from a distance; (*fig: de beaucoup*) by far

lointain, e [lwɛ̃tɛ̃, ɛn] *adj* faraway, distant; (*dans le futur, passé*) distant; (*cause, parent*) remote, distant ▷ *nm*: **dans le ~** in the distance

loir [lwaʀ] *nm* dormouse

Loire [lwaʀ] *nf*: **la ~** the (River) Loire

loisir [lwaziʀ] *nm*: **heures de ~** spare time; **loisirs** *nmpl* (*temps libre*) leisure *sg*; (*activités*) leisure activities; **avoir le ~ de faire** to have the time *ou* opportunity to do; **à ~** at leisure

londonien, ne [lɔ̃dɔnjɛ̃, jɛn] *adj* London *cpd*, of London ▷ *nm/f*: **L~, ne** Londoner

Londres [lɔ̃dʀ] *n* London

long, longue [lɔ̃, lɔ̃g] *adj* long ▷ *adv*: **en savoir ~** to know a great deal ▷ *nm*: **de 3 m de ~** 3 m long, 3 m in length; **ne pas faire ~ feu** not to last long; **(tout) le ~ de** (all) along; **tout au ~ de** (*année, vie*) throughout; **de ~ en large** (*marcher*) to and fro, up and down; *voir aussi* **longue**

longer [lɔ̃ʒe] *vt* to go (*ou* walk *ou* drive) along(side); (*suj: mur, route*) to border

longiligne [lɔ̃ʒiliɲ] *adj* long-limbed

longitude [lɔ̃ʒityd] *nf* longitude

longtemps [lɔ̃tɑ̃] *adv* (for) a long time, (for) long; **avant ~** before long; **pour** *ou* **pendant ~** for a long time; **mettre ~ à faire** to take a long time to do; **il en a pour ~?** will he be long?

longue [lɔ̃g] *adj voir* **long** ▷ *nf*: **à la ~** in the end; **longuement** *adv* (*longtemps*) for a long time; (*en détail*) at length

longueur [lɔ̃gœʀ] *nf* length; **longueurs** *nfpl* (*fig: d'un film etc*) tedious parts; **en ~** lengthwise; **tirer en ~** to drag on; **à ~ de journée** all day long

loquet [lɔkɛ] *nm* latch

lorgner [lɔʀɲe] *vt* to eye; (*fig*) to have one's eye on

lors [lɔʀ]: **~ de** *prép* at the time of; during

lorsque [lɔʀsk] *conj* when, as

losange [lozɑ̃ʒ] *nm* diamond

lot [lo] *nm* (*part*) share; (*de loterie*) prize; (*fig: destin*) fate, lot; (*Comm, Inform*) batch; **le gros ~** the jackpot

loterie [lɔtʀi] *nf* lottery

lotion [losjɔ̃] *nf* lotion; **lotion après rasage** aftershave (lotion)

lotissement [lɔtismɑ̃] *nm* housing development; (*parcelle*) plot, lot

loto [lɔto] *nm* lotto

lotte [lɔt] *nf* monkfish

louanges [lwɑ̃ʒ] *nfpl* praise *sg*

loubard [lubaʀ] (*fam*) *nm* lout

louche [luʃ] *adj* shady, fishy, dubious ▷ *nf* ladle; **loucher** *vi* to squint

louer [lwe] *vt* (*maison: suj: propriétaire*) to let, rent (out); (: *locataire*) to rent; (*voiture etc: entreprise*) to hire out (BRIT), rent (out); (: *locataire*) to hire, rent; (*réserver*) to book; (*faire l'éloge de*) to praise; **"à ~"** "to let" (BRIT), "for rent" (US); **je voudrais ~ une voiture** I'd like to hire (BRIT) *ou* rent (US) a car

loup [lu] *nm* wolf; **jeune ~** young go-getter

loupe [lup] *nf* magnifying glass; **à la ~** in minute detail

louper [lupe] (*fam*) *vt* (*manquer*) to miss; (*examen*) to flunk

lourd, e [luʀ, luʀd] *adj, adv* heavy; **c'est trop ~** it's too heavy; **~ de** (*conséquences, menaces*) charged with; **il fait ~** the weather is close, it's sultry; **lourdaud, e** (*péj*) *adj* clumsy; **lourdement** *adv* heavily

loutre [lutʀ] *nf* otter

louveteau, x [luv(ə)to] *nm* wolf-cub; (*scout*) cub (scout)

louvoyer [luvwaje] *vi* (*fig*) to hedge, evade the issue

loyal, e, -aux [lwajal, o] *adj* (*fidèle*) loyal, faithful; (*fair-play*) fair; **loyauté** *nf* loyalty, faithfulness; fairness

loyer [lwaje] *nm* rent

lu, e [ly] *pp de* **lire**

lubie [lybi] *nf* whim, craze

lubrifiant [lybʀifjɑ̃] *nm* lubricant

lubrifier [lybʀifje] *vt* to lubricate

lubrique [lybʀik] *adj* lecherous

lucarne [lykaʀn] *nf* skylight

lucide [lysid] *adj* lucid; (*accidenté*) conscious

lucratif, -ive [lykʀatif, iv] *adj* lucrative, profitable; **à but non ~** non profit-making

lueur [lɥœʀ] *nf* (*pâle*) (faint) light; (*chatoyante*) glimmer *no pl*; (*fig*) glimmer; gleam

luge [lyʒ] *nf* sledge (BRIT), sled (US)

lugubre [lygybʀ] *adj* gloomy, dismal

○ **MOT-CLÉ**

lui [lɥi] *pron* **1** (*objet indirect: mâle*) (to) him; (: *femelle*) (to) her; (: *chose, animal*) (to) it; **je lui ai parlé** I have spoken to him (*ou* to her); **il lui a offert un cadeau** he gave him (*ou* her) a present

2 (*après préposition, comparatif: personne*) him; (: *chose, animal*) it; **elle est contente de lui** she is pleased with him; **je la connais mieux que lui** I know her better than he does; I know her better than him; **ce livre est à lui** this book is his, this is his book; **c'est à lui de jouer** it's his turn *ou* go

3 (*sujet, forme emphatique*) he; **lui, il est à Paris** HE is in Paris; **c'est lui qui l'a fait** HE did it

4 (*objet, forme emphatique*) him; **c'est lui que j'attends** I'm waiting for HIM
5: lui-même himself; itself

luire [lɥiʀ] *vi* to shine; (*en rougeoyant*) to glow
lumière [lymjɛʀ] *nf* light; **mettre en ~** (*fig*) to highlight; **lumière du jour** daylight
luminaire [lyminɛʀ] *nm* lamp, light
lumineux, -euse [lyminø, øz] *adj* luminous; (*éclairé*) illuminated; (*ciel, couleur*) bright; (*rayon*) of light, light *cpd*; (*fig: regard*) radiant
lunatique [lynatik] *adj* whimsical, temperamental
lundi [lœ̃di] *nm* Monday; **on est ~** it's Monday; **le(s) ~(s)** on Mondays; **"à ~"** "see you on Monday"; **lundi de Pâques** Easter Monday
lune [lyn] *nf* moon; **lune de miel** honeymoon
lunette [lynɛt] *nf:* **~s** *nfpl* glasses, spectacles; (*protectrices*) goggles; **lunette arrière** (*Auto*) rear window; **lunettes de soleil** sunglasses; **lunettes noires** dark glasses
lustre [lystʀ] *nm* (*de plafond*) chandelier; (*fig: éclat*) lustre; **lustrer** *vt* to shine
luth [lyt] *nm* lute
lutin [lytɛ̃] *nm* imp, goblin
lutte [lyt] *nf* (*conflit*) struggle; (*sport*) wrestling; **lutter** *vi* to fight, struggle
luxe [lyks] *nm* luxury; **de ~** luxury *cpd*
Luxembourg [lyksɑ̃buʀ] *nm:* **le ~** Luxembourg
luxer [lykse] *vt:* **se ~ l'épaule** to dislocate one's shoulder
luxueux, -euse [lyksɥø, øz] *adj* luxurious
lycée [lise] *nm* ≈ secondary school; **lycéen, ne** *nm/f* secondary school pupil
Lyon [ljɔ̃] *n* Lyons
lyophilisé, e [ljɔfilize] *adj* (*café*) freeze-dried
lyrique [liʀik] *adj* lyrical; (*Opéra*) lyric; **artiste ~** opera singer
lys [lis] *nm* lily

m

M *abr* = **Monsieur**
m' [m] *pron voir* **me**
ma [ma] *adj voir* **mon**
macaron [makaʀɔ̃] *nm* (*gâteau*) macaroon; (*insigne*) (round) badge
macaronis [makaʀɔni] *nmpl* macaroni *sg*; **~ au fromage** *ou* **en gratin** macaroni cheese (*BRIT*), macaroni and cheese (*US*)
macédoine [masedwan] *nf:* **~ de fruits** fruit salad; **~ de légumes** mixed vegetables; **la M~** Macedonia
macérer [maseʀe] *vi, vt* to macerate; (*dans du vinaigre*) to pickle
mâcher [mɑʃe] *vt* to chew; **ne pas ~ ses mots** not to mince one's words
machin [maʃɛ̃] (*fam*) *nm* thing(umajig); (*personne*): **M~(e)** *nm(f)* what's-his(*ou* her)-name
machinal, e, -aux [maʃinal, o] *adj* mechanical, automatic
machination [maʃinasjɔ̃] *nf* frame-up
machine [maʃin] *nf* machine; (*locomotive*) engine; **machine à laver/coudre** washing/sewing machine; **machine à sous** fruit machine
mâchoire [maʃwaʀ] *nf* jaw
mâchonner [maʃɔne] *vt* to chew (at)
maçon [masɔ̃] *nm* builder; (*poseur de briques*) bricklayer; **maçonnerie** *nf* (*murs*) brickwork; (*pierres*) masonry, stonework

Madagascar [madagaskaʀ] *nf*
Madagascar

Madame [madam] (*pl* **Mesdames**) *nf:*
~ **Dupont** Mrs Dupont; **occupez-vous
de ~/Monsieur/Mademoiselle** please
serve this lady/gentleman/(young) lady;
bonjour ~/Monsieur/Mademoiselle
good morning; (*ton déférent*) good morning
Madam/Sir/Madam; (*le nom est connu*) good
morning Mrs/Mr/Miss X; **~/Monsieur/
Mademoiselle!** (*pour appeler*) Madam/Sir/
Miss!; **~/Monsieur/Mademoiselle** (*sur lettre*)
Dear Madam/Sir/Madam; **chère ~/cher
Monsieur/chère Mademoiselle** Dear Mrs/
Mr/Miss X; **Mesdames** Ladies; **mesdames,
mesdemoiselles, messieurs** ladies and
gentlemen

madeleine [madlɛn] *nf* madeleine, *small
sponge cake*

Mademoiselle [madmwazɛl] (*pl
Mesdemoiselles*) *nf* Miss; *voir aussi*
Madame

madère [madɛʀ] *nm* Madeira (wine)

Madrid [madʀid] *n* Madrid

magasin [magazɛ̃] *nm* (*boutique*) shop;
(*entrepôt*) warehouse; **en ~** (*Comm*) in
stock

magazine [magazin] *nm* magazine

Maghreb [magʀɛb] *nm:* **le ~** North Africa;
maghrébin, e *adj* North African ▷ *nm/f:*
Maghrébin, e North African

magicien, ne [maʒisjɛ̃, jɛn] *nm/f*
magician

magie [maʒi] *nf* magic; **magique** *adj* magic;
(*enchanteur*) magical

magistral, e, -aux [maʒistʀal, o] *adj* (*œuvre,
adresse*) masterly; (*ton*) authoritative; **cours
~** lecture

magistrat [maʒistʀa] *nm* magistrate

magnétique [maɲetik] *adj* magnetic

magnétophone [maɲetɔfɔn] *nm* tape
recorder; **magnétophone à cassettes**
cassette recorder

magnétoscope [maɲetɔskɔp] *nm* video-
tape recorder

magnifique [maɲifik] *adj*
magnificent

magret [magʀɛ] *nm:* **~ de canard** duck
steaklet

mai [mɛ] *nm* May

maigre [mɛgʀ] *adj* (very) thin, skinny; (*viande*)
lean; (*fromage*) low-fat; (*végétation*) thin,
sparse; (*fig*) poor, meagre, skimpy; **jours ~s**
days of abstinence, fish days; **maigreur** *nf*
thinness; **maigrir** *vi* to get thinner, lose
weight; **maigrir de 2 kilos** to lose 2 kilos

mail [mɛl] *nm* e-mail

maille [maj] *nf* stitch; **maille à l'endroit/
l'envers** plain/purl stitch

maillet [majɛ] *nm* mallet

maillon [majɔ̃] *nm* link

maillot [majo] *nm* (*aussi:* **~ de corps**) vest; (*de
sportif*) jersey; **maillot de bain** swimming *ou*
bathing (BRIT) costume, swimsuit; (*d'homme*)
(swimming *ou* bathing (BRIT)) trunks *pl*

main [mɛ̃] *nf* hand; **à la ~** (*tenir, avoir*) in one's
hand; (*faire, tricoter etc*) by hand; **se donner la
~** to hold hands; **donner** *ou* **tendre la ~ à qn**
to hold out one's hand to sb; **se serrer la ~** to
shake hands; **serrer la ~ à qn** to shake hands
with sb; **sous la ~** to *ou* at hand; **haut les ~s!**
hands up!; **attaque à ~ armée** armed attack;
à remettre en ~s propres to be delivered
personally; **mettre la dernière ~ à** to put the
finishing touches to; **se faire/perdre la ~** to
get one's hand in/lose one's touch; **avoir qch
bien en ~** to have (got) the hang of sth; **main-
d'œuvre** *nf* manpower, labour; **mainmise** *nf*
(*fig*): **mainmise sur** complete hold on; **mains
libres** *adj inv* (*téléphone, kit*) hands-free

maint, e [mɛ̃, mɛ̃t] *adj* many a; **~s** many; **à
~es reprises** time and (time) again

maintenant [mɛ̃t(ə)nɑ̃] *adv* now;
(*actuellement*) nowadays

maintenir [mɛ̃t(ə)niʀ] *vt* (*retenir, soutenir*)
to support; (*contenir: foule etc*) to hold back;
(*conserver, affirmer*) to maintain; **se maintenir**
vi (*prix*) to keep steady; (*amélioration*) to persist

maintien [mɛ̃tjɛ̃] *nm* (*sauvegarde*)
maintenance; (*attitude*) bearing

maire [mɛʀ] *nm* mayor; **mairie** *nf* (*bâtiment*)
town hall; (*administration*) town council

mais [mɛ] *conj* but; **~ non!** of course not!; **~**

m

enfin but after all; (*indignation*) look here!
maïs [mais] *nm* maize (BRIT), corn (US)
maison [mɛzɔ̃] *nf* house; (*chez-soi*) home;
(*Comm*) firm ▷ *adj inv* (*Culin*) home-made;
(*fig*) in-house, own; **à la ~** at home; (*direction*)
home; **maison de repos** convalescent home;
maison de retraite old people's home;
maison close *ou* **de passe** brothel; **maison
de santé** mental home; **maison des jeunes**
≈ youth club; **maison mère** parent company
maître, -esse [mɛtʀ, mɛtʀɛs] *nm/f*
master (mistress); (*Scol*) teacher,
schoolmaster(-mistress) ▷ *nm* (*peintre etc*)
master; (*titre*): **M~** Maître, *term of address gen
for a barrister* ▷ *adj* (*principal, essentiel*) main;
être ~ de (*soi, situation*) to be in control of; **une
~sse femme** a managing woman; **maître
chanteur** blackmailer; **maître d'école**
schoolmaster; **maître d'hôtel** (*domestique*)
butler; (*d'hôtel*) head waiter; **maître
nageur** lifeguard; **maîtresse** *nf* (*amante*)
mistress; **maîtresse (d'école)** teacher,
(school)mistress; **maîtresse de maison**
hostess; (*ménagère*) housewife
maîtrise [mɛtʀiz] *nf* (*aussi*: **~ de soi**)
self-control, self-possession; (*habileté*) skill,
mastery; (*suprématie*) mastery, command;
(*diplôme*) ≈ master's degree; **maîtriser** *vt*
(*cheval, incendie*) to (bring under) control;
(*sujet*) to master; (*émotion*) to control, master;
se maîtriser to control o.s.
majestueux, -euse [maʒɛstɥø, øz] *adj*
majestic
majeur, e [maʒœʀ] *adj* (*important*) major; (*Jur*)
of age ▷ *nm* (*doigt*) middle finger; **en ~e partie**
for the most part; **la ~e partie de** most of
majorer [maʒɔʀe] *vt* to increase
majoritaire [maʒɔʀitɛʀ] *adj* majority *cpd*
majorité [maʒɔʀite] *nf* (*gén*) majority; (*parti*)
party in power; **en ~** mainly; **avoir la ~** to have
the majority
majuscule [maʒyskyl] *adj, nf*: **(lettre) ~**
capital (letter)
mal [mal, mo] (*pl* **maux**) *nm* (*opposé au bien*)
evil; (*tort, dommage*) harm; (*douleur physique*)
pain, ache; (*maladie*) illness, sickness *no pl*
▷ *adv* badly; **~ à l'aise**
to be uncomfortable; **être ~ avec qn** to
be on bad terms with sb; **il a ~ compris** he
misunderstood; **se sentir** *ou* **se trouver ~**
to feel ill *ou* unwell; **dire/penser du ~ de** to
speak/think ill of; **ne voir aucun ~ à** to see
no harm in, see nothing wrong in; **faire ~ à
qn** to hurt sb; **se faire ~** to hurt o.s.; **avoir
du ~ à faire qch** to have trouble doing sth; **se
donner du ~ pour faire qch** to go to a lot of
trouble to do sth; **ça fait ~** it hurts; **j'ai ~ au
dos** my back hurts; **avoir ~ à la tête/à la
gorge/aux dents** to have a headache/a sore

throat/toothache; **avoir le ~ du pays** to be
homesick; *voir aussi* **cœur; maux; mal de mer**
seasickness; **mal en point** in a bad state
malade [malad] *adj* ill, sick; (*poitrine, jambe*)
bad; (*plante*) diseased ▷ *nm/f* invalid, sick
person; (*à l'hôpital etc*) patient; **tomber ~** to
fall ill; **être ~ du cœur** to have heart trouble
ou a bad heart; **malade mental** mentally ill
person; **maladie** *nf* (*spécifique*) disease, illness;
(*mauvaise santé*) illness, sickness; **maladif, -ive**
adj sickly; (*curiosité, besoin*) pathological
maladresse [maladʀɛs] *nf* clumsiness *no pl*;
(*gaffe*) blunder
maladroit, e [maladʀwa, wat] *adj* clumsy
malaise [malɛz] *nm* (*Méd*) feeling of faintness;
(*fig*) uneasiness, malaise; **avoir un ~** to feel
faint
Malaisie [malɛzi] *nf*: **la ~** Malaysia
malaria [malaʀja] *nf* malaria
malaxer [malakse] *vt* (*pétrir*) to knead;
(*mélanger*) to mix
malbouffe [malbuf] (*fam*) *nf*: **la ~** junk food
malchance [malʃɑ̃s] *nf* misfortune, ill luck *no
pl*; **par ~** unfortunately; **malchanceux, -euse**
adj unlucky
mâle [mɑl] *adj* (*aussi* Élec, Tech) male; (*viril: voix,
traits*) manly ▷ *nm* male
malédiction [malediksjɔ̃] *nf* curse
mal...: **malentendant, e** *nm/f*: **les
malentendants** the hard of hearing;
malentendu *nm* misunderstanding; **il
y a eu un malentendu** there's been a
misunderstanding; **malfaçon** *nf* fault;
malfaisant, e *adj* evil, harmful; **malfaiteur**
nm lawbreaker, criminal; (*voleur*) burglar, thief;
malfamé, e *adj* disreputable
malgache [malgaʃ] *adj* Madagascan,
Malagasy ▷ *nm/f*: **M~** Madagascan, Malagasy
▷ *nm* (*Ling*) Malagasy
malgré [malgʀe] *prép* in spite of, despite; **~
tout** all the same
malheur [malœʀ] *nm* (*situation*) adversity,
misfortune; (*événement*) misfortune; (:
très grave) disaster, tragedy; **faire un ~** to
be a smash hit; **malheureusement** *adv*
unfortunately; **malheureux, -euse** *adj* (*triste*)
unhappy, miserable; (*infortuné, regrettable*)
unfortunate; (*malchanceux*) unlucky;
(*insignifiant*) wretched ▷ *nm/f* poor soul
malhonnête [malɔnɛt] *adj* dishonest;
malhonnêteté *nf* dishonesty
malice [malis] *nf* mischievousness;
(*méchanceté*): **par ~** out of malice *ou* spite; **sans
~** guileless; **malicieux, -euse** *adj* mischievous
▌ Attention à ne pas traduire *malicieux*
par *malicious*.
malin, -igne [malɛ̃, maliɲ] *adj* (*futé: f gén:
aussi*: **maline**) smart, shrewd; (*Méd*) malignant
malingre [malɛ̃gʀ] *adj* puny

malle [mal] *nf* trunk; **mallette** *nf* (small) suitcase; (*porte-documents*) attaché case

malmener [malmǝne] *vt* to manhandle; (*fig*) to give a rough handling to

malodorant, e [malɔdɔʀɑ̃, ɑ̃t] *adj* foul-*ou* ill-smelling

malpoli, e [malpɔli] *adj* impolite

malsain, e [malsɛ̃, ɛn] *adj* unhealthy

malt [malt] *nm* malt

Malte [malt] *nf* Malta

maltraiter [maltʀete] *vt* to manhandle, ill-treat

malveillance [malvɛjɑ̃s] *nf* (*animosité*) ill will; (*intention de nuire*) malevolence

malversation [malvɛʀsasjɔ̃] *nf* embezzlement

maman [mamɑ̃] *nf* mum(my), mother

mamelle [mamɛl] *nf* teat

mamelon [mam(ǝ)lɔ̃] *nm* (*Anat*) nipple

mamie [mami] (*fam*) *nf* granny

mammifère [mamifɛʀ] *nm* mammal

mammouth [mamut] *nm* mammoth

manche [mɑ̃ʃ] *nf* (*de vêtement*) sleeve; (*d'un jeu, tournoi*) round; (*Géo*): **la M~** the Channel ▷ *nm* (*d'outil, casserole*) handle; (*de pelle, pioche etc*) shaft; **à ~s courtes/longues** short-/long-sleeved; **manche à balai** broomstick; (*Inform, Aviat*) joystick *m inv*

manchette [mɑ̃ʃɛt] *nf* (*de chemise*) cuff; (*coup*) forearm blow; (*titre*) headline

manchot [mɑ̃ʃo] *nm* one-armed man; armless man; (*Zool*) penguin

mandarine [mɑ̃daʀin] *nf* mandarin (orange), tangerine

mandat [mɑ̃da] *nm* (*postal*) postal *ou* money order; (*d'un député etc*) mandate; (*procuration*) power of attorney, proxy; (*Police*) warrant; **mandat d'arrêt** warrant for arrest; **mandat de perquisition** search warrant; **mandataire** *nm/f* (*représentant*) representative; (*Jur*) proxy

manège [manɛʒ] *nm* riding school; (*à la foire*) roundabout, merry-go-round; (*fig*) game, ploy

manette [manɛt] *nf* lever, tap; **manette de jeu** joystick

mangeable [mɑ̃ʒabl] *adj* edible, eatable

mangeoire [mɑ̃ʒwaʀ] *nf* trough, manger

manger [mɑ̃ʒe] *vt* to eat; (*ronger: suj: rouille etc*) to eat into *ou* away ▷ *vi* to eat; **donner à ~ à** (*enfant*) to feed; **est-ce qu'on peut ~ quelque chose?** can we have something to eat?

mangue [mɑ̃g] *nf* mango

maniable [manjabl] *adj* (*outil*) handy; (*voiture, voilier*) easy to handle

maniaque [manjak] *adj* finicky, fussy ▷ *nm/f* (*méticuleux*) fusspot; (*fou*) maniac

manie [mani] *nf* (*tic*) odd habit; (*obsession*) mania; **avoir la ~ de** to be obsessive about

manier [manje] *vt* to handle

manière [manjɛʀ] *nf* (*façon*) way, manner; **manières** *nfpl* (*attitude*) manners; (*chichis*) fuss *sg*; **de ~ à** so as to; **de cette ~** in this way *ou* manner; **d'une certaine ~** in a way; **de toute ~** in any case; **d'une ~ générale** generally speaking, as a general rule

maniéré, e [manjeʀe] *adj* affected

manifestant, e [manifɛstɑ̃, ɑ̃t] *nm/f* demonstrator

manifestation [manifɛstasjɔ̃] *nf* (*de joie, mécontentement*) expression, demonstration; (*symptôme*) outward sign; (*culturelle etc*) event; (*Pol*) demonstration

manifeste [manifɛst] *adj* obvious, evident ▷ *nm* manifesto; **manifester** *vt* (*volonté, intentions*) to show, indicate; (*joie, peur*) to express, show ▷ *vi* to demonstrate; **se manifester** *vi* (*émotion*) to show *ou* express itself; (*difficultés*) to arise; (*symptômes*) to appear

manigancer [manigɑ̃se] *vt* to plot

manipulation [manipylasjɔ̃] *nf* handling; (*Pol, génétique*) manipulation

manipuler [manipyle] *vt* to handle; (*fig*) to manipulate

manivelle [manivɛl] *nf* crank

mannequin [mankɛ̃] *nm* (*Couture*) dummy; (*Mode*) model

manœuvre [manœvʀ] *nf* (*gén*) manoeuvre (BRIT), maneuver (US) ▷ *nm* labourer; **manœuvrer** *vt* to manoeuvre (BRIT), maneuver (US); (*levier, machine*) to operate ▷ *vi* to manoeuvre

manoir [manwaʀ] *nm* manor *ou* country house

manque [mɑ̃k] *nm* (*insuffisance*): **~ de** lack of; (*vide*) emptiness, gap; (*Méd*) withdrawal; **être en état de ~** to suffer withdrawal symptoms

manqué, e [mɑ̃ke] *adj* failed; **garçon ~** tomboy

manquer [mɑ̃ke] *vi* (*faire défaut*) to be lacking; (*être absent*) to be missing; (*échouer*) to fail ▷ *vt* to miss ▷ *vb impers*: **il (nous) manque encore 10 euros** we are still 10 euros short; **il manque des pages (au livre)** there are some pages missing (from the book); **il/cela me manque** I miss him/this; **~ à** (*règles etc*) to be in breach of, fail to observe; **~ de** to lack; **je ne ~ai pas de le lui dire** I'll be sure to tell him; **il a manqué (de) se tuer** he very nearly got killed

mansarde [mɑ̃saʀd] *nf* attic; **mansardé, e** *adj*: **chambre mansardée** attic room

manteau, x [mɑ̃to] *nm* coat

manucure [manykyʀ] *nf* manicurist

manuel, le [manɥɛl] *adj* manual ▷ *nm* (*ouvrage*) manual, handbook

manufacture [manyfaktyʀ] *nf* factory; **manufacturé, e** *adj* manufactured

manuscrit, e [manyskʀi, it] *adj* handwritten

▷ *nm* manuscript

manutention [manytɑ̃sjɔ̃] *nf* (*Comm*) handling

mappemonde [mapmɔ̃d] *nf* (*plane*) map of the world; (*sphère*) globe

maquereau, x [makʀo] *nm* (*Zool*) mackerel *inv*; (*fam*) pimp

maquette [makɛt] *nf* (*à échelle réduite*) (scale) model; (*d'une page illustrée*) paste-up

maquillage [makijaʒ] *nm* making up; (*crème etc*) make-up

maquiller [makije] *vt* (*personne, visage*) to make up; (*truquer: passeport, statistique*) to fake; (: *voiture volée*) to do over (*respray etc*); **se maquiller** *vi* to make up (one's face)

maquis [maki] *nm* (*Géo*) scrub; (*Mil*) maquis, underground fighting *no pl*

maraîcher, -ère [maʀeʃe, ɛʀ] *adj*: **cultures maraîchères** market gardening *sg* ▷ *nm/f* market gardener

marais [maʀɛ] *nm* marsh, swamp

marasme [maʀasm] *nm* stagnation, slump

marathon [maʀatɔ̃] *nm* marathon

marbre [maʀbʀ] *nm* marble

marc [maʀ] *nm* (*de raisin, pommes*) marc

marchand, e [maʀʃɑ̃, ɑ̃d] *nm/f* shopkeeper, tradesman(-woman); (*au marché*) stallholder; (*de vins, charbon*) merchant ▷ *adj*: **prix/valeur ~(e)** market price/value; **marchand de fruits** fruiterer (*BRIT*), fruit seller (*US*); **marchand de journaux** newsagent; **marchand de légumes** greengrocer (*BRIT*), produce dealer (*US*); **marchand de poissons** fishmonger (*BRIT*), fish seller (*US*); **marchander** *vi* to bargain, haggle; **marchandise** *nf* goods *pl*, merchandise *no pl*

marche [maʀʃ] *nf* (*d'escalier*) step; (*activité*) walking; (*promenade, trajet, allure*) walk; (*démarche*) walk, gait; (*Mil etc, Mus*) march; (*fonctionnement*) running; (*des événements*) course; **dans le sens de la ~** (*Rail*) facing the engine; **en ~** (*monter etc*) while the vehicle is moving *ou* in motion; **mettre en ~** to start; **se mettre en ~** (*personne*) to get moving; (*machine*) to start; **être en état de ~** to be in working order; **marche à suivre** (correct) procedure; **marche arrière** reverse (gear); **faire marche arrière** to reverse; (*fig*) to backtrack, back-pedal

marché [maʀʃe] *nm* market; (*transaction*) bargain, deal; **faire du ~ noir** to buy and sell on the black market; **marché aux puces** flea market

marcher [maʀʃe] *vi* to walk; (*Mil*) to march; (*aller: voiture, train, affaires*) to go; (*prospérer*) to go well; (*fonctionner*) to work, run; (*fam: consentir*) to go along, agree; (: *croire naïvement*) to be taken in; **faire ~ qn** (*taquiner*) to pull sb's leg; (*tromper*) to lead sb up the garden path;

comment est-ce que ça marche? how does this work?; **marcheur, -euse** *nm/f* walker

mardi [maʀdi] *nm* Tuesday; **Mardi gras** Shrove Tuesday

mare [maʀ] *nf* pond; (*flaque*) pool

marécage [maʀekaʒ] *nm* marsh, swamp; **marécageux, -euse** *adj* marshy

maréchal, -aux [maʀeʃal, o] *nm* marshal

marée [maʀe] *nf* tide; (*poissons*) fresh (sea) fish; **marée haute/basse** high/low tide; **marée noire** oil slick

marelle [maʀɛl] *nf*: **(jouer à) la ~** (to play) hopscotch

margarine [maʀgaʀin] *nf* margarine

marge [maʀʒ] *nf* margin; **en ~ de** (*fig*) on the fringe of; **marge bénéficiaire** profit margin

marginal, e, -aux [maʀʒinal, o] *nm/f* (*original*) eccentric; (*déshérité*) dropout

marguerite [maʀgəʀit] *nf* marguerite, (oxeye) daisy; (*d'imprimante*) daisy-wheel

mari [maʀi] *nm* husband

mariage [maʀjaʒ] *nm* marriage; (*noce*) wedding; **mariage civil/religieux** registry office (*BRIT*) *ou* civil wedding/church wedding

marié, e [maʀje] *adj* married ▷ *nm* (bride)groom; **les ~s** the bride and groom; **les (jeunes) ~s** the newly-weds

marier [maʀje] *vt* to marry; (*fig*) to blend; **se ~ (avec)** to marry, get married (to)

marin, e [maʀɛ̃, in] *adj* sea *cpd*, marine ▷ *nm* sailor

marine [maʀin] *adj voir* **marin** ▷ *adj inv* navy (blue) ▷ *nm* (*Mil*) marine ▷ *nf* navy; **marine marchande** merchant navy

mariner [maʀine] *vt*: **faire ~** to marinade

marionnette [maʀjɔnɛt] *nf* puppet

maritalement [maʀitalmã] *adv*: **vivre ~** to live as husband and wife

maritime [maʀitim] *adj* sea *cpd*, maritime

mark [maʀk] *nm* mark

marmelade [maʀməlad] *nf* stewed fruit, compote; **marmelade d'oranges** marmalade

marmite [maʀmit] *nf* (cooking-)pot

marmonner [maʀmɔne] *vt, vi* to mumble, mutter

marmotter [maʀmɔte] *vt* to mumble

Maroc [maʀɔk] *nm*: **le ~** Morocco; **marocain, e** [maʀɔkɛ̃, ɛn] *adj* Moroccan ▷ *nm/f*: **Marocain, e** Moroccan

maroquinerie [maʀɔkinʀi] *nf* (*articles*) fine leather goods *pl*; (*boutique*) shop selling fine leather goods

marquant, e [maʀkɑ̃, ɑ̃t] *adj* outstanding

marque [maʀk] *nf* mark; (*Comm: de nourriture*) brand; (: *de voiture, produits manufacturés*) make; (*de disques*) label; **de ~** (*produits*) high-class; (*visiteur etc*) distinguished, well-known; **une grande ~ de vin** a well-known brand of wine; **marque de fabrique** trademark;

marque déposée registered trademark
marquer [maʀke] vt to mark; (*inscrire*) to write down; (*bétail*) to brand; (*Sport: but etc*) to score; (: *joueur*) to mark; (*accentuer: taille etc*) to emphasize; (*manifester: refus, intérêt*) to show ▷ vi (*événement*) to stand out, be outstanding; (*Sport*) to score; **~ les points** to keep the score
marqueterie [maʀkɛtʀi] nf inlaid work, marquetry
marquis [maʀki] nm marquis, marquess
marraine [maʀɛn] nf godmother
marrant, e [maʀɑ̃, ɑ̃t] (*fam*) adj funny
marre [maʀ] (*fam*) adv: **en avoir ~ de** to be fed up with
marrer [maʀe]: **se ~** (*fam*) vi to have a (good) laugh
marron [maʀɔ̃] nm (*fruit*) chestnut ▷ adj inv brown; **marrons glacés** candied chestnuts; **marronnier** nm chestnut (tree)
mars [maʀs] nm March
Marseille [maʀsɛj] n Marseilles
marteau, x [maʀto] nm hammer; **être ~** (*fam*) to be nuts; **marteau-piqueur** nm pneumatic drill
marteler [maʀtəle] vt to hammer
martien, ne [maʀsjɛ̃, jɛn] adj Martian, of ou from Mars
martyr, e [maʀtiʀ] nm/f martyr ▷ adj: **enfants ~s** battered children; **martyre** nm martyrdom; (*fig: sens affaibli*) agony, torture; **martyriser** vt (*Rel*) to martyr; (*fig*) to bully; (*enfant*) to batter, beat
marxiste [maʀksist] adj, nm/f Marxist
mascara [maskaʀa] nm mascara
masculin, e [maskylɛ̃, in] adj masculine; (*sexe, population*) male; (*équipe, vêtements*) men's; (*viril*) manly ▷ nm masculine
masochiste [mazɔʃist] adj masochistic
masque [mask] nm mask; **masque de beauté** face pack ou mask; **masque de plongée** diving mask; **masquer** vt (*cacher: paysage, porte*) to hide, conceal; (*dissimuler: vérité, projet*) to mask, obscure
massacre [masakʀ] nm massacre, slaughter; **massacrer** vt to massacre, slaughter; (*fam: texte etc*) to murder
massage [masaʒ] nm massage
masse [mas] nf mass; (*Élec*) earth; (*maillet*) sledgehammer; (*péj*): **la ~** the masses pl; **une ~ de** (*fam*) masses ou loads of; **en ~** adv (*acheter*) in bulk; (*en foule*) en masse ▷ adj (*exécutions, production*) mass cpd
masser [mase] vt (*assembler: gens*) to gather; (*pétrir*) to massage; **se masser** vi (*foule*) to gather; **masseur, -euse** nm/f masseur(-euse)
massif, -ive [masif, iv] adj (*porte*) solid, massive; (*visage*) heavy, large; (*bois, or*) solid; (*dose*) massive; (*déportations etc*) mass cpd ▷ nm (*montagneux*) massif; (*de fleurs*) clump, bank; **le**

M~ Central the Massif Central
massue [masy] nf club, bludgeon
mastic [mastik] nm (*pour vitres*) putty; (*pour fentes*) filler
mastiquer [mastike] vt (*aliment*) to chew, masticate
mat, e [mat] adj (*couleur, métal*) mat(t); (*bruit, son*) dull ▷ adj inv (*Échecs*): **être ~** to be checkmate
mât [mɑ] nm (*Navig*) mast; (*poteau*) pole, post
match [matʃ] nm match; **faire ~ nul** to draw; **match aller** first leg; **match retour** second leg, return match
matelas [mat(ə)lɑ] nm mattress; **matelas pneumatique** air bed ou mattress
matelot [mat(ə)lo] nm sailor, seaman
mater [mate] vt (*personne*) to bring to heel, subdue; (*révolte*) to put down
matérialiser [mateʀjalize]: **se matérialiser** vi to materialize
matérialiste [mateʀjalist] adj materialistic
matériau [mateʀjo] nm material; **matériaux** nmpl material(s)
matériel, le [mateʀjɛl] adj material ▷ nm equipment no pl; (*de camping etc*) gear no pl; (*Inform*) hardware
maternel, le [mateʀnɛl] adj (*amour, geste*) motherly, maternal; (*grand-père, oncle*) maternal; **maternelle** nf (*aussi*: **école maternelle**) (state) nursery school
maternité [mateʀnite] nf (*établissement*) maternity hospital; (*état de mère*) motherhood, maternity; (*grossesse*) pregnancy; **congé de ~** maternity leave
mathématique [matematik] adj mathematical; **mathématiques** nfpl (*science*) mathematics sg
maths [mat] (*fam*) nfpl maths
matière [matjɛʀ] nf matter; (*Comm, Tech*) material, matter no pl; (*fig: d'un livre etc*) subject matter, material; (*Scol*) subject; **en ~ de** as regards; **matières grasses** fat content sg; **matières premières** raw materials
Matignon [matiɲɔ̃] nm: **(l'hôtel) ~** the French Prime Minister's residence
matin [matɛ̃] nm, adv morning; **le ~** (*pendant le matin*) in the morning; **demain/hier/dimanche ~** tomorrow/yesterday/Sunday morning; **tous les ~s** every morning; **une heure du ~** one o'clock in the morning; **du ~ au soir** from morning till night; **de bon** ou **grand ~** early in the morning; **matinal, e, -aux** adj (*toilette, gymnastique*) morning cpd; **être matinal** (*personne*) to be up early; to be an early riser; **matinée** nf morning; (*spectacle*) matinée
matou [matu] nm tom(cat)
matraque [matʀak] nf (*de policier*) truncheon (BRIT), billy (US)

matricule [matrikyl] nm (Mil) regimental number; (Admin) reference number

matrimonial, e, -aux [matrimɔnjal, jo] adj marital, marriage cpd

maudit, e [modi, -it] (fam) adj (satané) blasted, confounded

maugréer [mogree] vi to grumble

maussade [mosad] adj sullen; (temps) gloomy

mauvais, e [mɔvɛ, ɛz] adj bad; (faux): **le ~ numéro/moment** the wrong number/ moment; (méchant, malveillant) malicious, spiteful ▷ adv: **il fait ~** the weather is bad; **sentir ~** to have a nasty smell, smell nasty; **la mer est ~e** the sea is rough; **mauvais joueur** bad loser; **mauvaise herbe** weed; **mauvaise langue** gossip, scandalmonger (BRIT); **mauvaise plaisanterie** nasty trick

mauve [mov] adj mauve

maux [mo] nmpl de **mal**

maximum [maksimɔm] adj, nm maximum; **au ~** (le plus possible) as much as one can; (tout au plus) at the (very) most ou maximum; **faire le ~** to do one's level best

mayonnaise [majɔnɛz] nf mayonnaise

mazout [mazut] nm (fuel) oil

me, m' [m(ə)] pron (direct: téléphoner, attendre etc) me; (indirect: parler, donner etc) (to) me; (réfléchi) myself

mec [mɛk] (fam) nm bloke, guy

mécanicien, ne [mekanisjɛ̃, jɛn] nm/f mechanic; (Rail) (train ou engine) driver; **pouvez-vous nous envoyer un ~?** can you send a mechanic?

mécanique [mekanik] adj mechanical ▷ nf (science) mechanics sg; (mécanisme) mechanism; **ennui ~** engine trouble no pl

mécanisme [mekanism] nm mechanism

méchamment [meʃamɑ̃] adv nastily, maliciously, spitefully

méchanceté [meʃɑ̃ste] nf nastiness, maliciousness; **dire des ~s à qn** to say spiteful things to sb

méchant, e [meʃɑ̃, ɑ̃t] adj nasty, malicious, spiteful; (enfant: pas sage) naughty; (animal) vicious

mèche [mɛʃ] nf (de cheveux) lock; (de lampe, bougie) wick; (d'un explosif) fuse; **se faire faire des ~s** to have highlights put in one's hair; **de ~ avec** in league with

méchoui [meʃwi] nm barbecue of a whole roast sheep

méconnaissable [mekɔnɛsabl] adj unrecognizable

méconnaître [mekɔnɛtr] vt (ignorer) to be unaware of; (mésestimer) to misjudge

mécontent, e [mekɔ̃tɑ̃, ɑ̃t] adj: **~ (de)** discontented ou dissatisfied ou displeased (with); (contrarié) annoyed (at);

mécontentement nm dissatisfaction, discontent, displeasure; (irritation) annoyance

Mecque [mɛk] nf: **la ~** Mecca

médaille [medaj] nf medal

médaillon [medajɔ̃] nm (bijou) locket

médecin [med(ə)sɛ̃] nm doctor

médecine [med(ə)sin] nf medicine

média [medja] nmpl: **les ~** the media; **médiatique** adj media cpd

médical, e, -aux [medikal, o] adj medical; **passer une visite ~e** to have a medical

médicament [medikamɑ̃] nm medicine, drug

médiéval, e, -aux [medjeval, o] adj medieval

médiocre [medjɔkr] adj mediocre, poor

méditer [medite] vi to meditate

Méditerranée [mediterane] nf: **la (mer) ~** the Mediterranean (Sea); **méditerranéen, ne** adj Mediterranean ▷ nm/f: **Méditerranéen, ne** native ou inhabitant of a Mediterranean country

méduse [medyz] nf jellyfish

méfait [mefɛ] nm (faute) misdemeanour, wrongdoing; **méfaits** nmpl (ravages) ravages, damage sg

méfiance [mefjɑ̃s] nf mistrust, distrust

méfiant, e [mefjɑ̃, jɑ̃t] adj mistrustful, distrustful

méfier [mefje]: **se méfier** vi to be wary; to be careful; **se ~ de** to mistrust, distrust, be wary of

mégaoctet [megaɔktɛ] nm megabyte

mégarde [megard] nf: **par ~** (accidentellement) accidentally; (par erreur) by mistake

mégère [meʒɛr] nf shrew

mégot [mego] (fam) nm cigarette end

meilleur, e [mɛjœr] adj, adv better ▷ nm: **le ~** the best; **le ~ des deux** the better of the two; **il fait ~ qu'hier** it's better weather than yesterday; **meilleur marché** (inv) cheaper

mél [mɛl] nm e-mail

mélancolie [melɑ̃kɔli] nf melancholy, gloom; **mélancolique** adj melancholic, melancholy

mélange [melɑ̃ʒ] nm mixture; **mélanger** vt to mix; (vins, couleurs) to blend; (mettre en désordre) to mix up, muddle (up)

mêlée [mele] nf mêlée, scramble; (Rugby) scrum(mage)

mêler [mele] vt (unir) to mix; (embrouiller) to muddle (up), mix up; **se mêler** vi to mix, mingle; **se ~ à** (personne: se joindre) to join; (: s'associer à) to mix with; **se ~ de** (suj: personne) to meddle with, interfere in; **mêle-toi de ce qui te regarde** ou **de tes affaires!** mind your own business!

mélodie [melɔdi] nf melody; **mélodieux, -euse** adj melodious

melon [m(ə)lɔ̃] nm (Bot) (honeydew) melon;

(*aussi*: **chapeau ~**) bowler (hat)

membre [mɑ̃bʀ] *nm* (*Anat*) limb; (*personne, pays, élément*) member ▷ *adj* member *cpd*

mémé [meme] (*fam*) *nf* granny

 MOT-CLÉ

même [mɛm] *adj* **1** (*avant le nom*) same; **en même temps** at the same time; **ils ont les mêmes goûts** they have the same *ou* similar tastes

2 (*après le nom: renforcement*): **il est la loyauté même** he is loyalty itself; **ce sont ses paroles mêmes** they are his very words

▷ *pron*: **le(la) même** the same one

▷ *adv* **1** (*renforcement*): **il n'a même pas pleuré** he didn't even cry; **même lui l'a dit** even HE said it; **ici même** at this very place; **même si** even if

2: **à même**: **à même la bouteille** straight from the bottle; **à même la peau** next to the skin; **être à même de faire** to be in a position to do, be able to do

3: **de même**: **faire de même** to do likewise; **lui de même** so does (*ou* did *ou* is) he; **de même que** just as; **il en va de même pour** the same goes for

mémoire [memwaʀ] *nf* memory ▷ *nm* (*Scol*) dissertation, paper; **mémoires** *nmpl* (*souvenirs*) memoirs; **à la ~ de** to the *ou* in memory of; **de ~** from memory; **mémoire morte** read-only memory, ROM; **mémoire vive** random access memory, RAM

mémorable [memɔʀabl] *adj* memorable, unforgettable

menace [mənas] *nf* threat; **menacer** *vt* to threaten

ménage [menaʒ] *nm* (*travail*) housework; (*couple*) (married) couple; (*famille, Admin*) household; **faire le ~** to do the housework; **ménagement** *nm* care and attention; **ménager, -ère** *adj* household *cpd*, domestic ▷ *vt* (*traiter: personne*) to handle with tact; (*utiliser*) to use sparingly; (*prendre soin de*) to take (great) care of, look after; (*organiser*) to arrange; **ménagère** *nf* housewife

mendiant, e [mɑ̃djɑ̃, jɑ̃t] *nm/f* beggar

mendier [mɑ̃dje] *vi* to beg ▷ *vt* to beg (for)

mener [m(ə)ne] *vt* to lead; (*enquête*) to conduct; (*affaires*) to manage ▷ *vi*: **~ à/dans** (*emmener*) to take to/into; **~ qch à bien** to see sth through (to a successful conclusion), complete sth successfully

meneur, -euse [mənœʀ, øz] *nm/f* leader; (*péj*) agitator

méningite [menɛ̃ʒit] *nf* meningitis *no pl*

ménopause [menopoz] *nf* menopause

menottes [mənɔt] *nfpl* handcuffs

mensonge [mɑ̃sɔ̃ʒ] *nm* lie; (*action*) lying *no pl*; **mensonger, -ère** *adj* false

mensualité [mɑ̃sɥalite] *nf* (*traite*) monthly payment

mensuel, le [mɑ̃sɥɛl] *adj* monthly

mensurations [mɑ̃syʀasjɔ̃] *nfpl* measurements

mental, e, -aux [mɑ̃tal, o] *adj* mental; **mentalité** *nf* mentality

menteur, -euse [mɑ̃tœʀ, øz] *nm/f* liar

menthe [mɑ̃t] *nf* mint

mention [mɑ̃sjɔ̃] *nf* (*annotation*) note, comment; (*Scol*) grade; **~ bien** ≈ grade B, ≈ good pass; (*Université*) ≈ upper 2nd class pass (*BRIT*), ≈ pass with (high) honors (*US*); (*Admin*): **"rayer les ~s inutiles"** "delete as appropriate"; **mentionner** *vt* to mention

mentir [mɑ̃tiʀ] *vi* to lie

menton [mɑ̃tɔ̃] *nm* chin

menu, e [məny] *adj* (*personne*) slim, slight; (*frais, difficulté*) minor ▷ *adv* (*couper, hacher*) very fine ▷ *nm* menu; **~ touristique/ gastronomique** economy/gourmet's menu

menuiserie [mənɥizʀi] *nf* (*métier*) joinery, carpentry; (*passe-temps*) woodwork; **menuisier** *nm* joiner, carpenter

méprendre [mepʀɑ̃dʀ]: **se méprendre** *vi*: **se ~ sur** to be mistaken (about)

mépris [mepʀi] *nm* (*dédain*) contempt, scorn; **au ~ de** regardless of, in defiance of; **méprisable** *adj* contemptible, despicable; **méprisant, e** *adj* scornful; **méprise** *nf* mistake, error; **mépriser** *vt* to scorn, despise; (*gloire, danger*) to scorn, spurn

mer [mɛʀ] *nf* sea; (*marée*) tide; **en ~** at sea; **en haute** *ou* **pleine ~** off shore, on the open sea; **la ~ du Nord/Rouge/Noire/Morte** the North/Red/Black/Dead Sea

mercenaire [mɛʀsənɛʀ] *nm* mercenary, hired soldier

mercerie [mɛʀsəʀi] *nf* (*boutique*) haberdasher's shop (*BRIT*), notions store (*US*)

merci [mɛʀsi] *excl* thank you ▷ *nf*: **à la ~ de qn/qch** at sb's mercy/the mercy of sth; **~ beaucoup** thank you very much; **~ de** thank you for; **sans ~** merciless(ly)

mercredi [mɛʀkʀədi] *nm* Wednesday; **~ des Cendres** Ash Wednesday; *voir aussi* **lundi**

mercure [mɛʀkyʀ] *nm* mercury

merde [mɛʀd] (*fam!*) *nf* shit (!) ▷ *excl* (*bloody*) hell (!)

mère [mɛʀ] *nf* mother; **mère célibataire** single parent, unmarried mother; **mère de famille** housewife, mother

merguez [mɛʀgɛz] *nf* merguez sausage (*type of spicy sausage from N Africa*)

méridional, e, -aux [meʀidjɔnal, o] *adj* southern ▷ *nm/f* Southerner

meringue [məʀɛ̃g] *nf* meringue

m

mérite [meʀit] nm merit; **avoir du ~ (à faire qch)** to deserve credit (for doing sth); **mériter** vt to deserve

merle [mɛʀl] nm blackbird

merveille [mɛʀvɛj] nf marvel, wonder; **faire ~** to work wonders; **à ~** perfectly, wonderfully; **merveilleux, -euse** adj marvellous, wonderful

mes [me] adj voir **mon**

mésange [mezɑ̃ʒ] nf tit(mouse)

mésaventure [mezavɑ̃tyʀ] nf misadventure, misfortune

Mesdames [medam] nfpl de **Madame**

Mesdemoiselles [medmwazɛl] nfpl de **Mademoiselle**

mesquin, e [mɛskɛ̃, in] adj mean, petty; **mesquinerie** nf meanness; (procédé) mean trick

message [mesaʒ] nm message; **est-ce que je peux laisser un ~?** can I leave a message?; **~ SMS** text message; **messager, -ère** nm/f messenger; **messagerie** nf (Internet): **messagerie électronique** e-mail; **messagerie vocale** (service) voice mail; **messagerie instantanée** instant messenger

messe [mɛs] nf mass; **aller à la ~** to go to mass

Messieurs [mesjø] nmpl de **Monsieur**

mesure [m(ə)zyʀ] nf (évaluation, dimension) measurement; (récipient) measure; (Mus: cadence) time, tempo; (: division) bar; (retenue) moderation; (disposition) measure, step; **sur ~** (costume) made-to-measure; **dans la ~ où** insofar as, inasmuch as; **à ~ que** as; **être en ~ de** to be in a position to; **dans une certaine ~** to a certain extent

mesurer [məzyʀe] vt to measure; (juger) to weigh up, assess; (modérer: ses paroles etc) to moderate

métal, -aux [metal, o] nm metal; **métallique** adj metallic

météo [meteo] nf (bulletin) weather report

météorologie [meteoʀɔlɔʒi] nf meteorology

méthode [metɔd] nf method; (livre, ouvrage) manual, tutor

méticuleux, -euse [metikylø, øz] adj meticulous

métier [metje] nm (profession: gén) job; (: manuel) trade; (artisanal) craft; (technique, expérience) (acquired) skill ou technique; (aussi: **~ à tisser**) (weaving) loom

métis, se [metis] adj, nm/f half-caste, half-breed

métrage [metʀaʒ] nm: **long/moyen/court ~** full-length/medium-length/short film

mètre [mɛtʀ] nm metre; (règle) (metre) rule; (ruban) tape measure; **métrique** adj metric

métro [metʀo] nm underground (BRIT), subway

métropole [metʀɔpɔl] nf (capitale) metropolis; (pays) home country

mets [mɛ] nm dish

metteur [metœʀ] nm: **~ en scène** (Théâtre) producer; (Cinéma) director

 MOT-CLÉ

mettre [mɛtʀ] vt **1** (placer) to put; **mettre en bouteille/en sac** to bottle/put in bags ou sacks

2 (vêtements: revêtir) to put on; (: porter) to wear; **mets ton gilet** put your cardigan on; **je ne mets plus mon manteau** I no longer wear my coat

3 (faire fonctionner: chauffage, électricité) to put on; (: réveil, minuteur) to set; (installer: gaz, eau) to put in, lay on; **mettre en marche** to start up

4 (consacrer): **mettre du temps à faire qch** to take time to do sth ou over sth

5 (noter, écrire) to say, put (down); **qu'est-ce qu'il a mis sur la carte?** what did he say ou write on the card?; **mettez au pluriel ...** put ... into the plural

6 (supposer): **mettons que ...** let's suppose ou say that ...

7: **y mettre du sien** to pull one's weight

se mettre vi **1** (se placer): **vous pouvez vous mettre là** you can sit (ou stand) there; **où ça se met?** where does it go?; **se mettre au lit** to get into bed; **se mettre au piano** to sit down at the piano; **se mettre de l'encre sur les doigts** to get ink on one's fingers

2 (s'habiller): **se mettre en maillot de bain** to get into ou put on a swimsuit; **n'avoir rien à se mettre** to have nothing to wear

3: **se mettre à** to begin, start; **se mettre à faire** to begin ou start doing ou to do; **se mettre au piano** to start learning the piano; **se mettre au régime** to go on a diet; **se mettre au travail/à l'étude** to get down to work/one's studies

meuble [mœbl] nm piece of furniture; **des ~s** furniture; **meublé** nm furnished flatlet (BRIT) ou room; **meubler** vt to furnish

meuf [mœf] nf (fam) woman

meugler [møgle] vi to low, moo

meule [møl] nf (de foin, blé) stack; (de fromage) round; (à broyer) millstone

meunier [mønje] nm miller

meurs etc [mœʀ] vb voir **mourir**

meurtre [mœʀtʀ] nm murder; **meurtrier, -ière** adj (arme etc) deadly; (fureur, instincts) murderous ▷ nm/f murderer(-eress)

meurtrir [mœʀtʀiʀ] vt to bruise; (fig) to wound

meus etc [mœ] vb voir **mouvoir**

meute [møt] *nf* pack

mexicain, e [mɛksikɛ̃, ɛn] *adj* Mexican ▷ *nm/f*: **M~, e** Mexican

Mexico [mɛksiko] *n* Mexico City

Mexique [mɛksik] *nm*: **le ~** Mexico

mi [mi] *nm* (*Mus*) E; (*en chantant la gamme*) mi ▷ *préfixe*: **mi...** half(-); mid-; **à la mi-janvier** in mid-January; **à mi-jambes/corps** (up *ou* down) to the knees/waist; **à mi-hauteur** halfway up

miauler [mjole] *vi* to mew

miche [miʃ] *nf* round *ou* cob loaf

mi-chemin [miʃmɛ̃]: **à ~** *adv* halfway, midway

mi-clos, e [miklo, kloz] *adj* half-closed

micro [mikro] *nm* mike, microphone; (*Inform*) micro

microbe [mikrɔb] *nm* germ, microbe

micro...: **micro-onde** *nf*: **four à micro-ondes** microwave oven; **micro-ordinateur** *nm* microcomputer; **microscope** *nm* microscope; **microscopique** *adj* microscopic

midi [midi] *nm* midday, noon; (*moment du déjeuner*) lunchtime; (*sud*) south; **à ~** at 12 (o'clock) *ou* midday *ou* noon; **le M~** the South (of France), the Midi

mie [mi] *nf* crumb (of the loaf)

miel [mjɛl] *nm* honey; **mielleux, -euse** *adj* (*personne*) unctuous, syrupy

mien, ne [mjɛ̃, mjɛn] *pron*: **le(la) ~(ne), les ~(ne)s** mine; **les ~s** my family

miette [mjɛt] *nf* (*de pain, gâteau*) crumb; (*fig: de la conversation etc*) scrap; **en ~s** in pieces *ou* bits

○ **MOT-CLÉ**

mieux [mjø] *adv* **1** (*d'une meilleure façon*): **mieux (que)** better (than); **elle travaille/mange mieux** she works/eats better; **aimer mieux** to prefer; **elle va mieux** she is better; **de mieux en mieux** better and better

2 (*de la meilleure façon*) best; **ce que je connais le mieux** what I know best; **les livres les mieux faits** the best-made books ▷ *adj* **1** (*plus à l'aise, en meilleure forme*) better; **se sentir mieux** to feel better

2 (*plus satisfaisant*) better; **c'est mieux ainsi** it's better like this; **c'est le mieux des deux** it's the better of the two; **le(la) mieux, les mieux** the best; **demandez-lui, c'est le mieux** ask him, it's the best thing

3 (*plus joli*) better-looking; **il est mieux que son frère** (*plus beau*) he's better-looking than his brother; (*plus gentil*) he's nicer than his brother; **il est mieux sans moustache** he looks better without a moustache

4: **au mieux** at best; **au mieux avec** on the best of terms with; **pour le mieux** for the best

▷ *nm* **1** (*progrès*) improvement

2: **de mon/ton mieux** as best I/you can (*ou* could); **faire de son mieux** to do one's best

mignon, ne [miɲɔ̃, ɔn] *adj* sweet, cute

migraine [migrɛn] *nf* headache; (*Méd*) migraine

mijoter [miʒɔte] *vt* to simmer; (*préparer avec soin*) to cook lovingly; (*fam: tramer*) to plot, cook up ▷ *vi* to simmer

milieu, x [miljø] *nm* (*centre*) middle; (*Bio, Géo*) environment; (*entourage social*) milieu; (*provenance*) background; (*pègre*): **le ~** the underworld; **au ~ de** in the middle of; **au beau ou en plein ~ (de)** right in the middle (of); **un juste ~** a happy medium

militaire [militɛr] *adj* military, army *cpd* ▷ *nm* serviceman

militant, e [militɑ̃, ɑ̃t] *adj, nm/f* militant

militer [milite] *vi* to be a militant

mille [mil] *num* a *ou* one thousand ▷ *nm* (*mesure*): **~ (marin)** nautical mile; **mettre dans le ~** (*fig*) to be bang on target; **millefeuille** *nm* cream *ou* vanilla slice; **millénaire** *nm* millennium ▷ *adj* thousand-year-old; (*fig*) ancient; **mille-pattes** *nm inv* centipede

millet [mijɛ] *nm* millet

milliard [miljar] *nm* milliard, thousand million (*BRIT*), billion (*US*); **milliardaire** *nm/f* multimillionaire (*BRIT*), billionaire (*US*)

millier [milje] *nm* thousand; **un ~ (de)** a thousand or so, about a thousand; **par ~s** in (their) thousands, by the thousand

milligramme [miligram] *nm* milligramme

millimètre [milimɛtr] *nm* millimetre

million [miljɔ̃] *nm* million; **deux ~s de** two million; **millionnaire** *nm/f* millionaire

mime [mim] *nm/f* (*acteur*) mime(r) ▷ *nm* (*art*) mime, miming; **mimer** *vt* to mime; (*singer*) to mimic, take off

minable [minabl] *adj* (*décrépit*) shabby(-looking); (*médiocre*) pathetic

mince [mɛ̃s] *adj* thin; (*personne, taille*) slim, slender; (*fig: profit, connaissances*) slight, small, weak ▷ *excl*: **~ alors!** drat it!, darn it! (*US*); **minceur** *nf* thinness; (*d'une personne*) slimness, slenderness; **mincir** *vi* to get slimmer

mine [min] *nf* (*physionomie*) expression, look; (*allure*) exterior, appearance; (*de crayon*) lead; (*gisement, explosif, fig: source*) mine; **avoir bonne ~** (*personne*) to look well; (*ironique*) to look an utter idiot; **avoir mauvaise ~** to look unwell *ou* poorly; **faire ~ de faire** to make a pretence of doing; **~ de rien** although you wouldn't think so

miner [mine] *vt* (*saper*) to undermine, erode; (*Mil*) to mine

minerai [minrɛ] *nm* ore

minéral, e, -aux [mineʀal, o] *adj, nm* mineral

minéralogique [mineʀalɔʒik] *adj*: **plaque ~** number (BRIT) *ou* license (US) plate; **numéro ~** registration (BRIT) *ou* license (US) number

minet, te [mine, ɛt] *nm/f* (*chat*) pussy-cat; (*péj*) young trendy

mineur, e [minœʀ] *adj* minor ⊳ *nm/f* (*Jur*) minor, person under age ⊳ *nm* (*travailleur*) miner

miniature [minjatyʀ] *adj, nf* miniature

minibus [minibys] *nm* minibus

minier, -ière [minje, jɛʀ] *adj* mining

mini-jupe [miniʒyp] *nf* mini-skirt

minime [minim] *adj* minor, minimal

minimessage [minimesaʒ] *nm* text message

minimiser [minimize] *vt* to minimize; (*fig*) to play down

minimum [minimɔm] *adj, nm* minimum; **au ~** (*au moins*) at the very least

ministère [ministɛʀ] *nm* (*aussi Rel*) ministry; (*cabinet*) government

ministre [ministʀ] *nm* (*aussi Rel*) minister; **ministre d'État** senior minister *ou* secretary

Minitel® [minitɛl] *nm* videotext terminal and service

● **MINITEL®**
●
●
● **Minitel®** is a public information system
● provided by France-Télécom to telephone
● subscribers since the early 80s. Among
● the services available are a computerized
● telephone directory and information on
● travel timetables, stock-market news
● and situations vacant. Subscribers pay for
● their time on screen as part of their phone
● bill. Although this information is now
● also available on the Internet, the special
● Minitel® screens, terminals and keyboards
● are still very much a part of French daily life.

minoritaire [minɔʀitɛʀ] *adj* minority

minorité [minɔʀite] *nf* minority; **être en ~ to** be in the *ou* a minority

minuit [minɥi] *nm* midnight

minuscule [minyskyl] *adj* minute, tiny ⊳ *nf*: **(lettre) ~** small letter

minute [minyt] *nf* minute; **à la ~** (just) this instant; (*faire*) there and then; **minuter** *vt* to time; **minuterie** *nf* time switch

minutieux, -euse [minysjø, jøz] *adj* (*personne*) meticulous; (*travail*) minutely detailed

mirabelle [miʀabɛl] *nf* (cherry) plum

miracle [miʀakl] *nm* miracle

mirage [miʀaʒ] *nm* mirage

mire [miʀ] *nf*: **point de ~** (*fig*) focal point

miroir [miʀwaʀ] *nm* mirror

miroiter [miʀwate] *vi* to sparkle, shimmer; **faire ~ qch à qn** to paint sth in glowing colours for sb, dangle sth in front of sb's eyes

mis, e [mi, miz] *pp de* **mettre** ⊳ *adj*: **bien ~** well-dressed

mise [miz] *nf* (*argent: au jeu*) stake; (*tenue*) clothing, attire; **être de ~** to be acceptable *ou* in season; **mise à jour** updating; **mise au point** (*fig*) clarification; **mise de fonds** capital outlay; **mise en plis** set; **mise en scène** production

miser [mize] *vt* (*enjeu*) to stake, bet; **~ sur** (*cheval, numéro*) to bet on; (*fig*) to bank *ou* count on

misérable [mizeʀabl] *adj* (*lamentable, malheureux*) pitiful, wretched; (*pauvre*) poverty-stricken; (*insignifiant, mesquin*) miserable ⊳ *nm/f* wretch

misère [mizɛʀ] *nf* (extreme) poverty, destitution; **misères** *nfpl* (*malheurs*) woes, miseries; (*ennuis*) little troubles; **salaire de ~** starvation wage

missile [misil] *nm* missile

mission [misjɔ̃] *nf* mission; **partir en ~** (*Admin, Pol*) to go on an assignment; **missionnaire** *nm/f* missionary

mité, e [mite] *adj* moth-eaten

mi-temps [mitɑ̃] *nf inv* (*Sport: période*) half; (: *pause*) half-time; **à ~** part-time

miteux, -euse [mitø, øz] *adj* (*lieu*) seedy

mitigé, e [mitiʒe] *adj*: **sentiments ~s** mixed feelings

mitoyen, ne [mitwajɛ̃, jɛn] *adj* (*mur*) common, party *cpd*; **maisons ~nes** semi-detached houses; (*plus de deux*) terraced (BRIT) *ou* row (US) houses

mitrailler [mitʀaje] *vt* to machine-gun; (*fig*) to pelt, bombard; (: *photographier*) to take shot after shot of; **mitraillette** *nf* submachine gun; **mitrailleuse** *nf* machine gun

mi-voix [mivwa]: **à ~** *adv* in a low *ou* hushed voice

mixage [miksaʒ] *nm* (*Cinéma*) (sound) mixing

mixer [miksœʀ] *nm* (food) mixer

mixte [mikst] *adj* (*gén*) mixed; (*Scol*) mixed, coeducational; **cuisinière ~** combined gas and electric cooker (BRIT) *ou* stove (US)

mixture [mikstyʀ] *nf* mixture; (*fig*) concoction

Mlle (*pl ~s*) *abr* = **Mademoiselle**

MM *abr* = **Messieurs**

Mme (*pl ~s*) *abr* = **Madame**

mobile [mɔbil] *adj* mobile; (*pièce de machine*) moving ⊳ *nm* (*motif*) motive; (*œuvre d'art*) mobile; **(téléphone) ~** mobile (phone)

mobilier, -ière [mɔbilje, jɛʀ] *nm* furniture

mobiliser [mɔbilize] *vt* to mobilize

mocassin [mɔkasɛ̃] *nm* moccasin

moche [mɔʃ] (*fam*) *adj* (*laid*) ugly; (*mauvais*)

rotten

modalité [mɔdalite] *nf* form, mode

mode [mɔd] *nf* fashion ▷ *nm* (*manière*) form, mode; (*Ling*) mood; (*Mus, Inform*) mode; **à la ~** fashionable, in fashion; **mode d'emploi** directions *pl* (for use); **mode de paiement** method of payment; **mode de vie** lifestyle

modèle [mɔdɛl] *adj, nm* model; (*qui pose: de peintre*) sitter; **modèle déposé** registered design; **modèle réduit** small-scale model; **modeler** *vt* to model

modem [mɔdɛm] *nm* modem

modéré, e [mɔdeʀe] *adj, nm/f* moderate

modérer [mɔdeʀe] *vt* to moderate; **se modérer** *vi* to restrain o.s.

moderne [mɔdɛʀn] *adj* modern ▷ *nm* (*style*) modern style; (*meubles*) modern furniture; **moderniser** *vt* to modernize

modeste [mɔdɛst] *adj* modest; **modestie** *nf* modesty

modifier [mɔdifje] *vt* to modify, alter; **se modifier** *vi* to alter

modique [mɔdik] *adj* modest

module [mɔdyl] *nm* module

moelle [mwal] *nf* marrow

moelleux, -euse [mwalø, øz] *adj* soft; (*gâteau*) light and moist

mœurs [mœʀ] *nfpl* (*conduite*) morals; (*manières*) manners; (*pratiques sociales, mode de vie*) habits

moi [mwa] *pron* me; (*emphatique*): **~, je ...** for my part, I ...; I myself ...; **c'est ~ qui l'ai fait** I did it, it was me who did it; **apporte-le-~** bring it to me; **à ~ -mine;** (*dans un jeu*) my turn; **moi-même** *pron* myself; (*emphatique*) I myself

moindre [mwɛ̃dʀ] *adj* lesser; lower; **le(la) ~, les ~s** the least, the slightest; **merci — c'est la ~ des choses!** thank you — it's a pleasure!

moine [mwan] *nm* monk, friar

moineau, x [mwano] *nm* sparrow

⊙ **MOT-CLÉ**

moins [mwɛ̃] *adv* **1** (*comparatif*): **moins (que)** less (than); **moins grand que** less tall than, not as tall as; **il a 3 ans de moins que moi** he's 3 years younger than me; **moins je travaille, mieux je me porte** the less I work, the better I feel

2 (*superlatif*): **le moins** (the) least; **c'est ce que j'aime le moins** it's what I like (the) least; **le(la) moins doué(e)** the least gifted; **au moins, du moins** at least; **pour le moins** at the very least

3: **moins de** (*quantité*) less (than); (*nombre*) fewer (than); **moins de sable/d'eau** less sand/water; **moins de livres/gens** fewer books/people; **moins de 2 ans** less than 2 years; **moins de midi** not yet midday

4: **de moins, en moins: 100 euros/3 jours de moins** 100 euros/3 days less; **3 livres en moins** 3 books fewer; **3 books too few; de l'argent en moins** less money; **le soleil en moins** but for the sun, minus the sun; **de moins en moins** less and less

5: **à moins de, à moins que** unless; **à moins de faire** unless we do (*ou* he does *etc*); **à moins que tu ne fasses** unless you do; **à moins d'un accident** barring any accident

▷ *prép*: **4 moins 2** 4 minus 2; **il est moins 5** it's 5 to; **il fait moins 5** it's 5 (degrees) below (freezing), it's minus 5

---

mois [mwa] *nm* month

moisi [mwazi] *nm* mould, mildew; **odeur de ~** musty smell; **moisir** *vi* to go mouldy; **moisissure** *nf* mould *no pl*

moisson [mwasɔ̃] *nf* harvest; **moissonner** *vt* to harvest, reap; **moissonneuse** *nf* (*machine*) harvester

moite [mwat] *adj* sweaty, sticky

moitié [mwatje] *nf* half; **la ~** half; **la ~ de** half (of); **la ~ du temps** half the time; **à la ~ de** halfway through; **à ~** (*avant le verbe*) half; (*avant l'adjectif*) half-; **à ~ prix** (at) half-price

molaire [mɔlɛʀ] *nf* molar

molester [mɔlɛste] *vt* to manhandle, maul (about)

molle [mɔl] *adj voir* **mou; mollement** *adv* (*péj: travailler*) sluggishly; (*protester*) feebly

mollet [mɔlɛ] *nm* calf ▷ *adj m*: **œuf ~** soft-boiled egg

molletonné, e [mɔltɔne] *adj* fleece-lined

mollir [mɔliʀ] *vi* (*fléchir*) to relent; (*substance*) to go soft

mollusque [mɔlysk] *nm* mollusc

môme [mom] (*fam*) *nm/f* (*enfant*) brat

moment [mɔmɑ̃] *nm* moment; **ce n'est pas le ~** this is not the (right) time; **au même ~** at the same time; (*instant*) at the same moment; **pour un bon ~** for a good while; **pour le ~** for the moment, for the time being; **au ~ de** at the time of; **au ~ où** just as; **à tout ~** (*peut arriver etc*) at any time *ou* moment; (*constamment*) constantly, continually; **en ce ~** at the moment; at present; **sur le ~** at the time; **par ~s** now and then, at times; **d'un ~ à l'autre** any time (now); **du ~ où** *ou* **que** seeing that, since; **momentané, e** *adj* temporary, momentary; **momentanément** *adv* (*court instant*) for a short while

momie [mɔmi] *nf* mummy

mon, ma [mɔ̃, ma] (*pl* **mes**) *adj* my

Monaco [mɔnako] *nm* Monaco

monarchie [mɔnaʀʃi] *nf* monarchy

monastère [mɔnastɛʀ] *nm* monastery

mondain, e [mɔ̃dɛ̃, ɛn] *adj* (*vie*) society *cpd*

monde [mɔ̃d] *nm* world; (*haute société*): **le ~**

m

(high) society; **il y a du ~** (*beaucoup de gens*) there are a lot of people; (*quelques personnes*) there are some people; **beaucoup/peu de ~** many/few people; **mettre au ~** to bring into the world; **pas le moins du ~** not in the least; **mondial, e, -aux** *adj* (*population*) world *cpd*; (*influence*) world-wide; **mondialement** *adv* throughout the world; **mondialisation** *nf* globalization

monégasque [mɔnegask] *adj* Monegasque, of *ou* from Monaco ▷ *nm/f*: **M~** Monegasque, person from *ou* inhabitant of Monaco

monétaire [mɔnetɛʀ] *adj* monetary

moniteur, -trice [mɔnitœʀ, tʀis] *nm/f* (*Sport*) instructor(-tress); (*de colonie de vacances*) supervisor ▷ *nm* (*écran*) monitor

monnaie [mɔnɛ] *nf* (*Écon, gén: moyen d'échange*) currency; (*petites pièces*): **avoir de la ~** to have (some) change; **une pièce de ~** a coin; **faire de la ~** to get (some) change; **avoir/faire la ~ de 20 euros** to have change of/get change for 20 euros; **rendre à qn la ~ (sur 20 euros)** to give sb the change (out of *ou* from 20 euros); **gardez la ~** keep the change; **désolé, je n'ai pas de ~** sorry, I don't have any change; **avez-vous de la ~?** do you have any change?

monologue [mɔnɔlɔg] *nm* monologue, soliloquy; **monologuer** *vi* to soliloquize

monopole [mɔnɔpɔl] *nm* monopoly

monotone [mɔnɔtɔn] *adj* monotonous

Monsieur [məsjø] (*pl* **Messieurs**) *titre* Mr ▷ *nm* (*homme quelconque*): **un/le monsieur** a/the gentleman; **~, ...** (*en tête de lettre*) Dear Sir, ...; *voir aussi* **Madame**

monstre [mɔ̃stʀ] *nm* monster ▷ *adj* (*fam: colossal*) monstrous; **un travail ~** a fantastic amount of work; **monstrueux, -euse** *adj* monstrous

mont [mɔ̃] *nm*: **par ~s et par vaux** up hill and down dale; **le Mont Blanc** Mont Blanc

montage [mɔ̃taʒ] *nm* (*assemblage: d'appareil*) assembly; (*Photo*) photomontage; (*Cinéma*) editing

montagnard, e [mɔ̃taɲaʀ, aʀd] *adj* mountain *cpd* ▷ *nm/f* mountain-dweller

montagne [mɔ̃taɲ] *nf* (*cime*) mountain; (*région*): **la ~** the mountains *pl*; **montagnes russes** big dipper *sg*, switchback *sg*; **montagneux, -euse** *adj* mountainous; (*basse montagne*) hilly

montant, e [mɔ̃tɑ̃, ɑ̃t] *adj* rising; **pull à col ~** high-necked jumper ▷ *nm* (*somme, total*) (sum) total, (total) amount; (*de fenêtre*) upright; (*de lit*) post

monte-charge [mɔ̃tʃaʀʒ] *nm inv* goods lift, hoist

montée [mɔ̃te] *nf* (*des prix, hostilités*) rise; (*escalade*) climb; (*côte*) hill; **au milieu de la ~**

halfway up

monter [mɔ̃te] *vt* (*escalier, côte*) to go (*ou* come) up; (*valise, paquet*) to take (*ou* bring) up; (*étagère*) to raise; (*tente, échafaudage*) to put up; (*machine*) to assemble; (*Cinéma*) to edit; (*Théâtre*) to put on, stage; (*société etc*) to set up ▷ *vi* to go (*ou* come) up; (*prix, niveau, température*) to go up, rise; (*passager*) to get on; **~ à cheval** (*faire du cheval*) to ride (a horse); **~ sur** to climb up onto; **~ sur** *ou* **à un arbre/une échelle** to climb (up) a tree/ladder; **se monter à** (*frais etc*) to add up to, come to

montgolfière [mɔ̃gɔlfjɛʀ] *nf* hot-air balloon

montre [mɔ̃tʀ] *nf* watch; **contre la ~** (*Sport*) against the clock

Montréal [mɔ̃ʀeal] *n* Montreal

montrer [mɔ̃tʀe] *vt* to show; **~ qch à qn** to show sb sth; **pouvez-vous me ~ où c'est?** can you show me where it is?

monture [mɔ̃tyʀ] *nf* (*cheval*) mount; (*de lunettes*) frame; (*d'une bague*) setting

monument [mɔnymɑ̃] *nm* monument; **monument aux morts** war memorial

moquer [mɔke]: **se moquer de** *vt* to make fun of, laugh at; (*fam: se désintéresser de*) not to care about; (*tromper*): **se ~ de qn** to take sb for a ride

moquette [mɔkɛt] *nf* fitted carpet

moqueur, -euse [mɔkœʀ, øz] *adj* mocking

moral, e, -aux [mɔʀal, o] *adj* moral ▷ *nm* morale; **avoir le ~** (*fam*) to be in good spirits; **avoir le ~ à zéro** (*fam*) to be really down; **morale** *nf* (*mœurs*) morals *pl*; (*valeurs*) moral standards *pl*, morality; (*d'une fable etc*) moral; **faire la morale à** to lecture, preach at; **moralité** *nf* morality; (*de fable*) moral

morceau, x [mɔʀso] *nm* piece, bit; (*d'une œuvre*) passage, extract; (*Mus*) piece; (*Culin: de viande*) cut; (*de sucre*) lump; **mettre en ~x** to pull to pieces *ou* bits; **manger un ~** to have a bite (to eat)

morceler [mɔʀsəle] *vt* to break up, divide up

mordant, e [mɔʀdɑ̃, ɑ̃t] *adj* (*ton, remarque*) scathing, cutting; (*ironie, froid*) biting ▷ *nm* (*style*) bite, punch

mordiller [mɔʀdije] *vt* to nibble at, chew at

mordre [mɔʀdʀ] *vt* to bite ▷ *vi* (*poisson*) to bite; **~ sur** (*fig*) to go over into, overlap into; **~ à l'hameçon** to bite, rise to the bait

mordu, e [mɔʀdy] (*fam*) *nm/f* enthusiast; **un ~ de jazz** a jazz fanatic

morfondre [mɔʀfɔ̃dʀ]: **se morfondre** *vi* to mope

morgue [mɔʀg] *nf* (*arrogance*) haughtiness; (*lieu: de la police*) morgue; (: *à l'hôpital*) mortuary

morne [mɔʀn] *adj* dismal, dreary

morose [mɔʀoz] *adj* sullen, morose

mors [mɔʀ] *nm* bit

morse [mɔʀs] *nm* (*Zool*) walrus; (*Tél*) Morse (code)

morsure [mɔʀsyʀ] *nf* bite

mort[1] [mɔʀ] *nf* death

mort[2], **e** [mɔʀ, mɔʀt] *pp de* **mourir** ▷ *adj* dead ▷ *nm/f* (*défunt*) dead man *ou* woman; (*victime*): **il y a eu plusieurs ~s** several people were killed, there were several killed; **~ de peur/ fatigue** frightened to death/dead tired

mortalité [mɔʀtalite] *nf* mortality, death rate

mortel, le [mɔʀtɛl] *adj* (*poison etc*) deadly, lethal; (*accident, blessure*) fatal; (*silence, ennemi*) deadly; (*péché*) mortal; (*fam: ennuyeux*) deadly boring

mort-né, e [mɔʀne] *adj* (*enfant*) stillborn

mortuaire [mɔʀtɥɛʀ] *adj*: **avis ~** death announcement

morue [mɔʀy] *nf* (*Zool*) cod *inv*

mosaïque [mɔzaik] *nf* mosaic

Moscou [mɔsku] *n* Moscow

mosquée [mɔske] *nf* mosque

mot [mo] *nm* word; (*message*) line, note; **~ à ~** word for word; **mot de passe** password; **mots croisés** crossword (puzzle) *sg*

motard [mɔtaʀ] *nm* (*cause*) biker; (*policier*) motorcycle cop

motel [mɔtɛl] *nm* motel

moteur, -trice [mɔtœʀ, tʀis] *adj* (*Anat, Physiol*) motor; (*Tech*) driving; (*Auto*): **à 4 roues motrices** 4-wheel drive ▷ *nm* engine, motor; **à ~** power-driven, motor *cpd*; **moteur de recherche** search engine

motif [mɔtif] *nm* (*cause*) motive; (*décoratif*) design, pattern, motif; **sans ~** groundless

motivation [mɔtivasjɔ̃] *nf* motivation

motiver [mɔtive] *vt* to motivate; (*justifier*) to justify, account for

moto [mɔto] *nf* (*motor*)bike; **motocycliste** *nm/f* motorcyclist

motorisé, e [mɔtɔʀize] *adj* (*personne*) having transport *ou* a car

motrice [mɔtʀis] *adj voir* **moteur**

motte [mɔt] *nf*: **~ de terre** lump of earth, clod (of earth); **motte de beurre** lump of butter

mou (mol), molle [mu, mɔl] *adj* soft; (*personne*) lethargic; (*protestations*) weak ▷ *nm*: **avoir du mou** to be slack

mouche [muʃ] *nf* fly

moucher [muʃe]: **se moucher** *vi* to blow one's nose

moucheron [muʃʀɔ̃] *nm* midge

mouchoir [muʃwaʀ] *nm* handkerchief, hanky; **mouchoir en papier** tissue, paper hanky

moudre [mudʀ] *vt* to grind

moue [mu] *nf* pout; **faire la ~** to pout; (*fig*) to pull a face

mouette [mwɛt] *nf* (*sea*)gull

moufle [mufl] *nf* (*gant*) mitt(en)

mouillé, e [muje] *adj* wet

mouiller [muje] *vt* (*humecter*) to wet, moisten; (*tremper*): **~ qn/qch** to make sb/sth wet ▷ *vi* (*Navig*) to lie *ou* be at anchor; **se mouiller** to get wet; (*fam: prendre des risques*) to commit o.s.

moulant, e [mulɑ̃, ɑ̃t] *adj* figure-hugging

moule [mul] *nf* mussel ▷ *nm* (*Culin*) mould; **moule à gâteaux** *nm* cake tin (ʙʀɪᴛ) *ou* pan (ᴜs)

mouler [mule] *vt* (*suj: vêtement*) to hug, fit closely round

moulin [mulɛ̃] *nm* mill; **moulin à café** coffee mill; **moulin à eau** watermill; **moulin à légumes** (vegetable) shredder; **moulin à paroles** (*fig*) chatterbox; **moulin à poivre** pepper mill; **moulin à vent** windmill

moulinet [muline] *nm* (*de canne à pêche*) reel; (*mouvement*): **faire des ~s avec qch** to whirl sth around

moulinette® [mulinɛt] *nf* (vegetable) shredder

moulu, e [muly] *pp de* **moudre**

mourant, e [muʀɑ̃, ɑ̃t] *adj* dying

mourir [muʀiʀ] *vi* to die; (*civilisation*) to die out; **~ de froid/faim** to die of exposure/ hunger; **~ de faim/d'ennui** (*fig*) to be starving/bored to death; **~ d'envie de faire** to be dying to do

mousse [mus] *nf* (*Bot*) moss; (*de savon*) lather; (*écume: sur eau, bière*) froth, foam; (*Culin*) mousse ▷ *nm* (*Navig*) ship's boy; **mousse à raser** shaving foam

mousseline [muslin] *nf* muslin; **pommes ~** mashed potatoes

mousser [muse] *vi* (*bière, détergent*) to foam; (*savon*) to lather; **mousseux, -euse** *adj* frothy ▷ *nm*: (*vin*) **mousseux** sparkling wine

mousson [musɔ̃] *nf* monsoon

moustache [mustaʃ] *nf* moustache; **moustaches** *nfpl* (*du chat*) whiskers *pl*; **moustachu, e** *adj* with a moustache

moustiquaire [mustikɛʀ] *nf* mosquito net

moustique [mustik] *nm* mosquito

moutarde [mutaʀd] *nf* mustard

mouton [mutɔ̃] *nm* sheep *inv*; (*peau*) sheepskin; (*Culin*) mutton

mouvement [muvmɑ̃] *nm* movement; (*fig: impulsion*) gesture; **avoir un bon ~** to make a nice gesture; **en ~** in motion; on the move; **mouvementé, e** *adj* (*vie, poursuite*) eventful; (*réunion*) turbulent

mouvoir [muvwaʀ]: **se mouvoir** *vi* to move

moyen, ne [mwajɛ̃, jɛn] *adj* average; (*tailles, prix*) medium; (*de grandeur moyenne*) medium-sized ▷ *nm* (*façon*) means *sg*, way; **moyens** *nmpl* (*capacités*) means; **très ~** (*résultats*) pretty poor; **je n'en ai pas les ~s** I can't afford it; **au ~ de** by means of; **par tous les ~s** by every possible means, every possible way; **par**

m

ses propres ~s all by oneself; **moyen âge** Middle Ages pl; **moyen de transport** means of transport

moyennant [mwajɛnɑ̃] prép (somme) for; (service, conditions) in return for; (travail, effort) with

moyenne [mwajɛn] nf average; (Math) mean; (Scol) pass mark; **en ~** on (an) average; **moyenne d'âge** average age

Moyen-Orient [mwajɛnɔʀjɑ̃] nm: **le ~** the Middle East

moyeu, x [mwajø] nm hub

MST sigle f (= maladie sexuellement transmissible) STD

mû, mue [my] pp de **mouvoir**

muer [mɥe] vi (oiseau, mammifère) to moult; (serpent) to slough; (jeune garçon): **il mue** his voice is breaking

muet, te [mɥɛ, mɥɛt] adj dumb; (fig): **~ d'admiration** etc speechless with admiration etc; (Cinéma) silent ▷ nm/f mute

mufle [myfl] nm muzzle; (fam: goujat) boor

mugir [myʒiʀ] vi (taureau) to bellow; (vache) to low; (fig) to howl

muguet [mygɛ] nm lily of the valley

mule [myl] nf (Zool) (she-)mule

mulet [mylɛ] nm (Zool) (he-)mule

multinationale [myltinasjɔnal] nf multinational

multiple [myltipl] adj multiple, numerous; (varié) many, manifold; **multiplication** nf multiplication; **multiplier** vt to multiply; **se multiplier** vi to multiply

municipal, e, -aux [mynisipal, o] adj (élections, stade) municipal; (conseil) town cpd; **piscine/bibliothèque ~e** public swimming pool/library; **municipalité** nf (ville) municipality; (conseil) town council

munir [myniʀ] vt: **~ qch de** to equip sth with; **se ~ de** to arm o.s. with

munitions [mynisjɔ̃] nfpl ammunition sg

mur [myʀ] nm wall; **mur du son** sound barrier

mûr, e [myʀ] adj ripe; (personne) mature

muraille [myʀaj] nf (high) wall

mural, e, -aux [myʀal, o] adj wall cpd; (art) mural

mûre [myʀ] nf blackberry

muret [myʀɛ] nm low wall

mûrir [myʀiʀ] vi (fruit, blé) to ripen; (abcès) to come to a head; (fig: idée, personne) to mature ▷ vt (projet) to nurture; (personne) to (make) mature

murmure [myʀmyʀ] nm murmur; **murmurer** vi to murmur

muscade [myskad] nf (aussi: **noix (de) ~**) nutmeg

muscat [myska] nm (raisins) muscat grape; (vin) muscatel (wine)

muscle [myskl] nm muscle; **musclé, e** adj

muscular; (fig) strong-arm

museau, x [myzo] nm muzzle; (Culin) brawn

musée [myze] nm museum; (de peinture) art gallery

museler [myz(ə)le] vt to muzzle; **muselière** nf muzzle

musette [myzɛt] nf (sac) lunchbag

musical, e, -aux [myzikal, o] adj musical

music-hall [myzikol] nm (salle) variety theatre; (genre) variety

musicien, ne [myzisjɛ̃, jɛn] adj musical ▷ nm/f musician

musique [myzik] nf music

⊙ **FÊTE DE LA MUSIQUE**
⊙
⊙ The **Fête de la Musique** is a music festival
⊙ which takes place every year on 21 June.
⊙ Throughout France, local musicians
⊙ perform free of charge in parks, streets and
⊙ squares.

musulman, e [myzylmɑ̃, an] adj, nm/f Moslem, Muslim

mutation [mytasjɔ̃] nf (Admin) transfer

muter [myte] vt to transfer, move

mutilé, e [mytile] nm/f disabled person (through loss of limbs)

mutiler [mytile] vt to mutilate, maim

mutin, e [mytɛ̃, in] adj (air, ton) mischievous, impish ▷ nm/f (Mil, Navig) mutineer; **mutinerie** nf mutiny

mutisme [mytism] nm silence

mutuel, le [mytɥɛl] adj mutual; **mutuelle** nf voluntary insurance premiums for back-up health cover

myope [mjɔp] adj short-sighted

myosotis [mjɔzɔtis] nm forget-me-not

myrtille [miʀtij] nf bilberry

mystère [mistɛʀ] nm mystery; **mystérieux, -euse** adj mysterious

mystifier [mistifje] vt to fool

mythe [mit] nm myth

mythologie [mitɔlɔʒi] nf mythology

n' [n] adv voir **ne**

nacre [nakʀ] nf mother of pearl

nage [naʒ] nf swimming; (manière) style of swimming, stroke; **traverser/s'éloigner à la ~** to swim across/away; **en ~** bathed in sweat; **nageoire** nf fin; **nager** vi to swim; **nageur, -euse** nm/f swimmer

naïf, -ïve [naif, naiv] adj naïve

nain, e [nɛ̃, nɛn] nm/f dwarf

naissance [nɛsɑ̃s] nf birth; **donner ~ à** to give birth to; (fig) to give rise to; **lieu de ~** place of birth

naître [nɛtʀ] vi to be born; (fig): **~ de** to arise from, be born out of; **il est né en 1960** he was born in 1960; **faire ~** (fig) to give rise to, arouse

naïveté [naivte] nf naïvety

nana [nana] (fam) nf (fille) chick, bird (BRIT)

nappe [nap] nf tablecloth; (de pétrole, gaz) layer; **napperon** nm table-mat

naquit etc [naki] vb voir **naître**

narguer [naʀge] vt to taunt

narine [naʀin] nf nostril

natal, e [natal] adj native; **natalité** nf birth rate

natation [natasjɔ̃] nf swimming

natif, -ive [natif, iv] adj native

nation [nasjɔ̃] nf nation; **national, e, -aux** adj national; **nationale** nf: **(route) nationale** ≈ A road (BRIT), ≈ state highway (US);

nationaliser vt to nationalize; **nationalisme** nm nationalism; **nationalité** nf nationality

natte [nat] nf (cheveux) plait; (tapis) mat

naturaliser [natyʀalize] vt to naturalize

nature [natyʀ] nf nature ▷ adj, adv (Culin) plain, without seasoning or sweetening; (café, thé) black, without sugar; (yaourt) natural; **payer en ~** to pay in kind; **nature morte** still life; **naturel, le** adj (gén, aussi enfant) natural ▷ nm (absence d'affectation) naturalness; (caractère) disposition, nature; **naturellement** adv naturally; (bien sûr) of course

naufrage [nofʀaʒ] nm (ship)wreck; **faire ~** to be shipwrecked

nausée [noze] nf nausea; **avoir la ~** to feel sick

nautique [notik] adj nautical, water cpd; **sports ~s** water sports

naval, e [naval] adj naval; (industrie) shipbuilding

navet [navɛ] nm turnip; (péj: film) rubbishy film

navette [navɛt] nf shuttle; **faire la ~ (entre)** to go to and fro ou shuttle (between)

navigateur [navigatœʀ] nm (Navig) seafarer; (Inform) browser

navigation [navigasjɔ̃] nf navigation, sailing

naviguer [navige] vi to navigate, sail; **~ sur Internet** to browse the Internet

navire [naviʀ] nm ship

navrer [navʀe] vt to upset, distress; **je suis navré** I'm so sorry

ne, n' [n(ə)] adv voir **pas**; **plus**; **jamais** etc; (sans valeur négative: non traduit): **c'est plus loin que je ne le croyais** it's further than I thought

né, e [ne] pp (voir naître): **né en 1960** born in 1960; **née Scott** née Scott

néanmoins [neɑ̃mwɛ̃] adv nevertheless

néant [neɑ̃] nm nothingness; **réduire à ~** to bring to nought; (espoir) to dash

nécessaire [neseseʀ] adj necessary ▷ nm necessary; (sac) kit; **je vais faire le ~** I'll see to it; **nécessaire de couture** sewing kit; **nécessaire de toilette** toilet bag; **nécessité** nf necessity; **nécessiter** vt to require

néerlandais, e [neɛʀlɑ̃dɛ, ɛz] adj Dutch

nef [nɛf] nf (d'église) nave

néfaste [nefast] adj (nuisible) harmful; (funeste) ill-fated

négatif, -ive [negatif, iv] adj negative ▷ nm (Photo) negative

négligé, e [negliʒe] adj (en désordre) slovenly ▷ nm (tenue) negligee

négligeable [negliʒabl] adj negligible

négligent, e [negliʒɑ̃, ɑ̃t] adj careless, negligent

négliger [negliʒe] vt (tenue) to be careless

about; (*avis, précautions*) to disregard; (*épouse, jardin*) to neglect; **~ de faire** to fail to do, not bother to do

négociant, e [negɔsjɑ̃, jɑ̃t] *nm/f* merchant

négociation [negɔsjasjɔ̃] *nf* negotiation

négocier [negɔsje] *vi, vt* to negotiate

nègre [nɛgʀ] (*péj*) *nm* (*écrivain*) ghost (writer)

neige [nɛʒ] *nf* snow; **neiger** *vi* to snow

nénuphar [nenyfaʀ] *nm* water-lily

néon [neɔ̃] *nm* neon

néo-zélandais, e [neozelɑ̃dɛ, ɛz] *adj* New Zealand *cpd* ▷ *nm/f*: **Néo-Zélandais, e** New Zealander

Népal [nepal] *nm*: **le ~** Nepal

nerf [nɛʀ] *nm* nerve; **être sur les ~s** to be all keyed up; **nerveux, -euse** *adj* nervous; (*irritable*) touchy, nervy; (*voiture*) nippy, responsive; **nervosité** *nf* excitability, tenseness; (*irritabilité passagère*) irritability, nerviness

n'est-ce pas? [nɛspɑ] *adv* isn't it?, won't you? etc, *selon le verbe qui précède*

Net [nɛt] *nm* (*Internet*): **le ~** the Net

net, nette [nɛt] *adj* (*sans équivoque, distinct*) clear; (*évident: amélioration, différence*) marked, distinct; (*propre*) neat, clean; (*Comm: prix, salaire*) net ▷ *adv* (*refuser*) flatly ▷ *nm*: **mettre au ~** to copy out; **s'arrêter ~** to stop dead; **nettement** *adv* clearly, distinctly; (*incontestablement*) decidedly; **netteté** *nf* clearness

nettoyage [netwajaʒ] *nm* cleaning; **nettoyage à sec** dry cleaning

nettoyer [netwaje] *vt* to clean

neuf¹ [nœf] *num* nine

neuf², neuve [nœf, nœv] *adj* new; **remettre à ~** to do up (as good as new), refurbish; **quoi de ~?** what's new?

neutre [nøtʀ] *adj* neutral; (*Ling*) neuter

neuve [nœv] *adj voir* **neuf²**

neuvième [nœvjɛm] *num* ninth

neveu, x [n(ə)vø] *nm* nephew

New York [njujɔʀk] *n* New York

nez [ne] *nm* nose; **~ à ~ avec** face to face with; **avoir du ~** to have flair

ni [ni] *conj*: **ni … ni** neither … nor; **je n'aime ni les lentilles ni les épinards** I like neither lentils nor spinach; **il n'a dit ni oui ni non** he didn't say either yes or no; **elles ne sont venues ni l'une ni l'autre** neither of them came; **il n'a rien vu ni entendu** he didn't see or hear anything

niche [niʃ] *nf* (*du chien*) kennel; (*de mur*) recess, niche; **nicher** *vi* to nest

nid [ni] *nm* nest; **nid de poule** pothole

nièce [njɛs] *nf* niece

nier [nje] *vt* to deny

Nil [nil] *nm*: **le ~** the Nile

n'importe [nɛ̃pɔʀt] *adv*: **n'importe qui/quoi/où** anybody/anything/anywhere; **n'importe quand** any time; **n'importe quel/quelle** any; **n'importe lequel/laquelle** any (one); **n'importe comment** (*sans soin*) carelessly

niveau, x [nivo] *nm* level; (*des élèves, études*) standard; **niveau de vie** standard of living

niveler [niv(ə)le] *vt* to level

noble [nɔbl] *adj* noble; **noblesse** *nf* nobility; (*d'une action etc*) nobleness

noce [nɔs] *nf* wedding; (*gens*) wedding party (*ou guests pl*); **faire la ~** (*fam*) to go on a binge; **noces d'argent/d'or/de diamant** silver/golden/diamond wedding (anniversary)

nocif, -ive [nɔsif, iv] *adj* harmful

nocturne [nɔktyʀn] *adj* nocturnal ▷ *nf* late-night opening

Noël [nɔɛl] *nm* Christmas

nœud [nø] *nm* knot; (*ruban*) bow; **nœud papillon** bow tie

noir, e [nwaʀ] *adj* black; (*obscur, sombre*) dark ▷ *nm/f* black man/woman ▷ *nm*: **dans le ~** in the dark; **travail au ~** moonlighting; **travailler au ~** to work on the side; **noircir** *vt, vi* to blacken; **noire** *nf* (*Mus*) crotchet (BRIT), quarter note (US)

noisette [nwazɛt] *nf* hazelnut

noix [nwa] *nf* walnut; (*Culin*): **une ~ de beurre** a knob of butter; **à la ~** (*fam*) worthless; **noix de cajou** cashew nut; **noix de coco** coconut; **noix muscade** nutmeg

nom [nɔ̃] *nm* name; (*Ling*) noun; **nom de famille** surname; **nom de jeune fille** maiden name

nomade [nɔmad] *nm/f* nomad

nombre [nɔ̃bʀ] *nm* number; **venir en ~** to come in large numbers; **depuis ~ d'années** for many years; **au ~ de mes amis** among my friends; **nombreux, -euse** *adj* many, numerous; (*avec nom sg: foule etc*) large; **peu nombreux** few; **de nombreux cas** many cases

nombril [nɔ̃bʀi(l)] *nm* navel

nommer [nɔme] *vt* to name; (*élire*) to appoint, nominate; **se nommer**; **il se nomme Pascal** his name's Pascal, he's called Pascal

non [nɔ̃] *adv* (*réponse*) no; (*avec loin, sans, seulement*) not; **~ (pas) que** not that; **moi ~ plus** neither do I, I don't either; **c'est bon ~?** (*exprimant le doute*) it's good, isn't it?; **je pense que ~** I don't think so

non alcoolisé, e [nɔ̃alkɔlize] *adj* non alcoholic

nonchalant, e [nɔ̃ʃalɑ̃, ɑ̃t] *adj* nonchalant

non-fumeur, -euse [nɔ̃fymœʀ, øz] *nm/f* non-smoker

non-sens [nɔ̃sɑ̃s] *nm* absurdity

nord [nɔʀ] nm North ▷ adj northern; north; **au ~** (situation) in the north; (direction) to the north; **au ~ de** (to the) north of; **nord-africain, e** adj North-African ▷ nm/f: **Nord-Africain, e** North-African; **nord-est** nm North-East; **nord-ouest** nm North-West

normal, e, -aux [nɔʀmal, o] adj normal; **c'est tout à fait ~** it's perfectly natural; **vous trouvez ça ~?** does it seem right to you?; **normale** nf: **la normale** the norm, the average; **normalement** adv (en général) normally

normand, e [nɔʀmã, ãd] adj of Normandy ▷ nm/f: **N~, e** (de Normandie) Norman

Normandie [nɔʀmãdi] nf Normandy

norme [nɔʀm] nf norm; (Tech) standard

Norvège [nɔʀvɛʒ] nf Norway; **norvégien, ne** adj Norwegian ▷ nm/f: **Norvégien, ne** Norwegian ▷ nm (Ling) Norwegian

nos [no] adj voir **notre**

nostalgie [nɔstalʒi] nf nostalgia; **nostalgique** adj nostalgic

notable [nɔtabl] adj (fait) notable, noteworthy; (marqué) noticeable, marked ▷ nm prominent citizen

notaire [nɔtɛʀ] nm solicitor

notamment [nɔtamã] adv in particular, among others

note [nɔt] nf (écrite, Mus) note; (Scol) mark (BRIT), grade; (facture) bill; **note de service** memorandum

noter [nɔte] vt (écrire) to write down; (remarquer) to note, notice; (devoir) to mark, grade

notice [nɔtis] nf summary, short article; (brochure) leaflet, instruction book

notifier [nɔtifje] vt: **~ qch à qn** to notify sb of sth, notify sth to sb

notion [nɔsjɔ̃] nf notion, idea

notoire [nɔtwaʀ] adj widely known; (en mal) notorious

notre [nɔtʀ] (pl nos) adj our

nôtre [notʀ] pron: **le ~, la ~, les ~s** ours ▷ adj ours; **les ~s** ours; (alliés etc) our own people; **soyez des ~s** join us

nouer [nwe] vt to tie, knot; (fig: alliance etc) to strike up

noueux, -euse [nwø, øz] adj gnarled

nourrice [nuʀis] nf (gardienne) child-minder

nourrir [nuʀiʀ] vt to feed; (fig: espoir) to harbour, nurse; **nourrissant, e** adj nourishing, nutritious; **nourrisson** nm (unweaned) infant; **nourriture** nf food

nous [nu] pron (sujet) we; (objet) us; **nous-mêmes** pron ourselves

nouveau (nouvel), -elle, x [nuvo, nuvɛl] adj new ▷ nm: **y a-t-il du nouveau?** is there anything new on this? ▷ nm/f new pupil (ou employee); **de nouveau, à nouveau** again;

nouveau venu, nouvelle venue newcomer; **nouveaux mariés** newly-weds; **nouveau-né, e** nm/f newborn baby; **nouveauté** nf novelty; (objet) new thing ou article

nouvel [nuvɛl] adj voir **nouveau**; **Nouvel An** New Year

nouvelle [nuvɛl] adj voir **nouveau** ▷ nf (piece of) news sg; (Littérature) short story; **les ~s** (Presse, TV) the news; **je suis sans ~s de lui** I haven't heard from him; **Nouvelle-Calédonie** nf New Caledonia; **Nouvelle-Zélande** nf New Zealand

novembre [nɔvãbʀ] nm November

● **NOVEMBRE**
●
● **Le 11 novembre** is a public holiday in
● France commemorating the signing of the
● armistice, near Compiègne, at the end of
● World War I.

noyade [nwajad] nf drowning no pl

noyau, x [nwajo] nm (de fruit) stone; (Bio, Physique) nucleus; (fig: centre) core

noyer [nwaje] nm walnut (tree); (bois) walnut ▷ vt to drown; (moteur) to flood; **se noyer** vi to be drowned, drown; (suicide) to drown o.s.

nu, e [ny] adj naked; (membres) naked, bare; (pieds, mains, chambre, fil électrique) bare ▷ nm (Art) nude; **tout nu** stark naked; **se mettre nu** to strip

nuage [nɥaʒ] nm cloud; **nuageux, -euse** adj cloudy

nuance [nɥãs] nf (de couleur, sens) shade; **il y a une ~ (entre)** there's a slight difference (between); **nuancer** vt (opinion) to bring some reservations ou qualifications to

nucléaire [nykleɛʀ] adj nuclear ▷ nm: **le ~** nuclear energy

nudiste [nydist] nm/f nudist

nuée [nɥe] nf: **une ~ de** a cloud ou host ou swarm of

nuire [nɥiʀ] vi to be harmful; **~ à** to harm, do damage to; **nuisible** adj harmful; **animal nuisible** pest

nuit [nɥi] nf night; **il fait ~** it's dark; **cette ~** (hier) last night; (aujourd'hui) tonight; **de ~** (vol, service) night cpd; **nuit blanche** sleepless night

nul, nulle [nyl] adj (aucun) no; (minime) nil, non-existent; (non valable) null; (péj): **être ~ (en)** to be useless ou hopeless (at) ▷ pron none, no one; **match ou résultat ~** draw; **~le part** nowhere; **nullement** adv by no means

numérique [nymeʀik] adj numerical; (affichage, son, télévision) digital

numéro [nymeʀo] nm number; (spectacle) act, turn; (Presse) issue, number; **numéro de téléphone** (tele)phone number; **numéro**

vert ≈ freefone® number (*BRIT*), ≈ toll-free number (*US*); **numéroter** *vt* to number

nuque [nyk] *nf* nape of the neck

nu-tête [nytɛt] *adj inv, adv* bareheaded

nutritif, -ive [nytʀitif, iv] *adj* (*besoins, valeur*) nutritional; (*nourrissant*) nutritious

nylon [nilɔ̃] *nm* nylon

oasis [ɔazis] *nf* oasis

obéir [ɔbeiʀ] *vi* to obey; **~ à** to obey; **obéissance** *nf* obedience; **obéissant, e** *adj* obedient

obèse [ɔbɛz] *adj* obese; **obésité** *nf* obesity

objecter [ɔbʒɛkte] *vt*: **~ que** to object that; **objecteur** *nm*: **objecteur de conscience** conscientious objector

objectif, -ive [ɔbʒɛktif, iv] *adj* objective ▷ *nm* objective; (*Photo*) lens *sg*, objective

objection [ɔbʒɛksjɔ̃] *nf* objection

objectivité [ɔbʒɛktivite] *nf* objectivity

objet [ɔbʒɛ] *nm* object; (*d'une discussion, recherche*) subject; **être** *ou* **faire l'~ de** (*discussion*) to be the subject of; (*soins*) to be given *ou* shown; **sans ~** purposeless; (*craintes*) groundless; **(bureau des) ~s trouvés** lost property *sg* (*BRIT*), lost-and-found *sg* (*US*); **objet d'art** objet d'art; **objets de valeur** valuables; **objets personnels** personal items

obligation [ɔbligasjɔ̃] *nf* obligation; (*Comm*) bond, debenture; **obligatoire** *adj* compulsory, obligatory; **obligatoirement** *adv* necessarily; (*fam: sans aucun doute*) inevitably

obliger [ɔbliʒe] *vt* (*contraindre*): **~ qn à faire** to force *ou* oblige sb to do; **je suis bien obligé (de le faire)** I have to (do it)

oblique [ɔblik] *adj* oblique; **en ~** diagonally

oblitérer [ɔbliteʀe] *vt* (*timbre-poste*) to cancel

obnubiler [ɔbnybile] *vt* to obsess

obscène [ɔpsɛn] *adj* obscene
obscur, e [ɔpskyʀ] *adj* dark; (*méconnu*) obscure; **obscurcir** *vt* to darken; (*fig*) to obscure; **s'obscurcir** *vi* to grow dark; **obscurité** *nf* darkness; **dans l'obscurité** in the dark, in darkness
obsédé, e [ɔpsede] *nm/f*: **un ~ de jazz** a jazz fanatic; **obsédé sexuel** sex maniac
obséder [ɔpsede] *vt* to obsess, haunt
obsèques [ɔpsɛk] *nfpl* funeral *sg*
observateur, -trice [ɔpsɛʀvatœʀ, tʀis] *adj* observant, perceptive ▷ *nm/f* observer
observation [ɔpsɛʀvasjɔ̃] *nf* observation; (*d'un règlement etc*) observance; (*reproche*) reproof; **être en ~** (*Méd*) to be under observation
observatoire [ɔpsɛʀvatwaʀ] *nm* observatory
observer [ɔpsɛʀve] *vt* (*regarder*) to observe, watch; (*scientifiquement; aussi règlement etc*) to observe; (*surveiller*) to watch; (*remarquer*) to observe, notice; **faire ~ qch à qn** (*dire*) to point out sth to sb
obsession [ɔpsesjɔ̃] *nf* obsession
obstacle [ɔpstakl] *nm* obstacle; (*Équitation*) jump, hurdle; **faire ~ à** (*projet*) to hinder, put obstacles in the path of
obstiné, e [ɔpstine] *adj* obstinate
obstiner [ɔpstine]: **s'obstiner** *vi* to insist, dig one's heels in; **s'~ à faire** to persist (obstinately) in doing
obstruer [ɔpstʀye] *vt* to block, obstruct
obtenir [ɔptəniʀ] *vt* to obtain, get; (*résultat*) to achieve, obtain; **~ de pouvoir faire** to obtain permission to do
obturateur [ɔptyʀatœʀ] *nm* (*Photo*) shutter
obus [ɔby] *nm* shell
occasion [ɔkazjɔ̃] *nf* (*aubaine, possibilité*) opportunity; (*circonstance*) occasion; (*Comm: article non neuf*) secondhand buy; (: *acquisition avantageuse*) bargain; **à plusieurs ~s** on several occasions; **à l'~** sometimes, on occasions; **d'~** secondhand; **occasionnel, le** *adj* (*non régulier*) occasional
occasionner [ɔkazjɔne] *vt* to cause
occident [ɔksidɑ̃] *nm*: **l'O~** the West; **occidental, e, -aux** *adj* western; (*Pol*) Western ▷ *nm/f* Westerner
occupation [ɔkypasjɔ̃] *nf* occupation
occupé, e [ɔkype] *adj* (*personne*) busy; (*place, sièges*) taken; (*toilettes*) engaged; (*Mil, Pol*) occupied; **la ligne est ~e** the line's engaged (BRIT) *ou* busy (US)
occuper [ɔkype] *vt* to occupy; (*poste*) to hold; **s'occuper de** (*être responsable de*) to be in charge of; (*se charger de: affaire*) to take charge of, deal with; (: *clients etc*) to attend to; **s'~ (à qch)** to occupy o.s. *ou* keep o.s. busy (with sth)
occurrence [ɔkyʀɑ̃s] *nf*: **en l'~** in this case

océan [ɔseɑ̃] *nm* ocean
octet [ɔktɛ] *nm* byte
octobre [ɔktɔbʀ] *nm* October
oculiste [ɔkylist] *nm/f* eye specialist
odeur [ɔdœʀ] *nf* smell
odieux, -euse [ɔdjø, jøz] *adj* hateful
odorant, e [ɔdɔʀɑ̃, ɑ̃t] *adj* sweet-smelling, fragrant
odorat [ɔdɔʀa] *nm* (sense of) smell
œil [œj] (*pl* **yeux**) *nm* eye; **avoir un ~ au beurre noir** *ou* **poché** to have a black eye; **à l'~** (*fam*) for free; **à l'~ nu** with the naked eye; **ouvrir l'~** (*fig*) to keep one's eyes open *ou* an eye out; **fermer les yeux (sur)** (*fig*) to turn a blind eye (to); **les yeux fermés** (*aussi fig*) with one's eyes shut
œillères [œjɛʀ] *nfpl* blinkers (BRIT), blinders (US)
œillet [œjɛ] *nm* (*Bot*) carnation
œuf [œf, *pl* ø] *nm* egg; **œuf à la coque** boiled egg; **œuf au plat** fried egg; **œuf dur** hard-boiled egg; **œuf de Pâques** Easter egg; **œufs brouillés** scrambled eggs
œuvre [œvʀ] *nf* (*tâche*) task, undertaking; (*livre, tableau etc*) work; (*ensemble de la production artistique*) works *pl* ▷ *nm* (*Constr*): **le gros ~** the shell; **mettre en ~** (*moyens*) to make use of; **œuvre de bienfaisance** charity; **œuvre d'art** work of art
offense [ɔfɑ̃s] *nf* insult; **offenser** *vt* to offend, hurt; **s'offenser de qch** to take offence (BRIT) *ou* offense (US) at sth
offert, e [ɔfɛʀ, ɛʀt] *pp de* **offrir**
office [ɔfis] *nm* (*agence*) bureau, agency; (*Rel*) service ▷ *nm ou nf* (*pièce*) pantry; **faire ~ de** to act as; **d'~** automatically; **office du tourisme** tourist bureau
officiel, le [ɔfisjɛl] *adj, nm/f* official
officier [ɔfisje] *nm* officer
officieux, -euse [ɔfisjø, jøz] *adj* unofficial
offrande [ɔfʀɑ̃d] *nf* offering
offre [ɔfʀ] *nf* offer; (*aux enchères*) bid; (*Admin: soumission*) tender; (*Écon*): **l'~ et la demande** supply and demand; **"~s d'emploi"** "situations vacant"; **offre d'emploi** job advertised; **offre publique d'achat** takeover bid
offrir [ɔfʀiʀ] *vt*: **~ (à qn)** to offer (to sb); (*faire cadeau de*) to give (to sb); **s'offrir** *vt* (*vacances, voiture*) to treat o.s. to; **~ (à qn) de faire qch** to offer to do sth (for sb); **~ à boire à qn** (*chez soi*) to offer sb a drink; **je vous offre un verre** I'll buy you a drink
OGM *sigle m* (= *organisme génétiquement modifié*) GMO
oie [wa] *nf* (*Zool*) goose
oignon [ɔɲɔ̃] *nm* onion; (*de tulipe etc*) bulb
oiseau, x [wazo] *nm* bird; **oiseau de proie** bird of prey
oisif, -ive [wazif, iv] *adj* idle

oléoduc [ɔleɔdyk] *nm* (oil) pipeline

olive [ɔliv] *nf* (*Bot*) olive; **olivier** *nm* olive (tree)

OLP *sigle f* (= *Organisation de libération de la Palestine*) PLO

olympique [ɔlɛ̃pik] *adj* Olympic

ombragé, e [ɔ̃braʒe] *adj* shaded, shady

ombre [ɔ̃br] *nf* (*espace non ensoleillé*) shade; (*ombre portée, tache*) shadow; **à l'~** in the shade; **dans l'~** (*fig*) in the dark; **ombre à paupières** eyeshadow

omelette [ɔmlɛt] *nf* omelette; **omelette norvégienne** baked Alaska

omettre [ɔmɛtr] *vt* to omit, leave out

omoplate [ɔmɔplat] *nf* shoulder blade

🔵 **MOT-CLÉ**

on [ɔ̃] *pron* **1** (*indéterminé*) you, one; **on peut le faire ainsi** you *ou* one can do it like this, it can be done like this

2 (*quelqu'un*): **on les a attaqués** they were attacked; **on vous demande au téléphone** there's a phone call for you, you're wanted on the phone

3 (*nous*) we; **on va y aller demain** we're going tomorrow

4 (*les gens*) they; **autrefois, on croyait ...** they used to believe ...

5: **on ne peut plus** *adv*: **on ne peut plus stupide** as stupid as can be

---

oncle [ɔ̃kl] *nm* uncle

onctueux, -euse [ɔ̃ktɥø, øz] *adj* creamy, smooth

onde [ɔ̃d] *nf* wave; **~s courtes/moyennes** short/medium wave *sg*; **grandes ~s** long wave *sg*

ondée [ɔ̃de] *nf* shower

on-dit [ɔ̃di] *nm inv* rumour

onduler [ɔ̃dyle] *vi* to undulate; (*cheveux*) to wave

onéreux, -euse [ɔnerø, øz] *adj* costly

ongle [ɔ̃gl] *nm* nail

ont [ɔ̃] *vb voir* **avoir**

ONU *sigle f* (= *Organisation des Nations Unies*) UN

onze ['ɔ̃z] *num* eleven; **onzième** *num* eleventh

OPA *sigle f* = **offre publique d'achat**

opaque [ɔpak] *adj* opaque

opéra [ɔpera] *nm* opera; (*édifice*) opera house

opérateur, -trice [ɔperatœr, tris] *nm/f* operator; **opérateur (de prise de vues)** cameraman

opération [ɔperasjɔ̃] *nf* operation; (*Comm*) dealing

opératoire [ɔperatwar] *adj* (*choc etc*) post-operative

opérer [ɔpere] *vt* (*personne*) to operate on; (*faire, exécuter*) to carry out, make ▷ *vi* (*remède*: faire effet*) to act, work; (*Méd*) to operate; **s'opérer** *vi* (*avoir lieu*) to occur, take place; **se faire ~** to have an operation

opérette [ɔperet] *nf* operetta, light opera

opinion [ɔpinjɔ̃] *nf* opinion; **l'opinion (publique)** public opinion

opportun, e [ɔpɔrtœ̃, yn] *adj* timely, opportune; **opportuniste** *nm/f* opportunist

opposant, e [ɔpozɑ̃, ɑ̃t] *nm/f* opponent

opposé, e [ɔpoze] *adj* (*direction*) opposite; (*faction*) opposing; (*opinions, intérêts*) conflicting; (*contre*): **~ à** opposed to, against ▷ *nm*: **l'~** the other *ou* opposite side (*ou* direction); (*contraire*) the opposite; **à l'~** (*fig*) on the other hand; **à l'~ de** (*fig*) contrary to, unlike

opposer [ɔpoze] *vt* (*personnes, équipes*) to oppose; (*couleurs*) to contrast; **s'opposer** *vi* (*équipes*) to confront each other; (*opinions*) to conflict; (*couleurs, styles*) to contrast; **s'~ à** (*interdire*) to oppose; **~ qch à** (*comme obstacle, défense*) to set sth against; (*comme objection*) to put sth forward against

opposition [ɔpozisjɔ̃] *nf* opposition; **par ~ à** as opposed to; **entrer en ~ avec** to come into conflict with; **faire ~ à un chèque** to stop a cheque

oppressant, e [ɔpresɑ̃, ɑ̃t] *adj* oppressive

oppresser [ɔprese] *vt* to oppress; **oppression** *nf* oppression

opprimer [ɔprime] *vt* to oppress

opter [ɔpte] *vi*: **~ pour** to opt for

opticien, ne [ɔptisjɛ̃, jɛn] *nm/f* optician

optimisme [ɔptimism] *nm* optimism; **optimiste** *nm/f* optimist ▷ *adj* optimistic

option [ɔpsjɔ̃] *nf* option; **matière à ~** (*Scol*) optional subject

optique [ɔptik] *adj* (*nerf*) optic; (*verres*) optical ▷ *nf* (*fig: manière de voir*) perspective

or [ɔr] *nm* gold ▷ *conj* now, but; **en or** (*objet*) gold *cpd*; **une affaire en or** a real bargain; **il croyait gagner or il a perdu** he was sure he would win and yet he lost

orage [ɔraʒ] *nm* (thunder)storm; **orageux, -euse** *adj* stormy

oral, e, -aux [ɔral, o] *adj, nm* oral; **par voie ~e** (*Méd*) orally

orange [ɔrɑ̃ʒ] *nf* orange ▷ *adj inv* orange; **orangé, e** *adj* orangey, orange-coloured; **orangeade** *nf* orangeade; **oranger** *nm* orange tree

orateur [ɔratœr] *nm* speaker

orbite [ɔrbit] *nf* (*Anat*) (eye-)socket; (*Physique*) orbit

Orcades [ɔrkad] *nfpl*: **les ~** the Orkneys, the Orkney Islands

orchestre [ɔrkɛstr] *nm* orchestra; (*de jazz*) band; (*places*) stalls *pl* (BRIT), orchestra (US)

orchidée [ɔrkide] *nf* orchid

ordinaire [ɔʀdinɛʀ] *adj* ordinary; *(qualité)* standard; *(péj: commun)* common ▷ *nm* ordinary; *(menus)* everyday fare ▷ *nf (essence)* ≈ two-star (petrol) (BRIT), ≈ regular gas (US); **d'~** usually, normally; **comme à l'~** as usual

ordinateur [ɔʀdinatœʀ] *nm* computer; **ordinateur individuel** *ou* **personnel** personal computer; **ordinateur portable** laptop (computer)

ordonnance [ɔʀdɔnɑ̃s] *nf (Méd)* prescription; *(Mil)* orderly, batman (BRIT); **pouvez-vous me faire une ~?** can you write me a prescription?

ordonné, e [ɔʀdɔne] *adj* tidy, orderly

ordonner [ɔʀdɔne] *vt (agencer)* to organize, arrange; *(donner un ordre)*: **~ à qn de faire** to order sb to do; *(Rel)* to ordain; *(Méd)* to prescribe

ordre [ɔʀdʀ] *nm* order; *(propreté et soin)* orderliness, tidiness; *(nature)*: **d'~ pratique** of a practical nature; **ordres** *nmpl (Rel)* holy orders; **mettre en ~** to tidy (up), put in order; **par ~ alphabétique/d'importance** in alphabetical order/in order of importance; **à l'~ de qn** payable to sb; **être aux ~s de qn/sous les ~s de qn** to be at sb's disposal/under sb's command; **jusqu'à nouvel ~** until further notice; **de premier ~** first-rate; **ordre du jour** *(d'une réunion)* agenda; **à l'ordre du jour** *(fig)* topical; **ordre publique** law and order

ordure [ɔʀdyʀ] *nf* filth *no pl*; **ordures** *nfpl (balayures, déchets)* rubbish *sg*, refuse *sg*; **ordures ménagères** household refuse

oreille [ɔʀɛj] *nf* ear; **avoir de l'~** to have a good ear (for music)

oreiller [ɔʀeje] *nm* pillow

oreillons [ɔʀɛjɔ̃] *nmpl* mumps *sg*

ores [ɔʀ]: **d'~ et déjà** *adv* already

orfèvrerie [ɔʀfɛvʀəʀi] *nf* goldsmith's *(ou* silversmith's) trade; *(ouvrage)* gold *(ou* silver) plate

organe [ɔʀgan] *nm* organ; *(porte-parole)* representative, mouthpiece

organigramme [ɔʀganigʀam] *nm (tableau hiérarchique)* organization chart; *(schéma)* flow chart

organique [ɔʀganik] *adj* organic

organisateur, -trice [ɔʀganizatœʀ, tʀis] *nm/f* organizer

organisation [ɔʀganizasjɔ̃] *nf* organization; **Organisation des Nations Unies** United Nations (Organization)

organiser [ɔʀganize] *vt* to organize; *(mettre sur pied: service etc)* to set up; **s'organiser** to get organized

organisme [ɔʀganism] *nm (Bio)* organism; *(corps, Admin)* body

organiste [ɔʀganist] *nm/f* organist

orgasme [ɔʀgasm] *nm* orgasm, climax

orge [ɔʀʒ] *nf* barley

orgue [ɔʀg] *nm* organ

orgueil [ɔʀgœj] *nm* pride; **orgueilleux, -euse** *adj* proud

oriental, e, -aux [ɔʀjɑ̃tal, -o] *adj (langue, produit)* oriental; *(frontière)* eastern

orientation [ɔʀjɑ̃tasjɔ̃] *nf (de recherches)* orientation; *(d'une maison etc)* aspect; *(d'un journal)* leanings *pl*; **avoir le sens de l'~** to have a (good) sense of direction; **orientation professionnelle** careers advisory service

orienté, e [ɔʀjɑ̃te] *adj (fig: article, journal)* slanted; **bien/mal ~** *(appartement)* well/badly positioned; **~ au sud** facing south, with a southern aspect

orienter [ɔʀjɑ̃te] *vt (tourner: antenne)* to direct, turn; *(personne, recherches)* to direct; *(fig: élève)* to orientate; **s'orienter** *(se repérer)* to find one's bearings; **s'~ vers** *(fig)* to turn towards

origan [ɔʀigɑ̃] *nm* oregano

originaire [ɔʀiʒinɛʀ] *adj*: **être ~ de** to be a native of

original, e, -aux [ɔʀiʒinal, o] *adj* original; *(bizarre)* eccentric ▷ *nm/f* eccentric ▷ *nm (document etc, Art)* original

origine [ɔʀiʒin] *nf* origin; **origines** *nfpl (d'une personne)* origins; **d'~ *(pays)*** of origin; **d'~ suédoise** of Swedish origin; *(pneus etc)* original; **à l'~** originally; **originel, le** *adj* original

orme [ɔʀm] *nm* elm

ornement [ɔʀnəmɑ̃] *nm* ornament

orner [ɔʀne] *vt* to decorate, adorn

ornière [ɔʀnjɛʀ] *nf* rut

orphelin, e [ɔʀfəlɛ̃, in] *adj* orphan(ed) ▷ *nm/f* orphan; **orphelin de mère/de père** motherless/fatherless; **orphelinat** *nm* orphanage

orteil [ɔʀtɛj] *nm* toe; **gros ~** big toe

orthographe [ɔʀtɔgʀaf] *nf* spelling

ortie [ɔʀti] *nf* (stinging) nettle

os [ɔs] *nm* bone; **os à moelle** marrowbone

osciller [ɔsile] *vi (au vent etc)* to rock; *(fig)*: **~ entre** to waver *ou* fluctuate between

osé, e [oze] *adj* daring, bold

oseille [ozɛj] *nf* sorrel

oser [oze] *vi, vt* to dare; **~ faire** to dare (to) do

osier [ozje] *nm* willow; **d'~, en ~** wicker(work)

osseux, -euse [ɔsø, øz] *adj* bony; *(tissu, maladie, greffe)* bone *cpd*

otage [ɔtaʒ] *nm* hostage; **prendre qn comme ~** to take sb hostage

OTAN *sigle f* (= *Organisation du traité de l'Atlantique Nord*) NATO

otarie [ɔtaʀi] *nf* sea-lion

ôter [ote] *vt* to remove; *(soustraire)* to take away; **~ qch à qn** to take sth (away) from sb; **~ qch de** to remove sth from

otite [ɔtit] *nf* ear infection

ou [u] *conj* or; **ou ... ou** either ... or; **ou bien** or (else)

MOT-CLÉ

où [u] *pron relatif* **1** (*position, situation*) where, that (*souvent omis*); **la chambre où il était** the room (that) he was in, the room where he was; **la ville où je l'ai rencontré** the town where I met him; **la pièce d'où il est sorti** the room he came out of; **le village d'où je viens** the village I come from; **les villes par où il est passé** the towns he went through **2** (*temps, état*) that (*souvent omis*); **le jour où il est parti** the day (that) he left; **au prix où c'est** at the price it is
▷ *adv* **1** (*interrogation*) where; **où est-il/va-t-il?** where is he/is he going?; **par où?** which way?; **d'où vient que ...?** how come ...?
2 (*position*) where; **je sais où il est** I know where he is; **où que l'on aille** wherever you go

ouate ['wat] *nf* cotton wool (BRIT), cotton (US)
oubli [ubli] *nm* (*acte*): **l'~ de** forgetting; (*trou de mémoire*) lapse of memory; (*négligence*) omission, oversight; **tomber dans l'~** to sink into oblivion
oublier [ublije] *vt* to forget; (*laisser quelque part: chapeau etc*) to leave behind; (*ne pas voir: erreurs etc*) to miss; **j'ai oublié ma clé/mon passeport** I've forgotten my key/passport
ouest [wɛst] *nm* west ▷ *adj inv* west; (*région*) western; **à l'~** in the west; (*direction*) (to the) west, westwards; **à l'~ de** (to the) west of
ouf ['uf] *excl* phew!
oui ['wi] *adv* yes
ouï-dire ['widiR]: **par ~** *adv* by hearsay
ouïe [wi] *nf* hearing; **ouïes** *nfpl* (*de poisson*) gills
ouragan [uRagã] *nm* hurricane
ourlet [uRlɛ] *nm* hem
ours [uRs] *nm* bear; **ours blanc/brun** polar/brown bear; **ours (en peluche)** teddy (bear)
oursin [uRsɛ̃] *nm* sea urchin
ourson [uRsɔ̃] *nm* (bear-)cub
ouste [ust] *excl* hop it!
outil [uti] *nm* tool; **outiller** *vt* to equip
outrage [utRaʒ] *nm* insult; **outrage à la pudeur** indecent conduct *no pl*
outrance [utRãs]: **à ~** *adv* excessively, to excess
outre [utR] *prép* besides ▷ *adv*: **passer ~ à** to disregard, take no notice of; **en ~** besides, moreover; **~ mesure** to excess; (*manger, boire*) immoderately; **outre-Atlantique** *adv* across the Atlantic; **outre-mer** *adv* overseas
ouvert, e [uvɛR, ɛRt] *pp de* **ouvrir** ▷ *adj* open; (*robinet, gaz etc*) on; **ouvertement** *adv* openly;

ouverture *nf* opening; (*Mus*) overture; **heures d'ouverture** (*Comm*) opening hours; **ouverture d'esprit** open-mindedness
ouvrable [uvRabl] *adj*: **jour ~** working day, weekday
ouvrage [uvRaʒ] *nm* (*tâche, de tricot etc*) work *no pl*; (*texte, livre*) work
ouvre-boîte(s) [uvRəbwat] *nm inv* tin (BRIT) *ou* can opener
ouvre-bouteille(s) [uvRəbutɛj] *nm inv* bottle-opener
ouvreuse [uvRøz] *nf* usherette
ouvrier, -ière [uvRije, ijɛR] *nm/f* worker ▷ *adj* working-class; (*conflit*) industrial; (*mouvement*) labour *cpd*; **classe ouvrière** working class
ouvrir [uvRiR] *vt* (*gén*) to open; (*brèche, passage, Méd: abcès*) to open up; (*commencer l'exploitation de, créer*) to open (up); (*eau, électricité, chauffage, robinet*) to turn on ▷ *vi* to open; to open up; **s'ouvrir** *vi* to open; **s'~ à qn** to open one's heart to sb; **est-ce ouvert au public?** is it open to the public?; **quand est-ce que le musée est ouvert?** when is the museum open?; **à quelle heure ouvrez-vous?** what time do you open?; **~ l'appétit à qn** to whet sb's appetite
ovaire [ovɛR] *nm* ovary
ovale [ɔval] *adj* oval
OVNI [ɔvni] *sigle m* (= *objet volant non identifié*) UFO
oxyder [ɔkside]: **s'oxyder** *vi* to become oxidized
oxygène [ɔksiʒɛn] *nm* oxygen
oxygéné, e [ɔksiʒene] *adj*: **eau ~e** hydrogen peroxide
ozone [ozon] *nf* ozone; **la couche d'~** the ozone layer

P

pacifique [pasifik] *adj* peaceful ▷ *nm*: **le P~, l'océan P~** the Pacific (Ocean)

pack [pak] *nm* pack

pacotille [pakɔtij] *nf* cheap junk

PACS *sigle m* (= *pacte civil de solidarité*) contract of civil partnership; **pacser: se pacser** *vi* to sign a contract of civil partnership

pacte [pakt] *nm* pact, treaty

pagaille [pagaj] *nf* mess, shambles *sg*

page [paʒ] *nf* page ▷ *nm* page (boy); **à la ~** (*fig*) up-to-date; **page d'accueil** (*Inform*) home page; **page Web** (*Inform*) web page

paiement [pɛmɑ̃] *nm* payment

païen, ne [pajɛ̃, pajɛn] *adj*, *nm/f* pagan, heathen

paillasson [pajasɔ̃] *nm* doormat

paille [paj] *nf* straw

pain [pɛ̃] *nm* (*substance*) bread; (*unité*) loaf (of bread); (*morceau*) ~ **de savon** *etc* bar of soap *etc*; **pain au chocolat** chocolate-filled pastry; **pain aux raisins** currant bun; **pain bis/complet** brown/wholemeal (BRIT) *ou* wholewheat (US) bread; **pain d'épice** ≈ gingerbread; **pain de mie** sandwich loaf; **pain grillé** toast

pair, e [pɛʀ] *adj* (*nombre*) even ▷ *nm* peer; **aller de ~** to go hand in hand *ou* together; **jeune fille au ~** au pair; **paire** *nf* pair

paisible [pezibl] *adj* peaceful, quiet

paix [pɛ] *nf* peace; **faire/avoir la ~** to make/have peace; **fiche-lui la ~!** (*fam*) leave him alone!

Pakistan [pakistɑ̃] *nm*: **le ~** Pakistan

palais [palɛ] *nm* palace; (*Anat*) palate

pâle [pɑl] *adj* pale; **bleu ~** pale blue

Palestine [palɛstin] *nf*: **la ~** Palestine

palette [palɛt] *nf* (*de peintre*) palette; (*produits*) range

pâleur [pɑlœʀ] *nf* paleness

palier [palje] *nm* (*d'escalier*) landing; (*fig*) level, plateau; **par ~s** in stages

pâlir [pɑliʀ] *vi* to turn *ou* go pale; (*couleur*) to fade

pallier [palje] *vt* to offset, make up for

palme [palm] *nf* (*de plongeur*) flipper; **palmé, e** *adj* (*pattes*) webbed

palmier [palmje] *nm* palm tree; (*gâteau*) heart-shaped biscuit made of flaky pastry

pâlot, te [pɑlo, ɔt] *adj* pale, peaky

palourde [paluʀd] *nf* clam

palper [palpe] *vt* to feel, finger

palpitant, e [palpitɑ̃, ɑ̃t] *adj* thrilling

palpiter [palpite] *vi* (*cœur, pouls*) to beat; (: *plus fort*) to pound, throb

paludisme [palydism] *nm* malaria

pamphlet [pɑ̃flɛ] *nm* lampoon, satirical tract

pamplemousse [pɑ̃pləmus] *nm* grapefruit

pan [pɑ̃] *nm* section, piece ▷ *excl* bang!

panache [panaʃ] *nm* plume; (*fig*) spirit, panache

panaché, e [panaʃe] *adj*: **glace ~e** mixed-flavour ice cream ▷ *nm* (*bière*) shandy

pancarte [pɑ̃kaʀt] *nf* sign, notice

pancréas [pɑ̃kʀeas] *nm* pancreas

pané, e [pane] *adj* fried in breadcrumbs

panier [panje] *nm* basket; **mettre au ~** to chuck away; **panier à provisions** shopping basket; **panier-repas** *nm* packed lunch

panique [panik] *nf*, *adj* panic; **paniquer** *vi* to panic

panne [pan] *nf* breakdown; **être/tomber en ~** to have broken down/break down; **être en ~ d'essence** *ou* **sèche** to have run out of petrol (BRIT) *ou* gas (US); **ma voiture est en ~** my car has broken down; **panne d'électricité** *ou* **de courant** power cut *ou* failure

panneau, x [pano] *nm* (*écriteau*) sign, notice; **panneau d'affichage** notice board; **panneau de signalisation** roadsign; **panneau indicateur** signpost

panoplie [panɔpli] *nf* (*jouet*) outfit; (*fig*) array

panorama [panɔʀama] *nm* panorama

panse [pɑ̃s] *nf* paunch

pansement [pɑ̃smɑ̃] *nm* dressing, bandage; **pansement adhésif** sticking plaster

pantacourt [pɑ̃takuʀ] *nm* three-quarter length trousers *pl*

pantalon [pɑ̃talɔ̃] *nm* trousers *pl*, pair of trousers; **pantalon de ski** ski pants *pl*

p

panthère [pɑ̃tɛʀ] *nf* panther
pantin [pɑ̃tɛ̃] *nm* puppet
pantoufle [pɑ̃tufl] *nf* slipper
paon [pɑ̃] *nm* peacock
papa [papa] *nm* dad(dy)
pape [pap] *nm* pope
paperasse [papʀas] (*péj*) *nf* bumf *no pl*,
papers *pl*; **paperasserie** (*péj*) *nf* paperwork *no pl*; (*tracasserie*) red tape *no pl*
papeterie [papɛtʀi] *nf* (*magasin*) stationer's (shop)
papi *nm* (*fam*) granddad
papier [papje] *nm* paper; (*article*) article;
papiers *nmpl* (*aussi*: **~s d'identité**)
(identity) papers; **papier à lettres** writing paper, notepaper; **papier (d')aluminium** aluminium (BRIT) *ou* aluminum (US) foil, tinfoil; **papier calque** tracing paper; **papier de verre** sandpaper; **papier hygiénique** *ou* **(de) toilette** toilet paper; **papier journal** newspaper; **papier peint** wallpaper
papillon [papijɔ̃] *nm* butterfly; (*fam: contravention*) (parking) ticket; **papillon de nuit** moth
papillote [papijɔt] *nf:* **en ~** cooked in tinfoil
papoter [papote] *vi* to chatter
paquebot [pak(ə)bo] *nm* liner
pâquerette [pɑkʀɛt] *nf* daisy
Pâques [pɑk] *nm, nfpl* Easter

paquet [pakɛ] *nm* packet; (*colis*) parcel; (*fig: tas*): **~ de** pile *ou* heap of; **un ~ de cigarettes, s'il vous plaît** a packet of cigarettes, please; **paquet-cadeau** *nm*: **pouvez-vous me faire un paquet-cadeau, s'il vous plaît?** can you gift-wrap it for me, please?
par [paʀ] *prép* by; **finir** *etc* **~ to** end *etc* with; **~ amour** out of love; **passer ~ Lyon/la côte** to go via *ou* through Lyons/along the coast; **~ la fenêtre** (*jeter, regarder*) out of the window; **3 ~ jour/personne** 3 a *ou* per day/person; **2 ~ 2** in twos; **~ ici** this way; (*dans le coin*) round here; **~-ci, ~-là** here and there; **~ temps de pluie** in wet weather
parabolique [paʀabɔlik] *adj*: **antenne ~** parabolic *ou* dish aerial
parachute [paʀaʃyt] *nm* parachute;
parachutiste *nm/f* parachutist; (*Mil*) paratrooper
parade [paʀad] *nf* (*spectacle, défilé*) parade; (*Escrime, Boxe*) parry
paradis [paʀadi] *nm* heaven, paradise

paradoxe [paʀadɔks] *nm* paradox
paraffine [paʀafin] *nf* paraffin
parages [paʀaʒ] *nmpl*: **dans les ~ (de)** in the area *ou* vicinity (of)
paragraphe [paʀagʀaf] *nm* paragraph
paraître [paʀɛtʀ] *vb +attrib* to seem, look, appear ▷ *vi* to appear; (*être visible*) to show; (*Presse, Édition*) to be published, come out, appear ▷ *vb impers*: **il paraît que** it seems *ou* appears that, they say that
parallèle [paʀalɛl] *adj* parallel; (*non officiel*) unofficial ▷ *nm* (*comparaison*): **faire un ~ entre** to draw a parallel between ▷ *nf* parallel (line)
paralyser [paʀalize] *vt* to paralyse
paramédical, e, -aux [paʀamedikal, o] *adj*: **personnel ~** paramedics *pl*, paramedical workers *pl*
paraphrase [paʀafʀɑz] *nf* paraphrase
parapluie [paʀaplɥi] *nm* umbrella
parasite [paʀazit] *nm* parasite; **parasites** *nmpl* (*Tél*) interference *sg*
parasol [paʀasɔl] *nm* parasol, sunshade
paratonnerre [paʀatɔnɛʀ] *nm* lightning conductor
parc [paʀk] *nm* (*public*) park, gardens *pl*; (*de château etc*) grounds *pl*; (*d'enfant*) playpen; **parc à thème** theme park; **parc d'attractions** amusement park; **parc de stationnement** car park
parcelle [paʀsɛl] *nf* fragment, scrap; (*de terrain*) plot, parcel
parce que [paʀsk(ə)] *conj* because
parchemin [paʀʃəmɛ̃] *nm* parchment
parc(o)mètre [paʀkmɛtʀ] *nm* parking meter
parcourir [paʀkuʀiʀ] *vt* (*trajet, distance*) to cover; (*article, livre*) to skim *ou* glance through; (*lieu*) to go all over, travel up and down; (*suj: frisson*) to run through
parcours [paʀkuʀ] *nm* (*trajet*) journey; (*itinéraire*) route
par-dessous [paʀd(ə)su] *prép, adv* under(neath)
pardessus [paʀdəsy] *nm* overcoat
par-dessus [paʀd(ə)sy] *prép* over (the top of) ▷ *adv* over (the top); **~ le marché** on top of all that; **~ tout** above all; **en avoir ~ la tête** to have had enough
par-devant [paʀd(ə)vɑ̃] *adv* (*passer*) round the front
pardon [paʀdɔ̃] *nm* forgiveness *no pl* ▷ *excl* sorry!; (*pour interpeller etc*) excuse me!; **demander ~ à qn (de)** to apologize to sb (for); **je vous demande ~** I'm sorry; (*pour interpeller*) excuse me; **pardonner** *vt* to forgive; **pardonner qch à qn** to forgive sb for sth
pare...: **pare-brise** *nm inv* windscreen (BRIT), windshield (US); **pare-chocs** *nm inv* bumper;

pare-feu *nm inv* (*de foyer*) fireguard; (*Inform*) firewall

pareil, le [paʀɛj] *adj* (*identique*) the same, alike; (*similaire*) similar; (*tel*): **un courage/ livre ~** such courage/a book, courage/a book like this; **de ~s livres** such books; **faire ~ to** do the same (thing); **~ à** the same as; (*similaire*) similar to; **sans ~** unparalleled, unequalled

parent, e [paʀɑ̃, ɑ̃t] *nm/f*: **un(e) ~(e)** a relative *ou* relation; **parents** *nmpl* (*père et mère*) parents; **parenté** *nf* (*lien*) relationship

parenthèse [paʀɑ̃tɛz] *nf* (*ponctuation*) bracket, parenthesis; (*digression*) parenthesis, digression; **entre ~s** in brackets; (*fig*) incidentally

paresse [paʀɛs] *nf* laziness; **paresseux, -euse** *adj* lazy

parfait, e [paʀfɛ, ɛt] *adj* perfect ▷ *nm* (*Ling*) perfect (tense); **parfaitement** *adv* perfectly ▷ *excl* (most) certainly

parfois [paʀfwa] *adv* sometimes

parfum [paʀfœ̃] *nm* (*produit*) perfume, scent; (*odeur: de fleur*) scent, fragrance; (*goût*) flavour; **quels ~s avez-vous?** what flavours do you have?; **parfumé, e** *adj* (*fleur, fruit*) fragrant; (*femme*) perfumed; **parfumé au café** coffee-flavoured; **parfumer** *vt* (*suj: odeur, bouquet*) to perfume; (*crème, gâteau*) to flavour; **parfumerie** *nf* (*produits*) perfumes *pl*; (*boutique*) perfume shop

pari [paʀi] *nm* bet; **parier** *vt* to bet

Paris [paʀi] *n* Paris; **parisien, ne** *adj* Parisian; (*Géo, Admin*) Paris *cpd* ▷ *nm/f*: **Parisien, ne** Parisian

parité [paʀite] *nf* (*Pol*): **~ hommes- femmes** balanced representation of men and women

parjure [paʀʒyʀ] *nm* perjury

parking [paʀkiŋ] *nm* (*lieu*) car park

 Attention à ne pas traduire **parking** par le mot anglais **parking**.

parlant, e [paʀlɑ̃, ɑ̃t] *adj* (*regard*) eloquent; (*Cinéma*) talking

parlement [paʀləmɑ̃] *nm* parliament; **parlementaire** *adj* parliamentary ▷ *nm/f* member of parliament

parler [paʀle] *vi* to speak, talk; (*avouer*) to talk; **~ (à qn) de** to talk *ou* speak (to sb) about; **~ le/en français** to speak French/in French; **~ affaires** to talk business; **sans ~ de** (*fig*) not to mention, to say nothing of; **tu parles!** (*fam: bien sûr*) you bet!; **parlez-vous français?** do you speak French?; **je ne parle pas anglais** I don't speak English; **est-ce que je peux ~ à ...?** can I speak to ...?

parloir [paʀlwaʀ] *nm* (*de prison, d'hôpital*) visiting room

parmi [paʀmi] *prép* among(st)

paroi [paʀwa] *nf* wall; (*cloison*) partition

paroisse [paʀwas] *nf* parish

parole [paʀɔl] *nf* (*faculté*): **la ~** speech; (*mot, promesse*) word; **paroles** *nfpl* (*Mus*) words, lyrics; **tenir ~** to keep one's word; **prendre la ~** to speak; **demander la ~** to ask for permission to speak; **je te crois sur ~** I'll take your word for it

parquet [paʀkɛ] *nm* (*parquet*) floor; (*Jur*): **le ~** the Public Prosecutor's department

parrain [paʀɛ̃] *nm* godfather; **parrainer** *vt* (*suj: entreprise*) to sponsor

pars [paʀ] *vb voir* **partir**

parsemer [paʀsəme] *vt* (*suj: feuilles, papiers*) to be scattered over; **~ qch de** to scatter sth with

part [paʀ] *nf* (*qui revient à qn*) share; (*fraction, partie*) part; **à ~** *adv* (*séparément*) separately; (*de côté*) aside ▷ *prép* apart from, except for; **prendre ~ à** (*débat etc*) to take part in; (*soucis, douleur de qn*) to share in; **faire ~ de qch à qn** to announce sth to sb, inform sb of sth; **pour ma ~** as for me, as far as I'm concerned; **à ~ entière** full; **de la ~ de** (*au nom de*) on behalf of; (*donné par*) from; **de toute(s) ~(s)** from all sides *ou* quarters; **de ~ et d'autre** on both sides, on either side; **d'une ~ ... d'autre ~** on the one hand ... on the other hand; **d'autre ~** (*de plus*) moreover; **faire la ~ des choses** to make allowances

partage [paʀtaʒ] *nm* (*fractionnement*) dividing up; (*répartition*) sharing (out) *no pl*, share-out

partager [paʀtaʒe] *vt* to share; (*distribuer, répartir*) to share (out); (*morceler, diviser*) to divide (up); **se partager** *vt* (*héritage etc*) to share between themselves (*ou* ourselves)

partenaire [paʀtənɛʀ] *nm/f* partner

parterre [paʀtɛʀ] *nm* (*de fleurs*) (flower) bed; (*Théâtre*) stalls *pl*

parti [paʀti] *nm* (*Pol*) party; (*décision*) course of action; (*personne à marier*) match; **tirer ~ de** to take advantage of, turn to good account; **prendre ~ (pour/contre)** to take sides *ou* a stand (for/against); **parti pris** bias

partial, e, -aux [paʀsjal, jo] *adj* biased, partial

participant, e [paʀtisipɑ̃, ɑ̃t] *nm/f* participant; (*à un concours*) entrant

participation [paʀtisipasjɔ̃] *nf* participation; (*financière*) contribution

participer [paʀtisipe]: **~ à** *vt* (*course, réunion*) to take part in; (*frais etc*) to contribute to; (*chagrin, succès de qn*) to share (in)

particularité [paʀtikylaʀite] *nf* (distinctive) characteristic

particulier, -ière [paʀtikylje, jɛʀ] *adj* (*spécifique*) particular; (*spécial*) special, particular; (*personnel, privé*) private; (*étrange*) peculiar, odd ▷ *nm* (*individu: Admin*) private individual; **~ à** peculiar to; **en ~** (*surtout*) in particular, particularly; (*en privé*) in private; **particulièrement** *adv* particularly

partie [paʀti] *nf* (*gén*) part; (*Jur etc: protagonistes*) party; (*de cartes, tennis etc*) game; **une ~ de pêche** a fishing party *ou* trip; **en ~** partly, in part; **faire ~ de** (*suj: chose*) to be part of; **prendre qn à ~** to take sb to task; **en grande ~** largely, in the main; **partie civile** (*Jur*) party claiming damages in a criminal case

partiel, le [paʀsjɛl] *adj* partial ▷ *nm* (*Scol*) class exam

partir [paʀtiʀ] *vi* (*gén*) to go; (*quitter*) to go, leave; (*tache*) to go, come out; **~ de** (*lieu: quitter*) to leave; (: *commencer à*) to start from; **~ pour/à** (*lieu, pays etc*) to leave for/go off to; **à ~ de** from; **le train/le bus part à quelle heure?** what time does the train/bus leave?

partisan, e [paʀtizã, an] *nm/f* partisan ▷ *adj*: **être ~ de qch/de faire** to be in favour of sth/doing

partition [paʀtisjɔ̃] *nf* (*Mus*) score

partout [paʀtu] *adv* everywhere; **~ où il allait** everywhere *ou* wherever he went

paru [paʀy] *pp de* **paraître**

parution [paʀysjɔ̃] *nf* publication

parvenir [paʀvəniʀ] **~ à** *vt* (*atteindre*) to reach; (*réussir*) **~ à faire** to manage to do, succeed in doing; **faire ~ qch à qn** to have sth sent to sb

pas¹ [pɑ] *nm* (*enjambée, Danse*) step; (*allure, mesure*) pace; (*bruit*) (foot)step; (*trace*) footprint; **~ à ~** step by step; **au ~** at walking pace; **marcher à grands ~** to stride along; **à ~ de loup** stealthily; **faire les cent ~** to pace up and down; **faire le premier ~** to make the first move; **sur le ~ de la porte** on the doorstep

⊙ **MOT-CLÉ**

pas² [pɑ] *adv* **1** (*en corrélation avec ne, non etc*) not; **il ne pleure pas** (*habituellement*) he does not *ou* doesn't cry; (*maintenant*) he's not *ou* isn't crying; **il n'a pas pleuré/ne pleurera pas** he did not *ou* didn't/will not *ou* won't cry; **ils n'ont pas de voiture/d'enfants** they don't have *ou* haven't got a car/any children; **il m'a dit de ne pas le faire** he told me not to do it; **non pas que ...** not that ...

2 (*employé sans ne etc*): **pas moi** not me, I don't (*ou* can't *etc*); **elle travaille, (mais) lui pas** *ou* **pas lui** she works but he doesn't *ou* does not; **une pomme pas mûre** an unripe apple; **pas du tout** not at all; **pas de sucre, merci** no sugar, thanks; **ceci est à vous**

ou pas? is this yours or not?, is this yours or isn't it?

3 : **pas mal** (*joli: personne, maison*) not bad; **pas mal fait** not badly done *ou* made; **comment ça va? — pas mal** how are things? — not bad; **pas mal de** quite a lot of

passage [pɑsaʒ] *nm* (*fait de passer*) *voir* **passer**; (*lieu, prix de la traversée, extrait*) passage; (*chemin*) way; **de ~** (*touristes*) passing through; **passage à niveau** level crossing; **passage clouté** pedestrian crossing; **passage interdit** no entry; **passage souterrain** subway (BRIT), underpass

passager, -ère [pɑsaʒe, ɛʀ] *adj* passing ▷ *nm/f* passenger

passant, e [pɑsã, ãt] *adj* (*rue, endroit*) busy ▷ *nm/f* passer-by; **en ~** in passing

passe [pɑs] *nf* (*Sport, Navig*) pass; **être en ~ de faire** to be on the way to doing; **être dans une mauvaise ~** to be going through a rough patch

passé, e [pɑse] *adj* (*révolu*) past; (*dernier: semaine etc*) last; (*couleur*) faded ▷ *prép* after ▷ *nm* past; (*Ling*) past (tense); **~ de mode** out of fashion; **passé composé** perfect (tense); **passé simple** past historic (tense)

passe-partout [pɑspaʀtu] *nm inv* master *ou* skeleton key ▷ *adj inv* all-purpose

passeport [pɑspɔʀ] *nm* passport

passer [pɑse] *vi* (*aller*) to go; (*voiture, piétons: défiler*) to pass (by), go by; (*facteur, laitier etc*) to come, call; (*pour rendre visite*) to call *ou* drop in; (*film, émission*) to be on; (*temps, jours*) to pass, go by; (*couleur*) to fade; (*mode*) to die out; (*douleur*) to pass, go away; (*Scol*): **~ dans la classe supérieure** to go up to the next class ▷ *vt* (*frontière, rivière etc*) to cross; (*douane*) to go through; (*examen*) to sit, take; (*visite médicale etc*) to have; (*journée, temps*) to spend; (*enfiler: vêtement*) to slip on; (*film, pièce*) to show, put on; (*disque*) to play, put on; (*commande*) to place; (*marché, accord*) to agree on; **se passer** *vi* (*avoir lieu: scène, action*) to take place; (*se dérouler: entretien etc*) to go; (*s'écouler: semaine etc*) to pass, go by; (*arriver*): **que s'est-il passé?** what happened?; **~ qch à qn** (*sel etc*) to pass sth to sb; (*prêter*) to lend sb sth; (*lettre, message*) to pass sth on to sb; (*tolérer*) to let sb get away with sth; **~ par** to go through; **~ avant qch/qn** (*fig*) to come before sth/sb; **~ un coup de fil à qn** (*fam*) to give sb a ring; **laisser ~** (*air, lumière, personne*) to let through; (*occasion*) to let slip, miss; (*erreur*) to overlook; **~ à la radio/télévision** to be on the radio/on television; **~ à table** to sit down to eat; **~ au salon** to go into the sitting-room; **~ son tour** to miss one's turn; **~ la seconde** (*Auto*) to change into second; **~**

le balai/l'aspirateur to sweep up/hoover; **je vous passe M. Dupont** (*je vous mets en communication avec lui*) I'm putting you through to Mr Dupont; (*je lui passe l'appareil*) here is Mr Dupont, I'll hand you over to Mr Dupont; **se ~ de** to go *ou* do without

passerelle [pasʀɛl] *nf* footbridge; (*de navire, avion*) gangway

passe-temps [pastɑ̃] *nm inv* pastime

passif, -ive [pasif, iv] *adj* passive

passion [pasjɔ̃] *nf* passion; **passionnant, e** *adj* fascinating; **passionné, e** *adj* (*personne*) passionate; (*récit*) impassioned; **être passionné de** to have a passion for; **passionner** *vt* (*personne*) to fascinate, grip

passoire [paswaʀ] *nf* sieve; (*à légumes*) colander; (*à thé*) strainer

pastèque [pastɛk] *nf* watermelon

pasteur [pastœʀ] *nm* (*protestant*) minister, pastor

pastille [pastij] *nf* (*à sucer*) lozenge, pastille

patate [patat] *nf* (*fam: pomme de terre*) spud; **patate douce** sweet potato

patauger [patoʒe] *vi* to splash about

pâte [pat] *nf* (*à tarte*) pastry; (*à pain*) dough; (*à frire*) batter; **pâtes** *nfpl* (*macaroni etc*) pasta *sg*; **pâte à modeler** modelling clay, Plasticine® (*BRIT*); **pâte brisée** shortcrust pastry; **pâte d'amandes** almond paste, marzipan; **pâte de fruits** crystallized fruit *no pl*; **pâte feuilletée** puff *ou* flaky pastry

pâté [pate] *nm* (*charcuterie*) pâté; (*tache*) ink blot; **pâté de maisons** block (of houses); **pâté (de sable)** sandpie; **pâté en croûte** ≈ pork pie

pâtée [pate] *nf* mash, feed

patente [patɑ̃t] *nf* (*Comm*) trading licence

paternel, le [patɛʀnɛl] *adj* (*amour, soins*) fatherly; (*ligne, autorité*) paternal

pâteux, -euse [patø, øz] *adj* pasty; (*langue*) coated

pathétique [patetik] *adj* moving

patience [pasjɑ̃s] *nf* patience

patient, e [pasjɑ̃, jɑ̃t] *adj, nm/f* patient; **patienter** *vi* to wait

patin [patɛ̃] *nm* skate; (*sport*) skating; **patins (à glace)** (ice) skates; **patins à roulettes** roller skates

patinage [patinaʒ] *nm* skating

patiner [patine] *vi* to skate; (*roue, voiture*) to spin; **se patiner** *vi* (*meuble, cuir*) to acquire a sheen; **patineur, -euse** *nm/f* skater; **patinoire** *nf* skating rink, (ice) rink

pâtir [patiʀ]: **~ de** *vt* to suffer because of

pâtisserie [patisʀi] *nf* (*boutique*) cake shop; (*gâteau*) cake, pastry; (*à la maison*) pastry- *ou* cake-making, baking; **pâtissier, -ière** *nm/f* pastrycook

patois [patwa] *nm* dialect, patois

patrie [patʀi] *nf* homeland

patrimoine [patʀimwan] *nm* (*culture*) heritage

patriotique [patʀijɔtik] *adj* patriotic

patron, ne [patʀɔ̃, ɔn] *nm/f* boss; (*Rel*) patron saint ▷ *nm* (*Couture*) pattern; **patronat** *nm* employers *pl*; **patronner** *vt* to sponsor, support

patrouille [patʀuj] *nf* patrol

patte [pat] *nf* (*jambe*) leg; (*pied: de chien, chat*) paw; (: *d'oiseau*) foot

pâturage [patyʀaʒ] *nm* pasture

paume [pom] *nf* palm

paumé, e [pome] (*fam*) *nm/f* drop-out

paupière [popjɛʀ] *nf* eyelid

pause [poz] *nf* (*arrêt*) break; (*en parlant, Mus*) pause

pauvre [povʀ] *adj* poor; **les pauvres** *nmpl* the poor; **pauvreté** *nf* (*état*) poverty

pavé, e [pave] *adj* (*cour*) paved; (*chaussée*) cobbled ▷ *nm* (*bloc*) paving stone; cobblestone

pavillon [pavijɔ̃] *nm* (*de banlieue*) small (detached) house; pavilion; (*drapeau*) flag

payant, e [pɛjɑ̃, ɑ̃t] *adj* (*spectateurs etc*) paying; (*fig: entreprise*) profitable; (*effort*) which pays off; **c'est ~** you have to pay, there is a charge

paye [pɛj] *nf* pay, wages *pl*

payer [peje] *vt* (*créancier, employé, loyer*) to pay; (*achat, réparations, fig: faute*) to pay for ▷ *vi* to pay; (*métier*) to be well-paid; (*tactique etc*) to pay off; **il me l'a fait ~ 10 euros** he charged me 10 euros for it; **~ qch à qn** to buy sth for sb, buy sb sth; **se ~ la tête de qn** (*fam*) to take the mickey out of sb; **est-ce que je peux ~ par carte de crédit?** can I pay by credit card?

pays [pei] *nm* country; (*région*) region; **du ~** local

paysage [peizaʒ] *nm* landscape

paysan, ne [peizɑ̃, an] *nm/f* farmer; (*péj*) peasant ▷ *adj* (*agricole*) farming; (*rural*) country

Pays-Bas [peiba] *nmpl*: **les ~** the Netherlands

PC *nm* (*Inform*) PC

PDA *sigle m* (= *personal digital assistant*) PDA

PDG *sigle m* = **président directeur général**

péage [peaʒ] *nm* toll; (*endroit*) tollgate

peau, x [po] *nf* skin; **gants de ~** fine leather gloves; **être bien/mal dans sa ~** to be quite at ease/ill-at-ease; **peau de chamois** (*chiffon*) chamois leather, shammy

pêche [pɛʃ] nf (fruit) peach; (sport, activité) fishing; (poissons pêchés) catch; **pêche à la ligne** (en rivière) angling

péché [peʃe] nm sin

pécher [peʃe] vi (Rel) to sin

pêcher [peʃe] nm peach tree ▷ vi to go fishing ▷ vt (attraper) to catch; (être pêcheur de) to fish for

pécheur, -eresse [peʃœr, peʃrɛs] nm/f sinner

pêcheur [pɛʃœr] nm fisherman; (à la ligne) angler

pédagogie [pedagɔʒi] nf educational methods pl, pedagogy; **pédagogique** adj educational

pédale [pedal] nf pedal

pédalo [pedalo] nm pedal-boat

pédant, e [pedã, ãt] (péj) adj pedantic

pédestre [pedɛstr] adj: **randonnée ~** ramble; **sentier ~** pedestrian footpath

pédiatre [pedjatr] nm/f paediatrician, child specialist

pédicure [pedikyr] nm/f chiropodist

pègre [pɛgr] nf underworld

peigne [pɛɲ] nm comb; **peigner** vt to comb (the hair of); **se peigner** vi to comb one's hair; **peignoir** nm dressing gown; **peignoir de bain** bathrobe

peindre [pɛ̃dr] vt to paint; (fig) to portray, depict

peine [pɛn] nf (affliction) sorrow, sadness no pl; (mal, effort) trouble no pl, effort; (difficulté) difficulty; (Jur) sentence; **avoir de la ~** to be sad; **faire de la ~ à qn** to distress ou upset sb; **prendre la ~ de faire** to go to the trouble of doing; **se donner de la ~** to make an effort; **ce n'est pas la ~ de faire** there's no point in doing, it's not worth doing; **à ~** scarcely, barely; **à ~ ... que** hardly ... than, no sooner ... than; **peine capitale** capital punishment; **peine de mort** death sentence ou penalty; **peiner** vi (personne) to work hard; (moteur, voiture) to labour ▷ vt to grieve, sadden

peintre [pɛ̃tr] nm painter; **peintre en bâtiment** painter (and decorator)

peinture [pɛ̃tyr] nf painting; (matière) paint; (surfaces peintes: aussi: **~s**) paintwork; **"~ fraîche"** "wet paint"

péjoratif, -ive [peʒɔratif, iv] adj pejorative, derogatory

Pékin [pekɛ̃] n Beijing

pêle-mêle [pɛlmɛl] adv higgledy-piggledy

peler [pəle] vt, vi to peel

pèlerin [pɛlrɛ̃] nm pilgrim

pèlerinage [pɛlrinaʒ] nm pilgrimage

pelle [pɛl] nf shovel; (d'enfant, de terrassier) spade

pellicule [pelikyl] nf film; **pellicules** nfpl (Méd) dandruff sg; **je voudrais une ~ de 36 poses** I'd like a 36-exposure film

pelote [p(ə)lɔt] nf (de fil, laine) ball; **pelote basque** pelota

peloton [p(ə)lɔtɔ̃] nm group, squad; (Cyclisme) pack

pelotonner [p(ə)lɔtɔne]: **se pelotonner** vi to curl (o.s.) up

pelouse [p(ə)luz] nf lawn

peluche [p(ə)lyʃ] nf: **(animal en) ~** fluffy animal, soft toy; **chien/lapin en ~** fluffy dog/rabbit

pelure [p(ə)lyr] nf peeling, peel no pl

pénal, e, -aux [penal, o] adj penal; **pénalité** nf penalty

penchant [pɑ̃ʃɑ̃] nm (tendance) tendency, propensity; (faible) liking, fondness

pencher [pɑ̃ʃe] vi to tilt, lean over ▷ vt to tilt; **se pencher** vi to lean over; (se baisser) to bend down; **se ~ sur** (fig: problème) to look into; **~ pour** to be inclined to favour

pendant [pɑ̃dɑ̃] prép (au cours de) during; (indique la durée) for; **~ que** while

pendentif [pɑ̃dɑ̃tif] nm pendant

penderie [pɑ̃dri] nf wardrobe

pendre [pɑ̃dr] vt, vi to hang; **se ~** (se suicider) to hang o.s.; **~ qch à** (mur) to hang sth (up) on; (plafond) to hang sth (up) from

pendule [pɑ̃dyl] nf clock ▷ nm pendulum

pénétrer [penetre] vi, vt to penetrate; **~ dans** to enter

pénible [penibl] adj (travail) hard; (sujet) painful; (personne) tiresome; **péniblement** adv with difficulty

péniche [peniʃ] nf barge

pénicilline [penisilin] nf penicillin

péninsule [penɛ̃syl] nf peninsula

pénis [penis] nm penis

pénitence [penitɑ̃s] nf (peine) penance; (repentir) penitence; **pénitencier** nm penitentiary

pénombre [penɔ̃br] nf (faible clarté) half-light; (obscurité) darkness

pensée [pɑ̃se] nf thought; (démarche, doctrine) thinking no pl; (fleur) pansy; **en ~** in one's mind

penser [pɑ̃se] vi, vt to think; **~ à** (ami, vacances) to think of ou about; (réfléchir à: problème, offre) to think about ou over; (prévoir) to think of; **faire ~ à** to remind one of; **~ faire qch** to be thinking of doing sth, intend to do sth; **pensif, -ive** adj pensive, thoughtful

pension [pɑ̃sjɔ̃] nf (allocation) pension; (prix du logement) board and lodgings, bed and board; (école) boarding school; **pension alimentaire** (de divorcée) maintenance allowance, alimony; **pension complète** full board; **pension de famille** boarding house, guesthouse; **pensionnaire** nm/f (Scol) boarder; **pensionnat** nm boarding school

pente [pɑ̃t] nf slope; **en ~** sloping

Pentecôte [pɑ̃tkot] *nf*: **la ~** Whitsun (BRIT),
Pentecost
pénurie [penyʀi] *nf* shortage
pépé [pepe] (*fam*) *nm* grandad
pépin [pepɛ̃] *nm* (*Bot: graine*) pip; (*ennui*) snag,
hitch
pépinière [pepinjɛʀ] *nf* nursery
perçant, e [pɛʀsɑ̃, ɑ̃t] *adj* (*cri*) piercing, shrill;
(*regard*) piercing
percepteur, -trice [pɛʀsɛptœʀ, tʀis] *nm/f*
tax collector
perception [pɛʀsɛpsjɔ̃] *nf* perception;
(*bureau*) tax office
percer [pɛʀse] *vt* to pierce; (*ouverture etc*) to
make; (*mystère, énigme*) to penetrate ▷ *vi* to
break through; **perceuse** *nf* drill
percevoir [pɛʀsəvwaʀ] *vt* (*distinguer*) to
perceive, detect; (*taxe, impôt*) to collect; (*revenu,
indemnité*) to receive
perche [pɛʀʃ] *nf* (*bâton*) pole
percher [pɛʀʃe] *vt, vi* to perch; **se percher** *vi*
to perch; **perchoir** *nm* perch
perçois *etc* [pɛʀswa] *vb voir* **percevoir**
perçu, e [pɛʀsy] *pp de* **percevoir**
percussion [pɛʀkysjɔ̃] *nf* percussion
percuter [pɛʀkyte] *vt* to strike; (*suj: véhicule*)
to crash into
perdant, e [pɛʀdɑ̃, ɑ̃t] *nm/f* loser
perdre [pɛʀdʀ] *vt* to lose; (*gaspiller: temps,
argent*) to waste; (*personne: moralement etc*) to
ruin ▷ *vi* to lose; (*sur une vente etc*) to lose out;
se perdre *vi* (*s'égarer*) to get lost, lose one's
way; (*denrées*) to go to waste; **j'ai perdu mon
portefeuille/passeport** I've lost my wallet/
passport; **je me suis perdu** (*et je le suis encore*)
I'm lost; (*et je ne le suis plus*) I got lost
perdrix [pɛʀdʀi] *nf* partridge
perdu, e [pɛʀdy] *pp de* **perdre** ▷ *adj* (*isolé*)
out-of-the-way; (*Comm: emballage*) non-
returnable; (*malade*): **il est ~** there's no hope
left for him; **à vos moments ~s** in your spare
time
père [pɛʀ] *nm* father; **père de famille** father;
le père Noël Father Christmas
perfection [pɛʀfɛksjɔ̃] *nf* perfection; **à
la ~** to perfection; **perfectionné, e** *adj*
sophisticated; **perfectionner** *vt* to improve,
perfect; **se perfectionner en anglais** to
improve one's English
perforer [pɛʀfɔʀe] *vt* (*poinçonner*) to punch
performant, e [pɛʀfɔʀmɑ̃, ɑ̃t] *adj*: **très ~**
high-performance *cpd*
perfusion [pɛʀfyzjɔ̃] *nf*: **faire une ~ à qn** to
put sb on a drip
péril [peʀil] *nm* peril
périmé, e [peʀime] *adj* (*Admin*) out-of-date,
expired
périmètre [peʀimɛtʀ] *nm* perimeter
période [peʀjɔd] *nf* period; **périodique**

adj periodic ▷ *nm* periodical; **garniture** *ou*
serviette périodique sanitary towel (BRIT)
ou napkin (US)
périphérique [peʀifeʀik] *adj* (*quartiers*)
outlying ▷ *nm* (*Auto*): **boulevard ~** ring road
(BRIT), beltway (US)
périr [peʀiʀ] *vi* to die, perish
périssable [peʀisabl] *adj* perishable
perle [pɛʀl] *nf* pearl; (*de plastique, métal, sueur*)
bead
permanence [pɛʀmanɑ̃s] *nf* permanence;
(*local*) (*duty*) office; **assurer une ~** (*service
public, bureaux*) to operate *ou* maintain a basic
service; **être de ~** to be on call *ou* duty; **en ~**
continuously
permanent, e [pɛʀmanɑ̃, ɑ̃t] *adj* permanent;
(*spectacle*) continuous; **permanente** *nf* perm
perméable [pɛʀmeabl] *adj* (*terrain*)
permeable; **~ à** (*fig*) receptive *ou* open to
permettre [pɛʀmɛtʀ] *vt* to allow, permit; **~ à
qn de faire/qch** to allow sb to do/sth; **se ~ de
faire** to take the liberty of doing
permis [pɛʀmi] *nm* permit, licence; **permis
de conduire** driving licence (BRIT), driver's
license (US); **permis de construire** planning
permission (BRIT), building permit (US);
permis de séjour residence permit; **permis
de travail** work permit
permission [pɛʀmisjɔ̃] *nf* permission; (*Mil*)
leave; **avoir la ~ de faire** to have permission
to do; **en ~** on leave
Pérou [peʀu] *nm* Peru
perpétuel, le [pɛʀpetɥɛl] *adj* perpetual;
perpétuité *nf*: **à perpétuité** for life; **être
condamné à perpétuité** to receive a life
sentence
perplexe [pɛʀplɛks] *adj* perplexed, puzzled
perquisitionner [pɛʀkizisjɔne] *vi* to carry
out a search
perron [peʀɔ̃] *nm* steps *pl* (*leading to entrance*)
perroquet [peʀɔke] *nm* parrot
perruche [peʀyʃ] *nf* budgerigar (BRIT), budgie
(BRIT), parakeet (US)
perruque [peʀyk] *nf* wig
persécuter [pɛʀsekyte] *vt* to persecute
persévérer [pɛʀseveʀe] *vi* to persevere
persil [pɛʀsi] *nm* parsley
Persique [pɛʀsik] *adj*: **le golfe ~** the (Persian)
Gulf
persistant, e [pɛʀsistɑ̃, ɑ̃t] *adj* persistent
persister [pɛʀsiste] *vi* to persist; **~ à faire qch**
to persist in doing sth
personnage [pɛʀsɔnaʒ] *nm* (*individu*)
character, individual; (*célébrité*) important
person; (*de roman, film*) character; (*Peinture*)
figure
personnalité [pɛʀsɔnalite] *nf* personality;
(*personnage*) prominent figure
personne [pɛʀsɔn] *nf* person ▷ *pron* nobody,

P

no one; (*avec négation en anglais*) anybody, anyone; **personne âgée** elderly person; **personnel, le** *adj* personal; (*égoïste*) selfish ▷ *nm* staff, personnel; **personnellement** *adv* personally

perspective [pɛʀspɛktiv] *nf* (*Art*) perspective; (*vue*) view; (*point de vue*) viewpoint, angle; (*chose envisagée*) prospect; **en ~** in prospect

perspicace [pɛʀspikas] *adj* clear-sighted, gifted with (*ou* showing) insight; **perspicacité** *nf* clear-sightedness

persuader [pɛʀsɥade] *vt*: **~ qn (de faire)** to persuade sb (to do); **persuasif, -ive** *adj* persuasive

perte [pɛʀt] *nf* loss; (*de temps*) waste; (*fig: morale*) ruin; **à ~ de vue** as far as the eye can (*ou* could) see; **pertes blanches** (vaginal) discharge *sg*

pertinent, e [pɛʀtinɑ̃, ɑ̃t] *adj* apt, relevant

perturbation [pɛʀtyʀbasjɔ̃] *nf*: **perturbation (atmosphérique)** atmospheric disturbance

perturber [pɛʀtyʀbe] *vt* to disrupt; (*Psych*) to perturb, disturb

pervers, e [pɛʀvɛʀ, ɛʀs] *adj* perverted

pervertir [pɛʀvɛʀtiʀ] *vt* to pervert

pesant, e [pəzɑ̃, ɑ̃t] *adj* heavy; (*fig: présence*) burdensome

pèse-personne [pɛzpɛʀsɔn] *nm* (bathroom) scales *pl*

peser [pəze] *vt* to weigh ▷ *vi* to weigh; (*fig: avoir de l'importance*) to carry weight; **~ lourd** to be heavy

pessimiste [pesimist] *adj* pessimistic ▷ *nm/f* pessimist

peste [pɛst] *nf* plague

pétale [petal] *nm* petal

pétanque [petɑ̃k] *nf type of bowls*

● **PÉTANQUE**
●
● **Pétanque** is a version of the game
● of 'boules', played on a variety of hard
● surfaces. Standing with their feet together,
● players throw steel bowls at a wooden
● jack. **Pétanque** originated in the South
● of France and is still very much associated
● with that area.

pétard [petaʀ] *nm* banger (*BRIT*), firecracker

péter [pete] *vi* (*fam: casser*) to bust; (*fam!*) to fart (*!*)

pétillant, e [petijɑ̃, ɑ̃t] *adj* (*eau etc*) sparkling

pétiller [petije] *vi* (*feu*) to crackle; (*champagne*) to bubble; (*yeux*) to sparkle

petit, e [p(ə)ti, it] *adj* small; (*avec nuance affective*) little; (*voyage*) short, little; (*bruit etc*) faint, slight ▷ *nm/f* (*petit enfant*) little boy/girl,

child; **petits** *nmpl* (*d'un animal*) young *no pl*; **faire des ~s** to have kittens (*ou* puppies *etc*); **la classe des ~s** the infant class; **les tout-~s** the little ones, the tiny tots (*fam*); **~ à ~** bit by bit, gradually; **petit(e) ami(e)** boyfriend/girlfriend; **petit déjeuner** breakfast; **le petit déjeuner est à quelle heure?** what time is breakfast?; **petit four** petit four; **petit pain** (bread) roll; **les petites annonces** the small ads; **petits pois** (garden) peas; **petite-fille** *nf* granddaughter; **petit-fils** *nm* grandson

pétition [petisjɔ̃] *nf* petition

petits-enfants [pətizɑ̃fɑ̃] *nmpl* grandchildren

pétrin [petʀɛ̃] *nm* (*fig*): **dans le ~** (*fam*) in a jam *ou* fix

pétrir [petʀiʀ] *vt* to knead

pétrole [petʀɔl] *nm* oil; (*pour lampe, réchaud etc*) paraffin (oil); **pétrolier, -ière** *nm* oil tanker

> ⬛ Attention à ne pas traduire **pétrole** par le mot anglais **petrol**.

🅞 **MOT-CLÉ**

peu [pø] *adv* **1** (*modifiant verbe, adjectif, adverbe*): **il boit peu** he doesn't drink (very) much; **il est peu bavard** he's not very talkative; **peu avant/après** shortly before/afterwards
2 (*modifiant nom*): **peu de: peu de gens/d'arbres** few *ou* not (very) many people/trees; **il a peu d'espoir** he hasn't (got) much hope, he has little hope; **pour peu de temps** for (only) a short while
3: **peu à peu** little by little; **à peu près** just about, more or less; **à peu près 10 kg/10 euros** approximately 10 kg/10 euros
▷ *nm* **1**: **le peu de gens qui** the few people who; **le peu de sable qui** what little sand, the little sand which
2: **un peu** a little; **un petit peu** a little bit; **un peu d'espoir** a little hope; **elle est un peu bavarde** she's quite *ou* rather talkative; **un peu plus de** slightly more than; **un peu moins de** slightly less than; (*avec pluriel*) slightly fewer than
▷ *pron*: **peu le savent** few know (it); **de peu** (only) just

peuple [pœpl] *nm* people; **peupler** *vt* (*pays, région*) to populate; (*étang*) to stock; (*suj: hommes, poissons*) to inhabit

peuplier [pøplije] *nm* poplar (tree)

peur [pœʀ] *nf* fear; **avoir ~ (de/de faire/que)** to be frightened *ou* afraid (of/of doing/that); **faire ~ à** to frighten; **de ~ de/que** for fear of/that; **peureux, -euse** *adj* fearful, timorous

peut [pø] *vb voir* **pouvoir**

peut-être [pøtɛtʀ] *adv* perhaps, maybe; **~ que** perhaps, maybe; **~ bien qu'il fera/est** he may well do/be

phare [faʀ] nm (en mer) lighthouse; (de véhicule) headlight

pharmacie [faʀmasi] nf (magasin) chemist's (BRIT), pharmacy; (de salle de bain) medicine cabinet; **pharmacien, ne** nm/f pharmacist, chemist (BRIT)

phénomène [fenɔmɛn] nm phenomenon

philosophe [filɔzɔf] nm/f philosopher ▷ adj philosophical

philosophie [filɔzɔfi] nf philosophy

phobie [fɔbi] nf phobia

phoque [fɔk] nm seal

phosphorescent, e [fɔsfɔʀesɑ̃, ɑ̃t] adj luminous

photo [fɔto] nf photo(graph); **prendre en ~** to take a photo of; **pourriez-vous nous prendre en ~, s'il vous plaît?** would you take a picture of us, please?; **faire de la ~** to take photos; **photo d'identité** passport photograph; **photocopie** nf photocopy; **photocopier** vt to photocopy; **photocopieuse** nf photocopier; **photographe** nm/f photographer; **photographie** nf (technique) photography; (cliché) photograph; **photographier** vt to photograph

phrase [fʀɑz] nf sentence

physicien, ne [fizisjɛ̃, jɛn] nm/f physicist

physique [fizik] adj physical ▷ nm physique ▷ nf physics sg; **au ~** physically; **physiquement** adv physically

pianiste [pjanist] nm/f pianist

piano [pjano] nm piano; **pianoter** vi to tinkle away (at the piano)

pic [pik] nm (instrument) pick(axe); (montagne) peak; (Zool) woodpecker; **à ~** vertically; (fig: tomber, arriver) just at the right time

pichet [piʃɛ] nm jug

picorer [pikɔʀe] vt to peck

pie [pi] nf magpie

pièce [pjɛs] nf (d'un logement) room; (Théâtre) play; (de machine) part; (de monnaie) coin; (document) document; (fragment, de collection) piece; **dix euros ~** ten euros each; **vendre à la ~** to sell separately; **travailler à la ~** to do piecework; **un maillot une ~** a one-piece swimsuit; **un deux-~s cuisine** a two-room(ed) flat (BRIT) ou apartment (US) with kitchen; **pièce à conviction** exhibit; **pièce d'eau** ornamental lake ou pond; **pièce de rechange** spare (part); **pièce d'identité: avez-vous une pièce d'identité?** have you got any (means of) identification?; **pièce jointe** (Comput) attachment; **pièce montée** tiered cake; **pièces détachées** spares, (spare) parts; **pièces justificatives** supporting documents

pied [pje] nm foot; (de table) leg; (de lampe) base; **~s nus** ou **nus-~s** barefoot; **à ~** on foot;

au **~ de la lettre** literally; **avoir ~** to be able to touch the bottom, not to be out of one's depth; **avoir le ~ marin** to be a good sailor; **sur ~** (debout, rétabli) up and about; **mettre sur ~** (entreprise) to set up; **c'est le ~** (fam) it's brilliant; **mettre les ~s dans le plat** (fam) to put one's foot in it; **il se débrouille comme un ~** (fam) he's completely useless; **pied-noir** nm Algerian-born Frenchman

piège [pjɛʒ] nm trap; **prendre au ~** to trap; **piéger** vt (avec une bombe) to booby-trap; **lettre/voiture piégée** letter-/car-bomb

piercing [pjɛʀsiŋ] nm body piercing

pierre [pjɛʀ] nf stone; **pierre tombale** tombstone; **pierreries** nfpl gems, precious stones

piétiner [pjetine] vi (trépigner) to stamp (one's foot); (fig) to be at a standstill ▷ vt to trample on

piéton, ne [pjetɔ̃, ɔn] nm/f pedestrian; **piétonnier, -ière** adj: **rue** ou **zone piétonnière** pedestrian precinct

pieu, x [pjø] nm post; (pointu) stake

pieuvre [pjœvʀ] nf octopus

pieux, -euse [pjø, pjøz] adj pious

pigeon [piʒɔ̃] nm pigeon

piger [piʒe] (fam) vi, vt to understand

pigiste [piʒist] nm/f freelance(r)

pignon [piɲɔ̃] nm (de mur) gable

pile [pil] nf (tas) pile; (Élec) battery ▷ adv (fam: s'arrêter etc) dead; **à deux heures ~** at two on the dot; **jouer à ~ ou face** to toss up (for it); **~ ou face?** heads or tails?

piler [pile] vt to crush, pound

pilier [pilje] nm pillar

piller [pije] vt to pillage, plunder, loot

pilote [pilɔt] nm pilot; (de voiture) driver ▷ adj pilot cpd; **pilote de course** racing driver; **pilote de ligne** airline pilot; **piloter** vt (avion) to pilot, fly; (voiture) to drive

pilule [pilyl] nf pill; **prendre la ~** to be on the pill

piment [pimɑ̃] nm (aussi: **~ rouge**) chilli; (fig) spice, piquancy; **~ doux** pepper, capsicum; **pimenté, e** adj (plat) hot, spicy

pin [pɛ̃] nm pine

pinard [pinaʀ] (fam) nm (cheap) wine, plonk (BRIT)

pince [pɛ̃s] nf (outil) pliers pl; (de homard, crabe) pincer, claw; (Couture: pli) dart; **pince à épiler** tweezers pl; **pince à linge** clothes peg (BRIT) ou pin (US)

pincé, e [pɛ̃se] adj (air) stiff

pinceau, x [pɛ̃so] nm (paint)brush

pincer [pɛ̃se] vt to pinch; (fam) to nab

pinède [pinɛd] nf pinewood, pine forest

pingouin [pɛ̃gwɛ̃] nm penguin

ping-pong® [piŋpɔ̃g] nm table tennis

pinson [pɛ̃sɔ̃] nm chaffinch

p

pintade [pɛ̃tad] nf guinea-fowl

pion [pjɔ̃] nm (Échecs) pawn; (Dames) piece; (Scol) supervisor

pionnier [pjɔnje] nm pioneer

pipe [pip] nf pipe; **fumer la ~** to smoke a pipe

piquant, e [pikɑ̃, ɑ̃t] adj (barbe, rosier etc) prickly; (saveur, sauce) hot, pungent; (détail) titillating; (froid) biting ▷ nm (épine) thorn, prickle; (fig) spiciness, spice

pique [pik] nf pike; (fig) cutting remark ▷ nm (Cartes) spades pl

pique-nique [piknik] nm picnic; **pique-niquer** vi to have a picnic

piquer [pike] vt (suj: guêpe, fumée, orties) to sting; (: moustique) to bite; (: barbe) to prick; (: froid) to bite; (Méd) to give a jab to; (: chien, chat) to put to sleep; (intérêt) to arouse; (fam: voler) to pinch ▷ vi (avion) to go into a dive

piquet [pikɛ] nm (pieu) post, stake; (de tente) peg

piqûre [pikyʀ] nf (d'épingle) prick; (d'ortie) sting; (de moustique) bite; (Méd) injection, shot (US); **faire une ~ à qn** to give sb an injection

pirate [piʀat] nm, adj pirate; **pirate de l'air** hijacker

pire [piʀ] adj worse; (superlatif): **le(la) ~ ...** the worst ... ▷ nm: **le ~ (de)** the worst (of); **au ~** at (the very) worst

pis [pi] nm (de vache) udder ▷ adj, adv worse; **de mal en ~** from bad to worse

piscine [pisin] nf (swimming) pool; **piscine couverte** indoor (swimming) pool

pissenlit [pisɑ̃li] nm dandelion

pistache [pistaʃ] nf pistachio (nut)

piste [pist] nf (d'un animal, sentier) track, trail; (indice) lead; (de stade) track; (de cirque) ring; (de danse) floor; (de patinage) rink; (de ski) run; (Aviat) runway; **piste cyclable** cycle track

pistolet [pistɔlɛ] nm (arme) pistol, gun; (à peinture) spray gun; **pistolet-mitrailleur** nm submachine gun

piston [pistɔ̃] nm (Tech) piston; **avoir du ~** (fam) to have friends in the right places; **pistonner** vt (candidat) to pull strings for

piteux, -euse [pitø, øz] adj pitiful, sorry (avant le nom); **en ~ état** in a sorry state

pitié [pitje] nf pity; **il me fait ~** I feel sorry for him; **avoir ~ de** (compassion) to pity, feel sorry for; (merci) to have pity ou mercy on

pitoyable [pitwajabl] adj pitiful

pittoresque [pitɔʀɛsk] adj picturesque

PJ sigle f (= police judiciaire) ≈ CID (BRIT), ≈ FBI (US)

placard [plakaʀ] nm (armoire) cupboard; (affiche) poster, notice

place [plas] nf (emplacement, classement) place; (de ville, village) square; (espace libre) room, space; (de parking) space; (siège: de train, cinéma, voiture) seat; (emploi) job; **en ~** (mettre) in its place; **sur ~** on the spot; **faire ~ à** to give way to; **ça prend de la ~** it takes up a lot of room ou space; **à la ~ de** in place of, instead of; **à votre ~ ...** if I were you ...; **je voudrais réserver deux ~s** I'd like to book two seats; **la ~ est prise?** is this seat taken?; **se mettre à la ~ de qn** to put o.s. in sb's place ou in sb's shoes

placé, e [plase] adj: **haut ~** (fig) high-ranking; **être bien/mal ~** (spectateur) to have a good/a poor seat; (concurrent) to be in a good/bad position; **il est bien ~ pour le savoir** he is in a position to know

placement [plasmɑ̃] nm (Finance) investment; **agence ou bureau de ~** employment agency

placer [plase] vt to place; (convive, spectateur) to seat; (argent) to place, invest; **se ~ au premier rang** to go and stand (ou sit) in the first row

plafond [plafɔ̃] nm ceiling

plage [plaʒ] nf beach; **plage arrière** (Auto) parcel ou back shelf

plaider [plede] vi (avocat) to plead ▷ vt to plead; **~ pour** (fig) to speak for; **plaidoyer** nm (Jur) speech for the defence; (fig) plea

plaie [plɛ] nf wound

plaignant, e [plɛɲɑ̃, ɑ̃t] nm/f plaintiff

plaindre [plɛ̃dʀ] vt to pity, feel sorry for; **se plaindre** vi (gémir) to moan; (protester): **se ~ (à qn) (de)** to complain (to sb) (about); (souffrir): **se ~ de** to complain of

plaine [plɛn] nf plain

plain-pied [plɛ̃pje] adv: **de ~ (avec)** on the same level (as)

plainte [plɛ̃t] nf (gémissement) moan, groan; (doléance) complaint; **porter ~** to lodge a complaint

plaire [plɛʀ] vi to be a success, be successful; **ça plaît beaucoup aux jeunes** it's very popular with young people; **~ à: cela me plaît** I like it; **se ~ quelque part** to like being somewhere ou like it somewhere; **s'il vous plaît** please

plaisance [plɛzɑ̃s] nf (aussi: **navigation de ~**) (pleasure) sailing, yachting

plaisant, e [plɛzɑ̃, ɑ̃t] adj pleasant; (histoire, anecdote) amusing

plaisanter [plɛzɑ̃te] vi to joke; **plaisanterie** nf joke

plaisir [pleziʀ] nm pleasure; **faire ~ à qn** (délibérément) to be nice to sb, please sb; **ça me fait ~** I like (doing) it; **j'espère que ça te fera ~** I hope you'll like it; **pour le ~** for pleasure

plaît [plɛ] vb voir **plaire**

plan, e [plɑ̃, an] adj flat ▷ nm plan; (fig) level, plane; (Cinéma) shot; **au premier/second ~** in the foreground/middle distance; **à l'arrière ~** in the background; **plan d'eau** lake

planche [plɑ̃ʃ] nf (pièce de bois) plank,

(wooden) board; (*illustration*) plate; **planche
à repasser** ironing board; **planche (à
roulettes)** skateboard; **planche (à voile)**
(*sport*) windsurfing

plancher [plɑ̃ʃe] *nm* floor; floorboards *pl* ▷ *vi*
(*fam*) to work hard

planer [plane] *vi* to glide; (*fam: rêveur*) to have
one's head in the clouds; **~ sur** (*fig: danger*) to
hang over

planète [planɛt] *nf* planet

planeur [plancer] *nm* glider

planifier [planifje] *vt* to plan

planning [planiŋ] *nm* programme, schedule;
planning familial family planning

plant [plɑ̃] *nm* seedling, young plant

plante [plɑ̃t] *nf* plant; **la plante du pied**
the sole (of the foot); **plante verte** *ou*
d'appartement house plant

planter [plɑ̃te] *vt* (*plante*) to plant; (*enfoncer*)
to hammer *ou* drive in; (*tente*) to put up, pitch;
(*fam: personne*) to dump; **se planter** (*fam: se
tromper*) to get it wrong

plaque [plak] *nf* plate; (*de verglas, d'eczéma*)
patch; (*avec inscription*) plaque; **plaque
chauffante** hotplate; **plaque de chocolat**
bar of chocolate; **plaque tournante** (*fig*)
centre

plaqué, e [plake] *adj*: **~ or/argent** gold-/silver-
plated

plaquer [plake] *vt* (*Rugby*) to bring down;
(*fam: laisser tomber*) to drop

plaquette [plakɛt] *nf* (*de chocolat*) bar; (*beurre*)
pack(et); **plaquette de frein** brake pad

plastique [plastik] *adj, nm* plastic; **plastiquer**
vt to blow up (*with a plastic bomb*)

plat, e [pla, -at] *adj* flat; (*cheveux*) straight;
(*style*) flat, dull ▷ *nm* (*récipient, Culin*) dish; (*d'un
repas*) course; **à ~ ventre** face down; **à ~** (*pneu,
batterie*) flat; (*fam: personne*) dead beat; **plat
cuisiné** pre-cooked meal; **plat de résistance**
main course; **plat du jour** dish of the day

platane [platan] *nm* plane tree

plateau, x [plato] *nm* (*support*) tray; (*Géo*)
plateau; (*Cinéma*) set; **plateau à fromages**
cheese board

plate-bande [platbɑ̃d] *nf* flower bed

plate-forme [platfɔrm] *nf* platform; **plate-
forme de forage/pétrolière** drilling/oil rig

platine [platin] *nm* platinum ▷ *nf* (*d'un tourne-
disque*) turntable; **platine laser** compact disc
ou CD player

plâtre [plɑtr] *nm* (*matériau*) plaster; (*statue*)
plaster statue; (*Méd*) (plaster) cast; **avoir un
bras dans le ~** to have an arm in plaster

plein, e [plɛ̃, plɛn] *adj* full ▷ *nm*: **faire le ~**
(**d'essence**) to fill up (with petrol); **à ~es
mains** (*ramasser*) in handfuls; **à ~ temps**
full-time; **en ~ air** in the open air; **en ~ soleil**
in direct sunlight; **en ~e nuit/rue** in the

middle of the night/street; **en ~ jour** in broad
daylight; **le ~, s'il vous plaît** fill it up, please

pleurer [plœre] *vi* to cry; (*yeux*) to water ▷ *vt*
to mourn (for); **~ sur** to lament (over), to
bemoan

pleurnicher [plœrniʃe] *vi* to snivel, whine

pleurs [plœr] *nmpl*: **en ~** in tears

pleut [plø] *vb voir* **pleuvoir**

pleuvoir [pløvwar] *vb impers* to rain ▷ *vi*
(*coups*) to rain down; (*critiques, invitations*) to
shower down; **il pleut** it's raining; **il pleut des
cordes** it's pouring (down), it's raining cats
and dogs

pli [pli] *nm* fold; (*de jupe*) pleat; (*de pantalon*)
crease

pliant, e [plijɑ̃, plijɑ̃t] *adj* folding

plier [plije] *vt* to fold; (*pour ranger*) to fold up;
(*genou, bras*) to bend ▷ *vi* to bend; (*fig*) to yield;
se ~ à to submit to

plisser [plise] *vt* (*jupe*) to put pleats in; (*yeux*)
to screw up; (*front*) to crease

plomb [plɔ̃] *nm* (*métal*) lead; (*d'une cartouche*)
(lead) shot; (*Pêche*) sinker; (*Élec*) fuse; **sans ~**
(*essence etc*) unleaded

plomberie [plɔ̃bri] *nf* plumbing

plombier [plɔ̃bje] *nm* plumber

plonge [plɔ̃ʒ] *nf* washing-up

plongeant, e [plɔ̃ʒɑ̃, ɑ̃t] *adj* (*vue*) from above;
(*décolleté*) plunging

plongée [plɔ̃ʒe] *nf* (*Sport*) diving *no pl*; (*sans
scaphandre*) skin diving; **~ sous-marine** diving

plongeoir [plɔ̃ʒwar] *nm* diving board

plongeon [plɔ̃ʒɔ̃] *nm* dive

plonger [plɔ̃ʒe] *vi* to dive ▷ *vt*: **~ qch dans** to
plunge sth into; **se ~ dans** (*études, lecture*) to
bury *ou* immerse o.s. in; **plongeur** *nm* diver

plu [ply] *pp de* **plaire**; *de* **pleuvoir**

pluie [plɥi] *nf* rain

plume [plym] *nf* feather; (*pour écrire*) (pen)
nib; (*fig*) pen

plupart [plypar]: **la ~** *pron* the majority, most
(of them); **la ~ des** most, the majority of; **la ~
du temps/d'entre nous** most of the time/of
us; **pour la ~** for the most part, mostly

pluriel [plyrjɛl] *nm* plural

plus¹ [ply] *vb voir* **plaire**

⊙ **MOT-CLÉ**

plus² [ply] *adv* **1** (*forme négative*): **ne ... plus**
no more, no longer; **je n'ai plus d'argent**
I've got no more money *ou* no money left; **il
ne travaille plus** he's no longer working, he
doesn't work any more

2 [ply, plyz + *voyelle*] (*comparatif*) more, ...+er;
(*superlatif*): **le plus** the most, the ...+est;
plus grand/intelligent (que) bigger/more
intelligent (than); **le plus grand/intelligent**
the biggest/most intelligent; **tout au plus** at

the very most

3 [plys, plyz + *voyelle*] (*davantage*) more; **il travaille plus (que)** he works more (than); **plus il travaille, plus il est heureux** the more he works, the happier he is; **plus de 10 personnes/3 heures** more than *ou* over 10 people/3 hours; **3 heures de plus que** 3 hours more than; **de plus** what's more, moreover; **il a 3 ans de plus que moi** he's 3 years older than me; **3 kilos en plus** 3 kilos more; **en plus de** in addition to; **de plus en plus** more and more; **plus ou moins** more or less; **ni plus ni moins** no more, no less

▷ *prép* [plys]: **4 plus 2** 4 plus 2

plusieurs [plyzjœR] *dét, pron* several; **ils sont ~** there are several of them

plus-value [plyvaly] *nf* (*bénéfice*) surplus

plutôt [plyto] *adv* rather; **je préfère ~ celui-ci** I'd rather have this one; **~ que (de) faire** rather than *ou* instead of doing

pluvieux, -euse [plyvjø, jøz] *adj* rainy, wet

PME *sigle f* (= *petite(s) et moyenne(s) entreprise(s)*) small business(es)

PMU *sigle m* (= *Pari mutuel urbain*) *system of betting on horses*; (*café*) betting agency

PNB *sigle m* (= *produit national brut*) GNP

pneu [pnø] *nm* tyre (BRIT), tire (US); **j'ai un ~ crevé** I've got a flat tyre

pneumonie [pnømɔni] *nf* pneumonia

poche [pɔʃ] *nf* pocket; (*sous les yeux*) bag, pouch; **argent de ~** pocket money

pochette [pɔʃɛt] *nf* (*d'aiguilles etc*) case; (*mouchoir*) breast pocket handkerchief; (*sac à main*) clutch bag; **pochette de disque** record sleeve

poêle [pwal] *nm* stove ▷ *nf*: **~ (à frire)** frying pan

poème [pɔɛm] *nm* poem

poésie [pɔezi] *nf* (*poème*) poem; (*art*): **la ~** poetry

poète [pɔɛt] *nm* poet

poids [pwa] *nm* weight; (*Sport*) shot; **vendre au ~** to sell by weight; **perdre/prendre du ~** to lose/put on weight; **poids lourd** (*camion*) lorry (BRIT), truck (US)

poignant, e [pwaɲɑ̃, ɑ̃t] *adj* poignant

poignard [pwaɲaR] *nm* dagger; **poignarder** *vt* to stab, knife

poigne [pwaɲ] *nf* grip; **avoir de la ~** (*fig*) to rule with a firm hand

poignée [pwaɲe] *nf* (*de sel etc, fig*) handful; (*de couvercle, porte*) handle; **poignée de main** handshake

poignet [pwaɲɛ] *nm* (*Anat*) wrist; (*de chemise*) cuff

poil [pwal] *nm* (*Anat*) hair; (*de pinceau, brosse*) bristle; (*de tapis*) strand; (*pelage*) coat; **à ~** (*fam*) starkers; **au ~** (*fam*) hunky-

dory; **poilu, e** *adj* hairy

poinçonner [pwɛ̃sɔne] *vt* (*bijou*) to hallmark; (*billet*) to punch

poing [pwɛ̃] *nm* fist; **coup de ~** punch

point [pwɛ̃] *nm* point; (*endroit*) spot; (*marque, signe*) dot; (: *de ponctuation*) full stop, period (US); (*Couture, Tricot*) stitch ▷ *adv* = **pas²**; **faire le ~** (*fig*) to take stock (of the situation); **sur le ~ de faire** (just) about to do; **à tel ~ que** so much so that; **mettre au ~** (*procédé*) to develop; (*affaire*) to settle; **à ~** (*Culin: viande*) medium; **à ~ (nommé)** just at the right time; **deux ~s** colon; **point de côté** stitch (*pain*); **point d'exclamation/d'interrogation** exclamation/question mark; **point de repère** landmark; (*dans le temps*) point of reference; **point de vente** retail outlet; **point de vue** viewpoint; (*fig: opinion*) point of view; **point faible** weak spot; **point final** full stop, period (US); **point mort: au point mort** (*Auto*) in neutral; **points de suspension** suspension points

pointe [pwɛ̃t] *nf* point; (*clou*) tack; (*fig*): **une ~ de** a hint of; **être à la ~ de** (*fig*) to be in the forefront of; **sur la ~ des pieds** on tiptoe; **en ~** pointed, tapered; **de ~** (*technique etc*) leading; **heures de ~** peak hours

pointer [pwɛ̃te] *vt* (*diriger: canon, doigt*): **~ sur qch** to point at sth ▷ *vi* (*employé*) to clock in

pointillé [pwɛ̃tije] *nm* (*trait*) dotted line

pointilleux, -euse [pwɛ̃tijø, øz] *adj* particular, pernickety

pointu, e [pwɛ̃ty] *adj* pointed; (*voix*) shrill; (*analyse*) precise

pointure [pwɛ̃tyR] *nf* size

point-virgule [pwɛ̃viRgyl] *nm* semi-colon

poire [pwaR] *nf* pear; (*fam: péj*) mug

poireau, x [pwaRo] *nm* leek

poirier [pwaRje] *nm* pear tree

pois [pwa] *nm* (*Bot*) pea; (*sur une étoffe*) dot, spot; **~ chiche** chickpea; **à ~** (*cravate etc*) spotted, polka-dot *cpd*

poison [pwazɔ̃] *nm* poison

poisseux, -euse [pwasø, øz] *adj* sticky

poisson [pwasɔ̃] *nm* fish *gén inv*; (*Astrol*): **P~s** Pisces; **~ d'avril** April fool; (*blague*) April Fool's Day trick; *see note*; **poisson rouge** goldfish; **poissonnerie** *nf* fish-shop; **poissonnier, -ière** *nm/f* fishmonger (BRIT), fish merchant (US)

● **POISSON D'AVRIL**
●
● The traditional April Fools' Day prank in
● France involves attaching a cut-out paper
● fish, known as a 'poisson d'avril', to the back
● of one's victim, without being caught.

poitrine [pwatRin] *nf* chest; (*seins*) bust,

bosom; (*Culin*) breast
poivre [pwavʀ] *nm* pepper
poivron [pwavʀɔ̃] *nm* pepper, capsicum
polaire [pɔlɛʀ] *adj* polar
pôle [pol] *nm* (*Géo, Élec*) pole; **le ~ Nord/Sud**
   the North/South Pole
poli, e [pɔli] *adj* polite; (*lisse*) smooth
police [pɔlis] *nf* police; **police judiciaire**
   ≈ Criminal Investigation Department (*BRIT*),
   ≈ Federal Bureau of Investigation (*US*); **police**
   secours ≈ emergency services *pl* (*BRIT*),
   ≈ paramedics *pl* (*US*); **policier, -ière** *adj* police
   cpd ▷ *nm* policeman; (*aussi*: **roman policier**)
   detective novel
polir [pɔliʀ] *vt* to polish
politesse [pɔlitɛs] *nf* politeness
politicien, ne [pɔlitisjɛ̃, jɛn] (*péj*) *nm/f*
   politician
politique [pɔlitik] *adj* political ▷ *nf* politics *sg*;
   (*mesures, méthode*) policies *pl*
politiquement [pɔlitikmɑ̃] *adv* politically; **~**
   correct politically correct
pollen [pɔlɛn] *nm* pollen
polluant, e [pɔlɥɑ̃, ɑ̃t] *adj* polluting ▷ *nm*
   (*produit*): **~** pollutant; **non ~** non-polluting
polluer [pɔlɥe] *vt* to pollute; **pollution** *nf*
   pollution
polo [pɔlo] *nm* (*chemise*) polo shirt
Pologne [pɔlɔɲ] *nf*: **la ~** Poland; **polonais,**
   e *adj* Polish ▷ *nm/f*: **Polonais, e** Pole ▷ *nm*
   (*Ling*) Polish
poltron, ne [pɔltʀɔ̃, ɔn] *adj* cowardly
polycopier [pɔlikɔpje] *vt* to duplicate
Polynésie [pɔlinezi] *nf*: **la ~** Polynesia; **la ~**
   française French Polynesia
polyvalent, e [pɔlivalɑ̃, ɑ̃t] *adj* (*rôle*) varied;
   (*salle*) multi-purpose
pommade [pɔmad] *nf* ointment, cream
pomme [pɔm] *nf* apple; **tomber dans**
   les ~s (*fam*) to pass out; **pomme d'Adam**
   Adam's apple; **pomme de pin** pine *ou* fir cone;
   pomme de terre potato
pommette [pɔmɛt] *nf* cheekbone
pommier [pɔmje] *nm* apple tree
pompe [pɔ̃p] *nf* pump; (*faste*) pomp (and
   ceremony); **pompe (à essence)** petrol
   pump; **pompes funèbres** funeral parlour *sg*,
   undertaker's *sg*; **pomper** *vt* to pump; (*aspirer*)
   to pump up; (*absorber*) to soak up
pompeux, -euse [pɔ̃pø, øz] *adj* pompous
pompier [pɔ̃pje] *nm* fireman
pompiste [pɔ̃pist] *nm/f* petrol (*BRIT*) *ou* gas
   (*US*) pump attendant
poncer [pɔ̃se] *vt* to sand (down)
ponctuation [pɔ̃ktɥasjɔ̃] *nf* punctuation
ponctuel, le [pɔ̃ktɥɛl] *adj* punctual
pondéré, e [pɔ̃deʀe] *adj* level-headed,
   composed
pondre [pɔ̃dʀ] *vt* to lay

poney [pɔnɛ] *nm* pony
pont [pɔ̃] *nm* bridge; (*Navig*) deck; **faire**
   le ~ to take the extra day off; *see note*; **pont**
   suspendu suspension bridge; **pont-levis** *nm*
   drawbridge

PONT

The expression 'faire le pont' refers to the
practice of taking a Monday or Friday off
to make a long weekend if a public holiday
falls on a Tuesday or Thursday. The French
commonly take an extra day off work to
give four consecutive days' holiday at
'l'Ascension', 'le 14 juillet' and 'le 15 août'.

pop [pɔp] *adj inv* pop
populaire [pɔpylɛʀ] *adj* popular;
   (*manifestation*) mass *cpd*; (*milieux, quartier*)
   working-class; (*expression*) vernacular
popularité [pɔpylaʀite] *nf* popularity
population [pɔpylasjɔ̃] *nf* population
populeux, -euse [pɔpylø, øz] *adj* densely
   populated
porc [pɔʀ] *nm* pig; (*Culin*) pork
porcelaine [pɔʀsəlɛn] *nf* porcelain, china;
   piece of china(ware)
porc-épic [pɔʀkepik] *nm* porcupine
porche [pɔʀʃ] *nm* porch
porcherie [pɔʀʃəʀi] *nf* pigsty
pore [pɔʀ] *nm* pore
porno [pɔʀno] *adj* porno ▷ *nm* porn
port [pɔʀ] *nm* harbour, port; (*ville*) port; (*de*
   l'uniforme etc) wearing; (*pour lettre*) postage;
   (*pour colis, aussi*: *posture*) carriage; **port**
   d'arme (*Jur*) carrying of a firearm; **port payé**
   postage paid
portable [pɔʀtabl] *adj* (*portatif*) portable;
   (*téléphone*) mobile ▷ *nm* (*Comput*) laptop
   (computer); (*téléphone*) mobile (phone)
portail [pɔʀtaj] *nm* gate
portant, e [pɔʀtɑ̃, ɑ̃t] *adj*: **bien/mal ~** in
   good/poor health
portatif, -ive [pɔʀtatif, iv] *adj* portable
porte [pɔʀt] *nf* door; (*de ville, jardin*) gate;
   mettre à la ~ to throw out; **porte-avions**
   nm inv aircraft carrier; **porte-bagages**
   nm inv luggage rack; **porte-bonheur** *nm*
   inv lucky charm; **porte-clefs** *nm inv* key
   ring; **porte-documents** *nm inv* attaché *ou*
   document case
porté, e [pɔʀte] *adj*: **être ~ à faire** to be
   inclined to do; **être ~ sur qch** to be keen on
   sth; **portée** *nf* (*d'une arme*) range; (*fig*: *effet*)
   impact, import; (: *capacité*) scope, capability;
   (*de chatte etc*) litter; (*Mus*) stave, staff; **à/hors**
   de portée (de) within/out of reach (of); **à**
   portée de (la) main within (arm's) reach; **à**
   la portée de qn (*fig*) at sb's level, within sb's

capabilities

porte...: portefeuille nm wallet;
portemanteau, x nm (cintre) coat hanger; (au
mur) coat rack; **porte-monnaie** nm inv purse;
porte-parole nm inv spokesman

porter [pɔʀte] vt to carry; (sur soi: vêtement,
barbe, bague) to wear; (fig: responsabilité etc)
to bear, carry; (inscription, nom, fruits) to bear;
(coup) to deal; (attention) to turn; (apporter): ~
qch à qn to take sth to sb ▷ vi (voix) to carry;
(coup, argument) to hit home; **se porter** vi (se
sentir): **se ~ bien/mal** to be well/unwell; **~ sur**
(recherches) to be concerned with; **se faire ~
malade** to report sick

porteur, -euse [pɔʀtœʀ, øz] nm/f (de
bagages) porter; (de chèque) bearer

porte-voix [pɔʀtəvwa] nm inv megaphone

portier [pɔʀtje] nm doorman

portière [pɔʀtjɛʀ] nf door

portion [pɔʀsjɔ̃] nf (part) portion, share;
(partie) portion, section

porto [pɔʀto] nm port (wine)

portrait [pɔʀtʀɛ] nm (peinture) portrait;
(photo) photograph; **portrait-robot** nm
Identikit® ou photo-fit® picture

portuaire [pɔʀtɥɛʀ] adj port cpd,
harbour cpd

portugais, e [pɔʀtyɡɛ, ɛz] adj Portuguese
▷ nm/f: **P~, e** Portuguese ▷ nm (Ling)
Portuguese

Portugal [pɔʀtyɡal] nm: **le ~** Portugal

pose [poz] nf (de moquette) laying; (attitude, d'un
modèle) pose; (Photo) exposure

posé, e [poze] adj serious

poser [poze] vt to put; (installer: moquette,
carrelage) to lay; (rideaux, papier peint) to hang;
(question) to ask; (principe, conditions) to lay
ou set down; (difficulté) to pose; (formuler:
problème) to formulate ▷ vi (modèle) to pose;
se poser vi (oiseau, avion) to land; (question)
to arise; **~ qch (sur)** (déposer) to put sth down
(on); **~ qch sur/quelque part** (placer) to put
sth on/somewhere; **~ sa candidature à un
poste** to apply for a post

positif, -ive [pozitif, iv] adj positive

position [pozisjɔ̃] nf position; **prendre ~** (fig)
to take a stand

posologie [pozɔlɔʒi] nf dosage

posséder [posede] vt to own, possess;
(qualité, talent) to have, possess; (sexuellement)
to possess; **possession** nf ownership no pl,
possession; **prendre possession de qch** to
take possession of sth

possibilité [posibilite] nf possibility;
possibilités nfpl (potentiel) potential sg

possible [posibl] adj possible; (projet,
entreprise) feasible ▷ nm: **faire son ~** to do all
one can, do one's utmost; **le plus/moins de
livres ~** as many/few books as possible; **le**
plus vite ~ as quickly as possible; **aussitôt/
dès que ~** as soon as possible

postal, e, -aux [postal, o] adj postal

poste¹ [post] nf (service) post, postal service;
(administration, bureau) post office; **mettre à
la ~** to post; **poste restante** poste restante
(BRIT), general delivery (US)

poste² [post] nm (fonction, Mil) post; (Tél)
extension; (de radio etc) set; **poste (de police)**
police station; **poste de secours** first-aid
post; **poste d'essence** filling station; **poste
d'incendie** fire point; **poste de pilotage**
cockpit, flight deck

poster [poste] vt to post; **où est-ce que je
peux ~ ces cartes postales?** where can I post
these cards?

postérieur, e [posterjœʀ] adj (date) later;
(partie) back ▷ nm (fam) behind

postuler [postyle] vi: **~ à** ou **pour un emploi**
to apply for a job

pot [po] nm (en verre) jar; (en terre) pot; (en
plastique, carton) carton; (en métal) tin;
(fam: chance) luck; **avoir du ~** (fam) to be
lucky; **boire** ou **prendre un ~** (fam) to have
a drink; **petit ~ (pour bébé)** (jar of) baby
food; **~ catalytique** catalytic converter; **pot
d'échappement** exhaust pipe

potable [potabl] adj: **eau (non) ~**
(non-)drinking water

potage [potaʒ] nm soup; **potager, -ère**
adj: **(jardin) potager** kitchen ou vegetable
garden

pot-au-feu [potofø] nm inv (beef) stew

pot-de-vin [podvɛ̃] nm bribe

pote [pot] (fam) nm pal

poteau, x [poto] nm post; **poteau indicateur**
signpost

potelé, e [pɔt(ə)le] adj plump, chubby

potentiel, le [pɔtɑ̃sjɛl] adj, nm potential

poterie [pɔtʀi] nf pottery; (objet) piece of
pottery

potier, -ière [pɔtje, jɛʀ] nm/f potter

potiron [pɔtiʀɔ̃] nm pumpkin

pou, x [pu] nm louse

poubelle [pubɛl] nf (dust)bin

pouce [pus] nm thumb

poudre [pudʀ] nf powder; (fard) (face)
powder; (explosif) gunpowder; **en ~: café en
~** instant coffee; **lait en ~** dried ou powdered
milk; **poudreuse** nf powder snow; **poudrier**
nm (powder) compact

pouffer [pufe] vi: **~ (de rire)** to burst out
laughing

poulailler [pulaje] nm henhouse

poulain [pulɛ̃] nm foal; (fig) protégé

poule [pul] nf hen; (Culin) (boiling) fowl; **poule
mouillée** coward

poulet [pulɛ] nm chicken; (fam) cop

poulie [puli] nf pulley

pouls [pu] *nm* pulse; **prendre le ~ de qn** to feel sb's pulse

poumon [pumɔ̃] *nm* lung

poupée [pupe] *nf* doll

pour [puʀ] *prép* for ▷ *nm*: **le ~ et le contre** the pros and cons; **~ faire** (so as) to do, in order to do; **~ avoir fait** for having done; **~ que** so that, in order that; **fermé ~ (cause de) travaux** closed for refurbishment *ou* alterations; **c'est ~ ça que …** that's why …; **~ quoi faire?** what for?; **~ 20 euros d'essence** 20 euros' worth of petrol; **~ cent** per cent; **~ ce qui est de** as for

pourboire [puʀbwaʀ] *nm* tip; **combien de ~ est-ce qu'il faut laisser?** how much should I tip?

pourcentage [puʀsɑ̃taʒ] *nm* percentage

pourchasser [puʀʃase] *vt* to pursue

pourparlers [puʀpaʀle] *nmpl* talks, negotiations

pourpre [puʀpʀ] *adj* crimson

pourquoi [puʀkwa] *adv, conj* why ▷ *nm inv*: **le ~ (de)** the reason (for)

pourrai *etc* [puʀe] *vb voir* **pouvoir**

pourri, e [puʀi] *adj* rotten

pourrir [puʀiʀ] *vi* to rot; *(fruit)* to go rotten *ou* bad ▷ *vt* to rot; *(fig)* to spoil thoroughly; **pourriture** *nf* rot

poursuite [puʀsɥit] *nf* pursuit, chase; **poursuites** *nfpl* (*Jur*) legal proceedings

poursuivre [puʀsɥivʀ] *vt* to pursue, chase (after); *(obséder)* to haunt; *(Jur)* to bring proceedings against, prosecute; *(: au civil)* to sue; *(but)* to strive towards; *(continuer: études etc)* to carry on with, continue; **se poursuivre** *vi* to go on, continue

pourtant [puʀtɑ̃] *adv* yet; **c'est ~ facile** (and) yet it's easy

pourtour [puʀtuʀ] *nm* perimeter

pourvoir [puʀvwaʀ] *vt*: **~ qch/qn de** to equip sth/sb with ▷ *vi*: **~ à** to provide for; **pourvu, e** *adj*: **pourvu de** equipped with; **pourvu que** *(si)* provided that, so long as; *(espérons que)* let's hope (that)

pousse [pus] *nf* growth; *(bourgeon)* shoot

poussée [puse] *nf* thrust; *(d'acné)* eruption; *(fig: prix)* upsurge

pousser [puse] *vt* to push; *(émettre: cri, soupir)* to give; *(stimuler: élève)* to urge on; *(poursuivre: études, discussion)* to carry on (further) ▷ *vi* to push; *(croître)* to grow; **se pousser** *vi* to move over; **~ qn à** *(inciter)* to urge *ou* press sb to; *(acculer)* to drive sb to; **faire ~** *(plante)* to grow

poussette [puset] *nf* push chair (BRIT), stroller (US)

poussière [pusjɛʀ] *nf* dust; **poussiéreux, -euse** *adj* dusty

poussin [pusɛ̃] *nm* chick

poutre [putʀ] *nf* beam

 MOT-CLÉ

pouvoir [puvwaʀ] *nm* power; *(Pol: dirigeants)*: **le pouvoir** those in power; **les pouvoirs publics** the authorities; **pouvoir d'achat** purchasing power
▷ *vb semi-aux* **1** *(être en état de)* can, be able to; **je ne peux pas le réparer** I can't *ou* I am not able to repair it; **déçu de ne pas pouvoir le faire** disappointed not to be able to do it
2 *(avoir la permission)* can, may, be allowed to; **vous pouvez aller au cinéma** you can *ou* may go to the pictures
3 *(probabilité, hypothèse)* may, might, could; **il a pu avoir un accident** he may *ou* might *ou* could have had an accident; **il aurait pu le dire!** he might *ou* could have said (so)!
▷ *vb impers* may, might, could; **il peut arriver que** it may *ou* might *ou* could happen that; **il pourrait pleuvoir** it might rain
▷ *vt* can, be able to; **j'ai fait tout ce que j'ai pu** I did all I could; **je n'en peux plus** *(épuisé)* I'm exhausted; *(à bout)* I can't take any more
▷ *vi*: **se pouvoir**: **il se peut que** it may *ou* might be that; **cela se pourrait** that's quite possible

prairie [pʀeʀi] *nf* meadow

praline [pʀalin] *nf* sugared almond

praticable [pʀatikabl] *adj* passable, practicable

pratiquant, e [pʀatikɑ̃, ɑ̃t] *nm/f* (regular) churchgoer

pratique [pʀatik] *nf* practice ▷ *adj* practical; **pratiquement** *adv* *(pour ainsi dire)* practically, virtually; **pratiquer** *vt* to practise; *(l'équitation, la pêche)* to go in for; *(le golf, football)* to play; *(intervention, opération)* to carry out

pré [pʀe] *nm* meadow

préalable [pʀealabl] *adj* preliminary; **au ~** beforehand

préambule [pʀeɑ̃byl] *nm* preamble; *(fig)* prelude; **sans ~** straight away

préau [pʀeo] *nm* (*Scol*) covered playground

préavis [pʀeavi] *nm* notice

précaution [pʀekosjɔ̃] *nf* precaution; **avec ~** cautiously; **par ~** as a precaution

précédemment [pʀesedamɑ̃] *adv* before, previously

précédent, e [pʀesedɑ̃, ɑ̃t] *adj* previous ▷ *nm* precedent; **sans ~** unprecedented; **le jour ~** the day before, the previous day

précéder [pʀesede] *vt* to precede

prêcher [pʀeʃe] *vt* to preach

précieux, -euse [pʀesjø, jøz] *adj* precious; *(aide, conseil)* invaluable

précipice [pʀesipis] *nm* drop, chasm

précipitamment [pʀesipitamɑ̃] adv hurriedly, hastily

précipitation [pʀesipitasjɔ̃] nf (hâte) haste

précipité, e [pʀesipite] adj hurried, hasty

précipiter [pʀesipite] vt (hâter: départ) to hasten; (faire tomber): **~ qn/qch du haut de** to throw ou hurl sb/sth off ou from; **se précipiter** vi to speed up; **se ~ sur/vers** to rush at/towards

précis, e [pʀesi, iz] adj precise; (mesures) accurate, precise; **à 4 heures ~es** at 4 o'clock sharp; **précisément** adv precisely; **préciser** vt (expliquer) to be more specific about, clarify; (spécifier) to state, specify; **se préciser** vi to become clear(er); **précision** nf precision; (détail) point ou detail; **demander des précisions** to ask for further explanation

précoce [pʀekɔs] adj early; (enfant) precocious

préconçu, e [pʀekɔ̃sy] adj preconceived

préconiser [pʀekɔnize] vt to advocate

prédécesseur [pʀedesesœʀ] nm predecessor

prédilection [pʀedilɛksjɔ̃] nf: **avoir une ~ pour** to be partial to

prédire [pʀediʀ] vt to predict

prédominer [pʀedɔmine] vi to predominate

préface [pʀefas] nf preface

préfecture [pʀefɛktyʀ] nf prefecture; **préfecture de police** police headquarters pl

préférable [pʀefeʀabl] adj preferable

préféré, e [pʀefeʀe] adj, nm/f favourite

préférence [pʀefeʀɑ̃s] nf preference; **de ~** preferably

préférer [pʀefeʀe] vt: **~ qn/qch (à)** to prefer sb/sth (to), like sb/sth better (than); **~ faire** to prefer to do; **je préférerais du thé** I would rather have tea, I'd prefer tea

préfet [pʀefɛ] nm prefect

préhistorique [pʀeistɔʀik] adj prehistoric

préjudice [pʀeʒydis] nm (matériel) loss; (moral) harm no pl; **porter ~ à** to harm, be detrimental to; **au ~ de** at the expense of

préjugé [pʀeʒyʒe] nm prejudice; **avoir un ~ contre** to be prejudiced ou biased against

prélasser [pʀelase]: **se prélasser** vi to lounge

prélèvement [pʀelɛvmɑ̃] nm (montant) deduction; **faire un ~ de sang** to take a blood sample

prélever [pʀel(ə)ve] vt (échantillon) to take; **~ (sur)** (montant) to deduct (from); (argent: sur son compte) to withdraw (from)

prématuré, e [pʀematyʀe] adj premature ▷ nm premature baby

premier, -ière [pʀəmje, jɛʀ] adj first; (rang) front; (fig: objectif) basic; **le ~ venu** the first person to come along; **de ~ ordre** first-rate; **Premier ministre** Prime Minister; **première** nf (Scol) year 12 (BRIT), eleventh grade (US); (Aviat, Rail etc) first class; **premièrement** adv firstly

prémonition [pʀemɔnisjɔ̃] nf premonition

prenant, e [pʀənɑ̃, ɑ̃t] adj absorbing, engrossing

prénatal, e [pʀenatal] adj (Méd) antenatal

prendre [pʀɑ̃dʀ] vt to take; (repas) to have; (se procurer) to get; (malfaiteur, poisson) to catch; (passager) to pick up; (personnel) to take on; (traiter: personne) to handle; (voix, ton) to put on; (ôter): **~ qch à** to take sth from; (coincer): **se ~ les doigts dans** to get one's fingers caught in ▷ vi (liquide, ciment) to set; (greffe, vaccin) to take; (feu: foyer) to go; (se diriger): **~ à gauche** to turn (to the) left; **~ froid** to catch cold; **se ~ pour** to think one is; **s'en ~ à** to attack; **se ~ d'amitié pour** to befriend; **s'y ~** (procéder) to set about it

preneur [pʀənœʀ] nm: **être/trouver ~** to be willing to buy/find a buyer

prénom [pʀenɔ̃] nm first ou Christian name

préoccupation [pʀeɔkypasjɔ̃] nf (souci) concern; (idée fixe) preoccupation

préoccuper [pʀeɔkype] vt (inquiéter) to worry; (absorber) to preoccupy; **se ~ de** to be concerned with

préparatifs [pʀepaʀatif] nmpl preparations

préparation [pʀepaʀasjɔ̃] nf preparation

préparer [pʀepaʀe] vt to prepare; (café, thé) to make; (examen) to prepare for; (voyage, entreprise) to plan; **se préparer** vi (orage, tragédie) to brew, be in the air; **~ qch à qn** (surprise etc) to have sth in store for sb; **se ~ (à qch/faire)** to prepare (o.s.) ou get ready (for sth/to do)

prépondérant, e [pʀepɔ̃deʀɑ̃, ɑ̃t] adj major, dominating

préposé, e [pʀepoze] nm/f employee; (facteur) postman

préposition [pʀepozisjɔ̃] nf preposition

près [pʀɛ] adv near, close; **~ de** near (to), close to; (environ) nearly, almost; **de ~** closely; **à 5 kg ~** to within about 5 kg; **il n'est pas à 10 minutes ~** he can spare 10 minutes; **est-ce qu'il y a une banque ~ d'ici?** is there a bank nearby?

présage [pʀezaʒ] nm omen

presbyte [pʀɛsbit] adj long-sighted

presbytère [pʀɛsbitɛʀ] nm presbytery

prescription [pʀɛskʀipsjɔ̃] nf prescription

prescrire [pʀɛskʀiʀ] vt to prescribe

présence [pʀezɑ̃s] nf presence; (au bureau, à l'école) attendance

présent, e [pʀezɑ̃, ɑ̃t] adj, nm present; **à ~ (que)** now (that)

présentation [pʀezɑ̃tasjɔ̃] nf presentation; (de nouveau venu) introduction; (allure) appearance; **faire les ~s** to do the introductions

présenter [pʀezɑ̃te] vt to present; (excuses, condoléances) to offer; (invité, conférencier):

~ qn (à) to introduce sb (to) ▷ vi: **~ bien** to have a pleasing appearance; **se présenter** vi (*occasion*) to arise; **se ~ à** (*examen*) to sit; (*élection*) to stand at, run for; **je vous présente Nadine** this is Nadine, could I introduce you to Nadine?

préservatif [pʀezɛʀvatif] *nm* condom, sheath

préserver [pʀezɛʀve] *vt*: **~ de** (*protéger*) to protect from

président [pʀezidɑ̃] *nm* (*Pol*) president; (*d'une assemblée, Comm*) chairman; **président directeur général** chairman and managing director; **présidentielles** *nfpl* presidential elections

présider [pʀezide] *vt* to preside over; (*dîner*) to be the guest of honour at

presque [pʀɛsk] *adv* almost, nearly; **~ personne** hardly anyone; **~ rien** hardly anything; **~ pas** hardly (at all); **~ pas (de)** hardly any

presqu'île [pʀɛskil] *nf* peninsula

pressant, e [pʀesɑ̃, ɑ̃t] *adj* urgent

presse [pʀɛs] *nf* press; (*affluence*): **heures de ~** busy times

pressé, e [pʀese] *adj* in a hurry; (*travail*) urgent; **orange ~e** freshly-squeezed orange juice

pressentiment [pʀesɑ̃timɑ̃] *nm* foreboding, premonition

pressentir [pʀesɑ̃tiʀ] *vt* to sense

presse-papiers [pʀɛspapje] *nm inv* paperweight

presser [pʀese] *vt* (*fruit, éponge*) to squeeze; (*bouton*) to press; (*allure*) to speed up; (*inciter*): **~ qn de faire** to urge *ou* press sb to do ▷ vi to be urgent; **se presser** vi (*se hâter*) to hurry (up); **se ~ contre qn** to squeeze up against sb; **le temps presse** there's not much time; **rien ne presse** there's no hurry

pressing [pʀesiŋ] *nm* (*magasin*) dry-cleaner's

pression [pʀesjɔ̃] *nf* pressure; (*bouton*) press stud; (*fam: bière*) draught beer; **faire ~ sur** to put pressure on; **sous ~** pressurized, under pressure; (*fig*) under pressure; **pression artérielle** blood pressure

prestataire [pʀɛstatɛʀ] *nm/f* supplier

prestation [pʀɛstasjɔ̃] *nf* (*allocation*) benefit; (*d'une entreprise*) service provided; (*d'un artiste*) performance

prestidigitateur, -trice [pʀɛstidiʒitatœʀ, tʀis] *nm/f* conjurer

prestige [pʀɛstiʒ] *nm* prestige; **prestigieux, -euse** *adj* prestigious

présumer [pʀezyme] *vt*: **~ que** to presume *ou* assume that

prêt, e [pʀɛ, pʀɛt] *adj* ready ▷ *nm* (*somme*) loan; **quand est-ce que mes photos seront ~es?** when will my photos be ready?; **prêt-à-**

porter *nm* ready-to-wear *ou* off-the-peg (*BRIT*) clothes *pl*

prétendre [pʀetɑ̃dʀ] *vt* (*affirmer*): **~ que** to claim that; (*avoir l'intention de*): **~ faire qch** to mean *ou* intend to do sth; **prétendu, e** *adj* (*supposé*) so-called

> Attention à ne pas traduire **prétendre** par **to pretend**.

prétentieux, -euse [pʀetɑ̃sjø, jøz] *adj* pretentious

prétention [pʀetɑ̃sjɔ̃] *nf* claim; (*vanité*) pretentiousness

prêter [pʀete] *vt* (*livres, argent*): **~ qch (à)** to lend sth (to); (*supposer*): **~ à qn** (*caractère, propos*) to attribute to sb; **pouvez-vous me ~ de l'argent?** can you lend me some money?

prétexte [pʀetɛkst] *nm* pretext, excuse; **sous aucun ~** on no account; **prétexter** *vt* to give as a pretext *ou* an excuse

prêtre [pʀɛtʀ] *nm* priest

preuve [pʀœv] *nf* proof; (*indice*) proof, evidence *no pl*; **faire ~ de** to show; **faire ses ~s** to prove o.s. (*ou* itself)

prévaloir [pʀevalwaʀ] *vi* to prevail

prévenant, e [pʀev(ə)nɑ̃, ɑ̃t] *adj* thoughtful, kind

prévenir [pʀev(ə)niʀ] *vt* (*éviter: catastrophe etc*) to avoid, prevent; (*anticiper: désirs, besoins*) to anticipate; **~ qn (de)** (*avertir*) to warn sb (about); (*informer*) to tell *ou* inform sb (about)

préventif, -ive [pʀevɑ̃tif, iv] *adj* preventive

prévention [pʀevɑ̃sjɔ̃] *nf* prevention; **prévention routière** road safety

prévenu, e [pʀev(ə)ny] *nm/f* (*Jur*) defendant, accused

prévision [pʀevizjɔ̃] *nf*: **~s** predictions; (*Écon*) forecast *sg*; **en ~ de** in anticipation of; **prévisions météorologiques** weather forecast *sg*

prévoir [pʀevwaʀ] *vt* (*anticiper*) to foresee; (*s'attendre à*) to expect, reckon on; (*organiser: voyage etc*) to plan; (*envisager*) to allow; **comme prévu** as planned; **prévoyant, e** *adj* gifted with (*ou* showing) foresight; **prévu, e** *pp de* **prévoir**

prier [pʀije] *vi* to pray ▷ *vt* (*Dieu*) to pray to; (*implorer*) to beg; (*demander*): **~ qn de faire** to ask sb to do; **se faire ~** to need coaxing *ou* persuading; **je vous en prie** (*allez-y*) please do; (*de rien*) don't mention it; **prière** *nf* prayer; **"prière de ..."** "please ..."

primaire [pʀimɛʀ] *adj* primary ▷ *nm* (*Scol*) primary education

prime [pʀim] *nf* (*bonus*) bonus; (*subvention*) premium; (*Comm: cadeau*) free gift; (*Assurances, Bourse*) premium ▷ *adj*: **de ~ abord** at first glance; **primer** *vt* (*récompenser*) to award a prize to ▷ *vi* to dominate; to be most important

P

primevère [pʀimvɛʀ] nf primrose
primitif, -ive [pʀimitif, iv] adj primitive; (originel) original
prince [pʀɛ̃s] nm prince; **princesse** nf princess
principal, e, -aux [pʀɛ̃sipal, o] adj principal, main ▷ nm (Scol) principal, head(master); (essentiel) main thing
principe [pʀɛ̃sip] nm principle; **par ~** on principle; **en ~** (habituellement) as a rule; (théoriquement) in principle
printemps [pʀɛ̃tɑ̃] nm spring
priorité [pʀijɔʀite] nf priority; (Auto) right of way; **priorité à droite** right of way to vehicles coming from the right
pris, e [pʀi, pʀiz] pp de **prendre** ▷ adj (place) taken; (mains) full; (personne) busy; **avoir le nez/la gorge ~(e)** to have a stuffy nose/a hoarse throat; **être ~ de panique** to be panic-stricken
prise [pʀiz] nf (d'une ville) capture; (Pêche, Chasse) catch; (point d'appui ou pour empoigner) hold; (Élec: fiche) plug; (: femelle) socket; **être aux ~s avec** to be grappling with; **prise de courant** power point; **prise de sang** blood test; **prise multiple** adaptor
priser [pʀize] vt (estimer) to prize, value
prison [pʀizɔ̃] nf prison; **aller/être en ~** to go to/be in prison ou jail; **prisonnier, -ière** nm/f prisoner ▷ adj captive
privé, e [pʀive] adj private; (en punition): **tu es ~ de télé!** no TV for you! ▷ nm (Comm) private sector; **en ~** in private
priver [pʀive] vt: **~ qn de** to deprive sb of; **se priver de** to go ou do without
privilège [pʀivilɛʒ] nm privilege
prix [pʀi] nm price; (récompense, Scol) prize; **hors de ~** exorbitantly priced; **à aucun ~** not at any price; **à tout ~** at all costs
probable [pʀɔbabl] adj likely, probable; **probablement** adv probably
problème [pʀɔblɛm] nm problem
procédé [pʀɔsede] nm (méthode) process; (comportement) behaviour no pl
procéder [pʀɔsede] vi to proceed; (moralement) to behave; **~ à** to carry out
procès [pʀɔsɛ] nm trial; (poursuites) proceedings pl; **être en ~ avec** to be involved in a lawsuit with
processus [pʀɔsesys] nm process
procès-verbal, -aux [pʀɔsɛvɛʀbal, o] nm (de réunion) minutes pl; (aussi: **P.-V.**) parking ticket
prochain, e [pʀɔʃɛ̃, ɛn] adj next; (proche: départ, arrivée) impending ▷ nm fellow man; **la ~e fois/semaine ~e** next time/week; **prochainement** adv soon, shortly
proche [pʀɔʃ] adj nearby; (dans le temps) imminent; (parent, ami) close; **proches** nmpl

(parents) close relatives; **être ~ (de)** to be near, be close (to)
proclamer [pʀɔklame] vt to proclaim
procuration [pʀɔkyʀasjɔ̃] nf proxy
procurer [pʀɔkyʀe] vt: **~ qch à qn** (fournir) to obtain sth for sb; (causer: plaisir etc) to bring sb sth; **se procurer** vt to get; **procureur** nm public prosecutor
prodige [pʀɔdiʒ] nm marvel, wonder; (personne) prodigy; **prodiguer** vt (soins, attentions): **prodiguer qch à qn** to give sb sth
producteur, -trice [pʀɔdyktœʀ, tʀis] nm/f producer
productif, -ive [pʀɔdyktif, iv] adj productive
production [pʀɔdyksjɔ̃] nf production; (rendement) output
productivité [pʀɔdyktivite] nf productivity
produire [pʀɔdɥiʀ] vt to produce; **se produire** vi (événement) to happen, occur; (acteur) to perform, appear
produit [pʀɔdɥi] nm product; **produit chimique** chemical; **produits agricoles** farm produce sg; **produits de beauté** beauty products, cosmetics; **produits d'entretien** cleaning products
prof [pʀɔf] (fam) nm teacher
proférer [pʀɔfeʀe] vt to utter
professeur, e [pʀɔfesœʀ] nm/f teacher; (de faculté) (university) lecturer; (: titulaire d'une chaire) professor
profession [pʀɔfesjɔ̃] nf occupation; **~ libérale** (liberal) profession; **sans ~** unemployed; **professionnel, le** adj, nm/f professional
profil [pʀɔfil] nm profile; **de ~** in profile
profit [pʀɔfi] nm (avantage) benefit, advantage; (Comm, Finance) profit; **au ~ de** in aid of; **tirer ~ de** to profit from; **profitable** adj (utile) beneficial; (lucratif) profitable; **profiter** vi: **profiter de** (situation, occasion) to take advantage of; (vacances, jeunesse etc) to make the most of
profond, e [pʀɔfɔ̃, ɔ̃d] adj deep; (sentiment, intérêt) profound; **profondément** adv deeply; **il dort profondément** he is sound asleep; **profondeur** nf depth; **l'eau a quelle profondeur?** how deep is the water?
programme [pʀɔgʀam] nm programme; (Scol) syllabus, curriculum; (Inform) program; **programmer** vt (émission) to schedule; (Inform) to program; **programmeur, -euse** nm/f programmer
progrès [pʀɔgʀɛ] nm progress no pl; **faire des ~** to make progress; **progresser** vi to progress; **progressif, -ive** adj progressive
proie [pʀwɑ] nf prey no pl
projecteur [pʀɔʒɛktœʀ] nm (pour film) projector; (de théâtre, cirque) spotlight
projectile [pʀɔʒɛktil] nm missile

projection [pʀɔʒɛksjɔ̃] nf projection; (séance) showing

projet [pʀɔʒɛ] nm plan; (ébauche) draft; **projet de loi** bill; **projeter** vt (envisager) to plan; (film, photos) to project; (ombre, lueur) to throw, cast; (jeter) to throw up (ou off ou out)

prolétaire [pʀɔletɛʀ] adj, nmf proletarian

prolongement [pʀɔlɔ̃ʒmɑ̃] nm extension; **dans le ~ de** running on from

prolonger [pʀɔlɔ̃ʒe] vt (débat, séjour) to prolong; (délai, billet, rue) to extend; **se prolonger** vi to go on

promenade [pʀɔm(ə)nad] nf walk (ou drive ou ride); **faire une ~** to go for a walk; **une ~ en voiture/à vélo** a drive/(bicycle) ride

promener [pʀɔm(ə)ne] vt (chien) to take out for a walk; (doigts, regard): **~ qch sur** to run sth over; **se promener** vi to go for (ou be out for) a walk

promesse [pʀɔmɛs] nf promise

promettre [pʀɔmɛtʀ] vt to promise ▷ vi to be ou look promising; **~ à qn de faire** to promise sb that one will do

promiscuité [pʀɔmiskɥite] nf (chambre) lack of privacy

promontoire [pʀɔmɔ̃twaʀ] nm headland

promoteur, -trice [pʀɔmɔtœʀ, tʀis] nm/f: **promoteur (immobilier)** property developer (BRIT), real estate promoter (US)

promotion [pʀɔmosjɔ̃] nf promotion; **en ~** on special offer

promouvoir [pʀɔmuvwaʀ] vt to promote

prompt, e [pʀɔ̃(pt), pʀɔ̃(p)t] adj swift, rapid

prôner [pʀone] vt (préconiser) to advocate

pronom [pʀɔnɔ̃] nm pronoun

prononcer [pʀɔnɔ̃se] vt to pronounce; (dire) to utter; (discours) to deliver; **se prononcer** vi to be pronounced; **comment est-ce que ça se prononce?** how do you pronounce ou say it?; **se ~ (sur)** (se décider) to reach a decision (on ou about), give a verdict (on); **prononciation** nf pronunciation

pronostic [pʀɔnɔstik] nm (Méd) prognosis; (fig: aussi: **~s**) forecast

propagande [pʀɔpagɑ̃d] nf propaganda

propager [pʀɔpaʒe] vt to spread; **se propager** vi to spread

prophète [pʀɔfɛt] nm prophet

prophétie [pʀɔfesi] nf prophecy

propice [pʀɔpis] adj favourable

proportion [pʀɔpɔʀsjɔ̃] nf proportion; **toute(s) ~(s) gardée(s)** making due allowance(s)

propos [pʀɔpo] nm (intention) intention, aim; (sujet): **à quel ~?** what about? ▷ nmpl (paroles) talk no pl, remarks; **à ~ de** about, regarding; **à tout ~** for the slightest thing ou reason; **à ~** by the way; (opportunément) at the right moment

proposer [pʀɔpoze] vt to propose; **~ qch**

(à qn) (suggérer) to suggest sth (to sb), propose sth (to sb); (offrir) to offer (sb) sth; **se ~ (pour faire)** to offer one's services (to do); **proposition** (suggestion) nf proposal, suggestion; (Ling) clause

propre [pʀɔpʀ] adj clean; (net) neat, tidy; (possessif) own; (sens) literal; (particulier): **~ à** peculiar to; (approprié): **~ à** suitable for ▷ nm: **recopier au ~** to make a fair copy of; **proprement** adv (avec propreté) cleanly; **le village proprement dit** the village itself; **à proprement parler** strictly speaking; **propreté** nf cleanliness

propriétaire [pʀɔpʀijetɛʀ] nm/f owner; (pour le locataire) landlord(-lady)

propriété [pʀɔpʀijete] nf property; (droit) ownership

propulser [pʀɔpylse] vt to propel

prose [pʀoz] nf (style) prose

prospecter [pʀɔspɛkte] vt to prospect; (Comm) to canvass

prospectus [pʀɔspɛktys] nm leaflet

prospère [pʀɔspɛʀ] adj prosperous; **prospérer** vi to prosper

prosterner [pʀɔstɛʀne]: **se prosterner** vi to bow low, prostrate o.s.

prostituée [pʀɔstitɥe] nf prostitute

prostitution [pʀɔstitysjɔ̃] nf prostitution

protecteur, -trice [pʀɔtɛktœʀ, tʀis] adj protective; (air, ton: péj) patronizing ▷ nm/f protector

protection [pʀɔtɛksjɔ̃] nf protection; (d'un personnage influent: aide) patronage

protéger [pʀɔteʒe] vt to protect; **se ~ de/ contre** to protect o.s. from

protège-slip [pʀɔtɛʒslip] nm panty liner

protéine [pʀɔtein] nf protein

protestant, e [pʀɔtɛstɑ̃, ɑ̃t] adj, nm/f Protestant

protestation [pʀɔtɛstasjɔ̃] nf (plainte) protest

protester [pʀɔtɛste] vi: **~ (contre)** to protest (against ou about); **~ de** (son innocence) to protest

prothèse [pʀɔtɛz] nf: **prothèse dentaire** denture

protocole [pʀɔtɔkɔl] nm (fig) etiquette

proue [pʀu] nf bow(s pl), prow

prouesse [pʀuɛs] nf feat

prouver [pʀuve] vt to prove

provenance [pʀɔv(ə)nɑ̃s] nf origin; **avion en ~ de** plane (arriving) from

provenir [pʀɔv(ə)niʀ]: **~ de** vt to come from

proverbe [pʀɔvɛʀb] nm proverb

province [pʀɔvɛ̃s] nf province

proviseur [pʀɔvizœʀ] nm ≈ head(teacher) (BRIT), ≈ principal (US)

provision [pʀɔvizjɔ̃] nf (réserve) stock, supply;

provisions *nfpl* (*vivres*) provisions, food *no pl*

provisoire [pʀɔvizwaʀ] *adj* temporary;
provisoirement *adv* temporarily

provocant, e [pʀɔvɔkɑ̃, ɑ̃t] *adj* provocative

provoquer [pʀɔvɔke] *vt* (*défier*) to provoke;
(*causer*) to cause, bring about; (*inciter*): ~ **qn à**
to incite sb to

proxénète [pʀɔksenɛt] *nm* procurer

proximité [pʀɔksimite] *nf* nearness,
closeness; (*dans le temps*) imminence,
closeness; **à ~** near *ou* close by; **à ~ de** near
(to), close to

prudemment [pʀydamɑ̃] *adv* carefully;
wisely, sensibly

prudence [pʀydɑ̃s] *nf* carefulness; **avec ~**
carefully; **par ~** as a precaution

prudent, e [pʀydɑ̃, ɑ̃t] *adj* (*pas téméraire*)
careful; (: *en général*) safety-conscious; (*sage,
conseillé*) wise, sensible; **c'est plus ~** it's wiser

prune [pʀyn] *nf* plum

pruneau, x [pʀyno] *nm* prune

prunier [pʀynje] *nm* plum tree

PS *sigle m* = **parti socialiste**

pseudonyme [psødɔnim] *nm* (*gén*) fictitious
name; (*d'écrivain*) pseudonym, pen name

psychanalyse [psikanaliz] *nf*
psychoanalysis

psychiatre [psikjatʀ] *nm/f* psychiatrist;
psychiatrique *adj* psychiatric

psychique [psiʃik] *adj* psychological

psychologie [psikɔlɔʒi] *nf* psychology;
psychologique *adj* psychological;
psychologue *nm/f* psychologist

pu [py] *pp de* **pouvoir**

puanteur [pɥɑ̃tœʀ] *nf* stink, stench

pub [pyb] *nf* (*fam: annonce*) ad, advert;
(*pratique*) advertising

public, -ique [pyblik] *adj* public; (*école,
instruction*) state *cpd* ▷ *nm* public; (*assistance*)
audience; **en ~** in public

publicitaire [pyblisitɛʀ] *adj* advertising *cpd*;
(*film*) publicity *cpd*

publicité [pyblisite] *nf* (*méthode, profession*)
advertising; (*annonce*) advertisement;
(*révélations*) publicity

publier [pyblije] *vt* to publish

publipostage [pyblipɔstaʒ] *nm* mailing *m*

publique [pyblik] *adj voir* **public**

puce [pys] *nf* flea; (*Inform*) chip; **carte à ~**
smart card; (**marché aux**) **~s** flea market *sg*

pudeur [pydœʀ] *nf* modesty; **pudique** *adj*
(*chaste*) modest; (*discret*) discreet

puer [pɥe] (*péj*) *vi* to stink

puéricultrice [pɥeʀikyltʀis] *nf* p(a)ediatric
nurse

puéril, e [pɥeʀil] *adj* childish

puis [pɥi] *vb voir* **pouvoir** ▷ *adv* then

puiser [pɥize] *vt*: ~ (**dans**) to draw (from)

puisque [pɥisk] *conj* since

puissance [pɥisɑ̃s] *nf* power; **en ~** *adj*
potential

puissant, e [pɥisɑ̃, ɑ̃t] *adj* powerful

puits [pɥi] *nm* well

pull(-over) [pyl(ɔvɛʀ)] *nm* sweater

pulluler [pylyle] *vi* to swarm

pulpe [pylp] *nf* pulp

pulvériser [pylveʀize] *vt* to pulverize;
(*liquide*) to spray

punaise [pynɛz] *nf* (*Zool*) bug; (*clou*) drawing
pin (BRIT), thumbtack (US)

punch [pɔ̃ʃ] *nm* (*boisson*) punch

punir [pyniʀ] *vt* to punish; **punition** *nf*
punishment

pupille [pypij] *nf* (*Anat*) pupil ▷ *nm/f* (*enfant*)
ward

pupitre [pypitʀ] *nm* (*Scol*) desk

pur, e [pyʀ] *adj* pure; (*vin*) undiluted; (*whisky*)
neat; **en ~e perte** to no avail; **c'est de la folie
~e** it's sheer madness

purée [pyʀe] *nf*: ~ (**de pommes de terre**)
mashed potatoes *pl*; **purée de marrons**
chestnut purée

purement [pyʀmɑ̃] *adv* purely

purgatoire [pyʀgatwaʀ] *nm* purgatory

purger [pyʀʒe] *vt* (*Méd, Pol*) to purge; (*Jur:
peine*) to serve

pur-sang [pyʀsɑ̃] *nm inv* thoroughbred

pus [py] *nm* pus

putain [pytɛ̃] (*fam!*) *nf* whore (!)

puzzle [pœzl] *nm* jigsaw (puzzle)

P.-V. [peve] *sigle m* = **procès-verbal**

pyjama [piʒama] *nm* pyjamas *pl* (BRIT),
pajamas *pl* (US)

pyramide [piʀamid] *nf* pyramid

Pyrénées [piʀene] *nfpl*: **les ~** the Pyrenees

QI *sigle m* (= *quotient intellectuel*) IQ

quadragénaire [k(w)adʀaʒenɛʀ] *nm/f* man/ woman in his/her forties

quadruple [k(w)adʀypl] *nm*: **le ~ de** four times as much as

quai [ke] *nm* (*de port*) quay; (*de gare*) platform; **être à ~** (*navire*) to be alongside; **de quel ~ part le train pour Paris?** which platform does the Paris train go from?

qualification [kalifikasjɔ̃] *nf* (*aptitude*) qualification

qualifier [kalifje] *vt* to qualify; **se qualifier** *vi* to qualify; **~ qch/qn de** to describe sth/sb as

qualité [kalite] *nf* quality

quand [kɑ̃] *conj, adv* when; **~ je serai riche** when I'm rich; **~ même** all the same; **~ même, il exagère!** really, he overdoes it!; **~ bien même** even though

quant [kɑ̃]: **~ à** *prép* (*pour ce qui est de*) as for, as to; (*au sujet de*) regarding

quantité [kɑ̃tite] *nf* quantity, amount; (*grand nombre*): **une** *ou* **des ~(s) de** a great deal of

quarantaine [kaʀɑ̃tɛn] *nf* (*Méd*) quarantine; **avoir la ~** (*âge*) to be around forty; **une ~ (de)** forty or so, about forty

quarante [kaʀɑ̃t] *num* forty

quart [kaʀ] *nm* (*fraction*) quarter; (*surveillance*) watch; **un ~ de vin** a quarter

litre of wine; **le ~ de** a quarter of; **quart d'heure** quarter of an hour; **quarts de finale** quarter finals

quartier [kaʀtje] *nm* (*de ville*) district, area; (*de bœuf*) quarter; (*de fruit*) piece; **cinéma de ~** local cinema; **avoir ~ libre** (*fig*) to be free; **quartier général** headquarters *pl*

quartz [kwaʀts] *nm* quartz

quasi [kazi] *adv* almost, nearly; **quasiment** *adv* almost, nearly; **quasiment jamais** hardly ever

quatorze [katɔʀz] *num* fourteen

quatorzième [katɔʀzjɛm] *num* fourteenth

quatre [katʀ] *num* four; **à ~ pattes** on all fours; **se mettre en ~ pour qn** to go out of one's way for sb; **~ à ~** (*monter, descendre*) four at a time; **quatre-vingt-dix** *num* ninety; **quatre-vingts** *num* eighty; **quatrième** *num* fourth ▷ *nf* (*Scol*) year 9 (*BRIT*), eighth grade (*US*)

quatuor [kwatɥɔʀ] *nm* quartet(te)

 MOT-CLÉ

que [kə] *conj* **1** (*introduisant complétive*) that; **il sait que tu es là** he knows (that) you're here; **je veux que tu acceptes** I want you to accept; **il a dit que oui** he said he would (*ou* it was *etc*)

2 (*reprise d'autres conjonctions*): **quand il rentrera et qu'il aura mangé** when he gets back and (when) he has eaten; **si vous y allez et que vous ...** if you go there and if you ...

3 (*en tête de phrase: hypothèse, souhait etc*): **qu'il le veuille ou non** whether he likes it or not; **qu'il fasse ce qu'il voudra!** let him do as he pleases!

4 (*après comparatif*) than, as; *voir aussi* **plus**; **aussi**; **autant** *etc*

5 (*seulement*): **ne ... que** only; **il ne boit que de l'eau** he only drinks water

6 (*temps*): **il y a 4 ans qu'il est parti** it is 4 years since he left, he left 4 years ago

▷ *adv* (*exclamation*): **qu'il** *ou* **qu'est-ce qu'il est bête/court vite!** he's so silly!/he runs so fast!; **que de livres!** what a lot of books!

▷ *pron* **1** (*relatif: personne*) whom; (: *chose*) that, which; **l'homme que je vois** the man (whom) I see; **le livre que tu vois** the book (that *ou* which) you see; **un jour que j'étais ...** a day when I was ...

2 (*interrogatif*) what; **que fais-tu?**, **qu'est-ce que tu fais?** what are you doing?; **qu'est-ce que c'est?** what is it?, what's that?; **que faire?** what can one do?

Québec [kebɛk] *n*: **le ~** Quebec; **québecois, e** *adj* Quebec ▷ *nm/f*: **Québecois, e** Quebecker

▷ *nm* (*Ling*) Quebec French

 MOT-CLÉ

quel, quelle [kɛl] *adj* **1** (*interrogatif: personne*)
who; (: *chose*) what; **quel est cet homme?**
who is this man?; **quel est ce livre?** what
is this book?; **quel livre/homme?** what
book/man?; (*parmi un certain choix*) which
book/man?; **quels acteurs préférez-vous?**
which actors do you prefer?; **dans quels pays
êtes-vous allé?** which ou what countries did
you go to?
2 (*exclamatif*): **quelle surprise!** what a
surprise!
3: **quel que soit le coupable** whoever is
guilty; **quel que soit votre avis** whatever
your opinion

quelconque [kɛlkɔ̃k] *adj* (*indéfini*): **un
ami/prétexte ~** some friend/pretext or
other; (*médiocre: repas*) indifferent, poor; (*laid:
personne*) plain-looking

 MOT-CLÉ

quelque [kɛlk] *adj* **1** (*au singulier*) some; (*au
pluriel*) a few, some; (*tournure interrogative*) any;
quelque espoir some hope; **il a quelques
amis** he has a few ou some friends; **a-t-il
quelques amis?** does he have any friends?; **les
quelques livres qui** the few books which; **20
kg et quelque(s)** a bit over 20 kg
2: **quelque ... que**: **quelque livre qu'il
choisisse** whatever (ou whichever) book he
chooses
3: **quelque chose** something; (*tournure
interrogative*) anything; **quelque chose
d'autre** something else; anything else;
quelque part somewhere; anywhere; **en
quelque sorte** as it were
▷ *adv* **1** (*environ*): **quelque 100 mètres** some
100 metres
2: **quelque peu** rather, somewhat

quelquefois [kɛlkəfwa] *adv* sometimes
quelques-uns, -unes [kɛlkəzœ̃, yn] *pron* a
few, some
quelqu'un [kɛlkœ̃] *pron* someone, somebody;
(+ *tournure interrogative*) anyone, anybody;
quelqu'un d'autre someone ou somebody
else; (+ *tournure interrogative*) anybody else
qu'en dira-t-on [kɑ̃diʀatɔ̃] *nm inv*: **le qu'en
dira-t-on** gossip, what people say
querelle [kəʀɛl] *nf* quarrel; **quereller: se
quereller** *vi* to quarrel
qu'est-ce que [kɛskə] *vb + conj voir* **que**
qu'est-ce qui [kɛski] *vb + conj voir* **qui**
question [kɛstjɔ̃] *nf* question; (*fig*) matter,

issue; **il a été ~ de** we (*ou* they) spoke about;
de quoi est-il ~? what is it about?; **il n'en
est pas ~** there's no question of it; **en ~** in
question; **hors de ~** out of the question;
remettre en ~ to question; **questionnaire**
nm questionnaire; **questionner** *vt* to
question
quête [kɛt] *nf* collection; (*recherche*) quest,
search; **faire la ~** (*à l'église*) to take the
collection; (*artiste*) to pass the hat round
quetsche [kwɛtʃ] *nf* kind of dark-red plum
queue [kø] *nf* tail; (*fig: du classement*) bottom;
(: *de poêle*) handle; (: *de fruit, feuille*) stalk; (: *de
train, colonne, file*) rear; **faire la ~** to queue (up)
(*BRIT*), line up (*US*); **queue de cheval** ponytail;
queue de poisson (*Auto*): **faire une queue de
poisson à qn** to cut in front of sb

 MOT-CLÉ

qui [ki] *pron* **1** (*interrogatif: personne*) who; (:
chose): **qu'est-ce qui est sur la table?** what
is on the table?; **qui est-ce qui?** who?; **qui est-
ce que?** who?; **à qui est ce sac?** whose bag is
this?; **à qui parlais-tu?** who were you talking
to?, to whom were you talking?; **chez qui
allez-vous?** whose house are you going to?
2 (*relatif: personne*) who; (+*prép*) whom; **l'ami
de qui je vous ai parlé** the friend I told you
about; **la dame chez qui je suis allé** the lady
whose house I went to
3 (*sans antécédent*): **amenez qui vous voulez**
bring who you like; **qui que ce soit** whoever
it may be

quiconque [kikɔ̃k] *pron* (*celui qui*) whoever,
anyone who; (*n'importe qui*) anyone, anybody
quille [kij] *nf*: **(jeu de) ~s** skittles *sg* (*BRIT*),
bowling (*US*)
quincaillerie [kɛ̃kajʀi] *nf* (*ustensiles*)
hardware; (*magasin*) hardware shop
quinquagénaire [kɛ̃kaʒenɛʀ] *nm/f* man/
woman in his/her fifties
quinquennat [kɛ̃kena] *nm five year term of
office (of French President)*
quinte [kɛ̃t] *nf*: **~ (de toux)** coughing fit
quintuple [kɛ̃typl] *nm*: **le ~ de** five times as
much as
quinzaine [kɛ̃zɛn] *nf*: **une ~ (de)** about
fifteen, fifteen or so; **une ~ (de jours)** a
fortnight (*BRIT*), two weeks
quinze [kɛ̃z] *num* fifteen; **dans ~ jours** in a
fortnight's (time), in two weeks' (time)
quinzième [kɛ̃zjɛm] *num* fifteenth
quiproquo [kipʀɔko] *nm* misunderstanding
quittance [kitɑ̃s] *nf* (*reçu*) receipt
quitte [kit] *adj*: **être ~ envers qn** to be no
longer in sb's debt; (*fig*) to be quits with sb; **~ à
faire** even if it means doing

quitter [kite] *vt* to leave; (*vêtement*) to take off;
se quitter *vi* (*couples, interlocuteurs*) to part;
ne quittez pas (*au téléphone*) hold the line
qui-vive [kiviv] *nm*: **être sur le ~** to be on
the alert

 MOT-CLÉ

quoi [kwa] *pron interrog* **1** what; **quoi de neuf?**
what's new?; **quoi?** (*qu'est-ce que tu dis?*) what?
2 (*avec prép*) **à quoi tu penses?** what are you
thinking about?; **de quoi parlez-vous?** what
are you talking about?; **à quoi bon?** what's
the use?
▷ *pron rel*: **as-tu de quoi écrire?** do you have
anything to write with?; **il n'y a pas de quoi**
(please) don't mention it; **il n'y a pas de quoi
rire** there's nothing to laugh about
▷ *pron* (*locutions*): **quoi qu'il arrive** whatever
happens; **quoi qu'il en soit** be that as it may;
quoi que ce soit anything at all
▷ *excl* what!

quoique [kwak] *conj* (al)though
quotidien, ne [kɔtidjɛ̃, jɛn] *adj* daily;
(*banal*) everyday ▷ *nm* (*journal*) daily (paper);
quotidiennement *adv* daily

r

r. *abr* = **route**; **rue**
rab [ʀab] (*fam*) *nm* (*nourriture*) extra; **est-ce
qu'il y a du ~?** are there any seconds?
rabâcher [ʀabaʃe] *vt* to keep on repeating
rabais [ʀabɛ] *nm* reduction, discount;
rabaisser *vt* (*dénigrer*) to belittle; (*rabattre:
prix*) to reduce
Rabat [ʀaba(t)] *n* Rabat
rabattre [ʀabatʀ] *vt* (*couvercle, siège*) to pull
down; (*déduire*) to reduce; **se rabattre** *vi*
(*se refermer: couvercle*) to fall shut; (*véhicule,
coureur*) to cut in; **se ~ sur** to fall back on
rabbin [ʀabɛ̃] *nm* rabbi
rabougri, e [ʀabugʀi] *adj* stunted
raccommoder [ʀakɔmɔde] *vt* to mend,
repair
raccompagner [ʀakɔ̃paɲe] *vt* to take *ou*
see back
raccord [ʀakɔʀ] *nm* link; (*retouche*) touch up;
raccorder *vt* to join (up), link up; (*suj: pont etc*)
to connect, link
raccourci [ʀakuʀsi] *nm* short cut
raccourcir [ʀakuʀsiʀ] *vt* to shorten ▷ *vi*
(*jours*) to grow shorter, draw in
raccrocher [ʀakʀɔʃe] *vt* (*tableau*) to hang
back up; (*récepteur*) to put down ▷ *vi* (*Tél*) to
hang up, ring off
race [ʀas] *nf* race; (*d'animaux, fig*) breed; **de ~**
purebred, pedigree
rachat [ʀaʃa] *nm* buying; (*du même objet*)

r

buying back

racheter [Raʃ(ə)te] vt (*article perdu*) to buy another; (*après avoir vendu*) to buy back; (*d'occasion*) to buy; (*Comm: part, firme*) to buy up; (*davantage*): **~ du lait/3 œufs** to buy more milk/another 3 eggs *ou* 3 more eggs; **se racheter** vi (*fig*) to make amends

racial, e, -aux [Rasjal, jo] adj racial

racine [Rasin] nf root; **racine carrée/ cubique** square/cube root

racisme [Rasism] nm racism

raciste [Rasist] adj, nm/f racist

racket [Raket] nm racketeering no pl

raclée [Rakle] (*fam*) nf hiding, thrashing

racler [Rakle] vt (*surface*) to scrape; **se ~ la gorge** to clear one's throat

racontars [Rakɔ̃tar] nmpl story, lie

raconter [Rakɔ̃te] vt: **~ (à qn)** (*décrire*) to relate (to sb), tell (sb) about; (*dire de mauvaise foi*) to tell (sb); **~ une histoire** to tell a story

radar [Radar] nm radar

rade [Rad] nf (*natural*) harbour; **rester en ~** (*fig*) to be left stranded

radeau, x [Rado] nm raft

radiateur [Radjatœr] nm radiator, heater; (*Auto*) radiator; **radiateur électrique** electric heater *ou* fire

radiation [Radjasjɔ̃] nf (*Physique*) radiation

radical, e, -aux [Radikal, o] adj radical

radieux, -euse [Radjø, jøz] adj radiant

radin, e [Radɛ̃, in] (*fam*) adj stingy

radio [Radjo] nf radio; (*Méd*) X-ray ▷ nm radio operator; **à la ~** on the radio; **radioactif, -ive** adj radioactive; **radiocassette** nm cassette radio, radio cassette player; **radiographie** nf radiography; (*photo*) X-ray photograph; **radiophonique** adj radio cpd; **radio-réveil** (*pl* **radios-réveils**) nm radio alarm clock

radis [Radi] nm radish

radoter [Radɔte] vi to ramble on

radoucir [Radusir]: **se radoucir** vi (*temps*) to become milder; (*se calmer*) to calm down

rafale [Rafal] nf (*vent*) gust (of wind); (*tir*) burst of gunfire

raffermir [Rafermir] vt to firm up

raffiner [Rafine] vt to refine; **raffinerie** nf refinery

raffoler [Rafɔle]: **~ de** vt to be very keen on

rafle [Rafl] nf (*de police*) raid; **rafler** (*fam*) vt to swipe, nick

rafraîchir [RafreʃiR] vt (*atmosphère, température*) to cool (down); (*aussi:* **mettre à ~**) to chill; (*fig: rénover*) to brighten up; **se rafraîchir** vi (*temps*) to grow cooler; (*en se lavant*) to freshen up; (*en buvant*) to refresh o.s.; **rafraîchissant, e** adj refreshing; **rafraîchissement** nm (*boisson*) cool drink; **rafraîchissements** nmpl (*boissons, fruits etc*) refreshments

rage [Raʒ] nf (*Méd*): **la ~** rabies; (*fureur*) rage, fury; **faire ~** to rage; **rage de dents** (raging) toothache

ragot [Rago] (*fam*) nm malicious gossip no pl

ragoût [Ragu] nm stew

raide [Rɛd] adj stiff; (*câble*) taut, tight; (*escarpé*) steep; (*droit: cheveux*) straight; (*fam: sans argent*) flat broke; (*osé*) daring, bold ▷ adv (*en pente*) steeply; **~ mort** stone dead; **raideur** nf (*rigidité*) stiffness; **avec raideur** (*répondre*) stiffly, abruptly; **raidir** vt (*muscles*) to stiffen; **se raidir** vi (*tissu*) to stiffen; (*personne*) to tense up; (*: se préparer moralement*) to brace o.s.; (*fig: position*) to harden

raie [Rɛ] nf (*Zool*) skate, ray; (*rayure*) stripe; (*des cheveux*) parting

raifort [Rɛfɔr] nm horseradish

rail [Raj] nm rail; (*chemins de fer*) railways pl; **par ~** by rail

railler [Raje] vt to scoff at, jeer at

rainure [Renyr] nf groove

raisin [Rɛzɛ̃] nm (*aussi:* **~s**) grapes pl; **raisins secs** raisins

raison [Rɛzɔ̃] nf reason; **avoir ~** to be right; **donner ~ à qn** to agree with sb; (*événement*) to prove sb right; **perdre la ~** to become insane; **se faire une ~** to learn to live with it; **~ de plus** all the more reason; **à plus forte ~** all the more so; **en ~ de** because of; **à ~ de** at the rate of; **sans ~** for no reason; **raison sociale** corporate name; **raisonnable** adj reasonable, sensible

raisonnement [Rɛzɔnmɑ̃] nm (*façon de réfléchir*) reasoning; (*argumentation*) argument

raisonner [Rɛzɔne] vi (*penser*) to reason; (*argumenter, discuter*) to argue ▷ vt (*personne*) to reason with

rajeunir [Raʒœnir] vt (*suj: coiffure, robe*): **~ qn** to make sb look younger; (*fig: personnel*) to inject new blood into ▷ vi to become (*ou* look) younger

rajouter [Raʒute] vt to add

rajuster [Raʒyste] vt (*vêtement*) to straighten, tidy; (*salaires*) to adjust

ralenti [Ralɑ̃ti] nm: **au ~** (*fig*) at a slower pace; **tourner au ~** (*Auto*) to tick over, idle

ralentir [Ralɑ̃tir] vt to slow down

râler [Rɑle] vi to groan; (*fam*) to grouse, moan (and groan)

rallier [Ralje] vt (*rejoindre*) to rejoin; (*gagner à sa cause*) to win over

rallonge [Ralɔ̃ʒ] nf (*de table*) (extra) leaf

rallonger [Ralɔ̃ʒe] vt to lengthen

rallye [Rali] nm rally; (*Pol*) march

ramassage [Ramasaʒ] nm: **ramassage scolaire** school bus service

ramasser [Ramase] vt (*objet tombé ou par terre, fam*) to pick up; (*recueillir: copies, ordures*) to collect; (*récolter*) to gather; **ramassis** (*péj*) nm (*de voyous*) bunch; (*d'objets*) jumble

rambarde [ʀɑ̃baʀd] *nf* guardrail

rame [ʀam] *nf* (*aviron*) oar; (*de métro*) train; (*de papier*) ream

rameau, x [ʀamo] *nm* (small) branch; **les Rameaux** (*Rel*) Palm Sunday *sg*

ramener [ʀam(ə)ne] *vt* to bring back; (*reconduire*) to take back; **~ qch à** (*réduire à*) to reduce sth to

ramer [ʀame] *vi* to row

ramollir [ʀamɔliʀ] *vt* to soften; **se ramollir** *vi* to go soft

rampe [ʀɑ̃p] *nf* (*d'escalier*) banister(s *pl*); (*dans un garage*) ramp; (*Théâtre*): **la ~** the footlights *pl*; **rampe de lancement** launching pad

ramper [ʀɑ̃pe] *vi* to crawl

rancard [ʀɑ̃kaʀ] (*fam*) *nm* (*rendez-vous*) date

rancart [ʀɑ̃kaʀ] *nm*: **mettre au ~** (*fam*) to scrap

rance [ʀɑ̃s] *adj* rancid

rancœur [ʀɑ̃kœʀ] *nf* rancour

rançon [ʀɑ̃sɔ̃] *nf* ransom

rancune [ʀɑ̃kyn] *nf* grudge, rancour; **garder ~ à qn (de qch)** to bear sb a grudge (for sth); **sans ~!** no hard feelings!; **rancunier, -ière** *adj* vindictive, spiteful

randonnée [ʀɑ̃dɔne] *nf* (*pédestre*) walk, ramble; (: *en montagne*) hike, hiking *no pl*; **la ~** (*activité*) hiking, walking; **une ~ à cheval** a pony trek

rang [ʀɑ̃] *nm* (*rangée*) row; (*grade, classement*) rank; **rangs** *nmpl* (*Mil*) ranks; **se mettre en ~s** to get into *ou* form rows; **au premier ~** in the first row; (*fig*) ranking first

rangé, e [ʀɑ̃ʒe] *adj* (*vie*) well-ordered; (*personne*) steady

rangée [ʀɑ̃ʒe] *nf* row

ranger [ʀɑ̃ʒe] *vt* (*mettre de l'ordre dans*) to tidy up; (*classer, grouper*) to order, arrange; (*mettre à sa place*) to put away; (*fig: classer*): **~ qn/qch parmi** to rank sb/sth among; **se ranger** *vi* (*véhicule, conducteur*) to pull over *ou* in; (*piéton*) to step aside; (*s'assagir*) to settle down; **se ~ à** (*avis*) to come round to

ranimer [ʀanime] *vt* (*personne*) to bring round; (*douleur, souvenir*) to revive; (*feu*) to rekindle

rapace [ʀapas] *nm* bird of prey

râpe [ʀɑp] *nf* (*Culin*) grater; **râper** *vt* (*Culin*) to grate

rapide [ʀapid] *adj* fast; (*prompt: coup d'œil, mouvement*) quick ▷ *nm* express (train); (*de cours d'eau*) rapid; **rapidement** *adv* fast; quickly

rapiécer [ʀapjese] *vt* to patch

rappel [ʀapɛl] *nm* (*Théâtre*) curtain call; (*Méd: vaccination*) booster; (*deuxième avis*) reminder; **rappeler** *vt* to call back; (*ambassadeur, Mil*) to recall; (*faire se souvenir*): **rappeler qch à qn** to

remind sb of sth; **se rappeler** *vt* (*se souvenir de*) to remember, recall; **pouvez-vous rappeler plus tard?** can you call back later?

rapport [ʀapɔʀ] *nm* (*lien, analogie*) connection; (*compte rendu*) report; (*profit*) yield, return; **rapports** *nmpl* (*entre personnes, pays*) relations; **avoir ~ à** to have something to do with; **être/se mettre en ~ avec qn** to be/get in touch with sb; **par ~ à** in relation to; **rapports (sexuels)** (sexual) intercourse *sg*; **rapport qualité-prix** value (for money)

rapporter [ʀapɔʀte] *vt* (*rendre, ramener*) to bring back; (*bénéfice*) to yield, bring in; (*mentionner, répéter*) to report ▷ *vi* (*investissement*) to give a good return *ou* yield; (*activité*) to be very profitable; **se ~ à** to relate to

rapprochement [ʀapʀɔʃmɑ̃] *nm* (*de nations*) reconciliation; (*rapport*) parallel

rapprocher [ʀapʀɔʃe] *vt* (*deux objets*) to bring closer together; (*fig: ennemis, partis etc*) to bring together; (*comparer*) to establish a parallel between; (*chaise d'une table*): **~ qch (de)** to bring sth closer (to); **se rapprocher** *vi* to draw closer *ou* nearer; **se ~ de** to come closer to; (*présenter une analogie avec*) to be close to

raquette [ʀakɛt] *nf* (*de tennis*) racket; (*de ping-pong*) bat

rare [ʀɑʀ] *adj* rare; **se faire ~** to become scarce; **rarement** *adv* rarely, seldom

ras, e [ʀɑ, ʀɑz] *adj* (*poil, herbe*) short; (*tête*) close-cropped ▷ *adv* short; **en ~e campagne** in open country; **à ~ bords** to the brim; **en avoir ~ le bol** (*fam*) to be fed up

raser [ʀɑze] *vt* (*barbe, cheveux*) to shave off; (*menton, personne*) to shave; (*fam: ennuyer*) to bore; (*démolir*) to raze (to the ground); (*frôler*) to graze, skim; **se raser** *vi* to shave; (*fam*) to be bored (to tears); **rasoir** *nm* razor

rassasier [ʀasazje] *vt*: **être rassasié** to have eaten one's fill

rassemblement [ʀasɑ̃bləmɑ̃] *nm* (*groupe*) gathering; (*Pol*) union

rassembler [ʀasɑ̃ble] *vt* (*réunir*) to assemble, gather; (*documents, notes*) to gather together, collect; **se rassembler** *vi* to gather

rassurer [ʀasyʀe] *vt* to reassure; **se rassurer** *vi* to reassure o.s.; **rassure-toi** don't worry

rat [ʀa] *nm* rat

rate [ʀat] *nf* spleen

raté, e [ʀate] *adj* (*tentative*) unsuccessful, failed ▷ *nm/f* (*fam: personne*) failure

râteau, x [ʀɑto] *nm* rake

rater [ʀate] *vi* (*affaire, projet etc*) to go wrong, fail ▷ *vt* (*fam: cible, train, occasion*) to miss; (*plat*) to spoil; (*fam: examen*) to fail; **nous avons raté notre train** we missed our train

ration [ʀasjɔ̃] *nf* ration

RATP *sigle f* (= *Régie autonome des transports parisiens*) Paris transport authority

rattacher [Rataʃe] *vt* (*animal, cheveux*) to tie up again; (*fig: relier*): **~ qch à** to link sth with

rattraper [Ratrape] *vt* (*fugitif*) to recapture; (*empêcher de tomber*) to catch (hold of); (*atteindre, rejoindre*) to catch up with; (*réparer: erreur*) to make up for; **se rattraper** *vi* to make up for it; **se ~ (à)** (*se raccrocher*) to stop o.s. falling (by catching hold of)

rature [Ratyr] *nf* deletion, erasure

rauque [Rok] *adj* (*voix*) hoarse

ravages [Ravaʒ] *nmpl*: **faire des ~** to wreak havoc

ravi, e [Ravi] *adj*: **être ~ de/que** to be delighted with/that

ravin [Ravɛ̃] *nm* gully, ravine

ravir [Ravir] *vt* (*enchanter*) to delight; **à ~** *adv* beautifully

raviser [Ravize]: **se raviser** *vi* to change one's mind

ravissant, e [Ravisɑ̃, ɑ̃t] *adj* delightful

ravisseur, -euse [Ravisœr, øz] *nm/f* abductor, kidnapper

ravitailler [Ravitaje] *vt* (*en vivres, munitions*) to provide with fresh supplies; (*avion*) to refuel; **se ~ (en)** to get fresh supplies (of)

raviver [Ravive] *vt* (*feu, douleur*) to revive; (*couleurs*) to brighten up

rayé, e [Reje] *adj* (*à rayures*) striped

rayer [Reje] *vt* (*érafler*) to scratch; (*barrer*) to cross out; (*d'une liste*) to cross off

rayon [Rejɔ̃] *nm* (*de soleil etc*) ray; (*Géom*) radius; (*de roue*) spoke; (*étagère*) shelf; (*de grand magasin*) department; **dans un ~ de** within a radius of; **rayon de soleil** sunbeam; **rayons X** X-rays

rayonnement [Rejɔnmɑ̃] *nm* (*fig: d'une culture*) influence

rayonner [Rejɔne] *vi* (*fig*) to shine forth; (*personne: de joie, de beauté*) to be radiant; (*touriste*) to go touring (*from one base*)

rayure [Rejyr] *nf* (*motif*) stripe; (*éraflure*) scratch; **à ~s** striped

raz-de-marée [Radmare] *nm inv* tidal wave

ré [Re] *nm* (*Mus*) D; (*en chantant la gamme*) re

réaction [Reaksjɔ̃] *nf* reaction

réadapter [Readapte]: **se réadapter (à)** *vi* to readjust (to)

réagir [Reaʒir] *vi* to react

réalisateur, -trice [Realizatœr, tris] *nm/f* (*TV, Cinéma*) director

réalisation [Realizasjɔ̃] *nf* realization; (*cinéma*) production; **en cours de ~** under way

réaliser [Realize] *vt* (*projet, opération*) to carry out, realize; (*rêve, souhait*) to realize, fulfil; (*exploit*) to achieve; (*film*) to produce; (*se rendre compte de*) to realize; **se réaliser** *vi* to be realized

réaliste [Realist] *adj* realistic

réalité [Realite] *nf* reality; **en ~** in (actual) fact; **dans la ~** in reality

réanimation [Reanimasjɔ̃] *nf* resuscitation; **service de ~** intensive care unit

rébarbatif, -ive [Rebarbatif, iv] *adj* forbidding

rebattu, e [R(ə)baty] *adj* hackneyed

rebelle [Rəbɛl] *nm/f* rebel ▷ *adj* (*troupes*) rebel; (*enfant*) rebellious; (*mèche etc*) unruly

rebeller [R(ə)bele]: **se rebeller** *vi* to rebel

rebondir [R(ə)bɔ̃dir] *vi* (*ballon: au sol*) to bounce; (*: contre un mur*) to rebound; (*fig*) to get moving again

rebord [R(ə)bɔr] *nm* edge; **le ~ de la fenêtre** the windowsill

rebours [R(ə)bur]: **à ~** *adv* the wrong way

rebrousser [R(ə)bruse] *vt*: **~ chemin** to turn back

rebuter [Rəbyte] *vt* to put off

récalcitrant, e [Rekalsitrɑ̃, ɑ̃t] *adj* refractory

récapituler [Rekapityle] *vt* to recapitulate, sum up

receler [R(ə)səle] *vt* (*produit d'un vol*) to receive; (*fig*) to conceal; **receleur, -euse** *nm/f* receiver

récemment [Resamɑ̃] *adv* recently

recensement [R(ə)sɑ̃smɑ̃] *nm* (*population*) census

recenser [R(ə)sɑ̃se] *vt* (*population*) to take a census of; (*inventorier*) to list

récent, e [Resɑ̃, ɑ̃t] *adj* recent

récépissé [Resepise] *nm* receipt

récepteur [Reseptœr] *nm* receiver

réception [Resepsjɔ̃] *nf* receiving *no pl*; (*accueil*) reception, welcome; (*bureau*) reception desk; (*réunion mondaine*) reception, party; **réceptionniste** *nm/f* receptionist

recette [R(ə)sɛt] *nf* recipe; (*Comm*) takings *pl*; **recettes** *nfpl* (*Comm: rentrées*) receipts; **faire ~** (*spectacle, exposition*) to be a winner

recevoir [R(ə)səvwar] *vt* to receive; (*client, patient*) to see; **être reçu** (*à un examen*) to pass

rechange [R(ə)ʃɑ̃ʒ]: **de ~** *adj* (*pièces, roue*) spare; (*fig: solution*) alternative; **des vêtements de ~** a change of clothes

recharge [R(ə)ʃarʒ] *nf* refill; **rechargeable** *adj* (*stylo etc*) refillable; **recharger** *vt* (*stylo*) to refill; (*batterie*) to recharge

réchaud [Reʃo] *nm* (*portable*) stove

réchauffer [Reʃofe] *vt* (*plat*) to reheat; (*mains, personne*) to warm; **se réchauffer** *vi* (*température*) to get warmer; (*personne*) to warm o.s. (up)

rêche [Rɛʃ] *adj* rough

recherche [R(ə)ʃɛrʃ] *nf* (*action*) search; (*raffinement*) studied elegance; (*scientifique etc*): **la ~** research; **recherches** *nfpl* (*de la police*) investigations; (*scientifiques*) research *sg*; **la ~ de** the search for; **être à la ~ de qch** to be looking for sth

recherché, e [R(ə)ʃɛRʃe] adj (rare, demandé) much sought-after; (raffiné: style) mannered; (: tenue) elegant

rechercher [R(ə)ʃɛRʃe] vt (objet égaré, personne) to look for; (causes, nouveau procédé) to try to find; (bonheur, compliments) to seek

rechute [R(ə)ʃyt] nf (Méd) relapse

récidiver [Residive] vi to commit a subsequent offence; (fig) to do it again

récif [Resif] nm reef

récipient [Resipjɑ̃] nm container

réciproque [Resiprɔk] adj reciprocal

récit [Resi] nm story; **récital** nm recital; **réciter** vt to recite

réclamation [Reklɑmɑsjɔ̃] nf complaint; **(service des) ~s** complaints department

réclame [Reklɑm] nf ad, advert(isement); **en ~** on special offer; **réclamer** vt to ask for; (revendiquer) to claim, demand ▷ vi to complain

réclusion [Reklyzjɔ̃] nf imprisonment

recoin [Rəkwɛ̃] nm nook, corner

reçois etc [Rəswa] vb voir **recevoir**

récolte [Rekɔlt] nf harvesting, gathering; (produits) harvest, crop; **récolter** vt to harvest, gather (in); (fig) to collect

recommandé [R(ə)kɔmɑ̃de] nm (Postes): **en ~** by registered mail

recommander [R(ə)kɔmɑ̃de] vt to recommend; (Postes) to register

recommencer [R(ə)kɔmɑ̃se] vt (reprendre: lutte, séance) to resume, start again; (refaire: travail, explications) to start afresh, start (over) again ▷ vi to start again; (récidiver) to do it again

récompense [Rekɔ̃pɑ̃s] nf reward; (prix) award; **récompenser** vt: **récompenser qn (de** ou **pour)** to reward sb (for)

réconcilier [Rekɔ̃silje] vt to reconcile; **se réconcilier (avec)** to make up (with)

reconduire [R(ə)kɔ̃dɥiʀ] vt (raccompagner) to take ou see back; (renouveler) to renew

réconfort [Rekɔ̃fɔʀ] nm comfort; **réconforter** vt (consoler) to comfort

reconnaissance [R(ə)kɔnɛsɑ̃s] nf (gratitude) gratitude, gratefulness; (action de reconnaître) recognition; (Mil) reconnaissance, recce; **reconnaissant, e** adj grateful; **je vous serais reconnaissant de bien vouloir ...** I would be most grateful if you would (kindly) ...

reconnaître [R(ə)kɔnɛtʀ] vt to recognize; (Mil: lieu) to reconnoitre; (Jur: enfant, torts) to acknowledge; **~ que** to admit ou acknowledge that; **~ qn/qch à** (l'identifier grâce à) to recognize sb/sth by; **reconnu, e** adj (indiscuté, connu) recognized

reconstituer [R(ə)kɔ̃stitɥe] vt (événement, accident) to reconstruct; (fresque, vase brisé) to piece together, reconstitute

reconstruire [R(ə)kɔ̃stʀɥiʀ] vt to rebuild

reconvertir [R(ə)kɔ̃vɛʀtiʀ]: **se reconvertir dans** vr (un métier, une branche) to go into

record [R(ə)kɔʀ] nm, adj record

recoupement [R(ə)kupmɑ̃] nm: **par ~** by cross-checking

recouper [R(ə)kupe]: **se recouper** vi (témoignages) to tie ou match up

recourber [R(ə)kuʀbe]: **se recourber** vi to curve (up), bend (up)

recourir [R(ə)kuʀiʀ]: **~ à** vt (ami, agence) to turn ou appeal to; (force, ruse, emprunt) to resort to

recours [R(ə)kuʀ] nm: **avoir ~ à** = **recourir à**; **en dernier ~** as a last resort

recouvrer [R(ə)kuvʀe] vt (vue, santé etc) to recover, regain

recouvrir [R(ə)kuvʀiʀ] vt (couvrir à nouveau) to re-cover; (couvrir entièrement, aussi fig) to cover

récréation [RekReɑsjɔ̃] nf (Scol) break

recroqueviller [R(ə)kʀɔk(ə)vije]: **se recroqueviller** vi (personne) to huddle up

recrudescence [R(ə)kʀydesɑ̃s] nf fresh outbreak

recruter [R(ə)kʀyte] vt to recruit

rectangle [Rektɑ̃gl] nm rectangle; **rectangulaire** adj rectangular

rectificatif [Rektifikatif] nm correction

rectifier [Rektifje] vt (calcul, adresse, paroles) to correct; (erreur) to rectify

rectiligne [Rektilin] adj straight

recto [Rekto] nm front (of a page); **~ verso** on both sides (of the page)

reçu, e [R(ə)sy] pp de **recevoir** ▷ adj (candidat) successful; (admis, consacré) accepted ▷ nm (Comm) receipt; **je peux avoir un ~, s'il vous plaît?** can I have a receipt, please?

recueil [Rəkœj] nm collection; **recueillir** vt to collect; (voix, suffrages) to win; (accueillir: réfugiés, chat) to take in; **se recueillir** vi to gather one's thoughts, meditate

recul [R(ə)kyl] nm (éloignement) distance; (déclin) decline; **être en ~** to be on the decline; **avec du ~** with hindsight; **avoir un mouvement de ~** to recoil; **prendre du ~** to stand back; **reculé, e** adj remote; **reculer** vi to move back, back away; (Auto) to reverse, back (up); (fig) to (be on the) decline ▷ vt to move back; (véhicule) to reverse, back (up); (date, décision) to postpone; **reculer devant** (danger, difficulté) to shrink from; **reculons: à reculons** adv backwards

récupérer [RekypeRe] vt to recover, get back; (heures de travail) to make up; (déchets) to salvage ▷ vi to recover

récurer [RekyRe] vt to scour; **poudre à ~** scouring powder

reçut [Rəsy] vb voir **recevoir**
recycler [R(ə)sikle] vt (Tech) to recycle; **se recycler** vi to retrain
rédacteur, -trice [Redaktœr, tris] nm/f (journaliste) writer; subeditor; (d'ouvrage de référence) editor, compiler
rédaction [Redaksjɔ̃] nf writing; (rédacteurs) editorial staff; (Scol: devoir) essay, composition
redescendre [R(ə)desɑ̃dR] vi to go back down ▷ vt (pente etc) to go down
rédiger [Rediʒe] vt to write; (contrat) to draw up
redire [R(ə)diR] vt to repeat; **trouver à ~ à** to find fault with
redoubler [R(ə)duble] vi (tempête, violence) to intensify; (Scol) to repeat a year; **~ de patience/prudence** to be doubly patient/careful
redoutable [R(ə)dutabl] adj formidable, fearsome
redouter [R(ə)dute] vt to dread
redressement [R(ə)dResmɑ̃] nm (économique) recovery
redresser [R(ə)dRese] vt (relever) to set upright; (pièce tordue) to straighten out; (situation, économie) to put right; **se redresser** vi (personne) to sit (ou stand) up (straight); (économie) to recover
réduction [Redyksjɔ̃] nf reduction; **y a-t-il une ~ pour les étudiants?** is there a reduction for students?
réduire [Reduir] vt to reduce; (prix, dépenses) to cut, reduce; **réduit** nm (pièce) tiny room
rééducation [Reedykasjɔ̃] nf (d'un membre) re-education; (de délinquants, d'un blessé) rehabilitation
réel, le [Reel] adj real; **réellement** adv really
réexpédier [Reekspedje] vt (à l'envoyeur) to return, send back; (au destinataire) to send on, forward
refaire [R(ə)fɛR] vt to do again; (faire de nouveau: sport) to take up again; (réparer, restaurer) to do up
réfectoire [RefɛktwaR] nm refectory
référence [Referɑ̃s] nf reference; **références** nfpl (recommandations) reference sg
référer [Refere] : **se référer à** vt to refer to
refermer [R(ə)fɛRme] vt to close ou shut again; **se refermer** vi (porte) to close ou shut (again)
refiler [R(ə)file] vi (fam) to palm off
réfléchi, e [Reflefi] adj (caractère) thoughtful; (action) well-thought-out; (Ling) reflexive; **c'est tout ~** my mind's made up
réfléchir [ReflefiR] vt to reflect ▷ vi to think; **~ à** to think about
reflet [R(ə)flɛ] nm reflection; (sur l'eau etc) sheen no pl, glint; **refléter** vt to reflect; **se refléter** vi to be reflected

réflexe [Reflɛks] nm, adj reflex
réflexion [Reflɛksjɔ̃] nf (de la lumière etc) reflection; (fait de penser) thought; (remarque) remark; **~ faite, à la ~** on reflection
réflexologie [Reflɛksɔlɔʒi] nf reflexology
réforme [RefɔRm] nf reform; (Rel): **la R~** the Reformation; **réformer** vt to reform; (Mil) to declare unfit for service
refouler [R(ə)fule] vt (envahisseurs) to drive back; (larmes) to force back; (désir, colère) to repress
refrain [R(ə)fRɛ̃] nm refrain, chorus
refréner [RəfRene], **réfréner** [RefRene] vt to curb, check
réfrigérateur [RefRiʒeRatœR] nm refrigerator, fridge
refroidir [R(ə)fRwadiR] vt to cool; (fig: personne) to put off ▷ vi to cool (down); **se refroidir** vi (temps) to get cooler ou colder; (fig: ardeur) to cool (off); **refroidissement** nm (grippe etc) chill
refuge [R(ə)fyʒ] nm refuge; **réfugié, e** adj, nm/f refugee; **réfugier: se réfugier** vi to take refuge
refus [R(ə)fy] nm refusal; **ce n'est pas de ~** I won't say no, it's welcome; **refuser** vt to refuse; (Scol: candidat) to fail; **refuser qch à qn** to refuse sb sth; **refuser du monde** to have to turn people away; **se refuser à faire** to refuse to do
regagner [R(ə)gaɲe] vt (faveur) to win back; (lieu) to get back to
régal [Regal] nm treat; **régaler: se régaler** vi to have a delicious meal; (fig) to enjoy o.s.
regard [R(ə)gaR] nm (coup d'œil) look, glance; (expression) look (in one's eye); **au ~ de** (loi, morale) from the point of view of; **en ~ de** in comparison with
regardant, e [R(ə)gaRdɑ̃, ɑ̃t] adj (économe) tight-fisted; **peu ~ (sur)** very free (about)
regarder [R(ə)gaRde] vt to look at; (film, télévision, match) to watch; (concerner) to concern ▷ vi to look; **ne pas ~ à la dépense** to spare no expense; **~ qn/qch comme** to regard sb/sth as
régie [Reʒi] nf (Comm, Industrie) state-owned company; (Théâtre, Cinéma) production; (Radio, TV) control room
régime [Reʒim] nm (Pol) régime; (Méd) diet; (Admin: carcéral, fiscal etc) system; (de bananes, dattes) bunch; **se mettre au/suivre un ~** to go on/be on a diet
régiment [Reʒimɑ̃] nm regiment
région [Reʒjɔ̃] nf region; **régional, e, -aux** adj regional
régir [ReʒiR] vt to govern
régisseur [ReʒisœR] nm (d'un domaine) steward; (Cinéma, TV) assistant director; (Théâtre) stage manager

registre [ʀəʒistʀ] nm register

réglage [ʀeglaʒ] nm adjustment

règle [ʀɛgl] nf (instrument) ruler; (loi) rule; **règles** nfpl (menstruation) period sg; **en ~** (papiers d'identité) in order; **en ~ générale** as a (general) rule

réglé, e [ʀegle] adj (vie) well-ordered; (arrangé) settled

règlement [ʀɛgləmɑ̃] nm (paiement) settlement; (arrêté) regulation; (règles, statuts) regulations pl, rules pl; **réglementaire** adj conforming to the regulations; (tenue) regulation cpd; **réglementation** nf (règles) regulations; **réglementer** vt to regulate

régler [ʀegle] vt (conflit, facture) to settle; (personne) to settle up with; (mécanisme, machine) to regulate, adjust; (thermostat etc) to set, adjust

réglisse [ʀeglis] nf liquorice

règne [ʀɛɲ] nm (d'un roi etc, fig) reign; **le ~ végétal/animal** the vegetable/animal kingdom; **régner** vi (roi) to rule, reign; (fig) to reign

regorger [ʀ(ə)gɔʀʒe] vi: **~ de** to overflow with, be bursting with

regret [ʀ(ə)gʀɛ] nm regret; **à ~** with regret; **sans ~** with no regrets; **regrettable** adj regrettable; **regretter** vt to regret; (personne) to miss; **je regrette mais ...** I'm sorry but ...

regrouper [ʀ(ə)gʀupe] vt (grouper) to group together; (contenir) to include, comprise; **se regrouper** vi to gather (together)

régulier, -ière [ʀegylje, jɛʀ] adj (gén) regular; (vitesse, qualité) steady; (égal: couche, ligne) even; (Transports: ligne, service) scheduled, regular; (légal) lawful, in order; (honnête) straight, on the level; **régulièrement** adv regularly; (uniformément) evenly

rehausser [ʀəose] vt (relever) to heighten, raise; (fig: souligner) to set off, enhance

rein [ʀɛ̃] nm kidney; **reins** nmpl (dos) back sg

reine [ʀɛn] nf queen

reine-claude [ʀɛnklod] nf greengage

réinscriptible [ʀeɛ̃skʀiptibl] adj (CD, DVD) rewritable

réinsertion [ʀeɛ̃sɛʀsjɔ̃] nf (de délinquant) reintegration, rehabilitation

réintégrer [ʀeɛ̃tegʀe] vt (lieu) to return to; (fonctionnaire) to reinstate

rejaillir [ʀ(ə)ʒajiʀ] vi to splash up; **~ sur** (fig: scandale) to rebound on; (: gloire) to be reflected on

rejet [ʀəʒɛ] nm rejection; **rejeter** vt (relancer) to throw back; (écarter) to reject; (déverser) to throw out, discharge; (vomir) to bring ou throw up; **rejeter la responsabilité de qch sur qn** to lay the responsibility for sth at sb's door

rejoindre [ʀ(ə)ʒwɛ̃dʀ] vt (famille, régiment) to rejoin, return to; (lieu) to get (back) to; (suj: route etc) to meet, join; (rattraper) to catch up (with); **se rejoindre** vi to meet; **je te rejoins à la gare** I'll see ou meet you at the station

réjouir [ʀeʒwiʀ] vt to delight; **se ~ (de qch/de faire)** to be delighted (about sth/to do); **réjouissances** nfpl (fête) festivities

relâche [ʀəlɑʃ] nm ou nf: **sans ~** without respite ou a break; **relâché, e** adj loose, lax; **relâcher** vt (libérer) to release; (desserrer) to loosen; **se relâcher** vi (discipline) to become slack ou lax; (élève etc) to slacken off

relais [ʀ(ə)lɛ] nm (Sport): **(course de) ~** relay (race); **prendre le ~ (de)** to take over (from); **relais routier** ≈ transport café (BRIT), ≈ truck stop (US)

relancer [ʀ(ə)lɑ̃se] vt (balle) to throw back; (moteur) to restart; (fig) to boost, revive; (harceler): **~ qn** to pester sb

relatif, -ive [ʀ(ə)latif, iv] adj relative

relation [ʀ(ə)lasjɔ̃] nf (rapport) relation(ship); (connaissance) acquaintance; **relations** nfpl (rapports) relations; (connaissances) connections; **être/entrer en ~(s) avec** to be/get in contact with

relaxer [ʀəlakse]: **se relaxer** vi to relax

relayer [ʀ(ə)leje] vt (collaborateur, coureur etc) to relieve; **se relayer** vi (dans une activité) to take it in turns

reléguer [ʀ(ə)lege] vt to relegate

relevé, e [ʀəl(ə)ve] adj (manches) rolled-up; (sauce) highly-seasoned ▷ nm (de compteur) reading; **relevé bancaire** ou **de compte** bank statement

relève [ʀəlɛv] nf (personne) relief; **prendre la ~** to take over

relever [ʀəl(ə)ve] vt (meuble) to stand up again; (personne tombée) to help up; (vitre, niveau de vie) to raise; (inf) to turn up; (style) to elevate; (plat, sauce) to season; (sentinelle, équipe) to relieve; (fautes) to pick out; (défi) to accept, take up; (noter: adresse etc) to take down, note; (: plan) to sketch; (compteur) to read; (ramasser: cahiers) to collect, take in; **se relever** vi (se remettre debout) to get up; **~ de** (maladie) to be recovering from; (être du ressort de) to be a matter for; (fig) to pertain to; **~ qn de** (fonctions) to relieve sb of; **~ la tête** to look up

relief [ʀəljɛf] nm relief; **mettre en ~** (fig) to bring out, highlight

relier [ʀəlje] vt to link up; (livre) to bind; **~ qch à** to link sth to th

religieux, -euse [ʀ(ə)liʒjø, jøz] adj religious ▷ nm monk

religion [ʀ(ə)liʒjɔ̃] nf religion

relire [ʀ(ə)liʀ] vt (à nouveau) to reread, read again; (vérifier) to read over

reluire [ʀ(ə)lɥiʀ] vi to gleam

remanier [ʀ(ə)manje] vt to reshape, recast;

(*Pol*) to reshuffle

remarquable [ʀ(ə)maʀkabl] *adj* remarkable

remarque [ʀ(ə)maʀk] *nf* remark; (*écrite*) note

remarquer [ʀ(ə)maʀke] *vt* (*voir*) to notice;
 se remarquer *vi* to be noticeable; **faire ~ (à
 qn) que** to point out (to sb) that; **faire ~ qch
 (à qn)** to point sth out (to sb); **remarquez, ...**
 mind you ...; **se faire ~** to draw attention to o.s.

rembourrer [ʀɑ̃buʀe] *vt* to stuff

remboursement [ʀɑ̃buʀsəmɑ̃] *nm* (*de
 dette, d'emprunt*) repayment; (*de frais*) refund;
 rembourser *vt* to pay back, repay; (*frais, billet
 etc*) to refund; **se faire rembourser** to get a
 refund

remède [ʀ(ə)mɛd] *nm* (*médicament*) medicine;
 (*traitement, fig*) remedy, cure

remémorer [ʀ(ə)memɔʀe]: **se remémorer** *vt*
 to recall, recollect

remerciements [ʀəmɛʀsimɑ̃] *nmpl* thanks;
 (avec) tous mes ~ (with) grateful *ou* many
 thanks

remercier [ʀ(ə)mɛʀsje] *vt* to thank;
 (*congédier*) to dismiss; **~ qn de/d'avoir fait** to
 thank sb for/for having done

remettre [ʀ(ə)mɛtʀ] *vt* (*replacer*) to put back;
 (*vêtement*) to put back on; (*ajouter*) to add;
 (*ajourner*): **~ qch (à)** to postpone sth (until); **se
 remettre** *vi*: **se ~ (de)** to recover (from); **~ qch
 à qn** (*donner: lettre, clé etc*) to hand over sth to
 sb; (: *prix, décoration*) to present sb with sth; **se
 ~ à faire qch** to start doing sth again; **s'en ~ à**
 to leave it (up) to

remise [ʀ(ə)miz] *nf* (*rabais*) discount; (*local*)
 shed; **remise de peine** reduction of sentence;
 remise des prix prize-giving; **remise en
 cause** *ou* **question** calling into question,
 challenging; **remise en jeu** (*Football*) throw-in

remontant [ʀ(ə)mɔ̃tɑ̃] *nm* tonic, pick-me-up

remonte-pente [ʀ(ə)mɔ̃tpɑ̃t] *nm* ski-lift

remonter [ʀ(ə)mɔ̃te] *vi* to go back up; (*prix,
 température*) to go up again ▷ *vt* (*pente*) to go
 up; (*fleuve*) to sail (*ou* swim *etc*) up; (*manches,
 pantalon*) to roll up; (*col*) to turn up; (*niveau,
 limite*) to raise; (*fig: personne*) to buck up; (*qch
 de démonté*) to put back together, reassemble;
 (*montre*) to wind up; **~ le moral à qn** to raise
 sb's spirits; **~ à** (*dater de*) to date *ou* go back to

remords [ʀ(ə)mɔʀ] *nm* remorse *no pl*; **avoir
 des ~** to feel remorse

remorque [ʀ(ə)mɔʀk] *nf* trailer; **remorquer**
 vt to tow; **remorqueur** *nm* tug(boat)

remous [ʀəmu] *nm* (*d'un navire*) (back)wash *no
 pl*; (*de rivière*) swirl, eddy ▷ *nmpl* (*fig*) stir *sg*

remparts [ʀɑ̃paʀ] *nmpl* walls, ramparts

remplaçant, e [ʀɑ̃plasɑ̃, ɑ̃t] *nm/f*
 replacement, stand-in; (*Scol*) supply teacher

remplacement [ʀɑ̃plasmɑ̃] *nm*
 replacement; **faire des ~s** (*professeur*) to do
 supply teaching; (*secrétaire*) to temp

remplacer [ʀɑ̃plase] *vt* to replace; **~ qch/qn
 par** to replace sth/sb with

rempli, e [ʀɑ̃pli] *adj* (*emploi du temps*) full,
 busy; **~ de** full of, filled with

remplir [ʀɑ̃pliʀ] *vt* to fill (up); (*questionnaire*)
 to fill out *ou* up; (*obligations, fonction, condition*)
 to fulfil; **se remplir** *vi* to fill up

remporter [ʀɑ̃pɔʀte] *vt* (*marchandise*) to take
 away; (*fig*) to win, achieve

remuant, e [ʀəmɥɑ̃, ɑ̃t] *adj* restless

remue-ménage [ʀ(ə)mymenaʒ] *nm inv*
 commotion

remuer [ʀəmɥe] *vt* to move; (*café, sauce*) to
 stir ▷ *vi* to move; **se remuer** *vi* to move; (*fam:
 s'activer*) to get a move on

rémunérer [ʀemyneʀe] *vt* to remunerate

renard [ʀ(ə)naʀ] *nm* fox

renchérir [ʀɑ̃ʃeʀiʀ] *vi* (*fig*): **~ (sur)** (*en paroles*)
 to add something (to)

rencontre [ʀɑ̃kɔ̃tʀ] *nf* meeting; (*imprévue*)
 encounter; **aller à la ~ de qn** to go and meet
 sb; **rencontrer** *vt* to meet; (*mot, expression*)
 to come across; (*difficultés*) to meet with; **se
 rencontrer** *vi* to meet

rendement [ʀɑ̃dmɑ̃] *nm* (*d'un travailleur, d'une
 machine*) output; (*d'un champ*) yield

rendez-vous [ʀɑ̃devu] *nm* appointment;
 (*d'amoureux*) date; (*lieu*) meeting place; **donner
 ~ à qn** to arrange to meet sb; **avoir/prendre ~
 (avec)** to have/make an appointment (with);
 j'ai ~ avec ... I have an appointment with ...;
 je voudrais prendre ~ I'd like to make an
 appointment

rendre [ʀɑ̃dʀ] *vt* (*restituer*) to give back, return;
 (*invitation*) to return, repay; (*vomir*) to bring up;
 (*exprimer, traduire*) to render; (*faire devenir*): **~ qn
 célèbre/qch possible** to make sb famous/sth
 possible; **se rendre** *vi* (*capituler*) to surrender,
 give o.s. up; (*aller*): **se ~ quelque part** to go
 somewhere; **~ la monnaie à qn** to give sb his
 change; **se ~ compte de qch** to realize sth

rênes [ʀɛn] *nfpl* reins

renfermé, e [ʀɑ̃fɛʀme] *adj* (*fig*) withdrawn
 ▷ *nm*: **sentir le ~** to smell stuffy

renfermer [ʀɑ̃fɛʀme] *vt* to contain

renforcer [ʀɑ̃fɔʀse] *vt* to reinforce; **renfort**:
 renforts *nmpl* reinforcements; **à grand
 renfort de** with a great deal of

renfrogné, e [ʀɑ̃fʀɔɲe] *adj* sullen

renier [ʀənje] *vt* (*personne*) to disown,
 repudiate; (*foi*) to renounce

renifler [ʀ(ə)nifle] *vi, vt* to sniff

renne [ʀɛn] *nm* reindeer *inv*

renom [ʀənɔ̃] *nm* reputation; (*célébrité*)
 renown; **renommé, e** *adj* celebrated,
 renowned; **renommée** *nf* fame

renoncer [ʀ(ə)nɔ̃se]: **~ à** *vt* to give up; **~ à
 faire** to give up the idea of doing

renouer [ʀənwe] *vt*: **~ avec** (*habitude*) to take

up again

renouveler [ʀ(ə)nuv(ə)le] *vt* to renew; (*exploit, méfait*) to repeat; **se renouveler** *vi* (*incident*) to recur, happen again; **renouvellement** *nm* (*remplacement*) renewal

rénover [ʀenɔve] *vt* (*immeuble*) to renovate, do up; (*quartier*) to redevelop

renseignement [ʀɑ̃sɛɲmɑ̃] *nm* information *no pl*, piece of information; **(guichet des) ~s** information office; **(service des) ~s** (*Tél*) directory enquiries (BRIT), information (US)

renseigner [ʀɑ̃sɛɲe] *vt*: **~ qn (sur)** to give information to sb (about); **se renseigner** *vi* to ask for information, make inquiries

rentabilité [ʀɑ̃tabilite] *nf* profitability

rentable [ʀɑ̃tabl] *adj* profitable

rente [ʀɑ̃t] *nf* private income; (*pension*) pension

rentrée [ʀɑ̃tʀe] *nf*: **~ (d'argent)** cash *no pl* coming in; **la ~ (des classes)** the start of the new school year

rentrer [ʀɑ̃tʀe] *vi* (*revenir chez soi*) to go (*ou* come) (back) home; (*entrer de nouveau*) to go (*ou* come) back in; (*entrer*) to go (*ou* come) in; (*air, clou: pénétrer*) to go in; (*revenu*) to come in ▷ *vt* to bring in; (*véhicule*) to put away; (*chemise dans pantalon etc*) to tuck in; (*griffes*) to draw in; **~ le ventre** to pull in one's stomach; **~ dans** (*heurter*) to crash into; **~ dans l'ordre** to be back to normal; **~ dans ses frais** to recover one's expenses; **je rentre mardi** I'm going *ou* coming home on Tuesday

renverse [ʀɑ̃vɛʀs]: **à la ~** *adv* backwards

renverser [ʀɑ̃vɛʀse] *vt* (*faire tomber: chaise, verre*) to knock over, overturn; (*liquide, contenu*) to spill, upset; (*piéton*) to knock down; (*retourner*) to turn upside down; (*: ordre des mots etc*) to reverse; (*fig: gouvernement etc*) to overthrow; (*fam: stupéfier*) to bowl over; **se renverser** *vi* (*verre, vase*) to fall over; (*contenu*) to spill

renvoi [ʀɑ̃vwa] *nm* (*d'employé*) dismissal; (*d'élève*) expulsion; (*référence*) cross-reference; (*éructation*) belch; **renvoyer** *vt* to send back; (*congédier*) to dismiss; (*élève: définitivement*) to expel; (*lumière*) to reflect; (*ajourner*): **renvoyer qch (à)** to put sth off *ou* postpone sth (until)

repaire [ʀ(ə)pɛʀ] *nm* den

répandre [ʀepɑ̃dʀ] *vt* (*renverser*) to spill; (*étaler, diffuser*) to spread; (*odeur*) to give off; **se répandre** *vi* to spill; (*se propager*) to spread; **répandu, e** *adj* (*opinion, usage*) widespread

réparation [ʀepaʀasjɔ̃] *nf* repair

réparer [ʀepaʀe] *vt* to repair; (*fig: offense*) to make up for, atone for; (*: oubli, erreur*) to put right; **où est-ce que je peux le faire ~?** where can I get it fixed?

repartie [ʀepaʀti] *nf* retort; **avoir de la ~** to be quick at repartee

repartir [ʀ(ə)paʀtiʀ] *vi* to leave again; (*voyageur*) to set off again; (*fig*) to get going again; **~ à zéro** to start from scratch (again)

répartir [ʀepaʀtiʀ] *vt* (*pour attribuer*) to share out; (*pour disperser, disposer*) to divide up; (*poids*) to distribute; **se répartir** *vt* (*travail, rôles*) to share out between themselves; **répartition** *nf* (*des richesses etc*) distribution

repas [ʀ(ə)pɑ] *nm* meal

repassage [ʀ(ə)pɑsaʒ] *nm* ironing

repasser [ʀ(ə)pɑse] *vi* to come (*ou* go) back ▷ *vt* (*vêtement, tissu*) to iron; (*examen*) to retake, resit; (*film*) to show again; (*leçon: revoir*) to go over (again)

repentir [ʀəpɑ̃tiʀ] *nm* repentance; **se repentir** *vi* to repent; **se ~ d'avoir fait qch** (*regretter*) to regret having done sth

répercussions [ʀepɛʀkysjɔ̃] *nfpl* (*fig*) repercussions

répercuter [ʀepɛʀkyte]: **se répercuter** *vi* (*bruit*) to reverberate; (*fig*): **se ~ sur** to have repercussions on

repère [ʀ(ə)pɛʀ] *nm* mark; (*monument, événement*) landmark

repérer [ʀ(ə)peʀe] *vt* (*fam: erreur, personne*) to spot; (*: endroit*) to locate; **se repérer** *vi* to find one's way about

répertoire [ʀepɛʀtwaʀ] *nm* (*liste*) (alphabetical) list; (*carnet*) index notebook; (*Inform*) folder, directory; (*d'un artiste*) repertoire

répéter [ʀepete] *vt* to repeat; (*préparer: leçon*) to learn, go over; (*Théâtre*) to rehearse; **se répéter** *vi* (*redire*) to repeat o.s.; (*se reproduire*) to be repeated, recur; **pouvez-vous ~, s'il vous plaît?** can you repeat that, please?

répétition [ʀepetisjɔ̃] *nf* repetition; (*Théâtre*) rehearsal; **~ générale** (final) dress rehearsal

répit [ʀepi] *nm* respite; **sans ~** without letting up

replier [ʀ(ə)plije] *vt* (*rabattre*) to fold down *ou* over; **se replier** *vi* (*troupes, armée*) to withdraw, fall back; (*sur soi-même*) to withdraw into o.s.

réplique [ʀeplik] *nf* (*repartie, fig*) reply; (*Théâtre*) line; (*copie*) replica; **répliquer** *vi* to reply; (*riposter*) to retaliate

répondeur [ʀepɔ̃dœʀ] *nm*: **~ (automatique)** (*Tél*) answering machine

répondre [ʀepɔ̃dʀ] *vi* to answer, reply; (*freins*) to respond; **~ à** to reply to, answer; (*affection, salut*) to return; (*provocation*) to respond to; (*correspondre à: besoin*) to answer; (*: conditions*) to meet; (*: description*) to match; (*avec impertinence*): **~ à qn** to answer sb back; **~ de** to answer for

réponse [ʀepɔ̃s] *nf* answer, reply; **en ~ à** in reply to

reportage [ʀ(ə)pɔʀtaʒ] *nm* report

reporter[1] [ʀəpɔʀtɛʀ] *nm* reporter

reporter² [ʀəpɔʀte] *vt* (*ajourner*): ~ **qch (à)** to postpone sth (until); (*transférer*): ~ **qch sur** to transfer sth to; **se reporter à** (*époque*) to think back to; (*document*) to refer to

repos [ʀ(ə)po] *nm* rest; (*tranquillité*) peace (and quiet); (*Mil*): ~! stand at ease!; **ce n'est pas de tout ~!** it's no picnic!

reposant, e [ʀ(ə)pozã, ãt] *adj* restful

reposer [ʀ(ə)poze] *vt* (*verre, livre*) to put down; (*délasser*) to rest ▷ *vi*: **laisser ~** (*pâte*) to leave to stand; **se reposer** *vi* to rest; **se ~ sur qn** to rely on sb; ~ **sur** (*fig*) to rest on

repoussant, e [ʀ(ə)pusã, ãt] *adj* repulsive

repousser [ʀ(ə)puse] *vi* to grow again ▷ *vt* to repel, repulse; (*offre*) to turn down, reject; (*personne*) to push back; (*différer*) to put back

reprendre [ʀ(ə)pʀãdʀ] *vt* (*objet prêté, donné*) to take back; (*prisonnier, ville*) to recapture; (*firme, entreprise*) to take over; (*le travail*) to resume; (*emprunter: argument, idée*) to take up, use; (*refaire: article etc*) to go over again; (*vêtement*) to alter; (*réprimander*) to tell off; (*corriger*) to correct; (*chercher*): **je viendrai te ~ à 4 h** I'll come and fetch you at 4; (*se resservir de*): ~ **du pain/un œuf** to take (*ou* eat) more bread/another egg ▷ *vi* (*classes, pluie*) to start (up) again; (*activités, travaux, combats*) to resume, start up again; (*affaires*) to pick up; (*dire*): **reprit-il** he went on; ~ **des forces** to recover one's strength; ~ **courage** to take new heart; ~ **la route** to resume one's journey, set off again; ~ **haleine** *ou* **son souffle** to get one's breath back

représentant, e [ʀ(ə)pʀezãtã, ãt] *nm/f* representative

représentation [ʀ(ə)pʀezãtasjɔ̃] *nf* (*symbole, image*) representation; (*spectacle*) performance

représenter [ʀ(ə)pʀezãte] *vt* to represent; (*donner: pièce, opéra*) to perform; **se représenter** *vt* (*se figurer*) to imagine

répression [ʀepʀesjɔ̃] *nf* repression

réprimer [ʀepʀime] *vt* (*émotions*) to suppress; (*peuple etc*) to repress

repris [ʀ(ə)pʀi] *nm*: ~ **de justice** ex-prisoner, ex-convict

reprise [ʀ(ə)pʀiz] *nf* (*recommencement*) resumption; (*économique*) recovery; (*TV*) repeat; (*Comm*) trade-in, part exchange; (*raccommodage*) mend; **à plusieurs ~s** on several occasions

repriser [ʀ(ə)pʀize] *vt* (*chaussette, lainage*) to darn; (*tissu*) to mend

reproche [ʀ(ə)pʀɔʃ] *nm* (*remontrance*) reproach; **faire des ~s à qn** to reproach sb; **sans ~(s)** beyond reproach; **reprocher** *vt*: **reprocher qch à qn** to reproach *ou* blame sb for sth; **reprocher qch à** (*critiquer*) to have sth against

reproduction [ʀ(ə)pʀɔdyksjɔ̃] *nf* reproduction

reproduire [ʀ(ə)pʀɔdɥiʀ] *vt* to reproduce; **se reproduire** *vi* (*Bio*) to reproduce; (*recommencer*) to recur, re-occur

reptile [ʀɛptil] *nm* reptile

république [ʀepyblik] *nf* republic

répugnant, e [ʀepyɲã, ãt] *adj* disgusting

répugner [ʀepyɲe] ~ **à** *vt* : ~ **à qn** to repel *ou* disgust sb; ~ **à faire** to be loath *ou* reluctant to do

réputation [ʀepytasjɔ̃] *nf* reputation; **réputé, e** *adj* renowned

requérir [ʀəkeʀiʀ] *vt* (*nécessiter*) to require, call for

requête [ʀəkɛt] *nf* request

requin [ʀəkɛ̃] *nm* shark

requis, e [ʀəki, iz] *adj* required

RER *sigle m* (= *réseau express régional*) Greater Paris high-speed train service

rescapé, e [ʀɛskape] *nm/f* survivor

rescousse [ʀɛskus] *nf*: **aller à la ~ de qn** to go to sb's aid *ou* rescue

réseau, x [ʀezo] *nm* network

réservation [ʀezɛʀvasjɔ̃] *nf* booking, reservation; **j'ai confirmé ma ~ par fax/e-mail** I confirmed my booking by fax/e-mail

réserve [ʀezɛʀv] *nf* (*retenue*) reserve; (*entrepôt*) storeroom; (*restriction, d'Indiens*) reservation; (*de pêche, chasse*) preserve; **de ~** (*provisions etc*) in reserve

réservé, e [ʀezɛʀve] *adj* reserved; **chasse/pêche ~e** private hunting/fishing

réserver [ʀezɛʀve] *vt* to reserve; (*chambre, billet etc*) to book, reserve; (*fig: destiner*) to have in store; (*garder*): ~ **qch pour/à** to keep *ou* save sth for; **je voudrais ~ une chambre pour deux personnes** I'd like to book a double room; **j'ai réservé une table au nom de ...** I booked a table in the name of ...

réservoir [ʀezɛʀvwaʀ] *nm* tank

résidence [ʀezidãs] *nf* residence; **résidence secondaire** second home; **résidence universitaire** hall of residence (BRIT), dormitory (US); **résidentiel, le** *adj* residential; **résider** *vi*: **résider à/dans/en** to reside in; **résider dans** (*fig*) to lie in

résidu [ʀezidy] *nm* residue *no pl*

résigner [ʀeziɲe]: **se ~ (à qch/à faire)** to resign o.s. (to sth/to doing)

résilier [ʀezilje] *vt* to terminate

résistance [ʀezistãs] *nf* resistance; (*de réchaud, bouilloire: fil*) element

résistant, e [ʀezistã, ãt] *adj* (*personne*) robust, tough; (*matériau*) strong, hard-wearing

résister [ʀeziste] *vi* to resist; ~ **à** (*assaut, tentation*) to resist; (*supporter: gel etc*) to withstand; (*désobéir à*) to stand up to, oppose

résolu, e [ʀezɔly] *pp de* **résoudre** ▷ *adj*: **être ~ à qch/faire** to be set upon sth/doing

résolution [Rezɔlysjɔ̃] nf (fermeté, décision) resolution; (d'un problème) solution

résolve etc [Rezɔlv] vb voir **résoudre**

résonner [Rezɔne] vi (cloche, pas) to reverberate, resound; (salle) to be resonant

résorber [RezɔRbe]: **se résorber** vi (fig: chômage) to be reduced; (: déficit) to be absorbed

résoudre [Rezudr] vt to solve; **se ~ à faire** to bring o.s. to do

respect [Rεspε] nm respect; **tenir en ~ to** keep at bay; **présenter ses ~s à qn** to pay one's respects to sb; **respecter** vt to respect; **respectueux, -euse** adj respectful

respiration [Rεspirasjɔ̃] nf breathing no pl

respirer [Rεspire] vi to breathe; (fig: se détendre) to get one's breath; (: se rassurer) to breathe again ▷ vt to breathe (in), inhale; (manifester: santé, calme etc) to exude

resplendir [RεsplɑdiR] vi to shine; (fig): **~ (de)** to be radiant (with)

responsabilité [Rεspɔ̃sabilite] nf responsibility; (légale) liability

responsable [Rεspɔ̃sabl] adj responsible ▷ nm/f (coupable) person responsible; (personne compétente) person in charge; (de parti, syndicat) official; **~ de** responsible for

ressaisir [R(ə)seziR]: **se ressaisir** vi to regain one's self-control

ressasser [R(ə)sase] vt to keep going over

ressemblance [R(ə)sɑblɑs] nf resemblance, similarity, likeness

ressemblant, e [R(ə)sɑblɑ, ɑ̃t] adj (portrait) lifelike, true to life

ressembler [R(ə)sɑble]: **~ à** vt to be like, resemble; (visuellement) to look like; **se ressembler** vi to be (ou look) alike

ressentiment [R(ə)sɑtimɑ̃] nm resentment

ressentir [R(ə)sɑtiR] vt to feel; **se ~ de** to feel (ou show) the effects of

resserrer [R(ə)seRe] vt (nœud, boulon) to tighten (up); (fig: liens) to strengthen

resservir [R(ə)seRviR] vi to do ou serve again; **~ qn (d'un plat)** to give sb a second helping (of a dish); **se ~ de** (plat) to take a second helping of; (outil etc) to use again

ressort [RəsɔR] nm (pièce) spring; (énergie) spirit; (recours): **en dernier ~** as a last resort; (compétence): **être du ~ de** to fall within the competence of

ressortir [RəsɔRtiR] vi to go (ou come) out (again); (contraster) to stand out; **~ de** to emerge from; **faire ~** (fig: souligner) to bring out

ressortissant, e [R(ə)sɔRtisɑ, ɑ̃t] nm/f national

ressources [R(ə)suRs] nfpl (moyens) resources

ressusciter [Resysite] vt (fig) to revive, bring back ▷ vi to rise (from the dead)

restant, e [Rεstɑ, ɑ̃t] adj remaining ▷ nm:

le ~ (de) the remainder (of); **un ~ de** (de trop) some left-over

restaurant [RεstɔRɑ] nm restaurant; **pouvez-vous m'indiquer un bon ~?** can you recommend a good restaurant?

restauration [RεstɔRasjɔ̃] nf restoration; (hôtellerie) catering; **restauration rapide** fast food

restaurer [RεstɔRe] vt to restore; **se restaurer** vi to have something to eat

reste [Rεst] nm (restant): **le ~ (de)** the rest (of); (de trop): **un ~ (de)** some left-over; **restes** nmpl (nourriture) left-overs; (d'une cité etc, dépouille mortelle) remains; **du ~, au ~** besides, moreover

rester [Rεste] vi to stay, remain; (subsister) to remain, be left; (durer) to last, live on ▷ vb impers: **il reste du pain/2 œufs** there's some bread/there are 2 eggs left (over); **restons-en là** let's leave it at that; **il me reste assez de temps** I have enough time left; **il ne me reste plus qu'à ...** I've just got to ...

restituer [Rεstitɥe] vt (objet, somme): **~ qch (à qn)** to return sth (to sb)

restreindre [RεstRɛ̃dR] vt to restrict, limit

restriction [Rεstriksjɔ̃] nf restriction

résultat [Rezylta] nm result; **résultats** nmpl (d'examen, d'élection) results pl

résulter [Rezylte]: **~ de** vt to result from, be the result of

résumé [Rezyme] nm summary, résumé; **en ~** in brief; (pour conclure) to sum up

résumer [Rezyme] vt (texte) to summarize; (récapituler) to sum up

> Attention à ne pas traduire **résumer** par to resume.

résurrection [RezyRεksjɔ̃] nf resurrection

rétablir [RetabliR] vt to restore, re-establish; **se rétablir** vi (guérir) to recover; (silence, calme) to return, be restored; **rétablissement** nm restoring; (guérison) recovery

retaper [R(ə)tape] (fam) vt (maison, voiture etc) to do up; (revigorer) to buck up

retard [R(ə)taR] nm (d'une personne attendue) lateness no pl; (sur l'horaire, un programme) delay; (fig: scolaire, mental etc) backwardness; **en ~ (de 2 heures)** (2 hours) late; **avoir du ~** to be late; (sur un programme) to be behind (schedule); **prendre du ~** (train, avion) to be delayed; **sans ~** without delay; **désolé d'être en ~** sorry I'm late; **le vol a deux heures de ~** the flight is two hours late

retardataire [R(ə)taRdatεR] nm/f latecomer

retardement [R(ə)taRdəmɑ̃]: **à ~** adj delayed action cpd; **bombe à ~** time bomb

retarder [R(ə)taRde] vt to delay; (montre) to put back ▷ vi (montre) to be slow; **~ qn (d'une heure)** (sur un horaire) to delay sb (an hour); **~ qch (de 2 jours)** (départ, date) to put sth back

(2 days)

retenir [Rət(ə)niʀ] *vt* (*garder, retarder*) to keep, detain; (*maintenir: objet qui glisse, fig: colère, larmes*) to hold back; (*se rappeler*) to retain; (*réserver*) to reserve; (*accepter: proposition etc*) to accept; (*fig: empêcher d'agir*): **~ qn (de faire)** to hold sb back (from doing); (*prélever*): **~ qch (sur)** to deduct sth (from); **se retenir** *vi* (*se raccrocher*): **se ~ à** to hold onto; (*se contenir*): **se ~ de faire** to restrain o.s. from doing; **~ son souffle** to hold one's breath

retentir [R(ə)tātiʀ] *vi* to ring out; **retentissant, e** *adj* resounding

retenue [Rət(ə)ny] *nf* (*prélèvement*) deduction; (*Scol*) detention; (*modération*) (self-)restraint

réticence [Retisās] *nf* hesitation, reluctance *no pl*; **réticent, e** *adj* hesitant, reluctant

rétine [Retin] *nf* retina

retiré, e [R(ə)tiRe] *adj* (*vie*) secluded; (*lieu*) remote

retirer [R(ə)tiRe] *vt* (*vêtement, lunettes*) to take off, remove; (*argent, plainte*) to withdraw; (*reprendre: bagages, billets*) to collect, pick up; (*extraire*): **~ qch de** to take sth out of, remove sth from

retomber [R(ə)tɔ̃be] *vi* (*à nouveau*) to fall again; (*atterrir: après un saut etc*) to land; (*échoir*): **~ sur qn** to fall on sb

rétorquer [RetɔRke] *vt*: **~ (à qn) que** to retort (to sb) that

retouche [R(ə)tuʃ] *nf* (*sur vêtement*) alteration; **retoucher** *vt* (*photographie*) to touch up; (*texte, vêtement*) to alter

retour [R(ə)tuR] *nm* return; **au ~** (*en route*) on the way back; **à mon ~** when I get/got back; **être de ~ (de)** to be back (from); **par ~ du courrier** by return of post; **quand serons-nous de ~?** when do we get back?

retourner [R(ə)tuRne] *vt* (*dans l'autre sens: matelas, crêpe etc*) to turn (over); (: *sac, vêtement*) to turn inside out; (*fam: bouleverser*) to shake; (*renvoyer, restituer*): **~ qch à qn** to return sth to sb ▷ *vi* (*aller, revenir*): **~ quelque part/à** to go back ou return somewhere/to; **se retourner** *vi* (*tourner la tête*) to turn round; **~ à** (*état, activité*) to return to, go back to; **se ~ contre** (*fig*) to turn against

retrait [R(ə)tRε] *nm* (*d'argent*) withdrawal; **en ~** set back; **retrait du permis (de conduire)** disqualification from driving (BRIT), revocation of driver's license (US)

retraite [R(ə)tRεt] *nf* (*d'un employé*) retirement; (*revenu*) pension; (*d'une armée, Rel*) retreat; **prendre sa ~** to retire; **retraite anticipée** early retirement; **retraité, e** *adj* retired ▷ *nm/f* pensioner

retrancher [R(ə)tRɑ̃ʃe] *vt* (*nombre, somme*):

~ qch de to take ou deduct sth from; **se ~ derrière/dans** to take refuge behind/in

rétrécir [RetResiR] *vt* (*vêtement*) to take in ▷ *vi* to shrink; **se rétrécir** (*route, vallée*) to narrow

rétro [Retro] *adj inv*: **la mode ~** the nostalgia vogue

rétroprojecteur [RetropRɔʒεktœR] *nm* overhead projector

rétrospective [Retrɔspεktiv] *nf* (*Art*) retrospective; (*Cinéma*) season, retrospective; **rétrospectivement** *adv* in retrospect

retrousser [R(ə)tRuse] *vt* to roll up

retrouvailles [R(ə)tRuvɑj] *nfpl* reunion *sg*

retrouver [R(ə)tRuve] *vt* (*fugitif, objet perdu*) to find; (*calme, santé*) to regain; (*revoir*) to see again; (*rejoindre*) to meet (again), join; **se retrouver** *vi* to meet; (*s'orienter*) to find one's way; **se ~ quelque part** to find o.s. somewhere; **s'y ~** (*y voir clair*) to make sense of it; (*rentrer dans ses frais*) to break even; **je ne retrouve plus mon portefeuille** I can't find my wallet (BRIT) ou billfold (US)

rétroviseur [RetRɔvizœR] *nm* (rear-view) mirror

réunion [Reynjɔ̃] *nf* (*séance*) meeting

réunir [ReyniR] *vt* (*rassembler*) to gather together; (*inviter: amis, famille*) to have round, have in; (*cumuler: qualités etc*) to combine; (*rapprocher: ennemis*) to bring together (again), reunite; (*rattacher: parties*) to join (together); **se réunir** *vi* (*se rencontrer*) to meet

réussi, e [Reysi] *adj* successful

réussir [ReysiR] *vi* to succeed, be successful; (*à un examen*) to pass ▷ *vt* to make a success of; **~ à faire** to succeed in doing; **~ à qn** (*être bénéfique à*) to agree with sb; **réussite** *nf* success; (*Cartes*) patience

revaloir [R(ə)valwaR] *vt*: **je vous revaudrai cela** I'll repay you some day; (*en mal*) I'll pay you back for this

revanche [R(ə)vɑ̃ʃ] *nf* revenge; (*sport*) revenge match; **en ~** on the other hand

rêve [Rεv] *nm* dream; **de ~** dream *cpd*; **faire un ~** to have a dream

réveil [Revεj] *nm* waking up *no pl*; (*fig*) awakening; (*pendule*) alarm (clock); **au ~** on waking (up); **réveiller** *vt* (*personne*) to wake up; (*fig*) to awaken, revive; **se réveiller** *vi* to wake up; **pouvez-vous me réveiller à 7 heures, s'il vous plaît?** could I have an alarm call at 7am, please?

réveillon [Revεjɔ̃] *nm* Christmas Eve; (*de la Saint-Sylvestre*) New Year's Eve; **réveillonner** *vi* to celebrate Christmas Eve (*ou* New Year's Eve)

révélateur, -trice [RevelatœR, tRis] *adj*: **~ (de qch)** revealing (sth)

révéler [Revele] *vt* to reveal; **se révéler** *vi* to be revealed, reveal itself ▷ *vb +attrib*: **se ~**

difficile/aisé to prove difficult/easy
revenant, e [R(ə)vənã, ãt] nm/f ghost
revendeur, -euse [R(ə)vãdœR, øz] nm/f
(détaillant) retailer; (de drogue) (drug-)dealer
revendication [R(ə)vãdikasjɔ̃] nf claim,
demand
revendiquer [R(ə)vãdike] vt to claim,
demand; (responsabilité) to claim
revendre [R(ə)vãdR] vt (d'occasion) to resell;
(détailler) to sell; **à ~** (en abondance) to spare
revenir [Rəv(ə)niR] vi to come back; (coûter):
~ cher/à 100 euros (à qn) to cost (sb) a
lot/100 euros; **~ à** (reprendre: études, projet) to
return to, go back to; (équivaloir à) to amount
to; **~ à qn** (part, honneur) to go to sb, be sb's;
(souvenir, nom) to come back to sb; **~ sur**
(question, sujet) to go back over; (engagement)
to go back on; **~ à soi** to come round; **n'en**
pas ~: je n'en reviens pas I can't get over
it; **~ sur ses pas** to retrace one's steps; **cela**
revient à dire que/au même it amounts to
saying that/the same thing; **faire ~** (Culin)
to brown
revenu [Rəv(ə)ny] nm income; **revenus** nmpl
income sg
rêver [Reve] vi, vt to dream; **~ de/à** to dream of
réverbère [ReveRbɛR] nm street lamp ou light;
réverbérer vt to reflect
revers [R(ə)vɛR] nm (de feuille, main) back;
(d'étoffe) wrong side; (de pièce, médaille) back,
reverse; (Tennis, Ping-Pong) backhand; (de veste)
lapel; (fig: échec) setback
revêtement [R(ə)vɛtmã] nm (des sols)
flooring; (de chaussée) surface
revêtir [R(ə)vetiR] vt (habit) to don, put on;
(prendre: importance, apparence) to take on; **~**
qch de to cover sth with
rêveur, -euse [RevœR, øz] adj dreamy ▷ nm/f
dreamer
revient [Rəvjɛ̃] vb voir **revenir**
revigorer [R(ə)vigoRe] vt (air frais) to
invigorate, brace up; (repas, boisson) to revive,
buck up
revirement [R(ə)viRmã] nm change of mind;
(d'une situation) reversal
réviser [Revize] vt to revise; (machine) to
overhaul, service
révision [Revizjɔ̃] nf revision; (de voiture)
servicing no pl
revivre [R(ə)vivR] vi (reprendre des forces) to
come alive again ▷ vt (épreuve, moment) to
relive
revoir [RəvwaR] vt to see again; (réviser) to
revise ▷ nm: **au ~** goodbye
révoltant, e [Revoltã, ãt] adj revolting,
appalling
révolte [Revolt] nf rebellion, revolt
révolter [Revolte] vt to revolt; **se révolter**
(contre) to rebel (against)

révolu, e [Revoly] adj past; (Admin): **âgé de 18**
ans ~s over 18 years of age
révolution [Revolysjɔ̃] nf revolution;
révolutionnaire adj, nm/f revolutionary
revolver [RevolvɛR] nm gun; (à barillet)
revolver
révoquer [Revoke] vt (fonctionnaire) to
dismiss; (arrêt, contrat) to revoke
revue [R(ə)vy] nf review; (périodique) review,
magazine; (de music-hall) variety show; **passer**
en ~ (mentalement) to go through
rez-de-chaussée [Red(ə)ʃose] nm inv ground
floor
RF sigle f = **République française**
Rhin [Rɛ̃] nm Rhine
rhinocéros [RinoseRos] nm rhinoceros
Rhône [Ron] nm Rhone
rhubarbe [RybaRb] nf rhubarb
rhum [Rom] nm rum
rhumatisme [Rymatism] nm
rheumatism no pl
rhume [Rym] nm cold; **rhume de cerveau**
head cold; **le rhume des foins** hay fever
ricaner [Rikane] vi (avec méchanceté) to
snigger; (bêtement) to giggle
riche [Riʃ] adj rich; (personne, pays) rich,
wealthy; **~ en** rich in; **richesse** nf wealth;
(fig: de sol, musée etc) richness; **richesses** nfpl
(ressources, argent) wealth sg; (fig: trésors)
treasures
ricochet [Rikoʃɛ] nm: **faire des ~s** to skip
stones
ride [Rid] nf wrinkle
rideau, x [Rido] nm curtain; **rideau de fer**
(boutique) metal shutter(s)
rider [Ride] vt to wrinkle; **se rider** vi to
become wrinkled
ridicule [Ridikyl] adj ridiculous ▷ nm:
le ~ ridicule; **ridiculiser** vt to ridicule; **se**
ridiculiser vi to make a fool of o.s.

⊙ **MOT-CLÉ**

rien [Rjɛ̃] pron 1: **(ne) ... rien** nothing, tournure
négative + anything; **qu'est-ce que vous avez?**
— rien what have you got? — nothing; **il n'a**
rien dit/fait he said/did nothing; he hasn't
said/done anything; **n'avoir peur de rien** to
be afraid ou frightened of nothing, not to be
afraid ou frightened of anything; **il n'a rien**
(n'est pas blessé) he's all right; **ça ne fait rien** it
doesn't matter; **de rien!** not at all!
2: **rien de: rien d'intéressant** nothing
interesting; **rien d'autre** nothing else; **rien du**
tout nothing at all
3: **rien que** just, only; nothing but; **rien que**
pour lui faire plaisir only ou just to please
him; **rien que la vérité** nothing but the truth;
rien que cela that alone

▷ *nm*: **un petit rien** (*cadeau*) a little something; **des riens** trivia *pl*; **un rien de** a hint of; **en un rien de temps** in no time at all

rieur, -euse [ʀ(i)jœʀ, ʀ(i)jøz] *adj* cheerful
rigide [ʀiʒid] *adj* stiff; (*fig*) rigid; strict
rigoler [ʀigɔle] *vi* (*fam: rire*) to laugh; (*s'amuser*) to have (some) fun; (*plaisanter*) to be joking *ou* kidding; **rigolo, -ote** (*fam*) *adj* funny ▷ *nm/f* comic; (*péj*) fraud, phoney
rigoureusement [ʀiguʀøzmɑ̃] *adv* (*vrai*) absolutely; (*interdit*) strictly
rigoureux, -euse [ʀiguʀø, øz] *adj* rigorous; (*hiver*) hard, harsh
rigueur [ʀigœʀ] *nf* rigour; **"tenue de soirée de ~"** "formal dress only"; **à la ~** at a pinch; **tenir ~ à qn de qch** to hold sth against sb
rillettes [ʀijɛt] *nfpl* potted meat (*made from pork or goose*)
rime [ʀim] *nf* rhyme
rinçage [ʀɛ̃saʒ] *nm* rinsing (out); (*opération*) rinse
rincer [ʀɛ̃se] *vt* to rinse; (*récipient*) to rinse out
ringard, e [ʀɛ̃gaʀ, aʀd] (*fam*) *adj* old-fashioned
riposter [ʀipɔste] *vi* to retaliate ▷ *vt*: **~ que** to retort that
rire [ʀiʀ] *vi* to laugh; (*se divertir*) to have fun ▷ *nm* laugh; **le ~** laughter; **~ de** to laugh at; **pour ~** (*pas sérieusement*) for a joke *ou* a laugh
risible [ʀizibl] *adj* laughable
risque [ʀisk] *nm* risk; **le ~** danger; **à ses ~s et périls** at his own risk; **risqué, e** *adj* risky; (*plaisanterie*) risqué, daring; **risquer** *vt* to risk; (*allusion, question*) to venture, hazard; **ça ne risque rien** it's quite safe; **risquer de**: **il risque de se tuer** he could get himself killed; **ce qui risque de se produire** what might *ou* could well happen; **il ne risque pas de recommencer** there's no chance of him doing that again; **se risquer à faire** (*tenter*) to venture *ou* dare to do
rissoler [ʀisɔle] *vi, vt*: **(faire) ~** to brown
ristourne [ʀistuʀn] *nf* discount
rite [ʀit] *nm* rite; (*fig*) ritual
rivage [ʀivaʒ] *nm* shore
rival, e, -aux [ʀival, o] *adj, nm/f* rival; **rivaliser** *vi*: **rivaliser avec** (*personne*) to rival, vie with; **rivalité** *nf* rivalry
rive [ʀiv] *nf* shore; (*de fleuve*) bank; **riverain, e** *nm/f* riverside (*ou* lakeside) resident; (*d'une route*) local resident
rivière [ʀivjɛʀ] *nf* river
riz [ʀi] *nm* rice; **rizière** *nf* paddy-field, ricefield
RMI *sigle m* (= *revenu minimum d'insertion*) ≈ income support (BRIT), ≈ welfare (US)
RN *sigle f* = **route nationale**
robe [ʀɔb] *nf* dress; (*de juge*) robe; (*pelage*) coat; **robe de chambre** dressing gown; **robe**

de mariée wedding dress; **robe de soirée** evening dress
robinet [ʀɔbinɛ] *nm* tap (BRIT), faucet (US)
robot [ʀɔbo] *nm* robot; **robot de cuisine** food processor
robuste [ʀɔbyst] *adj* robust, sturdy; **robustesse** *nf* robustness, sturdiness
roc [ʀɔk] *nm* rock
rocade [ʀɔkad] *nf* bypass
rocaille [ʀɔkaj] *nf* loose stones *pl*; (*jardin*) rockery, rock garden
roche [ʀɔʃ] *nf* rock
rocher [ʀɔʃe] *nm* rock
rocheux, -euse [ʀɔʃø, øz] *adj* rocky
rodage [ʀɔdaʒ] *nm*: **en ~** running in
rôder [ʀode] *vi* to roam about; (*de façon suspecte*) to lurk (about *ou* around); **rôdeur, -euse** *nm/f* prowler
rogne [ʀɔɲ] (*fam*) *nf*: **être en ~** to be in a temper
rogner [ʀɔɲe] *vt* to clip; **~ sur** (*fig*) to cut down *ou* back on
rognons [ʀɔɲɔ̃] *nmpl* (Culin) kidneys
roi [ʀwa] *nm* king; **la fête des Rois, les Rois** Twelfth Night
rôle [ʀol] *nm* role, part
rollers [ʀɔlœʀ] *nmpl* Rollerblades®
romain, e [ʀɔmɛ̃, ɛn] *adj* Roman ▷ *nm/f*: **R~, e** Roman
roman, e [ʀɔmɑ̃, an] *adj* (Archit) Romanesque ▷ *nm* novel; **roman policier** detective story
romancer [ʀɔmɑ̃se] *vt* (*agrémenter*) to romanticize; **romancier, -ière** *nm/f* novelist; **romanesque** *adj* (*amours, aventures*) storybook *cpd*; (*sentimental: personne*) romantic
roman-feuilleton [ʀɔmɑ̃fœjtɔ̃] *nm* serialized novel
romanichel, le [ʀɔmaniʃɛl] (*péj*) *nm/f* gipsy
romantique [ʀɔmɑ̃tik] *adj* romantic
romarin [ʀɔmaʀɛ̃] *nm* rosemary
Rome [ʀɔm] *n* Rome
rompre [ʀɔ̃pʀ] *vt* to break; (*entretien, fiançailles*) to break off ▷ *vi* (*fiancés*) to break it off; **se rompre** *vi* to break; **rompu, e** *adj* (*fourbu*) exhausted
ronces [ʀɔ̃s] *nfpl* brambles
ronchonner [ʀɔ̃ʃɔne] (*fam*) *vi* to grouse, grouch
rond, e [ʀɔ̃, ʀɔ̃d] *adj* round; (*joues, mollets*) well-rounded; (*fam: ivre*) tight ▷ *nm* (*cercle*) ring; (*fam: sou*): **je n'ai plus un ~** I haven't a penny left; **en ~** (*s'asseoir, danser*) in a ring; **ronde** *nf* (*gén: de surveillance*) rounds *pl*, patrol; (*danse*) round (dance); (Mus) semibreve (BRIT), whole note (US); **à la ronde** (*alentour*): **à 10 km à la ronde** for 10 km round; **rondelet, te** *adj* plump
rondelle [ʀɔ̃dɛl] *nf* (*tranche*) slice, round; (Tech) washer

rond-point [ʀɔ̃pwɛ̃] *nm* roundabout
ronflement [ʀɔ̃fləmɑ̃] *nm* snore, snoring
ronfler [ʀɔ̃fle] *vi* to snore; *(moteur, poêle)* to hum
ronger [ʀɔ̃ʒe] *vt* to gnaw (at); *(suj: vers, rouille)* to eat into; **se ~ les ongles** to bite one's nails; **se ~ les sangs** to worry o.s. sick; **rongeur** *nm* rodent
ronronner [ʀɔ̃ʀɔne] *vi* to purr
rosbif [ʀɔsbif] *nm*: **du ~** roasting beef; *(cuit)* roast beef
rose [ʀoz] *nf* rose ▷ *adj* pink; **rose bonbon** *adj inv* candy pink
rosé, e [ʀoze] *adj* pinkish; **(vin) ~** rosé
roseau, x [ʀozo] *nm* reed
rosée [ʀoze] *nf* dew
rosier [ʀozje] *nm* rosebush, rose tree
rossignol [ʀɔsiɲɔl] *nm* (*Zool*) nightingale
rotation [ʀɔtasjɔ̃] *nf* rotation
roter [ʀɔte] *(fam) vi* to burp, belch
rôti [ʀoti] *nm*: **du ~** roasting meat; *(cuit)* roast meat; **un ~ de bœuf/porc** a joint of beef/pork
rotin [ʀɔtɛ̃] *nm* rattan (cane); **fauteuil en ~** cane (arm)chair
rôtir [ʀotiʀ] *vi, vt (aussi*: **faire ~**) to roast; **rôtisserie** *nf (restaurant)* steakhouse; *(traiteur)* roast meat shop; **rôtissoire** *nf* (roasting) spit
rotule [ʀɔtyl] *nf* kneecap
rouage [ʀwaʒ] *nm* cog(wheel), gearwheel; **les ~s de l'État** the wheels of State
roue [ʀu] *nf* wheel; **roue de secours** spare wheel
rouer [ʀwe] *vt*: **~ qn de coups** to give sb a thrashing
rouge [ʀuʒ] *adj, nm/f* red ▷ *nm* red; **(vin) ~** red wine; **sur la liste ~** ex-directory *(BRIT)*, unlisted *(US)*; **passer au ~** *(signal)* to go red; *(automobiliste)* to go through a red light; **rouge à joue** blusher; **rouge (à lèvres)** lipstick; **rouge-gorge** *nm* robin (redbreast)
rougeole [ʀuʒɔl] *nf* measles *sg*
rougeoyer [ʀuʒwaje] *vi* to glow red
rouget [ʀuʒɛ] *nm* mullet
rougeur [ʀuʒœʀ] *nf* redness; *(Méd: tache)* red blotch
rougir [ʀuʒiʀ] *vi* to turn red; *(de honte, timidité)* to blush, flush; *(de plaisir, colère)* to flush
rouille [ʀuj] *nf* rust; **rouillé, e** *adj* rusty; **rouiller** *vt* to rust ▷ *vi* to rust, go rusty
roulant, e [ʀulɑ̃, ɑ̃t] *adj (meuble)* on wheels; *(tapis etc)* moving; **escalier ~** escalator
rouleau, x [ʀulo] *nm* roll; *(à mise en plis, à peinture, vague)* roller; **rouleau à pâtisserie** rolling pin
roulement [ʀulmɑ̃] *nm (rotation)* rotation; *(bruit)* rumbling *no pl*, rumble; **travailler par ~** to work on a rota *(BRIT) ou* rotation *(US)* basis; **roulement (à billes)** ball bearings *pl*;

roulement de tambour drum roll
rouler [ʀule] *vt* to roll; *(papier, tapis)* to roll up; *(Culin: pâte)* to roll out; *(fam: duper)* to do, con ▷ *vi (bille, boule)* to roll; *(voiture, train)* to go, run; *(automobiliste)* to drive; *(bateau)* to roll; **se ~ dans** *(boue)* to roll in; *(couverture)* to roll o.s. (up) in
roulette [ʀulɛt] *nf (de table, fauteuil)* castor; *(de dentiste)* drill; *(jeu)* roulette; **à ~s** on castors; **ça a marché comme sur des ~s** *(fam)* it went off very smoothly
roulis [ʀuli] *nm* roll(ing)
roulotte [ʀulɔt] *nf* caravan
roumain, e [ʀumɛ̃, ɛn] *adj* Rumanian ▷ *nm/f*: **R~, e** Rumanian
Roumanie [ʀumani] *nf* Rumania
rouquin, e [ʀukɛ̃, in] *(péj) nm/f* redhead
rouspéter [ʀuspete] *(fam) vi* to moan
rousse [ʀus] *adj voir* **roux**
roussir [ʀusiʀ] *vt* to scorch ▷ *vi (Culin)*: **faire ~** to brown
route [ʀut] *nf* road; *(fig: chemin)* way; *(itinéraire, parcours)* route; *(fig: voie)* road, path; **il y a 3h de ~** it's a 3-hour ride *ou* journey; **en ~** on the way; **en ~!** let's go!; **mettre en ~** to start up; **se mettre en ~** to set off; **quelle ~ dois-je prendre pour aller à ...?** which road do I take for ...?; **route nationale** ≈ A road *(BRIT)*, ≈ state highway *(US)*; **routier, -ière** *adj* road *cpd* ▷ *nm (camionneur)* (long-distance) lorry *(BRIT) ou* truck *(US)* driver; *(restaurant)* ≈ transport café *(BRIT)*, ≈ truck stop *(US)*
routine [ʀutin] *nf* routine; **routinier, -ière** *(péj) adj (activité)* humdrum; *(personne)* addicted to routine
rouvrir [ʀuvʀiʀ] *vt, vi* to reopen, open again; **se rouvrir** *vi* to reopen, open again
roux, rousse [ʀu, ʀus] *adj* red; *(personne)* red-haired ▷ *nm/f* redhead
royal, e, -aux [ʀwajal, o] *adj* royal; *(cadeau etc)* fit for a king
royaume [ʀwajom] *nm* kingdom; *(fig)* realm; **le Royaume-Uni** the United Kingdom
royauté [ʀwajote] *nf (régime)* monarchy
ruban [ʀybɑ̃] *nm* ribbon; **ruban adhésif** adhesive tape
rubéole [ʀybeɔl] *nf* German measles *sg*, rubella
rubis [ʀybi] *nm* ruby
rubrique [ʀybʀik] *nf (titre, catégorie)* heading; *(Presse: article)* column
ruche [ʀyʃ] *nf* hive
rude [ʀyd] *adj (au toucher)* rough; *(métier, tâche)* hard, tough; *(climat)* severe, harsh; *(bourru)* harsh, rough; *(fruste: manières)* rugged, tough; *(fam: fameux)* jolly good; **rudement** *(fam) adv (très)* terribly
rudimentaire [ʀydimɑ̃tɛʀ] *adj* rudimentary, basic

rudiments [ʀydimã] *nmpl*: **avoir des ~ d'anglais** to have a smattering of English
rue [ʀy] *nf* street
ruée [ʀɥe] *nf* rush
ruelle [ʀɥɛl] *nf* alley(-way)
ruer [ʀɥe] *vi* (*cheval*) to kick out; **se ruer** *vi*: **se ~ sur** to pounce on; **se ~ vers/dans/hors de** to rush *ou* dash towards/into/out of
rugby [ʀygbi] *nm* rugby (football)
rugir [ʀyʒiʀ] *vi* to roar
rugueux, -euse [ʀygø, øz] *adj* rough
ruine [ʀɥin] *nf* ruin; **ruiner** *vt* to ruin; **ruineux, -euse** *adj* ruinous
ruisseau, x [ʀɥiso] *nm* stream, brook
ruisseler [ʀɥis(ə)le] *vi* to stream
rumeur [ʀymœʀ] *nf* (*nouvelle*) rumour; (*bruit confus*) rumbling
ruminer [ʀymine] *vt* (*herbe*) to ruminate; (*fig*) to ruminate on *ou* over, chew over
rupture [ʀyptyʀ] *nf* (*séparation, désunion*) break-up, split; (*de négociations etc*) breakdown; (*de contrat*) breach; (*dans continuité*) break
rural, e, -aux [ʀyʀal, o] *adj* rural, country *cpd*
ruse [ʀyz] *nf*: **la ~** cunning, craftiness; (*pour tromper*) trickery; **une ~** a trick, a ruse; **rusé, e** *adj* cunning, crafty
russe [ʀys] *adj* Russian ▷ *nm/f*: **R~** Russian ▷ *nm* (*Ling*) Russian
Russie [ʀysi] *nf*: **la ~** Russia
rustine® [ʀystin] *nf* rubber repair patch (for bicycle tyre)
rustique [ʀystik] *adj* rustic
rythme [ʀitm] *nm* rhythm; (*vitesse*) rate; (: *de la vie*) pace, tempo; **rythmé, e** *adj* rhythmic(al)

s' [s] *pron voir* **se**
sa [sa] *adj voir* **son¹**
sable [sɑbl] *nm* sand
sablé [sɑble] *nm* shortbread biscuit
sabler [sɑble] *vt* (*contre le verglas*) to grit; **~ le champagne** to drink champagne
sabot [sabo] *nm* clog; (*de cheval*) hoof; **sabot de frein** brake shoe
saboter [sabɔte] *vt* to sabotage; (*bâcler*) to make a mess of, botch
sac [sak] *nm* bag; (*à charbon etc*) sack; **mettre à ~** to sack; **sac à dos** rucksack; **sac à main** handbag; **sac de couchage** sleeping bag; **sac de voyage** travelling bag
saccadé, e [sakade] *adj* jerky; (*respiration*) spasmodic
saccager [sakaʒe] *vt* (*piller*) to sack; (*dévaster*) to create havoc in
saccharine [sakaʀin] *nf* saccharin
sachet [saʃɛ] *nm* (small) bag; (*de sucre, café*) sachet; **du potage en ~** packet soup; **sachet de thé** tea bag
sacoche [sakɔʃ] *nf* (*gén*) bag; (*de bicyclette*) saddlebag
sacré, e [sakʀe] *adj* sacred; (*fam: satané*) blasted; (: *fameux*): **un ~ toupet** a heck of a cheek
sacrement [sakʀəmã] *nm* sacrament
sacrifice [sakʀifis] *nm* sacrifice; **sacrifier** *vt* to sacrifice

sacristie [sakʀisti] *nf* (*catholique*) sacristy; (*protestante*) vestry

sadique [sadik] *adj* sadistic

safran [safʀɑ̃] *nm* saffron

sage [saʒ] *adj* wise; (*enfant*) good

sage-femme [saʒfam] *nf* midwife

sagesse [saʒɛs] *nf* wisdom

Sagittaire [saʒitɛʀ] *nm*: **le ~** Sagittarius

Sahara [saaʀa] *nm*: **le ~** the Sahara (desert)

saignant, e [sɛɲɑ̃, ɑ̃t] *adj* (*viande*) rare

saigner [seɲe] *vi* to bleed ▷ *vt* to bleed; (*animal*) to kill (by bleeding); **~ du nez** to have a nosebleed

saillir [sajiʀ] *vi* to project, stick out; (*veine, muscle*) to bulge

sain, e [sɛ̃, sɛn] *adj* healthy; **~ et sauf** safe and sound, unharmed; **~ d'esprit** sound in mind, sane

saindoux [sɛ̃du] *nm* lard

saint, e [sɛ̃, sɛ̃t] *adj* holy ▷ *nm/f* saint; **le Saint Esprit** the Holy Spirit *ou* Ghost; **la Sainte Vierge** the Blessed Virgin; **la Saint-Sylvestre** New Year's Eve; **sainteté** *nf* holiness

sais *etc* [sɛ] *vb voir* **savoir**

saisie [sezi] *nf* seizure; **saisie (de données)** (data) capture

saisir [seziʀ] *vt* to take hold of, grab; (*fig: occasion; comprendre*) to grasp; (*entendre*) to get, catch; (*données*) to capture; (*Culin*) to fry quickly; (*Jur: biens, publication*) to seize; **saisissant, e** *adj* startling, striking

saison [sɛzɔ̃] *nf* season; **haute/basse/morte ~** high/low/slack season; **saisonnier, -ière** *adj* seasonal

salade [salad] *nf* (*Bot*) lettuce *etc*; (*Culin*) (green) salad; (*fam: confusion*) tangle, muddle; **salade composée** mixed salad; **salade de fruits** fruit salad; **saladier** *nm* (salad) bowl

salaire [salɛʀ] *nm* (*annuel, mensuel*) salary; (*hebdomadaire, journalier*) pay, wages *pl*; **salaire minimum interprofessionnel de croissance** index-linked guaranteed minimum wage

salarié, e [salaʀje] *nm/f* salaried employee; wage-earner

salaud [salo] (*fam!*) *nm* sod (!), bastard (!)

sale [sal] *adj* dirty, filthy; (*fam: mauvais*) nasty

salé, e [sale] *adj* (*mer, goût*) salty; (*Culin: amandes, beurre etc*) salted; (: *gâteaux*) savoury; (*fam: grivois*) spicy; (: *facture*) steep

saler [sale] *vt* to salt

saleté [salte] *nf* (*état*) dirtiness; (*crasse*) dirt, filth; (*tache etc*) dirt *no pl*; (*fam: méchanceté*) dirty trick; (: *camelote*) rubbish *no pl*; (: *obscénité*) filthy thing (to say)

salière [saljɛʀ] *nf* saltcellar

salir [saliʀ] *vt* to (make) dirty; (*fig: quelqu'un*) to soil the reputation of; **se salir** *vi* to get dirty; **salissant, e** *adj* (*tissu*) which shows the dirt; (*travail*) dirty, messy

salle [sal] *nf* room; (*d'hôpital*) ward; (*de restaurant*) dining room; (*d'un cinéma*) auditorium; (: *public*) audience; **salle à manger** dining room; **salle d'attente** waiting room; **salle de bain(s)** bathroom; **salle de classe** classroom; **salle de concert** concert hall; **salle d'eau** shower-room; **salle d'embarquement** (*à l'aéroport*) departure lounge; **salle de jeux** (*pour enfants*) playroom; **salle de séjour** living room; **salle des ventes** saleroom

salon [salɔ̃] *nm* lounge, sitting room; (*mobilier*) lounge suite; (*exposition*) exhibition, show; **salon de coiffure** hairdressing salon; **salon de thé** tearoom

salope [salɔp] (*fam!*) *nf* bitch (!); **saloperie** (*fam!*) *nf* (*action*) dirty trick; (*chose sans valeur*) rubbish *no pl*

salopette [salɔpɛt] *nf* dungarees *pl*; (*d'ouvrier*) overall(s)

salsifis [salsifi] *nm* salsify

salubre [salybʀ] *adj* healthy, salubrious

saluer [salɥe] *vt* (*pour dire bonjour, fig*) to greet; (*pour dire au revoir*) to take one's leave; (*Mil*) to salute

salut [saly] *nm* (*geste*) wave; (*parole*) greeting; (*Mil*) salute; (*sauvegarde*) safety; (*Rel*) salvation ▷ *excl* (*fam: bonjour*) hi (there); (: *au revoir*) see you, bye

salutations [salytasjɔ̃] *nfpl* greetings; **Veuillez agréer, Monsieur, mes ~ distinguées** yours faithfully

samedi [samdi] *nm* Saturday

SAMU [samy] *sigle m* (= *service d'assistance médicale d'urgence*) ≈ ambulance (service) (BRIT), ≈ paramedics *pl* (US)

sanction [sɑ̃ksjɔ̃] *nf* sanction; **sanctionner** *vt* (*loi, usage*) to sanction; (*punir*) to punish

sandale [sɑ̃dal] *nf* sandal

sandwich [sɑ̃dwi(t)ʃ] *nm* sandwich; **je voudrais un ~ au jambon/fromage** I'd like a ham/cheese sandwich

sang [sɑ̃] *nm* blood; **en ~** covered in blood; **se faire du mauvais ~** to fret, get in a state; **sang-froid** *nm* calm, sangfroid; **de sang-froid** in cold blood; **sanglant, e** *adj* bloody

sangle [sɑ̃gl] *nf* strap

sanglier [sɑ̃glije] *nm* (wild) boar

sanglot [sɑ̃glo] *nm* sob; **sangloter** *vi* to sob

sangsue [sɑ̃sy] *nf* leech

sanguin, e [sɑ̃gɛ̃, in] *adj* blood *cpd*

sanitaire [sanitɛʀ] *adj* health *cpd*; **sanitaires** *nmpl* (*lieu*) bathroom *sg*

sans [sɑ̃] *prép* without; **un pull ~ manches** a sleeveless jumper; **~ faute** without fail; **~ arrêt** without a break; **~ ça** (*fam*) otherwise; **~ qu'il s'en aperçoive** without him *ou* his noticing; **sans-abri** *nmpl* homeless; **sans-**

emploi nm/f inv unemployed person; **les sans-emploi** the unemployed; **sans-gêne** adj inv inconsiderate

santé [sɑ̃te] nf health; **en bonne ~** in good health; **boire à la ~ de qn** to drink (to) sb's health; **à ta/votre ~!** cheers!

saoudien, ne [saudjɛ̃, jɛn] adj Saudi Arabian
▷ nm/f: **S~, ne** Saudi Arabian

saoul, e [su, sul] adj = **soûl**

saper [sape] vt to undermine, sap

sapeur-pompier [sapœʀpɔ̃pje] nm fireman

saphir [safiʀ] nm sapphire

sapin [sapɛ̃] nm fir (tree); (bois) fir; **sapin de Noël** Christmas tree

sarcastique [saʀkastik] adj sarcastic

Sardaigne [saʀdɛɲ] nf: **la ~** Sardinia

sardine [saʀdin] nf sardine

SARL sigle f (= société à responsabilité limitée) ≈ plc (BRIT), ≈ Inc. (US)

sarrasin [saʀazɛ̃] nm buckwheat

satané, e [satane] (fam) adj confounded

satellite [satelit] nm satellite

satin [satɛ̃] nm satin

satire [satiʀ] nf satire; **satirique** adj satirical

satisfaction [satisfaksjɔ̃] nf satisfaction

satisfaire [satisfɛʀ] vt to satisfy; **~ à** (conditions) to meet; **satisfaisant, e** adj (acceptable) satisfactory; **satisfait, e** adj satisfied; **satisfait de** happy ou satisfied with

saturer [satyʀe] vt to saturate

sauce [sos] nf sauce; (avec un rôti) gravy; **sauce tomate** tomato sauce; **saucière** nf sauceboat

saucisse [sosis] nf sausage

saucisson [sosisɔ̃] nm (slicing) sausage

sauf, sauve [sof, sov] adj unharmed, unhurt; (fig: honneur) intact, saved ▷ prép except; **laisser la vie sauve à qn** to spare sb's life; **~ si** (à moins que) unless; **~ erreur** if I'm not mistaken; **~ avis contraire** unless you hear to the contrary

sauge [soʒ] nf sage

saugrenu, e [sogʀəny] adj preposterous

saule [sol] nm willow (tree)

saumon [somɔ̃] nm salmon inv

saupoudrer [sopudʀe] vt: **~ qch de** to sprinkle sth with

saur [sɔʀ] adj m: **hareng ~** smoked herring, kipper

saut [so] nm jump; (discipline sportive) jumping; **faire un ~ chez qn** to pop over to sb's (place); **saut à l'élastique** bungee jumping; **saut à la perche** pole vaulting; **saut en hauteur/longueur** high/long jump; **saut périlleux** somersault

sauter [sote] vi to jump, leap; (exploser) to blow up, explode; (: fusibles) to blow; (se détacher) to pop out (ou off) ▷ vt to jump (over), leap (over); (fig: omettre) to skip, miss

(out); **faire ~** to blow up; (Culin) to sauté; **~ à la corde** to skip; **~ au cou de qn** to fly into sb's arms; **~ sur une occasion** to jump at an opportunity; **~ aux yeux** to be (quite) obvious

sauterelle [sotʀɛl] nf grasshopper

sautiller [sotije] vi (oiseau) to hop; (enfant) to skip

sauvage [sovaʒ] adj (gén) wild; (peuplade) savage; (farouche: personne) unsociable; (barbare) wild, savage; (non officiel) unauthorized, unofficial; **faire du camping ~** to camp in the wild ▷ nm/f savage; (timide) unsociable type

sauve [sov] adj f voir **sauf**

sauvegarde [sovgaʀd] nf safeguard; (Inform) backup; **sauvegarder** vt to safeguard; (Inform: enregistrer) to save; (: copier) to back up

sauve-qui-peut [sovkipø] excl run for your life!

sauver [sove] vt to save; (porter secours à) to rescue; (récupérer) to salvage, rescue; **se sauver** vi (s'enfuir) to run away; (fam: partir) to be off; **sauvetage** nm rescue; **sauveteur** nm rescuer; **sauvette: à la sauvette** adv (se marier etc) hastily, hurriedly; **sauveur** nm saviour (BRIT), savior (US)

savant, e [savɑ̃, ɑ̃t] adj scholarly, learned ▷ nm scientist

saveur [savœʀ] nf flavour; (fig) savour

savoir [savwaʀ] vt to know; (être capable de): **il sait nager** he can swim ▷ nm knowledge; **se savoir** vi (être connu) to be known; **je ne sais pas** I don't know; **je ne sais pas parler français** I don't speak French; **savez-vous où je peux ...?** do you know where I can ...?; **je n'en sais rien** I (really) don't know; **à ~** that is, namely; **faire ~ qch à qn** to let sb know sth; **pas que je sache** not as far as I know

savon [savɔ̃] nm (produit) soap; (morceau) bar of soap; (fam): **passer un ~ à qn** to give sb a good dressing-down; **savonner** vt to soap; **savonnette** nf bar of soap

savourer [savuʀe] vt to savour; **savoureux, -euse** adj tasty; (fig: anecdote) spicy, juicy

saxo(phone) [saksɔ(fɔn)] nm sax(ophone)

scabreux, -euse [skabʀø, øz] adj risky; (indécent) improper, shocking

scandale [skɑ̃dal] nm scandal; **faire un ~** (scène) to make a scene; (Jur) to create a disturbance; **faire ~** to scandalize people; **scandaleux, -euse** adj scandalous, outrageous

scandinave [skɑ̃dinav] adj Scandinavian ▷ nm/f: **S~** Scandinavian

Scandinavie [skɑ̃dinavi] nf Scandinavia

scarabée [skaʀabe] nm beetle

scarlatine [skaʀlatin] nf scarlet fever

scarole [skaʀɔl] nf endive

sceau, x [so] nm seal

sceller [sele] vt to seal
scénario [senaʀjo] nm scenario
scène [sɛn] nf (gén) scene; (estrade, fig: théâtre) stage; **entrer en ~** to come on stage; **mettre en ~** (Théâtre) to stage; (Cinéma) to direct; **faire une ~ (à qn)** to make a scene (with sb); **scène de ménage** domestic scene
sceptique [sɛptik] adj sceptical
schéma [ʃema] nm (diagramme) diagram, sketch; **schématique** adj diagrammatic(al), schematic; (fig) oversimplified
sciatique [sjatik] nf sciatica
scie [si] nf saw
sciemment [sjamɑ̃] adv knowingly
science [sjɑ̃s] nf science; (savoir) knowledge; **sciences humaines/sociales** social sciences; **sciences naturelles** (Scol) natural science sg, biology sg; **sciences po** political science ou studies pl; **science-fiction** nf science fiction; **scientifique** adj scientific ▷ nm/f scientist; (étudiant) science student
scier [sje] vt to saw; (retrancher) to saw off; **scierie** nf sawmill
scintiller [sɛ̃tije] vi to sparkle; (étoile) to twinkle
sciure [sjyʀ] nf: **~ (de bois)** sawdust
sclérose [skleʀoz] nf: **sclérose en plaques** multiple sclerosis
scolaire [skɔlɛʀ] adj school cpd; **scolariser** vt to provide with schooling/schools; **scolarité** nf schooling
scooter [skutœʀ] nm (motor) scooter
score [skɔʀ] nm score
scorpion [skɔʀpjɔ̃] nm (signe): **le S~** Scorpio
scotch [skɔtʃ] nm (whisky) scotch, whisky; **S~®** (adhésif) Sellotape® (BRIT), Scotch® tape (US)
scout, e [skut] adj, nm scout
script [skʀipt] nm (écriture) printing; (Cinéma) (shooting) script
scrupule [skʀypyl] nm scruple
scruter [skʀyte] vt to scrutinize; (l'obscurité) to peer into
scrutin [skʀytɛ̃] nm (vote) ballot; (ensemble des opérations) poll
sculpter [skylte] vt to sculpt; (bois) to carve; **sculpteur** nm sculptor; **sculpture** nf sculpture
SDF sigle m: **sans domicile fixe** homeless person; **les ~** the homeless

MOT-CLÉ

se [sə], **s'** pron **1** (emploi réfléchi) oneself; (: masc) himself; (: fém) herself; (: sujet non humain) itself; (: pl) themselves; **se savonner** to soap o.s.
2 (réciproque) one another, each other; **ils s'aiment** they love one another ou each other
3 (passif): **cela se répare facilement** it is easily repaired
4 (possessif): **se casser la jambe/se laver les mains** to break one's leg/wash one's hands

séance [seɑ̃s] nf (d'assemblée) meeting, session; (de tribunal) sitting, session; (musicale, Cinéma, Théâtre) performance
seau, x [so] nm bucket, pail
sec, sèche [sɛk, sɛʃ] adj dry; (raisins, figues) dried; (cœur: insensible) hard, cold ▷ nm: **tenir au ~** to keep in a dry place ▷ adv hard; **je le bois ~** I drink it straight ou neat; **à ~** (puits) dried up
sécateur [sekatœʀ] nm secateurs pl (BRIT), shears pl
sèche [sɛʃ] adj f voir **sec**; **sèche-cheveux** nm inv hair-drier; **sèche-linge** nm inv tumble dryer; **sèchement** adv (répondre) drily
sécher [seʃe] vt to dry; (dessécher: peau, blé) to dry (out); (: étang) to dry up; (fam: cours) to skip ▷ vi to dry; to dry out; to dry up; (fam: candidat) to be stumped; **se sécher** (après le bain) to dry o.s.; **sécheresse** nf dryness; (absence de pluie) drought; **séchoir** nm drier
second, e¹ [s(ə)gɔ̃, ɔ̃d] adj second ▷ nm (assistant) second in command; (Navig) first mate ▷ nf (Scol) year 11 (BRIT), tenth grade (US); (Aviat, Rail etc) second class; **voyager en ~e** to travel second-class; **secondaire** adj secondary; **seconde²** nf second; **seconder** vt to assist
secouer [s(ə)kwe] vt to shake; (passagers) to rock; (traumatiser) to shake (up)
secourir [s(ə)kuʀiʀ] vt (venir en aide à) to assist, aid; **secourisme** nm first aid; **secouriste** nm/f first-aid worker
secours [s(ə)kuʀ] nm help, aid, assistance ▷ nmpl aid sg; **au ~!** help!; **appeler au ~** to shout ou call for help; **porter ~ à qn** to give sb assistance, help sb; **les premiers ~** first aid sg

ÉQUIPES DE SECOURS

Emergency phone numbers can be dialled free from public phones. For the police ('la police') dial 17; for medical services ('le SAMU') dial 15; for the fire brigade ('les sapeurs pompiers'), dial 18.

secousse [s(ə)kus] nf jolt, bump; (électrique) shock; (fig: psychologique) jolt, shock
secret, -ète [səkʀɛ, ɛt] adj secret; (fig: renfermé) reticent, reserved ▷ nm secret; (discrétion absolue): **le ~** secrecy; **en ~** in secret, secretly; **secret professionel** professional secrecy
secrétaire [s(ə)kʀetɛʀ] nm/f secretary ▷ nm (meuble) writing desk; **secrétaire de direction** private ou personal secretary; **secrétaire**

d'État junior minister; **secrétariat** nm
(profession) secretarial work; (bureau) office;
(: d'organisation internationale) secretariat

secteur [sɛktœʀ] nm sector; (zone) area;
(Élec): **branché sur ~** plugged into the mains
(supply)

section [sɛksjɔ̃] nf section; (de parcours
d'autobus) fare stage; (Mil: unité) platoon;
sectionner vt to sever

sécu [seky] abr f = **sécurité sociale**

sécurité [sekyʀite] nf (absence de danger)
safety; (absence de troubles) security; **système
de ~** security system; **être en ~** to be safe; **la
sécurité routière** road safety; **la sécurité
sociale** ≈ (the) Social Security (BRIT), ≈ Welfare
(US)

sédentaire [sedɑ̃tɛʀ] adj sedentary

séduction [sedyksjɔ̃] nf seduction; (charme,
attrait) appeal, charm

séduire [seduiʀ] vt to charm; (femme: abuser
de) to seduce; **séduisant, e** adj (femme)
seductive; (homme, offre) very attractive

ségrégation [segʀegasjɔ̃] nf segregation

seigle [sɛgl] nm rye

seigneur [sɛɲœʀ] nm lord

sein [sɛ̃] nm breast; (entrailles) womb; **au ~ de**
(équipe, institution) within

séisme [seism] nm earthquake

seize [sɛz] num sixteen; **seizième** num
sixteenth

séjour [seʒuʀ] nm stay; (pièce) living room;
séjourner vi to stay

sel [sɛl] nm salt; (fig: piquant) spice

sélection [selɛksjɔ̃] nf selection;
sélectionner vt to select

self-service [sɛlfsɛʀvis] adj, nm self-service

selle [sɛl] nf saddle; **selles** nfpl (Méd) stools;
seller vt to saddle

selon [s(ə)lɔ̃] prép according to; (en se
conformant à) in accordance with; **~ que**
according to whether; **~ moi** as I see it

semaine [s(ə)mɛn] nf week; **en ~** during the
week, on weekdays

semblable [sɑ̃blabl] adj similar; (de ce genre):
de ~s mésaventures such mishaps ▷ nm
fellow creature ou man; **~ à** similar to, like

semblant [sɑ̃blɑ̃] nm: **un ~ de ...** a semblance
of ...; **faire ~ (de faire)** to pretend (to do)

sembler [sɑ̃ble] vb +attrib to seem ▷ vb impers:
il semble (bien) que/inutile de it (really)
seems ou appears that/useless to; **il me
semble que** it seems to me that; **comme bon
lui semble** as he sees fit

semelle [s(ə)mɛl] nf sole; (intérieure) insole,
inner sole

semer [s(ə)me] vt to sow; (fig: éparpiller)
to scatter; (: confusion) to spread; (fam:
poursuivants) to lose, shake off; **semé de**
(difficultés) riddled with

semestre [s(ə)mɛstʀ] nm half-year; (Scol)
semester

séminaire [seminɛʀ] nm seminar

semi-remorque [səmiʀəmɔʀk] nm
articulated lorry (BRIT), semi(trailer) (US)

semoule [s(ə)mul] nf semolina

sénat [sena] nm senate; **sénateur** nm senator

Sénégal [senegal] nm: **le ~** Senegal

sens [sɑ̃s] nm (Physiol,) sense; (signification)
meaning, sense; (direction) direction; **à mon
~** to my mind; **dans le ~ des aiguilles d'une
montre** clockwise; **dans le ~ contraire des
aiguilles d'une montre** anticlockwise; **dans
le mauvais ~** (aller) the wrong way, in the
wrong direction; **le bon ~** common sense;
sens dessus dessous upside down; **sens
interdit/unique** one-way street

sensation [sɑ̃sasjɔ̃] nf sensation; **à ~** (péj)
sensational; **faire ~** to cause ou create
a sensation; **sensationnel, le** adj (fam)
fantastic, terrific

sensé, e [sɑ̃se] adj sensible

sensibiliser [sɑ̃sibilize] vt: **~ qn à** to make sb
sensitive to

sensibilité [sɑ̃sibilite] nf sensitivity

sensible [sɑ̃sibl] adj sensitive; (aux sens)
perceptible; (appréciable: différence, progrès)
appreciable, noticeable; **~ à** sensitive to;
sensiblement adv (à peu près): **ils sont
sensiblement du même âge** they are
approximately the same age; **sensiblerie** nf
sentimentality

Attention à ne pas traduire **sensible** par
le mot anglais **sensible**.

sensuel, le [sɑ̃sɥɛl] adj (personne) sensual;
(musique) sensuous

sentence [sɑ̃tɑ̃s] nf (jugement) sentence

sentier [sɑ̃tje] nm path

sentiment [sɑ̃timɑ̃] nm feeling; **recevez
mes ~s respectueux** (personne nommée)
yours sincerely; (personne non nommée)
yours faithfully; **sentimental, e, -aux** adj
sentimental; (vie, aventure) love cpd

sentinelle [sɑ̃tinɛl] nf sentry

sentir [sɑ̃tiʀ] vt (par l'odorat) to smell; (par le
goût) to taste; (au toucher, fig) to feel; (répandre
une odeur de) to smell of; (: ressemblance) to
smell like ▷ vi to smell; **~ mauvais** to smell
bad; **se ~ bien** to feel good; **se ~ mal** (être
indisposé) to feel unwell ou ill; **se ~ le courage/
la force de faire** to feel brave/strong enough
to do; **il ne peut pas le ~** (fam) he can't stand
him; **je ne me sens pas bien** I don't feel well

séparation [separasjɔ̃] nf separation;
(cloison) division, partition

séparé, e [separe] adj (distinct) separate;
(époux) separated; **séparément** adv
separately

séparer [separe] vt to separate; (désunir) to

drive apart; (*détacher*): **~ qch de** to pull sth (off)
from; **se séparer** *vi* (*époux, amis*) to separate,
part; (*se diviser: route etc*) to divide; **se ~ de**
(*époux*) to separate *ou* part from; (*employé, objet*
personnel) to part with

sept [sɛt] *num* seven; **septante** (BELGIQUE,
SUISSE) *adj inv* seventy

septembre [sɛptɑ̃bʁ] *nm* September

septicémie [sɛptisemi] *nf* blood poisoning,
septicaemia

septième [sɛtjɛm] *num* seventh

séquelles [sekɛl] *nfpl* after-effects; (*fig*)
aftermath *sg*

serbe [sɛʁb(ə)] *adj* Serbian

Serbie [sɛʁbi] *nf*: **la ~** Serbia

serein, e [səʁɛ̃, ɛn] *adj* serene

sergent [sɛʁʒɑ̃] *nm* sergeant

série [seʁi] *nf* series *inv*; (*de clés, casseroles,*
outils) set; (*catégorie: Sport*) rank; **en ~** in quick
succession; (*Comm*) mass *cpd*; **de ~** (*voiture*)
standard; **hors ~** (*Comm*) custom-built; **série**
noire (crime) thriller

sérieusement [seʁjøzmɑ̃] *adv* seriously

sérieux, -euse [seʁjø, jøz] *adj* serious; (*élève,*
employé) reliable, responsible; (*client, maison*)
reliable, dependable ▷ *nm* seriousness; (*d'une*
entreprise etc) reliability; **garder son ~** to keep
a straight face; **prendre qch/qn au ~** to take
sth/sb seriously

serin [s(ə)ʁɛ̃] *nm* canary

seringue [s(ə)ʁɛ̃g] *nf* syringe

serment [sɛʁmɑ̃] *nm* (*juré*) oath; (*promesse*)
pledge, vow

sermon [sɛʁmɔ̃] *nm* sermon

séropositif, -ive [seʁopozitif, iv] *adj* (*Méd*)
HIV positive

serpent [sɛʁpɑ̃] *nm* snake; **serpenter** *vi* to
wind

serpillière [sɛʁpijɛʁ] *nf* floorcloth

serre [sɛʁ] *nf* (*Agr*) greenhouse; **serres** *nfpl*
(*griffes*) claws, talons

serré, e [seʁe] *adj* (*habits*) tight; (*fig: lutte,*
match) tight, close-fought; (*passagers etc*)
(tightly) packed; (*réseau*) dense; **avoir le cœur**
~ to have a heavy heart

serrer [seʁe] *vt* (*tenir*) to grip *ou* hold tight;
(*comprimer, coincer*) to squeeze; (*poings,*
mâchoires) to clench; (*suj: vêtement*) to be too
tight for; (*ceinture, nœud, vis*) to tighten ▷ *vi*: **~**
à droite to keep *ou* get over to the right

serrure [seʁyʁ] *nf* lock; **serrurier** *nm*
locksmith

sert *etc* [sɛʁ] *vb voir* **servir**

servante [sɛʁvɑ̃t] *nf* (maid)servant

serveur, -euse [sɛʁvœʁ, øz] *nm/f* waiter
(waitress)

serviable [sɛʁvjabl] *adj* obliging, willing to
help

service [sɛʁvis] *nm* service; (*assortiment de*
vaisselle) set, service; (*bureau: de la vente etc*)
department, section; (*travail*) duty; **premier**
~ (*série de repas*) first sitting; **être de ~** to be on
duty; **faire le ~** to serve; **rendre un ~ à qn** to
do sb a favour; (*objet: s'avérer utile*) to come in
useful *ou* handy for sb; **mettre en ~** to put into
service *ou* operation; **~ compris/non compris**
service included/not included; **hors ~** out of
order; **service après vente** after sales service;
service d'ordre police (*ou* stewards) in charge
of maintaining order; **service militaire**
military service; *see note*; **services secrets**
secret service *sg*

SERVICE MILITAIRE

Until 1997, French men over the age of 18
who were passed as fit, and who were not
in full-time higher education, were required
to do ten months' "service militaire".
Conscientious objectors were required to
do two years' community service.
Since 1997, military service has been
suspended in France. However, all sixteen-
year-olds, both male and female, are
required to register for a compulsory one-
day training course, the "JAPD" ("journée
d'appel de préparation à la défense"), which
covers basic information on the principles
and organization of defence in France, and
also advises on career opportunities in the
military and in the voluntary sector. Young
people must attend the training day before
their eighteenth birthday.

serviette [sɛʁvjɛt] *nf* (*de table*) (table) napkin,
serviette; (*de toilette*) towel; (*porte-documents*)
briefcase; **serviette hygiénique** sanitary
towel

servir [sɛʁviʁ] *vt* to serve; (*au restaurant*) to
wait on; (*au magasin*) to serve, attend to ▷ *vi*
(*Tennis*) to serve; (*Cartes*) to deal; **se servir** *vi*
(*prendre d'un plat*) to help o.s.; **vous êtes servi?**
are you being served?; **~ à qn** (*diplôme, livre*) to
be of use to sb; **~ à qch/faire** (*outil etc*) to be
used for sth/doing; **ça ne sert à rien** it's no
use; **~ (à qn) de** to serve as (for sb); **se ~ de**
(*plat*) to help o.s. to; (*voiture, outil, relations*) to
use; **sers-toi!** help yourself!

serviteur [sɛʁvitœʁ] *nm* servant

ses [se] *adj voir* **son¹**

seuil [sœj] *nm* doorstep; (*fig*) threshold

seul, e [sœl] *adj* (*sans compagnie*) alone;
(*unique*): **un ~ livre** only one book, a single
book ▷ *adv* (*vivre*) alone, on one's own ▷ *nm,*
nf: **il en reste un(e) ~(e)** there's only one
left; **le ~ livre** the only book; **parler tout ~**
to talk to oneself; **faire qch (tout) ~** to do
sth (all) on one's own *ou* (all) by oneself; **à**

lui (tout) ~ single-handed, on his own; **se sentir ~** to feel lonely; **seulement** adv only; **non seulement ... mais aussi** ou **encore** not only ... but also

sève [sɛv] nf sap

sévère [sevɛʀ] adj severe

sexe [sɛks] nm sex; (organes génitaux) genitals, sex organs; **sexuel, le** adj sexual

shampooing [ʃɑ̃pwɛ̃] nm shampoo

Shetland [ʃɛtlɑ̃d] n: **les îles ~** the Shetland Islands, Shetland

short [ʃɔʀt] nm (pair of) shorts pl

 MOT-CLÉ

si [si] adv **1** (oui) yes; **"Paul n'est pas venu"** — **"si!"** "Paul hasn't come" — "yes, he has!"; **je vous assure que si**
I assure you he did ou she is etc
2 (tellement) so; **si gentil/rapidement** so kind/fast; **(tant et) si bien que** so much so that; **si rapide qu'il soit** however fast he may be
▷ conj if; **si tu veux** if you want; **je me demande si** I wonder if ou whether; **si seulement** if only
▷ nm (Mus) B; (en chantant la gamme) ti

Sicile [sisil] nf: **la ~** Sicily

SIDA [sida] sigle m (= syndrome immuno-déficitaire acquis) AIDS sg

sidéré, e [sideʀe] adj staggered

sidérurgie [sideʀyʀʒi] nf steel industry

siècle [sjɛkl] nm century

siège [sjɛʒ] nm seat; (d'entreprise) head office; (d'organisation) headquarters pl; (Mil) siege; **siège social** registered office; **siéger** vi to sit

sien, ne [sjɛ̃, sjɛn] pron: **le(la) ~(ne), les ~(ne)s** (homme) his; (femme) hers; (chose, animal) its

sieste [sjɛst] nf (afternoon) snooze ou nap; **faire la ~** to have a snooze ou nap

sifflement [sifləmɑ̃] nm: **un ~** a whistle

siffler [sifle] vi (gén) to whistle; (en respirant) to wheeze; (serpent, vapeur) to hiss ▷ vt (chanson) to whistle; (chien etc) to whistle for; (fille) to whistle at; (pièce, orateur) to hiss, boo; (fin du match, départ) to blow one's whistle for; (fam: verre) to guzzle

sifflet [siflɛ] nm whistle; **coup de ~** whistle

siffloter [siflɔte] vi, vt to whistle

sigle [sigl] nm acronym

signal, -aux [siɲal, o] nm signal; (indice, écriteau) sign; **donner le ~ de** to give the signal for; **signal d'alarme** alarm signal; **signalement** nm description, particulars pl

signaler [siɲale] vt to indicate; (personne: faire un signe) to signal; (vol, perte) to report; (faire remarquer): **~ qch à qn/(à qn) que** to point out

sth to sb/(to sb) that; **je voudrais ~ un vol** I'd like to report a theft

signature [siɲatyʀ] nf signature; (action) signing

signe [siɲ] nm sign; (Typo) mark; **faire un ~ de la main** to give a sign with one's hand; **faire ~ à qn** (fig: contacter) to get in touch with sb; **faire ~ à qn d'entrer** to motion (to) sb to come in; **signer** vt to sign; **se signer** vi to cross o.s.; **où dois-je signer?** where do I sign?

significatif, -ive [siɲifikatif, iv] adj significant

signification [siɲifikasjɔ̃] nf meaning

signifier [siɲifje] vt (vouloir dire) to mean; (faire connaître): **~ qch (à qn)** to make sth known (to sb)

silence [silɑ̃s] nm silence; (Mus) rest; **garder le ~** to keep silent, say nothing; **silencieux, -euse** adj quiet, silent ▷ nm silencer

silhouette [silwɛt] nf outline, silhouette; (allure) figure

sillage [sijaʒ] nm wake

sillon [sijɔ̃] nm furrow; (de disque) groove; **sillonner** vt to criss-cross

simagrées [simagʀe] nfpl fuss sg

similaire [similɛʀ] adj similar; **similicuir** nm imitation leather; **similitude** nf similarity

simple [sɛ̃pl] adj simple; (non multiple) single ▷ nm: **~ messieurs/dames** men's/ladies' singles sg ▷ nm/f: **~ d'esprit** simpleton

simplicité [sɛ̃plisite] nf simplicity; **en toute ~** quite simply

simplifier [sɛ̃plifje] vt to simplify

simuler [simyle] vt to sham, simulate

simultané, e [simyltane] adj simultaneous

sincère [sɛ̃sɛʀ] adj sincere; **sincèrement** adv sincerely; (pour parler franchement) honestly, really; **sincérité** nf sincerity

Singapour [sɛ̃gapuʀ] nm Singapore

singe [sɛ̃ʒ] nm monkey; (de grande taille) ape; **singer** vt to ape, mimic; **singeries** nfpl antics

singulariser [sɛ̃gylaʀize] vt: **se singulariser** vi to call attention to o.s.

singularité [sɛ̃gylaʀite] nf peculiarity

singulier, -ière [sɛ̃gylje, jɛʀ] adj remarkable, singular ▷ nm singular

sinistre [sinistʀ] adj sinister ▷ nm (incendie) blaze; (catastrophe) disaster; (Assurances) damage (giving rise to a claim); **sinistré, e** adj disaster-stricken ▷ nm/f disaster victim

sinon [sinɔ̃] conj (autrement, sans quoi) otherwise, or else; (sauf) except, other than; (si ce n'est) if not

sinueux, -euse [sinɥø, øz] adj winding

sinus [sinys] nm (Anat) sinus; (Géom) sine; **sinusite** nf sinusitis

sirène [siʀɛn] nf siren; **sirène d'alarme** fire alarm; (en temps de guerre) air-raid siren

sirop [siʀo] nm (à diluer: de fruit etc) syrup;

(*pharmaceutique*) syrup, mixture; **~ pour la toux** cough mixture

siroter [sirɔte] *vt* to sip

sismique [sismik] *adj* seismic

site [sit] *nm* (*paysage, environnement*) setting; (*d'une ville etc: emplacement*) site; **site (pittoresque)** beauty spot; **sites touristiques** places of interest; **site Web** (*Inform*) website

sitôt [sito] *adv*: **~ parti** as soon as he *etc* had left; **~ que** as soon as; **pas de ~** not for a long time

situation [situasjɔ̃] *nf* situation; (*d'un édifice, d'une ville*) position, location; **situation de famille** marital status

situé, e [situe] *adj* situated

situer [situe] *vt* to site, situate; (*en pensée*) to set, place; **se situer** *vi* to be situated

six [sis] *num* six; **sixième** *num* sixth ▷ *nf* (*Scol*) year 7 (*BRIT*), sixth grade (*US*)

skaï® [skaj] *nm* Leatherette®

ski [ski] *nm* (*objet*) ski; (*sport*) skiing; **faire du ~** to ski; **ski de fond** cross-country skiing; **ski nautique** water-skiing; **ski de piste** downhill skiing; **ski de randonnée** cross-country skiing; **skier** *vi* to ski; **skieur, -euse** *nm/f* skier

slip [slip] *nm* (*sous-vêtement*) pants *pl*, briefs *pl*; (*de bain: d'homme*) trunks *pl*; (: *du bikini*) (bikini) briefs *pl*

slogan [slɔgã] *nm* slogan

Slovaquie [slɔvaki] *nf*: **la ~** Slovakia

SMIC [smik] *sigle m* = **salaire minimum interprofessionnel de croissance**

smoking [smɔkiŋ] *nm* dinner *ou* evening suit

SMS *sigle m* (= *short message service*) (*service*) SMS; (*message*) text message

SNCF *sigle f* (= *Société nationale des chemins de fer français*) French railways

snob [snɔb] *adj* snobbish ▷ *nm/f* snob; **snobisme** *nm* snobbery, snobbishness

sobre [sɔbʀ] *adj* (*personne*) temperate, abstemious; (*élégance, style*) sober

sobriquet [sɔbʀikɛ] *nm* nickname

social, e, -aux [sɔsjal, jo] *adj* social

socialisme [sɔsjalism] *nm* socialism; **socialiste** *nm/f* socialist

société [sɔsjete] *nf* society; (*sportive*) club; (*Comm*) company; **la ~ de consommation** the consumer society; **société anonyme** ≈ limited (*BRIT*) *ou* incorporated (*US*) company

sociologie [sɔsjɔlɔʒi] *nf* sociology

socle [sɔkl] *nm* (*de colonne, statue*) plinth, pedestal; (*de lampe*) base

socquette [sɔkɛt] *nf* ankle sock

sœur [sœʀ] *nf* sister; (*religieuse*) nun, sister

soi [swa] *pron* oneself; **en ~** (*intrinsèquement*) in itself; **cela va de ~** that *ou* it goes without saying; **soi-disant** *adj inv* so-called ▷ *adv* supposedly

soie [swa] *nf* silk; **soierie** *nf* (*tissu*) silk

soif [swaf] *nf* thirst; **avoir ~** to be thirsty; **donner ~ à qn** to make sb thirsty

soigné, e [swaɲe] *adj* (*tenue*) well-groomed, neat; (*travail*) careful, meticulous

soigner [swaɲe] *vt* (*malade, maladie: suj: docteur*) to treat; (*suj: infirmière, mère*) to nurse, look after; (*travail, détails*) to take care over; (*jardin, invités*) to look after; **soigneux, -euse** *adj* (*propre*) tidy, neat; (*appliqué*) painstaking, careful

soi-même [swamɛm] *pron* oneself

soin [swɛ̃] *nm* (*application*) care; (*propreté, ordre*) tidiness, neatness; **soins** *nmpl* (*à un malade, blessé*) treatment *sg*, medical attention *sg*; (*hygiène*) care *sg*; **prendre ~ de** to take care of, look after; **prendre ~ de faire** to take care to do; **les premiers ~s** first aid *sg*

soir [swaʀ] *nm* evening; **ce ~** this evening, tonight; **à ce ~!** see you this evening (*ou* tonight)!; **sept/dix heures du ~** seven in the evening/ten at night; **demain ~** tomorrow evening, tomorrow night; **soirée** *nf* evening; (*réception*) party

soit¹ [swa] *vb voir* **être** ▷ *conj* (*à savoir*) namely; (*ou*): **~ ... ~** either ... or; **~ que ... ~ que** *ou* **ou que** whether ... or whether

soit² [swat] *adv* so be it, very well

soixantaine [swasãtɛn] *nf*: **une ~ (de)** sixty or so, about sixty; **avoir la ~** (*âge*) to be around sixty

soixante [swasãt] *num* sixty; **soixante-dix** *num* seventy

soja [sɔʒa] *nm* soya; (*graines*) soya beans *pl*; **germes de ~** beansprouts

sol [sɔl] *nm* ground; (*de logement*) floor; (*Agr*) soil; (*Mus*) G; (: *en chantant la gamme*) so(h)

solaire [sɔlɛʀ] *adj* (*énergie etc*) solar; (*crème etc*) sun *cpd*

soldat [sɔlda] *nm* soldier

solde [sɔld] *nf* pay ▷ *nm* (*Comm*) balance; **soldes** *nm ou f pl* (*articles*) sale goods; (*vente*) sales; **en ~** at sale price; **solder** *vt* (*marchandise*) to sell at sale price, sell off

sole [sɔl] *nf* sole *inv* (*fish*)

soleil [sɔlɛj] *nm* sun; (*lumière*) sun(light); (*temps ensoleillé*) sun(shine); **il fait du ~** it's sunny; **au ~** in the sun

solennel, le [sɔlanɛl] *adj* solemn

solfège [sɔlfɛʒ] *nm* musical theory

solidaire [sɔlidɛʀ] *adj*: **être ~s** to show solidarity, stand *ou* stick together; **être ~ de** (*collègues*) to stand by; **solidarité** *nf* solidarity; **par solidarité (avec)** in sympathy (with)

solide [sɔlid] *adj* solid; (*mur, maison, meuble*) solid, sturdy; (*connaissances, argument*) sound; (*personne, estomac*) robust, sturdy ▷ *nm* solid

soliste [sɔlist] *nm/f* soloist

solitaire [sɔlitɛʀ] *adj* (*sans compagnie*) solitary,

s

lonely; (*lieu*) lonely ▷ *nm/f* (*ermite*) recluse; (*fig: ours*) loner

solitude [sɔlityd] *nf* loneliness; (*tranquillité*) solitude

solliciter [sɔlisite] *vt* (*personne*) to appeal to; (*emploi, faveur*) to seek

sollicitude [sɔlisityd] *nf* concern

soluble [sɔlybl] *adj* soluble

solution [sɔlysjɔ̃] *nf* solution; **solution de facilité** easy way out

solvable [sɔlvabl] *adj* solvent

sombre [sɔ̃bʀ] *adj* dark; (*fig*) gloomy; **sombrer** *vi* (*bateau*) to sink; **sombrer dans** (*misère, désespoir*) to sink into

sommaire [sɔmɛʀ] *adj* (*simple*) basic; (*expéditif*) summary ▷ *nm* summary

somme [sɔm] *nf* (*Math*) sum; (*quantité*) amount; (*argent*) sum, amount ▷ *nm*: **faire un ~** to have a (short) nap; **en ~** all in all; **~ toute** all in all

sommeil [sɔmɛj] *nm* sleep; **avoir ~** to be sleepy; **sommeiller** *vi* to doze

sommet [sɔmɛ] *nm* top; (*d'une montagne*) summit, top; (*fig: de la perfection, gloire*) height

sommier [sɔmje] *nm* (bed) base

somnambule [sɔmnɑ̃byl] *nm/f* sleepwalker

somnifère [sɔmnifɛʀ] *nm* sleeping drug *no pl* (*ou* pill)

somnoler [sɔmnɔle] *vi* to doze

somptueux, -euse [sɔ̃ptɥø, øz] *adj* sumptuous

son¹, sa [sɔ̃, sa] (*pl* **ses**) *adj* (*antécédent humain: mâle*) his; (: *femelle*) her; (: *valeur indéfinie*) one's, his/her; (*antécédent non humain*) its

son² [sɔ̃] *nm* sound; (*de blé*) bran

sondage [sɔ̃daʒ] *nm*: **sondage (d'opinion)** (opinion) poll

sonde [sɔ̃d] *nf* (*Navig*) lead *ou* sounding line; (*Méd*) probe; (*Tech: de forage*) borer, driller

sonder [sɔ̃de] *vt* (*Navig*) to sound; (*Tech*) to bore, drill; (*fig: personne*) to sound out; **~ le terrain** (*fig*) to test the ground

songe [sɔ̃ʒ] *nm* dream; **songer** *vi*: **songer à** (*penser à*) to think over; (*envisager*) to consider, think of; **songer que** to think that; **songeur, -euse** *adj* pensive

sonnant, e [sɔnɑ̃, ɑ̃t] *adj*: **à 8 heures ~es** on the stroke of 8

sonné, e [sɔne] *adj* (*fam*) cracked; **il est midi ~** it's gone twelve

sonner [sɔne] *vi* to ring ▷ *vt* (*cloche*) to ring; (*glas, tocsin*) to sound; (*portier, infirmière*) to ring for; **~ faux** (*instrument*) to sound out of tune; (*rire*) to ring false

sonnerie [sɔnʀi] *nf* (*son*) ringing; (*sonnette*) bell; (*de portable*) ringtone; **sonnerie d'alarme** alarm bell

sonnette [sɔnɛt] *nf* bell; **sonnette d'alarme** alarm bell

sonore [sɔnɔʀ] *adj* (*voix*) sonorous, ringing; (*salle*) resonant; (*film, signal*) sound *cpd*; **sonorisation** *nf* (*équipement: de salle de conférences*) public address system, P.A. system; (: *de discothèque*) sound system; **sonorité** *nf* (*de piano, violon*) tone; (*d'une salle*) acoustics *pl*

sophistiqué, e [sɔfistike] *adj* sophisticated

sorbet [sɔʀbɛ] *nm* water ice, sorbet

sorcier [sɔʀsje] *nm* sorcerer

sordide [sɔʀdid] *adj* (*lieu*) squalid; (*action*) sordid

sort [sɔʀ] *nm* (*destinée*) fate; (*condition*) lot; (*magique*) curse, spell; **tirer au ~** to draw lots

sorte [sɔʀt] *nf* sort, kind; **de la ~** in that way; **de (telle) ~ que** so that; **en quelque ~** in a way; **faire en ~ que** to see to it that; **quelle ~ de ...?** what kind of ...?

sortie [sɔʀti] *nf* (*issue*) way out, exit; (*remarque drôle*) sally; (*promenade*) outing; (*le soir: au restaurant etc*) night out; (*Comm: d'un disque*) release; (: *d'un livre*) publication; (: *d'un modèle*) launching; **où est la ~?** where's the exit?; **sortie de bain** (*vêtement*) bathrobe

sortilège [sɔʀtilɛʒ] *nm* (magic) spell

sortir [sɔʀtiʀ] *vi* (*gén*) to come out; (*partir, se promener, aller au spectacle*) to go out; (*numéro gagnant*) to come up ▷ *vt* (*gén*) to take out; (*produit, modèle*) to bring out; (*fam: dire*) to come out with; **~ avec qn** to be going out with sb; **s'en ~** (*malade*) to pull through; (*d'une difficulté etc*) to get through; **~ de** (*endroit*) to go (*ou* come) out of, leave; (*provenir de*) to come from; (*compétence*) to be outside

sosie [sɔzi] *nm* double

sot, sotte [so, sɔt] *adj* silly, foolish ▷ *nm/f* fool; **sottise** *nf* (*caractère*) silliness, foolishness; (*action*) silly *ou* foolish thing

sou [su] *nm*: **près de ses ~s** tight-fisted; **sans le ~** penniless

soubresaut [subʀəso] *nm* start; (*cahot*) jolt

souche [suʃ] *nf* (*d'arbre*) stump; (*de carnet*) counterfoil (BRIT), stub

souci [susi] *nm* (*inquiétude*) worry; (*préoccupation*) concern; (*Bot*) marigold; **se faire du ~** to worry; **soucier: se soucier de** *vt* to care about; **soucieux, -euse** *adj* concerned, worried

soucoupe [sukup] *nf* saucer; **soucoupe volante** flying saucer

soudain, e [sudɛ̃, ɛn] *adj* (*douleur, mort*) sudden ▷ *adv* suddenly, all of a sudden

Soudan [sudɑ̃] *nm*: **le ~** Sudan

soude [sud] *nf* soda

souder [sude] *vt* (*avec fil à souder*) to solder; (*par soudure autogène*) to weld; (*fig*) to bind together

soudure [sudyʀ] *nf* soldering; welding; (*joint*) soldered joint; weld

souffle [sufl] *nm* (*en expirant*) breath; (*en soufflant*) puff, blow; (*respiration*) breathing; (*d'explosion, de ventilateur*) blast; (*du vent*) blowing; **être à bout de ~** to be out of breath; **un ~ d'air** a breath of air

soufflé, e [sufle] *adj* (*fam: stupéfié*) staggered ▷ *nm* (*Culin*) soufflé

souffler [sufle] *vi* (*gén*) to blow; (*haleter*) to puff (and blow) ▷ *vt* (*feu, bougie*) to blow out; (*chasser: poussière etc*) to blow away; (*Tech: verre*) to blow; (*dire*): **~ qch à qn** to whisper sth to sb

souffrance [sufʀɑ̃s] *nf* suffering; **en ~** (*affaire*) pending

souffrant, e [sufʀɑ̃, ɑ̃t] *adj* unwell

souffre-douleur [sufʀədulœʀ] *nm inv* butt, underdog

souffrir [sufʀiʀ] *vi* to suffer, be in pain ▷ *vt* to suffer, endure; (*supporter*) to bear, stand; **~ de** (*maladie, froid*) to suffer from; **elle ne peut pas le ~** she can't stand *ou* bear him

soufre [sufʀ] *nm* sulphur

souhait [swɛ] *nm* wish; **tous nos ~s pour la nouvelle année** (our) best wishes for the New Year; **à vos ~s!** bless you!; **souhaitable** *adj* desirable

souhaiter [swete] *vt* to wish for; **~ la bonne année à qn** to wish sb a happy New Year; **~ que** to hope that

soûl, e [su, sul] *adj* drunk ▷ *nm*: **tout son ~** to one's heart's content

soulagement [sulaʒmɑ̃] *nm* relief

soulager [sulaʒe] *vt* to relieve

soûler [sule] *vt*: **~ qn** to get sb drunk; (*suj: boisson*) to make sb drunk; (*fig*) to make sb's head spin *ou* reel; **se soûler** *vi* to get drunk

soulever [sul(ə)ve] *vt* to lift; (*poussière*) to send up; (*enthousiasme*) to arouse; (*question, débat*) to raise; **se soulever** *vi* (*peuple*) to rise up; (*personne couchée*) to lift o.s. up

soulier [sulje] *nm* shoe

souligner [suliɲe] *vt* to underline; (*fig*) to emphasize, stress

soumettre [sumɛtʀ] *vt* (*pays*) to subject, subjugate; (*rebelle*) to put down, subdue; **~ qch à qn** (*projet etc*) to submit sth to sb; **se soumettre (à)** to submit (to)

soumis, e [sumi, iz] *adj* submissive; **soumission** *nf* submission

soupçon [supsɔ̃] *nm* suspicion; (*petite quantité*): **un ~ de** a hint *ou* touch of; **soupçonner** *vt* to suspect; **soupçonneux, -euse** *adj* suspicious

soupe [sup] *nf* soup

souper [supe] *vi* to have supper ▷ *nm* supper

soupeser [supəze] *vt* to weigh in one's hand(s); (*fig*) to weigh up

soupière [supjɛʀ] *nf* (soup) tureen

soupir [supiʀ] *nm* sigh; **pousser un ~ de**

soulagement to heave a sigh of relief

soupirer [supiʀe] *vi* to sigh

souple [supl] *adj* supple; (*fig: règlement, caractère*) flexible; (: *démarche, taille*) lithe, supple; **souplesse** *nf* suppleness; (*de caractère*) flexibility

source [suʀs] *nf* (*point d'eau*) spring; (*d'un cours d'eau, fig*) source; **de bonne ~** on good authority

sourcil [suʀsi] *nm* (eye)brow; **sourciller** *vi*: **sans sourciller** without turning a hair *ou* batting an eyelid

sourd, e [suʀ, suʀd] *adj* deaf; (*bruit*) muffled; (*douleur*) dull ▷ *nm/f* deaf person; **faire la ~e oreille** to turn a deaf ear; **sourdine** *nf* (*Mus*) mute; **en sourdine** softly, quietly; **sourd-muet, sourde-muette** *adj* deaf-and-dumb ▷ *nm/f* deaf-mute

souriant, e [suʀjɑ̃, jɑ̃t] *adj* cheerful

sourire [suʀiʀ] *nm* smile ▷ *vi* to smile; **~ à qn** to smile at sb; (*fig: plaire à*) to appeal to sb; (*suj: chance*) to smile on sb; **garder le ~** to keep smiling

souris [suʀi] *nf* mouse

sournois, e [suʀnwa, waz] *adj* deceitful, underhand

sous [su] *prép* under; **~ la pluie** in the rain; **~ terre** underground; **~ peu** shortly, before long; **sous-bois** *nm inv* undergrowth

souscrire [suskʀiʀ]: **~ à** *vt* to subscribe to

sous...: **sous-directeur, -trice** *nm/f* assistant manager(-manageress); **sous-entendre** *vt* to imply, infer; **sous-entendu, e** *adj* implied ▷ *nm* innuendo, insinuation; **sous-estimer** *vt* to underestimate; **sous-jacent, e** *adj* underlying; **sous-louer** *vt* to sublet; **sous-marin, e** *adj* (*flore, faune*) submarine; (*pêche*) underwater ▷ *nm* submarine; **sous-pull** *nm* thin poloneck jersey; **soussigné, e** *adj*: **je soussigné** I the undersigned; **sous-sol** *nm* basement; **sous-titre** *nm* subtitle

soustraction [sustʀaksjɔ̃] *nf* subtraction

soustraire [sustʀɛʀ] *vt* to subtract, take away; (*dérober*): **~ qch à qn** to remove sth from sb; **se soustraire à** (*autorité etc*) to elude, escape from

sous...: **sous-traitant** *nm* sub-contractor; **sous-traiter** *vt* to sub-contract; **sous-vêtements** *nmpl* underwear *sg*

soutane [sutan] *nf* cassock, soutane

soute [sut] *nf* hold

soutenir [sut(ə)niʀ] *vt* to support; (*assaut, choc*) to stand up to, withstand; (*intérêt, effort*) to keep up; (*assurer*): **~ que** to maintain that; **soutenu, e** *adj* (*efforts*) sustained, unflagging; (*style*) elevated

souterrain, e [suteʀɛ̃, ɛn] *adj* underground ▷ *nm* underground passage

soutien [sutjɛ̃] *nm* support; **soutien-gorge**

S

nm bra

soutirer [sutiʀe] *vt*: **~ qch à qn** to squeeze *ou* get sth out of sb

souvenir [suv(ə)niʀ] *nm* (*réminiscence*) memory; (*objet*) souvenir ▷ *vb*: **se ~ de** to remember; **se ~ que** to remember that; **en ~ de** in memory *ou* remembrance of; **avec mes affectueux/meilleurs ~s, ...** with love from, .../regards, ...

souvent [suvɑ̃] *adv* often; **peu ~** seldom, infrequently

souverain, e [suv(ə)ʀɛ̃, ɛn] *nm/f* sovereign, monarch

soyeux, -euse [swajø, øz] *adj* silky

spacieux, -euse [spasjø, jøz] *adj* spacious, roomy

spaghettis [spageti] *nmpl* spaghetti *sg*

sparadrap [spaʀadʀa] *nm* sticking plaster (*BRIT*), Bandaid® (*US*)

spatial, e, -aux [spasjal, jo] *adj* (*Aviat*) space *cpd*

speaker, ine [spikœʀ, kʀin] *nm/f* announcer

spécial, e, -aux [spesjal, jo] *adj* special; (*bizarre*) peculiar; **spécialement** *adv* especially, particularly; (*tout exprès*) specially; **spécialiser**: **se spécialiser** *vi* to specialize; **spécialiste** *nm/f* specialist; **spécialité** *nf* speciality; (*branche*) special field

spécifier [spesifje] *vt* to specify, state

spécimen [spesimɛn] *nm* specimen

spectacle [spɛktakl] *nm* (*scène*) sight; (*représentation*) show; (*industrie*) show business; **spectaculaire** *adj* spectacular

spectateur, -trice [spɛktatœʀ, tʀis] *nm/f* (*Cinéma etc*) member of the audience; (*Sport*) spectator; (*d'un événement*) onlooker, witness

spéculer [spekyle] *vi* to speculate

spéléologie [speleɔlɔʒi] *nf* potholing

sperme [spɛʀm] *nm* semen, sperm

sphère [sfɛʀ] *nf* sphere

spirale [spiʀal] *nf* spiral

spirituel, le [spiʀitɥɛl] *adj* spiritual; (*fin, piquant*) witty

splendide [splɑ̃did] *adj* splendid

spontané, e [spɔ̃tane] *adj* spontaneous; **spontanéité** *nf* spontaneity

sport [spɔʀ] *nm* sport ▷ *adj inv* (*vêtement*) casual; **faire du ~** to do sport; **sports d'hiver** winter sports; **sportif, -ive** *adj* (*journal, association, épreuve*) sports *cpd*; (*allure, démarche*) athletic; (*attitude, esprit*) sporting

spot [spɔt] *nm* (*lampe*) spot(light); (*annonce*); **spot (publicitaire)** commercial (break)

square [skwaʀ] *nm* public garden(s)

squelette [skəlɛt] *nm* skeleton; **squelettique** *adj* scrawny

SRAS [sʀas] *sigle m* (= *syndrome respiratoire aigu sévère*) SARS

Sri Lanka [sʀilɑ̃ka] *nm*: **le ~** Sri Lanka

stabiliser [stabilize] *vt* to stabilize

stable [stabl] *adj* stable, steady

stade [stad] *nm* (*Sport*) stadium; (*phase, niveau*) stage

stage [staʒ] *nm* (*cours*) training course; **~ de formation (professionnelle)** vocational (training) course; **~ de perfectionnement** advanced training course; **stagiaire** *nm/f, adj* trainee

> Attention à ne pas traduire *stage* par le mot anglais *stage*.

stagner [stagne] *vi* to stagnate

stand [stɑ̃d] *nm* (*d'exposition*) stand; (*de foire*) stall; **stand de tir** (*à la foire, Sport*) shooting range

standard [stɑ̃daʀ] *adj inv* standard ▷ *nm* switchboard; **standardiste** *nm/f* switchboard operator

standing [stɑ̃diŋ] *nm* standing; **de grand ~** luxury

starter [staʀtɛʀ] *nm* (*Auto*) choke

station [stasjɔ̃] *nf* station; (*de bus*) stop; (*de villégiature*) resort; **station de ski** ski resort; **station de taxis** taxi rank (*BRIT*) *ou* stand (*US*); **stationnement** *nm* parking; **stationner** *vi* to park; **station-service** *nf* service station

statistique [statistik] *nf* (*science*) statistics *sg*; (*rapport, étude*) statistic ▷ *adj* statistical

statue [staty] *nf* statue

statu quo [statykwo] *nm* status quo

statut [staty] *nm* status; **statuts** *nmpl* (*Jur, Admin*) statutes; **statutaire** *adj* statutory

Sté *abr* = **société**

steak [stɛk] *nm* steak; **~ haché** hamburger

sténo(graphie) [steno(gʀafi)] *nf* shorthand

stérile [steʀil] *adj* sterile

stérilet [steʀilɛ] *nm* coil, loop

stériliser [steʀilize] *vt* to sterilize

stimulant [stimylɑ̃] *nm* (*fig*) stimulus, incentive; (*physique*) stimulant

stimuler [stimyle] *vt* to stimulate

stipuler [stipyle] *vt* to stipulate

stock [stɔk] *nm* stock; **stocker** *vt* to stock

stop [stɔp] *nm* (*Auto: écriteau*) stop sign; (: *feu arrière*) brake-light; **faire du ~** (*fam*) to hitch(hike); **stopper** *vt, vi* to stop, halt

store [stɔʀ] *nm* blind; (*de magasin*) shade, awning

strabisme [stʀabism] *nm* squinting

strapontin [stʀapɔ̃tɛ̃] *nm* jump *ou* foldaway seat

stratégie [stʀateʒi] *nf* strategy; **stratégique** *adj* strategic

stress [stʀɛs] *nm* stress; **stressant, e** *adj* stressful; **stresser** *vt*: **stresser qn** to make sb (feel) tense

strict, e [stʀikt] *adj* strict; (*tenue, décor*) severe, plain; **le ~ nécessaire/minimum** the bare essentials/minimum

strident, e [stʀidɑ̃, ɑ̃t] *adj* shrill, strident

strophe [stʀɔf] *nf* verse, stanza

structure [stʀyktyʀ] *nf* structure; **~s d'accueil** reception facilities

studieux, -euse [stydjø, jøz] *adj* studious

studio [stydjo] *nm* (*logement*) (one-roomed) flatlet (BRIT) *ou* apartment (US); (*d'artiste, TV etc*) studio

stupéfait, e [stypefɛ, ɛt] *adj* astonished

stupéfiant, e [stypefjɑ̃, jɑ̃t] *adj* (*étonnant*) stunning, astounding ▷ *nm* (*Méd*) drug, narcotic

stupéfier [stypefje] *vt* (*étonner*) to stun, astonish

stupeur [stypœʀ] *nf* astonishment

stupide [stypid] *adj* stupid; **stupidité** *nf* stupidity; (*parole, acte*) stupid thing (to do *ou* say)

style [stil] *nm* style

stylé, e [stile] *adj* well-trained

styliste [stilist] *nm/f* designer

stylo [stilo] *nm*: **~ (à encre)** (fountain) pen; **stylo (à) bille** ball-point pen

su, e [sy] *pp de* **savoir** ▷ *nm*: **au su de** with the knowledge of

suave [sɥav] *adj* sweet

subalterne [sybaltɛʀn] *adj* (*employé, officier*) junior; (*rôle*) subordinate, subsidiary ▷ *nm/f* subordinate

subconscient [sypkɔ̃sjɑ̃] *nm* subconscious

subir [sybiʀ] *vt* (*affront, dégâts*) to suffer; (*opération, châtiment*) to undergo

subit, e [sybi, it] *adj* sudden; **subitement** *adv* suddenly, all of a sudden

subjectif, -ive [sybʒɛktif, iv] *adj* subjective

subjonctif [sybʒɔ̃ktif] *nm* subjunctive

subjuguer [sybʒyge] *vt* to captivate

submerger [sybmɛʀʒe] *vt* to submerge; (*fig*) to overwhelm

subordonné, e [sybɔʀdɔne] *adj, nm/f* subordinate

subrepticement [sybʀɛptismɑ̃] *adv* surreptitiously

subside [sybzid] *nm* grant

subsidiaire [sybzidjɛʀ] *adj*: **question ~** deciding question

subsister [sybziste] *vi* (*rester*) to remain, subsist; (*survivre*) to live on

substance [sypstɑ̃s] *nf* substance

substituer [sypstitɥe] *vt*: **~ qn/qch à** to substitute sb/sth for; **se ~ à qn** (*évincer*) to substitute o.s. for sb

substitut [sypstity] *nm* (*succédané*) substitute

subterfuge [syptɛʀfyʒ] *nm* subterfuge

subtil, e [syptil] *adj* subtle

subvenir [sybvəniʀ] **~ à** *vt* to meet

subvention [sybvɑ̃sjɔ̃] *nf* subsidy, grant; **subventionner** *vt* to subsidize

suc [syk] *nm* (*Bot*) sap; (*de viande, fruit*) juice

succéder [syksede]: **~ à** *vt* to succeed; **se succéder** *vi* (*accidents, années*) to follow one another

succès [syksɛ] *nm* success; **avoir du ~** to be a success, be successful; **à ~** successful; **succès de librairie** bestseller

successeur [syksesœʀ] *nm* successor

successif, -ive [syksesif, iv] *adj* successive

succession [syksesjɔ̃] *nf* (*série, Pol*) succession; (*Jur: patrimoine*) estate, inheritance

succomber [sykɔ̃be] *vi* to die, succumb; (*fig*): **~ à** to succumb to

succulent, e [sykylɑ̃, ɑ̃t] *adj* (*repas, mets*) delicious

succursale [sykyʀsal] *nf* branch

sucer [syse] *vt* to suck; **sucette** *nf* (*bonbon*) lollipop; (*de bébé*) dummy (BRIT), pacifier (US)

sucre [sykʀ] *nm* (*substance*) sugar; (*morceau*) lump of sugar, sugar lump *ou* cube; **sucre d'orge** barley sugar; **sucre en morceaux/ cristallisé/en poudre** lump/granulated/ caster sugar; **sucre glace** icing sugar (BRIT), confectioner's sugar (US); **sucré, e** *adj* (*produit alimentaire*) sweetened; (*au goût*) sweet; **sucrer** *vt* (*thé, café*) to sweeten, put sugar in; **sucreries** *nfpl* (*bonbons*) sweets, sweet things; **sucrier** *nm* (*récipient*) sugar bowl

sud [syd] *nm*: **le ~** the south ▷ *adj inv* south; (*côte*) south, southern; **au ~** (*situation*) in the south; (*direction*) to the south; **au ~ de** (to the) south of; **sud-africain, e** *adj* South African ▷ *nm/f*: **Sud-Africain, e** South African; **sud-américain, e** *adj* South American ▷ *nm/f*: **Sud-Américain, e** South American; **sud-est** *nm, adj inv* south-east; **sud-ouest** *nm, adj inv* south-west

Suède [sɥɛd] *nf*: **la ~** Sweden; **suédois, e** *adj* Swedish ▷ *nm/f*: **Suédois, e** Swede ▷ *nm* (*Ling*) Swedish

suer [sɥe] *vi* to sweat; (*suinter*) to ooze; **sueur** *nf* sweat; **en sueur** sweating, in a sweat; **donner des sueurs froides à qn** to put sb in(to) a cold sweat

suffire [syfiʀ] *vi* (*être assez*): **~ (à qn/pour qch/pour faire)** to be enough *ou* sufficient (for sb/for sth/to do); **il suffit d'une négligence ...** it only takes one act of carelessness ...; **il suffit qu'on oublie pour que ...** one only needs to forget for ...; **ça suffit!** that's enough!

suffisamment [syfizamɑ̃] *adv* sufficiently, enough; **~ de** sufficient, enough

suffisant, e [syfizɑ̃, ɑ̃t] *adj* sufficient; (*résultats*) satisfactory; (*vaniteux*) self-important, bumptious

suffixe [syfiks] *nm* suffix

suffoquer [syfɔke] *vt* to choke, suffocate; (*stupéfier*) to stagger, astound ▷ *vi* to choke, suffocate

s

suffrage [syfʀaʒ] nm (Pol: voix) vote
suggérer [sygʒeʀe] vt to suggest;
suggestion nf suggestion
suicide [sɥisid] nm suicide; **suicider: se
suicider** vi to commit suicide
suie [sɥi] nf soot
suisse [sɥis] adj Swiss ▷ nm: **S~** Swiss pl
inv ▷ nf: **la S~** Switzerland; **la S~ romande/
allemande** French-speaking/German-
speaking Switzerland
suite [sɥit] nf (continuation: d'énumération etc)
rest, remainder; (: de feuilleton) continuation;
(: film etc sur le même thème) sequel; (série)
series, succession; (conséquence) result; (ordre,
liaison logique) coherence; (appartement, Mus)
suite; (escorte) retinue, suite; **suites** nfpl
(d'une maladie etc) effects; **prendre la ~ de**
(directeur etc) to succeed, take over from;
donner ~ à (requête, projet) to follow up; **faire
~ à** to follow; **(faisant) ~ à votre lettre du ...**
further to your letter of the ...; **de ~** (d'affilée)
in succession; (immédiatement) at once; **par
la ~** afterwards, subsequently; **à la ~** one
after the other; **à la ~ de** (derrière) behind; (en
conséquence de) following
suivant, e [sɥivɑ̃, ɑ̃t] adj next, following
▷ prép (selon) according to; **au ~!** next!
suivi, e [sɥivi] adj (effort, qualité) consistent;
(cohérent) coherent; **très/peu ~** (cours) well-
/poorly-attended
suivre [sɥivʀ] vt (gén) to follow; (Scol: cours)
to attend; (comprendre) to keep up with;
(Comm: article) to continue to stock ▷ vi to
follow; (élève: assimiler) to keep up; **se suivre**
vi (accidents etc) to follow one after the
other; **faire ~** (lettre) to forward; **"à ~"** "to be
continued"
sujet, te [syʒɛ, ɛt] adj: **être ~ à** (vertige
etc) to be liable ou subject to ▷ nm/f (d'un
souverain) subject ▷ nm subject; **au ~ de**
about; **sujet de conversation** topic ou subject
of conversation; **sujet d'examen** (Scol)
examination question
super [sypɛʀ] (fam) adj inv terrific, great,
fantastic, super
superbe [sypɛʀb] adj magnificent, superb
superficie [sypɛʀfisi] nf (surface) area
superficiel, le [sypɛʀfisjɛl] adj superficial
superflu, e [sypɛʀfly] adj superfluous
supérieur, e [sypeʀjœʀ] adj (lèvre, étages,
classes) upper; (plus élevé: température,
niveau, enseignement): **~ (à)** higher (than);
(meilleur: qualité, produit): **~ (à)** superior (to);
(excellent, hautain) superior ▷ nm, nf superior;
supériorité nf superiority
supermarché [sypɛʀmaʀʃe] nm
supermarket
superposer [sypɛʀpoze] vt (faire chevaucher)
to superimpose; **lits superposés** bunk beds

superpuissance [sypɛʀpɥisɑ̃s] nf superpower
superstitieux, -euse [sypɛʀstisjø, jøz] adj
superstitious
superviser [sypɛʀvize] vt to supervise
supplanter [syplɑ̃te] vt to supplant
suppléant, e [sypleɑ̃, -ɑ̃t] adj (professeur)
supply cpd; (juge, fonctionnaire) deputy cpd
▷ nm/f (professeur) supply teacher
suppléer [syplee] vt (ajouter: mot manquant
etc) to supply, provide; (compenser: lacune) to fill
in; **~ à** to make up for
supplément [syplemɑ̃] nm supplement;
(de frites etc) extra portion; **un ~ de travail**
extra ou additional work; **payer un ~** to pay
an additional charge; **le vin est en ~** wine
is extra; **supplémentaire** adj additional,
further; (train, bus) relief cpd, extra
supplications [syplikasjɔ̃] nfpl pleas,
entreaties
supplice [syplis] nm torture no pl
supplier [syplije] vt to implore, beseech
support [sypɔʀ] nm support; (publicitaire)
medium; (audio-visuel) aid
supportable [sypɔʀtabl] adj (douleur)
bearable
supporter¹ [sypɔʀtɛʀ] nm supporter, fan
supporter² [sypɔʀte] vt (conséquences,
épreuve) to bear, endure; (défauts, personne)
to put up with; (suj: chose: chaleur etc) to
withstand; (: personne: chaleur, vin) to be able
to take

Attention à ne pas traduire **supporter**
par **to support**.

supposer [sypoze] vt to suppose; (impliquer)
to presuppose; **à ~ que** supposing (that)
suppositoire [sypozitwaʀ] nm suppository
suppression [sypʀesjɔ̃] nf (voir supprimer)
cancellation; removal; deletion
supprimer [sypʀime] vt (congés, service
d'autobus etc) to cancel; (emplois, privilèges,
témoin gênant) to do away with; (cloison, cause,
anxiété) to remove; (clause, mot) to delete
suprême [sypʀɛm] adj supreme

 MOT-CLÉ

sur [syʀ] prép **1** (position) on; (par-dessus) over;
(au-dessus) above; **pose-le sur la table** put it
on the table; **je n'ai pas d'argent sur moi** I
haven't any money on me
2 (direction) towards; **en allant sur Paris**
going towards Paris; **sur votre droite** on ou
to your right
3 (à propos de) on, about; **un livre/une
conférence sur Balzac** a book/lecture on ou
about Balzac
4 (proportion) out of; **un sur 10** one in 10; (Scol)
one out of 10

5 (*mesures*) by; **4 m sur 2** 4 m by 2
6 (*succession*): **avoir accident sur accident** to have one accident after the other

sûr, e [syʀ] *adj* sure, certain; (*digne de confiance*) reliable; (*sans danger*) safe; (*diagnostic, goût*) reliable; **le plus ~ est de** the safest thing is to; **sûr de soi** self-assured, self-confident

surcharge [syʀʃaʀ3] *nf* (*de passagers, marchandises*) excess load; **surcharger** *vt* to overload

surcroît [syʀkʀwa] *nm*: **un ~ de** additional +*nom*; **par** *ou* **de ~** moreover; **en ~** in addition

surdité [syʀdite] *nf* deafness

sûrement [syʀmã] *adv* (*certainement*) certainly; (*sans risques*) safely

surenchère [syʀãʃɛʀ] *nf* (*aux enchères*) higher bid; **surenchérir** *vi* to bid higher; (*fig*) to try and outbid each other

surestimer [syʀɛstime] *vt* to overestimate

sûreté [syʀte] *nf* (*sécurité*) safety; (*exactitude: de renseignements etc*) reliability; (*d'un geste*) steadiness; **mettre en ~** to put in a safe place; **pour plus de ~** as an extra precaution, to be on the safe side

surf [sœʀf] *nm* surfing

surface [syʀfas] *nf* surface; (*superficie*) surface area; **une grande ~** a supermarket; **faire ~** to surface; **en ~** near the surface; (*fig*) superficially

surfait, e [syʀfɛ, ɛt] *adj* overrated

surfer [syʀfe] *vi*: **~ sur Internet** to surf *ou* browse the Internet

surgelé, e [syʀ3əle] *adj* (deep-)frozen ▷ *nm*: **les ~s** (deep-)frozen food

surgir [syʀ3iʀ] *vi* to appear suddenly; (*fig: problème, conflit*) to arise

sur...: **surhumain, e** *adj* superhuman; **sur-le-champ** *adv* immediately; **surlendemain** *nm*: **le surlendemain (soir)** two days later (in the evening); **le surlendemain de** two days after; **surmenage** *nm* overwork(ing); **surmener**: **se surmener** *vi* to overwork

surmonter [syʀmɔ̃te] *vt* (*vaincre*) to overcome; (*être au-dessus de*) to top

surnaturel, le [syʀnatyʀɛl] *adj, nm* supernatural

surnom [syʀnɔ̃] *nm* nickname

surnombre [syʀnɔ̃bʀ] *nm*: **être en ~** to be too many (*ou* one too many)

surpeuplé, e [syʀpœple] *adj* overpopulated

surplace [syʀplas] *nm*: **faire du ~** to mark time

surplomber [syʀplɔ̃be] *vt, vi* to overhang

surplus [syʀply] *nm* (*Comm*) surplus; (*reste*): **~ de bois** wood left over

surprenant, e [syʀpʀənã, ãt] *adj* amazing

surprendre [syʀpʀãdʀ] *vt* (*étonner*) to surprise; (*tomber sur: intrus etc*) to catch;

(*entendre*) to overhear

surpris, e [syʀpʀi, iz] *adj*: **~ (de/que)** surprised (at/that); **surprise** *nf* surprise; **faire une surprise à qn** to give sb a surprise; **surprise-partie** *nf* party

sursaut [syʀso] *nm* start, jump; **~ de** (*énergie, indignation*) sudden fit *ou* burst of; **en ~** with a start; **sursauter** *vi* to (give a) start, jump

sursis [syʀsi] *nm* (*Jur: gén*) suspended sentence; (*fig*) reprieve

surtout [syʀtu] *adv* (*avant tout, d'abord*) above all; (*spécialement, particulièrement*) especially; **~, ne dites rien!** whatever you do don't say anything!; **~ pas!** certainly *ou* definitely not!; **~ que...** especially as ...

surveillance [syʀvɛjãs] *nf* watch; (*Police, Mil*) surveillance; **sous ~ médicale** under medical supervision

surveillant, e [syʀvɛjã, ãt] *nm/f* (*de prison*) warder; (*Scol*) monitor

surveiller [syʀveje] *vt* (*enfant, élèves, bagages*) to watch, keep an eye on; (*prisonnier, suspect*) to keep (a) watch on; (*territoire, bâtiment*) to (keep) watch over; (*travaux, cuisson*) to supervise; (*Scol: examen*) to invigilate; **~ son langage/sa ligne** to watch one's language/figure

survenir [syʀvəniʀ] *vi* (*incident, retards*) to occur, arise; (*événement*) to take place

survêtement [syʀvɛtmã] *nm* tracksuit

survie [syʀvi] *nf* survival; **survivant, e** *nm/f* survivor; **survivre** *vi* to survive; **survivre à** (*accident etc*) to survive

survoler [syʀvɔle] *vt* to fly over; (*fig: livre*) to skim through

survolté, e [syʀvɔlte] *adj* (*fig*) worked up

sus [sy(s)]: **en ~ de** *prép* in addition to, over and above; **en ~** in addition

susceptible [sysɛptibl] *adj* touchy, sensitive; **~ de faire** (*hypothèse*) liable to do

susciter [sysite] *vt* (*admiration*) to arouse; (*ennuis*): **~ (à qn)** to create (for sb)

suspect, e [syspɛ(kt), ɛkt] *adj* suspicious; (*témoignage, opinions*) suspect ▷ *nm/f* suspect; **suspecter** *vt* to suspect; (*honnêteté de qn*) to question, have one's suspicions about

suspendre [syspãdʀ] *vt* (*accrocher: vêtement*): **~ qch (à)** to hang sth up (on); (*interrompre, démettre*) to suspend

suspendu, e [syspãdy] *adj* (*accroché*): **~ à** hanging on (*ou* from); (*perché*): **~ au-dessus de** suspended over

suspens [syspã]: **en ~** *adv* (*affaire*) in abeyance; **tenir en ~** to keep in suspense

suspense [syspɛns, syspãs] *nm* suspense

suspension [syspãsjɔ̃] *nf* suspension; (*lustre*) light fitting *ou* fitment

suture [sytyʀ] *nf* (*Méd*): **point de ~** stitch

svelte [svɛlt] *adj* slender, svelte

SVP *abr* (= s'il vous plaît) please
sweat [swit] *nm* (*fam*) sweatshirt
sweat-shirt [switʃœʀt] (*pl* ~**s**) *nm* sweatshirt
syllabe [si(l)lab] *nf* syllable
symbole [sɛ̃bɔl] *nm* symbol; **symbolique**
  adj symbolic(al); (*geste, offrande*) token *cpd*;
  symboliser *vt* to symbolize
symétrique [simetʀik] *adj* symmetrical
sympa [sɛ̃pa] (*fam*) *adj inv* nice; **sois ~, prête-**
  le moi be a pal and lend it to me
sympathie [sɛ̃pati] *nf* (*inclination*) liking;
  (*affinité*) friendship; (*condoléances*) sympathy;
  j'ai beaucoup de ~ pour lui I like him a lot;
  sympathique *adj* nice, friendly

  ▮ Attention à ne pas traduire *sympathique*
     par *sympathetic*.

sympathisant, e [sɛ̃patizɑ̃, ɑ̃t] *nm/f*
  sympathizer
sympathiser [sɛ̃patize] *vi* (*voisins etc*:
  s'entendre) to get on (*BRIT*) ou along (*US*) (well)
symphonie [sɛ̃fɔni] *nf* symphony
symptôme [sɛ̃ptom] *nm* symptom
synagogue [sinagɔg] *nf* synagogue
syncope [sɛ̃kɔp] *nf* (*Méd*) blackout; **tomber**
  en ~ to faint, pass out
syndic [sɛ̃dik] *nm* (*d'immeuble*) managing
  agent
syndical, e, -aux [sɛ̃dikal, o] *adj* (trade)
  union *cpd*; **syndicaliste** *nm/f* trade unionist
syndicat [sɛ̃dika] *nm* (*d'ouvriers, employés*)
  (trade) union; **syndicat d'initiative** tourist
  office; **syndiqué, e** *adj* belonging to a (trade)
  union; **syndiquer: se syndiquer** *vi* to form a
  trade union; (*adhérer*) to join a trade union
synonyme [sinɔnim] *adj* synonymous ▷ *nm*
  synonym; **~ de** synonymous with
syntaxe [sɛ̃taks] *nf* syntax
synthèse [sɛ̃tɛz] *nf* synthesis
synthétique [sɛ̃tetik] *adj* synthetic
Syrie [siʀi] *nf*: **la ~** Syria
systématique [sistematik] *adj* systematic
système [sistɛm] *nm* system; **le ~ D**
  resourcefulness

t

t' [t] *pron voir* **te**
ta [ta] *adj voir* **ton¹**
tabac [taba] *nm* tobacco; (*magasin*)
  tobacconist's (shop)
tabagisme [tabaʒism] *nm*: **tabagisme**
  passif passive smoking
table [tabl] *nf* table; **à ~!** dinner *etc* is ready!;
  se mettre à ~ to sit down to eat; **mettre la ~**
  to lay the table; **une ~ pour 4, s'il vous plaît**
  a table for 4, please; **table à repasser** ironing
  board; **table de cuisson** hob; **table de nuit** *ou*
  de chevet bedside table; **table des matières**
  (table of) contents *pl*; **table d'orientation**
  viewpoint indicator; **table roulante** trolley
  (*BRIT*), tea wagon (*US*)
tableau, x [tablo] *nm* (*peinture*) painting;
  (*reproduction, fig*) picture; (*panneau*) board;
  (*schéma*) table, chart; **tableau d'affichage**
  notice board; **tableau de bord** dashboard;
  (*Aviat*) instrument panel; **tableau noir**
  blackboard
tablette [tablɛt] *nf* (*planche*) shelf; **tablette**
  de chocolat bar of chocolate
tablier [tablije] *nm* apron
tabou [tabu] *nm* taboo
tabouret [tabuʀɛ] *nm* stool
tac [tak] *nm*: **il m'a répondu du ~ au ~** he
  answered me right back
tache [taʃ] *nf* (*saleté*) stain, mark; (*Art, de*
  couleur, lumière) spot; **tache de rousseur**

freckle

tâche [tɑʃ] nf task

tacher [taʃe] vt to stain, mark

tâcher [tɑʃe] vi: **~ de faire** to try ou endeavour to do

tacheté, e [taʃte] adj spotted

tact [takt] nm tact; **avoir du ~** to be tactful

tactique [taktik] adj tactical ▷ nf (technique) tactics sg; (plan) tactic

taie [tɛ] nf: **~ (d'oreiller)** pillowslip, pillowcase

taille [tɑj] nf cutting; (d'arbre etc) pruning; (milieu du corps) waist; (hauteur) height; (grandeur) size; **de ~ à faire** capable of doing; **de ~** sizeable; **taille-crayon(s)** nm pencil sharpener

tailler [tɑje] vt (pierre, diamant) to cut; (arbre, plante) to prune; (vêtement) to cut out; (crayon) to sharpen

tailleur [tɑjœʀ] nm (couturier) tailor; (vêtement) suit; **en ~** (assis) cross-legged

taillis [tɑji] nm copse

taire [tɛʀ] vi: **faire ~ qn** to make sb be quiet; **se taire** vi to be silent ou quiet; **taisez-vous!** be quiet!

Taiwan [tajwan] nf Taiwan

talc [talk] nm talc, talcum powder

talent [talɑ̃] nm talent

talkie-walkie [tokiwoki] nm walkie-talkie

talon [talɔ̃] nm heel; (de chèque, billet) stub, counterfoil (BRIT); **talons plats/aiguilles** flat/stiletto heels

talus [taly] nm embankment

tambour [tɑ̃buʀ] nm (Mus, aussi Tech) drum; (musicien) drummer; (porte) revolving door(s pl); **tambourin** nm tambourine

Tamise [tamiz] nf: **la ~** the Thames

tamisé, e [tamize] adj (fig) subdued, soft

tampon [tɑ̃pɔ̃] nm (de coton, d'ouate) wad, pad; (amortisseur) buffer; (bouchon) plug, stopper; (cachet, timbre) stamp; (mémoire) ~ (Inform) buffer; **tampon (hygiénique)** tampon; **tamponner** vt (timbres) to stamp; (heurter) to crash ou ram into; **tamponneuse** adj f: **autos tamponneuses** dodgems

tandem [tɑ̃dɛm] nm tandem

tandis [tɑ̃di]: **~ que** conj while

tanguer [tɑ̃ge] vi to pitch (and toss)

tant [tɑ̃] adv so much; **~ de** (sable, eau) so much; (gens, livres) so many; **~ que** as long as; (autant que) as much as; **~ mieux** that's great; (avec une certaine réserve) so much the better; **~ pis** too bad; (conciliant) never mind; **~ bien que mal** as well as can be expected

tante [tɑ̃t] nf aunt

tantôt [tɑ̃to] adv (parfois): **~ ... ~** now ... now; (cet après-midi) this afternoon

taon [tɑ̃] nm horsefly

tapage [tapaʒ] nm uproar, din

tapageur, -euse [tapaʒœʀ, øz] adj noisy; (voyant) loud, flashy

tape [tap] nf slap

tape-à-l'œil [tapalœj] adj inv flashy, showy

taper [tape] vt (porte) to bang, slam; (enfant) to slap; (dactylographier) to type (out); (fam: emprunter): **~ qn de 10 euros** to touch sb for 10 euros ▷ vi (soleil) to beat down; **se taper** vt (repas) to put away; (fam: corvée) to get landed with; **~ sur qn** to thump sb; (fig) to run sb down; **~ sur un clou** to hit a nail; **~ sur la table** to bang on the table; **~ à** (porte etc) to knock on; **~ dans** (se servir) to dig into; **~ des mains/pieds** to clap one's hands/stamp one's feet; **~ (à la machine)** to type

tapi, e [tapi] adj (blotti) crouching; (caché) hidden away

tapis [tapi] nm carpet; (petit) rug; **tapis de sol** (de tente) groundsheet; **tapis de souris** (Inform) mouse mat; **tapis roulant** (pour piétons) moving walkway; (pour bagages) carousel

tapisser [tapise] vt (avec du papier peint) to paper; (recouvrir): **~ qch (de)** to cover sth (with); **tapisserie** nf (tenture, broderie) tapestry; (papier peint) wallpaper; **tapissier-décorateur** nm interior decorator

tapoter [tapɔte] vt (joue, main) to pat; (objet) to tap

taquiner [takine] vt to tease

tard [taʀ] adv late; **plus ~** later (on); **au plus ~** at the latest; **sur le ~** late in life; **il est trop ~** it's too late

tarder [taʀde] vi (chose) to be a long time coming; (personne): **~ à faire** to delay doing; **il me tarde d'être** I am longing to be; **sans (plus) ~** without (further) delay

tardif, -ive [taʀdif, iv] adj late

tarif [taʀif] nm: **~ des consommations** price list; **~s postaux/douaniers** postal/customs rates; **~ des taxis** taxi fares; **~ plein/réduit** (train) full/reduced fare; (téléphone) peak/off-peak rate

tarir [taʀiʀ] vi to dry up, run dry

tarte [taʀt] nf tart; **~ aux fraises** strawberry tart; **~ Tatin** ≈ apple upside-down tart

tartine [taʀtin] nf slice of bread; **tartine de miel** slice of bread and honey; **tartiner** vt to spread; **fromage à tartiner** cheese spread

tartre [taʀtʀ] nm (des dents) tartar; (de bouilloire) fur, scale

tas [tɑ] nm heap, pile; (fig): **un ~ de** heaps of, lots of; **en ~** in a heap ou pile; **formé sur le ~** trained on the job

tasse [tɑs] nf cup; **tasse à café** coffee cup

tassé, e [tɑse] adj: **bien ~** (café etc) strong

tasser [tɑse] vt (terre, neige) to pack down; (entasser): **~ qch dans** to cram sth into; **se tasser** vi (se serrer) to squeeze up; (s'affaisser) to settle; (fig) to settle down

t

tâter [tɑte] vt to feel; (fig) to try out; **se tâter** (hésiter) to be in two minds; **~ de** (prison etc) to have a taste of

tatillon, ne [tatijɔ̃, ɔn] adj pernickety

tâtonnement [tɑtɔnmɑ̃] nm: **par ~s** (fig) by trial and error

tâtonner [tɑtɔne] vi to grope one's way along

tâtons [tɑtɔ̃]: **à ~** adv: **chercher/avancer à ~** to grope around for/grope one's way forward

tatouage [tatwaʒ] nm tattoo

tatouer [tatwe] vt to tattoo

taudis [todi] nm hovel, slum

taule [tol] (fam) nf nick (fam), prison

taupe [top] nf mole

taureau, x [tɔro] nm bull; (signe): **le T~** Taurus

taux [to] nm rate; (d'alcool) level; **taux d'intérêt** interest rate

taxe [taks] nf tax; (douanière) duty; **toutes ~s comprises** inclusive of tax; **la boutique hors ~s** the duty-free shop; **taxe à la valeur ajoutée** value-added tax; **taxe de séjour** tourist tax

taxer [takse] vt (personne) to tax; (produit) to put a tax on, tax

taxi [taksi] nm taxi; (chauffeur: fam) taxi driver; **pouvez-vous m'appeler un ~, s'il vous plaît?** can you call me a taxi, please?

Tchécoslovaquie [tʃekɔslɔvaki] nf Czechoslovakia; **tchèque** adj Czech ▷ nm/f: **Tchèque** Czech ▷ nm (Ling) Czech; **la République tchèque** the Czech Republic

Tchétchénie [tʃetʃeni] nf: **la ~** Chechnya

te, t' [tə] pron you; (réfléchi) yourself

technicien, ne [tɛknisjɛ̃, jɛn] nm/f technician

technico-commercial, e, -aux [tɛknikokɔmɛʀsjal, jo] adj: **agent ~** sales technician

technique [tɛknik] adj technical ▷ nf technique; **techniquement** adv technically

techno [tɛkno] nf (Mus) techno (music)

technologie [tɛknɔlɔʒi] nf technology; **technologique** adj technological

teck [tɛk] nm teak

tee-shirt [tiʃœʀt] nm T-shirt, tee-shirt

teindre [tɛ̃dʀ] vt to dye; **se ~ les cheveux** to dye one's hair; **teint, e** adj dyed ▷ nm (du visage) complexion; (momentané) colour ▷ nf shade; **grand teint** colourfast

teinté, e [tɛ̃te] adj: **~ de** (fig) tinged with

teinter [tɛ̃te] vt (verre, papier) to tint; (bois) to stain

teinture [tɛ̃tyʀ] nf dye; **teinture d'iode** tincture of iodine; **teinturerie** nf dry cleaner's; **teinturier** nm dry cleaner

tel, telle [tɛl] adj (pareil) such; (comme): **~ un/ des ...** like a/like ...; (indéfini) such-and-such a; (intensif): **un ~/de ~s ...** such (a)/such ...; **rien de ~** nothing like it; **~ que** like, such as; **~ quel**

as it is ou stands (ou was etc); **venez ~ jour** come on such-and-such a day

télé [tele] (fam) nf TV; **à la ~** on TV ou telly

télé...: **télécabine** nf (benne) cable car; **télécarte** nf phonecard; **téléchargeable** adj downloadable; **téléchargement** nm (action) downloading; (fichier) download; **télécharger** vt to download; **télécommande** nf remote control; **télécopieur** nm fax machine; **télédistribution** nf cable TV; **télégramme** nm telegram; **télégraphier** vt to telegraph, cable; **téléguider** vt to radio-control; **télématique** nf telematics sg; **téléobjectif** nm telephoto lens sg; **télépathie** nf telepathy; **téléphérique** nm cable car

téléphone [telefɔn] nm telephone; **avoir le ~** to be on the (tele)phone; **au ~** on the phone; **téléphoner** vi to make a phone call; **téléphoner à** to phone, call up; **est-ce que je peux téléphoner d'ici?** can I make a call from here?; **téléphonique** adj (tele)phone cpd

télé...: **téléréalité** nf reality TV

télescope [telɛskɔp] nm telescope

télescoper [telɛskɔpe] vt to smash up; **se télescoper** (véhicules) to concertina

télé...: **téléscripteur** nm teleprinter; **télésiège** nm chairlift; **téléski** nm ski-tow; **téléspectateur, -trice** nm/f (television) viewer; **télétravail** nm telecommuting; **télévente** nf telesales; **téléviseur** nm television set; **télévision** nf television; **à la télévision** on television; **télévision numérique** digital TV; **télévision par câble/ satellite** cable/satellite television

télex [telɛks] nm telex

telle [tɛl] adj voir **tel**; **tellement** adv (tant) so much; (si) so; **tellement de** (sable, eau) so much; (gens, livres) so many; **il s'est endormi tellement il était fatigué** he was so tired (that) he fell asleep; **pas tellement** not (all) that much; not (all) that +adjectif

téméraire [temeʀɛʀ] adj reckless, rash

témoignage [temwaɲaʒ] nm (Jur: déclaration) testimony no pl, evidence no pl; (rapport, récit) account; (fig: d'affection etc: cadeau) token, mark; (: geste) expression

témoigner [temwaɲe] vt (intérêt, gratitude) to show ▷ vi (Jur) to testify, give evidence; **~ de** to bear witness to, testify to

témoin [temwɛ̃] nm witness ▷ adj: **appartement ~** show flat (BRIT); **être ~ de** to witness; **témoin oculaire** eyewitness

tempe [tɑ̃p] nf temple

tempérament [tɑ̃peʀamɑ̃] nm temperament, disposition; **à ~** (vente) on deferred (payment) terms; (achat) by instalments, hire purchase cpd

température [tɑ̃peʀatyʀ] nf temperature; **avoir** ou **faire de la ~** to be running ou have a temperature

tempête [tɑ̃pɛt] *nf* storm; **tempête de sable/neige** sand/snowstorm

temple [tɑ̃pl] *nm* temple; (*protestant*) church

temporaire [tɑ̃pɔʀɛʀ] *adj* temporary

temps [tɑ̃] *nm* (*atmosphérique*) weather; (*durée*) time; (*époque*) time, times *pl*; (*Ling*) tense; (*Mus*) beat; (*Tech*) stroke; **un ~ de chien** (*fam*) rotten weather; **quel ~ fait-il?** what's the weather like?; **il fait beau/mauvais ~** the weather is fine/bad; **avoir le ~/tout son ~** to have time/plenty of time; **en ~ de paix/guerre** in peacetime/wartime; **en ~ utile** *ou* **voulu** in due time *ou* course; **ces derniers ~** lately; **dans quelque ~** in a (little) while; **de ~ en ~, de ~ à autre** from time to time; **à ~** (*partir, arriver*) in time; **à ~ complet, à plein ~** full-time; **à ~ partiel, à mi-~** part-time; **dans le ~** at one time; **temps d'arrêt** pause, halt; **temps libre** free *ou* spare time; **temps mort** (*Comm*) slack period

tenable [t(ə)nabl] *adj* bearable

tenace [tənas] *adj* persistent

tenant, e [tənɑ̃, ɑ̃t] *nm/f* (*Sport*): **~ du titre** title-holder

tendance [tɑ̃dɑ̃s] *nf* tendency; (*opinions*) leanings *pl*, sympathies *pl*; (*évolution*) trend; **avoir ~ à** to have a tendency to, tend to

tendeur [tɑ̃dœʀ] *nm* (*attache*) elastic strap

tendre [tɑ̃dʀ] *adj* tender; (*bois, roche, couleur*) soft ▷ *vt* (*élastique, peau*) to stretch; (*corde*) to tighten; (*muscle*) to tense; (*fig: piège*) to set, lay; (*donner*): **~ qch à qn** to hold sth out to sb; (*offrir*) to offer sb sth; **se tendre** *vi* (*corde*) to tighten; (*relations*) to become strained; **~ à qch/à faire** to tend towards sth/to do; **~ l'oreille** to prick up one's ears; **~ la main/le bras** to hold out one's hand/stretch out one's arm; **tendrement** *adv* tenderly; **tendresse** *nf* tenderness

tendu, e [tɑ̃dy] *pp de* **tendre** ▷ *adj* (*corde*) tight; (*muscles*) tensed; (*relations*) strained

ténèbres [tenɛbʀ] *nfpl* darkness *sg*

teneur [tənœʀ] *nf* content; (*d'une lettre*) terms *pl*, content

tenir [t(ə)niʀ] *vt* to hold; (*magasin, hôtel*) to run; (*promesse*) to keep ▷ *vi* to hold; (*neige, gel*) to last; **se tenir** *vi* (*avoir lieu*) to be held, take place; (*être: personne*) to stand; **~ à** (*personne, objet*) to be attached to; (*réputation*) to care about; **~ à faire** to be determined to do; **~ de** (*ressembler à*) to take after; **ça ne tient qu'à lui** it is entirely up to him; **~ qn pour** to regard sb as; **~ qch de qn** (*histoire*) to have heard *ou* learnt sth from sb; (*qualité, défaut*) to have inherited *ou* got sth from sb; **~ dans** to fit into; **~ compte de qch** to take sth into account; **~ les comptes** to keep the books; **~ bon** to stand fast; **~ le coup** to hold out; **~ au chaud**

(*café, plat*) to keep hot; **un manteau qui tient chaud** a warm coat; **tiens/tenez, voilà le stylo** there's the pen!; **tiens, voilà Alain!** look, here's Alain!; **tiens!** (*surprise*) really?; **se ~ droit** to stand (*ou* sit) up straight; **bien se ~** to behave well; **se ~ à qch** to hold on to sth; **s'en ~ à qch** to confine o.s. to sth

tennis [tenis] *nm* tennis; (*court*) tennis court ▷ *nm ou fpl* (*aussi*: **chaussures de ~**) tennis *ou* gym shoes; **tennis de table** table tennis; **tennisman** *nm* tennis player

tension [tɑ̃sjɔ̃] *nf* tension; (*Méd*) blood pressure; **avoir de la ~** to have high blood pressure

tentation [tɑ̃tasjɔ̃] *nf* temptation

tentative [tɑ̃tativ] *nf* attempt

tente [tɑ̃t] *nf* tent

tenter [tɑ̃te] *vt* (*éprouver, attirer*) to tempt; (*essayer*): **~ qch/de faire** to attempt *ou* try sth/to do; **~ sa chance** to try one's luck

tenture [tɑ̃tyʀ] *nf* hanging

tenu, e [t(ə)ny] *pp de* **tenir** ▷ *adj* (*maison, comptes*): **bien ~** well-kept; (*obligé*): **~ de faire** obliged to do ▷ *nf* (*vêtements*) clothes *pl*; (*comportement*) (good) manners *pl*, good behaviour; (*d'une maison*) upkeep; **en petite ~e** scantily dressed *ou* clad

ter [tɛʀ] *adj*: **16 ~** 16b *ou* B

terme [tɛʀm] *nm* term; (*fin*) end; **à court/long ~** *adj* short-/long-term ▷ *adv* in the short/long term; **avant ~** (*Méd*) prematurely; **mettre un ~ à** to put an end *ou* a stop to; **en bons ~s** on good terms

terminaison [tɛʀminɛzɔ̃] *nf* (*Ling*) ending

terminal, -aux [tɛʀminal, o] *nm* terminal; **terminale** *nf* (*Scol*) ≈ year 13 (*BRIT*), ≈ twelfth grade (*US*)

terminer [tɛʀmine] *vt* to finish; **se terminer** *vi* to end; **quand est-ce que le spectacle se termine?** when does the show finish?

terne [tɛʀn] *adj* dull

ternir [tɛʀniʀ] *vt* to dull; (*fig*) to sully, tarnish; **se ternir** *vi* to become dull

terrain [tɛʀɛ̃] *nm* (*sol, fig*) ground; (*Comm: étendue de terre*) land *no pl*; (*parcelle*) plot (of land); (*à bâtir*) site; **sur le ~** (*fig*) on the field; **terrain d'aviation** airfield; **terrain de camping** campsite; **terrain de football/rugby** football/rugby pitch (*BRIT*) *ou* field (*US*); **terrain de golf** golf course; **terrain de jeu** games field; (*pour les petits*) playground; **terrain de sport** sports ground; **terrain vague** waste ground *no pl*

terrasse [tɛʀas] *nf* terrace; **à la ~** (*café*) outside; **terrasser** *vt* (*adversaire*) to floor; (*suj: maladie etc*) to strike down

terre [tɛʀ] *nf* (*gén, aussi Élec*) earth; (*substance*) soil, earth; (*opposé à mer*) land *no pl*; (*contrée*) land; **terres** *nfpl* (*terrains*) lands, land *sg*; **en ~**

(pipe, poterie) clay cpd; **à ~ ou par ~** *(mettre, être, s'asseoir)* on the ground *(ou* floor); *(jeter, tomber)* to the ground, down; **terre à terre** adj inv *(considération, personne)* down-to-earth; **terre cuite** terracotta; **la terre ferme** dry land; **terre glaise** clay

terreau [tɛʁo] nm compost

terre-plein [tɛʁplɛ̃] nm platform; *(sur chaussée)* central reservation

terrestre [tɛʁɛstʁ] adj *(surface)* earth's, of the earth; *(Bot, Zool, Mil)* land cpd; *(Rel)* earthly

terreur [tɛʁœʁ] nf terror no pl

terrible [tɛʁibl] adj terrible, dreadful; *(fam)* terrific; **pas ~** nothing special

terrien, ne [tɛʁjɛ̃, jɛn] adj: **propriétaire ~** landowner ▷ nm/f *(non martien etc)* earthling

terrier [tɛʁje] nm burrow, hole; *(chien)* terrier

terrifier [tɛʁifje] vt to terrify

terrine [tɛʁin] nf *(récipient)* terrine; *(Culin)* pâté

territoire [tɛʁitwaʁ] nm territory

terroriser [tɛʁɔʁize] vt to terrorize

terrorisme [tɛʁɔʁism] nm terrorism; **terroriste** nm/f terrorist

tertiaire [tɛʁsjɛʁ] adj tertiary ▷ nm *(Écon)* service industries pl

tes [te] adj voir **ton'**

test [tɛst] nm test

testament [tɛstamã] nm *(Jur)* will; *(Rel)* Testament; *(fig)* legacy

tester [tɛste] vt to test

testicule [tɛstikyl] nm testicle

tétanos [tetanos] nm tetanus

têtard [tɛtaʁ] nm tadpole

tête [tɛt] nf head; *(cheveux)* hair no pl; *(visage)* face; **de ~** *(comme adj: wagon etc)* front cpd; *(comme adv: calculer)* in one's head, mentally; **perdre la ~** *(fig: s'affoler)* to lose one's head; (: *devenir fou)* to go off one's head; **tenir ~ à qn** to stand up to sb; **la ~ en bas** with one's head down; **la ~ la première** *(tomber)* headfirst; **faire une ~** *(Football)* to head the ball; **faire la ~** *(fig)* to sulk; **en ~** at the front; *(Sport)* in the lead; **à la ~ de** at the head of; **à ~ reposée** in a more leisurely moment; **n'en faire qu'à sa ~** to do as one pleases; **en avoir par-dessus la ~** to be fed up; **en ~ à ~** in private, alone together; **de la ~ aux pieds** from head to toe; **tête de lecture** *(playback)* head; **tête de liste** *(Pol)* chief candidate; **tête de mort** skull and crossbones; **tête de série** *(Tennis)* seeded player, seed; **tête de Turc** *(fig)* whipping boy *(BRIT)*, butt; **tête-à-queue** nm inv: **faire un tête-à-queue** to spin round

téter [tete] vt: **~ (sa mère)** to suck at one's mother's breast, feed

tétine [tetin] nf teat; *(sucette)* dummy *(BRIT)*, pacifier *(US)*

têtu, e [tety] adj stubborn, pigheaded

texte [tɛkst] nm text; *(morceau choisi)* passage

textile [tɛkstil] adj textile cpd ▷ nm textile; **le ~** the textile industry

Texto® [tɛksto] nm text message

texture [tɛkstyʁ] nf texture

TGV sigle m *(= train à grande vitesse)* high-speed train

thaïlandais, e [tajlɑ̃dɛ, ɛz] adj Thai ▷ nm/f: **T~, e** Thai

Thaïlande [tailɑ̃d] nf Thailand

thé [te] nm tea; **~ au citron** lemon tea; **~ au lait** tea with milk; **prendre le ~** to have tea; **faire le ~** to make the tea

théâtral, e, -aux [teatʁal, o] adj theatrical

théâtre [teatʁ] nm theatre; *(péj: simulation)* playacting; *(fig: lieu)* **le ~ de** the scene of; **faire du ~** to act

théière [tejɛʁ] nf teapot

thème [tɛm] nm theme; *(Scol: traduction)* prose *(composition)*

théologie [teɔlɔʒi] nf theology

théorie [teɔʁi] nf theory; **théorique** adj theoretical

thérapie [teʁapi] nf therapy

thermal, e, -aux [tɛʁmal, o] adj: **station ~e** spa; **cure ~e** water cure

thermomètre [tɛʁmɔmɛtʁ] nm thermometer

thermos® [tɛʁmos] nm ou nf: **(bouteille) thermos** vacuum ou Thermos® flask

thermostat [tɛʁmɔsta] nm thermostat

thèse [tɛz] nf thesis

thon [tɔ̃] nm tuna *(fish)*

thym [tɛ̃] nm thyme

Tibet [tibɛ] nm: **le ~** Tibet

tibia [tibja] nm shinbone, tibia; *(partie antérieure de la jambe)* shin

TIC sigle fpl *(= technologies de l'information et de la communication)* ICT sg

tic [tik] nm tic, *(nervous)* twitch; *(de langage etc)* mannerism

ticket [tikɛ] nm ticket; **ticket de caisse** receipt; **je peux avoir un ticket de caisse, s'il vous plaît?** can I have a receipt, please?

tiède [tjɛd] adj lukewarm; *(vent, air)* mild, warm; **tiédir** vi to cool; *(se réchauffer)* to grow warmer

tien, ne [tjɛ̃, tjɛn] pron: **le(la) ~(ne), les ~(ne)s** yours; **à la ~e!** cheers!

tiens [tjɛ̃] vb, excl voir **tenir**

tiercé [tjɛʁse] nm system of forecast betting giving first 3 horses

tiers, tierce [tjɛʁ, tjɛʁs] adj third ▷ nm *(Jur)* third party; *(fraction)* third; **le tiers monde** the Third World

tige [tiʒ] nf stem; *(baguette)* rod

tignasse [tiɲas] *(péj)* nf mop of hair

tigre [tigʁ] nm tiger; **tigré, e** adj *(rayé)* striped; *(tacheté)* spotted; *(chat)* tabby; **tigresse** nf tigress

tilleul [tijœl] nm lime (tree), linden (tree); (boisson) lime(-blossom) tea

timbre [tɛ̃bʀ] nm (tampon) stamp; (aussi: ~-poste) (postage) stamp; (Mus: de voix, instrument) timbre, tone

timbré, e [tɛ̃bʀe] (fam) adj cracked

timide [timid] adj shy; (timoré) timid; **timidement** adv shyly; timidly; **timidité** nf shyness; timidity

tintamarre [tɛ̃tamaʀ] nm din, uproar

tinter [tɛ̃te] vi to ring, chime; (argent, clefs) to jingle

tique [tik] nf (parasite) tick

tir [tiʀ] nm (sport) shooting; (fait ou manière de tirer) firing no pl; (rafale) fire; (stand) shooting gallery; **tir à l'arc** archery

tirage [tiʀaʒ] nm (action) printing; (Photo) print; (de journal) circulation; (de livre: nombre d'exemplaires) (print) run; (: édition) edition; (de loterie) draw; **par ~ au sort** by drawing lots

tire [tiʀ] nf: **vol à la ~** pickpocketing

tiré, e [tiʀe] adj (traits) drawn; **~ par les cheveux** far-fetched

tire-bouchon [tiʀbuʃɔ̃] nm corkscrew

tirelire [tiʀliʀ] nf moneybox

tirer [tiʀe] vt (gén) to pull; (trait, rideau, carte, conclusion, chèque) to draw; (langue) to stick out; (en faisant feu: balle, coup) to fire; (: animal) to shoot; (journal, livre, photo) to print; (Football: corner etc) to take ▷ vi (faire feu) to fire; (faire du tir, Football) to shoot; **se tirer** vi (fam) to push off; **s'en ~** (éviter le pire) to get off; (survivre) to pull through; (se débrouiller) to manage; **~ qch de** (extraire) to take ou pull sth out of; **~ qn de** (embarras etc) to help ou get sb out of; **~ sur** (corde) to pull on ou at; (faire feu sur) to shoot ou fire at; (pipe) to draw on; (approcher de: couleur) to verge ou border on; **~ à l'arc/la carabine** to shoot with a bow and arrow/with a rifle; **~ à sa fin** to be drawing to a close; **~ qch au clair** to clear sth up; **~ au sort** to draw lots; **~ parti de** to take advantage of; **~ profit de** to profit from; **~ les cartes** to read ou tell the cards

tiret [tiʀɛ] nm dash

tireur [tiʀœʀ] nm gunman; **tireur d'élite** marksman

tiroir [tiʀwaʀ] nm drawer; **tiroir-caisse** nm till

tisane [tizan] nf herb tea

tisser [tise] vt to weave

tissu [tisy] nm fabric, material, cloth no pl; (Anat, Bio) tissue; **tissu-éponge** nm (terry) towelling no pl

titre [titʀ] nm (gén) title; (de journal) headline; (diplôme) qualification; (Comm) security; **en ~** (champion) official; **à juste ~** rightly; **à quel ~?** on what grounds?; **à aucun ~** on no account; **au même ~ (que)** in the same way (as); **à ~**

d'information for (your) information; **à ~ gracieux** free of charge; **à ~ d'essai** on a trial basis; **à ~ privé** in a private capacity; **titre de propriété** title deed; **titre de transport** ticket

tituber [titybe] vi to stagger (along)

titulaire [titylɛʀ] adj (Admin) with tenure ▷ nm/f (de permis) holder; **être ~ de** (diplôme, permis) to hold

toast [tost] nm slice ou piece of toast; (de bienvenue) (welcoming) toast; **porter un ~ à qn** to propose ou drink a toast to sb

toboggan [tɔbɔgɑ̃] nm slide; (Auto) flyover

toc [tɔk] excl: **~, ~** knock knock ▷ nm: **en ~** fake

tocsin [tɔksɛ̃] nm alarm (bell)

tohu-bohu [tɔybɔy] nm hubbub

toi [twa] pron you

toile [twal] nf (tableau) canvas; **de** ou **en ~** (pantalon) cotton; (sac) canvas; **la T~** (Internet) the Web; **toile cirée** oilcloth; **toile d'araignée** cobweb; **toile de fond** (fig) backdrop

toilette [twalɛt] nf (habits) outfit; **toilettes** nfpl (w.-c.) toilet sg; **faire sa ~** to have a wash, get washed; **articles de ~** toiletries; **où sont les ~?** where's the toilet?

toi-même [twamɛm] pron yourself

toit [twa] nm roof; **toit ouvrant** sunroof

toiture [twatyʀ] nf roof

Tokyo [tɔkjo] n Tokyo

tôle [tol] nf (plaque) steel ou iron sheet; **tôle ondulée** corrugated iron

tolérable [tɔleʀabl] adj tolerable

tolérant, e [tɔleʀɑ̃, ɑ̃t] adj tolerant

tolérer [tɔleʀe] vt to tolerate; (Admin: hors taxe etc) to allow

tollé [tɔ(l)le] nm outcry

tomate [tɔmat] nf tomato; **~s farcies** stuffed tomatoes

tombe [tɔ̃b] nf (sépulture) grave; (avec monument) tomb

tombeau, x [tɔ̃bo] nm tomb

tombée [tɔ̃be] nf: **à la ~ de la nuit** at nightfall

tomber [tɔ̃be] vi to fall; (fièvre, vent) to drop; **laisser ~** (objet) to drop; (personne) to let down; (activité) to give up; **laisse ~!** forget it!; **faire ~** to knock over; **~ sur** (rencontrer) to bump into; **~ de fatigue/sommeil** to drop from exhaustion/be falling asleep on one's feet; **ça tombe bien** that's come at the right time; **il est bien tombé** he's been lucky; **~ à l'eau** (projet) to fall through; **~ en panne** to break down

tombola [tɔ̃bɔla] nf raffle

tome [tɔm] nm volume

ton¹, ta [tɔ̃, ta] (pl **tes**) adj your

ton² [tɔ̃] nm (gén) tone; (couleur) shade, tone; **de bon ~** in good taste

tonalité [tɔnalite] nf (au téléphone) dialling tone

tondeuse [tɔ̃døz] nf (à gazon) (lawn)mower;

(*du coiffeur*) clippers *pl*; (*pour les moutons*) shears *pl*

tondre [tɔ̃dʀ] *vt* (*pelouse, herbe*) to mow; (*haie*) to cut, clip; (*mouton, toison*) to shear; (*cheveux*) to crop

tongs [tɔ̃g] *nfpl* flip-flops

tonifier [tɔnifje] *vt* (*peau, organisme*) to tone up

tonique [tɔnik] *adj* fortifying ▷ *nm* tonic

tonne [tɔn] *nf* metric ton, tonne

tonneau, x [tɔno] *nm* (*à vin, cidre*) barrel; **faire des ~x** (*voiture, avion*) to roll over

tonnelle [tɔnɛl] *nf* bower, arbour

tonner [tɔne] *vi* to thunder; **il tonne** it is thundering, there's some thunder

tonnerre [tɔnɛʀ] *nm* thunder

tonus [tɔnys] *nm* energy

top [tɔp] *nm*: **au 3ème ~** at the 3rd stroke ▷ *adj*: **~ secret** top secret

topinambour [tɔpinãbuʀ] *nm* Jerusalem artichoke

torche [tɔʀʃ] *nf* torch

torchon [tɔʀʃɔ̃] *nm* cloth; (*à vaisselle*) tea towel *ou* cloth

tordre [tɔʀdʀ] *vt* (*chiffon*) to wring; (*barre, fig: visage*) to twist; **se tordre** *vi*: **se ~ le poignet/ la cheville** to twist one's wrist/ankle; **se ~ de douleur/rire** to be doubled up with pain/ laughter; **tordu, e** *adj* bent; (*fig*) crazy

tornade [tɔʀnad] *nf* tornado

torrent [tɔʀã] *nm* mountain stream

torsade [tɔʀsad] *nf*: **un pull à ~s** a cable sweater

torse [tɔʀs] *nm* chest; (*Anat, Sculpture*) torso; **~ nu** stripped to the waist

tort [tɔʀ] *nm* (*défaut*) fault; **torts** *nmpl* (*Jur*) fault *sg*; **avoir ~** to be wrong; **être dans son ~** to be in the wrong; **donner ~ à qn** to lay the blame on sb; **causer du ~ à qn** to harm sb; **à ~** wrongly; **à ~ et à travers** wildly

torticolis [tɔʀtikɔli] *nm* stiff neck

tortiller [tɔʀtije] *vt* to twist; (*moustache*) to twirl; **se tortiller** *vi* to wriggle; (*en dansant*) to wiggle

tortionnaire [tɔʀsjɔnɛʀ] *nm* torturer

tortue [tɔʀty] *nf* tortoise; (*d'eau douce*) terrapin; (*d'eau de mer*) turtle

tortueux, -euse [tɔʀtɥø, øz] *adj* (*rue*) twisting; (*fig*) tortuous

torture [tɔʀtyʀ] *nf* torture; **torturer** *vt* to torture; (*fig*) to torment

tôt [to] *adv* early; **~ ou tard** sooner or later; **si ~** so early; (*déjà*) so soon; **plus ~** earlier; **au plus ~** at the earliest

total, e, -aux [tɔtal, o] *adj, nm* total; **au ~** in total; (*fig*) on the whole; **faire le ~** to work out the total; **totalement** *adv* totally; **totaliser** *vt* to total; **totalitaire** *adj* totalitarian; **totalité** *nf*: **la totalité de** all (of); the whole

+*sg*; **en totalité** entirely

toubib [tubib] (*fam*) *nm* doctor

touchant, e [tuʃã, ãt] *adj* touching

touche [tuʃ] *nf* (*de piano, de machine à écrire*) key; (*de téléphone*) button; (*Peinture etc*) stroke, touch; (*fig: de nostalgie*) touch; (*Football: aussi*: **remise en ~**) throw-in; (*aussi*: **ligne de ~**) touch-line; **touche dièse** (*de téléphone, clavier*) hash key

toucher [tuʃe] *nm* touch ▷ *vt* to touch; (*palper*) to feel; (*atteindre: d'un coup de feu etc*) to hit; (*concerner*) to concern, affect; (*contacter*) to reach, contact; (*recevoir: récompense*) to receive, get; (*: salaire*) to draw, get; (*: chèque*) to cash; **se toucher** (*être en contact*) to touch; **au ~** to the touch; **~ à** to touch; (*concerner*) to have to do with, concern; **je vais lui en ~ un mot** I'll have a word with him about it; **~ au but** (*fig*) to near one's goal; **~ à sa fin** to be drawing to a close

touffe [tuf] *nf* tuft

touffu, e [tufy] *adj* thick, dense

toujours [tuʒuʀ] *adv* always; (*encore*) still; (*constamment*) forever; **~ plus** more and more; **pour ~** forever; **~ est-il que** the fact remains that; **essaie ~** (you can) try anyway

toupie [tupi] *nf* (spinning) top

tour¹ [tuʀ] *nf* tower; (*immeuble*) high-rise block (BRIT) *ou* building (US); (*Échecs*) castle, rook; **tour de contrôle** *nf* control tower; **la tour Eiffel** the Eiffel Tower

tour² [tuʀ] *nm* (*excursion*) trip; (*à pied*) stroll, walk; (*en voiture*) run, ride; (*Sport: aussi*: **~ de piste**) lap; (*d'être servi ou de jouer etc*) turn; (*de roue etc*) revolution; (*Pol: aussi*: **~ de scrutin**) ballot; (*ruse, de prestidigitation*) trick; (*de potier*) wheel; (*à bois, métaux*) lathe; (*circonférence*): **de 3 m de ~** 3 m round, with a circumference *ou* girth of 3 m; **faire le ~ de** to go round; (*à pied*) to walk round; **c'est au ~ de Renée** it's Renée's turn; **à ~ de rôle, ~ à ~** in turn; **tour de chant** *nm* song recital; **tour de force** tour de force; **tour de garde** *nm* spell of duty; **tour d'horizon** *nm* (*fig*) general survey; **tour de taille/tête** *nm* waist/head measurement; **un 33 tours** an LP; **un 45 tours** a single

tourbe [tuʀb] *nf* peat

tourbillon [tuʀbijɔ̃] *nm* whirlwind; (*d'eau*) whirlpool; (*fig*) whirl, swirl; **tourbillonner** *vi* to whirl (round)

tourelle [tuʀɛl] *nf* turret

tourisme [tuʀism] *nm* tourism; **agence de ~** tourist agency; **faire du ~** to go touring; (*en ville*) to go sightseeing; **touriste** *nm/f* tourist; **touristique** *adj* tourist *cpd*; (*région*) touristic

tourment [tuʀmã] *nm* torment; **tourmenter** *vt* to torment; **se tourmenter** to fret, worry o.s.

tournage [tuʀnaʒ] *nm* (*Cinéma*) shooting

tournant [tuʀnã] *nm* (*de route*) bend; (*fig*)

turning point

tournée [tuʀne] *nf* (*du facteur etc*) round; (*d'artiste, politicien*) tour; (*au café*) round (of drinks)

tourner [tuʀne] *vt* to turn; (*sauce, mélange*) to stir; (*Cinéma: faire les prises de vues*) to shoot; (: *produire*) to make ▷ *vi* to turn; (*moteur*) to run; (*taximètre*) to tick away; (*lait etc*) to turn (*sour*); **se tourner** *vi* to turn round; **tournez à gauche/droite au prochain carrefour** turn left/right at the next junction; **mal ~** to go wrong; **~ autour de** to go round; (*péj*) to hang round; **~ à/en** to turn into; **~ qn en ridicule** to ridicule sb; **~ le dos à** (*mouvement*) to turn one's back on; (*position*) to have one's back to; **~ de l'œil** to pass out; **se ~ vers** to turn towards; (*fig*) to turn to; **se ~ les pouces** to twiddle one's thumbs

tournesol [tuʀnəsɔl] *nm* sunflower

tournevis [tuʀnəvis] *nm* screwdriver

tournoi [tuʀnwa] *nm* tournament

tournure [tuʀnyʀ] *nf* (*Ling*) turn of phrase; (*évolution*): **la ~ de qch** the way sth is developing; **tournure d'esprit** turn *ou* cast of mind

tourte [tuʀt] *nf* pie

tourterelle [tuʀtəʀɛl] *nf* turtledove

tous [tu] *adj, pron voir* **tout**

Toussaint [tusɛ̃] *nf*: **la ~** All Saints' Day

⬤ **TOUSSAINT**
⬤
⬤ **La Toussaint**, 1 November, or All Saints'
⬤ Day, is a public holiday in France. People
⬤ traditionally visit the graves of friends and
⬤ relatives to lay chrysanthemums on them.

tousser [tuse] *vi* to cough

🔘 **MOT-CLÉ**

tout, e [tu, tut] (*mpl* **tous**, *fpl* **toutes**) *adj*
 1 (*avec article singulier*) all; **tout le lait** all the milk; **toute la nuit** all night, the whole night; **tout le livre** the whole book; **tout un pain** a whole loaf; **tout le temps** all the time; the whole time; **tout le monde** everybody; **c'est tout le contraire** it's quite the opposite
 2 (*avec article pluriel*) every, all; **tous les livres** all the books; **toutes les nuits** every night; **toutes les fois** every time; **toutes les trois/deux semaines** every third/other *ou* second week, every three/two weeks; **tous les deux** both *ou* each of us (*ou* them *ou* you); **toutes les trois** all three of us (*ou* them *ou* you)
 3 (*sans article*): **à tout âge** at any age; **pour toute nourriture, il avait ...** his only food was ...
 ▷ *pron* everything, all; **il a tout fait**

he's done everything; **je les vois tous** I can see them all *ou* all of them; **nous y sommes tous allés** all of us went, we all went; **c'est tout** that's all; **en tout** in all; **tout ce qu'il sait** all he knows
 ▷ *nm* whole; **le tout** all of it (*ou* them); **le tout est de ...** the main thing is to ...; **pas du tout** not at all
 ▷ *adv* **1** (*très, complètement*) very; **tout près** very near; **le tout premier** the very first; **tout seul** all alone; **le livre tout entier** the whole book; **tout en haut** right at the top; **tout droit** straight ahead
 2: **tout en** while; **tout en travaillant** while working, as he *etc* works *ou* worked
 3: **tout d'abord** first of all; **tout à coup** suddenly; **tout à fait** absolutely; **tout à l'heure** a short while ago; (*futur*) in a short while, shortly; **à tout à l'heure!** see you later!; **tout de même** all the same; **tout de suite** immediately, straight away; **tout simplement** quite simply

toutefois [tutfwa] *adv* however

toutes [tut] *adj, pron voir* **tout**

tout-terrain [tuteʀɛ̃] *adj*: **vélo ~** mountain bike; **véhicule ~** four-wheel drive

toux [tu] *nf* cough

toxicomane [tɔksikɔman] *nm/f* drug addict

toxique [tɔksik] *adj* toxic

trac [tʀak] *nm* (*au théâtre, en public*) stage fright; (*aux examens*) nerves *pl*; **avoir le ~** (*au théâtre, en public*) to have stage fright; (*aux examens*) to be feeling nervous

tracasser [tʀakase] *vt* to worry, bother; **se tracasser** to worry

trace [tʀas] *nf* (*empreintes*) tracks *pl*; (*marques, aussi fig*) mark; (*quantité infime, indice, vestige*) trace; **traces de pas** footprints

tracer [tʀase] *vt* to draw; (*piste*) to open up

tract [tʀakt] *nm* tract, pamphlet

tracteur [tʀaktœʀ] *nm* tractor

traction [tʀaksjɔ̃] *nf*: **~ avant/arrière** front-wheel/rear-wheel drive

tradition [tʀadisjɔ̃] *nf* tradition; **traditionnel, le** *adj* traditional

traducteur, -trice [tʀadyktœʀ, tʀis] *nm/f* translator

traduction [tʀadyksjɔ̃] *nf* translation

traduire [tʀadɥiʀ] *vt* to translate; (*exprimer*) to convey; **~ qn en justice** to bring sb before the courts; **pouvez-vous me ~ ceci?** can you translate this for me?

trafic [tʀafik] *nm* traffic; **trafic d'armes** arms dealing; **trafiquant, e** *nm/f* trafficker; (*d'armes*) dealer; **trafiquer** (*péj*) *vt* (*vin*) to doctor; (*moteur, document*) to tamper with

tragédie [tʀaʒedi] *nf* tragedy; **tragique** *adj* tragic

t

trahir [tʀaiʀ] vt to betray; **trahison** nf
betrayal; (Jur) treason

train [tʀɛ̃] nm (Rail) train; (allure) pace; **être
en ~ de faire qch** to be doing sth; **c'est bien
le ~ pour ...?** is this the train for ...?; **train
d'atterrissage** undercarriage; **train de vie**
lifestyle; **train électrique** (jouet) (electric)
train set

traîne [tʀɛn] nf (de robe) train; **être à la ~** to
lag behind

traîneau, x [tʀɛno] nm sleigh, sledge

traîner [tʀene] vt (remorque) to pull; (enfant,
chien) to drag ou trail along ▷ vi (robe, manteau)
to trail; (être en désordre) to lie around; (aller
lentement) to dawdle (along); (vagabonder, agir
lentement) to hang about; (durer) to drag on;
se traîner vi: **se ~ par terre** to crawl (on the
ground); **~ les pieds** to drag one's feet

train-train [tʀɛ̃tʀɛ̃] nm humdrum routine

traire [tʀɛʀ] vt to milk

trait [tʀɛ] nm (ligne) line; (de dessin) stroke;
(caractéristique) feature, trait; **traits** nmpl (du
visage) features; **d'un ~** (boire) in one gulp; **de
~** (animal) draught; **avoir ~ à** to concern; **trait
d'union** hyphen

traitant, e [tʀɛtɑ̃, ɑ̃t] adj (shampooing)
medicated; **votre médecin ~** your usual ou
family doctor

traite [tʀɛt] nf (Comm) draft; (Agr) milking;
d'une ~ without stopping

traité [tʀɛte] nm treaty

traitement [tʀɛtmɑ̃] nm treatment;
(salaire) salary; **traitement de données**
data processing; **traitement de texte** word
processing; (logiciel) word processing package

traiter [tʀɛte] vt to treat; (qualifier): **~ qn
d'idiot** to call sb a fool ▷ vi to deal; **~ de** to
deal with

traiteur [tʀɛtœʀ] nm caterer

traître, -esse [tʀɛtʀ, tʀɛtʀɛs] adj (dangereux)
treacherous ▷ nm traitor

trajectoire [tʀaʒɛktwaʀ] nf path

trajet [tʀaʒɛ] nm (parcours, voyage) journey;
(itinéraire) route; (distance à parcourir) distance;
il y a une heure de ~ the journey takes one
hour

trampoline [tʀɑ̃pɔlin] nm trampoline

tramway [tʀamwɛ] nm tram(way); (voiture)
tram(car) (BRIT), streetcar (US)

tranchant, e [tʀɑ̃ʃɑ̃, ɑ̃t] adj sharp; (fig)
peremptory ▷ nm (d'un couteau) cutting edge;
(de la main) edge; **à double ~** double-edged

tranche [tʀɑ̃ʃ] nf (morceau) slice; (arête) edge; **~
d'âge/de salaires** age/wage bracket

tranché, e [tʀɑ̃ʃe] adj (couleurs) distinct;
(opinions) clear-cut

trancher [tʀɑ̃ʃe] vt to cut, sever ▷ vi to take a
decision; **~ avec** to contrast sharply with

tranquille [tʀɑ̃kil] adj quiet; (rassuré) easy in

one's mind, with one's mind at rest; **se tenir
~** (enfant) to be quiet; **laisse-moi/laisse-ça ~**
leave me/it alone; **avoir la conscience ~** to
have a clear conscience; **tranquillisant** nm
tranquillizer; **tranquillité** nf peace (and
quiet); (d'esprit) peace of mind

transférer [tʀɑ̃sfeʀe] vt to transfer;
transfert nm transfer

transformation [tʀɑ̃sfɔʀmasjɔ̃] nf change,
alteration; (radicale) transformation; (Rugby)
conversion; **transformations** nfpl (travaux)
alterations

transformer [tʀɑ̃sfɔʀme] vt to change;
(radicalement) to transform; (vêtement) to
alter; (matière première, appartement, Rugby) to
convert; **(se) ~ en** to turn into

transfusion [tʀɑ̃sfyzjɔ̃] nf: **~ sanguine** blood
transfusion

transgénique [tʀɑ̃sʒenik] adj transgenic

transgresser [tʀɑ̃sgʀese] vt to contravene

transi, e [tʀɑ̃zi] adj numb (with cold), chilled
to the bone

transiger [tʀɑ̃ziʒe] vi to compromise

transit [tʀɑ̃zit] nm transit; **transiter** vi to
pass in transit

transition [tʀɑ̃zisjɔ̃] nf transition;
transitoire adj transitional

transmettre [tʀɑ̃smɛtʀ] vt (passer): **~ qch
à qn** to pass sth on to sb; (Tech, Tél, Méd)
to transmit; (TV, Radio: retransmettre) to
broadcast; **transmission** nf transmission

transparent, e [tʀɑ̃spaʀɑ̃, ɑ̃t] adj
transparent

transpercer [tʀɑ̃spɛʀse] vt (froid, pluie) to go
through, pierce; (balle) to go through

transpiration [tʀɑ̃spiʀasjɔ̃] nf perspiration

transpirer [tʀɑ̃spiʀe] vi to perspire

transplanter [tʀɑ̃splɑ̃te] vt (Méd, Bot) to
transplant

transport [tʀɑ̃spɔʀ] nm transport;
transports en commun public transport sg;
transporter vt to carry, move; (Comm) to
transport, convey; **transporteur** nm haulage
contractor (BRIT), trucker (US)

transvaser [tʀɑ̃svaze] vt to decant

transversal, e, -aux [tʀɑ̃svɛʀsal, o] adj (rue)
which runs across; **coupe ~e** cross section

trapèze [tʀapɛz] nm (au cirque) trapeze

trappe [tʀap] nf trap door

trapu, e [tʀapy] adj squat, stocky

traquenard [tʀaknaʀ] nm trap

traquer [tʀake] vt to track down; (harceler)
to hound

traumatiser [tʀomatize] vt to traumatize

travail, -aux [tʀavaj] nm (gén) work; (tâche,
métier) work no pl, job; (Écon, Méd) labour; **être
sans ~** (employé) to be unemployed; voir aussi
travaux; **travail (au) noir** moonlighting

travailler [tʀavaje] vi to work; (bois) to warp

▷ *vt* (*bois, métal*) to work; (*objet d'art, discipline*) to work on; **cela le travaille** it is on his mind; **travailleur, -euse** *adj* hard-working ▷ *nm/f* worker; **travailleur social** social worker; **travailliste** *adj* ≈ Labour *cpd*

travaux [tʀavo] *nmpl* (*de réparation, agricoles etc*) work *sg*; (*sur route*) roadworks *pl*; (*de construction*) building (work); **travaux des champs** farmwork *sg*; **travaux dirigés** (*Scol*) tutorial *sg*; **travaux forcés** hard labour *no pl*; **travaux manuels** (*Scol*) handicrafts; **travaux ménagers** housework *no pl*; **travaux pratiques** (*Scol*) practical work; (*en laboratoire*) lab work

travers [tʀavɛʀ] *nm* fault, failing; **en ~ (de)** across; **au ~ (de)/à ~** through; **de ~** (*nez, bouche*) crooked; (*chapeau*) askew; **comprendre de ~** to misunderstand; **regarder de ~** (*fig*) to look askance at

traverse [tʀavɛʀs] *nf* (*de voie ferrée*) sleeper; **chemin de ~** shortcut

traversée [tʀavɛʀse] *nf* crossing; **combien de temps dure la ~?** how long does the crossing take?

traverser [tʀavɛʀse] *vt* (*gén*) to cross; (*ville, tunnel, aussi: percer, fig*) to go through; (*suj: ligne, trait*) to run across

traversin [tʀavɛʀsɛ̃] *nm* bolster

travesti [tʀavɛsti] *nm* transvestite

trébucher [tʀebyʃe] *vi*: **~ (sur)** to stumble (over), trip (against)

trèfle [tʀɛfl] *nm* (*Bot*) clover; (*Cartes: couleur*) clubs *pl*; (*: carte*) club; **~ à quatre feuilles** four-leaf clover

treize [tʀɛz] *num* thirteen; **treizième** *num* thirteenth

tréma [tʀema] *nm* diaeresis

tremblement [tʀɑ̃bləmɑ̃] *nm*: **tremblement de terre** earthquake

trembler [tʀɑ̃ble] *vi* to tremble, shake; **~ de** (*froid, fièvre*) to shiver *ou* tremble with; (*peur*) to shake *ou* tremble with; **~ pour qn** to fear for sb

trémousser [tʀemuse]: **se trémousser** *vi* to jig about, wriggle about

trempé, e [tʀɑ̃pe] *adj* soaking (wet), drenched; (*Tech*) tempered

tremper [tʀɑ̃pe] *vt* to soak, drench; (*aussi*: **faire ~, mettre à ~**) to soak; (*plonger*): **~ qch dans** to dip sth in(to) ▷ *vi* to soak; (*fig*): **~ dans** to be involved *ou* have a hand in; **se tremper** *vi* to have a quick dip

tremplin [tʀɑ̃plɛ̃] *nm* springboard; (*Ski*) ski-jump

trentaine [tʀɑ̃tɛn] *nf*: **une ~ (de)** thirty or so, about thirty; **avoir la ~** (*âge*) to be around thirty

trente [tʀɑ̃t] *num* thirty; **être sur son ~ et un** to be wearing one's Sunday best; **trentième** *num* thirtieth

trépidant, e [tʀepidɑ̃, ɑ̃t] *adj* (*fig: rythme*) pulsating; (*: vie*) hectic

trépigner [tʀepiɲe] *vi* to stamp (one's feet)

très [tʀɛ] *adv* very; much +*pp*, highly +*pp*

trésor [tʀezɔʀ] *nm* treasure; **Trésor (public)** public revenue; **trésorerie** *nf* (*gestion*) accounts *pl*; (*bureaux*) accounts department; **difficultés de trésorerie** cash problems, shortage of cash *ou* funds; **trésorier, -ière** *nm/f* treasurer

tressaillir [tʀesajiʀ] *vi* to shiver, shudder

tressauter [tʀesote] *vi* to start, jump

tresse [tʀɛs] *nf* braid, plait; **tresser** *vt* (*cheveux*) to braid, plait; (*fil, jonc*) to plait; (*corbeille*) to weave; (*corde*) to twist

tréteau, x [tʀeto] *nm* trestle

treuil [tʀœj] *nm* winch

trêve [tʀɛv] *nf* (*Mil, Pol*) truce; (*fig*) respite; **~ de ...** enough of this ...

tri [tʀi] *nm*: **faire le ~ (de)** to sort out; **le (bureau de) ~** (*Postes*) the sorting office

triangle [tʀijɑ̃gl] *nm* triangle; **triangulaire** *adj* triangular

tribord [tʀibɔʀ] *nm*: **à ~** to starboard, on the starboard side

tribu [tʀiby] *nf* tribe

tribunal, -aux [tʀibynal, o] *nm* (*Jur*) court; (*Mil*) tribunal

tribune [tʀibyn] *nf* (*estrade*) platform, rostrum; (*débat*) forum; (*d'église, de tribunal*) gallery; (*de stade*) stand

tribut [tʀiby] *nm* tribute

tributaire [tʀibytɛʀ] *adj*: **être ~ de** to be dependent on

tricher [tʀiʃe] *vi* to cheat; **tricheur, -euse** *nm/f* cheat(er)

tricolore [tʀikɔlɔʀ] *adj* three-coloured; (*français*) red, white and blue

tricot [tʀiko] *nm* (*technique, ouvrage*) knitting *no pl*; (*vêtement*) jersey, sweater; **~ de peau** vest; **tricoter** *vt* to knit

tricycle [tʀisikl] *nm* tricycle

trier [tʀije] *vt* to sort out; (*Postes, fruits*) to sort

trimestre [tʀimɛstʀ] *nm* (*Scol*) term; (*Comm*) quarter; **trimestriel, le** *adj* quarterly; (*Scol*) end-of-term

trinquer [tʀɛ̃ke] *vi* to clink glasses

triomphe [tʀijɔ̃f] *nm* triumph; **triompher** *vi* to triumph, win; **triompher de** to triumph over, overcome

tripes [tʀip] *nfpl* (*Culin*) tripe *sg*

triple [tʀipl] *adj* triple ▷ *nm*: **le ~ (de)** (*comparaison*) three times as much (as); **en ~ exemplaire** in triplicate; **tripler** *vi, vt* to triple, treble

triplés, -ées [tʀiple] *nm/fpl* triplets

tripoter [tʀipɔte] *vt* to fiddle with

triste [tʀist] *adj* sad; (*couleur, temps, journée*) dreary; (*péj*): **~ personnage/affaire** sorry individual/affair; **tristesse** nf sadness

trivial, e, -aux [tʀivjal, jo] adj coarse, crude; (commun) mundane

troc [tʀɔk] nm barter

trognon [tʀɔɲɔ̃] nm (de fruit) core; (de légume) stalk

trois [tʀwɑ] num three; **troisième** num third ▷ nf (Scol) year 10 (BRIT), ninth grade (US); **le troisième âge** (période de vie) one's retirement years; (personnes âgées) senior citizens pl

trombe [tʀɔ̃b] nf: **des ~s d'eau** a downpour; **en ~** like a whirlwind

trombone [tʀɔ̃bɔn] nm (Mus) trombone; (de bureau) paper clip

trompe [tʀɔ̃p] nf (d'éléphant) trunk; (Mus) trumpet, horn

tromper [tʀɔ̃pe] vt to deceive; (vigilance, poursuivants) to elude; **se tromper** vi to make a mistake, be mistaken; **se ~ de voiture/jour** to take the wrong car/get the day wrong; **se ~ de 3 cm/20 euros** to be out by 3 cm/20 euros; **je me suis trompé de route** I took the wrong road

trompette [tʀɔ̃pɛt] nf trumpet; **en ~** (nez) turned-up

trompeur, -euse [tʀɔ̃pœʀ, øz] adj deceptive

tronc [tʀɔ̃] nm (Bot, Anat) trunk; (d'église) collection box

tronçon [tʀɔ̃sɔ̃] nm section; **tronçonner** vt to saw up; **tronçonneuse** nf chainsaw

trône [tʀon] nm throne

trop [tʀo] adv (+vb) too much; (+adjectif, adverbe) too; **~ (nombreux)** too many; **~ peu (nombreux)** too few; **~ (souvent)** too often; **~ (longtemps)** (for) too long; **~ de** (nombre) too many; (quantité) too much; **de ~, en ~: des livres en ~** a few books too many; **du lait en ~** too much milk; **3 livres/3 euros de ~** 3 books too many/3 euros too much; **ça coûte ~ cher** it's too expensive

tropical, e, -aux [tʀɔpikal, o] adj tropical

tropique [tʀɔpik] nm tropic

trop-plein [tʀoplɛ̃] nm (tuyau) overflow ou outlet (pipe); (liquide) overflow

troquer [tʀɔke] vt: **~ qch contre** to barter ou trade sth for; (fig) to swap sth for

trot [tʀo] nm trot; **trotter** vi to trot

trottinette [tʀɔtinɛt] nf (child's) scooter

trottoir [tʀɔtwaʀ] nm pavement (BRIT), sidewalk (US); **faire le ~** (péj) to walk the streets; **trottoir roulant** moving walkway, travellator

trou [tʀu] nm hole; (fig) gap; (Comm) deficit; **trou d'air** air pocket; **trou de mémoire** blank, lapse of memory

troublant, e [tʀublɑ̃, ɑ̃t] adj disturbing

trouble [tʀubl] adj (liquide) cloudy; (image, photo) blurred; (affaire) shady, murky ▷ adv: **voir ~** to have blurred vision ▷ nm agitation;

troubles nmpl (Pol) disturbances, troubles, unrest sg; (Méd) trouble sg, disorders; **trouble-fête** nm spoilsport

troubler [tʀuble] vt to disturb; (liquide) to make cloudy; (intriguer) to bother; **se troubler** vi (personne) to become flustered ou confused

trouer [tʀue] vt to make a hole (ou holes) in

trouille [tʀuj] (fam) nf: **avoir la ~** to be scared to death

troupe [tʀup] nf troop; **troupe (de théâtre)** (theatrical) company

troupeau, x [tʀupo] nm (de moutons) flock; (de vaches) herd

trousse [tʀus] nf case, kit; (d'écolier) pencil case; **aux ~s de** (fig) on the heels ou tail of; **trousse à outils** toolkit; **trousse de toilette** toilet bag

trousseau, x [tʀuso] nm (de mariée) trousseau; **trousseau de clefs** bunch of keys

trouvaille [tʀuvaj] nf find

trouver [tʀuve] vt to find; (rendre visite): **aller/venir ~ qn** to go/come and see sb; **se trouver** vi (être) to be; **je trouve que** I find ou think that; **~ à boire/critiquer** to find something to drink/criticize; **se ~ mal** to pass out

truand [tʀyɑ̃] nm gangster; **truander** vt: **se faire truander** to be swindled

truc [tʀyk] nm (astuce) way, trick; (de cinéma, prestidigitateur) trick, effect; (chose) thing, thingumajig; **avoir le ~** to have the knack; **c'est pas mon ~** (fam) it's not really my thing

truffe [tʀyf] nf truffle; (nez) nose

truffé, e [tʀyfe] adj (Culin) garnished with truffles; **~ de** (fig: citations) peppered with; (: fautes) riddled with; (: pièges) bristling with

truie [tʀɥi] nf sow

truite [tʀɥit] nf trout inv

truquage [tʀykaʒ] nm special effects pl

truquer [tʀyke] vt (élections, serrure, dés) to fix

TSVP sigle (= tournez svp) PTO

TTC sigle (= toutes taxes comprises) inclusive of tax

tu¹ [ty] pron you; **dire tu à qn** to use the "tu" form to sb

tu², e [ty] pp de **taire**

tuba [tyba] nm (Mus) tuba; (Sport) snorkel

tube [tyb] nm tube; (chanson) hit

tuberculose [tybɛʀkyloz] nf tuberculosis

tuer [tɥe] vt to kill; **se tuer** vi to be killed; (suicide) to kill o.s.; **se ~ au travail** (fig) to work o.s. to death; **tuerie** nf slaughter no pl

tue-tête [tytɛt]: **à ~** adv at the top of one's voice

tueur [tɥœʀ] nm killer; **tueur à gages** hired killer

tuile [tɥil] nf tile; (fam) spot of bad luck, blow

tulipe [tylip] nf tulip

tuméfié, e [tymefje] adj puffed-up, swollen

tumeur [tymœʀ] nf growth, tumour

tumulte [tymylt] *nm* commotion;
tumultueux, -euse *adj* stormy, turbulent
tunique [tynik] *nf* tunic
Tunis [tynis] *n* Tunis
Tunisie [tynizi] *nf*: **la ~** Tunisia; **tunisien, ne**
adj Tunisian ▷ *nm/f*: **Tunisien, ne** Tunisian
tunnel [tynɛl] *nm* tunnel; **le ~ sous la
Manche** the Channel Tunnel
turbulent, e [tyʀbylɑ̃, ɑ̃t] *adj* boisterous,
unruly
turc, turque [tyʀk] *adj* Turkish ▷ *nm/f*: **T~,
Turque** Turk/Turkish woman ▷ *nm* (*Ling*)
Turkish
turf [tyʀf] *nm* racing; **turfiste** *nm/f* racegoer
Turquie [tyʀki] *nf*: **la ~** Turkey
turquoise [tyʀkwaz] *nf* turquoise ▷ *adj inv*
turquoise
tutelle [tytɛl] *nf* (*Jur*) guardianship; (*Pol*)
trusteeship; **sous la ~ de** (*fig*) under the
supervision of
tuteur [tytœʀ] *nm* (*Jur*) guardian; (*de plante*)
stake, support
tutoyer [tytwaje] *vt*: **~ qn** to address sb as "tu"
tuyau, x [tɥijo] *nm* pipe; (*flexible*) tube; (*fam*)
tip; **tuyau d'arrosage** hosepipe; **tuyau
d'échappement** exhaust pipe; **tuyauterie**
nf piping *no pl*
TVA *sigle f* (= *taxe à la valeur ajoutée*) VAT
tympan [tɛ̃pɑ̃] *nm* (*Anat*) eardrum
type [tip] *nm* type; (*fam*) chap, guy ▷ *adj*
typical, classic
typé, e [tipe] *adj* ethnic
typique [tipik] *adj* typical
tyran [tiʀɑ̃] *nm* tyrant; **tyrannique** *adj*
tyrannical
tzigane [dzigan] *adj* gipsy, tzigane

ulcère [ylsɛʀ] *nm* ulcer
ultérieur, e [ylteʀjœʀ] *adj* later, subsequent;
remis à une date ~e postponed to a later
date; **ultérieurement** *adv* later, subsequently
ultime [yltim] *adj* final

 MOT-CLÉ

un, une [œ̃, yn] *art indéf* a; (*devant voyelle*) an;
un garçon/vieillard a boy/an old man; **une
fille** a girl
▷ *pron* one; **l'un des meilleurs** one of the
best; **l'un ..., l'autre** (the) one ..., the other;
les uns ..., les autres some ..., others; **l'un et
l'autre** both
(of them); **l'un ou l'autre** either (of them);
l'un l'autre each other; **les
uns les autres** one another; **pas un seul** not a
single one; **un par un** one by one
▷ *num* one; **un pamplemousse seulement**
one grapefruit only, just one grapefruit
▷ *nf*: **la une** (*Presse*) the front page

unanime [ynanim] *adj* unanimous;
unanimité *nf*: **à l'unanimité** unanimously
uni, e [yni] *adj* (*ton, tissu*) plain; (*surface*)
smooth, even; (*famille*) close(-knit); (*pays*)
united
unifier [ynifje] *vt* to unite, unify
uniforme [ynifɔʀm] *adj* uniform; (*surface*,

ton) even ▷ *nm* uniform; **uniformiser** *vt*
(*systèmes*) to standardize
union [ynjɔ̃] *nf* union; **union de**
   consommateurs consumers' association;
   union libre: **vivre en union libre** (*en*
   concubinage) to cohabit; **Union européenne**
   European Union; **Union soviétique** Soviet
   Union
unique [ynik] *adj* (*seul*) only; (*exceptionnel*)
   unique; (*le même*): **un prix/système ~** a
   single price/system; **fils/fille ~** only son/
   daughter, only child; **sens ~** one-way street;
   uniquement *adv* only, solely; (*juste*) only,
   merely
unir [yniʀ] *vt* (*nations*) to unite; (*en mariage*)
   to unite, join together; **s'unir** *vi* to unite; (*en*
   mariage) to be joined together
unitaire [ynitɛʀ] *adj*: **prix ~** unit price
unité [ynite] *nf* unit; (*harmonie, cohésion*) unity
univers [ynivɛʀ] *nm* universe; **universel, le**
   adj universal
universitaire [ynivɛʀsitɛʀ] *adj* university
   cpd; (*diplôme, études*) academic, university *cpd*
   ▷ *nm/f* academic
université [ynivɛʀsite] *nf* university
urbain, e [yʀbɛ̃, ɛn] *adj* urban, city *cpd*,
   town *cpd*; **urbanisme** *nm* town planning
urgence [yʀʒɑ̃s] *nf* urgency; (*Méd etc*)
   emergency; **d'~** *adj* emergency *cpd* ▷ *adv* as a
   matter of urgency; **(service des) ~s** casualty
urgent, e [yʀʒɑ̃, ɑ̃t] *adj* urgent
urine [yʀin] *nf* urine; **urinoir** *nm* (public)
   urinal
urne [yʀn] *nf* (*électorale*) ballot box; (*vase*) urn
urticaire [yʀtikɛʀ] *nf* nettle rash
us [ys] *nmpl*: **us et coutumes** (habits and)
   customs
usage [yzaʒ] *nm* (*emploi, utilisation*) use;
   (*coutume*) custom; **à l'~** with use; **à l'~ de** (*pour*)
   for (use of); **en ~** in use; **hors d'~** out of service;
   à ~ interne (*Méd*) to be taken (internally); **à ~**
   externe (*Méd*) for external use only; **usagé, e**
   adj (*usé*) worn; **usager, -ère** *nm/f* user
usé, e [yze] *adj* worn; (*banal: argument etc*)
   hackneyed
user [yze] *vt* (*outil*) to wear down; (*vêtement*) to
   wear out; (*matière*) to wear away; (*consommer:*
   charbon etc) to use; **s'user** *vi* (*tissu, vêtement*) to
   wear out; **~ de** (*moyen, procédé*) to use, employ;
   (*droit*) to exercise
usine [yzin] *nf* factory
usité, e [yzite] *adj* common
ustensile [ystɑ̃sil] *nm* implement; **ustensile**
   de cuisine kitchen utensil
usuel, le [yzɥɛl] *adj* everyday, common
usure [yzyʀ] *nf* wear
utérus [yteʀys] *nm* uterus, womb
utile [ytil] *adj* useful
utilisation [ytilizasjɔ̃] *nf* use

utiliser [ytilize] *vt* to use
utilitaire [ytilitɛʀ] *adj* utilitarian
utilité [ytilite] *nf* usefulness *no pl*; **de peu d'~**
   of little use *ou* help
utopie [ytɔpi] *nf* utopia

V

va [va] *vb voir* **aller**

vacance [vakɑ̃s] *nf* (*Admin*) vacancy; **vacances** *nfpl* holiday(s *pl* (BRIT)), vacation *sg* (US); **les grandes ~s** the summer holidays; **prendre des/ses ~s** to take a holiday/one's holiday(s); **aller en ~s** to go on holiday; **je suis ici en ~s** I'm here on holiday; **vacancier, -ière** *nm/f* holiday-maker

vacant, e [vakɑ̃, ɑ̃t] *adj* vacant

vacarme [vakaʀm] *nm* (*bruit*) racket

vaccin [vaksɛ̃] *nm* vaccine; (*opération*) vaccination; **vaccination** *nf* vaccination; **vacciner** *vt* to vaccinate; **être vacciné contre qch** (*fam*) to be cured of sth

vache [vaʃ] *nf* (*Zool*) cow; (*cuir*) cowhide ▷ *adj* (*fam*) rotten, mean; **vachement** (*fam*) *adv* (*très*) really; (*pleuvoir, travailler*) a hell of a lot; **vacherie** *nf* (*action*) dirty trick; (*remarque*) nasty remark

vaciller [vasije] *vi* to sway, wobble; (*bougie, lumière*) to flicker; (*fig*) to be failing, falter

va-et-vient [vaevjɛ̃] *nm inv* (*de personnes, véhicules*) comings and goings *pl*, to-ings and fro-ings *pl*

vagabond [vagabɔ̃] *nm* (*rôdeur*) tramp, vagrant; (*voyageur*) wanderer; **vagabonder** *vi* to roam, wander

vagin [vaʒɛ̃] *nm* vagina

vague [vag] *nf* wave ▷ *adj* vague; (*regard*) faraway; (*manteau, robe*) loose(-fitting);

(*quelconque*): **un ~ bureau/cousin** some office/cousin or other; **vague de fond** ground swell; **vague de froid** cold spell

vaillant, e [vajɑ̃, ɑ̃t] *adj* (*courageux*) gallant; (*robuste*) hale and hearty

vain, e [vɛ̃, vɛn] *adj* vain; **en ~** in vain

vaincre [vɛ̃kʀ] *vt* to defeat; (*fig*) to conquer, overcome; **vaincu, e** *nm/f* defeated party; **vainqueur** *nm* victor; (*Sport*) winner

vaisseau, x [vɛso] *nm* (*Anat*) vessel; (*Navig*) ship, vessel; **vaisseau spatial** spaceship

vaisselier [vɛsəlje] *nm* dresser

vaisselle [vɛsɛl] *nf* (*service*) crockery; (*plats etc à laver*) (dirty) dishes *pl*; **faire la ~** to do the washing-up (BRIT) *ou* the dishes

valable [valabl] *adj* valid; (*acceptable*) decent, worthwhile

valet [valɛ] *nm* manservant; (*Cartes*) jack

valeur [valœʀ] *nf* (*gén*) value; (*mérite*) worth, merit; (*Comm: titre*) security; **valeurs** *nfpl* (*morales*) values; **mettre en ~** (*détail*) to highlight; (*objet décoratif*) to show off to advantage; **avoir de la ~** to be valuable; **sans ~** worthless; **prendre de la ~** to go up *ou* gain in value

valide [valid] *adj* (*en bonne santé*) fit; (*valable*) valid; **valider** *vt* to validate

valise [valiz] *nf* (suit)case; **faire ses ~s** to pack one's bags

vallée [vale] *nf* valley

vallon [valɔ̃] *nm* small valley

valoir [valwaʀ] *vi* (*être valable*) to hold, apply ▷ *vt* (*prix, valeur, effort*) to be worth; (*causer*): **~ qch à qn** to earn sb sth; **se valoir** *vi* to be of equal merit; (*péj*) to be two of a kind; **faire ~** (*droits, prérogatives*) to assert; **se faire ~** to make the most of o.s.; **à ~ sur** to be deducted from; **vaille que vaille** somehow or other; **cela ne me dit rien qui vaille** I don't like the look of it at all; **ce climat ne me vaut rien** this climate doesn't suit me; **~ le coup** *ou* **la peine** to be worth the trouble *ou* worth it; **~ mieux: il vaut mieux se taire** it's better to say nothing; **ça ne vaut rien** it's worthless; **que vaut ce candidat?** how good is this applicant?

valse [vals] *nf* waltz

vandalisme [vɑ̃dalism] *nm* vandalism

vanille [vanij] *nf* vanilla

vanité [vanite] *nf* vanity; **vaniteux, -euse** *adj* vain, conceited

vanne [van] *nf* gate; (*fig*) joke

vannerie [vanʀi] *nf* basketwork

vantard, e [vɑ̃taʀ, aʀd] *adj* boastful

vanter [vɑ̃te] *vt* to speak highly of, praise; **se vanter** *vi* to boast, brag; **se ~ de** to pride o.s. on; (*péj*) to boast of

vapeur [vapœʀ] *nf* steam; (*émanation*) vapour, fumes *pl*; **vapeurs** *nfpl* (*bouffées*) vapours; **à ~** steam-powered, steam *cpd*; **cuit à la ~**

steamed; **vaporeux, -euse** adj (flou) hazy, misty; (léger) filmy; **vaporisateur** nm spray; **vaporiser** vt (parfum etc) to spray

varappe [vaʁap] nf rock climbing

vareuse [vaʁøz] nf (blouson) pea jacket; (d'uniforme) tunic

variable [vaʁjabl] adj variable; (temps, humeur) changeable; (divers: résultats) varied, various

varice [vaʁis] nf varicose vein

varicelle [vaʁisɛl] nf chickenpox

varié, e [vaʁje] adj varied; (divers) various; **hors d'œuvre ~s** selection of hors d'œuvres

varier [vaʁje] vi to vary; (temps, humeur) to change ▷ vt to vary; **variété** nf variety; **variétés** nfpl: **spectacle/émission de variétés** variety show

variole [vaʁjɔl] nf smallpox

Varsovie [vaʁsɔvi] n Warsaw

vas [va] vb voir **aller**; **~-y!** [vazi] go on!

vase [vɑz] nm vase ▷ nf silt, mud; **vaseux, -euse** adj silty, muddy; (fig: confus) woolly, hazy; (: fatigué) woozy

vasistas [vazistas] nm fanlight

vaste [vast] adj vast, immense

vautour [votuʁ] nm vulture

vautrer [votʁe] vb: **se ~ dans/sur** to wallow in/sprawl on

va-vite [vavit]: **à la ~** adv in a rush ou hurry

VDQS sigle (= vin délimité de qualité supérieure) label guaranteeing the quality of wine

veau, x [vo] nm (Zool) calf; (Culin) veal; (peau) calfskin

vécu, e [veky] pp de **vivre**

vedette [vədɛt] nf (artiste etc) star; (canot) motor boat; (police) launch

végétal, e, -aux [veʒetal, o] adj vegetable ▷ nm vegetable, plant; **végétalien, ne** adj, nm/f vegan

végétarien, ne [veʒetaʁjɛ̃, jɛn] adj, nm/f vegetarian; **avez-vous des plats ~s?** do you have any vegetarian dishes?

végétation [veʒetasjɔ̃] nf vegetation; **végétations** nfpl (Méd) adenoids

véhicule [veikyl] nm vehicle; **véhicule utilitaire** commercial vehicle

veille [vɛj] nf (état) wakefulness; (jour): **la ~ (de)** the day before; **la ~ au soir** the previous evening; **à la ~ de** on the eve of; **la ~ de Noël** Christmas Eve; **la ~ du jour de l'An** New Year's Eve

veillée [veje] nf (soirée) evening; (réunion) evening gathering; **veillée (funèbre)** wake

veiller [veje] vi to stay up ▷ vt (malade, mort) to watch over, sit up with; **~ à** to attend to, see to; **~ à ce que** to make sure that; **~ sur** to watch over; **veilleur** nm: **veilleur de nuit** night watchman; **veilleuse** nf (lampe) night light; (Auto) sidelight; (flamme) pilot light

veinard, e [venaʁ, aʁd] nm/f lucky devil

veine [vɛn] nf (Anat, du bois etc) vein; (filon) vein, seam; (fam: chance): **avoir de la ~** to be lucky

véliplanchiste [veliplɑ̃ʃist] nm/f windsurfer

vélo [velo] nm bike, cycle; **faire du ~** to go cycling; **vélomoteur** nm moped

velours [v(ə)luʁ] nm velvet; **velours côtelé** corduroy; **velouté, e** adj velvety ▷ nm: **velouté de tomates** cream of tomato soup

velu, e [vəly] adj hairy

vendange [vɑ̃dɑ̃ʒ] nf (aussi: **~s**) grape harvest; **vendanger** vi to harvest the grapes

vendeur, -euse [vɑ̃dœʁ, øz] nm/f shop assistant ▷ nm (Jur) vendor, seller

vendre [vɑ̃dʁ] vt to sell; **~ qch à qn** to sell sb sth; **"à ~"** "for sale"

vendredi [vɑ̃dʁədi] nm Friday; **vendredi saint** Good Friday

vénéneux, -euse [venenø, øz] adj poisonous

vénérien, ne [veneʁjɛ̃, jɛn] adj venereal

vengeance [vɑ̃ʒɑ̃s] nf vengeance no pl, revenge no pl

venger [vɑ̃ʒe] vt to avenge; **se venger** vi to avenge o.s.; **se ~ de qch** to avenge o.s. for sth, take one's revenge for sth; **se ~ de qn** to take revenge on sb; **se ~ sur** to take revenge on

venimeux, -euse [vənimø, øz] adj poisonous, venomous; (fig: haineux) venomous, vicious

venin [vənɛ̃] nm venom, poison

venir [v(ə)niʁ] vi to come; **~ de** to come from; **~ de faire: je viens d'y aller/de le voir** I've just been there/seen him; **s'il vient à pleuvoir** if it should rain; **j'en viens à croire que** I have come to believe that; **où veux-tu en ~?** what are you getting at?; **faire ~** (docteur, plombier) to call (out)

vent [vɑ̃] nm wind; **il y a du ~** it's windy; **c'est du ~** it's all hot air; **dans le ~** (fam) trendy

vente [vɑ̃t] nf sale; **la ~** (activité) selling; (secteur) sales pl; **mettre en ~** (produit) to put on sale; (maison, objet personnel) to put up for sale; **vente aux enchères** auction sale; **vente de charité** jumble sale

venteux, -euse [vɑ̃tø, øz] adj windy

ventilateur [vɑ̃tilatœʁ] nm fan

ventiler [vɑ̃tile] vt to ventilate

ventouse [vɑ̃tuz] nf (de caoutchouc) suction pad

ventre [vɑ̃tʁ] nm (Anat) stomach; (légèrement péj) belly; (utérus) womb; **avoir mal au ~** to have stomach ache (BRIT) ou a stomach ache (US)

venu, e [v(ə)ny] pp de **venir** ▷ adj: **bien ~** timely; **mal ~** out of place; **être mal ~ à ou de faire** to have no grounds for doing, be in no position to do

ver [vɛʁ] nm worm; (des fruits etc) maggot; (du

bois) woodworm *no pl*; *voir aussi* **vers**; **ver à soie** silkworm; **ver de terre** earthworm; **ver luisant** glow-worm; **ver solitaire** tapeworm

verbe [vɛʀb] *nm* verb

verdâtre [vɛʀdɑtʀ] *adj* greenish

verdict [vɛʀdik(t)] *nm* verdict

verdir [vɛʀdiʀ] *vi, vt* to turn green; **verdure** *nf* greenery

véreux, -euse [veʀø, øz] *adj* worm-eaten; (*malhonnête*) shady, corrupt

verge [vɛʀʒ] *nf* (*Anat*) penis

verger [vɛʀʒe] *nm* orchard

verglacé, e [vɛʀglase] *adj* icy, iced-over

verglas [vɛʀglɑ] *nm* (black) ice

véridique [veʀidik] *adj* truthful

vérification [veʀifikasjɔ̃] *nf* (*action*) checking *no pl*; (*contrôle*) check

vérifier [veʀifje] *vt* to check; (*corroborer*) to confirm, bear out

véritable [veʀitabl] *adj* real; (*ami, amour*) true; **un ~ désastre** an absolute disaster

vérité [veʀite] *nf* truth; **en ~** really, actually

verlan [vɛʀlɑ̃] *nm* (*fam*) (back) slang

vermeil, le [vɛʀmɛj] *adj* ruby red

vermine [vɛʀmin] *nf* vermin *pl*

vermoulu, e [vɛʀmuly] *adj* worm-eaten

verni, e [vɛʀni] *adj* (*fam*) lucky; **cuir ~** patent leather

vernir [vɛʀniʀ] *vt* (*bois, tableau, ongles*) to varnish; (*poterie*) to glaze; **vernis** *nm* (*enduit*) varnish, glaze; (*fig*) veneer; **vernis à ongles** nail polish *ou* varnish; **vernissage** *nm* (*d'une exposition*) preview

vérole [veʀɔl] *nf* (*variole*) smallpox

verre [vɛʀ] *nm* glass; (*de lunettes*) lens *sg*; **boire** *ou* **prendre un ~** to have a drink; **verres de contact** contact lenses; **verrière** *nf* (*paroi vitrée*) glass wall; (*toit vitré*) glass roof

verrou [veʀu] *nm* (*targette*) bolt; **mettre qn sous les ~s** to put sb behind bars; **verrouillage** *nm* locking; **verrouillage centralisé** central locking; **verrouiller** *vt* (*porte*) to bolt; (*ordinateur*) to lock

verrue [veʀy] *nf* wart

vers [vɛʀ] *nm* line ⊳ *nmpl* (*poésie*) verse *sg* ⊳ *prép* (*en direction de*) toward(s); (*près de*) around (about); (*temporel*) about, around

versant [vɛʀsɑ̃] *nm* slopes *pl*, side

versatile [vɛʀsatil] *adj* fickle, changeable

verse [vɛʀs]: **à ~** *adv*: **il pleut à ~** it's pouring (with rain)

Verseau [vɛʀso] *nm*: **le ~** Aquarius

versement [vɛʀsəmɑ̃] *nm* payment; **en 3 ~s** in 3 instalments

verser [vɛʀse] *vt* (*liquide, grains*) to pour; (*larmes, sang*) to shed; (*argent*) to pay; **~ qch sur un compte** to pay sth into an account

version [vɛʀsjɔ̃] *nf* version; (*Scol*) translation (*into the mother tongue*); **film en ~ originale**

film in the original language

verso [vɛʀso] *nm* back; **voir au ~** see over(leaf)

vert, e [vɛʀ, vɛʀt] *adj* green; (*vin*) young; (*vigoureux*) sprightly ⊳ *nm* green; **les V~s** (*Pol*) the Greens

vertèbre [vɛʀtɛbʀ] *nf* vertebra

vertement [vɛʀtəmɑ̃] *adv* (*réprimander*) sharply

vertical, e, -aux [vɛʀtikal, o] *adj* vertical; **verticale** *nf* vertical; **à la verticale** vertically; **verticalement** *adv* vertically

vertige [vɛʀtiʒ] *nm* (*peur du vide*) vertigo; (*étourdissement*) dizzy spell; (*fig*) fever; **vertigineux, -euse** *adj* breathtaking

vertu [vɛʀty] *nf* virtue; **en ~ de** in accordance with; **vertueux, -euse** *adj* virtuous

verve [vɛʀv] *nf* witty eloquence; **être en ~** to be in brilliant form

verveine [vɛʀvɛn] *nf* (*Bot*) verbena, vervain; (*infusion*) verbena tea

vésicule [vezikyl] *nf* vesicle; **vésicule biliaire** gall-bladder

vessie [vesi] *nf* bladder

veste [vɛst] *nf* jacket; **veste droite/croisée** single-/double-breasted jacket

vestiaire [vɛstjɛʀ] *nm* (*au théâtre etc*) cloakroom; (*de stade etc*) changing-room (BRIT), locker-room (US)

vestibule [vɛstibyl] *nm* hall

vestige [vɛstiʒ] *nm* relic; (*fig*) vestige; **vestiges** *nmpl* (*de ville*) remains

vestimentaire [vɛstimɑ̃tɛʀ] *adj* (*détail*) of dress; (*élégance*) sartorial; **dépenses ~s** clothing expenditure

veston [vɛstɔ̃] *nm* jacket

vêtement [vɛtmɑ̃] *nm* garment, item of clothing; **vêtements** *nmpl* clothes

vétérinaire [veteʀinɛʀ] *nm/f* vet, veterinary surgeon

vêtir [vetiʀ] *vt* to clothe, dress

vêtu, e [vety] *pp de* **vêtir** ⊳ *adj*: **~ de** dressed in, wearing

vétuste [vetyst] *adj* ancient, timeworn

veuf, veuve [vœf, vœv] *adj* widowed ⊳ *nm* widower

veuve [vœv] *nf* widow

vexant, e [vɛksɑ̃, ɑ̃t] *adj* (*contrariant*) annoying; (*blessant*) hurtful

vexation [vɛksasjɔ̃] *nf* humiliation

vexer [vɛkse] *vt*: **~ qn** to hurt sb's feelings; **se vexer** *vi* to be offended

viable [vjabl] *adj* viable; (*économie, industrie etc*) sustainable

viande [vjɑ̃d] *nf* meat; **je ne mange pas de ~** I don't eat meat

vibrer [vibʀe] *vi* to vibrate; (*son, voix*) to be vibrant; (*fig*) to be stirred; **faire ~** to (cause to) vibrate; (*fig*) to stir, thrill

v

vice [vis] nm vice; (défaut) fault ▷ préfixe: **~...** vice-; **vice de forme** legal flaw ou irregularity

vicié, e [visje] adj (air) polluted, tainted; (Jur) invalidated

vicieux, -euse [visjø, jøz] adj (pervers) lecherous; (rétif) unruly ▷ nm/f lecher

vicinal, e, -aux [visinal, o] adj: **chemin ~** by-road, byway

victime [viktim] nf victim; (d'accident) casualty

victoire [viktwaʀ] nf victory

victuailles [viktɥaj] nfpl provisions

vidange [vidɑ̃ʒ] nf (d'un fossé, réservoir) emptying; (Auto) oil change; (de lavabo: bonde) waste outlet; **vidanges** nfpl (matières) sewage sg; **vidanger** vt to empty

vide [vid] adj empty ▷ nm (Physique) vacuum; (espace) (empty) space, gap; (futilité, néant) void; **avoir peur du ~** to be afraid of heights; **emballé sous ~** vacuum packed; **à ~** (sans occupants) empty; (sans charge) unladen

vidéo [video] nf video ▷ adj: **cassette ~** video cassette; **jeu ~** video game; **vidéoclip** nm music video; **vidéoconférence** nf videoconference

vide-ordures [vidɔʀdyʀ] nm inv (rubbish) chute

vider [vide] vt to empty; (Culin: volaille, poisson) to gut, clean out; **se vider** vi to empty; **~ les lieux** to quit ou vacate the premises; **videur** nm (de boîte de nuit) bouncer, doorman

vie [vi] nf life; **être en ~** to be alive; **sans ~** lifeless; **à ~** for life; **que faites-vous dans la ~?** what do you do?

vieil [vjɛj] adj m voir **vieux**; **vieillard** nm old man; **vieille** adj, nf voir **vieux**; **vieilleries** nfpl old things; **vieillesse** nf old age; **vieillir** vi (prendre de l'âge) to grow old; (population, vin) to age; (doctrine, auteur) to become dated ▷ vt to age; **vieillissement** nm growing old; ageing

Vienne [vjɛn] nf Vienna

viens [vjɛ̃] vb voir **venir**

vierge [vjɛʀʒ] adj virgin; (page) clean, blank ▷ nf virgin; (signe): **la V~** Virgo

Vietnam, Viet-Nam [vjɛtnam] nm Vietnam; **vietnamien, ne** adj Vietnamese ▷ nm/f: **Vietnamien, ne** Vietnamese

vieux, vieil, vieille [vjø, vjɛj] adj old ▷ nm/f old man (woman); **les vieux** nmpl old people; **un petit ~** a little old man; **mon ~/ma vieille** (fam) old man/girl; **prendre un coup de ~** to put years on; **vieux garçon** bachelor; **vieux jeu** adj inv old-fashioned

vif, vive [vif, viv] adj (animé) lively; (alerte, brusque, aigu) sharp; (lumière, couleur) bright; (air) crisp; (vent, émotion) keen; (fort: regret, déception) great, deep; (vivant): **brûlé ~** burnt alive; **de vive voix** personally; **avoir l'esprit**

~ to be quick-witted; **piquer qn au ~** to cut sb to the quick; **à ~** (plaie) open; **avoir les nerfs à ~** to be on edge

vigne [viɲ] nf (plante) vine; (plantation) vineyard; **vigneron** nm wine grower

vignette [viɲɛt] nf (Admin) ≈ (road) tax disc (BRIT), ≈ license plate sticker (US); (de médicament) price label (used for reimbursement)

vignoble [viɲɔbl] nm (plantation) vineyard; (vignes d'une région) vineyards pl

vigoureux, -euse [viguʀø, øz] adj vigorous, robust

vigueur [vigœʀ] nf vigour; **entrer en ~** to come into force; **en ~** current

vilain, e [vilɛ̃, ɛn] adj (laid) ugly; (affaire, blessure) nasty; (pas sage: enfant) naughty; **vilain mot** naughty ou bad word

villa [villa] nf (detached) house; **~ en multipropriété** time-share villa

village [vilaʒ] nm village; **villageois, e** adj village cpd ▷ nm/f villager

ville [vil] nf town; (importante) city; (administration): **la ~** the (town) council, the local authority; **ville d'eaux** spa; **ville nouvelle** new town

vin [vɛ̃] nm wine; **avoir le ~ gai** to get happy after a few drinks; **vin d'honneur** reception (with wine and snacks); **vin de pays** local wine; **vin ordinaire** ou **de table** table wine

vinaigre [vinɛgʀ] nm vinegar; **vinaigrette** nf vinaigrette, French dressing

vindicatif, -ive [vɛ̃dikatif, iv] adj vindictive

vingt [vɛ̃] num twenty; **~-quatre heures sur ~-quatre** twenty-four hours a day, round the clock; **vingtaine** nf: **une vingtaine (de)** about twenty, twenty or so; **vingtième** num twentieth

vinicole [vinikɔl] adj wine cpd, wine-growing

vinyle [vinil] nm vinyl

viol [vjɔl] nm (d'une femme) rape; (d'un lieu sacré) violation

violacé, e [vjɔlase] adj purplish, mauvish

violemment [vjɔlamɑ̃] adv violently

violence [vjɔlɑ̃s] nf violence

violent, e [vjɔlɑ̃, ɑ̃t] adj violent; (remède) drastic

violer [vjɔle] vt (femme) to rape; (sépulture, loi, traité) to violate

violet, te [vjɔlɛ, ɛt] adj, nm purple, mauve; **violette** nf (fleur) violet

violon [vjɔlɔ̃] nm violin; (fam: prison) lock-up; **violon d'Ingres** hobby; **violoncelle** nm cello; **violoniste** nm/f violinist

vipère [vipɛʀ] nf viper, adder

virage [viraʒ] nm (d'un véhicule) turn; (d'une route, piste) bend

virée [vire] nf trip; (à pied) walk; (longue) walking tour; (dans les cafés) tour

virement [viʀmɑ̃] nm (Comm) transfer
virer [viʀe] vt (Comm): **~ qch (sur)** to transfer sth (into); (fam: expulser): **~ qn** to kick sb out ▷ vi to turn; (Chimie) to change colour; **~ au bleu/rouge** to turn blue/red; **~ de bord** to tack
virevolter [viʀvɔlte] vi to twirl around
virgule [viʀgyl] nf comma; (Math) point
viril, e [viʀil] adj (propre à l'homme) masculine; (énergique, courageux) manly, virile
virtuel, le [viʀtɥɛl] adj potential; (théorique) virtual
virtuose [viʀtɥoz] nm/f (Mus) virtuoso; (gén) master
virus [viʀys] nm virus
vis¹ [vi] vb voir **voir**; **vivre**
vis² [vis] nf screw
visa [viza] nm (sceau) stamp; (validation de passeport) visa
visage [vizaʒ] nm face
vis-à-vis [vizavi] prép: **~ de qn** to(wards) sb; **en ~** facing each other
visées [vize] nfpl (intentions) designs
viser [vize] vi to aim ▷ vt to aim at; (concerner) to be aimed ou directed at; (apposer un visa sur) to stamp, visa; **~ à qch/faire** to aim at sth/at doing ou to do
visibilité [vizibilite] nf visibility
visible [vizibl] adj visible; (disponible): **est-il ~?** can he see me?, will he see visitors?
visière [vizjɛʀ] nf (de casquette) peak; (qui s'attache) eyeshade
vision [vizjɔ̃] nf vision; (sens) (eye)sight, vision; (fait de voir): **la ~ de** the sight of; **visionneuse** nf viewer
visiophone [vizjɔfɔn] nm videophone
visite [vizit] nf visit; **~ médicale** medical examination; **~ accompagnée** ou **guidée** guided tour; **la ~ guidée commence à quelle heure?** what time does the guided tour start?; **faire une ~ à qn** to call on sb, pay sb a visit; **rendre ~ à qn** to visit sb, pay sb a visit; **être en ~ (chez qn)** to be visiting (sb); **avoir de la ~** to have visitors; **heures de ~** (hôpital, prison) visiting hours
visiter [vizite] vt to visit; **visiteur, -euse** nm/f visitor
vison [vizɔ̃] nm mink
visser [vise] vt: **~ qch** (fixer, serrer) to screw sth on
visuel, le [vizɥɛl] adj visual
vital, e, -aux [vital, o] adj vital
vitamine [vitamin] nf vitamin
vite [vit] adv (rapidement) quickly, fast; (sans délai) quickly; (sous peu) soon; **~!** quick!; **faire ~** to be quick; **le temps passe ~** time flies
vitesse [vitɛs] nf speed; (Auto: dispositif) gear; **prendre de la ~** to pick up ou gather speed; **à toute ~** at full ou top speed; **en ~** (rapidement) quickly; (en hâte) in a hurry

⬤ **LIMITE DE VITESSE**
⬤
⬤ The speed limit in France is 50 km/h in
⬤ built-up areas, 90 km/h on main roads, and
⬤ 130 km/h on motorways (110 km/h when
⬤ it is raining).

viticulteur [vitikyltœʀ] nm wine grower
vitrage [vitʀaʒ] nm: **double ~** double glazing
vitrail, -aux [vitʀaj, o] nm stained-glass window
vitre [vitʀ] nf (window) pane; (de portière, voiture) window; **vitré, e** adj glass cpd
vitrine [vitʀin] nf (shop) window; (petite armoire) display cabinet; **en ~** in the window
vivable [vivabl] adj (personne) livable-with; (maison) fit to live in
vivace [vivas] adj (arbre, plante) hardy; (fig) indestructible, inveterate
vivacité [vivasite] nf liveliness, vivacity
vivant, e [vivɑ̃, ɑ̃t] adj (qui vit) living, alive; (animé) lively; (preuve, exemple) living ▷ nm: **du ~ de qn** in sb's lifetime; **les ~s** the living
vive [viv] adj voir **vif** ▷ vb voir **vivre** ▷ excl: **~ le roi!** long live the king!; **vivement** adv deeply ▷ excl: **vivement les vacances!** roll on the holidays!
vivier [vivje] nm (étang) fish tank; (réservoir) fishpond
vivifiant, e [vivifjɑ̃, jɑ̃t] adj invigorating
vivoter [vivɔte] vi (personne) to scrape a living, get by; (fig: affaire etc) to struggle along
vivre [vivʀ] vi, vt to live; (période) to live through; **vivres** nmpl provisions, food supplies; **~ de** to live on; **il vit encore** he is still alive; **se laisser ~** to take life as it comes; **ne plus ~** (être anxieux) to live on one's nerves; **il a vécu** (eu une vie aventureuse) he has seen life; **être facile à ~** to be easy to get on with; **faire ~ qn** (pourvoir à sa subsistance) to provide (a living) for sb
vlan [vlɑ̃] excl wham!, bang!
VO [veo] nf: **film en VO** film in the original version; **en VO sous-titrée** in the original version with subtitles
vocabulaire [vɔkabylɛʀ] nm vocabulary
vocation [vɔkasjɔ̃] nf vocation, calling
vœu, x [vø] nm wish; (promesse) vow; **faire ~ de** to take a vow of; **tous nos ~x de bonne année, meilleurs ~x** best wishes for the New Year
vogue [vɔg] nf fashion, vogue; **en ~** in fashion, in vogue
voici [vwasi] prép (pour introduire, désigner) here is +sg, here are +pl; **et ~ que ...** and now it (ou he) ...; voir aussi **voilà**
voie [vwa] nf way; (Rail) track, line; (Auto) lane;

être en bonne ~ to be going well; **mettre qn sur la ~** to put sb on the right track; **pays en ~ de développement** developing country; **être en ~ d'achèvement/de rénovation** to be nearing completion/in the process of renovation; **par ~ buccale** ou **orale** orally; **route à ~ unique** single-track road; **route à 2/3 ~s** 2-/3-lane road; **voie de garage** (Rail) siding; **voie express** expressway; **voie ferrée** track; **railway line** (BRIT), **railroad** (US); **la voie lactée** the Milky Way; **la voie publique** the public highway

voilà [vwala] *prép (en désignant)* there is +sg, there are +pl; **les ~** ou **voici** here ou there they are; **en ~** ou **voici un** here's one, there's one; **voici mon frère et ~ ma sœur** this is my brother and that's my sister; **~** ou **voici deux ans** two years ago; **~** ou **voici deux ans que** it's two years since; **et ~!** there we are!; **~ tout** that's all; **~** ou **voici** (*en offrant etc*) there ou here you are; **tiens! ~ Paul** look! there's Paul

voile [vwal] *nm* veil; (*tissu léger*) net ▷ *nf* sail; (*sport*) sailing; **voiler** *vt* to veil; (*fausser: roue*) to buckle; (: *bois*) to warp; **se voiler** *vi* (*lune, regard*) to mist over; (*voix*) to become husky; (*roue, disque*) to buckle; (*planche*) to warp; **voilier** *nm* sailing ship; (*de plaisance*) sailing boat; **voilure** *nf* (*de voilier*) sails *pl*

voir [vwaʀ] *vi, vt* to see; **se voir** *vi* (*être visible*) to show; (*se fréquenter*) to see each other; (*se produire*) to happen; **cela se voit** (*c'est visible*) that's obvious, it shows; **faire ~ qch à qn** to show sb sth; **en faire ~ à qn** (*fig*) to give sb a hard time; **ne pas pouvoir ~ qn** not to be able to stand sb; **voyons!** let's see now; (*indignation etc*) come on!; **ça n'a rien à ~ avec lui** that has nothing to do with him

voire [vwaʀ] *adv* even

voisin, e [vwazɛ̃, in] *adj* (*proche*) neighbouring; (*contigu*) next; (*ressemblant*) connected ▷ *nm/f* neighbour; **voisinage** *nm* (*proximité*) proximity; (*environs*) vicinity; (*quartier, voisins*) neighbourhood

voiture [vwatyʀ] *nf* car; (*wagon*) coach, carriage; **voiture de course** racing car; **voiture de sport** sports car

voix [vwa] *nf* voice; (*Pol*) vote; **à haute ~** aloud; **à ~ basse** in a low voice; **à 2/4 ~** (*Mus*) in 2/4 parts; **avoir ~ au chapitre** to have a say in the matter

vol [vɔl] *nm* (*d'oiseau, d'avion*) flight; (*larcin*) theft; **~ régulier** scheduled flight; **à ~ d'oiseau** as the crow flies; **au ~: attraper qch au ~** to catch sth as it flies past; **en ~** in flight; **je voudrais signaler un ~** I'd like to report a theft; **vol à main armée** armed robbery; **vol à voile** gliding; **vol libre** hang-gliding

volage [vɔlaʒ] *adj* fickle

volaille [vɔlɑj] *nf* (*oiseaux*) poultry *pl*; (*viande*) poultry *no pl*; (*oiseau*) fowl

volant, e [vɔlɑ̃, ɑ̃t] *adj voir* **feuille** *etc* ▷ *nm* (*d'automobile*) (steering) wheel; (*de commande*) wheel; (*objet lancé*) shuttlecock; (*bande de tissu*) flounce

volcan [vɔlkɑ̃] *nm* volcano

volée [vɔle] *nf* (*Tennis*) volley; **à la ~: rattraper à la ~** to catch in mid-air; **à toute ~** (*sonner les cloches*) vigorously; (*lancer un projectile*) with full force

voler [vɔle] *vi* (*avion, oiseau, fig*) to fly; (*voleur*) to steal ▷ *vt* (*objet*) to steal; (*personne*) to rob; **~ qch à qn** to steal sth from sb; **on m'a volé mon portefeuille** my wallet (BRIT) ou billfold (US) has been stolen; **il ne l'a pas volé** he asked for it!

volet [vɔlɛ] *nm* (*de fenêtre*) shutter; (*de feuillet, document*) section

voleur, -euse [vɔlœʀ, øz] *nm/f* thief ▷ *adj* thieving; **"au ~!"** "stop thief!"

volontaire [vɔlɔ̃tɛʀ] *adj* (*acte, enrôlement, prisonnier*) voluntary; (*oubli*) intentional; (*caractère, personne: décidé*) self-willed ▷ *nm/f* volunteer

volonté [vɔlɔ̃te] *nf* (*faculté de vouloir*) will; (*énergie, fermeté*) will(power); (*souhait, désir*) wish; **à ~** as much as one likes; **bonne ~** goodwill, willingness; **mauvaise ~** lack of goodwill, unwillingness

volontiers [vɔlɔ̃tje] *adv* (*avec plaisir*) willingly, gladly; (*habituellement, souvent*) readily, willingly; **voulez-vous boire quelque chose? — ~!** would you like something to drink? — yes, please!

volt [vɔlt] *nm* volt

volte-face [vɔltəfas] *nf inv:* **faire ~** to turn round

voltige [vɔltiʒ] *nf* (*Équitation*) trick riding; (*au cirque*) acrobatics *sg*; **voltiger** *vi* to flutter (about)

volubile [vɔlybil] *adj* voluble

volume [vɔlym] *nm* volume; (*Géom: solide*) solid; **volumineux, -euse** *adj* voluminous, bulky

volupté [vɔlypte] *nf* sensual delight ou pleasure

vomi [vɔmi] *nm* vomit; **vomir** *vi* to vomit, be sick ▷ *vt* to vomit, bring up; (*fig*) to belch out, spew out; (*exécrer*) to loathe, abhor

vorace [vɔʀas] *adj* voracious

vos [vo] *adj voir* **votre**

vote [vɔt] *nm* vote; **vote par correspondance/procuration** postal/proxy vote; **voter** *vi* to vote ▷ *vt* (*projet de loi*) to vote for; (*loi, réforme*) to pass

votre [vɔtʀ] (*pl* **vos**) *adj* your

vôtre [votʀ] *pron:* **le ~, la ~, les ~s** yours; **les ~s** (*fig*) your family ou folks; **à la ~** (*toast*) your (good) health!

vouer [vwe] vt: **~ sa vie à** (*étude, cause etc*) to devote one's life to; **~ une amitié éternelle à qn** to vow undying friendship to sb

○ **MOT-CLÉ**

vouloir [vulwaʀ] nm: **le bon vouloir de qn** sb's goodwill; sb's pleasure
▷ vt **1** (*exiger, désirer*) to want; **vouloir faire/que qn fasse** to want to do/sb to do; **voulez-vous du thé?** would you like ou do you want some tea?; **que me veut-il?** what does he want with me?; **sans le vouloir** (*involontairement*) without meaning to, unintentionally; **je voudrais ceci/faire** I would ou I'd like this/to do; **le hasard a voulu que ...** as fate would have it ...; **la tradition veut que ...** it is a tradition that ...
2 (*consentir*): **je veux bien** (*bonne volonté*) I'll be happy to; (*concession*) fair enough, that's fine; **je peux le faire, si vous voulez** I can do it if you like; **oui, si on veut** (*en quelque sorte*) yes, if you like; **veuillez attendre** please wait; **veuillez agréer ...** (*formule épistolaire: personne nommée*) yours sincerely; (*personne non nommée*) yours faithfully
3: **en vouloir à qn** to bear sb a grudge; **s'en vouloir (de)** to be annoyed with o.s. (for); **il en veut à mon argent** he's after my money
4: **vouloir de**: **l'entreprise ne veut plus de lui** the firm doesn't want him any more; **elle ne veut pas de son aide** she doesn't want his help
5: **vouloir dire** to mean

voulu, e [vuly] adj (*requis*) required, requisite; (*délibéré*) deliberate, intentional; *voir aussi* **vouloir**

vous [vu] pron you; (*objet indirect*) (to) you; (*réfléchi: sg*) yourself; (: *pl*) yourselves; (*réciproque*) each other ▷ nm: **employer le ~** (*vouvoyer*) to use the "vous" form; **~-même** yourself; **~-mêmes** yourselves

vouvoyer [vuvwaje] vt: **~ qn** to address sb as "vous"

voyage [vwajaʒ] nm journey, trip; (*fait de voyager*): **le ~** travel(ling); **partir/être en ~** to go off/be away on a journey ou trip; **faire bon ~** to have a good journey; **votre ~ s'est bien passé?** how was your journey?; **voyage d'affaires/d'agrément** business/pleasure trip; **voyage de noces** honeymoon; **nous sommes en voyage de noces** we're on honeymoon; **voyage organisé** package tour

voyager [vwajaʒe] vi to travel; **voyageur, -euse** nm/f traveller; (*passager*) passenger; **voyageur de commerce** sales representative, commercial traveller

voyant, e [vwajɑ̃, ɑ̃t] adj (*couleur*) loud, gaudy

▷ nm (*signal*) (warning) light

voyelle [vwajɛl] nf vowel

voyou [vwaju] nm hooligan

vrac [vʀak]: **en ~** adv (*au détail*) loose; (*en gros*) in bulk; (*en désordre*) in a jumble

vrai, e [vʀɛ] adj (*véridique: récit, faits*) true; (*non factice, authentique*) real; **à ~ dire** to tell the truth; **vraiment** adv really; **vraisemblable** adj likely; (*excuse*) convincing; **vraisemblablement** adj probably; **vraisemblance** nf likelihood; (*romanesque*) verisimilitude

vrombir [vʀɔ̃biʀ] vi to hum

VRP sigle m (= *voyageur, représentant, placier*) sales rep (*fam*)

VTT sigle m (= *vélo tout-terrain*) mountain bike

vu, e [vy] pp de **voir** ▷ adj: **bien/mal vu** (*fig: personne*) popular/unpopular; (: *chose*) approved/disapproved of ▷ prép (*en raison de*) in view of; **vu que** in view of the fact that

vue [vy] nf (*fait de voir*): **la ~ de** the sight of; (*sens, faculté*) (eye)sight; (*panorama, image, photo*) view; **vues** nfpl (*idées*) views; (*dessein*) designs; **hors de ~** out of sight; **avoir en ~** to have in mind; **tirer à ~** to shoot on sight; **à ~ d'œil** visibly; **à première ~** at first sight; **de ~** by sight; **perdre de ~** to lose sight of; **en ~** (*visible*) in sight; (*célèbre*) in the public eye; **en ~ de faire** with a view to doing; **perdre la ~** to lose one's (eye)sight; **avoir ~ sur** (*suj: fenêtre*) to have a view of; **vue d'ensemble** overall view

vulgaire [vylgɛʀ] adj (*grossier*) vulgar, coarse; (*ordinaire*) commonplace, mundane; (*péj: quelconque*): **de ~s touristes** common tourists; (*Bot, Zool: non latin*) common; **vulgariser** vt to popularize

vulnérable [vylneʀabl] adj vulnerable

W X

wagon [vagɔ̃] *nm* (*de voyageurs*) carriage; (*de marchandises*) truck, wagon; **wagon-lit** *nm* sleeper, sleeping car; **wagon-restaurant** *nm* restaurant *ou* dining car

wallon, ne [walɔ̃, ɔn] *adj* Walloon ▷ *nm* (*Ling*) Walloon ▷ *nm/f*: **W~, ne** Walloon

watt [wat] *nm* watt

w-c *sigle mpl* (= *water-closet(s)*) toilet

Web [wɛb] *nm inv*: **le ~** the (World Wide) Web; **webmaster** [-mastœʀ], **webmestre** [-mɛstʀ] *nm/f* webmaster

week-end [wikɛnd] *nm* weekend

western [wɛstɛʀn] *nm* western

whisky [wiski] (*pl* **whiskies**) *nm* whisky

xénophobe [gzenɔfɔb] *adj* xenophobic ▷ *nm/f* xenophobe

xérès [gzeʀɛs] *nm* sherry

xylophone [gzilɔfɔn] *nm* xylophone

y [i] *adv* (*à cet endroit*) there; (*dessus*) on it (*ou* them); (*dedans*) in it (*ou* them) ▷ *pron* (*about ou on ou of*) it (*d'après le verbe employé*); **j'y pense** I'm thinking about it; **ça y est!** that's it!; *voir aussi* **aller**; **avoir**

yacht [jɔt] *nm* yacht

yaourt [jauʀt] *nm* yoghourt; **~ nature/aux fruits** plain/fruit yogurt

yeux [jø] *nmpl de* **œil**

yoga [jɔga] *nm* yoga

yoghourt [jɔguʀt] *nm* = **yaourt**

yougoslave [jugɔslav] (*Histoire*) *adj* Yugoslav(ian) ▷ *nm/f*: **Y~** Yugoslav

Yougoslavie [jugɔslavi] *nf* (*Histoire*) Yugoslavia; **l'ex-~** the former Yugoslavia

zapper [zape] *vi* to zap

zapping [zapiŋ] *nm*: **faire du ~** to flick through the channels

zèbre [zɛbʀ(ə)] *nm* (*Zool*) zebra; **zébré, e** *adj* striped, streaked

zèle [zɛl] *nm* zeal; **faire du ~** (*péj*) to be over-zealous; **zélé, e** *adj* zealous

zéro [zeʀo] *nm* zero, nought (BRIT); **au-dessous de ~** below zero (Centigrade) *ou* freezing; **partir de ~** to start from scratch; **trois (buts) à ~** 3 (goals to) nil

zeste [zɛst] *nm* peel, zest

zézayer [zezeje] *vi* to have a lisp

zigzag [zigzag] *nm* zigzag; **zigzaguer** *vi* to zigzag

Zimbabwe [zimbabwe] *nm*: **le ~** Zimbabwe

zinc [zɛ̃g] *nm* (*Chimie*) zinc

zipper [zipe] *vt* (*Inform*) to zip

zizi [zizi] *nm* (*langage enfantin*) willy

zodiaque [zɔdjak] *nm* zodiac

zona [zona] *nm* shingles *sg*

zone [zon] *nf* zone, area; (*fam: quartiers pauvres*): **la ~** the slums; **zone bleue** ≈ restricted parking area; **zone industrielle** industrial estate

zoo [zo(o)] *nm* zoo

zoologie [zɔɔlɔʒi] *nf* zoology; **zoologique** *adj* zoological

zut [zyt] *excl* dash (it)! (BRIT), nuts! (US)

ENGLISH | FRENCH
ANGLAIS | FRANÇAIS

A [eɪ] n (Mus) la m

○ **KEYWORD**

a [eɪ, ə] (before vowel or silent h **an**) indef art
1 un(e); **a book** un livre; **an apple** une pomme;
she's a doctor elle est médecin
2 (instead of the number "one") un(e); **a year ago**
il y a un an; **a hundred/thousand** etc **pounds**
cent/mille etc livres
3 (in expressing ratios, prices etc): **3 a day/week**
3 par jour/semaine; **10 km an hour** 10 km à
l'heure; **£5 a person** 5£ par personne; **30p a
kilo** 30p le kilo

A2 n (BRIT: Scol) deuxième partie de l'examen
équivalent au baccalauréat
A.A. n abbr (BRIT: = Automobile Association)
≈ ACF m; (= Alcoholics Anonymous) AA
A.A.A. n abbr (= American Automobile
Association) ≈ ACF m
aback [ə'bæk] adv: **to be taken ~** être
décontenancé(e)
abandon [ə'bændən] vt abandonner
abattoir ['æbətwɑːʳ] n (BRIT) abattoir m
abbey ['æbɪ] n abbaye f
abbreviation [əbriːvɪ'eɪʃən] n abréviation f
abdomen ['æbdəmən] n abdomen m
abduct [æb'dʌkt] vt enlever
abide [ə'baɪd] vt souffrir, supporter; **I can't ~**

it/him je ne le supporte pas; **abide by** vt fus
observer, respecter
ability [ə'bɪlɪtɪ] n compétence f; capacité f;
(skill) talent m
able ['eɪbl] adj compétent(e); **to be ~ to do sth**
pouvoir faire qch, être capable de faire qch
abnormal [æb'nɔːməl] adj anormal(e)
aboard [ə'bɔːd] adv à bord ▷ prep à bord de;
(train) dans
abolish [ə'bɔlɪʃ] vt abolir
abolition [æbə'lɪʃən] n abolition f
abort [ə'bɔːt] vt (Med) faire avorter; (Comput,
fig) abandonner; **abortion** [ə'bɔːʃən] n
avortement m; **to have an abortion** se faire
avorter

○ **KEYWORD**

about [ə'baut] adv **1** (approximately) environ,
à peu près; **about a hundred/thousand** etc
environ cent/mille etc, une centaine (de)/un
millier (de) etc; **it takes about 10 hours** ça
prend environ or à peu près 10 heures; **at
about 2 o'clock** vers 2 heures; **I've just about
finished** j'ai presque fini
2 (referring to place) çà et là, de-ci de-là; **to
run about** courir çà et là; **to walk about** se
promener, aller et venir; **they left all their
things lying about** ils ont laissé traîner
toutes leurs affaires
3: **to be about to do sth** être sur le point de
faire qch
▷ prep **1** (relating to) au sujet de, à propos de;
a book about London un livre sur Londres;
what is it about? de quoi s'agit-il?; **we talked
about it** nous en avons parlé; **what** or **how
about doing this?** et si nous faisions ceci?
2 (referring to place) dans; **to walk about the
town** se promener dans la ville

above [ə'bʌv] adv au-dessus ▷ prep au-
dessus de; (more than) plus de; **mentioned ~**
mentionné ci-dessus; **~ all** par-dessus tout,
surtout
abroad [ə'brɔːd] adv à l'étranger
abrupt [ə'brʌpt] adj (steep, blunt) abrupt(e);
(sudden, gruff) brusque
abscess ['æbsɪs] n abcès m
absence ['æbsəns] n absence f
absent ['æbsənt] adj absent(e); **absent-
minded** adj distrait(e)
absolute ['æbsəluːt] adj absolu(e);
absolutely [æbsə'luːtlɪ] adv absolument
absorb [əb'zɔːb] vt absorber; **to be ~ed in a
book** être plongé(e) dans un livre; **absorbent
cotton** n (US) coton m hydrophile; **absorbing**
adj absorbant(e); (book, film etc) captivant(e)
abstain [əb'steɪn] vi: **to ~ (from)** s'abstenir
(de)

abstract ['æbstrækt] *adj* abstrait(e)
absurd [əb'sə:d] *adj* absurde
abundance [ə'bʌndəns] *n* abondance *f*
abundant [ə'bʌndənt] *adj* abondant(e)
abuse *n* [ə'bju:s] (*insults*) insultes *fpl*, injures *fpl*; (*ill-treatment*) mauvais traitements *mpl*; (*of power etc*) abus *m* ▷ *vt* [ə'bju:z] (*insult*) insulter; (*ill-treat*) malmener; (*power etc*) abuser de;
  abusive *adj* grossier(-ière), injurieux(-euse)
abysmal [ə'bizməl] *adj* exécrable; (*ignorance etc*) sans bornes
academic [ækə'dɛmik] *adj* universitaire; (*person: scholarly*) intellectuel(-le); (*pej: issue*) oiseux(-euse), purement théorique ▷ *n* universitaire *m/f*; **academic year** (*University*) année *f* universitaire; (*Scol*) année scolaire
academy [ə'kædəmi] *n* (*learned body*) académie *f*; (*school*) collège *m*; **~ of music** conservatoire *m*
accelerate [æk'sɛləreit] *vt, vi* accélérer; **acceleration** [æksɛlə'reifən] *n* accélération *f*; **accelerator** *n* (BRIT) accélérateur *m*
accent ['æksɛnt] *n* accent *m*
accept [ək'sɛpt] *vt* accepter; **acceptable** *adj* acceptable; **acceptance** *n* acceptation *f*
access ['æksɛs] *n* accès *m*; **to have ~ to** (*information, library etc*) avoir accès à, pouvoir utiliser *or* consulter; (*person*) avoir accès auprès de; **accessible** [æk'sɛsəbl] *adj* accessible
accessory [æk'sɛsəri] *n* accessoire *m*; **~ to** (*Law*) accessoire à
accident ['æksidənt] *n* accident *m*; (*chance*) hasard *m*; **I've had an ~** j'ai eu un accident; **by ~** (*by chance*) par hasard; (*not deliberately*) accidentellement; **accidental** [æksi'dɛntl] *adj* accidentel(le); **accidentally** [æksi'dɛntəli] *adv* accidentellement; **Accident and Emergency Department** *n* (BRIT) service *m* des urgences; **accident insurance** *n* assurance *f* accident
acclaim [ə'kleim] *vt* acclamer ▷ *n* acclamations *fpl*
accommodate [ə'kɔmədeit] *vt* loger, recevoir; (*oblige, help*) obliger; (*car etc*) contenir
accommodation (US **accommodations**) [ə kɔmə'deifən(z)] *n(pl)* logement *m*
accompaniment [ə'kʌmpənimənt] *n* accompagnement *m*
accompany [ə'kʌmpəni] *vt* accompagner
accomplice [ə'kʌmplis] *n* complice *m/f*
accomplish [ə'kʌmplif] *vt* accomplir; **accomplishment** *n* (*skill: gen pl*) talent *m*; (*completion*) accomplissement *m*; (*achievement*) réussite *f*
accord [ə'kɔ:d] *n* accord *m* ▷ *vt* accorder; **of his own ~** de son plein gré; **accordance** *n*: **in accordance with** conformément à; **according: according to** *prep* selon;

accordingly *adv* (*appropriately*) en conséquence; (*as a result*) par conséquent
account [ə'kaunt] *n* (Comm) compte *m*; (*report*) compte rendu, récit *m*; **accounts** *npl* (Comm: *records*) comptabilité *f*, comptes; **of no ~** sans importance; **on ~** acompte; **to buy sth on ~** acheter qch à crédit; **on no ~** en aucun cas; **on ~ of** à cause de; **to take into ~, take ~ of** tenir compte de; **account for** *vt fus* (*explain*) expliquer, rendre compte de; (*represent*) représenter; **accountable** *adj*: **accountable (to)** responsable (devant); **accountant** *n* comptable *m/f*; **account number** *n* numéro *m* de compte
accumulate [ə'kju:mjuleit] *vt* accumuler, amasser ▷ *vi* s'accumuler, s'amasser
accuracy ['ækjurəsi] *n* exactitude *f*, précision *f*
accurate ['ækjurit] *adj* exact(e), précis(e); (*device*) précis; **accurately** *adv* avec précision
accusation [ækju'zeifən] *n* accusation *f*
accuse [ə'kju:z] *vt*: **to ~ sb (of sth)** accuser qn (de qch); **accused** *n* (Law) accusé(e)
accustomed [ə'kʌstəmd] *adj*: **~ to** habitué(e) *or* accoutumé(e) à
ace [eis] *n* as *m*
ache [eik] *n* mal *m*, douleur *f* ▷ *vi* (*be sore*) faire mal, être douloureux(-euse); **my head ~s** j'ai mal à la tête
achieve [ə'tfi:v] *vt* (*aim*) atteindre; (*victory, success*) remporter, obtenir; **achievement** *n* exploit *m*, réussite *f*; (*of aims*) réalisation *f*
acid ['æsid] *adj, n* acide (*m*)
acknowledge [ək'nɔlidʒ] *vt* (*also*: **~ receipt of**) accuser réception de; (*fact*) reconnaître; **acknowledgement** *n* (*of letter*) accusé *m* de réception
acne ['ækni] *n* acné *m*
acorn ['eikɔ:n] *n* gland *m*
acoustic [ə'ku:stik] *adj* acoustique
acquaintance [ə'kweintəns] *n* connaissance *f*
acquire [ə'kwaiəʳ] *vt* acquérir; **acquisition** [ækwi'zifən] *n* acquisition *f*
acquit [ə'kwit] *vt* acquitter; **to ~ o.s. well** s'en tirer très honorablement
acre ['eikəʳ] *n* acre *f* (= 4047 *m²*)
acronym ['ækrənim] *n* acronyme *m*
across [ə'krɔs] *prep* (*on the other side*) de l'autre côté de; (*crosswise*) en travers de ▷ *adv* de l'autre côté; en travers; **to run/swim ~** traverser en courant/à la nage; **~ from** en face de
acrylic [ə'krilik] *adj, n* acrylique (*m*)
act [ækt] *n* acte *m*, action *f*; (Theat: *part of play*) acte; (: *of performer*) numéro *m*; (Law) loi *f* ▷ *vi* agir; (Theat) jouer; (*pretend*) jouer la comédie ▷ *vt* (*role*) jouer, tenir; **to catch sb in the ~** prendre qn sur le fait *or* en flagrant

délit; **to ~ as** servir de; **act up** (inf) ▷ vi (person) se conduire mal; (knee, back, injury) jouer des tours; (machine) être capricieux(-ieuse);

acting adj suppléant(e), par intérim ▷ n (activity): **to do some acting** faire du théâtre (or du cinéma)

action ['ækʃən] n action f; (Mil) combat(s) m(pl); (Law) procès m, action en justice; **out of ~** hors de combat; (machine etc) hors d'usage; **to take ~** agir, prendre des mesures; **action replay** n (BRIT TV) ralenti m

activate ['æktɪveɪt] vt (mechanism) actionner, faire fonctionner

active ['æktɪv] adj actif(-ive); (volcano) en activité; **actively** adv activement; (discourage) vivement

activist ['æktɪvɪst] n activiste m/f

activity [æk'tɪvɪtɪ] n activité f; **activity holiday** n vacances actives

actor ['æktəʳ] n acteur m

actress ['æktrɪs] n actrice f

actual ['æktjuəl] adj réel(le), véritable; (emphatic use) lui-même (elle-même)

> Be careful not to translate **actual** by the French word **actuel**.

actually ['æktjuəlɪ] adv réellement, véritablement; (in fact) en fait

> Be careful not to translate **actually** by the French word **actuellement**.

acupuncture ['ækjupʌŋktʃəʳ] n acupuncture f

acute [ə'kjuːt] adj aigu(ë); (mind, observer) pénétrant(e)

A.D. adv abbr (= Anno Domini) ap. J.-C.

ad [æd] n abbr = **advertisement**

adamant ['ædəmənt] adj inflexible

adapt [ə'dæpt] vt adapter ▷ vi: **to ~ (to)** s'adapter (à); **adapter, adaptor** n (Elec) adaptateur m; (for several plugs) prise f multiple

add [æd] vt ajouter; (figures: also: **to ~ up**) additionner ▷ vi (fig): **it doesn't ~ up** cela ne rime à rien; **add up to** vt fus (Math) s'élever à; (fig: mean) signifier

addict ['ædɪkt] n toxicomane m/f; (fig) fanatique m/f; **addicted** [ə'dɪktɪd] adj: **to be addicted to** (drink, drugs) être adonné(e) à; (fig: football etc) être un(e) fanatique de; **addiction** [ə'dɪkʃən] n (Med) dépendance f; **addictive** [ə'dɪktɪv] adj qui crée une dépendance

addition [ə'dɪʃən] n (adding up) addition f; (thing added) ajout m; **in ~** de plus, de surcroît; **in ~ to** en plus de; **additional** adj supplémentaire

additive ['ædɪtɪv] n additif m

address [ə'drɛs] n adresse f; (talk) discours m, allocution f ▷ vt adresser; (speak to) s'adresser à; **my ~ is ...** mon adresse, c'est ...; **address book** n carnet m d'adresses

adequate ['ædɪkwɪt] adj (enough) suffisant(e); (satisfactory) satisfaisant(e)

adhere [əd'hɪəʳ] vi: **to ~ to** adhérer à; (fig: rule, decision) se tenir à

adhesive [əd'hiːzɪv] n adhésif m; **adhesive tape** n (BRIT) ruban m adhésif; (US Med) sparadrap m

adjacent [ə'dʒeɪsənt] adj adjacent(e), contigu(ë); **~ to** adjacent à

adjective ['ædʒɛktɪv] n adjectif m

adjoining [ə'dʒɔɪnɪŋ] adj voisin(e), adjacent(e), attenant(e)

adjourn [ə'dʒəːn] vt ajourner ▷ vi suspendre la séance; lever la séance; clore la session

adjust [ə'dʒʌst] vt (machine) ajuster, régler; (prices, wages) rajuster ▷ vi: **to ~ (to)** s'adapter (à); **adjustable** adj réglable; **adjustment** n (of machine) ajustage m, réglage m; (of prices, wages) rajustement m; (of person) adaptation f

administer [əd'mɪnɪstəʳ] vt administrer; **administration** [ədmɪnɪs'treɪʃən] n (management) administration f; (government) gouvernement m; **administrative** [ə d'mɪnɪstrətɪv] adj administratif(-ive)

administrator [əd'mɪnɪstreɪtəʳ] n administrateur(-trice)

admiral ['ædmərəl] n amiral m

admiration [ædmə'reɪʃən] n admiration f

admire [əd'maɪəʳ] vt admirer; **admirer** n (fan) admirateur(-trice)

admission [əd'mɪʃən] n admission f; (to exhibition, night club etc) entrée f; (confession) aveu m

admit [əd'mɪt] vt laisser entrer; admettre; (agree) reconnaître, admettre; (crime) reconnaître avoir commis; **"children not ~ted"** "entrée interdite aux enfants"; **admit to** vt fus reconnaître, avouer; **admittance** n admission f, (droit m d')entrée f; **admittedly** adv il faut en convenir

adolescent [ædəu'lɛsnt] adj, n adolescent(e)

adopt [ə'dɔpt] vt adopter; **adopted** adj adoptif(-ive), adopté(e); **adoption** [ə'dɔpʃən] n adoption f

adore [ə'dɔːʳ] vt adorer

adorn [ə'dɔːn] vt orner

Adriatic (Sea) [eɪdrɪ'ætɪk-] n, adj: **the Adriatic (Sea)** la mer Adriatique, l'Adriatique f

adrift [ə'drɪft] adv à la dérive

adult ['ædʌlt] n adulte m/f ▷ adj (grown-up) adulte; (for adults) pour adultes; **adult education** n éducation f des adultes

adultery [ə'dʌltərɪ] n adultère m

advance [əd'vɑːns] n avance f ▷ vt avancer ▷ vi s'avancer; **in ~** en avance, d'avance; **to make ~s to sb** (gen) faire des propositions à qn; (amorously) faire des avances à qn; **~ booking** location f; **~ notice, ~ warning** préavis m; (verbal) avertissement m; **do l**

need to book in ~? est-ce qu'il faut réserver à l'avance?; **advanced** adj avancé(e); (Scol: studies) supérieur(e)

advantage [əd'vɑːntɪdʒ] n (also Tennis) avantage m; **to take ~ of** (person) exploiter; (opportunity) profiter de

advent ['ædvənt] n avènement m, venue f; **A~** (Rel) avent m

adventure [əd'vɛntʃəʳ] n aventure f; **adventurous** [əd'vɛntʃərəs] adj aventureux(-euse)

adverb ['ædvəːb] n adverbe m

adversary ['ædvəsərɪ] n adversaire m/f

adverse ['ædvəːs] adj adverse; (effect) négatif(-ive); (weather, publicity) mauvais(e); (wind) contraire

advert ['ædvəːt] n abbr (BRIT) = advertisement

advertise ['ædvətaɪz] vi faire de la publicité or de la réclame; (in classified ads etc) mettre une annonce ▷ vt faire de la publicité or de la réclame pour; (in classified ads etc) mettre une annonce pour vendre; **to ~ for** (staff) recruter par (voie d')annonce; **advertisement** [əd'vəːtɪsmənt] n (Comm) publicité f, réclame f; (in classified ads etc) annonce f; **advertiser** n annonceur m; **advertising** n publicité f

advice [əd'vaɪs] n conseils mpl; (notification) avis m; **a piece of ~** un conseil; **to take legal ~** consulter un avocat

advisable [əd'vaɪzəbl] adj recommandable, indiqué(e)

advise [əd'vaɪz] vt conseiller; **to ~ sb of sth** aviser or informer qn de qch; **to ~ against sth/doing sth** déconseiller qch/conseiller de ne pas faire qch; **adviser, advisor** n conseiller(-ère); **advisory** adj consultatif(-ive)

advocate n ['ædvəkɪt] (lawyer) avocat (plaidant); (upholder) défenseur m, avocat(e) ▷ vt ['ædvəkeɪt] recommander, prôner; **to be an ~ of** être partisan(e) de

Aegean [iː'dʒiːən] n, adj: **the ~ (Sea)** la mer Égée, l'Égée f

aerial ['ɛərɪəl] n antenne f ▷ adj aérien(ne)

aerobics [ɛə'rəubɪks] n aérobic m

aeroplane ['ɛərəpleɪn] n (BRIT) avion m

aerosol ['ɛərəsɔl] n aérosol m

affair [ə'fɛəʳ] n affaire f; (also: **love ~**) liaison f; aventure f

affect [ə'fɛkt] vt affecter; (subj: disease) atteindre; **affected** adj affecté(e); **affection** n affection f; **affectionate** adj affectueux(-euse)

afflict [ə'flɪkt] vt affliger

affluent ['æfluənt] adj (person, family, surroundings) aisé(e), riche; **the ~ society** la société d'abondance

afford [ə'fɔːd] vt (behaviour) se permettre; (provide) fournir, procurer; **can we ~ a car?**

avons-nous de quoi acheter or les moyens d'acheter une voiture?; **affordable** adj abordable

Afghanistan [æf'gænɪstæn] n Afghanistan m

afraid [ə'freɪd] adj effrayé(e); **to be ~ of** or **to** avoir peur de; **I am ~ that** je crains que + sub; **I'm ~ so/not** oui/non, malheureusement

Africa ['æfrɪkə] n Afrique f; **African** adj africain(e) ▷ n Africain(e); **African-American** adj afro-américain(e) ▷ n Afro-Américain(e)

after ['ɑːftəʳ] prep, adv après ▷ conj après que; **it's quarter ~ two** (US) il est deux heures et quart; **~ having done/~ he left** après avoir fait/après son départ; **to name sb ~ sb** donner à qn le nom de qn; **to ask ~ sb** demander des nouvelles de qn; **what/who are you ~?** que/qui cherchez-vous?; **~ you!** après vous!; **~ all** après tout; **after-effects** npl (of disaster, radiation, drink etc) répercussions fpl; (of illness) séquelles fpl, suites fpl; **aftermath** n conséquences fpl; **afternoon** n après-midi m or f; **after-shave (lotion)** n lotion f après-rasage; **aftersun (lotion/cream)** n après-soleil m inv; **afterwards** (US **afterward**) adv après

again [ə'gɛn] adv de nouveau, encore (une fois); **to do sth ~** refaire qch; **~ and ~** à plusieurs reprises

against [ə'gɛnst] prep contre; (compared to) par rapport à

age [eɪdʒ] n âge m ▷ vt, vi vieillir; **he is 20 years of ~** il a 20 ans; **to come of ~** atteindre sa majorité; **it's been ~s since I saw you** ça fait une éternité que je ne t'ai pas vu; **~d 10** âgé(e) de 10 ans; **age group** n tranche f d'âge; **age limit** n limite f d'âge

agency ['eɪdʒənsɪ] n agence f

agenda [ə'dʒɛndə] n ordre m du jour

Be careful not to translate **agenda** by the French word **agenda**.

agent ['eɪdʒənt] n agent m; (firm) concessionnaire m

aggravate ['ægrəveɪt] vt (situation) aggraver; (annoy) exaspérer, agacer

aggression [ə'grɛʃən] n agression f

aggressive [ə'grɛsɪv] adj agressif(-ive)

agile ['ædʒaɪl] adj agile

agitated ['ædʒɪteɪtɪd] adj inquiet(-ète)

AGM n abbr (= annual general meeting) AG f

ago [ə'gəu] adv: **2 days ~** il y a 2 jours; **not long ~** il n'y a pas longtemps; **how long ~?** il y a combien de temps (de cela)?

agony ['ægənɪ] n (pain) douleur f atroce; (distress) angoisse f; **to be in ~** souffrir le martyre

agree [ə'griː] vt (price) convenir de ▷ vi: **to ~ with** (person) être d'accord avec; (statements etc) concorder avec; (Ling) s'accorder avec; **to ~ to do** accepter de or consentir à faire;

to ~ **to sth** consentir à qch; **to ~ that** (admit) convenir or reconnaître que; **garlic doesn't ~ with me** je ne supporte pas l'ail; **agreeable** adj (pleasant) agréable; (willing) consentant(e), d'accord; **agreed** adj (time, place) convenu(e); **agreement** n accord m; **in agreement** d'accord

agricultural [ægrɪ'kʌltʃərəl] adj agricole

agriculture ['ægrɪkʌltʃəʳ] n agriculture f

ahead [ə'hɛd] adv en avant; devant; **go right** or **straight ~** (direction) allez tout droit; **go ~!** (permission) allez-y!; **~ of** devant; (fig: schedule etc) en avance sur; **~ of time** en avance

aid [eɪd] n aide f; (device) appareil m ▷ vt aider; **in ~ of** en faveur de

aide [eɪd] n (person) assistant(e)

AIDS [eɪdz] n abbr (= acquired immune (or immuno-)deficiency syndrome) SIDA m

ailing ['eɪlɪŋ] adj (person) souffreteux(euse); (economy) malade

ailment ['eɪlmənt] n affection f

aim [eɪm] vt: **to ~ sth (at)** (gun, camera) braquer or pointer qch (sur); (missile) lancer qch (à or contre or en direction de); (remark, blow) destiner or adresser qch (à) ▷ vi (also: **to take ~**) viser ▷ n (objective) but m; (skill): **his ~ is bad** il vise mal; **to ~ at** viser; (fig) viser (à); **to ~ to do** avoir l'intention de faire

ain't [eɪnt] (inf) = **am not**; **aren't**; **isn't**

air [ɛəʳ] n air m ▷ vt aérer; (idea, grievance, views) mettre sur le tapis ▷ cpd (currents, attack etc) aérien(ne); **to throw sth into the ~** (ball etc) jeter qch en l'air; **by ~** par avion; **to be on the ~** (Radio, TV: programme) être diffusé(e); (: station) émettre; **airbag** n airbag m; **airbed** n (BRIT) matelas m pneumatique; **airborne** adj (plane) en vol; **as soon as the plane was airborne** dès que l'avion eut décollé; **air-conditioned** adj climatisé(e), à air conditionné; **air conditioning** n climatisation f; **aircraft** n inv avion m; **airfield** n terrain m d'aviation; **Air Force** n Armée f de l'air; **air hostess** n (BRIT) hôtesse f de l'air; **airing cupboard** n (BRIT) placard qui contient la chaudière et dans lequel on met le linge à sécher; **airlift** n pont aérien; **airline** n ligne aérienne, compagnie aérienne; **airliner** n avion m de ligne; **airmail** n: **by airmail** par avion; **airplane** n (US) avion m; **airport** n aéroport m; **air raid** n attaque aérienne; **airsick** adj: **to be airsick** avoir le mal de l'air; **airspace** n espace m aérien; **airstrip** n terrain m d'atterrissage; **air terminal** n aérogare f; **airtight** adj hermétique; **air-traffic controller** n aiguilleur m du ciel; **airy** adj bien aéré(e); (manners) dégagé(e)

aisle [aɪl] n (of church: central) allée f centrale; (: side) nef f latérale, bas-côté m; (in theatre, supermarket) allée f; (on plane) couloir m; **aisle seat** n place f côté couloir

ajar [ə'dʒɑːʳ] adj entrouvert(e)

à la carte [ælæ'kɑːt] adv à la carte

alarm [ə'lɑːm] n alarme f ▷ vt alarmer; **alarm call** n coup m de fil pour réveiller; **could I have an alarm call at 7 am, please?** pouvez-vous me réveiller à 7 heures, s'il vous plaît?; **alarm clock** n réveille-matin m inv, réveil m; **alarmed** adj (frightened) alarmé(e); (protected by an alarm) protégé(e) par un système d'alarme; **alarming** adj alarmant(e)

Albania [æl'beɪnɪə] n Albanie f

albeit [ɔːl'biːɪt] conj bien que + sub, encore que + sub

album ['ælbəm] n album m

alcohol ['ælkəhɔl] n alcool m; **alcohol-free** adj sans alcool; **alcoholic** [ælkə'hɔlɪk] adj, n alcoolique (m/f)

alcove ['ælkəuv] n alcôve f

ale [eɪl] n bière f

alert [ə'ləːt] adj alerte, vif (vive); (watchful) vigilant(e) ▷ n alerte f ▷ vt alerter; **on the ~** sur le qui-vive; (Mil) en état d'alerte

algebra ['ældʒɪbrə] n algèbre m

Algeria [æl'dʒɪərɪə] n Algérie f

Algerian [æl'dʒɪərɪən] adj algérien(ne) ▷ n Algérien(ne)

Algiers [æl'dʒɪəz] n Alger

alias ['eɪlɪəs] adv alias ▷ n faux nom, nom d'emprunt

alibi ['ælɪbaɪ] n alibi m

alien ['eɪlɪən] n (from abroad) étranger(-ère); (from outer space) extraterrestre ▷ adj: **~ (to)** étranger(-ère) (à); **alienate** vt aliéner; (subj: person) s'aliéner

alight [ə'laɪt] adj en feu ▷ vi mettre pied à terre; (passenger) descendre; (bird) se poser

align [ə'laɪn] vt aligner

alike [ə'laɪk] adj semblable, pareil(le) ▷ adv de même; **to look ~** se ressembler

alive [ə'laɪv] adj vivant(e); (active) plein(e) de vie

KEYWORD

all [ɔːl] adj (singular) tout(e); (plural) tous (toutes); **all day** toute la journée; **all night** toute la nuit; **all men** tous les hommes; **all five** tous les cinq; **all the books** tous les livres; **all his life** toute sa vie

▷ pron **1** tout; **I ate it all, I ate all of it** j'ai tout mangé; **all of us went** nous y sommes tous allés; **all of the boys went** tous les garçons y sont allés; **is that all?** c'est tout?; (in shop) ce sera tout?

2 (in phrases): **above all** surtout, par-dessus tout; **after all** après tout; **at all**: **not at all** (in answer to question) pas du tout; (in answer to thanks) je vous en prie!; **I'm not at all tired** je ne suis pas du tout fatigué(e); **anything at all**

will do n'importe quoi fera l'affaire; **all in all** tout bien considéré, en fin de compte ▷ *adv*: **all alone** tout(e) seul(e); **it's not as hard as all that** ce n'est pas si difficile que ça; **all the more/the better** d'autant plus/ mieux; **all but** presque, pratiquement; **the score is 2 all** le score est de 2 partout

Allah [ˈælə] *n* Allah *m*

allegation [ælɪˈɡeɪʃən] *n* allégation *f*

alleged [əˈlɛdʒd] *adj* prétendu(e); **allegedly** *adv* à ce que l'on prétend, paraît-il

allegiance [əˈliːdʒəns] *n* fidélité *f*, obéissance *f*

allergic [əˈlɜːdʒɪk] *adj*: **~ to** allergique à; **I'm ~ to penicillin** je suis allergique à la pénicilline

allergy [ˈælədʒɪ] *n* allergie *f*

alleviate [əˈliːvɪeɪt] *vt* soulager, adoucir

alley [ˈælɪ] *n* ruelle *f*

alliance [əˈlaɪəns] *n* alliance *f*

allied [ˈælaɪd] *adj* allié(e)

alligator [ˈælɪɡeɪtər] *n* alligator *m*

all-in [ˈɔːlɪn] *adj, adv* (BRIT: *charge*) tout compris

allocate [ˈæləkeɪt] *vt* (*share out*) répartir, distribuer; **to ~ sth to** (*duties*) assigner *or* attribuer qch à; (*sum, time*) allouer qch à

allot [əˈlɔt] *vt* (*share out*) répartir, distribuer; **to ~ sth to** (*time*) allouer qch à; (*duties*) assigner qch à

all-out [ˈɔːlaut] *adj* (*effort etc*) total(e)

allow [əˈlau] *vt* (*practice, behaviour*) permettre, autoriser; (*sum to spend etc*) accorder, allouer; (*sum, time estimated*) compter, prévoir; (*claim, goal*) admettre; (*concede*): **to ~ that** convenir que; **to ~ sb to do** permettre à qn de faire, autoriser qn à faire; **he is ~ed to ...** on lui permet de ...; **allow for** *vt fus* tenir compte de; **allowance** *n* (*money received*) allocation *f*; (: *from parent etc*) subside *m*; (: *for expenses*) indemnité *f*; (US: *pocket money*) argent *m* de poche; (*Tax*) somme *f* déductible du revenu imposable, abattement *m*; **to make allowances for** (*person*) essayer de comprendre; (*thing*) tenir compte de

all right *adv* (*feel, work*) bien; (*as answer*) d'accord

ally *n* [ˈælaɪ] allié *m* ▷ *vt* [əˈlaɪ]: **to ~ o.s. with** s'allier avec

almighty [ɔːlˈmaɪtɪ] *adj* tout(e)-puissant(e); (*tremendous*) énorme

almond [ˈɑːmənd] *n* amande *f*

almost [ˈɔːlməust] *adv* presque

alone [əˈləun] *adj, adv* seul(e); **to leave sb ~** laisser qn tranquille; **to leave sth ~** ne pas toucher à qch; **let ~ ...** sans parler de ...; encore moins ...

along [əˈlɔŋ] *prep* le long de ▷ *adv*: **is he coming ~ with us?** vient-il avec nous?; **he was hopping/limping ~** il venait *or* avançait

en sautillant/boitant; **~ with** avec, en plus de; (*person*) en compagnie de; **all ~** (*all the time*) depuis le début; **alongside** *prep* (*along*) le long de; (*beside*) à côté de ▷ *adv* bord à bord; côte à côte

aloof [əˈluːf] *adj* distant(e) ▷ *adv*: **to stand ~** se tenir à l'écart *or* à distance

aloud [əˈlaud] *adv* à haute voix

alphabet [ˈælfəbɛt] *n* alphabet *m*

Alps [ælps] *npl*: **the ~** les Alpes *fpl*

already [ɔːlˈrɛdɪ] *adv* déjà

alright [ˈɔːlˈraɪt] *adv* (BRIT) = **all right**

also [ˈɔːlsəu] *adv* aussi

altar [ˈɔltər] *n* autel *m*

alter [ˈɔltər] *vt, vi* changer; **alteration** [ɔltəˈreɪʃən] *n* changement *m*, modification *f*; **alterations** *npl* (*Sewing*) retouches *fpl*; (*Archit*) modifications *fpl*

alternate *adj* [ɔlˈtəːnɪt] alterné(e), alternant(e), alternatif(-ive); (US) = **alternative** ▷ *vi* [ˈɔltəːneɪt] alterner; **to ~ with** alterner avec; **on ~ days** un jour sur deux, tous les deux jours

alternative [ɔlˈtəːnətɪv] *adj* (*solution, plan*) autre, de remplacement; (*lifestyle*) parallèle ▷ *n* (*choice*) alternative *f*; (*other possibility*) autre possibilité *f*; **~ medicine** médecine alternative, médecine douce; **alternatively** *adv*: **alternatively one could ...** une autre *or* l'autre solution serait de ...

although [ɔːlˈðəu] *conj* bien que + *sub*

altitude [ˈæltɪtjuːd] *n* altitude *f*

altogether [ɔːltəˈɡɛðər] *adv* entièrement, tout à fait; (*on the whole*) tout compte fait; (*in all*) en tout

aluminium [æljuˈmɪnɪəm] (BRIT **aluminum**) [əˈluːmɪnəm] (US) *n* aluminium *m*

always [ˈɔːlweɪz] *adv* toujours

Alzheimer's (disease) [ˈæltshaɪməz-] *n* maladie *f* d'Alzheimer

am [æm] *vb* *see* **be**

a.m. *adv abbr* (= *ante meridiem*) du matin

amalgamate [əˈmælɡəmeɪt] *vt, vi* fusionner

amass [əˈmæs] *vt* amasser

amateur [ˈæmətər] *n* amateur *m*

amaze [əˈmeɪz] *vt* stupéfier; **to be ~d (at)** être stupéfait(e) (de); **amazed** *adj* stupéfait(e); **amazement** *n* surprise *f*, étonnement *m*; **amazing** *adj* étonnant(e), incroyable; (*bargain, offer*) exceptionnel(le)

Amazon [ˈæməzən] *n* (*Geo*) Amazone *f*

ambassador [æmˈbæsədər] *n* ambassadeur *m*

amber [ˈæmbər] *n* ambre *m*; **at ~** (BRIT Aut) à l'orange

ambiguous [æmˈbɪɡjuəs] *adj* ambigu(ë)

ambition [æmˈbɪʃən] *n* ambition *f*; **ambitious** [æmˈbɪʃəs] *adj* ambitieux(-euse)

ambulance [ˈæmbjuləns] *n* ambulance *f*;

a

call an ~! appelez une ambulance!
ambush ['æmbuʃ] n embuscade f ▷ vt tendre
une embuscade à
amen ['ɑː'mɛn] excl amen
amend [ə'mɛnd] vt (law) amender; (text)
corriger; **to make ~s** réparer ses torts, faire
amende honorable; **amendment** n (to law)
amendement m; (to text) correction f
amenities [ə'miːnɪtɪz] npl aménagements
mpl, équipements mpl
America [ə'mɛrɪkə] n Amérique f; **American**
adj américain(e) ▷ n Américain(e); **American**
football n (BRIT) football m américain
amicable ['æmɪkəbl] adj amical(e); (Law) à
l'amiable
amid(st) [ə'mɪd(st)] prep parmi, au milieu de
ammunition [æmju'nɪʃən] n munitions fpl
amnesty ['æmnɪstɪ] n amnistie f
among(st) [ə'mʌŋ(st)] prep parmi, entre
amount [ə'maunt] n (sum of money) somme
f; (total) montant m; (quantity) quantité f;
nombre m ▷ vi: **to ~ to** (total) s'élever à; (be
same as) équivaloir à, revenir à
amp(ère) ['æmp(ɛəᵣ)] n ampère m
ample ['æmpl] adj ample, spacieux(-euse);
(enough): **this is ~** c'est largement suffisant;
to have ~ time/room avoir bien assez de
temps/place
amplifier ['æmplɪfaɪəᵣ] n amplificateur m
amputate ['æmpjuteɪt] vt amputer
Amtrak ['æmtræk] (US) n société mixte
de transports ferroviaires interurbains pour
voyageurs
amuse [ə'mjuːz] vt amuser; **amusement**
n amusement m; (pastime) distraction f;
amusement arcade n salle f de jeu;
amusement park n parc m d'attractions
amusing [ə'mjuːzɪŋ] adj amusant(e),
divertissant(e)
an [æn, ən, n] indef art see **a**
anaemia [ə'niːmɪə] (US anemia) n anémie f
anaemic [ə'niːmɪk] (US anemic) adj
anémique
anaesthetic [ænɪs'θɛtɪk] (US anesthetic) n
anesthésique m
analog(ue) ['ænələɡ] adj (watch, computer)
analogique
analogy [ə'nælədʒɪ] n analogie f
analyse ['ænəlaɪz] (US analyze) vt
analyser; **analysis** (pl analyses) [ə'nælə
sɪs, -siːz] n analyse f; **analyst** ['ænə
lɪst] n (political analyst etc) analyste
m/f; (US) psychanalyste m/f
analyze ['ænəlaɪz] vt (US) = analyse
anarchy ['ænəkɪ] n anarchie f
anatomy [ə'nætəmɪ] n anatomie f
ancestor ['ænsɪstəᵣ] n ancêtre m, aïeul m
anchor ['æŋkəᵣ] n ancre f ▷ vi (also: **to drop**
~) jeter l'ancre, mouiller ▷ vt mettre à l'ancre;

(fig): **to ~ sth to** fixer qch à
anchovy ['æntʃəvɪ] n anchois m
ancient ['eɪnʃənt] adj ancien(ne),
antique; (person) d'un âge vénérable; (car)
antédiluvien(ne)
and [ænd] conj et; **~ so on** et ainsi de suite;
try ~ come tâchez de venir; **come ~ sit here**
venez vous asseoir ici; **he talked ~ talked** il
a parlé pendant des heures; **better ~ better**
de mieux en mieux; **more ~ more** de plus
en plus
Andorra [æn'dɔːrə] n (principauté f
d')Andorre f
anemia etc [ə'niːmɪə] (US) = **anaemia** etc
anesthetic [ænɪs'θɛtɪk] (US) = **anaesthetic**
angel ['eɪndʒəl] n ange m
anger ['æŋɡəᵣ] n colère f
angina [æn'dʒaɪnə] n angine f de poitrine
angle ['æŋɡl] n angle m; **from their ~** de leur
point de vue
angler ['æŋɡləᵣ] n pêcheur(-euse) à la ligne
Anglican ['æŋɡlɪkən] adj, n anglican(e)
angling ['æŋɡlɪŋ] n pêche f à la ligne
angrily ['æŋɡrɪlɪ] adv avec colère
angry ['æŋɡrɪ] adj en colère, furieux(-euse);
(wound) enflammé(e); **to be ~ with sb/at sth**
être furieux contre qn/de qch; **to get ~** se
fâcher, se mettre en colère
anguish ['æŋɡwɪʃ] n angoisse f
animal ['ænɪməl] n animal m ▷ adj
animal(e)
animated ['ænɪmeɪtɪd] adj animé(e)
animation [ænɪ'meɪʃən] n (of person) entrain
m; (of street, Cine) animation f
aniseed ['ænɪsiːd] n anis m
ankle ['æŋkl] n cheville f
annex ['ænɛks] n (BRIT: also: **~e**) annexe f ▷ vt
[ə'nɛks] annexer
anniversary [ænɪ'vɜːsərɪ] n anniversaire m
announce [ə'nauns] vt annoncer; (birth,
death) faire part de; **announcement** n
annonce f; (for births etc: in newspaper)
avis m de faire-part; (: letter, card) faire-
part m; **announcer** n (Radio, TV: between
programmes) speaker(ine); (: in a programme)
présentateur(-trice)
annoy [ə'nɔɪ] vt agacer, ennuyer, contrarier;
don't get ~ed! ne vous fâchez pas!; **annoying**
adj agaçant(e), contrariant(e)
annual ['ænjuəl] adj annuel(le) ▷ n (Bot)
plante annuelle; (book) album m; **annually** adv
annuellement
annum ['ænəm] n see **per**
anonymous [ə'nɔnɪməs] adj anonyme
anorak ['ænəræk] n anorak m
anorexia [ænə'rɛksɪə] n (also: **~ nervosa**)
anorexie f
anorexic [ænə'rɛksɪk] adj, n anorexique (m/f)
another [ə'nʌðəᵣ] adj: **~ book** (one more) un

autre livre, encore un livre, un livre de plus; (a different one) un autre livre ▷ pron un(e) autre, encore un(e), un(e) de plus; see also **one**

answer ['ɑːnsəʳ] n réponse f; (to problem) solution f ▷ vi répondre ▷ vt (reply to) répondre à; (problem) résoudre; (prayer) exaucer; **in ~ to your letter** suite à or en réponse à votre lettre; **to ~ the phone** répondre (au téléphone); **to ~ the bell** or **the door** aller or venir ouvrir (la porte); **answer back** vi répondre, répliquer; **answerphone** n (esp BRIT) répondeur m (téléphonique)

ant [ænt] n fourmi f

Antarctic [ænt'ɑːktɪk] n: **the ~** l'Antarctique m

antelope ['æntɪləup] n antilope f

antenatal ['æntɪ'neɪtl] adj prénatal(e)

antenna (pl **~e**) [æn'tɛnə, -niː] n antenne f

anthem ['ænθəm] n: **national ~** hymne national

anthology [æn'θɔlədʒɪ] n anthologie f

anthrax ['ænθræks] n anthrax m

anthropology [ænθrə'pɔlədʒɪ] n anthropologie f

anti ['æntɪ] prefix anti-; **antibiotic** ['æntɪbaɪ'ɔtɪk] n antibiotique m; **antibody** ['æntɪbɔdɪ] n anticorps m

anticipate [æn'tɪsɪpeɪt] vt s'attendre à, prévoir; (wishes, request) aller au devant de, devancer; **anticipation** [æntɪsɪ'peɪʃən] n attente f

anticlimax ['æntɪ'klaɪmæks] n déception f

anticlockwise ['æntɪ'klɔkwaɪz] (BRIT) adv dans le sens inverse des aiguilles d'une montre

antics ['æntɪks] npl singeries fpl

anti : **antidote** ['æntɪdəut] n antidote m, contrepoison m; **antifreeze** ['æntɪfriːz] n antigel m; **anti-globalization** n antimondialisation f; **antihistamine** [æntɪ'hɪstəmɪn] n antihistaminique m; **antiperspirant** [æntɪ'pəːspɪrənt] n déodorant m

antique [æn'tiːk] n (ornament) objet m d'art ancien; (furniture) meuble ancien ▷ adj ancien(ne); **antique shop** n magasin m d'antiquités

antiseptic [æntɪ'sɛptɪk] adj, n antiseptique (m)

antisocial ['æntɪ'səuʃəl] adj (unfriendly) peu liant(e), insociable; (against society) antisocial(e)

antlers ['æntləz] npl bois mpl, ramure f

anxiety [æŋ'zaɪətɪ] n anxiété f; (keenness): **~ to do** grand désir or impatience f de faire

anxious ['æŋkʃəs] adj (très) inquiet(-ète); (always worried) anxieux(-euse); (worrying) angoissant(e); (keen): **~ to do/that** qui tient

beaucoup à faire/à ce que + sub; impatient(e) de faire/que + sub

 KEYWORD

any ['ɛnɪ] adj **1** (in questions etc: singular) du, de l', de la; (: plural) des; **do you have any butter/children/ink?** avez-vous du beurre/des enfants/de l'encre?

2 (with negative) de, d'; **I don't have any money/books** je n'ai pas d'argent/de livres

3 (no matter which) n'importe quel(le); (each and every) tout(e), chaque; **choose any book you like** vous pouvez choisir n'importe quel livre; **any teacher you ask will tell you** n'importe quel professeur vous le dira

4 (in phrases): **in any case** de toute façon; **any day now** d'un jour à l'autre; **at any moment** à tout moment, d'un instant à l'autre; **at any rate** en tout cas; **any time** n'importe quand; **he might come (at) any time** il pourrait venir n'importe quand; **come (at) any time** venez quand vous voulez

▷ pron **1** (in questions etc) en; **have you got any?** est-ce que vous en avez?; **can any of you sing?** est-ce que parmi vous il y en a qui savent chanter?

2 (with negative) en; **I don't have any (of them)** je n'en ai pas, je n'en ai aucun

3 (no matter which one(s)) n'importe lequel (or laquelle); (anybody) n'importe qui; **take any of those books (you like)** vous pouvez prendre n'importe lequel de ces livres

▷ adv **1** (in questions etc): **do you want any more soup/sandwiches?** voulez-vous encore de la soupe/des sandwichs?; **are you feeling any better?** est-ce que vous vous sentez mieux?

2 (with negative): **I can't hear him any more** je ne l'entends plus; **don't wait any longer** n'attendez pas plus longtemps; **anybody** pron n'importe qui; (in interrogative sentences) quelqu'un; (in negative sentences): **I don't see anybody** je ne vois personne; **if anybody should phone ...** si quelqu'un téléphone ...; **anyhow** adv quoi qu'il en soit; (haphazardly) n'importe comment; **do it anyhow you like** faites-le comme vous voulez; **she leaves things just anyhow** elle laisse tout traîner; **I shall go anyhow** j'irai de toute façon; **anyone** pron = **anybody**; **anything** pron (no matter what) n'importe quoi; (in questions) quelque chose; (with negative) ne ... rien; **can you see anything?** tu vois quelque chose?; **if anything happens to me ...** s'il m'arrive quoi que ce soit ...; **you can say anything you like** vous pouvez dire ce que vous voulez; **anything will do** n'importe quoi fera l'affaire; **he'll eat anything** il mange de tout; **anytime**

adv (at any moment) d'un moment à l'autre; (whenever) n'importe quand; **anyway** adv de toute façon; **anyway, I couldn't come even if I wanted to** de toute façon, je ne pouvais pas venir même si je le voulais; **I shall go anyway** j'irai quand même; **why are you phoning, anyway?** au fait, pourquoi tu me téléphones?; **anywhere** adv n'importe où; (in interrogative sentences) quelque part; (in negative sentences): **I can't see him anywhere** je ne le vois nulle part; **can you see him anywhere?** tu le vois quelque part?; **put the books down anywhere** pose les livres n'importe où; **anywhere in the world** (no matter where) n'importe où dans le monde

apart [ə'pɑːt] adv (to one side) à part; de côté; à l'écart; (separately) séparément; **to take/pull ~** démonter; **10 miles/a long way ~** à 10 miles/très éloignés l'un de l'autre; **~ from** prep à part, excepté

apartment [ə'pɑːtmənt] n (us) appartement m, logement m; (room) chambre f; **apartment building** n (us) immeuble m; maison divisée en appartements

apathy ['æpəθɪ] n apathie f, indifférence f

ape [eɪp] n (grand) singe ▷ vt singer

aperitif [ə'pɛrɪtɪf] n apéritif m

aperture ['æpətʃuər] n orifice m, ouverture f; (Phot) ouverture (du diaphragme)

APEX ['eɪpɛks] n abbr (Aviat: = advance purchase excursion) APEX m

apologize [ə'pɔlədʒaɪz] vi: **to ~ (for sth to sb)** s'excuser (de qch auprès de qn), présenter des excuses (à qn pour qch)

apology [ə'pɔlədʒɪ] n excuses fpl

apostrophe [ə'pɔstrəfɪ] n apostrophe f

appal [ə'pɔːl] (us **appall**) vt consterner, atterrer; horrifier; **appalling** adj épouvantable; (stupidity) consternant(e)

apparatus [æpə'reɪtəs] n appareil m, dispositif m; (in gymnasium) agrès mpl

apparent [ə'pærənt] adj apparent(e); **apparently** adv apparemment

appeal [ə'piːl] vi (Law) faire or interjeter appel ▷ n (Law) appel m; (request) appel; prière f; (charm) attrait m, charme m; **to ~ for** demander (instamment); implorer; **to ~ to** (beg) faire appel à; (be attractive) plaire à; **it doesn't ~ to me** cela ne m'attire pas; **appealing** adj (attractive) attrayant(e)

appear [ə'pɪər] vi apparaître, se montrer; (Law) comparaître; (publication) paraître, sortir, être publié(e); (seem) paraître, sembler; **it would ~ that** il semble que; **to ~ in Hamlet** jouer dans Hamlet; **to ~ on TV** passer à la télé; **appearance** n apparition f; parution f; (look, aspect) apparence f, aspect m

appendices [ə'pɛndɪsiːz] npl of **appendix**

appendicitis [əpɛndɪ'saɪtɪs] n appendicite f

appendix (pl **appendices**) [ə'pɛndɪks, -siːz] n appendice m

appetite ['æpɪtaɪt] n appétit m

appetizer ['æpɪtaɪzər] n (food) amuse-gueule m; (drink) apéritif m

applaud [ə'plɔːd] vt, vi applaudir

applause [ə'plɔːz] n applaudissements mpl

apple ['æpl] n pomme f; **apple pie** n tarte f aux pommes

appliance [ə'plaɪəns] n appareil m

applicable [ə'plɪkəbl] adj applicable; **to be ~ to** (relevant) valoir pour

applicant ['æplɪkənt] n: **~ (for)** candidat(e) (à)

application [æplɪ'keɪʃən] n application f; (for a job, a grant etc) demande f; candidature f; **application form** n formulaire m de demande

apply [ə'plaɪ] vt: **to ~ (to)** (paint, ointment) appliquer (sur); (law, etc) appliquer (à) ▷ vi: **to ~ to** (ask) s'adresser à; (be suitable for, relevant to) s'appliquer à; **to ~ (for)** (permit, grant) faire une demande (en vue d'obtenir); (job) poser sa candidature (pour), faire une demande d'emploi (concernant); **to ~ o.s. to** s'appliquer à

appoint [ə'pɔɪnt] vt (to post) nommer, engager; (date, place) fixer, désigner; **appointment** n (to post) nomination f; (job) poste m; (arrangement to meet) rendez-vous m; **to have an appointment** avoir un rendez-vous; **to make an appointment (with)** prendre rendez-vous (avec); **I'd like to make an appointment** je voudrais prendre rendez-vous

appraisal [ə'preɪzl] n évaluation f

appreciate [ə'priːʃɪeɪt] vt (like) apprécier, faire cas de; (be grateful for) être reconnaissant(e) de; (be aware of) comprendre, se rendre compte de ▷ vi (Finance) prendre de la valeur; **appreciation** [əpriːʃɪ'eɪʃən] n appréciation f; (gratitude) reconnaissance f; (Finance) hausse f, valorisation f

apprehension [æprɪ'hɛnʃən] n appréhension f, inquiétude f

apprehensive [æprɪ'hɛnsɪv] adj inquiet(-ète), appréhensif(-ive)

apprentice [ə'prɛntɪs] n apprenti m

approach [ə'prəʊtʃ] vi approcher ▷ vt (come near) approcher de; (ask, apply to) s'adresser à; (subject, passer-by) aborder ▷ n approche f; accès m, abord m; démarche f (intellectuelle)

appropriate adj [ə'prəʊprɪɪt] (tool etc) qui convient, approprié(e); (moment, remark) opportun(e) ▷ vt [ə'prəʊprɪeɪt] (take) s'approprier

approval [ə'pruːvəl] n approbation f; **on ~** (Comm) à l'examen

approve [ə'pruːv] vt approuver; **approve of**

vt fus (thing) approuver; *(person)*: **they don't ~ of her** ils n'ont pas bonne opinion d'elle
approximate [ə'prɒksɪmɪt] *adj* approximatif(-ive); **approximately** *adv* approximativement
Apr. *abbr* = **April**
apricot ['eɪprɪkɒt] *n* abricot *m*
April ['eɪprəl] *n* avril *m*; **April Fools' Day** *n* le premier avril

● **APRIL FOOLS' DAY**
●
● **April Fools' Day** est le 1er avril, à l'occasion
● duquel on fait des farces de toutes sortes.
● Les victimes de ces farces sont les "April
● fools". Traditionnellement, on n'est censé
● faire des farces que jusqu'à midi.

apron ['eɪprən] *n* tablier *m*
apt [æpt] *adj (suitable)* approprié(e); *(likely)*: **~ to do** susceptible de faire; ayant tendance à faire
aquarium [ə'kwɛərɪəm] *n* aquarium *m*
Aquarius [ə'kwɛərɪəs] *n* le Verseau
Arab ['ærəb] *n* Arabe *m/f* ▷ *adj* arabe
Arabia [ə'reɪbɪə] *n* Arabie *f*; **Arabian** *adj* arabe; **Arabic** ['ærəbɪk] *adj, n* arabe *(m)*
arbitrary ['ɑ:bɪtrərɪ] *adj* arbitraire
arbitration [ɑ:bɪ'treɪʃən] *n* arbitrage *m*
arc [ɑ:k] *n* arc *m*
arcade [ɑ:'keɪd] *n* arcade *f*; *(passage with shops)* passage *m*, galerie *f*; *(with games)* salle *f* de jeu
arch [ɑ:tʃ] *n* arche *f*; *(of foot)* cambrure *f*, voûte *f* plantaire ▷ *vt* arquer, cambrer
archaeology [ɑ:kɪ'ɔlədʒɪ] *(US* **archeology**) *n* archéologie *f*
archbishop [ɑ:tʃ'bɪʃəp] *n* archevêque *m*
archeology [ɑ:kɪ'ɔlədʒɪ] *(US)* = **archaeology**
architect ['ɑ:kɪtɛkt] *n* architecte *m*; **architectural** [ɑ:kɪ'tɛktʃərəl] *adj* architectural(e); **architecture** *n* architecture *f*
archive ['ɑ:kaɪv] *n (often pl)* archives *fpl*
Arctic ['ɑ:ktɪk] *adj* arctique ▷ *n*: **the ~** l'Arctique *m*
are [ɑ:ʳ] *vb see* **be**
area ['ɛərɪə] *n (Geom)* superficie *f*; *(zone)* région *f*; *(: smaller)* secteur *m*; *(in room)* coin *m*; *(knowledge, research)* domaine *m*; **area code** *(US) n (Tel)* indicatif *m* de zone
arena [ə'ri:nə] *n* arène *f*
aren't [ɑ:nt] = **are not**
Argentina [ɑ:dʒən'ti:nə] *n* Argentine *f*; **Argentinian** [ɑ:dʒən'tɪnɪən] *adj* argentin(e) ▷ *n* Argentin(e)
arguably ['ɑ:gjuəblɪ] *adv*: **it is ~ ...** on peut soutenir que c'est ...
argue ['ɑ:gju:] *vi (quarrel)* se disputer; *(reason)* argumenter; **to ~ that** objecter *or* alléguer que, donner comme argument que

argument ['ɑ:gjumənt] *n (quarrel)* dispute *f*, discussion *f*; *(reasons)* argument *m*
Aries ['ɛərɪz] *n* le Bélier
arise *(pt* **arose**, *pp* **~n)** [ə'raɪz, ə'rəuz, ə'rɪzn] *vi* survenir, se présenter
arithmetic [ə'rɪθmətɪk] *n* arithmétique *f*
arm [ɑ:m] *n* bras *m* ▷ *vt* armer; **arms** *npl (weapons, Heraldry)* armes *fpl*; **~ in ~** bras dessus bras dessous; **armchair** ['ɑ:mtʃɛəʳ] *n* fauteuil *m*
armed [ɑ:md] *adj* armé(e); **armed forces** *npl*: **the armed forces** les forces armées; **armed robbery** *n* vol *m* à main armée
armour *(US* **armor)** ['ɑ:məʳ] *n* armure *f*; *(Mil: tanks)* blindés *mpl*
armpit ['ɑ:mpɪt] *n* aisselle *f*
armrest ['ɑ:mrɛst] *n* accoudoir *m*
army ['ɑ:mɪ] *n* armée *f*
A road *n (BRIT)* ≈ route nationale
aroma [ə'rəumə] *n* arôme *m*; **aromatherapy** *n* aromathérapie *f*
arose [ə'rəuz] *pt of* **arise**
around [ə'raund] *adv* (tout) autour; *(nearby)* dans les parages ▷ *prep* autour de; *(near)* près de; *(fig: about)* environ; *(: date, time)* vers; **is he ~?** est-il dans les parages *or* là?
arouse [ə'rauz] *vt (sleeper)* éveiller; *(curiosity, passions)* éveiller, susciter; *(anger)* exciter
arrange [ə'reɪndʒ] *vt* arranger; **to ~ to do sth** prévoir de faire qch; **arrangement** *n* arrangement *m*; **arrangements** *npl (plans etc)* arrangements *mpl*, dispositions *fpl*
array [ə'reɪ] *n (of objects)* déploiement *m*, étalage *m*
arrears [ə'rɪəz] *npl* arriéré *m*; **to be in ~ with one's rent** devoir un arriéré de loyer
arrest [ə'rɛst] *vt* arrêter; *(sb's attention)* retenir, attirer ▷ *n* arrestation *f*; **under ~** en état d'arrestation
arrival [ə'raɪvl] *n* arrivée *f*; **new ~** nouveau venu/nouvelle venue; *(baby)* nouveau-né(e)
arrive [ə'raɪv] *vi* arriver; **arrive at** *vt fus (decision, solution)* parvenir à
arrogance ['ærəgəns] *n* arrogance *f*
arrogant ['ærəgənt] *adj* arrogant(e)
arrow ['ærəu] *n* flèche *f*
arse [ɑ:s] *n (BRIT infl!)* cul *m (!)*
arson ['ɑ:sn] *n* incendie criminel
art [ɑ:t] *n* art *m*; **Arts** *npl (Scol)* les lettres *fpl*; **art college** *n* école *f* des beaux-arts
artery ['ɑ:tərɪ] *n* artère *f*
art gallery *n* musée *m* d'art; *(saleroom)* galerie *f* de peinture
arthritis [ɑ:'θraɪtɪs] *n* arthrite *f*
artichoke ['ɑ:tɪtʃəuk] *n* artichaut *m*; **Jerusalem ~** topinambour *m*
article ['ɑ:tɪkl] *n* article *m*
articulate *adj* [ɑ:'tɪkjulɪt] *(person)* qui s'exprime clairement et aisément; *(speech)*

bien articulé(e), prononcé(e) clairement
▷ vb [ɑ:'tɪkjuleɪt] ▷ vi articuler, parler
distinctement ▷ vt articuler

artificial [ɑ:tɪ'fɪʃəl] adj artificiel(le)

artist ['ɑ:tɪst] n artiste m/f; **artistic** [ɑ:'tɪstɪk]
adj artistique

art school n ≈ école f des beaux-arts

KEYWORD

as [æz] conj **1** (time: moment) comme, alors que;
à mesure que; **he came in as I was leaving**
il est arrivé comme je partais; **as the years
went by** à mesure que les années passaient;
as from tomorrow à partir de demain
2 (since, because) comme, puisque; **he left
early as he had to be home by 10** comme il or
puisqu'il devait être de retour avant 10h, il est
parti de bonne heure
3 (referring to manner, way) comme; **do as you
wish** faites comme vous voudrez; **as she said**
comme elle disait
▷ adv **1** (in comparisons): **as big as** aussi grand
que; **twice as big as** deux fois plus grand que;
as much or **many as** autant que; **as much
money/many books as** autant d'argent/de
livres que; **as soon as** dès que
2 (concerning): **as for** or **to that** quant à cela,
pour ce qui est de cela
3: **as if** or **though** comme si; **he looked as if
he was ill** il avait l'air d'être malade; see also
long; **such**; **well**
▷ prep (in the capacity of) en tant que, en qualité
de; **he works as a driver** il travaille comme
chauffeur; **as chairman of the company,
he ...** en tant que président de la société, il ...;
he gave me it as a present il me l'a offert, il
m'en a fait cadeau

a.s.a.p. abbr = **as soon as possible**

asbestos [æz'bɛstəs] n asbeste m, amiante m

ascent [ə'sɛnt] n (climb) ascension f

ash [æʃ] n (dust) cendre f; (also: **~ tree**) frêne m

ashamed [ə'ʃeɪmd] adj honteux(-euse),
confus(e); **to be ~ of** avoir honte de

ashore [ə'ʃɔ:ʳ] adv à terre

ashtray ['æʃtreɪ] n cendrier m

Ash Wednesday n mercredi m des Cendres

Asia ['eɪʃə] n Asie f; **Asian** n (from Asia)
Asiatique m/f; (BRIT: from Indian subcontinent)
Indo-Pakistanais(-e) ▷ adj asiatique; indo-
pakistanais(-e)

aside [ə'saɪd] adv de côté; à l'écart ▷ n
aparté m

ask [ɑ:sk] vt demander; (invite) inviter; **to ~ sb
sth/to do sth** demander à qn qch/de faire
qch; **to ~ sb about sth** questionner qn au
sujet de qch; se renseigner auprès de qn au
sujet de qch; **to ~ (sb) a question** poser une

question (à qn); **to ~ sb out to dinner** inviter
qn au restaurant; **ask for** vt fus demander;
it's just ~ing for trouble or **for it** ce serait
chercher des ennuis

asleep [ə'sli:p] adj endormi(e); **to fall ~**
s'endormir

AS level n abbr (= Advanced Subsidiary level)
première partie de l'examen équivalent au
baccalauréat

asparagus [əs'pærəgəs] n asperges fpl

aspect ['æspɛkt] n aspect m; (direction in which
a building etc faces) orientation f, exposition f

aspirations [æspə'reɪʃənz] npl (hopes,
ambition) aspirations fpl

aspire [əs'paɪəʳ] vi: **to ~ to** aspirer à

aspirin ['æsprɪn] n aspirine f

ass [æs] n âne m; (inf) imbécile m/f; (US inf!)
cul m (!)

assassin [ə'sæsɪn] n assassin m; **assassinate**
vt assassiner

assault [ə'sɔ:lt] n (Mil) assaut m; (gen: attack)
agression f ▷ vt attaquer; (sexually) violenter

assemble [ə'sɛmbl] vt assembler ▷ vi
s'assembler, se rassembler

assembly [ə'sɛmblɪ] n (meeting)
rassemblement m; (parliament) assemblée f;
(construction) assemblage m

assert [ə'sə:t] vt affirmer, déclarer; (authority)
faire valoir; (innocence) protester de; **assertion**
[ə'sə:ʃən] n assertion f, affirmation f

assess [ə'sɛs] vt évaluer, estimer; (tax,
damages) établir or fixer le montant de; (person)
juger la valeur de; **assessment** n évaluation f,
estimation f; (of tax) fixation f

asset ['æsɛt] n avantage m, atout m; (person)
atout; **assets** npl (Comm) capital m; avoir(s)
m(pl); actif m

assign [ə'saɪn] vt (date) fixer, arrêter; **to ~ sth
to** (task) assigner qch à; (resources) affecter qch
à; **assignment** n (task) mission f; (homework)
devoir m

assist [ə'sɪst] vt aider, assister; **assistance** n
aide f, assistance f; **assistant** n assistant(e),
adjoint(e); (BRIT: also: **shop assistant**)
vendeur(-euse)

associate adj, n [ə'səuʃɪɪt] associé(e) ▷ vb
[ə'səuʃɪeɪt] ▷ vt associer ▷ vi: **to ~ with sb**
fréquenter qn

association [əsəusɪ'eɪʃən] n association f

assorted [ə'sɔ:tɪd] adj assorti(e)

assortment [ə'sɔ:tmənt] n assortiment m;
(of people) mélange m

assume [ə'sju:m] vt supposer; (responsibilities
etc) assumer; (attitude, name) prendre, adopter

assumption [ə'sʌmpʃən] n supposition f,
hypothèse f; (of power) assomption f, prise f

assurance [ə'ʃuərəns] n assurance f

assure [ə'ʃuəʳ] vt assurer

asterisk ['æstərɪsk] n astérisque m

asthma ['æsmə] n asthme m
astonish [ə'stɒnɪʃ] vt étonner, stupéfier;
  astonished adj étonné(e); **to be astonished
  at** être étonné(e) de; **astonishing** adj
  étonnant(e), stupéfiant(e); **I find it
  astonishing that ...** je trouve incroyable
  que ... + sub; **astonishment** n (grand)
  étonnement, stupéfaction f
astound [ə'staund] vt stupéfier, sidérer
astray [ə'streɪ] adv: **to go ~** s'égarer; (fig)
  quitter le droit chemin; **to lead ~** (morally)
  détourner du droit chemin
astrology [əs'trɒlədʒɪ] n astrologie f
astronaut ['æstrənɔ:t] n astronaute m/f
astronomer [əs'trɒnəmər] n astronome m
astronomical [æstrə'nɒmɪkl] adj
  astronomique
astronomy [əs'trɒnəmɪ] n astronomie f
astute [əs'tju:t] adj astucieux(-euse),
  malin(-igne)
asylum [ə'saɪləm] n asile m; **asylum seeker**
  [-si:kər] n demandeur(-euse) d'asile

◯ **KEYWORD**

at [æt] prep **1** (referring to position, direction) à;
  at the top au sommet; **at home/school** à la
  maison or chez soi/à l'école; **at the baker's** à
  la boulangerie, chez le boulanger; **to look at
  sth** regarder qch
  2 (referring to time): **at 4 o'clock** à 4 heures; **at
  Christmas** à Noël; **at night** la nuit; **at times**
  par moments, parfois
  3 (referring to rates, speed etc) à; **at £1 a kilo** une
  livre le kilo; **two at a time** deux à la fois; **at 50
  km/h** à 50 km/h
  4 (referring to manner): **at a stroke** d'un seul
  coup; **at peace** en paix
  5 (referring to activity): **to be at work** (in the
  office etc) être au travail; (working) travailler; **to
  play at cowboys** jouer aux cowboys; **to be
  good at sth** être bon en qch
  6 (referring to cause): **shocked/surprised/
  annoyed at sth** choqué par/étonné de/agacé
  par qch; **I went at his suggestion** j'y suis allé
  sur son conseil
  7 (symbol) arobase f

ate [eɪt] pt of **eat**
atheist ['eɪθɪɪst] n athée m/f
Athens ['æθɪnz] n Athènes
athlete ['æθli:t] n athlète m/f
athletic [æθ'letɪk] adj athlétique; **athletics** n
  athlétisme m
Atlantic [ət'læntɪk] adj atlantique ▷ n: **the ~
  (Ocean)** l'(océan m) Atlantique m
atlas ['ætləs] n atlas m
A.T.M. n abbr (= Automated Telling Machine)
  guichet m automatique

atmosphere ['ætməsfɪər] n (air) atmosphère
  f; (fig: of place etc) atmosphère, ambiance f
atom ['ætəm] n atome m; **atomic** [ə'tɒmɪk]
  adj atomique; **atom(ic) bomb** n bombe f
  atomique
A to Z® n (map) plan m des rues
atrocity [ə'trɒsɪtɪ] n atrocité f
attach [ə'tætʃ] vt (gen) attacher; (document,
  letter) joindre; **to be ~ed to sb/sth** (to like)
  être attaché à qn/qch; **attachment** n
  (tool) accessoire m; (Comput) fichier m joint;
  (love): **attachment (to)** affection f (pour),
  attachement m (à)
attack [ə'tæk] vt attaquer; (task etc) s'attaquer
  à ▷ n attaque f; **heart ~** crise f cardiaque;
  attacker n attaquant m; agresseur m
attain [ə'teɪn] vt (also: **to ~ to**) parvenir à,
  atteindre; (knowledge) acquérir
attempt [ə'tempt] n tentative f ▷ vt essayer,
  tenter
attend [ə'tend] vt (course) suivre; (meeting,
  talk) assister à; (school, church) aller à,
  fréquenter; (patient) soigner, s'occuper de;
  attend to vt fus (needs, affairs etc) s'occuper de;
  (customer) s'occuper de, servir; **attendance**
  n (being present) présence f; (people present)
  assistance f; **attendant** n employé(e);
  gardien(ne) ▷ adj concomitant(e), qui
  accompagne or s'ensuit

  ▌Be careful not to translate **to attend** by
   the French word **attendre**.

attention [ə'tenʃən] n attention f ▷ excl
  (Mil) garde-à-vous!; **for the ~ of** (Admin) à
  l'attention de
attic ['ætɪk] n grenier m, combles mpl
attitude ['ætɪtju:d] n attitude f
attorney [ə'tə:nɪ] n (us: lawyer) avocat m;
  Attorney General n (BRIT) ≈ procureur
  général; (us) ≈ garde m des Sceaux, ministre m
  de la Justice
attract [ə'trækt] vt attirer; **attraction**
  [ə'trækʃən] n (gen pl: pleasant things)
  attraction f, attrait m; (Physics) attraction;
  (fig: towards sb, sth) attirance f; **attractive** adj
  séduisant(e), attrayant(e)
attribute n ['ætrɪbju:t] attribut m ▷ vt
  [ə'trɪbju:t]: **to ~ sth to** attribuer qch à
aubergine ['əubəʒi:n] n aubergine f
auburn ['ɔ:bən] adj auburn inv, châtain
  roux inv
auction ['ɔ:kʃən] n (also: **sale by ~**) vente f aux
  enchères ▷ vt (also: **to sell by ~**) vendre aux
  enchères
audible ['ɔ:dɪbl] adj audible
audience ['ɔ:dɪəns] n (people) assistance f,
  public m; (on radio) auditeurs mpl; (at theatre)
  spectateurs mpl; (interview) audience f
audit ['ɔ:dɪt] vt vérifier
audition [ɔ:'dɪʃən] n audition f

auditor ['ɔːdɪtə^r] *n* vérificateur *m* des comptes
auditorium [ɔːdɪ'tɔːrɪəm] *n* auditorium *m*, salle *f* de concert *or* de spectacle
Aug. *abbr* = **August**
August ['ɔːgəst] *n* août *m*
aunt [ɑːnt] *n* tante *f*; **auntie, aunty** *n* diminutive of **aunt**
au pair ['əu'pɛə^r] *n* (also: ~ **girl**) jeune fille *f* au pair
aura ['ɔːrə] *n* atmosphère *f*; (of person) aura *f*
austerity [ɔs'tɛrɪtɪ] *n* austérité *f*
Australia [ɔs'treɪlɪə] *n* Australie *f*; **Australian** *adj* australien(ne) ▷ *n* Australien(ne)
Austria ['ɔstrɪə] *n* Autriche *f*; **Austrian** *adj* autrichien(ne) ▷ *n* Autrichien(ne)
authentic [ɔː'θɛntɪk] *adj* authentique
author ['ɔːθə^r] *n* auteur *m*
authority [ɔː'θɔrɪtɪ] *n* autorité *f*; (permission) autorisation (formelle); **the authorities** les autorités *fpl*, l'administration *f*
authorize ['ɔːθəraɪz] *vt* autoriser
auto ['ɔːtəu] *n* (us) auto *f*, voiture *f*; **autobiography** [ɔːtəbaɪ'ɔgrəfɪ] *n* autobiographie *f*; **autograph** ['ɔːtəgrɑːf] *n* autographe *m* ▷ *vt* signer, dédicacer; **automatic** [ɔːtə'mætɪk] *adj* automatique ▷ *n* (gun) automatique *m*; (car) voiture *f* à transmission automatique; **automatically** *adv* automatiquement; **automobile** ['ɔːtəməbiːl] *n* (us) automobile *f*; **autonomous** [ɔː'tɔnəməs] *adj* autonome; **autonomy** [ɔː'tɔnəmɪ] *n* autonomie *f*
autumn ['ɔːtəm] *n* automne *m*
auxiliary [ɔːg'zɪlɪərɪ] *adj, n* auxiliaire (*m/f*)
avail [ə'veɪl] *vt*: **to ~ o.s. of** user de; profiter de ▷ *n*: **to no ~** sans résultat, en vain, en pure perte
availability [əveɪlə'bɪlɪtɪ] *n* disponibilité *f*
available [ə'veɪləbl] *adj* disponible
avalanche ['ævəlɑːnʃ] *n* avalanche *f*
Ave. *abbr* = **avenue**
avenue ['ævənjuː] *n* avenue *f*; (fig) moyen *m*
average ['ævərɪdʒ] *n* moyenne *f* ▷ *adj* moyen(ne) ▷ *vt* (a certain figure) atteindre *or* faire *etc* en moyenne; **on ~** en moyenne
avert [ə'vəːt] *vt* (danger) prévenir, écarter; (one's eyes) détourner
avid ['ævɪd] *adj* avide
avocado [ævə'kɑːdəu] *n* (BRIT: also: ~ **pear**) avocat *m*
avoid [ə'vɔɪd] *vt* éviter
await [ə'weɪt] *vt* attendre
awake [ə'weɪk] *adj* éveillé(e) ▷ *vb* (pt **awoke**, pp **awoken**) ▷ *vt* éveiller ▷ *vi* s'éveiller; **to be ~** être réveillé(e)
award [ə'wɔːd] *n* (for bravery) récompense *f*; (prize) prix *m*; (Law: damages) dommages-intérêts *mpl* ▷ *vt* (prize) décerner; (Law: damages) accorder

aware [ə'wɛə^r] *adj*: **~ of** (conscious) conscient(e) de; (informed) au courant de; **to become ~ of/that** prendre conscience de/que; se rendre compte de/que; **awareness** *n* conscience *f*, connaissance *f*
away [ə'weɪ] *adv* (au) loin; (movement): **she went ~** elle est partie ▷ *adj* (not in, not here) absent(e); **far ~** (au) loin; **two kilometres ~** à (une distance de) deux kilomètres, à deux kilomètres de distance; **two hours ~ by car** à deux heures de voiture *or* de route; **the holiday was two weeks ~** il restait deux semaines jusqu'aux vacances; **he's ~ for a week** il est parti (pour) une semaine; **to take sth ~ from sb** prendre qch à qn; **to take sth ~ from sth** (subtract) ôter qch de qch; **to work/pedal ~** travailler/pédaller à cœur joie; **to fade ~** (colour) s'estomper; (sound) s'affaiblir
awe [ɔː] *n* respect mêlé de crainte, effroi mêlé d'admiration; **awesome** ['ɔːsəm] (us) *adj* (inf: excellent) génial(e)
awful ['ɔːfəl] *adj* affreux(-euse); **an ~ lot of** énormément de; **awfully** *adv* (very) terriblement, vraiment
awkward ['ɔːkwəd] *adj* (clumsy) gauche, maladroit(e); (inconvenient) peu pratique; (embarrassing) gênant
awoke [ə'wəuk] *pt* of **awake**
awoken [ə'wəukən] *pp* of **awake**
axe [æks] (us **ax**) *n* hache *f* ▷ *vt* (project etc) abandonner; (jobs) supprimer
axle ['æksl] *n* essieu *m*
ay(e) [aɪ] *excl* (yes) oui
azalea [ə'zeɪlɪə] *n* azalée *f*

B [bi:] *n* (*Mus*): **B** si *m*

B.A. *abbr* (*Scol*) = **Bachelor of Arts**

baby ['beɪbɪ] *n* bébé *m*; **baby carriage** *n* (*us*) voiture *f* d'enfant; **baby-sit** *vi* garder les enfants; **baby-sitter** *n* baby-sitter *m*/*f*; **baby wipe** *n* lingette *f* (*pour bébé*)

bachelor ['bætʃələ'] *n* célibataire *m*; **B~ of Arts/Science (BA/BSc)** ≈ licencié(e) ès *or* en lettres/sciences

back [bæk] *n* (*of person, horse*) dos *m*; (*of hand*) dos, revers *m*; (*of house*) derrière *m*; (*of car, train*) arrière *m*; (*of chair*) dossier *m*; (*of page*) verso *m*; (*of crowd*) fond *m*: **can the people at the ~ hear me properly?** est-ce que les gens du fond peuvent m'entendre?; (*Football*) arrière *m*; **~ to front** à l'envers ▷ *vt* (*financially*) soutenir (financièrement); (*candidate: also:* **~ up**) soutenir, appuyer; (*horse: at races*) parier *or* miser sur; (*car*) (faire) reculer ▷ *vi* reculer; (*car etc*) faire marche arrière ▷ *adj* (*in compounds*) de derrière, à l'arrière; **~ seat/wheel** (*Aut*) siège *m*/roue *f* arrière *inv*; **~ payments/rent** arriéré *m* de paiements/loyer; **~ garden/room** jardin/pièce sur l'arrière ▷ *adv* (*not forward*) en arrière; (*returned*): **he's ~** il est rentré, il est de retour; **he ran ~** il est revenu en courant; (*restitution*): **throw the ball ~** renvoie la balle; **can I have it ~?** puis-je le ravoir?, peux-tu me le rendre?; (*again*): **he called ~** il a rappelé;

back down *vi* rabattre de ses prétentions; **back out** *vi* (*of promise*) se dédire; **back up** *vt* (*person*) soutenir; (*Comput*) faire une copie de sauvegarde de; **backache** *n* mal *m* au dos; **backbencher** (*BRIT*) *n* membre du parlement sans portefeuille; **backbone** *n* colonne vertébrale, épine dorsale; **back door** *n* porte *f* de derrière; **backfire** *vi* (*Aut*) pétarader; (*plans*) mal tourner; **backgammon** *n* trictrac *m*; **background** *n* arrière-plan *m*; (*of events*) situation *f*, conjoncture *f*; (*basic knowledge*) éléments *mpl* de base; (*experience*) formation *f*; **family background** milieu familial; **backing** *n* (*fig*) soutien *m*, appui *m*; **backlog** *n*: **backlog of work** travail *m* en retard; **backpack** *n* sac *m* à dos; **backpacker** *n* randonneur(-euse); **backslash** *n* barre oblique inversée; **backstage** *adv* dans les coulisses; **backstroke** *n* dos crawlé; **backup** *adj* (*train, plane*) supplémentaire, de réserve; (*Comput*) de sauvegarde ▷ *n* (*support*) appui *m*, soutien *m*; (*Comput: also:* **backup file**) sauvegarde *f*; **backward** *adj* (*movement*) en arrière; (*person, country*) arriéré(e), attardé(e); **backwards** *adv* (*move, go*) en arrière; (*read a list*) à l'envers, à rebours; (*fall*) à la renverse; (*walk*) à reculons; **backyard** *n* arrière-cour *f*

bacon ['beɪkən] *n* bacon *m*, lard *m*

bacteria [bæk'tɪərɪə] *npl* bactéries *fpl*

bad [bæd] *adj* mauvais(e); (*child*) vilain(e); (*mistake, accident*) grave; (*meat, food*) gâté(e), avarié(e); **his ~ leg** sa jambe malade; **to go ~** (*meat, food*) se gâter; (*milk*) tourner

bade [bæd] *pt of* **bid**

badge [bædʒ] *n* insigne *m*; (*of policeman*) plaque *f*; (*stick-on, sew-on*) badge *m*

badger ['bædʒə'] *n* blaireau *m*

badly ['bædlɪ] *adv* (*work, dress etc*) mal; **to reflect ~ on sb** donner une mauvaise image de qn; **~ wounded** grièvement blessé; **he needs it ~** il en a absolument besoin; **~ off** *adj, adv* dans la gêne

bad-mannered ['bæd'mænəd] *adj* mal élevé(e)

badminton ['bædmɪntən] *n* badminton *m*

bad-tempered ['bæd'tempəd] *adj* (*by nature*) ayant mauvais caractère; (*on one occasion*) de mauvaise humeur

bag [bæg] *n* sac *m*; **~s of** (*inf: lots of*) des tas de; **baggage** *n* bagages *mpl*; **baggage allowance** *n* franchise *f* de bagages; **baggage reclaim** *n* (*at airport*) livraison *f* des bagages; **baggy** *adj* avachi(e), qui fait des poches; **bagpipes** *npl* cornemuse *f*

bail [beɪl] *n* caution *f* ▷ *vt* (*prisoner: also:* **grant ~ to**) mettre en liberté sous caution; (*boat: also:* **~ out**) écoper; **to be released on ~** être libéré(e) sous caution; **bail out** *vt* (*prisoner*) payer la caution de

b

bait [beɪt] n appât m ▷ vt appâter; (fig: tease) tourmenter

bake [beɪk] vt (faire) cuire au four ▷ vi (bread etc) cuire (au four); (make cakes etc) faire de la pâtisserie; **baked beans** npl haricots blancs à la sauce tomate; **baked potato** n pomme f de terre en robe des champs; **baker** n boulanger m; **bakery** n boulangerie f; **baking** n (process) cuisson f; **baking powder** n levure f (chimique)

balance ['bæləns] n équilibre m; (Comm: sum) solde m; (remainder) reste m; (scales) balance f ▷ vt mettre or faire tenir en équilibre; (pros and cons) peser; (budget) équilibrer; (account) balancer; (compensate) compenser, contrebalancer; **~ of trade/payments** balance commerciale/des comptes or paiements; **balanced** adj (personality, diet) équilibré(e); (report) objectif(-ive); **balance sheet** n bilan m

balcony ['bælkənɪ] n balcon m; **do you have a room with a ~?** avez-vous une chambre avec balcon?

bald [bɔːld] adj chauve; (tyre) lisse

ball [bɔːl] n boule f; (football) ballon m; (for tennis, golf) balle f; (dance) bal m; **to play ~** jouer au ballon (or à la balle); (fig) coopérer

ballerina [bælə'riːnə] n ballerine f

ballet ['bæleɪ] n ballet m; (art) danse f (classique); **ballet dancer** n danseur(-euse) de ballet

balloon [bə'luːn] n ballon m

ballot ['bælət] n scrutin m

ballpoint (pen) ['bɔːlpɔɪnt-] n stylo m à bille

ballroom ['bɔːlrum] n salle f de bal

Baltic [bɔːltɪk] n: **the ~ (Sea)** la (mer) Baltique

bamboo [bæm'buː] n bambou m

ban [bæn] n interdiction f ▷ vt interdire

banana [bə'nɑːnə] n banane f

band [bænd] n bande f; (at a dance) orchestre m; (Mil) musique f, fanfare f

bandage ['bændɪdʒ] n bandage m, pansement m ▷ vt (wound, leg) mettre un pansement or un bandage sur

Band-Aid® ['bændeɪd] n (us) pansement adhésif

B. & B. n abbr = **bed and breakfast**

bandit ['bændɪt] n bandit m

bang [bæŋ] n détonation f; (of door) claquement m; (blow) coup (violent) ▷ vt frapper (violemment); (door) claquer ▷ vi détoner; claquer

Bangladesh [bæŋglə'dɛʃ] n Bangladesh m

Bangladeshi [bæŋglə'dɛʃɪ] adj du Bangladesh ▷ n habitant(e) du Bangladesh

bangle ['bæŋgl] n bracelet m

bangs [bæŋz] npl (us: fringe) frange f

banish ['bænɪʃ] vt bannir

banister(s) ['bænɪstə(z)] n(pl) rampe f (d'escalier)

banjo (pl **~es** or **~s**) ['bændʒəu] n banjo m

bank [bæŋk] n banque f; (of river, lake) bord m, rive f; (of earth) talus m, remblai m ▷ vi (Aviat) virer sur l'aile; **bank on** vt fus miser or tabler sur; **bank account** n compte m en banque; **bank balance** n solde m bancaire; **bank card** (BRIT) n carte f d'identité bancaire; **bank charges** npl (BRIT) frais mpl de banque; **banker** n banquier m; **bank holiday** n (BRIT) jour férié (où les banques sont fermées); voir encadré; **banking** n opérations fpl bancaires; profession f de banquier; **bank manager** n directeur m d'agence (bancaire); **banknote** n billet m de banque

● **BANK HOLIDAY**
●
● Le terme **bank holiday** s'applique au
● Royaume-Uni aux jours fériés pendant
● lesquels banques et commerces sont
● fermés. Les principaux **bank holidays** à
● part Noël et Pâques se situent au mois de
● mai et fin août, et contrairement aux pays
● de tradition catholique, ne coïncident pas
● nécessairement avec une fête religieuse.

bankrupt ['bæŋkrʌpt] adj en faillite; **to go ~** faire faillite; **bankruptcy** n faillite f

bank statement n relevé m de compte

banner ['bænər] n bannière f

bannister(s) ['bænɪstə(z)] n(pl) = **banister(s)**

banquet ['bæŋkwɪt] n banquet m, festin m

baptism ['bæptɪzəm] n baptême m

baptize [bæp'taɪz] vt baptiser

bar [bɑːr] n (pub) bar m; (counter) comptoir m, bar; (rod: of metal etc) barre f; (of window etc) barreau m; (of chocolate) tablette f, plaque f; (fig: obstacle) obstacle m; (prohibition) mesure f d'exclusion; (Mus) mesure f ▷ vt (road) barrer; (person) exclure; (activity) interdire; **~ of soap** savonnette f; **behind ~s** (prisoner) derrière les barreaux; **the B~** (Law) le barreau; **~ none** sans exception

barbaric [bɑː'bærɪk] adj barbare

barbecue ['bɑːbɪkjuː] n barbecue m

barbed wire ['bɑːbd-] n fil m de fer barbelé

barber ['bɑːbər] n coiffeur m (pour hommes); **barber's (shop)** (us **barber (shop)**) n salon m de coiffure (pour hommes)

bar code n code m à barres, code-barre m

bare [bɛər] adj nu(e) ▷ vt mettre à nu, dénuder; (teeth) montrer; **barefoot** adj, adv nu-pieds, (les) pieds nus; **barely** adv à peine

bargain ['bɑːgɪn] n (transaction) marché m; (good buy) affaire f, occasion f ▷ vi (haggle) marchander; (negotiate) négocier, traiter; **into the ~** par-dessus le marché; **bargain for** vt fus (*inf*): **he got more than he ~ed for!** il en a eu pour son argent!

barge [bɑːdʒ] *n* péniche *f*; **barge in** *vi* (*walk in*) faire irruption; (*interrupt talk*) intervenir mal à propos

bark [bɑːk] *n* (*of tree*) écorce *f*; (*of dog*) aboiement *m* ▷ *vi* aboyer

barley ['bɑːlɪ] *n* orge *f*

barmaid ['bɑːmeɪd] *n* serveuse *f* (de bar), barmaid *f*

barman ['bɑːmən] *n* serveur *m* (de bar), barman *m*

barn [bɑːn] *n* grange *f*

barometer [bə'rɒmɪtər] *n* baromètre *m*

baron ['bærən] *n* baron *m*; **baroness** *n* baronne *f*

barracks ['bærəks] *npl* caserne *f*

barrage ['bærɑːʒ] *n* (*Mil*) tir *m* de barrage; (*dam*) barrage *m*; (*of criticism*) feu *m*

barrel ['bærəl] *n* tonneau *m*; (*of gun*) canon *m*

barren ['bærən] *adj* stérile

barrette [bə'rɛt] (*US*) *n* barrette *f*

barricade [bærɪ'keɪd] *n* barricade *f*

barrier ['bærɪər] *n* barrière *f*

barring ['bɑːrɪŋ] *prep* sauf

barrister ['bærɪstər] *n* (*BRIT*) avocat (plaidant)

barrow ['bærəu] *n* (*cart*) charrette *f* à bras

bartender ['bɑːtɛndər] *n* (*US*) serveur *m* (de bar), barman *m*

base [beɪs] *n* base *f* ▷ *vt* (*opinion, belief*): **to ~ sth on** baser *or* fonder qch sur ▷ *adj* vil(e), bas(se)

baseball ['beɪsbɔːl] *n* base-ball *m*; **baseball cap** *n* casquette *f* de base-ball

Basel [bɑːl] *n* = **Basle**

basement ['beɪsmənt] *n* sous-sol *m*

bases ['beɪsiːz] *npl of* **basis**

bash [bæʃ] *vt* (*inf*) frapper, cogner

basic ['beɪsɪk] *adj* (*precautions, rules*) élémentaire; (*principles, research*) fondamental(e); (*vocabulary, salary*) de base; (*minimal*) réduit(e) au minimum, rudimentaire; **basically** *adv* (*in fact*) en fait; (*essentially*) fondamentalement; **basics** *npl*: **the basics** l'essentiel *m*

basil ['bæzl] *n* basilic *m*

basin ['beɪsn] *n* (*vessel, also Geo*) cuvette *f*, bassin *m*; (*BRIT: for food*) bol *m*; (*also*: **wash~**) lavabo *m*

basis (*pl* **bases**) ['beɪsɪs, -siːz] *n* base *f*; **on a part-time/trial ~** à temps partiel/à l'essai

basket ['bɑːskɪt] *n* corbeille *f*; (*with handle*) panier *m*; **basketball** *n* basket-ball *m*

Basle [bɑːl] *n* Bâle

Basque [bæsk] *adj* basque ▷ *n* Basque *m/f*; **the ~ Country** le Pays basque

bass [beɪs] *n* (*Mus*) basse *f*

bastard ['bɑːstəd] *n* enfant naturel(le),

bâtard(e); (*inf!*) salaud *m* (!)

bat [bæt] *n* chauve-souris *f*; (*for baseball etc*) batte *f*; (*BRIT: for table tennis*) raquette *f* ▷ *vt*: **he didn't ~ an eyelid** il n'a pas sourcillé *or* bronché

batch [bætʃ] *n* (*of bread*) fournée *f*; (*of papers*) liasse *f*; (*of applicants, letters*) paquet *m*

bath (*pl* **~s**) [bɑːθ, bɑːðz] *n* bain *m*; (*bathtub*) baignoire *f* ▷ *vt* baigner, donner un bain à; **to have a ~** prendre un bain; *see also* **baths**

bathe [beɪð] *vi* se baigner ▷ *vt* baigner; (*wound etc*) laver

bathing ['beɪðɪŋ] *n* baignade *f*; **bathing costume** (*US* **bathing suit**) *n* maillot *m* (de bain)

bath: **bathrobe** *n* peignoir *m* de bain; **bathroom** *n* salle *f* de bains; **baths** [bɑːðz] *npl* (*BRIT: also*: **swimming baths**) piscine *f*; **bath towel** *n* serviette *f* de bain; **bathtub** *n* baignoire *f*

baton ['bætən] *n* bâton *m*; (*Mus*) baguette *f*; (*club*) matraque *f*

batter ['bætər] *vt* battre ▷ *n* pâte *f* à frire; **battered** *adj* (*hat, pan*) cabossé(e); **battered wife/child** épouse/enfant maltraité(e) *or* martyr(e)

battery ['bætərɪ] *n* (*for torch, radio*) pile *f*; (*Aut, Mil*) batterie *f*; **battery farming** *n* élevage *m* en batterie

battle ['bætl] *n* bataille *f*, combat *m* ▷ *vi* se battre, lutter; **battlefield** *n* champ *m* de bataille

bay [beɪ] *n* (*of sea*) baie *f*; (*BRIT: for parking*) place *f* de stationnement; (*for loading*) aire *f* de chargement; **B~ of Biscay** golfe *m* de Gascogne; **to hold sb at ~** tenir qn à distance *or* en échec

bay leaf *n* laurier *m*

bazaar [bə'zɑːr] *n* (*shop, market*) bazar *m*; (*sale*) vente *f* de charité

BBC *n abbr* (= *British Broadcasting Corporation*) office de la radiodiffusion et télévision britannique

B.C. *adv abbr* (= *before Christ*) av. J.-C.

● KEYWORD

be [biː] (*pt* **was, were**, *pp* **been**) *aux vb* **1** (*with present participle: forming continuous tenses*): **what are you doing?** que faites-vous?; **they're coming tomorrow** ils viennent demain; **I've been waiting for you for 2 hours** je t'attends depuis 2 heures

2 (*with pp: forming passives*) être; **to be killed** être tué(e); **the box had been opened** la boîte avait été ouverte; **he was nowhere to be seen** on ne le voyait nulle part

3 (*in tag questions*): **it was fun, wasn't it?** c'était drôle, n'est-ce pas?; **he's good-**

looking, isn't he? il est beau, n'est-ce pas?; **she's back, is she?** elle est rentrée, n'est-ce pas or alors?

4 (+to +infinitive): **the house is to be sold** (necessity) la maison doit être vendue; (future) la maison va être vendue; **he's not to open it** il ne doit pas l'ouvrir

▷ vb + complement 1 (gen) être; **I'm English** je suis anglais(e); **I'm tired** je suis fatigué(e); **I'm hot/cold** j'ai chaud/froid; **he's a doctor** il est médecin; **be careful/good/quiet!** faites attention/soyez sages/taisez-vous!; **2 and 2 are 4** 2 et 2 font 4

2 (of health) aller; **how are you?** comment allez-vous?; **I'm better now** je vais mieux maintenant; **he's very ill** il est très malade 3 (of age) avoir; **how old are you?** quel âge avez-vous?; **I'm sixteen (years old)** j'ai seize ans

4 (cost) coûter; **how much was the meal?** combien a coûté le repas?; **that'll be £5, please** ça fera 5 livres, s'il vous plaît; **this shirt is £17** cette chemise coûte 17 livres ▷ vi 1 (exist, occur etc) être, exister; **the prettiest girl that ever was** la fille la plus jolie qui ait jamais existé; **is there a God?** y a-t-il un dieu?; **be that as it may** quoi qu'il en soit; **so be it** soit

2 (referring to place) être, se trouver; **I won't be here tomorrow** je ne serai pas là demain 3 (referring to movement) aller; **where have you been?** où êtes-vous allé(s)?

▷ impers vb 1 (referring to time) être; **it's 5 o'clock** il est 5 heures; **it's the 28th of April** c'est le 28 avril

2 (referring to distance): **it's 10 km to the village** le village est à 10 km

3 (referring to the weather) faire; **it's too hot/cold** il fait trop chaud/froid; **it's windy today** il y a du vent aujourd'hui

4 (emphatic): **it's me/the postman** c'est moi/le facteur; **it was Maria who paid the bill** c'est Maria qui a payé la note

beach [biːtʃ] n plage f ▷ vt échouer
beacon ['biːkən] n (lighthouse) fanal m; (marker) balise f
bead [biːd] n perle f; (of dew, sweat) goutte f; **beads** npl (necklace) collier m
beak [biːk] n bec m
beam [biːm] n (Archit) poutre f; (of light) rayon m ▷ vi rayonner
bean [biːn] n haricot m; (of coffee) grain m; **beansprouts** npl pousses fpl or germes mpl de soja
bear [bɛəʳ] n ours m ▷ vb (pt **bore**, pp **borne**) ▷ vt porter; (endure) supporter, rapporter ▷ vi: **to ~ right/left** obliquer à droite/gauche, se diriger vers la droite/gauche

beard [bɪəd] n barbe f
bearer ['bɛərəʳ] n porteur m; (of passport etc) titulaire m/f
bearing ['bɛərɪŋ] n maintien m, allure f; (connection) rapport m; (Tech): **(ball) bearings** npl roulement m (à billes)
beast [biːst] n bête f; (inf: person) brute f
beat [biːt] n battement m; (Mus) temps m, mesure f; (of policeman) ronde f ▷ vt, vi (pt ~, pp ~en) battre; **off the ~en track** hors des chemins or sentiers battus; **to ~ it** (inf) ficher le camp; **beat up** vt (inf: person) tabasser; **beating** n raclée f
beautiful ['bjuːtɪful] adj beau (belle); **beautifully** adv admirablement
beauty ['bjuːtɪ] n beauté f; **beauty parlour** (us **beauty parlor**) [-'pɑːləʳ] n institut m de beauté; **beauty salon** n institut m de beauté; **beauty spot** n (on skin) grain m de beauté; (BRIT Tourism) site naturel (d'une grande beauté)
beaver ['biːvəʳ] n castor m
became [bɪ'keɪm] pt of **become**
because [bɪ'kɔz] conj parce que; **~ of** prep à cause de
beckon ['bɛkən] vt (also: **~ to**) faire signe (de venir) à
become [bɪ'kʌm] vi devenir; **to ~ fat/thin** grossir/maigrir; **to ~ angry** se mettre en colère
bed [bɛd] n lit m; (of flowers) parterre m; (of coal, clay) couche f; (of sea, lake) fond m; **to go to ~** aller se coucher; **bed and breakfast** n (terms) chambre et petit déjeuner; (place) ≈ chambre f d'hôte; voir encadré; **bedclothes** npl couvertures fpl et draps mpl; **bedding** n literie f; **bed linen** n draps mpl de lit (et taies fpl d'oreillers), literie f; **bedroom** n chambre f (à coucher); **bedside** n: **at sb's bedside** au chevet de qn; **bedside lamp** n lampe f de chevet; **bedside table** n table f de chevet; **bedsit(ter)** n (BRIT) chambre meublée, studio m; **bedspread** n couvre-lit m, dessus-de-lit m; **bedtime** n: **it's bedtime** c'est l'heure de se coucher

● BED AND BREAKFAST

Un **bed and breakfast** est une petite pension dans une maison particulière ou une ferme où l'on peut louer une chambre avec petit déjeuner compris pour un prix modique par rapport à ce que l'on paierait dans un hôtel. Ces établissements sont communément appelés "B & B", et sont signalés par une pancarte dans le jardin ou au-dessus de la porte.

bee [biː] n abeille f

beech [biːtʃ] *n* hêtre *m*

beef [biːf] *n* bœuf *m*; **roast ~** rosbif *m*; **beefburger** *n* hamburger *m*; **Beefeater** *n* hallebardier *m* (de la tour de Londres)

been [biːn] *pp of* **be**

beer [bɪəʳ] *n* bière *f*; **beer garden** *n* (BRIT) jardin *m* d'un pub (*où l'on peut emmener ses consommations*)

beet [biːt] *n* (*vegetable*) betterave *f*; (US: *also*: **red ~**) betterave (potagère)

beetle [ˈbiːtl] *n* scarabée *m*, coléoptère *m*

beetroot [ˈbiːtruːt] *n* (BRIT) betterave *f*

before [bɪˈfɔːʳ] *prep* (*of time*) avant; (*of space*) devant ▷ *conj* avant que + *sub*; avant de ▷ *adv* avant; **~ going** avant de partir; **~ she goes** avant qu'elle (ne) parte; **the week ~** la semaine précédente *or* d'avant; **I've never seen it ~** c'est la première fois que je le vois; **beforehand** *adv* au préalable, à l'avance

beg [bɛg] *vi* mendier ▷ *vt* mendier; (*forgiveness, mercy etc*) demander; (*entreat*) supplier; **to ~ sb to do sth** supplier qn de faire qch; *see also* **pardon**

began [bɪˈgæn] *pt of* **begin**

beggar [ˈbɛgəʳ] *n* mendiant(e)

begin [bɪˈgɪn] (*pt* **began**, *pp* **begun**) *vt, vi* commencer; **to ~ doing** *or* **to do sth** commencer à faire qch; **beginner** *n* débutant(e); **beginning** *n* commencement *m*, début *m*

begun [bɪˈgʌn] *pp of* **begin**

behalf [bɪˈhɑːf] *n*: **on ~ of**, (US) **in ~ of** (*representing*) de la part de; (*for benefit of*) pour le compte de; **on my/his ~** de ma/sa part

behave [bɪˈheɪv] *vi* se conduire, se comporter; (*well: also*: **~ o.s.**) se conduire bien *or* comme il faut; **behaviour** (US **behavior**) *n* comportement *m*, conduite *f*

behind [bɪˈhaɪnd] *prep* derrière; (*time*) en retard sur; (*supporting*): **to be ~ sb** soutenir qn ▷ *adv* derrière; en retard ▷ *n* derrière *m*; **~ the scenes** dans les coulisses; **to be ~ (schedule) with sth** être en retard dans qch

beige [beɪʒ] *adj* beige

Beijing [ˈbeɪˈdʒɪŋ] *n* Pékin

being [ˈbiːɪŋ] *n* être *m*; **to come into ~** prendre naissance

belated [bɪˈleɪtɪd] *adj* tardif(-ive)

belch [bɛltʃ] *vi* avoir un renvoi, roter ▷ *vt* (*also*: **~ out**: *smoke etc*) vomir, cracher

Belgian [ˈbɛldʒən] *adj* belge, de Belgique ▷ *n* Belge *m/f*

Belgium [ˈbɛldʒəm] *n* Belgique *f*

belief [bɪˈliːf] *n* (*opinion*) conviction *f*; (*trust, faith*) foi *f*

believe [bɪˈliːv] *vt, vi* croire, estimer; **to ~ in** (*God*) croire en; (*ghosts, method*) croire à; **believer** *n* (*in idea, activity*) partisan(e); (*Rel*)

bell [bɛl] *n* cloche *f*; (*small*) clochette *f*, grelot *m*; (*on door*) sonnette *f*; (*electric*) sonnerie *f*

bellboy [ˈbɛlbɔɪ] (US **bellhop** [ˈbɛlhɔp]) *n* groom *m*, chasseur *m*

bellow [ˈbɛləu] *vi* (*bull*) meugler; (*person*) brailler

bell pepper *n* (*esp* US) poivron *m*

belly [ˈbɛlɪ] *n* ventre *m*; **belly button** (*inf*) *n* nombril *m*

belong [bɪˈlɔŋ] *vi*: **to ~ to** appartenir à; (*club etc*) faire partie de; **this book ~s here** ce livre va ici, la place de ce livre est ici; **belongings** *npl* affaires *fpl*, possessions *fpl*

beloved [bɪˈlʌvɪd] *adj* (bien-)aimé(e), chéri(e)

below [bɪˈləu] *prep* sous, au-dessous de ▷ *adv* en dessous; en contre-bas; **see ~** voir plus bas *or* plus loin *or* ci-dessous

belt [bɛlt] *n* ceinture *f*; (*Tech*) courroie *f* ▷ *vt* (*thrash*) donner une raclée à; **beltway** *n* (US *Aut*) route *f* de ceinture; (: *motorway*) périphérique *m*

bemused [bɪˈmjuːzd] *adj* médusé(e)

bench [bɛntʃ] *n* banc *m*; (*in workshop*) établi *m*; **the B~** (*Law: judges*) la magistrature, la Cour

bend [bɛnd] *vb* (*pt, pp* **bent**) ▷ *vt* courber; (*leg, arm*) plier ▷ *vi* se courber ▷ *n* (BRIT: *in road*) virage *m*, tournant *m*; (*in pipe, river*) coude *m*; **bend down** *vi* se baisser; **bend over** *vi* se pencher

beneath [bɪˈniːθ] *prep* sous, au-dessous de; (*unworthy of*) indigne de ▷ *adv* dessous, au-dessous, en bas

beneficial [bɛnɪˈfɪʃəl] *adj*: **~ (to)** salutaire (pour), bénéfique (à)

benefit [ˈbɛnɪfɪt] *n* avantage *m*, profit *m*; (*allowance of money*) allocation *f* ▷ *vt* faire du bien à, profiter à ▷ *vi*: **he'll ~ from it** cela lui fera du bien, il y gagnera *or* s'en trouvera bien

Benelux [ˈbɛnɪlʌks] *n* Bénélux *m*

benign [bɪˈnaɪn] *adj* (*person, smile*) bienveillant(e), affable; (*Med*) bénin(-igne)

bent [bɛnt] *pt, pp of* **bend** ▷ *n* inclination *f*, penchant *m* ▷ *adj*: **to be ~ on** être résolu(e) à

bereaved [bɪˈriːvd] *n*: **the ~** la famille du disparu

beret [ˈbɛreɪ] *n* béret *m*

Berlin [bəːˈlɪn] *n* Berlin

Bermuda [bəːˈmjuːdə] *n* Bermudes *fpl*

Bern [bəːn] *n* Berne *f*

berry [ˈbɛrɪ] *n* baie *f*

berth [bəːθ] *n* (*bed*) couchette *f*; (*for ship*) poste *m* d'amarrage, mouillage *m* ▷ *vi* (*in harbour*) venir à quai; (*at anchor*) mouiller

beside [bɪˈsaɪd] *prep* à côté de; (*compared with*) par rapport à; **that's ~ the point** ça n'a rien à voir; **to be ~ o.s. (with anger)** être hors de soi; **besides** *adv* en outre, de plus ▷ *prep* en plus de; *(except)* excepté

best [bɛst] *adj* meilleur(e) ▷ *adv* le mieux; **the ~ part of** *(quantity)* le plus clair de, la plus grande partie de; **at ~** au mieux; **to make the ~ of sth** s'accommoder de qch (du mieux que l'on peut); **to do one's ~** faire de son mieux; **to the ~ of my knowledge** pour autant que je sache; **to the ~ of my ability** du mieux que je pourrai; **best-before date** *n* date *f* de limite d'utilisation *or* de consommation; **best man** *(irreg)* *n* garçon *m* d'honneur; **bestseller** *n* best-seller *m*, succès *m* de librairie

bet [bɛt] *n* pari *m* ▷ *vt, vi* (*pt, pp* **~** *or* **~ted**) parier; **to ~ sb sth** parier qch à qn

betray [bɪ'treɪ] *vt* trahir

better ['bɛtər] *adj* meilleur(e) ▷ *adv* mieux ▷ *vt* améliorer ▷ *n*: **to get the ~ of** triompher de, l'emporter sur; **you had ~ do it** vous feriez mieux de le faire; **he thought ~ of it** il s'est ravisé; **to get ~** *(Med)* aller mieux; *(improve)* s'améliorer

betting ['bɛtɪŋ] *n* paris *mpl*; **betting shop** *n* (*BRIT*) bureau *m* de paris

between [bɪ'twiːn] *prep* entre ▷ *adv* au milieu, dans l'intervalle

beverage ['bɛvərɪdʒ] *n* boisson *f* (*gén sans alcool*)

beware [bɪ'wɛər] *vi*: **to ~ (of)** prendre garde (à); **"~ of the dog"** *(attention)* chien méchant"

bewildered [bɪ'wɪldəd] *adj* dérouté(e), ahuri(e)

beyond [bɪ'jɔnd] *prep* (*in space, time*) au-delà de; *(exceeding)* au-dessus de ▷ *adv* au-delà; **~ doubt** hors de doute; **~ repair** irréparable

bias ['baɪəs] *n* (*prejudice*) préjugé *m*, parti pris; *(preference)* prévention *f*; **bias(s)ed** *adj* partial(e), montrant un parti pris

bib [bɪb] *n* bavoir *m*

Bible ['baɪbl] *n* Bible *f*

bicarbonate of soda [baɪ'kɑːbənɪt-] *n* bicarbonate *m* de soude

biceps ['baɪsɛps] *n* biceps *m*

bicycle ['baɪsɪkl] *n* bicyclette *f*; **bicycle pump** *n* pompe *f* à vélo

bid [bɪd] *n* offre *f*; (*at auction*) enchère *f*; *(attempt)* tentative *f* ▷ *vb* (*pt* **~** *or* **bade**, *pp* **~** *or* **~den**) ▷ *vi* faire une enchère *or* offre ▷ *vt* faire une enchère *or* offre de; **to ~ sb good day** souhaiter le bonjour à qn; **bidder** *n*: **the highest bidder** le plus offrant

bidet ['biːdeɪ] *n* bidet *m*

big [bɪg] *adj* (*in height: person, building, tree*) grand(e); *(in bulk, amount: person, parcel, book)* gros(se); **bigheaded** *adj* prétentieux(-euse);

big toe *n* gros orteil

bike [baɪk] *n* vélo *m*; **bike lane** *n* piste *f* cyclable

bikini [bɪ'kiːnɪ] *n* bikini *m*

bilateral [baɪ'lætərl] *adj* bilatéral(e)

bilingual [baɪ'lɪŋgwəl] *adj* bilingue

bill [bɪl] *n* note *f*, facture *f*; (*in restaurant*) addition *f*, note *f*; *(Pol)* projet *m* de loi; *(us: banknote)* billet *m* (de banque); *(notice)* affiche *f*; *(of bird)* bec *m*; **put it on my ~** mettez-le sur mon compte; **"post no ~s"** "défense d'afficher"; **to fit** *or* **fill the ~** *(fig)* faire l'affaire; **billboard** (*us*) *n* panneau *m* d'affichage; **billfold** ['bɪlfəuld] *n* (*us*) portefeuille *m*

billiards ['bɪljədz] *n* (jeu *m* de) billard *m*

billion ['bɪljən] *n* (*BRIT*) billion *m* (*million de millions*); (*us*) milliard *m*

bin [bɪn] *n* boîte *f*; (*BRIT: also*: **dust~**, **litter~**) poubelle *f*; *(for coal)* coffre *m*

bind (*pt, pp* **bound**) [baɪnd, baund] *vt* attacher; *(book)* relier; *(oblige)* obliger, contraindre ▷ *n* (*inf: nuisance*) scie *f*

binge [bɪndʒ] *n* (*inf*): **to go on a ~** faire la bringue

bingo ['bɪŋgəu] *n* sorte de jeu de loto pratiqué dans des établissements publics

binoculars [bɪ'nɔkjuləz] *npl* jumelles *fpl*

bio... [baɪə'] *prefix*: **biochemistry** *n* biochimie *f*; **biodegradable** ['baɪəudɪ'greɪdəbl] *adj* biodégradable; **biography** [baɪ'ɔgrəfɪ] *n* biographie *f*; **biological** *adj* biologique; **biology** [baɪ'ɔlədʒɪ] *n* biologie *f*; **biometric** [baɪə'mɛtrɪk] *adj* biométrique

birch [bəːtʃ] *n* bouleau *m*

bird [bəːd] *n* oiseau *m*; (*BRIT inf: girl*) nana *f*; **bird flu** *n* grippe *f* aviaire; **bird of prey** *n* oiseau *m* de proie; **birdwatching** *n* ornithologie *f* (*d'amateur*)

Biro® ['baɪərəu] *n* stylo *m* à bille

birth [bəːθ] *n* naissance *f*; **to give ~ to** donner naissance à, mettre au monde; *(subj: animal)* mettre bas; **birth certificate** *n* acte *m* de naissance; **birth control** *n* (*policy*) limitation *f* des naissances; *(methods)* méthode(s) contraceptive(s); **birthday** n anniversaire m ▷ cpd (cake, card etc) d'anniversaire; **birthmark** n envie f, tache f de vin; **birthplace** n lieu m de naissance

biscuit ['bɪskɪt] n (BRIT) biscuit m; (US) petit pain au lait

bishop ['bɪʃəp] n évêque m; (Chess) fou m

bistro ['bi:strəu] n petit restaurant m, bistrot m

bit [bɪt] pt of **bite** ▷ n morceau m; (Comput) bit m, élément m binaire; (of tool) mèche f; (of horse) mors m; **a ~ of** un peu de; **a ~ mad/dangerous** un peu fou/risqué; **~ by ~** petit à petit

bitch [bɪtʃ] n (dog) chienne f; (inf!) salope f (!), garce f

bite [baɪt] vt, vi (pt **bit**, pp **bitten**) mordre; (insect) piquer ▷ n morsure f; (insect bite) piqûre f; (mouthful) bouchée f; **let's have a ~ (to eat)** mangeons un morceau; **to ~ one's nails** se ronger les ongles

bitten ['bɪtn] pp of **bite**

bitter ['bɪtəʳ] adj amer(-ère); (criticism) cinglant(e); (icy: weather, wind) glacial(e) ▷ n (BRIT: beer) bière f (à forte teneur en houblon)

bizarre [bɪ'zɑːʳ] adj bizarre

black [blæk] adj noir(e) ▷ n (colour) noir m; (person) **B~** noir(e) ▷ vt (BRIT Industry) boycotter; **to give sb a ~ eye** pocher l'œil à qn, faire un œil au beurre noir à qn; **to be in the ~** (in credit) avoir un compte créditeur; **~ and blue** (bruised) couvert(e) de bleus; **black out** vi (faint) s'évanouir; **blackberry** n mûre f; **blackbird** n merle m; **blackboard** n tableau noir; **black coffee** n café noir; **blackcurrant** n cassis m; **black ice** n verglas m; **blackmail** n chantage m ▷ vt faire chanter, soumettre au chantage; **black market** n marché noir; **blackout** n panne f d'électricité; (in wartime) black-out m; (TV) interruption f d'émission; (fainting) syncope f; **black pepper** n poivre noir; **black pudding** n boudin (noir); **Black Sea** n: **the Black Sea** la mer Noire

bladder ['blædəʳ] n vessie f

blade [bleɪd] n lame f; (of propeller) pale f; **a ~ of grass** un brin d'herbe

blame [bleɪm] n faute f, blâme m ▷ vt: **to ~ sb/sth for sth** attribuer à qn/qch la responsabilité de qch; reprocher qch à qn/qch; **I'm not to ~** ce n'est pas ma faute

bland [blænd] adj (taste, food) doux (douce), fade

blank [blæŋk] adj blanc (blanche); (look) sans expression, dénué(e) d'expression ▷ n espace m vide, blanc m; (cartridge) cartouche f à blanc; **his mind was a ~** il avait la tête vide

blanket ['blæŋkɪt] n couverture f; (of snow, cloud) couche f

blast [blɑːst] n explosion f; (shock wave) souffle

m; (of air, steam) bouffée f ▷ vt faire sauter or exploser

blatant ['bleɪtənt] adj flagrant(e), criant(e)

blaze [bleɪz] n (fire) incendie m; (fig) flamboiement m ▷ vi (fire) flamber; (fig) flamboyer, resplendir ▷ vt: **to ~ a trail** (fig) montrer la voie; **in a ~ of publicity** à grand renfort de publicité

blazer ['bleɪzəʳ] n blazer m

bleach [bli:tʃ] n (also: **household ~**) eau f de Javel ▷ vt (linen) blanchir; **bleachers** npl (US Sport) gradins mpl (en plein soleil)

bleak [bli:k] adj morne, désolé(e); (weather) triste, maussade; (smile) lugubre; (prospect, future) morose

bled [bled] pt, pp of **bleed**

bleed (pt, pp **bled**) [bli:d, bled] vt saigner; (brakes, radiator) purger ▷ vi saigner; **my nose is ~ing** je saigne du nez

blemish ['blɛmɪʃ] n défaut m; (on reputation) tache f

blend [blɛnd] n mélange m ▷ vt mélanger ▷ vi (colours etc: also: **~ in**) se mélanger, se fondre, s'allier; **blender** n (Culin) mixeur m

bless (pt, pp **~ed** or **blest**) [blɛs, blɛst] vt bénir; **~ you!** (after sneeze) à tes souhaits!; **blessing** n bénédiction f; (godsend) bienfait m

blew [blu:] pt of **blow**

blight [blaɪt] vt (hopes etc) anéantir, briser

blind [blaɪnd] adj aveugle ▷ n (for window) store m ▷ vt aveugler; **the blind** npl les aveugles mpl; **blind alley** n impasse f; **blindfold** n bandeau m ▷ adj, adv les yeux bandés ▷ vt bander les yeux à

blink [blɪŋk] vi cligner des yeux; (light) clignoter

bliss [blɪs] n félicité f, bonheur m sans mélange

blister ['blɪstəʳ] n (on skin) ampoule f, cloque f; (on paintwork) boursouflure f ▷ vi (paint) se boursoufler, se cloquer

blizzard ['blɪzəd] n blizzard m, tempête f de neige

bloated ['bləutɪd] adj (face) bouffi(e); (stomach, person) gonflé(e)

blob [blɔb] n (drop) goutte f; (stain, spot) tache f

block [blɔk] n bloc m; (in pipes) obstruction f; (toy) cube m; (of buildings) pâté m (de maisons) ▷ vt bloquer; (fig) faire obstacle à; **the sink is ~ed** l'évier est bouché; **~ of flats** (BRIT) immeuble (locatif); **mental ~** blocage m; **block up** vt boucher; **blockade** [blɔ'keɪd] n blocus m ▷ vt faire le blocus de; **blockage** n obstruction f; **blockbuster** n (film, book) grand succès; **block capitals** npl majuscules fpl d'imprimerie; **block letters** npl majuscules fpl

blog [blɔg] n blog m, blogue m

bloke [bləuk] n (BRIT inf) type m

blond(e) [blɔnd] adj, n blond(e)

blood [blʌd] n sang m; **blood donor** n

donneur(-euse) de sang; **blood group** n groupe sanguin; **blood poisoning** n empoisonnement m du sang; **blood pressure** n tension (artérielle); **bloodshed** n effusion f de sang, carnage m; **bloodshot** adj: **bloodshot eyes** yeux injectés de sang; **bloodstream** n sang m, système sanguin; **blood test** n analyse f de sang; **blood transfusion** n transfusion f de sang; **blood type** n groupe sanguin; **blood vessel** n vaisseau sanguin; **bloody** adj sanglant(e); (BRIT inf!): **this bloody ...** ce foutu ..., ce putain de ... (!) ▷ adv: **bloody strong/good** (BRIT: inf!) vachement or sacrément fort/bon

bloom [blu:m] n fleur f ▷ vi être en fleur

blossom ['blɔsəm] n fleur(s) f(pl) ▷ vi être en fleurs; (fig) s'épanouir

blot [blɔt] n tache f ▷ vt tacher; (ink) sécher

blouse [blauz] n (feminine garment) chemisier m, corsage m

blow [bləu] n coup m ▷ vb (pt **blew**, pp **~n**) ▷ vi souffler ▷ vt (instrument) jouer de; (fuse) faire sauter; **to ~ one's nose** se moucher; **blow away** vi s'envoler ▷ vt chasser, faire s'envoler; **blow out** vi (fire, flame) s'éteindre; (tyre) éclater; (fuse) sauter; **blow up** vi exploser, sauter ▷ vt faire sauter; (tyre) gonfler; (Phot) agrandir; **blow-dry** n (hairstyle) brushing m

blown [bləun] pp of **blow**

blue [blu:] adj bleu(e); (depressed) triste; **~ film/joke** film m/histoire f pornographique; **out of the ~** (fig) à l'improviste, sans qu'on s'y attende; **bluebell** n jacinthe f des bois; **blueberry** n myrtille f, airelle f; **blue cheese** n (fromage) bleu m; **blues** npl: **the blues** (Mus) le blues; **to have the blues** (inf: feeling) avoir le cafard; **bluetit** n mésange bleue

bluff [blʌf] vi bluffer ▷ n bluff m; **to call sb's ~** mettre qn au défi d'exécuter ses menaces

blunder ['blʌndə'] n gaffe f, bévue f ▷ vi faire une gaffe or une bévue

blunt [blʌnt] adj (knife) émoussé(e), peu tranchant(e); (pencil) mal taillé(e); (person) brusque, ne mâchant pas ses mots

blur [blə:'] n (shape): **to become a ~** devenir flou ▷ vt brouiller, rendre flou(e); **blurred** adj flou(e)

blush [blʌʃ] vi rougir ▷ n rougeur f; **blusher** n rouge m à joues

board [bɔ:d] n (wooden) planche f; (on wall) panneau m; (for chess etc) plateau m; (cardboard) carton m; (committee) conseil m, comité m; (in firm) conseil d'administration; (Naut, Aviat): **on ~** à bord ▷ vt (ship) monter à bord de; (train) monter dans; **full ~** (BRIT) pension complète; **half ~** (BRIT) demi-pension f; **~ and lodging** n chambre f avec pension; **to go by the ~** (hopes, principles) être abandonné(e); **board game** n jeu m de

société; **boarding card** n (Aviat, Naut) carte f d'embarquement; **boarding pass** n (BRIT) = **boarding card**; **boarding school** n internat m, pensionnat m; **board room** n salle f du conseil d'administration

boast [bəust] vi: **to ~ (about or of)** se vanter (de)

boat [bəut] n bateau m; (small) canot m; barque f

bob [bɔb] vi (boat, cork on water: also: **~ up and down**) danser, se balancer

bobby pin ['bɔbɪ-] n (us) pince f à cheveux

body ['bɔdɪ] n corps m; (of car) carrosserie f; (fig: society) organe m, organisme m; **body-building** n body-building m, culturisme m; **bodyguard** n garde m du corps; **bodywork** n carrosserie f

bog [bɔg] n tourbière f ▷ vt: **to get ~ged down (in)** (fig) s'enliser (dans)

bogus ['bəugəs] adj bidon inv; fantôme

boil [bɔɪl] vt (faire) bouillir ▷ vi bouillir ▷ n (Med) furoncle m; **to come to the** or (us) **a ~** bouillir; **boil down** vi (fig): **to ~ down to** se réduire or ramener à; **boil over** vi déborder; **boiled egg** n œuf m à la coque; **boiled potatoes** n pommes fpl à l'anglaise or à l'eau; **boiler** n chaudière f; **boiling** ['bɔɪlɪŋ] adj: **I'm boiling (hot)** (inf) je crève de chaud; **boiling point** n point m d'ébullition

bold [bəuld] adj hardi(e), audacieux(-euse); (pej) effronté(e); (outline, colour) franc (franche), tranché(e), marqué(e)

bollard ['bɔləd] n (BRIT Aut) borne lumineuse or de signalisation

bolt [bəult] n verrou m; (with nut) boulon m ▷ adv: **~ upright** droit(e) comme un piquet ▷ vt (door) verrouiller; (food) engloutir ▷ vi se sauver, filer (comme une flèche); (horse) s'emballer

bomb [bɔm] n bombe f ▷ vt bombarder; **bombard** [bɔm'bɑːd] vt bombarder; **bomber** n (Aviat) bombardier m; (terrorist) poseur m de bombes; **bomb scare** n alerte f à la bombe

bond [bɔnd] n lien m; (binding promise) engagement m, obligation f; (Finance) obligation; **bonds** npl (chains) chaînes fpl; **in ~** (of goods) en entrepôt

bone [bəun] n os m; (of fish) arête f ▷ vt désosser; ôter les arêtes de

bonfire ['bɔnfaɪə'] n feu m (de joie); (for rubbish) feu

bonnet ['bɔnɪt] n bonnet m; (BRIT: of car) capot m

bonus ['bəunəs] n (money) prime f; (advantage) avantage m

boo [bu:] excl hou!, peuh! ▷ vt huer

book [buk] n livre m; (of stamps, tickets etc) carnet m; (Comm): **books** npl comptes mpl, comptabilité f ▷ vt (ticket) prendre; (seat, room) réserver; (*football player*) prendre le nom de, donner un carton à; **I ~ed a table in the name of ...** j'ai réservé une table au nom de ...; **book in** *vi* (BRIT: *at hotel*) prendre sa chambre; **book up** *vt* réserver; **the hotel is ~ed up** l'hôtel est complet; **bookcase** *n* bibliothèque *f* (*meuble*); **booking** *n* (BRIT) réservation *f*; **I confirmed my booking by fax/e-mail** j'ai confirmé ma réservation par fax/e-mail; **booking office** *n* (BRIT) bureau *m* de location; **book-keeping** *n* comptabilité *f*; **booklet** *n* brochure *f*; **bookmaker** *n* bookmaker *m*; **bookmark** *n* (*for book*) marque-page *m*; (*Comput*) signet *m*; **bookseller** *n* libraire *m/f*; **bookshelf** *n* (*single*) étagère *f* (à livres); (*bookcase*) bibliothèque *f*; **bookshop, bookstore** *n* librairie *f*

boom [buːm] *n* (*noise*) grondement *m*; (*in prices, population*) forte augmentation; (*busy period*) boom *m*, vague *f* de prospérité ▷ *vi* gronder; prospérer

boost [buːst] *n* stimulant *m*, remontant *m* ▷ *vt* stimuler

boot [buːt] *n* botte *f*; (*for hiking*) chaussure *f* (de marche); (*ankle boot*) bottine *f*; (BRIT: *of car*) coffre *m* ▷ *vt* (*Comput*) lancer, mettre en route; **to ~** (*in addition*) par-dessus le marché, en plus

booth [buːð] *n* (*at fair*) baraque (foraine); (*of telephone etc*) cabine *f*; (*also:* **voting ~**) isoloir *m*

booze [buːz] (*inf*) *n* boissons *fpl* alcooliques, alcool *m*

border ['bɔːdəʳ] *n* bordure *f*; bord *m*; (*of a country*) frontière *f*; **borderline** *n* (*fig*) ligne *f* de démarcation

bore [bɔːʳ] *pt of* **bear** ▷ *vt* (*person*) ennuyer, raser; (*hole*) percer; (*well, tunnel*) creuser ▷ *n* (*person*) raseur(-euse); (*boring thing*) barbe *f*; (*of gun*) calibre *m*; **bored** *adj*: **to be bored** s'ennuyer; **boredom** *n* ennui *m*

boring ['bɔːrɪŋ] *adj* ennuyeux(-euse)

born [bɔːn] *adj*: **to be ~** naître; **I was ~ in 1960** je suis né en 1960

borne [bɔːn] *pp of* **bear**

borough ['bʌrə] *n* municipalité *f*

borrow ['bɔrəu] *vt*: **to ~ sth (from sb)** emprunter qch (à qn)

Bosnia(-Herzegovina) ['bɔːsnɪə(hɛrzə'gəuvi:nə)] *n* Bosnie-Herzégovine *f*; **Bosnian** ['bɔznɪən] *adj* bosniaque, bosnien(ne) ▷ *n* Bosniaque *m/f*, Bosnien(ne)

bosom ['buzəm] *n* poitrine *f*; (*fig*) sein *m*

boss [bɔs] *n* patron(ne) ▷ *vt* (*also:* **~ about**, **~ around**) mener à la baguette; **bossy** *adj* autoritaire

both [bəuθ] *adj* les deux, l'un(e) et l'autre ▷ *pron*: **~ (of them)** les deux, tous (toutes) (les) deux, l'un(e) et l'autre; **~ of us went, we ~ went** nous y sommes allés tous les deux ▷ *adv*: **~ A and B** A et B

bother ['bɔðəʳ] *vt* (*worry*) tracasser; (*needle, bait*) importuner, ennuyer; (*disturb*) déranger ▷ *vi* (*also:* **~ o.s.**) se tracasser, se faire du souci ▷ *n* (*trouble*) ennuis *mpl*; **to ~ doing** prendre la peine de faire; **don't ~** ce n'est pas la peine; **it's no ~** aucun problème

bottle ['bɔtl] *n* bouteille *f*; (*baby's*) biberon *m*; (*of perfume, medicine*) flacon *m* ▷ *vt* mettre en bouteille(s); **bottle bank** *n* conteneur *m* (de bouteilles); **bottle-opener** *n* ouvre-bouteille *m*

bottom ['bɔtəm] *n* (*of container, sea etc*) fond *m*; (*buttocks*) derrière *m*; (*of page, list*) bas *m*; (*of mountain, tree, hill*) pied *m* ▷ *adj* (*shelf, step*) du bas

bought [bɔːt] *pt, pp of* **buy**

boulder ['bəuldəʳ] *n* gros rocher (*gén lisse, arrondi*)

bounce [bauns] *vi* (*ball*) rebondir; (*cheque*) être refusé (*étant sans provision*) ▷ *vt* faire rebondir ▷ *n* (*rebound*) rebond *m*; **bouncer** *n* (*inf: at dance, club*) videur *m*

bound [baund] *pt, pp of* **bind** ▷ *n* (*gen pl*) limite *f*; (*leap*) bond *m* ▷ *vi* (*leap*) bondir ▷ *vt* (*limit*) borner ▷ *adj*: **to be ~ to do sth** (*obliged*) être obligé(e) *or* avoir obligation de faire qch; **he's ~ to fail** (*likely*) il est sûr d'échouer, son échec est inévitable *or* assuré; **~ by** (*law, regulation*) engagé(e) par; **~ for** à destination de; **out of ~s** dont l'accès est interdit

boundary ['baundrɪ] *n* frontière *f*

bouquet ['bukeɪ] *n* bouquet *m*

bourbon ['buəbən] *n* (US: *also:* **~ whiskey**) bourbon *m*

bout [baut] *n* période *f*; (*of malaria etc*) accès *m*, crise *f*, attaque *f*; (*Boxing etc*) combat *m*, match *m*

boutique [buː'tiːk] *n* boutique *f*

bow¹ [bəu] *n* nœud *m*; (*weapon*) arc *m*; (*Mus*) archet *m*

bow² [bau] *n* (*with body*) révérence *f*, inclination *f* (du buste *or* corps); (*Naut: also:* **~s**) proue *f* ▷ *vi* faire une révérence, s'incliner

bowels [bauəlz] *npl* intestins *mpl*; (*fig*) entrailles *fpl*

bowl [bəul] *n* (*for eating*) bol *m*; (*for washing*) cuvette *f*; (*ball*) boule *f* ▷ *vi* (*Cricket*) lancer (la balle); **bowler** *n* (*Cricket*) lanceur *m* (de la balle); (BRIT: *also:* **bowler hat**) (chapeau *m*) melon *m*; **bowling** *n* (*game*) jeu *m* de boules, jeu de quilles; **bowling alley** *n* bowling *m*; **bowling green** *n* terrain *m* de boules (*gazonné et carré*); **bowls** *n* (jeu *m* de) boules *fpl*

bow tie [bəu-] *n* nœud *m* papillon

box [bɔks] *n* boîte *f*; (*also:* **cardboard ~**) carton *m*; (*Theat*) loge *f* ▷ *vt* mettre en boîte ▷ *vi* boxer, faire de la boxe; **boxer** ['bɔksəʳ] *n* (*person*) boxeur *m*; **boxer shorts** *npl* caleçon *m*;

boxing ['bɔksɪŋ] n (sport) boxe f; **Boxing Day** n (BRIT) le lendemain de Noël; voir encadré; **boxing gloves** npl gants mpl de boxe; **boxing ring** n ring m; **box junction** n (BRIT Aut) zone f (de carrefour) d'accès réglementé; **box office** n bureau m de location

○ **BOXING DAY**
○
○
○ **Boxing Day** est le lendemain de Noël, férié
○ en Grande-Bretagne. Ce nom vient d'une
○ coutume du XIXe siècle qui consistait à
○ donner des cadeaux de Noël (dans des
○ boîtes) à ses employés etc le 26 décembre.

boy [bɔɪ] n garçon m; **boy band** n boys band m
boycott ['bɔɪkɔt] n boycottage m ▷ vt boycotter
boyfriend ['bɔɪfrɛnd] n (petit) ami
bra [brɑ:] n soutien-gorge m
brace [breɪs] n (support) attache f, agrafe f; (BRIT: also: ~**s**: on teeth) appareil m (dentaire); (tool) vilebrequin m ▷ vt (support) consolider, soutenir; **braces** npl (BRIT: for trousers) bretelles fpl; **to ~ o.s.** (fig) se préparer mentalement
bracelet ['breɪslɪt] n bracelet m
bracket ['brækɪt] n (Tech) tasseau m, support m; (group) classe f, tranche f; (also: **brace ~**) accolade f; (also: **round ~**) parenthèse f; (also: **square ~**) crochet m ▷ vt mettre entre parenthèses; **in ~s** entre parenthèses or crochets
brag [bræg] vi se vanter
braid [breɪd] n (trimming) galon m; (of hair) tresse f, natte f
brain [breɪn] n cerveau m; **brains** npl (intellect, food) cervelle f
braise [breɪz] vt braiser
brake [breɪk] n frein m ▷ vt, vi freiner; **brake light** n feu m de stop
bran [bræn] n son m
branch [brɑ:ntʃ] n branche f; (Comm) succursale f; (: of bank) agence f; **branch off** vi (road) bifurquer; **branch out** vi diversifier ses activités
brand [brænd] n marque (commerciale) ▷ vt (cattle) marquer (au fer rouge); **brand name** n nom m de marque; **brand-new** adj tout(e) neuf (neuve), flambant neuf (neuve)
brandy ['brændɪ] n cognac m
brash [bræʃ] adj effronté(e)
brass [brɑ:s] n cuivre m (jaune), laiton m; **the ~** (Mus) les cuivres; **brass band** n fanfare f
brat [bræt] n (pej) mioche m/f, môme m/f
brave [breɪv] adj courageux(-euse), brave ▷ vt braver, affronter; **bravery** n bravoure f, courage m
brawl [brɔ:l] n rixe f, bagarre f

Brazil [brə'zɪl] n Brésil m; **Brazilian** adj brésilien(ne) ▷ n Brésilien(ne)
breach [bri:tʃ] vt ouvrir une brèche dans ▷ n (gap) brèche f; (breaking): **~ of contract** rupture f de contrat; **~ of the peace** attentat m à l'ordre public
bread [brɛd] n pain m; **breadbin** n (BRIT) boîte f or huche f à pain; **breadbox** n (US) boîte f or huche f à pain; **breadcrumbs** npl miettes fpl de pain; (Culin) chapelure f, panure f
breadth [brɛtθ] n largeur f
break [breɪk] (pt broke, pp broken) vt casser, briser; (promise) rompre; (law) violer ▷ vi se casser, se briser; (weather) tourner; (storm) éclater; (day) se lever ▷ n (gap) brèche f; (fracture) cassure f; (rest) interruption f, arrêt m; (: short) pause f; (: at school) récréation f; (chance) chance f, occasion f favorable; **to ~ one's leg** etc se casser la jambe etc; **to ~ a record** battre un record; **to ~ the news to sb** annoncer la nouvelle à qn; **break down** vt (door etc) enfoncer; (figures, data) décomposer, analyser ▷ vi s'effondrer; (Med) faire une dépression (nerveuse); (Aut) tomber en panne; **my car has broken down** ma voiture est en panne; **break in** vt (horse etc) dresser ▷ vi (burglar) entrer par effraction; (interrupt) interrompre; **break into** vt fus (house) s'introduire or pénétrer par effraction dans; **break off** vi (speaker) s'interrompre; (branch) se rompre ▷ vt (talks, engagement) rompre; **break out** vi éclater, se déclarer; (prisoner) s'évader; **to ~ out in spots** se couvrir de boutons; **break up** vi (partnership) cesser, prendre fin; (marriage) se briser; (crowd, meeting) se séparer; (ship) se disloquer; (Scol: pupils) être en vacances; (line) couper; **the line's** or **you're ~ing up** ça coupe ▷ vt fracasser, casser; (fight etc) interrompre, faire cesser; (marriage) désunir; **breakdown** n (Aut) panne f; (in communications, marriage) rupture f; (Med: also: **nervous breakdown**) dépression (nerveuse); (of figures) ventilation f, répartition f; **breakdown truck** (US) **breakdown van** n dépanneuse f
breakfast ['brɛkfəst] n petit déjeuner m; **what time is ~?** le petit déjeuner est à quelle heure?
break: **break-in** n cambriolage m; **breakthrough** n percée f
breast [brɛst] n (of woman) sein m; (chest) poitrine f; (of chicken, turkey) blanc m; **breast-feed** vt, vi (irreg: like feed) allaiter; **breast-stroke** n brasse f
breath [brɛθ] n haleine f, souffle m; **to take a deep ~** respirer à fond; **out of ~** à bout de souffle, essoufflé(e)
Breathalyser® ['brɛθəlaɪzəʳ] (BRIT) n alcootest m

breathe [briːð] *vt, vi* respirer; **breathe in** *vi* inspirer ▷ *vt* aspirer; **breathe out** *vt, vi* expirer; **breathing** *n* respiration *f*

breath: **breathless** *adj* essoufflé(e), haletant(e); **breathtaking** *adj* stupéfiant(e), à vous couper le souffle; **breath test** *n* alcootest *m*

bred [brɛd] *pt, pp of* **breed**

breed [briːd] *(pt, pp* **bred**) *vt* élever, faire l'élevage de ▷ *vi* se reproduire ▷ *n* race *f*, variété *f*

breeze [briːz] *n* brise *f*

breezy ['briːzɪ] *adj* (*day, weather*) venteux(-euse); (*manner*) désinvolte; (*person*) jovial(e)

brew [bruː] *vt* (*tea*) faire infuser; (*beer*) brasser ▷ *vi* (*fig*) se préparer, couver; **brewery** *n* brasserie *f* (*fabrique*)

bribe [braɪb] *n* pot-de-vin *m* ▷ *vt* acheter, soudoyer; **bribery** *n* corruption *f*

bric-a-brac ['brɪkəbræk] *n* bric-à-brac *m*

brick [brɪk] *n* brique *f*; **bricklayer** *n* maçon *m*

bride [braɪd] *n* mariée *f*, épouse *f*; **bridegroom** *n* marié *m*, époux *m*; **bridesmaid** *n* demoiselle *f* d'honneur

bridge [brɪdʒ] *n* pont *m*; (*Naut*) passerelle *f* (*de commandement*); (*of nose*) arête *f*; (*Cards, Dentistry*) bridge *m* ▷ *vt* (*gap*) combler

bridle ['braɪdl] *n* bride *f*

brief [briːf] *adj* bref (brève) ▷ *n* (*Law*) dossier *m*, cause *f*; (*gen*) tâche *f* ▷ *vt* mettre au courant; **briefs** *npl* slip *m*; **briefcase** *n* serviette *f*, porte-documents *m inv*; **briefing** *n* instructions *fpl*; (*Press*) briefing *m*; **briefly** *adv* brièvement

brigadier [brɪgəˈdɪər] *n* brigadier général

bright [braɪt] *adj* brillant(e); (*room, weather*) clair(e); (*person: clever*) intelligent(e), doué(e); (: *cheerful*) gai(e); (*idea*) génial(e); (*colour*) vif (vive)

brilliant ['brɪljənt] *adj* brillant(e); (*light, sunshine*) éclatant(e); (*inf: great*) super

brim [brɪm] *n* bord *m*

brine [braɪn] *n* (*Culin*) saumure *f*

bring (*pt, pp* **brought**) [brɪŋ, brɔːt] *vt* (*thing*) apporter; (*person*) amener; **bring about** *vt* provoquer, entraîner; **bring back** *vt* rapporter; (*person*) ramener; **bring down** *vt* (*lower*) abaisser; (*shoot down*) abattre; (*government*) faire s'effondrer; **bring in** *vt* (*person*) faire entrer; (*object*) rentrer; (*Pol: legislation*) introduire; (*produce: income*) rapporter; **bring on** *vt* (*illness, attack*) provoquer; (*player, substitute*) amener; **bring out** *vt* sortir; (*meaning*) faire ressortir, mettre en relief; **bring up** *vt* élever; (*carry up*) monter; (*question*) soulever; (*food: vomit*) vomir, rendre

brink [brɪŋk] *n* bord *m*

brisk [brɪsk] *adj* vif (vive); (*abrupt*) brusque; (*trade etc*) actif(-ive)

bristle ['brɪsl] *n* poil *m* ▷ *vi* se hérisser

Brit [brɪt] *n abbr* (*inf: = British person*) Britannique *m/f*

Britain ['brɪtən] *n* (*also:* **Great ~**) la Grande-Bretagne

British ['brɪtɪʃ] *adj* britannique ▷ *npl*: **the ~** les Britanniques *mpl*; **British Isles** *npl*: **the British Isles** les îles *fpl* Britanniques

Briton ['brɪtən] *n* Britannique *m/f*

Brittany ['brɪtənɪ] *n* Bretagne *f*

brittle ['brɪtl] *adj* cassant(e), fragile

B road *n* (*BRIT*) ≈ route départementale

broad [brɔːd] *adj* large; (*distinction*) général(e); (*accent*) prononcé(e); **in ~ daylight** en plein jour; **broadband** *n* transmission *f* à haut débit; **broad bean** *n* fève *f*; **broadcast** *n* émission *f* ▷ *vb* (*pt, pp* **broadcast**) ▷ *vt* (*Radio*) radiodiffuser; (*TV*) téléviser ▷ *vi* émettre; **broaden** *vt* élargir; **to broaden one's mind** élargir ses horizons ▷ *vi* s'élargir; **broadly** *adv* en gros, généralement; **broad-minded** *adj* large d'esprit

broccoli ['brɔkəlɪ] *n* brocoli *m*

brochure ['brəuʃjuər] *n* prospectus *m*, dépliant *m*

broil [brɔɪl] (*us*) *vt* rôtir

broiler ['brɔɪlər] *n* (*fowl*) poulet *m* (*à rôtir*); (*us: grill*) gril *m*

broke [brəuk] *pt of* **break** ▷ *adj* (*inf*) fauché(e)

broken ['brəukn] *pp of* **break** ▷ *adj* (*stick, leg etc*) cassé(e); (*machine: also:* **~ down**) fichu(e); **in ~ French/English** dans un français/anglais approximatif *or* hésitant

broker ['brəukər] *n* courtier *m*

bronchitis [brɔŋˈkaɪtɪs] *n* bronchite *f*

bronze [brɔnz] *n* bronze *m*

brooch [brəutʃ] *n* broche *f*

brood [bruːd] *n* couvée *f* ▷ *vi* (*person*) méditer (sombrement), ruminer

broom [brum] *n* balai *m*; (*Bot*) genêt *m*

Bros. *abbr* (*Comm: = brothers*) Frères

broth [brɔθ] *n* bouillon *m* de viande et de légumes

brothel ['brɔθl] *n* maison close, bordel *m*

brother ['brʌðər] *n* frère *m*; **brother-in-law** *n* beau-frère *m*

brought [brɔːt] *pt, pp of* **bring**

brow [brau] *n* front *m*; (*eyebrow*) sourcil *m*; (*of hill*) sommet *m*

brown [braun] *adj* brun(e), marron *inv*; (*hair*) châtain *inv*; (*tanned*) bronzé(e) ▷ *n* (*colour*) brun *m*, marron *m* ▷ *vt* brunir; (*Culin*) faire dorer, faire roussir; **brown bread** *n* pain *m* bis

Brownie ['braunɪ] *n* jeannette *f* éclaireuse (cadette)

brown rice *n* riz *m* complet

brown sugar n cassonade f

browse [brauz] vi (in shop) regarder (sans acheter); **to ~ through a book** feuilleter un livre; **browser** n (Comput) navigateur m

bruise [bru:z] n bleu m, ecchymose f, contusion f ▷ vt contusionner, meurtrir

brunette [bru:'nɛt] n (femme) brune

brush [brʌʃ] n brosse f; (for painting) pinceau m; (for shaving) blaireau m; (quarrel) accrochage m, prise f de bec ▷ vt brosser; (also: **~ past, ~ against**) effleurer, frôler

Brussels ['brʌslz] n Bruxelles

Brussels sprout [-spraut] n chou m de Bruxelles

brutal ['bru:tl] adj brutal(e)

B.Sc. n abbr = **Bachelor of Science**

BSE n abbr (= bovine spongiform encephalopathy) ESB f, BSE f

bubble ['bʌbl] n bulle f ▷ vi bouillonner, faire des bulles; (sparkle, fig) pétiller; **bubble bath** n bain moussant; **bubble gum** n chewing-gum m; **bubblejet printer** ['bʌbldʒɛt-] n imprimante f à bulle d'encre

buck [bʌk] n mâle m (d'un lapin, lièvre, daim etc); (us inf) dollar m ▷ vi ruer, lancer une ruade; **to pass the ~ (to sb)** se décharger de la responsabilité (sur qn)

bucket ['bʌkɪt] n seau m

buckle ['bʌkl] n boucle f ▷ vt (belt etc) boucler, attacher ▷ vi (warp) tordre, gauchir; (: wheel) se voiler

bud [bʌd] n bourgeon m; (of flower) bouton m ▷ vi bourgeonner; (flower) éclore

Buddhism ['budɪzəm] n bouddhisme m

Buddhist ['budɪst] adj bouddhiste ▷ n Bouddhiste m/f

buddy ['bʌdɪ] n (us) copain m

budge [bʌdʒ] vt faire bouger ▷ vi bouger

budgerigar ['bʌdʒərɪgɑ:'] n perruche f

budget ['bʌdʒɪt] n budget m ▷ vi: **to ~ for sth** inscrire qch au budget

budgie ['bʌdʒɪ] n = **budgerigar**

buff [bʌf] adj (couleur f) chamois m ▷ n (inf: enthusiast) mordu(e)

buffalo (pl ~ or **~es**) ['bʌfələu] n (brit) buffle m; (us) bison m

buffer ['bʌfə'] n tampon m; (Comput) mémoire f tampon

buffet n ['bufeɪ] (food brit: bar) buffet m ▷ vt ['bʌfɪt] secouer, ébranler; **buffet car** n (brit Rail) voiture-bar f

bug [bʌg] n (bedbug etc) punaise f; (esp us: any insect) insecte m, bestiole f; (fig: germ) virus m, microbe m; (spy device) dispositif m d'écoute (électronique), micro clandestin; (Comput: of program) erreur f ▷ vt (room) poser des micros dans; (inf: annoy) embêter

buggy ['bʌgɪ] n poussette f

build [bɪld] n (of person) carrure f, charpente

f ▷ vt (pt, pp **built**) construire, bâtir; **build up** vt accumuler, amasser; (business) développer; (reputation) bâtir; **builder** n entrepreneur m; **building** n (trade) construction f; (structure) bâtiment m, construction; (: residential, offices) immeuble m; **building site** n chantier m (de construction); **building society** n (brit) société f de crédit immobilier

built [bɪlt] pt, pp of **build**; **built-in** adj (cupboard) encastré(e); (device) incorporé(e); intégré(e); **built-up** adj: **built-up area** zone urbanisée

bulb [bʌlb] n (Bot) bulbe m, oignon m; (Elec) ampoule f

Bulgaria [bʌl'gɛərɪə] n Bulgarie f; **Bulgarian** adj bulgare ▷ n Bulgare m/f

bulge [bʌldʒ] n renflement m, gonflement m ▷ vi faire saillie; présenter un renflement; (pocket, file): **to be bulging with** être plein(e) à craquer de

bulimia [bə'lɪmɪə] n boulimie f

bulimic [bju:'lɪmɪk] adj, n boulimique (m/f)

bulk [bʌlk] n masse f, volume m; **in ~** (Comm) en gros, en vrac; **the ~ of** la plus grande or grosse partie de; **bulky** adj volumineux(-euse), encombrant(e)

bull [bul] n taureau m; (male elephant, whale) mâle m

bulldozer ['buldəuzə'] n bulldozer m

bullet ['bulɪt] n balle f (de fusil etc)

bulletin ['bulɪtɪn] n bulletin m, communiqué m; (also: **news ~**) (bulletin d')informations fpl; **bulletin board** n (Comput) messagerie f (électronique)

bullfight ['bulfaɪt] n corrida f, course f de taureaux; **bullfighter** n torero m; **bullfighting** n tauromachie f

bully ['bulɪ] n brute f, tyran m ▷ vt tyranniser, rudoyer

bum [bʌm] n (inf: brit: backside) derrière m; (: esp us: tramp) vagabond(e), traîne-savates m/f inv; (: idler) glandeur m

bumblebee ['bʌmblbi:] n bourdon m

bump [bʌmp] n (blow) coup m, choc m; (jolt) cahot m; (on road etc, on head) bosse f ▷ vt heurter, cogner; (car) emboutir; **bump into** vt fus rentrer dans, tamponner; (inf: meet) tomber sur; **bumper** n pare-chocs m inv ▷ adj: **bumper crop/harvest** récolte/moisson exceptionnelle; **bumpy** adj (road) cahoteux(-euse); **it was a bumpy flight/ride** on a été secoués dans l'avion/la voiture

bun [bʌn] n (cake) petit gâteau; (bread) petit pain au lait; (of hair) chignon m

bunch [bʌntʃ] n (of flowers) bouquet m; (of keys) trousseau m; (of bananas) régime m; (of people) groupe m; **bunches** npl (in hair) couettes fpl; **~ of grapes** grappe f de raisin

bundle ['bʌndl] n paquet m ▷ vt (also: **~ up**)

faire un paquet de; (*put*): **to ~ sth/sb into** fourrer *or* enfourner qch/qn dans

bungalow ['bʌŋgələu] *n* bungalow *m*

bungee jumping ['bʌndʒi:'dʒʌmpɪŋ] *n* saut *m* à l'élastique

bunion ['bʌnjən] *n* oignon *m* (*au pied*)

bunk [bʌŋk] *n* couchette *f*; **bunk beds** *npl* lits superposés

bunker ['bʌŋkər] *n* (*coal store*) soute *f* à charbon; (*Mil, Golf*) bunker *m*

bunny ['bʌnɪ] *n* (*also*: **~ rabbit**) lapin *m*

buoy [bɔɪ] *n* bouée *f*; **buoyant** *adj* (*ship*) flottable; (*carefree*) gai(e), plein(e) d'entrain; (*Comm: market, economy*) actif(-ive)

burden ['bə:dn] *n* fardeau *m*, charge *f* ▷ *vt* charger; (*oppress*) accabler, surcharger

bureau (*pl* **~x**) ['bjuərəu, -z] *n* (*BRIT: writing desk*) bureau *m*, secrétaire *m*; (*US: chest of drawers*) commode *f*; (*office*) bureau, office *m*

bureaucracy [bjuə'rɔkrəsɪ] *n* bureaucratie *f*

bureaucrat ['bjuərəkræt] *n* bureaucrate *m/f*, rond-de-cuir *m*

bureau de change [-də'ʃɑ̃ʒ] (*pl* **bureaux de change**) *n* bureau *m* de change

bureaux ['bjuərəuz] *npl of* **bureau**

burger ['bə:gər] *n* hamburger *m*

burglar ['bə:glər] *n* cambrioleur *m*; **burglar alarm** *n* sonnerie *f* d'alarme; **burglary** *n* cambriolage *m*

Burgundy ['bə:gəndɪ] *n* Bourgogne *f*

burial ['bɛrɪəl] *n* enterrement *m*

burn [bə:n] *vt, vi* (*pt, pp* **~ed** *or* **~t**) brûler ▷ *n* brûlure *f*; **burn down** *vt* incendier, détruire par le feu; **burn out** *vt* (*writer etc*): **to ~ o.s. out** s'user (à force de travailler); **burning** *adj* (*building, forest*) en flammes; (*issue, question*) brûlant(e); (*ambition*) dévorant(e)

Burns' Night [bə:nz-] *n* fête écossaise à la mémoire du poète Robert Burns

● **Burns Night** est une fête qui a lieu le 25
● janvier, à la mémoire du poète écossais
● Robert Burns (1759 - 1796), à l'occasion de
● laquelle les Écossais partout dans le monde
● organisent un souper, en général arrosé
● de whisky. Le plat principal est toujours le
● haggis, servi avec de la purée de pommes
● de terre et de la purée de rutabagas. On
● apporte le haggis au son des cornemuses
● et au cours du repas on lit des poèmes de
● Burns et on chante ses chansons.

burnt [bə:nt] *pt, pp of* **burn**

burp [bə:p] (*inf*) *n* rot *m* ▷ *vi* roter

burrow ['bʌrəu] *n* terrier *m* ▷ *vi* (*rabbit*) creuser un terrier; (*rummage*) fouiller

burst [bə:st] (*pt, pp* **~**) *vt* faire éclater; (*river: banks etc*) rompre ▷ *vi* éclater; (*tyre*) crever ▷ *n* explosion *f*; (*also*: **~ pipe**) fuite *f* (*due à une rupture*); **a ~ of enthusiasm/energy** un accès d'enthousiasme/d'énergie; **to ~ into flames** s'enflammer soudainement; **to ~ out laughing** éclater de rire; **to ~ into tears** fondre en larmes; **to ~ open** s'ouvrir violemment *or* soudainement; **to be ~ing with** (*container*) être plein(e) (à craquer) de, regorger de; (*fig*) être débordant(e) de; **burst into** *vt fus* (*room etc*) faire irruption dans

bury ['bɛrɪ] *vt* enterrer

bus (*pl* **~es**) [bʌs, 'bʌsɪz] *n* autobus *m*; **bus conductor** *n* receveur(-euse) *m/f* de bus

bush [buʃ] *n* buisson *m*; (*scrub land*) brousse *f*; **to beat about the ~** tourner autour du pot

business ['bɪznɪs] *n* (*matter, firm*) affaire *f*; (*trading*) affaires *fpl*; (*job, duty*) travail *m*; **to be away on ~** être en déplacement d'affaires; **it's none of my ~** cela ne me regarde pas, ce ne sont pas mes affaires; **he means ~** il ne plaisante pas, il est sérieux; **business class** *n* (*on plane*) classe *f* affaires; **businesslike** *adj* sérieux(-euse), efficace; **businessman** (*irreg*) *n* homme *m* d'affaires; **business trip** *n* voyage *m* d'affaires; **businesswoman** (*irreg*) *n* femme *f* d'affaires

busker ['bʌskər] *n* (*BRIT*) artiste ambulant(e)

bus: **bus pass** *n* carte *f* de bus; **bus shelter** *n* abribus *m*; **bus station** *n* gare routière; **bus-stop** *n* arrêt *m* d'autobus

bust [bʌst] *n* buste *m*; (*measurement*) tour *m* de poitrine ▷ *adj* (*inf: broken*) fichu(e), fini(e); **to go ~** faire faillite

bustling ['bʌslɪŋ] *adj* (*town*) très animé(e)

busy ['bɪzɪ] *adj* occupé(e); (*shop, street*) très fréquenté(e); (*US: telephone, line*) occupé ▷ *vt*: **to ~ o.s.** s'occuper; **busy signal** *n* (*US*) tonalité *f* occupé *inv*

but [bʌt] *conj* mais; **I'd love to come, but I'm busy** j'aimerais venir mais je suis occupé; **he's not English but French** il n'est pas anglais mais français; **but that's far too expensive!** mais c'est bien trop cher!
▷ *prep* (*apart from, except*) sauf, excepté; **nothing but** rien d'autre que; **we've had nothing but trouble** nous n'avons eu que des ennuis; **no-one but him can do it** lui seul peut le faire; **who but a lunatic would do such a thing?** qui sinon un fou ferait une chose pareille?; **but for you/your help** sans toi/ton aide; **anything but that** tout sauf *or* excepté ça, tout mais pas ça
▷ *adv* (*just, only*) ne ... que; **she's but a child** elle n'est qu'une enfant; **had I but known**

si seulement j'avais su; **I can but try** je peux toujours essayer; **all but finished** pratiquement terminé

butcher ['butʃəʳ] n boucher m ▷ vt massacrer; (cattle etc for meat) tuer; **butcher's (shop)** n boucherie f

butler ['bʌtləʳ] n maître m d'hôtel

butt [bʌt] n (cask) gros tonneau; (of gun) crosse f; (of cigarette) mégot m; (BRIT fig: target) cible f ▷ vt donner un coup de tête à

butter ['bʌtəʳ] n beurre m ▷ vt beurrer; **buttercup** n bouton m d'or

butterfly ['bʌtəflaɪ] n papillon m; (Swimming: also: ~ **stroke**) brasse f papillon

buttocks ['bʌtəks] npl fesses fpl

button ['bʌtn] n bouton m; (us: badge) pin m ▷ vt (also: ~ **up**) boutonner ▷ vi se boutonner

buy [baɪ] (pt, pp **bought**) vt acheter ▷ n achat m; **to ~ sb sth/sth from sb** acheter qch à qn; **to ~ sb a drink** offrir un verre or à boire à qn; **can I ~ you a drink?** je vous offre un verre?; **where can I ~ some postcards?** où est-ce que je peux acheter des cartes postales?; **buy out** vt (partner) désintéresser; **buy up** vt acheter en bloc, rafler; **buyer** n acheteur(-euse) m/f

buzz [bʌz] n bourdonnement m; (inf: phone call): **to give sb a ~** passer un coup de fil à qn ▷ vi bourdonner; **buzzer** n timbre m électrique

⊘ KEYWORD

by [baɪ] prep **1** (referring to cause, agent) par, de; **killed by lightning** tué par la foudre; **surrounded by a fence** entouré d'une barrière; **a painting by Picasso** un tableau de Picasso

2 (referring to method, manner, means): **by bus/car** en autobus/voiture; **by train** par le or en train; **to pay by cheque** payer par chèque; **by moonlight/candlelight** à la lueur de la lune/d'une bougie; **by saving hard, he ...** à force d'économiser, il ...

3 (via, through) par; **we came by Dover** nous sommes venus par Douvres

4 (close to, past) à côté de; **the house by the school** la maison à côté de l'école; **a holiday by the sea** des vacances au bord de la mer; **she went by me** elle est passée à côté de moi; **I go by the post office every day** je passe devant la poste tous les jours

5 (with time: not later than) avant; (: during): **by daylight** à la lumière du jour; **by night** la nuit, de nuit; **by 4 o'clock** avant 4 heures; **by this time tomorrow** d'ici demain à la même heure; **by the time I got here it was too late** lorsque je suis arrivé il était déjà trop tard

6 (amount) à; **by the kilo/metre** au kilo/au mètre; **paid by the hour** payé à l'heure

7 (Math: measure): **to divide/multiply by 3** diviser/multiplier par 3; **a room 3 metres by 4** une pièce de 3 mètres sur 4; **it's broader by a metre** c'est plus large d'un mètre

8 (according to) d'après, selon; **it's 3 o'clock by my watch** il est 3 heures à ma montre; **it's all right by me** je n'ai rien contre

9: **(all) by oneself** etc tout(e) seul(e) ▷ adv **1** see **go**; **pass** etc

2: **by and by** un peu plus tard, bientôt; **by and large** dans l'ensemble

bye(-bye) ['baɪ('baɪ)] excl au revoir!, salut!

by-election ['baɪɪlɛkʃən] n (BRIT) élection (législative) partielle

bypass ['baɪpɑːs] n rocade f; (Med) pontage m ▷ vt éviter

byte [baɪt] n (Comput) octet m

C [si:] n (Mus): **C** do m
cab [kæb] n taxi m; (of train, truck) cabine f
cabaret ['kæbəreɪ] n (show) spectacle m de cabaret
cabbage ['kæbɪdʒ] n chou m
cabin ['kæbɪn] n (house) cabane f, hutte f; (on ship) cabine f; (on plane) compartiment m; **cabin crew** n (Aviat) équipage m
cabinet ['kæbɪnɪt] n (Pol) cabinet m; (furniture) petit meuble à tiroirs et rayons; (also: **display ~**) vitrine f, petite armoire vitrée; **cabinet minister** n ministre m (membre du cabinet)
cable ['keɪbl] n câble m ⊳ vt câbler, télégraphier; **cable car** n téléphérique m; **cable television** n télévision f par câble
cactus (pl **cacti**) ['kæktəs, -taɪ] n cactus m
café ['kæfeɪ] n ≈ café(-restaurant) m (sans alcool)
cafeteria [kæfɪ'tɪərɪə] n cafétéria f
caffein(e) ['kæfi:n] n caféine f
cage [keɪdʒ] n cage f
cagoule [kə'gu:l] n K-way® m
Cairo ['kaɪərəʊ] n le Caire
cake [keɪk] n gâteau m; **~ of soap** savonnette f
calcium ['kælsɪəm] n calcium m
calculate ['kælkjuleɪt] vt calculer; (estimate: chances, effect) évaluer; **calculation** [kælkju'leɪʃən] n calcul m; **calculator** n

calculatrice f
calendar ['kæləndər] n calendrier m
calf (pl **calves**) [kɑ:f, kɑ:vz] n (of cow) veau m; (of other animals) petit m; (also: **~skin**) veau m, vachette f; (Anat) mollet m
calibre (US **caliber**) ['kælɪbər] n calibre m
call [kɔ:l] vt appeler; (meeting) convoquer ⊳ vi appeler; (visit: also: **~ in**, **~ round**) passer ⊳ n (shout) appel m, cri m; (also: **telephone ~**) coup m de téléphone; **to be on ~** être de permanence; **to be ~ed** s'appeler; **can I make a ~ from here?** est-ce que je peux téléphoner d'ici?; **call back** vi (return) repasser; (Tel) rappeler ⊳ vt (Tel) rappeler; **can you ~ back later?** pouvez-vous rappeler plus tard?; **call for** vt fus (demand) demander; (fetch) passer prendre; **call in** vt (doctor, expert, police) appeler, faire venir; **call off** vt annuler; **call on** vt fus (visit) rendre visite à, passer voir; (request): **to ~ on sb to do** inviter qn à faire; **call out** vi pousser un cri or des cris; **call up** vt (Mil) appeler, mobiliser; (Tel) appeler; **callbox** n (BRIT) cabine f téléphonique; **call centre** (US **call center**) n centre m d'appels; **caller** n (Tel) personne f qui appelle; (visitor) visiteur m
callous ['kæləs] adj dur(e), insensible
calm [kɑ:m] adj calme ⊳ n calme m ⊳ vt calmer, apaiser; **calm down** vi se calmer, s'apaiser ⊳ vt calmer, apaiser; **calmly** ['kɑ:mlɪ] adv calmement, avec calme
Calor gas® ['kælər-] n (BRIT) butane m, butagaz® m
calorie ['kælərɪ] n calorie f
calves [kɑ:vz] npl of **calf**
Cambodia [kæm'bəudɪə] n Cambodge m
camcorder ['kæmkɔ:dər] n caméscope m
came [keɪm] pt of **come**
camel ['kæməl] n chameau m
camera ['kæmərə] n appareil-photo m; (Cine, TV) caméra f; **in ~** à huis clos, en privé; **cameraman** n caméraman m; **camera phone** n téléphone m avec appareil photo numérique intégré
camouflage ['kæməflɑ:ʒ] n camouflage m ⊳ vt camoufler
camp [kæmp] n camp m ⊳ vi camper ⊳ adj (man) efféminé(e)
campaign [kæm'peɪn] n (Mil, Pol etc) campagne f ⊳ vi (also fig) faire campagne; **campaigner** n: **campaigner for** partisan(e) de; **campaigner against** opposant(e) à
camp: **campbed** n (BRIT) lit m de camp; **camper** n campeur(-euse); (vehicle) camping-car m; **campground** (US) n (terrain m de) camping m; **camping** n camping m; **to go camping** faire du camping; **campsite** n (terrain m de)

camping *m*
campus ['kæmpəs] *n* campus *m*
can¹ [kæn] *n* (*of milk, oil, water*) bidon *m*;
(*tin*) boîte *f* (de conserve) ▷ *vt* mettre en
conserve

⊙ **KEYWORD**

can² [kæn] (*negative* **cannot, can't**, *conditional
and pt* **could**) *aux vb* **1** (*be able to*) pouvoir;
you can do it if you try vous pouvez le
faire si vous essayez; **I can't hear you** je ne
t'entends pas
2 (*know how to*) savoir; **I can swim/play
tennis/drive** je sais nager/jouer au tennis/
conduire; **can you speak French?** parlez-
vous français?
3 (*may*) pouvoir; **can I use your phone?** puis-
je me servir de votre téléphone?
4 (*expressing disbelief, puzzlement etc*): **it can't
be true!** ce n'est pas possible!; **what CAN he
want?** qu'est-ce qu'il peut bien vouloir?
5 (*expressing possibility, suggestion etc*): **he
could be in the library** il est peut-être
dans la bibliothèque; **she could have been
delayed** il se peut qu'elle ait été retardée

Canada ['kænədə] *n* Canada *m*; **Canadian**
[kə'neɪdɪən] *adj* canadien(ne) ▷ *n*
Canadien(ne)
canal [kə'næl] *n* canal *m*
canary [kə'nɛərɪ] *n* canari *m*, serin *m*
cancel ['kænsəl] *vt* annuler; (*train*) supprimer;
(*party, appointment*) décommander; (*cross
out*) barrer, rayer; (*cheque*) faire opposition
à; **I would like to ~ my booking** je voudrais
annuler ma réservation; **cancellation**
[kænsə'leɪʃən] *n* annulation *f*; suppression *f*
Cancer ['kænsər] *n* (*Astrology*) le Cancer
cancer ['kænsər] *n* cancer *m*
candidate ['kændɪdeɪt] *n* candidat(e)
candle ['kændl] *n* bougie *f*; (*in church*)
cierge *m*; **candlestick** *n* (*also:* **candle
holder**) bougeoir *m*; (*bigger, ornate*)
chandelier *m*
candy ['kændɪ] *n* sucre candi; (*US*) bonbon *m*;
candy bar (*US*) *n* barre *f* chocolatée;
candyfloss *n* (*BRIT*) barbe *f* à papa
cane [keɪn] *n* canne *f*; (*for baskets, chairs etc*)
rotin *m* ▷ *vt* (*BRIT Scol*) administrer des coups
de bâton à
canister ['kænɪstər] *n* boîte *f* (*gén en métal*); (*of
gas*) bombe *f*
cannabis ['kænəbɪs] *n* (*drug*) cannabis *m*
canned ['kænd] *adj* (*food*) en boîte, en
conserve; (*inf: music*) enregistré(e); (*BRIT inf:
drunk*) bourré(e); (*US inf: worker*) mis(e) à la
porte
cannon (*pl ~ or ~s*) ['kænən] *n* (*gun*)

canon *m*
cannot ['kænɔt] = **can not**
canoe [kə'nuː] *n* pirogue *f*; (*Sport*) canoë *m*;
canoeing *n* (*sport*) canoë *m*
canon ['kænən] *n* (*clergyman*) chanoine *m*;
(*standard*) canon *m*
can-opener [-'əupnər] *n* ouvre-boîte *m*
can't [kɑːnt] = **can not**
canteen [kæn'tiːn] *n* (*eating place*) cantine *f*;
(*BRIT: of cutlery*) ménagère *f*
canter ['kæntər] *vi* aller au petit galop
canvas ['kænvəs] *n* toile *f*
canvass ['kænvəs] *vi* (*Pol*): **to ~ for** faire
campagne pour ▷ *vt* (*citizens, opinions*) sonder
canyon ['kænjən] *n* cañon *m*, gorge
(profonde)
cap [kæp] *n* casquette *f*; (*for swimming*) bonnet
m de bain; (*of pen*) capuchon *m*; (*of bottle*)
capsule *f*; (*BRIT: contraceptive: also:* **Dutch ~**)
diaphragme *m* ▷ *vt* (*outdo*) surpasser; (*put limit
on*) plafonner
capability [keɪpə'bɪlɪtɪ] *n* aptitude *f*,
capacité *f*
capable ['keɪpəbl] *adj* capable
capacity [kə'pæsɪtɪ] *n* (*of container*) capacité *f*,
contenance *f*; (*ability*) aptitude *f*
cape [keɪp] *n* (*garment*) cape *f*; (*Geo*) cap *m*
caper ['keɪpər] *n* (*Culin: gen pl*) câpre *f*; (*prank*)
farce *f*
capital ['kæpɪtl] *n* (*also:* **~ city**) capitale *f*;
(*money*) capital *m*; (*also:* **~ letter**) majuscule *f*;
capitalism *n* capitalisme *m*; **capitalist** *adj, n*
capitaliste *m/f*; **capital punishment** *n* peine
capitale
Capitol ['kæpɪtl] *n*: **the ~** le Capitole
Capricorn ['kæprɪkɔːn] *n* le Capricorne
capsize [kæp'saɪz] *vt* faire chavirer ▷ *vi*
chavirer
capsule ['kæpsjuːl] *n* capsule *f*
captain ['kæptɪn] *n* capitaine *m*
caption ['kæpʃən] *n* légende *f*
captivity [kæp'tɪvɪtɪ] *n* captivité *f*
capture ['kæptʃər] *vt* (*prisoner, animal*)
capturer; (*town*) prendre; (*attention*) capter;
(*Comput*) saisir ▷ *n* capture *f*; (*of data*) saisie *f*
de données
car [kɑːr] *n* voiture *f*, auto *f*; (*US Rail*) wagon
m, voiture
carafe [kə'ræf] *n* carafe *f*
caramel ['kærəməl] *n* caramel *m*
carat ['kærət] *n* carat *m*
caravan ['kærəvæn] *n* caravane *f*; **caravan
site** *n* (*BRIT*) camping *m* pour caravanes
carbohydrate [kɑːbəu'haɪdreɪt] *n* hydrate *m*
de carbone; (*food*) féculent *m*
carbon ['kɑːbən] *n* carbone *m*; **carbon
dioxide** [-daɪ'ɔksaɪd] *n* gaz *m* carbonique,
dioxyde *m* de carbone; **carbon monoxide**
[-mɔ'nɔksaɪd] *n* oxyde *m* de carbone

car boot sale n voir encadré

carburettor (US **carburetor**) [kɑːbjuˈrɛtə^r] n
carburateur m

card [kɑːd] n carte f; (material) carton m;
cardboard n carton m; **card game** n jeu m
de cartes

cardigan [ˈkɑːdɪɡən] n cardigan m

cardinal [ˈkɑːdɪnl] adj cardinal(e);
(importance) capital(e) ▷ n cardinal m

cardphone [ˈkɑːdfəʊn] n téléphone m à carte
(magnétique)

care [kɛə^r] n soin m, attention f; (worry) souci
m ▷ vi: **to ~ about** (feel interest for) se soucier
de, s'intéresser à; (person: love) être attaché(e)
à; **in sb's ~** à la garde de qn, confié à qn; **~ of** (on
letter) chez; **to take ~ (to do)** faire attention
(à faire); **to take ~ of** vt s'occuper de; **I don't ~**
ça m'est bien égal, peu m'importe; **I couldn't**
~ less cela m'est complètement égal, je m'en
fiche complètement; **care for** vt fus s'occuper
de; (like) aimer

career [kəˈrɪə^r] n carrière f ▷ vi (also: **~ along**)
aller à toute allure

care: **carefree** adj sans souci, insouciant(e);
careful adj soigneux(-euse); (cautious)
prudent(e); **(be) careful!** (fais) attention!;
carefully adv avec soin, soigneusement;
prudemment; **caregiver** (US) n (professional)
travailleur social; (unpaid) personne qui
s'occupe d'un proche qui est malade; **careless**
adj négligent(e); (heedless) insouciant(e);
carelessness n manque m de soin,
négligence f; insouciance f; **carer** [ˈkɛərə^r]
n (professional) travailleur social; (unpaid)
personne qui s'occupe d'un proche qui est malade;
caretaker n gardien(ne), concierge m/f

car-ferry [ˈkɑːfɛrɪ] n (on sea) ferry(-boat) m;
(on river) bac m

cargo (pl **~es**) [ˈkɑːɡəʊ] n cargaison f,
chargement m

car hire n (BRIT) location f de voitures

Caribbean [kærɪˈbiːən] adj, n: **the ~ (Sea)** la
mer des Antilles or des Caraïbes

caring [ˈkɛərɪŋ] adj (person) bienveillant(e);
(society, organization) humanitaire

carnation [kɑːˈneɪʃən] n œillet m

carnival [ˈkɑːnɪvl] n (public celebration)
carnaval m; (US: funfair) fête foraine

carol [ˈkærəl] n: **(Christmas) ~** chant m de
Noël

carousel [kærəˈsɛl] n (for luggage) carrousel m;
(US) manège m

car park (BRIT) n parking m, parc m de
stationnement

carpenter [ˈkɑːpɪntə^r] n charpentier m;
(joiner) menuisier m

carpet [ˈkɑːpɪt] n tapis m ▷ vt recouvrir (d'un
tapis); **fitted ~** (BRIT) moquette f

car rental n (US) location f de voitures

carriage [ˈkærɪdʒ] n (BRIT Rail) wagon m;
(horse-drawn) voiture f; (of goods) transport m;
(: cost) port m; **carriageway** n (BRIT: part of
road) chaussée f

carrier [ˈkærɪə^r] n transporteur m,
camionneur m; (company) entreprise f de
transport; (Med) porteur(-euse); **carrier bag** n
(BRIT) sac m en papier or en plastique

carrot [ˈkærət] n carotte f

carry [ˈkærɪ] vt (subj: person) porter; (: vehicle)
transporter; (involve: responsibilities etc)
comporter, impliquer; (Med: disease) être
porteur de ▷ vi (sound) porter; **to get carried**
away (fig) s'emballer, s'enthousiasmer; **carry**
on vi (continue) continuer ▷ vt (conduct:
business) diriger; (: conversation) entretenir;
(continue: business, conversation) continuer; **to**
~ on with sth/doing continuer qch/à faire;
carry out vt (orders) exécuter; (investigation)
effectuer

cart [kɑːt] n charrette f ▷ vt (inf) transporter

carton [ˈkɑːtən] n (box) carton m; (of yogurt)
pot m (en carton)

cartoon [kɑːˈtuːn] n (Press) dessin m
(humoristique); (satirical) caricature f; (comic
strip) bande dessinée; (Cine) dessin animé

cartridge [ˈkɑːtrɪdʒ] n (for gun, pen)
cartouche f

carve [kɑːv] vt (meat: also: **~ up**) découper;
(wood, stone) tailler, sculpter; **carving** n (in
wood etc) sculpture f

car wash n station f de lavage (de voitures)

case [keɪs] n cas m; (Law) affaire f, procès m;
(box) caisse f, boîte f; (for glasses) étui m; (BRIT:
also: **suit~**) valise f; **in ~ of** en cas de; **in ~ he** au
cas où il; **just in ~** à tout hasard; **in any ~** en
tout cas, de toute façon

cash [kæʃ] n argent m; (Comm) (argent m)
liquide m ▷ vt encaisser; **to pay (in) ~** payer
(en argent) comptant or en espèces; **~ with**
order/on delivery (Comm) payable or
paiement à la commande/livraison; **I haven't**
got any ~ je n'ai pas de liquide; **cashback** n
(discount) remise f; (at supermarket etc) retrait
m (à la caisse); **cash card** n carte f de retrait;
cash desk n (BRIT) caisse f; **cash dispenser** n
distributeur m automatique de billets

cashew [kæˈʃuː] n (also: **~ nut**) noix f de cajou

cashier [kæ'ʃɪəʳ] n caissier(-ère)
cashmere ['kæʃmɪəʳ] n cachemire m
cash point n distributeur m automatique
de billets
cash register n caisse enregistreuse
casino [kə'si:nəʊ] n casino m
casket ['kɑ:skɪt] n coffret m; (US: coffin)
cercueil m
casserole ['kæsərəʊl] n (pot) cocotte f; (food)
ragoût m (en cocotte)
cassette [kæ'sɛt] n cassette f; **cassette
player** n lecteur m de cassettes
cast [kɑ:st] (vb: pt, pp ~) vt (throw) jeter;
(shadow: lit) projeter; (: fig) jeter; (glance) jeter
▷ n (Theat) distribution f; (also: **plaster ~**)
plâtre m; **to ~ sb as Hamlet** attribuer à qn le
rôle d'Hamlet; **to ~ one's vote** voter, exprimer
son suffrage; **to ~ doubt on** jeter un doute
sur; **cast off** vi (Naut) larguer les amarres;
(Knitting) arrêter les mailles
castanets [kæstə'nɛts] npl castagnettes fpl
caster sugar ['kɑ:stə-] n (BRIT) sucre m
semoule
cast-iron ['kɑ:staɪən] adj (lit) de or en fonte;
(fig: will) de fer; (alibi) en béton
castle ['kɑ:sl] n château m; (fortress) château-
fort m; (Chess) tour f
casual ['kæʒjul] adj (by chance) de hasard,
fait(e) au hasard, fortuit(e); (irregular: work etc)
temporaire; (unconcerned) désinvolte; **~ wear**
vêtements mpl sport inv
casualty ['kæʒjultɪ] n accidenté(e),
blessé(e); (dead) victime f, mort(e); (BRIT: Med:
department) urgences fpl
cat [kæt] n chat m
Catalan ['kætəlæn] adj catalan(e)
catalogue (US **catalog**) ['kætəlɔg] n
catalogue m ▷ vt cataloguer
catalytic converter [kætə'lɪtɪkkən'və:təʳ] n
pot m catalytique
cataract ['kætərækt] n (also Med) cataracte f
catarrh [kə'tɑ:ʳ] n rhume m chronique,
catarrhe f
catastrophe [kə'tæstrəfɪ] n catastrophe f
catch [kætʃ] (pt, pp **caught**) vt attraper;
(person: by surprise) prendre, surprendre;
(understand) saisir; (get entangled) accrocher
▷ vi (fire) prendre; (get entangled) s'accrocher
▷ n (fish etc) prise f; (hidden problem) attrape
f; (Tech) loquet m; cliquet m; **to ~ sb's
attention** or **eye** attirer l'attention de qn; **to
~ fire** prendre feu; **to ~ sight of** apercevoir;
catch up vi (with work) se rattraper,
combler son retard ▷ vt (also: **~ up with**)
rattraper; **catching** ['kætʃɪŋ] adj (Med)
contagieux(-euse)
category ['kætɪgərɪ] n catégorie f
cater ['keɪtəʳ] vi: **to ~ for** (BRIT: needs) satisfaire,
pourvoir à; (: readers, consumers) s'adresser à,

pourvoir aux besoins de; (Comm: parties etc)
préparer des repas pour
caterpillar ['kætəpɪləʳ] n chenille f
cathedral [kə'θi:drəl] n cathédrale f
Catholic ['kæθəlɪk] (Rel) adj catholique ▷ n
catholique m/f
Catseye® ['kæts'aɪ] n (BRIT Aut) (clou m à)
catadioptre m
cattle ['kætl] npl bétail m, bestiaux mpl
catwalk ['kætwɔ:k] n passerelle f; (for models)
podium m (de défilé de mode)
caught [kɔ:t] pt, pp of **catch**
cauliflower ['kɔlɪflauəʳ] n chou-fleur m
cause [kɔ:z] n cause f ▷ vt causer
caution ['kɔ:ʃən] n prudence f; (warning)
avertissement m ▷ vt avertir, donner un
avertissement à; **cautious** adj prudent(e)
cave [keɪv] n caverne f, grotte f; **cave in** vi (roof
etc) s'effondrer
caviar(e) ['kævɪɑ:ʳ] n caviar m
cavity ['kævɪtɪ] n cavité f; (Med) carie f
cc abbr (= cubic centimetre) cm³; (on letter etc)
= **carbon copy**
CCTV n abbr = **closed-circuit television**
CD n abbr (= compact disc) CD m; **CD burner** n
graveur m de CD; **CD player** n platine f laser;
CD-ROM [si:di:'rɔm] n abbr (= compact disc
read-only memory) CD-ROM m inv; **CD writer** n
graveur m de CD
cease [si:s] vt, vi cesser; **ceasefire** n cessez-
le-feu m
cedar ['si:dəʳ] n cèdre m
ceilidh ['keɪlɪ] n bal m folklorique écossais or
irlandais
ceiling ['si:lɪŋ] n (also fig) plafond m
celebrate ['sɛlɪbreɪt] vt, vi célébrer;
celebration [sɛlɪ'breɪʃən] n célébration f
celebrity [sɪ'lɛbrɪtɪ] n célébrité f
celery ['sɛlərɪ] n céleri m (en branches)
cell [sɛl] n (gen) cellule f; (Elec) élément m (de
pile)
cellar ['sɛlə] n cave f
cello ['tʃɛləʊ] n violoncelle m
Cellophane® ['sɛləfeɪn] n cellophane® f
cellphone ['sɛlfəʊn] n téléphone m cellulaire
Celsius ['sɛlsɪəs] adj Celsius inv
Celtic ['kɛltɪk, 'sɛltɪk] adj celte, celtique
cement [sə'mɛnt] n ciment m
cemetery ['sɛmɪtrɪ] n cimetière m
censor ['sɛnsəʳ] n censeur m ▷ vt censurer;
censorship n censure f
census ['sɛnsəs] n recensement m
cent [sɛnt] n (unit of dollar, euro) cent m (= un
centième du dollar, de l'euro); see also **per**
centenary [sɛn'ti:nərɪ] (US **centennial**)
[sɛn'tɛnɪəl] n centenaire m
center ['sɛntəʳ] (US) = **centre**
centi... [sɛntɪ] prefix: **centigrade** adj
centigrade; **centimetre** (US **centimeter**) n

centimètre *m*; **centipede** ['sɛntɪpiːd] *n* mille-pattes *m inv*

central ['sɛntrəl] *adj* central(e); **Central America** *n* Amérique centrale; **central heating** *n* chauffage central; **central reservation** *n* (*BRIT Aut*) terre-plein central

centre (*US* **center**) ['sɛntəʳ] *n* centre *m* ▷ *vt* centrer; **centre-forward** *n* (*Sport*) avant-centre *m*; **centre-half** *n* (*Sport*) demi-centre *m*

century ['sɛntjʊrɪ] *n* siècle *m*; **in the twentieth ~** au vingtième siècle

CEO *n abbr* (*US*) = **chief executive officer**

ceramic [sɪˈræmɪk] *adj* céramique

cereal ['siːrɪəl] *n* céréale *f*

ceremony ['sɛrɪmənɪ] *n* cérémonie *f*; **to stand on ~** faire des façons

certain ['səːtən] *adj* certain(e); **to make ~ of** s'assurer de; **for ~** certainement, sûrement; **certainly** *adv* certainement; **certainty** *n* certitude *f*

certificate [səˈtɪfɪkɪt] *n* certificat *m*

certify ['səːtɪfaɪ] *vt* certifier; (*award diploma to*) conférer un diplôme *etc* à; (*declare insane*) déclarer malade mental(e)

cf. *abbr* (= *compare*) cf., voir

CFC *n abbr* (= *chlorofluorocarbon*) CFC *m*

chain [tʃeɪn] *n* (*gen*) chaîne *f* ▷ *vt* (*also*: **~ up**) enchaîner, attacher (avec une chaîne); **chain-smoke** *vi* fumer cigarette sur cigarette

chair [tʃɛəʳ] *n* chaise *f*; (*armchair*) fauteuil *m*; (*of university*) chaire *f*; (*of meeting*) présidence *f* ▷ *vt* (*meeting*) présider; **chairlift** *n* télésiège *m*; **chairman** *n* président *m*; **chairperson** *n* président(e); **chairwoman** *n* présidente *f*

chalet ['ʃæleɪ] *n* chalet *m*

chalk [tʃɔːk] *n* craie *f*; **chalkboard** (*US*) *n* tableau noir

challenge ['tʃælɪndʒ] *n* défi *m* ▷ *vt* défier; (*statement, right*) mettre en question, contester; **to ~ sb to do** mettre qn au défi de faire; **challenging** *adj* (*task, career*) qui représente un défi *or* une gageure; (*tone, look*) de défi, provocateur(-trice)

chamber ['tʃeɪmbəʳ] *n* chambre *f*; (*BRIT Law*: *gen pl*) cabinet *m*; **~ of commerce** chambre de commerce; **chambermaid** *n* femme *f* de chambre

champagne [ʃæm'peɪn] *n* champagne *m*

champion ['tʃæmpɪən] *n* (*also of cause*) champion(ne); **championship** *n* championnat *m*

chance [tʃɑːns] *n* (*luck*) hasard *m*; (*opportunity*) occasion *f*, possibilité *f*; (*hope, likelihood*) chance *f*; (*risk*) risque *m* ▷ *vt* risquer ▷ *adj* fortuit(e), de hasard; **to take a ~** prendre un risque; **by ~** par hasard; **to ~ it** risquer le coup, essayer

chancellor ['tʃɑːnsələʳ] *n* chancelier *m*; **Chancellor of the Exchequer** [-ɪksˈtʃɛkəʳ]

(*BRIT*) *n* chancelier *m* de l'Échiquier

chandelier [ʃændəˈlɪəʳ] *n* lustre *m*

change [tʃeɪndʒ] *vt* (*alter, replace*: *Comm*: *money*) changer; (*switch, substitute*: *hands, trains, clothes, one's name etc*) changer de ▷ *vi* (*gen*) changer; (*change clothes*) se changer; (*be transformed*): **to ~ into** se changer *or* transformer en ▷ *n* changement *m*; (*money*) monnaie *f*; **to ~ gear** (*Aut*) changer de vitesse; **to ~ one's mind** changer d'avis; **a ~ of clothes** des vêtements de rechange; **for a ~** pour changer; **do you have ~ for £10?** vous avez la monnaie de 10 livres?; **where can I ~ some money?** où est-ce que je peux changer de l'argent?; **keep the ~!** gardez la monnaie!; **change over** *vi* (*swap*) échanger; (*change*: *drivers etc*) changer; (*change sides*: *players etc*) changer de côté; **to ~ over from sth to sth** passer de qch à qch; **changeable** *adj* (*weather*) variable; **change machine** *n* distributeur *m* de monnaie; **changing room** *n* (*BRIT*: *in shop*) salon m d'essayage; (: *Sport*) vestiaire *m*

channel ['tʃænl] *n* (*TV*) chaîne *f*; (*waveband, groove, fig*: *medium*) canal *m*; (*of river, sea*) chenal *m* ▷ *vt* canaliser; **the (English) C~** la Manche; **Channel Islands** *npl*: **the Channel Islands** les îles *fpl* Anglo-Normandes; **Channel Tunnel** *n*: **the Channel Tunnel** le tunnel sous la Manche

chant [tʃɑːnt] *n* chant *m*; (*Rel*) psalmodie *f* ▷ *vt* chanter, scander

chaos ['keɪɔs] *n* chaos *m*

chaotic [keɪˈɔtɪk] *adj* chaotique

chap [tʃæp] *n* (*BRIT inf*: *man*) type *m*

chapel ['tʃæpl] *n* chapelle *f*

chapped [tʃæpt] *adj* (*skin, lips*) gercé(e)

chapter ['tʃæptəʳ] *n* chapitre *m*

character ['kærɪktəʳ] *n* caractère *m*; (*in novel, film*) personnage *m*; (*eccentric person*) numéro *m*, phénomène *m*; **characteristic** ['kærɪktəˈrɪstɪk] *adj, n* caractéristique (*f*); **characterize** ['kærɪktəraɪz] *vt* caractériser

charcoal ['tʃɑːkəʊl] *n* charbon *m* de bois; (*Art*) charbon

charge [tʃɑːdʒ] *n* (*accusation*) accusation *f*; (*Law*) inculpation *f*; (*cost*) prix (demandé) ▷ *vt* (*gun, battery, Mil*: *enemy*) charger; (*customer, sum*) faire payer ▷ *vi* foncer; **charges** *npl* (*costs*) frais *mpl*; (*BRIT Tel*): **to reverse the ~s** téléphoner en PCV; **to take ~ of** se charger de; **to be in ~ of** être responsable de, s'occuper de; **to ~ sb (with)** (*Law*) inculper qn (de); **charge card** *n* carte *f* de client (*émise par un grand magasin*); **charger** *n* (*also*: **battery charger**) chargeur *m*

charismatic [kærɪzˈmætɪk] *adj* charismatique

charity ['tʃærɪtɪ] *n* charité *f*; (*organization*) institution *f* charitable *or* de bienfaisance, œuvre f (de charité); **charity shop** n (BRIT) boutique vendant des articles d'occasion au profit d'une organisation caritative

charm [tʃɑːm] n charme m; (on bracelet) breloque f ▷ vt charmer, enchanter; **charming** adj charmant(e)

chart [tʃɑːt] n tableau m, diagramme m; graphique m; (map) carte marine ▷ vt dresser or établir la carte de; (sales, progress) établir la courbe de; **charts** npl (Mus) hit-parade m; **to be in the ~s** (record, pop group) figurer au hit-parade

charter ['tʃɑːtər] vt (plane) affréter ▷ n (document) charte f; **chartered accountant** n (BRIT) expert-comptable m; **charter flight** n charter m

chase [tʃeɪs] vt poursuivre, pourchasser; (also: **~ away**) chasser ▷ n poursuite f, chasse f

chat [tʃæt] vi (also: **have a ~**) bavarder, causer; (on Internet) chatter ▷ n conversation f; **chat up** vt (BRIT inf: girl) baratiner; **chat room** n (Internet) forum m de discussion; **chat show** n (BRIT) talk-show m

chatter ['tʃætər] vi (person) bavarder, papoter ▷ n bavardage m, papotage m; **my teeth are ~ing** je claque des dents

chauffeur ['ʃəʊfər] n chauffeur m (de maître)

chauvinist ['ʃəʊvɪnɪst] n (also: **male ~**) phallocrate m, macho m; (nationalist) chauvin(e)

cheap [tʃiːp] adj bon marché inv, pas cher (chère); (reduced: ticket) à prix réduit; (: fare) réduit(e); (joke) facile, d'un goût douteux; (poor quality) à bon marché, de qualité médiocre ▷ adv à bon marché, pour pas cher; **can you recommend a ~ hotel/restaurant, please?** pourriez-vous m'indiquer un hôtel/restaurant bon marché?; **cheap day return** n billet m d'aller et retour réduit (valable pour la journée); **cheaply** adv à bon marché, à bon compte

cheat [tʃiːt] vi tricher; (in exam) copier ▷ vt tromper, duper; **to ~ sb out of sth** escroquer qch à qn ▷ n tricheur(-euse) m/f; escroc m; **cheat on** vt fus tromper

Chechnya [tʃɪtʃˈnjɑː] n Tchétchénie f

check [tʃɛk] vt vérifier; (passport, ticket) contrôler; (halt) enrayer; (restrain) maîtriser ▷ vi (official etc) se renseigner ▷ n vérification f; contrôle m; (curb) frein m; (BRIT: bill) addition f; (US) = **cheque**; (pattern: gen pl) carreaux mpl; **to ~ with sb** demander à qn; **check in** vi (in hotel) remplir sa fiche (d'hôtel); (at airport) se présenter à l'enregistrement ▷ vt (luggage) (faire) enregistrer; **check off** vt (tick off) cocher; **check out** vi (in hotel) régler sa note ▷ vt (investigate: story) vérifier; **check up** vi: **to ~ up (on sth)** vérifier (qch); **to ~ up on sb** se renseigner sur le compte de qn; **checkbook** (US) = **chequebook**; **checked** adj

(pattern, cloth) à carreaux; **checkers** n (US) jeu m de dames; **check-in** n (also: **check-in desk**: at airport) enregistrement m; **checking account** n (US) compte courant; **checklist** n liste f de contrôle; **checkmate** n échec et mat m; **checkout** n (in supermarket) caisse f; **checkpoint** n contrôle m; **checkroom** (US) n consigne f; **checkup** n (Med) examen médical, check-up m

cheddar ['tʃedər] n (also: **~ cheese**) cheddar m

cheek [tʃiːk] n joue f; (impudence) toupet m, culot m; **what a ~!** quel toupet!; **cheekbone** n pommette f; **cheeky** adj effronté(e), culotté(e)

cheer [tʃɪər] vt acclamer, applaudir; (gladden) réjouir, réconforter ▷ vi applaudir ▷ n (gen pl) acclamations fpl, applaudissements mpl; bravos mpl, hourras mpl; **~s!** à la vôtre!; **cheer up** vi se dérider, reprendre courage ▷ vt remonter le moral à or de, dérider, égayer; **cheerful** adj gai(e), joyeux(-euse)

cheerio [tʃɪərɪˈəʊ] excl (BRIT) salut!, au revoir!

cheerleader ['tʃɪəliːdər] n membre d'un groupe de majorettes qui chantent et dansent pour soutenir leur équipe pendant les matchs de football américain

cheese [tʃiːz] n fromage m; **cheeseburger** n cheeseburger m; **cheesecake** n tarte f au fromage

chef [ʃɛf] n chef (cuisinier)

chemical ['kemɪkl] adj chimique ▷ n produit m chimique

chemist ['kemɪst] n (BRIT: pharmacist) pharmacien(ne); (scientist) chimiste m/f; **chemistry** n chimie f; **chemist's (shop)** n (BRIT) pharmacie f

cheque (US **check**) [tʃɛk] n chèque m; **chequebook** (US **checkbook**) n chéquier m, carnet m de chèques; **cheque card** n (BRIT) carte f (d'identité) bancaire

cherry ['tʃerɪ] n cerise f; (also: **~ tree**) cerisier m

chess [tʃes] n échecs mpl

chest [tʃest] n poitrine f; (box) coffre m, caisse f

chestnut ['tʃesnʌt] n châtaigne f; (also: **~ tree**) châtaignier m

chest of drawers n commode f

chew [tʃuː] vt mâcher; **chewing gum** n chewing-gum m

chic [ʃiːk] adj chic inv, élégant(e)

chick [tʃɪk] n poussin m; (inf) pépée f

chicken ['tʃɪkɪn] n poulet m; (inf: coward) poule mouillée; **chicken out** vi (inf) se dégonfler; **chickenpox** n varicelle f

chickpea ['tʃɪkpiː] n pois m chiche

chief [tʃiːf] n chef m ▷ adj principal(e); **chief executive** (US **chief executive officer**) n directeur(-trice) général(e); **chiefly** adv principalement, surtout

child (pl **~ren**) [tʃaɪld, 'tʃɪldrən] n enfant

m/f; **child abuse** *n* maltraitance *f* d'enfants; (*sexual*) abus *mpl* sexuels sur des enfants; **child benefit** *n* (*BRIT*) ≈ allocations familiales; **childbirth** *n* accouchement *m*; **child-care** *n* (*for working parents*) garde *f* des enfants (*pour les parents qui travaillent*); **childhood** *n* enfance *f*; **childish** *adj* puéril(e), enfantin(e); **child minder** *n* (*BRIT*) garde *f* d'enfants; **children** ['tʃɪldrən] *npl of* **child**

Chile ['tʃɪlɪ] *n* Chili *m*

chill [tʃɪl] *n* (*of water*) froid *m*; (*of air*) fraîcheur *f*; (*Med*) refroidissement *m*, coup *m* de froid ▷ *vt* (*person*) faire frissonner; (*Culin*) mettre au frais, rafraîchir; **chill out** *vi* (*inf: esp US*) se relaxer

chil(l)i ['tʃɪlɪ] *n* piment *m* (rouge)

chilly ['tʃɪlɪ] *adj* froid(e), glacé(e); (*sensitive to cold*) frileux(-euse)

chimney ['tʃɪmnɪ] *n* cheminée *f*

chimpanzee [tʃɪmpæn'zi:] *n* chimpanzé *m*

chin [tʃɪn] *n* menton *m*

China ['tʃaɪnə] *n* Chine *f*

china ['tʃaɪnə] *n* (*material*) porcelaine *f*; (*crockery*) vaisselle *f* en) porcelaine

Chinese [tʃaɪ'ni:z] *adj* chinois(e) ▷ *n* (*pl inv*) Chinois(e); (*Ling*) chinois *m*

chip [tʃɪp] *n* (*gen pl: Culin: BRIT*) frite *f*; (: *US: also:* **potato ~**) chip *m*; (*of wood*) copeau *m*; (*of glass, stone*) éclat *m*; (*also:* **micro~**) puce *f*; (*in gambling*) fiche *f* ▷ *vt* (*cup, plate*) ébrécher; **chip shop** *n* (*BRIT*) friterie *f*

● **CHIP SHOP**
●
● Un **chip shop**, que l'on appelle également
● un "fish-and-chip shop", est un magasin
● où l'on vend des plats à emporter. Les
● **chip shops** sont d'ailleurs à l'origine des
● "takeaways". On y achète en particulier
● du poisson frit et des frites, mais on y
● trouve également des plats traditionnels
● britanniques ("steak pies", saucisses, etc).
● Tous les plats étaient à l'origine emballés
● dans du papier journal. Dans certains
● de ces magasins, on peut s'asseoir pour
● consommer sur place.

chiropodist [kɪ'rɔpədɪst] *n* (*BRIT*) pédicure *m/f*

chisel ['tʃɪzl] *n* ciseau *m*

chives [tʃaɪvz] *npl* ciboulette *f*, civette *f*

chlorine ['klɔ:ri:n] *n* chlore *m*

choc-ice ['tʃɔkaɪs] *n* (*BRIT*) esquimau® *m*

chocolate ['tʃɔklɪt] *n* chocolat *m*

choice [tʃɔɪs] *n* choix *m* ▷ *adj* de choix

choir ['kwaɪəʳ] *n* chœur *m*, chorale *f*

choke [tʃəuk] *vi* étouffer ▷ *vt* étrangler; étouffer; (*block*) boucher, obstruer ▷ *n* (*Aut*) starter *m*

cholesterol [kə'lɛstərɔl] *n* cholestérol *m*

choose (*pt* **chose**, *pp* **chosen**) [tʃu:z, tʃəuz, 'tʃəuzn] *vt* choisir; **to ~ to do** décider de faire, juger bon de faire

chop [tʃɔp] *vt* (*wood*) couper (à la hache); (*Culin: also:* **~ up**) couper (fin), émincer, hacher (en morceaux) ▷ *n* (*Culin*) côtelette *f*; **chop down** *vt* (*tree*) abattre; **chop off** *vt* trancher; **chopsticks** ['tʃɔpstɪks] *npl* baguettes *fpl*

chord [kɔ:d] *n* (*Mus*) accord *m*

chore [tʃɔ:ʳ] *n* travail *m* de routine; **household ~s** travaux *mpl* du ménage

chorus ['kɔ:rəs] *n* chœur *m*; (*repeated part of song, also fig*) refrain *m*

chose [tʃəuz] *pt of* **choose**

chosen ['tʃəuzn] *pp of* **choose**

Christ [kraɪst] *n* Christ *m*

christen ['krɪsn] *vt* baptiser; **christening** *n* baptême *m*

Christian ['krɪstɪən] *adj, n* chrétien(ne); **Christianity** [krɪstɪ'ænɪtɪ] *n* christianisme *m*; **Christian name** *n* prénom *m*

Christmas ['krɪsməs] *n* Noël *m or f*; **happy or merry ~!** joyeux Noël!; **Christmas card** *n* carte *f* de Noël; **Christmas carol** *n* chant *m* de Noël; **Christmas Day** *n* le jour de Noël; **Christmas Eve** *n* la veille de Noël; la nuit de Noël; **Christmas pudding** *n* (*esp BRIT*) Christmas pudding *m*; **Christmas tree** *n* arbre *m* de Noël

chrome [krəum] *n* chrome *m*

chronic ['krɔnɪk] *adj* chronique

chrysanthemum [krɪ'sænθəməm] *n* chrysanthème *m*

chubby ['tʃʌbɪ] *adj* potelé(e), rondelet(te)

chuck [tʃʌk] *vt* (*inf*) lancer, jeter; (*BRIT: also:* **~ up**: *job*) lâcher; **chuck out** *vt* (*inf: person*) flanquer dehors or à la porte; (: *rubbish etc*) jeter

chuckle ['tʃʌkl] *vi* glousser

chum [tʃʌm] *n* copain (copine)

chunk [tʃʌŋk] *n* gros morceau

church [tʃə:tʃ] *n* église *f*; **churchyard** *n* cimetière *m*

churn [tʃə:n] *n* (*for butter*) baratte *f*; (*also:* **milk ~**) (grand) bidon à lait

chute [ʃu:t] *n* goulotte *f*; (*also:* **rubbish ~**) vide-ordures *m inv*; (*BRIT: children's slide*) toboggan *m*

chutney ['tʃʌtnɪ] *n* chutney *m*

CIA *n abbr* (= *Central Intelligence Agency*) CIA *f*

CID *n abbr* (= *Criminal Investigation Department*) ≈ P.J. *f*

cider ['saɪdəʳ] *n* cidre *m*

cigar [sɪ'gɑ:ʳ] *n* cigare *m*

cigarette [sɪgə'rɛt] *n* cigarette *f*; **cigarette lighter** *n* briquet *m*

cinema ['sɪnəmə] *n* cinéma *m*

cinnamon ['sɪnəmən] *n* cannelle *f*

circle ['sə:kl] *n* cercle *m*; (*in cinema*) balcon *m* ▷ *vi* faire or décrire des cercles ▷ *vt* (*surround*) entourer, encercler; (*move round*) faire le tour de, tourner autour de

circuit ['sə:kɪt] n circuit m; (lap) tour m

circular ['sə:kjulər] adj circulaire ▷ n circulaire f; (as advertisement) prospectus m

circulate ['sə:kjuleɪt] vi circuler ▷ vt faire circuler; **circulation** [sə:kju'leɪʃən] n circulation f; (of newspaper) tirage m

circumstances ['sə:kəmstənsɪz] npl circonstances fpl; (financial condition) moyens mpl, situation financière

circus ['sə:kəs] n cirque m

cite [saɪt] vt citer

citizen ['sɪtɪzn] n (Pol) citoyen(ne); (resident): **the ~s of this town** les habitants de cette ville; **citizenship** n citoyenneté f; (BRIT: Scol) ≈ éducation f civique

citrus fruits ['sɪtrəs-] npl agrumes mpl

city ['sɪtɪ] n (grande) ville f; **the C~** la Cité de Londres (centre des affaires); **city centre** n centre ville m; **city technology college** n (BRIT) établissement m d'enseignement technologique (situé dans un quartier défavorisé)

civic ['sɪvɪk] adj civique; (authorities) municipal(e)

civil ['sɪvɪl] adj civil(e); (polite) poli(e), civil(e); **civilian** [sɪ'vɪlɪən] adj, n civil(e)

civilization [sɪvɪlaɪ'zeɪʃən] n civilisation f

civilized ['sɪvɪlaɪzd] adj civilisé(e); (fig) où règnent les bonnes manières

civil: **civil law** n code civil; (study) droit civil; **civil rights** npl droits mpl civiques; **civil servant** n fonctionnaire m/f; **Civil Service** n fonction publique, administration f; **civil war** n guerre civile

CJD n abbr (= Creutzfeldt-Jakob disease) MCJ f

claim [kleɪm] vt (rights etc) revendiquer; (compensation) réclamer; (assert) déclarer, prétendre ▷ vi (for insurance) faire une déclaration de sinistre ▷ n revendication f; prétention f; (right) droit m; **(insurance) ~** demande f d'indemnisation, déclaration f de sinistre; **claim form** n (gen) formulaire m de demande

clam [klæm] n palourde f

clamp [klæmp] n crampon m; (on workbench) valet m; (on car) sabot m de Denver ▷ vt attacher; (car) mettre un sabot à; **clamp down on** vt fus sévir contre, prendre des mesures draconiennes à l'égard de

clan [klæn] n clan m

clap [klæp] vi applaudir

claret ['klærət] n (vin m de) bordeaux m (rouge)

clarify ['klærɪfaɪ] vt clarifier

clarinet [klærɪ'nɛt] n clarinette f

clarity ['klærɪtɪ] n clarté f

clash [klæʃ] n (sound) choc m, fracas m; (with police) affrontement m; (fig) conflit m ▷ vi se heurter; être or entrer en conflit; (colours) jurer;

(dates, events) tomber en même temps

clasp [klɑːsp] n (of necklace, bag) fermoir m ▷ vt serrer, étreindre

class [klɑːs] n (gen) classe f; (group, category) catégorie f ▷ vt classer, classifier

classic ['klæsɪk] adj classique ▷ n (author, work) classique m; **classical** adj classique

classification [klæsɪfɪ'keɪʃən] n classification f

classify ['klæsɪfaɪ] vt classifier, classer

classmate ['klɑːsmeɪt] n camarade m/f de classe

classroom ['klɑːsrum] n (salle f de) classe f; **classroom assistant** n assistant(-e) d'éducation

classy ['klɑːsɪ] (inf) adj classe (inf)

clatter ['klætər] n cliquetis m ▷ vi cliqueter

clause [klɔːz] n clause f; (Ling) proposition f

claustrophobic [klɔːstrə'fəubɪk] adj (person) claustrophobe; (place) où l'on se sent claustrophobe

claw [klɔː] n griffe f; (of bird of prey) serre f; (of lobster) pince f

clay [kleɪ] n argile f

clean [kliːn] adj propre; (clear, smooth) net(te); (record, reputation) sans tache; (joke, story) correct(e) ▷ vt nettoyer; **clean up** vt nettoyer; (fig) remettre de l'ordre dans; **cleaner** n (person) nettoyeur(-euse), femme f de ménage; (product) détachant m; **cleaner's** n (also: **dry cleaner's**) teinturier m; **cleaning** n nettoyage m

cleanser ['klɛnzər] n (for face) démaquillant m

clear [klɪər] adj clair(e); (glass, plastic) transparent(e); (road, way) libre, dégagé(e); (profit, majority) net(te); (conscience) tranquille; (skin) frais (fraîche); (sky) dégagé(e) ▷ vt (road) dégager, déblayer; (table) débarrasser; (room etc: of people) faire évacuer; (cheque) compenser; (Law: suspect) innocenter; (obstacle) franchir or sauter sans heurter ▷ vi (weather) s'éclaircir; (fog) se dissiper ▷ adv: **~ of** à distance de, à l'écart de; **to ~ the table** débarrasser la table, desservir; **clear away** vt (things, clothes etc) enlever, retirer; **to ~ away the dishes** débarrasser la table; **clear up** vt ranger, mettre en ordre; (mystery) éclaircir, résoudre; **clearance** n (removal) déblayage m; (permission) autorisation f; **clear-cut** adj précis(e), nettement défini(e); **clearing** n (in forest) clairière f; **clearly** adv clairement; (obviously) de toute évidence; **clearway** n (BRIT) route f à stationnement interdit

clench [klɛntʃ] vt serrer

clergy ['klə:dʒɪ] n clergé m

clerk [klɑːk, US klə:rk] n (BRIT) employé(e) de bureau; (US: salesman/woman) vendeur(-euse)

clever ['klɛvər] adj (intelligent) intelligent(e); (skilful) habile, adroit(e); (device, arrangement) ingénieux(-euse), astucieux(-euse)

cliché ['kli:ʃeɪ] *n* cliché *m*

click [klɪk] *vi* (*Comput*) cliquer ▷ *vt*: **to ~ one's tongue** faire claquer sa langue; **to ~ one's heels** claquer des talons; **to ~ on an icon** cliquer sur une icône

client ['klaɪənt] *n* client(e)

cliff [klɪf] *n* falaise *f*

climate ['klaɪmɪt] *n* climat *m*; **climate change** *n* changement *m* climatique

climax ['klaɪmæks] *n* apogée *m*, point culminant; (*sexual*) orgasme *m*

climb [klaɪm] *vi* grimper, monter; (*plane*) prendre de l'altitude ▷ *vt* (*stairs*) monter; (*mountain*) escalader; (*tree*) grimper à ▷ *n* montée *f*, escalade *f*; **to ~ over a wall** passer par dessus un mur; **climb down** *vi* (re)descendre; (*BRIT fig*) rabattre de ses prétentions; **climber** *n* (*also*: **rock climber**) grimpeur(-euse), varappeur(-euse); (*plant*) plante grimpante; **climbing** *n* (*also*: **rock climbing**) escalade *f*, varappe *f*

clinch [klɪntʃ] *vt* (*deal*) conclure, sceller

cling (*pt, pp* **clung**) [klɪŋ, klʌŋ] *vi*: **to ~ (to)** se cramponner (à), s'accrocher (à); (*clothes*) coller (à)

Clingfilm® ['klɪŋfɪlm] *n* film *m* alimentaire

clinic ['klɪnɪk] *n* clinique *f*; centre médical

clip [klɪp] *n* (*for hair*) barrette *f*; (*also*: **paper ~**) trombone *m*; (*TV, Cinema*) clip *m* ▷ *vt* (*also*: **~ together**: *papers*) attacher; (*hair, nails*) couper; (*hedge*) tailler; **clipping** *n* (*from newspaper*) coupure *f* de journal

cloak [kləʊk] *n* grande cape ▷ *vt* (*fig*) masquer, cacher; **cloakroom** *n* (*for coats etc*) vestiaire *m*; (*BRIT: W.C.*) toilettes *fpl*

clock [klɔk] *n* (*large*) horloge *f*; (*small*) pendule *f*; **clock in** *or* **on** (*BRIT*) *vi* (*with card*) pointer (en arrivant); (*start work*) commencer à travailler; **clock off** *or* **out** (*BRIT*) *vi* (*with card*) pointer (en partant); (*leave work*) quitter le travail; **clockwise** *adv* dans le sens des aiguilles d'une montre; **clockwork** *n* rouages *mpl*, mécanisme *m*; (*of clock*) mouvement *m* (d'horlogerie) ▷ *adj* (*toy, train*) mécanique

clog [klɔg] *n* sabot *m* ▷ *vt* boucher, encrasser ▷ *vi* (*also*: **~ up**) se boucher, s'encrasser

clone [kləʊn] *n* clone *m* ▷ *vt* cloner

close¹ [kləʊs] *adj* (*near*): **~ (to)** près (de), proche (de); (*contact, link, watch*) étroit(e); (*examination*) attentif(-ive), minutieux(-euse); (*contest*) très serré(e); (*weather*) lourd(e), étouffant(e) ▷ *adv* près, à proximité; **~ to** *prep* près de; **~ by, ~ at hand** *adj, adv* tout(e) près; **a ~ friend** un ami intime; **to have a ~ shave** (*fig*) l'échapper belle

close² [kləʊz] *vt* fermer ▷ *vi* (*shop etc*) fermer; (*lid, door etc*) se fermer; (*end*) se terminer, se conclure ▷ *n* (*end*) conclusion *f*; **what time**

do you ~? à quelle heure fermez-vous?; **close down** *vi* fermer (*définitivement*); **closed** *adj* (*shop etc*) fermé(e)

closely ['kləʊslɪ] *adv* (*examine, watch*) de près

closet ['klɔzɪt] *n* (*cupboard*) placard *m*, réduit *m*

close-up ['kləʊsʌp] *n* gros plan

closing time *n* heure *f* de fermeture

closure ['kləʊʒə*] *n* fermeture *f*

clot [klɔt] *n* (*of blood, milk*) caillot *m*; (*inf: person*) ballot *m* ▷ *vi* (*: external bleeding*) se coaguler

cloth [klɔθ] *n* (*material*) tissu *m*, étoffe *f*; (*BRIT*: *also*: **tea ~**) torchon *m*; lavette *f*; (*also*: **table~**) nappe *f*

clothes [kləʊðz] *npl* vêtements *mpl*, habits *mpl*; **clothes line** *n* corde *f* (à linge); **clothes peg** (*US* **clothes pin**) *n* pince *f* à linge

clothing ['kləʊðɪŋ] *n* = **clothes**

cloud [klaʊd] *n* nuage *m*; **cloud over** *vi* se couvrir; (*fig*) s'assombrir; **cloudy** *adj* nuageux(-euse), couvert(e); (*liquid*) trouble

clove [kləʊv] *n* clou *m* de girofle; **a ~ of garlic** une gousse d'ail

clown [klaʊn] *n* clown *m* ▷ *vi* (*also*: **~ about**, **~ around**) faire le clown

club [klʌb] *n* (*society*) club *m*; (*weapon*) massue *f*, matraque *f*; (*also*: **golf ~**) club ▷ *vt* matraquer ▷ *vi*: **to ~ together** s'associer; **clubs** *npl* (*Cards*) trèfle *m*; **club class** *n* (*Aviat*) classe *f* club

clue [klu:] *n* indice *m*; (*in crosswords*) définition *f*; **I haven't a ~** je n'en ai pas la moindre idée

clump [klʌmp] *n*: **~ of trees** bouquet *m* d'arbres

clumsy ['klʌmzɪ] *adj* (*person*) gauche, maladroit(e); (*object*) malcommode, peu maniable

clung [klʌŋ] *pt, pp of* **cling**

cluster ['klʌstə*] *n* (*petit*) groupe; (*of flowers*) grappe *f* ▷ *vi* se rassembler

clutch [klʌtʃ] *n* (*Aut*) embrayage *m*; (*grasp*): **~es** étreinte *f*, prise *f* ▷ *vt* (*grasp*) agripper; (*hold tightly*) serrer fort; (*hold on to*) se cramponner à

cm *abbr* (= *centimetre*) cm

Co. *abbr* = **company, county**

c/o *abbr* (= *care of*) c/o, aux bons soins de

coach [kəʊtʃ] *n* (*bus*) autocar *m*; (*horse-drawn*) diligence *f*; (*of train*) voiture *f*, wagon *m*; (*Sport: trainer*) entraîneur(-euse); (*school*: *tutor*) répétiteur(-trice) ▷ *vt* (*Sport*) entraîner; (*student*) donner des leçons particulières à; **coach station** (*BRIT*) *n* gare routière; **coach trip** *n* excursion *f* en car

coal [kəʊl] *n* charbon *m*

coalition [kəʊə'lɪʃən] *n* coalition *f*

coarse [kɔ:s] *adj* grossier(-ère), rude; (*vulgar*) vulgaire

coast [kəʊst] *n* côte *f* ▷ *vi* (*car, cycle*) descendre en roue libre; **coastal** *adj* côtier(-ère); **coastguard** *n* garde-côte *m*; **coastline** *n* côte *f*, littoral *m*

coat [kəut] n manteau m; (of animal) pelage m, poil m; (of paint) couche f ▷ vt couvrir, enduire; **coat hanger** n cintre m; **coating** n couche f, enduit m

coax [kəuks] vt persuader par des cajoleries

cob [kɔb] n see **corn**

cobbled ['kɔbld] adj pavé(e)

cobweb ['kɔbwɛb] n toile f d'araignée

cocaine [kə'keɪn] n cocaïne f

cock [kɔk] n (rooster) coq m; (male bird) mâle m ▷ vt (gun) armer; **cockerel** n jeune coq m

cockney ['kɔkni] n cockney m/f (habitant des quartiers populaires de l'East End de Londres), ≈ faubourien(ne)

cockpit ['kɔkpɪt] n (in aircraft) poste m de pilotage, cockpit m

cockroach ['kɔkrəutʃ] n cafard m, cancrelat m

cocktail ['kɔkteɪl] n cocktail m

cocoa ['kəukəu] n cacao m

coconut ['kəukənʌt] n noix f de coco

C.O.D. abbr = **cash on delivery**

cod [kɔd] n morue fraîche, cabillaud m

code [kəud] n code m; (Tel: area code) indicatif m

coeducational ['kəuɛdju'keɪʃənl] adj mixte

coffee ['kɔfɪ] n café m; **coffee bar** n (BRIT) café m; **coffee bean** n grain m de café; **coffee break** n pause-café f; **coffee maker** n cafetière f; **coffeepot** n cafetière f; **coffee shop** n café m; **coffee table** n (petite) table basse

coffin ['kɔfɪn] n cercueil m

cog [kɔg] n (wheel) roue dentée; (tooth) dent f (d'engrenage)

cognac ['kɔnjæk] n cognac m

coherent [kəu'hɪərənt] adj cohérent(e)

coil [kɔɪl] n rouleau m, bobine f; (contraceptive) stérilet m ▷ vt enrouler

coin [kɔɪn] n pièce f (de monnaie) ▷ vt (word) inventer

coincide [kəuɪn'saɪd] vi coïncider; **coincidence** [kəu'ɪnsɪdəns] n coïncidence f

Coke® [kəuk] n coca m

coke [kəuk] n (coal) coke m

colander ['kɔləndər] n passoire f (à légumes)

cold [kəuld] adj froid(e) ▷ n froid m; (Med) rhume m; **it's ~** il fait froid; **to be ~** (person) avoir froid; **to catch a ~** s'enrhumer, attraper un rhume; **in ~ blood** de sang-froid; **cold cuts** (us) npl viandes froides; **cold sore** n bouton m de fièvre

coleslaw ['kəulslɔ:] n sorte de salade de chou cru

colic ['kɔlɪk] n colique(s) f(pl)

collaborate [kə'læbəreɪt] vi collaborer

collapse [kə'læps] vi s'effondrer, s'écrouler; (Med) avoir un malaise ▷ n effondrement m, écroulement m; (of government) chute f

collar ['kɔlər] n (of coat, shirt) col m; (for dog) collier m; **collarbone** n clavicule f

colleague ['kɔli:g] n collègue m/f

collect [kə'lɛkt] vt rassembler; (pick up) ramasser; (as a hobby) collectionner; (BRIT: call for) (passer) prendre; (mail) faire la levée de, ramasser; (money owed) encaisser; (donations, subscriptions) recueillir ▷ vi (people) se rassembler; (dust, dirt) s'amasser; **to call ~** (us Tel) téléphoner en PCV; **collection** [kə'lɛkʃən] n collection f; (of mail) levée f; (for money) collecte f, quête f; **collective** [kə'lɛktɪv] adj collectif(-ive); **collector** n collectionneur m

college ['kɔlɪdʒ] n collège m; (of technology, agriculture etc) institut m

collide [kə'laɪd] vi: **to ~ (with)** entrer en collision (avec)

collision [kə'lɪʒən] n collision f, heurt m

cologne [kə'ləun] n (also: **eau de ~**) eau f de cologne

colon ['kəulən] n (sign) deux-points mpl; (Med) côlon m

colonel ['kə:nl] n colonel m

colonial [kə'ləunɪəl] adj colonial(e)

colony ['kɔləni] n colonie f

colour etc (us **color** etc) ['kʌlər] n couleur f ▷ vt colorer; (dye) teindre; (paint) peindre; (with crayons) colorier; (news) fausser, exagérer ▷ vi (blush) rougir; **I'd like a different ~** je le voudrais dans un autre coloris; **colour in** vt colorier; **colour-blind** adj daltonien(ne); **coloured** adj coloré(e); (photo) en couleur; **colour film** n (for camera) pellicule f (en) couleur; **colourful** adj coloré(e), vif (vive); (personality) pittoresque, haut(e) en couleurs; **colouring** n colorant m; (complexion) teint m; **colour television** n télévision f (en) couleur

column ['kɔləm] n colonne f; (fashion column, sports column etc) rubrique f

coma ['kəumə] n coma m

comb [kəum] n peigne m ▷ vt (hair) peigner; (area) ratisser, passer au peigne fin

combat ['kɔmbæt] n combat m ▷ vt combattre, lutter contre

combination [kɔmbɪ'neɪʃən] n (gen) combinaison f

combine vb [kəm'baɪn] ▷ vt combiner ▷ vi s'associer; (Chem) se combiner ▷ n ['kɔmbaɪn] (Econ) trust m; **to ~ sth with sth** (one quality with another) joindre ou allier qch à qch

come (pt **came**, pp **~**) [kʌm, keɪm] vi
1 (movement towards) venir; **to ~ running** arriver en courant; **he's ~ here to work** il est venu ici pour travailler; **~ with me** suivez-moi
2 (arrive) arriver; **to ~ home** rentrer (chez soi ou à la maison); **we've just ~ from Paris** nous arrivons de Paris
3 (reach): **to ~ to** (decision etc) parvenir à, arriver à; **the bill came to £40** la note s'est élevée à 40 livres
4 (occur): **an idea came to me** il m'est venu

une idée

5 (*be, become*): **to ~ loose/undone** se défaire/desserrer; **I've ~ to like him** j'ai fini par bien l'aimer; **come across** *vt fus* rencontrer par hasard, tomber sur; **come along** *vi* (BRIT: *pupil, work*) faire des progrès, avancer; **come back** *vi* revenir; **come down** *vi* descendre; (*prices*) baisser; (*buildings*) s'écrouler; (: *be demolished*) être démoli(e); **come from** *vt fus* (*source*) venir de; (*place*) venir de, être originaire de; **come in** *vi* entrer; (*train*) arriver; (*fashion*) entrer en vogue; (*on deal etc*) participer; **come off** *vi* (*button*) se détacher; (*attempt*) réussir; **come on** *vi* (*lights, electricity*) s'allumer; (*central heating*) se mettre en marche; (*pupil, work, project*) faire des progrès, avancer; **~ on!** viens!; allons!, allez!; **come out** *vi* sortir; (*sun*) se montrer; (*book*) paraître; (*stain*) s'enlever; (*strike*) cesser le travail, se mettre en grève; **come round** *vi* (*after faint, operation*) revenir à soi, reprendre connaissance; **come to** *vi* revenir à soi; **come up** *vi* monter; (*sun*) se lever; (*problem*) se poser; (*event*) survenir; (*in conversation*) être soulevé; **come up with** *vt fus* (*money*) fournir; **he came up with an idea** il a eu une idée, il a proposé quelque chose

comeback ['kʌmbæk] *n* (*Theat etc*) rentrée *f*

comedian [kə'miːdɪən] *n* (*comic*) comique *m*; (*Theat*) comédien *m*

comedy ['kɒmɪdɪ] *n* comédie *f*; (*humour*) comique *m*

comet ['kɒmɪt] *n* comète *f*

comfort ['kʌmfət] *n* confort *m*, bien-être *m*; (*solace*) consolation *f*, réconfort *m* ▷ *vt* consoler, réconforter; **comfortable** *adj* confortable; (*person*) à l'aise; (*financially*) aisé(e); (*patient*) dont l'état est stationnaire; **comfort station** *n* (*US*) toilettes *fpl*

comic ['kɒmɪk] *adj* (*also*: **~al**) comique ▷ *n* (*person*) comique *m*; (BRIT: *magazine: for children*) magazine *m* de bandes dessinées *or* de BD; (: *for adults*) illustré *m*; **comic book** (*US*) *n* (*for children*) magazine *m* de bandes dessinées *or* de BD; (*for adults*) illustré *m*; **comic strip** *n* bande dessinée

comma ['kɒmə] *n* virgule *f*

command [kə'mɑːnd] *n* ordre *m*, commandement *m*; (*Mil: authority*) commandement; (*mastery*) maîtrise *f* ▷ *vt* (*troops*) commander; **to ~ sb to do** donner l'ordre *or* commander à qn de faire; **commander** *n* (*Mil*) commandant *m*

commemorate [kə'mɛməreɪt] *vt* commémorer

commence [kə'mɛns] *vt, vi* commencer; **commencement** (*US*) *n* (*University*) remise *f* des diplômes

commend [kə'mɛnd] *vt* louer; (*recommend*) recommander

comment ['kɒmɛnt] *n* commentaire *m* ▷ *vi*: **to ~ on** faire des remarques sur; **"no ~"** je n'ai rien à déclarer"; **commentary** ['kɒmən ntərɪ] *n* commentaire *m*; (*Sport*) reportage *m* (en direct); **commentator** ['kɒmənteɪtəʳ] *n* commentateur *m*; (*Sport*) reporter *m*

commerce ['kɒmɜːs] *n* commerce *m*

commercial [kə'mɜːʃəl] *adj* commercial(e) ▷ *n* (*Radio, TV*) annonce *f* publicitaire, spot *m* (publicitaire); **commercial break** *n* (*Radio, TV*) spot *m* (publicitaire)

commission [kə'mɪʃən] *n* (*committee, fee*) commission *f* ▷ *vt* (*work of art*) commander, charger un artiste de l'exécution de; **out of ~** (*machine*) hors service; **commissioner** *n* (*Police*) préfet *m* (de police)

commit [kə'mɪt] *vt* (*act*) commettre; (*resources*) consacrer; (*to sb's care*) confier (à); **to ~ o.s. (to do)** s'engager (à faire); **to ~ suicide** se suicider; **commitment** *n* engagement *m*; (*obligation*) responsabilité(s) (*fpl*)

committee [kə'mɪtɪ] *n* comité *m*; commission *f*

commodity [kə'mɒdɪtɪ] *n* produit *m*, marchandise *f*, article *m*

common ['kɒmən] *adj* (*gen*) commun(e); (*usual*) courant(e) ▷ *n* terrain communal; **commonly** *adv* communément, généralement; couramment; **commonplace** *adj* banal(e), ordinaire; **Commons** *npl* (BRIT *Pol*): **the (House of) Commons** la chambre des Communes; **common sense** *n* bon sens; **Commonwealth** *n*: **the Commonwealth** le Commonwealth

communal ['kɒmjuːnl] *adj* (*life*) communautaire; (*for common use*) commun(e)

commune *n* ['kɒmjuːn] (*group*) communauté *f* ▷ *vi* [kə'mjuːn]: **to ~ with** (*nature*) communier avec

communicate [kə'mjuːnɪkeɪt] *vt* communiquer, transmettre ▷ *vi*: **to ~ (with)** communiquer (avec)

communication [kəmjuːnɪ'keɪʃən] *n* communication *f*

communion [kə'mjuːnɪən] *n* (*also*: **Holy C~**) communion *f*

communism ['kɒmjunɪzəm] *n* communisme *m*; **communist** *adj, n* communiste *m/f*

community [kə'mjuːnɪtɪ] *n* communauté *f*; **community centre** (*US* **community center**) *n* foyer socio-éducatif, centre *m* de loisirs; **community service** *n* ≈ travail *m* d'intérêt général, TIG *m*

commute [kə'mjuːt] *vi* faire le trajet journalier (*de son domicile à un lieu de travail assez éloigné*) ▷ *vt* (*Law*) commuer; **commuter** *n* banlieusard(e) (*qui fait un trajet journalier pour se rendre à son travail*)

compact adj [kəm'pækt] compact(e) ▷ n ['kɔmpækt] (also: **powder ~**) poudrier m; **compact disc** n disque compact; **compact disc player** n lecteur m de disques compacts

companion [kəm'pænjən] n compagnon (compagne)

company ['kʌmpənɪ] n compagnie f; **to keep sb ~** tenir compagnie à qn; **company car** n voiture f de fonction; **company director** n administrateur(-trice)

comparable ['kɔmpərəbl] adj comparable

comparative [kəm'pærətɪv] adj (study) comparatif(-ive); (relative) relatif(-ive); **comparatively** adv (relatively) relativement

compare [kəm'pɛəʳ] vt: **to ~ sth/sb with** or **to** comparer qch/qn avec or à ▷ vi: **to ~ (with)** se comparer (à); être comparable (à); **comparison** [kəm'pærɪsn] n comparaison f

compartment [kəm'pɑːtmənt] n (also Rail) compartiment m; **a non-smoking ~** un compartiment non-fumeurs

compass ['kʌmpəs] n boussole f; **compasses** npl (Math) compas m

compassion [kəm'pæʃən] n compassion f, humanité f

compatible [kəm'pætɪbl] adj compatible

compel [kəm'pɛl] vt contraindre, obliger; **compelling** adj (fig: argument) irrésistible

compensate ['kɔmpənseɪt] vt indemniser, dédommager ▷ vi: **to ~ for** compenser; **compensation** [kɔmpən'seɪʃən] n compensation f; (money) dédommagement m, indemnité f

compete [kəm'piːt] vi (take part) concourir; (vie): **to ~ (with)** rivaliser (avec), faire concurrence (à)

competent ['kɔmpɪtənt] adj compétent(e), capable

competition [kɔmpɪ'tɪʃən] n (contest) compétition f, concours m; (Econ) concurrence f

competitive [kəm'pɛtɪtɪv] adj (Econ) concurrentiel(le); (sports) de compétition; (person) qui a l'esprit de compétition

competitor [kəm'pɛtɪtəʳ] n concurrent(e)

complacent [kəm'pleɪsnt] adj (trop) content(e) de soi

complain [kəm'pleɪn] vi: **to ~ (about)** se plaindre (de); (in shop etc) réclamer (au sujet de); **complaint** n plainte f; (in shop etc) réclamation f; (Med) affection f

complement n ['kɔmplɪmənt] n complément m; (esp of ship's crew etc) effectif complet ▷ vt (enhance) compléter; **complementary** [kɔmplɪ'mɛntərɪ] adj complémentaire

complete [kəm'pliːt] adj complet(-ète); (finished) achevé(e) ▷ vt achever, parachever; (set, group) compléter; (a form) remplir; **completely** adv complètement; **completion**

[kəm'pliːʃən] n achèvement m; (of contract) exécution f

complex ['kɔmplɛks] adj complexe ▷ n (Psych, buildings etc) complexe m

complexion [kəm'plɛkʃən] n (of face) teint m

compliance [kəm'plaɪəns] n (submission) docilité f; (agreement): **~ with** le fait de se conformer à; **in ~ with** en conformité avec, conformément à

complicate ['kɔmplɪkeɪt] vt compliquer; **complicated** adj compliqué(e); **complication** [kɔmplɪ'keɪʃən] n complication f

compliment n ['kɔmplɪmənt] compliment m ▷ vt ['kɔmplɪmɛnt] complimenter; **complimentary** [kɔmplɪ'mɛntərɪ] adj flatteur(-euse); (free) à titre gracieux

comply [kəm'plaɪ] vi: **to ~ with** se soumettre à, se conformer à

component [kəm'pəunənt] adj composant(e), constituant(e) ▷ n composant m, élément m

compose [kəm'pəuz] vt composer; (form): **to be ~d of** se composer de; **to ~ o.s.** se calmer, se maîtriser; **composer** n (Mus) compositeur m; **composition** [kɔmpə'zɪʃən] n composition f

composure [kəm'pəuʒəʳ] n calme m, maîtrise f de soi

compound ['kɔmpaund] n (Chem, Ling) composé m; (enclosure) enclos m, enceinte f ▷ adj composé(e); (fracture) compliqué(e)

comprehension [kɔmprɪ'hɛnʃən] n compréhension f

comprehensive [kɔmprɪ'hɛnsɪv] adj (très) complet(-ète); **~ policy** (Insurance) assurance f tous risques; **comprehensive (school)** n (BRIT) école secondaire non sélective avec libre circulation d'une section à l'autre, ≈ CES m

> Be careful not to translate *comprehensive* by the French word *compréhensif*.

compress vt [kəm'prɛs] comprimer; (text, information) condenser ▷ n ['kɔmprɛs] (Med) compresse f

comprise [kəm'praɪz] vt (also: **be ~d of**) comprendre; (constitute) constituer, représenter

compromise ['kɔmprəmaɪz] n compromis m ▷ vt compromettre ▷ vi transiger, accepter un compromis

compulsive [kəm'pʌlsɪv] adj (Psych) compulsif(-ive); (book, film etc) captivant(e)

compulsory [kəm'pʌlsərɪ] adj obligatoire

computer [kəm'pjuːtəʳ] n ordinateur m; **computer game** n jeu m vidéo; **computer-generated** adj de synthèse; **computerize** vt (data) traiter par ordinateur; (system, office) informatiser; **computer programmer**

n programmeur(-euse); **computer programming** *n* programmation *f*; **computer science** *n* informatique *f*; **computer studies** *npl* informatique *f*; **computing** [kəm'pju:tɪŋ] *n* informatique *f*
con [kɔn] *vt* duper; (*cheat*) escroquer ▷ *n* escroquerie *f*
conceal [kən'si:l] *vt* cacher, dissimuler
concede [kən'si:d] *vt* concéder ▷ *vi* céder
conceited [kən'si:tɪd] *adj* vaniteux(-euse), suffisant(e)
conceive [kən'si:v] *vt*, *vi* concevoir
concentrate ['kɔnsəntreɪt] *vi* se concentrer ▷ *vt* concentrer
concentration [kɔnsən'treɪʃən] *n* concentration *f*
concept ['kɔnsɛpt] *n* concept *m*
concern [kən'sə:n] *n* affaire *f*; (*Comm*) entreprise *f*, firme *f*; (*anxiety*) inquiétude *f*, souci *m* ▷ *vt* (*worry*) inquiéter; (*involve*) concerner; (*relate to*) se rapporter à; **to be ~ed (about)** s'inquiéter (de), être inquiet(-ète) (au sujet de); **concerning** *prep* en ce qui concerne, à propos de
concert ['kɔnsət] *n* concert *m*; **concert hall** *n* salle *f* de concert
concerto [kən'tʃə:təu] *n* concerto *m*
concession [kən'sɛʃən] *n* (*compromise*) concession *f*; (*reduced price*) réduction *f*; **tax ~** dégrèvement fiscal; **"~s"** tarif réduit
concise [kən'saɪs] *adj* concis(e)
conclude [kən'klu:d] *vt* conclure; **conclusion** [kən'klu:ʒən] *n* conclusion *f*
concrete ['kɔŋkri:t] *n* béton *m* ▷ *adj* concret(-ète); (*Constr*) en béton
concussion [kən'kʌʃən] *n* (*Med*) commotion (cérébrale)
condemn [kən'dɛm] *vt* condamner
condensation [kɔndɛn'seɪʃən] *n* condensation *f*
condense [kən'dɛns] *vi* se condenser ▷ *vt* condenser
condition [kən'dɪʃən] *n* condition *f*; (*disease*) maladie *f* ▷ *vt* déterminer, conditionner; **on ~ that** à condition que + *sub*, à condition de; **conditional** [kən'dɪʃənl] *adj* conditionnel(le); **conditioner** *n* (*for hair*) baume démêlant; (*for fabrics*) assouplissant *m*
condo ['kɔndəu] *n* (*us inf*) = **condominium**
condom ['kɔndəm] *n* préservatif *m*
condominium [kɔndə'mɪnɪəm] *n* (*us: building*) immeuble *m* (en copropriété); (*: rooms*) appartement *m* (dans un immeuble en copropriété)
condone [kən'dəun] *vt* fermer les yeux sur, approuver (tacitement)
conduct *n* ['kɔndʌkt] conduite *f* ▷ *vt* [kə n'dʌkt] conduire; (*manage*) mener, diriger; (*Mus*) diriger; **to ~ o.s.** se conduire, se

comporter; **conducted tour** (*BRIT*) *n* voyage organisé; (*of building*) visite guidée; **conductor** *n* (*of orchestra*) chef *m* d'orchestre; (*on bus*) receveur *m*; (*us: on train*) chef *m* de train; (*Elec*) conducteur *m*
cone [kəun] *n* cône *m*; (*for ice-cream*) cornet *m*; (*Bot*) pomme *f* de pin, cône
confectionery [kən'fɛkʃənrɪ] *n* (*sweets*) confiserie *f*
confer [kən'fə:ʳ] *vt*: **to ~ sth on** conférer qch à ▷ *vi* conférer, s'entretenir
conference ['kɔnfərns] *n* conférence *f*
confess [kən'fɛs] *vt* confesser, avouer ▷ *vi* (*admit sth*) avouer; (*Rel*) se confesser; **confession** [kən'fɛʃən] *n* confession *f*
confide [kən'faɪd] *vi*: **to ~ in** s'ouvrir à, se confier à
confidence ['kɔnfɪdns] *n* confiance *f*; (*also*: **self-~**) assurance *f*, confiance en soi; (*secret*) confidence *f*; **in ~** (*speak, write*) en confidence, confidentiellement; **confident** *adj* (*self-assured*) sûr(e) de soi; (*sure*) sûr; **confidential** [kɔnfɪ'dɛnʃəl] *adj* confidentiel(le)
confine [kən'faɪn] *vt* limiter, borner; (*shut up*) confiner, enfermer; **confined** *adj* (*space*) restreint(e), réduit(e)
confirm [kən'fə:m] *vt* (*report, Rel*) confirmer; (*appointment*) ratifier; **confirmation** [kɔnfə'meɪʃən] *n* confirmation *f*; ratification *f*
confiscate ['kɔnfɪskeɪt] *vt* confisquer
conflict *n* ['kɔnflɪkt] conflit *m*, lutte *f* ▷ *vi* [kə n'flɪkt] (*opinions*) s'opposer, se heurter
conform [kən'fɔ:m] *vi*: **to ~ (to)** se conformer (à)
confront [kən'frʌnt] *vt* (*two people*) confronter; (*enemy, danger*) affronter, faire face à; (*problem*) faire face à; **confrontation** [kɔnfrən'teɪʃən] *n* confrontation *f*
confuse [kən'fju:z] *vt* (*person*) troubler; (*situation*) embrouiller; (*one thing with another*) confondre; **confused** *adj* (*person*) dérouté(e), désorienté(e); (*situation*) embrouillé(e); **confusing** *adj* peu clair(e), déroutant(e); **confusion** [kən'fju:ʒən] *n* confusion *f*
congestion [kən'dʒɛstʃən] *n* (*Med*) congestion *f*; (*fig: traffic*) encombrement *m*
congratulate [kən'grætjuleɪt] *vt*: **to ~ sb (on)** féliciter qn (de); **congratulations** [kə ngrætju'leɪʃənz] *npl*: **congratulations (on)** félicitations *fpl* (pour) ▷ *excl*: **congratulations!** (toutes mes) félicitations!
congregation [kɔŋgrɪ'geɪʃən] *n* assemblée *f* (des fidèles)
congress ['kɔŋgrɛs] *n* congrès *m*; (*Pol*): **C~** Congrès *m*; **congressman** *n* membre *m* du Congrès; **congresswoman** *n* membre *m* du Congrès
conifer ['kɔnɪfəʳ] *n* conifère *m*
conjugate ['kɔndʒugeɪt] *vt* conjuguer

conjugation [kɔndʒə'geɪʃən] *n* conjugaison *f*

conjunction [kən'dʒʌŋkʃən] *n* conjonction *f*; **in ~ with** (conjointement) avec

conjure ['kʌndʒəʳ] *vi* faire des tours de passe-passe

connect [kə'nɛkt] *vt* joindre, relier; (*Elec*) connecter; (*Tel: caller*) mettre en connexion; (: *subscriber*) brancher; (*fig*) établir un rapport entre, faire un rapprochement entre ▷ *vi* (*train*): **to ~ with** assurer la correspondance avec; **to be ~ed with** avoir un rapport avec; (*have dealings with*) avoir des rapports avec, être en relation avec; **connecting flight** *n* (vol *m* de) correspondance *f*; **connection** [kə'nɛkʃən] *n* relation *f*, lien *m*; (*Elec*) connexion *f*; (*Tel*) communication *f*; (*train etc*) correspondance *f*

conquer ['kɔŋkəʳ] *vt* conquérir; (*feelings*) vaincre, surmonter

conquest ['kɔŋkwɛst] *n* conquête *f*

cons [kɔnz] *npl see* **convenience**; **pro**

conscience ['kɔnʃəns] *n* conscience *f*

conscientious [kɔnʃɪ'ɛnʃəs] *adj* consciencieux(-euse)

conscious ['kɔnʃəs] *adj* conscient(e); (*deliberate: insult, error*) délibéré(e); **consciousness** *n* conscience *f*; (*Med*) connaissance *f*

consecutive [kən'sɛkjutɪv] *adj* consécutif(-ive); **on three ~ occasions** trois fois de suite

consensus [kən'sɛnsəs] *n* consensus *m*

consent [kən'sɛnt] *n* consentement *m* ▷ *vi*: **to ~ (to)** consentir (à)

consequence ['kɔnsɪkwəns] *n* suites *fpl*, conséquence *f*; (*significance*) importance *f*

consequently ['kɔnsɪkwəntlɪ] *adv* par conséquent, donc

conservation [kɔnsə'veɪʃən] *n* préservation *f*, protection *f*; (*also*: **nature ~**) défense *f* de l'environnement

conservative [kən'sə:vətɪv] *adj* conservateur(-trice); (*cautious*) prudent(e); **Conservative** *adj*, *n* (*BRIT Pol*) conservateur(-trice)

conservatory [kən'sə:vətrɪ] *n* (*room*) jardin *m* d'hiver; (*Mus*) conservatoire *m*

consider [kən'sɪdəʳ] *vt* (*study*) considérer, réfléchir à; (*take into account*) penser à, prendre en considération; (*regard, judge*) considérer, estimer; **to ~ doing sth** envisager de faire qch; **considerable** *adj* considérable; **considerably** *adv* nettement; **considerate** *adj* prévenant(e), plein(e) d'égards; **consideration** [kənsɪdə'reɪʃən] *n* considération *f*; (*reward*) rétribution *f*, rémunération *f*; **considering** *prep*: **considering (that)** étant donné (que)

consignment [kən'saɪnmənt] *n* arrivage *m*, envoi *m*

consist [kən'sɪst] *vi*: **to ~ of** consister en, se composer de

consistency [kən'sɪstənsɪ] *n* (*thickness*) consistance *f*; (*fig*) cohérence *f*

consistent [kən'sɪstənt] *adj* logique, cohérent(e)

consolation [kɔnsə'leɪʃən] *n* consolation *f*

console¹ [kən'səul] *vt* consoler

console² ['kɔnsəul] *n* console *f*

consonant ['kɔnsənənt] *n* consonne *f*

conspicuous [kən'spɪkjuəs] *adj* voyant(e), qui attire l'attention

conspiracy [kən'spɪrəsɪ] *n* conspiration *f*, complot *m*

constable ['kʌnstəbl] *n* (*BRIT*) ≈ agent *m* de police, gendarme *m*; **chief ~** ≈ préfet *m* de police

constant ['kɔnstənt] *adj* constant(e); incessant(e); **constantly** *adv* constamment, sans cesse

constipated ['kɔnstɪpeɪtɪd] *adj* constipé(e); **constipation** [kɔnstɪ'peɪʃən] *n* constipation *f*

constituency [kən'stɪtjuənsɪ] *n* (*Pol: area*) circonscription électorale; (: *electors*) électorat *m*

constitute ['kɔnstɪtjuːt] *vt* constituer

constitution [kɔnstɪ'tjuːʃən] *n* constitution *f*

constraint [kən'streɪnt] *n* contrainte *f*

construct [kən'strʌkt] *vt* construire; **construction** [kən'strʌkʃən] *n* construction *f*; **constructive** *adj* constructif(-ive)

consul ['kɔnsl] *n* consul *m*; **consulate** ['kɔnsjulɪt] *n* consulat *m*

consult [kən'sʌlt] *vt* consulter; **consultant** *n* (*Med*) médecin consultant; (*other specialist*) consultant *m*, (*expert-)conseil *m*; **consultation** [kɔnsəl'teɪʃən] *n* consultation *f*; **consulting room** *n* (*BRIT*) cabinet *m* de consultation

consume [kən'sjuːm] *vt* consommer; (*subj: flames, hatred, desire*) consumer; **consumer** *n* consommateur(-trice)

consumption [kən'sʌmpʃən] *n* consommation *f*

cont. *abbr* (= *continued*) suite

contact ['kɔntækt] *n* contact *m*; (*person*) connaissance *f*, relation *f* ▷ *vt* se mettre en contact *or* en rapport avec; **contact lenses** *npl* verres *mpl* de contact

contagious [kən'teɪdʒəs] *adj* contagieux(-euse)

contain [kən'teɪn] *vt* contenir; **to ~ o.s.** se contenir, se maîtriser; **container** *n* récipient *m*; (*for shipping etc*) conteneur *m*

contaminate [kən'tæmɪneɪt] *vt* contaminer

cont'd *abbr* (= *continued*) suite

contemplate ['kɔntəmpleɪt] *vt* contempler; (*consider*) envisager

contemporary [kən'tɛmpərərɪ] *adj*
contemporain(e); (*design, wallpaper*) moderne
▷ *n* contemporain(e)
contempt [kən'tɛmpt] *n* mépris *m*, dédain
m; **~ of court** (*Law*) outrage *m* à l'autorité de
la justice
contend [kən'tɛnd] *vt*: **to ~ that** soutenir
or prétendre que ▷ *vi*: **to ~ with** (*compete*)
rivaliser avec; (*struggle*) lutter avec
content [kən'tɛnt] *adj* content(e), satisfait(e)
▷ *vt* contenter, satisfaire ▷ *n* ['kɔntɛnt]
contenu *m*; (*of fat, moisture*) teneur *f*; **contents**
npl (*of container etc*) contenu *m*; **(table
of) ~s** table *f* des matières; **contented** *adj*
content(e), satisfait(e)
contest *n* ['kɔntɛst] combat *m*, lutte *f*;
(*competition*) concours *m* ▷ *vt* [kən'tɛst]
contester, discuter; (*compete for*) disputer;
(*Law*) attaquer; **contestant** [kən'tɛstənt] *n*
concurrent(e); (*in fight*) adversaire *m/f*
context ['kɔntɛkst] *n* contexte *m*
continent ['kɔntɪnənt] *n* continent *m*; **the
C~** (*BRIT*) l'Europe continentale; **continental**
[kɔntɪ'nɛntl] *adj* continental(e); **continental
breakfast** *n* café (*or* thé) complet;
continental quilt *n* (*BRIT*) couette *f*
continual [kən'tɪnjuəl] *adj* continuel(le);
continually *adv* continuellement, sans cesse
continue [kən'tɪnjuː] *vi* continuer ▷ *vt*
continuer; (*start again*) reprendre
continuity [kɔntɪ'njuːɪtɪ] *n* continuité *f*; (*TV
etc*) enchaînement *m*
continuous [kən'tɪnjuəs] *adj* continu(e),
permanent(e); (*Ling*) progressif(-ive);
continuous assessment (*BRIT*) *n* contrôle
continu; **continuously** *adv* (*repeatedly*)
continuellement; (*uninterruptedly*) sans
interruption
contour ['kɔntuəʳ] *n* contour *m*, profil *m*; (*also:
~ line*) courbe *f* de niveau
contraception [kɔntrə'sɛpʃən] *n*
contraception *f*
contraceptive [kɔntrə'sɛptɪv] *adj*
contraceptif(-ive), anticonceptionnel(le) ▷ *n*
contraceptif *m*
contract *n* ['kɔntrækt] contrat *m* ▷ *vb* [kə
n'trækt] ▷ *vi* (*become smaller*) se contracter,
se resserrer ▷ *vt* contracter; (*Comm*): **to ~ to
do sth** s'engager (par contrat) à faire qch;
contractor *n* entrepreneur *m*
contradict [kɔntrə'dɪkt] *vt* contredire;
contradiction [kɔntrə'dɪkʃən] *n*
contradiction *f*
contrary¹ ['kɔntrərɪ] *adj* contraire,
opposé(e) ▷ *n* contraire *m*; **on the ~** au
contraire; **unless you hear to the ~** sauf avis
contraire
contrary² [kən'trɛərɪ] *adj* (*perverse*)
contrariant(e), entêté(e)

contrast *n* ['kɔntrɑːst] contraste *m* ▷ *vt* [kə
n'trɑːst] mettre en contraste, contraster; **in ~
to** *or* **with** contrairement à, par
opposition à
contribute [kən'trɪbjuːt] *vi* contribuer ▷ *vt*:
to ~ £10/an article to donner 10 livres/un
article à; **to ~ to** (*gen*) contribuer à; (*newspaper*)
collaborer à; (*discussion*) prendre part à;
contribution [kɔntrɪ'bjuːʃən] *n* contribution
f; (*BRIT: for social security*) cotisation *f*; (*to
publication*) article *m*; **contributor** *n* (*to
newspaper*) collaborateur(-trice); (*of money,
goods*) donateur(-trice)
control [kən'trəul] *vt* (*process, machinery*)
commander; (*temper*) maîtriser; (*disease*)
enrayer ▷ *n* maîtrise *f*; (*power*) autorité *f*;
controls *npl* (*of machine etc*) commandes *fpl*;
(*on radio*) boutons *mpl* de réglage; **to be in ~
of** être maître de, maîtriser; (*in charge of*) être
responsable de; **everything is under ~** j'ai (*or
il a etc*) la situation en main; **the car went out
of ~** j'ai (*or il a etc*) perdu le contrôle du véhicule;
control tower *n* (*Aviat*) tour *f* de contrôle
controversial [kɔntrə'vəːʃl] *adj* discutable,
controversé(e)
controversy ['kɔntrəvəːsɪ] *n* controverse *f*,
polémique *f*
convenience [kən'viːnɪəns] *n* commodité *f*;
at your ~ quand *or* comme cela vous convient;
all modern ~s, **all mod cons** (*BRIT*) avec tout
le confort moderne, tout confort
convenient [kən'viːnɪənt] *adj* commode
convent ['kɔnvənt] *n* couvent *m*
convention [kən'vɛnʃən] *n* convention
f; (*custom*) usage *m*; **conventional** *adj*
conventionnel(le)
conversation [kɔnvə'seɪʃən] *n* conversation *f*
conversely [kɔn'vəːslɪ] *adv* inversement,
réciproquement
conversion [kən'vəːʃən] *n* conversion *f*; (*BRIT:
of house*) transformation *f*, aménagement *m*;
(*Rugby*) transformation *f*
convert *vt* [kən'vəːt] (*Rel, Comm*) convertir;
(*alter*) transformer; (*house*) aménager ▷ *n*
['kɔnvəːt] converti(e); **convertible** *adj*
convertible ▷ *n* (*voiture f*) décapotable *f*
convey [kən'veɪ] *vt* transporter; (*thanks*)
transmettre; (*idea*) communiquer; **conveyor
belt** *n* convoyeur *m* tapis roulant
convict *vt* [kən'vɪkt] déclarer (*or* reconnaître)
coupable ▷ *n* ['kɔnvɪkt] forçat *m*,
convict *m*; **conviction** [kən'vɪkʃən] *n* (*Law*)
condamnation *f*; (*belief*) conviction *f*
convince [kən'vɪns] *vt* convaincre, persuader;
convinced *adj*: **convinced of/that**
convaincu(e) de/que; **convincing** *adj*
persuasif(-ive), convaincant(e)
convoy ['kɔnvɔɪ] *n* convoi *m*
cook [kuk] *vt* (*faire*) cuire ▷ *vi* cuire; (*person*)

faire la cuisine ▷ n cuisinier(-ière); **cookbook** n livre m de cuisine; **cooker** n cuisinière f; **cookery** n cuisine f; **cookery book** n (BRIT) = **cookbook**; **cookie** n (US) biscuit m, petit gâteau sec; **cooking** n cuisine f

cool [kuːl] adj frais (fraîche); (not afraid) calme; (unfriendly) froid(e); (inf: trendy) cool inv (inf); (: great) super inv (inf) ▷ vt, vi rafraîchir, refroidir; **cool down** vi refroidir; (fig: person, situation) se calmer; **cool off** vi (become calmer) se calmer; (lose enthusiasm) perdre son enthousiasme

cop [kɔp] n (inf) flic m

cope [kəup] vi s'en sortir, tenir le coup; **to ~ with** (problem) faire face à

copper ['kɔpər] n cuivre m; (BRIT: inf: policeman) flic m

copy ['kɔpɪ] n copie f; (book etc) exemplaire m ▷ vt copier; (imitate) imiter; **copyright** n droit m d'auteur, copyright m

coral ['kɔrəl] n corail m

cord [kɔːd] n corde f; (fabric) velours côtelé; (Elec) cordon m (d'alimentation), fil m (électrique); **cords** npl (trousers) pantalon m de velours côtelé; **cordless** adj sans fil

corduroy ['kɔːdərɔɪ] n velours côtelé

core [kɔːr] n (of fruit) trognon m, cœur m; (fig: of problem etc) cœur ▷ vt enlever le trognon or le cœur de

coriander [kɔrɪ'ændər] n coriandre f

cork [kɔːk] n (material) liège m; (of bottle) bouchon m; **corkscrew** n tire-bouchon m

corn [kɔːn] n (BRIT: wheat) blé m; (US: maize) maïs m; (on foot) cor m; **~ on the cob** (Culin) épi m de maïs au naturel

corned beef ['kɔːnd-] n corned-beef m

corner ['kɔːnər] n coin m; (in road) tournant m, virage m; (Football) corner m ▷ vt (trap: prey) acculer; (fig) coincer; (Comm: market) accaparer ▷ vi prendre un virage; **corner shop** (BRIT) n magasin m du coin

cornflakes ['kɔːnfleɪks] npl cornflakes mpl

cornflour ['kɔːnflauər] n (BRIT) farine f de maïs, maïzena® f

cornstarch ['kɔːnstɑːtʃ] n (US) farine f de maïs, maïzena® f

Cornwall ['kɔːnwəl] n Cornouailles f

coronary ['kɔrənərɪ] n: **~ (thrombosis)** infarctus m (du myocarde), thrombose f coronaire

coronation [kɔrə'neɪʃən] n couronnement m

coroner ['kɔrənər] n coroner m, officier de police judiciaire chargé de déterminer les causes d'un décès

corporal ['kɔːpərl] n caporal m, brigadier m ▷ adj: **~ punishment** châtiment corporel

corporate ['kɔːpərɪt] adj (action, ownership) en commun; (Comm) de la société

corporation [kɔːpə'reɪʃən] n (of town) municipalité f, conseil municipal; (Comm) société f

corps [kɔːr, pl kɔːz] n corps m; **the diplomatic ~** le corps diplomatique; **the press ~** la presse

corpse [kɔːps] n cadavre m

correct [kə'rɛkt] adj (accurate) correct(e), exact(e); (proper) correct, convenable ▷ vt corriger; **correction** [kə'rɛkʃən] n correction f

correspond [kɔrɪs'pɔnd] vi correspondre; **to ~ to sth** (be equivalent to) correspondre à qch; **correspondence** n correspondance f; **correspondent** n correspondant(e); **corresponding** adj correspondant(e)

corridor ['kɔrɪdɔːr] n couloir m, corridor m

corrode [kə'rəud] vt corroder, ronger ▷ vi se corroder

corrupt [kə'rʌpt] adj corrompu(e); (Comput) altéré(e) ▷ vt corrompre; (Comput) altérer; **corruption** n corruption f; (Comput) altération f (de données)

Corsica ['kɔːsɪkə] n Corse f

cosmetic [kɔz'mɛtɪk] n produit m de beauté, cosmétique m ▷ adj (fig: reforms) symbolique, superficiel(le); **cosmetic surgery** n chirurgie f esthétique

cosmopolitan [kɔzmə'pɔlɪtn] adj cosmopolite

cost [kɔst] n coût m ▷ vb (pt, pp ~) ▷ vi coûter ▷ vt établir or calculer le prix de revient de; **costs** npl (Comm) frais mpl; (Law) dépens mpl; **how much does it ~?** combien ça coûte?; **to ~ sb time/effort** demander du temps/un effort à qn; **it ~ him his life/job** ça lui a coûté la vie/son emploi; **at all ~s** coûte que coûte, à tout prix

co-star ['kəustɑːr] n partenaire m/f

costly ['kɔstlɪ] adj coûteux(-euse)

cost of living n coût m de la vie

costume ['kɔstjuːm] n costume m; (BRIT: also: **swimming ~**) maillot m (de bain)

cosy (US **cozy**) ['kəuzɪ] adj (room, bed) douillet(te); **to be ~** (person) être bien (au chaud)

cot [kɔt] n (BRIT: child's) lit m d'enfant, petit lit; (US: campbed) lit de camp

cottage ['kɔtɪdʒ] n petite maison (à la campagne), cottage m; **cottage cheese** n fromage blanc (maigre)

cotton ['kɔtn] n coton m; (thread) fil m (de coton); **cotton on** vi (inf): **to ~ on (to sth)** piger (qch); **cotton bud** (BRIT) n coton-tige ® m; **cotton candy** (US) n barbe f à papa; **cotton wool** n (BRIT) ouate f, coton m hydrophile

couch [kautʃ] n canapé m; divan m

cough [kɔf] vi tousser ▷ n toux f; **I've got a ~** j'ai la toux; **cough mixture, cough syrup** n sirop m pour la toux

could [kud] pt of **can²**; **couldn't = could not**

council ['kaunsl] n conseil m; **city** or **town ~** conseil municipal; **council**

estate n (BRIT) (quartier m or zone f de) logements loués à/par la municipalité; **council house** n (BRIT) maison f (à loyer modéré) louée par la municipalité; **councillor** (US **councilor**) n conseiller(-ère); **council tax** n (BRIT) impôts locaux

counsel ['kaunsl] n conseil m; (lawyer) avocat(e) ▷ vt: **to ~ (sb to do sth)** conseiller (à qn de faire qch); **counselling** (US **counseling**) n (Psych) aide psychosociale; **counsellor** (US **counselor**) n conseiller(-ère); (US Law) avocat m

count [kaunt] vt, vi compter ▷ n compte m; (nobleman) comte m; **count in** vt (inf): **to ~ sb in on sth** inclure qn dans qch; **count on** vt fus compter sur; **countdown** n compte m à rebours

counter ['kauntəʳ] n comptoir m; (in post office, bank) guichet m; (in game) jeton m ▷ vt aller à l'encontre de, opposer ▷ adv: **~ to** à l'encontre de; contrairement à; **counterclockwise** (US) adv en sens inverse des aiguilles d'une montre

counterfeit ['kauntəfɪt] n faux m, contrefaçon f ▷ vt contrefaire ▷ adj faux (fausse)

counterpart ['kauntəpɑ:t] n (of person) homologue m/f

countess ['kauntɪs] n comtesse f

countless ['kauntlɪs] adj innombrable

country ['kʌntrɪ] n pays m; (native land) patrie f; (as opposed to town) campagne f; (region) région f, pays; **country and western (music)** n musique f country; **country house** n manoir m, (petit) château; **countryside** n campagne f

county ['kauntɪ] n comté m

coup [ku:, pl ku:z] n (achievement) beau coup; (also: **~ d'état**) coup d'État

couple ['kʌpl] n couple m; **a ~ of** (two) deux; (a few) deux ou trois

coupon ['ku:pɔn] n (voucher) bon m de réduction; (detachable form) coupon m détachable, coupon-réponse m

courage ['kʌrɪdʒ] n courage m; **courageous** [kə'reɪdʒəs] adj courageux(-euse)

courgette [kuə'ʒɛt] n (BRIT) courgette f

courier ['kurɪəʳ] n messager m, courrier m; (for tourists) accompagnateur(-trice)

course [kɔ:s] n cours m; (of ship) route f; (for golf) terrain m; (part of meal) plat m; **of ~** adv bien sûr; **(no,) of ~ not!** bien sûr que non!, évidemment que non!; **~ of treatment** (Med) traitement m

court [kɔ:t] n cour f; (Law) cour, tribunal m; (Tennis) court m ▷ vt (woman) courtiser, faire la cour à; **to take to ~** actionner or poursuivre en justice

courtesy ['kə:təsɪ] n courtoisie f, politesse f; **(by) ~ of** avec l'aimable autorisation de;

courtesy bus, courtesy coach n navette gratuite

court: **court-house** ['kɔ:thaus] n (US) palais m de justice; **courtroom** ['kɔ:trum] n salle f de tribunal; **courtyard** ['kɔ:tjɑ:d] n cour f

cousin ['kʌzn] n cousin(e); **first ~** cousin(e) germain(e)

cover ['kʌvəʳ] vt couvrir; (Press: report on) faire un reportage sur; (feelings, mistake) cacher; (include) englober; (discuss) traiter ▷ n (of book, Comm) couverture f; (of pan) couvercle m; (over furniture) housse f; (shelter) abri m; **covers** npl (on bed) couvertures; **to take ~** se mettre à l'abri; **under ~** à l'abri; **under ~ of darkness** à la faveur de la nuit; **under separate ~** (Comm) sous pli séparé; **cover up** vi: **to ~ up for sb** (fig) couvrir qn; **coverage** n (in media) reportage m; **cover charge** n couvert m (supplément à payer); **cover-up** n tentative f pour étouffer une affaire

cow [kau] n vache f ▷ vt effrayer, intimider

coward ['kauəd] n lâche m/f; **cowardly** adj lâche

cowboy ['kaubɔɪ] n cow-boy m

cozy ['kəuzɪ] adj (US) = **cosy**

crab [kræb] n crabe m

crack [kræk] n (split) fente f, fissure f; (in cup, bone) fêlure f; (in wall) lézarde f; (noise) craquement m, coup (sec); (Drugs) crack m ▷ vt fendre, fissurer; fêler; lézarder; (whip) faire claquer; (nut) casser; (problem) résoudre; (code) déchiffrer ▷ cpd (athlete) de première classe, d'élite; **crack down on** vt fus (crime) sévir contre, réprimer; **cracked** adj (cup, bone) fêlé(e); (broken) cassé(e); (wall) lézardé(e); (surface) craquelé(e); (inf) toqué(e), timbré(e); **cracker** n (also: **Christmas cracker**) pétard m; (biscuit) biscuit (salé), craquelin m

crackle ['krækl] vi crépiter, grésiller

cradle ['kreɪdl] n berceau m

craft [krɑ:ft] n métier (artisanal); (cunning) ruse f, astuce f; (boat: pl inv) embarcation f, barque f; (plane: pl inv) appareil m; **craftsman** (irreg) n artisan m ouvrier (qualifié); **craftsmanship** n métier m, habileté f

cram [kræm] vt (fill): **to ~ sth with** bourrer qch de; (put): **to ~ sth into** fourrer qch dans ▷ vi (for exams) bachoter

cramp [kræmp] n crampe f; **I've got ~ in my leg** j'ai une crampe à la jambe; **cramped** adj à l'étroit, très serré(e)

cranberry ['krænbərɪ] n canneberge f

crane [kreɪn] n grue f

crap [kræp] n (inf!: nonsense) conneries fpl (!); (!: excrement) merde f (!)

crash [kræʃ] n (noise) fracas m; (of car, plane) collision f; (of business) faillite f ▷ vt (plane) écraser ▷ vi (plane) s'écraser; (two cars) se percuter, s'emboutir; (business) s'effondrer;

to ~ **into** se jeter or se fracasser contre; **crash course** n cours intensif; **crash helmet** n casque (protecteur)

crate [kreɪt] n cageot m; (for bottles) caisse f

crave [kreɪv] vt, vi: **to ~ (for)** avoir une envie irrésistible de

crawl [krɔːl] vi ramper; (vehicle) avancer au pas ▷ n (Swimming) crawl m

crayfish ['kreɪfɪʃ] n (pl inv: freshwater) écrevisse f; (saltwater) langoustine f

crayon ['kreɪən] n crayon m (de couleur)

craze [kreɪz] n engouement m

crazy ['kreɪzɪ] adj fou (folle); **to be ~ about sb/sth** (inf) être fou de qn/qch

creak [kriːk] vi (hinge) grincer; (floor, shoes) craquer

cream [kriːm] n crème f ▷ adj (colour) crème inv; **cream cheese** n fromage m à la crème, fromage blanc; **creamy** adj crémeux(-euse)

crease [kriːs] n pli m ▷ vt froisser, chiffonner ▷ vi se froisser, se chiffonner

create [kriː'eɪt] vt créer; **creation** [kriː'eɪʃən] n création f; **creative** adj créatif(-ive); **creator** n créateur(-trice)

creature ['kriːtʃəʳ] n créature f

crèche [krɛʃ] n garderie f, crèche f

credentials [krɪ'dɛnʃlz] npl (references) références fpl; (identity papers) pièce f d'identité

credibility [krɛdɪ'bɪlɪtɪ] n crédibilité f

credible ['krɛdɪbl] adj digne de foi, crédible

credit ['krɛdɪt] n crédit m; (recognition) honneur m; (Scol) unité f de valeur ▷ vt (Comm) créditer; (believe: also: **give ~ to**) ajouter foi à, croire; **credits** npl (Cine) générique m; **to be in ~** (person, bank account) être créditeur(-trice); **to ~ sb with** (fig) prêter or attribuer à qn; **credit card** n carte f de crédit; **do you take credit cards?** acceptez-vous les cartes de crédit?

creek [kriːk] n (inlet) crique f, anse f; (US: stream) ruisseau m, petit cours d'eau

creep (pt, pp **crept**) [kriːp, krɛpt] vi ramper

cremate [krɪ'meɪt] vt incinérer

crematorium (pl **crematoria**) [krɛmə'tɔːrɪə m, -'tɔːrɪə] n four m crématoire

crept [krɛpt] pt, pp of **creep**

crescent ['krɛsnt] n croissant m; (street) rue f (en arc de cercle)

cress [krɛs] n cresson m

crest [krɛst] n crête f; (of coat of arms) timbre m

crew [kruː] n équipage m; (Cine) équipe f (de tournage); **crew-neck** n col ras

crib [krɪb] n lit m d'enfant; (for baby) berceau m ▷ vt (inf) copier

cricket ['krɪkɪt] n (insect) grillon m, cri-cri m inv; (game) cricket m; **cricketer** n joueur m de cricket

crime [kraɪm] n crime m; **criminal** ['krɪmɪnl] adj, n criminel(le)

crimson ['krɪmzn] adj cramoisi(e)

cringe [krɪndʒ] vi avoir un mouvement de recul

cripple ['krɪpl] n boiteux(-euse), infirme m/f ▷ vt (person) estropier, paralyser; (ship, plane) immobiliser; (production, exports) paralyser

crisis (pl **crises**) ['kraɪsɪs, -siːz] n crise f

crisp [krɪsp] adj croquant(e); (weather) vif (vive); (manner etc) brusque; **crisps** (BRIT) npl (pommes fpl) chips fpl; **crispy** adj croustillant(e)

criterion (pl **criteria**) [kraɪ'tɪərɪən, -'tɪərɪə] n critère m

critic ['krɪtɪk] n critique m/f; **critical** adj critique; **criticism** ['krɪtɪsɪzəm] n critique f; **criticize** ['krɪtɪsaɪz] vt critiquer

Croat ['krəuæt] adj, n = **Croatian**

Croatia [krəu'eɪʃə] n Croatie f; **Croatian** adj croate ▷ n Croate m/f; (Ling) croate m

crockery ['krɔkərɪ] n vaisselle f

crocodile ['krɔkədaɪl] n crocodile m

crocus ['krəukəs] n crocus m

croissant ['krwasã] n croissant m

crook [kruk] n escroc m; (of shepherd) houlette f; **crooked** ['krukɪd] adj courbé(e), tordu(e); (action) malhonnête

crop [krɔp] n (produce) culture f; (amount produced) récolte f; (riding crop) cravache f ▷ vt (hair) tondre; **crop up** vi surgir, se présenter, survenir

cross [krɔs] n croix f; (Biol) croisement m ▷ vt (street etc) traverser; (arms, legs, Biol) croiser; (cheque) barrer ▷ adj en colère, fâché(e); **cross off** or **out** vt barrer, rayer; **cross over** vi traverser; **cross-Channel ferry** ['krɔs'tʃænl-] n ferry m qui fait la traversée de la Manche; **crosscountry (race)** n cross-(country) m; **crossing** n (sea passage) traversée f; (also: pedestrian crossing) passage clouté; **how long does the crossing take?** combien de temps dure la traversée?; **crossing guard** (US) n contractuel qui fait traverser la rue aux enfants; **crossroads** n carrefour m; **crosswalk** n (US) passage clouté; **crossword** n mots mpl croisés

crotch [krɔtʃ] n (of garment) entrejambe m; (Anat) entrecuisse m

crouch [krautʃ] vi s'accroupir; (hide) se tapir; (before springing) se ramasser

crouton ['kruːtɔn] n croûton m

crow [krəu] n (bird) corneille f; (of cock) chant m du coq, cocorico m ▷ vi (cock) chanter

crowd [kraud] n foule f ▷ vt bourrer, remplir ▷ vi affluer, s'attrouper, s'entasser; **crowded** adj bondé(e), plein(e)

crown [kraun] n couronne f; (of head) sommet m de la tête; (of hill) sommet m ▷ vt (also tooth) couronner; **crown jewels** npl joyaux mpl de la Couronne

crucial ['kruːʃl] adj crucial(e), décisif(-ive)

crucifix ['kru:sɪfɪks] n crucifix m
crude [kru:d] adj (materials) brut(e); non raffiné(e); (basic) rudimentaire, sommaire; (vulgar) cru(e), grossier(-ière); **crude (oil)** n (pétrole) brut m
cruel ['kruəl] adj cruel(le); **cruelty** n cruauté f
cruise [kru:z] n croisière f ▷ vi (ship) croiser; (car) rouler; (aircraft) voler
crumb [krʌm] n miette f
crumble ['krʌmbl] vt émietter ▷ vi (plaster etc) s'effriter; (land, earth) s'ébouler; (building) s'écrouler, crouler; (fig) s'effondrer
crumpet ['krʌmpɪt] n petite crêpe (épaisse)
crumple ['krʌmpl] vt froisser, friper
crunch [krʌntʃ] vt croquer; (underfoot) faire craquer, écraser; faire crisser ▷ n (fig) instant m or moment m critique, moment de vérité; **crunchy** adj croquant(e), croustillant(e)
crush [krʌʃ] n (crowd) foule f, cohue f; (love): **to have a ~ on sb** avoir le béguin pour qn; (drink): **lemon ~** citron pressé ▷ vt écraser; (crumple) froisser; (grind, break up: garlic, ice) piler; (: grapes) presser; (hopes) anéantir
crust [krʌst] n croûte f; **crusty** adj (bread) croustillant(e); (inf: person) revêche, bourru(e)
crutch [krʌtʃ] n béquille f; (also: **crotch**) entrejambe m
cry [kraɪ] vi pleurer; (shout: also: **~ out**) crier ▷ n cri m; **cry out** vi (call out, shout) pousser un cri ▷ vt crier
crystal ['krɪstl] n cristal m
cub [kʌb] n petit m (d'un animal); (also: **~ scout**) louveteau m
Cuba ['kju:bə] n Cuba m
cube [kju:b] n cube m ▷ vt (Math) élever au cube
cubicle ['kju:bɪkl] n (in hospital) box m; (at pool) cabine f
cuckoo ['kuku:] n coucou m
cucumber ['kju:kʌmbə'] n concombre m
cuddle ['kʌdl] vt câliner, caresser ▷ vi se blottir l'un contre l'autre
cue [kju:] n queue f de billard; (Theat etc) signal m
cuff [kʌf] n (BRIT: of shirt, coat etc) poignet m, manchette f; (US: on trousers) revers m; (blow) gifle f; **off the ~** adv à l'improviste; **cufflinks** n boutons m de manchette
cuisine [kwɪ'zi:n] n cuisine f
cul-de-sac ['kʌldəsæk] n cul-de-sac m, impasse f
cull [kʌl] vt sélectionner ▷ n (of animals) abattage sélectif
culminate ['kʌlmɪneɪt] vi: **to ~ in** finir or se terminer par; (lead to) mener à
culprit ['kʌlprɪt] n coupable m/f
cult [kʌlt] n culte m
cultivate ['kʌltɪveɪt] vt cultiver
cultural ['kʌltʃərəl] adj culturel(le)

culture ['kʌltʃə'] n culture f
cumin ['kʌmɪn] n (spice) cumin m
cunning ['kʌnɪŋ] n ruse f, astuce f ▷ adj rusé(e), malin(-igne); (clever: device, idea) astucieux(-euse)
cup [kʌp] n tasse f; (prize, event) coupe f; (of bra) bonnet m
cupboard ['kʌbəd] n placard m
cup final n (BRIT Football) finale f de la coupe
curator [kjuə'reɪtə'] n conservateur m (d'un musée etc)
curb [kə:b] vt refréner, mettre un frein à ▷ n (fig) frein m; (us) bord m du trottoir
curdle ['kə:dl] vi (se) cailler
cure [kjuə'] vt guérir; (Culin: salt) saler; (: smoke) fumer; (: dry) sécher ▷ n remède m
curfew ['kə:fju:] n couvre-feu m
curiosity [kjuərɪ'ɔsɪtɪ] n curiosité f
curious ['kjuərɪəs] adj curieux(-euse); **I'm ~ about him** il m'intrigue
curl [kə:l] n boucle f (de cheveux) ▷ vt, vi boucler; (tightly) friser; **curl up** vi s'enrouler; (person) se pelotonner; **curler** n bigoudi m, rouleau m; **curly** adj bouclé(e); (tightly curled) frisé(e)
currant ['kʌrnt] n raisin m de Corinthe, raisin sec; (fruit) groseille f
currency ['kʌrnsɪ] n monnaie f; **to gain ~** (fig) s'accréditer
current ['kʌrnt] n courant m ▷ adj (common) courant(e); (tendency, price, event) actuel(le); **current account** n (BRIT) compte courant; **current affairs** npl (questions fpl d')actualité f; **currently** adv actuellement
curriculum (pl **~s** or **curricula**) [kə'rɪkjulə m, -lə] n programme m d'études; **curriculum vitae** [-'vi:taɪ] n curriculum vitae (CV) m
curry ['kʌrɪ] n curry m ▷ vt: **to ~ favour with** chercher à gagner la faveur or à s'attirer les bonnes grâces de; **curry powder** n poudre f de curry
curse [kə:s] vi jurer, blasphémer ▷ vt maudire ▷ n (spell) malédiction f; (problem, scourge) fléau m; (swearword) juron m
cursor ['kə:sə'] n (Comput) curseur m
curt [kə:t] adj brusque, sec(-sèche)
curtain ['kə:tn] n rideau m
curve [kə:v] n courbe f; (in the road) tournant m, virage m ▷ vi se courber; (road) faire une courbe; **curved** adj courbe
cushion ['kuʃən] n coussin m ▷ vt (fall, shock) amortir
custard ['kʌstəd] n (for pouring) crème anglaise
custody ['kʌstədɪ] n (of child) garde f; (for offenders): **to take sb into ~** placer qn en détention préventive
custom ['kʌstəm] n coutume f, usage m; (Comm) clientèle f

customer ['kʌstəmər] n client(e)

customized ['kʌstəmaɪzd] adj
personnalisé(e); (car etc) construit(e) sur
commande

customs ['kʌstəmz] npl douane f; **customs
officer** n douanier m

cut [kʌt] vb (pt, pp **~**) ▷ vt couper; (meat)
découper; (reduce) réduire ▷ vi couper ▷ n
(gen) coupure f; (of clothes) coupe f; (in salary
etc) réduction f; (of meat) morceau m; **to ~ a
tooth** percer une dent; **to ~ one's finger** se
couper le doigt; **to get one's hair ~** se faire
couper les cheveux; **I've ~ myself** je me suis
coupé; **cut back** vt (plants) tailler; (production,
expenditure) réduire; **cut down** vt (tree)
abattre; (reduce) réduire; **cut off** vt couper;
(fig) isoler; **cut out** vt (picture etc) découper;
(remove) supprimer; **cut up** vt découper;
cutback n réduction f

cute [kju:t] adj mignon(ne), adorable

cutlery ['kʌtlərɪ] n couverts mpl

cutlet ['kʌtlɪt] n côtelette f

cut-price ['kʌt'praɪs] (us **cut-rate** ['kʌt'reɪt])
adj au rabais, à prix réduit

cutting ['kʌtɪŋ] adj (fig) cinglant(e) ▷ n (BRIT:
from newspaper) coupure f (de journal); (from
plant) bouture f

CV n abbr = **curriculum vitae**

cwt abbr = **hundredweight(s)**

cyberspace ['saɪbəspeɪs] n cyberespace m

cycle ['saɪkl] n cycle m; (bicycle) bicyclette f,
vélo m ▷ vi faire de la bicyclette; **cycle hire** n
location f de vélos; **cycle lane, cycle path** n
piste f cyclable; **cycling** n cyclisme m; **cyclist**
n cycliste m/f

cyclone ['saɪkləun] n cyclone m

cylinder ['sɪlɪndər] n cylindre m

cymbals ['sɪmblz] npl cymbales fpl

cynical ['sɪnɪkl] adj cynique

Cypriot ['sɪprɪət] adj cypriote, chypriote ▷ n
Cypriote m/f, Chypriote m/f

Cyprus ['saɪprəs] n Chypre f

cyst [sɪst] n kyste m; **cystitis** [sɪs'taɪtɪs] n
cystite f

czar [zɑ:'] n tsar m

Czech [tʃɛk] adj tchèque ▷ n Tchèque m/f;
(Ling) tchèque m; **Czech Republic** n: **the
Czech Republic** la République tchèque

D [di:] n (Mus): **D** ré m

dab [dæb] vt (eyes, wound) tamponner; (paint,
cream) appliquer (par petites touches or
rapidement)

dad, daddy [dæd, 'dædɪ] n papa m

daffodil ['dæfədɪl] n jonquille f

daft [dɑ:ft] adj (inf) idiot(e), stupide

dagger ['dægə'] n poignard m

daily ['deɪlɪ] adj quotidien(ne), journalier(-ière)
▷ adv tous les jours

dairy ['dɛərɪ] n (shop) crémerie f, laiterie f;
(on farm) laiterie; **dairy produce** n produits
laitiers

daisy ['deɪzɪ] n pâquerette f

dam [dæm] n (wall) barrage m; (water)
réservoir m, lac m de retenue ▷ vt endiguer

damage ['dæmɪdʒ] n dégâts mpl, dommages
mpl; (fig) tort m ▷ vt endommager, abîmer;
(fig) faire du tort à; **damages** npl (Law)
dommages-intérêts mpl

damn [dæm] vt condamner; (curse) maudire
▷ n (inf): **I don't give a ~** je m'en fous ▷ adj
(inf: also: **~ed**): **this ~ ...** ce sacré or foutu ...; **~
(it)!** zut!

damp [dæmp] adj humide ▷ n humidité f ▷ vt
(also: **~en**: cloth, rag) humecter; (: enthusiasm
etc) refroidir

dance [dɑ:ns] n danse f; (ball) bal m ▷ vi
danser; **dance floor** n piste f de danse;
dancer n danseur(-euse); **dancing** n danse f

dandelion ['dændɪlaɪən] n pissenlit m
dandruff ['dændrəf] n pellicules fpl
D & T n abbr (BRIT: Scol) = **design and
technology**
Dane [deɪn] n Danois(e)
danger ['deɪndʒər] n danger m; ~! (on sign)
danger!; **in** ~ en danger; **he was in** ~ **of
falling** il risquait de tomber; **dangerous** adj
dangereux(-euse)
dangle ['dæŋgl] vt balancer ▷ vi pendre, se
balancer
Danish ['deɪnɪʃ] adj danois(e) ▷ n (Ling)
danois m
dare [dɛər] vt: **to** ~ **sb to do** défier qn or
mettre qn au défi de faire ▷ vi: **to** ~ **(to) do
sth** oser faire qch; **I** ~ **say he'll turn up** il est
probable qu'il viendra; **daring** adj hardi(e),
audacieux(-euse) ▷ n audace f, hardiesse f
dark [dɑːk] adj (night, room) obscur(e), sombre;
(colour, complexion) foncé(e), sombre ▷ n: **in
the** ~ dans le noir; **to be in the** ~ **about** (fig)
ignorer tout de; **after** ~ après la tombée
de la nuit; **darken** vt obscurcir, assombrir
▷ vi s'obscurcir, s'assombrir; **darkness** n
obscurité f; **darkroom** n chambre noire
darling ['dɑːlɪŋ] adj, n chéri(e)
dart [dɑːt] n fléchette f; (in sewing) pince f ▷ vi:
to ~ **towards** se précipiter or s'élancer vers;
dartboard n cible f (de jeu de fléchettes);
darts n jeu m de fléchettes
dash [dæʃ] n (sign) tiret m; (small quantity)
goutte f, larme f ▷ vt (throw) jeter or lancer
violemment; (hopes) anéantir ▷ vi: **to** ~
towards se précipiter or se ruer vers
dashboard ['dæʃbɔːd] n (Aut) tableau m de
bord
data ['deɪtə] npl données fpl; **database** n base
f de données; **data processing** n traitement
m (électronique) de l'information
date [deɪt] n date f; (with sb) rendez-vous m;
(fruit) datte f ▷ vt dater; (person) sortir avec; ~
of birth date de naissance; **to** ~ adv à ce jour;
out of ~ périmé(e); **up to** ~ à la page, mis(e) à
jour, moderne; **dated** adj démodé(e)
daughter ['dɔːtər] n fille f; **daughter-in-law** n
belle-fille f, bru f
daunting ['dɔːntɪŋ] adj décourageant(e),
intimidant(e)
dawn [dɔːn] n aube f, aurore f ▷ vi (day) se
lever, poindre; **it ~ed on him that ...** il lui vint
à l'esprit que ...
day [deɪ] n jour m; (as duration) journée f; (period
of time, age) époque f, temps m; **the** ~ **before**
la veille, le jour précédent; **the** ~ **after, the
following** ~ le lendemain, le jour suivant; **the
** ~ **before yesterday** avant-hier; **the** ~ **after
tomorrow** après-demain; **by** ~ de jour; **day-
care centre** ['deɪkɛə-] n (for elderly etc) centre
m d'accueil de jour; (for children) garderie f;

daydream vi rêver (tout éveillé); **daylight**
n (lumière f du) jour m; **day return** n (BRIT)
billet m d'aller-retour (valable pour la journée);
daytime n jour m, journée f; **day-to-day** adj
(routine, expenses) journalier(-ière); **day trip** n
excursion f (d'une journée)
dazed [deɪzd] adj abruti(e)
dazzle ['dæzl] vt éblouir, aveugler; **dazzling**
adj (light) aveuglant(e), éblouissant(e); (fig)
éblouissant(e)
DC abbr (Elec) = **direct current**
dead [dɛd] adj mort(e); (numb) engourdi(e),
insensible; (battery) à plat ▷ adv (completely)
absolument, complètement; (exactly) juste; **he
was shot** ~ il a été tué d'un coup de revolver; ~
tired éreinté(e), complètement fourbu(e); **to
stop** ~ s'arrêter pile or net; **the line is** ~ (Tel)
la ligne est coupée; **dead end** n impasse f;
deadline n date f or heure f limite; **deadly** adj
mortel(le); (weapon) meurtrier(-ière); **Dead
Sea** n: **the Dead Sea** la mer Morte
deaf [dɛf] adj sourd(e); **deafen** vt rendre
sourd(e); **deafening** adj assourdissant(e)
deal [diːl] n affaire f, marché m ▷ vt (pt, pp
~t) (blow) porter; (cards) donner, distribuer;
a great ~ **of** beaucoup de; **deal with** vt
fus (handle) s'occuper or se charger de; (be
about: book etc) traiter de; **dealer** n (Comm)
marchand m; (Cards) donneur m; **dealings** npl
(in goods, shares) opérations fpl, transactions
fpl; (relations) relations fpl, rapports mpl
dealt [dɛlt] pt, pp of **deal**
dean [diːn] n (Rel, BRIT Scol) doyen m; (US Scol)
conseiller principal (conseillère principale)
d'éducation
dear [dɪər] adj cher (chère); (expensive) cher,
coûteux(-euse) ▷ n: **my** ~ mon cher (ma chère)
▷ excl: ~ **me!** mon Dieu!; **D** ~ **Sir/Madam** (in
letter) Monsieur/Madame; **D** ~ **Mr/Mrs X** Cher
Monsieur X (Chère Madame X); **dearly** adv
(love) tendrement; (pay) cher
death [dɛθ] n mort f; (Admin) décès m; **death
penalty** n peine f de mort; **death sentence** n
condamnation f à mort
debate [dɪ'beɪt] n discussion f, débat m ▷ vt
discuter, débattre
debit ['dɛbɪt] n débit m ▷ vt: **to** ~ **a sum to sb**
or **to sb's account** porter une somme au débit
de qn, débiter qn d'une somme; **debit card** n
carte f de paiement
debris ['dɛbriː] n débris mpl, décombres mpl
debt [dɛt] n dette f; **to be in** ~ avoir des dettes,
être endetté(e)
debut ['deɪbjuː] n début(s) m(pl)
Dec. abbr (= December) déc
decade ['dɛkeɪd] n décennie f, décade f
decaffeinated [dɪ'kæfɪneɪtɪd] adj
décaféiné(e)
decay [dɪ'keɪ] n (of building) délabrement m;

(also: **tooth ~**) carie f (dentaire) ▷ vi (rot) se décomposer, pourrir; (: teeth) se carier

deceased [dɪ'si:st] n: **the ~** le (la) défunt(e)

deceit [dɪ'si:t] n tromperie f, supercherie f; **deceive** [dɪ'si:v] vt tromper

December [dɪ'sɛmbə'] n décembre m

decency ['di:sənsɪ] n décence f

decent ['di:sənt] adj (proper) décent(e), convenable

deception [dɪ'sɛpʃən] n tromperie f

deceptive [dɪ'sɛptɪv] adj trompeur(-euse)

decide [dɪ'saɪd] vt (subj: person) décider; (question, argument) trancher, régler ▷ vi se décider, décider; **to ~ to do/that** décider de faire/que; **to ~ on** décider, se décider pour

decimal ['dɛsɪməl] adj décimal(e) ▷ n décimale f

decision [dɪ'sɪʒən] n décision f

decisive [dɪ'saɪsɪv] adj décisif(-ive); (manner, person) décidé(e), catégorique

deck [dɛk] n (Naut) pont m; (of cards) jeu m; (record deck) platine f; (of bus): **top ~** impériale f; **deckchair** n chaise longue

declaration [dɛklə'reɪʃən] n déclaration f

declare [dɪ'klɛə'] vt déclarer

decline [dɪ'klaɪn] n (decay) déclin m; (lessening) baisse f ▷ vt refuser, décliner ▷ vi décliner; (business) baisser

decorate ['dɛkəreɪt] vt (adorn, give a medal to) décorer; (paint and paper) peindre et tapisser; **decoration** [dɛkə'reɪʃən] n (medal etc, adornment) décoration f; **decorator** n peintre m en bâtiment

decrease n ['di:kri:s] diminution f ▷ vt, vi [di:'kri:s] diminuer

decree [dɪ'kri:] n (Pol, Rel) décret m; (Law) arrêt m, jugement m

dedicate ['dɛdɪkeɪt] vt consacrer; (book etc) dédier; **dedicated** adj (person) dévoué(e); (Comput) spécialisé(e), dédié(e); **dedicated word processor** station f de traitement de texte; **dedication** [dɛdɪ'keɪʃən] n (devotion) dévouement m; (in book) dédicace f

deduce [dɪ'dju:s] vt déduire, conclure

deduct [dɪ'dʌkt] vt: **to ~ sth (from)** déduire qch (de), retrancher qch (de); **deduction** [dɪ'dʌkʃən] n (deducting, deducing) déduction f; (from wage etc) prélèvement m, retenue f

deed [di:d] n action f, acte m; (Law) acte notarié, contrat m

deem [di:m] vt (formal) juger, estimer

deep [di:p] adj profond(e); (voice) grave ▷ adv: **spectators stood 20 ~** il y avait 20 rangs de spectateurs; **4 metres ~** de 4 mètres de profondeur; **how ~ is the water?** l'eau à quelle profondeur?; **deep-fry** vt faire frire (dans une friteuse); **deeply** adv profondément; (regret, interested) vivement

deer [dɪə'] n (pl inv): **(red) ~** cerf m; **(fallow) ~**

daim m; **(roe) ~** chevreuil m

default [dɪ'fɔ:lt] n (Comput: also: **~ value**) valeur f par défaut; **by ~** (Law) par défaut, par contumace; (Sport) par forfait

defeat [dɪ'fi:t] n défaite f ▷ vt (team, opponents) battre

defect n ['di:fɛkt] défaut m ▷ vi [dɪ'fɛkt]: **to ~ to the enemy/the West** passer à l'ennemi/l'Ouest; **defective** [dɪ'fɛktɪv] adj défectueux(-euse)

defence (us **defense**) [dɪ'fɛns] n défense f

defend [dɪ'fɛnd] vt défendre; **defendant** n défendeur(-deresse); (in criminal case) accusé(e), prévenu(e); **defender** n défenseur m

defense [dɪ'fɛns] (us) = **defence**

defensive [dɪ'fɛnsɪv] adj défensif(-ive) ▷ n: **on the ~** sur la défensive

defer [dɪ'fə:'] vt (postpone) différer, ajourner

defiance [dɪ'faɪəns] n défi m; **in ~ of** au mépris de; **defiant** [dɪ'faɪənt] adj provocant(e), de défi; (person) rebelle, intraitable

deficiency [dɪ'fɪʃənsɪ] n (lack) insuffisance f; (: Med) carence f; (flaw) faiblesse f; **deficient** [dɪ'fɪʃənt] adj (inadequate) insuffisant(e); **to be deficient in** manquer de

deficit ['dɛfɪsɪt] n déficit m

define [dɪ'faɪn] vt définir

definite ['dɛfɪnɪt] adj (fixed) défini(e), (bien) déterminé(e); (clear, obvious) net(te), manifeste; (certain) sûr(e); **he was ~ about it** il a été catégorique; **definitely** adv sans aucun doute

definition [dɛfɪ'nɪʃən] n définition f; (clearness) netteté f

deflate [di:'fleɪt] vt dégonfler

deflect [dɪ'flɛkt] vt détourner, faire dévier

defraud [dɪ'frɔ:d] vt: **to ~ sb of sth** escroquer qch à qn

defrost [di:'frɔst] vt (fridge) dégivrer; (frozen food) décongeler

defuse [di:'fju:z] vt désamorcer

defy [dɪ'faɪ] vt défier; (efforts etc) résister à; **it defies description** cela défie toute description

degree [dɪ'gri:] n degré m; (Scol) diplôme m (universitaire); **a (first) ~ in maths** (BRIT) une licence en maths; **by ~s** (gradually) par degrés; **to some ~** jusqu'à un certain point, dans une certaine mesure

dehydrated [di:haɪ'dreɪtɪd] adj déshydraté(e); (milk, eggs) en poudre

de-icer ['di:'aɪsə'] n dégivreur m

delay [dɪ'leɪ] vt retarder; (payment) différer ▷ vi s'attarder ▷ n délai m, retard m; **to be ~ed** être en retard

delegate n ['dɛlɪgɪt] délégué(e) ▷ vt ['dɛlɪgeɪt] déléguer

delete [dɪ'li:t] vt rayer, supprimer; (Comput)

effacer

deli ['dɛlɪ] n épicerie fine

deliberate adj [dɪ'lɪbərɪt] (intentional) délibéré(e); (slow) mesuré(e) ▷ vi [dɪ'lɪbəreɪt] délibérer, réfléchir; **deliberately** adv (on purpose) exprès, délibérément

delicacy ['dɛlɪkəsɪ] n délicatesse f; (choice food) mets fin or délicat, friandise f

delicate ['dɛlɪkɪt] adj délicat(e)

delicatessen [dɛlɪkə'tɛsn] n épicerie fine

delicious [dɪ'lɪʃəs] adj délicieux(-euse)

delight [dɪ'laɪt] n (grande) joie, grand plaisir ▷ vt enchanter; **she's a ~ to work with** c'est un plaisir de travailler avec elle; **to take ~ in** prendre grand plaisir à; **delighted** adj: **delighted (at** or **with sth)** ravi(e) (de qch); **to be delighted to do sth/that** être enchanté(e) or ravi(e) de faire qch/que; **delightful** adj (person) adorable; (meal, evening) merveilleux(-euse)

delinquent [dɪ'lɪŋkwənt] adj, n délinquant(e)

deliver [dɪ'lɪvər] vt (mail) distribuer; (goods) livrer; (message) remettre; (speech) prononcer; (Med: baby) mettre au monde; **delivery** n (of mail) distribution f; (of goods) livraison f; (of speaker) élocution f; (Med) accouchement m; **to take delivery of** prendre livraison de

delusion [dɪ'luːʒən] n illusion f

de luxe [də'lʌks] adj de luxe

delve [dɛlv] vi: **to ~ into** fouiller dans

demand [dɪ'mɑːnd] vt réclamer, exiger ▷ n exigence f; (claim) revendication f; (Econ) demande f; **in ~** demandé(e), recherché(e); **on ~** sur demande; **demanding** adj (person) exigeant(e); (work) astreignant(e)

⬛ Be careful not to translate **to demand** by the French word **demander**.

demise [dɪ'maɪz] n décès m

demo ['dɛməʊ] n abbr (inf) = demonstration (protest) manif f; (Comput) démonstration f

democracy [dɪ'mɔkrəsɪ] n démocratie f; **democrat** ['dɛməkræt] n démocrate m/f; **democratic** [dɛmə'krætɪk] adj démocratique

demolish [dɪ'mɔlɪʃ] vt démolir

demolition [dɛmə'lɪʃən] n démolition f

demon ['diːmən] n démon m

demonstrate ['dɛmənstreɪt] vt démontrer, prouver; (show) faire une démonstration de ▷ vi: **to ~ (for/against)** manifester (en faveur de/contre); **demonstration** [dɛmən'streɪʃən] n démonstration f; (Pol etc) manifestation f; **demonstrator** n (Pol etc) manifestant(e)

demote [dɪ'məʊt] vt rétrograder

den [dɛn] n (of lion) tanière f; (room) repaire m

denial [dɪ'naɪəl] n (of accusation) démenti m; (of rights, guilt, truth) dénégation f

denim ['dɛnɪm] n jean m; **denims** npl (blue-)jeans mpl

Denmark ['dɛnmɑːk] n Danemark m

denomination [dɪnɔmɪ'neɪʃən] n (money) valeur f; (Rel) confession f

denounce [dɪ'naʊns] vt dénoncer

dense [dɛns] adj dense; (inf: stupid) obtus(e)

density ['dɛnsɪtɪ] n densité f; **single-/double- ~ disk** (Comput) disquette f (à) simple/double densité

dent [dɛnt] n bosse f ▷ vt (also: **make a ~ in**) cabosser

dental ['dɛntl] adj dentaire; **dental floss** [-flɔs] n fil m dentaire; **dental surgery** n cabinet m de dentiste

dentist ['dɛntɪst] n dentiste m/f

dentures ['dɛntʃəz] npl dentier msg

deny [dɪ'naɪ] vt nier; (refuse) refuser

deodorant [diː'əʊdərənt] n déodorant m

depart [dɪ'pɑːt] vi partir; **to ~ from** (fig: differ from) s'écarter de

department [dɪ'pɑːtmənt] n (Comm) rayon m; (Scol) section f; (Pol) ministère m, département m; **department store** n grand magasin

departure [dɪ'pɑːtʃər] n départ m; (fig): **a new ~** une nouvelle voie; **departure lounge** n salle f de départ

depend [dɪ'pɛnd] vi: **to ~ (up)on** dépendre de; (rely on) compter sur; **it ~s** cela dépend; **~ing on the result ...** selon le résultat ...; **dependant** n personne f à charge; **dependent** adj: **to be dependent (on)** dépendre (de) ▷ n = **dependant**

depict [dɪ'pɪkt] vt (in picture) représenter; (in words) (dé)peindre, décrire

deport [dɪ'pɔːt] vt déporter, expulser

deposit [dɪ'pɔzɪt] n (Chem, Comm, Geo) dépôt m; (of ore, oil) gisement m; (part payment) arrhes fpl, acompte m; (on bottle etc) consigne f; (for hired goods etc) cautionnement m, garantie f ▷ vt déposer; **deposit account** n compte m sur livret

depot ['dɛpəʊ] n dépôt m; (us: Rail) gare f

depreciate [dɪ'priːʃɪeɪt] vi se déprécier, se dévaloriser

depress [dɪ'prɛs] vt déprimer, abaisser; (press down) appuyer sur, abaisser; (wages etc) faire baisser; **depressed** adj (person) déprimé(e); (area) en déclin, touché(e) par le sous-emploi; **depressing** adj déprimant(e); **depression** [dɪ'prɛʃən] n dépression f

deprive [dɪ'praɪv] vt: **to ~ sb of** priver qn de; **deprived** adj déshérité(e)

dept. abbr (= department) dép, dépt

depth [dɛpθ] n profondeur f; **to be in the ~s of despair** être au plus profond du désespoir; **to be out of one's ~** (BRIT: swimmer) ne plus avoir pied; (fig) être dépassé(e), nager

deputy ['dɛpjutɪ] n (second in command) adjoint(e); (Pol) député m; (us: also: **~ sheriff**) shérif adjoint ▷ adj: **~ head**

(Scol) directeur(-trice) adjoint(e), sous-directeur(-trice)

derail [dɪ'reɪl] vt: **to be ~ed** dérailler

derelict ['dɛrɪlɪkt] adj abandonné(e), à l'abandon

derive [dɪ'raɪv] vt: **to ~ sth from** tirer qch de; trouver qch dans ▷ vi: **to ~ from** provenir de, dériver de

descend [dɪ'sɛnd] vt, vi descendre; **to ~ from** descendre de, être issu(e) de; **to ~ to** s'abaisser à; **descendant** n descendant(e); **descent** n descente f; (origin) origine f

describe [dɪs'kraɪb] vt décrire; **description** [dɪs'krɪpʃən] n description f; (sort) sorte f, espèce f

desert n ['dɛzət] désert m ▷ vb [dɪ'zə:t] ▷ vt déserter, abandonner ▷ vi (Mil) déserter; **deserted** [dɪ'zə:tɪd] adj désert(e)

deserve [dɪ'zə:v] vt mériter

design [dɪ'zaɪn] n (sketch) plan m, dessin m; (layout, shape) conception f, ligne f; (pattern) dessin, motif(s) m(pl); (of dress, car) modèle m; (art) design m, stylisme m; (intention) dessein m ▷ vt dessiner; (plan) concevoir; **design and technology** n (BRIT: Scol) technologie f

designate vt ['dɛzɪgneɪt] désigner ▷ adj ['dɛzɪgnɪt] désigné(e)

designer [dɪ'zaɪnə'] n (Archit, Art) dessinateur(-trice); (Industry) concepteur m, designer m; (Fashion) styliste m/f

desirable [dɪ'zaɪərəbl] adj (property, location, purchase) attrayant(e)

desire [dɪ'zaɪə'] n désir m ▷ vt désirer, vouloir

desk [dɛsk] n (in office) bureau m; (for pupil) pupitre m; (BRIT: in shop, restaurant) caisse f; (in hotel, at airport) réception f; **desk-top publishing** ['dɛsktɔp-] n publication assistée par ordinateur, PAO f

despair [dɪs'pɛə'] n désespoir m ▷ vi: **to ~ of** désespérer de

despatch [dɪs'pætʃ] n, vt = **dispatch**

desperate ['dɛspərɪt] adj désespéré(e); (fugitive) prêt(e) à tout; **to be ~ for sth/to do sth** avoir désespérément besoin de qch/de faire qch; **desperately** adv désespérément; (very) terriblement, extrêmement; **desperation** [dɛspə'reɪʃən] n désespoir m; **in (sheer) desperation** en désespoir de cause

despise [dɪs'paɪz] vt mépriser

despite [dɪs'paɪt] prep malgré, en dépit de

dessert [dɪ'zə:t] n dessert m; **dessertspoon** n cuiller f à dessert

destination [dɛstɪ'neɪʃən] n destination f

destined ['dɛstɪnd] adj: **~ for London** à destination de Londres

destiny ['dɛstɪnɪ] n destinée f, destin m

destroy [dɪs'trɔɪ] vt détruire; (injured horse) abattre; (dog) faire piquer

destruction [dɪs'trʌkʃən] n destruction f

destructive [dɪs'trʌktɪv] adj destructeur(-trice)

detach [dɪ'tætʃ] vt détacher; **detached** adj (attitude) détaché(e); **detached house** n pavillon m maison(nette) (individuelle)

detail ['di:teɪl] n détail m ▷ vt raconter en détail, énumérer; **in ~** en détail; **detailed** adj détaillé(e)

detain [dɪ'teɪn] vt retenir; (in captivity) détenir

detect [dɪ'tɛkt] vt déceler, percevoir; (Med, Police) dépister; (Mil, Radar, Tech) détecter; **detection** [dɪ'tɛkʃən] n découverte f; **detective** n policier m; **private detective** détective privé; **detective story** n roman policier

detention [dɪ'tɛnʃən] n détention f; (Scol) retenue f, consigne f

deter [dɪ'tə:'] vt dissuader

detergent [dɪ'tə:dʒənt] n détersif m, détergent m

deteriorate [dɪ'tɪərɪəreɪt] vi se détériorer, se dégrader

determination [dɪtə:mɪ'neɪʃən] n détermination f

determine [dɪ'tə:mɪn] vt déterminer; **to ~ to do** résoudre de faire, se déterminer à faire; **determined** adj (person) déterminé(e), décidé(e); **determined to do** bien décidé à faire

deterrent [dɪ'tɛrənt] n effet m de dissuasion; force f de dissuasion

detest [dɪ'tɛst] vt détester, avoir horreur de

detour ['di:tuə'] n détour m; (US Aut: diversion) déviation f

detract [dɪ'trækt] vt: **to ~ from** (quality, pleasure) diminuer; (reputation) porter atteinte à

detrimental [dɛtrɪ'mɛntl] adj: **~ to** préjudiciable or nuisible à

devastating ['dɛvəsteɪtɪŋ] adj dévastateur(-trice); (news) accablant(e)

develop [dɪ'vɛləp] vt (gen) développer; (disease) commencer à souffrir de; (resources) mettre en valeur, exploiter; (land) aménager ▷ vi se développer; (situation, disease: evolve) évoluer; (facts, symptoms: appear) se manifester, se produire; **can you ~ this film?** pouvez-vous développer cette pellicule?; **developing country** n pays m en voie de développement; **development** n développement m; (of land) exploitation f; (new fact, event) rebondissement m, fait(s) nouveau(x)

device [dɪ'vaɪs] n (apparatus) appareil m, dispositif m

devil ['dɛvl] n diable m; démon m

devious ['di:vɪəs] adj (person) sournois(e), dissimulé(e)

devise [dɪ'vaɪz] vt imaginer, concevoir

devote [dɪ'vəut] vt: **to ~ sth to** consacrer qch

à; **devoted** adj dévoué(e); **to be devoted to** être dévoué(e) or très attaché(e) à; (book etc) être consacré(e) à; **devotion** n dévouement m, attachement m; (Rel) dévotion f, piété f

devour [dɪˈvauər] vt dévorer

devout [dɪˈvaut] adj pieux(-euse), dévot(e)

dew [djuː] n rosée f

diabetes [daɪəˈbiːtiːz] n diabète m

diabetic [daɪəˈbɛtɪk] n diabétique m/f ▷ adj (person) diabétique

diagnose [daɪəgˈnəuz] vt diagnostiquer

diagnosis (pl **diagnoses**) [daɪəgˈnəusɪs, -siːz] n diagnostic m

diagonal [daɪˈægənl] adj diagonal(e) ▷ n diagonale f

diagram [ˈdaɪəgræm] n diagramme m, schéma m

dial [ˈdaɪəl] n cadran m ▷ vt (number) faire, composer

dialect [ˈdaɪəlɛkt] n dialecte m

dialling code [ˈdaɪəlɪŋ-] (US **dial code**) n indicatif m (téléphonique); **what's the ~ for Paris?** quel est l'indicatif de Paris?

dialling tone [ˈdaɪəlɪŋ-] (US **dial tone**) n tonalité f

dialogue (US **dialog**) [ˈdaɪəlɔg] n dialogue m

diameter [daɪˈæmɪtər] n diamètre m

diamond [ˈdaɪəmənd] n diamant m; (shape) losange m; **diamonds** npl (Cards) carreau m

diaper [ˈdaɪəpər] n (US) couche f

diarrhoea (US **diarrhea**) [daɪəˈriːə] n diarrhée f

diary [ˈdaɪərɪ] n (daily account) journal m; (book) agenda m

dice [daɪs] n (pl inv) dé m ▷ vt (Culin) couper en dés or en cubes

dictate [dɪkˈteɪt] vt dicter; **dictation** [dɪkˈteɪʃən] n dictée f

dictator [dɪkˈteɪtər] n dictateur m

dictionary [ˈdɪkʃənrɪ] n dictionnaire m

did [dɪd] pt of **do**

didn't [ˈdɪdnt] = **did not**

die [daɪ] vi mourir; **to be dying for sth** avoir une envie folle de qch; **to be dying to do sth** mourir d'envie de faire qch; **die down** vi se calmer, s'apaiser; **die out** vi disparaître, s'éteindre

diesel [ˈdiːzl] n (vehicle) diesel m; (also: ~ **oil**) carburant m diesel, gas-oil m

diet [ˈdaɪət] n alimentation f; (restricted food) régime m ▷ vi (also: **be on a ~**) suivre un régime

differ [ˈdɪfər] vi: **to ~ from sth** (be different) être différent(e) de qch, différer de qch; **to ~ from sb over sth** ne pas être d'accord avec qn au sujet de qch; **difference** n différence f; (quarrel) différend m, désaccord m; **different** adj différent(e); **differentiate** [dɪfəˈrɛnʃɪeɪt] vi: **to differentiate between**

faire une différence entre; **differently** adv différemment

difficult [ˈdɪfɪkəlt] adj difficile; **difficulty** n difficulté f

dig [dɪg] vt (pt, pp **dug**) (hole) creuser; (garden) bêcher ▷ n (prod) coup m de coude; (fig: remark) coup de griffe or de patte; (Archaeology) fouille f; **to ~ one's nails into** enfoncer ses ongles dans; **dig up** vt déterrer

digest vt [daɪˈdʒɛst] digérer ▷ n [ˈdaɪdʒɛst] sommaire m, résumé m; **digestion** [dɪˈdʒɛstʃən] n digestion f

digit [ˈdɪdʒɪt] n (number) chiffre m (de 0 à 9); (finger) doigt m; **digital** adj (system, recording, radio) numérique, digital(e); (watch) à affichage numérique or digital; **digital camera** n appareil m photo numérique; **digital TV** n télévision f numérique

dignified [ˈdɪgnɪfaɪd] adj digne

dignity [ˈdɪgnɪtɪ] n dignité f

digs [dɪgz] npl (BRITinf) piaule f, chambre meublée

dilemma [daɪˈlɛmə] n dilemme m

dill [dɪl] n aneth m

dilute [daɪˈluːt] vt diluer

dim [dɪm] adj (light, eyesight) faible; (memory, outline) vague, indécis(e); (room) sombre; (inf: stupid) borné(e), obtus(e) ▷ vt (light) réduire, baisser; (US Aut) mettre en code, baisser

dime [daɪm] n (US) pièce f de 10 cents

dimension [daɪˈmɛnʃən] n dimension f

diminish [dɪˈmɪnɪʃ] vt, vi diminuer

din [dɪn] n vacarme m

dine [daɪn] vi dîner; **diner** n (person) dîneur(-euse); (US: eating place) petit restaurant

dinghy [ˈdɪŋgɪ] n youyou m; (inflatable) canot m pneumatique; (also: **sailing ~**) voilier m, dériveur m

dingy [ˈdɪndʒɪ] adj miteux(-euse), minable

dining car [ˈdaɪnɪŋ-] n (BRIT) voiture-restaurant f, wagon-restaurant m

dining room [ˈdaɪnɪŋ-] n salle f à manger

dining table [daɪnɪŋ-] n table f de (la) salle à manger

dinner [ˈdɪnər] n (evening meal) dîner m; (lunch) déjeuner m; (public) banquet m; **dinner jacket** n smoking m; **dinner party** n dîner m; **dinner time** n (evening) heure f du dîner; (midday) heure du déjeuner

dinosaur [ˈdaɪnəsɔːr] n dinosaure m

dip [dɪp] n (slope) déclivité f; (in sea) baignade f, bain m; (Culin) ≈ sauce f ▷ vt tremper, plonger; (BRIT Aut: lights) mettre en code, baisser ▷ vi plonger

diploma [dɪˈpləumə] n diplôme m

diplomacy [dɪˈpləuməsɪ] n diplomatie f

diplomat [ˈdɪpləmæt] n diplomate m; **diplomatic** [dɪpləˈmætɪk] adj diplomatique

dipstick ['dɪpstɪk] n (BRIT Aut) jauge f de niveau d'huile

dire [daɪə'] adj (poverty) extrême; (awful) affreux(-euse)

direct [daɪ'rɛkt] adj direct(e) ▷ vt (tell way) diriger, orienter; (letter, remark) adresser; (Cine, TV) réaliser; (Theat) mettre en scène; (order): **to ~ sb to do sth** ordonner à qn de faire qch ▷ adv directement; **can you ~ me to ...?** pouvez-vous m'indiquer le chemin de ...?; **direct debit** n (BRIT Banking) prélèvement m automatique

direction [dɪ'rɛkʃən] n direction f; **directions** npl (to a place) indications fpl; **~s for use** mode m d'emploi; **sense of ~** sens m de l'orientation

directly [dɪ'rɛktlɪ] adv (in straight line) directement, tout droit; (at once) tout de suite, immédiatement

director [dɪ'rɛktə'] n directeur m; (Theat) metteur m en scène; (Cine, TV) réalisateur(-trice)

directory [dɪ'rɛktərɪ] n annuaire m; (Comput) répertoire m; **directory enquiries** (US **directory assistance**) n (Tel: service) renseignements mpl

dirt [də:t] n saleté f; (mud) boue f; **dirty** adj sale; (joke) cochon(ne) ▷ vt salir

disability [dɪsə'bɪlɪtɪ] n invalidité f, infirmité f

disabled [dɪs'eɪbld] adj handicapé(e); (maimed) mutilé(e)

disadvantage [dɪsəd'vɑ:ntɪdʒ] n désavantage m, inconvénient m

disagree [dɪsə'gri:] vi (differ) ne pas concorder; (be against, think otherwise): **to ~ (with)** ne pas être d'accord (avec); **disagreeable** adj désagréable; **disagreement** n désaccord m, différend m

disappear [dɪsə'pɪə'] vi disparaître; **disappearance** n disparition f

disappoint [dɪsə'pɔɪnt] vt décevoir; **disappointed** adj déçu(e); **disappointing** adj décevant(e); **disappointment** n déception f

disapproval [dɪsə'pru:vəl] n désapprobation f

disapprove [dɪsə'pru:v] vi: **to ~ of** désapprouver

disarm [dɪs'ɑ:m] vt désarmer; **disarmament** [dɪs'ɑ:məmənt] n désarmement m

disaster [dɪ'zɑ:stə'] n catastrophe f, désastre m; **disastrous** adj désastreux(-euse)

disbelief ['dɪsbə'li:f] n incrédulité f

disc [dɪsk] n disque m; (Comput) = **disk**

discard [dɪs'kɑ:d] vt (old things) se débarrasser de; (fig) écarter, renoncer à

discharge vt [dɪs'tʃɑ:dʒ] (duties) s'acquitter de; (waste etc) déverser; décharger; (patient) renvoyer (chez lui); (employee, soldier) congédier, licencier ▷ n ['dɪstʃɑ:dʒ] (Elec, Med) émission f; (dismissal) renvoi m; licenciement m

discipline ['dɪsɪplɪn] n discipline f ▷ vt discipliner; (punish) punir

disc jockey n disque-jockey m (DJ)

disclose [dɪs'kləuz] vt révéler, divulguer

disco ['dɪskəu] n abbr discothèque f

discoloured [dɪs'kʌləd] (US **discolored**) adj décoloré(e), jauni(e)

discomfort [dɪs'kʌmfət] n malaise m, gêne f; (lack of comfort) manque m de confort

disconnect [dɪskə'nɛkt] vt (Elec, Radio) débrancher; (gas, water) couper

discontent [dɪskən'tɛnt] n mécontentement m

discontinue [dɪskən'tɪnju:] vt cesser, interrompre; **"~d"** (Comm) "fin de série"

discount n ['dɪskaunt] remise f, rabais m ▷ vt [dɪs'kaunt] (report etc) ne pas tenir compte de

discourage [dɪs'kʌrɪdʒ] vt décourager

discover [dɪs'kʌvə'] vt découvrir; **discovery** n découverte f

discredit [dɪs'krɛdɪt] vt (idea) mettre en doute; (person) discréditer

discreet [dɪs'kri:t] adj discret(-ète)

discrepancy [dɪs'krɛpənsɪ] n divergence f, contradiction f

discretion [dɪ'skrɛʃən] n discrétion f; **at the ~ of** à la discrétion de

discriminate [dɪs'krɪmɪneɪt] vi: **to ~ between** établir une distinction entre, faire la différence entre; **to ~ against** pratiquer une discrimination contre; **discrimination** [dɪskrɪmɪ'neɪʃən] n discrimination f; (judgment) discernement m

discuss [dɪ'skʌs] vt discuter de; (debate) discuter; **discussion** [dɪ'skʌʃən] n discussion f

disease [dɪ'zi:z] n maladie f

disembark [dɪsɪm'bɑ:k] vt, vi débarquer

disgrace [dɪs'greɪs] n honte f; (disfavour) disgrâce f ▷ vt déshonorer, couvrir de honte; **disgraceful** adj scandaleux(-euse), honteux(-euse)

disgruntled [dɪs'grʌntld] adj mécontent(e)

disguise [dɪs'gaɪz] n déguisement m ▷ vt déguiser; **in ~** déguisé(e)

disgust [dɪs'gʌst] n dégoût m, aversion f ▷ vt dégoûter, écœurer

disgusted [dɪs'gʌstɪd] adj dégoûté(e), écœuré(e)

disgusting [dɪs'gʌstɪŋ] adj dégoûtant(e)

dish [dɪʃ] n plat m; **to do** or **wash the ~es** faire la vaisselle; **dishcloth** n (for drying) torchon m; (for washing) lavette f

dishonest [dɪs'ɔnɪst] adj malhonnête

dishtowel ['dɪʃtauəl] n (US) torchon m (à vaisselle)

dishwasher ['dɪʃwɔʃə'] n lave-vaisselle m

disillusion [dɪsɪ'lu:ʒən] vt désabuser, désenchanter

disinfectant [dɪsɪn'fɛktənt] n désinfectant m

disintegrate [dɪs'ɪntɪgreɪt] vi se désintégrer

disk [dɪsk] n (Comput) disquette f; **single-/double-sided ~** disquette une face/double face; **disk drive** n lecteur m de disquette; **diskette** n (Comput) disquette f

dislike [dɪs'laɪk] n aversion f, antipathie f ▷ vt ne pas aimer

dislocate ['dɪsləkeɪt] vt disloquer, déboîter

disloyal [dɪs'lɔɪəl] adj déloyal(e)

dismal ['dɪzml] adj (gloomy) lugubre, maussade; (very bad) lamentable

dismantle [dɪs'mæntl] vt démonter

dismay [dɪs'meɪ] n consternation f ▷ vt consterner

dismiss [dɪs'mɪs] vt congédier, renvoyer; (idea) écarter; (Law) rejeter; **dismissal** n renvoi m

disobedient [dɪsə'bi:dɪənt] adj désobéissant(e), indiscipliné(e)

disobey [dɪsə'beɪ] vt désobéir à

disorder [dɪs'ɔ:də^r] n désordre m; (rioting) désordres mpl; (Med) troubles mpl

disorganized [dɪs'ɔ:gənaɪzd] adj désorganisé(e)

disown [dɪs'əun] vt renier

dispatch [dɪs'pætʃ] vt expédier, envoyer ▷ n envoi m, expédition f; (Mil, Press) dépêche f

dispel [dɪs'pɛl] vt dissiper, chasser

dispense [dɪs'pɛns] vt (medicine) préparer (et vendre); **dispense with** vt fus se passer de; **dispenser** n (device) distributeur m

disperse [dɪs'pə:s] vt disperser ▷ vi se disperser

display [dɪs'pleɪ] n (of goods) étalage m; affichage m; (Comput: information) visualisation f; (: device) visuel m; (of feeling) manifestation f ▷ vt montrer; (goods) mettre à l'étalage, exposer; (results, departure times) afficher; (pej) faire étalage de

displease [dɪs'pli:z] vt mécontenter, contrarier

disposable [dɪs'pəuzəbl] adj (pack etc) jetable; (income) disponible

disposal [dɪs'pəuzl] n (of rubbish) évacuation f, destruction f; (of property etc: by selling) vente f; (: by giving away) cession f; **at one's ~** à sa disposition

dispose [dɪs'pəuz] vi: **to ~ of** (unwanted goods) se débarrasser de, se défaire de; (problem) expédier; **disposition** [dɪspə'zɪʃən] n disposition f; (temperament) naturel m

disproportionate [dɪsprə'pɔ:ʃənət] adj disproportionné(e)

dispute [dɪs'pju:t] n discussion f; (also: **industrial ~**) conflit m ▷ vt (question) contester; (matter) discuter

disqualify [dɪs'kwɔlɪfaɪ] vt (Sport) disqualifier; **to ~ sb for sth/from doing** rendre qn inapte à qch/à faire

disregard [dɪsrɪ'gɑ:d] vt ne pas tenir compte de

disrupt [dɪs'rʌpt] vt (plans, meeting, lesson) perturber, déranger; **disruption** [dɪs'rʌpʃən] n perturbation f, dérangement m

dissatisfaction [dɪssætɪs'fækʃən] n mécontentement m, insatisfaction f

dissatisfied [dɪs'sætɪsfaɪd] adj: **~ (with)** insatisfait(e) (de)

dissect [dɪ'sɛkt] vt disséquer

dissent [dɪ'sɛnt] n dissentiment m, différence f d'opinion

dissertation [dɪsə'teɪʃən] n (Scol) mémoire m

dissolve [dɪ'zɔlv] vt dissoudre ▷ vi se dissoudre, fondre; **to ~ in(to) tears** fondre en larmes

distance ['dɪstns] n distance f; **in the ~** au loin

distant ['dɪstnt] adj lointain(e), éloigné(e); (manner) distant(e), froid(e)

distil (us **distill**) [dɪs'tɪl] vt distiller; **distillery** n distillerie f

distinct [dɪs'tɪŋkt] adj distinct(e); (clear) marqué(e); **as ~ from** par opposition à; **distinction** [dɪs'tɪŋkʃən] n distinction f; (in exam) mention f très bien; **distinctive** adj distinctif(-ive)

distinguish [dɪs'tɪŋgwɪʃ] vt distinguer; **to ~ o.s.** se distinguer; **distinguished** adj (eminent, refined) distingué(e)

distort [dɪs'tɔ:t] vt déformer

distract [dɪs'trækt] vt distraire, déranger; **distracted** adj (not concentrating) distrait(e); (worried) affolé(e); **distraction** [dɪs'trækʃən] n distraction f

distraught [dɪs'trɔ:t] adj éperdu(e)

distress [dɪs'trɛs] n détresse f ▷ vt affliger; **distressing** adj douloureux(-euse), pénible

distribute [dɪs'trɪbju:t] vt distribuer; **distribution** [dɪstrɪ'bju:ʃən] n distribution f; **distributor** n (gen: Tech) distributeur m; (Comm) concessionnaire m/f

district ['dɪstrɪkt] n (of country) région f; (of town) quartier m; (Admin) district m; **district attorney** n (us) ≈ procureur m de la République

distrust [dɪs'trʌst] n méfiance f, doute m ▷ vt se méfier de

disturb [dɪs'tə:b] vt troubler; (inconvenience) déranger; **disturbance** n dérangement m; (political etc) troubles mpl; **disturbed** adj (worried, upset) agité(e), troublé(e); **to be emotionally disturbed** avoir des problèmes affectifs; **disturbing** adj troublant(e), inquiétant(e)

ditch [dɪtʃ] n fossé m; (for irrigation) rigole f ▷ vt (inf) abandonner; (person) plaquer

ditto ['dɪtəu] adv idem

dive [daɪv] n plongeon m; (of submarine) plongée f ▷ vi plonger; **to ~ into** (bag etc) plonger la main dans; (place) se précipiter dans; **diver** n plongeur m

diverse [daɪ'vəːs] *adj* divers(e)

diversion [daɪ'vəːʃən] *n* (BRIT Aut) déviation *f*; (*distraction*, Mil) diversion *f*

diversity [daɪ'vəːsɪtɪ] *n* diversité *f*, variété *f*

divert [daɪ'vəːt] *vt* (BRIT: *traffic*) dévier; (*plane*) dérouter; (*train*, *river*) détourner

divide [dɪ'vaɪd] *vt* diviser; (*separate*) séparer
▷ *vi* se diviser; **divided highway** (US) *n* route *f* à quatre voies

divine [dɪ'vaɪn] *adj* divin(e)

diving ['daɪvɪŋ] *n* plongée (sous-marine); **diving board** *n* plongeoir *m*

division [dɪ'vɪʒən] *n* division *f*; (*separation*) séparation *f*; (Comm) service *m*

divorce [dɪ'vɔːs] *n* divorce *m* ▷ *vt* divorcer d'avec; **divorced** *adj* divorcé(e); **divorcee** [dɪvɔː'siː] *n* divorcé(e)

D.I.Y. *adj, n abbr* (BRIT) = **do-it-yourself**

dizzy ['dɪzɪ] *adj*: **I feel ~** la tête me tourne, j'ai la tête qui tourne

DJ *n abbr* = **disc jockey**

DNA *n abbr* (= deoxyribonucleic acid) ADN *m*

 KEYWORD

do [duː] (*pt* **did**, *pp* **done**) *n* (*inf: party etc*) soirée *f*, fête *f*
▷ *vb* **1** (*in negative constructions*) non traduit; **I don't understand** je ne comprends pas
2 (*to form questions*) non traduit; **didn't you know?** vous ne le saviez pas?; **what do you think?** qu'en pensez-vous?
3 (*for emphasis, in polite expressions*): **people do make mistakes sometimes** on peut toujours se tromper; **she does seem rather late** je trouve qu'elle est bien en retard; **do sit down/help yourself** asseyez-vous/servez-vous je vous en prie; **do take care!** faites bien attention à vous!
4 (*used to avoid repeating vb*): **she swims better than I do** elle nage mieux que moi; **do you agree? - yes, I do/no I don't** vous êtes d'accord? - oui/non; **she lives in Glasgow - so do I** elle habite Glasgow - moi aussi; **he didn't like it and neither did we** il n'a pas aimé ça, et nous non plus; **who broke it? - I did** qui l'a cassé? - c'est moi; **he asked me to help him and I did** il m'a demandé de l'aider, et c'est ce que j'ai fait
5 (*in question tags*): **you like him, don't you?** vous l'aimez bien, n'est-ce pas?; **I don't know him, do I?** je ne crois pas le connaître
▷ *vt* **1** (*gen: carry out, perform etc*) faire; (*visit: city, museum*) faire, visiter; **what are you doing tonight?** qu'est-ce que vous faites ce soir?; **what do you do?** (*job*) que faites-vous dans la vie?; **what can I do for you?** que puis-je faire pour vous?; **to do the cooking/washing-up** faire la cuisine/la vaisselle; **to do one's teeth/**

hair/nails se brosser les dents/se coiffer/se faire les ongles
2 (*Aut etc: distance*) faire; (: *speed*) faire du; **we've done 200 km already** nous avons déjà fait 200 km; **the car was doing 100** la voiture faisait du 100 (à l'heure); **he can do 100 in that car** il peut faire du 100 (à l'heure) dans cette voiture-là
▷ *vi* **1** (*act, behave*) faire; **do as I do** faites comme moi
2 (*get on, fare*) marcher; **the firm is doing well** l'entreprise marche bien; **he's doing well/badly at school** ça marche bien/mal pour lui à l'école; **how do you do?** comment allez-vous?; (*on being introduced*) enchanté(e)!
3 (*suit*) aller; **will it do?** est-ce que ça ira?
4 (*be sufficient*) suffire, aller; **will £10 do?** est-ce que 10 livres suffiront?; **that'll do** ça suffit, ça ira; **that'll do!** (*in annoyance*) ça va or suffit comme ça!; **to make do (with)** se contenter (de)

do up *vt* (*laces, dress*) attacher; (*buttons*) boutonner; (*zip*) fermer; (*renovate: room*) refaire; (: *house*) remettre à neuf

do with *vt fus* (*need*): **I could do with a drink/some help** quelque chose à boire/un peu d'aide ne serait pas de refus; **it could do with a wash** ça ne lui ferait pas de mal d'être lavé; (*be connected with*): **that has nothing to do with you** cela ne vous concerne pas; **I won't have anything to do with it** je ne veux pas m'en mêler

do without *vi* s'en passer; **if you're late for tea then you'll do without** si vous êtes en retard pour le dîner il faudra vous en passer
▷ *vt fus* se passer de; **I can do without a car** je peux me passer de voiture

dock [dɔk] *n* dock *m*; (*wharf*) quai *m*; (Law) banc *m* des accusés ▷ *vi* se mettre à quai; (Space) s'arrimer; **docks** *npl* (Naut) docks

doctor ['dɔktə'] *n* médecin *m*, docteur *m*; (PhD etc) docteur ▷ *vt* (*drink*) frelater; **call a ~!** appelez un docteur *or* un médecin!; **Doctor of Philosophy (PhD)** *n* (*degree*) doctorat *m*; (*person*) titulaire *m/f* d'un doctorat

document ['dɔkjumənt] *n* document *m*; **documentary** [dɔkju'mɛntərɪ] *adj, n* documentaire (*m*); **documentation** [dɔkjumən'teɪʃən] *n* documentation *f*

dodge [dɔdʒ] *n* truc *m*; combine *f* ▷ *vt* esquiver, éviter

dodgy ['dɔdʒɪ] *adj* (*inf: uncertain*) douteux(-euse); (: *shady*) louche

does [dʌz] *vb see* **do**

doesn't ['dʌznt] = **does not**

dog [dɔg] *n* chien(ne) ▷ *vt* (*follow closely*) suivre de près; (*fig: memory etc*) poursuivre, harceler; **doggy bag** ['dɔgɪ-] *n* petit sac pour emporter *les restes*

do-it-yourself ['du:ɪtjɔːˈsɛlf] *n* bricolage *m*

dole [dəʊl] *n* (BRIT: *payment*) allocation *f* de chômage; **on the ~** au chômage

doll [dɔl] *n* poupée *f*

dollar ['dɔlə*] *n* dollar *m*

dolphin ['dɔlfɪn] *n* dauphin *m*

dome [dəʊm] *n* dôme *m*

domestic [dəˈmɛstɪk] *adj* (*duty, happiness*) familial(e); (*policy, affairs, flight*) intérieur(e); (*animal*) domestique; **domestic appliance** *n* appareil ménager

dominant ['dɔmɪnənt] *adj* dominant(e)

dominate ['dɔmɪneɪt] *vt* dominer

domino ['dɔmɪnəʊ] (*pl* **~es**) *n* domino *m*; **dominoes** *n* (*game*) dominos *mpl*

donate [dəˈneɪt] *vt* faire don de, donner; **donation** [dəˈneɪʃən] *n* donation *f*, don *m*

done [dʌn] *pp* of **do**

donkey ['dɔŋkɪ] *n* âne *m*

donor ['dəʊnə*] *n* (*of blood etc*) donneur(-euse); (*to charity*) donateur(-trice); **donor card** *n* carte *f* de don d'organes

don't [dəʊnt] = **do not**

donut ['dəʊnʌt] (US) *n* = **doughnut**

doodle ['du:dl] *vi* griffonner, gribouiller

doom [du:m] *n* (*fate*) destin *m* ▷ *vt*: **to be ~ed to failure** être voué(e) à l'échec

door [dɔː*] *n* porte *f*; (*Rail, car*) portière *f*; **doorbell** *n* sonnette *f*; **door handle** *n* poignée *f* de porte; (*of car*) poignée de portière; **doorknob** *n* poignée *f* or bouton *m* de porte; **doorstep** *n* pas *m* de (la) porte, seuil *m*; **doorway** *n* (*embrasure f* de) porte *f*

dope [dəʊp] *n* (*inf: drug*) drogue *f*; (: *person*) andouille *f* ▷ *vt* (*horse etc*) doper

dormitory ['dɔːmɪtrɪ] *n* (BRIT) dortoir *m*; (US: *hall of residence*) résidence *f* universitaire

DOS [dɔs] *n abbr* (= *disk operating system*) DOS *m*

dosage ['dəʊsɪdʒ] *n* dose *f*; dosage *m*; (*on label*) posologie *f*

dose [dəʊs] *n* dose *f*

dot [dɔt] *n* point *m*; (*on material*) pois *m* ▷ *vt*: **~ted with** parsemé(e) de; **on the ~** à l'heure tapante; **dotcom** [dɔtˈkɔm] *n* point com *m*, pointcom *m*; **dotted line** ['dɔtɪd-] *n* ligne pointillée; **to sign on the dotted line** signer à l'endroit indiqué *or* sur la ligne pointillée

double ['dʌbl] *adj* double ▷ *adv* (*twice*): **to cost ~ (sth)** coûter le double *or* deux fois plus (que qch) ▷ *n* double *m*; (*Cine*) doublure *f* ▷ *vt* doubler; (*fold*) plier en deux ▷ *vi* doubler; **on the ~, at the ~** au pas de course; **double back** *vi* (*person*) revenir sur ses pas; **double bass** *n* contrebasse *f*; **double bed** *n* grand lit; **double-check** *vt, vi* revérifier; **double-click** *vi* (*Comput*) double-cliquer; **double-cross** *vt* doubler, trahir; **doubledecker** *n* autobus *m* à impériale; **double glazing** *n* (BRIT) double

vitrage *m*; **double room** *n* chambre *f* pour deux; **doubles** *n* (*Tennis*) double *m*; **double yellow lines** *npl* (BRIT: *Aut*) double bande jaune marquant l'interdiction de stationner

doubt [daʊt] *n* doute *m* ▷ *vt* douter de; **no ~** sans doute; **to ~ that** douter que + *sub*; **doubtful** *adj* douteux(-euse); (*person*) incertain(e); **doubtless** *adv* sans doute, sûrement

dough [dəʊ] *n* pâte *f*; **doughnut** (US **donut**) *n* beignet *m*

dove [dʌv] *n* colombe *f*

Dover ['dəʊvə*] *n* Douvres

down [daʊn] *n* (*fluff*) duvet *m* ▷ *adv* en bas, vers le bas; (*on the ground*) par terre ▷ *prep* en bas de; (*along*) le long de ▷ *vt* (*inf: drink*) siffler; **to walk ~ a hill** descendre une colline; **to run ~ the street** descendre la rue en courant; **~ with X!** à bas X!; **down-and-out** *n* (*tramp*) clochard(e); **downfall** *n* chute *f*; ruine *f*; **downhill** *adv*: **to go downhill** descendre; (*business*) péricliter

Downing Street ['daʊnɪŋ-] *n* (BRIT): **10 ~** résidence du Premier ministre

⬤ **DOWNING STREET**
⬤
⬤ **Downing Street** est une rue de
⬤ Westminster (à Londres) où se trouvent
⬤ la résidence officielle du Premier ministre
⬤ et celle du ministre des Finances. Le nom
⬤ **Downing Street** est souvent utilisé pour
⬤ désigner le gouvernement britannique.

down: **download** *vt* (*Comput*) télécharger; **downright** *adj* (*lie etc*) effronté(e); (*refusal*) catégorique

Down's syndrome [daʊnz-] *n* trisomie *f*

down: **downstairs** *adv* (*on or to ground floor*) au rez-de-chaussée; (*on or to floor below*) à l'étage inférieur; **down-to-earth** *adj* terre à terre *inv*; **downtown** *adv* en ville; **down under** *adv* en Australie *or* Nouvelle Zélande; **downward** ['daʊnwəd] *adj, adv* vers le bas; **downwards** ['daʊnwədz] *adv* vers le bas

doz. *abbr* = **dozen**

doze [dəʊz] *vi* sommeiller

dozen ['dʌzn] *n* douzaine *f*; **a ~ books** une douzaine de livres; **~s of** des centaines de

Dr. *abbr* (= *doctor*) Dr; (*in street names*) = **drive**

drab [dræb] *adj* terne, morne

draft [drɑːft] *n* (*of letter, school work*) brouillon *m*; (*of literary work*) ébauche *f*; (*Comm*) traite *f*; (US: *call-up*) conscription *f* ▷ *vt* faire le brouillon de; (*Mil: send*) détacher; *see also* **draught**

drag [dræg] *vt* traîner; (*river*) draguer ▷ *vi* traîner ▷ *n* (*inf*) casse-pieds *m/f*; (*women's clothing*): **in ~** (en) travesti; **to ~ and drop**

(Comput) glisser-poser

dragon ['drægn] n dragon m

dragonfly ['drægənflaɪ] n libellule f

drain [dreɪn] n égout m; (on resources) saignée f ▷ vt (land, marshes) drainer, assécher; (vegetables) égoutter; (reservoir etc) vider ▷ vi (water) s'écouler; **drainage** n (system) système m d'égouts; (act) drainage m; **drainpipe** n tuyau m d'écoulement

drama ['drɑːmə] n (art) théâtre m, art m dramatique; (play) pièce f; (event) drame m; **dramatic** [drə'mætɪk] adj (Theat) dramatique; (impressive) spectaculaire

drank [dræŋk] pt of **drink**

drape [dreɪp] vt draper; **drapes** npl (US) rideaux mpl

drastic ['dræstɪk] adj (measures) d'urgence, énergique; (change) radical(e)

draught (US **draft**) [drɑːft] n courant m d'air; **on ~** (beer) à la pression; **draught beer** n bière f (à la) pression; **draughts** n (BRIT: game) (jeu m de) dames fpl

draw [drɔː] (vb: pt **drew**, pp ~**n**) vt tirer; (picture) dessiner; (attract) attirer; (line, circle) tracer; (money) retirer; (wages) toucher ▷ vi (Sport) faire match nul ▷ n match nul; (lottery) loterie f, (: picking of ticket) tirage m au sort; **draw out** vi (lengthen) s'allonger ▷ vt (money) retirer; **draw up** vi (stop) s'arrêter ▷ vt (document) établir, dresser; (plan) formuler, dessiner; (chair) approcher; **drawback** n inconvénient m, désavantage m

drawer [drɔːʳ] n tiroir m

drawing ['drɔːɪŋ] n dessin m; **drawing pin** n (BRIT) punaise f; **drawing room** n salon m

drawn [drɔːn] pp of **draw**

dread [drɛd] n épouvante f, effroi m ▷ vt redouter, appréhender; **dreadful** adj épouvantable, affreux(-euse)

dream [driːm] n rêve m ▷ vt, vi (pt, pp ~**ed** or ~**t**) rêver; **dreamer** n rêveur(-euse)

dreamt [drɛmt] pt, pp of **dream**

dreary ['drɪərɪ] adj triste; monotone

drench [drɛntʃ] vt tremper

dress [drɛs] n robe f; (clothing) habillement m, tenue f ▷ vt habiller; (wound) panser ▷ vi: **to get ~ed** s'habiller; **dress up** vi s'habiller; (in fancy dress) se déguiser; **dress circle** n (BRIT) premier balcon; **dresser** n (furniture) vaisselier m; (: US) coiffeuse f, commode f; **dressing** n (Med) pansement m; (Culin) sauce f, assaisonnement m; **dressing gown** n (BRIT) robe f de chambre; **dressing room** n (Theat) loge f; (Sport) vestiaire m; **dressing table** n coiffeuse f; **dressmaker** n couturière f

drew [druː] pt of **draw**

dribble ['drɪbl] vi (baby) baver ▷ vt (ball) dribbler

dried [draɪd] adj (fruit, beans) sec (sèche); (eggs, milk) en poudre

drier ['draɪəʳ] n = **dryer**

drift [drɪft] n (of current etc) force f, direction f; (of snow) rafale f; coulée f; (: on ground) congère f; (general meaning) sens général ▷ vi (boat) aller à la dérive, dériver; (sand, snow) s'amonceler, s'entasser

drill [drɪl] n perceuse f; (bit) foret m; (of dentist) roulette f, fraise f; (Mil) exercice m ▷ vt percer; (troops) entraîner ▷ vi (for oil) faire un or des forage(s)

drink [drɪŋk] n boisson f; (alcoholic) verre m ▷ vt, vi (pt **drank**, pp **drunk**) boire; **to have a ~** boire quelque chose, boire un verre; **a ~ of water** un verre d'eau; **would you like a ~?** tu veux boire quelque chose?; **drink-driving** n conduite f en état d'ivresse; **drinker** n buveur(-euse); **drinking water** n eau f potable

drip [drɪp] n (drop) goutte f; (Med: device) goutte-à-goutte m inv; (: liquid) perfusion f ▷ vi tomber goutte à goutte; (tap) goutter

drive [draɪv] n promenade f or trajet m en voiture; (also: ~**way**) allée f; (energy) dynamisme m, énergie f; (push) effort (concerté); campagne f; (Comput: also: **disk ~**) lecteur m de disquette ▷ vb (pt **drove**, pp ~**n**) ▷ vt conduire; (nail) enfoncer; (push) chasser, pousser; (Tech: motor) actionner; entraîner ▷ vi (be at the wheel) conduire; (travel by car) aller en voiture; **left-/right-hand ~** (Aut) conduite f à gauche/droite; **to ~ sb mad** rendre qn fou (folle); **drive out** vt (force out) chasser; **drive-in** adj, n (esp US) drive-in m

driven ['drɪvn] pp of **drive**

driver ['draɪvəʳ] n conducteur(-trice); (of taxi, bus) chauffeur m; **driver's license** n (US) permis m de conduire

driveway ['draɪvweɪ] n allée f

driving ['draɪvɪŋ] n conduite f; **driving instructor** n moniteur m d'auto-école; **driving lesson** n leçon f de conduite; **driving licence** n (BRIT) permis m de conduire; **driving test** n examen m du permis de conduire

drizzle ['drɪzl] n bruine f, crachin m

droop [druːp] vi (flower) commencer à se faner; (shoulders, head) tomber

drop [drɔp] n (of liquid) goutte f; (fall) baisse f; (also: **parachute ~**) saut m ▷ vt laisser tomber; (voice, eyes, price) baisser; (passenger) déposer ▷ vi tomber; **drop in** vi (inf: visit): **to ~ in (on)** faire un saut (chez), passer (chez); **drop off** vi (sleep) s'assoupir ▷ vt (passenger) déposer; **drop out** vi (withdraw) se retirer; (student etc) abandonner, décrocher

drought [draut] n sécheresse f

drove [drəuv] pt of **drive**

drown [draun] vt noyer ▷ vi se noyer

drowsy ['drauzɪ] adj somnolent(e)

drug [drʌg] n médicament m; (narcotic) drogue f ▷ vt droguer; **to be on ~s** se droguer; **drug addict** n toxicomane m/f; **drug dealer** n revendeur(-euse) de drogue; **druggist** n (US) pharmacien(ne)-droguiste; **drugstore** n (US) pharmacie-droguerie f, drugstore m

drum [drʌm] n tambour m; (for oil, petrol) bidon m; **drums** npl (Mus) batterie f; **drummer** n (joueur m de) tambour m

drunk [drʌŋk] pp of **drink** ▷ adj ivre, soûl(e) ▷ n (also: **~ard**) ivrogne m/f; **to get ~** se soûler; **drunken** adj ivre, soûl(e); (rage, stupor) ivrogne, d'ivrogne

dry [draɪ] adj sec (sèche); (day) sans pluie ▷ vt sécher; (clothes) faire sécher ▷ vi sécher; **dry off** vi, vt sécher; **dry up** vi (river, supplies) se tarir; **dry-cleaner's** n teinturerie f; **dry-cleaning** n (process) nettoyage m à sec; **dryer** n (tumble-dryer) sèche-linge m inv; (for hair) sèche-cheveux m inv

DSS n abbr (BRIT) = **Department of Social Security**

DTP n abbr (= desktop publishing) PAO f

dual ['djuəl] adj double; **dual carriageway** n (BRIT) route f à quatre voies

dubious ['djuːbɪəs] adj hésitant(e), incertain(e); (reputation, company) douteux(-euse)

duck [dʌk] n canard m ▷ vi se baisser vivement, baisser subitement la tête

due [djuː] adj (money, payment) dû (due); (expected) attendu(e); (fitting) qui convient ▷ adv: **~ north** droit vers le nord; **~ to** (because of) en raison de; (caused by) dû à; **the train is ~ at 8 a.m.** le train est attendu à 8 h; **she is ~ back tomorrow** elle doit rentrer demain; **he is ~ £10** on lui doit 10 livres; **to give sb his** or **her ~** être juste envers qn

duel ['djuəl] n duel m

duet [djuːˈɛt] n duo m

dug [dʌg] pt, pp of **dig**

duke [djuːk] n duc m

dull [dʌl] adj (boring) ennuyeux(-euse); (not bright) morne, terne; (sound, pain) sourd(e); (weather, day) gris(e), maussade ▷ vt (pain, grief) atténuer; (mind, senses) engourdir

dumb [dʌm] adj muet(te); (stupid) bête

dummy ['dʌmɪ] n (tailor's model) mannequin m; (mock-up) factice m, maquette f; (BRIT: for baby) tétine f ▷ adj faux (fausse), factice

dump [dʌmp] n (also: **rubbish ~**) décharge (publique) trou m ▷ vt (put down) déposer; déverser; (get rid of) se débarrasser de; (Comput) lister

dumpling ['dʌmplɪŋ] n boulette f (de pâte)

dune [djuːn] n dune f

dungarees [dʌŋɡəˈriːz] npl bleu(s) m(pl); (for child, woman) salopette f

dungeon ['dʌndʒən] n cachot m

duplex ['djuːplɛks] n (US: also: **~ apartment**) duplex m

duplicate n ['djuːplɪkət] double m ▷ vt ['djuːplɪkeɪt] faire un double de; (on machine) polycopier; **in ~** en deux exemplaires, en double

durable ['djuərəbl] adj durable; (clothes, metal) résistant(e), solide

duration [djuəˈreɪʃən] n durée f

during ['djuərɪŋ] prep pendant, au cours de

dusk [dʌsk] n crépuscule m

dust [dʌst] n poussière f ▷ vt (furniture) essuyer, épousseter; (cake etc): **to ~ with** saupoudrer de; **dustbin** n (BRIT) poubelle f; **duster** n chiffon m; **dustman** n (BRIT: irreg) boueux m, éboueur m; **dustpan** n pelle f à poussière; **dusty** adj poussiéreux(-euse)

Dutch [dʌtʃ] adj hollandais(e), néerlandais(e) ▷ n (Ling) hollandais m, néerlandais m ▷ adv: **to go ~** or **dutch** (inf) partager les frais; **the Dutch** npl les Hollandais, les Néerlandais; **Dutchman** (irreg) n Hollandais m; **Dutchwoman** (irreg) n Hollandaise f

duty ['djuːtɪ] n devoir m; (tax) droit m, taxe f; **on ~** de service; (at night etc) de garde; **off ~** libre, pas de service or de garde; **duty-free** adj exempté(e) de douane, hors-taxe

duvet ['duːveɪ] n (BRIT) couette f

DVD n abbr (= digital versatile or video disc) DVD m; **DVD burner** n graveur m de DVD; **DVD player** n lecteur m de DVD; **DVD writer** n graveur m de DVD

dwarf (pl **dwarves**) [dwɔːf, dwɔːvz] n nain(e) ▷ vt écraser

dwell (pt, pp **dwelt**) [dwɛl, dwɛlt] vi demeurer; **dwell on** vt fus s'étendre sur

dwelt [dwɛlt] pt, pp of **dwell**

dwindle ['dwɪndl] vi diminuer, décroître

dye [daɪ] n teinture f ▷ vt teindre

dying ['daɪɪŋ] adj mourant(e), agonisant(e)

dynamic [daɪˈnæmɪk] adj dynamique

dynamite ['daɪnəmaɪt] n dynamite f

dyslexia [dɪsˈlɛksɪə] n dyslexie f

dyslexic [dɪsˈlɛksɪk] adj, n dyslexique m/f

e

E [iː] *n* (*Mus*): **E** mi *m*

E111 *n abbr* (= *form E111*) formulaire *m* E111

each [iːtʃ] *adj* chaque ▷ *pron* chacun(e); ~ **other** l'un l'autre; **they hate ~ other** ils se détestent (mutuellement); **they have 2 books ~** ils ont 2 livres chacun; **they cost £5 ~** ils coûtent 5 livres (la) pièce

eager ['iːgəʳ] *adj* (*person, buyer*) empressé(e); (*keen: pupil, worker*) enthousiaste; **to be ~ to do sth** (*impatient*) brûler de faire qch; (*keen*) désirer vivement faire qch; **to be ~ for** (*event*) désirer vivement; (*vengeance, affection, information*) être avide de

eagle ['iːgl] *n* aigle *m*

ear [ɪəʳ] *n* oreille *f*; (*of corn*) épi *m*; **earache** *n* mal *m* aux oreilles; **eardrum** *n* tympan *m*

earl [əːl] *n* comte *m*

earlier ['əːlɪəʳ] *adj* (*date etc*) plus rapproché(e); (*edition etc*) plus ancien(ne), antérieur(e) ▷ *adv* plus tôt

early ['əːlɪ] *adv* tôt, de bonne heure; (*ahead of time*) en avance; (*near the beginning*) au début ▷ *adj* précoce, qui se manifeste (*or* se fait) tôt *or* de bonne heure; (*Christians, settlers*) premier(-ière); (*reply*) rapide; (*death*) prématuré(e); (*work*) de jeunesse; **to have an ~ night/start** se coucher/partir tôt *or* de bonne heure; **in the ~ or ~ in the spring/19th century** au début *or* commencement du printemps/19ème siècle; **early retirement** *n* retraite anticipée

earmark ['ɪəmɑːk] *vt*: **to ~ sth for** réserver *or* destiner qch à

earn [əːn] *vt* gagner; (*Comm: yield*) rapporter; **to ~ one's living** gagner sa vie

earnest ['əːnɪst] *adj* sérieux(-euse) ▷ *n*: **in ~** *adv* sérieusement, pour de bon

earnings ['əːnɪŋz] *npl* salaire *m*; gains *mpl*; (*of company etc*) profits *mpl*, bénéfices *mpl*

ear: **earphones** *npl* écouteurs *mpl*; **earplugs** *npl* boules *fpl* Quiès®; (*to keep out water*) protège-tympans *mpl*; **earring** *n* boucle *f* d'oreille

earth [əːθ] *n* (*gen, also* BRIT *Elec*) terre *f* ▷ *vt* (BRIT *Elec*) relier à la terre; **earthquake** *n* tremblement *m* de terre, séisme *m*

ease [iːz] *n* facilité *f*, aisance *f*; (*comfort*) bien-être *m* ▷ *vt* (*soothe: mind*) tranquilliser; (*reduce: pain, problem*) atténuer; (: *tension*) réduire; (*loosen*) relâcher, détendre; (*help pass*): **to ~ sth in/out** faire pénétrer/sortir qch délicatement *or* avec douceur, faciliter la pénétration/la sortie de qch; **at ~** à l'aise; (*Mil*) au repos

easily ['iːzɪlɪ] *adv* facilement; (*by far*) de loin

east [iːst] *n* est *m* ▷ *adj* (*wind*) d'est; (*side*) est *inv* ▷ *adv* à l'est, vers l'est; **the E~** l'Orient *m*; (*Pol*) les pays *mpl* de l'Est; **eastbound** *adj* en direction de l'est; (*carriageway*) est *inv*

Easter ['iːstəʳ] *n* Pâques *fpl*; **Easter egg** *n* œuf *m* de Pâques

eastern ['iːstən] *adj* de l'est, oriental(e)

Easter Sunday *n* le dimanche de Pâques

easy ['iːzɪ] *adj* facile; (*manner*) aisé(e) ▷ *adv*: **to take it** *or* **things ~** (*rest*) ne pas se fatiguer; (*not worry*) ne pas (trop) s'en faire; **easy-going** *adj* accommodant(e), facile à vivre

eat (*pt* **ate**, *pp* **~en**) [iːt, eɪt, 'iːtn] *vt*, *vi* manger; **can we have something to ~?** est-ce qu'on peut manger quelque chose?; **eat out** *vi* manger au restaurant

eavesdrop ['iːvzdrɔp] *vi*: **to ~ (on)** écouter de façon indiscrète

e-book ['iːbuk] *n* livre *m* électronique

e-business ['iːbɪznɪs] *n* (*company*) entreprise *f* électronique; (*commerce*) commerce *m* électronique

EC *n abbr* (= *European Community*) CE *f*

eccentric [ɪk'sɛntrɪk] *adj*, *n* excentrique *m/f*

echo, echoes ['ɛkəu] *n* écho *m* ▷ *vt* répéter ▷ *vi* résonner; faire écho

eclipse [ɪ'klɪps] *n* éclipse *f*

eco-friendly [iːkəu'frɛndlɪ] *adj* non nuisible à *or* qui ne nuit pas à l'environnement

ecological [iːkə'lɔdʒɪkəl] *adj* écologique

ecology [ɪ'kɔlədʒɪ] *n* écologie *f*

e-commerce [iːkɔmə:s] *n* commerce *m* électronique

economic [iːkə'nɔmɪk] *adj* économique; (*profitable*) rentable; **economical** *adj*

économique; (*person*) économe; **economics** n
(*Scol*) économie f politique ▷ npl (*of project etc*)
côté m or aspect m économique
economist [ɪˈkɒnəmɪst] n économiste m/f
economize [ɪˈkɒnəmaɪz] vi économiser, faire
des économies
economy [ɪˈkɒnəmɪ] n économie f; **economy
class** n (*Aviat*) classe f touriste; **economy
class syndrome** n syndrome m de la classe
économique
ecstasy [ˈɛkstəsɪ] n extase f; (*Drugs*) ecstasy m;
ecstatic [ɛksˈtætɪk] adj extatique, en extase
eczema [ˈɛksɪmə] n eczéma m
edge [ɛdʒ] n bord m; (*of knife etc*) tranchant m,
fil m ▷ vt border; **on ~** (*fig*) crispé(e), tendu(e)
edgy [ˈɛdʒɪ] adj crispé(e), tendu(e)
edible [ˈɛdɪbl] adj comestible; (*meal*)
mangeable
Edinburgh [ˈɛdɪnbərə] n Édimbourg

edit [ˈɛdɪt] vt (*text, book*) éditer; (*report*)
préparer; (*film*) monter; (*magazine*)
diriger; (*newspaper*) être le rédacteur or
la rédactrice en chef de; **edition** [ɪˈdɪʃə
n] n édition f; **editor** n (*of newspaper*)
rédacteur(-trice), rédacteur(-trice) en chef;
(*of sb's work*) éditeur(-trice); (*also*: **film editor**)
monteur(-euse); **political/foreign editor**
rédacteur politique/au service étranger;
editorial [ɛdɪˈtɔːrɪəl] adj de la rédaction,
éditorial(e) ▷ n éditorial m
educate [ˈɛdjukeɪt] vt (*teach*) instruire; (*bring
up*) éduquer; **educated** [ˈɛdjukeɪtɪd] adj
(*person*) cultivé(e)
education [ɛdjuˈkeɪʃən] n éducation f;
(*studies*) études fpl; (*teaching*) enseignement m,
instruction f; **educational** adj pédagogique;
(*institution*) scolaire; (*game, toy*) éducatif(-ive)
eel [iːl] n anguille f
eerie [ˈɪərɪ] adj inquiétant(e), spectral(e),
surnaturel(le)
effect [ɪˈfɛkt] n effet m ▷ vt effectuer; **effects**
npl (*property*) effets, affaires fpl; **to take ~**
(*Law*) entrer en vigueur, prendre effet; (*drug*)
agir, faire son effet; **in ~** en fait; **effective** adj

efficace; (*actual*) véritable; **effectively** adv
efficacement; (*in reality*) effectivement, en fait
efficiency [ɪˈfɪʃənsɪ] n efficacité f; (*of machine,
car*) rendement m
efficient [ɪˈfɪʃənt] adj efficace; (*machine,
car*) d'un bon rendement; **efficiently** adv
efficacement
effort [ˈɛfət] n effort m; **effortless** adj sans
effort, aisé(e); (*achievement*) facile
e.g. adv abbr (= *exempli gratia*) par exemple,
p. ex.
egg [ɛg] n œuf m; **hard-boiled/soft-boiled
~** œuf dur/à la coque; **eggcup** n coquetier m;
egg plant (*us*) n aubergine f; **eggshell** n
coquille f d'œuf; **egg white** n blanc m d'œuf;
egg yolk n jaune m d'œuf
ego [ˈiːɡəu] n (*self-esteem*) amour-propre m;
(*Psych*) moi m
Egypt [ˈiːdʒɪpt] n Égypte f; **Egyptian**
[ɪˈdʒɪpʃən] adj égyptien(ne) ▷ n Égyptien(ne)
Eiffel Tower [ˈaɪfəl-] n tour f Eiffel
eight [eɪt] num huit; **eighteen** num dix-huit;
eighteenth num dix-huitième; **eighth** num
huitième; **eightieth** [ˈeɪtɪɪθ] num quatre-
vingtième
eighty [ˈeɪtɪ] num quatre-vingt(s)
Eire [ˈɛərə] n République f d'Irlande
either [ˈaɪðər] adj l'un ou l'autre; (*both, each*)
chaque ▷ pron: **~ (of them)** l'un ou l'autre
▷ adv non plus ▷ conj: **~ good or bad** soit
bon soit mauvais; **on ~ side** de chaque côté;
I don't like ~ je n'aime ni l'un ni l'autre; **no, I
don't ~** moi non plus; **which bike do you
want? - ~ will do** quel vélo voulez-vous?
- n'importe lequel; **answer with ~ yes or no**
répondez par oui ou par non
eject [ɪˈdʒɛkt] vt (*tenant etc*) expulser; (*object*)
éjecter
elaborate adj [ɪˈlæbərɪt] compliqué(e),
recherché(e), minutieux(-euse) ▷ vb
[ɪˈlæbəreɪt] ▷ vt élaborer ▷ vi entrer dans les
détails
elastic [ɪˈlæstɪk] adj, n élastique (m); **elastic
band** n (*BRIT*) élastique m
elbow [ˈɛlbəu] n coude m
elder [ˈɛldər] adj aîné(e) ▷ n (*tree*) sureau m;
one's ~s ses aînés; **elderly** adj âgé(e) ▷ npl:
the elderly les personnes âgées
eldest [ˈɛldɪst] adj, n: **the ~ (child)** l'aîné(e)
(des enfants)
elect [ɪˈlɛkt] vt élire; (*choose*): **to ~ to do** choisir
de faire ▷ adj: **the president ~** le président
désigné; **election** n élection f; **electoral** adj
électoral(e); **electorate** n électorat m
electric [ɪˈlɛktrɪk] adj électrique; **electrical**
adj électrique; **electric blanket** n couverture
chauffante; **electric fire** n (*BRIT*) radiateur
m électrique; **electrician** [ɪlɛkˈtrɪʃən] n
électricien m; **electricity** [ɪlɛkˈtrɪsɪtɪ] n

électricité f; **electric shock** n choc m or
décharge f électrique; **electrify** [ɪ'lɛktrɪfaɪ] vt
(Rail) électrifier; (audience) électriser
electronic [ɪlɛk'trɔnɪk] adj électronique;
electronic mail n courrier m électronique;
electronics n électronique f
elegance ['ɛlɪgəns] n élégance f
elegant ['ɛlɪgənt] adj élégant(e)
element ['ɛlɪmənt] n (gen) élément m; (of
heater, kettle etc) résistance f
elementary [ɛlɪ'mɛntərɪ] adj élémentaire;
(school, education) primaire; **elementary
school** n (US) école f primaire
elephant ['ɛlɪfənt] n éléphant m
elevate ['ɛlɪveɪt] vt élever
elevator ['ɛlɪveɪtər] n (in warehouse etc)
élévateur m, monte-charge m inv; (US: lift)
ascenseur m
eleven [ɪ'lɛvn] num onze; **eleventh** num
onzième
eligible ['ɛlɪdʒəbl] adj éligible; (for membership)
admissible; **an ~ young man** un beau parti;
to be ~ for sth remplir les conditions requises
pour qch
eliminate [ɪ'lɪmɪneɪt] vt éliminer
elm [ɛlm] n orme m
eloquent ['ɛləkwənt] adj éloquent(e)
else [ɛls] adv: **something ~** quelque chose
d'autre, autre chose; **somewhere ~** ailleurs,
autre part; **everywhere ~** partout ailleurs;
everyone ~ tous les autres; **nothing ~** rien
d'autre; **where ~?** à quel autre endroit?; **little
~** pas grand-chose d'autre; **elsewhere** adv
ailleurs, autre part
elusive [ɪ'luːsɪv] adj insaisissable
e-mail ['iːmeɪl] n abbr (= electronic mail) e-mail
m, courriel m ▷ vt: **to ~ sb** envoyer un e-mail
or un courriel à qn; **e-mail address** n adresse
f e-mail
embankment [ɪm'bæŋkmənt] n (of road,
railway) remblai m, talus m; (of river) berge f,
quai m; (dyke) digue f
embargo, embargoes [ɪm'baːgəu] n
(Comm, Naut) embargo m; (prohibition)
interdiction f
embark [ɪm'baːk] vi embarquer ▷ vt
embarquer; **to ~ on** (journey etc) commencer,
entreprendre; (fig) se lancer or s'embarquer
dans
embarrass [ɪm'bærəs] vt embarrasser, gêner;
embarrassed adj gêné(e); **embarrassing** adj
gênant(e), embarrassant(e); **embarrassment**
n embarras m, gêne f; (embarrassing thing,
person) source f d'embarras
embassy ['ɛmbəsɪ] n ambassade f
embrace [ɪm'breɪs] vt embrasser, étreindre;
(include) embrasser ▷ vi s'embrasser,
s'étreindre ▷ n étreinte f
embroider [ɪm'brɔɪdər] vt broder;

embroidery n broderie f
embryo ['ɛmbrɪəu] n (also fig) embryon m
emerald ['ɛmərəld] n émeraude f
emerge [ɪ'məːdʒ] vi apparaître; (from room,
car) surgir; (from sleep, imprisonment) sortir
emergency [ɪ'məːdʒənsɪ] n (crisis) cas m
d'urgence; (Med) urgence f; **in an ~** en cas
d'urgence; **state of ~** état m d'urgence;
emergency brake (US) n frein m à main;
emergency exit n sortie f de secours;
emergency landing n atterrissage forcé;
emergency room n (US: Med) urgences fpl;
emergency services npl: **the emergency
services** (fire, police, ambulance) les services
mpl d'urgence
emigrate ['ɛmɪgreɪt] vi émigrer; **emigration**
[ɛmɪ'greɪʃən] n émigration f
eminent ['ɛmɪnənt] adj éminent(e)
emissions [ɪ'mɪʃənz] npl émissions fpl
emit [ɪ'mɪt] vt émettre
emotion [ɪ'məuʃən] n sentiment m;
emotional adj (person) émotif(-ive), très
sensible; (needs) affectif(-ive); (scene)
émouvant(e); (tone, speech) qui fait appel aux
sentiments
emperor ['ɛmpərər] n empereur m
emphasis (pl **-ases**) ['ɛmfəsɪs, -siːz] n accent
m; **to lay** or **place ~ on sth** (fig) mettre l'accent
sur, insister sur
emphasize ['ɛmfəsaɪz] vt (syllable, word,
point) appuyer or insister sur; (feature)
souligner, accentuer
empire ['ɛmpaɪər] n empire m
employ [ɪm'plɔɪ] vt employer; **employee**
[ɪmplɔɪ'iː] n employé(e); **employer** n
employeur(-euse); **employment** n emploi m;
employment agency n agence for bureau m
de placement
empower [ɪm'pauər] vt: **to ~ sb to do**
autoriser or habiliter qn à faire
empress ['ɛmprɪs] n impératrice f
emptiness ['ɛmptɪnɪs] n vide m; (of area)
aspect m désertique
empty ['ɛmptɪ] adj vide; (street, area) désert(e);
(threat, promise) en l'air, vain(e) ▷ vt vider ▷ vi
se vider; (liquid) s'écouler; **empty-handed** adj
les mains vides
EMU n abbr (= European Monetary Union)
UME f
emulsion [ɪ'mʌlʃən] n émulsion f; (also: **~
paint**) peinture mate
enable [ɪ'neɪbl] vt: **to ~ sb to do** permettre à
qn de faire
enamel [ɪ'næməl] n émail m; (also: **~ paint**)
(peinture f) laque f
enchanting [ɪn'tʃaːntɪŋ] adj ravissant(e),
enchanteur(-eresse)
encl. abbr (on letters etc: = enclosed) ci-joint(e);
(= enclosure) PJ f

enclose [ɪnˈkləʊz] vt (land) clôturer; (space, object) entourer; (letter etc): **to ~ (with)** joindre (à); **please find ~d** veuillez trouver ci-joint

enclosure [ɪnˈkləʊʒəʳ] n enceinte f

encore [ɔŋˈkɔːʳ] excl, n bis (m)

encounter [ɪnˈkaʊntəʳ] n rencontre f ▷ vt rencontrer

encourage [ɪnˈkʌrɪdʒ] vt encourager; **encouragement** n encouragement m

encouraging [ɪnˈkʌrɪdʒɪŋ] adj encourageant(e)

encyclop(a)edia [ɛnsaɪkləʊˈpiːdɪə] n encyclopédie f

end [ɛnd] n fin f; (of table, street, rope etc) bout m, extrémité f ▷ vt terminer; (also: **bring to an ~, put an ~ to**) mettre fin à ▷ vi se terminer, finir; **in the ~** finalement; **on ~** (object) debout, dressé(e); **to stand on ~** (hair) se dresser sur la tête; **for hours on ~** pendant des heures (et des heures); **end up** vi: **to ~ up in** (condition) finir or se terminer par; (place) finir or aboutir à

endanger [ɪnˈdeɪndʒəʳ] vt mettre en danger; **an ~ed species** une espèce en voie de disparition

endearing [ɪnˈdɪərɪŋ] adj attachant(e)

endeavour (US **endeavor**) [ɪnˈdɛvəʳ] n effort m; (attempt) tentative f ▷ vt: **to ~ to do** tenter or s'efforcer de faire

ending [ˈɛndɪŋ] n dénouement m, conclusion f; (Ling) terminaison f

endless [ˈɛndlɪs] adj sans fin, interminable

endorse [ɪnˈdɔːs] vt (cheque) endosser; (approve) appuyer, approuver, sanctionner; **endorsement** n (approval) appui m, aval m; (BRIT: on driving licence) contravention f (portée au permis de conduire)

endurance [ɪnˈdjuərəns] n endurance f

endure [ɪnˈdjuəʳ] vt (bear) supporter, endurer ▷ vi (last) durer

enemy [ˈɛnəmɪ] adj, n ennemi(e)

energetic [ɛnəˈdʒɛtɪk] adj énergique; (activity) très actif(-ive), qui fait se dépenser (physiquement)

energy [ˈɛnədʒɪ] n énergie f

enforce [ɪnˈfɔːs] vt (law) appliquer, faire respecter

engaged [ɪnˈgeɪdʒd] adj (BRIT: busy, in use) occupé(e); (betrothed) fiancé(e); **to get ~** se fiancer; **the line's ~** la ligne est occupée; **engaged tone** n (BRIT Tel) tonalité f occupé inv

engagement [ɪnˈgeɪdʒmənt] n (undertaking) obligation f, engagement m; (appointment) rendez-vous m inv; (to marry) fiançailles fpl; **engagement ring** n bague f de fiançailles

engaging [ɪnˈgeɪdʒɪŋ] adj engageant(e), attirant(e)

engine [ˈɛndʒɪn] n (Aut) moteur m; (Rail) locomotive f

> Be careful not to translate **engine** by the French word **engin**.

engineer [ɛndʒɪˈnɪəʳ] n ingénieur m; (BRIT: repairer) dépanneur m; (Navy, US Rail) mécanicien m; **engineering** n engineering m, ingénierie f; (of bridges, ships) génie m; (of machine) mécanique f

England [ˈɪŋglənd] n Angleterre f

English [ˈɪŋglɪʃ] adj anglais(e) ▷ n (Ling) anglais m; **the ~** npl les Anglais; **English Channel** n: **the English Channel** la Manche; **Englishman** (irreg) n Anglais m; **Englishwoman** (irreg) n Anglaise f

engrave [ɪnˈgreɪv] vt graver

engraving [ɪnˈgreɪvɪŋ] n gravure f

enhance [ɪnˈhɑːns] vt rehausser, mettre en valeur

enjoy [ɪnˈdʒɔɪ] vt aimer, prendre plaisir à; (have benefit of: health, fortune) jouir de; (: success) connaître; **to ~ o.s.** s'amuser; **enjoyable** adj agréable; **enjoyment** n plaisir m

enlarge [ɪnˈlɑːdʒ] vt accroître; (Phot) agrandir ▷ vi: **to ~ on** (subject) s'étendre sur; **enlargement** n (Phot) agrandissement m

enlist [ɪnˈlɪst] vt recruter; (support) s'assurer ▷ vi s'engager

enormous [ɪˈnɔːməs] adj énorme

enough [ɪˈnʌf] adj: **~ time/books** assez or suffisamment de temps/livres ▷ adv: **big ~** assez or suffisamment grand ▷ pron: **have you got ~?** (en) avez-vous assez?; **~ to eat** assez à manger; **that's ~, thanks** cela suffit or c'est assez, merci; **I've had ~ of him** j'en ai assez de lui; **he has not worked ~** il n'a pas assez or suffisamment travaillé, il n'a pas travaillé assez or suffisamment; **... which, funnily** or **oddly ~ ...** qui, chose curieuse

enquire [ɪnˈkwaɪəʳ] vt, vi = **inquire**

enquiry [ɪnˈkwaɪərɪ] n = **inquiry**

enrage [ɪnˈreɪdʒ] vt mettre en fureur or en rage, rendre furieux(-euse)

enrich [ɪnˈrɪtʃ] vt enrichir

enrol (US **enroll**) [ɪnˈrəʊl] vt inscrire ▷ vi s'inscrire; **enrolment** (US **enrollment**) n inscription f

en route [ɔnˈruːt] adv en route, en chemin

en suite [ˈɔnswiːt] adj: **with ~ bathroom** avec salle de bains en attenante

ensure [ɪnˈʃuəʳ] vt assurer, garantir

entail [ɪnˈteɪl] vt entraîner, nécessiter

enter [ˈɛntəʳ] vt (room) entrer dans, pénétrer dans; (club, army) entrer à; (competition) s'inscrire à or pour; (sb for a competition) (faire) inscrire; (write down) inscrire, noter; (Comput) entrer, introduire ▷ vi entrer

enterprise [ˈɛntəpraɪz] n (company, undertaking) entreprise f; (initiative) (esprit *m* d')initiative *f*; **free ~** libre entreprise; **private ~** entreprise privée; **enterprising** *adj* entreprenant(e), dynamique; (*scheme*) audacieux(-euse)

entertain [ɛntə'teɪn] *vt* amuser, distraire; (*invite*) recevoir (à dîner); (*idea, plan*) envisager; **entertainer** *n* artiste *m/f* de variétés; **entertaining** *adj* amusant(e), distrayant(e); **entertainment** *n* (*amusement*) distraction *f*, divertissement *m*, amusement *m*; (*show*) spectacle *m*

enthusiasm [ɪn'θuːzɪæzəm] *n* enthousiasme *m*

enthusiast [ɪn'θuːzɪæst] *n* enthousiaste *m/f*; **enthusiastic** [ɪnθuːzɪ'æstɪk] *adj* enthousiaste; **to be enthusiastic about** être enthousiasmé(e) par

entire [ɪn'taɪəʳ] *adj* (tout) entier(-ère); **entirely** *adv* entièrement, complètement

entitle [ɪn'taɪtl] *vt*: **to ~ sb to sth** donner droit à qch à qn; **entitled** *adj* (*book*) intitulé(e); **to be entitled to do** avoir le droit de faire

entrance *n* ['ɛntrns] entrée *f* ▷ *vt* [ɪn'trɑːns] enchanter, ravir; **where's the ~?** où est l'entrée?; **to gain ~ to** (*university etc*) être admis à; **entrance examination** *n* examen *m* d'entrée or d'admission; **entrance fee** *n* (*to museum etc*) prix *m* d'entrée; (*to join club etc*) droit *m* d'inscription; **entrance ramp** *n* (*US Aut*) bretelle *f* d'accès; **entrant** *n* (*in race etc*) participant(e), concurrent(e); (*BRIT: in exam*) candidat(e)

entrepreneur ['ɔntrəprə'nəːʳ] *n* entrepreneur *m*

entrust [ɪn'trʌst] *vt*: **to ~ sth to** confier qch à

entry ['ɛntrɪ] *n* entrée *f*; (*in register, diary*) inscription *f*; **"no ~"** "défense d'entrer", "entrée interdite"; (*Aut*) "sens interdit"; **entry phone** *n* (*BRIT*) interphone *m* (à l'entrée d'un immeuble)

envelope ['ɛnvələup] *n* enveloppe *f*

envious ['ɛnvɪəs] *adj* envieux(-euse)

environment [ɪn'vaɪərnmənt] *n* (*social, moral*) milieu *m*; (*natural world*): **the ~** l'environnement *m*; **environmental** [ɪnvaɪərn'mɛntl] *adj* (*of surroundings*) du milieu; (*issue, disaster*) écologique; **environmentally** [ɪnvaɪərn'mɛntlɪ] *adv*: **environmentally sound/friendly** qui ne nuit pas à l'environnement

envisage [ɪn'vɪzɪdʒ] *vt* (*foresee*) prévoir

envoy ['ɛnvɔɪ] *n* envoyé(e); (*diplomat*) ministre *m* plénipotentiaire

envy ['ɛnvɪ] *n* envie *f* ▷ *vt* envier; **to ~ sb sth** envier qch à qn

epic ['ɛpɪk] *n* épopée *f* ▷ *adj* épique

epidemic [ɛpɪ'dɛmɪk] *n* épidémie *f*

epilepsy ['ɛpɪlɛpsɪ] *n* épilepsie *f*; **epileptic** *adj, n* épileptique *m/f*; **epileptic fit** *n* crise *f* d'épilepsie

episode ['ɛpɪsəud] *n* épisode *m*

equal ['iːkwl] *adj* égal(e) ▷ *vt* égaler; **~ to** (*task*) à la hauteur de; **equality** [iː'kwɔlɪtɪ] *n* égalité *f*; **equalize** *vt, vi* (*Sport*) égaliser; **equally** *adv* également; (*share*) en parts égales; (*treat*) de la même façon; (*pay*) autant; (*just as*) tout aussi

equation [ɪ'kweɪʃən] *n* (*Math*) équation *f*

equator [ɪ'kweɪtəʳ] *n* équateur *m*

equip [ɪ'kwɪp] *vt* équiper; **to ~ sb/sth with** équiper or munir qn/qch de; **equipment** *n* équipement *m*; (*electrical etc*) appareillage *m*, installation *f*

equivalent [ɪ'kwɪvəlnt] *adj* équivalent(e) ▷ *n* équivalent *m*; **to be ~ to** équivaloir à, être équivalent(e) à

ER *abbr* (*BRIT*: = *Elizabeth Regina*) la reine Élisabeth; (*US*: *Med*: = *emergency room*) urgences *fpl*

era ['ɪərə] *n* ère *f*, époque *f*

erase [ɪ'reɪz] *vt* effacer; **eraser** *n* gomme *f*

erect [ɪ'rɛkt] *adj* droit(e) ▷ *vt* construire; (*monument*) ériger, élever; (*tent etc*) dresser; **erection** [ɪ'rɛkʃən] *n* (*Physiol*) érection *f*; (*of building*) construction *f*

ERM *n abbr* (= *Exchange Rate Mechanism*) mécanisme *m* des taux de change

erode [ɪ'rəud] *vt* éroder; (*metal*) ronger

erosion [ɪ'rəuʒən] *n* érosion *f*

erotic [ɪ'rɔtɪk] *adj* érotique

errand ['ɛrnd] *n* course *f*, commission *f*

erratic [ɪ'rætɪk] *adj* irrégulier(-ière), inconstant(e)

error ['ɛrəʳ] *n* erreur *f*

erupt [ɪ'rʌpt] *vi* entrer en éruption; (*fig*) éclater; **eruption** [ɪ'rʌpʃən] *n* éruption *f*; (*of anger, violence*) explosion *f*

escalate ['ɛskəleɪt] *vi* s'intensifier; (*costs*) monter en flèche

escalator ['ɛskəleɪtəʳ] *n* escalier roulant

escape [ɪ'skeɪp] *n* évasion *f*, fuite *f*; (*of gas etc*) fuite ▷ *vi* s'échapper, fuir; (*from jail*) s'évader; (*fig*) s'en tirer; (*leak*) s'échapper ▷ *vt* échapper à; **to ~ from** (*person*) échapper à; (*place*) s'échapper de; (*fig*) fuir; **his name ~s me** son nom m'échappe

escort *vt* [ɪ'skɔːt] escorter ▷ *n* ['ɛskɔːt] (*Mil*) escorte *f*

especially [ɪ'spɛʃlɪ] *adv* (*particularly*) particulièrement; (*above all*) surtout

espionage ['ɛspɪɔnɑːʒ] *n* espionnage *m*

essay ['ɛseɪ] *n* (*Scol*) dissertation *f*; (*Literature*) essai *m*

essence ['ɛsns] *n* essence *f*; (*Culin*) extrait *m*

essential [ɪ'sɛnʃl] *adj* essentiel(le); (*basic*) fondamental(e); **essentials** *npl* éléments essentiels; **essentially** *adv* essentiellement

establish [ɪ'stæblɪʃ] *vt* établir; (*business*)

fonder, créer; (*one's power etc*) asseoir, affermir;
establishment *n* établissement *m*; (*founding*)
création *f*; (*institution*) établissement; **the**
Establishment les pouvoirs établis; l'ordre
établi

estate [ɪ'steɪt] *n* (*land*) domaine *m*, propriété
f; (*Law*) biens *mpl*, succession *f*; (BRIT: *also*:
housing ~) lotissement *m*; **estate agent** *n*
(BRIT) agent immobilier; **estate car** *n* (BRIT)
break *m*

estimate *n* ['ɛstɪmət] estimation *f*; (*Comm*)
devis *m* ▷ *vb* ['ɛstɪmeɪt] ▷ *vt* estimer

etc *abbr* (= *et cetera*) etc

eternal [ɪ'təːnl] *adj* éternel(le)

eternity [ɪ'təːnɪtɪ] *n* éternité *f*

ethical ['ɛθɪkl] *adj* moral(e); **ethics** ['ɛθɪks] *n*
éthique *f* ▷ *npl* moralité *f*

Ethiopia [iːθɪ'əupɪə] *n* Éthiopie *f*

ethnic ['ɛθnɪk] *adj* ethnique; (*clothes, food*)
folklorique, exotique, *propre aux minorités*
ethniques non-occidentales; **ethnic minority** *n*
minorité *f* ethnique

e-ticket ['iːtɪkɪt] *n* billet *m* électronique

etiquette ['ɛtɪkɛt] *n* convenances *fpl*,
étiquette *f*

EU *n abbr* (= *European Union*) UE *f*

euro ['juərəu] *n* (*currency*) euro *m*

Europe ['juərəp] *n* Europe *f*; **European** [juə
rə'piːən] *adj* européen(ne) ▷ *n* Européen(ne);
European Community *n* Communauté
européenne; **European Union** *n* Union
européenne

Eurostar® ['juərəustɑːʳ] *n* Eurostar® *m*

evacuate [ɪ'vækjueɪt] *vt* évacuer

evade [ɪ'veɪd] *vt* échapper à; (*question etc*)
éluder; (*duties*) se dérober à

evaluate [ɪ'væljueɪt] *vt* évaluer

evaporate [ɪ'væpəreɪt] *vi* s'évaporer; (*fig*:
hopes, fear) s'envoler; (*anger*) se dissiper

eve [iːv] *n*: **on the ~ of** à la veille de

even ['iːvn] *adj* (*level, smooth*) régulier(-ière);
(*equal*) égal(e); (*number*) pair(e) ▷ *adv* même; **~**
if même si + *indic*; **~ though** alors même que +
cond; **~ more** encore plus; **~ faster** encore plus
vite; **~ so** quand même; **not ~** pas même; **~ he**
was there même lui était là; **~ on Sundays**
même le dimanche; **to get ~ with sb** prendre
sa revanche sur qn

evening ['iːvnɪŋ] *n* soir *m*; (*as duration, event*)
soirée *f*; **in the ~** le soir; **evening class** *n*
cours *m* du soir; **evening dress** *n* (*man's*)
tenue *f* de soirée, smoking *m*; (*woman's*) robe
f de soirée

event [ɪ'vɛnt] *n* événement *m*; (*Sport*)
épreuve *f*; **in the ~ of** en cas de; **eventful** *adj*
mouvementé(e)

eventual [ɪ'vɛntʃuəl] *adj* final(e)

Be careful not to translate *eventual* by
the French word *éventuel*.

eventually [ɪ'vɛntʃuəlɪ] *adv* finalement

Be careful not to translate *eventually* by
the French word *éventuellement*.

ever ['ɛvəʳ] *adv* jamais; (*at all times*) toujours;
(*in questions*): **why ~ not?** mais enfin, pourquoi
pas?; **the best ~** le meilleur qu'on ait jamais vu;
have you ~ seen it? l'as-tu déjà vu?, as-tu eu
l'occasion *or* t'est-il arrivé de le voir?; **~ since**
(*as adv*) depuis; (*as conj*) depuis que; **~ so**
pretty si joli; **evergreen** *n* arbre *m* à feuilles
persistantes

KEYWORD

every ['ɛvrɪ] *adj* **1** (*each*) chaque; **every one of**
them tous (sans exception); **every shop in**
town was closed tous les magasins en ville
étaient fermés
2 (*all possible*) tous (toutes) les; **I gave you**
every assistance j'ai fait tout mon possible
pour vous aider; **I have every confidence in**
him j'ai entièrement *or* pleinement confiance
en lui; **we wish you every success** nous vous
souhaitons beaucoup de succès
3 (*showing recurrence*) tous les; **every day** tous
les jours, chaque jour; **every other car** une
voiture sur deux; **every other/third day** tous
les deux/trois jours; **every now and then**
de temps en temps; **everybody** = **everyone**
everyday *adj* (*expression*) courant(e), d'usage
courant; (*use*) courant; (*clothes, life*) de tous
les jours; (*occurrence, problem*) quotidien(ne);
everyone *pron* tout le monde, tous *pl*;
everything *pron* tout; **everywhere** *adv*
partout; **everywhere you go you meet ...** où
qu'on aille, on rencontre ...

evict [ɪ'vɪkt] *vt* expulser

evidence ['ɛvɪdns] *n* (*proof*) preuve(s) *f(pl)*; (*of*
witness) témoignage *m*; (*sign*): **to show ~ of**
donner des signes de; **to give ~** témoigner,
déposer

evident ['ɛvɪdnt] *adj* évident(e); **evidently**
adv de toute évidence; (*apparently*)
apparemment

evil ['iːvl] *adj* mauvais(e) ▷ *n* mal *m*

evoke [ɪ'vəuk] *vt* évoquer

evolution [iːvə'luːʃən] *n* évolution *f*

evolve [ɪ'vɔlv] *vt* élaborer ▷ *vi* évoluer, se
transformer

ewe [juː] *n* brebis *f*

ex [ɛks] *n* (*inf*): **my ex** mon ex

ex- [ɛks] *prefix* ex-

exact [ɪg'zækt] *adj* exact(e) ▷ *vt*: **to ~ sth**
(from) (*signature, confession*) extorquer qch
(à); (*apology*) exiger qch (de); **exactly** *adv*
exactement

exaggerate [ɪg'zædʒəreɪt] *vt, vi* exagérer;
exaggeration [ɪgzædʒə'reɪʃən] *n*

exagération f

exam [ɪgˈzæm] n abbr (Scol) = **examination**

examination [ɪgzæmɪˈneɪʃən] n (Scol, Med) examen m; **to take** or **sit an ~** (BRIT) passer un examen

examine [ɪgˈzæmɪn] vt (gen) examiner; (Scol, Law: person) interroger; **examiner** n examinateur(-trice)

example [ɪgˈzɑːmpl] n exemple m; **for ~** par exemple

exasperated [ɪgˈzɑːspəreɪtɪd] adj exaspéré(e)

excavate [ˈɛkskəveɪt] vt (site) fouiller, excaver; (object) mettre au jour

exceed [ɪkˈsiːd] vt dépasser; (one's powers) outrepasser; **exceedingly** adv extrêmement

excel [ɪkˈsɛl] vi exceller ▷ vt surpasser; **to ~ o.s.** se surpasser

excellence [ˈɛksələns] n excellence f

excellent [ˈɛksələnt] adj excellent(e)

except [ɪkˈsɛpt] prep (also: **~ for**, **~ing**) sauf, excepté, à l'exception de ▷ vt excepter; **~ if/when** sauf si/quand; **~ that** excepté que, si ce n'est que; **exception** [ɪkˈsɛpʃən] n exception f; **to take exception to** s'offusquer de; **exceptional** [ɪkˈsɛpʃənl] adj exceptionnel(le); **exceptionally** [ɪkˈsɛpʃənəlɪ] adv exceptionnellement

excerpt [ˈɛksəːpt] n extrait m

excess [ɪkˈsɛs] n excès m; **excess baggage** n excédent m de bagages; **excessive** adj excessif(-ive)

exchange [ɪksˈtʃeɪndʒ] n échange m; (also: **telephone ~**) central m ▷ vt: **to ~ (for)** échanger (contre); **could I ~ this, please?** est-ce que je peux échanger ceci, s'il vous plaît?; **exchange rate** n taux m de change

excite [ɪkˈsaɪt] vt exciter; **excited** adj (tout (toute)) excité(e); **to get excited** s'exciter; **excitement** n excitation f; **exciting** adj passionnant(e)

exclaim [ɪkˈskleɪm] vi s'exclamer; **exclamation** [ɛkskləˈmeɪʃən] n exclamation f; **exclamation mark** (us **exclamation point**) n point m d'exclamation

exclude [ɪkˈskluːd] vt exclure

excluding [ɪkˈskluːdɪŋ] prep: **~ VAT** la TVA non comprise

exclusion [ɪkˈskluːʒən] n exclusion f

exclusive [ɪkˈskluːsɪv] adj exclusif(-ive); (club, district) sélect(e); (item of news) en exclusivité; **~ of VAT** TVA non comprise; **exclusively** adv exclusivement

excruciating [ɪkˈskruːʃɪeɪtɪŋ] adj (pain) atroce, déchirant(e); (embarrassing) pénible

excursion [ɪkˈskəːʃən] n excursion f

excuse n [ɪkˈskjuːs] excuse f ▷ vt [ɪkˈskjuːz] (forgive) excuser; **to ~ sb from** (activity) dispenser qn de; **~ me!** excusez-moi!, pardon!;

now if you will ~ me, ... maintenant, si vous (le) permettez ...

ex-directory [ˈɛksdɪˈrɛktərɪ] adj (BRIT) sur la liste rouge

execute [ˈɛksɪkjuːt] vt exécuter; **execution** [ɛksɪˈkjuːʃən] n exécution f

executive [ɪgˈzɛkjutɪv] n (person) cadre m; (managing group) bureau m; (Pol) exécutif m ▷ adj exécutif(-ive); (position, job) de cadre

exempt [ɪgˈzɛmpt] adj: **~ from** exempté(e) or dispensé(e) de ▷ vt: **to ~ sb from** exempter or dispenser qn de

exercise [ˈɛksəsaɪz] n exercice m ▷ vt exercer; (patience etc) faire preuve de; (dog) promener ▷ vi (also: **to take ~**) prendre de l'exercice; **exercise book** n cahier m

exert [ɪgˈzəːt] vt exercer, employer; **to ~ o.s.** se dépenser; **exertion** [ɪgˈzəːʃən] n effort m

exhale [ɛksˈheɪl] vt exhaler ▷ vi expirer

exhaust [ɪgˈzɔːst] n (also: **~ fumes**) gaz mpl d'échappement; (also: **~ pipe**) tuyau m d'échappement ▷ vt épuiser; **exhausted** adj épuisé(e); **exhaustion** [ɪgˈzɔːstʃən] n épuisement m; **nervous exhaustion** fatigue nerveuse

exhibit [ɪgˈzɪbɪt] n (Art) pièce f or objet m exposé(e); (Law) pièce à conviction ▷ vt (Art) exposer; (courage, skill) faire preuve de; **exhibition** [ɛksɪˈbɪʃən] n exposition f

exhilarating [ɪgˈzɪləreɪtɪŋ] adj grisant(e), stimulant(e)

exile [ˈɛksaɪl] n exil m; (person) exilé(e) ▷ vt exiler

exist [ɪgˈzɪst] vi exister; **existence** n existence f; **existing** adj actuel(le)

exit [ˈɛksɪt] n sortie f ▷ vi (Comput, Theat) sortir; **where's the ~?** où est la sortie?; **exit ramp** n (us Aut) bretelle f d'accès

exotic [ɪgˈzɔtɪk] adj exotique

expand [ɪkˈspænd] vt (area) agrandir; (quantity) accroître ▷ vi (trade, etc) se développer, s'accroître; (gas, metal) se dilater

expansion [ɪkˈspænʃən] n (territorial, economic) expansion f; (of trade, influence etc) développement m; (of production) accroissement m; (of population) croissance f; (of gas, metal) expansion, dilatation f

expect [ɪkˈspɛkt] vt (anticipate) s'attendre à, s'attendre à ce que + sub; (count on) compter sur, escompter; (require) demander, exiger; (suppose) supposer; (await: also baby) attendre ▷ vi: **to be ~ing** (pregnant woman) être enceinte; **expectation** [ɛkspɛkˈteɪʃən] n (hope) attente f, espérance(s) f(pl); (belief) attente

expedition [ɛkspəˈdɪʃən] n expédition f

expel [ɪkˈspɛl] vt chasser, expulser; (Scol) renvoyer, exclure

expenditure [ɪkˈspɛndɪtʃəʳ] n (act of spending)

dépense f; (money spent) dépenses fpl
expense [ɪk'spɛns] n (high cost) coût m;
(spending) dépense f, frais mpl; **expenses**
npl frais mpl; dépenses; **at the ~ of** (fig) aux
dépens de; **expense account** n (note f de)
frais mpl
expensive [ɪk'spɛnsɪv] adj cher (chère),
coûteux(-euse)
experience [ɪk'spɪərɪəns] n expérience f ▷ vt
connaître; (feeling) éprouver; **experienced** adj
expérimenté(e)
experiment [ɪk'spɛrɪmənt] n expérience
f ▷ vi faire une expérience; **experimental**
[ɪkspɛrɪ'mɛntl] adj expérimental(e)
expert ['ɛkspəːt] adj expert(e) ▷ n expert m;
expertise [ɛkspəː'tiːz] n (grande)
compétence
expire [ɪk'spaɪər] vi expirer; **expiry** n
expiration f; **expiry date** n date f d'expiration;
(on label) à utiliser avant ...
explain [ɪk'spleɪn] vt expliquer; **explanation**
[ɛksplə'neɪʃən] n explication f
explicit [ɪk'splɪsɪt] adj explicite; (definite)
formel(le)
explode [ɪk'spləud] vi exploser
exploit n ['ɛksplɔɪt] exploit m ▷ vt [ɪk'splɔɪt]
exploiter; **exploitation** [ɛksplɔɪ'teɪʃən] n
exploitation f
explore [ɪk'splɔːr] vt explorer; (possibilities)
étudier, examiner; **explorer** n
explorateur(-trice)
explosion [ɪk'spləuʒən] n explosion f;
explosive [ɪk'spləusɪv] adj explosif(-ive) ▷ n
explosif m
export vt [ɛk'spɔːt] exporter ▷ n ['ɛkspɔːt]
exportation f ▷ cpd d'exportation; **exporter** n
exportateur m
expose [ɪk'spəuz] vt exposer; (unmask)
démasquer, dévoiler; **exposed** adj (land,
house) exposé(e); **exposure** [ɪk'spəuʒər] n
exposition f; (publicity) couverture f; (Phot:
speed) (temps m de) pose f; (: shot) pose; **to die
of exposure** (Med) mourir de froid
express [ɪk'sprɛs] adj (definite) formel(le),
exprès(-esse); (BRIT: letter etc) exprès inv ▷ n
(train) rapide m ▷ vt exprimer; **expression**
[ɪk'sprɛʃən] n expression f; **expressway** n
(US) voie f express (à plusieurs files)
exquisite [ɛk'skwɪzɪt] adj exquis(e)
extend [ɪk'stɛnd] vt (visit, street) prolonger,
remettre; (building) agrandir; (offer) présenter,
offrir; (hand, arm) tendre ▷ vi (land) s'étendre;
extension n (of visit, street) prolongation
f; (building) annexe f; (telephone: in offices)
poste m; (: in private house) téléphone m
supplémentaire; **extension cable, extension
lead** n (Elec) rallonge f; **extensive** adj
étendu(e), vaste; (damage, alterations)
considérable; (inquiries) approfondi(e)

extent [ɪk'stɛnt] n étendue f; **to some ~** dans
une certaine mesure; **to the ~ of ...** au point
de ...; **to what ~?** dans quelle mesure?, jusqu'à
quel point?; **to such an ~ that ...** à tel point
que ...
exterior [ɛk'stɪərɪər] adj extérieur(e) ▷ n
extérieur m
external [ɛk'stəːnl] adj externe
extinct [ɪk'stɪŋkt] adj (volcano) éteint(e);
(species) disparu(e); **extinction** n extinction f
extinguish [ɪk'stɪŋgwɪʃ] vt éteindre
extra ['ɛkstrə] adj supplémentaire, de plus
▷ adv (in addition) en plus ▷ n supplément m;
(perk) à-coté m; (Cine, Theat) figurant(e)
extract vt [ɪk'strækt] extraire; (tooth)
arracher; (money, promise) soutirer ▷ n
['ɛkstrækt] extrait m
extradite ['ɛkstrədaɪt] vt extrader
extraordinary [ɪk'strɔːdnrɪ] adj
extraordinaire
extravagance [ɪk'strævəgəns] n (excessive
spending) prodigalités fpl; (thing bought)
folie f, dépense excessive; **extravagant** adj
extravagant(e); (in spending: person) prodigue,
dépensier(-ière); (: tastes) dispendieux(-euse)
extreme [ɪk'striːm] adj, n extrême (m);
extremely adv extrêmement
extremist [ɪk'striːmɪst] adj, n extrémiste m/f
extrovert ['ɛkstrəvəːt] n extraverti(e)
eye [aɪ] n œil m ((yeux) pl); (of needle) trou
m, chas m ▷ vt examiner; **to keep an ~ on**
surveiller; **eyeball** n globe m oculaire;
eyebrow n sourcil m; **eyedrops** npl
gouttes fpl pour les yeux; **eyelash** n cil m;
eyelid n paupière f; **eyeliner** n eye-liner m;
eyeshadow n ombre f à paupières; **eyesight**
n vue f; **eye witness** n témoin m oculaire

F [ɛf] *n* (*Mus*): **F** fa *m*

fabric ['fæbrɪk] *n* tissu *m*

fabulous ['fæbjuləs] *adj* fabuleux(-euse); (*inf*: *super*) formidable, sensationnel(le)

face [feɪs] *n* visage *m*, figure *f*; (*expression*) air *m*; (*of clock*) cadran *m*; (*of cliff*) paroi *f*; (*of mountain*) face *f*; (*of building*) façade *f* ▷ *vt* faire face à; (*facts etc*) accepter; **~ down** (*person*) à plat ventre; (*card*) face en dessous; **to lose/save ~** perdre/sauver la face; **to pull a ~** faire une grimace; **in the ~ of** (*difficulties etc*) devant; **on the ~ of it** à première vue; **~ to ~** face à face; **face up to** *vt fus* faire face à, affronter; **face cloth** *n* (*BRIT*) gant *m* de toilette; **face pack** *n* (*BRIT*) masque *m* (de beauté)

facial ['feɪʃl] *adj* facial(e) ▷ *n* soin complet du visage

facilitate [fə'sɪlɪteɪt] *vt* faciliter

facilities [fə'sɪlɪtɪz] *npl* installations *fpl*, équipement *m*; **credit ~** facilités de paiement

fact [fækt] *n* fait *m*; **in ~** en fait

faction ['fækʃən] *n* faction *f*

factor ['fæktə^r] *n* facteur *m*; (*of sun cream*) indice *m* (de protection); **I'd like a ~ 15 suntan lotion** je voudrais une crème solaire d'indice 15

factory ['fæktərɪ] *n* usine *f*, fabrique *f*

factual ['fæktjuəl] *adj* basé(e) sur les faits

faculty ['fækəltɪ] *n* faculté *f*; (*us*: *teaching staff*) corps enseignant

fad [fæd] *n* (*personal*) manie *f*; (*craze*) engouement *m*

fade [feɪd] *vi* se décolorer, passer; (*light, sound*) s'affaiblir; (*flower*) se faner; **fade away** *vi* (*sound*) s'affaiblir

fag [fæg] *n* (*BRIT inf*: *cigarette*) clope *f*

Fahrenheit ['fɑːrənhaɪt] *n* Fahrenheit *m inv*

fail [feɪl] *vt* (*exam*) échouer à; (*candidate*) recaler; (*subj*: *courage, memory*) faire défaut à ▷ *vi* échouer; (*eyesight, health, light: also*: **be ~ing**) baisser, s'affaiblir; (*brakes*) lâcher; **to ~ to do sth** (*neglect*) négliger de *or* ne pas faire qch; (*be unable*) ne pas arriver *or* parvenir à faire qch; **without ~** à coup sûr; sans faute; **failing** *n* défaut *m* ▷ *prep* faute de; **failing that** à défaut, sinon; **failure** ['feɪljə^r] *n* échec *m*; (*person*) raté(e); (*mechanical etc*) défaillance *f*

faint [feɪnt] *adj* faible; (*recollection*) vague; (*mark*) à peine visible ▷ *n* évanouissement *m* ▷ *vi* s'évanouir; **to feel ~** défaillir; **faintest** *adj*: **I haven't the faintest idea** je n'en ai pas la moindre idée; **faintly** *adv* faiblement; (*vaguely*) vaguement

fair [fɛə^r] *adj* équitable, juste; (*hair*) blond(e); (*skin, complexion*) pâle, blanc (blanche); (*weather*) beau (belle); (*good enough*) assez bon(ne); (*sizeable*) considérable ▷ *adv*: **to play ~** jouer franc jeu ▷ *n* foire *f*; (*BRIT*: *funfair*) fête (foraine); **fairground** *n* champ *m* de foire; **fair-haired** *adj* (*person*) aux cheveux clairs, blond(e); **fairly** *adv* (*justly*) équitablement; (*quite*) assez; **fair trade** *n* commerce *m* équitable; **fairway** *n* (*Golf*) fairway *m*

fairy ['fɛərɪ] *n* fée *f*; **fairy tale** *n* conte *m* de fées

faith [feɪθ] *n* foi *f*; (*trust*) confiance *f*; (*sect*) culte *m*, religion *f*; **faithful** *adj* fidèle; **faithfully** *adv* fidèlement; **yours faithfully** (*BRIT*: *in letters*) veuillez agréer l'expression de mes salutations les plus distinguées

fake [feɪk] *n* (*painting etc*) faux *m*; (*person*) imposteur *m* ▷ *adj* faux (fausse) ▷ *vt* (*emotions*) simuler; (*painting*) faire un faux de

falcon ['fɔːlkən] *n* faucon *m*

fall [fɔːl] *n* chute *f*; (*decrease*) baisse *f*; (*us*: *autumn*) automne *m* ▷ *vi* (*pt* **fell**, *pp* **~en**) tomber; (*price, temperature, dollar*) baisser; **falls** *npl* (*waterfall*) chute *f* d'eau, cascade *f*; **to ~ flat** *vi* (*on one's face*) tomber de tout son long, s'étaler; (*joke*) tomber à plat; (*plan*) échouer; **fall apart** *vi* (*object*) tomber en morceaux; **fall down** *vi* (*person*) tomber; (*building*) s'effondrer, s'écrouler; **fall for** *vt fus* (*trick*) se laisser prendre à; (*person*) tomber amoureux(-euse) de; **fall off** *vi* tomber; (*diminish*) baisser, diminuer; **fall out** *vi* (*friends etc*) se brouiller; (*hair, teeth*) tomber; **fall over** *vi* tomber (par terre); **fall through** *vi* (*plan, project*) tomber à l'eau

fallen ['fɔːlən] pp of **fall**

fallout ['fɔːlaut] n retombées (radioactives)

false [fɔːls] adj faux (fausse); **under ~ pretences** sous un faux prétexte; **false alarm** n fausse alerte; **false teeth** npl (BRIT) fausses dents, dentier m

fame [feɪm] n renommée f, renom m

familiar [fə'mɪlɪə'] adj familier(-ière); **to be ~ with sth** connaître qch; **familiarize** [fə'mɪlɪəraɪz] vt: **to familiarize o.s. with** se familiariser avec

family ['fæmɪlɪ] n famille f; **family doctor** n médecin m de famille; **family planning** n planning familial

famine ['fæmɪn] n famine f

famous ['feɪməs] adj célèbre

fan [fæn] n (folding) éventail m; (Elec) ventilateur m; (person) fan m, admirateur(-trice); (Sport) supporter m/f ▷ vt éventer; (fire, quarrel) attiser

fanatic [fə'nætɪk] n fanatique m/f

fan belt n courroie f de ventilateur

fan club n fan-club m

fancy ['fænsɪ] n (whim) fantaisie f, envie f; (imagination) imagination f ▷ adj (luxury) de luxe; (elaborate: jewellery, packaging) fantaisie inv ▷ vt (feel like, want) avoir envie de; (imagine) imaginer; **to take a ~ to** se prendre d'affection pour; s'enticher de; **he fancies her** elle lui plaît; **fancy dress** n déguisement m, travesti m

fan heater n (BRIT) radiateur soufflant

fantasize ['fæntəsaɪz] vi fantasmer

fantastic [fæn'tæstɪk] adj fantastique

fantasy ['fæntəsɪ] n imagination f, fantaisie f; (unreality) fantasme m

fanzine ['fænziːn] n fanzine m

FAQ n abbr (= frequently asked question) FAQ f inv, faq f inv

far [fɑː'] adj (distant) lointain(e), éloigné(e) ▷ adv loin; **the ~ side/end** l'autre côté/bout; **it's not ~ (from here)** ce n'est pas loin (d'ici); **~ away**, **~ off** au loin, dans le lointain; **~ better** beaucoup mieux; **~ from** loin de; **by ~** de loin, de beaucoup; **go as ~ as the bridge** allez jusqu'au pont; **as ~ as I know** pour autant que je sache; **how ~ is it to ...?** combien y a-t-il jusqu'à ...?; **how ~ have you got with your work?** où en êtes-vous dans votre travail?

farce [fɑːs] n farce f

fare [fɛə'] n (on trains, buses) prix m du billet; (in taxi) prix de la course; (food) table f, chère f; **half ~** demi-tarif; **full ~** plein tarif

Far East n: **the ~** l'Extrême-Orient m

farewell [fɛə'wɛl] excl, n adieu m

farm [fɑːm] n ferme f ▷ vt cultiver; **farmer** n fermier(-ière); **farmhouse** n (maison f de) ferme f; **farming** n agriculture f; (of animals) élevage m; **farmyard** n cour f de ferme

far-reaching ['fɑː'riːtʃɪŋ] adj d'une grande portée

fart [fɑːt] (inf!) vi péter

farther ['fɑːðə'] adv plus loin ▷ adj plus éloigné(e), plus lointain(e)

farthest ['fɑːðɪst] superlative of **far**

fascinate ['fæsɪneɪt] vt fasciner, captiver; **fascinated** adj fasciné(e)

fascinating ['fæsɪneɪtɪŋ] adj fascinant(e)

fascination [fæsɪ'neɪʃən] n fascination f

fascist ['fæʃɪst] adj, n fasciste m/f

fashion ['fæʃən] n mode f; (manner) façon f, manière f ▷ vt façonner; **in ~** à la mode; **out of ~** démodé(e); **fashionable** adj à la mode; **fashion show** n défilé m de mannequins or de mode

fast [fɑːst] adj rapide; (clock): **to be ~** avancer; (dye, colour) grand or bon teint inv ▷ adv vite, rapidement; (stuck, held) solidement ▷ n jeûne m ▷ vi jeûner; **~ asleep** profondément endormi

fasten ['fɑːsn] vt attacher, fixer; (coat) attacher, fermer ▷ vi se fermer, s'attacher

fast food n fast food m, restauration f rapide

fat [fæt] adj gros(se) ▷ n graisse f; (on meat) gras m; (for cooking) matière grasse

fatal ['feɪtl] adj (mistake) fatal(e); (injury) mortel(le); **fatality** [fə'tælɪtɪ] n (road death etc) victime f, décès m; **fatally** adv fatalement; (injured) mortellement

fate [feɪt] n destin m; (of person) sort m

father ['fɑːðə'] n père m; **Father Christmas** n le Père Noël; **father-in-law** n beau-père m

fatigue [fə'tiːg] n fatigue f

fattening ['fætnɪŋ] adj (food) qui fait grossir

fatty ['fætɪ] adj (food) gras(se) ▷ n (inf) gros (grosse)

faucet ['fɔːsɪt] n (US) robinet m

fault [fɔːlt] n faute f; (defect) défaut m; (Geo) faille f ▷ vt trouver des défauts à, prendre en défaut; **it's my ~** c'est de ma faute; **to find ~ with** trouver à redire or à critiquer à; **at ~** fautif(-ive), coupable; **faulty** adj défectueux(-euse)

fauna ['fɔːnə] n faune f

favour etc (US **favor** etc) ['feɪvə'] n faveur f; (help) service m ▷ vt (proposition) être en faveur de; (pupil etc) favoriser; (team, horse) donner gagnant; **to do sb a ~** rendre un service à qn; **in ~ of** en faveur de; **to find ~ with sb** trouver grâce aux yeux de qn; **favourable** adj favorable; **favourite** ['feɪvrɪt] adj, n favori(te)

fawn [fɔːn] n (deer) faon m ▷ adj (also: **~-coloured**) fauve ▷ vi: **to ~ (up)on** flatter servilement

fax [fæks] n (document) télécopie f; (machine) télécopieur m ▷ vt envoyer par télécopie

FBI n abbr (US: = Federal Bureau of Investigation) FBI m

fear [fɪə'] n crainte f, peur f ▷ vt craindre; **for ~ of** de peur que + sub or de + infinitive; **fearful** adj craintif(-ive); (sight, noise) affreux(-euse), épouvantable; **fearless** adj intrépide

feasible ['fi:zəbl] adj faisable, réalisable

feast [fi:st] n festin m, banquet m; (Rel: also: **~ day**) fête f ▷ vi festoyer

feat [fi:t] n exploit m, prouesse f

feather ['fɛðə'] n plume f

feature ['fi:tʃə'] n caractéristique f; (article) chronique f, rubrique f ▷ vt (film) avoir pour vedette(s) ▷ vi figurer (en bonne place); **features** npl (of face) traits mpl; **a (special) ~ on sth/sb** un reportage sur qch/qn; **feature film** n long métrage

Feb. abbr (= February) fév

February ['fɛbruərɪ] n février m

fed [fɛd] pt, pp of **feed**

federal ['fɛdərəl] adj fédéral(e)

federation [fɛdə'reɪʃən] n fédération f

fed up adj: **to be ~ (with)** en avoir marre or plein le dos (de)

fee [fi:] n rémunération f; (of doctor, lawyer) honoraires mpl; (of school, college etc) frais mpl de scolarité; (for examination) droits mpl

feeble ['fi:bl] adj faible; (attempt, excuse) pauvre; (joke) piteux(-euse)

feed [fi:d] n (of animal) nourriture f, pâture f; (on printer) mécanisme m d'alimentation ▷ vt (pt, pp **fed**) (person) nourrir; (BRIT: baby: breastfeed) allaiter; (: with bottle) donner le biberon à; (horse etc) donner à manger à; (machine) alimenter; (data etc): **to ~ sth into** enregistrer qch dans; **feedback** n (Elec) effet m Larsen; (from person) réactions fpl

feel [fi:l] n (sensation) sensation f; (impression) impression f ▷ vt (pt, pp **felt**) (touch) toucher; (explore) tâter, palper; (cold, pain) sentir; (grief, anger) ressentir, éprouver; (think, believe): **to ~ (that)** trouver que; **to ~ hungry/cold** avoir faim/froid; **to ~ lonely/better** se sentir seul/ mieux; **I don't ~ well** je ne me sens pas bien; **it ~s soft** c'est doux au toucher; **to ~ like** (want) avoir envie de; **feeling** n (physical) sensation f; (emotion, impression) sentiment m; **to hurt sb's feelings** froisser qn

feet [fi:t] npl of **foot**

fell [fɛl] pt of **fall** ▷ vt (tree) abattre

fellow ['fɛləu] n type m; (comrade) compagnon m; (of learned society) membre m ▷ cpd: **their ~ prisoners/students** leurs camarades prisonniers/étudiants; **fellow citizen** n concitoyen(ne); **fellow countryman** n (irreg) compatriote m; **fellow men** npl semblables mpl; **fellowship** n (society) association f; (comradeship) amitié f, camaraderie f; (Scol) sorte de bourse universitaire

felony ['fɛlənɪ] n crime m, forfait m

felt [fɛlt] pt, pp of **feel** ▷ n feutre m; **felt-tip** n

(also: **felt-tip pen**) stylo-feutre m

female ['fi:meɪl] n (Zool) femelle f; (pej: woman) bonne femme ▷ adj (Biol) femelle; (sex, character) féminin(e); (vote etc) des femmes

feminine ['fɛmɪnɪn] adj féminin(e)

feminist ['fɛmɪnɪst] n féministe m/f

fence [fɛns] n barrière f ▷ vi faire de l'escrime; **fencing** n (sport) escrime m

fend [fɛnd] vi: **to ~ for o.s.** se débrouiller (tout seul); **fend off** vt (attack etc) parer; (questions) éluder

fender ['fɛndə'] n garde-feu m inv; (on boat) défense f; (US: of car) aile f

fennel ['fɛnl] n fenouil m

ferment vi [fə'mɛnt] fermenter ▷ n ['fə:mɛnt] (fig) agitation f, effervescence f

fern [fə:n] n fougère f

ferocious [fə'rəuʃəs] adj féroce

ferret ['fɛrɪt] n furet m

ferry ['fɛrɪ] n (small) bac m; (large: also: **~boat**) ferry(-boat m) m ▷ vt transporter

fertile ['fə:taɪl] adj fertile; (Biol) fécond(e); **fertilize** ['fə:tɪlaɪz] vt fertiliser; (Biol) féconder; **fertilizer** n engrais m

festival ['fɛstɪvəl] n (Rel) fête f; (Art, Mus) festival m

festive ['fɛstɪv] adj de fête; **the ~ season** (BRIT: Christmas) la période des fêtes

fetch [fɛtʃ] vt aller chercher; (BRIT: sell for) rapporter

fête [feɪt] n fête f, kermesse f

fetus ['fi:təs] n (US) = **foetus**

feud [fju:d] n querelle f, dispute f

fever ['fi:və'] n fièvre f; **feverish** adj fiévreux(-euse), fébrile

few [fju:] adj (not many) peu de ▷ pron peu; **a ~** (as adj) quelques; (as pron) quelques-uns(-unes); **quite a ~ ...** adj un certain nombre de ..., pas mal de ...; **in the past ~ days** ces derniers jours; **fewer** adj moins de; **fewest** adj le moins nombreux

fiancé [fɪ'ɑ̃:ŋseɪ] n fiancé m; **fiancée** n fiancée f

fiasco [fɪ'æskəu] n fiasco m

fib [fɪb] n bobard m

fibre (US **fiber**) ['faɪbə'] n fibre f; **fibreglass** (US **Fiberglass®**) n fibre f de verre

fickle ['fɪkl] adj inconstant(e), volage, capricieux(-euse)

fiction ['fɪkʃən] n romans mpl, littérature f romanesque; (invention) fiction f; **fictional** adj fictif(-ive)

fiddle ['fɪdl] n (Mus) violon m; (cheating) combine f; escroquerie f ▷ vt (BRIT: accounts) falsifier, maquiller; **fiddle with** vt fus tripoter

fidelity [fɪ'dɛlɪtɪ] n fidélité f

fidget ['fɪdʒɪt] vi se trémousser, remuer

field [fi:ld] n champ m; (fig) domaine m, champ m; (Sport: ground) terrain m; **field**

marshal n maréchal m

fierce [fɪəs] adj (look, animal) féroce, sauvage; (wind, attack, person) (très) violent(e); (fighting, enemy) acharné(e)

fifteen [fɪf'tiːn] num quinze; **fifteenth** num quinzième

fifth [fɪfθ] num cinquième

fiftieth ['fɪftɪɪθ] num cinquantième

fifty ['fɪftɪ] num cinquante; **fifty-fifty** adv moitié-moitié ▷ adj: **to have a fifty-fifty chance (of success)** avoir une chance sur deux (de réussir)

fig [fɪg] n figue f

fight [faɪt] n (between persons) bagarre f; (argument) dispute f; (Mil) combat m; (against cancer etc) lutte f ▷ vb (pt, pp **fought**) ▷ vt se battre contre; (cancer, alcoholism, emotion) combattre, lutter contre; (election) se présenter à ▷ vi se battre; (argue) se disputer; (fig): **to ~ (for/against)** lutter (pour/contre); **fight back** vi rendre les coups; (after illness) reprendre le dessus ▷ vt (tears) réprimer; **fight off** vt repousser; (disease, sleep, urge) lutter contre; **fighting** n combats mpl; (brawls) bagarres fpl

figure ['fɪgəʳ] n (Drawing, Geom) figure f; (number) chiffre m; (body, outline) silhouette f; (person's shape) ligne f, formes fpl; (person) personnage m ▷ vt (US: think) supposer ▷ vi (appear) figurer; (US: make sense) s'expliquer; **figure out** vt (understand) arriver à comprendre; (plan) calculer

file [faɪl] n (tool) lime f; (dossier) dossier m; (folder) dossier, chemise f; (: binder) classeur m; (Comput) fichier m; (row) file f ▷ vt (nails, wood) limer; (papers) classer; (Law: claim) faire enregistrer; déposer; **filing cabinet** n classeur m (meuble)

Filipino [fɪlɪ'piːnəu] adj philippin(e) ▷ n (person) Philippin(e)

fill [fɪl] vt remplir; (vacancy) pourvoir à ▷ n: **to eat one's ~** manger à sa faim; **to ~ with** remplir de; **fill in** vt (hole) boucher; (form) remplir; **fill out** vt (form, receipt) remplir; **fill up** vt remplir ▷ vi (Aut) faire le plein

fillet ['fɪlɪt] n filet m; **fillet steak** n filet m de bœuf, tournedos m

filling ['fɪlɪŋ] n (Culin) garniture f, farce f; (for tooth) plombage m; **filling station** n station-service f, station f d'essence

film [fɪlm] n film m; (Phot) pellicule f, film; (of powder, liquid) couche f, pellicule ▷ vt (scene) filmer ▷ vi tourner; **I'd like a 36-exposure ~** je voudrais une pellicule de 36 poses; **film star** n vedette f de cinéma

filter ['fɪltəʳ] n filtre m ▷ vt filtrer; **filter lane** n (BRIT Aut: at traffic lights) voie f de dégagement; (: on motorway) voie f de sortie

filth [fɪlθ] n saleté f; **filthy** adj sale,

dégoûtant(e); (language) ordurier(-ière), grossier(-ière)

fin [fɪn] n (of fish) nageoire f; (of shark) aileron m; (of diver) palme f

final ['faɪnl] adj final(e), dernier(-ière); (decision, answer) définitif(-ive) ▷ n (BRIT Sport) finale f; **finals** npl (Scol) examens mpl de dernière année; (US Sport) finale f; **finale** [fɪ'nɑːlɪ] n finale m; **finalist** n (Sport) finaliste m/f; **finalize** vt mettre au point; **finally** adv (eventually) enfin, finalement; (lastly) en dernier lieu

finance [faɪ'næns] n finance f ▷ vt financer; **finances** npl finances fpl; **financial** [faɪ'nænʃəl] adj financier(-ière); **financial year** n année f budgétaire

find [faɪnd] vt (pt, pp **found**) trouver; (lost object) retrouver ▷ n trouvaille f, découverte f; **to ~ sb guilty** (Law) déclarer qn coupable; **find out** vt se renseigner sur; (truth, secret) découvrir; (person) démasquer ▷ vi: **to ~ out about** (make enquiries) se renseigner sur; (by chance) apprendre; **findings** npl (Law) conclusions fpl, verdict m; (of report) constatations fpl

fine [faɪn] adj (weather) beau (belle); (excellent) excellent(e); (thin, subtle, not coarse) fin(e); (acceptable) bien inv ▷ adv (well) très bien; (small) fin, finement ▷ n (Law) amende f, contravention f ▷ vt (Law) condamner à une amende; donner une contravention à; **he's ~** il va bien; **the weather is ~** il fait beau; **fine arts** npl beaux-arts mpl

finger ['fɪŋgəʳ] n doigt m ▷ vt palper, toucher; **index ~** index m; **fingernail** n ongle m (de la main); **fingerprint** n empreinte digitale; **fingertip** n bout m du doigt

finish ['fɪnɪʃ] n fin f; (Sport) arrivée f; (polish etc) finition f ▷ vt finir, terminer ▷ vi finir, se terminer; **to ~ doing sth** finir de faire qch; **to ~ third** arriver or terminer troisième; **when does the show ~?** quand est-ce que le spectacle se termine?; **finish off** vt finir, terminer; (kill) achever; **finish up** vi, vt finir

Finland ['fɪnlənd] n Finlande f; **Finn** n Finnois(e), Finlandais(e); **Finnish** adj finnois(e), finlandais(e) ▷ n (Ling) finnois m

fir [fəːʳ] n sapin m

fire ['faɪəʳ] n feu m; (accidental) incendie m; (heater) radiateur m ▷ vt (discharge): **to ~ a gun** tirer un coup de feu; (fig: interest) enflammer, animer; (inf: dismiss) mettre à la porte, renvoyer ▷ vi (shoot) tirer, faire feu; **~!** au feu!; **on ~** en feu; **to set ~ to sth, set sth on ~** mettre le feu à qch; **fire alarm** n avertisseur m d'incendie; **firearm** n arme f à feu; **fire brigade** n (US **fire department**) (régiment m de sapeurs-)pompiers mpl; **fire engine** n (BRIT) pompe f à incendie; **fire**

escape n escalier m de secours; **fire exit** n issue f or sortie f de secours; **fire extinguisher** n extincteur m; **fireman** (irreg) n pompier m; **fireplace** n cheminée f; **fire station** n caserne f de pompiers; **fire truck** (US) n = **fire engine**; **firewall** n (Internet) pare-feu m; **firewood** n bois m de chauffage; **fireworks** npl (display) feu(x) m(pl) d'artifice

firm [fə:m] adj ferme ▷ n compagnie f, firme f; **firmly** adv fermement

first [fə:st] adj premier(-ière) ▷ adv (before other people) le premier, la première; (before other things) en premier, d'abord; (when listing reasons etc) en premier lieu, premièrement; (in the beginning) au début ▷ n (person: in race) premier(-ière); (BRIT Scol) mention f très bien; (Aut) première f; **the ~ of January** le premier janvier; **at ~** au commencement, au début; **~ of all** tout d'abord, pour commencer; **first aid** n premiers secours or soins; **first-aid kit** n trousse f à pharmacie; **first-class** adj (ticket etc) de première classe; (excellent) excellent(e), exceptionnel(le); (post) en tarif prioritaire; **first-hand** adj de première main; **first lady** n (US) femme f du président; **firstly** adv premièrement, en premier lieu; **first name** n prénom m; **first-rate** adj excellent(e)

fiscal ['fɪskl] adj fiscal(e); **fiscal year** n exercice financier

fish [fɪʃ] n (pl inv) poisson m ▷ vt, vi pêcher; **~ and chips** poisson frit et frites; **fisherman** (irreg) n pêcheur m; **fish fingers** npl (BRIT) bâtonnets de poisson (congelés); **fishing** n pêche f; **to go fishing** aller à la pêche; **fishing boat** n barque f de pêche; **fishing line** n ligne f (de pêche); **fishmonger** n (BRIT) marchand m de poisson; **fishmonger's (shop)** n (BRIT) poissonnerie f; **fish sticks** npl (US) = **fish fingers**; **fishy** adj (inf) suspect(e), louche

fist [fɪst] n poing m

fit [fɪt] adj (Med, Sport) en (bonne) forme; (proper) convenable; approprié(e) ▷ vt (subj: clothes) aller à; (put in, attach) installer, poser; (equip) équiper, garnir, munir; (suit) convenir à ▷ vi (clothes) aller; (parts) s'adapter; (in space, gap) entrer, s'adapter ▷ n (Med) accès m, crise f; (of anger) accès; (of hysterics, jealousy) crise; **~ to** (ready to) en état de; **~ for** (worthy) digne de; (capable) apte à; **to keep ~** se maintenir en forme; **this dress is a tight/good ~** cette robe est un peu juste/(me) va très bien; **a ~ of coughing** une quinte de toux; **by ~s and starts** par à-coups; **fit in** vi (add up) cadrer; (integrate) s'intégrer; (to new situation) s'adapter; **fitness** n (Med) forme f physique; **fitted** adj (jacket, shirt) ajusté(e); **fitted carpet** n moquette f; **fitted kitchen** n (BRIT) cuisine équipée; **fitted sheet** n drap-housse m; **fitting** adj approprié(e) ▷ n (of dress) essayage m; (of piece of equipment) pose f, installation f; **fitting room** n (in shop) cabine f d'essayage; **fittings** npl installations fpl

five [faɪv] num cinq; **fiver** n (inf: BRIT) billet m de cinq livres; (: US) billet de cinq dollars

fix [fɪks] vt (date, amount etc) fixer; (sort out) arranger; (mend) réparer; (make ready: meal, drink) préparer ▷ n: **to be in a ~** être dans le pétrin; **fix up** vt (meeting) arranger; **to ~ sb up with sth** faire avoir qch à qn; **fixed** adj (prices etc) fixe; **fixture** n installation f (fixe); (Sport) rencontre f (au programme)

fizzy ['fɪzɪ] adj pétillant(e), gazeux(-euse)

flag [flæg] n drapeau m; (also: **~stone**) dalle f ▷ vi faiblir; fléchir; **flag down** vt héler, faire signe (de s'arrêter) à; **flagpole** n mât m

flair [fleəʳ] n flair m

flak [flæk] n (Mil) tir antiaérien; (inf: criticism) critiques fpl

flake [fleɪk] n (of rust, paint) écaille f; (of snow, soap powder) flocon m ▷ vi (also: **~ off**) s'écailler

flamboyant [flæm'bɔɪənt] adj flamboyant(e), éclatant(e); (person) haut(e) en couleur

flame [fleɪm] n flamme f

flamingo [flə'mɪŋɡəʊ] n flamant m (rose)

flammable ['flæməbl] adj inflammable

flan [flæn] n (BRIT) tarte f

flank [flæŋk] n flanc m ▷ vt flanquer

flannel ['flænl] n (BRIT: also: **face ~**) gant m de toilette; (fabric) flanelle f

flap [flæp] n (of pocket, envelope) rabat m ▷ vt (wings) battre (de) ▷ vi (sail, flag) claquer

flare [fleəʳ] n (signal) signal lumineux; (Mil) fusée éclairante; (in skirt etc) évasement m; **flares** npl (trousers) pantalon m à pattes d'éléphant; **flare up** vi s'embraser; (fig: person) se mettre en colère, s'emporter; (: revolt) éclater

flash [flæʃ] n éclair m; (also: **news ~**) flash m (d'information); (Phot) flash ▷ vt (switch on) allumer (brièvement); (direct): **to ~ sth at** braquer qch sur; (send: message) câbler; (smile) lancer ▷ vi briller; jeter des éclairs; (light on ambulance etc) clignoter; **a ~ of lightning** un éclair; **in a ~** en un clin d'œil; **to ~ one's headlights** faire un appel de phares; **he ~ed by or past** il passa (devant nous) comme un éclair; **flashback** n flashback m, retour m en arrière; **flashbulb** n ampoule f de flash; **flashlight** n lampe f de poche

flask [flɑ:sk] n flacon m, bouteille f; (also: **vacuum ~**) bouteille f thermos®

flat [flæt] adj plat(e); (tyre) dégonflé(e), à plat; (beer) éventé(e); (battery) à plat; (denial) catégorique; (Mus) bémol inv; (: voice) faux (fausse) ▷ n (BRIT: apartment) appartement m; (Aut) crevaison f, pneu crevé; (Mus) bémol m; **~ out** (work) sans relâche; (race) à fond; **flatten**

vt (also: **flatten out**) aplatir; (crop) coucher; (house, city) raser

flatter ['flætə^r] vt flatter; **flattering** adj flatteur(-euse); (clothes etc) seyant(e)

flaunt [flɔːnt] vt faire étalage de

flavour etc (us **flavor** etc) ['fleɪvə^r] n goût m, saveur f; (of ice cream etc) parfum m ▷ vt parfumer, aromatiser; **vanilla-~ed** à l'arôme de vanille, vanillé(e); **what ~s do you have?** quels parfums avez-vous?; **flavouring** n arôme m (synthétique)

flaw [flɔː] n défaut m; **flawless** adj sans défaut

flea [fliː] n puce f; **flea market** n marché m aux puces

flee (pt, pp **fled**) [fliː, flɛd] vt fuir, s'enfuir de ▷ vi fuir, s'enfuir

fleece [fliːs] n (of sheep) toison f; (top) (laine f) polaire f ▷ vt (inf) voler, filouter

fleet [fliːt] n flotte f; (of lorries, cars etc) parc m; convoi m

fleeting ['fliːtɪŋ] adj fugace, fugitif(-ive); (visit) très bref (brève)

Flemish ['flɛmɪʃ] adj flamand(e) ▷ n (Ling) flamand m; **the ~** npl les Flamands

flesh [flɛʃ] n chair f

flew [fluː] pt of **fly**

flex [flɛks] n fil m or câble m électrique (souple) ▷ vt (knee) fléchir; (muscles) tendre; **flexibility** n flexibilité f; **flexible** adj flexible; (person, schedule) souple; **flexitime** (us **flextime**) n horaire m variable or à la carte

flick [flɪk] n petit coup; (with finger) chiquenaude f ▷ vt donner un petit coup à; (switch) appuyer sur; **flick through** vt fus feuilleter

flicker ['flɪkə^r] vi (light, flame) vaciller

flies [flaɪz] npl of **fly**

flight [flaɪt] n vol m; (escape) fuite f; (also: **~ of steps**) escalier m; **flight attendant** n steward m, hôtesse f de l'air

flimsy ['flɪmzɪ] adj peu solide; (clothes) trop léger(-ère); (excuse) pauvre, mince

flinch [flɪntʃ] vi tressaillir; **to ~ from** se dérober à, reculer devant

fling [flɪŋ] vt (pt, pp **flung**) jeter, lancer

flint [flɪnt] n silex m; (in lighter) pierre f (à briquet)

flip [flɪp] vt (throw) donner une chiquenaude à; (switch) appuyer sur; (us: pancake) faire sauter; **to ~ sth over** retourner qch

flip-flops ['flɪpflɔps] npl (esp BRIT) tongs fpl

flipper ['flɪpə^r] n (of animal) nageoire f; (for swimmer) palme f

flirt [fləːt] vi flirter ▷ n flirteur(-euse)

float [fləut] n flotteur m; (in procession) char m; (sum of money) réserve f ▷ vi flotter

flock [flɔk] n (of sheep) troupeau m; (of birds) vol m; (of people) foule f

flood [flʌd] n inondation f; (of letters, refugees

etc) flot m ▷ vt inonder ▷ vi (place) être inondé; (people): **to ~ into** envahir; **flooding** n inondation f; **floodlight** n projecteur m

floor [flɔː^r] n sol m; (storey) étage m; (of sea, valley) fond m ▷ vt (knock down) terrasser; (baffle) désorienter; **ground ~**, (us) **first ~** rez-de-chaussée m; **first ~**, (us) **second ~** premier étage; **what ~ is it on?** c'est à quel étage?; **floorboard** n planche f (du plancher); **flooring** n sol m; (wooden) plancher m; (covering) revêtement m de sol; **floor show** n spectacle m de variétés

flop [flɔp] n fiasco m ▷ vi (fail) faire fiasco; (fall) s'affaler, s'effondrer; **floppy** adj lâche, flottant(e) ▷ n (Comput: also: **floppy disk**) disquette f

flora ['flɔːrə] n flore f

floral ['flɔːrl] adj floral(e); (dress) à fleurs

florist ['flɔrɪst] n fleuriste m/f; **florist's (shop)** n magasin m or boutique f de fleuriste

flotation [fləu'teɪʃən] n (of shares) émission f; (of company) lancement m (en Bourse)

flour ['flauə^r] n farine f

flourish ['flʌrɪʃ] vi prospérer ▷ n (gesture) moulinet m

flow [fləu] n (of water, traffic etc) écoulement m; (tide, influx) flux m; (of blood, Elec) circulation f; (of river) courant m ▷ vi couler; (traffic) s'écouler; (robes, hair) flotter

flower ['flauə^r] n fleur f ▷ vi fleurir; **flower bed** n plate-bande f; **flowerpot** n pot m (à fleurs)

flown [fləun] pp of **fly**

fl. oz. abbr = **fluid ounce**

flu [fluː] n grippe f

fluctuate ['flʌktjueɪt] vi varier, fluctuer

fluent ['fluːənt] adj (speech, style) coulant(e), aisé(e); **he speaks ~ French, he's ~ in French** il parle le français couramment

fluff [flʌf] n duvet m; (on jacket, carpet) peluche f; **fluffy** adj duveteux(-euse); (toy) en peluche

fluid ['fluːɪd] n fluide m; (in diet) liquide m ▷ adj fluide; **fluid ounce** n (BRIT) = 0.028 l; 0.05 pints

fluke [fluːk] n coup m de veine

flung [flʌŋ] pt, pp of **fling**

fluorescent [fluə'rɛsnt] adj fluorescent(e)

fluoride ['fluəraɪd] n fluor m

flurry ['flʌrɪ] n (of snow) rafale f, bourrasque f; **a ~ of activity** un affairement soudain

flush [flʌʃ] n (on face) rougeur f; (fig: of youth etc) éclat m ▷ vt nettoyer à grande eau ▷ vi rougir ▷ adj (level): **~ with** au ras de, de niveau avec; **to ~ the toilet** tirer la chasse (d'eau)

flute [fluːt] n flûte f

flutter ['flʌtə^r] n (of panic, excitement) agitation f; (of wings) battement m ▷ vi (bird) battre des ailes, voleter

fly [flaɪ] n (insect) mouche f; (on trousers: also:

flies) braguette f ▷ vb (pt **flew**, pp **flown**) ▷ vt (plane) piloter; (passengers, cargo) transporter (par avion); (distance) parcourir ▷ vi voler; (passengers) aller en avion; (escape) s'enfuir, fuir; (flag) se déployer; **fly away, fly off** vi s'envoler; **fly-drive** n formule f avion plus voiture; **flying** n (activity) aviation f; (action) vol m ▷ adj: **flying visit** visite f éclair inv; **with flying colours** haut la main; **flying saucer** n soucoupe volante; **flyover** n (BRIT: overpass) pont routier

FM abbr (Radio: = frequency modulation) FM

foal [fəul] n poulain m

foam [fəum] n écume f; (on beer) mousse f; (also: ~ **rubber**) caoutchouc m mousse ▷ vi (liquid) écumer; (soapy water) mousser

focus ['fəukəs] n (pl **~es**) foyer m; (of interest) centre m ▷ vt (field glasses etc) mettre au point ▷ vi: **to ~ (on)** (with camera) régler la mise au point (sur); (with eyes) fixer son regard (sur); (fig: concentrate) se concentrer; **out of/in ~** (picture) flou(e)/net(te); (camera) pas au point/au point

foetus (US **fetus**) ['fiːtəs] n fœtus m

fog [fɔg] n brouillard m; **foggy** adj: **it's foggy** il y a du brouillard; **fog lamp** (US **fog light**) n (Aut) phare m anti-brouillard

foil [fɔil] vt déjouer, contrecarrer ▷ n feuille f de métal; (kitchen foil) papier m d'alu(minium); **to act as a ~ to** (fig) servir de repoussoir or de faire-valoir à

fold [fəuld] n (bend, crease) pli m; (Agr) parc m à moutons; (fig) bercail m ▷ vt plier; **to ~ one's arms** croiser les bras; **fold up** vi (map etc) se plier, se replier; (business) fermer boutique ▷ vt (map etc) plier, replier; **folder** n (for papers) chemise f; (: binder) classeur m; (Comput) dossier m; **folding** adj (chair, bed) pliant(e)

foliage ['fəuliɪdʒ] n feuillage m

folk [fəuk] npl gens mpl ▷ cpd folklorique; **folks** npl (inf: parents) famille f, parents mpl; **folklore** ['fəuklɔːʳ] n folklore m; **folk music** n musique f folklorique; (contemporary) musique folk, folk m; **folk song** n chanson f folklorique; (contemporary) chanson folk inv

follow ['fɔləu] vt suivre ▷ vi suivre; (result) s'ensuivre; **to ~ suit** (fig) faire de même; **follow up** vt (letter, offer) donner suite à; (case) suivre; **follower** n disciple m/f, partisan(e); **following** adj suivant(e) ▷ n partisans mpl, disciples mpl; **follow-up** n suite f; (on file, case) suivi m

fond [fɔnd] adj (memory, look) tendre, affectueux(-euse); (hopes, dreams) un peu fou (folle); **to be ~ of** aimer beaucoup

food [fuːd] n nourriture f; **food mixer** n mixeur m; **food poisoning** n intoxication f alimentaire; **food processor** n robot m de cuisine; **food stamp** n (US) bon m de nourriture (pour indigents)

fool [fuːl] n idiot(e); (Culin) mousse f de fruits ▷ vt berner, duper; **fool about, fool around** vi (pej: waste time) traînailler, glandouiller; (: behave foolishly) faire l'idiot or l'imbécile; **foolish** adj idiot(e), stupide; (rash) imprudent(e); **foolproof** adj (plan etc) infaillible

foot (pl **feet**) [fut, fiːt] n pied m; (of animal) patte f; (measure) pied (= 30.48 cm; 12 inches) ▷ vt (bill) payer; **on ~** à pied; **footage** n (Cine: length) ≈ métrage m; (: material) séquences fpl; **foot-and-mouth (disease)** [futənd'mauθ-] n fièvre aphteuse; **football** n (ball) ballon m (de football); (sport: BRIT) football m; (: US) football américain; **footballer** n (BRIT) = **football player**; **football match** n (BRIT) match m de foot(ball); **football player** n footballeur(-euse), joueur(-euse) de football; (US) joueur(-euse) de football américain; **footbridge** n passerelle f; **foothills** npl contreforts mpl; **foothold** n prise f (de pied); **footing** n (fig) position f; **to lose one's footing** perdre pied; **footnote** n note f (en bas de page); **footpath** n sentier m; **footprint** n trace f (de pied); **footstep** n pas m; **footwear** n chaussures fpl

○ **KEYWORD**

for [fɔːʳ] prep **1** (indicating destination, intention, purpose) pour; **the train for London** le train pour (or à destination de) Londres; **he left for Rome** il est parti pour Rome; **he went for the paper** il est allé chercher le journal; **is this for me?** c'est pour moi?; **it's time for lunch** c'est l'heure du déjeuner; **what's it for?** ça sert à quoi?; **what for?** (why) pourquoi?; (to what end) pour quoi faire?, à quoi bon?; **for sale** à vendre; **to pray for peace** prier pour la paix

2 (on behalf of, representing) pour; **the MP for Hove** le député de Hove; **to work for sb/sth** travailler pour qn/qch; **I'll ask him for you** je vais lui demander pour toi; **G for George** G comme Georges

3 (because of) pour; **for this reason** pour cette raison; **for fear of being criticized** de peur d'être critiqué

4 (with regard to) pour; **it's cold for July** il fait froid pour juillet; **a gift for languages** un don pour les langues

5 (in exchange for): **I sold it for £5** je l'ai vendu 5 livres; **to pay 50 pence for a ticket** payer un billet 50 pence

6 (in favour of) pour; **are you for or against us?** êtes-vous pour ou contre nous?; **I'm all for it** je suis tout à fait pour; **vote for X** votez pour X

7 (referring to distance) pendant, sur; **there**

are roadworks for **5 km** il y a des travaux sur or pendant 5 km; **we walked for miles** nous avons marché pendant des kilomètres **8** (*referring to time*) pendant; depuis; pour; **he was away for 2 years** il a été absent pendant 2 ans; **she will be away for a month** elle sera absente (pendant) un mois; **it hasn't rained for 3 weeks** ça fait 3 semaines qu'il ne pleut pas, il ne pleut pas depuis 3 semaines; **I have known her for years** je la connais depuis des années; **can you do it for tomorrow?** est-ce que tu peux le faire pour demain? **9** (*with infinitive clauses*): **it is not for me to decide** ce n'est pas à moi de décider; **it would be best for you to leave** le mieux serait que vous partiez; **there is still time for you to do it** vous avez encore le temps de le faire; **for this to be possible ...** pour que cela soit possible .. **10** (*in spite of*): **for all that** malgré cela, néanmoins; **for all his work/efforts** malgré tout son travail/tous ses efforts; **for all his complaints, he's very fond of her** il a beau se plaindre, il l'aime beaucoup ▷ *conj* (*since, as: rather formal*) car

forbid (*pt* **forbad(e)**, *pp* **~den**) [fə'bɪd, -'bæd, -'bɪdn] *vt* défendre, interdire; **to ~ sb to do** défendre *or* interdire à qn de faire; **forbidden** *adj* défendu(e)

force [fɔːs] *n* force *f* ▷ *vt* forcer; (*push*) pousser (de force); **to ~ o.s. to do** se forcer à faire; **in ~** (*being used: rule, law, prices*) en vigueur; (*in large numbers*) en force; **forced** *adj* forcé(e); **forceful** *adj* énergique

ford [fɔːd] *n* gué *m*

fore [fɔːʳ] *n*: **to the ~** en évidence; **forearm** *n* avant-bras *m inv*; **forecast** *n* prévision *f*; (*also*: **weather forecast**) prévisions *fpl* météorologiques, météo *f* ▷ *vt* (*irreg: like* **cast**) prévoir; **forecourt** *n* (*of garage*) devant *m*; **forefinger** *n* index *m*; **forefront** *n*: **in the forefront of** au premier rang *or* plan de; **foreground** *n* premier plan; **forehead** ['fɔrɪd] *n* front *m*

foreign ['fɔrɪn] *adj* étranger(-ère); (*trade*) extérieur(e); (*travel*) à l'étranger; **foreign currency** *n* devises étrangères; **foreigner** *n* étranger(-ère); **foreign exchange** *n* (*system*) change *m*; (*money*) devises *fpl*; **Foreign Office** *n* (BRIT) ministère *m* des Affaires étrangères; **Foreign Secretary** *n* (BRIT) ministre *m* des Affaires étrangères

fore: **foreman** (*irreg*) *n* (*in construction*) contremaître *m*; **foremost** *adj* le (la) plus en vue, premier(-ière) ▷ *adv*: **first and foremost** avant tout, tout d'abord; **forename** *n* prénom *m*

forensic [fə'rɛnsɪk] *adj*: **~ medicine** médecine

légale

foresee (*pt* **foresaw**, *pp* **~n**) [fɔː'siː, -'sɔː, -'siːn] *vt* prévoir; **foreseeable** *adj* prévisible

forest ['fɔrɪst] *n* forêt *f*; **forestry** *n* sylviculture *f*

forever [fə'rɛvəʳ] *adv* pour toujours; (*fig: endlessly*) continuellement

foreword ['fɔːwəːd] *n* avant-propos *m inv*

forfeit ['fɔːfɪt] *vt* perdre

forgave [fə'geɪv] *pt of* **forgive**

forge [fɔːdʒ] *n* forge *f* ▷ *vt* (*signature*) contrefaire; (*wrought iron*) forger; **to ~ money** (BRIT) fabriquer de la fausse monnaie; **forger** *n* faussaire *m*; **forgery** *n* faux *m*, contrefaçon *f*

forget (*pt* **forgot**, *pp* **forgotten**) [fə'gɛt, -'gɔt, -'gɔtn] *vt*, *vi* oublier; **I've forgotten my key/passport** j'ai oublié ma clé/mon passeport; **forgetful** *adj* distrait(e), étourdi(e)

forgive (*pt* **forgave**, *pp* **~n**) [fə'gɪv, -'geɪv, -'gɪvn] *vt* pardonner; **to ~ sb for sth/for doing sth** pardonner qch à qn/à qn de faire qch

forgot [fə'gɔt] *pt of* **forget**

forgotten [fə'gɔtn] *pp of* **forget**

fork [fɔːk] *n* (*for eating*) fourchette *f*; (*for gardening*) fourche *f*; (*of roads*) bifurcation *f* ▷ *vi* (*road*) bifurquer

forlorn [fə'lɔːn] *adj* (*deserted*) abandonné(e); (*hope, attempt*) désespéré(e)

form [fɔːm] *n* forme *f*; (*Scol*) classe *f*; (*questionnaire*) formulaire *m* ▷ *vt* former; (*habit*) contracter; **to ~ part of sth** faire partie de qch; **on top ~** en pleine forme

formal ['fɔːməl] *adj* (*offer, receipt*) en bonne et due forme; (*person*) cérémonieux(-euse); (*occasion, dinner*) officiel(le); (*garden*) à la française; (*clothes*) de soirée; **formality** [fɔː'mælɪtɪ] *n* formalité *f*

format ['fɔːmæt] *n* format *m* ▷ *vt* (*Comput*) formater

formation [fɔː'meɪʃən] *n* formation *f*

former ['fɔːməʳ] *adj* ancien(ne); (*before n*) précédent(e); **the ~ ... the latter** le premier ... le second, celui-là ... celui-ci; **formerly** *adv* autrefois

formidable ['fɔːmɪdəbl] *adj* redoutable

formula ['fɔːmjulə] *n* formule *f*

fort [fɔːt] *n* fort *m*

forthcoming [fɔːθ'kʌmɪŋ] *adj* qui va paraître *or* avoir lieu prochainement; (*character*) ouvert(e), communicatif(-ive); (*available*) disponible

fortieth ['fɔːtɪɪθ] *num* quarantième

fortify ['fɔːtɪfaɪ] *vt* (*city*) fortifier; (*person*) remonter

fortnight ['fɔːtnaɪt] *n* (BRIT) quinzaine *f*, quinze jours *mpl*; **fortnightly** *adj* bimensuel(le) ▷ *adv* tous les quinze jours

fortress ['fɔːtrɪs] *n* forteresse *f*

fortunate ['fɔːtʃənɪt] *adj* heureux(-euse);

(person) chanceux(-euse); **it is ~ that** c'est une chance que, il est heureux que; **fortunately** adv heureusement, par bonheur

fortune ['fɔːtʃən] n chance f; (wealth) fortune f; **fortune-teller** n diseuse f de bonne aventure

forty ['fɔːtɪ] num quarante

forum ['fɔːrəm] n forum m, tribune f

forward ['fɔːwəd] adj (movement, position) en avant, vers l'avant; (not shy) effronté(e); (in time) en avance ▷ adv (also: ~s) en avant ▷ n (Sport) avant m ▷ vt (letter) faire suivre; (parcel, goods) expédier; (fig) promouvoir, favoriser; **to move ~** avancer; **forwarding address** n adresse f de réexpédition

forward slash n barre f oblique

fossil ['fɔsl] adj, n fossile m

foster ['fɔstə^r] vt (encourage) encourager, favoriser; (child) élever (sans adopter); **foster child** n enfant élevé dans une famille d'accueil

foster parent n parent qui élève un enfant sans l'adopter

fought [fɔːt] pt, pp of **fight**

foul [faul] adj (weather, smell, food) infect(e); (language) ordurier(-ière) ▷ n (Football) faute f ▷ vt (dirty) salir, encrasser; **he's got a ~ temper** il a un caractère de chien; **foul play** n (Law) acte criminel

found [faund] pt, pp of **find** ▷ vt (establish) fonder; **foundation** [faun'deɪʃən] n (act) fondation f; (base) fondement m; (also: **foundation cream**) fond m de teint; **foundations** npl (of building) fondations fpl

founder ['faundə^r] n fondateur m ▷ vi couler, sombrer

fountain ['fauntɪn] n fontaine f; **fountain pen** n stylo m (à encre)

four [fɔː^r] num quatre; **on all ~s** à quatre pattes; **four-letter word** n obscénité f, gros mot; **four-poster** n (also: **four-poster bed**) lit m à baldaquin; **fourteen** num quatorze; **fourteenth** num quatorzième; **fourth** num quatrième ▷ n (Aut: also: **fourth gear**) quatrième f; **four-wheel drive** n (Aut: car) voiture f à quatre roues motrices

fowl [faul] n volaille f

fox [fɔks] n renard m ▷ vt mystifier

foyer ['fɔɪeɪ] n (in hotel) vestibule m; (Theat) foyer m

fraction ['frækʃən] n fraction f

fracture ['fræktʃə^r] n fracture f ▷ vt fracturer

fragile ['frædʒaɪl] adj fragile

fragment ['frægmənt] n fragment m

fragrance ['freɪgrəns] n parfum m

frail [freɪl] adj fragile, délicat(e); (person) frêle

frame [freɪm] n (of building) charpente f; (of human, animal) charpente, ossature f; (of picture) cadre m; (of door, window) encadrement m, chambranle m; (of spectacles: also: ~s) monture f ▷ vt (picture) encadrer; **~ of mind**

disposition f d'esprit; **framework** n structure f

France [frɑːns] n la France

franchise ['fræntʃaɪz] n (Pol) droit m de vote; (Comm) franchise f

frank [fræŋk] adj franc (franche) ▷ vt (letter) affranchir; **frankly** adv franchement

frantic ['fræntɪk] adj (hectic) frénétique; (distraught) hors de soi

fraud [frɔːd] n supercherie f, fraude f, tromperie f; (person) imposteur m

fraught [frɔːt] adj (tense: person) très tendu(e); (: situation) pénible; **~ with** (difficulties etc) chargé(e) de, plein(e) de

fray [freɪ] vt effilocher ▷ vi s'effilocher

freak [friːk] n (eccentric person) phénomène m; (unusual event) hasard m extraordinaire; (pej: fanatic): **health food ~** fana m/f or obsédé(e) de l'alimentation saine ▷ adj (storm) exceptionnel(le); (accident) bizarre

freckle ['frɛkl] n tache f de rousseur

free [friː] adj libre; (gratis) gratuit(e) ▷ vt (prisoner etc) libérer; (jammed object or person) dégager; **is this seat ~?** la place est libre?; **~ (of charge)** gratuitement; **freedom** n liberté f; **Freefone®** n numéro vert; **free gift** n prime f; **free kick** n (Sport) coup franc; **freelance** adj (journalist etc) indépendant(e), free-lance inv ▷ adv en free-lance; **freely** adv librement; (liberally) libéralement; **Freepost®** n (BRIT) port payé; **free-range** adj (egg) de ferme; (chicken) fermier; **freeway** n (US) autoroute f; **free will** n libre arbitre m; **of one's own free will** de son plein gré

freeze [friːz] vb (pt **froze**, pp **frozen**) ▷ vi geler ▷ vt geler; (food) congeler; (prices, salaries) bloquer, geler ▷ n gel m; (of prices, salaries) blocage m; **freezer** n congélateur m; **freezing** adj: **freezing (cold)** (room etc) glacial(e); (person, hands) gelé(e), glacé(e) ▷ n: **3 degrees below freezing** 3 degrés au-dessous de zéro; **it's freezing** il fait un froid glacial; **freezing point** n point m de congélation

freight [freɪt] n (goods) fret m, cargaison f; (money charged) fret, prix m du transport; **freight train** n (US) train m de marchandises

French [frɛntʃ] adj français(e) ▷ n (Ling) français m; **the ~** npl les Français; **what's the ~ (word) for ...?** comment dit-on ... en français?; **French bean** n (BRIT) haricot vert; **French bread** n pain m français; **French dressing** n (Culin) vinaigrette f; **French fried potatoes** (US **French fries**) npl (pommes de terre fpl) frites fpl; **Frenchman** (irreg) n Français m; **French stick** n ≈ baguette f; **French window** n porte-fenêtre f; **Frenchwoman** (irreg) n Française f

frenzy ['frɛnzɪ] n frénésie f

frequency ['friːkwənsɪ] n fréquence f

frequent adj ['friːkwənt] fréquent(e) ▷ vt

[frɪ'kwɛnt] fréquenter; **frequently**
['fri:kwəntlɪ] adv fréquemment

fresh [frɛʃ] adj frais (fraîche); (new) nouveau
(nouvelle); (cheeky) familier(-ière), culotté(e);
freshen vi (wind, air) fraîchir; **freshen up**
vi faire un brin de toilette; **fresher** n (BRIT
University: inf) bizuth m, étudiant(e) de
première année; **freshly** adv nouvellement,
récemment; **freshman** (US: irreg) n = **fresher**;
freshwater adj (fish) d'eau douce

fret [frɛt] vi s'agiter, se tracasser

Fri abbr (= Friday) ve

friction ['frɪkʃən] n friction f, frottement m

Friday ['fraɪdɪ] n vendredi m

fridge [frɪdʒ] n (BRIT) frigo m, frigidaire® m

fried [fraɪd] adj frit(e); ~ **egg** œuf m sur le plat

friend [frɛnd] n ami(e); **friendly** adj amical(e);
(kind) sympathique, gentil(le); (place)
accueillant(e); (Pol: country) ami(e) ▷ n (also:
friendly match) match amical; **friendship**
n amitié f

fries [fraɪz] (esp US) npl = **French fried
potatoes**

frigate ['frɪgɪt] n frégate f

fright [fraɪt] n peur f, effroi m; **to give sb
a ~** faire peur à qn; **to take ~** prendre peur,
s'effrayer; **frighten** vt effrayer, faire peur
à; **frightened** adj: **to be frightened (of)**
avoir peur (de); **frightening** adj effrayant(e);
frightful adj affreux(-euse)

frill [frɪl] n (of dress) volant m; (of shirt) jabot m

fringe [frɪndʒ] n (BRIT: of hair) frange f; (edge: of
forest etc) bordure f

Frisbee® ['frɪzbɪ] n Frisbee® m

fritter ['frɪtə'] n beignet m

frivolous ['frɪvələs] adj frivole

fro [frəu] see **to**

frock [frɒk] n robe f

frog [frɒg] n grenouille f; **frogman** (irreg) n
homme-grenouille m

◯ **KEYWORD**

from [frɒm] prep **1** (indicating starting place,
origin etc) de; **where do you come from?**,
where are you from? d'où venez-vous?;
where has he come from? d'où arrive-t-il?;
from London to Paris de Londres à Paris; **to
escape from sb/sth** échapper à qn/qch; **a
letter/telephone call from my sister** une
lettre/un appel de ma sœur; **to drink from
the bottle** boire à (même) la bouteille; **tell
him from me that ...** dites-lui de ma part
que ...

2 (indicating time) (à partir) de; **from one
o'clock to** or **until** or **till two** d'une heure à
deux heures; **from January (on)** à partir de
janvier

3 (indicating distance) de; **the hotel is one**
kilometre from the beach l'hôtel est à un
kilomètre de la plage

4 (indicating price, number etc) de; **prices range
from £10 to £50** les prix varient entre 10 livres
et 50 livres; **the interest rate was increased
from 9% to 10%** le taux d'intérêt est passé de
9% à 10%

5 (indicating difference) de; **he can't tell red
from green** il ne peut pas distinguer le rouge
du vert; **to be different from sb/sth** être
différent de qn/qch

6 (because of, on the basis of): **from what he
says** d'après ce qu'il dit; **weak from hunger**
affaibli par la faim

front [frʌnt] n (of house, dress) devant m; (of
coach, train) avant m; (promenade: also: **sea ~**)
bord m de mer; (Mil, Pol, Meteorology) front
m; (fig: appearances) contenance f, façade f
▷ adj de devant; (seat, wheel) avant inv ▷ vi: **in
~ (of)** devant; **front door** n porte f d'entrée;
(of car) portière f avant; **frontier** ['frʌntɪə'] n
frontière f; **front page** n première page; **front-
wheel drive** n traction f avant

frost [frɒst] n gel m, gelée f; (also: **hoar~**)
givre m; **frostbite** n gelures fpl; **frosting** n
(esp US: on cake) glaçage m; **frosty** adj (window)
couvert(e) de givre; (weather, welcome)
glacial(e)

froth [frɒθ] n mousse f; écume f

frown [fraun] n froncement m de sourcils ▷ vi
froncer les sourcils

froze [frəuz] pt of **freeze**

frozen ['frəuzn] pp of **freeze** ▷ adj (food)
congelé(e); (very cold: person: Comm: assets)
gelé(e)

fruit [fru:t] n (pl inv) fruit m; **fruit juice** n jus
m de fruit; **fruit machine** n (BRIT) machine f à
sous; **fruit salad** n salade f de fruits

frustrate [frʌs'treɪt] vt frustrer; **frustrated**
adj frustré(e)

fry (pt, pp **fried**) [fraɪ, -d] vt (faire) frire; **small ~**
le menu fretin; **frying pan** n poêle f (à frire)

ft. abbr = **foot**; **feet**

fudge [fʌdʒ] n (Culin) sorte de confiserie à base de
sucre, de beurre et de lait

fuel [fjuəl] n (for heating) combustible m; (for
engine) carburant m; **fuel tank** n (in vehicle)
réservoir m de or à carburant

fulfil (US **fulfill**) [ful'fɪl] vt (function, condition)
remplir; (order) exécuter; (wish, desire)
satisfaire, réaliser

full [ful] adj plein(e); (details, hotel, bus)
complet(-ète); (busy: day) chargé(e); (skirt)
ample, large ▷ adv: **to know ~ well that** savoir
fort bien que; **I'm ~ (up)** j'ai bien mangé; **~
employment/fare** plein emploi/tarif; **a ~
two hours** deux bonnes heures; **at ~ speed**
à toute vitesse; **in ~** (reproduce, quote, pay)

intégralement; (*write name etc*) en toutes lettres; **full-length** *adj* (*portrait*) en pied; (*coat*) long(ue); **full-length film** long métrage; **full moon** *n* pleine lune; **full-scale** *adj* (*model*) grandeur nature *inv*; (*search, retreat*) complet(-ète), total(e); **full stop** *n* point *m*; **full-time** *adj, adv* (*work*) à plein temps; **fully** *adv* entièrement, complètement; (*at least*)

fumble ['fʌmbl] *vi* fouiller, tâtonner; **fumble with** *vt fus* tripoter

fume [fjuːm] *vi* (*rage*) rager; **fumes** *npl* vapeurs *fpl*, émanations *fpl*, gaz *mpl*

fun [fʌn] *n* amusement *m*, divertissement *m*; **to have ~** s'amuser; **for ~** pour rire; **to make ~ of** se moquer de

function ['fʌŋkʃən] *n* fonction *f*; (*reception, dinner*) cérémonie *f*, soirée officielle ▷ *vi* fonctionner

fund [fʌnd] *n* caisse *f*, fonds *m*; (*source, store*) source *f*, mine *f*; **funds** *npl* (*money*) fonds *mpl*

fundamental [fʌndə'mɛntl] *adj* fondamental(e)

funeral ['fjuːnərəl] *n* enterrement *m*, obsèques *fpl* (*more formal occasion*); **funeral director** *n* entrepreneur *m* des pompes funèbres; **funeral parlour** [-'pɑːləʳ] *n* (*BRIT*) dépôt *m* mortuaire

funfair ['fʌnfɛəʳ] *n* (*BRIT*) fête (foraine)

fungus (*pl* **fungi**) ['fʌŋgəs, -gaɪ] *n* champignon *m*; (*mould*) moisissure *f*

funnel ['fʌnl] *n* entonnoir *m*; (*of ship*) cheminée *f*

funny ['fʌnɪ] *adj* amusant(e), drôle; (*strange*) curieux(-euse), bizarre

fur [fəːʳ] *n* fourrure *f*; (*BRIT*: *in kettle etc*) (dépôt *m* de) tartre *m*; **fur coat** *n* manteau *m* de fourrure

furious ['fjuərɪəs] *adj* furieux(-euse); (*effort*) acharné(e)

furnish ['fəːnɪʃ] *vt* meubler; (*supply*) fournir; **furnishings** *npl* mobilier *m*, articles *mpl* d'ameublement

furniture ['fəːnɪtʃəʳ] *n* meubles *mpl*, mobilier *m*; **piece of ~** meuble *m*

furry ['fəːrɪ] *adj* (*animal*) à fourrure; (*toy*) en peluche

further ['fəːðəʳ] *adj* supplémentaire, autre; nouveau (nouvelle) ▷ *adv* plus loin; (*more*) davantage; (*moreover*) de plus ▷ *vt* faire avancer *or* progresser, promouvoir; **further education** *n* enseignement *m* postscolaire (*recyclage, formation professionnelle*); **furthermore** *adv* de plus, en outre

furthest ['fəːðɪst] *superlative of* **far**

fury ['fjuərɪ] *n* fureur *f*

fuse (*US* **fuze**) [fjuːz] *n* fusible *m*; (*for bomb etc*) amorce *f*, détonateur *m* ▷ *vt, vi* (*metal*) fondre; (*BRIT*: *Elec*): **to ~ the lights** faire sauter les fusibles *or* les plombs; **fuse box** *n* boîte *f* à fusibles

fusion ['fjuːʒən] *n* fusion *f*

fuss [fʌs] *n* (*anxiety, excitement*) chichis *mpl*, façons *fpl*; (*commotion*) tapage *m*; (*complaining, trouble*) histoire(s) *f(pl)*; **to make a ~** faire des façons (*or* des histoires); **to make a ~ of sb** dorloter qn; **fussy** *adj* (*person*) tatillon(ne), difficile, chichiteux(-euse); (*dress, style*) tarabiscoté(e)

future ['fjuːtʃəʳ] *adj* futur(e) ▷ *n* avenir *m*; (*Ling*) futur *m*; **futures** *npl* (*Comm*) opérations *fpl* à terme; **in (the) ~** à l'avenir

fuze [fjuːz] *n, vt, vi* (*US*) = **fuse**

fuzzy ['fʌzɪ] *adj* (*Phot*) flou(e); (*hair*) crépu(e)

f

g [dʒiː]

G [dʒiː] n (Mus): **G** sol m

g. abbr (= gram) g

gadget ['gædʒɪt] n gadget m

Gaelic ['geɪlɪk] adj, n (Ling) gaélique (m)

gag [gæg] n (on mouth) bâillon m; (joke) gag m
▷ vt (prisoner etc) bâillonner

gain [geɪn] n (improvement) gain m; (profit) gain,
profit m ▷ vt gagner ▷ vi (watch) avancer; **to
~ from/by** gagner de/à; **to ~ on sb** (catch up)
rattraper qn; **to ~ 3lbs (in weight)** prendre 3
livres; **to ~ ground** gagner du terrain

gal. abbr = **gallon**

gala ['gɑːlə] n gala m

galaxy ['gæləksɪ] n galaxie f

gale [geɪl] n coup m de vent

gall bladder ['gɔːl-] n vésicule f biliaire

gallery ['gælərɪ] n (also: **art ~**) musée m; (:
private) galerie; (: in theatre) dernier balcon

gallon ['gælən] n gallon m (BRIT = 4.543 l; US =
3.785 l)

gallop ['gæləp] n galop m ▷ vi galoper

gallstone ['gɔːlstəʊn] n calcul m (biliaire)

gamble ['gæmbl] n pari m, risque calculé ▷ vt,
vi jouer; **to ~ on** (fig) miser sur; **gambler** n
joueur m; **gambling** n jeu m

game [geɪm] n jeu m; (event) match m; (of
tennis, chess, cards) partie f; (Hunting) gibier m
▷ adj (willing): **to be ~ (for)** être prêt(e) (à or
pour); **big ~** gros gibier; **games** npl (Scol) sport
m; (sport event) jeux; **games console** ['geɪmz-]

n console f de jeux vidéo; **game show** n jeu
télévisé

gammon ['gæmən] n (bacon) quartier m de
lard fumé; (ham) jambon fumé or salé

gang [gæŋ] n bande f; (of workmen) équipe f

gangster ['gæŋstər] n gangster m, bandit m

gap [gæp] n trou m; (in time) intervalle m;
(difference): **~ (between)** écart m (entre)

gape [geɪp] vi (person) être or rester bouche
bée; (hole, shirt) être ouvert(e)

gap year n année que certains étudiants prennent
pour voyager ou pour travailler avant d'entrer à
l'université

garage ['gærɑːʒ] n garage m; **garage sale** n
vide-grenier m

garbage ['gɑːbɪdʒ] n (us: rubbish) ordures
fpl, détritus mpl; (inf: nonsense) âneries fpl;
garbage can n (us) poubelle f, boîte f à
ordures; **garbage collector** n (us) éboueur m

garden ['gɑːdn] n jardin m; **gardens** npl
(public) jardin public; (private) parc m; **garden
centre** (BRIT) n pépinière f, jardinerie f;
gardener n jardinier m; **gardening** n
jardinage m

garlic ['gɑːlɪk] n ail m

garment ['gɑːmənt] n vêtement m

garnish ['gɑːnɪʃ] (Culin) vt garnir ▷ n
décoration f

garrison ['gærɪsn] n garnison f

gas [gæs] n gaz m; (us: gasoline) essence f
▷ vt asphyxier; **I can smell ~** ça sent le gaz;
gas cooker n (BRIT) cuisinière f à gaz; **gas
cylinder** n bouteille f de gaz; **gas fire** n (BRIT)
radiateur m à gaz

gasket ['gæskɪt] n (Aut) joint m de culasse

gasoline ['gæsəliːn] n (us) essence f

gasp [gɑːsp] n halètement m; (of shock etc): **she
gave a small ~ of pain** la douleur lui coupa le
souffle ▷ vi haleter; (fig) avoir le souffle coupé

gas: gas pedal n (us) accélérateur m; **gas
station** n (us) station-service f; **gas tank** n
(us Aut) réservoir m d'essence

gate [geɪt] n (of garden) portail m; (of field, at
level crossing) barrière f; (of building, town, at
airport) porte f

gateau (pl **~x**) ['gætəʊ, -z] n gros gâteau à
la crème

gatecrash ['geɪtkræʃ] vt s'introduire sans
invitation dans

gateway ['geɪtweɪ] n porte f

gather ['gæðər] vt (flowers, fruit) cueillir; (pick
up) ramasser; (assemble: objects) rassembler;
(: people) réunir; (: information) recueillir;
(understand) comprendre; (Sewing) froncer ▷ vi
(assemble) se rassembler; **to ~ speed** prendre
de la vitesse; **gathering** n rassemblement m

gauge [geɪdʒ] n (instrument) jauge f ▷ vt
jauger; (fig) juger de

gave [geɪv] pt of **give**

gay [geɪ] adj (homosexual) homosexuel(le);
(colour) gai, vif (vive)

gaze [geɪz] n regard m fixe ▷ vi: **to ~ at** vt fixer
du regard

GB abbr = **Great Britain**

GCSE n abbr (BRIT: = General Certificate of
Secondary Education) examen passé à l'âge de 16
ans sanctionnant les connaissances de l'élève

gear [gɪəʳ] n matériel m, équipement m; (Tech)
engrenage m; (Aut) vitesse f ▷ vt (fig: adapt)
adapter; **top** or (US) **high/low ~** quatrième
(or cinquième)/première vitesse; **in ~** en
prise; **gear up** vi: **to ~ up (to do)** se préparer
(à faire); **gear box** n boîte f de vitesse; **gear
lever** n levier m de vitesse; **gear shift** (US) n
= **gear lever**; **gear stick** (BRIT) n = **gear lever**

geese [giːs] npl of **goose**

gel [dʒɛl] n gelée f

gem [dʒɛm] n pierre précieuse

Gemini ['dʒɛmɪnaɪ] n les Gémeaux mpl

gender ['dʒɛndəʳ] n genre m; (person's sex)
sexe m

gene [dʒiːn] n (Biol) gène m

general ['dʒɛnərl] n général m ▷ adj
général(e); **in ~** en général; **general
anaesthetic** (US **general anesthetic**) n
anesthésie générale; **general election**
n élection(s) législative(s); **generalize** vi
généraliser; **generally** adv généralement;
general practitioner n généraliste m/f;
general store n épicerie f

generate ['dʒɛnəreɪt] vt engendrer;
(electricity) produire

generation [dʒɛnə'reɪʃən] n génération f; (of
electricity etc) production f

generator ['dʒɛnəreɪtəʳ] n générateur m

generosity [dʒɛnə'rɔsɪtɪ] n générosité f

generous ['dʒɛnərəs] adj généreux(-euse);
(copious) copieux(-euse)

genetic [dʒɪ'nɛtɪk] adj génétique; **~
engineering** ingénierie m génétique; **~
fingerprinting** système m d'empreinte
génétique; **genetically modified** adj (food
etc) génétiquement modifié(e); **genetics** n
génétique f

Geneva [dʒɪ'niːvə] n Genève

genitals ['dʒɛnɪtlz] npl organes génitaux

genius ['dʒiːnɪəs] n génie m

gent [dʒɛnt] n abbr (BRIT inf) = **gentleman**

gentle ['dʒɛntl] adj doux (douce); (breeze,
touch) léger(-ère)

gentleman (irreg) ['dʒɛntlmən] n monsieur
m; (well-bred man) gentleman m

gently ['dʒɛntlɪ] adv doucement

gents [dʒɛnts] n W.-C. mpl (pour hommes)

genuine ['dʒɛnjuɪn] adj véritable,
authentique; (person, emotion) sincère;
genuinely adv sincèrement, vraiment

geographic(al) [dʒɪə'græfɪk(l)] adj
géographique

geography [dʒɪ'ɔgrəfɪ] n géographie f

geology [dʒɪ'ɔlədʒɪ] n géologie f

geometry [dʒɪ'ɔmətrɪ] n géométrie f

geranium [dʒɪ'reɪnɪəm] n géranium m

geriatric [dʒɛrɪ'ætrɪk] adj gériatrique ▷ n
patient(e) gériatrique

germ [dʒəːm] n (Med) microbe m

German ['dʒəːmən] adj allemand(e) ▷ n
Allemand(e); (Ling) allemand m; **German
measles** n rubéole f

Germany ['dʒəːmənɪ] n Allemagne f

gesture ['dʒɛstʃəʳ] n geste m

○ **KEYWORD**

g

get [gɛt] (pt, pp **got**, pp **gotten** (US)) vi
1 (become, be) devenir; **to get old/tired**
devenir vieux/fatigué, vieillir/se fatiguer; **to
get drunk** s'enivrer; **to get dirty** se salir; **to
get married** se marier; **when do I get paid?**
quand est-ce que je serai payé?; **it's getting
late** il se fait tard

2 (go): **to get to/from** aller à/de; **to get
home** rentrer chez soi; **how did you get
here?** comment es-tu arrivé ici?

3 (begin) commencer or se mettre à; **to
get to know sb** apprendre à connaître qn;
I'm getting to like him je commence à
l'apprécier; **let's get going** or **started** allons-y

4 (modal aux vb): **you've got to do it** il faut que
vous le fassiez; **I've got to tell the police** je
dois le dire à la police

▷ vt **1**: **to get sth done** (do) faire qch; (have
done) faire faire qch; **to get sth/sb ready**
préparer qch/qn; **to get one's hair cut** se
faire couper les cheveux; **to get the car going**
or **to go** (faire) démarrer la voiture; **to get sb
to do sth** faire faire qch à qn

2 (obtain: money, permission, results) obtenir,
avoir; (buy) acheter; (find: job, flat) trouver;
(fetch: person, doctor, object) aller chercher; **to
get sth for sb** procurer qch à qn; **get me Mr
Jones, please** (on phone) passez-moi Mr Jones,
s'il vous plaît; **can I get you a drink?** est-ce
que je peux vous servir à boire?

3 (receive: present, letter) recevoir, avoir; (acquire:
reputation) avoir; (prize) obtenir; **what did you
get for your birthday?** qu'est-ce que tu as eu
pour ton anniversaire?; **how much did you
get for the painting?** combien avez-vous
vendu le tableau?

4 (catch) prendre, saisir, attraper; (hit: target
etc) atteindre; **to get sb by the arm/throat**
prendre or saisir or attraper qn par le bras/à la
gorge; **get him!** arrête-le!; **the bullet got him
in the leg** il a pris la balle dans la jambe

5 (take, move): **to get sth to sb** faire parvenir
qch à qn; **do you think we'll get it through**

the door? on arrivera à le faire passer par la porte?

6 (*catch, take: plane, bus etc*) prendre; **where do I get the train for Birmingham?** où prend-on le train pour Birmingham?

7 (*understand*) comprendre, saisir; (*hear*) entendre; **I've got it!** j'ai compris!; **I don't get your meaning** je ne vois *or* comprends pas ce que vous voulez dire; **I didn't get your name** je n'ai pas entendu votre nom

8 (*have, possess*): **to have got** avoir; **how many have you got?** vous en avez combien?

9 (*illness*) avoir; **I've got a cold** j'ai le rhume; **she got pneumonia and died** elle a fait une pneumonie et elle en est morte

get away *vi* partir, s'en aller; (*escape*) s'échapper

get away with *vt fus* (*punishment*) en être quitte pour; (*crime etc*) se faire pardonner

get back *vi* (*return*) rentrer

▷ *vt* récupérer, recouvrer; **when do we get back?** quand serons-nous de retour?

get in *vi* entrer; (*arrive home*) rentrer; (*train*) arriver

get into *vt fus* entrer dans; (*car, train etc*) monter dans; (*clothes*) mettre, enfiler, endosser; **to get into bed/a rage** se mettre au lit/en colère

get off *vi* (*from train etc*) descendre; (*depart: person, car*) s'en aller

▷ *vt* (*remove: clothes, stain*) enlever

▷ *vt fus* (*train, bus*) descendre de; **where do I get off?** où est-ce que je dois descendre?

get on *vi* (*at exam etc*) se débrouiller; (*agree*): **to get on (with)** s'entendre (avec); **how are you getting on?** comment ça va?

▷ *vt fus* monter dans; (*horse*) monter sur

get out *vi* sortir; (*of vehicle*) descendre

▷ *vt* sortir

get out of *vt fus* sortir de; (*duty etc*) échapper à, se soustraire à

get over *vt fus* (*illness*) se remettre de

get through *vi* (*Tel*) avoir la communication; **to get through to sb** atteindre qn

get up *vi* (*rise*) se lever

▷ *vt fus* monter

getaway ['gɛtəweɪ] *n* fuite *f*

Ghana ['gɑːnə] *n* Ghana *m*

ghastly ['gɑːstlɪ] *adj* atroce, horrible

ghetto ['gɛtəu] *n* ghetto *m*

ghost [gəust] *n* fantôme *m*, revenant *m*

giant ['dʒaɪənt] *n* géant(e) ▷ *adj* géant(e), énorme

gift [gɪft] *n* cadeau *m*; (*donation, talent*) don *m*; **gifted** *adj* doué(e); **gift shop** (*us* **gift store**) *n* boutique *f* de cadeaux; **gift token, gift voucher** *n* chèque-cadeau *m*

gig [gɪg] *n* (*inf: concert*) concert *m*

gigabyte ['dʒɪgəbaɪt] *n* gigaoctet *m*

gigantic [dʒaɪ'gæntɪk] *adj* gigantesque

giggle ['gɪgl] *vi* pouffer, ricaner sottement

gills [gɪlz] *npl* (*of fish*) ouïes *fpl*, branchies *fpl*

gilt [gɪlt] *n* dorure *f* ▷ *adj* doré(e)

gimmick ['gɪmɪk] *n* truc *m*

gin [dʒɪn] *n* gin *m*

ginger ['dʒɪndʒə'] *n* gingembre *m*

gipsy ['dʒɪpsɪ] *n* = **gypsy**

giraffe [dʒɪ'rɑːf] *n* girafe *f*

girl [gəːl] *n* fille *f*, fillette *f*; (*young unmarried woman*) jeune fille; (*daughter*) fille; **an English ~** une jeune Anglaise; **girl band** *n* girls band *m*; **girlfriend** *n* (*of girl*) amie *f*; (*of boy*) petite amie; **Girl Guide** *n* (*BRIT*) éclaireuse *f*; (*Roman Catholic*) guide *f*; **Girl Scout** *n* (*us*) = **Girl Guide**

gist [dʒɪst] *n* essentiel *m*

give [gɪv] *vb* (*pt* **gave**, *pp* **~n**) ▷ *vt* donner ▷ *vi* (*break*) céder; (*stretch: fabric*) se prêter; **to ~ sb sth, ~ sth to sb** donner qch à qn; (*gift*) offrir qch à qn; (*message*) transmettre qch à qn; **to ~ sb a call/kiss** appeler/embrasser qn; **to ~ a cry/sigh** pousser un cri/un soupir; **give away** *vt* donner; (*give free*) faire cadeau de; (*betray*) donner, trahir; (*disclose*) révéler; **give back** *vt* rendre; **give in** *vi* céder ▷ *vt* donner; **give out** *vt* (*food etc*) distribuer; **give up** *vi* renoncer ▷ *vt* renoncer à; **to ~ up smoking** arrêter de fumer; **to ~ o.s. up** se rendre

given ['gɪvn] *pp* of **give** ▷ *adj* (*fixed: time, amount*) donné(e), déterminé(e) ▷ *conj*: **~ the circumstances ...** étant donné les circonstances ..., vu les circonstances ...; **~ that ...** étant donné que ...

glacier ['glæsɪə'] *n* glacier *m*

glad [glæd] *adj* content(e); **gladly** ['glædlɪ] *adv* volontiers

glamorous ['glæmərəs] *adj* (*person*) séduisant(e); (*job*) prestigieux(-euse)

glamour (*us* **glamor**) ['glæmə'] *n* éclat *m*, prestige *m*

glance [glɑːns] *n* coup *m* d'œil ▷ *vi*: **to ~ at** jeter un coup d'œil à

gland [glænd] *n* glande *f*

glare [glɛə'] *n* (*of anger*) regard furieux; (*of light*) lumière éblouissante; (*of publicity*) feux *mpl* ▷ *vi* briller d'un éclat aveuglant; **to ~ at** lancer un regard *or* des regards furieux à; **glaring** *adj* (*mistake*) criant(e), qui saute aux yeux

glass [glɑːs] *n* verre *m*; **glasses** *npl* (*spectacles*) lunettes *fpl*

glaze [gleɪz] *vt* (*door*) vitrer; (*pottery*) vernir ▷ *n* vernis *m*

gleam [gliːm] *vi* luire, briller

glen [glɛn] *n* vallée *f*

glide [glaɪd] *vi* glisser; (*Aviat, bird*) planer; **glider** *n* (*Aviat*) planeur *m*

glimmer ['glɪmə'] *n* lueur *f*

glimpse [glɪmps] *n* vision passagère, aperçu

m ▷ *vt* entrevoir, apercevoir

glint [glɪnt] *vi* étinceler

glisten ['glɪsn] *vi* briller, luire

glitter ['glɪtəʳ] *vi* scintiller, briller

global ['gləʊbl] *adj* (*world-wide*) mondial(e); (*overall*) global(e); **globalization** *n* mondialisation *f*; **global warming** *n* réchauffement *m* de la planète

globe [gləʊb] *n* globe *m*

gloom [gluːm] *n* obscurité *f*; (*sadness*) tristesse *f*, mélancolie *f*; **gloomy** *adj* (*person*) morose; (*place, outlook*) sombre

glorious ['glɔːrɪəs] *adj* glorieux(-euse); (*beautiful*) splendide

glory ['glɔːrɪ] *n* gloire *f*; splendeur *f*

gloss [glɔs] *n* (*shine*) brillant *m*, vernis *m*; (*also:* **~ paint**) peinture brillante *or* laquée

glossary ['glɔsərɪ] *n* glossaire *m*, lexique *m*

glossy ['glɔsɪ] *adj* brillant(e), luisant(e) ▷ *n* (*also:* **~ magazine**) revue *f* de luxe

glove [glʌv] *n* gant *m*; **glove compartment** *n* (*Aut*) boîte *f* à gants, vide-poches *m inv*

glow [gləʊ] *vi* rougeoyer; (*face*) rayonner; (*eyes*) briller

glucose ['gluːkəʊs] *n* glucose *m*

glue [gluː] *n* colle *f* ▷ *vt* coller

GM *abbr* (= *genetically modified*) génétiquement modifié(e)

gm *abbr* (= *gram*) g

GMO *n abbr* (= *genetically modified organism*) OGM *m*

GMT *abbr* (= *Greenwich Mean Time*) GMT

gnaw [nɔː] *vt* ronger

go [gəʊ] *vb* (*pt* **went**, *pp* **gone**) ▷ *vi* aller; (*depart*) partir, s'en aller; (*work*) marcher; (*break*) céder; (*time*) passer; (*be sold*): **to go for £10** se vendre 10 livres; (*become*): **to go pale/mouldy** pâlir/moisir ▷ *n* (*pl* **goes**): **to have a go (at)** essayer (de faire); **to be on the go** être en mouvement; **whose go is it?** à qui est-ce de jouer?; **he's going to do it** il va le faire, il est sur le point de le faire; **to go for a walk** aller se promener; **to go dancing/shopping** aller danser/faire les courses; **to go and see sb, go to see sb** aller voir qn; **how did it go?** comment est-ce que ça s'est passé?; **to go round the back/by the shop** passer par derrière/devant le magasin; **... to go** (*us: food*) ... à emporter; **go ahead** *vi* (*take place*) avoir lieu; (*get going*) y aller; **go away** *vi* partir, s'en aller; **go back** *vi* rentrer; revenir; (*go again*) retourner; **go by** *vi* (*years, time*) passer, s'écouler ▷ *vt fus* s'en tenir à; (*believe*) en croire; **go down** *vi* descendre; (*number, price, amount*) baisser; (*ship*) couler; (*sun*) se coucher ▷ *vt fus* descendre; **go for** *vt fus* (*fetch*) aller chercher; (*like*) aimer; (*attack*) s'en prendre à; attaquer; **go in** *vi* entrer; **go into** *vt fus* entrer dans; (*investigate*) étudier, examiner; (*embark on*) se

lancer dans; **go off** *vi* partir, s'en aller; (*food*) se gâter; (*milk*) tourner; (*bomb*) sauter; (*alarm clock*) sonner; (*alarm*) se déclencher; (*lights etc*) s'éteindre; (*event*) se dérouler ▷ *vt fus* ne plus aimer; **the gun went off** le coup est parti; **go on** *vi* continuer; (*happen*) se passer; (*lights*) s'allumer ▷ *vt fus*: **to go on doing** continuer à faire; **go out** *vi* sortir; (*fire, light*) s'éteindre; (*tide*) descendre; **to go out with sb** sortir avec qn; **go over** *vi, vt fus* (*check*) revoir, vérifier; **go past** *vt fus*: **to go past sth** passer devant qch; **go round** *vi* (*circulate: news, rumour*) circuler; (*revolve*) tourner; (*suffice*) suffire (pour tout le monde); (*visit*): **to go round to sb's** passer chez qn; aller chez qn; (*make a detour*): **to go round (by)** faire un détour (par); **go through** *vt fus* (*town etc*) traverser; (*search through*) fouiller; (*suffer*) subir; **go up** *vi* monter; (*price*) augmenter ▷ *vt fus* gravir; **go with** *vt fus* aller avec; **go without** *vt fus* se passer de

go-ahead ['gəʊəhɛd] *adj* dynamique, entreprenant(e) ▷ *n* feu vert

goal [gəʊl] *n* but *m*; **goalkeeper** *n* gardien *m* de but; **goal-post** *n* poteau *m* de but

goat [gəʊt] *n* chèvre *f*

gobble ['gɔbl] *vt* (*also:* **~ down, ~ up**) engloutir

god [gɔd] *n* dieu *m*; **G~** Dieu; **godchild** *n* filleul(e); **goddaughter** *n* filleule *f*; **goddess** *n* déesse *f*; **godfather** *n* parrain *m*; **godmother** *n* marraine *f*; **godson** *n* filleul *m*

goggles ['gɔglz] *npl* (*for skiing etc*) lunettes (protectrices); (*for swimming*) lunettes de piscine

going ['gəʊɪŋ] *n* (*conditions*) état *m* du terrain ▷ *adj*: **the ~ rate** le tarif (en vigueur)

gold [gəʊld] *n* or *m* ▷ *adj* en or; (*reserves*) d'or; **golden** *adj* (*made of gold*) en or; (*gold in colour*) doré(e); **goldfish** *n* poisson *m* rouge; **goldmine** *n* mine *f* d'or; **gold-plated** *adj* plaqué(e) or *inv*

golf [gɔlf] *n* golf *m*; **golf ball** *n* balle *f* de golf; (*on typewriter*) boule *f*; **golf club** *n* club *m* de golf; (*stick*) club *m*, crosse *f* de golf; **golf course** *n* terrain *m* de golf; **golfer** *n* joueur(-euse) de golf

gone [gɔn] *pp of* **go**

gong [gɔŋ] *n* gong *m*

good [gʊd] *adj* bon(ne); (*kind*) gentil(le); (*child*) sage; (*weather*) beau (belle) ▷ *n* bien *m*; **goods** *npl* marchandise *f*, articles *mpl*; **~!** bon!, très bien!; **to be ~ at** être bon en; **to be ~ for** être bon pour; **it's no ~ complaining** cela ne sert à rien de se plaindre; **to make ~** (*deficit*) combler; (*losses*) compenser; **for ~** (*for ever*) pour de bon, une fois pour toutes; **would you be ~ enough to ...?** auriez-vous la bonté or l'amabilité de ...?; **is this any ~?** (*will it do?*) est-ce que ceci fera l'affaire?, est-ce que cela peut vous rendre service?; (*what's it like?*)

qu'est-ce que ça vaut?; **a ~ deal (of)** beaucoup (de); **a ~ many** beaucoup (de); **~ morning/ afternoon!** bonjour!; **~ evening!** bonsoir!; **~ night!** bonsoir!; (on going to bed) bonne nuit!; **goodbye** excl au revoir!; **to say goodbye to sb** dire au revoir à qn; **Good Friday** n Vendredi saint; **good-looking** adj beau (belle), bien inv; **good-natured** adj (person) qui a un bon naturel; **goodness** n (of person) bonté f; **for goodness sake!** je vous en prie!; **goodness gracious!** mon Dieu!; **goods train** n (BRIT) train m de marchandises; **goodwill** n bonne volonté

goose (pl **geese**) [guːs, giːs] n oie f

gooseberry ['guzbərɪ] n groseille f à maquereau; **to play ~** (BRIT) tenir la chandelle

goose bumps, goose pimples npl chair f de poule

gorge [gɔːdʒ] n gorge f ▷ vt: **to ~ o.s. (on)** se gorger (de)

gorgeous ['gɔːdʒəs] adj splendide, superbe

gorilla [gə'rɪlə] n gorille m

gosh (inf) [gɔʃ] excl mince alors!

gospel ['gɔspl] n évangile m

gossip ['gɔsɪp] n (chat) bavardages mpl; (malicious) commérage m, cancans mpl; (person) commère f ▷ vi bavarder; cancaner, faire des commérages; **gossip column** n (Press) échos mpl

got [gɔt] pt, pp of **get**

gotten ['gɔtn] (US) pp of **get**

gourmet ['guəmeɪ] n gourmet m, gastronome m/f

govern ['gʌvən] vt gouverner; (influence) déterminer; **government** n gouvernement m; (BRIT: ministers) ministère m; **governor** n (of colony, state, bank) gouverneur m; (of school, hospital etc) administrateur(-trice); (BRIT: of prison) directeur(-trice)

gown [gaun] n robe f; (of teacher, BRIT: of judge) toge f

G.P. n abbr (Med) = **general practitioner**

grab [græb] vt saisir, empoigner ▷ vi: **to ~ at** essayer de saisir

grace [greɪs] n grâce f ▷ vt (honour) honorer; (adorn) orner; **5 days' ~** un répit de 5 jours; **graceful** adj gracieux(-euse), élégant(e); **gracious** ['greɪʃəs] adj bienveillant(e)

grade [greɪd] n (Comm: quality) qualité f; (size) calibre m; (type) catégorie f; (in hierarchy) grade m, échelon m; (Scol) note f; (US: school class) classe f; (: gradient) pente f ▷ vt classer; (by size) calibrer; **grade crossing** n (US) passage m à niveau; **grade school** n (US) école f primaire

gradient ['greɪdɪənt] n inclinaison f, pente f

gradual ['grædjuəl] adj graduel(le), progressif(-ive); **gradually** adv peu à peu, graduellement

graduate n ['grædjuɪt] diplômé(e)

d'université; (US: of high school) diplômé(e) de fin d'études ▷ vi ['grædjueɪt] obtenir un diplôme d'université (or de fin d'études); **graduation** [grædju'eɪʃən] n cérémonie f de remise des diplômes

graffiti [grə'fiːtɪ] npl graffiti mpl

graft [grɑːft] n (Agr, Med) greffe f; (bribery) corruption f ▷ vt greffer; **hard ~** (BRIT: inf) boulot acharné

grain [greɪn] n (single piece) grain m; (no pl: cereals) céréales fpl; (US: corn) blé m

gram [græm] n gramme m

grammar ['græmər] n grammaire f; **grammar school** n (BRIT) ≈ lycée m

gramme [græm] n = **gram**

gran (inf) [græn] n (BRIT) mamie f (inf), mémé f (inf)

grand [grænd] adj magnifique, splendide; (gesture etc) noble; **grandad** (inf) n = **granddad**; **grandchild** (pl **~ren**) n petit-fils m, petite-fille f; **grandchildren** npl petits-enfants; **granddad** n (inf) papy m (inf), papi m (inf), pépé m (inf); **granddaughter** n petite-fille f; **grandfather** n grand-père m; **grandma** n (inf) = **gran**; **grandmother** n grand-mère f; **grandpa** n (inf) = **granddad**; **grandparents** npl grands-parents mpl; **grand piano** n piano m à queue; **Grand Prix** ['grɑ̃ː'priː] n (Aut) grand prix automobile; **grandson** n petit-fils m

granite ['grænɪt] n granit m

granny ['grænɪ] n (inf) = **gran**

grant [grɑːnt] vt accorder; (a request) accéder à; (admit) concéder ▷ n (Scol) bourse f; (Admin) subside m, subvention f; **to take sth for ~ed** considérer qch comme acquis; **to take sb for ~ed** considérer qn comme faisant partie du décor

grape [greɪp] n raisin m

grapefruit ['greɪpfruːt] n pamplemousse m

graph [grɑːf] n graphique m, courbe f; **graphic** ['græfɪk] adj graphique; (vivid) vivant(e); **graphics** n (art) arts mpl graphiques; (process) graphisme m ▷ npl (drawings) illustrations fpl

grasp [grɑːsp] vt saisir ▷ n (grip) prise f; (fig) compréhension f, connaissance f

grass [grɑːs] n herbe f; (lawn) gazon m; **grasshopper** n sauterelle f

grate [greɪt] n grille f de cheminée ▷ vi grincer ▷ vt (Culin) râper

grateful ['greɪtful] adj reconnaissant(e)

grater ['greɪtər] n râpe f

gratitude ['grætɪtjuːd] n gratitude f

grave [greɪv] n tombe f ▷ adj grave, sérieux(-euse)

gravel ['grævl] n gravier m

gravestone ['greɪvstəun] n pierre tombale

graveyard ['greɪvjɑːd] n cimetière m

gravity ['grævɪtɪ] n (Physics) gravité f;

pesanteur f; (seriousness) gravité

gravy ['greɪvɪ] n jus m (de viande), sauce f (au jus de viande)

gray [greɪ] adj (US) = **grey**

graze [greɪz] vi paître, brouter ▷ vt (touch lightly) frôler, effleurer; (scrape) écorcher ▷ n écorchure f

grease [gri:s] n (fat) graisse f; (lubricant) lubrifiant m ▷ vt graisser; lubrifier; **greasy** adj gras(se), graisseux(-euse); (hands, clothes) graisseux

great [greɪt] adj grand(e); (heat, pain etc) très fort(e), intense; (inf) formidable; **Great Britain** n Grande-Bretagne f; **great-grandfather** n arrière-grand-père m; **great-grandmother** n arrière-grand-mère f; **greatly** adv très, grandement; (with verbs) beaucoup

Greece [gri:s] n Grèce f

greed [gri:d] n (also: ~**iness**) avidité f; (for food) gourmandise f; **greedy** adj avide; (for food) gourmand(e)

Greek [gri:k] adj grec (grecque) ▷ n Grec (Grecque); (Ling) grec m

green [gri:n] adj vert(e); (inexperienced) (bien) jeune, naïf(-ïve); (ecological: product etc) écologique ▷ n (colour) vert m; (on golf course) green m; (stretch of grass) pelouse f; **greens** npl (vegetables) légumes verts; **green card** n (Aut) carte verte; (US: work permit) permis m de travail; **greengrocer** n (BRIT) marchand m de fruits et légumes; **greengrocer's (shop)** n magasin m de fruits et légumes; **greenhouse** n serre f; **greenhouse effect** n: **the greenhouse effect** l'effet m de serre

Greenland ['gri:nlənd] n Groenland m

green salad n salade verte

greet [gri:t] vt accueillir; **greeting** n salutation f; **Christmas/birthday greetings** souhaits mpl de Noël/de bon anniversaire; **greeting(s) card** n carte f de vœux

grew [gru:] pt of **grow**

grey (US **gray**) [greɪ] adj gris(e); (dismal) sombre; **grey-haired** adj aux cheveux gris; **greyhound** n lévrier m

grid [grɪd] n grille f; (Elec) réseau m; **gridlock** n (traffic jam) embouteillage m

grief [gri:f] n chagrin m, douleur f

grievance ['gri:vəns] n doléance f, grief m; (cause for complaint) grief

grieve [gri:v] vi avoir du chagrin; se désoler ▷ vt faire de la peine à, affliger; **to ~ for sb** pleurer qn

grill [grɪl] n (on cooker) gril m; (also: **mixed ~**) grillade(s) f(pl) ▷ vt (BRIT) griller; (inf: question) cuisiner

grille [grɪl] n grillage m; (Aut) calandre f

grim [grɪm] adj sinistre, lugubre; (serious, stern) sévère

grime [graɪm] n crasse f

grin [grɪn] n large sourire m ▷ vi sourire

grind [graɪnd] vb (pt, pp **ground**) ▷ vt écraser; (coffee, pepper etc) moudre; (US: meat) hacher ▷ n (work) corvée f

grip [grɪp] n (handclasp) poigne f; (control) prise f; (handle) poignée f; (holdall) sac m de voyage ▷ vt saisir, empoigner; (viewer, reader) captiver; **to come to ~s with** se colleter avec, en venir aux prises avec; **to ~ the road** (Aut) adhérer à la route; **gripping** adj prenant(e), palpitant(e)

grit [grɪt] n gravillon m; (courage) cran m ▷ vt (road) sabler; **to ~ one's teeth** serrer les dents

grits [grɪts] npl (US) gruau m de maïs

groan [grəun] n (of pain) gémissement m ▷ vi gémir

grocer ['grəusə'] n épicier m; **groceries** npl provisions fpl; **grocer's (shop), grocery** n épicerie f

groin [grɔɪn] n aine f

groom [gru:m] n (for horses) palefrenier m; (also: **bride~**) marié m ▷ vt (horse) panser; (fig): **to ~ sb for** former qn pour

groove [gru:v] n sillon m, rainure f

grope [grəup] vi tâtonner; **to ~ for** chercher à tâtons

gross [grəus] adj grossier(-ière); (Comm) brut(e); **grossly** adv (greatly) très, grandement

grotesque [grə'tɛsk] adj grotesque

ground [graund] pt, pp of **grind** ▷ n sol m, terre f; (land) terrain m, terres fpl; (Sport) terrain; (reason: gen pl) raison f; (US: also: ~**wire**) terre f ▷ vt (plane) empêcher de décoller, retenir au sol; (US Elec) équiper d'une prise de terre; **grounds** npl (gardens etc) parc m, domaine m; (of coffee) marc m; **on the ~, to the ~** par terre; **to gain/lose ~** gagner/perdre du terrain; **ground floor** n (BRIT) rez-de-chaussée m; **groundsheet** n (BRIT) tapis m de sol; **groundwork** n préparation f

group [gru:p] n groupe m ▷ vt (also: ~**together**) grouper ▷ vi (also: ~ **together**) se grouper

grouse [graus] n (pl inv: bird) grouse f (sorte de coq de bruyère) ▷ vi (complain) rouspéter, râler

grovel ['grɔvl] vi (fig): **to ~ (before)** ramper (devant)

grow (pt **grew**, pp ~**n**) [grəu, gru:, grəun] vi (plant) pousser, croître; (person) grandir; (increase) augmenter, se développer; (become) devenir; **to ~ rich/weak** s'enrichir/s'affaiblir ▷ vt cultiver, faire pousser; (hair, beard) laisser pousser; **grow on** vt fus: **that painting is ~ing on me** je finirai par aimer ce tableau; **grow up** vi grandir

growl [graul] vi grogner

grown [grəun] pp of **grow**; **grown-up** n adulte m/f, grande personne

growth [grəʊθ] n croissance f, développement m; (what has grown) pousse f, poussée f; (Med) grosseur f, tumeur f

grub [grʌb] n larve f; (inf: food) bouffe f

grubby ['grʌbɪ] adj crasseux(-euse)

grudge [grʌdʒ] n rancune f ▷ vt: **to ~ sb sth** (in giving) donner qch à qn à contre-cœur; (resent) reprocher qch à qn; **to bear sb a ~ (for)** garder rancune or en vouloir à qn (de)

gruelling (us **grueling**) ['gruəlɪŋ] adj exténuant(e)

gruesome ['gru:səm] adj horrible

grumble ['grʌmbl] vi rouspéter, ronchonner

grumpy ['grʌmpɪ] adj grincheux(-euse)

grunt [grʌnt] vi grogner

guarantee [gærən'ti:] n garantie f ▷ vt garantir

guard [gɑ:d] n garde f; (one man) garde m; (BRIT Rail) chef m de train; (safety device: on machine) dispositif m de sûreté; (also: **fire~**) garde-feu m inv ▷ vt garder, surveiller; (protect): **to ~ sb/sth (against or from)** protéger qn/qch (contre); **to be on one's ~** (fig) être sur ses gardes; **guardian** n gardien(ne); (of minor) tuteur(-trice)

guerrilla [gə'rɪlə] n guérillero m

guess [gɛs] vi deviner ▷ vt deviner; (estimate) évaluer; (us) croire, penser ▷ n supposition f, hypothèse f; **to take** or **have a ~** essayer de deviner

guest [gɛst] n invité(e); (in hotel) client(e); **guest house** n pension f; **guest room** n chambre f d'amis

guidance ['gaɪdəns] n (advice) conseils mpl

guide [gaɪd] n (person) guide m/f; (book) guide m; (also: **Girl G~**) éclaireuse f; (Roman Catholic) guide f ▷ vt guider; **is there an English-speaking ~?** est-ce que l'un des guides parle anglais?; **guidebook** n guide m; **guide dog** n chien m d'aveugle; **guided tour** n visite guidée; **what time does the guided tour start?** la visite guidée commence à quelle heure?; **guidelines** npl (advice) instructions générales, conseils mpl

guild [gɪld] n (History) corporation f; (sharing interests) cercle m, association f

guilt [gɪlt] n culpabilité f; **guilty** adj coupable

guinea pig ['gɪnɪ-] n cobaye m

guitar [gɪ'tɑ:ʳ] n guitare f; **guitarist** n guitariste m/f

gulf [gʌlf] n golfe m; (abyss) gouffre m

gull [gʌl] n mouette f

gulp [gʌlp] vi avaler sa salive; (from emotion) avoir la gorge serrée, s'étrangler ▷ vt (also: **~down**) avaler

gum [gʌm] n (Anat) gencive f; (glue) colle f; (also: **chewing-~**) chewing-gum m ▷ vt coller

gun [gʌn] n (small) revolver m, pistolet m; (rifle) fusil m, carabine f; (cannon) canon m; **gunfire** n fusillade f; **gunman** (irreg) n bandit armé; **gunpoint** n: **at gunpoint** sous la menace du pistolet (or fusil); **gunpowder** n poudre f à canon; **gunshot** n coup m de feu

gush [gʌʃ] vi jaillir; (fig) se répandre en effusions

gust [gʌst] n (of wind) rafale f

gut [gʌt] n intestin m, boyau m; **guts** npl (Anat) boyaux mpl; (inf: courage) cran m

gutter ['gʌtəʳ] n (of roof) gouttière f; (in street) caniveau m

guy [gaɪ] n (inf: man) type m; (also: **~rope**) corde f; (figure) effigie de Guy Fawkes

Guy Fawkes' Night [gaɪ'fɔ:ks-] n voir encadré

gym [dʒɪm] n (also: **~nasium**) gymnase m; (also: **~nastics**) gym f; **gymnasium** n gymnase m; **gymnast** n gymnaste m/f; **gymnastics** n, npl gymnastique f; **gym shoes** npl chaussures fpl de gym(nastique)

gynaecologist (us **gynecologist**) [gaɪnɪ'kɔlədʒɪst] n gynécologue m/f

gypsy ['dʒɪpsɪ] n gitan(e), bohémien(ne)

haberdashery [hæbə'dæʃərɪ] *n* (BRIT) mercerie *f*

habit ['hæbɪt] *n* habitude *f*; (*costume: Rel*) habit *m*

habitat ['hæbɪtæt] *n* habitat *m*

hack [hæk] *vt* hacher, tailler ▷ *n* (*pej: writer*) nègre *m*; **hacker** *n* (*Comput*) pirate *m* (informatique)

had [hæd] *pt, pp of* **have**

haddock (*pl ~ or ~s*) ['hædək] *n* églefin *m*; **smoked ~** haddock *m*

hadn't ['hædnt] = **had not**

haemorrhage (*US* **hemorrhage**) ['hɛmərɪdʒ] *n* hémorragie *f*

haemorrhoids (*US* **hemorrhoids**) ['hɛmərɔɪdz] *npl* hémorroïdes *fpl*

haggle ['hægl] *vi* marchander

Hague [heɪg] *n*: **The ~** La Haye

hail [heɪl] *n* grêle *f* ▷ *vt* (*call*) héler; (*greet*) acclamer ▷ *vi* grêler; **hailstone** *n* grêlon *m*

hair [hɛə'] *n* cheveux *mpl*; (*on body*) poils *mpl*; (*of animal*) pelage *m*; (*single hair: on head*) cheveu *m*; (: *on body, of animal*) poil *m*; **to do one's ~** se coiffer; **hairband** *n* (*elasticated*) bandeau *m*; (*plastic*) serre-tête *m*; **hairbrush** *n* brosse *f* à cheveux; **haircut** *n* coupe *f* (de cheveux); **hairdo** *n* coiffure *f*; **hairdresser** *n* coiffeur(-euse); **hairdresser's** *n* salon *m* de coiffure, coiffeur *m*; **hair dryer** *n* sèche-cheveux *m*, séchoir *m*; **hair gel** *n* gel

m pour cheveux; **hair spray** *n* laque *f* (pour les cheveux); **hairstyle** *n* coiffure *f*; **hairy** *adj* poilu(e), chevelu(e); (*inf: frightening*) effrayant(e)

hake (*pl ~ or ~s*) [heɪk] *n* colin *m*, merlu *m*

half [hɑːf] *n* (*pl* **halves**) moitié *f*; (*of beer: also: ~ pint*) ≈ demi *m*; (*Rail, bus: also: ~ fare*) demi-tarif *m*; (*Sport: of match*) mi-temps *f* ▷ *adj* demi(e) ▷ *adv* (à) moitié, à demi; **~ an hour** une demi-heure; **~ a dozen** une demi-douzaine; **~ a pound** une demi-livre, ≈ 250 g; **two and a ~** deux et demi; **to cut sth in ~** couper qch en deux; **half board** *n* (BRIT: *in hotel*) demi-pension *f*; **half-brother** *n* demi-frère *m*; **half day** *n* demi-journée *f*; **half fare** *n* demi-tarif *m*; **half-hearted** *adj* tiède, sans enthousiasme; **half-hour** *n* demi-heure *f*; **half-price** *adj* à moitié prix ▷ *adv* (*also*: **at half-price**) à moitié prix; **half term** *n* (BRIT Scol) vacances *fpl* (de demi-trimestre); **half-time** *n* mi-temps *f*; **halfway** *adv* à mi-chemin; **halfway through sth** au milieu de qch

hall [hɔːl] *n* salle *f*; (*entrance way: big*) hall *m*; (*small*) entrée *f*; (*US: corridor*) couloir *m*; (*mansion*) château *m*, manoir *m*

hallmark ['hɔːlmɑːk] *n* poinçon *m*; (*fig*) marque *f*

hallo [hə'ləu] *excl* = **hello**

hall of residence *n* (BRIT) pavillon *m* or résidence *f* universitaire

Halloween, Hallowe'en ['hæləu'iːn] *n* veille *f* de la Toussaint; *voir encadré*

● **HALLOWEEN**
●
● Selon la tradition, **Halloween** est la nuit
● des fantômes et des sorcières. En Écosse
● et aux États-Unis surtout (et de plus en
● plus en Angleterre) les enfants, pour fêter
● **Halloween**, se déguisent ce soir-là et ils
● vont ainsi de porte en porte en demandant
● de petits cadeaux (du chocolat, une pomme
● etc).

hallucination [həluːsɪ'neɪʃən] *n* hallucination *f*

hallway ['hɔːlweɪ] *n* (*entrance*) vestibule *m*; (*corridor*) couloir *m*

halo ['heɪləu] *n* (*of saint etc*) auréole *f*

halt [hɔːlt] *n* halte *f*, arrêt *m* ▷ *vt* faire arrêter; (*progress etc*) interrompre ▷ *vi* faire halte, s'arrêter

halve [hɑːv] *vt* (*apple etc*) partager *or* diviser en deux; (*reduce by half*) réduire de moitié

halves [hɑːvz] *npl of* **half**

ham [hæm] *n* jambon *m*

hamburger ['hæmbəːgə'] *n* hamburger *m*

hamlet ['hæmlɪt] *n* hameau *m*

hammer ['hæmə'] *n* marteau *m* ▷ *vt* (*nail*)

enfoncer; (*fig*) éreinter, démolir ▷ *vi* (*at door*)
frapper à coups redoublés; **to ~ a point home
to sb** faire rentrer qch dans la tête de qn
hammock ['hæmək] *n* hamac *m*
hamper ['hæmpər] *vt* gêner ▷ *n* panier *m*
(d'osier)
hamster ['hæmstər] *n* hamster *m*
hamstring ['hæmstrɪŋ] *n* (*Anat*) tendon *m*
du jarret
hand [hænd] *n* main *f*; (*of clock*) aiguille
f; (*handwriting*) écriture *f*; (*at cards*) jeu *m*;
(*worker*) ouvrier(-ière) ▷ *vt* passer, donner;
to give sb a ~ donner un coup de main à qn;
at ~ à portée de la main; **in ~** (*situation*) en
main; (*work*) en cours; **to be on ~** (*person*)
être disponible; (*emergency services*) se tenir
prêt(e) (à intervenir); **to ~** (*information etc*)
sous la main, à portée de la main; **on the
one ~ ..., on the other ~** d'une part ...,
d'autre part; **hand down** *vt* passer; (*tradition,
heirloom*) transmettre; (*us: sentence, verdict*)
prononcer; **hand in** *vt* remettre; **hand
out** *vt* distribuer; **hand over** *vt* remettre;
(*powers etc*) transmettre; **handbag** *n* sac *m*
à main; **hand baggage** *n* = **hand luggage**;
handbook *n*.manuel *m*; **handbrake** *n* frein *m*
à main; **handcuffs** *npl* menottes *fpl*; **handful**
n poignée *f*
handicap ['hændɪkæp] *n* handicap *m* ▷ *vt*
handicaper; **mentally/physically ~ped**
handicapé(e) mentalement/physiquement
handkerchief ['hæŋkətʃɪf] *n* mouchoir *m*
handle ['hændl] *n* (*of door etc*) poignée *f*; (*of cup
etc*) anse *f*; (*of knife etc*) manche *m*; (*of saucepan*)
queue *f*; (*for winding*) manivelle *f* ▷ *vt* toucher,
manier; (*deal with*) s'occuper de; (*treat: people*)
prendre; **"~ with care"** "fragile"; **to fly off the
~** s'énerver; **handlebar(s)** *n*(*pl*) guidon *m*
hand: **hand luggage** *n* bagages *mpl* à main;
handmade *adj* fait(e) à la main; **handout** *n*
(*money*) aide *f*, don *m*; (*leaflet*) prospectus *m*; (*at
lecture*) polycopié *m*; **hands-free** *adj* (*phone*)
mains libres *inv* ▷ *n* (*also*: **hands-free kit**) kit *m*
mains libres *inv*
handsome ['hænsəm] *adj* beau (belle);
(*profit*) considérable
handwriting ['hændraɪtɪŋ] *n* écriture *f*
handy ['hændɪ] *adj* (*person*) adroit(e); (*close at
hand*) sous la main; (*convenient*) pratique
hang (*pt, pp hung*) [hæŋ, hʌŋ] *vt* accrocher;
(*criminal: pt, pp* **~ed**) pendre ▷ *vi* pendre; (*hair,
drapery*) tomber ▷ *n*: **to get the ~ of (doing)
sth** (*inf*) attraper le coup pour faire qch; **hang
about, hang around** *vi* traîner; **hang down**
vi pendre; **hang on** *vi* (*wait*) attendre; **hang
out** *vt* (*washing*) étendre (dehors) ▷ *vi* (*inf: live*)
habiter, percher; (: *spend time*) traîner; **hang
round** *vi* = **hang around**; **hang up** *vi* (*Tel*)
raccrocher ▷ *vt* (*coat, painting etc*) accrocher,

suspendre
hanger ['hæŋər] *n* cintre *m*, portemanteau *m*
hang-gliding ['hæŋglaɪdɪŋ] *n* vol *m* libre *or*
sur aile delta
hangover ['hæŋəuvər] *n* (*after drinking*)
gueule *f* de bois
hankie, hanky ['hæŋkɪ] *n abbr*
= **handkerchief**
happen ['hæpən] *vi* arriver, se passer, se
produire; **what's ~ing?** que se passe-t-il?; **she
~ed to be free** il s'est trouvé (*or* se trouvait)
qu'elle était libre; **as it ~s** justement
happily ['hæpɪlɪ] *adv* heureusement;
(*cheerfully*) joyeusement
happiness ['hæpɪnɪs] *n* bonheur *m*
happy ['hæpɪ] *adj* heureux(-euse); **~ with**
(*arrangements etc*) satisfait(e) de; **to be ~ to do**
faire volontiers; **~ birthday!** bon anniversaire!
harass ['hærəs] *vt* accabler, tourmenter;
harassment *n* tracasseries *fpl*
harbour (*us* **harbor**) ['hɑːbər] *n* port *m* ▷ *vt*
héberger, abriter; (*hopes, suspicions*) entretenir
hard [hɑːd] *adj* dur(e); (*question, problem*)
difficile; (*facts, evidence*) concret(-ète) ▷ *adv*
(*work*) dur; (*think, try*) sérieusement; **to look
~ at** regarder fixement; (*thing*) regarder de
près; **no ~ feelings!** sans rancune!; **to be ~ of
hearing** être dur(e) d'oreille; **to be ~ done by**
être traité(e) injustement; **hardback** *n* livre
relié; **hardboard** *n* Isorel® *m*; **hard disk** *n*
(*Comput*) disque dur; **harden** *vt* durcir; (*fig*)
endurcir ▷ *vi* (*substance*) durcir
hardly ['hɑːdlɪ] *adv* (*scarcely*) à peine; (*harshly*)
durement; **~ anywhere/ever** presque nulle
part/jamais
hard: **hardship** *n* (*difficulties*) épreuves *fpl*;
(*deprivation*) privations *fpl*; **hard shoulder**
n (*BRIT Aut*) accotement stabilisé; **hard-up**
adj (*inf*) fauché(e); **hardware** *n* quincaillerie
f; (*Comput, Mil*) matériel *m*; **hardware shop**
(*us* **hardware store**) *n* quincaillerie *f*;
hard-working *adj* travailleur(-euse),
consciencieux(-euse)
hardy ['hɑːdɪ] *adj* robuste; (*plant*) résistant(e)
au gel
hare [hɛər] *n* lièvre *m*
harm [hɑːm] *n* mal *m*; (*wrong*) tort *m* ▷ *vt*
(*person*) faire du mal *or* du tort à; (*thing*)
endommager; **out of ~'s way** à l'abri du
danger, en lieu sûr; **harmful** *adj* nuisible;
harmless *adj* inoffensif(-ive)
harmony ['hɑːmənɪ] *n* harmonie *f*
harness ['hɑːnɪs] *n* harnais *m* ▷ *vt* (*horse*)
harnacher; (*resources*) exploiter
harp [hɑːp] *n* harpe *f* ▷ *vi*: **to ~ on about**
revenir toujours sur
harsh [hɑːʃ] *adj* (*hard*) dur(e); (*severe*) sévère;
(*unpleasant: sound*) discordant(e); (: *light*) cru(e)
harvest ['hɑːvɪst] *n* (*of corn*) moisson *f*; (*of*

fruit) récolte f; (of grapes) vendange f ▷ vt
moissonner; récolter; vendanger
has [hæz] vb see **have**
hasn't ['hæznt] = **has not**
hassle ['hæsl] n (inf: fuss) histoire(s) f(pl)
haste [heɪst] n hâte f, précipitation f; **hasten**
['heɪsn] vt hâter, accélérer ▷ vi se hâter,
s'empresser; **hastily** adv à la hâte; (leave)
précipitamment; **hasty** adj (decision, action)
hâtif(-ive); (departure, escape) précipité(e)
hat [hæt] n chapeau m
hatch [hætʃ] n (Naut: also: **~way**) écoutille f;
(BRIT: also: **service ~**) passe-plats m inv ▷ vi
éclore
hatchback ['hætʃbæk] n (Aut) modèle m avec
hayon arrière
hate [heɪt] vt haïr, détester ▷ n haine f;
hatred ['heɪtrɪd] n haine f
haul [hɔːl] vt traîner, tirer ▷ n (of fish) prise f; (of
stolen goods etc) butin m
haunt [hɔːnt] vt (subj: ghost, fear) hanter; (:
person) fréquenter ▷ n repaire m; **haunted** adj
(castle etc) hanté(e); (look) égaré(e), hagard(e)

○ KEYWORD

have [hæv] (pt, pp **had**) aux vb **1** (gen) avoir;
être; **to have eaten/slept** avoir mangé/
dormi; **to have arrived/gone** être arrivé(e)/
allé(e); **having finished** or **when he had
finished, he left** quand il a eu fini, il est parti;
we'd already eaten nous avions déjà mangé
2 (in tag questions): **you've done it, haven't
you?** vous l'avez fait, n'est-ce pas?
3 (in short answers and questions): **no I
haven't!/yes we have!** mais non!/mais si!;
so I have! ah oui!, oui c'est vrai!; **I've been
there before, have you?** j'y suis déjà allé, et
vous?
▷ modal aux vb (be obliged): **to have (got) to do
sth** devoir faire qch, être obligé(e) de faire qch;
she has (got) to do it elle doit le faire, il faut
qu'elle le fasse; **you haven't to tell her** vous
n'êtes pas obligé de le lui dire; (must not) ne le
lui dites surtout pas; **do you have to book?** il
faut réserver?
▷ vt **1** (possess) avoir; **he has (got) blue eyes/
dark hair** il a les yeux bleus/les cheveux bruns
2 (referring to meals etc): **to have breakfast**
prendre le petit déjeuner; **to have dinner/
lunch** dîner/déjeuner; **to have a drink**
prendre un verre; **to have a cigarette** fumer
une cigarette
3 (receive) avoir, recevoir; (obtain) avoir;
may I have your address? puis-je avoir
votre adresse?; **you can have it for £5** vous
pouvez l'avoir pour 5 livres; **I must have it for
tomorrow** il me le faut pour demain; **to have
a baby** avoir un bébé

4 (maintain, allow): **I won't have it!** ça ne se
passera pas comme ça!; **we can't have that**
nous ne tolérerons pas ça
5 (by sb else): **to have sth done** faire faire qch;
to have one's hair cut se faire couper les
cheveux; **to have sb do sth** faire faire qch à qn
6 (experience, suffer) avoir; **to have a cold/flu**
avoir un rhume/la grippe; **to have an
operation** se faire opérer; **she had her bag
stolen** elle s'est fait voler son sac
7 (+noun): **to have a swim/walk** nager/se
promener; **to have a bath/shower** prendre
un bain/une douche; **let's have a look**
regardons; **to have a meeting** se réunir; **to
have a party** organiser une fête; **let me have
a try** laissez-moi essayer

haven ['heɪvn] n port m; (fig) havre m
haven't ['hævnt] = **have not**
havoc ['hævək] n ravages mpl
Hawaii [hə'waɪː] n (îles fpl) Hawaï m
hawk [hɔːk] n faucon m
hawthorn ['hɔːθɔːn] n aubépine f
hay [heɪ] n foin m; **hay fever** n rhume m des
foins; **haystack** n meule f de foin
hazard ['hæzəd] n (risk) danger m, risque
m ▷ vt risquer, hasarder; **hazardous** adj
hasardeux(-euse), risqué(e); **hazard warning
lights** npl (Aut) feux mpl de détresse
haze [heɪz] n brume f
hazel ['heɪzl] n (tree) noisetier m ▷ adj (eyes)
noisette inv; **hazelnut** n noisette f
hazy ['heɪzɪ] adj brumeux(-euse); (idea) vague
he [hiː] pron il; **it is he who ...** c'est lui qui ...;
here he is le voici
head [hɛd] n tête f; (leader) chef m; (of school)
directeur(-trice); (of secondary school) proviseur
m ▷ vt (list) être en tête de; (group, company)
être à la tête de; **~s or tails** pile ou face; **~
first** la tête la première; **~ over heels in love**
follement or éperdument amoureux(-euse);
to ~ the ball faire une tête; **head for** vt fus
se diriger vers; (disaster) aller à; **head off** vt
(threat, danger) détourner; **headache** n mal
m de tête; **to have a headache** avoir mal
à la tête; **heading** n titre m; (subject title)
rubrique f; **headlamp** (BRIT) n = **headlight**;
headlight n phare m; **headline** n titre m;
head office n siège m, bureau m central;
headphones npl casque m (à écouteurs);
headquarters npl (of business) bureau or siège
central; (Mil) quartier général; **headroom**
n (in car) hauteur f de plafond; (under bridge)
hauteur limite; **headscarf** n foulard m;
headset n = **headphones**; **headteacher**
n directeur(-trice); (of secondary school)
proviseur m; **head waiter** n maître m d'hôtel
heal [hiːl] vt, vi guérir
health [hɛlθ] n santé f; **health care** n services

médicaux; **health centre** n (BRIT) centre m de santé; **health food** n aliment(s) naturel(s); **Health Service** n: **the Health Service** (BRIT) ≈ la Sécurité Sociale; **healthy** adj (person) en bonne santé; (climate, food, attitude etc) sain(e)

heap [hi:p] n tas m ▷ vt (also: ~ **up**) entasser, amonceler; **she ~ed her plate with cakes** elle a chargé son assiette de gâteaux; **~s (of)** (inf: lots) des tas (de)

hear (pt, pp **~d**) [hɪər, hɑ:d] vt entendre; (news) apprendre ▷ vi entendre; **to ~ about** entendre parler de; (have news of) avoir des nouvelles de; **to ~ from sb** recevoir des nouvelles de qn

heard [hɑ:d] pt, pp of **hear**

hearing ['hɪərɪŋ] n (sense) ouïe f; (of witnesses) audition f; (of a case) audience f; **hearing aid** n appareil m acoustique

hearse [hɑ:s] n corbillard m

heart [hɑ:t] n cœur m; **hearts** npl (Cards) cœur; **at ~** au fond; **by ~** (learn, know) par cœur; **to lose/take ~** perdre/prendre courage; **heart attack** n crise f cardiaque; **heartbeat** n battement m de cœur; **heartbroken** adj: **to be heartbroken** avoir beaucoup de chagrin; **heartburn** n brûlures fpl d'estomac; **heart disease** n maladie f cardiaque

hearth [hɑ:θ] n foyer m, cheminée f

heartless ['hɑ:tlɪs] adj (person) sans cœur, insensible; (treatment) cruel(le)

hearty ['hɑ:tɪ] adj chaleureux(-euse); (appetite) solide; (dislike) cordial(e); (meal) copieux(-euse)

heat [hi:t] n chaleur f; (Sport: also: **qualifying ~**) éliminatoire f ▷ vt chauffer; **heat up** vi (liquid) chauffer; (room) se réchauffer ▷ vt réchauffer; **heated** adj chauffé(e); (fig) passionné(e), échauffé(e), excité(e); **heater** n appareil m de chauffage; radiateur m; (in car) chauffage m; (water heater) chauffe-eau m

heather ['hɛðər] n bruyère f

heating ['hi:tɪŋ] n chauffage m

heatwave ['hi:tweɪv] n vague f de chaleur

heaven ['hɛvn] n ciel m, paradis m; (fig) paradis; **heavenly** adj céleste, divin(e)

heavily ['hɛvɪlɪ] adv lourdement; (drink, smoke) beaucoup; (sleep, sigh) profondément

heavy ['hɛvɪ] adj lourd(e); (work, rain, user, eater) gros(se); (drinker, smoker) grand(e); (schedule, week) chargé(e)

Hebrew ['hi:bru:] adj hébraïque ▷ n (Ling) hébreu m

Hebrides ['hɛbrɪdi:z] npl: **the ~** les Hébrides fpl

hectare ['hɛktɑ:ʳ] n (BRIT) hectare m

hectic ['hɛktɪk] adj (schedule) très chargé(e); (day) mouvementé(e); (lifestyle) trépidant(e)

he'd [hi:d] = **he would**; **he had**

hedge [hɛdʒ] n haie f ▷ vi se dérober ▷ vt: **to ~ one's bets** (fig) se couvrir

hedgehog ['hɛdʒhɔg] n hérisson m

heed [hi:d] vt (also: **take ~ of**) tenir compte de, prendre garde à

heel [hi:l] n talon m ▷ vt retalonner

hefty ['hɛftɪ] adj (person) costaud(e); (parcel) lourd(e); (piece, price) gros(se)

height [haɪt] n (of person) taille f, grandeur f; (of object) hauteur f; (of plane, mountain) altitude f; (high ground) hauteur, éminence f; (fig: of glory, fame, power) sommet m; (: of luxury, stupidity) comble m; **at the ~ of summer** au cœur de l'été; **heighten** vt hausser, surélever; (fig) augmenter

heir [ɛəʳ] n héritier m; **heiress** n héritière f

held [hɛld] pt, pp of **hold**

helicopter ['hɛlɪkɔptəʳ] n hélicoptère m

hell [hɛl] n enfer m; **oh ~!** (inf) merde!

he'll [hi:l] = **he will**; **he shall**

hello [hə'ləu] excl bonjour!; (to attract attention) hé!; (surprise) tiens!

helmet ['hɛlmɪt] n casque m

help [hɛlp] n aide f; (cleaner etc) femme f de ménage ▷ vt, vi aider; **~!** au secours!; **~ yourself** servez-vous; **can you ~ me?** pouvez-vous m'aider?; **can I ~ you?** (in shop) vous désirez?; **he can't ~ it** il n'y peut rien; **help out** vi aider ▷ vt: **to ~ sb out** aider qn; **helper** n aide m/f, assistant(e); **helpful** adj serviable, obligeant(e); (useful) utile; **helping** n portion f; **helpless** adj impuissant(e); (baby) sans défense; **helpline** n service m d'assistance téléphonique; (free) ≈ numéro vert

hem [hɛm] n ourlet m ▷ vt ourler

hemisphere ['hɛmɪsfɪəʳ] n hémisphère m

hemorrhage ['hɛmərɪdʒ] n (US) = **haemorrhage**

hemorrhoids ['hɛmərɔɪdz] npl (US) = **haemorrhoids**

hen [hɛn] n poule f; (female bird) femelle f

hence [hɛns] adv (therefore) d'où, de là; **2 years ~** d'ici 2 ans

hen night, hen party n soirée f entre filles (avant le mariage de l'une d'elles)

hepatitis [hɛpə'taɪtɪs] n hépatite f

her [hə:ʳ] pron (direct) la, l' + vowel or h mute; (indirect) lui; (stressed, after prep) elle ▷ adj son (sa), ses pl; see also **me**; **my**

herb [hə:b] n herbe f; **herbal** adj à base de plantes; **herbal tea** n tisane f

herd [hə:d] n troupeau m

here [hɪəʳ] adv ici; (time) alors ▷ excl tiens!, tenez!; **~!** (present) présent!; **~ is, ~ are** voici; **~ he/she is** le (la) voici

hereditary [hɪ'rɛdɪtrɪ] adj héréditaire

heritage ['hɛrɪtɪdʒ] n héritage m, patrimoine m

hernia ['hə:nɪə] n hernie f

hero (pl **~es**) ['hɪərəu] n héros m; **heroic** [hɪ'rəuɪk] adj héroïque

heroin ['hɛrəʊɪn] n héroïne f (drogue)
heroine ['hɛrəʊɪn] n héroïne f (femme)
heron ['hɛrən] n héron m
herring ['hɛrɪŋ] n hareng m
hers [həːz] pron le (la) sien(ne), les siens (siennes); see also **mine¹**
herself [həːˈsɛlf] pron (reflexive) se; (emphatic) elle-même; (after prep) elle; see also **oneself**
he's [hiːz] = **he is; he has**
hesitant ['hɛzɪtənt] adj hésitant(e), indécis(e)
hesitate ['hɛzɪteɪt] vi: **to ~ (about/to do)** hésiter (sur/à faire); **hesitation** [hɛzɪˈteɪʃən] n hésitation f
heterosexual ['hɛtərəʊˈsɛksjuəl] adj, n hétérosexuel(le)
hexagon ['hɛksəgən] n hexagone m
hey [heɪ] excl hé!
heyday ['heɪdeɪ] n: **the ~ of** l'âge m d'or de, les beaux jours de
HGV n abbr = **heavy goods vehicle**
hi [haɪ] excl salut!; (to attract attention) hé!
hibernate ['haɪbəneɪt] vi hiberner
hiccough, hiccup ['hɪkʌp] vi hoqueter ▷ n: **to have (the) ~s** avoir le hoquet
hid [hɪd] pt of **hide**
hidden ['hɪdn] pp of **hide** ▷ adj: **~ agenda** intentions non déclarées
hide [haɪd] n (skin) peau f ▷ vb (pt hid, pp hidden) ▷ vt cacher ▷ vi: **to ~ (from sb)** se cacher (de qn)
hideous ['hɪdɪəs] adj hideux(-euse), atroce
hiding ['haɪdɪŋ] n (beating) correction f, volée f de coups; **to be in ~** (concealed) se tenir caché(e)
hi-fi ['haɪfaɪ] adj, n abbr (= high fidelity) hi-fi f inv
high [haɪ] adj haut(e); (speed, respect, number) grand(e); (price) élevé(e); (wind) fort(e), violent(e); (voice) aigu(ë) ▷ adv haut, en haut; **20 m** ~ haut(e) de 20 m; **~ in the air** haut dans le ciel; **highchair** n (child's) chaise haute; **high-class** adj (neighbourhood, hotel) chic inv, de grand standing; **higher education** n études supérieures; **high heels** npl talons hauts, hauts talons; **high jump** n (Sport) saut m en hauteur; **highlands** ['haɪləndz] npl région montagneuse; **the Highlands** (in Scotland) les Highlands mpl; **highlight** n (fig: of event) point culminant ▷ vt (emphasize) faire ressortir, souligner; **highlights** npl (in hair) reflets mpl; **highlighter** n (pen) surligneur (lumineux); **highly** adv extrêmement, très; (unlikely) fort, (recommended, skilled, qualified) hautement; **to speak highly of** dire beaucoup de bien de; **highness** n: **His/Her Highness** son Altesse f; **high-rise** n (also: **high-rise block, high-rise building**) tour f (d'habitation); **high school** n lycée m; (US) établissement m d'enseignement supérieur; **high season** n (BRIT) haute saison; **high street** n (BRIT) grand-rue f; **high-tech**

(inf) adj de pointe; **highway** n (BRIT) route f; (US) route nationale; **Highway Code** n (BRIT) code m de la route
hijack ['haɪdʒæk] vt détourner (par la force); **hijacker** n auteur m d'un détournement d'avion, pirate m de l'air
hike [haɪk] vi faire des excursions à pied ▷ n excursion f à pied, randonnée f; **hiker** n promeneur(-euse), excursionniste m/f; **hiking** n excursions fpl à pied, randonnée f
hilarious [hɪˈlɛərɪəs] adj (behaviour, event) désopilant(e)
hill [hɪl] n colline f; (fairly high) montagne f; (on road) côte f; **hillside** n (flanc m de) coteau m; **hill walking** n randonnée f de basse montagne; **hilly** adj vallonné(e), montagneux(-euse)
him [hɪm] pron (direct) le, l' + vowel or h mute; (stressed, indirect, after prep) lui; see also **me**; **himself** pron (reflexive) se; (emphatic) lui-même; (after prep) lui; see also **oneself**
hind [haɪnd] adj de derrière
hinder ['hɪndər] vt gêner; (delay) retarder
hindsight ['haɪndsaɪt] n: **with (the benefit of) ~** avec du recul, rétrospectivement
Hindu ['hɪnduː] n Hindou(e); **Hinduism** n (Rel) hindouisme m
hinge [hɪndʒ] n charnière f ▷ vi: **to ~ on** dépendre de
hint [hɪnt] n allusion f; (advice) conseil m; (clue) indication f ▷ vt: **to ~ that** insinuer que ▷ vi: **to ~ at** faire une allusion à
hip [hɪp] n hanche f
hippie, hippy ['hɪpɪ] n hippie m/f
hippo ['hɪpəʊ] (pl ~s) n hippopotame m
hippopotamus [hɪpəˈpotəməs] (pl ~es or hippopotami) n hippopotame m
hippy ['hɪpɪ] n = **hippie**
hire ['haɪər] vt (BRIT: car, equipment) louer; (worker) embaucher, engager ▷ n location f; **for ~** à louer; (taxi) libre; **I'd like to ~ a car** je voudrais louer une voiture; **hire(d) car** n (BRIT) voiture f de location; **hire purchase** n (BRIT) achat m (or vente f) à tempérament or crédit
his [hɪz] pron le (la) sien(ne), les siens (siennes) ▷ adj son (sa), ses pl; see also **mine¹; my**
Hispanic [hɪsˈpænɪk] adj (in US) hispano-américain(e) ▷ n Hispano-Américain(e)
hiss [hɪs] vi siffler
historian [hɪˈstɔːrɪən] n historien(ne)
historic(al) [hɪˈstɔrɪk(l)] adj historique
history ['hɪstərɪ] n histoire f
hit [hɪt] vt (pt, pp ~) frapper; (reach: target) atteindre, toucher; (collide with: car) entrer en collision avec, heurter; (fig: affect) toucher ▷ n coup m; (success) succès m; (song) tube m; (to website) visite f; (on search engine) résultat m de recherche; **to ~ it off with sb** bien s'entendre

avec qn; **hit back** vi: **to ~ back at sb** prendre sa revanche sur qn

hitch [hɪtʃ] vt (fasten) accrocher, attacher; (also: **~ up**) remonter d'une saccade ▷ vi faire de l'autostop ▷ n (difficulty) anicroche f, contretemps m; **to ~ a lift** faire du stop; **hitch-hike** vi faire de l'auto-stop; **hitch-hiker** n auto-stoppeur(-euse); **hitch-hiking** n auto-stop m, stop m (inf)

hi-tech ['haɪtɛk] adj de pointe

hitman ['hɪtmæn] (irreg) n (inf) tueur m à gages

HIV n abbr (= human immunodeficiency virus) HIV m, VIH m; **~-negative/positive** séronégatif(-ive)/positif(-ive)

hive [haɪv] n ruche f

hoard [hɔːd] n (of food) provisions fpl, réserves fpl; (of money) trésor m ▷ vt amasser

hoarse [hɔːs] adj enroué(e)

hoax [həʊks] n canular m

hob [hɔb] n plaque chauffante

hobble ['hɔbl] vi boitiller

hobby ['hɔbɪ] n passe-temps favori

hobo ['həʊbəʊ] n (us) vagabond m

hockey ['hɔkɪ] n hockey m; **hockey stick** n crosse f de hockey

hog [hɔg] n porc (châtré) ▷ vt (fig) accaparer; **to go the whole ~** aller jusqu'au bout

Hogmanay [hɔgmə'neɪ] n réveillon m du jour de l'An, Saint-Sylvestre f; voir encadré

● **HOGMANAY**

●
● La Saint-Sylvestre ou "New Year's Eve" se
● nomme **Hogmanay** en Écosse. En cette
● occasion, la famille et les amis se réunissent
● pour entendre les douze coups de
● minuit et pour fêter le "first-footing", une
● coutume qui veut qu'on se rende chez
● ses amis et voisins en apportant quelque
● chose à boire (du whisky en général) et un
● morceau de charbon en gage de prospérité
● pour la nouvelle année.

hoist [hɔɪst] n palan m ▷ vt hisser

hold [həʊld] (pt, pp **held**) vt tenir; (contain) contenir; (meeting) tenir; (keep back) retenir; (believe) considérer; (possess) avoir ▷ vi (withstand pressure) tenir (bon); (be valid) valoir; (on telephone) attendre ▷ n prise f; (find) influence f; (Naut) cale f; **to catch** or **get (a) ~ of** saisir; **to get ~ of** (find) trouver; **~ the line!** (Tel) ne quittez pas!; **to ~ one's own** (fig) (bien) se défendre; **hold back** vt retenir; (secret) cacher; **hold on** vi tenir bon; (wait) attendre; **~ on!** (Tel) ne quittez pas!; **to ~ on to sth** (grasp) se cramponner à qch; (keep) conserver or garder qch; **hold out** vt offrir ▷ vi (resist): **to ~ out (against)** résister (devant), tenir bon

(devant); **hold up** vt (raise) lever; (support) soutenir; (delay) retarder; (: traffic) ralentir; (rob) braquer; **holdall** n (BRIT) fourre-tout m inv; **holder** n (container) support m; (of ticket, record) détenteur(-trice); (of office, title, passport etc) titulaire m/f

hole [həʊl] n trou m

holiday ['hɔlədɪ] n (BRIT: vacation) vacances fpl; (day off) jour m de congé; (public) jour férié; **to be on ~** être en vacances; **I'm here on ~** je suis ici en vacances; **holiday camp** n (also: **holiday centre**) camp m de vacances; **holiday job** n (BRIT) boulot m (inf) de vacances; **holiday-maker** n (BRIT) vacancier(-ière); **holiday resort** n centre m de villégiature or de vacances

Holland ['hɔlənd] n Hollande f

hollow ['hɔləʊ] adj creux(-euse); (fig) faux (fausse) ▷ n creux m; (in land) dépression f (de terrain), cuvette f ▷ vt: **to ~ out** creuser, évider

holly ['hɔlɪ] n houx m

Hollywood ['hɔlɪwʊd] n Hollywood

holocaust ['hɔləkɔːst] n holocauste m

holy ['həʊlɪ] adj saint(e); (bread, water) bénit(e); (ground) sacré(e)

home [həʊm] n foyer m, maison f; (country) pays natal, patrie f; (institution) maison ▷ adj de famille; (Econ, Pol) national(e), intérieur(e); (Sport: team) qui reçoit; (: match, win) sur leur (or notre) terrain ▷ adv chez soi, à la maison; au pays natal; (right in: nail etc) à fond; **at ~** chez soi, à la maison; **to go (or come)** ~ rentrer (chez soi), rentrer à la maison (or au pays); **make yourself at ~** faites comme chez vous; **home address** n domicile permanent; **homeland** n patrie f; **homeless** adj sans foyer, sans abri; **homely** adj (plain) simple, sans prétention; (welcoming) accueillant(e); **home-made** adj fait(e) à la maison; **home match** n match m à domicile; **Home Office** n (BRIT) ministère m de l'Intérieur; **home owner** n propriétaire occupant; **home page** n (Comput) page f d'accueil; **Home Secretary** n (BRIT) ministre m de l'Intérieur; **homesick** adj: **to be homesick** avoir le mal du pays; (missing one's family) s'ennuyer de sa famille; **home town** n ville natale; **homework** n devoirs mpl

homicide ['hɔmɪsaɪd] n (us) homicide m

homoeopathic (us **homeopathic**) [hə umɪə'pæθɪk] adj (medicine) homéopathique; (doctor) homéopathe

homoeopathy (us **homeopathy**) [hə umɪ'ɔpəθɪ] n homéopathie f

homosexual [hɔməʊ'sɛksjuəl] adj, n homosexuel(le)

honest ['ɔnɪst] adj honnête; (sincere) franc (franche); **honestly** adv honnêtement; franchement; **honesty** n honnêteté f

honey ['hʌnɪ] n miel m; **honeymoon** n

lune f de miel, voyage m de noces; **we're on honeymoon** nous sommes en voyage de noces; **honeysuckle** n chèvrefeuille m

Hong Kong ['hɔŋ'kɔŋ] n Hong Kong

honorary ['ɔnərərɪ] adj honoraire; (duty, title) honorifique; **~ degree** diplôme m honoris causa

honour (us **honor**) ['ɔnəʳ] vt honorer ▷ n honneur m; **to graduate with ~s** obtenir sa licence avec mention; **honourable** (us **honorable**) adj honorable; **honours degree** n (Scol) ≈ licence f avec mention

hood [hud] n capuchon m; (of cooker) hotte f; (BRIT Aut) capote f; (us Aut) capot m; **hoodie** ['hudɪ] n (top) sweat m à capuche

hoof (pl **~s** or **hooves**) [hu:f, hu:vz] n sabot m

hook [huk] n crochet m; (on dress) agrafe f; (for fishing) hameçon m ▷ vt accrocher; **off the ~** (Tel) décroché

hooligan ['hu:lɪgən] n voyou m

hoop [hu:p] n cerceau m

hooray [hu:'reɪ] excl = **hurray**

hoot [hu:t] vi (BRIT: Aut) klaxonner; (siren) mugir; (owl) hululer

Hoover® ['hu:vəʳ] n (BRIT) aspirateur m ▷ vt: **to hoover** (room) passer l'aspirateur dans; (carpet) passer l'aspirateur sur

hooves [hu:vz] npl of **hoof**

hop [hɔp] vi sauter; (on one foot) sauter à cloche-pied; (bird) sautiller

hope [həup] vt, vi espérer ▷ n espoir m; **I ~ so** je l'espère; **I ~ not** j'espère que non; **hopeful** adj (person) plein(e) d'espoir; (situation) prometteur(-euse), encourageant(e); **hopefully** adv (expectantly) avec espoir, avec optimisme; (one hopes) avec un peu de chance; **hopeless** adj désespéré(e); (useless) nul(le)

hops [hɔps] npl houblon m

horizon [hə'raɪzn] n horizon m; **horizontal** [hɔrɪ'zɔntl] adj horizontal(e)

hormone ['hɔ:məun] n hormone f

horn [hɔ:n] n corne f; (Mus) cor m; (Aut) klaxon m

horoscope ['hɔrəskəup] n horoscope m

horrendous [hə'rɛndəs] adj horrible, affreux(-euse)

horrible ['hɔrɪbl] adj horrible, affreux(-euse)

horrid ['hɔrɪd] adj (person) détestable; (weather, place, smell) épouvantable

horrific [hɔ'rɪfɪk] adj horrible

horrifying ['hɔrɪfaɪɪŋ] adj horrifiant(e)

horror ['hɔrəʳ] n horreur f; **horror film** n film m d'épouvante

hors d'œuvre [ɔ:'də:vrə] n hors d'œuvre m

horse [hɔ:s] n cheval m; **horseback: on horseback** adj, adv à cheval; **horse chestnut** n (nut) marron m (d'Inde); (tree) marronnier m (d'Inde); **horsepower** n puissance f (en chevaux); (unit) cheval-vapeur m (CV); **horse-**racing n courses fpl de chevaux; **horseradish** n raifort m; **horse riding** n (BRIT) équitation f

hose [həuz] n (also: **~pipe**) tuyau m; (also: **garden ~**) tuyau d'arrosage; **hosepipe** n tuyau m; (in garden) tuyau d'arrosage

hospital ['hɔspɪtl] n hôpital m; **in ~** à l'hôpital; **where's the nearest ~?** où est l'hôpital le plus proche?

hospitality [hɔspɪ'tælɪtɪ] n hospitalité f

host [həust] n hôte m; (TV, Radio) présentateur(-trice), animateur(-trice); (large number): **a ~ of** une foule de; (Rel) hostie f

hostage ['hɔstɪdʒ] n otage m

hostel ['hɔstl] n foyer m; (also: **youth ~**) auberge f de jeunesse

hostess ['həustɪs] n hôtesse f; (BRIT: also: **air ~**) hôtesse de l'air; (TV, Radio) animatrice f

hostile ['hɔstaɪl] adj hostile

hostility [hɔ'stɪlɪtɪ] n hostilité f

hot [hɔt] adj chaud(e); (as opposed to only warm) très chaud; (spicy) fort(e); (fig: contest) acharné(e); (topic) brûlant(e); (temper) violent(e), passionné(e); **to be ~** (person) avoir chaud; (thing) être (très) chaud; (weather) faire chaud; **hot dog** n hot-dog m

hotel [həu'tɛl] n hôtel m

hot-water bottle [hɔt'wɔ:tə-] n bouillotte f

hound [haund] vt poursuivre avec acharnement ▷ n chien courant

hour ['auəʳ] n heure f; **hourly** adj toutes les heures; (rate) horaire

house n [haus] maison f; (Pol) chambre f; (Theat) salle f; auditoire m ▷ vt [hauz] (person) loger, héberger; **on the ~** (fig) aux frais de la maison; **household** n (Admin etc) ménage m; (people) famille f, maisonnée f; **householder** n propriétaire m/f; (head of house) chef m de famille; **housekeeper** n gouvernante f; **housekeeping** n (work) ménage m; **housewife** (irreg) n ménagère f; femme f au foyer; **house wine** n cuvée f maison or du patron; **housework** n (travaux mpl du) ménage m

housing ['hauzɪŋ] n logement m; **housing development** (BRIT **housing estate**) n (blocks of flats) cité f; (houses) lotissement m

hover ['hɔvəʳ] vi planer; **hovercraft** n aéroglisseur m, hovercraft m

how [hau] adv comment; **~ are you?** comment allez-vous?; **~ do you do?** bonjour!; (on being introduced) enchanté(e); **~ long have you been here?** depuis combien de temps êtes-vous là?; **~ lovely/awful!** que or comme c'est joli/affreux!; **~ much time/many people?** combien de temps/gens?; **~ much does it cost?** ça coûte combien?; **~ old are you?** quel âge avez-vous?; **~ tall is he?** combien mesure-t-il?; **~ is school?** ça va à l'école?; **~ was the film?** comment était le film?

however [hauˈɛvəʳ] *conj* pourtant, cependant ▷ *adv*: **~ I do it** de quelque manière que je m'y prenne; **~ cold it is** même s'il fait très froid; **~ did you do it?** comment y êtes-vous donc arrivé?

howl [haul] *n* hurlement *m* ▷ *vi* hurler; (*wind*) mugir

H.P. *n abbr* (*BRIT*) = **hire purchase**

h.p. *abbr* (*Aut*) = **horsepower**

HQ *n abbr* (= *headquarters*) QG *m*

hr(s) *abbr* (= *hour(s)*) h

HTML *n abbr* (= *hypertext markup language*) HTML *m*

hubcap [ˈhʌbkæp] *n* (*Aut*) enjoliveur *m*

huddle [ˈhʌdl] *vi*: **to ~ together** se blottir les uns contre les autres

huff [hʌf] *n*: **in a ~** fâché(e)

hug [hʌg] *vt* serrer dans ses bras; (*shore, kerb*) serrer ▷ *n*: **to give sb a ~** serrer qn dans ses bras

huge [hjuːdʒ] *adj* énorme, immense

hull [hʌl] *n* (*of ship*) coque *f*

hum [hʌm] *vt* (*tune*) fredonner ▷ *vi* fredonner; (*insect*) bourdonner; (*plane, tool*) vrombir

human [ˈhjuːmən] *adj* humain(e) ▷ *n* (*also*: **~ being**) être humain

humane [hjuːˈmeɪn] *adj* humain(e), humanitaire

humanitarian [hjuːmænɪˈtɛərɪən] *adj* humanitaire

humanity [hjuːˈmænɪtɪ] *n* humanité *f*

human rights *npl* droits *mpl* de l'homme

humble [ˈhʌmbl] *adj* humble, modeste

humid [ˈhjuːmɪd] *adj* humide; **humidity** [hjuːˈmɪdɪtɪ] *n* humidité *f*

humiliate [hjuːˈmɪlɪeɪt] *vt* humilier

humiliating [hjuːˈmɪlɪeɪtɪŋ] *adj* humiliant(e)

humiliation [hjuːmɪlɪˈeɪʃən] *n* humiliation *f*

hummus [ˈhuməs] *n* houm(m)ous *m*

humorous [ˈhjuːmərəs] *adj* humoristique

humour (*US* **humor**) [ˈhjuːməʳ] *n* humour *m*; (*mood*) humeur *f* ▷ *vt* (*person*) faire plaisir à; se prêter aux caprices de

hump [hʌmp] *n* bosse *f*

hunch [hʌntʃ] *n* (*premonition*) intuition *f*

hundred [ˈhʌndrəd] *num* cent; **~s of** des centaines de; **hundredth** [-ɪdθ] *num* centième

hung [hʌŋ] *pt, pp of* **hang**

Hungarian [hʌŋˈgɛərɪən] *adj* hongrois(e) ▷ *n* Hongrois(e); (*Ling*) hongrois *m*

Hungary [ˈhʌŋgərɪ] *n* Hongrie *f*

hunger [ˈhʌŋgəʳ] *n* faim *f* ▷ *vi*: **to ~ for** avoir faim de, désirer ardemment

hungry [ˈhʌŋgrɪ] *adj* affamé(e); **to be ~** avoir faim; **~ for** (*fig*) avide de

hunt [hʌnt] *vt* (*seek*) chercher; (*Sport*) chasser ▷ *vi* (*search*): **to ~ for** chercher (partout); (*Sport*) chasser ▷ *n* (*Sport*) chasse *f*; **hunter** *n* chasseur *m*; **hunting** *n* chasse *f*

hurdle [ˈhəːdl] *n* (*Sport*) haie *f*; (*fig*) obstacle *m*

hurl [həːl] *vt* lancer (avec violence); (*abuse, insults*) lancer

hurrah, hurray [huˈrɑː, huˈreɪ] *excl* hourra!

hurricane [ˈhʌrɪkən] *n* ouragan *m*

hurry [ˈhʌrɪ] *n* hâte *f*, précipitation *f* ▷ *vi* se presser, se dépêcher ▷ *vt* (*person*) faire presser, faire se dépêcher; (*work*) presser; **to be in a ~** être pressé(e); **to do sth in a ~** faire qch en vitesse; **hurry up** *vi* se dépêcher

hurt [həːt] (*pt, pp* **~**) *vt* (*cause pain to*) faire mal à; (*injure, fig*) blesser ▷ *vi* faire mal ▷ *adj* blessé(e); **my arm ~s** j'ai mal au bras; **to ~ o.s.** se faire mal

husband [ˈhʌzbənd] *n* mari *m*

hush [hʌʃ] *n* calme *m*, silence *m* ▷ *vt* faire taire; **~!** chut!

husky [ˈhʌskɪ] *adj* (*voice*) rauque ▷ *n* chien *m* esquimau *or* de traîneau

hut [hʌt] *n* hutte *f*; (*shed*) cabane *f*

hyacinth [ˈhaɪəsɪnθ] *n* jacinthe *f*

hydrangea [haɪˈdreɪndʒə] *n* hortensia *m*

hydrofoil [ˈhaɪdrəfɔɪl] *n* hydrofoil *m*

hydrogen [ˈhaɪdrədʒən] *n* hydrogène *m*

hygiene [ˈhaɪdʒiːn] *n* hygiène *f*; **hygienic** [haɪˈdʒiːnɪk] *adj* hygiénique

hymn [hɪm] *n* hymne *m*; cantique *m*

hype [haɪp] *n* (*inf*) matraquage *m* publicitaire *or* médiatique

hypermarket [ˈhaɪpəmɑːkɪt] (*BRIT*) *n* hypermarché *m*

hyphen [ˈhaɪfn] *n* trait *m* d'union

hypnotize [ˈhɪpnətaɪz] *vt* hypnotiser

hypocrite [ˈhɪpəkrɪt] *n* hypocrite *m/f*

hypocritical [hɪpəˈkrɪtɪkl] *adj* hypocrite

hypothesis (*pl* **hypotheses**) [haɪˈpɔθɪsɪs, -siːz] *n* hypothèse *f*

hysterical [hɪˈstɛrɪkl] *adj* hystérique; (*funny*) hilarant(e)

hysterics [hɪˈstɛrɪks] *npl*: **to be in/have ~** (*anger, panic*) avoir une crise de nerfs; (*laughter*) attraper un fou rire

I [aɪ] *pron* je; *(before vowel)* j'; *(stressed)* moi

ice [aɪs] *n* glace *f*; *(on road)* verglas *m* ▷ *vt (cake)* glacer ▷ *vi (also:* **~ over**) geler; *(also:* **~ up**) se givrer; **iceberg** *n* iceberg *m*; **ice cream** *n* glace *f*; **ice cube** *n* glaçon *m*; **ice hockey** *n* hockey *m* sur glace

Iceland ['aɪslənd] *n* Islande *f*; **Icelander** *n* Islandais(e); **Icelandic** [aɪs'lændɪk] *adj* islandais(e) ▷ *n (Ling)* islandais *m*

ice: **ice lolly** *n* (BRIT) esquimau *m*; **ice rink** *n* patinoire *f*; **ice skating** *n* patinage *m* (sur glace)

icing ['aɪsɪŋ] *n* (Culin) glaçage *m*; **icing sugar** *n* (BRIT) sucre *m* glace

icon ['aɪkɔn] *n* icône *f*

ICT *n abbr* (BRIT: Scol: = information and communications technology) TIC *fpl*

icy ['aɪsɪ] *adj* glacé(e); *(road)* verglacé(e); *(weather, temperature)* glacial(e)

I'd [aɪd] = **I would**; **I had**

ID card *n* carte *f* d'identité

idea [aɪ'dɪə] *n* idée *f*

ideal [aɪ'dɪəl] *n* idéal *m* ▷ *adj* idéal(e); **ideally** [aɪ'dɪəlɪ] *adv (preferably)* dans l'idéal; *(perfectly)*: **he is ideally suited to the job** il est parfait pour ce poste

identical [aɪ'dɛntɪkl] *adj* identique

identification [aɪdɛntɪfɪ'keɪʃən] *n* identification *f*; **means of ~** pièce *f* d'identité

identify [aɪ'dɛntɪfaɪ] *vt* identifier

identity [aɪ'dɛntɪtɪ] *n* identité *f*; **identity card** *n* carte *f* d'identité; **identity theft** *n* usurpation *f* d'identité

ideology [aɪdɪ'ɔlədʒɪ] *n* idéologie *f*

idiom ['ɪdɪəm] *n (phrase)* expression *f* idiomatique; *(style)* style *m*

idiot ['ɪdɪət] *n* idiot(e), imbécile *m/f*

idle ['aɪdl] *adj (doing nothing)* sans occupation, désœuvré(e); *(lazy)* oisif(-ive), paresseux(-euse); *(unemployed)* au chômage; *(machinery)* au repos; *(question, pleasures)* vain(e), futile ▷ *vi (engine)* tourner au ralenti

idol ['aɪdl] *n* idole *f*

idyllic [ɪ'dɪlɪk] *adj* idyllique

i.e. *abbr* (= id est: that is) c. à d., c'est-à-dire

if [ɪf] *conj* si; **if necessary** si nécessaire, le cas échéant; **if so** si c'est le cas; **if not** sinon; **if only I could!** si seulement je pouvais!; *see also* **as; even**

ignite [ɪg'naɪt] *vt* mettre le feu à, enflammer ▷ *vi* s'enflammer

ignition [ɪg'nɪʃən] *n (Aut)* allumage *m*; **to switch on/off the ~** mettre/couper le contact

ignorance ['ɪgnərəns] *n* ignorance *f*

ignorant ['ɪgnərənt] *adj* ignorant(e); **to be ~ of** *(subject)* ne rien connaître en; *(events)* ne pas être au courant de

ignore [ɪg'nɔːʳ] *vt* ne tenir aucun compte de; *(mistake)* ne pas relever; *(person: pretend to not see)* faire semblant de ne pas reconnaître; (: *pay no attention to)* ignorer

ill [ɪl] *adj (sick)* malade; *(bad)* mauvais(e) ▷ *n* mal *m* ▷ *adv*: **to speak/think ~ of sb** dire/penser du mal de qn; **to be taken ~** tomber malade

I'll [aɪl] = **I will**; **I shall**

illegal [ɪ'liːgl] *adj* illégal(e)

illegible [ɪ'lɛdʒɪbl] *adj* illisible

illegitimate [ɪlɪ'dʒɪtɪmət] *adj* illégitime

ill health *n* mauvaise santé

illiterate [ɪ'lɪtərət] *adj* illettré(e)

illness ['ɪlnɪs] *n* maladie *f*

illuminate [ɪ'luːmɪneɪt] *vt (room, street)* éclairer; *(for special effect)* illuminer

illusion [ɪ'luːʒən] *n* illusion *f*

illustrate ['ɪləstreɪt] *vt* illustrer

illustration [ɪlə'streɪʃən] *n* illustration *f*

I'm [aɪm] = **I am**

image ['ɪmɪdʒ] *n* image *f*; *(public face)* image de marque

imaginary [ɪ'mædʒɪnərɪ] *adj* imaginaire

imagination [ɪmædʒɪ'neɪʃən] *n* imagination *f*

imaginative [ɪ'mædʒɪnətɪv] *adj* imaginatif(-ive); *(person)* plein(e) d'imagination

imagine [ɪ'mædʒɪn] *vt* s'imaginer; *(suppose)* imaginer, supposer

imbalance [ɪmˈbæləns] n déséquilibre m

imitate [ˈɪmɪteɪt] vt imiter; **imitation** [ɪmɪˈteɪʃən] n imitation f

immaculate [ɪˈmækjulət] adj impeccable; (Rel) immaculé(e)

immature [ɪməˈtjuər] adj (fruit) qui n'est pas mûr(e); (person) qui manque de maturité

immediate [ɪˈmiːdɪət] adj immédiat(e); **immediately** adv (at once) immédiatement; **immediately next to** juste à côté de

immense [ɪˈmɛns] adj immense, énorme; **immensely** adv (+adj) extrêmement; (+vb) énormément

immerse [ɪˈmɜːs] vt immerger, plonger; **to be ~d in** (fig) être plongé dans

immigrant [ˈɪmɪɡrənt] n immigrant(e); (already established) immigré(e); **immigration** [ɪmɪˈɡreɪʃən] n immigration f

imminent [ˈɪmɪnənt] adj imminent(e)

immoral [ɪˈmɔrl] adj immoral(e)

immortal [ɪˈmɔːtl] adj, n immortel(le)

immune [ɪˈmjuːn] adj: **~ (to)** immunisé(e) (contre); **immune system** n système m immunitaire

immunize [ˈɪmjunaɪz] vt immuniser

impact [ˈɪmpækt] n choc m, impact m; (fig) impact

impair [ɪmˈpɛər] vt détériorer, diminuer

impartial [ɪmˈpɑːʃl] adj impartial(e)

impatience [ɪmˈpeɪʃəns] n impatience f

impatient [ɪmˈpeɪʃənt] adj impatient(e); **to get** or **grow ~** s'impatienter

impeccable [ɪmˈpɛkəbl] adj impeccable, parfait(e)

impending [ɪmˈpɛndɪŋ] adj imminent(e)

imperative [ɪmˈpɛrətɪv] adj (need) urgent(e), pressant(e); (tone) impérieux(-euse) ▷ n (Ling) impératif m

imperfect [ɪmˈpəːfɪkt] adj imparfait(e); (goods etc) défectueux(-euse) ▷ n (Ling: also: **~ tense**) imparfait m

imperial [ɪmˈpɪərɪəl] adj impérial(e); (BRIT: measure) légal(e)

impersonal [ɪmˈpəːsənl] adj impersonnel(le)

impersonate [ɪmˈpəːsəneɪt] vt se faire passer pour; (Theat) imiter

impetus [ˈɪmpətəs] n impulsion f; (of runner) élan m

implant [ɪmˈplɑːnt] vt (Med) implanter; (fig: idea, principle) inculquer

implement n [ˈɪmplɪmənt] outil m, instrument m; (for cooking) ustensile m ▷ vt [ˈɪmplɪment] exécuter

implicate [ˈɪmplɪkeɪt] vt impliquer, compromettre

implication [ɪmplɪˈkeɪʃən] n implication f; **by ~** indirectement

implicit [ɪmˈplɪsɪt] adj implicite; (complete) absolu(e), sans réserve

imply [ɪmˈplaɪ] vt (hint) suggérer, laisser entendre; (mean) indiquer, supposer

impolite [ɪmpəˈlaɪt] adj impoli(e)

import vt [ɪmˈpɔːt] importer ▷ n [ˈɪmpɔːt] (Comm) importation f; (meaning) portée f, signification f

importance [ɪmˈpɔːtns] n importance f

important [ɪmˈpɔːtnt] adj important(e); **it's not ~** c'est sans importance, ce n'est pas important

importer [ɪmˈpɔːtər] n importateur(-trice)

impose [ɪmˈpəuz] vt imposer ▷ vi: **to ~ on sb** abuser de la gentillesse de qn; **imposing** adj imposant(e), impressionnant(e)

impossible [ɪmˈpɔsɪbl] adj impossible

impotent [ˈɪmpətnt] adj impuissant(e)

impoverished [ɪmˈpɔvərɪʃt] adj pauvre, appauvri(e)

impractical [ɪmˈpræktɪkl] adj pas pratique; (person) qui manque d'esprit pratique

impress [ɪmˈprɛs] vt impressionner, faire impression sur; (mark) imprimer, marquer; **to ~ sth on sb** faire bien comprendre qch à qn

impression [ɪmˈprɛʃən] n impression f; (of stamp, seal) empreinte f; (imitation) imitation f; **to be under the ~ that** avoir l'impression que

impressive [ɪmˈprɛsɪv] adj impressionnant(e)

imprison [ɪmˈprɪzn] vt emprisonner, mettre en prison; **imprisonment** n emprisonnement m; (period): **to sentence sb to 10 years' imprisonment** condamner qn à 10 ans de prison

improbable [ɪmˈprɔbəbl] adj improbable; (excuse) peu plausible

improper [ɪmˈprɔpər] adj (unsuitable) déplacé(e), de mauvais goût; (indecent) indécent(e); (dishonest) malhonnête

improve [ɪmˈpruːv] vt améliorer ▷ vi s'améliorer; (pupil etc) faire des progrès; **improvement** n amélioration f; (of pupil etc) progrès m

improvise [ˈɪmprəvaɪz] vt, vi improviser

impulse [ˈɪmpʌls] n impulsion f; **on ~** impulsivement, sur un coup de tête; **impulsive** [ɪmˈpʌlsɪv] adj impulsif(-ive)

 KEYWORD

in [ɪn] prep **1** (indicating place, position) dans; **in the house/the fridge** dans la maison/le frigo; **in the garden** dans le or au jardin; **in town** en ville; **in the country** à la campagne; **in school** à l'école; **in here/there** ici/là

2 (with place names: of town, region, country): **in London** à Londres; **in England** en Angleterre; **in Japan** au Japon; **in the United States** aux États-Unis

3 (indicating time: during): **in spring** au printemps; **in summer** en été; **in May/2005**

en mai/2005; **in the afternoon** (dans) l'après-midi; **at 4 o'clock in the afternoon** à 4 heures de l'après-midi

4 (indicating time: in the space of) en; (: future) dans; **I did it in 3 hours/days** je l'ai fait en 3 heures/jours; **I'll see you in 2 weeks** or **in 2 weeks' time** je te verrai dans 2 semaines

5 (indicating manner etc) à; **in a loud/soft voice** à voix haute/basse; **in pencil** au crayon; **in writing** par écrit; **in French** en français; **the boy in the blue shirt** le garçon à or avec la chemise bleue

6 (indicating circumstances): **in the sun** au soleil; **in the shade** à l'ombre; **in the rain** sous la pluie; **a change in policy** un changement de politique

7 (indicating mood, state): **in tears** en larmes; **in anger** sous le coup de la colère; **in despair** au désespoir; **in good condition** en bon état; **to live in luxury** vivre dans le luxe

8 (with ratios, numbers): **1 in 10 households, 1 household in 10** 1 ménage sur 10; **20 pence in the pound** 20 pence par livre sterling; **they lined up in twos** ils se mirent en rangs (deux) par deux; **in hundreds** par centaines

9 (referring to people, works) chez; **the disease is common in children** c'est une maladie courante chez les enfants; **in (the works of) Dickens** chez Dickens, dans (l'œuvre de) Dickens

10 (indicating profession etc) dans; **to be in teaching** être dans l'enseignement

11 (after superlative) de; **the best pupil in the class** le meilleur élève de la classe

12 (with present participle): **in saying this** en disant ceci

▷ adv: **to be in** (person: at home, work) être là; (train, ship, plane) être arrivé(e); (in fashion) être à la mode; **to ask sb in** inviter qn à entrer; **to run/limp** etc **in** entrer en courant/boitant etc ▷ n: **the ins and outs (of)** (of proposal, situation etc) les tenants et aboutissants (de)

inability [ɪnəˈbɪlɪtɪ] n incapacité f; **~ to pay** incapacité de payer

inaccurate [ɪnˈækjʊrət] adj inexact(e); (person) qui manque de précision

inadequate [ɪnˈædɪkwət] adj insuffisant(e), inadéquat(e)

inadvertently [ɪnədˈvɜːtntlɪ] adv par mégarde

inappropriate [ɪnəˈprəʊprɪət] adj inopportun(e), mal à propos; (word, expression) impropre

inaugurate [ɪˈnɔːɡjʊreɪt] vt inaugurer; (president, official) investir de ses fonctions

Inc. abbr = **incorporated**

incapable [ɪnˈkeɪpəbl] adj: **~ (of)** incapable (de)

incense n [ˈɪnsɛns] encens m ▷ vt [ɪnˈsɛns] (anger) mettre en colère

incentive [ɪnˈsɛntɪv] n encouragement m, raison f de se donner de la peine

inch [ɪntʃ] n pouce m (=25 mm; 12 in a foot); **within an ~ of** à deux doigts de; **he wouldn't give an ~** (fig) il n'a pas voulu céder d'un pouce

incidence [ˈɪnsɪdns] n (of crime, disease) fréquence f

incident [ˈɪnsɪdnt] n incident m

incidentally [ɪnsɪˈdɛntəlɪ] adv (by the way) à propos

inclination [ɪnklɪˈneɪʃən] n inclination f; (desire) envie f

incline n [ˈɪnklaɪn] pente f, plan incliné ▷ vb [ɪnˈklaɪn] ▷ vt incliner ▷ vi (surface) s'incliner; **to be ~d to do** (have a tendency to do) avoir tendance à faire

include [ɪnˈkluːd] vt inclure, comprendre; **service is/is not ~d** le service est compris/n'est pas compris; **including** prep y compris; **inclusion** n inclusion f; **inclusive** adj inclus(e), compris(e); **inclusive of tax** taxes comprises

income [ˈɪnkʌm] n revenu m; (from property etc) rentes fpl; **income support** n (BRIT) ≈ revenu m minimum d'insertion, RMI m; **income tax** n impôt m sur le revenu

incoming [ˈɪnkʌmɪŋ] adj (passengers, mail) à l'arrivée; (government, tenant) nouveau (nouvelle)

incompatible [ɪnkəmˈpætɪbl] adj incompatible

incompetence [ɪnˈkɒmpɪtns] n incompétence f, incapacité f

incompetent [ɪnˈkɒmpɪtnt] adj incompétent(e), incapable

incomplete [ɪnkəmˈpliːt] adj incomplet(-ète)

inconsistent [ɪnkənˈsɪstnt] adj qui manque de constance; (work) irrégulier(-ière); (statement) peu cohérent(e); **~ with** en contradiction avec

inconvenience [ɪnkənˈviːnjəns] n inconvénient m; (trouble) dérangement m ▷ vt déranger

inconvenient [ɪnkənˈviːnjənt] adj malcommode; (time, place) mal choisi(e), qui ne convient pas; (visitor) importun(e)

incorporate [ɪnˈkɔːpəreɪt] vt incorporer; (contain) contenir

incorrect [ɪnkəˈrɛkt] adj incorrect(e); (opinion, statement) inexact(e)

increase n [ˈɪnkriːs] augmentation f ▷ vi, vt [ɪnˈkriːs] augmenter; **increasingly** adv de plus en plus

incredible [ɪnˈkrɛdɪbl] adj incroyable; **incredibly** adv incroyablement

incur [ɪnˈkɜː] vt (expenses) encourir; (anger, risk) s'exposer à; (debt) contracter; (loss) subir

indecent [ɪnˈdiːsnt] adj indécent(e), inconvenant(e)

indeed [ɪnˈdiːd] adv (confirming, agreeing) en effet, effectivement; (for emphasis) vraiment; (furthermore) d'ailleurs; **yes ~!** certainement!

indefinitely [ɪnˈdɛfɪnɪtlɪ] adv (wait) indéfiniment

independence [ɪndɪˈpɛndns] n indépendance f; **Independence Day** n (US) fête de l'Indépendance américaine; voir encadré

● **INDEPENDENCE DAY**

● L'**Independence Day** est la fête nationale
● aux États-Unis, le 4 juillet. Il commémore
● l'adoption de la déclaration d'Indépendance,
● en 1776, écrite par Thomas Jefferson et
● proclamant la séparation des 13 colonies
● américaines de la Grande-Bretagne.

independent [ɪndɪˈpɛndnt] adj indépendant(e); (radio) libre; **independent school** n (BRIT) école privée

index [ˈɪndɛks] n (pl ~es) (in book) index m; (: in library etc) catalogue m (pl **indices**) (ratio, sign) indice m

India [ˈɪndɪə] n Inde f; **Indian** adj indien(ne) ▷ n Indien(ne); **(American) Indian** Indien(ne) (d'Amérique)

indicate [ˈɪndɪkeɪt] vt indiquer ▷ vi (BRIT Aut): **to ~ left/right** mettre son clignotant à gauche/à droite; **indication** [ɪndɪˈkeɪʃən] n indication f, signe m; **indicative** [ɪnˈdɪkətɪv] adj: **to be indicative of sth** être symptomatique de qch ▷ n (Ling) indicatif m; **indicator** n (sign) indicateur m; (Aut) clignotant m

indices [ˈɪndɪsiːz] npl of **index**

indict [ɪnˈdaɪt] vt accuser; **indictment** n accusation f

indifference [ɪnˈdɪfrəns] n indifférence f

indifferent [ɪnˈdɪfrənt] adj indifférent(e); (poor) médiocre, quelconque

indigenous [ɪnˈdɪdʒɪnəs] adj indigène

indigestion [ɪndɪˈdʒɛstʃən] n indigestion f, mauvaise digestion

indignant [ɪnˈdɪgnənt] adj: **~ (at sth/with sb)** indigné(e) (de qch/contre qn)

indirect [ɪndɪˈrɛkt] adj indirect(e)

indispensable [ɪndɪˈspɛnsəbl] adj indispensable

individual [ɪndɪˈvɪdjuəl] n individu m ▷ adj individuel(le); (characteristic) particulier(-ière), original(e); **individually** adv individuellement

Indonesia [ɪndəˈniːzɪə] n Indonésie f

indoor [ˈɪndɔːˈ] adj d'intérieur; (plant) d'appartement; (swimming pool) couvert(e); (sport, games) pratiqué(e) en salle; **indoors** [ɪnˈdɔːz] adv à l'intérieur

induce [ɪnˈdjuːs] vt (persuade) persuader; (bring about) provoquer; (labour) déclencher

indulge [ɪnˈdʌldʒ] vt (whim) céder à, satisfaire; (child) gâter ▷ vi: **to ~ in sth** (luxury) s'offrir qch, se permettre qch; (fantasies etc) se livrer à qch; **indulgent** adj indulgent(e)

industrial [ɪnˈdʌstrɪəl] adj industriel(le); (injury) du travail; (dispute) ouvrier(-ière); **industrial estate** n (BRIT) zone industrielle; **industrialist** n industriel m; **industrial park** n (US) zone industrielle

industry [ˈɪndəstrɪ] n industrie f; (diligence) zèle m, application f

inefficient [ɪnɪˈfɪʃənt] adj inefficace

inequality [ɪnɪˈkwɔlɪtɪ] n inégalité f

inevitable [ɪnˈɛvɪtəbl] adj inévitable; **inevitably** adv inévitablement, fatalement

inexpensive [ɪnɪkˈspɛnsɪv] adj bon marché inv

inexperienced [ɪnɪkˈspɪərɪənst] adj inexpérimenté(e)

inexplicable [ɪnɪkˈsplɪkəbl] adj inexplicable

infamous [ˈɪnfəməs] adj infâme, abominable

infant [ˈɪnfənt] n (baby) nourrisson m; (young child) petit(e) enfant

infantry [ˈɪnfəntrɪ] n infanterie f

infant school n (BRIT) classes fpl préparatoires (entre 5 et 7 ans)

infect [ɪnˈfɛkt] vt (wound) infecter; (person, blood) contaminer; **infection** [ɪnˈfɛkʃən] n infection f; (contagion) contagion f; **infectious** [ɪnˈfɛkʃəs] adj infectieux(-euse); (also fig) contagieux(-euse)

infer [ɪnˈfəːˈ] vt: **to ~ (from)** conclure (de), déduire (de)

inferior [ɪnˈfɪərɪəˈ] adj inférieur(e); (goods) de qualité inférieure ▷ n inférieur(e); (in rank) subalterne m/f

infertile [ɪnˈfəːtaɪl] adj stérile

infertility [ɪnfəˈtɪlɪtɪ] n infertilité f, stérilité f

infested [ɪnˈfɛstɪd] adj: **~ (with)** infesté(e) (de)

infinite [ˈɪnfɪnɪt] adj infini(e); (time, money) illimité(e); **infinitely** adv infiniment

infirmary [ɪnˈfəːmərɪ] n hôpital m; (in school, factory) infirmerie f

inflamed [ɪnˈfleɪmd] adj enflammé(e)

inflammation [ɪnfləˈmeɪʃən] n inflammation f

inflatable [ɪnˈfleɪtəbl] adj gonflable

inflate [ɪnˈfleɪt] vt (tyre, balloon) gonfler; (fig: exaggerate) grossir; (: increase) gonfler; **inflation** [ɪnˈfleɪʃən] n (Econ) inflation f

inflexible [ɪnˈflɛksɪbl] adj inflexible, rigide

inflict [ɪnˈflɪkt] vt: **to ~ on** infliger à

influence [ˈɪnfluəns] n influence f ▷ vt influencer; **under the ~ of alcohol** en état d'ébriété; **influential** [ɪnfluˈɛnʃl] adj influent(e)

influenza [ɪnfluˈɛnzə] n grippe f

influx ['ɪnflʌks] n afflux m

info (inf) ['ɪnfəu] n (= information) renseignements mpl

inform [ɪn'fɔ:m] vt: **to ~ sb (of)** informer or avertir qn (de) ▷ vi: **to ~ on sb** dénoncer qn, informer contre qn

informal [ɪn'fɔ:ml] adj (person, manner, party) simple; (visit, discussion) dénué(e) de formalités; (announcement, invitation) non officiel(le); (colloquial) familier(-ère)

information [ɪnfə'meɪʃən] n information(s) f(pl); renseignements mpl; (knowledge) connaissances fpl; **a piece of ~** un renseignement; **information office** n bureau m de renseignements; **information technology** n informatique f

informative [ɪn'fɔ:mətɪv] adj instructif(-ive)

infra-red [ɪnfrə'rɛd] adj infrarouge

infrastructure ['ɪnfrəstrʌktʃər] n infrastructure f

infrequent [ɪn'fri:kwənt] adj peu fréquent(e), rare

infuriate [ɪn'fjuərɪeɪt] vt mettre en fureur

infuriating [ɪn'fjuərɪeɪtɪŋ] adj exaspérant(e)

ingenious [ɪn'dʒi:njəs] adj ingénieux(-euse)

ingredient [ɪn'gri:dɪənt] n ingrédient m; (fig) élément m

inhabit [ɪn'hæbɪt] vt habiter; **inhabitant** n habitant(e)

inhale [ɪn'heɪl] vt inhaler; (perfume) respirer; (smoke) avaler ▷ vi (breathe in) aspirer; (in smoking) avaler la fumée; **inhaler** n inhalateur m

inherent [ɪn'hɪərənt] adj: **~ (in or to)** inhérent(e) (à)

inherit [ɪn'hɛrɪt] vt hériter (de); **inheritance** n héritage m

inhibit [ɪn'hɪbɪt] vt (Psych) inhiber; (growth) freiner; **inhibition** [ɪnhɪ'bɪʃən] n inhibition f

initial [ɪ'nɪʃl] adj initial(e) ▷ n initiale f ▷ vt parafer; **initials** npl initiales fpl; (as signature) parafe m; **initially** adv initialement, au début

initiate [ɪ'nɪʃɪeɪt] vt (start) entreprendre; amorcer; (enterprise) lancer; (person) initier; **to ~ proceedings against sb** (Law) intenter une action à qn, engager des poursuites contre qn

initiative [ɪ'nɪʃətɪv] n initiative f

inject [ɪn'dʒɛkt] vt injecter; (person): **to ~ sb with sth** faire une piqûre de qch à qn; **injection** [ɪn'dʒɛkʃən] n injection f, piqûre f

injure ['ɪndʒər] vt blesser; (damage: reputation etc) compromettre; **to ~ o.s.** se blesser; **injured** adj (person, leg etc) blessé(e); **injury** n blessure f; (wrong) tort m

injustice [ɪn'dʒʌstɪs] n injustice f

ink [ɪŋk] n encre f; **ink-jet printer** ['ɪŋkdʒɛt-] n imprimante f à jet d'encre

inland adj ['ɪnlənd] intérieur(e) ▷ adv [ɪn'lænd] à l'intérieur, dans les terres; **Inland**

Revenue n (BRIT) fisc m

in-laws ['ɪnlɔ:z] npl beaux-parents mpl; belle famille

inmate ['ɪnmeɪt] n (in prison) détenu(e); (in asylum) interné(e)

inn [ɪn] n auberge f

inner ['ɪnər] adj intérieur(e); **inner-city** adj (schools, problems) de quartiers déshérités

inning ['ɪnɪŋ] n (US: Baseball) tour m de batte; **innings** npl (Cricket) tour de batte

innocence ['ɪnəsns] n innocence f

innocent ['ɪnəsnt] adj innocent(e)

innovation [ɪnəu'veɪʃən] n innovation f

innovative ['ɪnəu'veɪtɪv] adj novateur(-trice); (product) innovant(e)

in-patient ['ɪnpeɪʃənt] n malade hospitalisé(e)

input ['ɪnput] n (contribution) contribution f; (resources) ressources fpl; (Comput) entrée f (de données); (: data) données fpl ▷ vt (Comput) introduire, entrer

inquest ['ɪnkwɛst] n enquête (criminelle); (coroner's) enquête judiciaire

inquire [ɪn'kwaɪər] vi demander ▷ vt demander; **to ~ about** s'informer de, se renseigner sur; **to ~ when/where/whether** demander quand/où/si; **inquiry** n demande f de renseignements; (Law) enquête f, investigation f; **"inquiries"** "renseignements"

ins. abbr = **inches**

insane [ɪn'seɪn] adj fou (folle); (Med) aliéné(e)

insanity [ɪn'sænɪtɪ] n folie f; (Med) aliénation (mentale)

insect ['ɪnsɛkt] n insecte m; **insect repellent** n crème f anti-insectes

insecure [ɪnsɪ'kjuər] adj (person) anxieux(-euse); (job) précaire; (building etc) peu sûr(e)

insecurity [ɪnsɪ'kjuərɪtɪ] n insécurité f

insensitive [ɪn'sɛnsɪtɪv] adj insensible

insert vt [ɪn'sə:t] insérer ▷ n ['ɪnsə:t] insertion f

inside ['ɪn'saɪd] n intérieur m ▷ adj intérieur(e) ▷ adv à l'intérieur, dedans ▷ prep à l'intérieur de; (of time): **~ 10 minutes** en moins de 10 minutes; **to go ~** rentrer; **inside lane** n (Aut: in Britain) voie f de gauche; (: in US, Europe) voie f de droite; **inside out** adv à l'envers; (know) à fond; **to turn sth inside out** retourner qch

insight ['ɪnsaɪt] n perspicacité f; (glimpse, idea) aperçu m

insignificant [ɪnsɪg'nɪfɪknt] adj insignifiant(e)

insincere [ɪnsɪn'sɪər] adj hypocrite

insist [ɪn'sɪst] vi insister; **to ~ on doing** insister pour faire; **to ~ on sth** exiger qch; **to ~ that** insister pour que + sub; (claim) maintenir or soutenir que; **insistent** adj insistant(e), pressant(e); (noise, action) ininterrompu(e)

insomnia [ɪnˈsɒmnɪə] n insomnie f
inspect [ɪnˈspɛkt] vt inspecter; (BRIT:
ticket) contrôler; **inspection** [ɪnˈspɛkʃən]
n inspection f; (BRIT: of tickets) contrôle m;
inspector n inspecteur(-trice); (BRIT: on buses,
trains) contrôleur(-euse)
inspiration [ɪnspəˈreɪʃən] n inspiration f;
inspire [ɪnˈspaɪər] vt inspirer; **inspiring** adj
inspirant(e)
instability [ɪnstəˈbɪlɪtɪ] n instabilité f
install (US instal) [ɪnˈstɔːl] vt installer;
installation [ɪnstəˈleɪʃən] n installation f
instalment (US installment) [ɪnˈstɔːlmə
nt] n (payment) acompte m, versement
partiel; (of TV serial etc) épisode m; **in ~s** (pay) à
tempérament; (receive) en plusieurs fois
instance [ˈɪnstəns] n exemple m; **for ~** par
exemple; **in the first ~** tout d'abord, en
premier lieu
instant [ˈɪnstənt] n instant m ▷ adj
immédiat(e), urgent(e); (coffee, food)
instantané(e), en poudre; **instantly** adv
immédiatement, tout de suite; **instant
messaging** n messagerie f instantanée
instead [ɪnˈstɛd] adv au lieu de cela; **~ of** au
lieu de; **~ of sb** à la place de qn
instinct [ˈɪnstɪŋkt] n instinct m; **instinctive**
adj instinctif(-ive)
institute [ˈɪnstɪtjuːt] n institut m ▷ vt
instituer, établir; (inquiry) ouvrir; (proceedings)
entamer
institution [ɪnstɪˈtjuːʃən] n institution f;
(school) établissement m (scolaire); (for care)
établissement (psychiatrique etc)
instruct [ɪnˈstrʌkt] vt: **to ~ sb in sth** enseigner
qch à qn; **to ~ sb to do** charger qn or ordonner
à qn de faire; **instruction** [ɪnˈstrʌkʃən]
n instruction f; **instructions** npl (orders)
directives fpl; **instructions for use** mode m
d'emploi; **instructor** n professeur m; (for skiing,
driving) moniteur m
instrument [ˈɪnstrumənt] n instrument m;
instrumental [ɪnstruˈmɛntl] adj (Mus)
instrumental(e); **to be instrumental in sth/
in doing sth** contribuer à qch/à faire qch
insufficient [ɪnsəˈfɪʃənt] adj insuffisant(e)
insulate [ˈɪnsjuleɪt] vt isoler; (against sound)
insonoriser; **insulation** [ɪnsjuˈleɪʃən] n
isolation f; (against sound) insonorisation f
insulin [ˈɪnsjulɪn] n insuline f
insult n [ˈɪnsʌlt] insulte f, affront m ▷ vt
[ɪnˈsʌlt] insulter, faire un affront à; **insulting**
adj insultant(e), injurieux(-euse)
insurance [ɪnˈʃuərəns] n assurance
f; **fire/life ~** assurance-incendie/-vie;
insurance company n compagnie f or société
f d'assurances; **insurance policy** n police f
d'assurance
insure [ɪnˈʃuər] vt assurer; **to ~ (o.s.) against**

(fig) parer à
intact [ɪnˈtækt] adj intact(e)
intake [ˈɪnteɪk] n (Tech) admission f;
(consumption) consommation f; (BRIT Scol): **an ~
of 200 a year** 200 admissions par an
integral [ˈɪntɪɡrəl] adj (whole) intégral(e);
(part) intégrant(e)
integrate [ˈɪntɪɡreɪt] vt intégrer ▷ vi
s'intégrer
integrity [ɪnˈtɛɡrɪtɪ] n intégrité f
intellect [ˈɪntəlɛkt] n intelligence f;
intellectual [ɪntəˈlɛktjuəl] adj, n
intellectuel(le)
intelligence [ɪnˈtɛlɪdʒəns] n intelligence f;
(Mil etc) informations fpl, renseignements mpl
intelligent [ɪnˈtɛlɪdʒənt] adj intelligent(e)
intend [ɪnˈtɛnd] vt (gift etc): **to ~ sth for**
destiner qch à; **to ~ to do** avoir l'intention
de faire
intense [ɪnˈtɛns] adj intense; (person)
véhément(e)
intensify [ɪnˈtɛnsɪfaɪ] vt intensifier
intensity [ɪnˈtɛnsɪtɪ] n intensité f
intensive [ɪnˈtɛnsɪv] adj intensif(-ive);
intensive care n: **to be in intensive care**
être en réanimation; **intensive care unit** n
service m de réanimation
intent [ɪnˈtɛnt] n intention f ▷ adj
attentif(-ive), absorbé(e); **to all ~s and
purposes** en fait, pratiquement; **to be ~ on
doing sth** être (bien) décidé à faire qch
intention [ɪnˈtɛnʃən] n intention f;
intentional adj intentionnel(le), délibéré(e)
interact [ɪntərˈækt] vi avoir une action
réciproque; (people) communiquer;
interaction [ɪntərˈækʃən] n interaction f;
interactive adj (Comput) interactif,
conversationnel(le)
intercept [ɪntəˈsɛpt] vt intercepter; (person)
arrêter au passage
interchange n [ˈɪntətʃeɪndʒ] (exchange)
échange m; (on motorway) échangeur m
intercourse [ˈɪntəkɔːs] n: **sexual ~** rapports
sexuels
interest [ˈɪntrɪst] n intérêt m; (Comm:
stake, share) participation f, intérêts mpl ▷ vt
intéresser; **interested** adj intéressé(e); **to
be interested in sth** s'intéresser à qch; **I'm
interested in going** ça m'intéresse d'y aller;
interesting adj intéressant(e); **interest rate**
n taux m d'intérêt
interface [ˈɪntəfeɪs] n (Comput) interface f
interfere [ɪntəˈfɪər] vi: **to ~ in** (quarrel)
s'immiscer dans; (other people's business) se
mêler de; **to ~ with** (object) tripoter, toucher à;
(plans) contrecarrer; (duty) être en conflit avec;
interference n (gen) ingérence f; (Radio, TV)
parasites mpl
interim [ˈɪntərɪm] adj provisoire; (post)

intérimaire ▷ n: **in the ~** dans l'intérim

interior [ɪnˈtɪərɪəʳ] n intérieur m ▷ adj intérieur(e); (minister, department) de l'intérieur; **interior design** n architecture f d'intérieur

intermediate [ɪntəˈmiːdɪət] adj intermédiaire; (Scol: course, level) moyen(ne)

intermission [ɪntəˈmɪʃən] n pause f; (Theat, Cine) entracte m

intern vt [ɪnˈtəːn] interner ▷ n [ˈɪntəːn] (US) interne m/f

internal [ɪnˈtəːnl] adj interne; (dispute, reform etc) intérieur(e); **Internal Revenue Service** n (US) fisc m

international [ɪntəˈnæʃənl] adj international(e) ▷ n (BRIT Sport) international m

Internet [ɪntəˈnɛt] n: **the ~** l'Internet m; **Internet café** n cybercafé m; **Internet Service Provider** n fournisseur m d'accès à Internet; **Internet user** n internaute m/f

interpret [ɪnˈtəːprɪt] vt interpréter ▷ vi servir d'interprète; **interpretation** [ɪntəːprɪˈteɪʃən] n interprétation f; **interpreter** n interprète m/f; **could you act as an interpreter for us?** pourriez-vous nous servir d'interprète?

interrogate [ɪnˈtɛrəugeɪt] vt interroger; (suspect etc) soumettre à un interrogatoire; **interrogation** [ɪntɛrəuˈgeɪʃən] n interrogation f; (by police) interrogatoire m

interrogative [ɪntəˈrɔgətɪv] adj interrogateur(-trice) ▷ n (Ling) interrogatif m

interrupt [ɪntəˈrʌpt] vt, vi interrompre; **interruption** [ɪntəˈrʌpʃən] n interruption f

intersection [ɪntəˈsɛkʃən] n (of roads) croisement m

interstate [ˈɪntəsteɪt] (US) n autoroute f (qui relie plusieurs États)

interval [ˈɪntəvl] n intervalle m; (BRIT: Theat) entracte m; (: Sport) mi-temps f; **at ~s** par intervalles

intervene [ɪntəˈviːn] vi (time) s'écouler (entre-temps); (event) survenir; (person) intervenir

interview [ˈɪntəvjuː] n (Radio, TV etc) interview f; (for job) entrevue f ▷ vt interviewer; avoir une entrevue avec; **interviewer** n (Radio, TV etc) interviewer m

intimate adj [ˈɪntɪmət] intime; (friendship) profond(e); (knowledge) approfondi(e) ▷ vt [ˈɪntɪmeɪt] suggérer, laisser entendre; (announce) faire savoir

intimidate [ɪnˈtɪmɪdeɪt] vt intimider

intimidating [ɪnˈtɪmɪdeɪtɪŋ] adj intimidant(e)

into [ˈɪntu] prep dans; **~ pieces/French** en morceaux/français

intolerant [ɪnˈtɔlərnt] adj: **~ (of)** intolérant(e) (de)

intranet [ɪnˈtrənɛt] n intranet m

intransitive [ɪnˈtrænsɪtɪv] adj intransitif(-ive)

intricate [ˈɪntrɪkət] adj complexe, compliqué(e)

intrigue [ɪnˈtriːg] n intrigue f ▷ vt intriguer; **intriguing** adj fascinant(e)

introduce [ɪntrəˈdjuːs] vt introduire; (TV show etc) présenter; **to ~ sb (to sb)** présenter qn (à qn); **to ~ sb to** (pastime, technique) initier qn à; **introduction** [ɪntrəˈdʌkʃən] n introduction f; (of person) présentation f; (to new experience) initiation f; **introductory** [ɪntrəˈdʌktərɪ] adj préliminaire, introductif(-ive)

intrude [ɪnˈtruːd] vi (person) être importun(e); **to ~ on** or **into** (conversation etc) s'immiscer dans; **intruder** n intrus(e)

intuition [ɪntjuːˈɪʃən] n intuition f

inundate [ˈɪnʌndeɪt] vt: **to ~ with** inonder de

invade [ɪnˈveɪd] vt envahir

invalid n [ˈɪnvəlɪd] malade m/f, (with disability) invalide m/f ▷ adj [ɪnˈvælɪd] (not valid) invalide, non valide

invaluable [ɪnˈvæljuəbl] adj inestimable, inappréciable

invariably [ɪnˈvɛərɪəblɪ] adv invariablement; **she is ~ late** elle est toujours en retard

invasion [ɪnˈveɪʒən] n invasion f

invent [ɪnˈvɛnt] vt inventer; **invention** [ɪnˈvɛnʃən] n invention f; **inventor** n inventeur(-trice)

inventory [ˈɪnvəntrɪ] n inventaire m

inverted commas [ɪnˈvəːtɪd-] npl (BRIT) guillemets mpl

invest [ɪnˈvɛst] vt investir ▷ vi: **to ~ in** placer de l'argent or investir dans; (fig: acquire) s'offrir, faire l'acquisition de

investigate [ɪnˈvɛstɪgeɪt] vt étudier, examiner; (crime) faire une enquête sur; **investigation** [ɪnvɛstɪˈgeɪʃən] n (of crime) enquête f, investigation f

investigator [ɪnˈvɛstɪgeɪtəʳ] n investigateur(-trice); **private ~** détective privé

investment [ɪnˈvɛstmənt] n investissement m, placement m

investor [ɪnˈvɛstəʳ] n épargnant(e); (shareholder) actionnaire m/f

invisible [ɪnˈvɪzɪbl] adj invisible

invitation [ɪnvɪˈteɪʃən] n invitation f

invite [ɪnˈvaɪt] vt inviter; (opinions etc) demander; **inviting** adj engageant(e), attrayant(e)

invoice [ˈɪnvɔɪs] n facture f ▷ vt facturer

involve [ɪnˈvɔlv] vt (entail) impliquer; (concern) concerner; (require) nécessiter; **to ~ sb in** (theft etc) impliquer qn dans; (activity, meeting) faire participer qn à; **involved** adj (complicated) complexe; **to be involved in** (take part) participer à; **involvement** n (personal role) rôle m; (participation) participation f; (enthusiasm) enthousiasme m

inward ['ɪnwəd] adj (movement) vers l'intérieur; (thought, feeling) profond(e), intime ▷ adv = **inwards**; **inwards** adv vers l'intérieur

IQ n abbr (= intelligence quotient) Q.I. m

IRA n abbr (= Irish Republican Army) IRA f

Iran [ɪ'rɑːn] n Iran m; **Iranian** [ɪ'reɪnɪən] adj iranien(ne) ▷ n Iranien(ne)

Iraq [ɪ'rɑːk] n Irak m; **Iraqi** adj irakien(ne) ▷ n Irakien(ne)

Ireland ['aɪələnd] n Irlande f

iris, irises ['aɪrɪs, -ɪz] n iris m

Irish ['aɪrɪʃ] adj irlandais(e) ▷ npl: **the ~** les Irlandais; **Irishman** (irreg) n Irlandais m; **Irishwoman** (irreg) n Irlandaise f

iron ['aɪən] n fer m; (for clothes) fer m à repasser ▷ adj de or en fer ▷ vt (clothes) repasser

ironic(al) [aɪ'rɒnɪk(l)] adj ironique; **ironically** adv ironiquement

ironing ['aɪənɪŋ] n (activity) repassage m; (clothes: ironed) linge repassé; (: to be ironed) linge à repasser; **ironing board** n planche f à repasser

irony ['aɪrənɪ] n ironie f

irrational [ɪ'ræʃənl] adj irrationnel(le); (person) qui n'est pas rationnel

irregular [ɪ'regjʊlər] adj irrégulier(-ière); (surface) inégal(e); (action, event) peu orthodoxe

irrelevant [ɪ'reləvənt] adj sans rapport, hors de propos

irresistible [ɪrɪ'zɪstɪbl] adj irrésistible

irresponsible [ɪrɪ'spɒnsɪbl] adj (act) irréfléchi(e); (person) qui n'a pas le sens des responsabilités

irrigation [ɪrɪ'geɪʃən] n irrigation f

irritable ['ɪrɪtəbl] adj irritable

irritate ['ɪrɪteɪt] vt irriter; **irritating** adj irritant(e); **irritation** [ɪrɪ'teɪʃən] n irritation f

IRS n abbr (US) = **Internal Revenue Service**

is [ɪz] vb see **be**

ISDN n abbr (= Integrated Services Digital Network) RNIS m

Islam ['ɪzlɑːm] n Islam m; **Islamic** [ɪz'lɑːmɪk] adj islamique

island ['aɪlənd] n île f; (also: **traffic ~**) refuge m (pour piétons); **islander** n habitant(e) d'une île, insulaire m/f

isle [aɪl] n île f

isn't ['ɪznt] = **is not**

isolated ['aɪsəleɪtɪd] adj isolé(e)

isolation [aɪsə'leɪʃən] n isolement m

ISP n abbr = **Internet Service Provider**

Israel ['ɪzreɪl] n Israël m; **Israeli** [ɪz'reɪlɪ] adj israélien(ne) ▷ n Israélien(ne)

issue ['ɪʃuː] n question f, problème m; (of banknotes) émission f; (of newspaper) numéro m; (of book) publication f, parution f ▷ vt (rations, equipment) distribuer; (orders) donner; (statement) publier, faire; (certificate, passport) délivrer; (banknotes, cheques, stamps) émettre, mettre en circulation; **at ~** en jeu, en cause; **to take ~ with sb (over sth)** exprimer son désaccord avec qn (sur qch)

IT n abbr = **information technology**

⊙ **KEYWORD**

it [ɪt] pron **1** (specific: subject) il (elle); (: direct object) le (la, l'); (: indirect object) lui; **it's on the table** c'est or il (or elle) est sur la table; **I can't find it** je n'arrive pas à le trouver; **give it to me** donne-le-moi

2 (after prep): **about/from/of it** en; **I spoke to him about it** je lui en ai parlé; **what did you learn from it?** qu'est-ce que vous en avez retiré?; **I'm proud of it** j'en suis fier; **in/to it** y; **put the book in it** mettez-y le livre; **he agreed to it** il y a consenti; **did you go to it?** (party, concert etc) est-ce que vous y êtes allé(s)?

3 (impersonal) il; ce, cela, ça; **it's raining** il pleut; **it's Friday tomorrow** demain, c'est vendredi or nous sommes, vendredi; **it's 6 o'clock** il est 6 heures; **how far is it? — it's 10 miles** c'est loin? — c'est à 10 miles; **who is it? — it's me** qui est-ce? — c'est moi

Italian [ɪ'tæljən] adj italien(ne) ▷ n Italien(ne); (Ling) italien m

italics [ɪ'tælɪks] npl italique m

Italy ['ɪtəlɪ] n Italie f

itch [ɪtʃ] n démangeaison f ▷ vi (person) éprouver des démangeaisons; (part of body) démanger; **I'm ~ing to do** l'envie me démange de faire; **itchy** adj: **my back is itchy** j'ai le dos qui me démange

it'd ['ɪtd] = **it would**; **it had**

item ['aɪtəm] n (gen) article m; (on agenda) question f, point m; (also: **news ~**) nouvelle f

itinerary [aɪ'tɪnərərɪ] n itinéraire m

it'll ['ɪtl] = **it will**; **it shall**

its [ɪts] adj son (sa), ses pl

it's [ɪts] = **it is**; **it has**

itself [ɪt'sɛlf] pron (reflexive) se; (emphatic) lui-même (elle-même)

ITV n abbr (BRIT: = Independent Television) chaîne de télévision commerciale

I've [aɪv] = **I have**

ivory ['aɪvərɪ] n ivoire m

ivy ['aɪvɪ] n lierre m

jab [dʒæb] *vt*: **to ~ sth into** enfoncer *or* planter qch dans ▷ *n* (*Med*: *inf*) piqûre *f*

jack [dʒæk] *n* (*Aut*) cric *m*; (*Cards*) valet *m*

jacket ['dʒækɪt] *n* veste *f*, veston *m*; (*of book*) couverture *f*, jaquette *f*; **jacket potato** *n* pomme *f* de terre en robe des champs

jackpot ['dʒækpɔt] *n* gros lot

Jacuzzi® [dʒə'ku:zɪ] *n* jacuzzi® *m*

jagged ['dʒægɪd] *adj* dentelé(e)

jail [dʒeɪl] *n* prison *f* ▷ *vt* emprisonner, mettre en prison; **jail sentence** *n* peine *f* de prison

jam [dʒæm] *n* confiture *f*; (*also*: **traffic ~**) embouteillage *m* ▷ *vt* (*passage etc*) encombrer, obstruer; (*mechanism, drawer etc*) bloquer, coincer; (*Radio*) brouiller ▷ *vi* (*mechanism, sliding part*) se coincer, se bloquer; (*gun*) s'enrayer; **to be in a ~** (*inf*) être dans le pétrin; **to ~ sth into** (*stuff*) entasser *or* comprimer qch dans; (*thrust*) enfoncer qch dans

Jamaica [dʒə'meɪkə] *n* Jamaïque *f*

jammed [dʒæmd] *adj* (*window etc*) coincé(e)

Jan *abbr* (= *January*) janv

janitor ['dʒænɪtə'] *n* (*caretaker*) concierge *m*

January ['dʒænjuərɪ] *n* janvier *m*

Japan [dʒə'pæn] *n* Japon *m*; **Japanese** [dʒæpə'niːz] *adj* japonais(e) ▷ *n* (*pl inv*) Japonais(e); (*Ling*) japonais *m*

jar [dʒɑ:'] *n* (*stone, earthenware*) pot *m*; (*glass*) bocal *m* ▷ *vi* (*sound*) produire un son grinçant *or* discordant; (*colours etc*) détonner, jurer

jargon ['dʒɑ:gən] *n* jargon *m*

javelin ['dʒævlɪn] *n* javelot *m*

jaw [dʒɔ:] *n* mâchoire *f*

jazz [dʒæz] *n* jazz *m*

jealous ['dʒɛləs] *adj* jaloux(-ouse); **jealousy** *n* jalousie *f*

jeans [dʒi:nz] *npl* jean *m*

Jello® ['dʒɛləu] (*us*) *n* gelée *f*

jelly ['dʒɛlɪ] *n* (*dessert*) gelée *f*; (*us: jam*) confiture *f*; **jellyfish** *n* méduse *f*

jeopardize ['dʒɛpədaɪz] *vt* mettre en danger *or* péril

jerk [dʒə:k] *n* secousse *f*, saccade *f*; (*of muscle*) spasme *m*; (*inf*) pauvre type *m* ▷ *vt* (*shake*) donner une secousse à; (*pull*) tirer brusquement ▷ *vi* (*vehicles*) cahoter

jersey ['dʒə:zɪ] *n* tricot *m*; (*fabric*) jersey *m*

Jesus ['dʒi:zəs] *n* Jésus

jet [dʒɛt] *n* (*of gas, liquid*) jet *m*; (*Aviat*) avion *m* à réaction, jet *m*; **jet lag** *n* décalage *m* horaire; **jet-ski** *vi* faire du jet-ski *or* scooter des mers

jetty ['dʒɛtɪ] *n* jetée *f*, digue *f*

Jew [dʒu:] *n* Juif *m*

jewel ['dʒu:əl] *n* bijou *m*, joyau *m*; (*in watch*) rubis *m*; **jeweller** (*us* **jeweler**) *n* bijoutier(-ière), joaillier *m*; **jeweller's (shop)** (*us* **jewelry store**) *n* bijouterie *f*, joaillerie *f*; **jewellery** (*us* **jewelry**) *n* bijoux *mpl*

Jewish ['dʒu:ɪʃ] *adj* juif (juive)

jigsaw ['dʒɪgsɔ:] *n* (*also*: **~ puzzle**) puzzle *m*

job [dʒɔb] *n* (*chore, task*) travail *m*, tâche *f*; (*employment*) emploi *m*, poste *m*, place *f*; **it's a good ~ that** ... c'est heureux *or* c'est une chance que ... + *sub*; **just the ~!** (c'est) juste *or* exactement ce qu'il faut!; **job centre** (*BRIT*) *n* ≈ ANPE *f*, ≈ Agence nationale pour l'emploi; **jobless** *adj* sans travail, au chômage

jockey ['dʒɔkɪ] *n* jockey *m* ▷ *vi*: **to ~ for position** manœuvrer pour être bien placé

jog [dʒɔg] *vt* secouer ▷ *vi* (*Sport*) faire du jogging; **to ~ sb's memory** rafraîchir la mémoire de qn; **jogging** *n* jogging *m*

join [dʒɔɪn] *vt* (*put together*) unir, assembler; (*become member of*) s'inscrire à; (*meet*) rejoindre, retrouver; (*queue*) se joindre à ▷ *vi* (*roads, rivers*) se rejoindre, se rencontrer ▷ *n* raccord *m*; **join in** *vi* se mettre de la partie ▷ *vt fus* se mêler à; **join up** *vi* (*meet*) se rejoindre; (*Mil*) s'engager

joiner ['dʒɔɪnə'] (*BRIT*) *n* menuisier *m*

joint [dʒɔɪnt] *n* (*Tech*) jointure *f*; joint *m*; (*Anat*) articulation *f*, jointure; (*BRIT Culin*) rôti *m*; (*inf: place*) boîte *f*; (*of cannabis*) joint ▷ *adj* commun(e); (*committee*) mixte, paritaire; (*winner*) ex aequo; **joint account** *n* compte joint; **jointly** *adv* ensemble, en commun

joke [dʒəuk] *n* plaisanterie *f*; (*also*: **practical ~**) farce *f* ▷ *vi* plaisanter; **to play a ~ on** jouer un tour à, faire une farce à; **joker** *n* (*Cards*) joker *m*

jolly ['dʒɔlɪ] *adj* gai(e), enjoué(e); (*enjoyable*)

amusant(e), plaisant(e) ▷ *adv* (BRIT *inf*) rudement, drôlement

jolt [dʒəʊlt] *n* cahot *m*, secousse *f*; (*shock*) choc *m* ▷ *vt* cahoter, secouer

Jordan [dʒɔːdən] *n* (*country*) Jordanie *f*

journal [ˈdʒəːnl] *n* journal *m*; **journalism** *n* journalisme *m*; **journalist** *n* journaliste *m/f*

journey [ˈdʒəːnɪ] *n* voyage *m*; (*distance covered*) trajet *m*; **the ~ takes two hours** le trajet dure deux heures; **how was your ~?** votre voyage s'est bien passé?

joy [dʒɔɪ] *n* joie *f*; **joyrider** *n* voleur(-euse) de voiture (*qui fait une virée dans le véhicule volé*); **joy stick** *n* (*Aviat*) manche *m* à balai; (*Comput*) manche à balai, manette *f* (de jeu)

Jr *abbr* = **junior**

judge [dʒʌdʒ] *n* juge *m* ▷ *vt* juger; (*estimate: weight, size etc*) apprécier; (*consider*) estimer

judo [ˈdʒuːdəʊ] *n* judo *m*

jug [dʒʌg] *n* pot *m*, cruche *f*

juggle [ˈdʒʌgl] *vi* jongler; **juggler** *n* jongleur *m*

juice [dʒuːs] *n* jus *m*; **juicy** *adj* juteux(-euse)

Jul *abbr* (= *July*) juil

July [dʒuːˈlaɪ] *n* juillet *m*

jumble [ˈdʒʌmbl] *n* fouillis *m* ▷ *vt* (*also*: **~ up**, **~ together**) mélanger, brouiller; **jumble sale** *n* (BRIT) vente *f* de charité

● **JUMBLE SALE**
●
● Les **jumble sales** ont lieu dans les églises,
● salles des fêtes ou halls d'écoles, et l'on
● y vend des articles de toutes sortes, en
● général bon marché et surtout d'occasion,
● pour collecter des fonds pour une œuvre
● de charité, une école (par exemple, pour
● acheter un ordinateur), ou encore une
● église (pour réparer un toit etc).

jumbo [ˈdʒʌmbəʊ] *adj* (*also*: **~ jet**) (avion) gros porteur (à réaction)

jump [dʒʌmp] *vi* sauter, bondir; (*with fear etc*) sursauter; (*increase*) monter en flèche ▷ *vt* sauter, franchir ▷ *n* saut *m*, bond *m*; (*with fear etc*) sursaut *m*; (*fence*) obstacle *m*; **to ~ the queue** (BRIT) passer avant son tour

jumper [ˈdʒʌmpəʳ] *n* (BRIT: *pullover*) pull-over *m*; (US: *pinafore dress*) robe-chasuble *f*

jump leads (US **jumper cables**) *npl* câbles *mpl* de démarrage

Jun. *abbr* = **June**; **junior**

junction [ˈdʒʌŋkʃən] *n* (BRIT: *of roads*) carrefour *m*; (*of rails*) embranchement *m*

June [dʒuːn] *n* juin *m*

jungle [ˈdʒʌŋgl] *n* jungle *f*

junior [ˈdʒuːnɪəʳ] *adj, n*: **he's ~ to me (by 2 years)**, **he's my ~ (by 2 years)** il est mon cadet (de 2 ans), il est plus jeune que moi (de 2 ans); **he's ~ to me** (*seniority*) il est en

dessous de moi (dans la hiérarchie), j'ai plus d'ancienneté que lui; **junior high school** *n* (US) ≈ collège *m* d'enseignement secondaire; *see also* **high school**; **junior school** *n* (BRIT) école *f* primaire, cours moyen

junk [dʒʌŋk] *n* (*rubbish*) camelote *f*; (*cheap goods*) bric-à-brac *m inv*; **junk food** *n* snacks vite prêts (*sans valeur nutritive*)

junkie [ˈdʒʌŋkɪ] *n* (*inf*) junkie *m*, drogué(e)

junk mail *n* prospectus *mpl*; (*Comput*) messages *mpl* publicitaires

Jupiter [ˈdʒuːpɪtəʳ] *n* (*planet*) Jupiter *f*

jurisdiction [dʒuərɪsˈdɪkʃən] *n* juridiction *f*; **it falls** *or* **comes within/outside our ~** cela est/n'est pas de notre compétence *or* ressort

jury [ˈdʒuərɪ] *n* jury *m*

just [dʒʌst] *adj* juste ▷ *adv*: **he's ~ done it/left** il vient de le faire/partir; **~ right/two o'clock** exactement *or* juste ce qu'il faut/deux heures; **we were ~ going** nous partions; **I was ~ about to phone** j'allais téléphoner; **~ as he was leaving** au moment *or* à l'instant précis où il partait; **~ before/enough/here** juste avant/assez/là; **it's ~ me/a mistake** ce n'est que moi/(rien) qu'une erreur; **~ missed/ caught** manqué/attrapé de justesse; **~ listen to this!** écoutez un peu ça!; **she's ~ as clever as you** elle est tout aussi intelligente que vous; **it's ~ as well that you ...** heureusement que vous ...; **~ a minute!**, **~ one moment!** un instant (s'il vous plaît)!

justice [ˈdʒʌstɪs] *n* justice *f*; (US: *judge*) juge *m* de la Cour suprême

justification [dʒʌstɪfɪˈkeɪʃən] *n* justification *f*

justify [ˈdʒʌstɪfaɪ] *vt* justifier

jut [dʒʌt] *vi* (*also*: **~ out**) dépasser, faire saillie

juvenile [ˈdʒuːvənaɪl] *adj* juvénile; (*court, books*) pour enfants ▷ *n* adolescent(e)

K, k [keɪ] *abbr* (= *one thousand*) K; (= *kilobyte*) Ko
kangaroo [kæŋɡəˈruː] *n* kangourou *m*
karaoke [kɑːrəˈəʊkɪ] *n* karaoké *m*
karate [kəˈrɑːtɪ] *n* karaté *m*
kebab [kəˈbæb] *n* kébab *m*
keel [kiːl] *n* quille *f*; **on an even ~** (*fig*) à flot
keen [kiːn] *adj* (*eager*) plein(e) d'enthousiasme; (*interest, desire, competition*) vif (vive); (*eye, intelligence*) pénétrant(e); (*edge*) effilé(e); **to be ~ to do** *or* **on doing sth** désirer vivement faire qch, tenir beaucoup à faire qch; **to be ~ on sth/sb** aimer beaucoup qch/qn
keep [kiːp] (*pt, pp* **kept**) *vt* (*retain, preserve*) garder; (*hold back*) retenir; (*shop, accounts, promise, diary*) tenir; (*support*) entretenir; (*chickens, bees, pigs etc*) élever ▷ *vi* (*food*) se conserver; (*remain: in a certain state or place*) rester ▷ *n* (*of castle*) donjon *m*; (*food etc*): **enough for his ~** assez pour (assurer) sa subsistance; **to ~ doing sth** (*continue*) continuer à faire qch; (*repeatedly*) ne pas arrêter de faire qch; **to ~ sb from doing/sth from happening** empêcher qn de faire *or* que qn (ne) fasse/que qch (n')arrive; **to ~ sb happy/a place tidy** faire que qn soit content/qu'un endroit reste propre; **to ~ sth to o.s.** garder qch pour soi, tenir qch secret; **to ~ sth from sb** cacher qch à qn; **to ~ time** (*clock*) être à l'heure, ne pas retarder; **for ~s** (*inf*) pour de bon, pour toujours; **keep away** *vt*: **to ~ sth/sb away**

from sb tenir qch/qn éloigné de qn ▷ *vi*: **to ~ away (from)** ne pas s'approcher (de); **keep back** *vt* (*crowds, tears, money*) retenir; (*conceal: information*): **to ~ sth back from sb** cacher qch à qn ▷ *vi* rester en arrière; **keep off** *vt* (*dog, person*) éloigner ▷ *vi*: **if the rain ~s off** s'il ne pleut pas; **~ your hands off!** pas touche! (*inf*); **"~ off the grass"** "pelouse interdite"; **keep on** *vi* continuer; **to ~ on doing** continuer à faire; **don't ~ on about it!** arrête (d'en parler)!; **keep out** *vt* empêcher d'entrer ▷ *vi* (*stay out*) rester en dehors; **"~ out"** "défense d'entrer"; **keep up** *vi* (*fig: in comprehension*) suivre ▷ *vt* continuer, maintenir; **to ~ up with sb** (*in work etc*) se maintenir au même niveau que qn; (*in race etc*) aller aussi vite que qn; **keeper** *n* gardien(ne); **keep-fit** *n* gymnastique *f* (d'entretien); **keeping** *n* (*care*) garde *f*; **in keeping with** en harmonie avec
kennel [ˈkɛnl] *n* niche *f*; **kennels** *npl* (*for boarding*) chenil *m*
Kenya [ˈkɛnjə] *n* Kenya *m*
kept [kɛpt] *pt, pp of* **keep**
kerb [kəːb] *n* (BRIT) bordure *f* du trottoir
kerosene [ˈkɛrəsiːn] *n* kérosène *m*
ketchup [ˈkɛtʃəp] *n* ketchup *m*
kettle [ˈkɛtl] *n* bouilloire *f*
key [kiː] *n* (*gen, Mus*) clé *f*; (*of piano, typewriter*) touche *f*; (*on map*) légende *f* ▷ *adj* (*factor, role, area*) clé *inv* ▷ *vt* (*also*: **~ in**: *text*) saisir; **can I have my ~?** je peux avoir ma clé?; **a ~ issue** un problème fondamental; **keyboard** *n* clavier *m*; **keyhole** *n* trou *m* de la serrure; **keyring** *n* porte-clés *m*
kg *abbr* (= *kilogram*) K
khaki [ˈkɑːkɪ] *adj, n* kaki *m*
kick [kɪk] *vt* donner un coup de pied à ▷ *vi* (*horse*) ruer ▷ *n* coup *m* de pied; (*inf: thrill*): **he does it for ~s** il le fait parce que ça l'excite, il le fait pour le plaisir; **to ~ the habit** (*inf*) arrêter; **kick off** *vi* (*Sport*) donner le coup d'envoi; **kick-off** *n* (*Sport*) coup *m* d'envoi
kid [kɪd] *n* (*inf: child*) gamin(e), gosse *m/f*; (*animal, leather*) chevreau *m* ▷ *vi* (*inf*) plaisanter, blaguer
kidnap [ˈkɪdnæp] *vt* enlever, kidnapper; **kidnapping** *n* enlèvement *m*
kidney [ˈkɪdnɪ] *n* (*Anat*) rein *m*; (*Culin*) rognon *m*; **kidney bean** *n* haricot *m* rouge
kill [kɪl] *vt* tuer ▷ *n* mise *f* à mort; **to ~ time** tuer le temps; **killer** *n* tueur(-euse); (*murderer*) meurtrier(-ière); **killing** *n* meurtre *m*; (*of group of people*) tuerie *f*, massacre *m*; (*inf*): **to make a killing** se remplir les poches, réussir un beau coup
kiln [kɪln] *n* four *m*
kilo [ˈkiːləʊ] *n* kilo *m*; **kilobyte** *n* (*Comput*) kilo-octet *m*; **kilogram(me)** *n* kilogramme *m*; **kilometre** (US **kilometer**) [ˈkɪləmiːtəʳ] *n*

kilomètre *m*; **kilowatt** *n* kilowatt *m*

kilt [kɪlt] *n* kilt *m*

kin [kɪn] *n see* **next-of-kin**

kind [kaɪnd] *adj* gentil(le), aimable ▷ *n* sorte *f*, espèce *f*; (*species*) genre *m*; **to be two of a ~** se ressembler; **in ~** (*Comm*) en nature; **~ of** (*inf: rather*) plutôt; **a ~ of** une sorte de; **what ~ of ...?** quelle sorte de ...?

kindergarten ['kɪndəɡɑːtn] *n* jardin *m* d'enfants

kindly ['kaɪndlɪ] *adj* bienveillant(e), plein(e) de gentillesse ▷ *adv* avec bonté; **will you ~ ...** auriez-vous la bonté *or* l'obligeance de ...

kindness ['kaɪndnɪs] *n* (*quality*) bonté *f*, gentillesse *f*

king [kɪŋ] *n* roi *m*; **kingdom** *n* royaume *m*; **kingfisher** *n* martin-pêcheur *m*; **king-size(d) bed** *n* grand lit (*de* 1,95 *m de large*)

kiosk ['kiːɔsk] *n* kiosque *m*; (*BRIT: also:* **telephone ~**) cabine *f* (téléphonique)

kipper ['kɪpər] *n* hareng fumé et salé

kiss [kɪs] *n* baiser *m* ▷ *vt* embrasser; **to ~ (each other)** s'embrasser; **kiss of life** *n* (*BRIT*) bouche à bouche *m*

kit [kɪt] *n* équipement *m*, matériel *m*; (*set of tools etc*) trousse *f*; (*for assembly*) kit *m*

kitchen ['kɪtʃɪn] *n* cuisine *f*

kite [kaɪt] *n* (*toy*) cerf-volant *m*

kitten ['kɪtn] *n* petit chat, chaton *m*

kitty ['kɪtɪ] *n* (*money*) cagnotte *f*

kiwi ['kiːwiː] *n* (*also:* **~ fruit**) kiwi *m*

km *abbr* (= *kilometre*) km

km/h *abbr* (= *kilometres per hour*) km/h

knack [næk] *n*: **to have the ~ (of doing)** avoir le coup (pour faire)

knee [niː] *n* genou *m*; **kneecap** *n* rotule *f*

kneel (*pt, pp* **knelt**) [niːl, nɛlt] *vi* (*also:* **~ down**) s'agenouiller

knelt [nɛlt] *pt, pp of* **kneel**

knew [njuː] *pt of* **know**

knickers ['nɪkəz] *npl* (*BRIT*) culotte *f* (de femme)

knife [naɪf] *n* (*pl* **knives**) couteau *m* ▷ *vt* poignarder, frapper d'un coup de couteau

knight [naɪt] *n* chevalier *m*; (*Chess*) cavalier *m*

knit [nɪt] *vt* tricoter ▷ *vi* tricoter; (*broken bones*) se ressouder; **to ~ one's brows** froncer les sourcils; **knitting** *n* tricot *m*; **knitting needle** *n* aiguille *f* à tricoter; **knitwear** *n* tricots *mpl*, lainages *mpl*

knives [naɪvz] *npl of* **knife**

knob [nɔb] *n* bouton *m*; (*BRIT*): **a ~ of butter** une noix de beurre

knock [nɔk] *vt* frapper; (*bump into*) heurter; (*fig: col*) dénigrer ▷ *vi* (*at door etc*): **to ~ at/on** frapper à/sur ▷ *n* coup *m*; **knock down** *vt* renverser; (*price*) réduire; **knock off** *vi* (*inf: finish*) s'arrêter (de travailler) ▷ *vt* (*vase, object*) faire tomber; (*inf: steal*) piquer; (*fig: from price*

etc): **to ~ off £10** faire une remise de 10 livres; **knock out** *vt* assommer; (*Boxing*) mettre k.-o.; (*in competition*) éliminer; **knock over** *vt* (*object*) faire tomber; (*pedestrian*) renverser; **knockout** *n* (*Boxing*) knock-out *m*, K.-O. *m*; **knockout competition** (*BRIT*) compétition *f* avec épreuves éliminatoires

knot [nɔt] *n* (*gen*) nœud *m* ▷ *vt* nouer

know [nəu] *vt* (*pt* **knew**, *pp* **~n**) savoir; (*person, place*) connaître; **to ~ that** savoir que; **to ~ how to do** savoir faire; **to ~ how to swim** savoir nager; **to ~ about/of sth** (*event*) être au courant de qch; (*subject*) connaître qch; **I don't ~** je ne sais pas; **do you ~ where I can ...?** savez-vous où je peux ...?; **know-all** *n* (*BRIT pej*) je-sais-tout *m/f*; **know-how** *n* savoir-faire *m*, technique *f*, compétence *f*; **knowing** *adj* (*look etc*) entendu(e); **knowingly** *adv* (*on purpose*) sciemment; (*smile, look*) d'un air entendu; **know-it-all** *n* (*US*) = **know-all**

knowledge ['nɔlɪdʒ] *n* connaissance *f*; (*learning*) connaissances, savoir *m*; **without my ~** à mon insu; **knowledgeable** *adj* bien informé(e)

known [nəun] *pp of* **know** ▷ *adj* (*thief, facts*) notoire; (*expert*) célèbre

knuckle ['nʌkl] *n* articulation *f* (des phalanges), jointure *f*

koala [kəuˈɑːlə] *n* (*also:* **~ bear**) koala *m*

Koran [kɔˈrɑːn] *n* Coran *m*

Korea [kəˈrɪə] *n* Corée *f*; **Korean** *adj* coréen(ne) ▷ *n* Coréen(ne)

kosher ['kəuʃər] *adj* kascher *inv*

Kosovar, Kosovan ['kɔsəvɑːr, 'kɔsəvən] *adj* kosovar(e)

Kosovo ['kɔsəvəu] *n* Kosovo *m*

Kuwait [kuˈweɪt] *n* Koweït *m*

L

L *abbr* (BRIT Aut: = *learner*) signale un conducteur débutant

l. *abbr* (= *litre*) l

lab [læb] *n abbr* (= *laboratory*) labo *m*

label ['leɪbl] *n* étiquette *f*; (*brand: of record*) marque *f* ▷ *vt* étiqueter

labor *etc* ['leɪbə'] (US) = **labour** *etc*

laboratory [lə'bɔrətərɪ] *n* laboratoire *m*

Labor Day *n* (US, CANADA) fête *f* du travail (*le premier lundi de septembre*)

● **LABOR DAY**
●
● La fête du Travail aux États-Unis et au
● Canada est fixée au premier lundi de
● septembre. Instituée par le Congrès en
● 1894 après avoir été réclamée par les
● mouvements ouvriers pendant douze
● ans, elle a perdu une grande partie de son
● caractère politique pour devenir un jour
● férié assez ordinaire et l'occasion de partir
● pour un long week-end avant la rentrée
● des classes.

labor union *n* (US) syndicat *m*

Labour ['leɪbə'] *n* (BRIT Pol: *also:* **the ~ Party**) le parti travailliste, les travaillistes *mpl*

labour (US **labor**) ['leɪbə'] *n* (*work*) travail *m*; (*workforce*) main-d'œuvre *f* ▷ *vi*: **to ~ (at)** travailler dur (à), peiner (sur) ▷ *vt*: **to ~ a point** insister sur un point; **in ~** (*Med*) en travail; **labourer** *n* manœuvre *m*; **farm labourer** ouvrier *m* agricole

lace [leɪs] *n* dentelle *f*; (*of shoe etc*) lacet *m* ▷ *vt* (*shoe: also:* **~ up**) lacer

lack [læk] *n* manque *m* ▷ *vt* manquer de; **through** *or* **for ~ of** faute de, par manque de; **to be ~ing** manquer, faire défaut; **to be ~ing in** manquer de

lacquer ['lækə'] *n* laque *f*

lacy ['leɪsɪ] *adj* (*of lace*) en dentelle; (*like lace*) comme de la dentelle

lad [læd] *n* garçon *m*, gars *m*

ladder ['lædə'] *n* échelle *f*; (BRIT: *in tights*) maille filée ▷ *vt*, *vi* (BRIT: *tights*) filer

ladle ['leɪdl] *n* louche *f*

lady ['leɪdɪ] *n* dame *f*; **"ladies and gentlemen …"** "Mesdames (et) Messieurs …"; **young ~** jeune fille *f*; (*married*) jeune femme *f*; **the ladies' (room)** les toilettes *fpl* des dames; **ladybird** (US **ladybug**) *n* coccinelle *f*

lag [læg] *n* retard *m* ▷ *vi* (*also:* **~ behind**) rester en arrière, traîner; (*fig*) rester à la traîne ▷ *vt* (*pipes*) calorifuger

lager ['lɑːgə'] *n* bière blonde

lagoon [lə'guːn] *n* lagune *f*

laid [leɪd] *pt*, *pp of* **lay**; **laid back** *adj* (*inf*) relaxe, décontracté(e)

lain [leɪn] *pp of* **lie**

lake [leɪk] *n* lac *m*

lamb [læm] *n* agneau *m*

lame [leɪm] *adj* (*also fig*) boiteux(-euse)

lament [lə'mɛnt] *n* lamentation *f* ▷ *vt* pleurer, se lamenter sur

lamp [læmp] *n* lampe *f*; **lamppost** *n* (BRIT) réverbère *m*; **lampshade** *n* abat-jour *m inv*

land [lænd] *n* (*as opposed to sea*) terre *f* (*ferme*); (*country*) pays *m*; (*soil*) terre; (*piece of land*) terrain *m*; (*estate*) terre(s), domaine(s) *m(pl)* ▷ *vi* (*from ship*) débarquer; (*Aviat*) atterrir; (*fig: fall*) (re)tomber ▷ *vt* (*passengers, goods*) débarquer; (*obtain*) décrocher; **to ~ sb with sth** (*inf*) coller qch à qn; **landing** *n* (*from ship*) débarquement *m*; (*Aviat*) atterrissage *m*; (*of staircase*) palier *m*; **landing card** *n* carte *f* de débarquement; **landlady** *n* propriétaire *f*, logeuse *f*; (*of pub*) patronne *f*; **landlord** *n* propriétaire *m*, logeur *m*; (*of pub etc*) patron *m*; **landmark** *n* (point *m* de) repère *m*; **to be a landmark** (*fig*) faire date *or* époque; **landowner** *n* propriétaire foncier *or* terrien; **landscape** *n* paysage *m*; **landslide** *n* (*Geo*) glissement *m* (de terrain); (*fig: Pol*) raz-de-marée (électoral)

lane [leɪn] *n* (*in country*) chemin *m*; (*Aut: of road*) voie *f*; (: *line of traffic*) file *f*; (*in race*) couloir *m*

language ['læŋgwɪdʒ] *n* langue *f*; (*way one speaks*) langage *m*; **what ~s do you speak?** quelles langues parlez-vous?; **bad ~**

grossièretés *fpl*, langage grossier; **language laboratory** *n* laboratoire *m* de langues; **language school** *n* école *f* de langue

lantern ['læntn] *n* lanterne *f*

lap [læp] *n* (*of track*) tour *m* (de piste); (*of body*): **in** *or* **on one's ~** sur les genoux ▷ *vt* (*also:* **~ up**) laper ▷ *vi* (*waves*) clapoter

lapel [lə'pɛl] *n* revers *m*

lapse [læps] *n* défaillance *f*; (*in behaviour*) écart *m* (de conduite) ▷ *vi* (*Law*) cesser d'être en vigueur; (*contract*) expirer; **to ~ into bad habits** prendre de mauvaises habitudes; **~ of time** laps *m* de temps, intervalle *m*

laptop (computer) ['læptɔp-] *n* portable *m*

lard [lɑːd] *n* saindoux *m*

larder ['lɑːdər] *n* garde-manger *m inv*

large [lɑːdʒ] *adj* grand(e); (*person, animal*) gros (grosse); **at ~** (*free*) en liberté; (*generally*) en général; pour la plupart; *see also* **by**; **largely** *adv* en grande partie; (*principally*) surtout; **large-scale** *adj* (*map, drawing etc*) à grande échelle; (*fig*) important(e)

lark [lɑːk] *n* (*bird*) alouette *f*; (*joke*) blague *f*, farce *f*

laryngitis [lærɪn'dʒaɪtɪs] *n* laryngite *f*

lasagne [lə'zænjə] *n* lasagne *f*

laser ['leɪzər] *n* laser *m*; **laser printer** *n* imprimante *f* laser

lash [læʃ] *n* coup *m* de fouet; (*also:* **eye~**) cil *m* ▷ *vt* fouetter; (*tie*) attacher; **lash out** *vi*: **to ~ out (at** *or* **against sb/sth)** attaquer violemment (qn/qch)

lass [læs] (*BRIT*) *n* (jeune) fille *f*

last [lɑːst] *adj* dernier(-ière) ▷ *adv* en dernier; (*most recently*) la dernière fois; (*finally*) finalement ▷ *vi* durer; **~ week** la semaine dernière; **~ night** (*evening*) hier soir; (*night*) la nuit dernière; **at ~** enfin; **~ but one** avant-dernier(-ière); **lastly** *adv* en dernier lieu, pour finir; **last-minute** *adj* de dernière minute

latch [lætʃ] *n* loquet *m*; **latch onto** *vt fus* (*cling to: person, group*) s'accrocher à; (*idea*) se mettre en tête

late [leɪt] *adj* (*not on time*) en retard; (*far on in day etc*) tardif(-ive); (*: edition, delivery*) dernier(-ière); (*dead*) défunt(e) ▷ *adv* tard; (*behind time, schedule*) en retard; **to be 10 minutes ~** avoir 10 minutes de retard; **sorry I'm ~** désolé d'être en retard; **it's too ~** il est trop tard; **of ~** dernièrement; **in ~ May** vers la fin (du mois) de mai, fin mai; **the ~ Mr X** feu M. X; **latecomer** *n* retardataire *m/f*; **lately** *adv* récemment; **later** *adj* (*date etc*) ultérieur(e); (*version etc*) plus récent(e) ▷ *adv* plus tard; **latest** ['leɪtɪst] *adj* tout(e) dernier(-ière); **at the latest** au plus tard

lather ['lɑːðər] *n* mousse *f* (de savon) ▷ *vt* savonner

Latin ['lætɪn] *n* latin *m* ▷ *adj* latin(e); **Latin America** *n* Amérique latine; **Latin American** *adj* latino-américain(e), d'Amérique latine ▷ *n* Latino-Américain(e)

latitude ['lætɪtjuːd] *n* (*also fig*) latitude *f*

latter ['lætər] *adj* deuxième, dernier(-ière) ▷ *n*: **the ~** ce dernier, celui-ci

laugh [lɑːf] *n* rire *m* ▷ *vi* rire; **(to do sth) for a ~** (faire qch) pour rire; **laugh at** *vt fus* se moquer de; (*joke*) rire de; **laughter** *n* rire *m*; (*of several people*) rires *mpl*

launch [lɔːntʃ] *n* lancement *m*; (*also:* **motor ~**) vedette *f* ▷ *vt* (*ship, rocket, plan*) lancer; **launch into** *vt fus* se lancer dans

launder ['lɔːndər] *vt* laver; (*fig: money*) blanchir

Launderette® [lɔːn'drɛt] (*BRIT*) (*US* **Laundromat®** ['lɔːndrəmæt]) *n* laverie *f* (automatique)

laundry ['lɔːndrɪ] *n* (*clothes*) linge *m*; (*business*) blanchisserie *f*; (*room*) buanderie *f*; **to do the ~** faire la lessive

lava ['lɑːvə] *n* lave *f*

lavatory ['lævətəri] *n* toilettes *fpl*

lavender ['lævəndər] *n* lavande *f*

lavish ['lævɪʃ] *adj* (*amount*) copieux(-euse); (*person: giving freely*): **~ with** prodigue de ▷ *vt*: **to ~ sth on sb** prodiguer qch à qn; (*money*) dépenser qch sans compter pour qn

law [lɔː] *n* loi *f*; (*science*) droit *m*; **lawful** *adj* légal(e), permis(e); **lawless** *adj* (*action*) illégal(e); (*place*) sans loi

lawn [lɔːn] *n* pelouse *f*; **lawnmower** *n* tondeuse *f* à gazon

lawsuit ['lɔːsuːt] *n* procès *m*

lawyer ['lɔːjər] *n* (*consultant, with company*) juriste *m*; (*for sales, wills etc*) ≈ notaire *m*; (*partner, in court*) ≈ avocat *m*

lax [læks] *adj* relâché(e)

laxative ['læksətɪv] *n* laxatif *m*

lay [leɪ] *pt of* **lie** ▷ *adj* laïque; (*not expert*) profane ▷ *vt* (*pt, pp* **laid**) poser, mettre; (*eggs*) pondre; (*trap*) tendre; (*plans*) élaborer; **to ~ the table** mettre la table; **lay down** *vt* poser; (*rules etc*) établir; **to ~ down the law** (*fig*) faire la loi; **lay off** *vt* (*workers*) licencier; (*provide: meal etc*) fournir; **lay out** *vt* (*design*) dessiner, concevoir; (*display*) disposer; (*spend*) dépenser; **lay-by** *n* (*BRIT*) aire *f* de stationnement (sur le bas-côté)

layer ['leɪər] *n* couche *f*

layman ['leɪmən] (*irreg*) *n* (*Rel*) laïque *m*; (*non-expert*) profane *m*

layout ['leɪaut] *n* disposition *f*, plan *m*, agencement *m*; (*Press*) mise *f* en page

lazy ['leɪzɪ] *adj* paresseux(-euse)

lb. *abbr* (*weight*) = **pound**

lead [liːd] *n* (*front position*) tête *f*; (*distance, time ahead*) avance *f*; (*clue*) piste *f*; (*Elec*) fil *m*; (*for dog*) laisse *f*; (*Theat*) rôle principal ▷ *vb* (*pt, pp* **led**) ▷ *vt* (*guide*) mener, conduire; (*be leader of*) être à la tête de ▷ vi (Sport) mener, être en tête; **to ~ to** (road, pipe) mener à, conduire à; (result in) conduire à; aboutir à; **to be in the ~** (Sport: in race) mener, être en tête; (: in match) mener (à la marque); **to ~ sb to do sth** amener qn à faire qch; **to ~ the way** montrer le chemin; **lead up to** vt conduire à; (in conversation) en venir à

lead² [lɛd] n (metal) plomb m; (in pencil) mine f

leader ['liːdəʳ] n (of team) chef m; (of party etc) dirigeant(e), leader m; (Sport: in league) leader; (: in race) coureur m de tête; **leadership** n (position) direction f; **under the leadership of ...** sous la direction de ...; **qualities of leadership** qualités fpl de chef or de meneur

lead-free ['lɛdfriː] adj sans plomb

leading ['liːdɪŋ] adj de premier plan; (main) principal(e); (in race) de tête

lead singer [liːd-] n (in pop group) (chanteur m) vedette f

leaf (pl **leaves**) [liːf, liːvz] n feuille f; (of table) rallonge f; **to turn over a new ~** (fig) changer de conduite or d'existence; **leaf through** vt (book) feuilleter

leaflet ['liːflɪt] n prospectus m, brochure f; (Pol, Rel) tract m

league [liːg] n ligue f; (Football) championnat m; **to be in ~ with** avoir partie liée avec, être de mèche avec

leak [liːk] n (out: also fig) fuite f ▷ vi (pipe, liquid etc) fuir; (shoes) prendre l'eau; (ship) faire eau ▷ vt (liquid) répandre; (information) divulguer

lean [liːn] adj maigre ▷ vb (pt, pp **~ed** or **~t**) ▷ vt: **to ~ sth on** appuyer qch sur ▷ vi (slope) pencher; (rest): **to ~ against** s'appuyer contre; être appuyé(e) contre; **to ~ on** s'appuyer sur; **lean forward** vi se pencher en avant; **lean over** vi se pencher; **leaning** n: **leaning (towards)** penchant m (pour)

leant [lɛnt] pt, pp of **lean**

leap [liːp] n bond m, saut m ▷ vi (pt, pp **~ed** or **~t**) bondir, sauter

leapt [lɛpt] pt, pp of **leap**

leap year n année f bissextile

learn (pt, pp **~ed** or **~t**) [ləːn, -t] vt, vi apprendre; **to ~ (how) to do sth** apprendre à faire qch; **to ~ about sth** (Scol) étudier qch; (hear, read) apprendre qch; **learner** n débutant(e); (BRIT: also: **learner driver**) (conducteur(-trice)) débutant(e); **learning** n savoir m

learnt [ləːnt] pp of **learn**

lease [liːs] n bail m ▷ vt louer à bail

leash [liːʃ] n laisse f

least [liːst] adj: **the ~** (+ noun) le (la) plus petit(e), le (la) moindre; (smallest amount of) le moins de ▷ pron: **(the) ~** le moins ▷ adv (+ verb) le moins; (+ adj): **the ~** le (la) moins; **the ~ money** le moins d'argent; **the ~ expensive** le (la) moins cher (chère); **the ~ possible effort** le moins d'effort possible; **at ~** au moins; (or rather) du moins; **you could at ~ have written** tu aurais au moins pu écrire; **not in the ~** pas le moins du monde

leather ['lɛðəʳ] n cuir m

leave [liːv] (vb: pt, pp **left**) vt laisser; (go away from) quitter; (forget) oublier ▷ vi partir, s'en aller ▷ n (time off) congé m; (Mil, also: consent) permission f; **what time does the train/bus ~?** le train/le bus part à quelle heure?; **to ~ sth to sb** (money etc) laisser qch à qn; **to be left** rester; **there's some milk left over** il reste du lait; **~ it to me!** laissez-moi faire!, je m'en occupe!; **on ~** en permission; **leave behind** vt (also fig) laisser; (forget) laisser, oublier; **leave out** vt oublier, omettre

leaves [liːvz] npl of **leaf**

Lebanon ['lɛbənən] n Liban m

lecture ['lɛktʃəʳ] n conférence f; (Scol) cours (magistral) ▷ vi donner des cours; enseigner ▷ vt (scold) sermonner, réprimander; **to give a ~ (on)** faire une conférence (sur), faire un cours (sur); **lecture hall** n amphithéâtre m; **lecturer** n (speaker) conférencier(-ière); (BRIT: at university) professeur m (d'université), prof m/f de fac (inf); **lecture theatre** n = **lecture hall**

> Be careful not to translate **lecture** by the French word **lecture**.

led [lɛd] pt, pp of **lead¹**

ledge [lɛdʒ] n (of window, on wall) rebord m; (of mountain) saillie f, corniche f

leek [liːk] n poireau m

left [lɛft] pt, pp of **leave** ▷ adj gauche ▷ adv à gauche ▷ n gauche f; **there are two ~** il en reste deux; **on the ~, to the ~** à gauche; **the L~** (Pol) la gauche; **left-hand** adj: **the left-hand side** la gauche; **left-hand drive** n (BRIT: vehicle) véhicule m avec la conduite à gauche; **left-handed** adj gaucher(-ère); (scissors etc) pour gauchers; **left-luggage locker** n (BRIT) (casier m à) consigne f automatique; **left-luggage (office)** n (BRIT) consigne f; **left-overs** npl restes mpl; **left-wing** adj (Pol) de gauche

leg [lɛg] n jambe f; (of animal) patte f; (of furniture) pied m; (Culin: of chicken) cuisse f; (of journey) étape f; **1st/2nd ~** (Sport) match m aller/retour; **~ of lamb** (Culin) gigot m d'agneau

legacy ['lɛgəsɪ] n (also fig) héritage m, legs m

legal ['liːgl] adj (permitted by law) légal(e); (relating to law) juridique; **legal holiday** (US) n jour férié; **legalize** vt légaliser; **legally** adv légalement

legend ['lɛdʒənd] n légende f; **legendary** ['lɛdʒəndərɪ] adj légendaire

leggings ['lɛgɪŋz] npl caleçon m

legible ['lɛdʒəbl] *adj* lisible

legislation [lɛdʒɪs'leɪʃən] *n* législation *f*

legislative ['lɛdʒɪslətɪv] *adj* législatif(-ive)

legitimate [lɪ'dʒɪtɪmət] *adj* légitime

leisure ['lɛʒəʳ] *n* (*free time*) temps libre, loisirs *mpl*; **at ~** (*tout*) à loisir; **at your ~** (*later*) à tête reposée; **leisure centre** *n* (BRIT) centre *m* de loisirs; **leisurely** *adj* tranquille, fait(e) sans se presser

lemon ['lɛmən] *n* citron *m*; **lemonade** *n* (*fizzy*) limonade *f*; **lemon tea** *n* thé *m* au citron

lend (*pt, pp* **lent**) [lɛnd, lɛnt] *vt*: **to ~ sth (to sb)** prêter qch (à qn); **could you ~ me some money?** pourriez-vous me prêter de l'argent?

length [lɛŋθ] *n* longueur *f*; (*section: of road, pipe etc*) morceau *m*, bout *m*; **~ of time** durée *f*; **it is 2 metres in ~** cela fait 2 mètres de long; **at ~** (*at last*) enfin, à la fin; (*lengthily*) longuement; **lengthen** *vt* allonger, prolonger ▷ *vi* s'allonger; **lengthways** *adv* dans le sens de la longueur, en long; **lengthy** *adj* (très) long (longue)

lens [lɛnz] *n* lentille *f*; (*of spectacles*) verre *m*; (*of camera*) objectif *m*

Lent [lɛnt] *n* carême *m*

lent [lɛnt] *pt, pp of* **lend**

lentil ['lɛntɪl] *n* lentille *f*

Leo ['liːəu] *n* le Lion

leopard ['lɛpəd] *n* léopard *m*

leotard ['liːətɑːd] *n* justaucorps *m*

leprosy ['lɛprəsɪ] *n* lèpre *f*

lesbian ['lɛzbɪən] *n* lesbienne *f* ▷ *adj* lesbien(ne)

less [lɛs] *adj* moins de ▷ *pron, adv* moins ▷ *prep*: **~ tax/10% discount** avant impôt/moins 10% de remise; **~ than that/you** moins que cela/vous; **~ than half** moins de la moitié; **~ than ever** moins que jamais; **~ and ~** de moins en moins; **the ~ he works ...** moins il travaille ...; **lessen** *vi* diminuer, s'amoindrir, s'atténuer ▷ *vt* diminuer, réduire, atténuer; **lesser** ['lɛsəʳ] *adj* moindre; **to a lesser extent** *or* **degree** à un degré moindre

lesson ['lɛsn] *n* leçon *f*; **to teach sb a ~** (*fig*) donner une bonne leçon à qn

let (*pt, pp* **~**) [lɛt] *vt* laisser; (BRIT: *lease*) louer; **to ~ sb do sth** laisser qn faire qch; **to ~ sb know sth** faire savoir qch à qn, prévenir qn de qch; **to ~ go** lâcher prise; **to ~ go of sth** , **to ~ sth go** lâcher qch; **~'s go** allons-y; **~ him come** qu'il vienne; **"to ~"** (BRIT) "à louer"; **let down** *vt* (*lower*) baisser; (BRIT: *tyre*) dégonfler; (*disappoint*) décevoir; **let in** *vt* laisser entrer; (*visitor etc*) faire entrer; **let off** *vt* (*allow to leave*) laisser partir; (*not punish*) ne pas punir; (*firework etc*) faire partir; (*bomb*) faire exploser; **let out** *vt* laisser sortir; (*scream*) laisser échapper; (BRIT: *rent out*) louer

lethal ['liːθl] *adj* mortel(le), fatal(e); (*weapon*)

meurtrier(-ère)

letter ['lɛtəʳ] *n* lettre *f*; **letterbox** *n* (BRIT) boîte *f* aux or à lettres

lettuce ['lɛtɪs] *n* laitue *f*, salade *f*

leukaemia (US **leukemia**) [luː'kiːmɪə] *n* leucémie *f*

level ['lɛvl] *adj* (*flat*) plat(e), plan(e), uni(e); (*horizontal*) horizontal(e) ▷ *n* niveau *m* ▷ *vt* niveler, aplanir; **"A" ~s** *npl* (BRIT) ≈ baccalauréat *m*; **to be ~ with** être au même niveau que; **to draw ~ with** (*runner, car*) arriver à la hauteur de, rattraper; **on the ~** (*fig: honest*) régulier(-ière); **level crossing** *n* (BRIT) passage *m* à niveau

lever ['liːvəʳ] *n* levier *m*; **leverage** *n* (*influence*): **leverage (on** *or* **with)** prise *f* (sur)

levy ['lɛvɪ] *n* taxe *f*, impôt *m* ▷ *vt* (*tax*) lever; (*fine*) infliger

liability [laɪə'bɪlətɪ] *n* responsabilité *f*; (*handicap*) handicap *m*

liable ['laɪəbl] *adj* (*subject*): **~ to** sujet(te) à, passible de; (*responsible*): **~ (for)** responsable (de); (*likely*): **~ to do** susceptible de faire

liaise [liː'eɪz] *vi*: **to ~ with** assurer la liaison avec

liar ['laɪəʳ] *n* menteur(-euse)

libel ['laɪbl] *n* diffamation *f*; (*document*) écrit *m* diffamatoire ▷ *vt* diffamer

liberal ['lɪbərl] *adj* libéral(e); (*generous*): **~ with** prodigue de, généreux(-euse) avec ▷ *n*: **L~** (*Pol*) libéral(e); **Liberal Democrat** *n* (BRIT) libéral(e)-démocrate *m/f*

liberate ['lɪbəreɪt] *vt* libérer

liberation [lɪbə'reɪʃən] *n* libération *f*

liberty ['lɪbətɪ] *n* liberté *f*; **to be at ~** (*criminal*) être en liberté; **at ~ to do** libre de faire; **to take the ~ of** prendre la liberté de, se permettre de

Libra ['liːbrə] *n* la Balance

librarian [laɪ'brɛərɪən] *n* bibliothécaire *m/f*

library ['laɪbrərɪ] *n* bibliothèque *f*

▌ Be careful not to translate *library* by the French word *librairie*.

Libya ['lɪbɪə] *n* Libye *f*

lice [laɪs] *npl of* **louse**

licence (US **license**) ['laɪsns] *n* autorisation *f*, permis *m*; (*Comm*) licence *f*; (*Radio, TV*) redevance *f*; (*also*: **driving ~**, US: *also*: **driver's license**) permis *m* (de conduire)

license ['laɪsns] *n* (US) = **licence**; **licensed** *adj* (*for alcohol*) patenté(e) pour la vente des spiritueux, qui a une patente de débit de boissons; (*car*) muni(e) de la vignette; **license plate** *n* (US Aut) plaque *f* minéralogique; **licensing hours** (BRIT) *npl* heures *fpl* d'ouvertures (*des pubs*)

lick [lɪk] *vt* lécher; (*inf: defeat*) écraser, flanquer une piquette or raclée à; **to ~ one's lips** (*fig*) se frotter les mains

lid [lɪd] *n* couvercle *m*; (*eyelid*) paupière *f*

lie [laɪ] n mensonge m ▷ vi (pt, pp **~d**) (tell lies) mentir; (pt **lay**, pp **lain**) (rest) être étendu(e) or allongé(e) or couché(e); (object: be situated) se trouver, être; **to ~ low** (fig) se cacher, rester caché(e); **to tell ~s** mentir; **lie about, lie around** vi (things) traîner; (BRIT: person) traînasser, flemmarder; **lie down** vi se coucher, s'étendre

Liechtenstein ['lɪktənstaɪn] n Liechtenstein m

lie-in ['laɪɪn] n (BRIT): **to have a ~** faire la grasse matinée

lieutenant [lef'tɛnənt, US luː'tɛnənt] n lieutenant m

life (pl **lives**) [laɪf, laɪvz] n vie f; **to come to ~** (fig) s'animer; **life assurance** n (BRIT) = **life insurance**; **lifeboat** n canot m or chaloupe f de sauvetage; **lifeguard** n surveillant m de baignade; **life insurance** n assurance-vie f; **life jacket** n gilet m or ceinture f de sauvetage; **lifelike** adj qui semble vrai(e) or vivant(e), ressemblant(e); (painting) réaliste; **life preserver** n (US) gilet m or ceinture f de sauvetage; **life sentence** n condamnation f à vie or à perpétuité; **lifestyle** n style m de vie; **lifetime** n: **in his lifetime** de son vivant

lift [lɪft] vt soulever, lever; (end) supprimer, lever ▷ vi (fog) se lever ▷ n (BRIT: elevator) ascenseur m; **to give sb a ~** (BRIT) emmener or prendre qn en voiture; **can you give me a ~ to the station?** pouvez-vous m'emmener à la gare?; **lift up** vt soulever; **lift-off** n décollage m

light [laɪt] n lumière f; (lamp) lampe f; (Aut: rear light) feu m; (: headlamp) phare m; (for cigarette etc): **have you got a ~?** avez-vous du feu? ▷ vt (pt, pp **~ed** or **lit**) (candle, cigarette, fire) allumer; (room) éclairer ▷ adj (room, colour) clair(e); (not heavy, also fig) léger(-ère); (not strenuous) peu fatigant(e); **lights** npl (traffic lights) feux mpl; **to come to ~** être dévoilé(e) or découvert(e); **in the ~ of** à la lumière de; étant donné; **light up** vi s'allumer; (face) s'éclairer; (smoke) allumer une cigarette or une pipe etc ▷ vt (illuminate) éclairer, illuminer; **light bulb** n ampoule f; **lighten** vt (light up) éclairer; (make lighter) éclaircir; (make less heavy) alléger; **lighter** n (also: **cigarette lighter**) briquet m; **light-hearted** adj gai(e), joyeux(-euse), enjoué(e); **lighthouse** n phare m; **lighting** n éclairage m; (in theatre) éclairages; **lightly** adv légèrement; **to get off lightly** s'en tirer à bon compte

lightning ['laɪtnɪŋ] n foudre f; (flash) éclair m

lightweight ['laɪtweɪt] adj (suit) léger(-ère) ▷ n (Boxing) poids léger

like [laɪk] vt aimer (bien) ▷ prep comme ▷ adj semblable, pareil(le) ▷ n: **the ~** (pej) (d')autres du même genre or acabit; **his ~s and dislikes**

ses goûts mpl or préférences fpl; **I would ~**, **I'd ~** je voudrais, j'aimerais; **would you ~ a coffee?** voulez-vous du café?; **to be/look ~ sb/sth** ressembler à qn/qch; **what's he ~?** comment est-il?; **what does it look ~?** de quoi est-ce que ça a l'air?; **what does it taste ~?** quel goût est-ce que ça a?; **that's just ~ him** c'est bien de lui, ça lui ressemble; **do it ~ this** fais-le comme ceci; **it's nothing ~ ...** ce n'est pas du tout comme ...; **likeable** adj sympathique, agréable

likelihood ['laɪklɪhud] n probabilité f

likely ['laɪklɪ] adj (result, outcome) probable; (excuse) plausible; **he's ~ to leave** il va sûrement partir, il risque fort de partir; **not ~!** (inf) pas de danger!

likewise ['laɪkwaɪz] adv de même, pareillement

liking ['laɪkɪŋ] n (for person) affection f; (for thing) penchant m, goût m; **to be to sb's ~** être au goût de qn, plaire à qn

lilac ['laɪlək] n lilas m

Lilo® ['laɪləu] n matelas m pneumatique

lily ['lɪlɪ] n lis m; **~ of the valley** muguet m

limb [lɪm] n membre m

limbo ['lɪmbəu] n: **to be in ~** (fig) être tombé(e) dans l'oubli

lime [laɪm] n (tree) tilleul m; (fruit) citron vert, lime f; (Geo) chaux f

limelight ['laɪmlaɪt] n: **in the ~** (fig) en vedette, au premier plan

limestone ['laɪmstəun] n pierre f à chaux; (Geo) calcaire m

limit ['lɪmɪt] n limite f ▷ vt limiter; **limited** adj limité(e), restreint(e); **to be limited to** se limiter à, ne concerner que

limousine ['lɪməziːn] n limousine f

limp [lɪmp] n: **to have a ~** boiter ▷ vi boiter ▷ adj mou (molle)

line [laɪn] n (gen) ligne f; (stroke) trait m; (wrinkle) ride f; (rope) corde f; (wire) fil m; (of poem) vers m; (row, series) rangée f; (of people) file f, queue f; (railway track) voie f; (Comm: series of goods) article(s) m(pl), ligne de produits; (work) métier m ▷ vt: **to ~ (with)** (clothes) doubler (de); (box) garnir or tapisser (de); (subj: trees, crowd) border; **to stand in ~** (US) faire la queue; **in his ~ of business** dans sa partie, dans son rayon; **to be in ~ for sth** (fig) être en lice pour qch; **in ~ with** en accord avec, en conformité avec; **in a ~** aligné(e); **line up** vi s'aligner, se mettre en rang(s); (in queue) faire la queue ▷ vt aligner; (event) prévoir; (find) trouver; **to have sb/sth ~d up** avoir qn/qch en vue or de prévu(e)

linear ['lɪnɪə^r] adj linéaire

linen ['lɪnɪn] n linge m (de corps or de maison); (cloth) lin m

liner ['laɪnə^r] n (ship) paquebot m de ligne; (for *bin*) sac-poubelle *m*

line-up ['laɪnʌp] *n* (*us*: *queue*) file *f*; (*also*: **police ~**) parade *f* d'identification; (*Sport*) (*composition f* de l')équipe *f*

linger ['lɪŋgəʳ] *vi* s'attarder; traîner; (*smell, tradition*) persister

lingerie ['lænʒəri:] *n* lingerie *f*

linguist ['lɪŋgwɪst] *n* linguiste *m/f*; **to be a good ~** être doué(e) pour les langues; **linguistic** *adj* linguistique

lining ['laɪnɪŋ] *n* doublure *f*; (*of brakes*) garniture *f*

link [lɪŋk] *n* (*connection*) lien *m*, rapport *m*; (*Internet*) lien; (*of a chain*) maillon *m* ▷ *vt* relier, lier, unir; **links** *npl* (*Golf*) (terrain *m* de) golf *m*; **link up** *vt* relier ▷ *vi* (*people*) se rejoindre; (*companies etc*) s'associer

lion ['laɪən] *n* lion *m*; **lioness** *n* lionne *f*

lip [lɪp] *n* lèvre *f*; (*of cup etc*) rebord *m*; **lipread** *vi* lire sur les lèvres; **lip salve** [-sælv] *n* pommade *f* pour les lèvres, pommade rosat; **lipstick** *n* rouge *m* à lèvres

liqueur [lɪ'kjuəʳ] *n* liqueur *f*

liquid ['lɪkwɪd] *n* liquide *m* ▷ *adj* liquide; **liquidizer** ['lɪkwɪdaɪzəʳ] *n* (*BRIT Culin*) mixer *m*

liquor ['lɪkəʳ] *n* spiritueux *m*, alcool *m*; **liquor store** (*us*) *n* magasin *m* de vins et spiritueux

Lisbon ['lɪzbən] *n* Lisbonne *f*

lisp [lɪsp] *n* zézaiement *m* ▷ *vi* zézayer

list [lɪst] *n* liste *f* ▷ *vt* (*write down*) inscrire; (*make list of*) faire la liste de; (*enumerate*) énumérer

listen ['lɪsn] *vi* écouter; **to ~ to** écouter; **listener** *n* auditeur(-trice)

lit [lɪt] *pt, pp of* **light**

liter ['li:təʳ] *n* (*us*) = **litre**

literacy ['lɪtərəsɪ] *n* degré *m* d'alphabétisation, fait *m* de savoir lire et écrire

literal ['lɪtərl] *adj* littéral(e); **literally** *adv* littéralement; (*really*) réellement

literary ['lɪtərərɪ] *adj* littéraire

literate ['lɪtərət] *adj* qui sait lire et écrire; (*educated*) instruit(e)

literature ['lɪtrɪtʃəʳ] *n* littérature *f*; (*brochures etc*) copie *f* publicitaire, prospectus *mpl*

litre (*us* **liter**) ['li:təʳ] *n* litre *m*

litter ['lɪtəʳ] *n* (*rubbish*) détritus *mpl*; (*dirtier*) ordures *fpl*; (*young animals*) portée *f*; **litter bin** *n* (*BRIT*) poubelle *f*; **littered** *adj*: **littered with** (*scattered*) jonché(e) de

little ['lɪtl] *adj* (*small*) petit(e); (*not much*): **~ milk** peu de lait ▷ *adv* peu; **a ~** un peu (de); **a ~ milk** un peu de lait; **a ~ bit** un peu; **as ~ as possible** le moins possible; **~ by ~** petit à petit, peu à peu; **little finger** *n* auriculaire *m*, petit doigt

live¹ [laɪv] *adj* (*animal*) vivant(e), en vie; (*wire*) sous tension; (*broadcast*) (transmis(e)) en direct; (*unexploded*) non explosé(e)

live² [lɪv] *vi* vivre; (*reside*) vivre, habiter; **to ~ in London** habiter (à) Londres; **where do you ~?** où habitez-vous?; **live together** vivre ensemble, cohabiter; **live up to** *vt fus* se montrer à la hauteur de

livelihood ['laɪvlɪhud] *n* moyens *mpl* d'existence

lively ['laɪvlɪ] *adj* vif (vive), plein(e) d'entrain; (*place, book*) vivant(e)

liven up ['laɪvn-] *vt* (*room etc*) égayer; (*discussion, evening*) animer ▷ *vi* s'animer

liver ['lɪvəʳ] *n* foie *m*

lives [laɪvz] *npl of* **life**

livestock ['laɪvstɔk] *n* cheptel *m*, bétail *m*

living ['lɪvɪŋ] *adj* vivant(e), en vie ▷ *n*: **to earn** *or* **make a ~** gagner sa vie; **living room** *n* salle *f* de séjour

lizard ['lɪzəd] *n* lézard *m*

load [ləud] *n* (*weight*) poids *m*; (*thing carried*) chargement *m*, charge *f*; (*Elec, Tech*) charge ▷ *vt* (*also*: **~ up**): **to ~ (with)** (*lorry, ship*) charger (de); (*gun, camera*) charger (avec); (*Comput*) charger; **a ~ of**, **~s of** (*fig*) un *or* des tas de, des masses de; **to talk a ~ of rubbish** (*inf*) dire des bêtises; **loaded** *adj* (*dice*) pipé(e); (*question*) insidieux(-euse); (*inf: rich*) bourré(e) de fric

loaf (*pl* **loaves**) [ləuf, ləuvz] *n* pain *m*, miche *f* ▷ *vi* (*also*: **~ about**, **~ around**) fainéanter, traîner

loan [ləun] *n* prêt *m* ▷ *vt* prêter; **on ~** prêté(e), en prêt

loathe [ləuð] *vt* détester, avoir en horreur

loaves [ləuvz] *npl of* **loaf**

lobby ['lɔbɪ] *n* hall *m*, entrée *f*; (*Pol*) groupe *m* de pression, lobby *m* ▷ *vt* faire pression sur

lobster ['lɔbstəʳ] *n* homard *m*

local ['ləukl] *adj* local(e) ▷ *n* (*BRIT: pub*) pub *m or* café *m* du coin; **the locals** *npl* les gens *mpl* du pays *or* du coin; **local anaesthetic** *n* anesthésie locale; **local authority** *n* collectivité locale, municipalité *f*; **local government** *n* administration locale *or* municipale; **locally** ['ləukəlɪ] *adv* localement; dans les environs *or* la région

locate [ləu'keɪt] *vt* (*find*) trouver, repérer; (*situate*) situer; **to be ~d in** être situé à *or* en

location [ləu'keɪʃən] *n* emplacement *m*; **on ~** (*Cine*) en extérieur

> Be careful not to translate *location* by the French word *location*.

loch [lɔx] *n* lac *m*, loch *m*

lock [lɔk] *n* (*of door, box*) serrure *f*; (*of canal*) écluse *f*; (*of hair*) mèche *f*, boucle *f* ▷ *vt* (*with key*) fermer à clé ▷ *vi* (*door etc*) fermer à clé; (*wheels*) se bloquer; **lock in** *vt* enfermer; **lock out** *vt* enfermer dehors; (*on purpose*) mettre à la porte; **lock up** *vt* (*person*) enfermer; (*house*) fermer à clé ▷ *vi* tout fermer (à clé)

locker ['lɔkəʳ] *n* casier *m*; (*in station*) consigne

f automatique; **locker-room** (US) *n* (Sport) vestiaire *m*

locksmith ['lɔksmɪθ] *n* serrurier *m*

locomotive [ləukə'məutɪv] *n* locomotive *f*

locum ['ləukəm] *n* (Med) suppléant(e) de médecin *etc*

lodge [lɔdʒ] *n* pavillon *m* (de gardien); (*also:* hunting ~) pavillon de chasse ▷ *vi* (*person*): **to ~ with** être logé(e) chez, être en pension chez; (*bullet*) se loger ▷ *vt* (*appeal etc*) présenter; déposer; **to ~ a complaint** porter plainte; **lodger** *n* locataire *m/f*; (*with room and meals*) pensionnaire *m/f*

lodging ['lɔdʒɪŋ] *n* logement *m*

loft [lɔft] *n* grenier *m*; (*apartment*) grenier aménagé (en appartement) (*gén dans ancien entrepôt ou fabrique*)

log [lɔg] *n* (*of wood*) bûche *f*; (Naut) livre *m* or journal *m* de bord; (*of car*) ≈ carte grise ▷ *vt* enregistrer; **log in, log on** *vi* (Comput) ouvrir une session, entrer dans le système; **log off, log out** *vi* (Comput) clore une session, sortir du système

logic ['lɔdʒɪk] *n* logique *f*; **logical** *adj* logique

logo ['ləugəu] *n* logo *m*

Loire [lwa:] *n*: **the (River) ~** la Loire

lollipop ['lɔlɪpɔp] *n* sucette *f*; **lollipop man/ lady** (BRIT: *irreg*) *n* contractuel qui fait traverser la rue aux enfants

lolly ['lɔlɪ] *n* (*inf: ice*) esquimau *m*; (: *lollipop*) sucette *f*

London ['lʌndən] *n* Londres; **Londoner** *n* Londonien(ne)

lone [ləun] *adj* solitaire

loneliness ['ləunlɪnɪs] *n* solitude *f*, isolement *m*

lonely ['ləunlɪ] *adj* seul(e); (*childhood etc*) solitaire; (*place*) solitaire, isolé(e)

long [lɔŋ] *adj* long (longue) ▷ *adv* longtemps ▷ *vi*: **to ~ for sth/to do sth** avoir très envie de qch/de faire qch, attendre qch avec impatience/attendre avec impatience de faire qch; **how ~ is this river/course?** quelle est la longueur de ce fleuve/la durée de ce cours?; **6 metres ~** (long) de 6 mètres; **6 months ~** qui dure 6 mois, de 6 mois; **all night ~** toute la nuit; **he no ~er comes** il ne vient plus; **I can't stand it any ~er** je ne peux plus le supporter; **~ before** longtemps avant; **before ~** (+ *future*) avant peu, dans peu de temps; (+ *past*) peu de temps après; **don't be ~!** fais vite!, dépêche-toi!; **I shan't be ~** je n'en ai pas pour longtemps; **at ~ last** enfin; **so** or **as ~ as** à condition que + *sub*; **long-distance** *adj* (*race*) de fond; (*call*) interurbain(e); **long-haul** *adj* (*flight*) long-courrier; **longing** *n* désir *m*, envie *f*; (*nostalgia*) nostalgie *f* ▷ *adj* plein(e) d'envie or de nostalgie

longitude ['lɔŋgɪtjuːd] *n* longitude *f*

long: **long jump** *n* saut *m* en longueur; **long-life** *adj* (*batteries etc*) longue durée *inv*; (*milk*) longue conservation; **long-sighted** *adj* (BRIT) presbyte; (*fig*) prévoyant(e); **long-standing** *adj* de longue date; **long-term** *adj* à long terme

loo [luː] *n* (BRIT *inf*) w.-c *mpl*, petit coin

look [luk] *vi* regarder; (*seem*) sembler, paraître, avoir l'air; (*building etc*): **to ~ south/on to the sea** donner au sud/sur la mer ▷ *n* regard *m*; (*appearance*) air *m*, allure *f*, aspect *m*; **looks** *npl* (*good looks*) physique *m*, beauté *f*; **to ~ like** ressembler à; **to have a ~** regarder; **to have a ~ at sth** jeter un coup d'œil à qch; **~ (here)!** (*annoyance*) écoutez!; **look after** *vt fus* s'occuper de; (*luggage etc: watch over*) garder, surveiller; **look around** *vi* regarder autour de soi; **look at** *vt fus* regarder; (*problem etc*) examiner; **look back** *vi*: **to ~ back at sth/sb** se retourner pour regarder qch/qn; **to ~ back on** (*event, period*) évoquer, repenser à; **look down on** *vt fus* (*fig*) regarder de haut, dédaigner; **look for** *vt fus* chercher; **we're ~ing for a hotel/restaurant** nous cherchons un hôtel/restaurant; **look forward to** *vt fus* attendre avec impatience; **~ing forward to hearing from you** (*in letter*) dans l'attente de vous lire; **look into** *vt fus* (*matter, possibility*) examiner, étudier; **look out** *vi* (*beware*): **to ~ out (for)** prendre garde (à), faire attention (à); **~ out!** attention!; **look out for** *vt fus* (*seek*) être à la recherche de; (*try to spot*) guetter; **look round** *vt fus* (*house, shop*) faire le tour de ▷ *vi* (*turn*) regarder derrière soi, se retourner; **look through** *vt fus* (*papers, book*) examiner; (: *briefly*) parcourir; **look up** *vi* lever les yeux; (*improve*) s'améliorer ▷ *vt* (*word*) chercher; **look up to** *vt fus* avoir du respect pour; **lookout** *n* (*tower etc*) poste *m* de guet; (*person*) guetteur *m*; **to be on the lookout (for)** guetter

loom [luːm] *vi* (*also:* ~ up) surgir; (*event*) paraître imminent(e); (*threaten*) menacer

loony ['luːnɪ] *adj*, *n* (*inf*) timbré(e), cinglé(e) *m/f*

loop [luːp] *n* boucle *f* ▷ *vt*: **to ~ sth round sth** passer qch autour de qch; **loophole** *n* (*fig*) porte *f* de sortie; échappatoire *f*

loose [luːs] *adj* (*knot, screw*) desserré(e); (*clothes*) vague, ample, lâche; (*hair*) dénoué(e), épars(e); (*not firmly fixed*) pas solide; (*morals, discipline*) relâché(e); (*translation*) approximatif(-ive) ▷ *n*: **to be on the ~** être en liberté; **~ connection** (Elec) mauvais contact; **to be at a ~ end** or (US) **at ~ ends** (*fig*) ne pas trop savoir quoi faire; **loosely** *adv* sans serrer; (*imprecisely*) approximativement; **loosen** *vt* desserrer, relâcher, défaire

loot [luːt] *n* butin *m* ▷ *vt* piller

lop-sided ['lɒp'saɪdɪd] *adj* de travers,
asymétrique

lord [lɔːd] *n* seigneur *m*; **L~ Smith** lord
Smith; **the L~** (*Rel*) le Seigneur; **my L~** (*to
noble*) Monsieur le comte/le baron; (*to judge*)
Monsieur le juge; (*to bishop*) Monseigneur;
good L~! mon Dieu!; **Lords** *npl* (*BRIT: Pol*): **the
(House of) Lords** (*BRIT*) la Chambre des Lords

lorry ['lɒrɪ] *n* (*BRIT*) camion *m*; **lorry driver** *n*
(*BRIT*) camionneur *m*, routier *m*

lose (*pt, pp* lost) [luːz, lɒst] *vt* perdre ▷ *vi*
perdre; **I've lost my wallet/passport**
j'ai perdu mon portefeuille/passeport; **to
~ (time)** (*clock*) retarder; **lose out** *vi* être
perdant(e); **loser** *n* perdant(e)

loss [lɒs] *n* perte *f*; **to make a ~** enregistrer
une perte; **to be at a ~** être perplexe *or*
embarrassé(e)

lost [lɒst] *pt, pp of* lose ▷ *adj* perdu(e); **to get
~** *vi* se perdre; **I'm ~** je me suis perdu; **~ and
found property** *n* (*US*) objets trouvés; **~ and
found** *n* (*US*) (bureau *m* des) objets trouvés;
lost property *n* (*BRIT*) objets trouvés; **lost
property office** *or* **department** (bureau *m*
des) objets trouvés

lot [lɒt] *n* (*at auctions, set*) lot *m*; (*destiny*)
sort *m*, destinée *f*; **the ~** (*everything*) le tout;
(*everyone*) tous *mpl*, toutes *fpl*; **a ~** beaucoup; **a ~ of**
beaucoup de; **~s of** des tas de; **to draw ~s (for
sth)** tirer (qch) au sort

lotion ['ləʊʃən] *n* lotion *f*

lottery ['lɒtərɪ] *n* loterie *f*

loud [laʊd] *adj* bruyant(e), sonore; (*voice*)
fort(e); (*condemnation etc*) vigoureux(-euse);
(*gaudy*) voyant(e), tapageur(-euse) ▷ *adv*
(*speak etc*) fort; **out ~** tout haut; **loudly** *adv*
fort, bruyamment; **loudspeaker** *n* haut-
parleur *m*

lounge [laʊndʒ] *n* salon *m*; (*of airport*) salle *f*;
(*BRIT: also*: **~ bar**) (salle de) café *m or* bar *m* ▷ *vi*
(*also*: **~ about** *or* **around**) se prélasser, paresser

louse (*pl* lice) [laʊs, laɪs] *n* pou *m*

lousy ['laʊzɪ] (*inf*) *adj* (*bad quality*) infect(e),
moche; **I feel ~** je suis mal fichu(e)

love [lʌv] *n* amour *m* ▷ *vt* aimer; (*caringly,
kindly*) aimer beaucoup; **I ~ chocolate** j'adore
le chocolat; **to ~ to do** aimer beaucoup
or adorer faire; **"15 ~" (**Tennis**)** "15 à rien *or*
zéro"; **to be/fall in ~ with** être/tomber
amoureux(-euse) de; **to make ~** faire l'amour;
~ from Anne, ~, Anne affectueusement,
Anne; **I ~ you** je t'aime; **love affair** *n* liaison
(amoureuse); **love life** *n* vie sentimentale

lovely ['lʌvlɪ] *adj* (*pretty*) ravissant(e); (*friend,
wife*) charmant(e); (*holiday, surprise*) très
agréable, merveilleux(-euse)

lover ['lʌvəʳ] *n* amant *m*; (*person in love*)
amoureux(-euse); (*amateur*): **a ~ of** un(e)
ami(e) de, un(e) amoureux(-euse) de

loving ['lʌvɪŋ] *adj* affectueux(-euse), tendre,
aimant(e)

low [ləʊ] *adj* bas (basse); (*quality*) mauvais(e),
inférieur(e) ▷ *adv* bas ▷ *n* (*Meteorology*)
dépression *f*; **to feel ~** se sentir déprimé(e);
he's very ~ (*ill*) il est bien bas *or* très affaibli;
to turn (down) ~ *vt* baisser; **to be ~ on**
(*supplies etc*) être à court de; **to reach a new**
or **an all-time ~** tomber au niveau le plus bas;
low-alcohol *adj* à faible teneur en alcool, peu
alcoolisé(e); **low-calorie** *adj* hypocalorique

lower ['ləʊəʳ] *adj* inférieur(e) ▷ *vt* baisser;
(*resistance*) diminuer; **to ~ o.s. to** s'abaisser à

low-fat ['ləʊ'fæt] *adj* maigre

loyal ['lɔɪəl] *adj* loyal(e), fidèle; **loyalty** *n*
loyauté *f*, fidélité *f*; **loyalty card** *n* carte *f* de
fidélité

L.P. *n abbr* = **long-playing record**

L-plates ['ɛlpleɪts] *npl* (*BRIT*) plaques *fpl*
(obligatoires) d'apprenti conducteur

Lt *abbr* (= lieutenant) Lt.

Ltd *abbr* (*Comm: company*: = limited) ≈ S.A.

luck [lʌk] *n* chance *f*; **bad ~** malchance *f*,
malheur *m*; **good ~!** bonne chance!; **bad
or hard *or* tough ~!** pas de chance!; **luckily**
adv heureusement, par bonheur; **lucky**
adj (*person*) qui a de la chance; (*coincidence*)
heureux(-euse); (*number etc*) qui porte bonheur

lucrative ['luːkrətɪv] *adj* lucratif(-ive),
rentable, qui rapporte

ludicrous ['luːdɪkrəs] *adj* ridicule, absurde

luggage ['lʌgɪdʒ] *n* bagages *mpl*; **our ~ hasn't
arrived** nos bagages ne sont pas arrivés;
could you send someone to collect our ~?
pourriez-vous envoyer quelqu'un chercher
nos bagages?; **luggage rack** *n* (*in train*) porte-
bagages *m inv*; (: *on car*) galerie *f*

lukewarm ['luːkwɔːm] *adj* tiède

lull [lʌl] *n* accalmie *f*; (*in conversation*) pause
f ▷ *vt*: **to ~ sb to sleep** bercer qn pour qu'il
s'endorme; **to be ~ed into a false sense of
security** s'endormir dans une fausse sécurité

lullaby ['lʌləbaɪ] *n* berceuse *f*

lumber ['lʌmbəʳ] *n* (*wood*) bois *m* de
charpente; (*junk*) bric-à-brac *m inv* ▷ *vt* (*BRIT
inf*): **to ~ sb with sth/sb** coller *or* refiler
qch/qn à qn

luminous ['luːmɪnəs] *adj* lumineux(-euse)

lump [lʌmp] *n* morceau *m*; (*in sauce*) grumeau
m; (*swelling*) grosseur *f* ▷ *vt* (*also*: **~ together**)
réunir, mettre en tas; **lump sum** *n* somme
globale *or* forfaitaire; **lumpy** *adj* (*sauce*)
qui a des grumeaux; (*bed*) défoncé(e), peu
confortable

lunatic ['luːnətɪk] *n* fou (folle), dément(e)
▷ *adj* fou (folle), dément(e)

lunch [lʌntʃ] *n* déjeuner *m* ▷ *vi* déjeuner;
lunch break, lunch hour *n* pause *f* de
midi, heure *f* du déjeuner; **lunchtime** *n*: **it's**

lunchtime c'est l'heure du déjeuner

lung [lʌŋ] *n* poumon *m*

lure [luəʳ] *n* (*attraction*) attrait *m*, charme *m*; (*in hunting*) appât *m*, leurre *m* ▷ *vt* attirer or persuader par la ruse

lurk [lə:k] *vi* se tapir, se cacher

lush [lʌʃ] *adj* luxuriant(e)

lust [lʌst] *n* (*sexual*) désir (sexuel); (*Rel*) luxure *f*; (*fig*): **~ for** soif *f* de

Luxembourg ['lʌksəmbə:g] *n* Luxembourg *m*

luxurious [lʌg'zjuərɪəs] *adj* luxueux(-euse)

luxury ['lʌkʃərɪ] *n* luxe *m* ▷ *cpd* de luxe

Lycra® ['laɪkrə] *n* Lycra® *m*

lying ['laɪɪŋ] *n* mensonge(s) *m(pl)* ▷ *adj* (*statement, story*) mensonger(-ère), faux (fausse); (*person*) menteur(-euse)

Lyons ['ljɔ̃] *n* Lyon

lyrics ['lɪrɪks] *npl* (*of song*) paroles *fpl*

m. *abbr* (= *metre*) m; (= *million*) M; (= *mile*) mi

M.A. *n abbr* (*Scol*) = **Master of Arts**

ma [mɑ:] (*inf*) *n* maman *f*

mac [mæk] *n* (*BRIT*) imper(méable *m*) *m*

macaroni [mækə'rəʊnɪ] *n* macaronis *mpl*

Macedonia [mæsɪ'dəʊnɪə] *n* Macédoine *f*; **Macedonian** [mæsɪ'dəʊnɪən] *adj* macédonien(ne) ▷ *n* Macédonien(ne); (*Ling*) macédonien *m*

machine [mə'ʃi:n] *n* machine *f* ▷ *vt* (*dress etc*) coudre à la machine; (*Tech*) usiner; **machine gun** *n* mitrailleuse *f*; **machinery** *n* machinerie *f*, machines *fpl*; (*fig*) mécanisme(s) *m(pl)*; **machine washable** *adj* (*garment*) lavable en machine

macho ['mætʃəʊ] *adj* macho *inv*

mackerel ['mækrl] *n* (*pl inv*) maquereau *m*

mackintosh ['mækɪntɔʃ] *n* (*BRIT*) imperméable *m*

mad [mæd] *adj* fou (folle); (*foolish*) insensé(e); (*angry*) furieux(-euse); **to be ~ (keen) about** or **on sth** (*inf*) être follement passionné de qch, être fou de qch

Madagascar [mædə'gæskəʳ] *n* Madagascar *m*

madam ['mædəm] *n* madame *f*

mad cow disease *n* maladie *f* des vaches folles

made [meɪd] *pt*, *pp of* **make**; **made-to-measure** *adj* (*BRIT*) fait(e) sur mesure;

made-up ['meɪdʌp] *adj* (*story*) inventé(e), fabriqué(e)

madly ['mædlɪ] *adv* follement; **~ in love** éperdument amoureux(-euse)

madman ['mædmən] (*irreg*) *n* fou *m*, aliéné *m*

madness ['mædnɪs] *n* folie *f*

Madrid [mə'drɪd] *n* Madrid

Mafia ['mæfɪə] *n* maf(f)ia *f*

mag [mæg] *n abbr* (BRIT *inf*: = *magazine*) magazine *m*

magazine [mægə'zi:n] *n* (*Press*) magazine *m*, revue *f*; (*Radio, TV*) magazine

maggot ['mægət] *n* ver *m*, asticot *m*

magic ['mædʒɪk] *n* magie *f* ▷ *adj* magique; **magical** *adj* magique; (*experience, evening*) merveilleux(-euse); **magician** [mə'dʒɪʃən] *n* magicien(ne)

magistrate ['mædʒɪstreɪt] *n* magistrat *m*; juge *m*

magnet ['mægnɪt] *n* aimant *m*; **magnetic** [mæg'netɪk] *adj* magnétique

magnificent [mæg'nɪfɪsnt] *adj* superbe, magnifique; (*splendid: robe, building*) somptueux(-euse), magnifique

magnify ['mægnɪfaɪ] *vt* grossir; (*sound*) amplifier; **magnifying glass** *n* loupe *f*

magpie ['mægpaɪ] *n* pie *f*

mahogany [mə'hɔgənɪ] *n* acajou *m*

maid [meɪd] *n* bonne *f*; (*in hotel*) femme *f* de chambre; **old ~** (*pej*) vieille fille

maiden name *n* nom *m* de jeune fille

mail [meɪl] *n* poste *f*; (*letters*) courrier *m* ▷ *vt* envoyer (par la poste); **by ~** par la poste; **mailbox** *n* (US: *also* Comput) boîte *f* aux lettres; **mailing list** *n* liste *f* d'adresses; **mailman** (*irreg*) *n* (US) facteur *m*; **mail-order** *n* vente *f* or achat *m* par correspondance

main [meɪn] *adj* principal(e) ▷ *n* (*pipe*) conduite principale, canalisation *f*; **the ~s** (*Elec*) le secteur; **the ~ thing** l'essentiel *m*; **in the ~** dans l'ensemble; **main course** *n* (Culin) plat *m* de résistance; **mainland** *n* continent *m*; **mainly** *adv* principalement, surtout; **main road** *n* grand axe, route nationale; **mainstream** *n* (*fig*) courant principal; **main street** *n* rue *f* principale

maintain [meɪn'teɪn] *vt* entretenir; (*continue*) maintenir, préserver; (*affirm*) soutenir; **maintenance** ['meɪntənəns] *n* entretien *m*; (*Law: alimony*) pension *f* alimentaire

maisonette [meɪzə'net] *n* (BRIT) appartement *m* en duplex

maize [meɪz] *n* (BRIT) maïs *m*

majesty ['mædʒɪstɪ] *n* majesté *f*; (*title*): **Your M~** Votre Majesté

major ['meɪdʒə'] *n* (Mil) commandant *m* ▷ *adj* (*important*) important(e); (*most important*) principal(e); (*Mus*) majeur(e) ▷ *vi* (US Scol): **to ~ (in)** se spécialiser (en)

Majorca [mə'jɔːkə] *n* Majorque *f*

majority [mə'dʒɔrɪtɪ] *n* majorité *f*

make [meɪk] *vt* (*pt, pp* **made**) faire; (*manufacture*) faire, fabriquer; (*earn*) gagner; (*decision*) prendre; (*friend*) se faire; (*speech*) faire, prononcer; (*cause to be*): **to ~ sb sad** *etc* rendre qn triste *etc*; (*force*): **to ~ sb do sth** obliger qn à faire qch, faire faire qch à qn; (*equal*): **2 and 2 ~ 4** 2 et 2 font 4 ▷ *n* (*manufacture*) fabrication *f*; (*brand*) marque *f*; **to ~ the bed** faire le lit; **to ~ a fool of sb** (*ridicule*) ridiculiser qn; (*trick*) avoir or duper qn; **to ~ a profit** faire un or des bénéfice(s); **to ~ a loss** essuyer une perte; **to ~ it** (*in time etc*) y arriver; (*succeed*) réussir; **what time do you ~ it?** quelle heure avez-vous?; **I ~ it £249** d'après mes calculs ça fait 249 livres; **to be made of** être en; **to ~ do with** se contenter de; se débrouiller avec; **make off** *vi* filer; **make out** *vt* (*write out: cheque*) faire; (*decipher*) déchiffrer; (*understand*) comprendre; (*see*) distinguer; (*claim, imply*) prétendre, vouloir faire croire; **make up** *vt* (*invent*) inventer, imaginer; (*constitute*) constituer; (*parcel, bed*) faire ▷ *vi* se réconcilier; (*with cosmetics*) se maquiller, se farder; **to be made up of** se composer de; **make up for** *vt fus* compenser; (*lost time*) rattraper; **makeover** ['meɪkəuvə'] *n* (*by beautician*) soins *mpl* de maquillage; (*change of image*) changement *m* d'image; **maker** *n* fabricant *m*; (*of film, programme*) réalisateur(-trice); **makeshift** *adj* provisoire, improvisé(e); **make-up** *n* maquillage *m*

making ['meɪkɪŋ] *n* (*fig*): **in the ~** en formation or gestation; **to have the ~s of** (*actor, athlete*) avoir l'étoffe de

malaria [mə'lɛərɪə] *n* malaria *f*, paludisme *m*

Malaysia [mə'leɪzɪə] *n* Malaisie *f*

male [meɪl] *n* (Biol, Elec) mâle *m* ▷ *adj* (*sex, attitude*) masculin(e); (*animal*) mâle; (*child etc*) du sexe masculin

malicious [mə'lɪʃəs] *adj* méchant(e), malveillant(e)

> Be careful not to translate *malicious* by the French word *malicieux*.

malignant [mə'lɪgnənt] *adj* (Med) malin(-igne)

mall [mɔːl] *n* (*also*: **shopping ~**) centre commercial

mallet ['mælɪt] *n* maillet *m*

malnutrition [mælnjuː'trɪʃən] *n* malnutrition *f*

malpractice [mæl'præktɪs] *n* faute professionnelle; négligence *f*

malt [mɔːlt] *n* malt *m* ▷ *cpd* (*whisky*) pur malt

Malta ['mɔːltə] *n* Malte *f*; **Maltese** [mɔːl'tiːz] *adj* maltais(e) ▷ *n* (*pl inv*) Maltais(e)

mammal ['mæml] *n* mammifère *m*

mammoth ['mæməθ] *n* mammouth *m* ▷ *adj* géant(e), monstre

man (pl **men**) [mæn, mɛn] n homme m;
(Sport) joueur m; (Chess) pièce f ▷ vt (Naut:
ship) garnir d'hommes; (machine) assurer le
fonctionnement de; (Mil: gun) servir; (: post)
être de service à; **an old ~** un vieillard; **~ and
wife** mari et femme

manage ['mænɪdʒ] vi se débrouiller; (succeed)
y arriver, réussir ▷ vt (business) gérer; (team,
operation) diriger; (control: ship) manier,
manœuvrer; (: person) savoir s'y prendre avec;
to ~ to do se débrouiller pour faire; (succeed)
réussir à faire; **manageable** adj maniable;
(task etc) faisable; (number) raisonnable;
management n (running) administration f,
direction f; (people in charge: of business, firm)
dirigeants mpl, cadres mpl; (: of hotel, shop,
theatre) direction; **manager** n (of business)
directeur m; (of institution etc) administrateur
m; (of department, unit) responsable m/f, chef
m; (of hotel etc) gérant m; (Sport) manager
m; (of artist) impresario m; **manageress** n
directrice f; (of hotel etc) gérante f; **managerial**
[mænɪ'dʒɪərɪəl] adj directorial(e); (skills)
de cadre, de gestion; **managing director** n
directeur général

mandarin ['mændərɪn] n (also: **~ orange**)
mandarine f

mandate ['mændeɪt] n mandat m

mandatory ['mændətərɪ] adj obligatoire

mane [meɪn] n crinière f

maneuver [mə'nu:vəʳ] (US) = **manoeuvre**

mangetout ['mɒnʒ'tu:] n mange-tout m inv

mango (pl **~es**) ['mæŋɡəʊ] n mangue f

man: manhole n trou m d'homme; **manhood**
n (age) âge m d'homme; (manliness) virilité f

mania ['meɪnɪə] n manie f; **maniac**
['meɪnɪæk] n maniaque m/f; (fig) fou (folle)

manic ['mænɪk] adj maniaque

manicure ['mænɪkjuəʳ] n manucure f

manifest ['mænɪfɛst] vt manifester ▷ adj
manifeste, évident(e)

manifesto [mænɪ'fɛstəʊ] n (Pol) manifeste m

manipulate [mə'nɪpjuleɪt] vt manipuler;
(system, situation) exploiter

man: mankind [mæn'kaɪnd] n humanité f,
genre humain; **manly** adj viril(e); **man-made**
adj artificiel(le); (fibre) synthétique

manner ['mænəʳ] n manière f, façon f;
(behaviour) attitude f, comportement m;
manners npl: (good) **~s** (bonnes) manières;
bad ~s mauvaises manières; **all ~ of** toutes
sortes de

manoeuvre (US **maneuver**) [mə'nu:vəʳ]
vt (move) manœuvrer; (manipulate: person)
manipuler; (: situation) exploiter ▷ n
manœuvre f

manpower ['mænpauəʳ] n main-d'œuvre f

mansion ['mænʃən] n château m, manoir m

manslaughter ['mænslɔ:təʳ] n homicide m

involontaire

mantelpiece ['mæntlpi:s] n cheminée f

manual ['mænjuəl] adj manuel(le) ▷ n
manuel m

manufacture [mænju'fæktʃəʳ] vt fabriquer
▷ n fabrication f; **manufacturer** n fabricant m

manure [mə'njuəʳ] n fumier m; (artificial)
engrais m

manuscript ['mænjuskrɪpt] n manuscrit m

many ['mɛnɪ] adj beaucoup de, de
nombreux(-euses) ▷ pron beaucoup, un grand
nombre; **a great ~** un grand nombre (de); **~ a ...**
bien des ..., plus d'un(e) ...

map [mæp] n carte f; (of town) plan m; **can
you show it to me on the ~?** pouvez-vous me
l'indiquer sur la carte?; **map out** vt tracer; (fig:
task) planifier

maple ['meɪpl] n érable m

Mar abbr = **March**

mar [mɑ:ʳ] vt gâcher, gâter

marathon ['mærəθən] n marathon m

marble ['mɑ:bl] n marbre m; (toy) bille f

March [mɑ:tʃ] n mars m

march [mɑ:tʃ] vi marcher au pas;
(demonstrators) défiler ▷ n marche f;
(demonstration) manifestation f

mare [mɛəʳ] n jument f

margarine [mɑ:dʒə'ri:n] n margarine f

margin ['mɑ:dʒɪn] n marge f; **marginal**
adj marginal(e); **marginal seat** (Pol) siège
disputé; **marginally** adv très légèrement,
sensiblement

marigold ['mærɪɡəʊld] n souci m

marijuana [mærɪ'wɑ:nə] n marijuana f

marina [mə'ri:nə] n marina f

marinade n [mærɪ'neɪd] marinade f

marinate ['mærɪneɪt] vt (faire) mariner

marine [mə'ri:n] adj marin(e) ▷ n fusilier
marin; (US) marine m

marital ['mærɪtl] adj matrimonial(e); **marital
status** n situation f de famille

maritime ['mærɪtaɪm] adj maritime

marjoram ['mɑ:dʒərəm] n marjolaine f

mark [mɑ:k] n marque f; (of skid etc) trace
f; (BRIT Scol) note f; (oven temperature): **(gas)
~ 4** thermostat m 4 ▷ vt (also Sport: player)
marquer; (stain) tacher; (BRIT Scol) corriger,
noter; **to ~ time** marquer le pas; **marked** adj
(obvious) marqué(e), net(te); **marker** n (sign)
jalon m; (bookmark) signet m

market ['mɑ:kɪt] n marché m ▷ vt (Comm)
commercialiser; **marketing** n marketing m;
marketplace n place f du marché; (Comm)
marché m; **market research** n étude f de
marché

marmalade ['mɑ:məleɪd] n confiture f
d'oranges

maroon [mə'ru:n] vt: **to be ~ed** être
abandonné(e); (fig) être bloqué(e) ▷ adj

(colour) bordeaux inv

marquee ['mɑːˈkiː] n chapiteau m

marriage ['mærɪdʒ] n mariage m; **marriage certificate** n extrait m d'acte de mariage

married ['mærɪd] adj marié(e); (life, love) conjugal(e)

marrow ['mærəu] n (of bone) moelle f; (vegetable) courge f

marry ['mærɪ] vt épouser, se marier avec; (subj: father, priest etc) marier ▷ vi (also: **get married**) se marier

Mars [mɑːz] n (planet) Mars f

Marseilles [mɑːˈseɪ] n Marseille

marsh [mɑːʃ] n marais m, marécage m

marshal ['mɑːʃl] n maréchal m; (US: fire, police) ≈ capitaine m; (for demonstration, meeting) membre m du service d'ordre ▷ vt rassembler

martyr ['mɑːtər] n martyr(e)

marvel ['mɑːvl] n merveille f ▷ vi: **to ~ (at)** s'émerveiller (de); **marvellous** (US **marvelous**) adj merveilleux(-euse)

Marxism ['mɑːksɪzəm] n marxisme m

Marxist ['mɑːksɪst] adj, n marxiste (m/f)

marzipan ['mɑːzɪpæn] n pâte f d'amandes

mascara [mæsˈkɑːrə] n mascara m

mascot ['mæskət] n mascotte f

masculine ['mæskjulɪn] adj masculin(e) ▷ n masculin m

mash [mæʃ] vt (Culin) faire une purée de; **mashed potato(es)** n(pl) purée f de pommes de terre

mask [mɑːsk] n masque m ▷ vt masquer

mason ['meɪsn] n (also: **stone~**) maçon m; (also: **free~**) franc-maçon m; **masonry** n maçonnerie f

mass [mæs] n multitude f, masse f; (Physics) masse; (Rel) messe f ▷ cpd (communication) de masse; (unemployment) massif(-ive) ▷ vi se masser; **masses** npl: **the ~es** les masses; **~es of** (inf) des tas de

massacre ['mæsəkər] n massacre m

massage ['mæsɑːʒ] n massage m ▷ vt masser

massive ['mæsɪv] adj énorme, massif(-ive)

mass media npl mass-media mpl

mass-produce ['mæsprəˈdjuːs] vt fabriquer en série

mast [mɑːst] n mât m; (Radio, TV) pylône m

master ['mɑːstər] n maître m; (in secondary school) professeur m; (in primary school) instituteur m; (title for boys): **M~ X** Monsieur X ▷ vt maîtriser; (learn) apprendre à fond; **M~ of Arts/Science (MA/MSc)** n ≈ titulaire m/f d'une maîtrise (en lettres/science); **M~ of Arts/Science degree (MA/MSc)** n ≈ maîtrise f; **mastermind** n esprit supérieur ▷ vt diriger, être le cerveau de; **masterpiece** n chef-d'œuvre m

masturbate ['mæstəbeɪt] vi se masturber

mat [mæt] n petit tapis; (also: **door~**)

paillasson m; (also: **table~**) set m de table ▷ adj = **matt**

match [mætʃ] n allumette f; (game) match m, partie f; (fig) égal(e) ▷ vt (also: **~ up**) assortir; (go well with) aller bien avec, s'assortir à; (equal) égaler, valoir ▷ vi être assorti(e); **to be a good ~** être bien assorti(e); **matchbox** n boîte f d'allumettes; **matching** adj assorti(e)

mate [meɪt] n (inf) copain (copine); (animal) partenaire m/f, mâle (femelle); (in merchant navy) second m ▷ vi s'accoupler

material [məˈtɪərɪəl] n (substance) matière f, matériau m; (cloth) tissu m, étoffe f; (information, data) données fpl ▷ adj matériel(le); (relevant: evidence) pertinent(e); **materials** npl (equipment) matériaux mpl

materialize [məˈtɪərɪəlaɪz] vi se matérialiser, se réaliser

maternal [məˈtəːnl] adj maternel(le)

maternity [məˈtəːnɪtɪ] n maternité f; **maternity hospital** n maternité f; **maternity leave** n congé m de maternité

math [mæθ] n (US: = mathematics) maths fpl

mathematical [mæθəˈmætɪkl] adj mathématique

mathematician [mæθəməˈtɪʃən] n mathématicien(ne)

mathematics [mæθəˈmætɪks] n mathématiques fpl

maths [mæθs] n abbr (BRIT: = mathematics) maths fpl

matinée ['mætɪneɪ] n matinée f

matron ['meɪtrən] n (in hospital) infirmière-chef f; (in school) infirmière f

matt [mæt] adj mat(e)

matter ['mætər] n question f; (Physics) matière f, substance f; (Med: pus) pus m ▷ vi importer; **matters** npl (affairs, situation) la situation; **it doesn't ~** cela n'a pas d'importance; (I don't mind) cela ne fait rien; **what's the ~?** qu'est-ce qu'il y a?, qu'est-ce qui ne va pas?; **no ~ what** quoi qu'il arrive; **as a ~ of course** tout naturellement; **as a ~ of fact** en fait; **reading ~** (BRIT) de quoi lire, de la lecture

mattress ['mætrɪs] n matelas m

mature [məˈtjuər] adj mûr(e); (cheese) fait(e); (wine) arrive(e) à maturité ▷ vi mûrir; (cheese, wine) se faire; **mature student** n étudiant(e) plus âgé(e) que la moyenne; **maturity** n maturité f

maul [mɔːl] vt lacérer

mauve [məuv] adj mauve

max abbr = **maximum**

maximize ['mæksɪmaɪz] vt (profits etc, chances) maximiser

maximum ['mæksɪməm] (pl **maxima**) adj maximum ▷ n maximum m

May [meɪ] n mai m

may [meɪ] (conditional **might**) vi (indicating

possibility): **he ~ come** il se peut qu'il vienne; (_be allowed to_): **~ I smoke?** puis-je fumer?; (_wishes_): **~ God bless you!** (que) Dieu vous bénisse!; **you ~ as well go** vous feriez aussi bien d'y aller

maybe ['meɪbiː] _adv_ peut-être; **~ he'll ...** peut-être qu'il ...

May Day _n_ le Premier mai

mayhem ['meɪhɛm] _n_ grabuge _m_

mayonnaise [meɪə'neɪz] _n_ mayonnaise _f_

mayor [mɛəʳ] _n_ maire _m_; **mayoress** _n_ (_female mayor_) maire _m_; (_wife of mayor_) épouse _f_ du maire

maze [meɪz] _n_ labyrinthe _m_, dédale _m_

MD _n abbr_ (_Comm_) = **managing director**

me [miː] _pron_ me, m' + _vowel or h mute_; (_stressed, after prep_) moi; **it's me** c'est moi; **he heard me** il m'a entendu; **give me a book** donnez-moi un livre; **it's for me** c'est pour moi

meadow ['mɛdəu] _n_ prairie _f_, pré _m_

meagre (_US_ **meager**) ['miːgəʳ] _adj_ maigre

meal [miːl] _n_ repas _m_; (_flour_) farine _f_; **mealtime** _n_ heure _f_ du repas

mean [miːn] _adj_ (_with money_) avare, radin(e); (_unkind_) mesquin(e), méchant(e); (_shabby_) misérable; (_average_) moyen(ne) ▷ _vt_ (_pt, pp_ **~t**) (_signify_) signifier, vouloir dire; (_refer to_) faire allusion à, parler de; (_intend_): **to ~ to do** avoir l'intention de faire ▷ _n_ moyenne _f_; **means** _npl_ (_way, money_) moyens _mpl_; **by ~s of** (_instrument_) au moyen de; **by all ~s** je vous en prie; **to be ~t for** être destiné(e) à; **do you ~ it?** vous êtes sérieux?; **what do you ~?** que voulez-vous dire?

meaning ['miːnɪŋ] _n_ signification _f_, sens _m_; **meaningful** _adj_ significatif(-ive); (_relationship_) valable; **meaningless** _adj_ dénué(e) de sens

meant [mɛnt] _pt, pp of_ **mean**

meantime ['miːntaɪm] _adv_ (_also_: **in the ~**) pendant ce temps

meanwhile ['miːnwaɪl] _adv_ = **meantime**

measles ['miːzlz] _n_ rougeole _f_

measure ['mɛʒəʳ] _vt, vi_ mesurer ▷ _n_ mesure _f_; (_ruler_) règle (graduée)

measurements ['mɛʒəməntz] _npl_ mesures _fpl_; **chest/hip ~** tour _m_ de poitrine/hanches

meat [miːt] _n_ viande _f_; **I don't eat ~** je ne mange pas de viande; **cold ~s** (_BRIT_) viandes froides; **meatball** _n_ boulette _f_ de viande

Mecca ['mɛkə] _n_ la Mecque

mechanic [mɪ'kænɪk] _n_ mécanicien _m_; **can you send a ~?** pouvez-vous nous envoyer un mécanicien?; **mechanical** _adj_ mécanique

mechanism ['mɛkənɪzəm] _n_ mécanisme _m_

medal ['mɛdl] _n_ médaille _f_; **medallist** (_US_ **medalist**) _n_ (_Sport_) médaillé(e)

meddle ['mɛdl] _vi_: **to ~ in** se mêler de, s'occuper de; **to ~ with** toucher à

media ['miːdɪə] _npl_ media _mpl_ ▷ _npl of_

medium

mediaeval [mɛdɪ'iːvl] _adj_ = **medieval**

mediate ['miːdɪeɪt] _vi_ servir d'intermédiaire

medical ['mɛdɪkl] _adj_ médical(e) ▷ _n_ (_also_: **~ examination**) visite médicale; (_private_) examen médical; **medical certificate** _n_ certificat médical

medicated ['mɛdɪkeɪtɪd] _adj_ traitant(e), médicamenteux(-euse)

medication [mɛdɪ'keɪʃən] _n_ (_drugs etc_) médication _f_

medicine ['mɛdsɪn] _n_ médecine _f_; (_drug_) médicament _m_

medieval [mɛdɪ'iːvl] _adj_ médiéval(e)

mediocre [miːdɪ'əukəʳ] _adj_ médiocre

meditate ['mɛdɪteɪt] _vi_: **to ~ (on)** méditer (sur)

meditation [mɛdɪ'teɪʃən] _n_ méditation _f_

Mediterranean [mɛdɪtə'reɪnɪən] _adj_ méditerranéen(ne); **the ~ (Sea)** la (mer) Méditerranée

medium ['miːdɪəm] _adj_ moyen(ne) ▷ _n_ (_pl_ **media**: _means_) moyen _m_; (_pl_ **~s**: _person_) médium _m_; **the happy ~** le juste milieu; **medium-sized** _adj_ de taille moyenne; **medium wave** _n_ (_Radio_) ondes moyennes, petites ondes

meek [miːk] _adj_ doux (douce), humble

meet (_pt, pp_ **met**) [miːt, mɛt] _vt_ rencontrer; (_by arrangement_) retrouver, rejoindre; (_for the first time_) faire la connaissance de; (_go and fetch_): **I'll ~ you at the station** j'irai te chercher à la gare; (_opponent, danger, problem_) faire face à; (_requirements_) satisfaire à, répondre à ▷ _vi_ (_friends_) se rencontrer; se retrouver; (_in session_) se réunir; (_join: lines, roads_) se joindre; **nice ~ing you** ravi d'avoir fait votre connaissance; **meet up** _vi_: **to ~ up with sb** rencontrer qn; **meet with** _vt fus_ (_difficulty_) rencontrer; **to ~ with success** être couronné(e) de succès; **meeting** _n_ (_of group of people_) réunion _f_; (_between individuals_) rendez-vous _m_; **she's at** _or_ **in a meeting** (_Comm_) elle est en réunion; **meeting place** _n_ lieu _m_ de (la) réunion; (_for appointment_) lieu de rendez-vous

megabyte ['mɛgəbaɪt] _n_ (_Comput_) méga-octet _m_

megaphone ['mɛgəfəun] _n_ porte-voix _m inv_

megapixel ['mɛgəpɪksl] _n_ mégapixel _m_

melancholy ['mɛlənkəlɪ] _n_ mélancolie _f_ ▷ _adj_ mélancolique

melody ['mɛlədɪ] _n_ mélodie _f_

melon ['mɛlən] _n_ melon _m_

melt [mɛlt] _vi_ fondre ▷ _vt_ faire fondre

member ['mɛmbəʳ] _n_ membre _m_; **Member of Congress** (_US_) _n_ membre _m_ du Congrès, ≈ député _m_; **Member of Parliament (MP)** _n_ (_BRIT_) député _m_; **Member of the European Parliament (MEP)** _n_ Eurodéputé _m_;

m

Member of the House of Representatives (MHR) n (us) membre m de la Chambre des représentants; **Member of the Scottish Parliament (MSP)** n (BRIT) député m au Parlement écossais; **membership** n (becoming a member) adhésion f; admission f; (the members) membres mpl, adhérents mpl; **membership card** n carte f de membre

memento [mə'mɛntəu] n souvenir m

memo ['mɛməu] n note f (de service)

memorable ['mɛmərəbl] adj mémorable

memorandum (pl **memoranda**) [mɛmə'rændəm, -ə] n note f (de service)

memorial [mɪ'mɔ:rɪəl] n mémorial m ▷ adj commémoratif(-ive)

memorize ['mɛməraɪz] vt apprendre or retenir par cœur

memory ['mɛmərɪ] n (also Comput) mémoire f; (recollection) souvenir m; **in ~ of** à la mémoire de; **memory card** n (for digital camera) carte f mémoire

men [mɛn] npl of **man**

menace ['mɛnɪs] n menace f; (inf: nuisance) peste f, plaie f ▷ vt menacer

mend [mɛnd] vt réparer; (darn) raccommoder, repriser ▷ n: **on the ~** en voie de guérison; **to ~ one's ways** s'amender

meningitis [mɛnɪn'dʒaɪtɪs] n méningite f

menopause ['mɛnəupɔ:z] n ménopause f

men's room (us) n: **the men's room** les toilettes fpl pour hommes

menstruation [mɛnstru'eɪʃən] n menstruation f

menswear ['mɛnzwɛəʳ] n vêtements mpl d'hommes

mental ['mɛntl] adj mental(e); **mental hospital** n hôpital m psychiatrique; **mentality** [mɛn'tælɪtɪ] n mentalité f; **mentally** adv: **to be mentally handicapped** être handicapé(e) mental(e); **the mentally ill** les malades mentaux

menthol ['mɛnθɔl] n menthol m

mention ['mɛnʃən] n mention f ▷ vt mentionner, faire mention de; **don't ~ it!** je vous en prie, il n'y a pas de quoi!

menu ['mɛnju:] n (set menu, Comput) menu m; (list of dishes) carte f; **could we see the ~?** est-ce qu'on peut voir la carte?

MEP n abbr = **Member of the European Parliament**

mercenary ['mə:sɪnərɪ] adj (person) intéressé(e), mercenaire ▷ n mercenaire m

merchandise ['mə:tʃəndaɪz] n marchandises fpl

merchant ['mə:tʃənt] n négociant m, marchand m; **merchant bank** n (BRIT) banque f d'affaires; **merchant navy** (us **merchant marine**) n marine marchande

merciless ['mə:sɪlɪs] adj impitoyable, sans pitié

mercury ['mə:kjurɪ] n mercure m

mercy ['mə:sɪ] n pitié f, merci f; (Rel) miséricorde f; **at the ~ of** à la merci de

mere [mɪəʳ] adj simple; (chance) pur(e); **a ~ two hours** seulement deux heures; **merely** adv simplement, purement

merge [mə:dʒ] vt unir; (Comput) fusionner, interclasser ▷ vi (colours, shapes, sounds) se mêler; (roads) se joindre; (Comm) fusionner; **merger** n (Comm) fusion f

meringue [mə'ræŋ] n meringue f

merit ['mɛrɪt] n mérite m, valeur f ▷ vt mériter

mermaid ['mə:meɪd] n sirène f

merry ['mɛrɪ] adj gai(e); **M~ Christmas!** joyeux Noël!; **merry-go-round** n manège m

mesh [mɛʃ] n mailles fpl

mess [mɛs] n désordre m, fouillis m, pagaille f; (muddle: of life) gâchis m; (: of economy) pagaille f; (dirt) saleté f; (Mil) mess m, cantine f; **to be (in) a ~** être en désordre; **to be/get o.s. in a ~** (fig) être/se mettre dans le pétrin; **mess about** or **around** (inf) vi perdre son temps; **mess up** vt (dirty) salir; (spoil) gâcher; **mess with** (inf) vt fus (challenge, confront) se frotter à; (interfere with) toucher à

message ['mɛsɪdʒ] n message m; **can I leave a ~?** est-ce que je peux laisser un message?; **are there any ~s for me?** est-ce que j'ai des messages?

messenger ['mɛsɪndʒəʳ] n messager m

Messrs, Messrs. ['mɛsəz] abbr (on letters: = messieurs) MM

messy ['mɛsɪ] adj (dirty) sale; (untidy) en désordre

met [mɛt] pt, pp of **meet**

metabolism [mɛ'tæbəlɪzəm] n métabolisme m

metal ['mɛtl] n métal m ▷ cpd en métal; **metallic** [mɛ'tælɪk] adj métallique

metaphor ['mɛtəfəʳ] n métaphore f

meteor ['mi:tɪəʳ] n météore m; **meteorite** ['mi:tɪəraɪt] n météorite m or f

meteorology [mi:tɪə'rɔlədʒɪ] n météorologie f

meter ['mi:təʳ] n (instrument) compteur m; (also: **parking ~**) parc(o)mètre m; (us: unit) = **metre** ▷ vt (us Post) affranchir à la machine

method ['mɛθəd] n méthode f; **methodical** [mɪ'θɔdɪkl] adj méthodique

methylated spirit ['mɛθɪleɪtɪd-] n (BRIT: also: **meths**) alcool m à brûler

meticulous [mɛ'tɪkjuləs] adj méticuleux(-euse)

metre (us **meter**) ['mi:təʳ] n mètre m

metric ['mɛtrɪk] adj métrique

metro ['mɛtrəu] n métro m

metropolitan [mɛtrə'pɔlɪtən] adj métropolitain(e); **the M~ Police** (BRIT) la

police londonienne
Mexican ['mɛksɪkən] *adj* mexicain(e) ▷ *n* Mexicain(e)
Mexico ['mɛksɪkəu] *n* Mexique *m*
mg *abbr* (= *milligram*) mg
mice [maɪs] *npl of* **mouse**
micro... [maɪkrəu] *prefix*: **microchip** *n* (*Elec*) puce *f*; **microphone** *n* microphone *m*; **microscope** *n* microscope *m*; **microwave** *n* (*also*: **microwave oven**) four *m* à micro-ondes
mid [mɪd] *adj*: **~ May** la mi-mai; **~ afternoon** le milieu de l'après-midi; **in ~ air** en plein ciel; **he's in his ~ thirties** il a dans les trente-cinq ans; **midday** *n* midi *m*
middle ['mɪdl] *n* milieu *m*; (*waist*) ceinture *f*, taille *f* ▷ *adj* du milieu; (*average*) moyen(ne); **in the ~ of the night** au milieu de la nuit; **middle-aged** *adj* d'un certain âge, ni vieux ni jeune; **Middle Ages** *npl*: **the Middle Ages** le moyen âge; **middle-class** *adj* bourgeois(e); **middle class(es)** *n(pl)*: **the middle class(es)** ≈ les classes moyennes; **Middle East** *n*: **the Middle East** le Proche-Orient, le Moyen-Orient; **middle name** *n* second prénom; **middle school** *n* (*US*) *école pour les enfants de 12 à 14 ans*, ≈ collège *m*; (*BRIT*) *école pour les enfants de 8 à 14 ans*
midge [mɪdʒ] *n* moucheron *m*
midget ['mɪdʒɪt] *n* nain(e)
midnight ['mɪdnaɪt] *n* minuit *m*
midst [mɪdst] *n*: **in the ~ of** au milieu de
midsummer [mɪd'sʌmər] *n* milieu *m* de l'été
midway [mɪd'weɪ] *adj, adv*: **~ (between)** à mi-chemin (entre); **~ through ...** au milieu de ..., en plein(e) ...
midweek [mɪd'wi:k] *adv* au milieu de la semaine, en pleine semaine
midwife (*pl* **midwives**) ['mɪdwaɪf, -vz] *n* sage-femme *f*
midwinter [mɪd'wɪntər] *n* milieu *m* de l'hiver
might [maɪt] *vb see* **may** ▷ *n* puissance *f*, force *f*; **mighty** *adj* puissant(e)
migraine ['mi:greɪn] *n* migraine *f*
migrant ['maɪɡrənt] *n* (*bird, animal*) migrateur *m*; (*person*) migrant(e) ▷ *adj* migrateur(-trice); migrant(e); (*worker*) saisonnier(-ière)
migrate [maɪ'greɪt] *vi* migrer
migration [maɪ'greɪʃən] *n* migration *f*
mike [maɪk] *n abbr* (= *microphone*) micro *m*
mild [maɪld] *adj* doux (douce); (*reproach, infection*) léger(-ère); (*illness*) bénin(-igne); (*interest*) modéré(e); (*taste*) peu relevé(e); **mildly** ['maɪldlɪ] *adv* doucement; légèrement; **to put it mildly** (*inf*) c'est le moins qu'on puisse dire
mile [maɪl] *n* mil(l)e *m* (= 1609 m); **mileage** *n* distance *f* en milles, ≈ kilométrage *m*; **mileometer** [maɪ'lɔmɪtər] *n* compteur *m* kilométrique; **milestone** *n* borne *f*; (*fig*)

jalon *m*
military ['mɪlɪtərɪ] *adj* militaire
militia [mɪ'lɪʃə] *n* milice *f*
milk [mɪlk] *n* lait *m* ▷ *vt* (*cow*) traire; (*fig: person*) dépouiller, plumer; (: *situation*) exploiter à fond; **milk chocolate** *n* chocolat *m* au lait; **milkman** (*irreg*) *n* laitier *m*; **milky** *adj* (*drink*) au lait; (*colour*) laiteux(-euse)
mill [mɪl] *n* moulin *m*; (*factory*) usine *f*, fabrique *f*; (*spinning mill*) filature *f*; (*flour mill*) minoterie *f* ▷ *vt* moudre, broyer ▷ *vi* (*also*: **~ about**) grouiller
millennium (*pl* **~s** *or* **millennia**) [mɪ'lɛnɪəm, -'lɛnɪə] *n* millénaire *m*
milli... ['mɪlɪ] *prefix* milli...; **milligram(me)** *n* milligramme *m*; **millilitre** (*US* **milliliter**) ['mɪlɪli:tər] *n* millilitre *m*; **millimetre** (*US* **millimeter**) *n* millimètre *m*
million ['mɪljən] *n* million *m*; **a ~ pounds** un million de livres sterling; **millionaire** [mɪljə'nɛər] *n* millionnaire *m*; **millionth** [-θ] *num* millionième
milometer [maɪ'lɔmɪtər] *n* = **mileometer**
mime [maɪm] *n* mime *m* ▷ *vt, vi* mimer
mimic ['mɪmɪk] *n* imitateur(-trice) ▷ *vt, vi* imiter, contrefaire
min. *abbr* (= *minute(s)*) mn.; (= *minimum*) min.
mince [mɪns] *vt* hacher ▷ *n* (*BRIT Culin*) viande hachée, hachis *m*; **mincemeat** *n* *hachis de fruits secs utilisés en pâtisserie;* (*US*) viande hachée, hachis *m*; **mince pie** *n* *sorte de tarte aux fruits secs*
mind [maɪnd] *n* esprit *m* ▷ *vt* (*attend to, look after*) s'occuper de; (*be careful*) faire attention à; (*object to*): **I don't ~ the noise** je ne crains pas le bruit, le bruit ne me dérange pas; **it is on my ~** cela me préoccupe; **to change one's ~** changer d'avis; **to my ~** à mon avis, selon moi; **to bear sth in ~** tenir compte de qch; **to have sb/sth in ~** avoir qn/qch en tête; **to make up one's ~** se décider; **do you ~ if ...?** est-ce que cela vous gêne si ...?; **I don't ~** cela ne me dérange pas; (*don't care*) ça m'est égal; **~ you, ...** remarquez, ...; **never ~** peu importe, ça ne fait rien; (*don't worry*) ne vous en faîtes pas; **"~ the step"** "attention à la marche"; **mindless** *adj* irréfléchi(e); (*violence, crime*) insensé(e); (*boring: job*) idiot(e)
mine¹ [maɪn] *pron* le (la) mien(ne), les miens (miennes); **a friend of ~** un de mes amis, un ami à moi; **this book is ~** ce livre est à moi
mine² [maɪn] *n* mine *f* ▷ *vt* (*coal*) extraire; (*ship, beach*) miner; **minefield** *n* champ *m* de mines; **miner** *n* mineur *m*
mineral ['mɪnərəl] *adj* minéral(e) ▷ *n* minéral *m*; **mineral water** *n* eau minérale
mingle ['mɪŋɡl] *vi*: **to ~ with** se mêler à
miniature ['mɪnətʃər] *adj* (*en*) miniature ▷ *n* miniature *f*

m

minibar ['mɪnɪbɑːʳ] n minibar m
minibus ['mɪnɪbʌs] n minibus m
minicab ['mɪnɪkæb] n (BRIT) taxi m
indépendant
minimal ['mɪnɪml] adj minimal(e)
minimize ['mɪnɪmaɪz] vt (reduce) réduire au
minimum; (play down) minimiser
minimum ['mɪnɪməm] n (pl **minima**)
minimum m ▷ adj minimum
mining ['maɪnɪŋ] n exploitation minière
miniskirt ['mɪnɪskəːt] n mini-jupe f
minister ['mɪnɪstəʳ] n (BRIT Pol) ministre m;
(Rel) pasteur m
ministry ['mɪnɪstrɪ] n (BRIT Pol) ministère m;
(Rel): **to go into the ~** devenir pasteur
minor ['maɪnəʳ] adj petit(e), de peu
d'importance; (Mus, poet, problem) mineur(e)
▷ n (Law) mineur(e)
minority [maɪ'nɔrɪtɪ] n minorité f
mint [mɪnt] n (plant) menthe f; (sweet) bonbon
m à la menthe ▷ vt (coins) battre; **the (Royal)
M~, the (US) M~** ≈ l'hôtel m de la Monnaie; **in ~
condition** à l'état de neuf
minus ['maɪnəs] n (also: **~ sign**) signe m moins
▷ prep moins; **12 – 6 equals 6** 12 moins 6 égal 6;
~ 24°C moins 24°C
minute¹ n ['mɪnɪt] minute f; **minutes** npl (of
meeting) procès-verbal m, compte rendu; **wait
a ~!** (attendez) un instant!; **at the last ~** à la
dernière minute
minute² adj [maɪ'njuːt] minuscule; (detailed)
minutieux(-euse); **in ~ detail** par le menu
miracle ['mɪrəkl] n miracle m
miraculous [mɪ'rækjuləs] adj
miraculeux(-euse)
mirage ['mɪrɑːʒ] n mirage m
mirror ['mɪrəʳ] n miroir m, glace f; (in car)
rétroviseur m
misbehave [mɪsbɪ'heɪv] vi mal se conduire
misc. abbr = **miscellaneous**
miscarriage ['mɪskærɪdʒ] n (Med) fausse
couche; **~ of justice** erreur f judiciaire
miscellaneous [mɪsɪ'leɪnɪəs] adj (items,
expenses) divers(es); (selection) varié(e)
mischief ['mɪstʃɪf] n (naughtiness) sottises
fpl; (playfulness) espièglerie f; (harm) mal m,
dommage m; (maliciousness) méchanceté f;
mischievous ['mɪstʃɪvəs] adj (playful,
naughty) coquin(e), espiègle
misconception ['mɪskən'sɛpʃən] n idée
fausse
misconduct [mɪs'kɔndʌkt] n inconduite f;
professional ~ faute professionnelle
miser ['maɪzəʳ] n avare m/f
miserable ['mɪzərəbl] adj (person, expression)
malheureux(-euse); (conditions) misérable;
(weather) maussade; (offer, donation) minable;
(failure) pitoyable
misery ['mɪzərɪ] n (unhappiness) tristesse f;

(pain) souffrances fpl; (wretchedness) misère f
misfortune [mɪs'fɔːtʃən] n malchance f,
malheur m
misgiving [mɪs'gɪvɪŋ] n (apprehension)
craintes fpl; **to have ~s about sth** avoir des
doutes quant à qch
misguided [mɪs'gaɪdɪd] adj malavisé(e)
mishap ['mɪshæp] n mésaventure f
misinterpret [mɪsɪn'təːprɪt] vt mal
interpréter
misjudge [mɪs'dʒʌdʒ] vt méjuger, se
méprendre sur le compte de
mislay [mɪs'leɪ] vt (irreg: like **lay**) égarer
mislead [mɪs'liːd] vt (irreg: like **lead**) induire
en erreur; **misleading** adj trompeur(-euse)
misplace [mɪs'pleɪs] vt égarer; **to be ~d** (trust
etc) être mal placé(e)
misprint ['mɪsprɪnt] n faute f d'impression
misrepresent [mɪsrɛprɪ'zɛnt] vt présenter
sous un faux jour
Miss [mɪs] n Mademoiselle
miss [mɪs] vt (fail to get, attend, see) manquer,
rater; (regret the absence of): **I ~ him/it** il/cela
me manque ▷ vi manquer ▷ n (shot) coup
manqué; **we ~ed our train** nous avons raté
notre train; **you can't ~ it** vous ne pouvez
pas vous tromper; **miss out** vt (BRIT) oublier;
miss out on vt fus (fun, party) rater, manquer;
(chance, bargain) laisser passer
missile ['mɪsaɪl] n (Aviat) missile m; (object
thrown) projectile m
missing ['mɪsɪŋ] adj manquant(e); (after
escape, disaster: person) disparu(e); **to go
~** disparaître; **~ in action** (Mil) porté(e)
disparu(e)
mission ['mɪʃən] n mission f; **on a ~ to sb**
en mission auprès de qn; **missionary** n
missionnaire m/f
misspell ['mɪs'spɛl] vt (irreg: like **spell**) mal
orthographier
mist [mɪst] n brume f ▷ vi (also: **~ over, ~ up**)
devenir brumeux(-euse); (BRIT: windows)
s'embuer
mistake [mɪs'teɪk] n erreur f, faute f ▷ vt
(irreg: like **take**) (meaning) mal comprendre;
(intentions) se méprendre sur; **to ~ for** prendre
pour; **by ~** par erreur, par inadvertance; **to
make a ~** (in writing) faire une faute; (in
calculating etc) faire une erreur; **there must be
some ~** il doit y avoir une erreur, se tromper;
mistaken pp of **mistake** ▷ adj (idea etc)
erroné(e); **to be mistaken** faire erreur, se
tromper
mister ['mɪstəʳ] n (inf) Monsieur m; see **Mr**
mistletoe ['mɪsltəu] n gui m
mistook [mɪs'tuk] pt of **mistake**
mistress ['mɪstrɪs] n maîtresse f; (BRIT: in
primary school) institutrice f; (: in secondary
school) professeur m

mistrust [mɪs'trʌst] vt se méfier de

misty ['mɪstɪ] adj brumeux(-euse); (glasses, window) embué(e)

misunderstand [mɪsʌndə'stænd] vt, vi (irreg: like **stand**) mal comprendre; **misunderstanding** n méprise f, malentendu m; **there's been a misunderstanding** il y a eu un malentendu

misunderstood [mɪsʌndə'stud] pt, pp of **misunderstand** ▷ adj (person) incompris(e)

misuse n [mɪs'juːs] mauvais emploi; (of power) abus m ▷ vt [mɪs'juːz] mal employer; abuser de

mitt(en) ['mɪt(n)] n moufle f; (fingerless) mitaine f

mix [mɪks] vt mélanger; (sauce, drink etc) préparer ▷ vi se mélanger; (socialize): **he doesn't ~ well** il est peu sociable ▷ n mélange m; **to ~ sth with sth** mélanger qch à qch; **cake ~** préparation f pour gâteau; **mix up** vt mélanger; (confuse) confondre; **to be ~ed up in sth** être mêlé(e) à qch or impliqué(e) dans qch; **mixed** adj (feelings, reactions) contradictoire; (school, marriage) mixte; **mixed grill** n (BRIT) assortiment m de grillades; **mixed salad** n salade f de crudités; **mixed-up** adj (person) désorienté(e), embrouillé(e); **mixer** n (for food) batteur m, mixeur m; (drink) boisson gazeuse (servant à couper un alcool); (person): **he is a good mixer** il est très sociable; **mixture** n assortiment m, mélange m; (Med) préparation f; **mix-up** n: **there was a mix-up** il y a eu confusion

ml abbr (= millilitre(s)) ml

mm abbr (= millimetre) mm

moan [məun] n gémissement m ▷ vi gémir; (inf: complain): **to ~ (about)** se plaindre (de)

moat [məut] n fossé m, douves fpl

mob [mɔb] n foule f; (disorderly) cohue f ▷ vt assaillir

mobile ['məubaɪl] adj mobile ▷ n (Art) mobile m; **mobile home** n caravane f; **mobile phone** n téléphone portatif

mobility [məu'bɪlɪtɪ] n mobilité f

mobilize ['məubɪlaɪz] vt, vi mobiliser

mock [mɔk] vt ridiculiser; (laugh at) se moquer de ▷ adj faux (fausse); **mocks** npl (BRIT: Scol) examens blancs; **mockery** n moquerie f, raillerie f

mod cons ['mɔd'kɔnz] npl abbr (BRIT) = **modern conveniences**; see **convenience**

mode [məud] n mode m; (of transport) moyen m

model ['mɔdl] n modèle m; (person: for fashion) mannequin m; (: for artist) modèle ▷ vt (with clay etc) modeler ▷ vi travailler comme mannequin ▷ adj (railway: toy) modèle réduit inv; (child, factory) modèle; **to ~ clothes** présenter des vêtements; **to ~ o.s. on** imiter

modem ['məudɛm] n modem m

moderate adj ['mɔdərət] modéré(e); (amount, change) peu important(e) ▷ vb ['mɔdəreɪt] ▷ vi se modérer, se calmer ▷ vt modérer; **moderation** [mɔdə'reɪʃən] n modération f, mesure f; **in ~** à dose raisonnable, pris(e) or pratiqué(e) modérément

modern ['mɔdən] adj moderne; **modernize** vt moderniser; **modern languages** npl langues vivantes

modest ['mɔdɪst] adj modeste; **modesty** n modestie f

modification [mɔdɪfɪ'keɪʃən] n modification f

modify ['mɔdɪfaɪ] vt modifier

module ['mɔdjuːl] n module m

mohair ['məuhɛəʳ] n mohair m

Mohammed [mə'hæmɛd] n Mahomet m

moist [mɔɪst] adj humide, moite; **moisture** ['mɔɪstʃəʳ] n humidité f; (on glass) buée f; **moisturizer** ['mɔɪstʃəraɪzəʳ] n crème hydratante

mold etc [məuld] n (US) = **mould** etc

mole [məul] n (animal, spy) taupe f; (spot) grain m de beauté

molecule ['mɔlɪkjuːl] n molécule f

molest [məu'lɛst] vt (assault sexually) attenter à la pudeur de

molten ['məultən] adj fondu(e); (rock) en fusion

mom [mɔm] n (US) = **mum**

moment ['məumənt] n moment m, instant m; **at the ~** en ce moment; **momentarily** ['məuməntrɪlɪ] adv momentanément; (US: soon) bientôt; **momentary** adj momentané(e), passager(-ère); **momentous** [məu'mɛntəs] adj important(e), capital(e)

momentum [məu'mɛntəm] n élan m, vitesse acquise; (fig) dynamique f; **to gather ~** prendre de la vitesse; (fig) gagner du terrain

mommy ['mɔmɪ] n (US: mother) maman f

Mon abbr (= Monday) l.

Monaco ['mɔnəkəu] n Monaco f

monarch ['mɔnək] n monarque m; **monarchy** n monarchie f

monastery ['mɔnəstərɪ] n monastère m

Monday ['mʌndɪ] n lundi m

monetary ['mʌnɪtərɪ] adj monétaire

money ['mʌnɪ] n argent m; **to make ~** (person) gagner de l'argent; (business) rapporter; **money belt** n ceinture-portefeuille f; **money order** n mandat m

mongrel ['mʌŋgrəl] n (dog) bâtard m

monitor ['mɔnɪtəʳ] n (TV, Comput) écran m, moniteur m ▷ vt contrôler; (foreign station) être à l'écoute de; (progress) suivre de près

monk [mʌŋk] n moine m

monkey ['mʌŋkɪ] n singe m

monologue ['mɔnəlɔg] n monologue m

monopoly [mə'nɔpəlɪ] n monopole m
monosodium glutamate [mɔnə'səʊdɪəm 'gluːtəmeɪt] n glutamate m de sodium
monotonous [mə'nɔtənəs] adj monotone
monsoon [mɔn'suːn] n mousson f
monster ['mɔnstər] n monstre m
month [mʌnθ] n mois m; **monthly** adj mensuel(le) ▷ adv mensuellement
Montreal [mɔntrɪ'ɔːl] n Montréal
monument ['mɔnjumənt] n monument m
mood [muːd] n humeur f, disposition f; **to be in a good/bad ~** être de bonne/mauvaise humeur; **moody** adj (variable) d'humeur changeante, lunatique; (sullen) morose, maussade
moon [muːn] n lune f; **moonlight** n clair m de lune
moor [mʊər] n lande f ▷ vt (ship) amarrer ▷ vi mouiller
moose [muːs] n (pl inv) élan m
mop [mɔp] n balai m à laver; (for dishes) lavette f à vaisselle ▷ vt éponger, essuyer; **~ of hair** tignasse f; **mop up** vt éponger
mope [məʊp] vi avoir le cafard, se morfondre
moped ['məʊpɛd] n cyclomoteur m
moral ['mɔrl] adj moral(e) ▷ n morale f; **morals** npl moralité f
morale [mɔ'rɑːl] n moral m
morality [mə'rælɪtɪ] n moralité f
morbid ['mɔːbɪd] adj morbide

🔵 **KEYWORD**

more [mɔːr] adj **1** (greater in number etc) plus (de), davantage (de); **more people/work (than)** plus de gens/de travail (que) **2** (additional) encore (de); **do you want (some) more tea?** voulez-vous encore du thé?; **is there any more wine?** reste-t-il du vin?; **I have no** or **I don't have any more money** je n'ai plus d'argent; **it'll take a few more weeks** ça prendra encore quelques semaines
▷ pron plus, davantage; **more than 10** plus de 10; **it cost more than we expected** cela a coûté plus que prévu; **I want more** j'en veux plus or davantage; **is there any more?** est-ce qu'il en reste?; **there's no more** il n'y en a plus; **a little more** un peu plus; **many/much more** beaucoup plus, bien davantage
▷ adv plus; **more dangerous/easily (than)** plus dangereux/facilement (que); **more and more expensive** de plus en plus cher; **more or less** plus ou moins; **more than ever** plus que jamais; **once more** encore une fois, une fois de plus

moreover [mɔː'rəʊvər] adv de plus
morgue [mɔːg] n morgue f

morning ['mɔːnɪŋ] n matin m; (as duration) matinée f ▷ cpd matinal(e); (paper) du matin; **in the ~** le matin; **7 o'clock in the ~** 7 heures du matin; **morning sickness** n nausées matinales
Moroccan [mə'rɔkən] adj marocain(e) ▷ n Marocain(e)
Morocco [mə'rɔkəʊ] n Maroc m
moron ['mɔːrɔn] n idiot(e), minus m/f
morphine ['mɔːfiːn] n morphine f
morris dancing ['mɔrɪs-] n (BRIT) danses folkloriques anglaises

⬤ **MORRIS DANCING**
⬤
⬤ Le **Morris dancing** est une danse
⬤ folklorique anglaise traditionnellement
⬤ réservée aux hommes. Habillés tout
⬤ en blanc et portant des clochettes, ils
⬤ exécutent différentes figures avec des
⬤ mouchoirs et de longs bâtons. Cette danse
⬤ est très populaire dans les fêtes de village.

Morse [mɔːs] n (also: **~ code**) morse m
mortal ['mɔːtl] adj, n mortel(le)
mortar ['mɔːtər] n mortier m
mortgage ['mɔːgɪdʒ] n hypothèque f; (loan) prêt m (or crédit m) hypothécaire ▷ vt hypothéquer
mortician [mɔː'tɪʃən] n (US) entrepreneur m de pompes funèbres
mortified ['mɔːtɪfaɪd] adj mort(e) de honte
mortuary ['mɔːtjʊərɪ] n morgue f
mosaic [məʊ'zeɪɪk] n mosaïque f
Moscow ['mɔskəʊ] n Moscou
Moslem ['mɔzləm] adj, n = **Muslim**
mosque [mɔsk] n mosquée f
mosquito (pl **~es**) [mɔs'kiːtəʊ] n moustique m
moss [mɔs] n mousse f
most [məʊst] adj (majority of) la plupart de; (greatest amount of) le plus de ▷ pron la plupart ▷ adv le plus; (very) très, extrêmement; **the ~ le plus; ~ fish** la plupart des poissons; **the ~ beautiful woman in the world** la plus belle femme du monde; **~ of** (with plural) la plupart de; (with singular) la plus grande partie de; **~ of them** la plupart d'entre eux; **~ of the time** la plupart du temps; **I saw ~** (a lot but not all) j'en ai vu la plupart; (more than anyone else) c'est moi qui en ai vu le plus; **at the (very) ~** au plus; **to make the ~ of** profiter au maximum de; **mostly** adv (chiefly) surtout, principalement; (usually) généralement
MOT n abbr (BRIT) = **Ministry of Transport**; **the ~ (test)** visite technique (annuelle) obligatoire des véhicules à moteur
motel [məʊ'tɛl] n motel m
moth [mɔθ] n papillon m de nuit; (in clothes)

mite f

mother ['mʌðəʳ] n mère f ▷ vt (pamper, protect) dorloter; **motherhood** n maternité f; **mother-in-law** n belle-mère f; **mother-of-pearl** n nacre f; **Mother's Day** n fête f des Mères; **mother-to-be** n future maman; **mother tongue** n langue maternelle

motif [məu'ti:f] n motif m

motion ['məuʃən] n mouvement m; (gesture) geste m; (at meeting) motion f ▷ vt, vi: **to ~ (to) sb to do** faire signe à qn de faire; **motionless** adj immobile, sans mouvement; **motion picture** n film m

motivate ['məutɪveɪt] vt motiver

motivation [məutɪ'veɪʃən] n motivation f

motive ['məutɪv] n motif m, mobile m

motor ['məutəʳ] n moteur m; (BRIT inf: vehicle) auto f; **motorbike** n moto f; **motorboat** n bateau m à moteur; **motorcar** n (BRIT) automobile f; **motorcycle** n moto f; **motorcyclist** n motocycliste m/f; **motoring** (BRIT) n tourisme m automobile; **motorist** n automobiliste m/f; **motor racing** n (BRIT) course f automobile; **motorway** n (BRIT) autoroute f

motto (pl ~es) ['mɔtəu] n devise f

mould (US **mold**) [məuld] n moule m; (mildew) moisissure f ▷ vt mouler, modeler; (fig) façonner; **mouldy** adj moisi(e); (smell) de moisi

mound [maund] n monticule m, tertre m

mount [maunt] n (hill) mont m, montagne f; (horse) monture f; (for picture) carton m de montage ▷ vt monter; (horse) monter à; (bike) monter sur; (picture) monter sur carton ▷ vi (inflation, tension) augmenter; **mount up** vi s'élever, monter; (bills, problems, savings) s'accumuler

mountain ['mauntɪn] n montagne f ▷ cpd de (la) montagne; **mountain bike** n VTT m, vélo m tout terrain; **mountaineer** n alpiniste m/f; **mountaineering** n alpinisme m; **mountainous** adj montagneux(-euse); **mountain range** n chaîne f de montagnes

mourn [mɔ:n] vt pleurer ▷ vi: **to ~ for sb** pleurer qn; **to ~ for sth** se lamenter sur qch; **mourner** n parent(e) or ami(e) du défunt; personne f en deuil or venue rendre hommage au défunt; **mourning** n deuil m; **in mourning** en deuil

mouse (pl **mice**) [maus, maɪs] n (also Comput) souris f; **mouse mat** n (Comput) tapis m de souris

moussaka [mu'sɑ:kə] n moussaka f

mousse [mu:s] n mousse f

moustache (US **mustache**) [məs'tɑ:ʃ] n moustache(s) f(pl)

mouth [mauθ, pl -ðz] n bouche f; (of dog, cat) gueule f; (of river) embouchure f; (of hole,

cave) ouverture f; **mouthful** n bouchée f; **mouth organ** n harmonica m; **mouthpiece** n (of musical instrument) bec m, embouchure f; (spokesperson) porte-parole m inv; **mouthwash** n eau f dentifrice

move [mu:v] n (movement) mouvement m; (in game) coup m; (: turn to play) tour m; (change of house) déménagement m; (change of job) changement m d'emploi ▷ vt déplacer, bouger; (emotionally) émouvoir; (Pol: resolution etc) proposer ▷ vi (gen) bouger, remuer; (traffic) circuler; (also: **~ house**) déménager; (in game) jouer; **can you ~ your car, please?** pouvez-vous déplacer votre voiture, s'il vous plaît?; **to ~ sb to do sth** pousser or inciter qn à faire qch; **to get a ~ on** se dépêcher, se remuer; **move back** vi revenir, retourner; **move in** vi (to a house) emménager; (police, soldiers) intervenir; **move off** vi s'éloigner, s'en aller; **move on** vi se remettre en route; **move out** vi (of house) déménager; **move over** vi se pousser, se déplacer; **move up** vi avancer; (employee) avoir de l'avancement; (pupil) passer dans la classe supérieure; **movement** n mouvement m

movie ['mu:vɪ] n film m; **movies** npl: **the ~s** le cinéma; **movie theater** (US) n cinéma m

moving ['mu:vɪŋ] adj en mouvement; (touching) émouvant(e)

mow (pt ~ed, pp ~ed or ~n) [məu, -d, -n] vt faucher; (lawn) tondre; **mower** n (also: **lawnmower**) tondeuse f à gazon

Mozambique [məuzəm'bi:k] n Mozambique m

MP n abbr (BRIT) = **Member of Parliament**

MP3 n mp3 m; **MP3 player** n lecteur m mp3

mpg n abbr = miles per gallon (30 mpg = 9,4 l. aux 100 km)

m.p.h. abbr = miles per hour (60 mph = 96 km/h)

Mr (US **Mr.**) ['mɪstəʳ] n: **Mr X** Monsieur X, M. X

Mrs (US **Mrs.**) ['mɪsɪz] n: **~ X** Madame X, Mme X

Ms (US **Ms.**) [mɪz] n (Miss or Mrs): **Ms X** Madame X, Mme X

MSP n abbr (= Member of the Scottish Parliament) député m au Parlement écossais

Mt abbr (Geo: = mount) Mt

much [mʌtʃ] adj beaucoup de ▷ adv, n or pron beaucoup; **we don't have ~ time** nous n'avons pas beaucoup de temps; **how ~ is it?** combien est-ce que ça coûte?; **it's not ~** ce n'est pas beaucoup; **too ~** trop (de); **so ~** tant (de); **I like it very/so ~** j'aime beaucoup/ tellement ça; **as ~ as** autant de; **that's ~ better** c'est beaucoup mieux

muck [mʌk] n (mud) boue f; (dirt) ordures fpl; **muck up** vt (inf: ruin) gâcher, esquinter; (: dirty) salir; (: exam, interview) se planter à; **mucky** adj (dirty) boueux(-euse), sale

mucus ['mju:kəs] n mucus m

mud [mʌd] n boue f

muddle ['mʌdl] n (mess) pagaille f, fouillis m; (mix-up) confusion f ▷ vt (also: ~ **up**) brouiller, embrouiller; **to get in a ~** (while explaining etc) s'embrouiller

muddy ['mʌdɪ] adj boueux(-euse)

mudguard ['mʌdgɑːd] n garde-boue m inv

muesli ['mjuːzlɪ] n muesli m

muffin ['mʌfɪn] n (roll) petit pain rond et plat; (cake) petit gâteau au chocolat ou aux fruits

muffled ['mʌfld] adj étouffé(e), voilé(e)

muffler ['mʌfləʳ] n (scarf) cache-nez m inv; (us Aut) silencieux m

mug [mʌg] n (cup) tasse f (sans soucoupe); (: for beer) chope f; (inf: face) bouille f; (: fool) poire f ▷ vt (assault) agresser; **mugger** ['mʌgəʳ] n agresseur m; **mugging** n agression f

muggy ['mʌgɪ] adj lourd(e), moite

mule [mjuːl] n mule f

multicoloured (us **multicolored**) ['mʌltɪkʌləd] adj multicolore

multimedia [mʌltɪ'miːdɪə] adj multimédia inv

multinational [mʌltɪ'næʃənl] n multinationale f ▷ adj multinational(e)

multiple ['mʌltɪpl] adj multiple ▷ n multiple m; **multiple choice (test)** n QCM m, questionnaire m à choix multiple; **multiple sclerosis** [-sklɪ'rəusɪs] n sclérose f en plaques

multiplex (cinema) ['mʌltɪplɛks-] n (cinéma m) multisalles m

multiplication [mʌltɪplɪ'keɪʃən] n multiplication f

multiply ['mʌltɪplaɪ] vt multiplier ▷ vi se multiplier

multistorey ['mʌltɪ'stɔːrɪ] adj (BRIT: building) à étages; (: car park) à étages or niveaux multiples

mum [mʌm] n (BRIT) maman f ▷ adj: **to keep ~** ne pas souffler mot

mumble ['mʌmbl] vt, vi marmotter, marmonner

mummy ['mʌmɪ] n (BRIT: mother) maman f; (embalmed) momie f

mumps [mʌmps] n oreillons mpl

munch [mʌntʃ] vt, vi mâcher

municipal [mjuː'nɪsɪpl] adj municipal(e)

mural ['mjuərl] n peinture murale

murder ['məːdəʳ] n meurtre m, assassinat m ▷ vt assassiner; **murderer** n meurtrier m, assassin m

murky ['məːkɪ] adj sombre, ténébreux(-euse); (water) trouble

murmur ['məːməʳ] n murmure m ▷ vt, vi murmurer

muscle ['mʌsl] n muscle m; (fig) force f; **muscular** ['mʌskjuləʳ] adj musculaire; (person, arm) musclé(e)

museum [mjuː'zɪəm] n musée m

mushroom ['mʌʃrum] n champignon m ▷ vi (fig) pousser comme un (or des) champignon(s)

music ['mjuːzɪk] n musique f; **musical** adj musical(e); (person) musicien(ne) ▷ n (show) comédie musicale; **musical instrument** n instrument m de musique; **musician** [mjuː'zɪʃən] n musicien(ne)

Muslim ['mʌzlɪm] adj, n musulman(e)

muslin ['mʌzlɪn] n mousseline f

mussel ['mʌsl] n moule f

must [mʌst] aux vb (obligation): **I ~ do it** je dois le faire, il faut que je le fasse; (probability): **he ~ be there by now** il doit y être maintenant, il y est probablement maintenant; (suggestion, invitation): **you ~ come and see me** il faut que vous veniez me voir ▷ n nécessité f, impératif m; **it's a ~** c'est indispensable; **I ~ have made a mistake** j'ai dû me tromper

mustache ['mʌstæʃ] n (us) = **moustache**

mustard ['mʌstəd] n moutarde f

mustn't ['mʌsnt] = **must not**

mute [mjuːt] adj, n muet(te)

mutilate ['mjuːtɪleɪt] vt mutiler

mutiny ['mjuːtɪnɪ] n mutinerie f ▷ vi se mutiner

mutter ['mʌtəʳ] vt, vi marmonner, marmotter

mutton ['mʌtn] n mouton m

mutual ['mjuːtʃuəl] adj mutuel(le), réciproque; (benefit, interest) commun(e)

muzzle ['mʌzl] n museau m; (protective device) muselière f; (of gun) gueule f ▷ vt museler

my [maɪ] adj mon (ma), mes pl; **my house/ car/gloves** ma maison/ma voiture/mes gants; **I've washed my hair/cut my finger** je me suis lavé les cheveux/coupé le doigt; **is this my pen or yours?** c'est mon stylo ou c'est le vôtre?

myself [maɪ'sɛlf] pron (reflexive) me; (emphatic) moi-même; (after prep) moi; see also **oneself**

mysterious [mɪs'tɪərɪəs] adj mystérieux(-euse)

mystery ['mɪstərɪ] n mystère m

mystical ['mɪstɪkl] adj mystique

mystify ['mɪstɪfaɪ] vt (deliberately) mystifier; (puzzle) ébahir

myth [mɪθ] n mythe m; **mythology** [mɪ'θɔlə-dʒɪ] n mythologie f

n/a *abbr* (= *not applicable*) n.a.

nag [næg] *vt* (*scold*) être toujours après, reprendre sans arrêt

nail [neɪl] *n* (*human*) ongle *m*; (*metal*) clou *m* ▷ *vt* clouer; **to ~ sth to sth** clouer qch à qch; **to ~ sb down to a date/price** contraindre qn à accepter *or* donner une date/un prix; **nailbrush** *n* brosse *f* à ongles; **nailfile** *n* lime *f* à ongles; **nail polish** *n* vernis *m* à ongles; **nail polish remover** *n* dissolvant *m*; **nail scissors** *npl* ciseaux *mpl* à ongles; **nail varnish** *n* (BRIT) = **nail polish**

naïve [naɪˈiːv] *adj* naïf(-ïve)

naked [ˈneɪkɪd] *adj* nu(e)

name [neɪm] *n* nom *m*; (*reputation*) réputation *f* ▷ *vt* nommer; (*identify: accomplice etc*) citer; (*price, date*) fixer, donner; **by ~** par son nom; de nom; **in the ~ of** au nom de; **what's your ~?** comment vous appelez-vous?, quel est votre nom?; **namely** *adv* à savoir

nanny [ˈnænɪ] *n* bonne *f* d'enfants

nap [næp] *n* (*sleep*) (petit) somme

napkin [ˈnæpkɪn] *n* serviette *f* (de table)

nappy [ˈnæpɪ] *n* (BRIT) couche *f*

narcotics [nɑːˈkɔtɪkz] *npl* (*illegal drugs*) stupéfiants *mpl*

narrative [ˈnærətɪv] *n* récit *m* ▷ *adj* narratif(-ive)

narrator [nəˈreɪtə'] *n* narrateur(-trice)

narrow [ˈnærəu] *adj* étroit(e); (*fig*) restreint(e),

limité(e) ▷ *vi* (*road*) devenir plus étroit, se rétrécir; (*gap, difference*) se réduire; **to have a ~ escape** l'échapper belle; **narrow down** *vt* restreindre; **narrowly** *adv*: **he narrowly missed injury/the tree** il a failli se blesser/rentrer dans l'arbre; **he only narrowly missed the target** il a manqué la cible de peu *or* de justesse; **narrow-minded** *adj* à l'esprit étroit, borné(e); (*attitude*) borné(e)

nasal [ˈneɪzl] *adj* nasal(e)

nasty [ˈnɑːstɪ] *adj* (*person: malicious*) méchant(e); (: *rude*) très désagréable; (*smell*) dégoûtant(e); (*wound, situation*) mauvais(e), vilain(e)

nation [ˈneɪʃən] *n* nation *f*

national [ˈnæʃənl] *adj* national(e) ▷ *n* (*abroad*) ressortissant(e); (*when home*) national(e); **national anthem** *n* hymne national; **national dress** *n* costume national; **National Health Service** *n* (BRIT) service national de santé, ≈ Sécurité Sociale; **National Insurance** *n* (BRIT) ≈ Sécurité Sociale; **nationalist** *adj*, *n* nationaliste *m/f*; **nationality** [næʃəˈnælɪtɪ] *n* nationalité *f*; **nationalize** *vt* nationaliser; **national park** *n* parc national; **National Trust** *n* (BRIT) ≈ Caisse *f* nationale des monuments historiques et des sites

● **NATIONAL TRUST**
●
● Le **National Trust** est un organisme
● indépendant, à but non lucratif, dont
● la mission est de protéger et de mettre
● en valeur les monuments et les sites
● britanniques en raison de leur intérêt
● historique ou de leur beauté naturelle.

nationwide [ˈneɪʃənwaɪd] *adj* s'étendant à l'ensemble du pays; (*problem*) à l'échelle du pays entier

native [ˈneɪtɪv] *n* habitant(e) du pays, autochtone *m/f* ▷ *adj* du pays, indigène; (*country*) natal(e); (*language*) maternel(le); (*ability*) inné(e); **Native American** *n* Indien(ne) d'Amérique ▷ *adj* amérindien(ne); **native speaker** *n* locuteur natif

NATO [ˈneɪtəu] *n abbr* (= *North Atlantic Treaty Organization*) OTAN *f*

natural [ˈnætʃrəl] *adj* naturel(le); **natural gas** *n* gaz naturel; **natural history** *n* histoire naturelle; **naturally** *adv* naturellement; **natural resources** *npl* ressources naturelles

nature [ˈneɪtʃə'] *n* nature *f*; **by ~** par tempérament, de nature; **nature reserve** *n* (BRIT) réserve naturelle

naughty [ˈnɔːtɪ] *adj* (*child*) vilain(e), pas sage

nausea [ˈnɔːsɪə] *n* nausée *f*

naval [ˈneɪvl] *adj* naval(e)

navel ['neɪvl] n nombril m

navigate ['nævɪgeɪt] vt (steer) diriger, piloter
▷ vi naviguer; (Aut) indiquer la route à suivre;
navigation [nævɪ'geɪʃən] n navigation f

navy ['neɪvɪ] n marine f

navy-blue ['neɪvɪ'bluː] adj bleu marine inv

Nazi ['nɑːtsɪ] n Nazi(e)

NB abbr (= nota bene) NB

near [nɪəʳ] adj proche ▷ adv près ▷ prep (also: ~
to) près de ▷ vt approcher de; **in the ~ future**
dans un proche avenir; **nearby** [nɪə'baɪ] adj
proche ▷ adv tout près; **nearly**
adv presque; **I nearly fell** j'ai failli tomber; **it's
not nearly big enough** ce n'est vraiment pas
assez grand, c'est loin d'être assez grand; **near-
sighted** adj myope

neat [niːt] adj (person, work) soigné(e); (room
etc) bien tenu(e) or rangé(e); (solution, plan)
habile; (spirits) pur(e); **neatly** adv avec soin or
ordre; (skilfully) habilement

necessarily ['nɛsɪsrɪlɪ] adv nécessairement;
not ~ pas nécessairement or forcément

necessary ['nɛsɪsrɪ] adj nécessaire; **if ~** si
besoin est, le cas échéant

necessity [nɪ'sɛsɪtɪ] n nécessité f; chose
nécessaire or essentielle

neck [nɛk] n cou m; (of horse, garment) encolure
f; (of bottle) goulot m; **~ and ~** à égalité;
necklace ['nɛklɪs] n collier m; **necktie**
['nɛktaɪ] n (esp US) cravate f

nectarine ['nɛktərɪn] n brugnon m,
nectarine f

need [niːd] n besoin m ▷ vt avoir besoin de; **to
~ to do** devoir faire; avoir besoin de faire; **you
don't ~ to go** vous n'avez pas besoin or vous
n'êtes pas obligé de partir; **a signature is ~ed**
il faut une signature; **there's no ~ to do ....** il
n'y a pas lieu de faire ..., il n'est pas nécessaire
de faire ...

needle ['niːdl] n aiguille f ▷ vt (inf) asticoter,
tourmenter

needless ['niːdlɪs] adj inutile; **~ to say, ...**
inutile de dire que ...

needlework ['niːdlwəːk] n (activity) travaux
mpl d'aiguille; (object) ouvrage m

needn't ['niːdnt] = need not

needy ['niːdɪ] adj nécessiteux(-euse)

negative ['nɛgətɪv] n (Phot, Elec) négatif m;
(Ling) terme m de négation ▷ adj négatif(-ive)

neglect [nɪ'glɛkt] vt négliger; (garden) ne
pas entretenir; (duty) manquer à ▷ n (of
person, duty, garden) le fait de négliger; **(state
of) ~** abandon m; **to ~ to do sth** négliger or
omettre de faire qch; **to ~ one's appearance**
se négliger

negotiate [nɪ'gəʊʃɪeɪt] vi négocier ▷ vt
négocier; (obstacle) franchir, négocier; **to
~ with sb for sth** négocier avec qn en vue
d'obtenir qch

negotiation [nɪgəʊʃɪ'eɪʃən] n négociation f,
pourparlers mpl

negotiator [nɪ'gəʊʃɪeɪtəʳ] n
négociateur(-trice)

neighbour (US **neighbor** etc) ['neɪbəʳ] n
voisin(e); **neighbourhood** n (place) quartier
m; (people) voisinage m; **neighbouring** adj
voisin(e), avoisinant(e)

neither ['naɪðəʳ] adj, pron aucun(e) (des deux),
ni l'un(e) ni l'autre ▷ conj: **~ do I** moi non plus
▷ adv: **~ good nor bad** ni bon ni mauvais; **~ of
them** ni l'un ni l'autre

neon ['niːɔn] n néon m

Nepal [nɪ'pɔːl] n Népal m

nephew ['nɛvjuː] n neveu m

nerve [nəːv] n nerf m; (bravery) sang-froid
m, courage m; (cheek) aplomb m, toupet m;
nerves npl (nervousness) nervosité f; **he gets
on my ~s** il m'énerve

nervous ['nəːvəs] adj nerveux(-euse); (anxious)
inquiet(-ète), plein(e) d'appréhension;
(timid) intimidé(e); **nervous breakdown** n
dépression nerveuse

nest [nɛst] n nid m ▷ vi (se) nicher, faire son nid

Net [nɛt] n (Comput): **the ~** (Internet) le Net

net [nɛt] n filet m; (fabric) tulle f ▷ adj net(te)
▷ vt (fish etc) prendre au filet; **netball** n
netball m

Netherlands ['nɛðələndz] npl: **the ~** les
Pays-Bas mpl

nett [nɛt] adj = **net**

nettle ['nɛtl] n ortie f

network ['nɛtwəːk] n réseau m

neurotic [njuə'rɔtɪk] adj névrosé(e)

neuter ['njuːtəʳ] adj neutre ▷ vt (cat etc)
châtrer, couper

neutral ['njuːtrəl] adj neutre ▷ n (Aut) point
mort

never ['nɛvəʳ] adv (ne ...) jamais; **I ~ went**
je n'y suis pas allé; **I've ~ been to Spain** je
ne suis jamais allé en Espagne; **~ again** plus
jamais; **~ in my life** jamais de ma vie; see
also **mind**; **never-ending** adj interminable;
nevertheless [nɛvəðə'lɛs] adv néanmoins,
malgré tout

new [njuː] adj nouveau (nouvelle); (brand
new) neuf (neuve); **New Age** n New
Age m; **newborn** adj nouveau-né(e);
newcomer ['njuːkʌməʳ] n nouveau venu
(nouvelle venue); **newly** adv nouvellement,
récemment

news [njuːz] n nouvelle(s) f(pl); (Radio, TV)
informations fpl, actualités fpl; **a piece of
~** une nouvelle; **news agency** n agence f
de presse; **newsagent** n (BRIT) marchand
m de journaux; **newscaster** n (Radio, TV)
présentateur(-trice); **news dealer** n (US)
marchand m de journaux; **newsletter**
n bulletin m; **newspaper** n journal m;

newsreader n = **newscaster**
newt [njuːt] n triton m
New Year n Nouvel An; **Happy ~!** Bonne
Année!; **New Year's Day** n le jour de l'An; **New
Year's Eve** n la Saint-Sylvestre
New York [-'jɔːk] n New York
New Zealand [-'ziːlənd] n Nouvelle-
Zélande f; **New Zealander** n Néo-
Zélandais(e)
next [nɛkst] adj (in time) prochain(e); (seat,
room) voisin(e), d'à côté; (meeting, bus stop)
suivant(e) ▷ adv la fois suivante; la prochaine
fois; (afterwards) ensuite; **~ to** prep à côté
de; **~ to nothing** presque rien; **~ time** adv la
prochaine fois; **the ~ day** le lendemain, le jour
suivant or d'après; **~ year** l'année prochaine; **~
please!** (at doctor's etc) au suivant!; **the week
after ~** dans deux semaines; **next door** adv à
côté ▷ adj (neighbour) d'à côté; **next-of-kin** n
parent m le plus proche
NHS n abbr (BRIT) = **National Health Service**
nibble ['nɪbl] vt grignoter
nice [naɪs] adj (holiday, trip, taste) agréable; (flat,
picture) joli(e); (person) gentil(le); (distinction,
point) subtil(e); **nicely** adv agréablement;
joliment; gentiment; subtilement
niche [niːʃ] n (Archit) niche f
nick [nɪk] n (indentation) encoche f; (wound)
entaille f; (BRIT inf): **in good ~** en bon état ▷ vt
(cut): **to ~ o.s.** se couper; (inf: steal) faucher,
piquer; **in the ~ of time** juste à temps
nickel ['nɪkl] n nickel m; (US) pièce f de 5 cents
nickname ['nɪkneɪm] n surnom m ▷ vt
surnommer
nicotine ['nɪkətiːn] n nicotine f
niece [niːs] n nièce f
Nigeria [naɪ'dʒɪərɪə] n Nigéria m or f
night [naɪt] n nuit f; (evening) soir m; **at ~** la
nuit; **by ~** de nuit; **last ~** (evening) hier soir;
(night-time) la nuit dernière; **night club** n
boîte f de nuit; **nightdress** n chemise f de nuit;
nightie ['naɪtɪ] n chemise f de nuit; **nightlife**
n vie f nocturne; **nightly** adj (news) du soir; (by
night) nocturne ▷ adv (every evening) tous les
soirs; (every night) toutes les nuits; **nightmare**
n cauchemar m; **night school** n cours mpl
du soir; **night shift** n équipe f de nuit; **night-
time** n nuit f
nil [nɪl] n (BRIT Sport) zéro m
nine [naɪn] num neuf; **nineteen** num dix-neuf;
nineteenth [naɪn'tiːnθ] num dix-neuvième;
ninetieth ['naɪntɪɪθ] num quatre-vingt-
dixième; **ninety** num quatre-vingt-dix
ninth [naɪnθ] num neuvième
nip [nɪp] vt pincer ▷ vi (BRIT inf): **to ~
out/down/up** sortir/descendre/monter
en vitesse
nipple ['nɪpl] n (Anat) mamelon m, bout m
du sein

nitrogen ['naɪtrədʒən] n azote m

🔵 **KEYWORD**

no [nəu] (pl **noes**) adv (opposite of "yes") non;
are you coming? — no (I'm not) est-ce que
vous venez? — non; **would you like some
more? — no thank you** vous en voulez
encore? — non merci
▷ adj (not any) (ne ...) pas de, (ne ...) aucun(e);
I have no money/books je n'ai pas d'argent/
de livres; **no student would have done it**
aucun étudiant ne l'aurait fait; **"no smoking"**
"défense de fumer"; **"no dogs"** "les chiens ne
sont pas admis"
▷ n non m

nobility [nəu'bɪlɪtɪ] n noblesse f
noble ['nəubl] adj noble
nobody ['nəubədɪ] pron (ne ...) personne
nod [nɔd] vi faire un signe de (la) tête (affirmatif
ou amical); (sleep) somnoler ▷ vt: **to ~ one's
head** faire un signe de (la) tête; (in agreement)
faire signe que oui ▷ n signe m de (la) tête; **nod
off** vi s'assoupir
noise [nɔɪz] n bruit m; **I can't sleep for the ~**
je n'arrive pas à dormir à cause du bruit; **noisy**
adj bruyant(e)
nominal ['nɔmɪnl] adj (rent, fee) symbolique;
(value) nominal(e)
nominate ['nɔmɪneɪt] vt (propose) proposer;
(appoint) nommer; **nomination** [nɔmɪ'neɪʃə
n] nomination f; **nominee** [nɔmɪ'niː] n
candidat agréé; personne nommée
none [nʌn] pron aucun(e); **~ of you** aucun
d'entre vous, personne parmi vous; **I have ~
left** je n'en ai plus; **he's ~ the worse for it** il ne
s'en porte pas plus mal
nonetheless ['nʌnðə'lɛs] adv néanmoins
non-fiction [nɔn'fɪkʃən] n littérature f non-
romanesque
nonsense ['nɔnsəns] n absurdités fpl, idioties
fpl; **~!** ne dites pas d'idioties!
non: **non-smoker** n non-fumeur m; **non-
smoking** adj non-fumeur; **non-stick** adj qui
n'attache pas
noodles ['nuːdlz] npl nouilles fpl
noon [nuːn] n midi m
no-one ['nəuwʌn] pron = **nobody**
nor [nɔːʳ] conj = **neither** ▷ adv see **neither**
norm [nɔːm] n norme f
normal ['nɔːml] adj normal(e); **normally** adv
normalement
Normandy ['nɔːməndɪ] n Normandie f
north [nɔːθ] n nord m ▷ adj nord inv; (wind)
du nord ▷ adv au or vers le nord; **North
Africa** n Afrique f du Nord; **North African** adj
nord-africain(e), d'Afrique du Nord ▷ n Nord-
Africain(e); **North America** n Amérique f du

Nord; **North American** n Nord-Américain(e)
▷ adj nord-américain(e), d'Amérique du
Nord; **northbound** ['nɔ:θbaund] adj (traffic)
en direction du nord; (carriageway) nord inv;
north-east n nord-est m; **northeastern** adj
(du) nord-est inv; **northern** ['nɔ:ðən] adj du
nord, septentrional(e); **Northern Ireland**
n Irlande f du Nord; **North Korea** n Corée
f du Nord; **North Pole** n: **the North Pole** le
pôle Nord; **North Sea** n: **the North Sea** la
mer du Nord; **north-west** n nord-ouest m;
northwestern ['nɔ:θ'westən] adj (du) nord-
ouest inv

Norway ['nɔ:weɪ] n Norvège f; **Norwegian**
[nɔ:'wi:dʒən] adj norvégien(ne) ▷ n
Norvégien(ne); (Ling) norvégien m

nose [nəuz] n nez m; (of dog, cat) museau
m; (fig) flair m; **nose about, nose around**
vi fouiner or fureter (partout); **nosebleed**
n saignement m de nez; **nosey** adj (inf)
curieux(-euse)

nostalgia [nɔs'tældʒɪə] n nostalgie f

nostalgic [nɔs'tældʒɪk] adj nostalgique

nostril ['nɔstrɪl] n narine f; (of horse) naseau m

nosy ['nəuzɪ] (inf) adj = **nosey**

not [nɔt] adv (ne ...) pas; **he is ~** or **isn't here** il
n'est pas ici; **you must ~** or **mustn't do that**
tu ne dois pas faire ça; **I hope ~** j'espère que
non; **~ at all** pas du tout; (after thanks) de rien;
it's too late, isn't it? c'est trop tard, n'est-ce
pas?; **~ yet/now** pas encore/maintenant; see
also **only**

notable ['nəutəbl] adj notable; **notably**
adv (particularly) en particulier; (markedly)
spécialement

notch [nɔtʃ] n encoche f

note [nəut] n note f; (letter) mot m; (banknote)
billet m ▷ vt (also: **~ down**) noter; (notice)
constater; **notebook** n carnet m; (for
shorthand etc) bloc-notes m; **noted** ['nəutɪd]
adj réputé(e); **notepad** n bloc-notes m;
notepaper n papier m à lettres

nothing ['nʌθɪŋ] n rien m; **he does ~** il ne fait
rien; **~ new** rien de nouveau; **for ~** (free) pour
rien, gratuitement; (in vain) pour rien; **~ at all**
rien du tout; **~ much** pas grand-chose

notice ['nəutɪs] n (announcement, warning) avis
m ▷ vt remarquer, s'apercevoir de; **advance
~** préavis m; **at short ~** dans un délai très
court; **until further ~** jusqu'à nouvel ordre; **to
give ~, hand in one's ~** (employee) donner sa
démission, démissionner; **to take ~ of** prêter
attention à; **to bring sth to sb's ~** porter qch à
la connaissance de qn; **noticeable** adj visible

notice board n (BRIT) panneau m d'affichage

notify ['nəutɪfaɪ] vt: **to ~ sb of sth** avertir qn
de qch

notion ['nəuʃən] n idée f; (concept) notion f;
notions npl (US: haberdashery) mercerie f

notorious [nəu'tɔ:rɪəs] adj notoire (souvent
en mal)

notwithstanding [nɔtwɪθ'stændɪŋ] adv
néanmoins ▷ prep en dépit de

nought [nɔ:t] n zéro m

noun [naun] n nom m

nourish ['nʌrɪʃ] vt nourrir; **nourishment** n
nourriture f

Nov. abbr (= November) nov

novel ['nɔvl] n roman m ▷ adj nouveau
(nouvelle), original(e); **novelist** n
romancier m; **novelty** n nouveauté f

November [nəu'vɛmbər] n novembre m

novice ['nɔvɪs] n novice m/f

now [nau] adv maintenant ▷ conj: **~ (that)**
maintenant (que); **right ~** tout de suite;
by ~ à l'heure qu'il est; **just ~: that's the
fashion just ~** c'est la mode en ce moment
or maintenant; **~ and then, ~ and again**
de temps en temps; **from ~ on** dorénavant;
nowadays ['nauədeɪz] adv de nos jours

nowhere ['nəuwɛər] adv (ne ...) nulle part

nozzle ['nɔzl] n (of hose) jet m, lance f; (of
vacuum cleaner) suceur m

nr abbr (BRIT) = **near**

nuclear ['nju:klɪər] adj nucléaire

nucleus (pl **nuclei**) ['nju:klɪəs, 'nju:klɪaɪ] n
noyau m

nude [nju:d] adj nu(e) ▷ n (Art) nu m; **in the ~**
(tout(e)) nu(e)

nudge [nʌdʒ] vt donner un (petit) coup de
coude à

nudist ['nju:dɪst] n nudiste m/f

nudity ['nju:dɪtɪ] n nudité f

nuisance ['nju:sns] n: **it's a ~** c'est (très)
ennuyeux or gênant; **he's a ~** il est assommant
or casse-pieds; **what a ~!** quelle barbe!

numb [nʌm] adj engourdi(e); (with fear)
paralysé(e)

number ['nʌmbər] n nombre m; (numeral)
chiffre m; (of house, car, telephone, newspaper)
numéro m ▷ vt numéroter; (amount to)
compter; **a ~ of** un certain nombre de; **they
were seven in ~** ils étaient (au nombre
de) sept; **to be ~ed among** compter
parmi; **number plate** n (BRIT Aut) plaque f
minéralogique or d'immatriculation; **Number
Ten** n (BRIT: 10 Downing Street) résidence du
Premier ministre

numerical [nju:'mɛrɪkl] adj numérique

numerous ['nju:mərəs] adj nombreux(-euse)

nun [nʌn] n religieuse f, sœur f

nurse [nə:s] n infirmière f; (also: **~maid**) bonne
f d'enfants ▷ vt (patient, cold) soigner

nursery ['nə:sərɪ] n (room) nursery f;
(institution) crèche f, garderie f; (for plants)
pépinière f; **nursery rhyme** n comptine f,
chansonnette f pour enfants; **nursery school**
n école maternelle; **nursery slope** n (BRIT Ski)

piste f pour débutants

nursing ['nə:sɪŋ] n (profession) profession f d'infirmière; (care) soins mpl; **nursing home** n clinique f; (for convalescence) maison f de convalescence or de repos; (for old people) maison de retraite

nurture ['nə:tʃə'] vt élever

nut [nʌt] n (of metal) écrou m; (fruit: walnut) noix f; (: hazelnut) noisette f; (: peanut) cacahuète f (terme générique en anglais)

nutmeg ['nʌtmɛg] n (noix f) muscade f

nutrient ['nju:trɪənt] n substance nutritive

nutrition [nju:'trɪʃən] n nutrition f, alimentation f

nutritious [nju:'trɪʃəs] adj nutritif(-ive), nourrissant(e)

nuts [nʌts] (inf) adj dingue

NVQ n abbr (BRIT) = **National Vocational Qualification**

nylon ['naɪlɔn] n nylon m ▷ adj de or en nylon

oak [əuk] n chêne m ▷ cpd de or en (bois de) chêne

O.A.P. n abbr (BRIT) = **old age pensioner**

oar [ɔ:'] n aviron m, rame f

oasis (pl oases) [əu'eɪsɪs, əu'eɪsi:z] n oasis f

oath [əuθ] n serment m; (swear word) juron m; **on** (BRIT) or **under ~** sous serment; assermenté(e)

oatmeal ['əutmi:l] n flocons mpl d'avoine

oats [əuts] n avoine f

obedience [ə'bi:dɪəns] n obéissance f

obedient [ə'bi:dɪənt] adj obéissant(e)

obese [əu'bi:s] adj obèse

obesity [əu'bi:sɪtɪ] n obésité f

obey [ə'beɪ] vt obéir à; (instructions, regulations) se conformer à ▷ vi obéir

obituary [ə'bɪtjuərɪ] n nécrologie f

object n ['ɔbdʒɪkt] objet m; (purpose) but m, objet; (Ling) complément m d'objet ▷ vi [ə b'dʒɛkt]: **to ~ to** (attitude) désapprouver; (proposal) protester contre, élever une objection contre; **I ~!** je proteste!; **he ~ed that ...** il a fait valoir or a objecté que ...; **money is no ~** l'argent n'est pas un problème; **objection** [əb'dʒɛkʃən] n objection f; **if you have no objection** si vous n'y voyez pas d'inconvénient; **objective** n objectif m ▷ adj objectif(-ive)

obligation [ɔblɪ'geɪʃən] n obligation f, devoir m; (debt) dette f (de reconnaissance)

obligatory [ə'blɪgətərɪ] *adj* obligatoire

oblige [ə'blaɪdʒ] *vt* (*force*): **to ~ sb to do** obliger *or* forcer qn à faire; (*do a favour*) rendre service à, obliger; **to be ~d to sb for sth** être obligé(e) à qn de qch

oblique [ə'bliːk] *adj* oblique; (*allusion*) indirect(e)

obliterate [ə'blɪtəreɪt] *vt* effacer

oblivious [ə'blɪvɪəs] *adj*: **~ of** oublieux(-euse) de

oblong ['ɔblɔŋ] *adj* oblong(ue) ▷ *n* rectangle *m*

obnoxious [əb'nɔkʃəs] *adj* odieux(-euse); (*smell*) nauséabond(e)

oboe ['əubəu] *n* hautbois *m*

obscene [əb'siːn] *adj* obscène

obscure [əb'skjuəʳ] *adj* obscur(e) ▷ *vt* obscurcir; (*hide: sun*) cacher

observant [əb'zəːvnt] *adj* observateur(-trice)

observation [ɔbzə'veɪʃən] *n* observation *f*; (*by police etc*) surveillance *f*

observatory [əb'zəːvətrɪ] *n* observatoire *m*

observe [əb'zəːv] *vt* observer; (*remark*) faire observer *or* remarquer; **observer** *n* observateur(-trice)

obsess [əb'sɛs] *vt* obséder; **obsession** [əb'sɛʃən] *n* obsession *f*; **obsessive** *adj* obsédant(e)

obsolete ['ɔbsəliːt] *adj* dépassé(e), périmé(e)

obstacle ['ɔbstəkl] *n* obstacle *m*

obstinate ['ɔbstɪnɪt] *adj* obstiné(e); (*pain, cold*) persistant(e)

obstruct [əb'strʌkt] *vt* (*block*) boucher, obstruer; (*hinder*) entraver; **obstruction** [əb'strʌkʃən] *n* obstruction *f*; (*to plan, progress*) obstacle *m*

obtain [əb'teɪn] *vt* obtenir

obvious ['ɔbvɪəs] *adj* évident(e), manifeste; **obviously** *adv* manifestement; (*of course*): **obviously!** bien sûr!; **obviously not!** évidemment pas!, bien sûr que non!

occasion [ə'keɪʒən] *n* occasion *f*; (*event*) événement *m*; **occasional** *adj* pris(e) (*or* fait(e) *etc*) de temps en temps; (*worker, spending*) occasionnel(le); **occasionally** *adv* de temps en temps, quelquefois

occult [ɔ'kʌlt] *adj* occulte ▷ *n*: **the ~** le surnaturel

occupant ['ɔkjupənt] *n* occupant *m*

occupation [ɔkju'peɪʃən] *n* occupation *f*; (*job*) métier *m*, profession *f*

occupy ['ɔkjupaɪ] *vt* occuper; **to ~ o.s. with** *or* **by doing** s'occuper à faire

occur [ə'kəːʳ] *vi* se produire; (*difficulty, opportunity*) se présenter; (*phenomenon, error*) se rencontrer; **to ~ to sb** venir à l'esprit de qn; **occurrence** [ə'kʌrəns] *n* (*existence*) présence *f*, existence *f*; (*event*) cas *m*, fait *m*

ocean ['əuʃən] *n* océan *m*

o'clock [ə'klɔk] *adv*: **it is 5 o'clock** il est 5 heures

Oct. *abbr* (= *October*) oct

October [ɔk'təubəʳ] *n* octobre *m*

octopus ['ɔktəpəs] *n* pieuvre *f*

odd [ɔd] *adj* (*strange*) bizarre, curieux(-euse); (*number*) impair(e); (*not of a set*) dépareillé(e); **60-~** 60 et quelques; **at ~ times** de temps en temps; **the ~ one out** l'exception *f*; **oddly** *adv* bizarrement, curieusement; **odds** *npl* (*in betting*) cote *f*; **it makes no odds** cela n'a pas d'importance; **odds and ends** de petites choses; **at odds** en désaccord

odometer [ɔ'dɔmɪtəʳ] *n* (*us*) odomètre *m*

odour (*us* **odor**) ['əudəʳ] *n* odeur *f*

Ⓞ **KEYWORD**

of [ɔv, əv] *prep* **1** (*gen*) de; **a friend of ours** un de nos amis; **a boy of 10** un garçon de 10 ans; **that was kind of you** c'était gentil de votre part

2 (*expressing quantity, amount, dates etc*) de; **a kilo of flour** un kilo de farine; **how much of this do you need?** combien vous en faut-il?; **there were three of them** (*people*) ils étaient 3; (*objects*) il y en avait 3; **three of us went** 3 d'entre nous y sont allé(e)s; **the 5th of July** le 5 juillet; **a quarter of 4** (*us*) 4 heures moins le quart

3 (*from, out of*) en, de; **a statue of marble** une statue de *or* en marbre; **made of wood** (fait) en bois

off [ɔf] *adj, adv* (*engine*) coupé(e); (*light, TV*) éteint(e); (*tap*) fermé(e); (*BRIT: food*) mauvais(e), avancé(e); (: *milk*) tourné(e); (*absent*) absent(e); (*cancelled*) annulé(e); (*removed*): **the lid was ~** le couvercle était retiré *or* n'était pas mis; (*away*): **to run/drive ~** partir en courant/en voiture ▷ *prep* de; **to be ~** (*to leave*) partir, s'en aller; **to be ~ sick** être absent pour cause de maladie; **a day ~** un jour de congé; **to have an ~ day** n'être pas en forme; **he had his coat ~** il avait enlevé son manteau; **10% ~** (*Comm*) 10% de rabais; **5 km ~ (the road)** à 5 km (de la route); **~ the coast** au large de la côte; **it's a long way ~** c'est loin (d'ici); **I'm ~ meat** je ne mange plus de viande; je n'aime plus la viande; **on the ~ chance** à tout hasard; **~ and on, on and ~** de temps à autre

offence (*us* **offense**) [ə'fɛns] *n* (*crime*) délit *m*, infraction *f*; **to take ~ at** se vexer de, s'offenser de

offend [ə'fɛnd] *vt* (*person*) offenser, blesser; **offender** *n* délinquant(e); (*against regulations*) contrevenant(e)

offense [ə'fɛns] *n* (*us*) = **offence**

offensive [ə'fɛnsɪv] *adj* offensant(e), choquant(e); (*smell etc*) très déplaisant(e); (*weapon*) offensif(-ive) ▷ *n* (*Mil*) offensive *f*

offer ['ɔfəʳ] *n* offre *f*, proposition *f* ▷ *vt* offrir, proposer; **"on ~"** (*Comm*) "en promotion"

offhand [ɔf'hænd] *adj* désinvolte ▷ *adv* spontanément

office ['ɔfɪs] *n* (*place*) bureau *m*; (*position*) charge *f*, fonction *f*; **doctor's ~** (*us*) cabinet (médical); **to take ~** entrer en fonctions; **office block** (*us* **office building**) *n* immeuble *m* de bureaux; **office hours** *npl* heures *fpl* de bureau; (*us Med*) heures de consultation

officer ['ɔfɪsəʳ] *n* (*Mil etc*) officier *m*; (*also:* **police ~**) agent *m* (de police); (*of organization*) membre *m* du bureau directeur

office worker *n* employé(e) de bureau

official [ə'fɪʃl] *adj* (*authorized*) officiel(le) ▷ *n* officiel *m*; (*civil servant*) fonctionnaire *m/f*; (*of railways, post office, town hall*) employé(e)

off: **off-licence** *n* (*BRIT: shop*) débit *m* de vins et de spiritueux; **off-line** *adj* (*Comput*) (en mode) autonome; (: *switched off*) non connecté(e); **off-peak** *adj* aux heures creuses; (*electricity, ticket*) au tarif heures creuses; **off-putting** *adj* (*BRIT: remark*) rébarbatif(-ive); (*person*) rebutant(e), peu engageant(e); **off-season** *adj*, *adv* hors-saison *inv*

offset ['ɔfsɛt] *vt* (*irreg: like* **set**) (*counteract*) contrebalancer, compenser

offshore [ɔf'ʃɔːʳ] *adj* (*breeze*) de terre; (*island*) proche du littoral; (*fishing*) côtier(-ière)

offside ['ɔf'saɪd] *adj* (*Sport*) hors jeu; (*Aut: in Britain*) de droite; (: *in US, Europe*) de gauche

offspring ['ɔfsprɪŋ] *n* progéniture *f*

often ['ɔfn] *adv* souvent; **how ~ do you go?** vous y allez tous les combien?; **every so ~** de temps en temps, de temps à autre

oh [əu] *excl* ô!, oh!, ah!

oil [ɔɪl] *n* huile *f*; (*petroleum*) pétrole *m*; (*for central heating*) mazout *m* ▷ *vt* (*machine*) graisser; **oil filter** *n* (*Aut*) filtre *m* à huile; **oil painting** *n* peinture *f* à l'huile; **oil refinery** *n* raffinerie *f* de pétrole; **oil rig** *n* derrick *m*; (*at sea*) plate-forme pétrolière; **oil slick** *n* nappe *f* de mazout; **oil tanker** *n* (*ship*) pétrolier *m*; (*truck*) camion-citerne *m*; **oil well** *n* puits *m* de pétrole; **oily** *adj* huileux(-euse); (*food*) gras(se)

ointment ['ɔɪntmənt] *n* onguent *m*

O.K., okay ['əu'keɪ] (*inf*) *excl* d'accord! ▷ *vt* approuver, donner son accord à ▷ *adj* (*not bad*) pas mal; **is it O.K.?, are you O.K.?** ça va?

old [əuld] *adj* vieux (vieille); (*person*) vieux, âgé(e); (*former*) ancien(ne), vieux; **how ~ are you?** quel âge avez-vous?; **he's 10 years ~** il a 10 ans, il est âgé de 10 ans; **~er brother/sister** frère/sœur aîné(e); **old age** *n* vieillesse *f*; **old-age pension** *n* (*BRIT*) (pension *f* de) retraite *f* (de la sécurité sociale); **old-age pensioner**

n (*BRIT*) retraité(e); **old-fashioned** *adj* démodé(e); (*person*) vieux jeu *inv*; **old people's home** *n* (*esp BRIT*) maison *f* de retraite

olive ['ɔlɪv] *n* (*fruit*) olive *f*; (*tree*) olivier *m* ▷ *adj* (*also:* **~-green**) (vert) olive *inv*; **olive oil** *n* huile *f* d'olive

Olympic [əu'lɪmpɪk] *adj* olympique; **the ~ Games, the ~s** les Jeux *mpl* olympiques

omelet(te) ['ɔmlɪt] *n* omelette *f*

omen ['əumən] *n* présage *m*

ominous ['ɔmɪnəs] *adj* menaçant(e), inquiétant(e); (*event*) de mauvais augure

omit [əu'mɪt] *vt* omettre

🅞 **KEYWORD**

on [ɔn] *prep* **1** (*indicating position*) sur; **on the table** sur la table; **on the wall** sur le *or* au mur; **on the left** à gauche

2 (*indicating means, method, condition etc*): **on foot** à pied; **on the train/plane** (*be*) dans le train/l'avion; (*go*) en train/avion; **on the telephone/radio/television** au téléphone/à la radio/à la télévision; **to be on drugs** se droguer; **on holiday** (*BRIT*), **on vacation** (*us*) en vacances

3 (*referring to time*): **on Friday** vendredi; **on Fridays** le vendredi; **on June 20th** le 20 juin; **a week on Friday** vendredi en huit; **on arrival** à l'arrivée; **on seeing this** en voyant cela

4 (*about, concerning*) sur, de; **a book on Balzac/physics** un livre sur Balzac/de physique

▷ *adv* **1** (*referring to dress*): **to have one's coat on** avoir (mis) son manteau; **to put one's coat on** mettre son manteau; **what's she got on?** qu'est-ce qu'elle porte?

2 (*referring to covering*): **screw the lid on tightly** vissez bien le couvercle

3 (*further, continuously*): **to walk** *etc* **on** continuer à marcher *etc*; **from that day on** depuis ce jour

▷ *adj* **1** (*in operation: machine*) en marche; (: *radio, TV, light*) allumé(e); (: *tap, gas*) ouvert(e); (: *brakes*) mis(e); **is the meeting still on?** (*not cancelled*) est-ce que la réunion a bien lieu?; (*in progress*) la réunion dure-t-elle encore?; **when is this film on?** quand passe ce film?

2 (*inf*): **that's not on!** (*not acceptable*) cela ne se fait pas!; (*not possible*) pas question!

once [wʌns] *adv* une fois; (*formerly*) autrefois ▷ *conj* une fois que + *sub*; **~ he had left/it was done** une fois qu'il fut parti/ que ce fut terminé; **at ~** tout de suite, immédiatement; (*simultaneously*) à la fois; **all at ~** *adv* tout d'un coup; **~ a week** une fois par semaine; **~ more** encore une fois; **~ and for all** une fois pour toutes; **~ upon a time there was ...** il y avait une fois ..., il était une fois ...

oncoming ['ɔnkʌmɪŋ] *adj* (*traffic*) venant en sens inverse

⬤ **KEYWORD**

one [wʌn] *num* un(e); **one hundred and fifty** cent cinquante; **one by one** un(e) à *or* par un(e); **one day** un jour
▷ *adj* **1** (*sole*) seul(e), unique; **the one book which** l'unique *or* le seul livre qui; **the one man who** le seul (homme) qui
2 (*same*) même; **they came in the one car** ils sont venus dans la même voiture
▷ *pron* **1**: **this one** celui-ci (celle-ci); **that one** celui-là (celle-là); **I've already got one/a red one** j'en ai déjà un(e)/un(e) rouge; **which one do you want?** lequel voulez-vous?
2: **one another** l'un(e) l'autre; **to look at one another** se regarder
3 (*impersonal*) on; **one never knows** on ne sait jamais; **to cut one's finger** se couper le doigt; **one needs to eat** il faut manger

one-off [wʌn'ɔf] (*BRIT inf*) *n* exemplaire *m* unique

oneself [wʌn'sɛlf] *pron* se; (*after prep, also emphatic*) soi-même; **to hurt ~** se faire mal; **to keep sth for ~** garder qch pour soi; **to talk to ~** se parler à soi-même; **by ~** tout seul

one: **one-shot** [wʌn'ʃɔt] (*US*) *n* = **one-off; one-sided** *adj* (*argument, decision*) unilatéral(e); **one-to-one** *adj* (*relationship*) univoque; **one-way** *adj* (*street, traffic*) à sens unique

ongoing ['ɔngəʊɪŋ] *adj* en cours; (*relationship*) suivi(e)

onion ['ʌnjən] *n* oignon *m*

on-line ['ɔnlaɪn] *adj* (*Comput*) en ligne; (: *switched on*) connecté(e)

onlooker ['ɔnlʊkəʳ] *n* spectateur(-trice)

only ['əʊnlɪ] *adv* seulement ▷ *adj* seul(e), unique ▷ *conj* seulement, mais; **an ~ child** un enfant unique; **not ~ ... but also** non seulement ... mais aussi; **I ~ took one** j'en ai seulement pris un, je n'en ai pris qu'un

on-screen [ɔn'skriːn] *adj* à l'écran

onset ['ɔnsɛt] *n* début *m*; (*of winter, old age*) approche *f*

onto ['ɔntu] *prep* = **on to**

onward(s) ['ɔnwəd(z)] *adv* (*move*) en avant; **from that time ~** à partir de ce moment

oops [ups] *excl* houp!

ooze [uːz] *vi* suinter

opaque [əʊ'peɪk] *adj* opaque

open ['əʊpn] *adj* ouvert(e); (*car*) découvert(e); (*road, view*) dégagé(e); (*meeting*) public(-ique); (*admiration*) manifeste ▷ *vt* ouvrir ▷ *vi* (*flower, eyes, door, debate*) s'ouvrir; (*shop, bank, museum*)

ouvrir; (*book etc: commence*) commencer, débuter; **is it ~ to public?** est-ce ouvert au public?; **what time do you ~?** à quelle heure ouvrez-vous?; **in the ~** (*air*) en plein air; **open up** *vt* ouvrir; (*blocked road*) dégager ▷ *vi* s'ouvrir; **open-air** *adj* en plein air; **opening** *n* ouverture *f*; (*opportunity*) occasion *f*; (*work*) débouché *m*; (*job*) poste vacant; **opening hours** *npl* heures *fpl* d'ouverture; **open learning** *n* enseignement universitaire à la carte, notamment par correspondance; (*distance learning*) télé-enseignement *m*; **openly** *adv* ouvertement; **open-minded** *adj* à l'esprit ouvert; **open-necked** *adj* à col ouvert; **open-plan** *adj* sans cloisons; **Open University** *n* (*BRIT*) *cours universitaires par correspondance*

⬤ **OPEN UNIVERSITY**
⬤
⬤ L'**Open University** a été fondée en 1969.
⬤ L'enseignement comprend des cours
⬤ (certaines plages horaires sont réservées
⬤ à cet effet à la télévision et à la radio), des
⬤ devoirs qui sont envoyés par l'étudiant à
⬤ son directeur ou sa directrice d'études, et
⬤ un séjour obligatoire en université d'été. Il
⬤ faut préparer un certain nombre d'unités
⬤ de valeur pendant une période de temps
⬤ déterminée et obtenir la moyenne à un
⬤ certain nombre d'entre elles pour recevoir le
⬤ diplôme visé.

opera ['ɔpərə] *n* opéra *m*; **opera house** *n* opéra *m*; **opera singer** *n* chanteur(-euse) d'opéra

operate ['ɔpəreɪt] *vt* (*machine*) faire marcher, faire fonctionner ▷ *vi* fonctionner; **to ~ on sb (for)** (*Med*) opérer qn (de)

operating room *n* (*US: Med*) salle *f* d'opération

operating theatre *n* (*BRIT: Med*) salle *f* d'opération

operation [ɔpə'reɪʃən] *n* opération *f*; (*of machine*) fonctionnement *m*; **to have an ~ (for)** se faire opérer (de); **to be in ~** (*machine*) être en service; (*system*) être en vigueur; **operational** *adj* opérationnel(le); (*ready for use*) en état de marche

operative ['ɔpərətɪv] *adj* (*measure*) en vigueur ▷ *n* (*in factory*) ouvrier(-ière)

operator ['ɔpəreɪtəʳ] *n* (*of machine*) opérateur(-trice); (*Tel*) téléphoniste *m/f*

opinion [ə'pɪnjən] *n* opinion *f*, avis *m*; **in my ~** à mon avis; **opinion poll** *n* sondage *m* d'opinion

opponent [ə'pəʊnənt] *n* adversaire *m/f*

opportunity [ɔpə'tjuːnɪtɪ] *n* occasion *f*; **to take the ~ to do** *or* **of doing** profiter de l'occasion pour faire

oppose [ə'pəuz] *vt* s'opposer à; **to be ~d
to sth** être opposé(e) à qch; **as ~d to** par
opposition à

opposite ['ɔpəzɪt] *adj* opposé(e); (*house etc*)
d'en face ▷ *adv* en face ▷ *prep* en face de ▷ *n*
opposé *m*, contraire *m*; (*of word*) contraire

opposition [ɔpə'zɪʃən] *n* opposition *f*

oppress [ə'prɛs] *vt* opprimer

opt [ɔpt] *vi*: **to ~ for** opter pour; **to ~ to do**
choisir de faire; **opt out** *vi*: **to ~ out of** choisir
de ne pas participer à or de ne pas faire

optician [ɔp'tɪʃən] *n* opticien(ne)

optimism ['ɔptɪmɪzəm] *n* optimisme *m*

optimist ['ɔptɪmɪst] *n* optimiste *m/f*;
optimistic [ɔptɪ'mɪstɪk] *adj* optimiste

optimum ['ɔptɪməm] *adj* optimum

option ['ɔpʃən] *n* choix *m*, option *f*;
(*Scol*) matière *f* à option; **optional** *adj*
facultatif(-ive)

or [ɔːʳ] *conj* ou; (*with negative*): **he hasn't seen
or heard anything** il n'a rien vu ni entendu; **or
else** sinon; ou bien

oral ['ɔːrəl] *adj* oral(e) ▷ *n* oral *m*

orange ['ɔrɪndʒ] *n* (*fruit*) orange *f* ▷ *adj*
orange *inv*; **orange juice** *n* jus *m* d'orange;
orange squash *n* orangeade *f*

orbit ['ɔːbɪt] *n* orbite *f* ▷ *vt* graviter autour de

orchard ['ɔːtʃəd] *n* verger *m*

orchestra ['ɔːkɪstrə] *n* orchestre *m*; (*us:
seating*) (fauteuils *mpl* d')orchestre

orchid ['ɔːkɪd] *n* orchidée *f*

ordeal [ɔː'diːl] *n* épreuve *f*

order ['ɔːdəʳ] *n* ordre *m*; (*Comm*) commande
f ▷ *vt* ordonner; (*Comm*) commander; **in
~** en ordre; (*of document*) en règle; **out of ~**
(*not in correct order*) en désordre; (*machine*)
hors service; (*telephone*) en dérangement;
a machine in working ~ une machine
en état de marche; **in ~ to do/that** pour
faire/que + *sub*; **could I ~ now, please?** je peux
commander, s'il vous plaît?; **to be on ~** être
en commande; **to ~ sb to do** ordonner à qn
de faire; **order form** *n* bon *m* de commande;
orderly *n* (*Mil*) ordonnance *f*; (*Med*) garçon
m de salle ▷ *adj* (*room*) en ordre; (*mind*)
méthodique; (*person*) qui a de l'ordre

ordinary ['ɔːdnrɪ] *adj* ordinaire, normal(e);
(*pej*) ordinaire, quelconque; **out of the ~**
exceptionnel(le)

ore [ɔːʳ] *n* minerai *m*

oregano [ɔrɪ'gɑːnəu] *n* origan *m*

organ ['ɔːgən] *n* organe *m*; (*Mus*) orgue *m*,
orgues *fpl*; **organic** [ɔː'gænɪk] *adj* organique;
(*crops etc*) biologique, naturel(le); **organism** *n*
organisme *m*

organization [ɔːgənaɪ'zeɪʃən] *n*
organisation *f*

organize ['ɔːgənaɪz] *vt* organiser; **organized**
['ɔːgənaɪzd] *adj* (*planned*) organisé(e);

(*efficient*) bien organisé; **organizer** *n*
organisateur(-trice)

orgasm ['ɔːgæzəm] *n* orgasme *m*

orgy ['ɔːdʒɪ] *n* orgie *f*

oriental [ɔːrɪ'ɛntl] *adj* oriental(e)

orientation [ɔːrɪen'teɪʃən] *n* (*attitudes*)
tendance *f*; (*in job*) orientation *f*; (*of building*)
orientation, exposition *f*

origin ['ɔrɪdʒɪn] *n* origine *f*

original [ə'rɪdʒɪnl] *adj* original(e); (*earliest*)
originel(le) ▷ *n* original *m*; **originally** *adv* (*at
first*) à l'origine

originate [ə'rɪdʒɪneɪt] *vi*: **to ~ from** être
originaire de; (*suggestion*) provenir de; **to ~ in**
(*custom*) prendre naissance dans, avoir son
origine dans

Orkney ['ɔːknɪ] *n* (*also*: **the ~s, the ~ Islands**)
les Orcades *fpl*

ornament ['ɔːnəmənt] *n* ornement *m*;
(*trinket*) bibelot *m*; **ornamental** [ɔːnə'mɛntl]
adj décoratif(-ive); (*garden*) d'agrément

ornate [ɔː'neɪt] *adj* très orné(e)

orphan ['ɔːfn] *n* orphelin(e)

orthodox ['ɔːθədɔks] *adj* orthodoxe

orthopaedic (*us* **orthopedic**) [ɔːθə'piːdɪk]
adj orthopédique

osteopath ['ɔstɪəpæθ] *n* ostéopathe *m/f*

ostrich ['ɔstrɪtʃ] *n* autruche *f*

other ['ʌðəʳ] *adj* autre ▷ *pron*: **the ~ (one)**
l'autre; **~s** (*other people*) d'autres ▷ *adv*: **~ than**
autrement que; à part; **the ~ day** l'autre jour;
otherwise *adv, conj* autrement

Ottawa ['ɔtəwə] *n* Ottawa

otter ['ɔtəʳ] *n* loutre *f*

ouch [autʃ] *excl* aïe!

ought (*pt* **~**) [ɔːt] *aux vb*: **I ~ to do it** je devrais le
faire, il faudrait que je le fasse; **this ~ to have
been corrected** cela aurait dû être corrigé; **he
~ to win** (*probability*) il devrait gagner

ounce [auns] *n* once *f* (28.35*g*; 16 *in a pound*)

our ['auəʳ] *adj* notre, nos *pl*; *see also* **my**; **ours**
pron le (la) nôtre, les nôtres; *see also* **mine**[1];
ourselves *pron pl* (*reflexive, after preposition*)
nous; (*emphatic*) nous-mêmes; *see also* **oneself**

oust [aust] *vt* évincer

out [aut] *adv* dehors; (*published, not at home etc*)
sorti(e); (*light, fire*) éteint(e); **~ there** là-bas;
he's ~ (*absent*) il est sorti; **to be ~ in one's
calculations** s'être trompé dans ses calculs;
to run/back *etc* **~** sortir en courant/en
reculant *etc*; **~ loud** *adv* à haute voix; **~ of**
prep (*outside*) en dehors de; (*because of: anger
etc*) par; (*from among*): **10 ~ of 10** 10 sur 10;
(*without*): **~ of petrol** sans essence, à court
d'essence; **~ of order** (*machine*) en panne; (*Tel:
line*) en dérangement; **outback** *n* (*in Australia*)
intérieur *m*; **outbound** *adj*: **outbound
(from/for)** en partance (de/pour); **outbreak**
n (*of violence*) éruption *f*, explosion *f*; (*of disease*)

de nombreux cas; **the outbreak of war south of the border** la guerre qui s'est déclarée au sud de la frontière; **outburst** n explosion f, accès m; **outcast** n exilé(e); (socially) paria m; **outcome** n issue f, résultat m; **outcry** n tollé (général); **outdated** adj démodé(e); **outdoor** adj de or en plein air; **outdoors** adv dehors; au grand air

outer ['autə'] adj extérieur(e); **outer space** n espace m cosmique

outfit ['autfɪt] n (clothes) tenue f

out: outgoing adj (president, tenant) sortant(e); (character) ouvert(e), extraverti(e); **outgoings** npl (BRIT: expenses) dépenses fpl; **outhouse** n appentis m, remise f

outing ['autɪŋ] n sortie f, excursion f

out: outlaw n hors-la-loi m inv ▷ vt (person) mettre hors la loi; (practice) proscrire; **outlay** n dépenses fpl; (investment) mise f de fonds; **outlet** n (for liquid etc) issue f, sortie f; (for emotion) exutoire m; (also: **retail outlet**) point m de vente; (US: Elec) prise f de courant; **outline** n (shape) contour m; (summary) esquisse f, grandes lignes ▷ vt (fig: theory, plan) exposer à grands traits; **outlook** n perspective f; (point of view) attitude f; **outnumber** vt surpasser en nombre; **out-of-date** adj (passport, ticket) périmé(e); (theory, idea) dépassé(e); (custom) désuet(-ète); (clothes) démodé(e); **out-of-doors** adv = **outdoors**; **out-of-the-way** adj loin de tout; **out-of-town** adj (shopping centre etc) en périphérie; **outpatient** n malade m/f en consultation externe; **outpost** n avant-poste m; **output** n rendement m, production f; (Comput) sortie f ▷ vt (Comput) sortir

outrage ['autreɪdʒ] n (anger) indignation f; (violent act) atrocité f, acte m de violence; (scandal) scandale m ▷ vt outrager; **outrageous** [aut'reɪdʒəs] adj atroce; (scandalous) scandaleux(-euse)

outright adv [aut'raɪt] complètement; (deny, refuse) catégoriquement; (ask) carrément; (kill) sur le coup ▷ adj ['autraɪt] complet(-ète); catégorique

outset ['autsɛt] n début m

outside [aut'saɪd] n extérieur m ▷ adj extérieur(e) ▷ adv (au) dehors, à l'extérieur ▷ prep hors de, à l'extérieur de; (in front of) devant; **at the ~** (fig) au plus or maximum; **outside lane** n (Aut: in Britain) voie f de droite; (: in US, Europe) voie de gauche; **outside line** n (Tel) ligne extérieure; **outsider** n (stranger) étranger(-ère)

out: outsize adj énorme; (clothes) grande taille inv; **outskirts** npl faubourgs mpl; **outspoken** adj très franc (franche); **outstanding** adj remarquable, exceptionnel(le); (unfinished: work, business)

en suspens, en souffrance; (debt) impayé(e); (problem) non réglé(e)

outward ['autwəd] adj (sign, appearances) extérieur(e); (journey) (d')aller; **outwards** adv (esp BRIT) = **outward**

outweigh [aut'weɪ] vt l'emporter sur

oval ['əuvl] adj, n ovale m

ovary ['əuvəri] n ovaire m

oven ['ʌvn] n four m; **oven glove** n gant m de cuisine; **ovenproof** adj allant au four; **oven-ready** adj prêt(e) à cuire

over ['əuvə'] adv (par-)dessus ▷ adj (or adv) (finished) fini(e), terminé(e); (too much) en plus ▷ prep sur; par-dessus; (above) au-dessus de; (on the other side of) de l'autre côté de; (more than) plus de; (during) pendant; (about, concerning): **they fell out ~ money/her** ils se sont brouillés pour des questions d'argent/à cause d'elle; **~ here** ici; **~ there** là-bas; **all ~** (everywhere) partout; **~ and ~ (again)** à plusieurs reprises; **~ and above** en plus de; **to ask sb ~** inviter qn (à passer); **to fall ~** tomber; **to turn sth ~** retourner qch

overall ['əuvərɔːl] adj (length) total(e); (study, impression) d'ensemble ▷ n (BRIT) blouse f ▷ adv [əuvər'ɔːl] dans l'ensemble, en général; **overalls** npl (boiler suit) bleus mpl (de travail)

overboard ['əuvəbɔːd] adv (Naut) par-dessus bord

overcame [əuvə'keɪm] pt of **overcome**

overcast ['əuvəkɑːst] adj couvert(e)

overcharge [əuvə'tʃɑːdʒ] vt: **to ~ sb for sth** faire payer qch trop cher à qn

overcoat ['əuvəkəut] n pardessus m

overcome [əuvə'kʌm] vt (irreg: like **come**) (defeat) triompher de; (difficulty) surmonter ▷ adj (emotionally) bouleversé(e); **~ with grief** accablé(e) de douleur

over: overcrowded adj bondé(e); (city, country) surpeuplé(e); **overdo** vt (irreg: like **do**) exagérer; (overcook) trop cuire; **to overdo it, to overdo things** (work too hard) en faire trop, se surmener; **overdone** [əuvə'dʌn] adj (vegetables, steak) trop cuit(e); **overdose** n dose excessive; **overdraft** n découvert m; **overdrawn** adj (account) à découvert; **overdue** adj en retard; (bill) impayé(e); (change) qui tarde; **overestimate** vt surestimer

overflow vi [əuvə'fləu] déborder ▷ n ['əuvəfləu] (also: **~ pipe**) tuyau m d'écoulement, trop-plein m

overgrown [əuvə'grəun] adj (garden) envahi(e) par la végétation

overhaul vt [əuvə'hɔːl] réviser ▷ n ['əuvəhɔːl] révision f

overhead adv [əuvə'hɛd] au-dessus ▷ adj, n ['əuvəhɛd] ▷ adj aérien(ne); (lighting) vertical(e) ▷ n (US) = **overheads**; **overhead**

projector n rétroprojecteur m; **overheads** npl (BRIT) frais généraux

over: **overhear** vt (irreg: like **hear**) entendre (par hasard); **overheat** vi (engine) chauffer; **overland** adj, adv par voie de terre; **overlap** vi se chevaucher; **overleaf** adv au verso; **overload** vt surcharger; **overlook** vt (have view of) donner sur; (miss) oublier, négliger; (forgive) fermer les yeux sur

overnight adv [əuvə'naɪt] (happen) durant la nuit; (fig) soudain ▷ adj ['əuvənaɪt] d'une (or de) nuit; soudain(e); **to stay ~ (with sb)** passer la nuit (chez qn); **overnight bag** n nécessaire m de voyage

overpass ['əuvəpɑːs] n (US: for cars) pont autoroutier; (: for pedestrians) passerelle f, pont m

overpower [əuvə'pauər] vt vaincre; (fig) accabler; **overpowering** adj irrésistible; (heat, stench) suffocant(e)

over: **overreact** [əuvəriː'ækt] vi réagir de façon excessive; **overrule** vt (decision) annuler; (claim) rejeter; (person) rejeter l'avis de; **overrun** vt (irreg: like **run**) (Mil: country etc) occuper; (time limit etc) dépasser ▷ vi dépasser le temps imparti

overseas [əuvə'siːz] adv outre-mer; (abroad) à l'étranger ▷ adj (trade) extérieur(e); (visitor) étranger(-ère)

oversee [əuvə'siː] vt (irreg: like **see**) surveiller

overshadow [əuvə'ʃædəu] vt (fig) éclipser

oversight ['əuvəsaɪt] n omission f, oubli m

oversleep [əuvə'sliːp] vi (irreg: like **sleep**) se réveiller (trop) tard

overspend [əuvə'spɛnd] vi (irreg: like **spend**) dépenser de trop

overt [əu'vəːt] adj non dissimulé(e)

overtake [əuvə'teɪk] vt (irreg: like **take**) dépasser; (BRIT: Aut) dépasser, doubler

over: **overthrow** vt (irreg: like **throw**) (government) renverser; **overtime** n heures fpl supplémentaires

overtook [əuvə'tuk] pt of **overtake**

over: **overturn** vt renverser; (decision, plan) annuler ▷ vi se retourner; **overweight** adj (person) trop gros(se); **overwhelm** vt (subj: emotion) accabler, submerger; (enemy, opponent) écraser; **overwhelming** adj (victory, defeat) écrasant(e); (desire) irrésistible

ow [au] excl aïe!

owe [əu] vt devoir; **to ~ sb sth, to ~ sth to sb** devoir qch à qn; **how much do I ~ you?** combien est-ce que je vous dois?; **owing to** prep à cause de, en raison de

owl [aul] n hibou m

own [əun] vt posséder ▷ adj propre; **a room of my ~** une chambre à moi, ma propre chambre; **to get one's ~ back** prendre sa revanche; **on one's ~** tout(e) seul(e); **own up** vi avouer;

owner n propriétaire m/f; **ownership** n possession f

ox (pl **oxen**) [ɔks, 'ɔksn] n bœuf m

Oxbridge ['ɔksbrɪdʒ] n (BRIT) les universités d'Oxford et de Cambridge

oxen ['ɔksən] npl of **ox**

oxygen ['ɔksɪdʒən] n oxygène m

oyster ['ɔɪstər] n huître f

oz. abbr = **ounce(s)**

ozone ['əuzəun] n ozone m; **ozone friendly** adj qui n'attaque pas or qui préserve la couche d'ozone; **ozone layer** n couche f d'ozone

o

p *abbr* (*BRIT*) = **penny; pence**

P.A. *n abbr* = **personal assistant; public address system**

p.a. *abbr* = **per annum**

pace [peɪs] *n* pas *m*; (*speed*) allure *f*; vitesse *f* ▷ *vi*: **to ~ up and down** faire les cent pas; **to keep ~ with** aller à la même vitesse que; (*events*) se tenir au courant de; **pacemaker** *n* (*Med*) stimulateur *m* cardiaque; (*Sport: also*: **pacesetter**) meneur(-euse) de train

Pacific [pəˈsɪfɪk] *n*: **the ~ (Ocean)** le Pacifique, l'océan *m* Pacifique

pacifier [ˈpæsɪfaɪəʳ] *n* (*US: dummy*) tétine *f*

pack [pæk] *n* paquet *m*; (*of hounds*) meute *f*; (*of thieves, wolves etc*) bande *f*; (*of cards*) jeu *m*; (*US: of cigarettes*) paquet; (*back pack*) sac *m* à dos ▷ *vt* (*goods*) empaqueter, emballer; (*in suitcase etc*) emballer; (*box*) remplir; (*cram*) entasser ▷ *vi*: **to ~ (one's bags)** faire ses bagages; **pack in** (*BRIT inf*) ▷ *vi* (*machine*) tomber en panne ▷ *vt* (*boyfriend*) plaquer; **~ it in!** laisse tomber!; **pack off** *vt*: **to ~ sb off to** expédier qn à; **pack up** *vi* (*BRIT inf: machine*) tomber en panne; (: *person*) se tirer ▷ *vt* (*belongings*) ranger; (*goods, presents*) empaqueter, emballer

package [ˈpækɪdʒ] *n* paquet *m*; (*also*: **~ deal**: *agreement*) marché global; (: *purchase*) forfait *m*; (*Comput*) progiciel *m* ▷ *vt* (*goods*) conditionner; **package holiday** *n* (*BRIT*) vacances organisées; **package tour** *n* voyage organisé

packaging [ˈpækɪdʒɪŋ] *n* (*wrapping materials*) emballage *m*

packed [pækt] *adj* (*crowded*) bondé(e); **packed lunch** (*BRIT*) *n* repas froid

packet [ˈpækɪt] *n* paquet *m*

packing [ˈpækɪŋ] *n* emballage *m*

pact [pækt] *n* pacte *m*, traité *m*

pad [pæd] *n* bloc(-notes *m*) *m*; (*to prevent friction*) tampon *m* ▷ *vt* rembourrer; **padded** *adj* (*jacket*) matelassé(e); (*bra*) rembourré(e)

paddle [ˈpædl] *n* (*oar*) pagaie *f*; (*US: for table tennis*) raquette *f* de ping-pong ▷ *vi* (*with feet*) barboter, faire trempette ▷ *vt*: **to ~ a canoe** *etc* pagayer; **paddling pool** *n* petit bassin

paddock [ˈpædək] *n* enclos *m*; (*Racing*) paddock *m*

padlock [ˈpædlɔk] *n* cadenas *m*

paedophile (*US* **pedophile**) [ˈpiːdəʊfaɪl] *n* pédophile *m*

page [peɪdʒ] *n* (*of book*) page *f*; (*also*: **~ boy**) groom *m*, chasseur *m*; (*at wedding*) garçon *m* d'honneur ▷ *vt* (*in hotel etc*) (faire) appeler

pager [ˈpeɪdʒəʳ] *n* bip *m* (*inf*), Alphapage® *m*

paid [peɪd] *pt, pp of* **pay** ▷ *adj* (*work, official*) rémunéré(e); (*holiday*) payé(e); **to put ~ to** (*BRIT*) mettre fin à, mettre par terre

pain [peɪn] *n* douleur *f*; (*inf: nuisance*) plaie *f*; **to be in ~** souffrir, avoir mal; **to take ~s to do** se donner du mal pour faire; **painful** *adj* douloureux(-euse); (*difficult*) difficile, pénible; **painkiller** *n* calmant *m*, analgésique *m*; **painstaking** [ˈpeɪnzteɪkɪŋ] *adj* (*person*) soigneux(-euse); (*work*) soigné(e)

paint [peɪnt] *n* peinture *f* ▷ *vt* peindre; **to ~ the door blue** peindre la porte en bleu; **paintbrush** *n* pinceau *m*; **painter** *n* peintre *m*; **painting** *n* peinture *f*; (*picture*) tableau *m*

pair [pɛəʳ] *n* (*of shoes, gloves etc*) paire *f*; (*of people*) couple *m*; **~ of scissors** (paire de) ciseaux *mpl*; **~ of trousers** pantalon *m*

pajamas [pəˈdʒɑːməz] *npl* (*US*) pyjama(s) *m(pl)*

Pakistan [pɑːkɪˈstɑːn] *n* Pakistan *m*; **Pakistani** *adj* pakistanais(e) ▷ *n* Pakistanais(e)

pal [pæl] *n* (*inf*) copain (copine)

palace [ˈpæləs] *n* palais *m*

pale [peɪl] *adj* pâle; **~ blue** *adj* bleu pâle *inv*

Palestine [ˈpælɪstaɪn] *n* Palestine *f*; **Palestinian** [pælɪsˈtɪnɪən] *adj* palestinien(ne) ▷ *n* Palestinien(ne)

palm [pɑːm] *n* (*Anat*) paume *f*; (*also*: **~ tree**) palmier *m* ▷ *vt*: **to ~ sth off on sb** (*inf*) refiler qch à qn

pamper [ˈpæmpəʳ] *vt* gâter, dorloter

pamphlet [ˈpæmflət] *n* brochure *f*

pan [pæn] *n* (*also*: **sauce~**) casserole *f*; (*also*:

frying ~) poêle *f*

pancake ['pænkeɪk] *n* crêpe *f*

panda ['pændə] *n* panda *m*

pane [peɪn] *n* carreau *m* (de fenêtre), vitre *f*

panel ['pænl] *n* (*of wood, cloth etc*) panneau *m*; (*Radio, TV*) panel *m*, invités *mpl*; (*for interview, exams*) jury *m*

panhandler ['pænhændlə^r] *n* (*US inf*) mendiant(e)

panic ['pænɪk] *n* panique *f*, affolement *m* ▷ *vi* s'affoler, paniquer

panorama [pænə'rɑːmə] *n* panorama *m*

pansy ['pænzɪ] *n* (*Bot*) pensée *f*

pant [pænt] *vi* haleter

panther ['pænθə^r] *n* panthère *f*

panties ['pæntɪz] *npl* slip *m*, culotte *f*

pantomime ['pæntəmaɪm] *n* (*BRIT*) spectacle *m* de Noël; *voir encadré*

⬤ **PANTOMIME**
⬤
⬤
⬤ Une **pantomime** (à ne pas confondre
⬤ avec le mot tel qu'on l'utilise en français),
⬤ que l'on appelle également de façon
⬤ familière "panto", est un genre de farce où
⬤ le personnage principal est souvent un
⬤ jeune garçon et où il y a toujours une "dame",
⬤ c'est-à-dire une vieille femme jouée par
⬤ un homme, et un méchant. La plupart du
⬤ temps, l'histoire est basée sur un conte de
⬤ fées comme Cendrillon ou Le Chat botté,
⬤ et le public est encouragé à participer en
⬤ prévenant le héros d'un danger imminent.
⬤ Ce genre de spectacle, qui s'adresse
⬤ surtout aux enfants, vise également un
⬤ public d'adultes au travers des nombreuses
⬤ plaisanteries faisant allusion à des faits
⬤ d'actualité.

pants [pænts] *n* (*BRIT: woman's*) culotte *f*, slip *m*; (: *man's*) slip *m*, caleçon *m*; (*US: trousers*) pantalon *m*

pantyhose ['pæntɪhəuz] (*US*) *npl* collant *m*

paper ['peɪpə^r] *n* papier *m*; (*also:* **wall~**) papier peint; (*also:* **news~**) journal *m*; (*academic essay*) article *m*; (*exam*) épreuve écrite ▷ *adj* en or de papier ▷ *vt* tapisser (de papier peint); **papers** *npl* (*also:* **identity ~s**) papiers *mpl* (d'identité); **paperback** *n* livre broché *or* non relié; (*small*) livre *m* de poche; **paper bag** *n* sac *m* en papier; **paper clip** *n* trombone *m*; **paper shop** *n* (*BRIT*) marchand *m* de journaux; **paperwork** *n* papiers *mpl*; (*pej*) paperasserie *f*

paprika ['pæprɪkə] *n* paprika *m*

par [pɑː^r] *n* pair *m*; (*Golf*) normale *f* du parcours; **on a ~ with** à égalité avec, au même niveau que

paracetamol [pærə'siːtəmɔl] (*BRIT*) *n* paracétamol *m*

parachute ['pærəʃuːt] *n* parachute *m*

parade [pə'reɪd] *n* défilé *m* ▷ *vt* (*fig*) faire étalage de ▷ *vi* défiler

paradise ['pærədaɪs] *n* paradis *m*

paradox ['pærədɔks] *n* paradoxe *m*

paraffin ['pærəfɪn] *n* (*BRIT*): **~ (oil)** pétrole (lampant)

paragraph ['pærəgrɑːf] *n* paragraphe *m*

parallel ['pærəlɛl] *adj*: **~ (with *or* to)** parallèle (à); (*fig*) analogue (à) ▷ *n* (*line*) parallèle *f*; (*fig, Geo*) parallèle *m*

paralysed ['pærəlaɪzd] *adj* paralysé(e)

paralysis (*pl* **paralyses**) [pə'rælɪsɪs, -siːz] *n* paralysie *f*

paramedic [pærə'mɛdɪk] *n* auxiliaire *m/f* médical(e)

paranoid ['pærənɔɪd] *adj* (*Psych*) paranoïaque; (*neurotic*) paranoïde

parasite ['pærəsaɪt] *n* parasite *m*

parcel ['pɑːsl] *n* paquet *m*, colis *m* ▷ *vt* (*also:* **~ up**) empaqueter

pardon ['pɑːdn] *n* pardon *m*; (*Law*) grâce *f* ▷ *vt* pardonner à; (*Law*) gracier; **~!** pardon!; **~ me!** (*after burping etc*) excusez-moi!; **I beg your ~!** (*I'm sorry*) pardon!, je suis désolé!; (**I beg your**) **~?**, (*US*) **~ me?** (*what did you say?*) pardon?

parent ['pɛərənt] *n* (*father*) père *m*; (*mother*) mère *f*; **parents** *npl* parents *mpl*; **parental** [pə'rɛntl] *adj* parental(e), des parents

Paris ['pærɪs] *n* Paris

parish ['pærɪʃ] *n* paroisse *f*; (*BRIT: civil*) ≈ commune *f*

Parisian [pə'rɪzɪən] *adj* parisien(ne), de Paris ▷ *n* Parisien(ne)

park [pɑːk] *n* parc *m*, jardin public ▷ *vt* garer ▷ *vi* se garer; **can I ~ here?** est-ce que je peux me garer ici?

parking ['pɑːkɪŋ] *n* stationnement *m*; **"no ~"** "stationnement interdit"; **parking lot** *n* (*US*) parking *m*, parc *m* de stationnement; **parking meter** *n* parc(o)mètre *m*; **parking ticket** *n* P.-V. *m*

⬤ Be careful not to translate *parking* by the French word *parking*.

parkway ['pɑːkweɪ] *n* (*US*) route *f* express (*en site vert ou aménagé*)

parliament ['pɑːləmənt] *n* parlement *m*; **parliamentary** [pɑːlə'mɛntərɪ] *adj* parlementaire

Parmesan [pɑːmɪ'zæn] *n* (*also:* **~ cheese**) Parmesan *m*

parole [pə'rəul] *n*: **on ~** en liberté conditionnelle

parrot ['pærət] *n* perroquet *m*

parsley ['pɑːslɪ] *n* persil *m*

parsnip ['pɑːsnɪp] *n* panais *m*

parson ['pɑːsn] *n* ecclésiastique *m*; (*Church of England*) pasteur *m*

part [pɑːt] *n* partie *f*; (*of machine*) pièce *f*; (*Theat*

p

etc) rôle *m*; (*of serial*) épisode *m*; (*us: in hair*) raie *f* ▷ *adv* = **partly** ▷ *vt* séparer ▷ *vi* (*people*) se séparer; (*crowd*) s'ouvrir; **to take ~ in** participer à, prendre part à; **to take sb's ~** prendre le parti de qn, prendre parti pour qn; **for my ~** en ce qui me concerne; **for the most ~** en grande partie; dans la plupart des cas; **in ~** en partie; **to take sth in good/bad ~** prendre qch du bon/mauvais côté; **part with** *vt fus* (*person*) se séparer de; (*possessions*) se défaire de

partial ['pɑ:ʃl] *adj* (*incomplete*) partiel(le); **to be ~ to** aimer, avoir un faible pour

participant [pɑ:'tɪsɪpənt] *n* (*in competition, campaign*) participant(e)

participate [pɑ:'tɪsɪpeɪt] *vi*: **to ~ (in)** participer (à), prendre part (à)

particle ['pɑ:tɪkl] *n* particule *f*; (*of dust*) grain *m*

particular [pə'tɪkjulər] *adj* (*specific*) particulier(-ière); (*special*) particulier, spécial(e); (*fussy*) difficile, exigeant(e); (*careful*) méticuleux(-euse); **in ~** en particulier, surtout; **particularly** *adv* particulièrement; (*in particular*) en particulier; **particulars** *npl* détails *mpl*; (*information*) renseignements *mpl*

parting ['pɑ:tɪŋ] *n* séparation *f*; (BRIT: *in hair*) raie *f*

partition [pɑ:'tɪʃən] *n* (*Pol*) partition *f*, division *f*; (*wall*) cloison *f*

partly ['pɑ:tlɪ] *adv* en partie, partiellement

partner ['pɑ:tnər] *n* (*Comm*) associé(e); (*Sport*) partenaire *m/f*; (*spouse*) conjoint(e); (*lover*) ami(e); (*at dance*) cavalier(-ière); **partnership** *n* association *f*

part of speech *n* (*Ling*) partie *f* du discours

partridge ['pɑ:trɪdʒ] *n* perdrix *f*

part-time ['pɑ:t'taɪm] *adj, adv* à mi-temps, à temps partiel

party ['pɑ:tɪ] *n* (*Pol*) parti *m*; (*celebration*) fête *f*; (: *formal*) réception *f*; (: *in evening*) soirée *f*; (*group*) groupe *m*; (*Law*) partie *f*

pass [pɑ:s] *vt* (*time, object*) passer; (*place*) passer devant; (*friend*) croiser; (*exam*) être reçu(e) à, réussir; (*overtake*) dépasser; (*approve*) approuver, accepter ▷ *vi* passer; (*Scol*) être reçu(e) *or* admis(e), réussir ▷ *n* (*permit*) laissez-passer *m inv*; (*membership card*) carte *f* d'accès *or* d'abonnement; (*in mountains*) col *m*; (*Sport*) passe *f*; (*Scol*: *also*: **~ mark**): **to get a ~** être reçu(e) (sans mention); **to ~ sb sth** passer qch à qn; **could you ~ the salt/oil, please?** pouvez-vous me passer le sel/l'huile, s'il vous plaît?; **to make a ~ at sb** (*inf*) faire des avances à qn; **pass away** *vi* mourir; **pass by** *vi* passer ▷ *vt* (*ignore*) négliger; **pass on** *vt* (*hand on*): **to ~ on (to)** transmettre (à); **pass out** *vi* s'évanouir; **pass over** *vt* (*ignore*) passer sous silence; **pass up** *vt* (*opportunity*) laisser passer; **passable** *adj*

(*road*) praticable; (*work*) acceptable

> Be careful not to translate *to pass an exam* by the French expression *passer un examen*.

passage ['pæsɪdʒ] *n* (*also*: **~way**) couloir *m*; (*gen, in book*) passage *m*; (*by boat*) traversée *f*

passenger ['pæsɪndʒər] *n* passager(-ère)

passer-by [pɑ:sə'baɪ] *n* passant(e)

passing place *n* (*Aut*) aire *f* de croisement

passion ['pæʃən] *n* passion *f*; **passionate** *adj* passionné(e); **passion fruit** *n* fruit *m* de la passion

passive ['pæsɪv] *adj* (*also* Ling) passif(-ive)

passport ['pɑ:spɔ:t] *n* passeport *m*; **passport control** *n* contrôle *m* des passeports; **passport office** *n* bureau *m* de délivrance des passeports

password ['pɑ:swə:d] *n* mot *m* de passe

past [pɑ:st] *prep* (*in front of*) devant; (*further than*) au delà de, plus loin que; après; (*later than*) après ▷ *adv*: **to run ~** passer en courant ▷ *adj* passé(e); (*president etc*) ancien(ne) ▷ *n* passé *m*; **he's ~ forty** il a dépassé la quarantaine, il a plus de *or* passé quarante ans; **ten/quarter ~ eight** huit heures dix/un *or* et quart; **for the ~ few/3 days** depuis quelques/3 jours; ces derniers/3 derniers jours

pasta ['pæstə] *n* pâtes *fpl*

paste [peɪst] *n* pâte *f*; (*Culin: meat*) pâté *m* (à tartiner); (: *tomato*) purée *f*, concentré *m*; (*glue*) colle *f* (de pâte) ▷ *vt* coller

pastel ['pæstl] *adj* pastel *inv* ▷ *n* (*Art: pencil*) (crayon *m*) pastel *m*; (: *drawing*) (dessin *m* au) pastel; (*colour*) ton *m* pastel *inv*

pasteurized ['pæstəraɪzd] *adj* pasteurisé(e)

pastime ['pɑ:staɪm] *n* passe-temps *m inv*, distraction *f*

pastor ['pɑ:stər] *n* pasteur *m*

past participle [-'pɑ:tɪsɪpl] *n* (*Ling*) participe passé

pastry ['peɪstrɪ] *n* pâte *f*; (*cake*) pâtisserie *f*

pasture ['pɑ:stʃər] *n* pâturage *m*

pasty¹ ['pæstɪ] petit pâté (en croûte)

pasty² ['peɪstɪ] *adj* (*complexion*) terreux(-euse)

pat [pæt] *vt* donner une petite tape à; (*dog*) caresser

patch [pætʃ] *n* (*of material*) pièce *f*; (*eye patch*) cache *m*; (*spot*) tache *f*; (*of land*) parcelle *f*; (*on tyre*) rustine *f* ▷ *vt* (*clothes*) rapiécer; **a bad ~** (BRIT) une période difficile; **patchy** *adj* inégal(e); (*incomplete*) fragmentaire

pâté ['pæteɪ] *n* pâté *m*, terrine *f*

patent ['peɪtnt, *us* 'pætnt] *n* brevet *m* (d'invention) ▷ *vt* faire breveter ▷ *adj* patent(e), manifeste

paternal [pə'tə:nl] *adj* paternel(le)

paternity leave [pə'tə:nɪtɪ-] *n* congé *m* de paternité

path [pɑ:θ] *n* chemin *m*, sentier *m*; (*in garden*)

allée f; (of missile) trajectoire f

pathetic [pəˈθɛtɪk] adj (pitiful) pitoyable; (very bad) lamentable, minable

pathway [ˈpɑːθweɪ] n chemin m, sentier m; (in garden) allée f

patience [ˈpeɪʃns] n patience f; (BRIT: Cards) réussite f

patient [ˈpeɪʃnt] n malade m/f; (of dentist etc) patient(e) ▷ adj patient(e)

patio [ˈpætɪəu] n patio m

patriotic [pætrɪˈɔtɪk] adj patriotique; (person) patriote

patrol [pəˈtrəul] n patrouille f ▷ vt patrouiller dans; **patrol car** n voiture f de police

patron [ˈpeɪtrən] n (in shop) client(e); (of charity) patron(ne); **~ of the arts** mécène m

patronizing [ˈpætrənaɪzɪŋ] adj condescendant(e)

pattern [ˈpætən] n (Sewing) patron m; (design) motif m; **patterned** adj à motifs

pause [pɔːz] n pause f, arrêt m ▷ vi faire une pause, s'arrêter

pave [peɪv] vt paver, daller; **to ~ the way for** ouvrir la voie à

pavement [ˈpeɪvmənt] n (BRIT) trottoir m; (US) chaussée f

pavilion [pəˈvɪlɪən] n pavillon m; (Sport) stand m

paving [ˈpeɪvɪŋ] n (material) pavé m, dalle f

paw [pɔː] n patte f

pawn [pɔːn] n (Chess, also fig) pion m ▷ vt mettre en gage; **pawnbroker** n prêteur m sur gages

pay [peɪ] n salaire m; (of manual worker) paie f ▷ vb (pt, pp **paid**) ▷ vt payer ▷ vi payer; (be profitable) être rentable; **can I ~ by credit card?** est-ce que je peux payer par carte de crédit?; **to ~ attention (to)** prêter attention (à); **to ~ sb a visit** rendre visite à qn; **to ~ one's respects to sb** présenter ses respects à qn; **pay back** vt rembourser; **pay for** vt fus payer; **pay in** vt verser; **pay off** vt (debts) régler, acquitter; (person) rembourser ▷ vi (scheme, decision) se révéler payant(e); **pay out** vt (money) payer, sortir de sa poche; **pay up** vt (amount) payer; **payable** adj payable; **to make a cheque payable to sb** établir un chèque à l'ordre de qn; **pay day** n jour m de paie; **pay envelope** n (US) paie f; **payment** n paiement m; (of bill) règlement m; (of deposit, cheque) versement m; **monthly payment** mensualité f; **payout** n (from insurance) dédommagement m; (in competition) prix m; **pay packet** n (BRIT) paie f; **pay phone** n cabine f téléphonique, téléphone public; **pay raise** n (US) = **pay rise**; **pay rise** n (BRIT) augmentation f (de salaire); **payroll** n registre m du personnel; **pay slip** n (BRIT) bulletin m de paie, feuille f de paie; **pay television** n

chaînes fpl payantes

PC n abbr = **personal computer**; (BRIT) = **police constable** ▷ adj abbr = **politically correct**

p.c. abbr = **per cent**

PDA n abbr (= personal digital assistant) agenda m électronique

PE n abbr (= physical education) EPS f

pea [piː] n (petit) pois

peace [piːs] n paix f; (calm) calme m, tranquillité f; **peaceful** adj paisible, calme

peach [piːtʃ] n pêche f

peacock [ˈpiːkɔk] n paon m

peak [piːk] n (mountain) pic m, cime f; (of cap) visière f; (fig: highest level) maximum m; (: of career, fame) apogée m; **peak hours** npl heures fpl d'affluence or de pointe

peanut [ˈpiːnʌt] n arachide f, cacahuète f; **peanut butter** n beurre m de cacahuète

pear [pɛər] n poire f

pearl [pəːl] n perle f

peasant [ˈpɛznt] n paysan(ne)

peat [piːt] n tourbe f

pebble [ˈpɛbl] n galet m, caillou m

peck [pɛk] vt (also: ~ at) donner un coup de bec à; (food) picorer ▷ n coup m de bec; (kiss) bécot m; **peckish** adj (BRIT inf): **I feel peckish** je mangerais bien quelque chose, j'ai la dent

peculiar [pɪˈkjuːlɪər] adj (odd) étrange, bizarre, curieux(-euse); (particular) particulier(-ière); **~ to** particulier à

pedal [ˈpɛdl] n pédale f ▷ vi pédaler

pedalo [ˈpɛdələu] n pédalo m

pedestal [ˈpɛdəstl] n piédestal m

pedestrian [pɪˈdɛstrɪən] n piéton m; **pedestrian crossing** n (BRIT) passage clouté; **pedestrianized** adj: **a pedestrianized street** une rue piétonne; **pedestrian precinct** (US **pedestrian zone**) n (BRIT) zone piétonne

pedigree [ˈpɛdɪɡriː] n ascendance f; (of animal) pedigree m ▷ cpd (animal) de race

pedophile [ˈpiːdəufaɪl] (US) n = **paedophile**

pee [piː] vi (inf) faire pipi, pisser

peek [piːk] vi jeter un coup d'œil (furtif)

peel [piːl] n pelure f, épluchure f; (of orange, lemon) écorce f ▷ vt peler, éplucher ▷ vi (paint etc) s'écailler; (wallpaper) se décoller; (skin) peler

peep [piːp] n (BRIT: look) coup d'œil furtif; (sound) pépiement m ▷ vi (BRIT) jeter un coup d'œil (furtif)

peer [pɪər] vi: **to ~ at** regarder attentivement, scruter ▷ n (noble) pair m; (equal) pair, égal(e)

peg [pɛɡ] n (for coat etc) patère f; (BRIT: also: **clothes ~**) pince f à linge

pelican [ˈpɛlɪkən] n pélican m; **pelican crossing** n (BRIT Aut) feu m à commande manuelle

pelt [pɛlt] vt: **to ~ sb (with)** bombarder qn (de)

▷ vi (rain) tomber à seaux; (inf: run) courir à toutes jambes ▷ n peau f

pelvis ['pɛlvɪs] n bassin m

pen [pɛn] n (for writing) stylo m; (for sheep) parc m

penalty ['pɛnltɪ] n pénalité f; sanction f; (fine) amende f; (Sport) pénalisation f; (Football) penalty m; (Rugby) pénalité f

pence [pɛns] npl of **penny**

pencil ['pɛnsl] n crayon m; **pencil in** vt noter provisoirement; **pencil case** n trousse f (d'écolier); **pencil sharpener** n taille-crayon(s) m inv

pendant ['pɛndnt] n pendentif m

pending ['pɛndɪŋ] prep en attendant ▷ adj en suspens

penetrate ['pɛnɪtreɪt] vt pénétrer dans; (enemy territory) entrer en

penfriend ['pɛnfrɛnd] n (BRIT) correspondant(e)

penguin ['pɛŋgwɪn] n pingouin m

penicillin [pɛnɪ'sɪlɪn] n pénicilline f

peninsula [pə'nɪnsjulə] n péninsule f

penis ['piːnɪs] n pénis m, verge f

penitentiary [pɛnɪ'tɛnʃərɪ] n (US) prison f

penknife ['pɛnnaɪf] n canif m

penniless ['pɛnɪlɪs] adj sans le sou

penny (pl **pennies** or **pence**) ['pɛnɪ, 'pɛnɪz, pɛns] n (BRIT) penny m; (US) cent m

penpal ['pɛnpæl] n correspondant(e)

pension ['pɛnʃən] n (from company) retraite f; **pensioner** n (BRIT) retraité(e)

pentagon ['pɛntəgən] n: **the P~** (US Pol) le Pentagone

penthouse ['pɛnthaus] n appartement m (de luxe) en attique

penultimate [pɪ'nʌltɪmət] adj pénultième, avant-dernier(-ière)

people ['piːpl] npl gens mpl; personnes fpl; (inhabitants) population f; (Pol) peuple m ▷ n (nation, race) peuple m; **several ~ came** plusieurs personnes sont venues; **~ say that ...** on dit or les gens disent que ...

pepper ['pɛpə'] n poivre m; (vegetable) poivron m ▷ vt (Culin) poivrer; **peppermint** n (sweet) pastille f de menthe

per [pə:'] prep par; **~ hour** (miles etc) à l'heure; (fee) (de) l'heure; **~ kilo** etc le kilo etc; **~ day/person** par jour/personne; **~ annum** per an

perceive [pə'siːv] vt percevoir; (notice) remarquer, s'apercevoir de

per cent adv pour cent

percentage [pə'sɛntɪdʒ] n pourcentage m

perception [pə'sɛpʃən] n perception f; (insight) sensibilité f

perch [pə:tʃ] n (fish) perche f; (for bird) perchoir m ▷ vi (se) percher

percussion [pə'kʌʃən] n percussion f

perennial [pə'rɛnɪəl] n (Bot) (plante f) vivace f,

plante pluriannuelle

perfect ['pə:fɪkt] adj parfait(e) ▷ n (also: **~ tense**) parfait m ▷ vt [pə'fɛkt] (technique, skill, work of art) parfaire; (method, plan) mettre au point; **perfection** [pə'fɛkʃən] n perfection f; **perfectly** ['pə:fɪktlɪ] adv parfaitement

perform [pə'fɔ:m] vt (carry out) exécuter; (concert etc) jouer, donner ▷ vi (actor, musician) jouer; **performance** n représentation f, spectacle m; (of an artist) interprétation f; (Sport: of car, engine) performance f; (of company, economy) résultats mpl; **performer** n artiste m/f

perfume ['pə:fju:m] n parfum m

perhaps [pə'hæps] adv peut-être

perimeter [pə'rɪmɪtə'] n périmètre m

period ['pɪərɪəd] n période f; (History) époque f; (Scol) cours m; (full stop) point m; (Med) règles fpl ▷ adj (costume, furniture) d'époque; **periodical** [pɪərɪ'ɔdɪkl] n périodique m; **periodically** adv périodiquement

perish ['pɛrɪʃ] vi périr, mourir; (decay) se détériorer

perjury ['pə:dʒərɪ] n (Law: in court) faux témoignage; (breach of oath) parjure m

perk [pə:k] n (inf) avantage m, à-côté m

perm [pə:m] n (for hair) permanente f

permanent ['pə:mənənt] adj permanent(e); **permanently** adv de façon permanente; (move abroad) définitivement; (open, closed) en permanence; (tired, unhappy) constamment

permission [pə'mɪʃən] n permission f, autorisation f

permit n ['pə:mɪt] permis m

perplex [pə'plɛks] vt (person) rendre perplexe

persecute ['pə:sɪkju:t] vt persécuter

persecution [pə:sɪ'kju:ʃən] n persécution f

persevere [pə:sɪ'vɪə'] vi persévérer

Persian ['pə:ʃən] adj persan(e); **the ~ Gulf** le golfe Persique

persist [pə'sɪst] vi: **to ~ (in doing)** persister (à faire), s'obstiner (à faire); **persistent** adj persistant(e), tenace

person ['pə:sn] n personne f; **in ~** en personne; **personal** adj personnel(le); **personal assistant** n secrétaire personnel(le); **personal computer** n ordinateur individuel, PC m; **personality** [pə:sə'nælɪtɪ] n personnalité f; **personally** adv personnellement; **to take sth personally** se sentir visé(e) par qch; **personal organizer** n agenda (personnel); (style Filofax®); (electronic) agenda électronique; **personal stereo** n Walkman® m, baladeur m

personnel [pə:sə'nɛl] n personnel m

perspective [pə'spɛktɪv] n perspective f

perspiration [pə:spɪ'reɪʃən] n transpiration f

persuade [pə'sweɪd] vt: **to ~ sb to do sth** persuader qn de faire qch, amener or décider qn à faire qch

persuasion [pə'sweɪʒən] n persuasion f; (creed) conviction f

persuasive [pə'sweɪsɪv] adj persuasif(-ive)

perverse [pə'və:s] adj pervers(e); (contrary) entêté(e), contrariant(e)

pervert n ['pə:və:t] perverti(e) ▷ vt [pə'və:t] pervertir; (words) déformer

pessimism ['pɛsɪmɪzəm] n pessimisme m

pessimist ['pɛsɪmɪst] n pessimiste m/f; **pessimistic** [pɛsɪ'mɪstɪk] adj pessimiste

pest [pɛst] n animal m (or insecte m) nuisible; (fig) fléau m

pester ['pɛstər] vt importuner, harceler

pesticide ['pɛstɪsaɪd] n pesticide m

pet [pɛt] n animal familier ▷ cpd (favourite) favori(e) ▷ vt (stroke) caresser, câliner; **teacher's ~** chouchou m du professeur; **~ hate** bête noire

petal ['pɛtl] n pétale m

petite [pə'ti:t] adj menu(e)

petition [pə'tɪʃən] n pétition f

petrified ['pɛtrɪfaɪd] adj (fig) mort(e) de peur

petrol ['pɛtrəl] n (BRIT) essence f; **I've run out of ~** je suis en panne d'essence

> Be careful not to translate **petrol** by the French word **pétrole**.

petroleum [pə'trəulɪəm] n pétrole m

petrol: **petrol pump** n (BRIT: in car, at garage) pompe f à essence; **petrol station** n (BRIT) station-service f; **petrol tank** n (BRIT) réservoir m d'essence

petticoat ['pɛtɪkəut] n jupon m

petty ['pɛtɪ] adj (mean) mesquin(e); (unimportant) insignifiant(e), sans importance

pew [pju:] n banc m (d'église)

pewter ['pju:tər] n étain m

phantom ['fæntəm] n fantôme m

pharmacist ['fɑ:məsɪst] n pharmacien(ne)

pharmacy ['fɑ:məsɪ] n pharmacie f

phase [feɪz] n phase f, période f; **phase in** vt introduire progressivement; **phase out** vt supprimer progressivement

Ph.D. abbr = **Doctor of Philosophy**

pheasant ['fɛznt] n faisan m

phenomena [fə'nɔmɪnə] npl of **phenomenon**

phenomenal [fɪ'nɔmɪnl] adj phénoménal(e)

phenomenon (pl **phenomena**) [fə'nɔmɪnən, -nə] n phénomène m

Philippines ['fɪlɪpi:nz] npl (also: **Philippine Islands**): **the ~** les Philippines fpl

philosopher [fɪ'lɔsəfər] n philosophe m

philosophical [fɪlə'sɔfɪkl] adj philosophique

philosophy [fɪ'lɔsəfɪ] n philosophie f

phlegm [flɛm] n flegme m

phobia ['fəubjə] n phobie f

phone [fəun] n téléphone m ▷ vt téléphoner à ▷ vi téléphoner; **to be on the ~** avoir le téléphone; (be calling) être au téléphone; **phone back** vt, vi rappeler; **phone up** vt téléphoner à ▷ vi téléphoner; **phone book** n annuaire m; **phone box** (US **phone booth**) n cabine f téléphonique; **phone call** n coup m de fil or de téléphone; **phonecard** n télécarte f; **phone number** n numéro m de téléphone

phonetics [fə'nɛtɪks] n phonétique f

phoney ['fəunɪ] adj faux (fausse), factice; (person) pas franc (franche)

photo ['fəutəu] n photo f; **photo album** n album m de photos; **photocopier** n copieur m; **photocopy** n photocopie f ▷ vt photocopier

photograph ['fəutəgræf] n photographie f ▷ vt photographier; **photographer** [fə'tɔgrəfər] n photographe m/f; **photography** [fə'tɔgrəfɪ] n photographie f

phrase [freɪz] n expression f; (Ling) locution f ▷ vt exprimer; **phrase book** n recueil m d'expressions (pour touristes)

physical ['fɪzɪkl] adj physique; **physical education** n éducation f physique; **physically** adv physiquement

physician [fɪ'zɪʃən] n médecin m

physicist ['fɪzɪsɪst] n physicien(ne)

physics ['fɪzɪks] n physique f

physiotherapist [fɪzɪəu'θɛrəpɪst] n kinésithérapeute m/f

physiotherapy [fɪzɪəu'θɛrəpɪ] n kinésithérapie f

physique [fɪ'zi:k] n (appearance) physique m; (health etc) constitution f

pianist ['pi:ənɪst] n pianiste m/f

piano [pɪ'ænəu] n piano m

pick [pɪk] n (tool: also: **~-axe**) pic m, pioche f ▷ vt choisir; (gather) cueillir; (remove) prendre; (lock) forcer; **~ take your ~** faites votre choix; **the ~ of** le (la) meilleur(e) de; **to ~ one's nose** se mettre les doigts dans le nez; **to ~ one's teeth** se curer les dents; **to ~ a quarrel with sb** chercher noise à qn; **pick on** vt fus (person) harceler; **pick out** vt choisir; (distinguish) distinguer; **pick up** vi (improve) remonter, s'améliorer ▷ vt ramasser; (collect) passer prendre; (Aut: give lift to) prendre; (learn) apprendre; (Radio) capter; **to ~ up speed** prendre de la vitesse; **to ~ o.s. up** se relever

pickle ['pɪkl] n (also: **~s**: as condiment) pickles mpl ▷ vt conserver dans du vinaigre or dans de la saumure; **in a ~** (fig) dans le pétrin

pickpocket ['pɪkpɔkɪt] n pickpocket m

pick-up ['pɪkʌp] n (also: **~ truck**) pick-up m inv

picnic ['pɪknɪk] n pique-nique m ▷ vi pique-niquer; **picnic area** n aire f de pique-nique

picture ['pɪktʃər] n (also TV) image f; (painting) peinture f, tableau m; (photograph) photo(graphie) f; (drawing) dessin m; (film) film m; (fig: description) description f ▷ vt (imagine) se représenter; **pictures** npl: **the ~s** (BRIT) le cinéma; **to take a ~ of sb/sth** prendre qn/qch en photo; **would you take a ~ of us, please?** pourriez-vous nous prendre en photo, s'il vous plaît?; **picture frame** n cadre m; **picture messaging** n picture messaging m, messagerie f d'images

picturesque [pɪktʃə'resk] adj pittoresque

pie [paɪ] n tourte f; (of fruit) tarte f; (of meat) pâté m en croûte

piece [piːs] n morceau m; (item): **a ~ of furniture/advice** un meuble/conseil ▷ vt: **to ~ together** rassembler; **to take to ~s** démonter

pie chart n graphique m à secteurs, camembert m

pier [pɪəʳ] n jetée f

pierce [pɪəs] vt percer, transpercer; **pierced** adj (ears) percé(e)

pig [pɪg] n cochon m, porc m; (pej: unkind person) mufle m; (: greedy person) goinfre m

pigeon ['pɪdʒən] n pigeon m

piggy bank ['pɪgɪ-] n tirelire f

pigsty ['pɪgstaɪ] n porcherie f

pigtail ['pɪgteɪl] n natte f, tresse f

pike [paɪk] n (fish) brochet m

pilchard ['pɪltʃəd] n pilchard m (sorte de sardine)

pile [paɪl] n (pillar, of books) pile f; (heap) tas m; (of carpet) épaisseur f; **pile up** vi (accumulate) s'entasser, s'accumuler ▷ vt (put in heap) empiler, entasser; (accumulate) accumuler; **piles** npl hémorroïdes fpl; **pile-up** n (Aut) télescopage m, collision f en série

pilgrim ['pɪlgrɪm] n pèlerin m

pilgrimage ['pɪlgrɪmɪdʒ] n pèlerinage m

pill [pɪl] n pilule f; **the ~** la pilule

pillar ['pɪləʳ] n pilier m

pillow ['pɪləu] n oreiller m; **pillowcase, pillowslip** n taie f d'oreiller

pilot ['paɪlət] n pilote m ▷ cpd (scheme etc) pilote, expérimental(e) ▷ vt piloter; **pilot light** n veilleuse f

pimple ['pɪmpl] n bouton m

PIN n abbr (= personal identification number) code

m confidentiel

pin [pɪn] n épingle f; (Tech) cheville f ▷ vt épingler; **~s and needles** fourmis fpl; **to ~ sb down** (fig) coincer qn; **to ~ sth on sb** (fig) mettre qch sur le dos de qn

pinafore ['pɪnəfɔːʳ] n tablier m

pinch [pɪntʃ] n pincement m; (of salt etc) pincée f ▷ vt pincer; (inf: steal) piquer, chiper ▷ vi (shoe) serrer; **at a ~** à la rigueur

pine [paɪn] n (also: ~ **tree**) pin m ▷ vi: **to ~ for** aspirer à, désirer ardemment

pineapple ['paɪnæpl] n ananas m

ping [pɪŋ] n (noise) tintement m; **ping-pong®** n ping-pong® m

pink [pɪŋk] adj rose ▷ n (colour) rose m

pinpoint ['pɪnpɔɪnt] vt indiquer (avec précision)

pint [paɪnt] n pinte f (BRIT = 0.57 l; US = 0.47 l); (BRIT inf) ≈ demi m, ≈ pot m

pioneer [paɪə'nɪəʳ] n pionnier m

pious ['paɪəs] adj pieux(-euse)

pip [pɪp] n (seed) pépin m; **pips** npl: **the ~s** (BRIT: time signal on radio) le top

pipe [paɪp] n tuyau m, conduite f; (for smoking) pipe f ▷ vt amener par tuyau; **pipeline** n (for gas) gazoduc m, pipeline m; (for oil) oléoduc m, pipeline; **piper** n (flautist) joueur(-euse) de pipeau; (of bagpipes) joueur(-euse) de cornemuse

pirate ['paɪərət] n pirate m ▷ vt (CD, video, book) pirater

Pisces ['paɪsiːz] n les Poissons mpl

piss [pɪs] vi (inf!) pisser (!); **pissed** (inf!) adj (BRIT: drunk) bourré(e); (US: angry) furieux(-euse)

pistol ['pɪstl] n pistolet m

piston ['pɪstən] n piston m

pit [pɪt] n trou m, fosse f; (also: **coal ~**) puits m de mine; (also: **orchestra ~**) fosse d'orchestre; (US: fruit stone) noyau m ▷ vt: **to ~ o.s. or one's wits against** se mesurer à

pitch [pɪtʃ] n (BRIT Sport) terrain m; (Mus) ton m; (fig: degree) degré m; (tar) poix f ▷ vt (throw) lancer; (tent) dresser ▷ vi (fall): **to ~ into/off** tomber dans/de; **pitch-black** adj noir(e) comme poix

pitfall ['pɪtfɔːl] n piège m

pith [pɪθ] n (of orange etc) intérieur m de l'écorce

pitiful ['pɪtɪful] adj (touching) pitoyable; (contemptible) lamentable

pity ['pɪtɪ] n pitié f ▷ vt plaindre; **what a ~!** quel dommage!

pizza ['piːtsə] n pizza f

placard ['plækɑːd] n affiche f; (in march) pancarte f

place [pleɪs] n endroit m, lieu m; (proper position, job, rank, seat) place f; (home): **at/to his ~** chez lui ▷ vt (position) placer, mettre; (identify) situer; reconnaître; **to take ~** avoir lieu; **to change ~s with sb** changer de place avec qn; **out of ~** (not suitable) déplacé(e), inopportun(e); **in the first ~** d'abord, en premier; **place mat** n set m de table; (in linen etc) napperon m; **placement** n (during studies) stage m

placid ['plæsɪd] adj placide

plague [pleɪg] n (Med) peste f ▷ vt (fig) tourmenter

plaice [pleɪs] n (pl inv) carrelet m

plain [pleɪn] adj (in one colour) uni(e); (clear) clair(e), évident(e); (simple) simple; (not handsome) quelconque, ordinaire ▷ adv franchement, carrément ▷ n plaine f; **plain chocolate** n chocolat m à croquer; **plainly** adv clairement; (frankly) carrément, sans détours

plaintiff ['pleɪntɪf] n plaignant(e)

plait [plæt] n tresse f, natte f

plan [plæn] n plan m; (scheme) projet m ▷ vt (think in advance) projeter; (prepare) organiser ▷ vi faire des projets; **to ~ to do** projeter de faire

plane [pleɪn] n (Aviat) avion m; (also: **~ tree**) platane m; (tool) rabot m; (Art, Math etc) plan m; (fig) niveau m, plan ▷ vt (with tool) raboter

planet ['plænɪt] n planète f

plank [plæŋk] n planche f

planning ['plænɪŋ] n planification f; **family ~** planning familial

plant [plɑːnt] n plante f; (machinery) matériel m; (factory) usine f ▷ vt planter; (bomb) déposer, poser; (microphone, evidence) cacher

plantation [plæn'teɪʃən] n plantation f

plaque [plæk] n plaque f

plaster ['plɑːstəʳ] n plâtre m; (also: **~ of Paris**) plâtre à mouler; (BRIT: also: **sticking ~**) pansement adhésif ▷ vt plâtrer; (cover): **to ~ with** couvrir de; **plaster cast** n (Med) plâtre m; (model, statue) moule m

plastic ['plæstɪk] n plastique m ▷ adj (made of plastic) en plastique; **plastic bag** n sac m en plastique; **plastic surgery** n chirurgie f esthétique

plate [pleɪt] n (dish) assiette f; (sheet of metal, on door: Phot) plaque f; (in book) gravure f; (dental) dentier m

plateau (pl **~s** or **~x**) ['plætəʊ, -z] n plateau m

platform ['plætfɔːm] n (at meeting) tribune f; (stage) estrade f; (Rail) quai m; (Pol) plateforme f

platinum ['plætɪnəm] n platine m

platoon [plə'tuːn] n peloton m

platter ['plætəʳ] n plat m

plausible ['plɔːzɪbl] adj plausible; (person) convaincant(e)

play [pleɪ] n jeu m; (Theat) pièce f (de théâtre) ▷ vt (game) jouer à; (team, opponent) jouer contre; (instrument) jouer de; (part, piece of music, note) jouer; (CD etc) passer ▷ vi jouer; **to ~ safe** ne prendre aucun risque; **play back** vt repasser, réécouter; **play up** vi (cause trouble) faire des siennes; **player** n joueur(-euse); (Mus) musicien(ne); **playful** adj enjoué(e); **playground** n cour f de récréation; (in park) aire f de jeux; **playgroup** n garderie f; **playing card** n carte f à jouer; **playing field** n terrain m de sport; **playschool** n = **playgroup**; **playtime** n (Scol) récréation f; **playwright** n dramaturge m

plc abbr (BRIT: = public limited company) ≈ SARL f

plea [pliː] n (request) appel m; (Law) défense f

plead [pliːd] vt plaider; (give as excuse) invoquer ▷ vi (Law) plaider; (beg): **to ~ with sb (for sth)** implorer qn (d'accorder qch); **to ~ guilty/not guilty** plaider coupable/non coupable

pleasant ['plɛznt] adj agréable

please [pliːz] excl s'il te (or vous) plaît ▷ vt plaire à ▷ vi (think fit): **do as you ~** faites comme il vous plaira; **~ yourself!** (inf) (faites) comme vous voulez!; **pleased** adj: **pleased (with)** content(e) (de); **pleased to meet you** enchanté (de faire votre connaissance)

pleasure ['plɛʒəʳ] n plaisir m; **"it's a ~"** "je vous en prie"

pleat [pliːt] n pli m

pledge [plɛdʒ] n (promise) promesse f ▷ vt promettre

plentiful ['plɛntɪful] adj abondant(e), copieux(-euse)

plenty ['plɛntɪ] n: **~ of** beaucoup de; (sufficient) (bien) assez de

pliers ['plaɪəz] npl pinces fpl

plight [plaɪt] n situation f critique

plod [plɔd] vi avancer péniblement; (fig) peiner

plonk [plɔŋk] (inf) n (BRIT: wine) pinard m, piquette f ▷ vt: **to ~ sth down** poser brusquement qch

plot [plɔt] n complot m, conspiration f; (of story, play) intrigue f; (of land) lot m de terrain, lopin m ▷ vt (mark out) tracer point par point; (Naut) pointer; (make graph of) faire le graphique de; (conspire) comploter ▷ vi comploter

plough (US **plow**) [plaʊ] n charrue f ▷ vt (earth) labourer; **to ~ money into** investir dans; **ploughman's lunch** n (BRIT) assiette froide avec du pain, du fromage et des pickles

plow [plaʊ] (US) = **plough**

ploy [plɔɪ] n stratagème m

pluck [plʌk] vt (fruit) cueillir; (musical instrument) pincer; (bird) plumer; **to ~ one's eyebrows** s'épiler les sourcils; **to ~ up courage** prendre son courage à deux mains

plug [plʌg] n (stopper) bouchon m, bonde f; (Elec) prise f de courant; (Aut: also: **spark(ing) ~**) bougie f ▷ vt (hole) boucher; (inf: advertise) faire du battage pour, matraquer; **plug in** vt (Elec) brancher; **plughole** n (BRIT) trou m

(d'écoulement)

plum [plʌm] n (fruit) prune f

plumber ['plʌmər] n plombier m

plumbing ['plʌmɪŋ] n (trade) plomberie f; (piping) tuyauterie f

plummet ['plʌmɪt] vi (person, object) plonger; (sales, prices) dégringoler

plump [plʌmp] adj rondelet(te), dodu(e), bien en chair; **plump for** vt fus (inf: choose) se décider pour

plunge [plʌndʒ] n plongeon m; (fig) chute f ▷ vt plonger ▷ vi (fall) tomber, dégringoler; (dive) plonger; **to take the ~** se jeter à l'eau

pluperfect [pluː'pəːfɪkt] n (Ling) plus-que-parfait m

plural ['pluərl] adj pluriel(le) ▷ n pluriel m

plus [plʌs] n (also: **~ sign**) signe m plus; (advantage) atout m ▷ prep plus; **ten/twenty ~** plus de dix/vingt

ply [plaɪ] n (of wool) fil m ▷ vt (a trade) exercer ▷ vi (ship) faire la navette; **to ~ sb with drink** donner continuellement à boire à qn; **plywood** n contreplaqué m

P.M. n abbr (BRIT) = **prime minister**

p.m. adv abbr (= post meridiem) de l'après-midi

PMS n abbr (= premenstrual syndrome) syndrome prémenstruel

PMT n abbr (= premenstrual tension) syndrome prémenstruel

pneumatic drill [njuː'mætɪk-] n marteau-piqueur m

pneumonia [njuː'məunɪə] n pneumonie f

poach [pəutʃ] vt (cook) pocher; (steal) pêcher (or chasser) sans permis ▷ vi braconner; **poached** adj (egg) poché(e)

P.O. Box n abbr = **post office box**

pocket ['pɔkɪt] n poche f ▷ vt empocher; **to be (£5) out of ~** en être de sa poche (pour 5 livres); **pocketbook** n (US: wallet) portefeuille m; **pocket money** n argent m de poche

pod [pɔd] n cosse f

podcast n podcast m

podiatrist [pɔ'diːətrɪst] n (US) pédicure m/f

podium ['pəudɪəm] n podium m

poem ['pəuɪm] n poème m

poet ['pəuɪt] n poète m; **poetic** [pəu'ɛtɪk] adj poétique; **poetry** n poésie f

poignant ['pɔɪnjənt] adj poignant(e)

point [pɔɪnt] n point m; (tip) pointe f; (in time) moment m; (in space) endroit m; (subject, idea) point, sujet m; (purpose) but m; (also: **decimal ~**): **2 ~ 3 (2.3)** 2 virgule 3 (2,3); (BRIT Elec: also: **power ~**) prise f (de courant) ▷ vt (show) indiquer; (gun etc): **to ~ sth at** braquer or diriger qch sur ▷ vi: **to ~ at** montrer du doigt; **points** npl (Rail) aiguillage m; **to make a ~ of doing sth** ne pas manquer de faire qch; **to get/miss the ~** comprendre/ne pas

comprendre; **to come to the ~** en venir au fait; **there's no ~ (in doing)** cela ne sert à rien (de faire), à quoi ça sert?; **to be on the ~ of doing sth** être sur le point de faire qch; **point out** vt (mention) faire remarquer, souligner; **point-blank** adv (fig) catégoriquement; (also: **at point-blank range**) à bout portant; **pointed** adj (shape) pointu(e); (remark) plein(e) de sous-entendus; **pointer** n (needle) aiguille f; (clue) indication f; (advice) tuyau m; **pointless** adj inutile, vain(e); **point of view** n point m de vue

poison ['pɔɪzn] n poison m ▷ vt empoisonner; **poisonous** adj (snake) venimeux(-euse); (substance, plant) vénéneux(-euse); (fumes) toxique

poke [pəuk] vt (jab with finger, stick etc) piquer; pousser du doigt; (put): **to ~ sth in(to)** fourrer or enfoncer qch dans; **poke about** vi fureter; **poke out** vi (stick out) sortir

poker ['pəukər] n tisonnier m; (Cards) poker m

Poland ['pəulənd] n Pologne f

polar ['pəulər] adj polaire; **polar bear** n ours blanc

Pole [pəul] n Polonais(e)

pole [pəul] n (of wood) mât m, perche f; (Elec) poteau m; (Geo) pôle m; **pole bean** n (US) haricot m (à rames); **pole vault** n saut m à la perche

police [pə'liːs] npl police f ▷ vt maintenir l'ordre dans; **police car** n voiture f de police; **police constable** n (BRIT) agent m de police; **police force** n police f, forces fpl de l'ordre; **policeman** (irreg) n agent m de police, policier m; **police officer** n agent m de police; **police station** n commissariat m de police; **policewoman** (irreg) n femme-agent f

policy ['pɔlɪsɪ] n politique f; (also: **insurance ~**) police f (d'assurance)

polio ['pəulɪəu] n polio f

Polish ['pəulɪʃ] adj polonais(e) ▷ n (Ling) polonais m

polish ['pɔlɪʃ] n (for shoes) cirage m; (for floor) cire f, encaustique f; (for nails) vernis m; (shine) éclat m, poli m; (fig: refinement) raffinement m ▷ vt (put polish on: shoes, wood) cirer; (make shiny) astiquer, faire briller; **polish off** vt (food) liquider; **polished** adj (fig) raffiné(e)

polite [pə'laɪt] adj poli(e); **politeness** n politesse f

political [pə'lɪtɪkl] adj politique; **politically** adv politiquement; **politically correct** politiquement correct(e)

politician [pɔlɪ'tɪʃən] n homme/femme politique, politicien(ne)

politics ['pɔlɪtɪks] n politique f

poll [pəul] n scrutin m, vote m; (also: **opinion ~**) sondage m (d'opinion) ▷ vt (votes) obtenir

pollen ['pɔlən] n pollen m

polling station n (BRIT) bureau m de vote

pollute [pə'luːt] vt polluer

pollution [pə'luːʃən] n pollution f

polo ['pəuləu] n polo m; **polo-neck** adj à col roulé ▷ n (sweater) pull m à col roulé; **polo shirt** n polo m

polyester [pɔlɪ'estəʳ] n polyester m

polystyrene [pɔlɪ'staɪriːn] n polystyrène m

polythene ['pɔlɪθiːn] n (BRIT) polyéthylène m; **polythene bag** n sac m en plastique

pomegranate ['pɔmɪgrænɪt] n grenade f

pompous ['pɔmpəs] adj pompeux(-euse)

pond [pɔnd] n étang m; (stagnant) mare f

ponder ['pɔndəʳ] vt considérer, peser

pony ['pəunɪ] n poney m; **ponytail** n queue f de cheval; **pony trekking** n (BRIT) randonnée f équestre or à cheval

poodle ['puːdl] n caniche m

pool [puːl] n (of rain) flaque f; (pond) mare f; (artificial) bassin m; (also: **swimming ~**) piscine f; (sth shared) fonds commun; (billiards) poule f ▷ vt mettre en commun; **pools** npl (football) ≈ loto sportif

poor [puəʳ] adj pauvre; (mediocre) médiocre, faible, mauvais(e) ▷ npl: **the ~** les pauvres mpl; **poorly** adv (badly) mal, médiocrement ▷ adj souffrant(e), malade

pop [pɔp] n (noise) bruit sec; (Mus) musique f pop; (inf: drink) soda m; (us inf: father) papa m ▷ vt (put) fourrer, mettre (rapidement) ▷ vi éclater; (cork) sauter; **pop in** vi entrer en passant; **pop out** vi sortir; **popcorn** n pop-corn m

pope [pəup] n pape m

poplar ['pɔpləʳ] n peuplier m

popper ['pɔpəʳ] n (BRIT) bouton-pression m

poppy ['pɔpɪ] n (wild) coquelicot m; (cultivated) pavot m

Popsicle® ['pɔpsɪkl] n (us) esquimau m (glace)

pop star n pop star f

popular ['pɔpjuləʳ] adj populaire; (fashionable) à la mode; **popularity** [pɔpju'lærɪtɪ] n popularité f

population [pɔpju'leɪʃən] n population f

pop-up adj (Comput: menu, window) pop up inv ▷ n pop up m inv, fenêtre f pop up

porcelain ['pɔːslɪn] n porcelaine f

porch [pɔːtʃ] n porche m; (us) véranda f

pore [pɔːʳ] n pore m ▷ vi: **to ~ over** s'absorber dans, être plongé(e) dans

pork [pɔːk] n porc m; **pork chop** n côte f de porc; **pork pie** n pâté m de porc en croûte

porn [pɔːn] adj (inf) porno ▷ n (inf) porno m; **pornographic** [pɔːnə'græfɪk] adj pornographique; **pornography** [pɔː'nɔgrəfɪ] n pornographie f

porridge ['pɔrɪdʒ] n porridge m

port [pɔːt] n (harbour) port m; (Naut: left side) bâbord m; (wine) porto m; (Comput) port m,

accès m; **~ of call** (port d')escale f

portable ['pɔːtəbl] adj portatif(-ive)

porter ['pɔːtəʳ] n (for luggage) porteur m; (doorkeeper) gardien(ne); portier m

portfolio [pɔːt'fəuliəu] n portefeuille m; (of artist) portfolio m

portion ['pɔːʃən] n portion f, part f

portrait ['pɔːtreɪt] n portrait m

portray [pɔː'treɪ] vt faire le portrait de; (in writing) dépeindre, représenter; (subj: actor) jouer

Portugal ['pɔːtjugl] n Portugal m

Portuguese [pɔːtju'giːz] adj portugais(e) ▷ n (pl inv) Portugais(e); (Ling) portugais m

pose [pəuz] n pose f ▷ vi poser; (pretend): **to ~ as** se faire passer pour ▷ vt poser; (problem) créer

posh [pɔʃ] adj (inf) chic inv

position [pə'zɪʃən] n position f; (job, situation) situation f ▷ vt mettre en place or en position

positive ['pɔzɪtɪv] adj positif(-ive); (certain) sûr(e), certain(e); (definite) formel(le), catégorique; **positively** adv (affirmatively, enthusiastically) de façon positive; (inf: really) carrément

possess [pə'zɛs] vt posséder; **possession** [pə'zɛʃən] n possession f; **possessions** npl (belongings) affaires fpl; **possessive** adj possessif(-ive)

possibility [pɔsɪ'bɪlɪtɪ] n possibilité f; (event) éventualité f

possible ['pɔsɪbl] adj possible; **as big as ~** aussi gros que possible; **possibly** adv (perhaps) peut-être; **I cannot possibly come** il m'est impossible de venir

post [pəust] n (BRIT: mail) poste f; (: letters, delivery) courrier m; (job, situation) poste m; (pole) poteau m ▷ vt (BRIT: send by post) poster; (: appoint): **to ~ to** affecter à; **where can I ~ these cards?** où est-ce que je peux poster ces cartes postales?; **postage** n tarifs mpl d'affranchissement; **postal** adj postal(e); **postal order** n mandat(-poste m) m; **postbox** n (BRIT) boîte f aux lettres (publique); **postcard** n carte postale; **postcode** n (BRIT) code postal

poster ['pəustəʳ] n affiche f

postgraduate ['pəust'grædjuət] n ≈ étudiant(e) de troisième cycle

postman ['pəustmən] (BRIT: irreg) n facteur m

postmark ['pəustmɑːk] n cachet m (de la poste)

post-mortem [pəust'mɔːtəm] n autopsie f

post office n (building) poste f; (organization): **the Post Office** les postes fpl

postpone [pəs'pəun] vt remettre (à plus tard), reculer

posture ['pɔstʃəʳ] n posture f; (fig) attitude f

postwoman ['pəust'wumən] (BRIT: irreg) n factrice f

pot [pɔt] n (for cooking) marmite f; casserole f; (teapot) théière f; (for coffee) cafetière f; (for plants, jam) pot m; (inf: marijuana) herbe f ▷ vt (plant) mettre en pot; **to go to ~** (inf) aller à vau-l'eau

potato (pl **~es**) [pə'teɪtəu] n pomme f de terre; **potato peeler** n épluche-légumes m

potent ['pəutnt] adj puissant(e); (drink) fort(e), très alcoolisé(e); (man) viril

potential [pə'tɛnʃl] adj potentiel(le) ▷ n potentiel m

pothole ['pɔthəul] n (in road) nid m de poule; (BRIT: underground) gouffre m, caverne f

pot plant n plante f d'appartement

potter ['pɔtə'] n potier m ▷ vi (BRIT): **to ~ around** or **about** bricoler; **pottery** n poterie f

potty ['pɔtɪ] n (child's) pot m

pouch [pautʃ] n (Zool) poche f; (for tobacco) blague f; (for money) bourse f

poultry ['pəultrɪ] n volaille f

pounce [pauns] vi: **to ~ (on)** bondir (sur), fondre (sur)

pound [paund] n livre f (weight = 453g, 16 ounces; money = 100 pence); (for dogs, cars) fourrière f ▷ vt (beat) bourrer de coups, marteler; (crush) piler, pulvériser ▷ vi (heart) battre violemment, taper; **pound sterling** n livre f sterling

pour [pɔː'] vt verser ▷ vi couler à flots; (rain) pleuvoir à verse; **to ~ sb a drink** verser or servir à boire à qn; **pour in** vi (people) affluer, se précipiter; (news, letters) arriver en masse; **pour out** vi (people) sortir en masse ▷ vt vider; (fig) déverser; (serve: a drink) verser; **pouring** adj: **pouring rain** pluie torrentielle

pout [paut] vi faire la moue

poverty ['pɔvətɪ] n pauvreté f, misère f

powder ['paudə'] n poudre f ▷ vt poudrer; **powdered milk** n lait m en poudre

power ['pauə'] n (strength, nation) puissance f, force f; (ability, Pol: of party, leader) pouvoir m; (of speech, thought) faculté f; (Elec) courant m; **to be in ~** être au pouvoir; **power cut** n (BRIT) coupure f de courant; **power failure** n panne f de courant; **powerful** adj puissant(e); (performance etc) très fort(e); **powerless** adj impuissant(e); **power point** n (BRIT) prise f de courant; **power station** n centrale f électrique

p.p. abbr (= per procurationem: by proxy) p.p.

PR n abbr = **public relations**

practical ['præktɪkl] adj pratique; **practical joke** n farce f; **practically** adv (almost) pratiquement

practice ['præktɪs] n pratique f; (of profession) exercice m; (at football etc) entraînement m; (business) cabinet m ▷ vt, vi (US) = **practise; in ~** (in reality) en pratique; **out of ~** rouillé(e)

practise (US **practice**) ['præktɪs] vt (work

at: piano, backhand etc) s'exercer à, travailler; (train for: sport) s'entraîner à; (a sport, religion, method) pratiquer; (profession) exercer ▷ vi s'exercer, travailler; (train) s'entraîner; (lawyer, doctor) exercer; **practising** (US **practicing**) adj (Christian etc) pratiquant(e); (lawyer) en exercice

practitioner [præk'tɪʃənə'] n praticien(ne)

pragmatic [præg'mætɪk] adj pragmatique

prairie ['prɛərɪ] n savane f

praise [preɪz] n éloge(s) m(pl), louange(s) f(pl) ▷ vt louer, faire l'éloge de

pram [præm] n (BRIT) landau m, voiture f d'enfant

prank [præŋk] n farce f

prawn [prɔːn] n crevette f (rose); **prawn cocktail** n cocktail m de crevettes

pray [preɪ] vi prier; **prayer** [prɛə'] n prière f

preach [priːtʃ] vi prêcher; **preacher** n prédicateur m; (US: clergyman) pasteur m

precarious [prɪ'kɛərɪəs] adj précaire

precaution [prɪ'kɔːʃən] n précaution f

precede [prɪ'siːd] vt, vi précéder; **precedent** ['prɛsɪdənt] n précédent m; **preceding** [prɪ'siːdɪŋ] adj qui précède (or précédait)

precinct ['priːsɪŋkt] n (US: district) circonscription f, arrondissement m; **pedestrian ~** (BRIT) zone piétonnière; **shopping ~** (BRIT) centre commercial

precious ['prɛʃəs] adj précieux(-euse)

precise [prɪ'saɪs] adj précis(e); **precisely** adv précisément

precision [prɪ'sɪʒən] n précision f

predator ['prɛdətə'] n prédateur m, rapace m

predecessor ['priːdɪsɛsə'] n prédécesseur m

predicament [prɪ'dɪkəmənt] n situation f difficile

predict [prɪ'dɪkt] vt prédire; **predictable** adj prévisible; **prediction** [prɪ'dɪkʃən] n prédiction f

predominantly [prɪ'dɔmɪnəntlɪ] adv en majeure partie; (especially) surtout

preface ['prɛfəs] n préface f

prefect ['priːfɛkt] n (BRIT: in school) élève chargé de certaines fonctions de discipline

prefer [prɪ'fəː'] vt préférer; **preferable** ['prɛfrəbl] adj préférable; **preferably** ['prɛfrəblɪ] adv de préférence; **preference** ['prɛfrəns] n préférence f

prefix ['priːfɪks] n préfixe m

pregnancy ['prɛgnənsɪ] n grossesse f

pregnant ['prɛgnənt] adj enceinte adj f; (animal) pleine

prehistoric ['priːhɪs'tɔrɪk] adj préhistorique

prejudice ['prɛdʒudɪs] n préjugé m; **prejudiced** adj (person) plein(e) de préjugés; (in a matter) partial(e)

preliminary [prɪ'lɪmɪnərɪ] adj préliminaire

prelude ['prɛljuːd] n prélude m

premature ['prɛmətʃuəʳ] *adj* prématuré(e)

premier ['prɛmɪəʳ] *adj* premier(-ière), principal(e) ▷ *n* (*Pol: Prime Minister*) premier ministre; (*Pol: President*) chef *m* de l'État

premiere ['prɛmɪɛəʳ] *n* première *f*

Premier League *n* première division

premises ['prɛmɪsɪz] *npl* locaux *mpl*; **on the ~** sur les lieux; sur place

premium ['pri:mɪəm] *n* prime *f*; **to be at a ~** (*fig: housing etc*) être très demandé(e), être rarissime

premonition [prɛmə'nɪʃən] *n* prémonition *f*

preoccupied [pri:'ɔkjupaɪd] *adj* préoccupé(e)

prepaid [pri:'peɪd] *adj* payé(e) d'avance

preparation [prɛpə'reɪʃən] *n* préparation *f*; **preparations** *npl* (*for trip, war*) préparatifs *mpl*

preparatory school *n* école primaire privée; (*US*) lycée privé

prepare [prɪ'pɛəʳ] *vt* préparer ▷ *vi*: **to ~ for** se préparer à

prepared [prɪ'pɛəd] *adj*: **~ for** préparé(e) à; **~ to** prêt(e) à

preposition [prɛpə'zɪʃən] *n* préposition *f*

prep school *n* = **preparatory school**

prerequisite [pri:'rɛkwɪzɪt] *n* condition *f* préalable

preschool ['pri:'sku:l] *adj* préscolaire; (*child*) d'âge préscolaire

prescribe [prɪ'skraɪb] *vt* prescrire

prescription [prɪ'skrɪpʃən] *n* (*Med*) ordonnance *f*; (*: medicine*) médicament *m* (obtenu sur ordonnance); **could you write me a ~?** pouvez-vous me faire une ordonnance?

presence ['prɛzns] *n* présence *f*; **in sb's ~** en présence de qn; **~ of mind** présence d'esprit

present ['prɛznt] *adj* présent(e); (*current*) présent, actuel(le) ▷ *n* cadeau *m*; (*actuality*) présent *m* ▷ *vt* [prɪ'zɛnt] présenter; (*prize, medal*): (*give*): **to ~ sb with sth** offrir qch à qn; **at ~** en ce moment; **to give sb a ~** offrir un cadeau à qn; **presentable** [prɪ'zɛntəbl] *adj* présentable; **presentation** [prɛzn'teɪʃən] *n* présentation *f*; (*ceremony*) remise *f* du cadeau (*or de la médaille etc*); **present-day** *adj* contemporain(e), actuel(le); **presenter** [prɪ'zɛntəʳ] *n* (*BRIT Radio, TV*) présentateur(-trice); **presently** *adv* (*soon*) tout à l'heure, bientôt; (*with verb in past*) peu après; (*at present*) en ce moment; **present participle** [-'pɑ:tɪsɪpl] *n* participe *m* présent

preservation [prɛzə'veɪʃən] *n* préservation *f*, conservation *f*

preservative [prɪ'zə:vətɪv] *n* agent *m* de conservation

preserve [prɪ'zə:v] *vt* (*keep safe*) préserver, protéger; (*maintain*) conserver, garder; (*food*) mettre en conserve ▷ *n* (*for game, fish*) réserve *f*; (*often pl: jam*) confiture *f*

preside [prɪ'zaɪd] *vi* présider

president ['prɛzɪdənt] *n* président(e); **presidential** [prɛzɪ'dɛnʃl] *adj* présidentiel(le)

press [prɛs] *n* (*tool, machine, newspapers*) presse *f*; (*for wine*) pressoir *m* ▷ *vt* (*push*) appuyer sur; (*squeeze*) presser, serrer; (*clothes: iron*) repasser; (*insist*): **to ~ sth on sb** presser qn d'accepter qch; (*urge, entreat*): **to ~ sb to do** *or* **into doing sth** pousser qn à faire qch ▷ *vi* appuyer; **we are ~ed for time** le temps nous manque; **to ~ for sth** faire pression pour obtenir qch; **press conference** *n* conférence *f* de presse; **pressing** *adj* urgent(e), pressant(e); **press stud** *n* (*BRIT*) bouton-pression *m*; **press-up** *n* (*BRIT*) traction *f*

pressure ['prɛʃəʳ] *n* pression *f*; (*stress*) tension *f*; **to put ~ on sb (to do sth)** faire pression sur qn (pour qu'il fasse qch); **pressure cooker** *n* cocotte-minute *f*; **pressure group** *n* groupe *m* de pression

prestige [prɛs'ti:ʒ] *n* prestige *m*

prestigious [prɛs'tɪdʒəs] *adj* prestigieux(-euse)

presumably [prɪ'zju:məblɪ] *adv* vraisemblablement

presume [prɪ'zju:m] *vt* présumer, supposer

pretence (*US* **pretense**) [prɪ'tɛns] *n* (*claim*) prétention *f*; **under false ~s** sous des prétextes fallacieux

pretend [prɪ'tɛnd] *vt* (*feign*) feindre, simuler ▷ *vi* (*feign*) faire semblant

pretense [prɪ'tɛns] *n* (*US*) = **pretence**

pretentious [prɪ'tɛnʃəs] *adj* prétentieux(-euse)

pretext ['pri:tɛkst] *n* prétexte *m*

pretty ['prɪtɪ] *adj* joli(e) ▷ *adv* assez

prevail [prɪ'veɪl] *vi* (*win*) l'emporter, prévaloir; (*be usual*) avoir cours; **prevailing** *adj* (*widespread*) courant(e), répandu(e); (*wind*) dominant(e)

prevalent ['prɛvələnt] *adj* répandu(e), courant(e)

prevent [prɪ'vɛnt] *vt*: **to ~ (from doing)** empêcher (de faire); **prevention** [prɪ'vɛnʃən] *n* prévention *f*; **preventive** *adj* préventif(-ive)

preview ['pri:vju:] *n* (*of film*) avant-première *f*

previous ['pri:vɪəs] *adj* (*last*) précédent(e); (*earlier*) antérieur(e); **previously** *adv* précédemment, auparavant

prey [preɪ] *n* proie *f* ▷ *vi*: **to ~ on** s'attaquer à; **it was ~ing on his mind** ça le rongeait *or* minait

price [praɪs] *n* prix *m* ▷ *vt* (*goods*) fixer le prix de; **priceless** *adj* sans prix, inestimable; **price list** *n* tarif *m*

prick [prɪk] *n* (*sting*) piqûre *f* ▷ *vt* piquer; **to ~ up one's ears** dresser *or* tendre l'oreille

prickly ['prɪklɪ] *adj* piquant(e), épineux(-euse); (*fig: person*) irritable

P

pride [praɪd] *n* fierté *f*; (*pej*) orgueil *m* ▷ *vt*: **to ~ o.s. on** se flatter de; s'enorgueillir de

priest [priːst] *n* prêtre *m*

primarily ['praɪmərɪlɪ] *adv* principalement, essentiellement

primary ['praɪmərɪ] *adj* primaire; (*first in importance*) premier(-ière), primordial(e) ▷ *n* (*us: election*) (élection *f*) primaire *f*; **primary school** *n* (BRIT) école *f* primaire

prime [praɪm] *adj* primordial(e), fondamental(e); (*excellent*) excellent(e) ▷ *vt* (*fig*) mettre au courant ▷ *n*: **in the ~ of life** dans la fleur de l'âge; **Prime Minister** *n* Premier ministre

primitive ['prɪmɪtɪv] *adj* primitif(-ive)

primrose ['prɪmrəuz] *n* primevère *f*

prince [prɪns] *n* prince *m*

princess [prɪn'sɛs] *n* princesse *f*

principal ['prɪnsɪpl] *adj* principal(e) ▷ *n* (*head teacher*) directeur *m*, principal *m*; **principally** *adv* principalement

principle ['prɪnsɪpl] *n* principe *m*; **in ~** en principe; **on ~** par principe

print [prɪnt] *n* (*mark*) empreinte *f*; (*letters*) caractères *mpl*; (*fabric*) imprimé *m*; (*Art*) gravure *f*, estampe *f*; (*Phot*) épreuve *f* ▷ *vt* imprimer; (*publish*) publier; (*write in capitals*) écrire en majuscules; **out of ~** épuisé(e); **print out** *vt* (*Comput*) imprimer; **printer** *n* (*machine*) imprimante *f*; (*person*) imprimeur *m*; **printout** *n* (*Comput*) sortie *f* imprimante

prior ['praɪər] *adj* antérieur(e), précédent(e); (*more important*) prioritaire ▷ *adv*: **~ to doing** avant de faire

priority [praɪ'ɔrɪtɪ] *n* priorité *f*; **to have** *or* **take ~ over sth/sb** avoir la priorité sur qch/qn

prison ['prɪzn] *n* prison *f* ▷ *cpd* pénitentiaire; **prisoner** *n* prisonnier(-ière); **prisoner of war** *n* prisonnier(-ière) de guerre

pristine ['prɪstiːn] *adj* virginal(e)

privacy ['prɪvəsɪ] *n* intimité *f*, solitude *f*

private ['praɪvɪt] *adj* (*not public*) privé(e); (*personal*) personnel(le); (*house, car, lesson*) particulier(-ière); (*quiet: place*) tranquille ▷ *n* soldat *m* de deuxième classe; **"~"** (*on envelope*) "personnelle"; (*on door*) "privé"; **in ~** en privé; **privately** *adv* en privé; (*within oneself*) intérieurement; **private property** *n* propriété privée; **private school** *n* école privée

privatize ['praɪvɪtaɪz] *vt* privatiser

privilege ['prɪvɪlɪdʒ] *n* privilège *m*

prize [praɪz] *n* prix *m* ▷ *adj* (*example, idiot*) parfait(e); (*bull, novel*) primé(e) ▷ *vt* priser, faire grand cas de; **prize-giving** *n* distribution *f* des prix; **prizewinner** *n* gagnant(e)

pro [prəu] *n* (*inf: Sport*) professionnel(le) ▷ *prep* pro ...; **pros** *npl*: **the ~s and cons** le pour et le contre

probability [prɔbə'bɪlɪtɪ] *n* probabilité *f*; **in all ~** très probablement

probable ['prɔbəbl] *adj* probable

probably ['prɔbəblɪ] *adv* probablement

probation [prə'beɪʃən] *n*: **on ~** (*employee*) à l'essai; (*Law*) en liberté surveillée

probe [prəub] *n* (*Med, Space*) sonde *f*; (*enquiry*) enquête *f*, investigation *f* ▷ *vt* sonder, explorer

problem ['prɔbləm] *n* problème *m*

procedure [prə'siːdʒər] *n* (*Admin, Law*) procédure *f*; (*method*) marche *f* à suivre, façon *f* de procéder

proceed [prə'siːd] *vi* (*go forward*) avancer; (*act*) procéder; (*continue*): **to ~ (with)** continuer, poursuivre; **to ~ to do** se mettre à faire; **proceedings** *npl* (*measures*) mesures *fpl*; (*Law: against sb*) poursuites *fpl*; (*meeting*) réunion *f*, séance *f*; (*records*) compte rendu; actes *mpl*; **proceeds** ['prəusiːdz] *npl* produit *m*, recette *f*

process ['prəusɛs] *n* processus *m*; (*method*) procédé *m* ▷ *vt* traiter

procession [prə'sɛʃən] *n* défilé *m*, cortège *m*; **funeral ~** (*on foot*) cortège funèbre; (*in cars*) convoi *m* mortuaire

proclaim [prə'kleɪm] *vt* déclarer, proclamer

prod [prɔd] *vt* pousser

produce *n* ['prɔdjuːs] (*Agr*) produits *mpl* ▷ *vt* [prə'djuːs] produire; (*show*) présenter; (*cause*) provoquer, causer; (*Theat*) monter, mettre en scène; (*TV: programme*) réaliser; (: *play, film*) mettre en scène; (*Radio: programme*) réaliser; (: *play*) mettre en ondes; **producer** *n* (*Theat*) metteur *m* en scène; (*Agr, Comm, Cine*) producteur *m*; (*TV: of programme*) réalisateur *m*; (: *of play, film*) metteur en scène; (*Radio: of programme*) réalisateur *m*; (: *of play*) metteur en ondes

product ['prɔdʌkt] *n* produit *m*; **production** [prə'dʌkʃən] *n* production *f*; (*Theat*) mise *f* en scène; **productive** [prə'dʌktɪv] *adj* productif(-ive); **productivity** [prɔdʌk'tɪvɪtɪ] *n* productivité *f*

Prof. [prɔf] *abbr* (= *professor*) Prof

profession [prə'fɛʃən] *n* profession *f*; **professional** *n* professionnel(le) ▷ *adj* professionnel(le); (*work*) de professionnel

professor [prə'fɛsər] *n* professeur *m* (*titulaire d'une chaire*); (*us: teacher*) professeur *m*

profile ['prəufaɪl] *n* profil *m*

profit ['prɔfɪt] *n* (*from trading*) bénéfice *m*; (*advantage*) profit *m* ▷ *vi*: **to ~ (by** *or* **from)** profiter (de); **profitable** *adj* lucratif(-ive), rentable

profound [prə'faund] *adj* profond(e)

programme (*us* **program**) ['prəugræm] *n* (*Comput: also BRIT*: **program**) programme *m*; (*Radio, TV*) émission *f* ▷ *vt* programmer; **programmer** (*us* **programer**) *n* programmeur(-euse); **programming** (us **programing**) n programmation f

progress n ['prəugrɛs] progrès m(pl) ▷ vi [prə'grɛs] progresser, avancer; **in ~** en cours; **progressive** [prə'grɛsɪv] adj progressif(-ive); (person) progressiste

prohibit [prə'hɪbɪt] vt interdire, défendre

project n ['prɔdʒɛkt] (plan) projet m, plan m; (venture) opération f, entreprise f; (Scol: research) étude f, dossier m ▷ vb [prə'dʒɛkt] ▷ vt projeter ▷ vi (stick out) faire saillie, s'avancer; **projection** [prə'dʒɛkʃən] n projection f; (overhang) saillie f; **projector** [prə'dʒɛktər] n projecteur m

prolific [prə'lɪfɪk] adj prolifique

prolong [prə'lɔŋ] vt prolonger

prom [prɔm] n abbr = **promenade** (us: ball) bal m d'étudiants; **the P~s** série de concerts de musique classique; voir encadré

● **PROM**
●
● En Grande-Bretagne, un **promenade**
● **concert** ou **prom** est un concert de
● musique classique, ainsi appelé car, à
● l'origine, le public restait debout et se
● promenait au lieu de rester assis. De nos
● jours, une partie du public reste debout,
● mais il y a également des places assises
● (plus chères). Les **Proms** les plus connus
● sont les Proms londoniens. La dernière
● séance (the "Last Night of the Proms") est
● un grand événement médiatique où se
● jouent des airs traditionnels et patriotiques.
● Aux États-Unis et au Canada, le **prom** ou
● **promenade** est un bal organisé par le lycée.

promenade [prɔmə'nɑːd] n (by sea) esplanade f, promenade f

prominent ['prɔmɪnənt] adj (standing out) proéminent(e); (important) important(e)

promiscuous [prə'mɪskjuəs] adj (sexually) de mœurs légères

promise ['prɔmɪs] n promesse f ▷ vt, vi promettre; **promising** adj prometteur(-euse)

promote [prə'məut] vt promouvoir; (new product) lancer; **promotion** [prə'məuʃən] n promotion f

prompt [prɔmpt] adj rapide ▷ n (Comput) message m (de guidage) ▷ vt (cause) entraîner, provoquer; (Theat) souffler (son rôle or ses répliques) à; **at 8 o'clock ~** à 8 heures précises; **to ~ sb to do** inciter or pousser qn à faire; **promptly** adv (quickly) rapidement, sans délai; (on time) ponctuellement

prone [prəun] adj (lying) couché(e) (face contre terre); **~ to** enclin(e) à

prong [prɔŋ] n (of fork) dent f

pronoun ['prəunaun] n pronom m

pronounce [prə'nauns] vt prononcer; **how do you ~ it?** comment est-ce que ça se prononce?

pronunciation [prənʌnsɪ'eɪʃən] n prononciation f

proof [pruːf] n preuve f ▷ adj: **~ against** à l'épreuve de

prop [prɔp] n support m, étai m; (fig) soutien m ▷ vt (also: **~ up**) étayer, soutenir; **props** npl accessoires mpl

propaganda [prɔpə'gændə] n propagande f

propeller [prə'pɛlər] n hélice f

proper ['prɔpər] adj (suited, right) approprié(e), bon (bonne); (seemly) correct(e), convenable; (authentic) vrai(e), véritable; (referring to place): **the village ~** le village proprement dit; **properly** adv correctement, convenablement; **proper noun** n nom m propre

property ['prɔpətɪ] n (possessions) biens mpl; (house etc) propriété f; (land) terres fpl, domaine m

prophecy ['prɔfɪsɪ] n prophétie f

prophet ['prɔfɪt] n prophète m

proportion [prə'pɔːʃən] n proportion f; (share) part f; partie f; **proportions** npl (size) dimensions fpl; **proportional, proportionate** adj proportionnel(le)

proposal [prə'pəuzl] n proposition f, offre f; (plan) projet m; (of marriage) demande f en mariage

propose [prə'pəuz] vt proposer, suggérer ▷ vi faire sa demande en mariage; **to ~ to do** avoir l'intention de faire

proposition [prɔpə'zɪʃən] n proposition f

proprietor [prə'praɪətər] n propriétaire m/f

prose [prəuz] n prose f; (Scol: translation) thème m

prosecute ['prɔsɪkjuːt] vt poursuivre; **prosecution** [prɔsɪ'kjuːʃən] n poursuites fpl judiciaires; (accusing side: in criminal case) accusation f; (: in civil case) la partie plaignante; **prosecutor** (lawyer) procureur m; (also: **public prosecutor**) ministère public; (us: plaintiff) plaignant(e)

prospect n ['prɔspɛkt] perspective f; (hope) espoir m, chances fpl ▷ vt, vi [prə'spɛkt] prospecter; **prospects** npl (for work etc) possibilités fpl d'avenir, débouchés mpl; **prospective** [prə'spɛktɪv] adj (possible) éventuel(le); (future) futur(e)

prospectus [prə'spɛktəs] n prospectus m

prosper ['prɔspər] vi prospérer; **prosperity** [prɔ'spɛrɪtɪ] n prospérité f; **prosperous** adj prospère

prostitute ['prɔstɪtjuːt] n prostituée f; **male ~** prostitué m

protect [prə'tɛkt] vt protéger; **protection** [prə'tɛkʃən] n protection f; **protective** adj

protecteur(-trice); *(clothing)* de protection
protein ['prəʊtiːn] *n* protéine *f*
protest *n* ['prəʊtɛst] protestation *f* ▷ *vb* [prə'tɛst] ▷ *vi*: **to ~ against/about** protester contre/à propos de; **to ~ (that)** protester que
Protestant ['prɒtɪstənt] *adj, n* protestant(e)
protester, protestor [prə'tɛstəʳ] *n (in demonstration)* manifestant(e)
protractor [prə'træktəʳ] *n (Geom)* rapporteur *m*
proud [praʊd] *adj* fier(-ère); *(pej)* orgueilleux(-euse)
prove [pruːv] *vt* prouver, démontrer ▷ *vi*: **to ~ correct** *etc* s'avérer juste *etc*; **to ~ o.s.** montrer ce dont on est capable
proverb ['prɒvəːb] *n* proverbe *m*
provide [prə'vaɪd] *vt* fournir; **to ~ sb with sth** fournir qch à qn; **provide for** *vt fus (person)* subvenir aux besoins de; *(future event)* prévoir; **provided** *conj*: **provided (that)** à condition que + *sub*; **providing** [prə'vaɪdɪŋ] *conj* à condition que + *sub*
province ['prɒvɪns] *n* province *f*; *(fig)* domaine *m*; **provincial** [prə'vɪnʃəl] *adj* provincial(e)
provision [prə'vɪʒən] *n (supplying)* fourniture *f*; approvisionnement *m*; *(stipulation)* disposition *f*; **provisions** *npl (food)* provisions *fpl*; **provisional** *adj* provisoire
provocative [prə'vɒkətɪv] *adj* provocateur(-trice), provocant(e)
provoke [prə'vəʊk] *vt* provoquer
prowl [praʊl] *vi (also:* **~ about, ~ around)** rôder
proximity [prɒk'sɪmɪtɪ] *n* proximité *f*
proxy ['prɒksɪ] *n*: **by ~** par procuration
prudent ['pruːdnt] *adj* prudent(e)
prune [pruːn] *n* pruneau *m* ▷ *vt* élaguer
pry [praɪ] *vi*: **to ~ into** fourrer son nez dans
PS *n abbr (= postscript)* PS *m*
pseudonym ['sjuːdənɪm] *n* pseudonyme *m*
PSHE *n abbr (BRIT: Scol: = personal, social and health education)* cours d'éducation personnelle, sanitaire et sociale préparant à la vie adulte
psychiatric [saɪkɪ'ætrɪk] *adj* psychiatrique
psychiatrist [saɪ'kaɪətrɪst] *n* psychiatre *m/f*
psychic ['saɪkɪk] *adj (also:* **~al)** *(méta)*psychique; *(person)* doué(e) de télépathie *or* d'un sixième sens
psychoanalysis *(pl* **-ses)** [saɪkəʊə'nælɪsɪs, -siːz] *n* psychanalyse *f*
psychological [saɪkə'lɒdʒɪkl] *adj* psychologique
psychologist [saɪ'kɒlədʒɪst] *n* psychologue *m/f*
psychology [saɪ'kɒlədʒɪ] *n* psychologie *f*
psychotherapy [saɪkəʊ'θɛrəpɪ] *n* psychothérapie *f*
pt *abbr* = **pint(s)**; **point(s)**

PTO *abbr (= please turn over)* TSVP
pub [pʌb] *n abbr (= public house)* pub *m*
puberty ['pjuːbətɪ] *n* puberté *f*
public ['pʌblɪk] *adj* public(-ique) ▷ *n* public *m*; **in ~** en public; **to make ~** rendre public
publication [pʌblɪ'keɪʃən] *n* publication *f*
public: **public company** *n* société *f* anonyme; **public convenience** *n (BRIT)* toilettes *fpl*; **public holiday** *n (BRIT)* jour férié; **public house** *n (BRIT)* pub *m*
publicity [pʌb'lɪsɪtɪ] *n* publicité *f*
publicize ['pʌblɪsaɪz] *vt (make known)* faire connaître, rendre public; *(advertise)* faire de la publicité pour
public: **public limited company** *n* ≈ société *f* anonyme (SA) *(cotée en Bourse)*; **publicly** *adv* publiquement, en public; **public opinion** *n* opinion publique; **public relations** *n or npl* relations publiques (RP); **public school** *n (BRIT)* école privée; *(US)* école publique; **public transport** *(US* **public transportation)** *n* transports *mpl* en commun
publish ['pʌblɪʃ] *vt* publier; **publisher** *n* éditeur *m*; **publishing** *n (industry)* édition *f*
pub lunch *n* repas *m* de bistrot
pudding ['pʊdɪŋ] *n (BRIT: dessert)* dessert *m*, entremets *m*; *(sweet dish)* pudding *m*, gâteau *m*
puddle ['pʌdl] *n* flaque *f* d'eau
puff [pʌf] *n* bouffée *f* ▷ *vt (also:* **~ out**: *sails, cheeks)* gonfler ▷ *vi (pant)* haleter; **puff pastry** *(US* **puff paste)** *n* pâte feuilletée
pull [pʊl] *n (tug):* **to give sth a ~** tirer sur qch ▷ *vt (trigger)* presser; *(strain: muscle, tendon)* se claquer ▷ *vi* tirer; **to ~ to pieces** mettre en morceaux; **to ~ one's punches** *(also fig)* ménager son adversaire; **to ~ one's weight** y mettre du sien; **to ~ o.s. together** se ressaisir; **to ~ sb's leg** *(fig)* faire marcher qn; **pull apart** *vt (break)* mettre en pièces, démantibuler; **pull away** *vi (vehicle: move off)* partir; *(draw back)* s'éloigner; **pull back** *vt (lever etc)* tirer sur; *(curtains)* ouvrir ▷ *vi (refrain)* s'abstenir; *(Mil: withdraw)* se retirer; **pull down** *vt* baisser, abaisser; *(house)* démolir; **pull in** *vi (Aut)* se ranger; *(Rail)* entrer en gare; **pull off** *vt* enlever, ôter; *(deal etc)* conclure; **pull out** *vi* démarrer, partir; *(Aut: come out of line)* déboîter ▷ *vt (from bag, pocket)* sortir; *(remove)* arracher; **pull over** *vi (Aut)* se ranger; **pull up** *vi (stop)* s'arrêter ▷ *vt* remonter; *(uproot)* déraciner, arracher
pulley ['pʊlɪ] *n* poulie *f*
pullover ['pʊləʊvəʳ] *n* pull-over *m*, tricot *m*
pulp [pʌlp] *n (of fruit)* pulpe *f*; *(for paper)* pâte *f* à papier
pulpit ['pʊlpɪt] *n* chaire *f*
pulse [pʌls] *n (of blood)* pouls *m*; *(of heart)* battement *m*; **pulses** *npl (Culin)* légumineuses *fpl*

puma ['pjuːmə] *n* puma *m*

pump [pʌmp] *n* pompe *f*; (*shoe*) escarpin *m* ▷ *vt* pomper; **pump up** *vt* gonfler

pumpkin ['pʌmpkɪn] *n* potiron *m*, citrouille *f*

pun [pʌn] *n* jeu *m* de mots, calembour *m*

punch [pʌntʃ] *n* (*blow*) coup *m* de poing; (*tool*) poinçon *m*; (*drink*) punch *m* ▷ *vt* (*make a hole in*) poinçonner, perforer; (*hit*): **to ~ sb/sth** donner un coup de poing à qn/sur qch; **punch-up** *n* (BRIT *inf*) bagarre *f*

punctual ['pʌŋktjuəl] *adj* ponctuel(le)

punctuation [pʌŋktjuˈeɪʃən] *n* ponctuation *f*

puncture ['pʌŋktʃə*r*] *n* (BRIT) crevaison *f* ▷ *vt* crever

punish ['pʌnɪʃ] *vt* punir; **punishment** *n* punition *f*, châtiment *m*

punk [pʌŋk] *n* (*person*: *also*: **~ rocker**) punk *m/f*; (*music*: *also*: **~ rock**) le punk; (US *inf*: *hoodlum*) voyou *m*

pup [pʌp] *n* chiot *m*

pupil ['pjuːpl] *n* élève *m/f*; (*of eye*) pupille *f*

puppet ['pʌpɪt] *n* marionnette *f*, pantin *m*

puppy ['pʌpɪ] *n* chiot *m*, petit chien

purchase ['pəːtʃɪs] *n* achat *m* ▷ *vt* acheter

pure [pjuə*r*] *adj* pur(e); **purely** *adv* purement

purify ['pjuərɪfaɪ] *vt* purifier, épurer

purity ['pjuərɪtɪ] *n* pureté *f*

purple ['pəːpl] *adj* violet(te); (*face*) cramoisi(e)

purpose ['pəːpəs] *n* intention *f*, but *m*; **on ~** exprès

purr [pəː*r*] *vi* ronronner

purse [pəːs] *n* (BRIT: *for money*) porte-monnaie *m inv*; (US: *handbag*) sac *m* (à main) ▷ *vt* serrer, pincer

pursue [pəˈsjuː] *vt* poursuivre

pursuit [pəˈsjuːt] *n* poursuite *f*; (*occupation*) occupation *f*, activité *f*

pus [pʌs] *n* pus *m*

push [puʃ] *n* poussée *f* ▷ *vt* pousser; (*button*) appuyer sur; (*fig*: *product*) mettre en avant, faire de la publicité pour ▷ *vi* pousser; **to ~ for** (*better pay, conditions*) réclamer; **push in** *vi* s'introduire de force; **push off** *vi* (*inf*) filer, ficher le camp; **push on** *vi* (*continue*) continuer; **push over** *vt* renverser; **push through** *vi* (*in crowd*) se frayer un chemin; **pushchair** *n* (BRIT) poussette *f*; **pusher** *n* (*also*: **drug pusher**) revendeur(-euse) (de drogue), ravitailleur(-euse) (en drogue); **push-up** *n* (US) traction *f*

pussy(-cat) ['pusɪ-] *n* (*inf*) minet *m*

put [put] (*pt, pp* **~**) [put] *vt* mettre; (*place*) poser, placer; (*say*) dire, exprimer; (*a question*) poser; (*case, view*) exposer, présenter; (*estimate*) estimer; **put aside** *vt* mettre de côté; **put away** *vt* (*store*) ranger; **put back** *vt* (*replace*) remettre, replacer; (*postpone*) remettre; **put by** *vt* (*money*) mettre de côté, économiser; **put down** *vt* (*parcel etc*) poser, déposer; (*in writing*) mettre par écrit, inscrire; (*suppress: revolt etc*) réprimer, écraser; (*attribute*) attribuer; (*animal*) abattre; (*cat, dog*) faire piquer; **put forward** *vt* (*ideas*) avancer, proposer; **put in** *vt* (*complaint*) soumettre; (*time, effort*) consacrer; **put off** *vt* (*postpone*) remettre à plus tard, ajourner; (*discourage*) dissuader; **put on** *vt* (*clothes, lipstick, CD*) mettre; (*light etc*) allumer; (*play etc*) monter; (*weight*) prendre; (*assume: accent, manner*) prendre; **put out** *vt* (*take outside*) mettre dehors; (*one's hand*) tendre; (*light etc*) éteindre; (*person: inconvenience*) déranger, gêner; **put through** *vt* (Tel: *caller*) mettre en communication; (: *call*) passer; (*plan*) faire accepter; **put together** *vt* mettre ensemble; (*assemble: furniture*) monter, assembler; (*meal*) préparer; **put up** *vt* (*raise*) lever, relever, remonter; (*hang*) accrocher; (*build*) construire, ériger; (*increase*) augmenter; (*accommodate*) loger; **put up with** *vt fus* supporter

putt [pʌt] *n* putt *m*; **putting green** *n* green *m*

puzzle ['pʌzl] *n* énigme *f*, mystère *m*; (*game*) jeu *m*, casse-tête *m*; (*jigsaw*) puzzle *m*; (*also*: **crossword ~**) mots croisés ▷ *vt* intriguer, rendre perplexe ▷ *vi*: **to ~ over** chercher à comprendre; **puzzled** *adj* perplexe; **puzzling** *adj* déconcertant(e), inexplicable

pyjamas [pɪˈdʒɑːməz] *npl* (BRIT) pyjama *m*

pylon ['paɪlən] *n* pylône *m*

pyramid ['pɪrəmɪd] *n* pyramide *f*

Pyrenees [pɪrəˈniːz] *npl* Pyrénées *fpl*

quack [kwæk] *n* (*of duck*) coin-coin *m inv*; (*pej: doctor*) charlatan *m*

quadruple [kwɔ'druːpl] *vt, vi* quadrupler

quail [kweɪl] *n* (*Zool*) caille *f* ▷ *vi*: **to ~ at** *or* **before** reculer devant

quaint [kweɪnt] *adj* bizarre; (*old-fashioned*) désuet(-ète); (*picturesque*) au charme vieillot, pittoresque

quake [kweɪk] *vi* trembler ▷ *n abbr* = **earthquake**

qualification [kwɔlɪfɪ'keɪʃən] *n* (*often pl: degree etc*) diplôme *m*; (*training*) qualification(s) *f(pl)*; (*ability*) compétence(s) *f(pl)*; (*limitation*) réserve *f*, restriction *f*

qualified ['kwɔlɪfaɪd] *adj* (*trained*) qualifié(e); (*professionally*) diplômé(e); (*fit, competent*) compétent(e), qualifié(e); (*limited*) conditionnel(le)

qualify ['kwɔlɪfaɪ] *vt* qualifier; (*modify*) atténuer, nuancer ▷ *vi*: **to ~ (as)** obtenir son diplôme (de); **to ~ (for)** remplir les conditions requises (pour); (*Sport*) se qualifier (pour)

quality ['kwɔlɪtɪ] *n* qualité *f*

qualm [kwɑːm] *n* doute *m*; scrupule *m*

quantify ['kwɔntɪfaɪ] *vt* quantifier

quantity ['kwɔntɪtɪ] *n* quantité *f*

quarantine ['kwɔrəntiːn] *n* quarantaine *f*

quarrel ['kwɔrl] *n* querelle *f*, dispute *f* ▷ *vi* se disputer, se quereller

quarry ['kwɔrɪ] *n* (*for stone*) carrière *f*; (*animal*) proie *f*, gibier *m*

quart [kwɔːt] *n* ≈ litre *m*

quarter ['kwɔːtəʳ] *n* quart *m*; (*of year*) trimestre *m*; (*district*) quartier *m*; (*US, CANADA: 25 cents*) (*pièce f de*) vingt-cinq cents *mpl* ▷ *vt* partager en quartiers *or* en quatre; (*Mil*) caserner, cantonner; **quarters** *npl* logement *m*; (*Mil*) quartiers *mpl*, cantonnement *m*; **a ~ of an hour** un quart d'heure; **quarter final** *n* quart *m* de finale; **quarterly** *adj* trimestriel(le) ▷ *adv* tous les trois mois

quartet(te) [kwɔː'tɛt] *n* quatuor *m*; (*jazz players*) quartette *m*

quartz [kwɔːts] *n* quartz *m*

quay [kiː] *n* (*also*: **~side**) quai *m*

queasy ['kwiːzɪ] *adj*: **to feel ~** avoir mal au cœur

Quebec [kwɪ'bɛk] *n* (*city*) Québec; (*province*) Québec *m*

queen [kwiːn] *n* (*gen*) reine *f*; (*Cards etc*) dame *f*

queer [kwɪəʳ] *adj* étrange, curieux(-euse); (*suspicious*) louche ▷ *n* (*inf: highly offensive*) homosexuel *m*

quench [kwɛntʃ] *vt*: **to ~ one's thirst** se désaltérer

query ['kwɪərɪ] *n* question *f* ▷ *vt* (*disagree with, dispute*) mettre en doute, questionner

quest [kwɛst] *n* recherche *f*, quête *f*

question ['kwɛstʃən] *n* question *f* ▷ *vt* (*person*) interroger; (*plan, idea*) mettre en question *or* en doute; **beyond ~** sans aucun doute; **out of the ~** hors de question; **questionable** *adj* discutable; **question mark** *n* point *m* d'interrogation; **questionnaire** [kwɛstʃə'nɛəʳ] *n* questionnaire *m*

queue [kjuː] (*BRIT*) *n* queue *f*, file *f* ▷ *vi* (*also*: **~ up**) faire la queue

quiche [kiːʃ] *n* quiche *f*

quick [kwɪk] *adj* rapide; (*mind*) vif (vive); (*agile*) agile, vif (vive) ▷ *n*: **cut to the ~** (*fig*) touché(e) au vif; **be ~!** dépêche-toi!; **quickly** *adv* (*fast*) vite, rapidement; (*immediately*) tout de suite

quid [kwɪd] *n* (*pl inv*: *BRIT inf*) livre *f*

quiet ['kwaɪət] *adj* tranquille, calme; (*voice*) bas(se); (*ceremony, colour*) discret(-ète) ▷ *n* tranquillité *f*, calme *m*; (*silence*) silence *m*; **quietly** *adv* tranquillement; (*silently*) silencieusement; (*discreetly*) discrètement

quilt [kwɪlt] *n* édredon *m*; (*continental quilt*) couette *f*

quirky ['kwɜːkɪ] *adj* singulier(-ère)

quit [kwɪt] (*pt, pp* ~ *or* **~ted**) *vt* quitter ▷ *vi* (*give up*) abandonner, renoncer; (*resign*) démissionner

quite [kwaɪt] *adv* (*rather*) assez, plutôt; (*entirely*) complètement, tout à fait; **~ a few of them** un assez grand nombre d'entre eux; **that's not ~ right** ce n'est pas tout à fait juste; **~ (so)!** exactement!

quits [kwɪts] *adj*: **~ (with)** quitte (envers); **let's call it ~** restons-en là

quiver ['kwɪvəʳ] *vi* trembler, frémir

quiz [kwɪz] *n* (*on TV*) jeu-concours *m* (télévisé); (*in magazine etc*) test *m* de connaissances ▷ *vt* interroger

quota ['kwəʊtə] *n* quota *m*

quotation [kwəʊ'teɪʃən] *n* citation *f*; (*estimate*) devis *m*; **quotation marks** *npl* guillemets *mpl*

quote [kwəʊt] *n* citation *f*; (*estimate*) devis *m* ▷ *vt* (*sentence, author*) citer; (*price*) donner, soumettre ▷ *vi*: **to ~ from** citer; **quotes** *npl* (*inverted commas*) guillemets *mpl*

Rabat [rə'bɑːt] *n* Rabat

rabbi ['ræbaɪ] *n* rabbin *m*

rabbit ['ræbɪt] *n* lapin *m*

rabies ['reɪbiːz] *n* rage *f*

RAC *n abbr* (BRIT: = *Royal Automobile Club*) ≈ ACF *m*

rac(c)oon [rə'kuːn] *n* raton *m* laveur

race [reɪs] *n* (*species*) race *f*; (*competition, rush*) course *f* ▷ *vt* (*person*) faire la course avec ▷ *vi* (*compete*) faire la course, courir; (*pulse*) battre très vite; **race car** *n* (US) = **racing car**; **racecourse** *n* champ *m* de courses; **racehorse** *n* cheval *m* de course; **racetrack** *n* piste *f*

racial ['reɪʃl] *adj* racial(e)

racing ['reɪsɪŋ] *n* courses *fpl*; **racing car** *n* (BRIT) voiture *f* de course; **racing driver** *n* (BRIT) pilote *m* de course

racism ['reɪsɪzəm] *n* racisme *m*; **racist** ['reɪsɪst] *adj, n* raciste *m/f*

rack [ræk] *n* (*for guns, tools*) râtelier *m*; (*for clothes*) portant *m*; (*for bottles*) casier *m*; (*also:* **luggage ~**) filet *m* à bagages; (*also:* **roof ~**) galerie *f*; (*also:* **dish ~**) égouttoir *m* ▷ *vt* tourmenter; **to ~ one's brains** se creuser la cervelle

racket ['rækɪt] *n* (*for tennis*) raquette *f*; (*noise*) tapage *m*, vacarme *m*; (*swindle*) escroquerie *f*

racquet ['rækɪt] *n* raquette *f*

radar ['reɪdɑːʳ] *n* radar *m*

radiation [ˌreɪdɪˈeɪʃən] n rayonnement m;
(radioactive) radiation f
radiator [ˈreɪdɪeɪtəʳ] n radiateur m
radical [ˈrædɪkl] adj radical(e)
radio [ˈreɪdɪəu] n radio f ▷ vt (person) appeler
par radio; **on the ~** à la radio; **radioactive**
adj radioactif(-ive); **radio station** n station
f de radio
radish [ˈrædɪʃ] n radis m
RAF n abbr (BRIT) = **Royal Air Force**
raffle [ˈræfl] n tombola f
raft [rɑːft] n (craft: also: **life ~**) radeau m; (logs)
train m de flottage
rag [ræg] n chiffon m; (pej: newspaper) feuille f,
torchon m; (for charity) attractions organisées par
les étudiants au profit d'œuvres de charité; **rags**
npl haillons mpl
rage [reɪdʒ] n (fury) rage f, fureur f ▷ vi (person)
être fou (folle) de rage; (storm) faire rage, être
déchaîné(e); **it's all the ~** cela fait fureur
ragged [ˈrægɪd] adj (edge) inégal(e), qui
accroche; (clothes) en loques; (appearance)
déguenillé(e)
raid [reɪd] n (Mil) raid m; (criminal) hold-up m
inv; (by police) descente f, rafle f ▷ vt faire un
raid sur or un hold-up dans or une descente
dans
rail [reɪl] n (on stair) rampe f; (on bridge, balcony)
balustrade f; (of ship) bastingage m; (for train)
rail m; **railcard** n (BRIT) carte f de chemin
de fer; **railing(s)** n(pl) grille f; **railway** (US
railroad) n chemin m de fer; (track) voie f
ferrée; **railway line** n (BRIT) ligne f de chemin
de fer; (track) voie ferrée; **railway station** n
(BRIT) gare f
rain [reɪn] n pluie f ▷ vi pleuvoir; **in the ~** sous
la pluie; **it's ~ing** il pleut; **rainbow** n arc-en-
ciel m; **raincoat** n imperméable m; **raindrop**
n goutte f de pluie; **rainfall** n chute f de pluie;
(measurement) hauteur f des précipitations;
rainforest n forêt tropicale; **rainy** adj
pluvieux(-euse)
raise [reɪz] n augmentation f ▷ vt (lift) lever;
hausser; (increase) augmenter; (morale)
remonter; (standards) améliorer; (a protest,
doubt) provoquer, causer; (a question) soulever;
(cattle, family) élever; (crop) faire pousser; (army,
funds) rassembler; (loan) obtenir; **to ~ one's
voice** élever la voix
raisin [ˈreɪzn] n raisin sec
rake [reɪk] n (tool) râteau m; (person) débauché
m ▷ vt (garden) ratisser
rally [ˈrælɪ] n (Pol etc) meeting m,
rassemblement m; (Aut) rallye m; (Tennis)
échange m ▷ vt rassembler, rallier; (support)
gagner ▷ vi (sick person) aller mieux; (Stock
Exchange) reprendre
RAM [ræm] n abbr (Comput: = random access
memory) mémoire vive

ram [ræm] n bélier m ▷ vt (push) enfoncer;
(crash into: vehicle) emboutir; (: lamppost etc)
percuter
Ramadan [ˌræməˈdæn] n Ramadan m
ramble [ˈræmbl] n randonnée f ▷ vi (walk)
se promener, faire une randonnée; (pej:
also: **~ on**) discourir, pérorer; **rambler** n
promeneur(-euse), randonneur(-euse);
rambling adj (speech) décousu(e); (house)
plein(e) de coins et de recoins; (Bot)
grimpant(e)
ramp [ræmp] n (incline) rampe f; (Aut)
dénivellation f; (in garage) pont m; **on/off ~** (US
Aut) bretelle f d'accès
rampage [ræmˈpeɪdʒ] n: **to be on the ~** se
déchaîner
ran [ræn] pt of **run**
ranch [rɑːntʃ] n ranch m
random [ˈrændəm] adj fait(e) or établi(e) au
hasard; (Comput, Math) aléatoire ▷ n: **at ~** au
hasard
rang [ræŋ] pt of **ring**
range [reɪndʒ] n (of mountains) chaîne f; (of
missile, voice) portée f; (of products) choix m,
gamme f; (also: **shooting ~**) champ m de tir;
(also: **kitchen ~**) fourneau m (de cuisine) ▷ vt
(place) mettre en rang, placer ▷ vi: **to ~ over**
couvrir; **to ~ from ... to** aller de ... à
ranger [ˈreɪndʒəʳ] n garde m forestier
rank [ræŋk] n rang m; (Mil) grade m; (BRIT:
also: **taxi ~**) station f de taxis ▷ vi: **to ~ among**
compter or se classer parmi ▷ adj (smell)
nauséabond(e); **the ~ and file** (fig) la masse,
la base
ransom [ˈrænsəm] n rançon f; **to hold sb to ~**
(fig) exercer un chantage sur qn
rant [rænt] vi fulminer
rap [ræp] n (music) rap m ▷ vt (door) frapper sur
or à; (table etc) taper sur
rape [reɪp] n viol m; (Bot) colza m ▷ vt violer
rapid [ˈræpɪd] adj rapide; **rapidly** adv
rapidement; **rapids** npl (Geo) rapides mpl
rapist [ˈreɪpɪst] n auteur m d'un viol
rapport [ræˈpɔːʳ] n entente f
rare [rɛəʳ] adj rare; (Culin: steak) saignant(e);
rarely adv rarement
rash [ræʃ] adj imprudent(e), irréfléchi(e) ▷ n
(Med) rougeur f, éruption f; (of events) série f
(noire)
rasher [ˈræʃəʳ] n fine tranche (de lard)
raspberry [ˈrɑːzbərɪ] n framboise f
rat [ræt] n rat m
rate [reɪt] n (ratio) taux m, pourcentage m;
(speed) vitesse f, rythme m; (price) tarif m ▷ vt
(price) évaluer, estimer; (people) classer; **rates**
npl (BRIT: property tax) impôts locaux; **to ~
sb/sth as** considérer qn/qch comme
rather [ˈrɑːðəʳ] adv (somewhat) assez, plutôt;
(to some extent) un peu; **it's ~ expensive**

c'est assez cher; (*too much*) c'est un peu cher;
there's ~ a lot il y en a beaucoup; **I would** or
I'd ~ go j'aimerais mieux or je préférerais partir;
or ~ (*more accurately*) ou plutôt
rating ['reɪtɪŋ] *n* (*assessment*) évaluation *f*;
(*score*) classement *m*; (*Finance*) cote *f*; **ratings**
npl (*Radio*) indice(s) *m*(*pl*) d'écoute; (*TV*)
Audimat®
ratio ['reɪʃɪəu] *n* proportion *f*; **in the ~ of 100
to 1** dans la proportion de 100 contre 1
ration ['ræʃən] *n* ration *f* ▷ *vt* rationner;
rations *npl* (*food*) vivres *mpl*
rational ['ræʃənl] *adj* raisonnable, sensé(e);
(*solution, reasoning*) logique; (*Med: person*)
lucide
rat race *n* foire *f* d'empoigne
rattle ['rætl] *n* (*of door, window*) battement
m; (*of coins, chain*) cliquetis *m*; (*of train, engine*)
bruit *m* de ferraille; (*for baby*) hochet *m*
▷ *vi* cliqueter; (*car, bus*): **to ~ along** rouler
en faisant un bruit de ferraille ▷ *vt* agiter
(bruyamment); (*inf: disconcert*) déconcertant
rave [reɪv] *vi* (*in anger*) s'emporter; (*with
enthusiasm*) s'extasier; (*Med*) délirer ▷ *n* (*inf:
party*) rave *f*, soirée *f* techno
raven ['reɪvən] *n* grand corbeau
ravine [rə'viːn] *n* ravin *m*
raw [rɔː] *adj* (*uncooked*) cru(e); (*not processed*)
brut(e); (*sore*) à vif, irrité(e); (*inexperienced*)
inexpérimenté(e); **~ materials** matières
premières
ray [reɪ] *n* rayon *m*; **~ of hope** lueur *f* d'espoir
razor ['reɪzəʳ] *n* rasoir *m*; **razor blade** *n* lame
f de rasoir
Rd *abbr* = **road**
RE *n abbr* (*BRIT*) = **religious education**
re [riː] *prep* concernant
reach [riːtʃ] *n* portée *f*, atteinte *f*; (*of river etc*)
étendue *f* ▷ *vt* atteindre, arriver à; (*conclusion,
decision*) parvenir à ▷ *vi* s'étendre; **out of/
within ~** (*object*) hors de/à portée; **reach out**
vt tendre ▷ *vi*: **to ~ out (for)** allonger le bras
(pour prendre)
react [riː'ækt] *vi* réagir; **reaction** [riː'ækʃən] *n*
réaction *f*; **reactor** [riː'æktəʳ] *n* réacteur *m*
read (*pt, pp* **~**) [riːd, rɛd] *vi* lire ▷ *vt* lire;
(*understand*) comprendre, interpréter; (*study*)
étudier; (*meter*) relever; (*subj: instrument etc*)
indiquer, marquer; **read out** *vt* lire à haute
voix; **reader** *n* lecteur(-trice)
readily ['rɛdɪlɪ] *adv* volontiers, avec
empressement; (*easily*) facilement
reading ['riːdɪŋ] *n* lecture *f*; (*understanding*)
interprétation *f*; (*on instrument*) indications *fpl*
ready ['rɛdɪ] *adj* prêt(e); (*willing*) prêt,
disposé(e); (*available*) disponible ▷ *n*: **at the ~**
(*Mil*) prêt à faire feu; **when will my photos be
~?** quand est-ce que mes photos seront prêtes?;
to get ~ (*as vi*) se préparer; (*as vt*) préparer;

ready-cooked *adj* précuit(e); **ready-made**
adj tout(e) faite(e)
real [rɪəl] *adj* (*world, life*) réel(le); (*genuine*)
véritable; (*proper*) vrai(e) ▷ *adv* (*US inf: very*)
vraiment; **real ale** *n* bière traditionnelle;
real estate *n* biens fonciers or immobiliers;
realistic [rɪə'lɪstɪk] *adj* réaliste; **reality**
[riː'ælɪtɪ] *n* réalité *f*
reality TV *n* téléréalité *f*
realization [rɪəlaɪ'zeɪʃən] *n* (*awareness*)
prise *f* de conscience; (*fulfilment: also: of asset*)
réalisation *f*
realize ['rɪəlaɪz] *vt* (*understand*) se rendre
compte de, prendre conscience de; (*a project,
Comm: asset*) réaliser
really ['rɪəlɪ] *adv* vraiment; **~?** vraiment?, c'est
vrai?
realm [rɛlm] *n* royaume *m*; (*fig*) domaine *m*
realtor ['rɪəltɔːʳ] *n* (*US*) agent immobilier
reappear [riːə'pɪəʳ] *vi* réapparaître, reparaître
rear [rɪəʳ] *adj* de derrière, arrière *inv*; (*Aut: wheel
etc*) arrière ▷ *n* arrière *m* ▷ *vt* (*cattle, family*)
élever ▷ *vi* (*also:* **~ up**: *animal*) se cabrer
rearrange [riːə'reɪndʒ] *vt* réarranger
rear: **rear-view mirror** *n* (*Aut*) rétroviseur *m*;
rear-wheel drive *n* (*Aut*) traction *f* arrière
reason ['riːzn] *n* raison *f* ▷ *vi*: **to ~ with
sb** raisonner qn, faire entendre raison à
qn; **it stands to ~ that** il va sans dire que;
reasonable *adj* raisonnable; (*not bad*)
acceptable; **reasonably** *adv* (*behave*)
raisonnablement; (*fairly*) assez; **reasoning** *n*
raisonnement *m*
reassurance [riːə'ʃuərəns] *n* (*factual*)
assurance *f*, garantie *f*; (*emotional*) réconfort *m*
reassure [riːə'ʃuəʳ] *vt* rassurer
rebate ['riːbeɪt] *n* (*on tax etc*) dégrèvement *m*
rebel *n* ['rɛbl] rebelle *m/f* ▷ *vi* [rɪ'bɛl] se
rebeller, se révolter; **rebellion** [rɪ'bɛljən] *n*
rébellion *f*, révolte *f*; **rebellious** [rɪ'bɛljəs] *adj*
rebelle
rebuild [riː'bɪld] *vt* (*irreg: like* **build**)
reconstruire
recall *vt* [rɪ'kɔːl] rappeler; (*remember*) se
rappeler, se souvenir de ▷ *n* ['riːkɔl] rappel *m*;
(*ability to remember*) mémoire *f*
rec'd *abbr of* **received**
receipt [rɪ'siːt] *n* (*document*) reçu *m*; (*for parcel
etc*) accusé *m* de réception; (*act of receiving*)
réception *f*; **receipts** *npl* (*Comm*) recettes *fpl*;
can I have a ~, please? je peux avoir un reçu,
s'il vous plaît?
receive [rɪ'siːv] *vt* recevoir; (*guest*) recevoir,
accueillir; **receiver** *n* (*Tel*) récepteur *m*,
combiné *m*; (*Radio*) récepteur *m*; (*of stolen goods*)
receleur *m*; (*for bankruptcies*) administrateur
m judiciaire
recent ['riːsnt] *adj* récent(e); **recently** *adv*
récemment

r

reception [rɪ'sɛpʃən] n réception f; (welcome) accueil m, réception; **reception desk** n réception f; **receptionist** n réceptionniste m/f
recession [rɪ'sɛʃən] n (Econ) récession f
recharge [ri:'tʃɑːdʒ] vt (battery) recharger
recipe ['rɛsɪpɪ] n recette f
recipient [rɪ'sɪpɪənt] n (of payment) bénéficiaire m/f; (of letter) destinataire m/f
recital [rɪ'saɪtl] n récital m
recite [rɪ'saɪt] vt (poem) réciter
reckless ['rɛkləs] adj (driver etc) imprudent(e); (spender etc) insouciant(e)
reckon ['rɛkən] vt (count) calculer, compter; (consider) considérer, estimer; (think): **I ~ (that)** ... je pense que ..., j'estime que ...
reclaim [rɪ'kleɪm] vt (land: from sea) assécher; (demand back) réclamer (le remboursement or la restitution de); (waste materials) récupérer
recline [rɪ'klaɪn] vi être allongé(e) or étendu(e)
recognition [rɛkəg'nɪʃən] n reconnaissance f; **transformed beyond ~** méconnaissable
recognize ['rɛkəgnaɪz] vt: **to ~ (by/as)** reconnaître (à/comme étant)
recollection [rɛkə'lɛkʃən] n souvenir m
recommend [rɛkə'mɛnd] vt recommander; **can you ~ a good restaurant?** pouvez-vous me conseiller un bon restaurant?; **recommendation** [rɛkəmɛn'deɪʃən] n recommandation f
reconcile ['rɛkənsaɪl] vt (two people) réconcilier; (two facts) concilier, accorder; **to ~ o.s. to** se résigner à
reconsider [ri:kən'sɪdər] vt reconsidérer
reconstruct [ri:kən'strʌkt] vt (building) reconstruire; (crime, system) reconstituer
record n ['rɛkɔːd] rapport m, récit m; (of meeting etc) procès-verbal m; (register) registre m; (file) dossier m; (Comput) article m; (also: **police ~**) casier m judiciaire; (Mus: disc) disque m; (Sport) record m ▷ adj record inv ▷ vt [rɪ'kɔːd] (set down) noter; (Mus: song etc) enregistrer; **public ~s** archives fpl; **in ~ time** dans un temps record; **recorded delivery** n (Brit Post): **to send sth recorded delivery** ≈ envoyer qch en recommandé; **recorder** n (Mus) flûte f à bec; **recording** n (Mus) enregistrement m; **record player** n tourne-disque m
recount [rɪ'kaunt] vt raconter
recover [rɪ'kʌvər] vt récupérer ▷ vi (from illness) se rétablir; (from shock) se remettre; **recovery** n récupération f; rétablissement m; (Econ) redressement m
recreate [ri:krɪ'eɪt] vt recréer
recreation [rɛkrɪ'eɪʃən] n (leisure) récréation f, détente f; **recreational drug** n drogue récréative; **recreational vehicle** n (US) camping-car m
recruit [rɪ'kru:t] n recrue f ▷ vt recruter; **recruitment** n recrutement m

rectangle ['rɛktæŋgl] n rectangle m; **rectangular** [rɛk'tæŋgjulər] adj rectangulaire
rectify ['rɛktɪfaɪ] vt (error) rectifier, corriger
rector ['rɛktər] n (Rel) pasteur m
recur [rɪ'kəːr] vi se reproduire; (idea, opportunity) se retrouver; (symptoms) réapparaître; **recurring** adj (problem) périodique, fréquent(e); (Math) périodique
recyclable [ri:'saɪkləbl] adj recyclable
recycle [ri:'saɪkl] vt, vi recycler
recycling [ri:'saɪklɪŋ] n recyclage m
red [rɛd] n rouge m; (Pol: pej) rouge m/f ▷ adj rouge; (hair) roux (rousse); **in the ~** (account) à découvert; (business) en déficit; **Red Cross** n Croix-Rouge f; **redcurrant** n groseille f (rouge)
redeem [rɪ'di:m] vt (debt) rembourser; (sth in pawn) dégager; (fig, also Rel) racheter
red: **red-haired** adj roux (rousse); **redhead** n roux (rousse); **red-hot** adj chauffé(e) au rouge, brûlant(e); **red light** n: **to go through a red light** (Aut) brûler un feu rouge; **red-light district** n quartier mal famé
red meat n viande f rouge
reduce [rɪ'dju:s] vt réduire; (lower) abaisser; **"~ speed now"** (Aut) "ralentir"; **to ~ sb to tears** faire pleurer qn; **reduced** adj réduit(e); **"greatly reduced prices"** "gros rabais"; **at a reduced price** (goods) au rabais; (ticket etc) à prix réduit; **reduction** [rɪ'dʌkʃən] n réduction f; (of price) baisse f; (discount) rabais m; réduction; **is there a reduction for children/students?** y a-t-il une réduction pour les enfants/les étudiants?
redundancy [rɪ'dʌndənsɪ] n (Brit) licenciement m, mise f au chômage
redundant [rɪ'dʌndnt] adj (Brit: worker) licencié(e), mis(e) au chômage; (detail, object) superflu(e); **to be made ~** (worker) être licencié, être mis au chômage
reed [ri:d] n (Bot) roseau m
reef [ri:f] n (at sea) récif m, écueil m
reel [ri:l] n bobine f; (Fishing) moulinet m; (Cine) bande f; (dance) quadrille écossais ▷ vi (sway) chanceler
ref [rɛf] n abbr (inf: = referee) arbitre m
refectory [rɪ'fɛktərɪ] n réfectoire m
refer [rɪ'fəːr] vt: **to ~ sb to** (inquirer, patient) adresser qn à; (reader: to text) renvoyer qn à ▷ vi: **to ~ to** (allude to) parler de, faire allusion à; (consult) se reporter à; (apply to) s'appliquer à
referee [rɛfə'ri:] n arbitre m; (Brit: for job application) répondant(e) ▷ vt arbitrer
reference ['rɛfrəns] n référence f, renvoi m; (mention) allusion f, mention f; (for job application: letter) références; lettre f de recommandation; **with ~ to** en ce qui concerne; (Comm: in letter) me référant à; **reference number** n (Comm) numéro m de

référence

refill vt [riːˈfɪl] remplir à nouveau; (pen, lighter etc) recharger ▷ n [ˈriːfɪl] (for pen etc) recharge f

refine [rɪˈfaɪn] vt (sugar, oil) raffiner; (taste) affiner; (idea, theory) peaufiner; **refined** adj (person, taste) raffiné(e); **refinery** n raffinerie f

reflect [rɪˈflɛkt] vt (light, image) réfléchir, refléter ▷ vi (think) réfléchir, méditer; **it ~s badly on him** cela le discrédite; **it ~s well on him** c'est tout à son honneur; **reflection** [rɪˈflɛkʃən] n réflexion f; (image) reflet m; **on reflection** réflexion faite

reflex [ˈriːflɛks] adj, n réflexe (m)

reform [rɪˈfɔːm] n réforme f ▷ vt réformer

refrain [rɪˈfreɪn] vi: **to ~ from doing** s'abstenir de faire ▷ n refrain m

refresh [rɪˈfrɛʃ] vt rafraîchir; (subj: food, sleep etc) redonner des forces à; **refreshing** adj (drink) rafraîchissant(e); (sleep) réparateur(-trice); **refreshments** npl rafraîchissements mpl

refrigerator [rɪˈfrɪdʒəreɪtəʳ] n réfrigérateur m, frigidaire m

refuel [riːˈfjʊəl] vi se ravitailler en carburant

refuge [ˈrɛfjuːdʒ] n refuge m; **to take ~ in** se réfugier dans; **refugee** [rɛfjuˈdʒiː] n réfugié(e)

refund n [ˈriːfʌnd] remboursement m ▷ vt [rɪˈfʌnd] rembourser

refurbish [riːˈfəːbɪʃ] vt remettre à neuf

refusal [rɪˈfjuːzəl] n refus m; **to have first ~ on sth** avoir droit de préemption sur qch

refuse¹ [ˈrɛfjuːs] n ordures fpl, détritus mpl

refuse² [rɪˈfjuːz] vt, vi refuser; **to ~ to do sth** refuser de faire qch

regain [rɪˈgeɪn] vt (lost ground) regagner; (strength) retrouver

regard [rɪˈgɑːd] n respect m, estime f, considération f ▷ vt considérer; **to give one's ~s to** faire ses amitiés à; **"with kindest ~s"** "bien amicalement"; **as ~s, with ~ to** en ce qui concerne; **regarding** prep en ce qui concerne; **regardless** adv quand même; **regardless of** sans se soucier de

regenerate [rɪˈdʒɛnəreɪt] vt régénérer ▷ vi se régénérer

reggae [ˈrɛgeɪ] n reggae m

regiment [ˈrɛdʒɪmənt] n régiment m

region [ˈriːdʒən] n région f; **in the ~ of** (fig) aux alentours de; **regional** adj régional(e)

register [ˈrɛdʒɪstəʳ] n registre m; (also: electoral ~) liste électorale ▷ vt enregistrer, inscrire; (birth) déclarer; (vehicle) immatriculer; (letter) envoyer en recommandé; (subj: instrument) marquer ▷ vi s'inscrire; (at hotel) signer le registre; (make impression) être (bien) compris(e); **registered** adj (BRIT: letter) recommandé(e)

registered trademark n marque déposée

registrar [ˈrɛdʒɪstrɑːʳ] n officier m de l'état civil

registration [rɛdʒɪsˈtreɪʃən] n (act) enregistrement m; (of student) inscription f; (BRIT Aut: also: ~ number) numéro m d'immatriculation

registry office [ˈrɛdʒɪstrɪ-] n (BRIT) bureau m de l'état civil; **to get married in a ~** ≈ se marier à la mairie

regret [rɪˈgrɛt] n regret m ▷ vt regretter; **regrettable** adj regrettable, fâcheux(-euse)

regular [ˈrɛgjʊləʳ] adj régulier(-ière); (usual) habituel(le), normal(e); (soldier) de métier; (Comm: size) ordinaire ▷ n (client etc) habitué(e); **regularly** adv régulièrement

regulate [ˈrɛgjʊleɪt] vt régler; **regulation** [rɛgjuˈleɪʃən] n (rule) règlement m; (adjustment) réglage m

rehabilitation [ˈriːəbɪlɪˈteɪʃən] n (of offender) réhabilitation f; (of addict) réadaptation f

rehearsal [rɪˈhəːsəl] n répétition f

rehearse [rɪˈhəːs] vt répéter

reign [reɪn] n règne m ▷ vi régner

reimburse [riːɪmˈbəːs] vt rembourser

rein [reɪn] n (for horse) rêne f

reincarnation [riːɪnkɑːˈneɪʃən] n réincarnation f

reindeer [ˈreɪndɪəʳ] n (pl inv) renne m

reinforce [riːɪnˈfɔːs] vt renforcer; **reinforcements** npl (Mil) renfort(s) m(pl)

reinstate [riːɪnˈsteɪt] vt rétablir, réintégrer

reject n [ˈriːdʒɛkt] (Comm) article m de rebut ▷ vt [rɪˈdʒɛkt] refuser; (idea) rejeter; **rejection** [rɪˈdʒɛkʃən] n rejet m, refus m

rejoice [rɪˈdʒɔɪs] vi: **to ~ (at or over)** se réjouir (de)

relate [rɪˈleɪt] vt (tell) raconter; (connect) établir un rapport entre ▷ vi: **to ~ to** (connect) se rapporter à; **to ~ to sb** (interact) entretenir des rapports avec qn; **related** adj apparenté(e); **related to** (subject) lié(e) à; **relating to** prep concernant

relation [rɪˈleɪʃən] n (person) parent(e); (link) rapport m, lien m; **relations** npl (relatives) famille f; **relationship** n rapport m, lien m; (personal ties) relations fpl, rapports; (also: **family relationship**) lien de parenté; (affair) liaison f

relative [ˈrɛlətɪv] n parent(e) ▷ adj relatif(-ive); (respective) respectif(-ive); **relatively** adv relativement

relax [rɪˈlæks] vi (muscle) se relâcher; (person: unwind) se détendre ▷ vt relâcher; (mind, person) détendre; **relaxation** [riːlækˈseɪʃən] n relâchement m; (of mind) détente f; (recreation) détente, délassement m; **relaxed** adj relâché(e); détendu(e); **relaxing** adj délassant(e)

relay [ˈriːleɪ] n (Sport) course f de relais ▷ vt

(*message*) retransmettre, relayer
release [rɪ'liːs] *n* (*from prison, obligation*)
libération *f*; (*of gas etc*) émission *f*; (*of film etc*)
sortie *f*; (*new recording*) disque *m* ▷ *vt* (*prisoner*)
libérer; (*book, film*) sortir; (*report, news*) rendre
public, publier; (*gas etc*) émettre, dégager;
(*free: from wreckage etc*) dégager; (*Tech: catch,
spring etc*) déclencher; (*let go: person, animal*)
relâcher; (: *hand, object*) lâcher; (: *grip, brake*)
desserrer
relegate ['rɛləɡeɪt] *vt* reléguer; (*BRIT Sport*): **to
be ~d** descendre dans une division inférieure
relent [rɪ'lɛnt] *vi* se laisser fléchir; **relentless**
adj implacable; (*non-stop*) continuel(le)
relevant ['rɛləvənt] *adj* (*question*)
pertinent(e); (*corresponding*) approprié(e);
(*fact*) significatif(-ive); (*information*) utile
reliable [rɪ'laɪəbl] *adj* (*person, firm*)
sérieux(-euse), fiable; (*method, machine*) fiable;
(*news, information*) sûr(e)
relic ['rɛlɪk] *n* (*Rel*) relique *f*; (*of the past*)
vestige *m*
relief [rɪ'liːf] *n* (*from pain, anxiety*) soulagement
m; (*help, supplies*) secours *m(pl)*; (*Art, Geo*)
relief *m*
relieve [rɪ'liːv] *vt* (*pain, patient*) soulager;
(*fear, worry*) dissiper; (*bring help*) secourir;
(*take over from: gen*) relayer; (: *guard*) relever;
to ~ sb of sth débarrasser qn de qch; **to ~ o.s.**
(*euphemism*) se soulager, faire ses besoins;
relieved *adj* soulagé(e)
religion [rɪ'lɪdʒən] *n* religion *f*
religious [rɪ'lɪdʒəs] *adj* religieux(-euse); (*book*)
de piété; **religious education** *n* instruction
religieuse
relish ['rɛlɪʃ] *n* (*Culin*) condiment *m*; (*enjoyment*)
délectation *f* ▷ *vt* (*food etc*) savourer; **to ~
doing** se délecter à faire
relocate [riːləu'keɪt] *vt* (*business*) transférer
▷ *vi* se transférer, s'installer *or* s'établir ailleurs
reluctance [rɪ'lʌktəns] *n* répugnance *f*
reluctant [rɪ'lʌktənt] *adj* peu disposé(e), qui
hésite; **reluctantly** *adv* à contrecœur, sans
enthousiasme
rely on [rɪ'laɪ-] *vt fus* (*be dependent on*)
dépendre de; (*trust*) compter sur
remain [rɪ'meɪn] *vi* rester; **remainder** *n* reste
m; (*Comm*) fin *f* de série; **remaining** *adj* qui
reste; **remains** *npl* restes *mpl*
remand [rɪ'mɑːnd] *n*: **on ~** en détention
préventive ▷ *vt*: **to be ~ed in custody** être
placé(e) en détention préventive
remark [rɪ'mɑːk] *n* remarque *f*, observation
f ▷ *vt* (faire) remarquer, dire; **remarkable** *adj*
remarquable
remarry [riː'mærɪ] *vi* se remarier
remedy ['rɛmədɪ] *n*: **~ (for)** remède *m* (contre
or à) ▷ *vt* remédier à
remember [rɪ'mɛmbər] *vt* se rappeler, se

souvenir de; (*send greetings*): **~ me to him**
saluez-le de ma part; **Remembrance
Day** [rɪ'mɛmbrəns-] *n* (*BRIT*) ≈ (le jour de)
l'Armistice *m*, ≈ le 11 novembre

● **REMEMBRANCE DAY**
●
● **Remembrance Day** ou **Remembrance
● Sunday** est le dimanche le plus proche du
● 11 novembre, jour où la Première Guerre
● mondiale a officiellement pris fin. Il rend
● hommage aux victimes des deux guerres
● mondiales. À cette occasion, on observe
● deux minutes de silence à 11h, heure de la
● signature de l'armistice avec l'Allemagne
● en 1918; certaines membres de la famille
● royale et du gouvernement déposent des
● gerbes de coquelicots au cénotaphe de
● Whitehall, et des couronnes sont placées
● sur les monuments aux morts dans toute
● la Grande-Bretagne; par ailleurs, les gens
● portent des coquelicots artificiels fabriqués
● et vendus par des membres de la légion
● britannique blessés au combat, au profit
● des blessés de guerre et de leur famille.

remind [rɪ'maɪnd] *vt*: **to ~ sb of sth** rappeler
qch à qn; **to ~ sb to do** faire penser à qn à
faire, rappeler à qn qu'il doit faire; **reminder** *n*
(*Comm: letter*) rappel *m*; (*note etc*) pense-bête
m; (*souvenir*) souvenir *m*
reminiscent [rɛmɪ'nɪsnt] *adj*: **~ of** qui
rappelle, qui fait penser à
remnant ['rɛmnənt] *n* reste *m*, restant *m*; (*of
cloth*) coupon *m*
remorse [rɪ'mɔːs] *n* remords *m*
remote [rɪ'məut] *adj* éloigné(e), lointain(e);
(*person*) distant(e); (*possibility*) vague; **remote
control** *n* télécommande *f*; **remotely** *adv* au
loin; (*slightly*) très vaguement
removal [rɪ'muːvəl] *n* (*taking away*)
enlèvement *m*; suppression *f*; (*BRIT: from
house*) déménagement *m*; (*from office:
dismissal*) renvoi *m*; (*of stain*) nettoyage *m*;
(*Med*) ablation *f*; **removal man** (*irreg*) *n* (*BRIT*)
déménageur *m*; **removal van** *n* (*BRIT*) camion
m de déménagement
remove [rɪ'muːv] *vt* enlever, retirer; (*employee*)
renvoyer; (*stain*) faire partir; (*abuse*) supprimer;
(*doubt*) chasser
Renaissance [rɪ'neɪsãs] *n*: **the ~** la
Renaissance
rename [riː'neɪm] *vt* rebaptiser
render ['rɛndər] *vt* rendre
rendezvous ['rɔndɪvuː] *n* rendez-vous *m inv*
renew [rɪ'njuː] *vt* renouveler; (*negotiations*)
reprendre; (*acquaintance*) renouer
renovate ['rɛnəveɪt] *vt* rénover; (*work of art*)
restaurer

renowned [rɪ'naʊnd] *adj* renommé(e)
rent [rɛnt] *pt, pp of* **rend** ▷ *n* loyer *m* ▷ *vt* louer; **rental** *n* (*for television, car*) (prix *m* de) location *f*
reorganize [riː'ɔːɡənaɪz] *vt* réorganiser
rep [rɛp] *n abbr* (*Comm*) = **representative**
repair [rɪ'pɛə^r] *n* réparation *f* ▷ *vt* réparer; **in good/bad ~** en bon/mauvais état; **where can I get this ~ed?** où est-ce que je peux faire réparer ceci?; **repair kit** *n* trousse *f* de réparations
repay [riː'peɪ] *vt* (*irreg: like* **pay**) (*money, creditor*) rembourser; (*sb's efforts*) récompenser; **repayment** *n* remboursement *m*
repeat [rɪ'piːt] *n* (*Radio, TV*) reprise *f* ▷ *vt* répéter; (*promise, attack, also Comm: order*) renouveler; (*Scol: a class*) redoubler ▷ *vi* répéter; **can you ~ that, please?** pouvez-vous répéter, s'il vous plaît?; **repeatedly** *adv* souvent, à plusieurs reprises; **repeat prescription** *n* (*BRIT*): **I'd like a repeat prescription** je voudrais renouveler mon ordonnance
repellent [rɪ'pɛlənt] *adj* repoussant(e) ▷ *n*: **insect ~** insectifuge *m*
repercussions [riːpə'kʌʃənz] *npl* répercussions *fpl*
repetition [rɛpɪ'tɪʃən] *n* répétition *f*
repetitive [rɪ'pɛtɪtɪv] *adj* (*movement, work*) répétitif(-ive); (*speech*) plein(e) de redites
replace [rɪ'pleɪs] *vt* (*put back*) remettre, replacer; (*take the place of*) remplacer; **replacement** *n* (*substitution*) remplacement *m*; (*person*) remplaçant(e)
replay ['riːpleɪ] *n* (*of match*) match rejoué; (*of tape, film*) répétition *f*
replica ['rɛplɪkə] *n* réplique *f*, copie exacte
reply [rɪ'plaɪ] *n* réponse *f* ▷ *vi* répondre
report [rɪ'pɔːt] *n* rapport *m*; (*Press etc*) reportage *m*; (*BRIT: also:* **school ~**) bulletin *m* (scolaire); (*of gun*) détonation *f* ▷ *vt* rapporter, faire un compte rendu de; (*Press etc*) faire un reportage sur; (*notify: accident*) signaler; (: *culprit*) dénoncer ▷ *vi* (*make a report*) faire un rapport; **I'd like to ~ a theft** je voudrais signaler un vol; (*present o.s.*): **to ~ (to sb)** se présenter (chez qn); **report card** *n* (*US, SCOTTISH*) bulletin *m* (scolaire); **reportedly** *adv*: **she is reportedly living in Spain** elle habiterait en Espagne; **he reportedly told them to ...** il leur aurait dit de ...; **reporter** *n* reporter *m*
represent [rɛprɪ'zɛnt] *vt* représenter; (*view, belief*) présenter, expliquer; (*describe*): **to ~ sth as** présenter or décrire qch comme; **representation** [rɛprɪzɛn'teɪʃən] *n* représentation *f*; **representative** *n* représentant(e); (*US Pol*) député *m* ▷ *adj* représentatif(-ive), caractéristique

repress [rɪ'prɛs] *vt* réprimer; **repression** [rɪ'prɛʃən] *n* répression *f*
reprimand ['rɛprɪmɑːnd] *n* réprimande *f* ▷ *vt* réprimander
reproduce [riːprə'djuːs] *vt* reproduire ▷ *vi* se reproduire; **reproduction** [riːprə'dʌkʃən] *n* reproduction *f*
reptile ['rɛptaɪl] *n* reptile *m*
republic [rɪ'pʌblɪk] *n* république *f*; **republican** *adj, n* républicain(e)
reputable ['rɛpjutəbl] *adj* de bonne réputation; (*occupation*) honorable
reputation [rɛpju'teɪʃən] *n* réputation *f*
request [rɪ'kwɛst] *n* demande *f*; (*formal*) requête *f* ▷ *vt*: **to ~ (of or from sb)** demander (à qn); **request stop** *n* (*BRIT: for bus*) arrêt facultatif
require [rɪ'kwaɪə^r] *vt* (*need: subj: person*) avoir besoin de; (: *thing, situation*) nécessiter, demander; (*want*) exiger; (*order*): **to ~ sb to do sth/sth of sb** exiger que qn fasse qch/qch de qn; **requirement** *n* (*need*) exigence *f*; besoin *m*; (*condition*) condition *f* (requise)
resat [riː'sæt] *pt, pp of* **resit**
rescue ['rɛskjuː] *n* (*from accident*) sauvetage *m*; (*help*) secours *mpl* ▷ *vt* sauver
research [rɪ'səːtʃ] *n* recherche(s) *f(pl)* ▷ *vt* faire des recherches sur
resemblance [rɪ'zɛmbləns] *n* ressemblance *f*
resemble [rɪ'zɛmbl] *vt* ressembler à
resent [rɪ'zɛnt] *vt* être contrarié(e) par; **resentful** *adj* irrité(e), plein(e) de ressentiment; **resentment** *n* ressentiment *m*
reservation [rɛzə'veɪʃən] *n* (*booking*) réservation *f*; **to make a ~ (in an hotel/a restaurant/on a plane)** réserver or retenir une chambre/une table/une place; **reservation desk** *n* (*US: in hotel*) réception *f*
reserve [rɪ'zəːv] *n* réserve *f*; (*Sport*) remplaçant(e) ▷ *vt* (*seats etc*) réserver, retenir; **reserved** *adj* réservé(e)
reservoir ['rɛzəvwɑː^r] *n* réservoir *m*
reshuffle [riː'ʃʌfl] *n*: **Cabinet ~** (*Pol*) remaniement ministériel
residence ['rɛzɪdəns] *n* résidence *f*; **residence permit** *n* (*BRIT*) permis *m* de séjour
resident ['rɛzɪdənt] *n* (*of country*) résident(e); (*of area, house*) habitant(e); (*in hotel*) pensionnaire ▷ *adj* résidant(e); **residential** [rɛzɪ'dɛnʃəl] *adj* de résidence; (*area*) résidentiel(le); (*course*) avec hébergement sur place
residue ['rɛzɪdjuː] *n* reste *m*; (*Chem, Physics*) résidu *m*
resign [rɪ'zaɪn] *vt* (*one's post*) se démettre de ▷ *vi* démissionner; **to ~ o.s. to** (*endure*) se résigner à; **resignation** [rɛzɪɡ'neɪʃən] *n* (*from post*) démission *f*; (*state of mind*) résignation *f*
resin ['rɛzɪn] *n* résine *f*

r

resist [rɪ'zɪst] vt résister à; **resistance** n résistance f

resit (BRIT) vt [ri:'sɪt] (pt, pp **resat**) (exam) repasser ▷ n ['ri:sɪt] deuxième session f (d'un examen)

resolution [rɛzə'lu:ʃən] n résolution f

resolve [rɪ'zɔlv] n résolution f ▷ vt (decide): **to ~ to do** résoudre or décider de faire; (problem) résoudre

resort [rɪ'zɔ:t] n (seaside town) station f balnéaire; (for skiing) station de ski; (recourse) recours m ▷ vi: **to ~ to** avoir recours à; **in the last ~** en dernier ressort

resource [rɪ'sɔ:s] n ressource f; **resourceful** adj ingénieux(-euse), débrouillard(e)

respect [rɪs'pɛkt] n respect m ▷ vt respecter; **respectable** adj respectable; (quite good: result etc) honorable; **respectful** adj respectueux(-euse); **respective** adj respectif(-ive); **respectively** adv respectivement

respite ['rɛspaɪt] n répit m

respond [rɪs'pɔnd] vi répondre; (react) réagir; **response** [rɪs'pɔns] n réponse f; (reaction) réaction f

responsibility [rɪspɔnsɪ'bɪlɪtɪ] n responsabilité f

responsible [rɪs'pɔnsɪbl] adj (liable): **~ (for)** responsable (de); (person) digne de confiance; (job) qui comporte des responsabilités; **responsibly** adv avec sérieux

responsive [rɪs'pɔnsɪv] adj (student, audience) réceptif(-ive); (brakes, steering) sensible

rest [rɛst] n repos m; (stop) arrêt m, pause f; (Mus) silence m; (support) support m, appui m; (remainder) reste m, restant m ▷ vi se reposer; (be supported): **to ~ on** appuyer or reposer sur ▷ vt (lean): **to ~ sth on/against** appuyer qch sur/contre; **the ~ of them** les autres

restaurant ['rɛstərɔŋ] n restaurant m; **restaurant car** n (BRIT Rail) wagon-restaurant m

restless ['rɛstlɪs] adj agité(e)

restoration [rɛstə'reɪʃən] n (of building) restauration f; (of stolen goods) restitution f

restore [rɪ'stɔ:ʳ] vt (building) restaurer; (sth stolen) restituer; (peace, health) rétablir; **to ~ to** (former state) ramener à

restrain [rɪs'treɪn] vt (feeling) contenir; (person): **to ~ (from doing)** retenir (de faire); **restraint** n (restriction) contrainte f; (moderation) retenue f; (of style) sobriété f

restrict [rɪs'trɪkt] vt restreindre, limiter; **restriction** [rɪs'trɪkʃən] n restriction f, limitation f

rest room n (US) toilettes fpl

restructure [ri:'strʌktʃəʳ] vt restructurer

result [rɪ'zʌlt] n résultat m ▷ vi: **to ~ in** aboutir à, se terminer par; **as a ~ of** à la suite de

resume [rɪ'zju:m] vt (work, journey) reprendre ▷ vi (work etc) reprendre

résumé ['reɪzju:meɪ] n (summary) résumé m; (US: curriculum vitae) curriculum vitae m inv

resuscitate [rɪ'sʌsɪteɪt] vt (Med) réanimer

retail ['ri:teɪl] adj de or au détail ▷ adv au détail; **retailer** n détaillant(e)

retain [rɪ'teɪn] vt (keep) garder, conserver

retaliation [rɪtælɪ'eɪʃən] n représailles fpl, vengeance f

retarded [rɪ'tɑ:dɪd] adj retardé(e)

retire [rɪ'taɪəʳ] vi (give up work) prendre sa retraite; (withdraw) se retirer, partir; (go to bed) (aller) se coucher; **retired** adj (person) retraité(e); **retirement** n retraite f

retort [rɪ'tɔ:t] vi riposter

retreat [rɪ'tri:t] n retraite f ▷ vi battre en retraite

retrieve [rɪ'tri:v] vt (sth lost) récupérer; (situation, honour) sauver; (error, loss) réparer; (Comput) rechercher

retrospect ['rɛtrəspɛkt] n: **in ~** rétrospectivement, après coup; **retrospective** [rɛtrə'spɛktɪv] adj rétrospectif(-ive); (law) rétroactif(-ive) ▷ n (Art) rétrospective f

return [rɪ'tə:n] n (going or coming back) retour m; (of sth stolen etc) restitution f; (Finance: from land, shares) rapport m ▷ cpd (journey) de retour; (BRIT: ticket) aller et retour; (match) retour ▷ vi (person etc: come back) revenir; (: go back) retourner ▷ vt rendre; (bring back) rapporter; (send back) renvoyer; (put back) remettre; (Pol: candidate) élire; **returns** npl (Comm) recettes fpl; (Finance) bénéfices mpl; **many happy ~s (of the day)!** bon anniversaire!; **by ~ (of post)** par retour (du courrier); **in ~ (for)** en échange (de); **a ~ (ticket) for ...** un billet aller et retour pour ...; **return ticket** n (esp BRIT) billet m aller-retour

reunion [ri:'ju:nɪən] n réunion f

reunite [ri:ju:'naɪt] vt réunir

revamp [ri:'væmp] vt (house) retaper; (firm) réorganiser

reveal [rɪ'vi:l] vt (make known) révéler; (display) laisser voir; **revealing** adj révélateur(-trice); (dress) au décolleté généreux or suggestif

revel ['rɛvl] vi: **to ~ in sth/in doing** se délecter de qch/à faire

revelation [rɛvə'leɪʃən] n révélation f

revenge [rɪ'vɛndʒ] n vengeance f; (in game etc) revanche f ▷ vt venger; **to take ~ (on)** se venger (sur)

revenue ['rɛvənju:] n revenu m

Reverend ['rɛvərənd] adj (in titles): **the ~ John Smith** (Anglican) le révérend John Smith; (Catholic) l'abbé (John) Smith; (Protestant) le pasteur (John) Smith

reversal [rɪ'və:sl] n (of opinion) revirement

m; (*of order*) renversement *m*; (*of direction*) changement *m*

reverse [rɪ'vəːs] *n* contraire *m*, opposé *m*; (*back*) dos *m*, envers *m*; (*of paper*) verso *m*; (*of coin*) revers *m*; (*Aut: also:* **~ gear**) marche f arrière ▷ *adj* (*order, direction*) opposé(e), inverse ▷ *vt* (*order, position*) changer, inverser; (*direction, policy*) changer complètement de; (*decision*) annuler; (*roles*) renverser ▷ *vi* (*BRIT Aut*) faire marche arrière; **reverse-charge call** *n* (*BRIT Tel*) communication f en PCV; **reversing lights** *npl* (*BRIT Aut*) feux *mpl* de marche arrière *or* de recul

revert [rɪ'vəːt] *vi*: **to ~ to** revenir à, retourner à

review [rɪ'vjuː] *n* revue f; (*of book, film*) critique f; (*of situation, policy*) examen *m*, bilan *m*; (*US: examination*) examen *m* ▷ *vt* passer en revue; faire la critique de; examiner

revise [rɪ'vaɪz] *vt* réviser, modifier; (*manuscript*) revoir, corriger ▷ *vi* (*study*) réviser; **revision** [rɪ'vɪʒən] *n* révision f

revival [rɪ'vaɪvəl] *n* reprise f; (*recovery*) rétablissement *m*; (*of faith*) renouveau *m*

revive [rɪ'vaɪv] *vt* (*person*) ranimer; (*custom*) rétablir; (*economy*) relancer; (*hope, courage*) raviver, faire renaître; (*play, fashion*) reprendre ▷ *vi* (*person*) reprendre connaissance; (*: from ill health*) se rétablir; (*hope etc*) renaître; (*activity*) reprendre

revolt [rɪ'vəult] *n* révolte f ▷ *vi* se révolter, se rebeller ▷ *vt* révolter, dégoûter; **revolting** *adj* dégoûtant(e)

revolution [rɛvə'luːʃən] *n* révolution f; (*of wheel etc*) tour *m*, révolution; **revolutionary** *adj, n* révolutionnaire (*m/f*)

revolve [rɪ'vɔlv] *vi* tourner

revolver [rɪ'vɔlvəʳ] *n* revolver *m*

reward [rɪ'wɔːd] *n* récompense f ▷ *vt*: **to ~ (for)** récompenser (de); **rewarding** *adj* (*fig*) qui (en) vaut la peine, gratifiant(e)

rewind [riː'waɪnd] *vt* (*irreg: like* **wind**) (*tape*) réembobiner

rewritable [riː'raɪtəbl] *adj* (*CD, DVD*) réinscriptible

rewrite [riː'raɪt] (*pt* **rewrote**, *pp* **rewritten**) *vt* récrire

rheumatism ['ruːmətɪzəm] *n* rhumatisme *m*

Rhine [raɪn] *n*: **the (River) ~** le Rhin

rhinoceros [raɪ'nɔsərəs] *n* rhinocéros *m*

Rhône [rəun] *n*: **the (River) ~** le Rhône

rhubarb ['ruːbɑːb] *n* rhubarbe f

rhyme [raɪm] *n* rime f; (*verse*) vers *mpl*

rhythm ['rɪðm] *n* rythme *m*

rib [rɪb] *n* (*Anat*) côte f

ribbon ['rɪbən] *n* ruban *m*; **in ~s** (*torn*) en lambeaux

rice [raɪs] *n* riz *m*; **rice pudding** *n* riz *m* au lait

rich [rɪtʃ] *adj* riche; (*gift, clothes*) somptueux(-euse); **to be ~ in sth** être riche en qch

rid [rɪd] (*pt, pp* **~**) *vt*: **to ~ sb of** débarrasser qn de; **to get ~ of** se débarrasser de

riddle ['rɪdl] *n* (*puzzle*) énigme f ▷ *vt*: **to be ~d with** être criblé(e) de; (*fig*) être en proie à

ride [raɪd] *n* promenade f, tour *m*; (*distance covered*) trajet *m* ▷ *vb* (*pt* **rode**, *pp* **ridden**) ▷ *vi* (*as sport*) monter (à cheval), faire du cheval; (*go somewhere: on horse, bicycle*) aller (à cheval *or* bicyclette etc); (*travel: on bicycle, motor cycle, bus*) rouler ▷ *vt* (*a horse*) monter; (*distance*) parcourir, faire; **to ~ a horse/bicycle** monter à cheval/à bicyclette; **to take sb for a ~** (*fig*) faire marcher qn; (*cheat*) rouler qn; **rider** *n* cavalier(-ière); (*in race*) jockey *m*; (*on bicycle*) cycliste *m/f*; (*on motorcycle*) motocycliste *m/f*

ridge [rɪdʒ] *n* (*of hill*) faîte *m*; (*of roof, mountain*) arête f; (*on object*) strie f

ridicule ['rɪdɪkjuːl] *n* ridicule *m*; dérision f ▷ *vt* ridiculiser, tourner en dérision; **ridiculous** [rɪ'dɪkjuləs] *adj* ridicule

riding ['raɪdɪŋ] *n* équitation f; **riding school** *n* manège *m*, école f d'équitation

rife [raɪf] *adj* répandu(e); **~ with** abondant(e) en

rifle ['raɪfl] *n* fusil *m* (à canon rayé) ▷ *vt* vider, dévaliser

rift [rɪft] *n* fente f, fissure f; (*fig: disagreement*) désaccord *m*

rig [rɪg] *n* (*also:* **oil ~**: *on land*) derrick *m*; (*: at sea*) plate-forme pétrolière ▷ *vt* (*election etc*) truquer

right [raɪt] *adj* (*true*) juste, exact(e); (*correct*) bon (bonne); (*suitable*) approprié(e), convenable; (*just*) juste, équitable; (*morally good*) bien inv; (*not left*) droit(e) ▷ *n* (*moral good*) bien *m*; (*title, claim*) droit *m*; (*not left*) droite f ▷ *adv* (*answer*) correctement; (*treat*) bien, comme il faut; (*not on the left*) à droite ▷ *vt* redresser ▷ *excl* bon!; **do you have the ~ time?** avez-vous l'heure juste *or* exacte?; **to be ~** (*person*) avoir raison; (*answer*) être juste *or* correct(e); **by ~s** en toute justice; **on the ~** à droite; **to be in the ~** avoir raison; **~ in the middle** en plein milieu; **~ away** immédiatement; **right angle** *n* (*Math*) angle droit; **rightful** *adj* (*heir*) légitime; **right-hand** *adj*: **the right-hand side** la droite; **right-hand drive** *n* (*BRIT*) conduite f à droite; (*vehicle*) véhicule *m* avec la conduite à droite; **right-handed** *adj* (*person*) droitier(-ière); **rightly** *adv* bien, correctement; (*with reason*) à juste titre; **right of way** *n* (*on path etc*) droit *m* de passage; (*Aut*) priorité f; **right-wing** *adj* (*Pol*) de droite

rigid ['rɪdʒɪd] *adj* rigide; (*principle, control*) strict(e)

rigorous ['rɪgərəs] *adj* rigoureux(-euse)

rim [rɪm] *n* bord *m*; (*of spectacles*) monture f; (*of* *wheel)* jante *f*

rind [raɪnd] *n (of bacon)* couenne *f; (of lemon etc)* écorce *f*, zeste *m; (of cheese)* croûte *f*

ring [rɪŋ] *n* anneau *m; (on finger)* bague *f; (also:* **wedding ~**) alliance *f; (of people, objects)* cercle *m; (of spies)* réseau *m; (of smoke etc)* rond *m; (arena)* piste *f*, arène *f; (for boxing)* ring *m; (sound of bell)* sonnerie *f ▷ vb (pt* **rang***, pp* **rung**) *▷ vi (telephone, bell)* sonner; *(person: by telephone)* téléphoner; *(ears)* bourdonner; *(also:* **~ out***: voice, words)* retentir *▷ vt (BRIT Tel: also:* **~ up**) téléphoner à, appeler; **to ~ the bell** sonner; **to give sb a ~** *(Tel)* passer un coup de téléphone or de fil à qn; **ring back** *vt, vi (BRIT Tel)* rappeler; **ring off** *vi (BRIT Tel)* raccrocher; **ring up** *(BRIT) ▷ vt (Tel)* téléphoner à, appeler; **ringing tone** *n (BRIT Tel)* tonalité *f* d'appel; **ringleader** *n (of gang)* chef *m*, meneur *m*; **ring road** *n (BRIT)* rocade *f; (motorway)* périphérique *m*; **ringtone** *n (on mobile)* sonnerie *f (de téléphone portable)*

rink [rɪŋk] *n (also:* **ice ~**) patinoire *f*

rinse [rɪns] *n* rinçage *m ▷ vt* rincer

riot ['raɪət] *n* émeute *f*, bagarres *fpl ▷ vi (demonstrators)* manifester avec violence; *(population)* se soulever, se révolter; **to run ~** se déchaîner

rip [rɪp] *n* déchirure *f ▷ vt* déchirer *▷ vi* se déchirer; **rip off** *vt (inf: cheat)* arnaquer; **rip up** *vt* déchirer

ripe [raɪp] *adj (fruit)* mûr(e); *(cheese)* fait(e)

rip-off ['rɪpɔf] *n (inf)*: **it's a ~!** c'est du vol manifeste!, c'est de l'arnaque!

ripple ['rɪpl] *n* ride *f*, ondulation *f; (of applause, laughter)* cascade *f ▷ vi* se rider, onduler

rise [raɪz] *n (slope)* côte *f*, pente *f; (hill)* élévation *f; (increase: in wages: BRIT)* augmentation *f; (: in prices, temperature)* hausse *f*, augmentation; *(fig: to power etc)* ascension *f ▷ vi (pt* **rose***, pp* **~n**) s'élever, monter; *(prices, numbers)* augmenter, monter; *(waters, river)* monter; *(sun, wind, person: from chair, bed)* se lever; *(also:* **~ up***: tower, building)* s'élever; *(: rebel)* se révolter; se rebeller; *(in rank)* s'élever; **to give ~ to** donner lieu à; **to ~ to the occasion** se montrer à la hauteur; **risen** ['rɪzn] *pp of* **rise**; **rising** *adj (increasing: number, prices)* en hausse; *(tide)* montant(e); *(sun, moon)* levant(e)

risk [rɪsk] *n* risque *m ▷ vt* risquer; **to take** or **run the ~ of doing** courir le risque de faire; **at ~** en danger; **at one's own ~** à ses risques et périls; **risky** *adj* risqué(e)

rite [raɪt] *n* rite *m*; **the last ~s** les derniers sacrements

ritual ['rɪtjuəl] *adj* rituel(le) *▷ n* rituel *m*

rival ['raɪvl] *n* rival(e); *(in business)* concurrent(e) *▷ adj* rival(e); qui fait concurrence *▷ vt (match)* égaler; **rivalry** *n* rivalité *f; (in business)* concurrence *f*

river ['rɪvəʳ] *n* rivière *f; (major: also fig)* fleuve *m ▷ cpd (port, traffic)* fluvial(e); **up/down ~** en amont/aval; **riverbank** *n* rive *f*, berge *f*

rivet ['rɪvɪt] *n* rivet *m ▷ vt (fig)* river, fixer

Riviera [rɪvɪ'ɛərə] *n*: **the (French) ~** la Côte d'Azur

road [rəud] *n* route *f; (in town)* rue *f; (fig)* chemin, voie *f ▷ cpd (accident)* de la route; **major/minor ~** route principale or à priorité/voie secondaire; **which ~ do I take for …?** quelle route dois-je prendre pour aller à …?; **roadblock** *n* barrage routier; **road map** *n* carte routière; **road rage** *n* comportement très agressif de certains usagers de la route; **road safety** *n* sécurité routière; **roadside** *n* bord *m* de la route, bas-côté *m*; **roadsign** *n* panneau *m* de signalisation; **road tax** *n (BRIT Aut)* taxe *f* sur les automobiles; **roadworks** *npl* travaux *mpl (de réfection des routes)*

roam [rəum] *vi* errer, vagabonder

roar [rɔːʳ] *n* rugissement *m; (of crowd)* hurlements *mpl; (of vehicle, thunder, storm)* grondement *m ▷ vi* rugir; hurler; gronder; **to ~ with laughter** rire à gorge déployée; **to do a ~ing trade** faire des affaires en or

roast [rəust] *n* rôti *m ▷ vt (meat)* (faire) rôtir; *(coffee)* griller, torréfier; **roast beef** *n* rôti *m* de bœuf, rosbif *m*

rob [rɔb] *vt (person)* voler; *(bank)* dévaliser; **to ~ sb of sth** voler or dérober qch à qn; *(fig: deprive)* priver qn de qch; **robber** *n* bandit *m*, voleur *m*; **robbery** *n* vol *m*

robe [rəub] *n (for ceremony etc)* robe *f; (also:* **bath~**) peignoir *m; (us: rug)* couverture *f ▷ vt* revêtir (d'une robe)

robin ['rɔbɪn] *n* rouge-gorge *m*

robot ['rəubɔt] *n* robot *m*

robust [rəu'bʌst] *adj* robuste; *(material, appetite)* solide

rock [rɔk] *n (substance)* roche *f*, roc *m; (boulder)* rocher *m*, roche; *(us: small stone)* caillou *m; (BRIT: sweet)* ≈ sucre *m* d'orge *f ▷ vt (swing gently: cradle)* balancer; *(: child)* bercer; *(shake)* ébranler, secouer *▷ vi* se balancer, être ébranlé(e) or secoué(e); **on the ~s** *(drink)* avec des glaçons; *(marriage etc)* en train de craquer; **rock and roll** *n* rock (and roll) *m*, rock'n'roll *m*; **rock climbing** *n* varappe *f*

rocket ['rɔkɪt] *n* fusée *f; (Mil)* fusée, roquette *f; (Culin)* roquette

rocking chair ['rɔkɪŋ-] *n* fauteuil *m* à bascule

rocky ['rɔkɪ] *adj (hill)* rocheux(-euse); *(path)* rocailleux(-euse)

rod [rɔd] *n (metallic)* tringle *f; (Tech)* tige *f; (wooden)* baguette *f; (also:* **fishing ~**) canne *f* à pêche

rode [rəud] *pt of* **ride**

rodent ['rəudnt] *n* rongeur *m*

rogue [rəug] *n* coquin(e)

role [rəʊl] n rôle m; **role-model** n modèle m
à émuler
roll [rəʊl] n rouleau m; (of banknotes) liasse
f; (also: **bread ~**) petit pain; (register) liste f;
(sound: of drums etc) roulement m ▷ vt rouler;
(also: **~ up**: string) enrouler; (also: **~ out**:
pastry) étendre au rouleau, abaisser ▷ vi
rouler; **roll over** vi se retourner; **roll up**
vi (inf: arrive) arriver, s'amener ▷ vt (carpet,
cloth, map) rouler; (sleeves) retrousser; **roller**
n rouleau m; (wheel) roulette f; (for road)
rouleau compresseur; (for hair) bigoudi m;
roller coaster n montagnes fpl russes; **roller
skates** npl patins mpl à roulettes; **roller-
skating** n patin m à roulettes; **to go roller-
skating** faire du patin à roulettes; **rolling pin**
n rouleau m à pâtisserie
ROM [rɔm] n abbr (Comput: = read-only memory)
mémoire morte, ROM f
Roman ['rəʊmən] adj romain(e) ▷ n
Romain(e); **Roman Catholic** adj, n
catholique (m/f)
romance [rə'mæns] n (love affair) idylle f;
(charm) poésie f; (novel) roman m à l'eau de rose
Romania etc [rəʊ'meɪnɪə] = **Rumania** etc
Roman numeral n chiffre romain
romantic [rə'mæntɪk] adj romantique; (novel,
attachment) sentimental(e)
Rome [rəʊm] n Rome
roof [ruːf] n toit m; (of tunnel, cave) plafond m
▷ vt couvrir (d'un toit); **the ~ of the mouth** la
voûte du palais; **roof rack** n (Aut) galerie f
rook [rʊk] n (bird) freux m; (Chess) tour f
room [ruːm] n (in house) pièce f; (also: **bed~**)
chambre f (à coucher); (in school etc) salle
f; (space) place f; **roommate** n camarade
m/f de chambre; **room service** n service
m des chambres (dans un hôtel); **roomy** adj
spacieux(-euse); (garment) ample
rooster ['ruːstəʳ] n coq m
root [ruːt] n (Bot, Math) racine f; (fig: of problem)
origine f, fond m ▷ vi (plant) s'enraciner
rope [rəʊp] n corde f; (Naut) cordage m ▷ vt
(tie up or together) attacher; (climbers: also: **~
together**) encorder; (area: also: **~ off**) interdire
l'accès de; (: divide off) séparer; **to know the ~s**
(fig) être au courant, connaître les ficelles
rose [rəʊz] pt of **rise** ▷ n rose f; (also: **~bush**)
rosier m
rosé ['rəʊzeɪ] n rosé m
rosemary ['rəʊzməri] n romarin m
rosy ['rəʊzɪ] adj rose; **a ~ future** un bel avenir
rot [rɔt] n (decay) pourriture f; (fig: pej: nonsense)
idioties fpl, balivernes fpl ▷ vt, vi pourrir
rota ['rəʊtə] n liste f, tableau m de service
rotate [rəʊ'teɪt] vt (revolve) faire tourner;
(change round: crops) alterner; (: jobs) faire à
tour de rôle ▷ vi (revolve) tourner
rotten ['rɔtn] adj (decayed) pourri(e);

(dishonest) corrompu(e); (inf: bad) mauvais(e),
moche; **to feel ~** (ill) être mal fichu(e)
rough [rʌf] adj (cloth, skin) rêche,
rugueux(-euse); (terrain) accidenté(e); (path)
rocailleux(-euse); (voice) rauque, rude;
(person, manner: coarse) rude, fruste; (: violent)
brutal(e); (district, weather) mauvais(e); (sea)
houleux(-euse); (plan) ébauché(e); (guess)
approximatif(-ive) ▷ n (Golf) rough m ▷ vt: **to
~ it** vivre à la dure; **to sleep ~** (Brit) coucher
à la dure; **roughly** adv (handle) rudement,
brutalement; (speak) avec brusquerie; (make)
grossièrement; (approximately) à peu près, en
gros
roulette [ruː'lɛt] n roulette f
round [raʊnd] adj rond(e) ▷ n rond m, cercle
m; (Brit: of toast) tranche f; (duty: of policeman,
milkman etc) tournée f; (: of doctor) visites fpl;
(game: of cards, in competition) partie f; (Boxing)
round m; (of talks) série f ▷ vt (corner) tourner
▷ prep autour de ▷ adv: **right ~, all ~** tout
autour; **~ of ammunition** cartouche f; **~ of
applause** applaudissements mpl; **~ of drinks**
tournée f; **~ of sandwiches** (Brit) sandwich
m; **the long way ~** (par) le chemin le plus long;
all (the) year ~ toute l'année; **it's just ~ the
corner** (fig) c'est tout près; **to go ~ to sb's
(house)** aller chez qn; **go ~ the back** passez
par derrière; **enough to go ~** assez pour tout
le monde; **she arrived ~ (about) noon** (Brit)
elle est arrivée vers midi; **~ the clock** 24 heures
sur 24; **round off** vt (speech etc) terminer;
round up vt rassembler; (criminals) effectuer
une rafle de; (prices) arrondir (au chiffre
supérieur); **roundabout** n (Brit Aut) rond-
point m (à sens giratoire); (at fair) manège
m (de chevaux de bois) ▷ adj (route, means)
détourné(e); **round trip** n (voyage m) aller et
retour m; **roundup** n rassemblement m; (of
criminals) rafle f
rouse [raʊz] vt (wake up) réveiller; (stir
up) susciter, provoquer; (interest) éveiller;
(suspicions) susciter, éveiller
route [ruːt] n itinéraire m; (of bus) parcours m;
(of trade, shipping) route f
routine [ruː'tiːn] adj (work) ordinaire,
courant(e); (procedure) d'usage ▷ n (habits)
habitudes fpl; (pej) train-train m; (Theat)
numéro m
row¹ [rəʊ] n (line) rangée f; (of people, seats,
Knitting) rang m; (behind one another: of cars,
people) file f ▷ vi (in boat) ramer; (as sport) faire
de l'aviron ▷ vt (boat) faire aller à la rame or à
l'aviron; **in a ~** (fig) d'affilée
row² [raʊ] n (noise) vacarme m; (dispute)
dispute f, querelle f; (scolding) réprimande f,
savon m ▷ vi (also: **to have a ~**) se disputer, se
quereller
rowboat ['rəʊbəʊt] n (US) canot m (à rames)

rowing ['rəʊɪŋ] *n* canotage *m*; (*as sport*) aviron *m*; **rowing boat** *n* (BRIT) canot *m* (à rames)

royal ['rɔɪəl] *adj* royal(e); **royalty** *n* (*royal persons*) (membres *mpl* de la) famille royale; (*payment: to author*) droits *mpl* d'auteur; (: *to inventor*) royalties *fpl*

rpm *abbr* (= *revolutions per minute*) t/mn (= *tours/minute*)

R.S.V.P. *abbr* (= *répondez s'il vous plaît*) RSVP

Rt. Hon. *abbr* (BRIT: = *Right Honourable*) titre donné aux députés de la Chambre des communes

rub [rʌb] *n*: **to give sth a ~** donner un coup de chiffon *or* de torchon à qch ▷ *vt* frotter; (*person*) frictionner; (*hands*) se frotter; **to ~ sb up** (BRIT) *or* **to ~ sb** (US) **the wrong way** prendre qn à rebrousse-poil; **rub in** *vt* (*ointment*) faire pénétrer; **rub off** *vi* partir; **rub out** *vt* effacer

rubber ['rʌbə^r] *n* caoutchouc *m*; (BRIT: *eraser*) gomme *f* (à effacer); **rubber band** *n* élastique *m*; **rubber gloves** *npl* gants *mpl* en caoutchouc

rubbish ['rʌbɪʃ] *n* (*from household*) ordures *fpl*; (*fig: pej*) choses *fpl* sans valeur; camelote *f*; (*nonsense*) bêtises *fpl*, idioties *fpl*; **rubbish bin** *n* (BRIT) boîte *f* à ordures, poubelle *f*; **rubbish dump** *n* (BRIT: *in town*) décharge publique, dépotoir *m*

rubble ['rʌbl] *n* décombres *mpl*; (*smaller*) gravats *mpl*; (*Constr*) blocage *m*

ruby ['ruːbɪ] *n* rubis *m*

rucksack ['rʌksæk] *n* sac m à dos

rudder ['rʌdə^r] *n* gouvernail *m*

rude [ruːd] *adj* (*impolite: person*) impoli(e); (: *word, manners*) grossier(-ière); (*shocking*) indécent(e), inconvenant(e)

ruffle ['rʌfl] *vt* (*hair*) ébouriffer; (*clothes*) chiffonner; (*fig: person*): **to get ~d** s'énerver

rug [rʌg] *n* petit tapis; (BRIT: *blanket*) couverture *f*

rugby ['rʌgbɪ] *n* (*also*: **~ football**) rugby *m*

rugged ['rʌgɪd] *adj* (*landscape*) accidenté(e); (*features, character*) rude

ruin ['ruːɪn] *n* ruine *f* ▷ *vt* ruiner; (*spoil: clothes*) abîmer; (: *event*) gâcher; **ruins** *npl* (*of building*) ruine(s)

rule [ruːl] *n* règle *f*; (*regulation*) règlement *m*; (*government*) autorité *f*, gouvernement *m* ▷ *vt* (*country*) gouverner; (*person*) dominer; (*decide*) décider ▷ *vi* commander; (*Law*): **as a ~** normalement, en règle générale; **rule out** *vt* exclure; **ruler** *n* (*sovereign*) souverain(e); (*leader*) chef *m* (d'État); (*for measuring*) règle *f*; **ruling** *adj* (*party*) au pouvoir; (*class*) dirigeant(e) ▷ *n* (*Law*) décision *f*

rum [rʌm] *n* rhum *m*

Rumania [ruːˈmeɪnɪə] *n* Roumanie *f*; **Rumanian** *adj* roumain(e) ▷ *n* Roumain(e); (*Ling*) roumain *m*

rumble ['rʌmbl] *n* grondement *m*; (*of stomach, pipe*) gargouillement *m* ▷ *vi* gronder; (*stomach, pipe*) gargouiller

rumour (US **rumor**) ['ruːmə^r] *n* rumeur *f*, bruit *m* (qui court) ▷ *vt*: **it is ~ed that** le bruit court que

rump steak *n* romsteck *m*

run [rʌn] *n* (*race*) course *f*; (*outing*) tour *m or* promenade *f* (en voiture); (*distance travelled*) parcours *m*, trajet *m*; (*series*) suite *f*, série *f*; (*Theat*) série de représentations; (*Ski*) piste *f*; (*Cricket, Baseball*) point *m*; (*in tights, stockings*) maille filée, échelle *f* ▷ *vb* (*pt* **ran**, *pp* **~**) ▷ *vt* (*business*) diriger; (*competition, course*) organiser; (*hotel, house*) tenir; (*race*) participer à; (*Comput: program*) exécuter; (*to pass: hand, finger*): **to ~ sth over** promener *or* passer qch sur; (*water, bath*) faire couler; (*Press: feature*) publier ▷ *vi* courir; (*pass: road etc*) passer; (*work: machine, factory*) marcher; (*bus, train*) circuler; (*continue: play*) se jouer, être à l'affiche; (: *contract*) être valide *or* en vigueur; (*flow: river, bath, nose*) couler; (*colours, washing*) déteindre; (*in election*) être candidat, se présenter; **at a ~** au pas de course; **to go for a ~** aller courir *or* faire un peu de course à pied; (*in car*) faire un tour *or* une promenade (en voiture); **there was a ~ on** (*meat, tickets*) les gens se sont rués sur; **in the long ~** à la longue; **on the ~** en fuite; **I'll ~ you to the station** je vais vous emmener *or* conduire à la gare; **to ~ a risk** courir un risque; **run after** *vt fus* (*to catch up*) courir après; (*chase*) poursuivre; **run away** *vi* s'enfuir; **run down** *vt* (*Aut: knock over*) renverser; (BRIT: *reduce: production*) réduire progressivement; (: *factory/shop*) réduire progressivement la production/l'activité de; (*criticize*) critiquer, dénigrer; **to be ~ down** (*tired*) être fatigué(e) *or* à plat; **run into** *vt fus* (*meet: person*) rencontrer par hasard; (: *trouble*) se heurter à; (*collide with*) heurter; **run off** *vi* s'enfuir ▷ *vt* (*water*) laisser s'écouler; (*copies*) tirer; **run out** *vi* (*person*) sortir en courant; (*liquid*) couler; (*lease*) expirer; (*money*) être épuisé(e); **run out of** *vt fus* se trouver à court de; **run over** *vt* (*Aut*) écraser ▷ *vt fus* (*revise*) revoir, reprendre; **run through** *vt fus* (*recap*) reprendre, revoir; (*play*) répéter; **run up** *vi*: **to ~ up against** (*difficulties*) se heurter à; **runaway** *adj* (*horse*) emballé(e); (*truck*) fou (folle); (*person*) fugitif(-ive); (*child*) fugueur(-euse)

rung [rʌŋ] *pp of* **ring** ▷ *n* (*of ladder*) barreau *m*

runner ['rʌnə^r] *n* (*in race: person*) coureur(-euse); (: *horse*) partant *m*; (*on sledge*) patin *m*; (*for drawer etc*) coulisseau *m*; **runner bean** *n* (BRIT) haricot *m* (à rames); **runner-up** *n* second(e)

running ['rʌnɪŋ] *n* (*in race etc*) course *f*; (*of*

business, organization) direction f, gestion f
▷ adj (water) courant(e); (commentary) suivi(e);
6 days ~ 6 jours de suite; **to be in/out of the ~
for sth** être/ne pas être sur les rangs pour qch
runny ['rʌnɪ] adj qui coule
run-up ['rʌnʌp] n (BRIT): **~ to sth** période f
précédant qch
runway ['rʌnweɪ] n (Aviat) piste f (d'envol or
d'atterrissage)
rupture ['rʌptʃəʳ] n (Med) hernie f
rural ['ruərl] adj rural(e)
rush [rʌʃ] n (of crowd, Comm: sudden demand)
ruée f; (hurry) hâte f; (of anger, joy) accès
m; (current) flot m; (Bot) jonc m ▷ vt (hurry)
transporter or envoyer d'urgence ▷ vi se
précipiter; **to ~ sth off** (do quickly) faire qch à
la hâte; **rush hour** n heures fpl de pointe or
d'affluence
Russia ['rʌʃə] n Russie f; **Russian** adj russe ▷ n
Russe m/f; (Ling) russe m
rust [rʌst] n rouille f ▷ vi rouiller
rusty ['rʌstɪ] adj rouillé(e)
ruthless ['ruːθlɪs] adj sans pitié, impitoyable
RV n abbr (US) = **recreational vehicle**
rye [raɪ] n seigle m

Sabbath ['sæbəθ] n (Jewish) sabbat m;
(Christian) dimanche m
sabotage ['sæbətɑːʒ] n sabotage m ▷ vt
saboter
saccharin(e) ['sækərɪn] n saccharine f
sachet ['sæʃeɪ] n sachet m
sack [sæk] n (bag) sac m ▷ vt (dismiss) renvoyer,
mettre à la porte; (plunder) piller, mettre à sac;
to get the ~ être renvoyé(e) or mis(e) à la porte
sacred ['seɪkrɪd] adj sacré(e)
sacrifice ['sækrɪfaɪs] n sacrifice m ▷ vt
sacrifier
sad [sæd] adj (unhappy) triste; (deplorable)
triste, fâcheux(-euse); (inf: pathetic: thing)
triste, lamentable; (: person) minable
saddle ['sædl] n selle f ▷ vt (horse) seller; **to be
~d with sth** (inf) avoir qch sur les bras
sadistic [sə'dɪstɪk] adj sadique
sadly ['sædlɪ] adv tristement; (unfortunately)
malheureusement; (seriously) fort
sadness ['sædnɪs] n tristesse f
s.a.e. n abbr (BRIT: = stamped addressed
envelope) enveloppe affranchie pour la réponse
safari [sə'fɑːrɪ] n safari m
safe [seɪf] adj (out of danger) hors de danger,
en sécurité; (not dangerous) sans danger;
(cautious) prudent(e); (sure: bet etc) assuré(e)
▷ n coffre-fort m; **could you put this in
the ~, please?** pourriez-vous mettre ceci
dans le coffre-fort?; **~ and sound** sain(e) et

sauf (*sauve*); **(just) to be on the ~ side** pour plus de sûreté, par précaution; **safely** adv (*assume, say*) sans risque d'erreur; (*drive, arrive*) sans accident; **safe sex** n rapports sexuels protégés

safety ['seifti] n sécurité f; **safety belt** n ceinture f de sécurité; **safety pin** n épingle f de sûreté or de nourrice

saffron ['sæfrən] n safran m

sag [sæg] vi s'affaisser, fléchir; (*hem, breasts*) pendre

sage [seidʒ] n (*herb*) sauge f; (*person*) sage m

Sagittarius [sædʒɪ'tɛərɪəs] n le Sagittaire

Sahara [sə'hɑːrə] n: **the ~ (Desert)** le (désert du) Sahara m

said [sɛd] pt, pp of **say**

sail [seil] n (*on boat*) voile f; (*trip*): **to go for a ~** faire un tour en bateau ▷ vt (*boat*) manœuvrer, piloter ▷ vi (*travel: ship*) avancer, naviguer; (*set off*) partir, prendre la mer; (*Sport*) faire de la voile; **they ~ed into Le Havre** ils sont entrés dans le port du Havre; **sailboat** n (*us*) bateau m à voiles, voilier m; **sailing** n (*Sport*) voile f; **to go sailing** faire de la voile; **sailing boat** n bateau m à voiles, voilier m; **sailor** n marin m, matelot m

saint [seint] n saint(e)

sake [seik] n: **for the ~ of** (*out of concern for*) pour (l'amour de), dans l'intérêt de; (*out of consideration for*) par égard pour

salad ['sæləd] n salade f; **salad cream** n (*BRIT*) (sorte f de) mayonnaise f; **salad dressing** n vinaigrette f

salami [sə'lɑːmɪ] n salami m

salary ['sælərɪ] n salaire m, traitement m

sale [seil] n vente f; (*at reduced prices*) soldes mpl; **sales** npl (*total amount sold*) chiffre m de ventes; **"for ~"** "à vendre"; **on ~** en vente; **sales assistant** (*us* **sales clerk**) n vendeur(-euse); **salesman** (*irreg*) n (*in shop*) vendeur m; **salesperson** (*irreg*) n (*in shop*) vendeur(-euse); **sales rep** n (*Comm*) représentant(e) m/f; **saleswoman** (*irreg*) n (*in shop*) vendeuse f

saline ['seilain] adj salin(e)

saliva [sə'laivə] n salive f

salmon ['sæmən] n (pl inv) saumon m

salon ['sælɔn] n salon m

saloon [sə'luːn] n (*us*) bar m; (*BRIT Aut*) berline f; (*ship's lounge*) salon m

salt [sɔːlt] n sel m ▷ vt saler; **saltwater** adj (*fish etc*) (d'eau) de mer; **salty** adj salé(e)

salute [sə'luːt] n salut m; (*of guns*) salve f ▷ vt saluer

salvage ['sælvidʒ] n (*saving*) sauvetage m; (*things saved*) biens sauvés or récupérés ▷ vt sauver, récupérer

Salvation Army [sæl'veiʃən-] n Armée f du Salut

same [seim] adj même ▷ pron: **the ~** le (la) même, les mêmes; **the ~ book as** le même livre que; **at the ~ time** en même temps; (*yet*) néanmoins; **all** or **just the ~** tout de même, quand même; **to do the ~** faire de même, en faire autant; **to do the ~ as sb** faire comme qn; **and the ~ to you!** et à vous de même!; (*after insult*) toi-même!

sample ['sɑːmpl] n échantillon m; (*Med*) prélèvement m ▷ vt (*food, wine*) goûter

sanction ['sæŋkʃən] n approbation f, sanction f ▷ vt cautionner, sanctionner; **sanctions** npl (*Pol*) sanctions

sanctuary ['sæŋktjuərɪ] n (*holy place*) sanctuaire m; (*refuge*) asile m; (*for wildlife*) réserve f

sand [sænd] n sable m ▷ vt (*also*: **~ down**: *wood etc*) poncer

sandal ['sændl] n sandale f

sand: sandbox n (*us: for children*) tas m de sable; **sandcastle** n château m de sable; **sand dune** n dune f de sable; **sandpaper** n papier m de verre; **sandpit** n (*BRIT: for children*) tas m de sable; **sands** npl plage f (de sable); **sandstone** ['sændstəun] n grès m

sandwich ['sændwitʃ] n sandwich m ▷ vt (*also*: **~ in**) intercaler; **~ed between** pris en sandwich entre; **cheese/ham ~** sandwich au fromage/jambon

sandy ['sændɪ] adj sablonneux(-euse); (*colour*) sable inv, blond roux inv

sane [sein] adj (*person*) sain(e) d'esprit; (*outlook*) sensé(e), sain(e)

sang [sæŋ] pt of **sing**

sanitary towel (*us* **sanitary napkin**) ['sænɪtəri-] n serviette f hygiénique

sanity ['sænɪtɪ] n santé mentale; (*common sense*) bon sens

sank [sæŋk] pt of **sink**

Santa Claus [sæntə'klɔːz] n le Père Noël

sap [sæp] n (*of plants*) sève f ▷ vt (*strength*) saper, miner

sapphire ['sæfaɪə'] n saphir m

sarcasm ['sɑːkæzm] n sarcasme m, raillerie f

sarcastic [sɑː'kæstɪk] adj sarcastique

sardine [sɑː'diːn] n sardine f

SASE n abbr (*us* = *self-addressed stamped envelope*) enveloppe affranchie pour la réponse

sat [sæt] pt, pp of **sit**

Sat. abbr (= *Saturday*) sa

satchel ['sætʃl] n cartable m

satellite ['sætəlaɪt] n satellite m; **satellite dish** n antenne f parabolique; **satellite television** n télévision f par satellite

satin ['sætɪn] n satin m ▷ adj en or de satin, satiné(e)

satire ['sætaɪə'] n satire f

satisfaction [sætɪs'fækʃən] n satisfaction f

satisfactory [sætɪs'fæktərɪ] adj satisfaisant(e)

satisfied ['sætɪsfaɪd] *adj* satisfait(e); **to be ~ with sth** être satisfait de qch

satisfy ['sætɪsfaɪ] *vt* satisfaire, contenter; (*convince*) convaincre, persuader

Saturday ['sætədɪ] *n* samedi *m*

sauce [sɔːs] *n* sauce *f*; **saucepan** *n* casserole *f*

saucer ['sɔːsəʳ] *n* soucoupe *f*

Saudi Arabia ['saʊdɪ-] *n* Arabie *f* Saoudite

sauna ['sɔːnə] *n* sauna *m*

sausage ['sɔsɪdʒ] *n* saucisse *f*; (*salami etc*) saucisson *m*; **sausage roll** *n* friand *m*

sautéed ['səʊteɪd] *adj* sauté(e)

savage ['sævɪdʒ] *adj* (*cruel, fierce*) brutal(e), féroce; (*primitive*) primitif(-ive), sauvage ▷ *n* sauvage *m/f* ▷ *vt* attaquer férocement

save [seɪv] *vt* (*person, belongings*) sauver; (*money*) mettre de côté, économiser; (*time*) (faire) gagner; (*keep*) garder; (*Comput*) sauvegarder; (*Sport: stop*) arrêter; (*avoid: trouble*) éviter ▷ *vi* (*also: ~ up*) mettre de l'argent de côté ▷ *n* (*Sport*) arrêt *m* (du ballon) ▷ *prep* sauf, à l'exception de

savings ['seɪvɪŋz] *npl* économies *fpl*; **savings account** *n* compte *m* d'épargne; **savings and loan association** (*us*) *n* ≈ société *f* de crédit immobilier

savoury (*us* **savory**) ['seɪvərɪ] *adj* savoureux(-euse); (*dish: not sweet*) salé(e)

saw [sɔː] *pt of* **see** ▷ *n* (*tool*) scie *f* ▷ *vt* (*pt* **~ed**, *pp* **~ed** *or* **~n**) scier; **sawdust** *n* sciure *f*

sawn [sɔːn] *pp of* **saw**

saxophone ['sæksəfəʊn] *n* saxophone *m*

say [seɪ] *n*: **to have one's ~** dire ce qu'on a à dire ▷ *vt* (*pt, pp* **said**) dire; **to have a ~** avoir voix au chapitre; **could you ~ that again?** pourriez-vous répéter ce que vous venez de dire?; **to ~ yes/no** dire oui/non; **my watch ~s 3 o'clock** ma montre indique 3 heures, il est 3 heures à ma montre; **that is to ~** c'est-à-dire, cela va sans dire, cela va de soi; **saying** *n* dicton *m*, proverbe *m*

scab [skæb] *n* croûte *f*; (*pej*) jaune *m*

scaffolding ['skæfəldɪŋ] *n* échafaudage *m*

scald [skɔːld] *n* brûlure *f* ▷ *vt* ébouillanter

scale [skeɪl] *n* (*of fish*) écaille *f*; (*Mus*) gamme *f*; (*of ruler, thermometer etc*) graduation *f*, échelle (graduée); (*of salaries, fees etc*) barème *m*; (*of map, also size, extent*) échelle ▷ *vt* (*mountain*) escalader; **scales** *npl* balance *f*; (*larger*) bascule *f*; (*also:* **bathroom ~s**) pèse-personne *m inv*; **~ of charges** tableau *m* des tarifs; **on a large ~** sur une grande échelle, en grand

scallion ['skæljən] *n* (*us: salad onion*) ciboule *f*

scallop ['skɔləp] *n* coquille *f* Saint-Jacques; (*Sewing*) feston *m*

scalp [skælp] *n* cuir chevelu ▷ *vt* scalper

scalpel ['skælpl] *n* scalpel *m*

scam [skæm] *n* (*inf*) arnaque *f*

scampi ['skæmpɪ] *npl* langoustines (frites),

scampi *mpl*

scan [skæn] *vt* (*examine*) scruter, examiner; (*glance at quickly*) parcourir; (*TV, Radar*) balayer ▷ *n* (*Med*) scanographie *f*

scandal ['skændl] *n* scandale *m*; (*gossip*) ragots *mpl*

Scandinavia [skændɪ'neɪvɪə] *n* Scandinavie *f*; **Scandinavian** *adj* scandinave ▷ *n* Scandinave *m/f*

scanner ['skænəʳ] *n* (*Radar, Med*) scanner *m*, scanographe *m*; (*Comput*) scanner, numériseur *m*

scapegoat ['skeɪpɡəʊt] *n* bouc *m* émissaire

scar [skɑːʳ] *n* cicatrice *f* ▷ *vt* laisser une cicatrice *or* une marque à

scarce [skɛəs] *adj* rare, peu abondant(e); **to make o.s. ~** (*inf*) se sauver; **scarcely** *adv* à peine, presque pas

scare [skɛəʳ] *n* peur *f*, panique *f* ▷ *vt* effrayer, faire peur à; **to ~ sb stiff** faire une peur bleue à qn; **bomb ~** alerte *f* à la bombe; **scarecrow** *n* épouvantail *m*; **scared** *adj*: **to be scared** avoir peur

scarf (*pl* **scarves**) [skɑːf, skɑːvz] *n* (*long*) écharpe *f*; (*square*) foulard *m*

scarlet ['skɑːlɪt] *adj* écarlate

scarves [skɑːvz] *npl of* **scarf**

scary ['skɛərɪ] *adj* (*inf*) effrayant(e); (*film*) qui fait peur

scatter ['skætəʳ] *vt* éparpiller, répandre; (*crowd*) disperser ▷ *vi* se disperser

scenario [sɪ'nɑːrɪəʊ] *n* scénario *m*

scene [siːn] *n* (*Theat, fig etc*) scène *f*; (*of crime, accident*) lieu(x) *m(pl)*, endroit *m*; (*sight, view*) spectacle *m*, vue *f*; **scenery** *n* (*Theat*) décor(s) *m(pl)*; (*landscape*) paysage *m*; **scenic** *adj* offrant de beaux paysages *or* panoramas

scent [sɛnt] *n* parfum *m*, odeur *f*; (*fig: track*) piste *f*

sceptical (*us* **skeptical**) ['skɛptɪkl] *adj* sceptique

schedule ['ʃɛdjuːl, *us* 'skɛdjuːl] *n* programme *m*, plan *m*; (*of trains*) horaire *m*; (*of prices etc*) barème *m*, tarif *m* ▷ *vt* prévoir; **on ~** à l'heure (prévue); à la date prévue; **to be ahead of/behind ~** avoir de l'avance/du retard; **scheduled flight** *n* vol régulier

scheme [skiːm] *n* plan *m*, projet *m*; (*plot*) complot *m*, combine *f*; (*arrangement*) arrangement *m*, classification *f*; (*pension scheme etc*) régime *m* ▷ *vt, vi* comploter, manigancer

schizophrenic [skɪtsə'frɛnɪk] *adj* schizophrène

scholar ['skɔləʳ] *n* érudit(e); (*pupil*) boursier(-ère); **scholarship** *n* érudition *f*; (*grant*) bourse *f* (d'études)

school [skuːl] *n* (*gen*) école *f*; (*secondary school*) collège *m*, lycée *m*; (*in university*) faculté *f*;

(us: university) université f ▷ cpd scolaire;
schoolbook n livre m scolaire or de classe;
schoolboy n écolier m; (at secondary school)
collégien m, lycéen m; **schoolchildren** npl
écoliers mpl; (at secondary school) collégiens
mpl, lycéens mpl; **schoolgirl** n écolière f; (at
secondary school) collégienne f, lycéenne f;
schooling n instruction f, études fpl;
schoolteacher n (primary) instituteur(-trice);
(secondary) professeur m
science ['saɪəns] n science f; **science fiction**
n science-fiction f; **scientific** [saɪən'tɪfɪk]
adj scientifique; **scientist** n scientifique m/f;
(eminent) savant m
sci-fi ['saɪfaɪ] n abbr (inf: = science fiction) SF f
scissors ['sɪzəz] npl ciseaux mpl; **a pair of ~**
une paire de ciseaux
scold [skəuld] vt gronder
scone [skɔn] n sorte de petit pain rond au lait
scoop [sku:p] n pelle f (à main); (for ice cream)
boule f à glace; (Press) reportage exclusif or à
sensation
scooter ['sku:tər] n (motor cycle) scooter m;
(toy) trottinette f
scope [skəup] n (capacity: of plan, undertaking)
portée f, envergure f; (: of person) compétence f,
capacités fpl; (opportunity) possibilités fpl
scorching ['skɔ:tʃɪŋ] adj torride, brûlant(e)
score [skɔ:r] n score m, décompte m des points;
(Mus) partition f ▷ vt (goal, point) marquer;
(success) remporter; (cut: leather, wood, card)
entailler, inciser ▷ vi marquer des points;
(Football) marquer un but; (keep score) compter
les points; **on that ~** sur ce chapitre, à cet
égard; **a ~ of** (twenty) vingt; **~s of** (fig) des tas
de; **to ~ 6 out of 10** obtenir 6 sur 10; **score
out** vt rayer, barrer, biffer; **scoreboard** n
tableau m; **scorer** n (Football) auteur m du but;
buteur m; (keeping score) marqueur m
scorn [skɔ:n] n mépris m, dédain m
Scorpio ['skɔ:pɪəu] n le Scorpion
scorpion ['skɔ:pɪən] n scorpion m
Scot [skɔt] n Écossais(e)
Scotch [skɔtʃ] n whisky m, scotch m
Scotch tape® (us) n scotch® m, ruban
adhésif
Scotland ['skɔtlənd] n Écosse f
Scots [skɔts] adj écossais(e); **Scotsman**
(irreg) n Écossais m; **Scotswoman** (irreg) n
Écossaise f; **Scottish** ['skɔtɪʃ] adj écossais(e);
Scottish Parliament n Parlement écossais
scout [skaut] n (Mil) éclaireur m; (also: **boy ~**)
scout m; **girl ~** (us) guide f
scowl [skaul] vi se renfrogner, avoir l'air
maussade; **to ~ at** regarder de travers
scramble ['skræmbl] n (rush) bousculade f,
ruée f ▷ vi grimper/descendre tant bien que
mal; **to ~ for** se bousculer or se disputer pour
(avoir); **to go scrambling** (Sport) faire du trial;

scrambled eggs npl œufs brouillés
scrap [skræp] n bout m, morceau m; (fight)
bagarre f; (also: **~ iron**) ferraille f ▷ vt jeter,
mettre au rebut; (fig) abandonner, laisser
tomber ▷ vi se bagarrer; **scraps** npl (waste)
déchets mpl; **scrapbook** n album m
scrape [skreɪp] vt, vi gratter, racler ▷ n: **to get
into a ~** s'attirer des ennuis; **scrape through**
vi (exam etc) réussir de justesse
scrap paper n papier m brouillon
scratch [skrætʃ] n égratignure f, rayure f; (on
paint) éraflure f; (from claw) coup m de griffe
▷ vt (rub) (se) gratter; (paint etc) érafler; (with
claw, nail) griffer ▷ vi (se) gratter; **to start
from ~** partir de zéro; **to be up to ~** être à la
hauteur; **scratch card** n carte f à gratter
scream [skri:m] n cri perçant, hurlement m
▷ vi crier, hurler
screen [skri:n] n écran m; (in room) paravent
m; (fig) écran, rideau m ▷ vt masquer, cacher;
(from the wind etc) abriter, protéger; (film)
projeter; (candidates etc) filtrer; **screening** n
(of film) projection f; (Med) test m (or tests) de
dépistage; **screenplay** n scénario m; **screen
saver** n (Comput) économiseur m d'écran
screw [skru:] n vis f ▷ vt (also: **~ in**) visser;
screw up vt (paper etc) froisser; **to ~ up
one's eyes** se plisser les yeux; **screwdriver** n
tournevis m
scribble ['skrɪbl] n gribouillage m ▷ vt
gribouiller, griffonner
script [skrɪpt] n (Cine etc) scénario m, texte m;
(writing) (écriture f) script m
scroll [skrəul] n rouleau m ▷ vt (Comput) faire
défiler (sur l'écran)
scrub [skrʌb] n (land) broussailles fpl ▷ vt
(floor) nettoyer à la brosse; (pan) récurer;
(washing) frotter
scruffy ['skrʌfɪ] adj débraillé(e)
scrum(mage) ['skrʌm(ɪdʒ)] n mêlée f
scrutiny ['skru:tɪnɪ] n examen minutieux
scuba diving ['sku:bə-] n plongée sous-
marine (autonome)
sculptor ['skʌlptər] n sculpteur m
sculpture ['skʌlptʃər] n sculpture f
scum [skʌm] n écume f, mousse f; (pej: people)
rebut m, lie f
scurry ['skʌrɪ] vi filer à toute allure; **to ~ off**
détaler, se sauver
sea [si:] n mer f ▷ cpd marin(e), de (la) mer,
maritime; **by** or **beside the ~** (holiday, town) au
bord de la mer; **by ~** par mer, en bateau; **out to
~** au large; **(out) at ~** en mer; **to be all at ~**
(fig) nager complètement; **seafood** n fruits mpl
de mer; **sea front** n bord m de mer; **seagull**
n mouette f
seal [si:l] n (animal) phoque m; (stamp) sceau
m, cachet m ▷ vt sceller; (envelope) coller; (:
with seal) cacheter; **seal off** vt (forbid entry to)

interdire l'accès de

sea level n niveau m de la mer

seam [si:m] n couture f; (of coal) veine f, filon m

search [sə:tʃ] n (for person, thing, Comput) recherche(s) f(pl); (of drawer, pockets) fouille f; (Law: at sb's home) perquisition f ▷ vt fouiller; (examine) examiner minutieusement; scruter ▷ vi: **to ~ for** chercher; **in ~ of** à la recherche de; **search engine** n (Comput) moteur m de recherche; **search party** n expédition f de secours

sea: **seashore** n rivage m, plage f, bord m de (la) mer; **seasick** adj: **to be seasick** avoir le mal de mer; **seaside** n bord m de mer; **seaside resort** n station f balnéaire

season ['si:zn] n saison f ▷ vt assaisonner, relever; **to be in/out of ~** être/ne pas être de saison; **seasonal** adj saisonnier(-ière); **seasoning** n assaisonnement m; **season ticket** n carte f d'abonnement

seat [si:t] n siège m; (in bus, train: place) place f; (buttocks) postérieur m; (of trousers) fond m ▷ vt faire asseoir, placer; (have room for) avoir des places assises pour, pouvoir accueillir; **I'd like to book two ~s** je voudrais réserver deux places; **to be ~ed** être assis; **seat belt** n ceinture f de sécurité; **seating** n sièges fpl, places assises

sea: **sea water** n eau f de mer; **seaweed** n algues fpl

sec. abbr (= second) sec

secluded [sɪˈkluːdɪd] adj retiré(e), à l'écart

second ['sɛkənd] num deuxième, second(e) ▷ adv (in race etc) en seconde position ▷ n (unit of time) seconde f; (Aut: also: **~ gear**) seconde; (Comm: imperfect) article m de second choix; (BRIT Scol) ≈ licence f avec mention ▷ vt (motion) appuyer; **seconds** npl (inf: food) rab m (inf); **secondary** adj secondaire; **secondary school** n collège m; lycée m; **second-class** adj de deuxième classe; (Rail) de seconde (classe); (Post) au tarif réduit; (pej) de qualité inférieure ▷ adv (Rail) en seconde; (Post) au tarif réduit; **secondhand** adj d'occasion; (information) de seconde main; **secondly** adv deuxièmement; **second-rate** adj de deuxième ordre, de qualité inférieure; **second thoughts** npl: **to have second thoughts** changer d'avis; **on second thoughts** or **thought** (us) à la réflexion

secrecy ['si:krəsɪ] n secret m

secret ['si:krɪt] adj secret(-ète) ▷ n secret m; **in ~** adv en secret, secrètement, en cachette

secretary ['sɛkrətrɪ] n secrétaire m/f; **S~ of State (for)** (Brit Pol) ministre m (de)

secretive ['si:krətɪv] adj réservé(e); (pej) cachottier(-ière), dissimulé(e)

secret service n services secrets

sect [sɛkt] n secte f

section ['sɛkʃən] n section f; (Comm) rayon m; (of document) section, article m, paragraphe m; (cut) coupe f

sector ['sɛktər] n secteur m

secular ['sɛkjulər] adj laïque

secure [sɪˈkjuər] adj (free from anxiety) sans inquiétude, sécurisé(e); (firmly fixed) solide, bien attaché(e) (or fermé(e) etc); (in safe place) en lieu sûr, en sûreté ▷ vt (fix) fixer, attacher; (get) obtenir, se procurer

security [sɪˈkjuərɪtɪ] n sécurité f, mesures fpl de sécurité; (for loan) caution f, garantie f; **securities** npl (Stock Exchange) valeurs fpl, titres mpl; **security guard** n garde chargé de la sécurité; (transporting money) convoyeur m de fonds

sedan [səˈdæn] n (us Aut) berline f

sedate [sɪˈdeɪt] adj calme; posé(e) ▷ vt donner des sédatifs à

sedative ['sɛdɪtɪv] n calmant m, sédatif m

seduce [sɪˈdjuːs] vt séduire; **seductive** [sɪˈdʌktɪv] adj séduisant(e); (smile) séducteur(-trice); (fig: offer) alléchant(e)

see [si:] vb (pt saw, pp **~n**) ▷ vt (gen) voir; (accompany): **to ~ sb to the door** reconduire or raccompagner qn jusqu'à la porte ▷ vi voir; **to ~ that** (ensure) veiller à ce que + sub, faire en sorte que + sub, s'assurer que; **~ you soon/later/tomorrow!** à bientôt/plus tard/demain!; **see off** vt accompagner (à la gare or à l'aéroport etc); **see out** vt (take to door) raccompagner à la porte; **see through** vt mener à bonne fin ▷ vt fus voir clair dans; **see to** vt fus s'occuper de, se charger de

seed [si:d] n graine f; (fig) germe m; (Tennis etc) tête f de série; **to go to ~** (plant) monter en graine; (fig) se laisser aller

seeing ['si:ɪŋ] conj: **~ (that)** vu que, étant donné que

seek (pt, pp sought) [si:k, sɔ:t] vt chercher, rechercher

seem [si:m] vi sembler, paraître; **there ~s to be ...** il semble qu'il y a ..., on dirait qu'il y a ...; **seemingly** adv apparemment

seen [si:n] pp of **see**

seesaw ['si:sɔ:] n (jeu m de) bascule f

segment ['sɛgmənt] n segment m; (of orange) quartier m

segregate ['sɛgrɪgeɪt] vt séparer, isoler

Seine [seɪn] n: **the (River) ~** la Seine

seize [si:z] vt (grasp) saisir, attraper; (take possession of) s'emparer de; (opportunity) saisir

seizure ['si:ʒər] n (Med) crise f, attaque f; (of power) prise f

seldom ['sɛldəm] adv rarement

select [sɪˈlɛkt] adj choisi(e), d'élite; (hotel, restaurant, club) chic inv, sélect inv ▷ vt sélectionner, choisir; **selection** n sélection f, choix m; **selective** adj sélectif(-ive); (school) à recrutement sélectif

self [sɛlf] n (pl **selves**): **the ~** le moi inv ▷ prefix auto-; **self-assured** adj sûr(e) de soi, plein(e) d'assurance; **self-catering** adj (BRIT: flat) avec cuisine, où l'on peut faire sa cuisine; (: holiday) en appartement (or chalet etc) loué; **self-centred** (US **self-centered**) adj égocentrique; **self-confidence** n confiance f en soi; **self-confident** adj sûr(e) de soi, plein(e) d'assurance; **self-conscious** adj timide, qui manque d'assurance; **self-contained** adj (BRIT: flat) avec entrée particulière, indépendant(e); **self-control** n maîtrise f de soi; **self-defence** (US **self-defense**) n autodéfense f; (Law) légitime défense f; **self-drive** adj (BRIT): **self-drive car** voiture f de location; **self-employed** adj qui travaille à son compte; **self-esteem** n amour-propre m; **self-indulgent** adj qui ne se refuse rien; **self-interest** n intérêt personnel; **selfish** adj égoïste; **self-pity** n apitoiement m sur soi-même; **self-raising** [sɛlf'reɪzɪŋ] (US **self-rising** [sɛlf'raɪzɪŋ]) adj: **self-raising flour** farine f pour gâteaux (avec levure incorporée); **self-respect** n respect m de soi, amour-propre m; **self-service** adj, n libre-service (m), self-service (m)

sell (pt, pp **sold**) [sɛl, səʊld] vt vendre ▷ vi se vendre; **to ~ at** or **for 10 euros** se vendre 10 euros; **sell off** vt liquider; **sell out** vi: **to ~ out (of sth)** (use up stock) vendre tout son stock (de qch); **sell-by date** n date f limite de vente; **seller** n vendeur(-euse), marchand(e)

Sellotape® ['sɛləʊteɪp] n (BRIT) scotch® m

selves [sɛlvz] npl of **self**

semester [sɪ'mɛstəʳ] n (esp US) semestre m

semi... ['sɛmɪ] prefix semi-, demi-; à demi, à moitié; **semicircle** n demi-cercle m; **semidetached (house)** n (BRIT) maison jumelée or jumelle; **semi-final** n demi-finale f

seminar ['sɛmɪnɑːʳ] n séminaire m

semi-skimmed ['sɛmɪ'skɪmd] adj demi-écrémé(e)

senate ['sɛnɪt] n sénat m; (US): **the S~** le Sénat; **senator** n sénateur m

send (pt, pp **sent**) [sɛnd, sɛnt] vt envoyer; **send back** vt renvoyer; **send for** vt fus (by post) se faire envoyer, commander par correspondance; **send in** vt (report, application, resignation) remettre; **send off** vt (goods) envoyer, expédier; (BRIT Sport: player) or renvoyer du terrain; **send on** vt (BRIT: letter) faire suivre; (luggage etc: in advance) (faire) expédier à l'avance; **send out** vt (invitation) envoyer (par la poste); (emit: light, heat, signal) émettre; **send up** vt (person, price) faire monter; (BRIT: parody) mettre en boîte, parodier; **sender** n expéditeur(-trice); **send-off** n: **a good send-off** des adieux chaleureux

senile ['siːnaɪl] adj sénile

senior ['siːnɪəʳ] adj (high-ranking) de haut niveau; (of higher rank): **to be ~ to sb** être le supérieur de qn; **senior citizen** n personne f du troisième âge; **senior high school** n (US) ≈ lycée m

sensation [sɛn'seɪʃən] n sensation f; **sensational** adj qui fait sensation; (marvellous) sensationnel(le)

sense [sɛns] n sens m; (feeling) sentiment m; (meaning) sens, signification f; (wisdom) bon sens ▷ vt sentir, pressentir; **it makes ~** c'est logique; **senseless** adj insensé(e), stupide; (unconscious) sans connaissance; **sense of humour** (US **sense of humor**) n sens m de l'humour

sensible ['sɛnsɪbl] adj sensé(e), raisonnable; (shoes etc) pratique

> Be careful not to translate *sensible* by the French word *sensible*.

sensitive ['sɛnsɪtɪv] adj: **~ (to)** sensible (à)

sensual ['sɛnsjuəl] adj sensuel(le)

sensuous ['sɛnsjuəs] adj voluptueux(-euse), sensuel(le)

sent [sɛnt] pt, pp of **send**

sentence ['sɛntns] n (Ling) phrase f; (Law: judgment) condamnation f, sentence f; (: punishment) peine f ▷ vt: **to ~ sb to death/to 5 years** condamner qn à mort/à 5 ans

sentiment ['sɛntɪmənt] n sentiment m; (opinion) opinion f, avis m; **sentimental** [sɛntɪ'mɛntl] adj sentimental(e)

Sep. abbr (= September) septembre

separate adj ['sɛprɪt] séparé(e); (organization) indépendant(e); (day, occasion, issue) différent(e) ▷ vb ['sɛpəreɪt] ▷ vt séparer; (distinguish) distinguer ▷ vi se séparer; **separately** adv séparément; **separates** npl (clothes) coordonnés mpl; **separation** [sɛpə'reɪʃən] n séparation f

September [sɛp'tɛmbəʳ] n septembre m

septic ['sɛptɪk] adj (wound) infecté(e); **septic tank** n fosse f septique

sequel ['siːkwl] n conséquence f; séquelles fpl; (of story) suite f

sequence ['siːkwəns] n ordre m, suite f; (in film) séquence f; (dance) numéro m

sequin ['siːkwɪn] n paillette f

Serb [səːb] adj, n = **Serbian**

Serbia ['səːbɪə] n Serbie f

Serbian ['səːbɪən] adj serbe ▷ n Serbe m/f; (Ling) serbe m

sergeant ['sɑːdʒənt] n sergent m; (Police) brigadier m

serial ['sɪərɪəl] n feuilleton m; **serial killer** n meurtrier m tuant en série; **serial number** n numéro m de série

series ['sɪərɪz] n série f; (Publishing) collection f

serious ['sɪərɪəs] adj sérieux(-euse); (accident

etc) grave; **seriously** *adv* sérieusement; *(hurt)* gravement

sermon ['səːmən] *n* sermon *m*

servant ['səːvənt] *n* domestique *m/f*; *(fig)* serviteur (servante)

serve [səːv] *vt (employer etc)* servir, être au service de; *(purpose)* servir à; *(customer, food, meal)* servir; *(subj: train)* desservir; *(apprenticeship)* faire, accomplir; *(prison term)* faire; purger ▷ *vi (Tennis)* servir; *(be useful)*: **to ~ as/for/to do** servir de/à/à faire ▷ *n (Tennis)* service *m*; **it ~s him right** c'est bien fait pour lui; **server** *n (Comput)* serveur *m*

service ['səːvɪs] *n (gen)* service *m*; *(Aut)* révision *f*; *(Rel)* office *m* ▷ *vt (car etc)* réviser; **services** *npl (Econ: tertiary sector)* (secteur *m*) tertiaire *m*, secteur des services; *(BRIT: on motorway)* station-service *f*; *(Mil)*: **the S~s** *npl* les forces armées; **to be of ~ to sb, to do sb a ~** rendre service à qn; **~ included/not included** service compris/non compris; **service area** *n (on motorway)* aire *f* de services; **service charge** *n (BRIT)* service *m*; **serviceman** *(irreg)* *n* militaire *m*; **service station** *n* station-service *f*

serviette [səːvɪˈɛt] *n (BRIT)* serviette *f* (de table)

session ['sɛʃən] *n (sitting)* séance *f*; **to be in ~** siéger, être en session *or* en séance

set [sɛt] *n* série *f*, assortiment *m*; *(of tools etc)* jeu *m*; *(Radio, TV)* poste *m*; *(Tennis)* set *m*; *(group of people)* cercle *m*, milieu *m*; *(Cine)* plateau *m*; *(Theat: stage)* scène *f*; (: *scenery)* décor *m*; *(Math)* ensemble *m*; *(Hairdressing)* mise *f* en plis ▷ *adj (fixed)* fixe, déterminé(e); *(ready)* prêt(e) ▷ *vb (pt, pp ~)* ▷ *vt (place)* mettre, poser, placer; *(fix, establish)* fixer; (: *record)* établir; *(assign: task, homework)* donner; *(exam)* composer; *(adjust)* régler; *(decide: rules etc)* fixer, choisir ▷ *vi (sun)* se coucher; *(jam, jelly, concrete)* prendre; *(bone)* se ressouder; **to be ~ on doing** être résolu(e) à faire; **to ~ to music** mettre en musique; **to ~ on fire** mettre le feu à; **to ~ free** libérer; **to ~ sth going** déclencher qch; **to ~ sail** partir, prendre la mer; **set aside** *vt* mettre de côté; *(time)* garder; **set down** *vt (subj: bus, train)* déposer; **set in** *vi (infection, bad weather)* s'installer; *(complications)* survenir, surgir; **set off** *vi* se mettre en route, partir ▷ *vt (bomb)* faire exploser; *(cause to start)* déclencher; *(show up well)* mettre en valeur, faire valoir; **set out** *vi*: **to ~ out (from)** partir (de) ▷ *vt (arrange)* disposer; *(state)* présenter, exposer; **to ~ out to do** entreprendre de faire; avoir pour but *or* intention de faire; **set up** *vt (organization)* fonder, créer; **setback** *n (hitch)* revers *m*, contretemps *m*; **set menu** *n* menu *m*

settee [sɛˈtiː] *n* canapé *m*

setting ['sɛtɪŋ] *n* cadre *m*; *(of jewel)* monture *f*; *(position: of controls)* réglage *m*

settle ['sɛtl] *vt (argument, matter, account)* régler; *(problem)* résoudre; *(Med: calm)* calmer ▷ *vi (bird, dust etc)* se poser; **to ~ for sth** accepter qch, se contenter de qch; **to ~ on sth** opter *or* se décider pour qch; **settle down** *vi (get comfortable)* s'installer; *(become calmer)* se calmer; se ranger; *(live quietly)* se fixer; **settle in** *vi* s'installer; **settle up** *vi*: **to ~ up with sb** régler (ce que l'on doit à) qn; **settlement** *n (payment)* règlement *m*; *(agreement)* accord *m*; *(village etc)* village *m*, hameau *m*

setup ['sɛtʌp] *n (arrangement)* manière *f* dont les choses sont organisées; *(situation)* situation *f*, allure *f* des choses

seven ['sɛvn] *num* sept; **seventeen** *num* dix-sept; **seventeenth** [sɛvnˈtiːnθ] *num* dix-septième; **seventh** *num* septième; **seventieth** ['sɛvntɪɪθ] *num* soixante-dixième; **seventy** *num* soixante-dix

sever ['sɛvər] *vt* couper, trancher; *(relations)* rompre

several ['sɛvərl] *adj, pron* plusieurs *pl*; **~ of us** plusieurs d'entre nous

severe [sɪˈvɪər] *adj (stern)* sévère, strict(e); *(serious)* grave, sérieux(-euse); *(plain)* sévère, austère

sew *(pt ~ed, pp ~n)* [səʊ, səʊd, səʊn] *vt, vi* coudre

sewage ['suːɪdʒ] *n* vidange(s) *f(pl)*

sewer ['suːər] *n* égout *m*

sewing ['səʊɪŋ] *n* couture *f*; *(item(s))* ouvrage *m*; **sewing machine** *n* machine *f* à coudre

sewn [səʊn] *pp of* **sew**

sex [sɛks] *n* sexe *m*; **to have ~ with** avoir des rapports (sexuels) avec; **sexism** ['sɛksɪzəm] *n* sexisme *m*; **sexist** *adj* sexiste; **sexual** ['sɛksjuəl] *adj* sexuel(le); **sexual intercourse** *n* rapports sexuels; **sexuality** [sɛksjuˈælɪtɪ] *n* sexualité *f*; **sexy** *adj* sexy *inv*

shabby ['ʃæbɪ] *adj* miteux(-euse); *(behaviour)* mesquin(e), méprisable

shack [ʃæk] *n* cabane *f*, hutte *f*

shade [ʃeɪd] *n* ombre *f*; *(for lamp)* abat-jour *m inv*; *(of colour)* nuance *f*, ton *m*; *(us: window shade)* store *m*; *(small quantity)*: **a ~ of** soupçon de ▷ *vt* abriter du soleil, ombrager; **shades** *npl (us: sunglasses)* lunettes *fpl* de soleil; **in the ~** à l'ombre; **a ~ smaller** un tout petit peu plus petit

shadow ['ʃædəʊ] *n* ombre *f* ▷ *vt (follow)* filer; **shadow cabinet** *n (BRIT Pol)* cabinet parallèle formé par le parti qui n'est pas au pouvoir

shady ['ʃeɪdɪ] *adj* ombragé(e); *(fig: dishonest)* louche, véreux(-euse)

shaft [ʃɑːft] *n (of arrow, spear)* hampe *f*; *(Aut, Tech)* arbre *m*; *(of mine)* puits *m*; *(of lift)* cage *f*; *(of light)* rayon *m*, trait *m*

s

shake [ʃeɪk] *vb* (*pt* **shook**, *pp* **~n**) ▷ *vt* secouer; (*bottle, cocktail*) agiter; (*house, confidence*) ébranler ▷ *vi* trembler; **to ~ one's head** (*in refusal etc*) dire or faire non de la tête; (*in dismay*) secouer la tête; **to ~ hands with sb** serrer la main à qn; **shake off** *vt* secouer; (*pursuer*) se débarrasser de; **shake up** *vt* secouer; **shaky** *adj* (*hand, voice*) tremblant(e); (*building*) branlant(e), peu solide

shall [ʃæl] *aux vb*: **I ~ go** j'irai; **~ I open the door?** j'ouvre la porte?; **I'll get the coffee, ~ I?** je vais chercher le café, d'accord?

shallow [ˈʃæləʊ] *adj* peu profond(e); (*fig*) superficiel(le), qui manque de profondeur

sham [ʃæm] *n* frime *f*

shambles [ˈʃæmblz] *n* confusion *f*, pagaïe *f*, fouillis *m*

shame [ʃeɪm] *n* honte *f* ▷ *vt* faire honte à; **it is a ~ (that/to do)** c'est dommage (que + *sub*/de faire); **what a ~!** quel dommage!; **shameful** *adj* honteux(-euse), scandaleux(-euse); **shameless** *adj* éhonté(e), effronté(e)

shampoo [ʃæmˈpuː] *n* shampooing *m* ▷ *vt* faire un shampooing à

shandy [ˈʃændɪ] *n* bière panachée

shan't [ʃɑːnt] = **shall not**

shape [ʃeɪp] *n* forme *f* ▷ *vt* façonner, modeler; (*sb's ideas, character*) former; (*sb's life*) déterminer ▷ *vi* (*also*: **~ up**: *events*) prendre tournure; (*: person*) faire des progrès, s'en sortir; **to take ~** prendre forme or tournure

share [ʃɛəʳ] *n* part *f*; (*Comm*) action *f* ▷ *vt* partager; (*have in common*) avoir en commun; **to ~ out (among** or **between)** partager (entre); **shareholder** *n* (BRIT) actionnaire *m/f*

shark [ʃɑːk] *n* requin *m*

sharp [ʃɑːp] *adj* (*razor, knife*) tranchant(e), bien aiguisé(e); (*point, voice*) aigu(ë); (*nose, chin*) pointu(e); (*outline, increase*) net(te); (*cold, pain*) vif (vive); (*taste*) piquant(e), âcre; (*Mus*) dièse; (*person: quick-witted*) vif (vive), éveillé(e); (*: unscrupulous*) malhonnête ▷ *n* (*Mus*) dièse *m* ▷ *adv*: **at 2 o'clock ~** à 2 heures pile or tapantes; **sharpen** *vt* aiguiser; (*pencil*) tailler; (*fig*) aviver; **sharpener** *n* (*also*: **pencil sharpener**) taille-crayon(s) *m inv*; **sharply** *adv* (*turn, stop*) brusquement; (*stand out*) nettement; (*criticize, retort*) sèchement, vertement

shatter [ˈʃætəʳ] *vt* briser; (*fig: upset*) bouleverser; (*: ruin*) briser, ruiner ▷ *vi* voler en éclats, se briser; **shattered** *adj* (*overwhelmed, grief-stricken*) bouleversé(e); (*inf: exhausted*) éreinté(e)

shave [ʃeɪv] *vt* raser ▷ *vi* se raser ▷ *n*: **to have a ~** se raser; **shaver** *n* (*also*: **electric shaver**) rasoir *m* électrique

shaving cream *n* crème *f* à raser

shaving foam *n* mousse *f* à raser

shavings [ˈʃeɪvɪŋz] *npl* (*of wood etc*) copeaux *mpl*

shawl [ʃɔːl] *n* châle *m*

she [ʃiː] *pron* elle

sheath [ʃiːθ] *n* gaine *f*, fourreau *m*, étui *m*; (*contraceptive*) préservatif *m*

shed [ʃɛd] *n* remise *f*, resserre *f* ▷ *vt* (*pt, pp* **~**) (*leaves, fur etc*) perdre; (*tears*) verser, répandre; (*workers*) congédier

she'd [ʃiːd] = **she had; she would**

sheep [ʃiːp] *n* (*pl inv*) mouton *m*; **sheepdog** *n* chien *m* de berger; **sheepskin** *n* peau *f* de mouton

sheer [ʃɪəʳ] *adj* (*utter*) pur(e), pur et simple; (*steep*) à pic, abrupt(e); (*almost transparent*) extrêmement fin(e) ▷ *adv* à pic, abruptement

sheet [ʃiːt] *n* (*on bed*) drap *m*; (*of paper*) feuille *f*; (*of glass, metal etc*) feuille, plaque *f*

sheik(h) [ʃeɪk] *n* cheik *m*

shelf (*pl* **shelves**) [ʃɛlf, ʃɛlvz] *n* étagère *f*, rayon *m*

shell [ʃɛl] *n* (*on beach*) coquillage *m*; (*of egg, nut etc*) coquille *f*; (*explosive*) obus *m*; (*of building*) carcasse *f* ▷ *vt* (*peas*) écosser; (*Mil*) bombarder (d'obus)

she'll [ʃiːl] = **she will; she shall**

shellfish [ˈʃɛlfɪʃ] *n* (*pl inv: crab etc*) crustacé *m*; (*: scallop etc*) coquillage *m* ▷ *npl* (*as food*) fruits *mpl* de mer

shelter [ˈʃɛltəʳ] *n* abri *m*, refuge *m* ▷ *vt* abriter, protéger; (*give lodging to*) donner asile à ▷ *vi* s'abriter, se mettre à l'abri; **sheltered** *adj* (*life*) retiré(e), à l'abri des soucis; (*spot*) abrité(e)

shelves [ʃɛlvz] *npl* of **shelf**

shelving [ˈʃɛlvɪŋ] *n* (*shelves*) rayonnage(s) *m(pl)*

shepherd [ˈʃɛpəd] *n* berger *m* ▷ *vt* (*guide*) guider, escorter; **shepherd's pie** *n* ≈ hachis *m* Parmentier

sheriff [ˈʃɛrɪf] (US) *n* shérif *m*

sherry [ˈʃɛrɪ] *n* xérès *m*, sherry *m*

she's [ʃiːz] = **she is; she has**

Shetland [ˈʃɛtlənd] *n* (*also*: **the ~s, the ~ Isles** or **Islands**) les îles *fpl* Shetland

shield [ʃiːld] *n* bouclier *m*; (*protection*) écran *m* de protection ▷ *vt*: **to ~ (from)** protéger (de or contre)

shift [ʃɪft] *n* (*change*) changement *m*; (*work period*) période *f* de travail; (*of workers*) équipe *f*, poste *m* ▷ *vt* déplacer, changer de place; (*remove*) enlever ▷ *vi* changer de place, bouger

shin [ʃɪn] *n* tibia *m*

shine [ʃaɪn] *n* éclat *m*, brillant *m* ▷ *vb* (*pt, pp* **shone**) ▷ *vi* briller ▷ *vt* (*torch*): **to ~ on** braquer sur; (*polish*: *pt, pp* **~d**) faire briller or reluire

shingles [ˈʃɪŋglz] *n* (*Med*) zona *m*

shiny [ˈʃaɪnɪ] *adj* brillant(e)

ship [ʃɪp] *n* bateau *m*; (*large*) navire *m* ▷ *vt* transporter (par mer); (*send*) expédier (par mer); **shipment** *n* cargaison *f*; **shipping**

n (*ships*) navires *mpl*; (*traffic*) navigation *f*; (*the industry*) industrie navale; (*transport*) transport *m*; **shipwreck** *n* épave *f*; (*event*) naufrage *m* ▷ *vt*: **to be shipwrecked** faire naufrage; **shipyard** *n* chantier naval

shirt [ʃəːt] *n* chemise *f*; (*woman's*) chemisier *m*; **in ~ sleeves** en bras de chemise

shit [ʃɪt] *excl* (*inf!*) merde (!)

shiver ['ʃɪvəʳ] *n* frisson *m* ▷ *vi* frissonner

shock [ʃɔk] *n* choc *m*; (*Elec*) secousse *f*, décharge *f*; (*Med*) commotion *f*, choc ▷ *vt* (*scandalize*) choquer, scandaliser; (*upset*) bouleverser; **shocking** *adj* (*outrageous*) choquant(e), scandaleux(-euse); (*awful*) épouvantable

shoe [ʃuː] *n* chaussure *f*, soulier *m*; (*also*: **horse~**) fer *m* à cheval ▷ *vt* (*pt, pp* **shod**) (*horse*) ferrer; **shoelace** *n* lacet *m* (de soulier); **shoe polish** *n* cirage *m*; **shoeshop** *n* magasin *m* de chaussures

shone [ʃɔn] *pt, pp of* **shine**

shook [ʃuk] *pt of* **shake**

shoot [ʃuːt] *n* (*on branch, seedling*) pousse *f* ▷ *vb* (*pt, pp* **shot**) ▷ *vt* (*game: hunt*) chasser; (: *aim at*) tirer; (: *kill*) abattre; (*person*) blesser/tuer d'un coup de fusil (*or de revolver*); (*execute*) fusiller; (*arrow*) tirer; (*gun*) tirer un coup de; (*Cine*) tourner ▷ *vi* (*with gun, bow*): **to ~ (at)** tirer (sur); (*Football*) shooter, tirer; **shoot down** *vt* (*plane*) abattre; **shoot up** *vi* (*fig: prices etc*) monter en flèche; **shooting** *n* (*shots*) coups *mpl* de feu; (*attack*) fusillade *f*; (*murder*) homicide *m* (*à l'aide d'une arme à feu*); (*Hunting*) chasse *f*

shop [ʃɔp] *n* magasin *m*; (*workshop*) atelier *m* ▷ *vi* (*also*: **go ~ping**) faire ses courses *or* ses achats; **shop assistant** *n* (*BRIT*) vendeur(-euse); **shopkeeper** *n* marchand(e), commerçant(e); **shoplifting** *n* vol *m* à l'étalage; **shopping** *n* (*goods*) achats *mpl*, provisions *fpl*; **shopping bag** *n* sac *m* (à provisions); **shopping centre** (*US* **shopping center**) *n* centre commercial; **shopping mall** *n* centre commercial; **shopping trolley** *n* (*BRIT*) Caddie® *m*; **shop window** *n* vitrine *f*

shore [ʃɔːʳ] *n* (*of sea, lake*) rivage *m*, rive *f* ▷ *vt*: **to ~ (up)** étayer; **on ~** à terre

short [ʃɔːt] *adj* (*not long*) court(e); (*soon finished*) court, bref (brève); (*person, step*) petit(e); (*curt*) brusque, sec (sèche); (*insufficient*) insuffisant(e) ▷ *n* (*also*: **~ film**) court métrage; (*Elec*) court-circuit *m*; **to be ~ of sth** être à court de *or* manquer de qch; **in ~** bref; en bref; **~ of doing** à moins de faire; **everything ~ of** tout sauf; **it is ~ for** c'est l'abréviation *or* le diminutif de; **to cut ~** (*speech, visit*) abréger, écourter; **to fall ~ of** ne pas être à la hauteur de; **to run ~ of** arriver à court de, venir à manquer de; **to stop ~** s'arrêter net;

to stop ~ of ne pas aller jusqu'à; **shortage** *n* manque *m*, pénurie *f*; **shortbread** *n* ≈ sablé *m*; **shortcoming** *n* défaut *m*; **short(crust) pastry** *n* (*BRIT*) pâte brisée; **shortcut** *n* raccourci *m*; **shorten** *vt* raccourcir; (*text, visit*) abréger; **shortfall** *n* déficit *m*; **shorthand** *n* (*BRIT*) sténo(graphie) *f*; **shortlist** *n* (*BRIT: for job*) liste *f* des candidats sélectionnés; **short-lived** *adj* de courte durée; **shortly** *adv* bientôt, sous peu; **shorts** *npl*: (**a pair of) shorts** un short; **short-sighted** *adj* (*BRIT*) myope; (*fig*) qui manque de clairvoyance; **short-sleeved** *adj* à manches courtes; **short story** *n* nouvelle *f*; **short-tempered** *adj* qui s'emporte facilement; **short-term** *adj* (*effect*) à court terme

shot [ʃɔt] *pt, pp of* **shoot** ▷ *n* coup *m* (de feu); (*try*) coup, essai *m*; (*injection*) piqûre *f*; (*Phot*) photo *f*; **to be a good/poor ~** (*person*) tirer bien/mal; **like a ~** comme une flèche; (*very readily*) sans hésiter; **shotgun** *n* fusil *m* de chasse

should [ʃud] *aux vb*: **I ~ go now** je devrais partir maintenant; **he ~ be there now** il devrait être arrivé maintenant; **I ~ go if I were you** si j'étais vous j'irais; **I ~ like to** j'aimerais bien, volontiers

shoulder ['ʃəuldəʳ] *n* épaule *f* ▷ *vt* (*fig*) endosser, se charger de; **shoulder blade** *n* omoplate *f*

shouldn't ['ʃudnt] = **should not**

shout [ʃaut] *n* cri *m* ▷ *vt* crier ▷ *vi* crier, pousser des cris

shove [ʃʌv] *vt* pousser; (*inf: put*): **to ~ sth in** fourrer *or* ficher qch dans ▷ *n* poussée *f*

shovel ['ʃʌvl] *n* pelle *f* ▷ *vt* pelleter, enlever (*or enfourner*) à la pelle

show [ʃəu] *n* (*of emotion*) manifestation *f*, démonstration *f*; (*semblance*) semblant *m*, apparence *f*; (*exhibition*) exposition *f*, salon *m*; (*Theat, TV*) spectacle *m*; (*Cine*) séance *f* ▷ *vb* (*pt* **~ed**, *pp* **~n**) ▷ *vt* montrer; (*film*) passer; (*courage etc*) faire preuve de, manifester; (*exhibit*) exposer ▷ *vi* se voir, être visible; **can you ~ me where it is, please?** pouvez-vous me montrer où c'est?; **to be on ~** être exposé(e); **it's just for ~** c'est juste pour l'effet; **show in** *vt* faire entrer; **show off** *vi* (*pej*) crâner ▷ *vt* (*display*) faire valoir; (*pej*) faire étalage de; **show out** *vt* reconduire à la porte; **show up** *vi* (*stand out*) ressortir; (*inf: turn up*) se montrer ▷ *vt* (*unmask*) démasquer, dénoncer; (*flaw*) faire ressortir; **show business** *n* le monde du spectacle

shower ['ʃauəʳ] *n* (*for washing*) douche *f*; (*rain*) averse *f*; (*of stones etc*) pluie *f*, grêle *f*; (*US: party*) réunion organisée pour la remise de cadeaux ▷ *vi* prendre une douche, se doucher ▷ *vt*: **to ~ sb with** (*gifts etc*) combler qn de; **to have** *or* **take a ~** prendre une douche, se doucher; **shower**

cap n bonnet m de douche; **shower gel** n gel m douche

showing ['ʃəʊɪŋ] n (of film) projection f

show jumping [-dʒʌmpɪŋ] n concours m hippique

shown [ʃəʊn] pp of **show**

show: **show-off** n (inf: person) crâneur(-euse), m'as-tu-vu(e); **showroom** n magasin m or salle f d'exposition

shrank [ʃræŋk] pt of **shrink**

shred [ʃrɛd] n (gen pl) lambeau m, petit morceau; (fig: of truth, evidence) parcelle f ▷ vt mettre en lambeaux, déchirer; (documents) détruire; (Culin: grate) râper; (: lettuce etc) couper en lanières

shrewd [ʃruːd] adj astucieux(-euse), perspicace; (business person) habile

shriek [ʃriːk] n cri perçant or aigu, hurlement m ▷ vt, vi hurler, crier

shrimp [ʃrɪmp] n crevette grise

shrine [ʃraɪn] n (place) lieu m de pèlerinage

shrink (pt **shrank**, pp **shrunk**) [ʃrɪŋk, ʃræŋk, ʃrʌŋk] vi rétrécir; (fig) diminuer; (also: ~ **away**) reculer ▷ vt (wool) (faire) rétrécir ▷ n (inf: pej) psychanalyste m/f; **to ~ from (doing) sth** reculer devant (la pensée de faire) qch

shrivel ['ʃrɪvl] (also: ~ **up**) vt ratatiner, flétrir ▷ vi se ratatiner, se flétrir

shroud [ʃraʊd] n linceul m ▷ vt: **~ed in mystery** enveloppé(e) de mystère

Shrove Tuesday ['ʃrəʊv-] n (le) Mardi gras

shrub [ʃrʌb] n arbuste m

shrug [ʃrʌg] n haussement m d'épaules ▷ vt, vi: **to ~ (one's shoulders)** hausser les épaules; **shrug off** vt faire fi de

shrunk [ʃrʌŋk] pp of **shrink**

shudder ['ʃʌdəʳ] n frisson m, frémissement m ▷ vi frissonner, frémir

shuffle ['ʃʌfl] vt (cards) battre; **to ~ (one's feet)** traîner les pieds

shun [ʃʌn] vt éviter, fuir

shut (pt, pp ~) [ʃʌt] vt fermer ▷ vi (se) fermer; **shut down** vt fermer définitivement ▷ vi fermer définitivement; **shut up** vi (inf: keep quiet) se taire ▷ vt (close) fermer; (silence) faire taire; **shutter** n volet m; (Phot) obturateur m

shuttle ['ʃʌtl] n navette f; (also: ~ **service**) (service m de) navette f; **shuttlecock** n volant m (de badminton)

shy [ʃaɪ] adj timide

siblings ['sɪblɪŋz] npl (formal) frères et sœurs mpl (de mêmes parents)

Sicily ['sɪsɪlɪ] n Sicile f

sick [sɪk] adj (ill) malade; (BRIT: vomiting): **to be ~** vomir; (humour) noir(e), macabre; **to feel ~** avoir envie de vomir, avoir mal au cœur; **to be ~ of** (fig) en avoir assez de; **sickening** adj (fig) écœurant(e), révoltant(e), répugnant(e); **sick leave** n congé m de maladie; **sickly** adj

maladif(-ive), souffreteux(-euse); (causing nausea) écœurant(e); **sickness** n maladie f; (vomiting) vomissement(s) m(pl)

side [saɪd] n côté m; (of lake, road) bord m; (of mountain) versant m; (fig: aspect) côté, aspect m; (team: Sport) équipe f; (TV: channel) chaîne f ▷ adj (door, entrance) latéral(e) ▷ vi: **to ~ with sb** prendre le parti de qn, se ranger du côté de qn; **by the ~ of** au bord de; **~ by ~** côte à côte; **to rock from ~ to ~** se balancer; **to take ~s (with)** prendre parti (pour); **sideboard** n buffet m; **sideboards** (BRIT), **sideburns** npl (whiskers) pattes fpl; **side effect** n effet m secondaire; **sidelight** n (Aut) veilleuse f; **sideline** n (Sport) (ligne f de) touche f; (fig) activité f secondaire; **side order** n garniture f; **side road** n petite route, route transversale; **side street** n rue transversale; **sidetrack** vt (fig) faire dévier de son sujet; **sidewalk** n (US) trottoir m; **sideways** adv de côté

siege [siːdʒ] n siège m

sieve [sɪv] n tamis m, passoire f ▷ vt tamiser, passer (au tamis)

sift [sɪft] vt passer au tamis or au crible; (fig) passer au crible

sigh [saɪ] n soupir m ▷ vi soupirer, pousser un soupir

sight [saɪt] n (faculty) vue f; (spectacle) spectacle m; (on gun) mire f ▷ vt apercevoir; **in ~** visible; (fig) en vue; **out of ~** hors de vue; **sightseeing** n tourisme m; **to go sightseeing** faire du tourisme

sign [saɪn] n (gen) signe m; (with hand etc) signe, geste m; (notice) panneau m, écriteau m; (also: road ~) panneau de signalisation ▷ vt signer; **where do I ~?** où dois-je signer?; **sign for** vt fus (item) signer le reçu pour; **sign in** vi signer le registre (en arrivant); **sign on** vi (BRIT: as unemployed) s'inscrire au chômage; (enrol) s'inscrire ▷ vt (employee) embaucher; **sign over** vt: **to ~ sth over to sb** céder qch par écrit à qn; **sign up** vi (Mil) s'engager; (for course) s'inscrire

signal ['sɪgnl] n signal m ▷ vi (Aut) mettre son clignotant ▷ vt (person) faire signe à; (message) communiquer par signaux

signature ['sɪgnətʃəʳ] n signature f

significance [sɪg'nɪfɪkəns] n signification f; importance f

significant [sɪg'nɪfɪkənt] adj significatif(-ive); (important) important(e), considérable

signify ['sɪgnɪfaɪ] vt signifier

sign language n langage m par signes

signpost ['saɪnpəʊst] n poteau indicateur

Sikh [siːk] adj, n Sikh m/f

silence ['saɪləns] n silence m ▷ vt faire taire, réduire au silence

silent ['saɪlnt] adj silencieux(-euse); (film) muet(te); **to keep** or **remain ~** garder le silence, ne rien dire

silhouette [sɪluːˈɛt] n silhouette f

silicon chip [ˈsɪlɪkən-] n puce f électronique

silk [sɪlk] n soie f ▷ cpd de or en soie

silly [ˈsɪlɪ] adj stupide, sot(te), bête

silver [ˈsɪlvəʳ] n argent m; (money) monnaie f (en pièces d'argent); (also: **~ware**) argenterie f ▷ adj (made of silver) d'argent, en argent; (in colour) argenté(e); **silver-plated** adj plaqué(e) argent

similar [ˈsɪmɪləʳ] adj: **~ (to)** semblable (à); **similarity** [sɪmɪˈlærɪtɪ] n ressemblance f, similarité f; **similarly** adv de la même façon, de même

simmer [ˈsɪməʳ] vi cuire à feu doux, mijoter

simple [ˈsɪmpl] adj simple; **simplicity** [sɪmˈplɪsɪtɪ] n simplicité f; **simplify** [ˈsɪmplɪfaɪ] vt simplifier; **simply** adv simplement; (without fuss) avec simplicité; (absolutely) absolument

simulate [ˈsɪmjuleɪt] vt simuler, feindre

simultaneous [sɪməlˈteɪnɪəs] adj simultané(e); **simultaneously** adv simultanément

sin [sɪn] n péché m ▷ vi pécher

since [sɪns] adv, prep depuis ▷ conj (time) depuis que; (because) puisque, étant donné que, comme; **~ then**, **ever ~** depuis ce moment-là

sincere [sɪnˈsɪəʳ] adj sincère; **sincerely** adv sincèrement; **Yours sincerely** (at end of letter) veuillez agréer, Monsieur (or Madame) l'expression de mes sentiments distingués or les meilleurs

sing (pt **sang**, pp **sung**) [sɪŋ, sæŋ, sʌŋ] vt, vi chanter

Singapore [sɪŋɡəˈpɔːʳ] n Singapour m

singer [ˈsɪŋəʳ] n chanteur(-euse)

singing [ˈsɪŋɪŋ] n (of person, bird) chant m

single [ˈsɪŋɡl] adj seul(e), unique; (unmarried) célibataire; (not double) simple ▷ n (BRIT: also: **~ ticket**) aller m (simple); (record) 45 tours m; **singles** npl (Tennis) simple m; **every ~ day** chaque jour sans exception; **single out** vt choisir; (distinguish) distinguer; **single bed** n lit m d'une personne or à une place; **single file** n: **in single file** en file indienne; **single-handed** adv tout(e) seul(e), sans (aucune) aide; **single-minded** adj résolu(e), tenace; **single parent** n parent unique (or célibataire); **single-parent family** famille monoparentale; **single room** n chambre f à un lit or pour une personne

singular [ˈsɪŋɡjuləʳ] adj singulier(-ière); (odd) singulier, étrange; (outstanding) remarquable; (Ling) (au) singulier, du singulier ▷ n (Ling) singulier m

sinister [ˈsɪnɪstəʳ] adj sinistre

sink [sɪŋk] n évier m; (washbasin) lavabo m ▷ vb (pt **sank**, pp **sunk**) ▷ vt (ship) (faire) couler, faire sombrer; (foundations) creuser ▷ vi couler, sombrer; (ground etc) s'affaisser; **to ~ into sth** (chair) s'enfoncer dans qch; **sink in** vi (explanation) rentrer (inf), être compris

sinus [ˈsaɪnəs] n (Anat) sinus m inv

sip [sɪp] n petite gorgée ▷ vt boire à petites gorgées

sir [səʳ] n monsieur m; **S~ John Smith** sir John Smith; **yes ~** oui Monsieur

siren [ˈsaɪərn] n sirène f

sirloin [ˈsəːlɔɪn] n (also: **~ steak**) aloyau m

sister [ˈsɪstəʳ] n sœur f; (nun) religieuse f, (bonne) sœur; (BRIT: nurse) infirmière f en chef; **sister-in-law** n belle-sœur f

sit (pt, pp **sat**) [sɪt, sæt] vi s'asseoir; (be sitting) être assis(e); (assembly) être en séance, siéger; (for painter) poser ▷ vt (exam) passer, se présenter à; **sit back** vi (in seat) bien s'installer, se carrer; **sit down** vi s'asseoir; **sit on** vt fus (jury, committee) faire partie de; **sit up** vi s'asseoir; (straight) se redresser; (not go to bed) rester debout, ne pas se coucher

sitcom [ˈsɪtkɔm] n abbr (TV: = situation comedy) sitcom f, comédie f de situation

site [saɪt] n emplacement m, site m; (also: **building ~**) chantier m ▷ vt placer

sitting [ˈsɪtɪŋ] n (of assembly etc) séance f; (in canteen) service m; **sitting room** n salon m

situated [ˈsɪtjueɪtɪd] adj situé(e)

situation [sɪtjuˈeɪʃən] n situation f; **"~s vacant/wanted"** (BRIT) "offres/demandes d'emploi"

six [sɪks] num six; **sixteen** num seize; **sixteenth** [sɪksˈtiːnθ] num seizième; **sixth** [sɪksθ] num sixième; **sixth form** n (BRIT) ≈ classes fpl de première et de terminale; **sixth-form college** n lycée n'ayant que des classes de première et de terminale; **sixtieth** [ˈsɪkstɪɪθ] num soixantième; **sixty** num soixante

size [saɪz] n dimensions fpl; (of person) taille f; (of clothing) taille f; (of shoes) pointure f; (of problem) ampleur f; (glue) colle f; **sizeable** adj assez grand(e); (amount, problem, majority) assez important(e)

sizzle [ˈsɪzl] vi grésiller

skate [skeɪt] n patin m; (fish: pl inv) raie f ▷ vi patiner; **skateboard** n skateboard m, planche f à roulettes; **skateboarding** n skateboard m; **skater** n patineur(-euse); **skating** n patinage m; **skating rink** n patinoire f

skeleton [ˈskɛlɪtn] n squelette m; (outline) schéma m

skeptical [ˈskɛptɪkl] (US) = **sceptical**

sketch [skɛtʃ] n (drawing) croquis m, esquisse f; (outline plan) aperçu m; (Theat) sketch m, saynète f ▷ vt esquisser, faire un croquis or une esquisse de; (plan etc) esquisser

skewer [ˈskjuːəʳ] n brochette f

ski [skiː] n ski m ⊳ vi skier, faire du ski; **ski boot**
n chaussure f de ski

skid [skɪd] n dérapage m ⊳ vi déraper

ski: **skier** n skieur(-euse); **skiing** n ski m; **to go
skiing** (aller) faire du ski

skilful (US **skillful**) ['skɪlful] adj habile,
adroit(e)

ski lift n remonte-pente m inv

skill [skɪl] n (ability) habileté f, adresse f, talent
m; (requiring training) compétences fpl; **skilled**
adj habile, adroit(e); (worker) qualifié(e)

skim [skɪm] vt (soup) écumer; (glide over) raser,
effleurer ⊳ vi: **to ~ through** (fig) parcourir;
skimmed milk (US **skim milk**) n lait écrémé

skin [skɪn] n peau f ⊳ vt (fruit etc) éplucher;
(animal) écorcher; **skinhead** n skinhead m;
skinny adj maigre, maigrichon(ne)

skip [skɪp] n petit bond or saut; (BRIT: container)
benne f ⊳ vi gambader, sautiller; (with rope)
sauter à la corde ⊳ vt (pass over) sauter

ski: **ski pass** n forfait-skieur(s) m; **ski pole** n
bâton m de ski

skipper ['skɪpər] n (Naut, Sport) capitaine m; (in
race) skipper m

skipping rope ['skɪpɪŋ-] (US **skip rope**) n
(BRIT) corde f à sauter

skirt [skəːt] n jupe f ⊳ vt longer, contourner

skirting board ['skəːtɪŋ-] n (BRIT) plinthe f

ski slope n piste f de ski

ski suit n combinaison f de ski

skull [skʌl] n crâne m

skunk [skʌŋk] n mouffette f

sky [skaɪ] n ciel m; **skyscraper** n gratte-ciel m
inv

slab [slæb] n (of stone) dalle f; (of meat, cheese)
tranche épaisse

slack [slæk] adj (loose) lâche, desserré(e);
(slow) stagnant(e); (careless) négligent(e), peu
sérieux(-euse) or consciencieux(-euse); **slacks**
npl pantalon m

slain [sleɪn] pp of **slay**

slam [slæm] vt (door) (faire) claquer; (throw)
jeter violemment, flanquer; (inf: criticize)
éreinter, démolir ⊳ vi claquer

slander ['slɑːndər] n calomnie f; (Law)
diffamation f

slang [slæŋ] n argot m

slant [slɑːnt] n inclinaison f; (fig) angle m,
point m de vue

slap [slæp] n claque f, gifle f; (on the back) tape
f ⊳ vt donner une claque or une gifle (or une
tape) à; **to ~ on** (paint) appliquer rapidement
⊳ adv (directly) tout droit, en plein

slash [slæʃ] vt entailler, taillader; (fig: prices)
casser

slate [sleɪt] n ardoise f ⊳ vt (fig: criticize)
éreinter, démolir

slaughter ['slɔːtər] n carnage m, massacre
m; (of animals) abattage m ⊳ vt (animal)

abattre; (people) massacrer; **slaughterhouse**
n abattoir m

Slav [slɑːv] adj slave

slave [sleɪv] n esclave m/f ⊳ vi (also: **~ away**)
trimer, travailler comme un forçat; **slavery** n
esclavage m

slay (pt **slew**, pp **slain**) [sleɪ, sluː, sleɪn] vt
(literary) tuer

sleazy ['sliːzɪ] adj miteux(-euse), minable

sled [slɛd] (US) = **sledge**

sledge [slɛdʒ] n luge f

sleek [sliːk] adj (hair, fur) brillant(e), luisant(e);
(car, boat) aux lignes pures or élégantes

sleep [sliːp] n sommeil m ⊳ vi (pt, pp **slept**)
dormir; **to go to ~** s'endormir; **sleep in** vi
(oversleep) se réveiller trop tard; (on purpose)
faire la grasse matinée; **sleep together**
vi (have sex) coucher ensemble; **sleeper** n
(person) dormeur(-euse); (BRIT Rail: on track)
traverse f; (: train) train-couchettes m; (:
berth) couchette f; **sleeping bag** n sac m
de couchage; **sleeping car** n wagon-lits m,
voiture-lits f; **sleeping pill** n somnifère m;
sleepover n nuit f chez un copain or une
copine; **we're having a sleepover at Jo's**
nous allons passer la nuit chez Jo; **sleepwalk**
vi marcher en dormant; **sleepy** adj (fig)
endormi(e)

sleet [sliːt] n neige fondue

sleeve [sliːv] n manche f; (of record) pochette f;
sleeveless adj (garment) sans manches

sleigh [sleɪ] n traîneau m

slender ['slɛndər] adj svelte, mince; (fig) faible,
ténu(e)

slept [slɛpt] pt, pp of **sleep**

slew [sluː] pt of **slay**

slice [slaɪs] n tranche f; (round) rondelle f;
(utensil) spatule f; (also: **fish ~**) pelle f à poisson
⊳ vt couper en tranches (or en rondelles)

slick [slɪk] adj (skilful) bien ficelé(e);
(salesperson) qui a du bagout ⊳ n (also: **oil ~**)
nappe f de pétrole, marée noire

slide [slaɪd] n (in playground) toboggan m;
(Phot) diapositive f; (BRIT: also: **hair ~**) barrette
f; (in prices) chute f, baisse f ⊳ vb (pt, pp **slid**)
⊳ vt (faire) glisser ⊳ vi glisser; **sliding** adj
(door) coulissant(e)

slight [slaɪt] adj (slim) mince, menu(e); (frail)
frêle; (trivial) faible, insignifiant(e); (small)
petit(e), léger(-ère) before n ⊳ n offense f,
affront m ⊳ vt (offend) blesser, offenser; **not in
the ~est** pas le moins du monde, pas du tout;
slightly adv légèrement, un peu

slim [slɪm] adj mince ⊳ vi maigrir; (diet)
suivre un régime amaigrissant; **slimming**
n amaigrissement m ⊳ adj (diet, pills)
amaigrissant(e), pour maigrir; (food) qui ne
fait pas grossir

slimy ['slaɪmɪ] adj visqueux(-euse), gluant(e)

sling [slɪŋ] n (Med) écharpe f; (for baby) porte-bébé m; (weapon) fronde f, lance-pierre m ▷ vt (pt, pp **slung**) lancer, jeter

slip [slɪp] n faux pas; (mistake) erreur f, bévue f; (underskirt) combinaison f; (of paper) petite feuille, fiche f ▷ vt (slide) glisser ▷ vi (slide) glisser; (move smoothly): **to ~ into/out of** se glisser or se faufiler dans/hors de; (decline) baisser; **to ~ sth on/off** enfiler/enlever qch; **to give sb the ~** fausser compagnie à qn; **a ~ of the tongue** un lapsus; **slip up** vi faire une erreur, gaffer

slipped disc [slɪpt-] n déplacement m de vertèbre

slipper ['slɪpəʳ] n pantoufle f

slippery ['slɪpərɪ] adj glissant(e)

slip road n (BRIT: to motorway) bretelle f d'accès

slit [slɪt] n fente f; (cut) incision f ▷ vt (pt, pp ~) fendre; couper, inciser

slog [slɔg] n (BRIT: effort) gros effort; (: work) tâche fastidieuse ▷ vi travailler très dur

slogan ['sləugən] n slogan m

slope [sləup] n pente f, côte f; (side of mountain) versant m; (slant) inclinaison f ▷ vi: **to ~ down** être or descendre en pente; **to ~ up** monter; **sloping** adj en pente, incliné(e); (handwriting) penché(e)

sloppy ['slɔpɪ] adj (work) peu soigné(e), bâclé(e); (appearance) négligé(e), débraillé(e)

slot [slɔt] n fente f ▷ vt: **to ~ sth into** encastrer or insérer qch dans; **slot machine** n (BRIT: vending machine) distributeur m (automatique), machine f à sous; (for gambling) appareil m or machine à sous

Slovakia [sləu'vækɪə] n Slovaquie f

Slovene [sləu'viːn] adj slovène ▷ n Slovène m/f; (Ling) slovène m

Slovenia [sləu'viːnɪə] n Slovénie f; **Slovenian** adj, n = **Slovene**

slow [sləu] adj lent(e); (watch): **to be ~** retarder ▷ adv lentement ▷ vt, vi ralentir; **"~"** (road sign) "ralentir"; **slow down** vi ralentir; **slowly** adv lentement; **slow motion** n: **in slow motion** au ralenti

slug [slʌg] n limace f; (bullet) balle f; **sluggish** adj (person) mou (molle), lent(e); (stream, engine, trading) lent(e)

slum [slʌm] n (house) taudis m; **slums** npl (area) quartiers mpl pauvres

slump [slʌmp] n baisse soudaine, effondrement m; (Econ) crise f ▷ vi s'effondrer, s'affaisser

slung [slʌŋ] pt, pp of **sling**

slur [sləːʳ] n (smear): ~ **(on)** atteinte f (à); insinuation f (contre) ▷ vt mal articuler

slush [slʌʃ] n neige fondue

sly [slaɪ] adj (person) rusé(e); (smile, expression, remark) sournois(e)

smack [smæk] n (slap) tape f; (on face) gifle f ▷ vt donner une tape à; (on face) gifler; (on bottom) donner la fessée à ▷ vi: **to ~ of** avoir des relents de, sentir

small [smɔːl] adj petit(e); **small ads** npl (BRIT) petites annonces; **small change** n petite or menue monnaie

smart [smɑːt] adj élégant(e), chic inv; (clever) intelligent(e); (quick) vif (vive), prompt(e) ▷ vi faire mal, brûler; **smartcard** n carte f à puce

smash [smæʃ] n (also: **~-up**) collision f, accident m; (Mus) succès foudroyant ▷ vt casser, briser, fracasser; (opponent) écraser; (Sport: record) pulvériser ▷ vi se briser, se fracasser; s'écraser; **smashing** adj (inf) formidable

smear [smɪəʳ] n (stain) tache f; (mark) trace f; (Med) frottis m ▷ vt enduire; (make dirty) salir; **smear test** n (BRIT Med) frottis m

smell [smɛl] n odeur f; (sense) odorat m ▷ vb (pt, pp **smelt** or **~ed**) ▷ vt sentir ▷ vi (pej) sentir mauvais; **smelly** adj qui sent mauvais, malodorant(e)

smelt [smɛlt] pt, pp of **smell**

smile [smaɪl] n sourire m ▷ vi sourire

smirk [sməːk] n petit sourire suffisant or affecté

smog [smɔg] n brouillard mêlé de fumée

smoke [sməuk] n fumée f ▷ vt, vi fumer; **do you mind if I ~?** ça ne vous dérange pas que je fume?; **smoke alarm** n détecteur m de fumée; **smoked** adj (bacon, glass) fumé(e); **smoker** n (person) fumeur(-euse); (Rail) wagon m fumeurs; **smoking** n: **"no smoking"** (sign) "défense de fumer"; **smoky** adj enfumé(e); (taste) fumé(e)

smooth [smuːð] adj lisse; (sauce) onctueux(-euse); (flavour, whisky) moelleux(-euse); (movement) régulier(-ière), sans à-coups or heurts; (flight) sans secousses; (pej: person) doucereux(-euse), mielleux(-euse) ▷ vt (also: ~ **out**) lisser, défroisser; (creases, difficulties) faire disparaître

smother ['smʌðəʳ] vt étouffer

SMS n abbr (= short text message service) SMS m; **SMS message** n message m SMS

smudge [smʌdʒ] n tache f, bavure f ▷ vt salir, maculer

smug [smʌg] adj suffisant(e), content(e) de soi

smuggle ['smʌgl] vt passer en contrebande or en fraude; **smuggling** n contrebande f

snack [snæk] n casse-croûte m inv; **snack bar** n snack(-bar) m

snag [snæg] n inconvénient m, difficulté f

snail [sneɪl] n escargot m

snake [sneɪk] n serpent m

snap [snæp] n (sound) claquement m, bruit sec; (photograph) photo f, instantané m ▷ adj

subit(e), fait(e) sans réfléchir ▷ vt (*fingers*)
faire claquer; (*break*) casser net ▷ vi se casser
net *or* avec un bruit sec; (*speak sharply*) parler
d'un ton brusque; **to ~ open/shut** s'ouvrir/se
refermer brusquement; **snap at** vt fus (*subj:
dog*) essayer de mordre; **snap up** vt sauter sur,
saisir; **snapshot** n photo f, instantané m
snarl [snɑːl] vi gronder
snatch [snætʃ] n (*small amount*) ▷ vt saisir
(*d'un geste vif*); (*steal*) voler; **to ~ some sleep**
arriver à dormir un peu
sneak [sniːk] (*us: pt* **snuck**) vi: **to ~ in/out**
entrer/sortir furtivement *or* à la dérobée ▷ n
(*inf: pej: informer*) faux jeton; **to ~ up on sb**
s'approcher de qn sans faire de bruit; **sneakers**
npl tennis mpl, baskets f pl
sneer [snɪər] vi ricaner; **to ~ at sb/sth** se
moquer de qn/qch avec mépris
sneeze [sniːz] vi éternuer
sniff [snɪf] vi renifler ▷ vt renifler, flairer; (*glue,
drug*) sniffer, respirer
snigger ['snɪɡər] vi ricaner
snip [snɪp] n (*cut*) entaille f; (*BRIT: inf: bargain*)
(bonne) occasion *or* affaire ▷ vt couper
sniper ['snaɪpər] n (*marksman*) tireur
embusqué
snob [snɔb] n snob m/f
snooker ['snuːkər] n sorte de jeu de billard
snoop [snuːp] vi: **to ~ about** fureter
snooze [snuːz] n petit somme ▷ vi faire un
petit somme
snore [snɔːr] vi ronfler ▷ n ronflement m
snorkel ['snɔːkl] n (*of swimmer*) tuba m
snort [snɔːt] n grognement m ▷ vi grogner;
(*horse*) renâcler
snow [snəu] n neige f ▷ vi neiger; **snowball**
n boule f de neige; **snowdrift** n congère f;
snowman (*irreg*) n bonhomme m de neige;
snowplough (us **snowplow**) n chasse-
neige m inv; **snowstorm** n tempête f de neige
snub [snʌb] vt repousser, snober ▷ n
rebuffade f
snug [snʌɡ] adj douillet(te), confortable;
(*person*) bien au chaud

 KEYWORD

so [səu] adv **1** (*thus, likewise*) ainsi, de cette
façon; **if so** si oui; **so do** *or* **have I** moi aussi;
it's 5 o'clock - so it is! il est 5 heures - en effet!
or c'est vrai!; **I hope/think so** je l'espère/le
crois; **so far** jusqu'ici, jusqu'à maintenant; (*in
past*) jusque-là

2 (*in comparisons etc: to such a degree*) si,
tellement; **so big (that)** si *or* tellement grand
(que); **she's not so clever as her brother** elle
n'est pas aussi intelligente que son frère
3: **so much** adj, adv tant (de); **I've got so
much work** j'ai tant de travail; **I love you so
much** je vous aime tant; **so many** tant (de)
4 (*phrases*): **10 or so** à peu près *or* environ 10;
so long! (*inf: goodbye*) au revoir!, à un de ces
jours!; **so (what)?** (*inf*) (bon) et alors?, et après?
▷ conj **1** (*expressing purpose*): **so as to do** pour
faire, afin de faire; **so (that)** pour que *or* afin
que + sub
2 (*expressing result*) donc, par conséquent; **so
that** si bien que, de (telle) sorte que; **so that's
the reason!** c'est donc (pour) çal; **so you
see, I could have gone** alors tu vois, j'aurais
pu y aller

soak [səuk] vt faire *or* laisser tremper; (*drench*)
tremper ▷ vi tremper; **soak up** vt absorber;
soaking adj (*also:* **soaking wet**) trempé(e)
so-and-so ['səuənsəu] n (*somebody*) un(e)
tel(le)
soap [səup] n savon m; **soap opera** n
feuilleton télévisé (*quotidienneté réaliste
ou embellie*); **soap powder** n lessive f,
détergent m
soar [sɔːr] vi monter (en flèche), s'élancer;
(*building*) s'élancer
sob [sɔb] n sanglot m ▷ vi sangloter
sober ['səubər] adj qui n'est pas (*or* plus) ivre;
(*serious*) sérieux(-euse), sensé(e); (*colour, style*)
sobre, discret(-ète); **sober up** vi se dégriser
so-called ['səu'kɔːld] adj soi-disant inv
soccer ['sɔkər] n football m
sociable ['səuʃəbl] adj sociable
social ['səuʃl] adj social(e); (*sociable*) sociable
▷ n (petite) fête; **socialism** n socialisme m;
socialist adj, n socialiste (m/f); **socialize** vi:
to socialize with (*meet often*) fréquenter;
(*get to know*) lier connaissance *or* parler
avec; **social life** n vie sociale; **socially** adv
socialement, en société; **social security** n
aide sociale; **social services** npl services
sociaux; **social work** n assistance sociale;
social worker n assistant(e) sociale(e)
society [sə'saɪətɪ] n société f; (*club*) société,
association f; (*also:* **high ~**) (haute) société,
grand monde
sociology [səusɪ'ɒlədʒɪ] n sociologie f
sock [sɔk] n chaussette f
socket ['sɔkɪt] n cavité f; (*Elec: also:* **wall ~**)
prise f de courant
soda ['səudə] n (*Chem*) soude f; (*also:* **~ water**)
eau f de Seltz; (*us: also:* **~ pop**) soda m
sodium ['səudɪəm] n sodium m
sofa ['səufə] n sofa m, canapé m; **sofa bed** n
canapé-lit m
soft [sɔft] adj (*not rough*) doux (douce); (*not
hard*) doux, mou (molle); (*not loud*) doux,
léger(-ère); (*kind*) doux, gentil(le); **soft drink**
n boisson non alcoolisée; **soft drugs** npl
drogues douces; **soften** ['sɔfn] vt (r)amollir;
(*fig*) adoucir ▷ vi se ramollir; (*fig*) s'adoucir;

softly adv doucement; (touch) légèrement; (kiss) tendrement; **software** n (Comput) logiciel m, software m

soggy ['sɔgɪ] adj (clothes) trempé(e); (ground) détrempé(e)

soil [sɔɪl] n (earth) sol m, terre f ▷ vt salir; (fig) souiller

solar ['səulə'] adj solaire; **solar power** n énergie f solaire; **solar system** n système m solaire

sold [səuld] pt, pp of **sell**

soldier ['səuldʒə'] n soldat m, militaire m

sold out adj (Comm) épuisé(e)

sole [səul] n (of foot) plante f; (of shoe) semelle f; (fish: pl inv) sole f ▷ adj seul(e), unique; **solely** adv seulement, uniquement

solemn ['sɔləm] adj solennel(le); (person) sérieux(-euse), grave

solicitor [sə'lɪsɪtə'] n (BRIT: for wills etc) ≈ notaire m; (: in court) ≈ avocat m

solid ['sɔlɪd] adj (not liquid) solide; (not hollow: mass) compact(e); (: metal, rock, wood) massif(-ive) ▷ n solide m

solitary ['sɔlɪtərɪ] adj solitaire

solitude ['sɔlɪtjuːd] n solitude f

solo ['səuləu] n solo m ▷ adv (fly) en solitaire; **soloist** n soliste m/f

soluble ['sɔljubl] adj soluble

solution [sə'luːʃən] n solution f

solve [sɔlv] vt résoudre

solvent ['sɔlvənt] adj (Comm) solvable ▷ n (Chem) (dis)solvant m

sombre (US **somber**) ['sɔmbə'] adj sombre, morne

KEYWORD

some [sʌm] adj 1 (a certain amount or number of): **some tea/water/ice cream** du thé/de l'eau/de la glace; **some children/apples** des enfants/pommes; **I've got some money but not much** j'ai de l'argent mais pas beaucoup

2 (certain: in contrasts): **some people say that ...** il y a des gens qui disent que ...; **some films were excellent, but most were mediocre** certains films étaient excellents, mais la plupart étaient médiocres

3 (unspecified): **some woman was asking for you** il y avait une dame qui vous demandait; **he was asking for some book (or other)** il demandait un livre quelconque; **some day** un de ces jours; **some day next week** un jour la semaine prochaine

▷ pron 1 (a certain number) quelques-un(e)s, certain(e)s; **I've got some** (books etc) j'en ai (quelques-uns); **some (of them) have been sold** certains ont été vendus

2 (a certain amount) un peu; **I've got some** (money, milk) j'en ai (un peu); **would you like**

some? est-ce que vous en voulez?, en voulez-vous?; **could I have some of that cheese?** pourrais-je avoir un peu de ce fromage?; **I've read some of the book** j'ai lu une partie du livre

▷ adv: **some 10 people** quelque 10 personnes, 10 personnes environ; **somebody** ['sʌmbədɪ] pron = **someone**; **somehow** adv d'une façon ou d'une autre; (for some reason) pour une raison ou une autre; **someone** pron quelqu'un; **someplace** adv (US) = **somewhere**; **something** pron quelque chose m; **something interesting** quelque chose d'intéressant; **something to do** quelque chose à faire; **sometime** adv (in future) un de ces jours, un jour ou l'autre; (in past): **sometime last month** au cours du mois dernier; **sometimes** adv quelquefois, parfois; **somewhat** adv quelque peu, un peu; **somewhere** adv quelque part; **somewhere else** ailleurs, autre part

son [sʌn] n fils m

song [sɔŋ] n chanson f; (of bird) chant m

son-in-law ['sʌnɪnlɔ:] n gendre m, beau-fils m

soon [suːn] adv bientôt; (early) tôt; **~ afterwards** peu après; see also **as**; **sooner** adv (time) plus tôt; (preference): **I would sooner do that** j'aimerais autant or je préférerais faire ça; **sooner or later** tôt ou tard

soothe [suːð] vt calmer, apaiser

sophisticated [sə'fɪstɪkeɪtɪd] adj raffiné(e), sophistiqué(e); (machinery) hautement perfectionné(e), très complexe

sophomore ['sɔfəmɔ:'] n (US) étudiant(e) de seconde année

soprano [sə'prɑːnəu] n (singer) soprano m/f

sorbet ['sɔːbeɪ] n sorbet m

sordid ['sɔːdɪd] adj sordide

sore [sɔː'] adj (painful) douloureux(-euse), sensible ▷ n plaie f

sorrow ['sɔrəu] n peine f, chagrin m

sorry ['sɔrɪ] adj désolé(e); (condition, excuse, tale) triste, déplorable; **~!** pardon!, excusez-moi!; **~?** pardon?; **to feel ~ for sb** plaindre qn

sort [sɔːt] n genre m, espèce f, sorte f; (make: of coffee, car etc) marque f ▷ vt (also: **~ out**: select which to keep) trier; (classify) classer; (tidy) ranger; **sort out** vt (problem) résoudre, régler

SOS n SOS m

so-so ['səusəu] adv comme ci comme ça

sought [sɔːt] pt, pp of **seek**

soul [səul] n âme f

sound [saund] adj (healthy) en bonne santé, sain(e); (safe, not damaged) solide, en bon état; (reliable, not superficial) sérieux(-euse), solide; (sensible) sensé(e) ▷ adv: **~ asleep** profondément endormi(e) ▷ n (noise, volume) son m; (louder) bruit m; (Geo) détroit m, bras *m* de mer ▷ *vt* (*alarm*) sonner ▷ *vi* sonner, retentir; (*fig: seem*) sembler (être); **to ~ like** ressembler à; **sound bite** *n* phrase toute faite (*pour être citée dans les médias*); **soundtrack** *n* (*of film*) bande *f* sonore

soup [su:p] *n* soupe *f*, potage *m*

sour ['sauə^r] *adj* aigre; **it's ~ grapes** c'est du dépit

source [sɔ:s] *n* source *f*

south [sauθ] *n* sud *m* ▷ *adj* sud *inv*; (*wind*) du sud ▷ *adv* au sud, vers le sud; **South Africa** *n* Afrique *f* du Sud; **South African** *adj* sud-africain(e) ▷ *n* Sud-Africain(e); **South America** *n* Amérique *f* du Sud; **South American** *adj* sud-américain(e) ▷ *n* Sud-Américain(e); **southbound** *adj* en direction du sud; (*carriageway*) sud *inv*; **south-east** *n* sud-est *m*; **southeastern** [sauθ'i:stən] *adj* du *or* au sud-est; **southern** ['sʌðən] *adj* (du) sud; méridional(e); **South Korea** *n* Corée *f* du Sud; **South of France** *n*: **the South of France** le Sud de la France, le Midi; **South Pole** *n* Pôle *m* Sud; **southward(s)** *adv* vers le sud; **south-west** *n* sud-ouest *m*; **southwestern** [sauθ'westən] *adj* du *or* au sud-ouest

souvenir [su:və'nɪə^r] *n* souvenir *m* (*objet*)

sovereign ['sɔvrɪn] *adj, n* souverain(e)

sow¹ [səu] (*pt* **~ed**, *pp* **~n**) *vt* semer

sow² *n* [sau] truie *f*

soya ['sɔɪə] (*us* **soy** [sɔɪ]) *n*: **~ bean** graine *f* de soja; **~ sauce** sauce *f* au soja

spa [spɑ:] *n* (*town*) station thermale; (*us: also*: **health ~**) établissement *m* de cure de rajeunissement

space [speɪs] *n* (*gen*) espace *m*; (*room*) place *f*; espace; (*length of time*) laps *m* de temps ▷ *cpd* spatial(e) ▷ *vt* (*also*: **~ out**) espacer; **spacecraft** *n* engin *or* vaisseau spatial; **spaceship** *n* = **spacecraft**

spacious ['speɪʃəs] *adj* spacieux(-euse), grand(e)

spade [speɪd] *n* (*tool*) bêche *f*, pelle *f*; (*child's*) pelle; **spades** *npl* (*Cards*) pique *m*

spaghetti [spə'gɛtɪ] *n* spaghetti *mpl*

Spain [speɪn] *n* Espagne *f*

spam [spæm] *n* (*Comput*) spam *m*

span [spæn] *n* (*of bird, plane*) envergure *f*; (*of arch*) portée *f*; (*in time*) espace *m* de temps, durée *f* ▷ *vt* enjamber, franchir; (*fig*) couvrir, embrasser

Spaniard ['spænjəd] *n* Espagnol(e)

Spanish ['spænɪʃ] *adj* espagnol(e), d'Espagne ▷ *n* (*Ling*) espagnol *m*; **the Spanish** *npl* les Espagnols

spank [spæŋk] *vt* donner une fessée à

spanner ['spænə^r] *n* (*BRIT*) clé *f* (de mécanicien)

spare [spɛə^r] *adj* de réserve, de rechange; (*surplus*) de *or* en trop, de reste ▷ *n* (*part*) pièce *f* de rechange, pièce détachée ▷ *vt* (*do without*) se passer de; (*afford to give*) donner, accorder, passer; (*not hurt*) épargner; **to ~** (*surplus*) en surplus, de trop; **spare part** *n* pièce *f* de rechange, pièce détachée; **spare room** *n* chambre *f* d'ami; **spare time** *n* moments *mpl* de loisir; **spare tyre** (*us* **spare tire**) *n* (*Aut*) pneu *m* de rechange; **spare wheel** *n* (*Aut*) roue *f* de secours

spark [spɑ:k] *n* étincelle *f*; **spark(ing) plug** *n* bougie *f*

sparkle ['spɑ:kl] *n* scintillement *m*, étincellement *m*, éclat *m* ▷ *vi* étinceler, scintiller

sparkling ['spɑ:klɪŋ] *adj* (*wine*) mousseux(-euse), pétillant(e); (*water*) pétillant(e), gazeux(-euse)

sparrow ['spærəu] *n* moineau *m*

sparse [spɑ:s] *adj* clairsemé(e)

spasm ['spæzəm] *n* (*Med*) spasme *m*

spat [spæt] *pt, pp of* **spit**

spate [speɪt] *n* (*fig*): **~ of** avalanche *f* or torrent *m* de

spatula ['spætjulə] *n* spatule *f*

speak (*pt* **spoke**, *pp* **spoken**) [spi:k, spəuk, 'spəukn] *vt* (*language*) parler; (*truth*) dire ▷ *vi* parler; (*make a speech*) prendre la parole; **to ~ to sb/of** *or* **about sth** parler à qn/de qch; **I don't ~ French** je ne parle pas français; **do you ~ English?** parlez-vous anglais?; **can I ~ to ...?** est-ce que je peux parler à ...?; **speaker** *n* (*in public*) orateur *m*; (*also*: **loudspeaker**) haut-parleur *m*; (*for stereo etc*) baffle *m*, enceinte *f*; (*Pol*): **the Speaker** (*BRIT*) le président de la Chambre des communes *or* des représentants; (*us*) le président de la Chambre

spear [spɪə^r] *n* lance *f* ▷ *vt* transpercer

special ['spɛʃl] *adj* spécial(e); **special delivery** *n* (*Post*): **by special delivery** en express; **special effects** *npl* (*Cine*) effets spéciaux; **specialist** *n* spécialiste *m/f*; **speciality** [spɛʃɪ'ælɪtɪ] *n* (*BRIT*) spécialité *f*; **specialize** *vi*: **to specialize (in)** se spécialiser (dans); **specially** *adv* spécialement, particulièrement; **special needs** *npl* (*BRIT*) difficultés *fpl* d'apprentissage scolaire; **special offer** *n* (*Comm*) réclame *f*; **special school** *n* (*BRIT*) établissement *m* d'enseignement spécialisé; **specialty** (*us*) = **speciality**

species ['spi:ʃi:z] *n* (*pl inv*) espèce *f*

specific [spə'sɪfɪk] *adj* (*not vague*) précis(e), explicite; (*particular*) particulier(-ière); **specifically** *adv* explicitement, précisément; (*intend, ask, design*) expressément, spécialement

specify ['spɛsɪfaɪ] *vt* spécifier, préciser

specimen ['spɛsɪmən] *n* spécimen *m*, échantillon *m*; (*Med: of blood*) prélèvement *m*; (: *of urine*) échantillon *m*

speck [spɛk] n petite tache, petit point; (particle) grain m

spectacle ['spɛktəkl] n spectacle m; **spectacles** npl (BRIT) lunettes fpl; **spectacular** [spɛk'tækjuləʳ] adj spectaculaire

spectator [spɛk'teɪtəʳ] n spectateur(-trice)

spectrum (pl **spectra**) ['spɛktrəm, -rə] n spectre m; (fig) gamme f

speculate ['spɛkjuleɪt] vi spéculer; (try to guess): **to ~ about** s'interroger sur

sped [spɛd] pt, pp of **speed**

speech [spiːtʃ] n (faculty) parole f; (talk) discours m, allocution f; (manner of speaking) façon f de parler, langage m; (enunciation) élocution f; **speechless** adj muet(te)

speed [spiːd] n vitesse f; (promptness) rapidité f ▷ vi (pt, pp **sped**: Aut: exceed speed limit) faire un excès de vitesse; **at full** or **top ~** à toute vitesse or allure; **speed up** (pt, pp **~ed up**) vi aller plus vite, accélérer vt accélérer; **speedboat** n vedette f, hors-bord m inv; **speeding** n (Aut) excès m de vitesse; **speed limit** n limitation f de vitesse, vitesse maximale permise; **speedometer** [spɪ'dɒmɪtəʳ] n compteur m (de vitesse); **speedy** adj rapide, prompt(e)

spell [spɛl] n (also: **magic ~**) sortilège m, charme m; (period of time) (courte) période ▷ vt (pt, pp **spelt** or **~ed**) (in writing) écrire, orthographier; (aloud) épeler; (fig) signifier; **to cast a ~ on sb** jeter un sort à qn; **he can't ~** il fait des fautes d'orthographe; **spell out** vt (explain): **to ~ sth out for sb** expliquer qch clairement à qn; **spellchecker** ['spɛltʃekəʳ] n (Comput) correcteur m or vérificateur m orthographique; **spelling** n orthographe f

spelt [spɛlt] pt, pp of **spell**

spend (pt, pp **spent**) [spɛnd, spɛnt] vt (money) dépenser; (time, life) passer; (devote) consacrer; **spending** n: **government spending** les dépenses publiques

spent [spɛnt] pt, pp of **spend** ▷ adj (cartridge, bullets) vide

sperm [spəːm] n spermatozoïde m; (semen) sperme m

sphere [sfɪəʳ] n sphère f; (fig) sphère, domaine m

spice [spaɪs] n épice f ▷ vt épicer

spicy ['spaɪsɪ] adj épicé(e), relevé(e); (fig) piquant(e)

spider ['spaɪdəʳ] n araignée f

spike [spaɪk] n pointe f; (Bot) épi m

spill (pt, pp **spilt** or **~ed**) [spɪl, -t, -d] vt renverser; répandre ▷ vi se répandre; **spill over** vi déborder

spin [spɪn] n (revolution of wheel) tour m; (Aviat) (chute f en) vrille f; (trip in car) petit tour, balade f; (on ball) effet m ▷ vb (pt, pp **spun**) ▷ vt (wool etc) filer; (wheel) faire tourner ▷ vi (turn) tourner, tournoyer

spinach ['spɪnɪtʃ] n épinards mpl

spinal ['spaɪnl] adj vertébral(e), spinal(e)

spinal cord n moelle épinière

spin doctor n (inf) personne employée pour présenter un parti politique sous un jour favorable

spin-dryer [spɪn'draɪəʳ] n (BRIT) essoreuse f

spine [spaɪn] n colonne vertébrale; (thorn) épine f, piquant m

spiral ['spaɪərl] n spirale f ▷ vi (fig: prices etc) monter en flèche

spire ['spaɪəʳ] n flèche f, aiguille f

spirit ['spɪrɪt] n (soul) esprit m, âme f; (ghost) esprit, revenant m; (mood) esprit, état m d'esprit; (courage) courage m, énergie f; **spirits** npl (drink) spiritueux mpl, alcool m; **in good ~s** de bonne humeur

spiritual ['spɪrɪtjuəl] adj spirituel(le); (religious) religieux(-euse)

spit [spɪt] n (for roasting) broche f; (spittle) crachat m; (saliva) salive f ▷ vi (pt, pp **spat**) cracher; (sound) crépiter; (rain) crachiner

spite [spaɪt] n rancune f, dépit m ▷ vt contrarier, vexer; **in ~ of** en dépit de, malgré; **spiteful** adj malveillant(e), rancunier(-ière)

splash [splæʃ] n (sound) plouf m; (of colour) tache f ▷ vt éclabousser ▷ vi (also: **~ about**) barboter, patauger; **splash out** vi (BRIT) faire une folie

splendid ['splɛndɪd] adj splendide, superbe, magnifique

splinter ['splɪntəʳ] n (wood) écharde f; (metal) éclat m ▷ vi (wood) se fendre; (glass) se briser

split [splɪt] n fente f, déchirure f; (fig: Pol) scission f ▷ vb (pt, pp **~**) ▷ vt fendre, déchirer; (party) diviser; (work, profits) partager, répartir ▷ vi (break) se fendre, se briser; (divide) se diviser; **split up** vi (couple) se séparer, rompre; (meeting) se disperser

spoil (pt, pp **~ed** or **~t**) [spɔɪl, -d, -t] vt (damage) abîmer; (mar) gâcher; (child) gâter

spoilt [spɔɪlt] pt, pp of **spoil** ▷ adj (child) gâté(e); (ballot paper) nul(le)

spoke [spəʊk] pt of **speak** ▷ n rayon m

spoken ['spəʊkn] pp of **speak**

spokesman ['spəʊksmən] (irreg) n porte-parole m inv

spokesperson ['spəʊkspəːsn] n porte-parole m inv

spokeswoman ['spəʊkswumən] (irreg) n porte-parole m inv

sponge [spʌndʒ] n éponge f; (Culin: also: **~ cake**) ≈ biscuit m de Savoie ▷ vt éponger ▷ vi: **to ~ off** or **on** vivre aux crochets de; **sponge bag** n (BRIT) trousse f de toilette

sponsor ['spɒnsəʳ] n (Radio, TV, Sport) sponsor m; (for application) parrain m, marraine f; (BRIT: for fund-raising event) donateur(-trice) ▷ vt sponsoriser, parrainer, faire un don à;

sponsorship n sponsoring m, parrainage m; dons mpl

spontaneous [spɒn'teɪnɪəs] adj spontané(e)

spooky ['spuːkɪ] adj (inf) qui donne la chair de poule

spoon [spuːn] n cuiller f; **spoonful** n cuillerée f

sport [spɔːt] n sport m; (person) chic type m/chic fille f ▷ vt (wear) arborer; **sport jacket** n (US) = **sports jacket**; **sports car** n voiture f de sport; **sports centre** (BRIT) n centre sportif; **sports jacket** n (BRIT) veste f de sport; **sportsman** (irreg) n sportif m; **sports utility vehicle** n véhicule m de loisirs (de type SUV); **sportswear** n vêtements mpl de sport; **sportswoman** (irreg) n sportive f; **sporty** adj sportif(-ive)

spot [spɒt] n tache f; (dot: on pattern) pois m; (pimple) bouton m; (place) endroit m, coin m; (small amount): **a ~ of** un peu de ▷ vt (notice) apercevoir, repérer; **on the ~** sur place, sur les lieux; (immediately) sur le champ; **spotless** adj immaculé(e); **spotlight** n projecteur m; (Aut) phare m auxiliaire

spouse [spauz] n époux (épouse)

sprain [spreɪn] n entorse f, foulure f ▷ vt: **to ~ one's ankle** se fouler or se tordre la cheville

sprang [spræŋ] pt of **spring**

sprawl [sprɔːl] vi s'étaler

spray [spreɪ] n jet m (en fines gouttelettes); (from sea) embruns mpl; (aerosol) vaporisateur m, bombe f; (for garden) pulvérisateur m; (of flowers) petit bouquet ▷ vt vaporiser, pulvériser; (crops) traiter

spread [spred] n (distribution) répartition f; (Culin) pâte f à tartiner; (inf: meal) festin m ▷ vb (pt, pp ~) ▷ vt (paste, contents) étendre, étaler; (rumour, disease) répandre, propager; (wealth) répartir ▷ vi s'étendre; se répandre; se propager; (stain) s'étaler; **spread out** vi (people) se disperser; **spreadsheet** n (Comput) tableur m

spree [spriː] n: **to go on a ~** faire la fête

spring [sprɪŋ] n (season) printemps m; (leap) bond m, saut m; (coiled metal) ressort m; (of water) source f ▷ vb (pt **sprang**, pp **sprung**) ▷ vi bondir, sauter; **spring up** vi (problem) se présenter, surgir; (plant, buildings) surgir de terre; **spring onion** n (BRIT) ciboule f, cive f

sprinkle ['sprɪŋkl] vt: **to ~ water** etc **on, ~ with water** etc asperger d'eau etc; **to ~ sugar** etc **on, ~ with sugar** etc saupoudrer de sucre etc

sprint [sprɪnt] n sprint m ▷ vi courir à toute vitesse; (Sport) sprinter

sprung [sprʌŋ] pp of **spring**

spun [spʌn] pt, pp of **spin**

spur [spəːʳ] n éperon m; (fig) aiguillon m ▷ vt (also: **~ on**) éperonner; aiguillonner; **on the ~ of the moment** sous l'impulsion du moment

spurt [spəːt] n jet m; (of blood) jaillissement m; (of energy) regain m, sursaut m ▷ vi jaillir, gicler

spy [spaɪ] n espion(ne) ▷ vi: **to ~ on** espionner, épier ▷ vt (see) apercevoir

sq. abbr = **square**

squabble ['skwɒbl] vi se chamailler

squad [skwɒd] n (Mil, Police) escouade f, groupe m; (Football) contingent m

squadron ['skwɒdrn] n (Mil) escadron m; (Aviat, Naut) escadrille f

squander ['skwɒndəʳ] vt gaspiller, dilapider

square [skwɛəʳ] n carré m; (in town) place f ▷ adj carré(e) ▷ vt (arrange) régler; arranger; (Math) élever au carré; (reconcile) concilier; **all ~** quitte; à égalité; **a ~ meal** un repas convenable; **2 metres ~** (de) 2 mètres sur 2; **1 ~ metre** 1 mètre carré; **square root** n racine carrée

squash [skwɒʃ] n (BRIT: drink): **lemon/orange ~** citronnade f/orangeade f; (Sport) squash m; (US: vegetable) courge f ▷ vt écraser

squat [skwɒt] adj petit(e) et épais(se), ramassé(e) ▷ vi (also: **~ down**) s'accroupir; **squatter** n squatter m

squeak [skwiːk] vi (hinge, wheel) grincer; (mouse) pousser un petit cri

squeal [skwiːl] vi pousser un or des cri(s) aigu(s) or perçant(s); (brakes) grincer

squeeze [skwiːz] n pression f ▷ vt presser; (hand, arm) serrer

squid [skwɪd] n calmar m

squint [skwɪnt] vi loucher

squirm [skwəːm] vi se tortiller

squirrel ['skwɪrəl] n écureuil m

squirt [skwəːt] vi jaillir, gicler ▷ vt faire gicler

Sr abbr = **senior**

Sri Lanka [srɪ'læŋkə] n Sri Lanka m

St abbr = **saint**; **street**

stab [stæb] n (with knife etc) coup m (de couteau etc); (of pain) lancée f; (inf: try): **to have a ~ at (doing) sth** s'essayer à (faire) qch ▷ vt poignarder

stability [stə'bɪlɪtɪ] n stabilité f

stable ['steɪbl] n écurie f ▷ adj stable

stack [stæk] n tas m, pile f ▷ vt empiler, entasser

stadium ['steɪdɪəm] n stade m

staff [stɑːf] n (workforce) personnel m; (BRIT Scol: also: **teaching ~**) professeurs mpl, enseignants mpl, personnel enseignant ▷ vt pourvoir en personnel

stag [stæg] n cerf m

stage [steɪdʒ] n scène f; (platform) estrade f; (point) étape f, stade m; (profession): **the ~** le théâtre ▷ vt (play) monter, mettre en scène; (demonstration) organiser; **in ~s** par étapes, par degrés

Be careful not to translate *stage* by the French word *stage*.

stagger ['stægə'] vi chanceler, tituber ▷ vt (person: amaze) stupéfier; (hours, holidays) étaler, échelonner; **staggering** adj (amazing) stupéfiant(e), renversant(e)

stagnant ['stægnənt] adj stagnant(e)

stag night, stag party n enterrement m de vie de garçon

stain [steɪn] n tache f; (colouring) colorant m ▷ vt tacher; (wood) teindre; **stained glass** n (decorative) verre coloré; (in church) vitraux mpl; **stainless steel** n inox m, acier m inoxydable

staircase ['stɛəkeɪs] n = **stairway**

stairs [stɛəz] npl escalier m

stairway ['stɛəweɪ] n escalier m

stake [steɪk] n pieu m, poteau m; (Comm: interest) intérêts mpl; (Betting) enjeu m ▷ vt risquer, jouer; (also: ~ **out**: area) marquer, délimiter; **to be at ~** être en jeu

stale [steɪl] adj (bread) rassis(e); (food) pas frais (fraîche); (beer) éventé(e); (smell) de renfermé; (air) confiné(e)

stalk [stɔ:k] n tige f ▷ vt traquer

stall [stɔ:l] n (BRIT: in street, market etc) éventaire m, étal m; (in stable) stalle f ▷ vt (Aut) caler; (fig: delay) retarder ▷ vi (Aut) caler; (fig) essayer de gagner du temps; **stalls** npl (BRIT: in cinema, theatre) orchestre m

stamina ['stæmɪnə] n vigueur f, endurance f

stammer ['stæmə'] n bégaiement m ▷ vi bégayer

stamp [stæmp] n timbre m; (also: **rubber ~**) tampon m; (mark, also fig) empreinte f; (on document) cachet m ▷ vi (also: ~ **one's foot**) taper du pied ▷ vt (letter) timbrer; (with rubber stamp) tamponner; **stamp out** vt (fire) piétiner; (crime) éradiquer; (opposition) éliminer; **stamped addressed envelope** n (BRIT) enveloppe affranchie pour la réponse

stampede [stæm'pi:d] n ruée f; (of cattle) débandade f

stance [stæns] n position f

stand [stænd] n (position) position f; (for taxis) station f (de taxis); (Comm) étalage m, stand m; (Sport: also: ~**s**) tribune f; (also: **music ~**) pupitre m ▷ vb (pt, pp **stood**) ▷ vi être or se tenir (debout); (rise) se lever, se mettre debout; (be placed) se trouver; (remain: offer etc) rester valable ▷ vt (place) mettre, poser; (tolerate, withstand) supporter; (treat, invite) offrir, payer; **to make a ~** prendre position; **to ~ for parliament** (BRIT) se présenter aux élections (comme candidat à la députation); **I can't ~ him** je ne peux pas le voir; **stand back** vi (move back) reculer, s'écarter; **stand by** vi (be ready) se tenir prêt(e) ▷ vt fus (opinion) s'en tenir à; (person) ne pas abandonner, soutenir; **stand down** vi (withdraw) se retirer; **stand for** vt fus (signify) représenter, signifier; (tolerate) supporter, tolérer; **stand in for** vt

fus remplacer; **stand out** vi (be prominent) ressortir; **stand up** vi (rise) se lever, se mettre debout; **stand up for** vt fus défendre; **stand up to** vt fus tenir tête à, résister à

standard ['stændəd] n (norm) norme f, étalon m; (level) niveau m (voulu); (criterion) critère m; (flag) étendard m ▷ adj (size etc) ordinaire, normal(e); (model, feature) standard inv; (practice) courant(e); (text) de base; **standards** npl (morals) morale f, principes mpl; **standard of living** n niveau m de vie

stand-by ticket n (Aviat) billet m stand-by

standing ['stændɪŋ] adj debout inv; (permanent) permanent(e) ▷ n réputation f, rang m, standing m; **of many years' ~** qui dure or existe depuis longtemps; **standing order** n (BRIT: at bank) virement m automatique, prélèvement m bancaire

stand: **standpoint** n point m de vue; **standstill** n: **at a standstill** à l'arrêt; (fig) au point mort; **to come to a standstill** s'immobiliser, s'arrêter

stank [stæŋk] pt of **stink**

staple ['steɪpl] n (for papers) agrafe f ▷ adj (food, crop, industry etc) de base principal(e) ▷ vt agrafer

star [stɑ:'] n étoile f; (celebrity) vedette f ▷ vt (Cine) avoir pour vedette; **stars** npl: **the ~s** (Astrology) l'horoscope m

starboard ['stɑ:bəd] n tribord m

starch [stɑ:tʃ] n amidon m; (in food) fécule f

stardom ['stɑ:dəm] n célébrité f

stare [stɛə'] n regard m fixe ▷ vi: **to ~ at** regarder fixement

stark [stɑ:k] adj (bleak) désolé(e), morne ▷ adv: **~ naked** complètement nu(e)

start [stɑ:t] n commencement m, début m; (of race) départ m; (sudden movement) sursaut m; (advantage) avance f, avantage m ▷ vt commencer; (cause: fight) déclencher; (rumour) donner naissance à; (fashion) lancer; (found: business, newspaper) lancer, créer; (engine) mettre en marche ▷ vi (begin) commencer; (begin journey) partir, se mettre en route; (jump) sursauter; **when does the film ~?** à quelle heure est-ce que le film commence?; **to ~ doing** or **to do sth** se mettre à faire qch; **start off** vi commencer; (leave) partir; **start out** vi (begin) commencer; (set out) partir; **start up** vi commencer; (car) démarrer ▷ vt (fight) déclencher; (business) créer; (car) mettre en marche; **starter** n (Aut) démarreur m; (Sport: official) starter m; (BRIT Culin) entrée f; **starting point** n point m de départ

startle ['stɑ:tl] vt faire sursauter; donner un choc à; **startling** adj surprenant(e), saisissant(e)

starvation [stɑ:'veɪʃən] n faim f, famine f

starve [stɑ:v] vi mourir de faim ▷ vt laisser

mourir de faim

state [steɪt] n état m; (Pol) État ▷ vt (declare) déclarer, affirmer; (specify) indiquer, spécifier; **States** npl: **the S~s** les États-Unis; **to be in a ~** être dans tous ses états; **stately home** n manoir m or château m (ouvert au public); **statement** n déclaration f; (Law) déposition f; **state school** n école publique; **statesman** (irreg) n homme m d'État

static ['stætɪk] n (Radio) parasites mpl; (also: **~ electricity**) électricité f statique ▷ adj statique

station ['steɪʃən] n gare f; (also: **police ~**) poste m or commissariat m (de police) ▷ vt placer, poster

stationary ['steɪʃnərɪ] adj à l'arrêt, immobile

stationer's (shop) n (BRIT) papeterie f

stationery ['steɪʃnərɪ] n papier m à lettres, petit matériel de bureau

station wagon n (US) break m

statistic [stə'tɪstɪk] n statistique f; **statistics** n (science) statistique f

statue ['stætjuː] n statue f

stature ['stætʃəʳ] n stature f; (fig) envergure f

status ['steɪtəs] n position f, situation f; (prestige) prestige m; (Admin, official position) statut m; **status quo** [-'kwəʊ] n: **the status quo** le statu quo

statutory ['stætjʊtrɪ] adj statutaire, prévu(e) par un article de loi

staunch [stɔːntʃ] adj sûr(e), loyal(e)

stay [steɪ] n (period of time) séjour m ▷ vi rester; (reside) loger; (spend some time) séjourner; **to ~ put** ne pas bouger; **to ~ the night** passer la nuit; **stay away** vi (from person, building) ne pas s'approcher; (from event) ne pas venir; **stay behind** vi rester en arrière; **stay in** vi (at home) rester à la maison; **stay on** vi rester; **stay out** vi (of house) ne pas rentrer; (strikers) rester en grève; **stay up** vi (at night) ne pas se coucher

steadily ['stɛdɪlɪ] adv (regularly) progressivement; (firmly) fermement; (walk) d'un pas ferme; (fixedly: look) sans détourner les yeux

steady ['stɛdɪ] adj stable, solide, ferme; (regular) constant(e), régulier(-ière); (person) calme, pondéré(e) ▷ vt assurer, stabiliser; (nerves) calmer; **a ~ boyfriend** un petit ami

steak [steɪk] n (meat) bifteck m, steak m; (fish, pork) tranche f

steal (pt **stole**, pp **stolen**) [stiːl, stəʊl, 'stəʊln] vt, vi voler; (move) se faufiler, se déplacer furtivement; **my wallet has been stolen** on m'a volé mon portefeuille

steam [stiːm] n vapeur f ▷ vt (Culin) cuire à la vapeur ▷ vi fumer; **steam up** vi (window) se couvrir de buée; **to get ~ed up about sth** (fig: inf) s'exciter à propos de qch; **steamy** adj

humide; (window) embué(e); (sexy) torride

steel [stiːl] n acier m ▷ cpd d'acier

steep [stiːp] adj raide, escarpé(e); (price) très élevé(e), excessif(-ive) ▷ vt (faire) tremper

steeple ['stiːpl] n clocher m

steer [stɪəʳ] vt diriger; (boat) gouverner; (lead: person) guider, conduire ▷ vi tenir le gouvernail; **steering** n (Aut) conduite f; **steering wheel** n volant m

stem [stɛm] n (of plant) tige f; (of glass) pied m ▷ vt contenir, endiguer; (attack, spread of disease) juguler

step [stɛp] n pas m; (stair) marche f; (action) mesure f, disposition f ▷ vi: **to ~ forward/ back** faire un pas en avant/arrière, avancer/ reculer; **steps** npl (BRIT) = **stepladder**; **to be in/out of ~ (with)** (fig) aller dans le sens (de)/être déphasé(e) (par rapport à); **step down** vi (fig) se retirer, se désister; **step in** vi (fig) intervenir; **step up** vt (production, sales) augmenter; (campaign, efforts) intensifier; **stepbrother** n demi-frère m; **stepchild** (pl **~ren**) n beau-fils m, belle-fille f; **stepdaughter** n belle-fille f; **stepfather** n beau-père m; **stepladder** n (BRIT) escabeau m; **stepmother** n belle-mère f; **stepsister** n demi-sœur f; **stepson** n beau-fils m

stereo ['stɛrɪəʊ] n (sound) stéréo f; (hi-fi) chaîne f stéréo ▷ adj (also: **~phonic**) stéréo(phonique)

stereotype ['stɪərɪətaɪp] n stéréotype m ▷ vt stéréotyper

sterile ['stɛraɪl] adj stérile; **sterilize** ['stɛrɪlaɪz] vt stériliser

sterling ['stəːlɪŋ] adj (silver) de bon aloi, fin(e) ▷ n (currency) livre f sterling inv

stern [stəːn] adj sévère ▷ n (Naut) arrière m, poupe f

steroid ['stɪərɔɪd] n stéroïde m

stew [stjuː] n ragoût m ▷ vt, vi cuire à la casserole

steward ['stjuːəd] n (Aviat, Naut, Rail) steward m; **stewardess** n hôtesse f

stick [stɪk] n bâton m; (for walking) canne f; (of chalk etc) morceau m ▷ vb (pt, pp **stuck**) ▷ vt (glue) coller; (thrust): **to ~ sth into** piquer or planter or enfoncer qch dans; (inf: put) mettre, fourrer; (: tolerate) supporter ▷ vi (adhere) tenir, coller; (remain) rester; (get jammed: door, lift) se bloquer; **stick out** vi dépasser, sortir; **stick up** vi dépasser, sortir; **stick up for** vt fus défendre; **sticker** n auto-collant m; **sticking plaster** n sparadrap m, pansement adhésif; **stick insect** n phasme m; **stick shift** n (US Aut) levier m de vitesses

sticky ['stɪkɪ] adj poisseux(-euse); (label) adhésif(-ive); (fig: situation) délicat(e)

stiff [stɪf] adj (gen) raide, rigide; (door, brush) dur(e); (difficult) difficile, ardu(e); (cold) froid(e), distant(e); (*strong, high*) fort(e), élevé(e) ▷ *adv*: **to be bored/scared/frozen** ~ s'ennuyer à mourir/être mort(e) de peur/froid

stifling ['staɪflɪŋ] *adj* (*heat*) suffocant(e)

stigma ['stɪgmə] *n* stigmate *m*

stiletto [stɪˈlɛtəu] *n* (*BRIT: also:* ~ **heel**) talon *m* aiguille

still [stɪl] *adj* immobile ▷ *adv* (*up to this time*) encore, toujours; (*even*) encore; (*nonetheless*) quand même, tout de même

stimulate ['stɪmjuleɪt] *vt* stimuler

stimulus (*pl* **stimuli**) ['stɪmjuləs, 'stɪmjulaɪ] *n* stimulant *m*; (*Biol, Psych*) stimulus *m*

sting [stɪŋ] *n* piqûre *f*; (*organ*) dard *m* ▷ *vt, vi* (*pt, pp* **stung**) piquer

stink [stɪŋk] *n* puanteur *f* ▷ *vi* (*pt* **stank**, *pp* **stunk**) puer, empester

stir [stəː'] *n* agitation *f*, sensation *f* ▷ *vt* remuer ▷ *vi* remuer, bouger; **stir up** *vt* (*trouble*) fomenter, provoquer; **stir-fry** *vt* faire sauter ▷ *n*: **vegetable stir-fry** légumes sautés à la poêle

stitch [stɪtʃ] *n* (*Sewing*) point *m*; (*Knitting*) maille *f*; (*Med*) point de suture; (*pain*) point de côté ▷ *vt* coudre, piquer; (*Med*) suturer

stock [stɔk] *n* réserve *f*, provision *f*; (*Comm*) stock *m*; (*Agr*) cheptel *m*, bétail *m*; (*Culin*) bouillon *m*; (*Finance*) valeurs *fpl*, titres *mpl*; (*descent, origin*) souche *f* ▷ *adj* (*fig: reply etc*) classique ▷ *vt* (*have in stock*) avoir, vendre; **in** ~ en stock, en magasin; **out of** ~ épuisé(e); **to take** ~ (*fig*) faire le point; ~**s and shares** valeurs (mobilières), titres; **stockbroker** ['stɔkbrəukə'] *n* agent *m* de change; **stock cube** *n* (*BRIT Culin*) bouillon-cube *m*; **stock exchange** *n* Bourse *f* (des valeurs); **stockholder** ['stɔkhəuldə'] *n* (*US*) actionnaire *m/f*

stocking ['stɔkɪŋ] *n* bas *m*

stock market *n* Bourse *f*, marché financier

stole [stəul] *pt of* **steal** ▷ *n* étole *f*

stolen ['stəuln] *pp of* **steal**

stomach ['stʌmək] *n* estomac *m*; (*abdomen*) ventre *m* ▷ *vt* supporter, digérer; **stomachache** *n* mal *m* à l'estomac *or* au ventre

stone [stəun] *n* pierre *f*; (*pebble*) caillou *m*, galet *m*; (*in fruit*) noyau *m*; (*Med*) calcul *m*; (*BRIT: weight*) = 6.348 kg; 14 pounds ▷ *cpd* de *or* en pierre ▷ *vt* (*person*) lancer des pierres sur, lapider; (*fruit*) dénoyauter

stood [stud] *pt, pp of* **stand**

stool [stuːl] *n* tabouret *m*

stoop [stuːp] *vi* (*also:* **have a** ~) être voûté(e); (*also:* ~ **down**: *bend*) se baisser, se courber

stop [stɔp] *n* arrêt *m*; (*in punctuation*) point *m* ▷ *vt* arrêter; (*break off*) interrompre; (*also:* **put a** ~ **to**) mettre fin à; (*prevent*) empêcher ▷ *vi* s'arrêter; (*rain, noise etc*) cesser, s'arrêter; **to** ~

doing sth cesser *or* arrêter de faire qch; **to** ~ **sb (from) doing sth** empêcher qn de faire qch; ~ **it!** arrête!; **stop by** *vi* s'arrêter (au passage); **stop off** *vi* faire une courte halte; **stopover** *n* halte *f*; (*Aviat*) escale *f*; **stoppage** *n* (*strike*) arrêt *m* de travail; (*obstruction*) obstruction *f*

storage ['stɔːrɪdʒ] *n* emmagasinage *m*

store [stɔː'] *n* (*stock*) provision *f*, réserve *f*; (*depot*) entrepôt *m*; (*BRIT: large shop*) grand magasin; (*US: shop*) magasin *m* ▷ *vt* emmagasiner; (*information*) enregistrer; **stores** *npl* (*food*) provisions; **who knows what is in** ~ **for us?** qui sait ce que l'avenir nous réserve *or* ce qui nous attend?; **storekeeper** *n* (*US*) commerçant(e)

storey (*US* **story**) ['stɔːrɪ] *n* étage *m*

storm [stɔːm] *n* tempête *f*; (*thunderstorm*) orage *m* ▷ *vi* (*fig*) fulminer ▷ *vt* prendre d'assaut; **stormy** *adj* orageux(-euse)

story ['stɔːrɪ] *n* histoire *f*; (*Press: article*) article *m*; (*US*) = **storey**

stout [staut] *adj* (*strong*) solide; (*fat*) gros(se), corpulent(e) ▷ *n* bière brune

stove [stəuv] *n* (*for cooking*) fourneau *m*; (: *small*) réchaud *m*; (*for heating*) poêle *m*

straight [streɪt] *adj* droit(e); (*hair*) raide; (*frank*) honnête, franc (franche); (*simple*) simple ▷ *adv* (tout) droit; (*drink*) sec, sans eau; **to put** *or* **get** ~ mettre en ordre, mettre de l'ordre dans; (*fig*) mettre au clair; ~ **away**, ~ **off** (*at once*) tout de suite; **straighten** *vt* ajuster; (*bed*) arranger; **straighten out** *vt* (*fig*) débrouiller; **straighten up** *vi* (*stand up*) se redresser; **straightforward** *adj* simple; (*frank*) honnête, direct(e)

strain [streɪn] *n* (*Tech*) tension *f*, pression *f*; (*physical*) effort *m*; (*mental*) tension (nerveuse); (*Med*) entorse *f*; (*breed: of plants*) variété *f*; (: *of animals*) race *f* ▷ *vt* (*fig: resources etc*) mettre à rude épreuve, grever; (*hurt: back etc*) se faire mal à; (*vegetables*) égoutter; **strains** *npl* (*Mus*) accords *mpl*, accents *mpl*; **strained** *adj* (*muscle*) froissé(e); (*laugh etc*) forcé(e), contraint(e); (*relations*) tendu(e); **strainer** *n* passoire *f*

strait [streɪt] *n* (*Geo*) détroit *m*; **straits** *npl*: **to be in dire** ~**s** (*fig*) avoir de sérieux ennuis

strand [strænd] *n* (*of thread*) fil *m*, brin *m*; (*of rope*) toron *m*; (*of hair*) mèche *f* ▷ *vt* (*boat*) échouer; **stranded** *adj* en rade, en plan

strange [streɪndʒ] *adj* (*not known*) inconnu(e); (*odd*) étrange, bizarre; **strangely** *adv* étrangement, bizarrement; *see also* **enough**; **stranger** *n* (*unknown*) inconnu(e); (*from somewhere else*) étranger(-ère)

strangle ['stræŋgl] *vt* étrangler

strap [stræp] *n* lanière *f*, courroie *f*, sangle *f*; (*of slip, dress*) bretelle *f*

strategic [strəˈtiːdʒɪk] *adj* stratégique

s

strategy ['strætɪdʒɪ] n stratégie f
straw [strɔ:] n paille f; **that's the last ~!** ça c'est le comble!
strawberry ['strɔːbərɪ] n fraise f
stray [streɪ] adj (animal) perdu(e), errant(e); (scattered) isolé(e) ▷ vi s'égarer; **~ bullet** balle perdue
streak [striːk] n bande f, filet m; (in hair) raie f ▷ vt zébrer, strier
stream [striːm] n (brook) ruisseau m; (current) courant m, flot m; (of people) défilé ininterrompu, flot ▷ vt (Scol) répartir par niveau ▷ vi ruisseler; **to ~ in/out** entrer/sortir à flots
street [striːt] n rue f; **streetcar** n (us) tramway m; **street light** n réverbère m; **street map**, **street plan** n plan m des rues
strength [strɛŋθ] n force f; (of girder, knot etc) solidité f; **strengthen** vt renforcer; (muscle) fortifier; (building, Econ) consolider
strenuous ['strɛnjuəs] adj vigoureux(-euse), énergique; (tiring) ardu(e), fatigant(e)
stress [strɛs] n (force, pressure) pression f; (mental strain) tension (nerveuse), stress m; (accent) accent m; (emphasis) insistance f ▷ vt insister sur, souligner; (syllable) accentuer; **stressed** adj (tense) stressé(e); (syllable) accentué(e); **stressful** adj (job) stressant(e)
stretch [strɛtʃ] n (of sand etc) étendue f ▷ vi s'étirer; (extend): **to ~ to** or **as far as** s'étendre jusqu'à ▷ vt tendre, étirer; (fig) pousser (au maximum); **at a ~** d'affilée; **stretch out** vi s'étendre ▷ vt (arm etc) allonger, tendre; (to spread) étendre
stretcher ['strɛtʃə'] n brancard m, civière f
strict [strɪkt] adj strict(e); **strictly** adv strictement
stride [straɪd] n grand pas, enjambée f ▷ vi (pt **strode**, pp **stridden**) marcher à grands pas
strike [straɪk] n grève f; (of oil etc) découverte f; (attack) raid m ▷ vb (pt, pp **struck**) ▷ vt frapper; (oil etc) trouver, découvrir; (make: agreement, deal) conclure ▷ vi faire grève; (attack) attaquer; (clock) sonner; **to go on** or **come out on ~** se mettre en grève, faire grève; **to ~ a match** frotter une allumette; **striker** n gréviste m/f; (Sport) buteur m; **striking** adj frappant(e), saisissant(e); (attractive) éblouissant(e)
string [strɪŋ] n ficelle f, fil m; (row: of beads) rang m; (Mus) corde f ▷ vt (pt, pp **strung**): **to ~ out** échelonner; **to ~ together** enchaîner; **the strings** npl (Mus) les instruments mpl à cordes; **to pull ~s** (fig) faire jouer le piston
strip [strɪp] n bande f; (Sport) tenue f ▷ vt (undress) déshabiller; (paint) décaper; (fig) dégarnir, dépouiller; (also: **~ down**: machine) démonter ▷ vi se déshabiller; **strip off** vt (paint etc) décaper ▷ vi (person) se déshabiller

stripe [straɪp] n raie f, rayure f; (Mil) galon m; **striped** adj rayé(e), à rayures
stripper ['strɪpə'] n strip-teaseuse f
strip-search ['strɪpsəːtʃ] vt: **to ~ sb** fouiller qn (en le faisant se déshabiller)
strive (pt **strove**, pp **~n**) [straɪv, strəuv, 'strɪvn] vi: **to ~ to do/for sth** s'efforcer de faire/d'obtenir qch
strode [strəud] pt of **stride**
stroke [strəuk] n coup m; (Med) attaque f; (Swimming: style) (sorte f de) nage f ▷ vt caresser; **at a ~** d'un (seul) coup
stroll [strəul] n petite promenade f ▷ vi flâner, se promener nonchalamment; **stroller** n (us: for child) poussette f
strong [strɔŋ] adj (gen) fort(e); (healthy) vigoureux(-euse); (heart, nerves) solide; **they are 50 ~** ils sont au nombre de 50; **stronghold** n forteresse f, fort m; (fig) bastion m; **strongly** adv fortement, avec force; vigoureusement; solidement
strove [strəuv] pt of **strive**
struck [strʌk] pt, pp of **strike**
structure ['strʌktʃə'] n structure f; (building) construction f
struggle ['strʌgl] n lutte f ▷ vi lutter, se battre
strung [strʌŋ] pt, pp of **string**
stub [stʌb] n (of cigarette) bout m, mégot m; (of ticket etc) talon m ▷ vt: **to ~ one's toe (on sth)** se heurter le doigt de pied (contre qch); **stub out** vt écraser
stubble ['stʌbl] n chaume m; (on chin) barbe f de plusieurs jours
stubborn ['stʌbən] adj têtu(e), obstiné(e), opiniâtre
stuck [stʌk] pt, pp of **stick** ▷ adj (jammed) bloqué(e), coincé(e)
stud [stʌd] n (on boots etc) clou m; (collar stud) bouton m de col; (earring) petite boucle d'oreille; (of horses: also: **~ farm**) écurie f, haras m; (also: **~ horse**) étalon m ▷ vt (fig): **~ded with** parsemé(e) or criblé(e) de
student ['stjuːdənt] n étudiant(e) ▷ adj (life) estudiantin(e), étudiant(e), d'étudiant; (residence, restaurant) universitaire; (loan, movement) étudiant; **student driver** n (us) (conducteur(-trice)) débutant(e); **students' union** n (BRIT: association) ≈ union f des étudiants; (: building) ≈ foyer m des étudiants
studio ['stjuːdɪəu] n studio m, atelier m; (TV etc) studio; **studio flat** (us **studio apartment**) n studio m
study ['stʌdɪ] n étude f; (room) bureau m ▷ vt étudier; (examine) examiner ▷ vi étudier, faire ses études
stuff [stʌf] n (gen) chose(s) f(pl), truc m; (belongings) affaires fpl, trucs; (substance) substance f ▷ vt rembourrer; (Culin) farcir; (inf: push) fourrer; **stuffing** n bourre f,

rembourrage m; (Culin) farce f; **stuffy** adj
(room) mal ventilé(e) or aéré(e); (ideas) vieux
jeu inv
stumble ['stʌmbl] vi trébucher; **to ~ across** or
on (fig) tomber sur
stump [stʌmp] n souche f; (of limb) moignon
m ▷ vt: **to be ~ed** sécher, ne pas savoir que
répondre
stun [stʌn] vt (blow) étourdir; (news)
abasourdir, stupéfier
stung [stʌŋ] pt, pp of **sting**
stunk [stʌŋk] pp of **stink**
stunned [stʌnd] adj assommé(e); (fig)
sidéré(e)
stunning ['stʌnɪŋ] adj (beautiful)
étourdissant(e); (news etc) stupéfiant(e)
stunt [stʌnt] n (in film) cascade f, acrobatie
f; (publicity) truc m publicitaire ▷ vt retarder,
arrêter
stupid ['stjuːpɪd] adj stupide, bête; **stupidity**
[stjuːˈpɪdɪtɪ] n stupidité f, bêtise f
sturdy ['stəːdɪ] adj (person, plant) robuste,
vigoureux(-euse); (object) solide
stutter ['stʌtə'] n bégaiement m ▷ vi bégayer
style [staɪl] n style m; (distinction) allure f,
cachet m, style; (design) modèle m; **stylish**
adj élégant(e), chic inv; **stylist** n (hair stylist)
coiffeur(-euse)
sub... [sʌb] prefix sub..., sous-; **subconscious**
adj subconscient(e)
subdued [səbˈdjuːd] adj (light) tamisé(e);
(person) qui a perdu de son entrain
subject n ['sʌbdʒɪkt] sujet m; (Scol) matière
f ▷ vt [səbˈdʒɛkt]: **to ~ to** soumettre à; **to
be ~ to** (law) être soumis(e) à; **subjective** [sə
bˈdʒɛktɪv] adj subjectif(-ive); **subject matter**
n (content) contenu m
subjunctive [səbˈdʒʌŋktɪv] n subjonctif m
submarine [sʌbməˈriːn] n sous-marin m
submission [səbˈmɪʃən] n soumission f
submit [səbˈmɪt] vt soumettre ▷ vi se
soumettre
subordinate [səˈbɔːdɪnət] adj (junior)
subalterne; (Grammar) subordonné(e) ▷ n
subordonné(e)
subscribe [səbˈskraɪb] vi cotiser; **to ~ to**
(opinion, fund) souscrire à; (newspaper)
s'abonner à; être abonné(e) à
subscription [səbˈskrɪpʃən] n (to magazine
etc) abonnement m
subsequent ['sʌbsɪkwənt] adj ultérieur(e),
suivant(e); **subsequently** adv par la suite
subside [səbˈsaɪd] vi (land) s'affaisser; (flood)
baisser; (wind, feelings) tomber
subsidiary [səbˈsɪdɪərɪ] adj subsidiaire;
accessoire; (Brit Scol: subject) complémentaire
▷ n filiale f
subsidize ['sʌbsɪdaɪz] vt subventionner
subsidy ['sʌbsɪdɪ] n subvention f

substance ['sʌbstəns] n substance f
substantial [səbˈstænʃl] adj substantiel(le);
(fig) important(e)
substitute ['sʌbstɪtjuːt] n (person)
remplaçant(e); (thing) succédané m ▷ vt: **to ~
sth/sb for** substituer qch/qn à, remplacer par
qch/qn; **substitution** n substitution f
subtitles ['sʌbtaɪtlz] npl (Cine) sous-titres mpl
subtle ['sʌtl] adj subtil(e)
subtract [səbˈtrækt] vt soustraire, retrancher
suburb ['sʌbəːb] n faubourg m; **the ~s** la
banlieue; **suburban** [səˈbəːbən] adj de
banlieue, suburbain(e)
subway ['sʌbweɪ] n (Brit: underpass) passage
souterrain; (us: railway) métro m
succeed [səkˈsiːd] vi réussir ▷ vt succéder à;
to ~ in doing réussir à faire
success [səkˈsɛs] n succès m; réussite f;
successful adj (business) prospère, qui
réussit; (attempt) couronné(e) de succès; **to
be successful (in doing)** réussir (à faire);
successfully adv avec succès
succession [səkˈsɛʃən] n succession f
successive [səkˈsɛsɪv] adj successif(-ive)
successor [səkˈsɛsə'] n successeur m
succumb [səˈkʌm] vi succomber
such [sʌtʃ] adj tel(telle); (of that kind): **~ a
book** un livre de ce genre or pareil, un tel livre;
(so much): **~ courage** un tel courage ▷ adv
si; **~ a long trip** un si long voyage; **~ a lot of**
tellement or tant de; **~ as** (like) tel (telle) que,
comme; **as ~** adv en tant que tel (telle), à
proprement parler; **such-and-such** adj tel ou
tel (telle ou telle)
suck [sʌk] vt sucer; (breast, bottle) téter
Sudan [suˈdɑːn] n Soudan m
sudden ['sʌdn] adj soudain(e), subit(e); **all
of a ~** soudain, tout à coup; **suddenly** adv
brusquement, tout à coup, soudain
sue [suː] vt poursuivre en justice, intenter un
procès à
suede [sweɪd] n daim m, cuir suédé
suffer ['sʌfə'] vt souffrir, subir; (bear) tolérer,
supporter, subir ▷ vi souffrir; **to ~ from**
(illness) souffrir de, avoir; **suffering** n
souffrance(s) f(pl)
suffice [səˈfaɪs] vi suffire
sufficient [səˈfɪʃənt] adj suffisant(e)
suffocate ['sʌfəkeɪt] vi suffoquer; étouffer
sugar ['ʃugə'] n sucre m ▷ vt sucrer
suggest [səˈdʒɛst] vt suggérer, proposer;
(indicate) sembler indiquer; **suggestion**
[səˈdʒɛstʃən] n suggestion f
suicide ['suɪsaɪd] n suicide m; **~ bombing**
attentat m suicide; see also **commit**; **suicide
bomber** n kamikaze m/f
suit [suːt] n (man's) costume m, complet m;
(woman's) tailleur m, ensemble m; (Cards)
couleur f; (lawsuit) procès m ▷ vt (subj: clothes,

hairstyle) aller à; (*be convenient for*) convenir à; (*adapt*): **to ~ sth to** adapter *or* approprier qch à; **well ~ed** (*couple*) faits l'un pour l'autre, très bien assortis; **suitable** *adj* qui convient; approprié(e), adéquat(e); **suitcase** *n* valise *f*

suite [swiːt] *n* (*of rooms, also Mus*) suite *f*; (*furniture*): **bedroom/dining room ~** (ensemble *m* de) chambre *f* à coucher/salle *f* à manger; **a three-piece ~** un salon (canapé et deux fauteuils)

sulfur ['sʌlfəʳ] (*US*) *n* = **sulphur**

sulk [sʌlk] *vi* bouder

sulphur (*US* **sulfur**) ['sʌlfəʳ] *n* soufre *m*

sultana [sʌl'tɑːnə] *n* (*fruit*) raisin (sec) de Smyrne

sum [sʌm] *n* somme *f*; (*Scol etc*) calcul *m*; **sum up** *vt* résumer ▷ *vi* résumer

summarize ['sʌməraɪz] *vt* résumer

summary ['sʌmərɪ] *n* résumé *m*

summer ['sʌməʳ] *n* été *m* ▷ *cpd* d'été, estival(e); **in (the) ~** en été, pendant l'été; **summer holidays** *npl* grandes vacances; **summertime** *n* (*season*) été *m*

summit ['sʌmɪt] *n* sommet *m*; (*also:* **~ conference**) (conférence *f* au) sommet *m*

summon ['sʌmən] *vt* appeler, convoquer; **to ~ a witness** citer *or* assigner un témoin

Sun. *abbr* (= *Sunday*) dim

sun [sʌn] *n* soleil *m*; **sunbathe** *vi* prendre un bain de soleil; **sunbed** *n* lit pliant; (*with sun lamp*) lit à ultra-violets; **sunblock** *n* écran *m* total; **sunburn** *n* coup *m* de soleil; **sunburned, sunburnt** *adj* bronzé(e), hâlé(e); (*painfully*) brûlé(e) par le soleil

Sunday ['sʌndɪ] *n* dimanche *m*

sunflower ['sʌnflauəʳ] *n* tournesol *m*

sung [sʌŋ] *pp of* **sing**

sunglasses ['sʌnglɑːsɪz] *npl* lunettes *fpl* de soleil

sunk [sʌŋk] *pp of* **sink**

sun: **sunlight** *n* (lumière *f* du) soleil *m*; **sun lounger** *n* chaise longue; **sunny** *adj* ensoleillé(e); **it is sunny** il fait (du) soleil, il y a du soleil; **sunrise** *n* lever *m* du soleil; **sun roof** *n* (*Aut*) toit ouvrant; **sunscreen** *n* crème *f* solaire; **sunset** *n* coucher *m* du soleil; **sunshade** *n* (*over table*) parasol *m*; **sunshine** *n* (lumière *f* du) soleil *m*; **sunstroke** *n* insolation *f*, coup *m* de soleil; **suntan** *n* bronzage *m*; **suntan lotion** *n* lotion *f* or lait *m* solaire; **suntan oil** *n* huile *f* solaire

super ['suːpəʳ] *adj* (*inf*) formidable

superb [suː'pəːb] *adj* superbe, magnifique

superficial [suːpə'fɪʃəl] *adj* superficiel(le)

superintendent [suːpərɪn'tɛndənt] *n* directeur(-trice); (*Police*) ≈ commissaire *m*

superior [suː'pɪərɪəʳ] *adj* supérieur(e); (*smug*) condescendant(e), méprisant(e) ▷ *n* supérieur(e)

superlative [suː'pəːlətɪv] *n* (*Ling*) superlatif *m*

supermarket ['suːpəmɑːkɪt] *n* supermarché *m*

supernatural [suːpə'nætʃərəl] *adj* surnaturel(le) ▷ *n*: **the ~** le surnaturel

superpower ['suːpəpauəʳ] *n* (*Pol*) superpuissance *f*

superstition [suːpə'stɪʃən] *n* superstition *f*

superstitious [suːpə'stɪʃəs] *adj* superstitieux(-euse)

superstore ['suːpəstɔːʳ] *n* (*BRIT*) hypermarché *m*, grande surface

supervise ['suːpəvaɪz] *vt* (*children etc*) surveiller; (*organization, work*) diriger; **supervision** [suːpə'vɪʒən] *n* surveillance *f*; (*monitoring*) contrôle *m*; (*management*) direction *f*; **supervisor** *n* surveillant(e); (*in shop*) chef *m* de rayon

supper ['sʌpəʳ] *n* dîner *m*; (*late*) souper *m*

supple ['sʌpl] *adj* souple

supplement *n* ['sʌplɪmənt] supplément *m* ▷ *vt* [sʌplɪ'mɛnt] ajouter à, compléter

supplier [sə'plaɪəʳ] *n* fournisseur *m*

supply [sə'plaɪ] *vt* (*provide*) fournir; (*equip*): **to ~ (with)** approvisionner *or* ravitailler (en); fournir (en) ▷ *n* provision *f*, réserve *f*; (*supplying*) approvisionnement *m*; **supplies** *npl* (*food*) vivres *mpl*; (*Mil*) subsistances *fpl*

support [sə'pɔːt] *n* (*moral, financial etc*) soutien *m*, appui *m*; (*Tech*) support *m*, soutien ▷ *vt* soutenir, supporter; (*financially*) subvenir aux besoins de; (*uphold*) être pour, être partisan de, appuyer; (*Sport: team*) être pour; **supporter** *n* (*Pol etc*) partisan(e); (*Sport*) supporter *m*

suppose [sə'pəuz] *vt, vi* supposer; imaginer; **to be ~d to do/be** être censé(e) faire/être; **supposedly** [sə'pəuzɪdlɪ] *adv* soi-disant; **supposing** *conj* si, à supposer que + *sub*

suppress [sə'prɛs] *vt* (*revolt, feeling*) réprimer; (*information*) faire disparaître; (*scandal, yawn*) étouffer

supreme [suː'priːm] *adj* suprême

surcharge ['səːtʃɑːdʒ] *n* surcharge *f*

sure [ʃuəʳ] *adj* (*gen*) sûr(e); (*definite, convinced*) sûr, certain(e); **~!** (*of course*) bien sûr!; **~ enough** effectivement; **to make ~ of sth/ that** s'assurer de qch/que, vérifier qch/que; **surely** *adv* sûrement; certainement

surf [səːf] *n* (*waves*) ressac *m* ▷ *vt*: **to ~ the Net** surfer sur Internet, surfer sur le net

surface ['səːfɪs] *n* surface *f* ▷ *vt* (*road*) poser un revêtement sur ▷ *vi* remonter à la surface; (*fig*) faire surface; **by ~ mail** par voie de terre; (*by sea*) par voie maritime

surfboard ['səːfbɔːd] *n* planche *f* de surf

surfer ['səːfəʳ] *n* (*in sea*) surfeur(-euse); **web** or **net ~** internaute *m/f*

surfing ['səːfɪŋ] *n* surf *m*

surge [səːdʒ] *n* (*of emotion*) vague *f* ▷ *vi* déferler

surgeon ['sə:dʒən] n chirurgien m

surgery ['sə:dʒərɪ] n chirurgie f; (BRIT: room) cabinet m (de consultation); (also: **~ hours**) heures fpl de consultation

surname ['sə:neɪm] n nom m de famille

surpass [sə:'pɑ:s] vt surpasser, dépasser

surplus ['sə:pləs] n surplus m, excédent m ▷ adj en surplus, de trop; (Comm) excédentaire

surprise [sə'praɪz] n (gen) surprise f; (astonishment) étonnement m ▷ vt surprendre, étonner; **surprised** adj (look, smile) surpris(e), étonné(e); **to be surprised** être surpris(e); **surprising** adj surprenant(e), étonnant(e); **surprisingly** adv (easy, helpful) étonnamment, étrangement; **(somewhat) surprisingly, he agreed** curieusement, il a accepté

surrender [sə'rɛndə'] n reddition f, capitulation f ▷ vi se rendre, capituler

surround [sə'raund] vt entourer; (Mil etc) encercler; **surrounding** adj environnant(e); **surroundings** npl environs mpl, alentours mpl

surveillance [sə:'veɪləns] n surveillance f

survey n ['sə:veɪ] enquête f, étude f; (in house buying etc) inspection f, (rapport m d')expertise f; (of land) levé m ▷ vt [sə:'veɪ] (situation) passer en revue; (examine carefully) inspecter; (building) expertiser; (land) faire le levé de; (look at) embrasser du regard; **surveyor** n (of building) expert m; (of land) (arpenteur m) géomètre m

survival [sə'vaɪvl] n survie f

survive [sə'vaɪv] vi survivre; (custom etc) subsister ▷ vt (accident etc) survivre à, réchapper de; (person) survivre à; **survivor** n survivant(e)

suspect adj, n ['sʌspɛkt] suspect(e) ▷ vt [sə s'pɛkt] soupçonner, suspecter

suspend [səs'pɛnd] vt suspendre; **suspended sentence** n (Law) condamnation f avec sursis; **suspenders** npl (BRIT) jarretelles fpl; (US) bretelles fpl

suspense [səs'pɛns] n attente f, incertitude f; (in film etc) suspense m; **to keep sb in ~** tenir qn en suspens, laisser qn dans l'incertitude

suspension [səs'pɛnʃən] n (gen, Aut) suspension f; (of driving licence) retrait m provisoire; **suspension bridge** n pont suspendu

suspicion [səs'pɪʃən] n soupçon(s) m(pl); **suspicious** adj (suspecting) soupçonneux(-euse), méfiant(e); (causing suspicion) suspect(e)

sustain [səs'teɪn] vt soutenir; (subj: food) nourrir, donner des forces à; (damage) subir; (injury) recevoir

SUV n abbr (esp US: = sports utility vehicle) SUV m, véhicule m de loisirs

swallow ['swɔləu] n (bird) hirondelle f ▷ vt avaler; (fig: story) gober

swam [swæm] pt of **swim**

swamp [swɔmp] n marais m, marécage m ▷ vt submerger

swan [swɔn] n cygne m

swap [swɔp] n échange m, troc m ▷ vt: **to ~ (for)** échanger (contre), troquer (contre)

swarm [swɔ:m] n essaim m ▷ vi (bees) essaimer; (people) grouiller; **to be ~ing with** grouiller de

sway [sweɪ] vi se balancer, osciller ▷ vt (influence) influencer

swear [swɛə'] (pt **swore**, pp **sworn**) vt, vi jurer; **swear in** vt assermenter; **swearword** n gros mot, juron m

sweat [swɛt] n sueur f, transpiration f ▷ vi suer

sweater ['swɛtə'] n tricot m, pull m

sweatshirt ['swɛtʃə:t] n sweat-shirt m

sweaty ['swɛtɪ] adj en sueur, moite or mouillé(e) de sueur

Swede [swi:d] n Suédois(e)

swede [swi:d] n (BRIT) rutabaga m

Sweden ['swi:dn] n Suède f; **Swedish** ['swi: dɪʃ] adj suédois(e) ▷ n (Ling) suédois m

sweep [swi:p] n (curve) grande courbe; (also: **chimney ~**) ramoneur m ▷ vb (pt, pp **swept**) ▷ vt balayer; (subj: current) emporter

sweet [swi:t] n (BRIT: pudding) dessert m; (candy) bonbon m ▷ adj doux (douce); (not savoury) sucré(e); (kind) gentil(le); (baby) mignon(ne); **sweetcorn** n maïs doux; **sweetener** ['swi:tnə'] n (Culin) édulcorant m; **sweetheart** n amoureux(-euse); **sweetshop** n (BRIT) confiserie f

swell [swɛl] n (of sea) houle f ▷ adj (US: inf: excellent) chouette ▷ vb (pt **~ed**, pp **swollen** or **~ed**) ▷ vt (increase) grossir, augmenter ▷ vi (increase) grossir, augmenter; (sound) s'enfler; (Med: also: **~ up**) enfler; **swelling** n (Med) enflure f; (: lump) grosseur f

swept [swɛpt] pt, pp of **sweep**

swerve [swə:v] vi (to avoid obstacle) faire une embardée or un écart; (off the road) dévier

swift [swɪft] n (bird) martinet m ▷ adj rapide, prompt(e)

swim [swɪm] n: **to go for a ~** aller nager or se baigner ▷ vb (pt **swam**, pp **swum**) ▷ vi nager; (Sport) faire de la natation; (fig: head, room) tourner ▷ vt traverser (à la nage); **to ~ a length** nager une longueur; **swimmer** n nageur(-euse); **swimming** n nage f, natation f; **swimming costume** n (BRIT) maillot m (de bain); **swimming pool** n piscine f; **swimming trunks** npl maillot m de bain; **swimsuit** n maillot m (de bain)

swing [swɪŋ] n (in playground) balançoire f;

s

(*movement*) balancement *m*, oscillations *fpl*; (*change in opinion etc*) revirement *m* ▷ *vb* (*pt, pp* **swung**) ▷ *vt* balancer, faire osciller; (*also*: **~ round**) tourner, faire virer ▷ *vi* se balancer, osciller; (*also*: **~ round**) virer, tourner; **to be in full ~** battre son plein

swipe card [swaɪp-] *n* carte *f* magnétique

swirl [swəːl] *vi* tourbillonner, tournoyer

Swiss [swɪs] *adj* suisse ▷ *n* (*pl inv*) Suisse(-esse)

switch [swɪtʃ] *n* (*for light, radio etc*) bouton *m*; (*change*) changement *m*, revirement *m* ▷ *vt* (*change*) changer; **switch off** *vt* éteindre; (*engine, machine*) arrêter; **could you ~ off the light?** pouvez-vous éteindre la lumière?; **switch on** *vt* allumer; (*engine, machine*) mettre en marche; **switchboard** *n* (*Tel*) standard *m*

Switzerland ['swɪtsələnd] *n* Suisse *f*

swivel ['swɪvl] *vi* (*also*: **~ round**) pivoter, tourner

swollen ['swəʊlən] *pp of* **swell**

swoop [swuːp] *n* (*by police etc*) rafle *f*, descente *f* ▷ *vi* (*bird: also*: **~ down**) descendre en piqué, piquer

swop [swɒp] *n, vt* = **swap**

sword [sɔːd] *n* épée *f*; **swordfish** *n* espadon *m*

swore [swɔːʳ] *pt of* **swear**

sworn [swɔːn] *pp of* **swear** ▷ *adj* (*statement, evidence*) donné(e) sous serment; (*enemy*) juré(e)

swum [swʌm] *pp of* **swim**

swung [swʌŋ] *pt, pp of* **swing**

syllable ['sɪləbl] *n* syllabe *f*

syllabus ['sɪləbəs] *n* programme *m*

symbol ['sɪmbl] *n* symbole *m*; **symbolic(al)** [sɪm'bɒlɪk(l)] *adj* symbolique

symmetrical [sɪ'mɛtrɪkl] *adj* symétrique

symmetry ['sɪmɪtrɪ] *n* symétrie *f*

sympathetic [sɪmpə'θetɪk] *adj* (*showing pity*) compatissant(e); (*understanding*) bienveillant(e), compréhensif(-ive); **~ towards** bien disposé(e) envers

Be careful not to translate *sympathetic* by the French word *sympathique*.

sympathize ['sɪmpəθaɪz] *vi*: **to ~ with sb** plaindre qn; (*in grief*) s'associer à la douleur de qn; **to ~ with sth** comprendre qch

sympathy ['sɪmpəθɪ] *n* (*pity*) compassion *f*

symphony ['sɪmfənɪ] *n* symphonie *f*

symptom ['sɪmptəm] *n* symptôme *m*; indice *m*

synagogue ['sɪnəɡɒɡ] *n* synagogue *f*

syndicate ['sɪndɪkɪt] *n* syndicat *m*, coopérative *f*; (*Press*) agence *f* de presse

syndrome ['sɪndrəʊm] *n* syndrome *m*

synonym ['sɪnənɪm] *n* synonyme *m*

synthetic [sɪn'θetɪk] *adj* synthétique

Syria ['sɪrɪə] *n* Syrie *f*

syringe [sɪ'rɪndʒ] *n* seringue *f*

syrup ['sɪrəp] *n* sirop *m*; (*BRIT: also*: **golden ~**) mélasse raffinée

system ['sɪstəm] *n* système *m*; (*Anat*) organisme *m*; **systematic** [sɪstə'mætɪk] *adj* systématique; méthodique; **systems analyst** *n* analyste-programmeur *m/f*

ta [tɑː] *excl* (BRIT *inf*) merci!
tab [tæb] *n* (*label*) étiquette *f*; (*on drinks can etc*) languette *f*; **to keep ~s on** (*fig*) surveiller
table ['teɪbl] *n* table *f* ▷ *vt* (BRIT: *motion etc*) présenter; **a ~ for 4, please** une table pour 4, s'il vous plaît; **to lay** *or* **set the ~** mettre le couvert *or* la table; **tablecloth** *n* nappe *f*; **table d'hôte** [tɑːblˈdəut] *adj* (*meal*) à prix fixe; **table lamp** *n* lampe décorative *or* de table; **tablemat** *n* (*for plate*) napperon *m*, set *m*; (*for hot dish*) dessous-de-plat *m inv*; **tablespoon** *n* cuiller *f* de service; (*also:* **tablespoonful:** *as measurement*) cuillerée *f* à soupe
tablet ['tæblɪt] *n* (*Med*) comprimé *m*; (*of stone*) plaque *f*
table tennis *n* ping-pong *m*, tennis *m* de table
tabloid ['tæblɔɪd] *n* (*newspaper*) quotidien *m* populaire
taboo [təˈbuː] *adj, n* tabou (*m*)
tack [tæk] *n* (*nail*) petit clou; (*fig*) direction *f* ▷ *vt* (*nail*) clouer; (*sew*) bâtir ▷ *vi* (*Naut*) tirer un *or* des bord(s); **to ~ sth on to (the end of) sth** (*of letter, book*) rajouter qch à la fin de qch
tackle ['tækl] *n* matériel *m*, équipement *m*; (*for lifting*) appareil *m* de levage; (*Football, Rugby*) plaquage *m* ▷ *vt* (*difficulty, animal, burglar*) s'attaquer à; (*person: challenge*) s'expliquer avec; (*Football, Rugby*) plaquer
tacky ['tækɪ] *adj* collant(e); (*paint*) pas sec (sèche); (*pej: poor-quality*) minable; (: *showing bad taste*) ringard(e)
tact [tækt] *n* tact *m*; **tactful** *adj* plein(e) de tact
tactics ['tæktɪks] *npl* tactique *f*
tactless ['tæktlɪs] *adj* qui manque de tact
tadpole ['tædpəul] *n* têtard *m*
taffy ['tæfɪ] *n* (US) (bonbon *m* au) caramel *m*
tag [tæg] *n* étiquette *f*
tail [teɪl] *n* queue *f*; (*of shirt*) pan *m* ▷ *vt* (*follow*) suivre, filer; **tails** *npl* (*suit*) habit *m*; *see also* **head**
tailor ['teɪlər] *n* tailleur *m* (*artisan*)
Taiwan ['taɪˈwɑːn] *n* Taïwan (*no article*); **Taiwanese** [taɪwəˈniːz] *adj* taïwanais(e) ▷ *n inv* Taïwanais(e)
take [teɪk] *vb* (*pt* **took**, *pp* **~n**) ▷ *vt* prendre; (*gain: prize*) remporter; (*require: effort, courage*) demander; (*tolerate*) accepter, supporter; (*hold: passengers etc*) contenir; (*accompany*) emmener, accompagner; (*bring, carry*) apporter, emporter; (*exam*) passer, se présenter à; **to ~ sth from** (*drawer etc*) prendre qch dans; (*person*) prendre qch à; **I ~ it that** je suppose que; **to be ~n ill** tomber malade; **it won't ~ long** ça ne prendra pas longtemps; **I was quite ~n with her/it** elle/cela m'a beaucoup plu; **take after** *vt fus* ressembler à; **take apart** *vt* démonter; **take away** *vt* (*carry off*) emporter; (*remove*) enlever; (*subtract*) soustraire; **take back** *vt* (*return*) rendre, rapporter; (*one's words*) retirer; **take down** *vt* (*building*) démolir; (*letter etc*) prendre, écrire; **take in** *vt* (*deceive*) tromper, rouler; (*understand*) comprendre, saisir; (*include*) couvrir, inclure; (*lodger*) prendre; (*dress, waistband*) reprendre; **take off** *vi* (*Aviat*) décoller ▷ *vt* (*remove*) enlever; **take on** *vt* (*work*) accepter, se charger de; (*employee*) prendre, embaucher; (*opponent*) accepter de se battre contre; **take out** *vt* sortir; (*remove*) enlever; (*invite*) sortir avec; **to ~ sth out of** (*out of drawer etc*) prendre qch dans; **to ~ sb out to a restaurant** emmener qn au restaurant; **take over** *vt* (*business*) reprendre ▷ *vi*: **to ~ over from sb** prendre la relève de qn; **take up** *vt* (*one's story*) reprendre; (*dress*) raccourcir; (*occupy: time, space*) prendre, occuper; (*engage in: hobby etc*) se mettre à; (*accept: offer, challenge*) accepter; **takeaway** (BRIT) *adj* (*food*) à emporter ▷ *n* (*shop, restaurant*) ≈ magasin *m* qui vend des plats à emporter; **taken** *pp of* **take**; **is this seat taken?** la place est-elle prise?;
takeoff *n* (*Aviat*) décollage *m*; **takeout** *adj*, *n* (US) = **takeaway**; **takeover** *n* (*Comm*) rachat *m*; **takings** *npl* (*Comm*) recette *f*
talc [tælk] *n* (*also:* **~um powder**) talc *m*
tale [teɪl] *n* (*story*) conte *m*, histoire *f*; (*account*) récit *m*; **to tell ~s** (*fig*) rapporter
talent ['tælnt] *n* talent *m*, don *m*; **talented** *adj*

doué(e), plein(e) de talent

talk [tɔ:k] n (a speech) causerie f, exposé m; (conversation) discussion f; (interview) entretien m; (gossip) racontars mpl (pej) ▷ vi parler; (chatter) bavarder; **talks** npl (Pol etc) entretiens mpl; **to ~ about** parler de; **to ~ sb out of/into doing** persuader qn de ne pas faire/de faire; **to ~ shop** parler métier or affaires; **talk over** vt discuter (de); **talk show** n (TV, Radio) émission-débat f

tall [tɔ:l] adj (person) grand(e); (building, tree) haut(e); **to be 6 feet ~** ≈ mesurer 1 mètre 80

tambourine [tæmbə'ri:n] n tambourin m

tame [teɪm] adj apprivoisé(e); (fig: story, style) insipide

tamper ['tæmpə¹] vi: **to ~ with** toucher à (en cachette ou sans permission)

tampon ['tæmpən] n tampon m hygiénique or périodique

tan [tæn] n (also: **sun~**) bronzage m ▷ vt, vi bronzer, brunir ▷ adj (colour) marron clair inv

tandem ['tændəm] n tandem m

tangerine [tændʒə'ri:n] n mandarine f

tangle ['tæŋgl] n enchevêtrement m; **to get in(to) a ~** s'emmêler

tank [tæŋk] n réservoir m; (for fish) aquarium m; (Mil) char m d'assaut, tank m

tanker ['tæŋkə¹] n (ship) pétrolier m, tanker m; (truck) camion-citerne m

tanned [tænd] adj bronzé(e)

tantrum ['tæntrəm] n accès m de colère

Tanzania [tænzə'nɪə] n Tanzanie f

tap [tæp] n (on sink etc) robinet m; (gentle blow) petite tape ▷ vt frapper or taper légèrement; (resources) exploiter, utiliser; (telephone) mettre sur écoute; **on ~** (fig: resources) disponible; **tap dancing** n claquettes fpl

tape [teɪp] n (for tying) ruban m; (also: **magnetic ~**) bande f (magnétique); (cassette) cassette f; (sticky) Scotch® m ▷ vt (record) enregistrer (au magnétoscope or sur cassette); (stick) coller avec du Scotch®; **tape measure** n mètre m à ruban; **tape recorder** n magnétophone m

tapestry ['tæpɪstrɪ] n tapisserie f

tar [tɑ:] n goudron m

target ['tɑ:gɪt] n cible f; (fig: objective) objectif m

tariff ['tærɪf] n (Comm) tarif m; (taxes) tarif douanier

tarmac ['tɑ:mæk] n (BRIT: on road) macadam m; (Aviat) aire f d'envol

tarpaulin [tɑ:'pɔ:lɪn] n bâche goudronnée

tarragon ['tærəgən] n estragon m

tart [tɑ:t] n (Culin) tarte f; (BRIT inf: pej: prostitute) poule f ▷ adj (flavour) âpre, aigrelet(te)

tartan ['tɑ:tn] n tartan m ▷ adj écossais(e)

tartar(e) sauce n sauce f tartare

task [tɑ:sk] n tâche f; **to take to ~** prendre à partie

taste [teɪst] n goût m; (fig: glimpse, idea) idée f, aperçu m ▷ vt goûter ▷ vi: **to ~ of** (fish etc) avoir le or un goût de; **you can ~ the garlic (in it)** on sent bien l'ail; **to have a ~ of sth** goûter (à) qch; **can I have a ~?** je peux goûter?; **to be in good/bad** or **poor ~** être de bon/mauvais goût; **tasteful** adj de bon goût; **tasteless** adj (food) insipide; (remark) de mauvais goût; **tasty** adj savoureux(-euse), délicieux(-euse)

tatters ['tætəz] npl: **in ~** (also: **tattered**) en lambeaux

tattoo [tə'tu:] n tatouage m; (spectacle) parade f militaire ▷ vt tatouer

taught [tɔ:t] pt, pp of **teach**

taunt [tɔ:nt] n raillerie f ▷ vt railler

Taurus ['tɔ:rəs] n le Taureau

taut [tɔ:t] adj tendu(e)

tax [tæks] n (on goods etc) taxe f; (on income) impôts mpl, contributions fpl ▷ vt taxer; imposer; (fig: patience etc) mettre à l'épreuve; **tax disc** n (BRIT Aut) vignette f (automobile); **tax-free** adj exempt(e) d'impôts

taxi ['tæksɪ] n taxi m ▷ vi (Aviat) rouler (lentement) au sol; **can you call me a ~, please?** pouvez-vous m'appeler un taxi, s'il vous plaît?; **taxi driver** n chauffeur m de taxi; **taxi rank** (BRIT), **taxi stand** n station f de taxis

tax payer [-peɪə¹] n contribuable m/f

tax return n déclaration f d'impôts or de revenus

TB n abbr = **tuberculosis**

tea [ti:] n thé m; (BRIT: snack: for children) goûter m; **high ~** (BRIT) collation combinant goûter et dîner; **tea bag** n sachet m de thé; **tea break** n (BRIT) pause-thé f

teach (pt, pp **taught**) [ti:tʃ, tɔ:t] vt: **to ~ sb sth, to ~ sth to sb** apprendre qch à qn; (in school etc) enseigner qch à qn ▷ vi enseigner; **teacher** n (in secondary school) professeur m; (in primary school) instituteur(-trice); **teaching** n enseignement m

tea: **tea cloth** n (BRIT) torchon m; **teacup** n tasse f à thé

tea leaves npl feuilles fpl de thé

team [ti:m] n équipe f; (of animals) attelage m; **team up** vi: **to ~ up (with)** faire équipe (avec)

teapot ['ti:pɔt] n théière f

tear¹ ['tɪə¹] n larme f; **in ~s** en larmes

tear² n [teə¹] déchirure f ▷ vb (pt **tore**, pp **torn**) ▷ vt déchirer ▷ vi se déchirer; **tear apart** vt (also fig) déchirer; **tear down** vt (building, statue) démolir; (poster, flag) arracher; **tear off** vt (sheet of paper etc) arracher; (one's clothes) enlever à toute vitesse; **tear up** vt (sheet of paper etc) déchirer, mettre en morceaux or pièces

tearful ['tɪəful] adj larmoyant(e)
tear gas ['tɪə-] n gaz m lacrymogène
tearoom ['tiːruːm] n salon m de thé
tease [tiːz] vt taquiner; (unkindly) tourmenter
tea: teaspoon n petite cuiller; (also:
teaspoonful: as measurement) ≈ cuillerée f à café; **teatime** n l'heure f du thé; **tea towel** n (BRIT) torchon m (à vaisselle)
technical ['tɛknɪkl] adj technique
technician [tɛk'nɪʃən] n technicien(ne)
technique [tɛk'niːk] n technique f
technology [tɛk'nɔlədʒɪ] n technologie f
teddy (bear) ['tɛdɪ-] n ours m (en peluche)
tedious ['tiːdɪəs] adj fastidieux(-euse)
tee [tiː] n (Golf) tee m
teen [tiːn] adj = **teenage** ▷ n (US) = **teenager**
teenage ['tiːneɪdʒ] adj (fashions etc) pour jeunes, pour adolescents; (child) qui est adolescent(e); **teenager** n adolescent(e)
teens [tiːnz] npl: **to be in one's ~** être adolescent(e)
teeth [tiːθ] npl of **tooth**
teetotal ['tiː'təutl] adj (person) qui ne boit jamais d'alcool
telecommunications ['tɛlɪkəmjuːnɪ'keɪʃənz] n télécommunications fpl
telegram ['tɛlɪgræm] n télégramme m
telegraph pole ['tɛlɪgrɑːf-] n poteau m télégraphique
telephone ['tɛlɪfəun] n téléphone m ▷ vt (person) téléphoner à; (message) téléphoner; **to be on the ~** (be speaking) être au téléphone; **telephone book** n = **telephone directory**; **telephone booth** (BRIT), **telephone box** n cabine f téléphonique; **telephone call** n appel m téléphonique; **telephone directory** n annuaire m (du téléphone); **telephone number** n numéro m de téléphone
telesales ['tɛlɪseɪlz] npl télévente f
telescope ['tɛlɪskəup] n télescope m
televise ['tɛlɪvaɪz] vt téléviser
television ['tɛlɪvɪʒən] n télévision f; **on ~** à la télévision; **television programme** n émission f de télévision
tell (pt, pp **told**) [tɛl, təuld] vt dire; (relate: story) raconter; (distinguish): **to ~ sth from** distinguer qch de ▷ vi (talk): **to ~ of** parler de; (have effect) se faire sentir, se voir; **to ~ sb to do** dire à qn de faire; **to ~ the time** (know how to) savoir lire l'heure; **tell off** vt réprimander, gronder; **teller** n (in bank) caissier(-ière)
telly ['tɛlɪ] n abbr (BRIT inf: = television) télé f
temp [tɛmp] n (BRIT = temporary worker) intérimaire m/f ▷ vi travailler comme intérimaire
temper ['tɛmpər] n (nature) caractère m; (mood) humeur f; (fit of anger) colère f ▷ vt (moderate) tempérer, adoucir; **to be in a ~** être

en colère; **to lose one's ~** se mettre en colère
temperament ['tɛmprəmənt] n (nature) tempérament m; **temperamental** [tɛmprə'mɛntl] adj capricieux(-euse)
temperature ['tɛmprətʃər] n température f; **to have** or **run a ~** avoir de la fièvre
temple ['tɛmpl] n (building) temple m; (Anat) tempe f
temporary ['tɛmpərərɪ] adj temporaire, provisoire; (job, worker) temporaire
tempt [tɛmpt] vt tenter; **to ~ sb into doing** induire qn à faire; **temptation** n tentation f; **tempting** adj tentant(e); (food) appétissant(e)
ten [tɛn] num dix
tenant ['tɛnənt] n locataire m/f
tend [tɛnd] vt s'occuper de ▷ vi: **to ~ to do** avoir tendance à faire; **tendency** ['tɛndənsɪ] n tendance f
tender ['tɛndər] adj tendre; (delicate) délicat(e); (sore) sensible ▷ n (Comm: offer) soumission f; (money): **legal ~** cours légal ▷ vt offrir
tendon ['tɛndən] n tendon m
tenner ['tɛnər] n (BRIT inf) billet m de dix livres
tennis ['tɛnɪs] n tennis m; **tennis ball** n balle f de tennis; **tennis court** n (court m de) tennis m; **tennis match** n match m de tennis; **tennis player** n joueur(-euse) de tennis; **tennis racket** n raquette f de tennis
tenor ['tɛnər] n (Mus) ténor m
tenpin bowling ['tɛnpɪn-] n (BRIT) bowling m (à 10 quilles)
tense [tɛns] adj tendu(e) ▷ n (Ling) temps m
tension ['tɛnʃən] n tension f
tent [tɛnt] n tente f
tentative ['tɛntətɪv] adj timide, hésitant(e); (conclusion) provisoire
tenth [tɛnθ] num dixième
tent: tent peg n piquet m de tente; **tent pole** n montant m de tente
tepid ['tɛpɪd] adj tiède
term [təːm] n terme m; (Scol) trimestre m ▷ vt appeler; **terms** npl (conditions) conditions fpl; (Comm) tarif m; **in the short/long ~** à court/long terme; **to come to ~s with** (problem) faire face à; **to be on good ~s with** bien s'entendre avec, être en bons termes avec
terminal ['təːmɪnl] adj (disease) dans sa phase terminale; (patient) incurable ▷ n (Elec) borne f; (for oil, ore etc, also Comput) terminal m; (also: **air ~**) aérogare f; (BRIT: also: **coach ~**) gare routière
terminate ['təːmɪneɪt] vt mettre fin à; (pregnancy) interrompre
termini ['təːmɪnaɪ] npl of **terminus**
terminology [təːmɪ'nɔlədʒɪ] n terminologie f
terminus (pl **termini**) ['təːmɪnəs, 'təːmɪnaɪ] n terminus m inv

terrace ['tɛrəs] n terrasse f; (BRIT: row of houses) rangée f de maisons (attenantes les unes aux autres); **the ~s** (BRIT Sport) les gradins mpl; **terraced** adj (garden) en terrasses; (in a row: house, cottage etc) attenant(e) aux maisons voisines

terrain [tɛ'reɪn] n terrain m (sol)

terrestrial [tɪ'rɛstrɪəl] adj terrestre

terrible ['tɛrɪbl] adj terrible, atroce; (weather, work) affreux(-euse), épouvantable; **terribly** adv terriblement; (very badly) affreusement mal

terrier ['tɛrɪər] n terrier m (chien)

terrific [tə'rɪfɪk] adj (very great) fantastique, incroyable, terrible; (wonderful) formidable, sensationnel(le)

terrified ['tɛrɪfaɪd] adj terrifié(e); **to be ~ of sth** avoir très peur de qch

terrify ['tɛrɪfaɪ] vt terrifier; **terrifying** adj terrifiant(e)

territorial [tɛrɪ'tɔːrɪəl] adj territorial(e)

territory ['tɛrɪtərɪ] n territoire m

terror ['tɛrər] n terreur f; **terrorism** n terrorisme m; **terrorist** n terroriste m/f; **terrorist attack** n attentat m terroriste

test [tɛst] n (trial, check) essai m; (: of courage etc) épreuve f; (Med) examen m; (Chem) analyse f; (Scol) interrogation f de contrôle; (also: **driving ~**) (examen du) permis m de conduire ▷ vt essayer; mettre à l'épreuve; examiner; analyser; faire subir une interrogation (de contrôle) à

testicle ['tɛstɪkl] n testicule m

testify ['tɛstɪfaɪ] vi (Law) témoigner, déposer; **to ~ to sth** (Law) attester qch

testimony ['tɛstɪmənɪ] n (Law) témoignage m, déposition f

test: **test match** n (Cricket, Rugby) match international; **test tube** n éprouvette f

tetanus ['tɛtənəs] n tétanos m

text [tɛkst] n texte m; (on mobile phone) texto m, SMS m inv ▷ vt (inf) envoyer un texto or SMS à; **textbook** n manuel m

textile ['tɛkstaɪl] n textile m

text message n texto m, SMS m inv

text messaging [-'mɛsɪdʒɪŋ] n messagerie textuelle

texture ['tɛkstʃər] n texture f; (of skin, paper etc) grain m

Thai [taɪ] adj thaïlandais(e) ▷ n Thaïlandais(e)

Thailand ['taɪlænd] n Thaïlande f

Thames [tɛmz] n: **the (River) ~** la Tamise

than [ðæn, ðən] conj que; (with numerals): **more ~ 10/once** plus de 10/d'une fois; **I have more/less ~ you** j'en ai plus/moins que toi; **she has more apples ~ pears** elle a plus de pommes que de poires; **it is better to phone ~ to write** il vaut mieux téléphoner (plutôt) qu'écrire; **she is older ~ you think** elle est plus âgée que tu le crois

thank [θæŋk] vt remercier, dire merci à; **thanks** npl remerciements mpl ▷ excl merci!; **~ you (very much)** merci (beaucoup); **~ God** Dieu merci; **~s to** prep grâce à; **thankfully** adv (fortunately) heureusement; **Thanksgiving (Day)** n jour m d'action de grâce; voir encadré

⊙ **KEYWORD**

that [ðæt] adj (demonstrative: pl **those**) ce, cet + vowel or h mute, cette f; **that man/woman/book** cet homme/cette femme/ce livre; (not this) cet homme-là/cette femme-là/ce livre-là; **that one** celui-là (celle-là) ▷ pron 1 (demonstrative: pl **those**) ce; (not this one) cela, ça; (that one) celui (celle); **who's that?** qui est-ce?; **what's that?** qu'est-ce que c'est?; **is that you?** c'est toi?; **I prefer this to that** je préfère ceci à cela or ça; **that's what he said** c'est or voilà ce qu'il a dit; **will you eat all that?** est-ce que tu vas manger tout ça?; **that is (to say)** c'est-à-dire, à savoir

2 (relative: subject) qui; (: object) que; (: after prep) lequel (laquelle), lesquels (lesquelles) pl; **the book that I read** le livre que j'ai lu; **the books that are in the library** les livres qui sont dans la bibliothèque; **all that I have** tout ce que j'ai; **the box that I put it in** la boîte dans laquelle je l'ai mis; **the people that I spoke to** les gens auxquels or à qui j'ai parlé

3 (relative: of time) où; **the day that he came** le jour où il est venu ▷ conj que; **he thought that I was ill** il pensait que j'étais malade ▷ adv (demonstrative): **I don't like it that much** ça ne me plaît pas tant que ça; **I didn't know it was that bad** je ne savais pas que c'était si or aussi mauvais; **it's about that high** c'est à peu près de cette hauteur

thatched [θætʃt] adj (roof) de chaume; **~ cottage** chaumière f

thaw [θɔː] n dégel m ▷ vi (ice) fondre; (food) dégeler ▷ vt (food) (faire) dégeler

○ **KEYWORD**

the [ðiː, ðə] def art **1** (gen) le, la f, l' + vowel or h mute, les pl (NB: à + le(s) = **au(x)**; de + le = **du**; de + les = **des**); **the boy/girl/ink** le garçon/la fille/l'encre; **the children** les enfants; **the history of the world** l'histoire du monde; **give it to the postman** donne-le au facteur; **to play the piano/flute** jouer du piano/de la flûte **2** (+ adj to form n) le, la f, l' + vowel or h mute, les pl; **the rich and the poor** les riches et les pauvres; **to attempt the impossible** tenter l'impossible
3 (in titles): **Elizabeth the First** Elisabeth première; **Peter the Great** Pierre le Grand **4** (in comparisons): **the more he works, the more he earns** plus il travaille, plus il gagne de l'argent

theatre (US **theater**) [ˈθɪətər] n théâtre m; (Med: also: **operating ~**) salle f d'opération
theft [θɛft] n vol m (larcin)
their [ðɛər] adj leur, leurs pl; see also **my**; **theirs** pron le (la) leur, les leurs; see also **mine**[1]
them [ðɛm, ðəm] pron (direct) les; (indirect) leur; (stressed, after prep) eux (elles); **give me a few of ~** donnez m'en quelques uns (or quelques unes); see also **me**
theme [θiːm] n thème m; **theme park** n parc m à thème
themselves [ðəmˈsɛlvz] pl pron (reflexive) se; (emphatic, after prep) eux-mêmes (elles-mêmes); **between ~** entre eux (elles); see also **oneself**
then [ðɛn] adv (at that time) alors, à ce moment-là; (next) puis, ensuite; (and also) et puis ▷ conj (therefore) alors, dans ce cas ▷ adj: **the ~ president** le président d'alors or de l'époque; **by ~** (past) à ce moment-là; (future) d'ici là; **from ~ on** dès lors; **until ~** jusqu'à ce moment-là, jusque-là
theology [θɪˈɒlədʒɪ] n théologie f
theory [ˈθɪərɪ] n théorie f
therapist [ˈθɛrəpɪst] n thérapeute m/f
therapy [ˈθɛrəpɪ] n thérapie f

○ **KEYWORD**

there [ðɛər] adv **1**: **there is**, **there are** il y a; **there are 3 of them** (people, things) il y en a 3; **there is no-one here/no bread left** il n'y a personne/il n'y a plus de pain; **there has been an accident** il y a eu un accident
2 (referring to place) là, là-bas; **it's there** c'est là(-bas); **in/on/up/down there** là-dedans/là-dessus/là-haut/en bas; **he went there on**

Friday il y est allé vendredi; **I want that book there** je veux ce livre-là; **there he is!** le voilà!
3: **there, there** (esp to child) allons, allons!

there: **thereabouts** adv (place) par là, près de là; (amount) environ, à peu près; **thereafter** adv par la suite; **thereby** adv ainsi; **therefore** adv donc, par conséquent
there's [ˈðɛəz] = **there is**; **there has**
thermal [ˈθəːml] adj thermique; **~ underwear** sous-vêtements mpl en Thermolactyl®
thermometer [θəˈmɒmɪtər] n thermomètre m
thermostat [ˈθəːməustæt] n thermostat m
these [ðiːz] pl pron ceux-ci (celles-ci) ▷ pl adj ces; (not those): **~ books** ces livres-ci
thesis (pl **theses**) [ˈθiːsɪs, ˈθiːsiːz] n thèse f
they [ðeɪ] pl pron ils (elles); (stressed) eux (elles); **~ say that ...** (it is said that) on dit que ...; **they'd** = **they had**; **they would**; **they'll** = **they shall**; **they will**; **they're** = **they are**; **they've** = **they have**
thick [θɪk] adj épais(se); (stupid) bête, borné(e) ▷ n: **in the ~ of** au beau milieu de, en plein cœur de; **it's 20 cm ~** ça a 20 cm d'épaisseur; **thicken** vi s'épaissir ▷ vt (sauce etc) épaissir; **thickness** n épaisseur f
thief (pl **thieves**) [θiːf, θiːvz] n voleur(-euse)
thigh [θaɪ] n cuisse f
thin [θɪn] adj mince; (skinny) maigre; (soup) peu épais(se); (hair, crowd) clairsemé(e) ▷ vt (also: **~ down**: sauce, paint) délayer
thing [θɪŋ] n chose f; (object) objet m; (contraption) truc m; **things** npl (belongings) affaires fpl; **the ~ is ...** c'est que ...; **the best ~ would be to** le mieux serait de; **how are ~s?** comment ça va?; **to have a ~ about** (be obsessed by) être obsédé(e) par; (hate) détester; **poor ~!** le (or la) pauvre!
think (pt, pp **thought**) [θɪŋk, θɔːt] vi penser, réfléchir ▷ vt penser, croire; (imagine) s'imaginer; **what did you ~ of them?** qu'avez-vous pensé d'eux?; **to ~ about sth/sb** penser à qch/qn; **I'll ~ about it** je vais y réfléchir; **to ~ of doing** avoir l'idée de faire; **I ~ so/not** je crois or pense que oui/non; **to ~ well of** avoir une haute opinion de; **think over** vt bien réfléchir à; **think up** vt inventer, trouver
third [θəːd] num troisième ▷ n (fraction) tiers m; (Aut) troisième (vitesse) f; (BRIT Scol: degree) ≈ licence f avec mention passable; **thirdly** adv troisièmement; **third party insurance** n (BRIT) assurance f au tiers; **Third World** n: **the Third World** le Tiers-Monde
thirst [θəːst] n soif f; **thirsty** adj qui a soif, assoiffé(e); (work) qui donne soif; **to be thirsty** avoir soif
thirteen [θəːˈtiːn] num treize; **thirteenth** [-ˈtiːnθ] num treizième

thirtieth ['θə:tɪɪθ] num trentième
thirty ['θə:tɪ] num trente

O **KEYWORD**

this [ðɪs] adj (demonstrative: pl **these**) ce, cet
+ vowel or h mute, cette f; **this man/woman/
book** cet homme/cette femme/ce livre; (not
that) cet homme-ci/cette femme-ci/ce livre-
ci; **this one** celui-ci (celle-ci)
▷ pron (demonstrative: pl **these**) ce; (not that
one) celui-ci (celle-ci), ceci; **who's this?** qui
est-ce?; **what's this?** qu'est-ce que c'est?; **I
prefer this to that** je préfère ceci à cela; **this
is where I live** c'est ici que j'habite; **this is
what he said** voici ce qu'il a dit; **this is Mr
Brown** (in introductions) je vous présente Mr
Brown; (in photo) c'est Mr Brown; (on telephone)
ici Mr Brown
▷ adv (demonstrative): **it was about this big**
c'était à peu près de cette grandeur or grand
comme ça; **I didn't know it was this bad** je
ne savais pas que c'était si or aussi mauvais

thistle ['θɪsl] n chardon m
thorn [θɔ:n] n épine f
thorough ['θʌrə] adj (search)
minutieux(-euse); (knowledge,
research) approfondi(e); (work, person)
consciencieux(-euse); (cleaning) à fond;
thoroughly adv (search) minutieusement;
(study) en profondeur; (clean) à fond; (very)
tout à fait
those [ðəuz] pl pron ceux-là (celles-là) ▷ pl adj
ces; (not these): **~ books** ces livres-là
though [ðəu] conj bien que + sub, quoique +
sub ▷ adv pourtant
thought [θɔ:t] pt, pp of **think** ▷ n pensée
f; (idea) idée f; (opinion) avis m; **thoughtful**
adj (deep in thought) pensif(-ive); (serious)
réfléchi(e); (considerate) prévenant(e);
thoughtless adj qui manque de
considération
thousand ['θauzənd] num mille; **one ~**
mille; **two ~** deux mille; **~s of** des milliers de;
thousandth num millième
thrash [θræʃ] vt rouer de coups; (as
punishment) donner une correction à; (inf:
defeat) battre à plate(s) couture(s)
thread [θrɛd] n fil m; (of screw) pas m, filetage
m ▷ vt (needle) enfiler
threat [θrɛt] n menace f; **threaten** vi (storm)
menacer ▷ vt: **to threaten sb with sth/to do**
menacer qn de qch/de faire; **threatening** adj
menaçant(e)
three [θri:] num trois; **three-dimensional** adj
à trois dimensions; **three-piece suite** n salon
m (canapé et deux fauteuils); **three-quarters**
npl trois-quarts mpl; **three-quarters full** aux

trois-quarts plein
threshold ['θrɛʃhəuld] n seuil m
threw [θru:] pt of **throw**
thrill [θrɪl] n (excitement) émotion f, sensation
forte; (shudder) frisson m ▷ vt (audience)
électriser; **thrilled** adj: **thrilled (with)** ravi(e)
de; **thriller** n film m (or roman m or pièce
f) à suspense; **thrilling** adj (book, play etc)
saisissant(e); (news, discovery) excitant(e)
thriving ['θraɪvɪŋ] adj (business, community)
prospère
throat [θrəut] n gorge f; **to have a sore ~**
avoir mal à la gorge
throb [θrɔb] vi (heart) palpiter; (engine) vibrer;
my head is ~bing j'ai des élancements dans
la tête
throne [θrəun] n trône m
through [θru:] prep à travers; (time) pendant,
durant; (by means of) par, par l'intermédiaire
de; (owing to) à cause de ▷ adj (ticket, train,
passage) direct(e) ▷ adv à travers; **(from)
Monday ~ Friday** (us) de lundi à vendredi;
to put sb ~ to sb (Tel) passer qn à qn; **to
be ~** (BRIT: Tel) avoir la communication; (esp
US: have finished) avoir fini; **"no ~ traffic"**
(US) "passage interdit"; **"no ~ road"** (BRIT)
"impasse"; **throughout** prep (place) partout
dans; (time) durant tout(e) le (la) ▷ adv partout
throw [θrəu] n jet m; (Sport) lancer m ▷ vt (pt
threw, pp **~n**) lancer, jeter; (Sport) lancer;
(rider) désarçonner; (fig) décontenancer; **to ~
a party** donner une réception; **throw away**
vt jeter; (money) gaspiller; **throw in** vt (Sport:
ball) remettre en jeu; (include) ajouter; **throw
off** vt se débarrasser de; **throw out** vt jeter;
(reject) rejeter; (person) mettre à la porte;
throw up vi vomir
thru [θru:] (US) = **through**
thrush [θrʌʃ] n (Zool) grive f
thrust [θrʌst] vt (pt, pp **~**) pousser
brusquement; (push in) enfoncer
thud [θʌd] n bruit sourd
thug [θʌg] n voyou m
thumb [θʌm] n (Anat) pouce m ▷ vt: **to ~ a
lift** faire de l'auto-stop, arrêter une voiture;
thumbtack n (US) punaise f (clou)
thump [θʌmp] n grand coup (sound) bruit
sourd ▷ vt cogner sur ▷ vi cogner, frapper
thunder ['θʌndə'] n tonnerre m ▷ vi
tonner; (train etc): **to ~ past** passer dans
un grondement or un bruit de tonnerre;
thunderstorm n orage m
Thur(s) abbr (= Thursday) jeu
Thursday ['θə:zdɪ] n jeudi m
thus [ðʌs] adv ainsi
thwart [θwɔ:t] vt contrecarrer
thyme [taɪm] n thym m
Tibet [tɪ'bɛt] n Tibet m
tick [tɪk] n (sound: of clock) tic-tac m; (mark)

coche f; (Zool) tique f; (BRIT inf): **in a ~** dans un instant ▷ vi faire tic-tac ▷ vt (item on list) cocher; **tick off** vt (item on list) cocher; (person) réprimander, attraper

ticket ['tɪkɪt] n billet m; (for bus, tube) ticket m; (in shop: on goods) étiquette f; (for library) carte f; (also: **parking ~**) contravention f, p.-v. m; **ticket barrier** n (BRIT: Rail) portillon m automatique; **ticket collector** n contrôleur(-euse); **ticket inspector** n contrôleur(-euse); **ticket machine** n billetterie f automatique; **ticket office** n guichet m, bureau m de vente des billets

tickle ['tɪkl] vi chatouiller ▷ vt chatouiller; **ticklish** adj (person) chatouilleux(-euse); (problem) épineux(-euse)

tide [taɪd] n marée f; (fig: of events) cours m

tidy ['taɪdɪ] adj (room) bien rangé(e); (dress, work) net (nette), soigné(e); (person) ordonné(e), qui a de l'ordre ▷ vt (also: **~ up**) ranger

tie [taɪ] n (string etc) cordon m; (BRIT: also: **neck~**) cravate f; (fig: link) lien m; (Sport: draw) égalité f de points; match nul ▷ vt (parcel) attacher; (ribbon) nouer ▷ vi (Sport) faire match nul; finir à égalité de points; **to ~ sth in a bow** faire un nœud à or avec qch; **to ~ a knot in sth** faire un nœud à qch; **tie down** vt (fig): **to ~ sb down to** contraindre qn à accepter; **to feel ~d down** (by relationship) se sentir coincé(e); **tie up** vt (parcel) ficeler; (dog, boat) attacher; (prisoner) ligoter; (arrangements) conclure; **to be ~d up** (busy) être pris(e) or occupé(e)

tier [tɪəʳ] n gradin m; (of cake) étage m

tiger ['taɪgəʳ] n tigre m

tight [taɪt] adj (rope) tendu(e), raide; (clothes) étroit(e), très juste; (budget, programme, bend) serré(e); (control) strict(e), sévère; (inf: drunk) ivre, rond(e) ▷ adv (squeeze) très fort; (shut) à bloc, hermétiquement; **hold ~!** accrochez-vous bien!; **tighten** vt (rope) tendre; (screw) resserrer; (control) renforcer ▷ vi se tendre; se resserrer; **tightly** adv (grasp) bien, très fort; **tights** npl (BRIT) collant m

tile [taɪl] n (on roof) tuile f; (on wall or floor) carreau m

till [tɪl] n caisse (enregistreuse) ▷ prep, conj = **until**

tilt [tɪlt] vt pencher, incliner ▷ vi pencher, être incliné(e)

timber ['tɪmbəʳ] n (material) bois m de construction

time [taɪm] n temps m; (epoch: often pl) époque f, temps; (by clock) heure f; (moment) moment m; (occasion, also Math) fois f; (Mus) mesure f ▷ vt (race) chronométrer; (programme) minuter; (visit) fixer; (remark etc) choisir le moment de; **a long ~** un long moment, longtemps;

four at a ~ quatre à la fois; **for the ~ being** pour le moment; **from ~ to ~** de temps en temps; **at ~s** parfois; **in ~** (soon enough) à temps; (after some time) avec le temps, à la longue; (Mus) en mesure; **in a week's ~** dans une semaine; **in no ~** en un rien de temps; **any ~** n'importe quand; **on ~** à l'heure; **5 ~s 5** 5 fois 5; **what ~ is it?** quelle heure est-il?; **what ~ is the museum/shop open?** à quelle heure ouvre le musée/magasin?; **to have a good ~** bien s'amuser; **time limit** n limite f de temps, délai m; **timely** adj opportun(e); **timer** n (in kitchen) compte-minutes m inv; (Tech) minuteur m; **time-share** n maison f/ appartement m en multipropriété; **timetable** n (Rail) (indicateur m) horaire m; (Scol) emploi m du temps; **time zone** n fuseau m horaire

timid ['tɪmɪd] adj timide; (easily scared) peureux(-euse)

timing ['taɪmɪŋ] n (Sport) chronométrage m; **the ~ of his resignation** le moment choisi pour sa démission

tin [tɪn] n étain m; (also: **~ plate**) fer-blanc m; (BRIT: can) boîte f (de conserve); (: for baking) moule m (à gâteau); (for storage) boîte f; **tinfoil** n papier m d'étain or d'aluminium

tingle ['tɪŋgl] vi picoter; (person) avoir des picotements

tinker ['tɪŋkəʳ]; **tinker with** vt fus bricoler, rafistoler

tinned [tɪnd] adj (BRIT: food) en boîte, en conserve

tin opener [-'əupnəʳ] n (BRIT) ouvre-boîte(s) m

tinsel ['tɪnsl] n guirlandes fpl de Noël (argentées)

tint [tɪnt] n teinte f; (for hair) shampooing colorant; **tinted** adj (hair) teint(e); (spectacles, glass) teinté(e)

tiny ['taɪnɪ] adj minuscule

tip [tɪp] n (end) bout m; (gratuity) pourboire m; (BRIT: for rubbish) décharge f; (advice) tuyau m ▷ vt (waiter) donner un pourboire à; (tilt) incliner; (overturn: also: **~ over**) renverser; (empty: also: **~ out**) déverser; **how much should I ~?** combien de pourboire est-ce qu'il faut laisser?; **tip off** vt prévenir, avertir

tiptoe ['tɪptəu] n: **on ~** sur la pointe des pieds

tire ['taɪəʳ] n (US) = **tyre** ▷ vt fatiguer ▷ vi se fatiguer; **tired** adj fatigué(e); **to be tired of** en avoir assez de, être las (lasse) de; **tire pressure** (US) = **tyre pressure**; **tiring** adj fatigant(e)

tissue ['tɪʃuː] n tissu m; (paper handkerchief) mouchoir m en papier, kleenex® m; **tissue paper** n papier m de soie

tit [tɪt] n (bird) mésange f; **to give ~ for tat** rendre coup pour coup

title ['taɪtl] n titre m

T-junction ['tiː'dʒʌŋkʃən] n croisement m en T

TM *n abbr* = **trademark**

○ KEYWORD

to [tuː, tə] *prep* **1** (*direction*) à; (*towards*) vers; envers; **to go to France/Portugal/London/ school** aller en France/au Portugal/à Londres/à l'école; **to go to Claude's/the doctor's** aller chez Claude/le docteur; **the road to Edinburgh** la route d'Édimbourg **2** (*as far as*) (jusqu')à; **to count to 10** compter jusqu'à 10; **from 40 to 50 people** de 40 à 50 personnes **3** (*with expressions of time*): **a quarter to 5** 5 heures moins le quart; **it's twenty to 3** il est 3 heures moins vingt **4** (*for, of*) de; **the key to the front door** la clé de la porte d'entrée; **a letter to his wife** une lettre (adressée) à sa femme **5** (*expressing indirect object*) à; **to give sth to sb** donner qch à qn; **to talk to sb** parler à qn; **to be a danger to sb** être dangereux(-euse) pour qn **6** (*in relation to*) à; **3 goals to 2** 3 (buts) à 2; **30 miles to the gallon** ≈ 9,4 litres aux cent (km) **7** (*purpose, result*): **to come to sb's aid** venir au secours de qn, porter secours à qn; **to sentence sb to death** condamner qn à mort; **to my surprise** à ma grande surprise ▷ *with vb* **1** (*simple infinitive*): **to go/eat** aller/manger **2** (*following another vb*): **to want/try/start to do** vouloir/essayer de/commencer à faire **3** (*with vb omitted*): **I don't want to** je ne veux pas **4** (*purpose, result*) pour; **I did it to help you** je l'ai fait pour vous aider **5** (*equivalent to relative clause*): **I have things to do** j'ai des choses à faire; **the main thing is to try** l'important est d'essayer **6** (*after adjective etc*): **ready to go** prêt(e) à partir; **too old/young to ...** trop vieux/jeune pour ... ▷ *adv*: **push/pull the door to** tirez/poussez la porte

toad [təud] *n* crapaud *m*; **toadstool** *n* champignon (vénéneux)

toast [təust] *n* (*Culin*) pain grillé, toast *m*; (*drink, speech*) toast ▷ *vt* (*Culin*) faire griller; (*drink to*) porter un toast à; **toaster** *n* grille-pain *m inv*

tobacco [tə'bækəu] *n* tabac *m*

toboggan [tə'bɔgən] *n* toboggan *m*; (*child's*) luge *f*

today [tə'deɪ] *adv, n* (*also fig*) aujourd'hui (*m*)

toddler ['tɔdlər] *n* enfant *m/f* qui commence à marcher, bambin *m*

toe [təu] *n* doigt *m* de pied, orteil *m*; (*of shoe*)

bout *m* ▷ *vt*: **to ~ the line** (*fig*) obéir, se conformer; **toenail** *n* ongle *m* de l'orteil

toffee ['tɔfɪ] *n* caramel *m*

together [tə'geðər] *adv* ensemble; (*at same time*) en même temps; **~ with** *prep* avec

toilet ['tɔɪlət] *n* (*BRIT: lavatory*) toilettes *fpl*, cabinets *mpl*; **to go to the ~** aller aux toilettes; **where's the ~?** où sont les toilettes?; **toilet bag** *n* (*BRIT*) nécessaire *m* de toilette; **toilet paper** *n* papier *m* hygiénique; **toiletries** *npl* articles *mpl* de toilette; **toilet roll** *n* rouleau *m* de papier hygiénique

token ['təukən] *n* (*sign*) marque *f*, témoignage *m*; (*metal disc*) jeton *m* ▷ *adj* (*fee, strike*) symbolique; **book/record ~** (*BRIT*) chèque-livre/-disque *m*

Tokyo ['təukjəu] *n* Tokyo

told [təuld] *pt, pp of* **tell**

tolerant ['tɔlərnt] *adj*: **~ (of)** tolérant(e) (à l'égard de)

tolerate ['tɔləreɪt] *vt* supporter

toll [təul] *n* (*tax, charge*) péage *m* ▷ *vi* (*bell*) sonner; **the accident ~ on the roads** le nombre des victimes de la route; **toll call** *n* (*US Tel*) appel *m* (à) longue distance; **toll-free** *adj* (*US*) gratuit(e) ▷ *adv* gratuitement

tomato [tə'mɑːtəu] (*pl ~es*) *n* tomate *f*; **tomato sauce** *n* sauce *f* tomate

tomb [tuːm] *n* tombe *f*; **tombstone** *n* pierre tombale

tomorrow [tə'mɔrəu] *adv, n* (*also fig*) demain (*m*); **the day after ~** après-demain; **a week ~** demain en huit; **~ morning** demain matin

ton [tʌn] *n* tonne *f* (*BRIT*: = 1016 kg; *US* = 907 kg; *metric* = 1000 kg); **~s of** (*inf*) des tas de

tone [təun] *n* ton *m*; (*of radio, BRIT Tel*) tonalité *f* ▷ *vi* (*also*: **~ in**) s'harmoniser; **tone down** *vt* (*colour, criticism*) adoucir

tongs [tɔŋz] *npl* pinces *fpl*; (*for coal*) pincettes *fpl*; (*for hair*) fer *m* à friser

tongue [tʌŋ] *n* langue *f*; **~ in cheek** *adv* ironiquement

tonic ['tɔnɪk] *n* (*Med*) tonique *m*; (*also*: **~ water**) Schweppes® *m*

tonight [tə'naɪt] *adv, n* cette nuit; (*this evening*) ce soir

tonne [tʌn] *n* (*BRIT: metric ton*) tonne *f*

tonsil ['tɔnsl] *n* amygdale *f*; **tonsillitis** [tɔnsɪ'laɪtɪs] *n*: **to have tonsillitis** avoir une angine or une amygdalite

too [tuː] *adv* (*excessively*) trop; (*also*) aussi; **~ much** (*as adv*) trop; (*as adj*) trop de; **~ many** *adj* trop de

took [tuk] *pt of* **take**

tool [tuːl] *n* outil *m*; **tool box** *n* boîte *f* à outils; **tool kit** *n* trousse *f* à outils

tooth (*pl* **teeth**) [tuːθ, tiːθ] *n* (*Anat, Tech*) dent *f*; **to brush one's teeth** se laver les dents; **toothache** *n* mal *m* de dents; **to have**

toothache avoir mal aux dents; **toothbrush** n brosse f à dents; **toothpaste** n (pâte f) dentifrice m; **toothpick** n cure-dent m

top [tɒp] n (of mountain, head) sommet m; (of page, ladder) haut m; (of box, cupboard, table) dessus m; (lid: of box, jar) couvercle m; (: of bottle) bouchon m; (toy) toupie f; (Dress: blouse etc) haut; (: of pyjamas) veste f ▷ adj du haut; (in rank) premier(-ière); (best) meilleur(e) ▷ vt (exceed) dépasser; (be first in) être en tête de; **from ~ to bottom** de fond en comble; **on ~ of** sur; (in addition to) en plus de; **over the ~** (inf: behaviour etc) qui dépasse les limites; **top up** (us **top off**) vt (bottle) remplir; (salary) compléter; **to ~ up one's mobile (phone)** recharger son compte; **top floor** n dernier étage; **top hat** n haut-de-forme m

topic ['tɒpɪk] n sujet m, thème m; **topical** adj d'actualité

topless ['tɒplɪs] adj (bather etc) aux seins nus

topping ['tɒpɪŋ] n (Culin) couche de crème, fromage etc qui recouvre un plat

topple ['tɒpl] vt renverser, faire tomber ▷ vi basculer; tomber

top-up ['tɒpʌp] n (for mobile phone) recharge f, minutes fpl; **top-up card** n (for mobile phone) recharge f

torch [tɔːtʃ] n torche f; (BRIT: electric) lampe f de poche

tore [tɔːʳ] pt of **tear²**

torment n ['tɔːmɛnt] tourment m ▷ vt [tɔː'mɛnt] tourmenter; (fig: annoy) agacer

torn [tɔːn] pp of **tear²**

tornado [tɔː'neɪdəʊ] (pl **~es**) n tornade f

torpedo [tɔː'piːdəʊ] (pl **~es**) n torpille f

torrent ['tɒrnt] n torrent m; **torrential** [tɒ'rɛnʃl] adj torrentiel(le)

tortoise ['tɔːtəs] n tortue f

torture ['tɔːtʃəʳ] n torture f ▷ vt torturer

Tory ['tɔːrɪ] adj, n (BRIT Pol) tory m/f, conservateur(-trice)

toss [tɒs] vt lancer, jeter; (BRIT: pancake) faire sauter; (head) rejeter en arrière ▷ vi: **to ~ up for sth** (BRIT) jouer qch à pile ou face; **to ~ a coin** jouer à pile ou face; **to ~ and turn** (in bed) se tourner et se retourner

total ['təʊtl] adj total(e) ▷ n total m ▷ vt (add up) faire le total de, additionner; (amount to) s'élever à

totalitarian [təʊtælɪ'tɛərɪən] adj totalitaire

totally ['təʊtəlɪ] adv totalement

touch [tʌtʃ] n contact m, toucher m; (sense, skill: of pianist etc) toucher ▷ vt (gen) toucher; (tamper with) toucher à; **a ~ of** (fig) un petit peu de; une touche de; **to get in ~ with** prendre contact avec; **to lose ~** (friends) se perdre de vue; **touch down** vi (Aviat) atterrir; (on sea) amerrir; **touchdown** n (Aviat) atterrissage m; (on sea) amerrissage m; (us Football) essai m;

touched adj (moved) touché(e); **touching** adj touchant(e), attendrissant(e); **touchline** n (Sport) (ligne f de) touche f; **touch-sensitive** adj (keypad) à effleurement; (screen) tactile

tough [tʌf] adj dur(e); (resistant) résistant(e), solide; (meat) dur, coriace; (firm) inflexible; (task, problem, situation) difficile

tour ['tʊəʳ] n voyage m; (also: **package ~**) voyage organisé; (of town, museum) tour m, visite f; (by band) tournée f ▷ vt visiter; **tour guide** n (person) guide m/f

tourism ['tʊərɪzm] n tourisme m

tourist ['tʊərɪst] n touriste m/f ▷ cpd touristique; **tourist office** n syndicat m d'initiative

tournament ['tʊənəmənt] n tournoi m

tour operator n (BRIT) organisateur m de voyages, tour-opérateur m

tow [təʊ] vt remorquer; (caravan, trailer) tracter; **"on ~"**, (us) **"in ~"** (Aut) "véhicule en remorque"; **tow away** vt (subj: police) emmener à la fourrière; (: breakdown service) remorquer

toward(s) [tə'wɔːd(z)] prep vers; (of attitude) envers, à l'égard de; (of purpose) pour

towel ['taʊəl] n serviette f (de toilette); **towelling** n (fabric) tissu-éponge m

tower ['taʊəʳ] n tour f; **tower block** n (BRIT) tour f (d'habitation)

town [taʊn] n ville f; **to go to ~** aller en ville; (fig) y mettre le paquet; **town centre** n (BRIT) centre m de la ville, centre-ville m; **town hall** n ≈ mairie f

tow truck n (us) dépanneuse f

toxic ['tɒksɪk] adj toxique

toy [tɔɪ] n jouet m; **toy with** vt fus jouer avec; (idea) caresser; **toyshop** n magasin m de jouets

trace [treɪs] n trace f ▷ vt (draw) tracer, dessiner; (follow) suivre la trace de; (locate) retrouver

tracing paper ['treɪsɪŋ-] n papier-calque m

track [træk] n (mark) trace f; (path: gen) chemin m, piste f; (: of bullet etc) trajectoire f; (: of suspect, animal) piste; (Rail) voie ferrée, rails mpl; (on tape, Comput, Sport) piste; (on CD) piste f; (on record) plage f ▷ vt suivre la trace or la piste de; **to keep ~ of** suivre; **track down** vt (prey) trouver et capturer; (sth lost) finir par retrouver; **tracksuit** n survêtement m

tractor ['træktəʳ] n tracteur m

trade [treɪd] n commerce m; (skill, job) métier m ▷ vi faire du commerce ▷ vt (exchange): **to ~ sth (for sth)** échanger qch (contre qch); **to ~ with/in** faire du commerce avec/le commerce de; **trade in** vt (old car etc) faire reprendre; **trademark** n marque f de fabrique; **trader** n commerçant(e), négociant(e); **tradesman** (irreg) n (shopkeeper) commerçant m; **trade**

union n syndicat m

trading ['treɪdɪŋ] n affaires fpl, commerce m

tradition [trə'dɪʃən] n tradition f; **traditional** adj traditionnel(le)

traffic ['træfɪk] n trafic m; (cars) circulation f ▷ vi: **to ~ in** (pej: liquor, drugs) faire le trafic de; **traffic circle** n (us) rond-point m; **traffic island** n refuge m (pour piétons); **traffic jam** n embouteillage m; **traffic lights** npl feux mpl (de signalisation); **traffic warden** n contractuel(le)

tragedy ['trædʒədɪ] n tragédie f

tragic ['trædʒɪk] adj tragique

trail [treɪl] n (tracks) trace f, piste f; (path) chemin m, piste; (of smoke etc) traînée f ▷ vt (drag) traîner, tirer; (follow) suivre ▷ vi traîner; (in game, contest) être en retard; **trailer** n (Aut) remorque f; (us) caravane f; (Cine) bande-annonce f

train [treɪn] n train m; (in underground) rame f; (of dress) traîne f; (BRIT: series): **~ of events** série f d'événements ▷ vt (apprentice, doctor etc) former; (Sport) entraîner; (dog) dresser; (memory) exercer; (point: gun etc): **to ~ sth on** braquer qch sur ▷ vi recevoir sa formation; (Sport) s'entraîner; **one's ~ of thought** le fil de sa pensée; **what time does the ~ from Paris get in?** à quelle heure arrive le train de Paris?; **is this the ~ for ...?** c'est bien le train pour...?; **trainee** [treɪ'niː] n stagiaire m/f; (in trade) apprenti(e); **trainer** n (Sport) entraîneur(-euse); (of dogs etc) dresseur(-euse); **trainers** npl (shoes) chaussures fpl de sport; **training** n formation f; (Sport) entraînement m; (of dog etc) dressage m; **in training** (Sport) à l'entraînement; (fit) en forme; **training course** n cours m de formation professionnelle; **training shoes** npl chaussures fpl de sport

trait [treɪt] n trait m (de caractère)

traitor ['treɪtə^r] n traître m

tram [træm] n (BRIT: also: **~car**) tram(way) m

tramp [træmp] n (person) vagabond(e), clochard(e); (inf: pej: woman): **to be a ~** être coureuse

trample ['træmpl] vt: **to ~ (underfoot)** piétiner

trampoline ['træmpəliːn] n trampoline m

tranquil ['træŋkwɪl] adj tranquille; **tranquillizer** (us **tranquilizer**) n (Med) tranquillisant m

transaction [træn'zækʃən] n transaction f

transatlantic ['trænzət'læntɪk] adj transatlantique

transcript ['trænskrɪpt] n transcription f (texte)

transfer n ['trænsfə^r] (gen, also Sport) transfert m; (Pol: of power) passation f; (of money) virement m; (picture, design)

décalcomanie f; (: stick-on) autocollant m ▷ vt [træns'fəː^r] transférer; passer; virer; **to ~ the charges** (BRIT Tel) téléphoner en P.C.V.

transform [træns'fɔːm] vt transformer; **transformation** n transformation f

transfusion [træns'fjuːʒən] n transfusion f

transit ['trænzɪt] n: **in ~** en transit

transition [træn'zɪʃən] n transition f

transitive ['trænzɪtɪv] adj (Ling) transitif(-ive)

translate [trænz'leɪt] vt: **to ~ (from/into)** traduire (du/en); **can you ~ this for me?** pouvez-vous me traduire ceci?; **translation** [trænz'leɪʃən] n traduction f; (Scol: as opposed to prose) version f; **translator** n traducteur(-trice)

transmission [trænz'mɪʃən] n transmission f

transmit [trænz'mɪt] vt transmettre; (Radio, TV) émettre; **transmitter** n émetteur m

transparent [træns'pærnt] adj transparent(e)

transplant n ['trænsplɑːnt] (Med) transplantation f

transport n ['trænspɔːt] transport m ▷ vt [træns'pɔːt] transporter; **transportation** [trænspɔː'teɪʃən] n (moyen m de) transport m

transvestite [trænz'vɛstaɪt] n travesti(e)

trap [træp] n (snare, trick) piège m; (carriage) cabriolet m ▷ vt prendre au piège; (confine) coincer

trash [træʃ] n (pej: goods) camelote f; (: nonsense) sottises fpl; (us: rubbish) ordures fpl; **trash can** n (us) poubelle f

trauma ['trɔːmə] n traumatisme m; **traumatic** [trɔː'mætɪk] adj traumatisant(e)

travel ['trævl] n voyage(s) m(pl) ▷ vi voyager; (news, sound) se propager ▷ vt (distance) parcourir; **travel agency** n agence f de voyages; **travel agent** n agent m de voyages; **travel insurance** n assurance-voyage f; **traveller** (us **traveler**) n voyageur(-euse); **traveller's cheque** (us **traveler's check**) n chèque m de voyage; **travelling** (us **traveling**) n voyage(s) m(pl); **travel-sick** adj: **to get travel-sick** avoir le mal de la route (or de mer or de l'air); **travel sickness** n mal m de la route (or de mer or de l'air)

tray [treɪ] n (for carrying) plateau m; (on desk) corbeille f

treacherous ['trɛtʃərəs] adj traître(sse); (ground, tide) dont il faut se méfier

treacle ['triːkl] n mélasse f

tread [trɛd] n (step) pas m; (sound) bruit m de pas; (of tyre) chape f, bande f de roulement ▷ vi (pt **trod**, pp **trodden**) marcher; **tread on** vt fus marcher sur

treasure ['trɛʒə^r] n trésor m ▷ vt (value) tenir beaucoup à; **treasurer** n trésorier(-ière)

treasury ['trɛʒərɪ] n: **the T~**, (us) **the T~ Department** ≈ le ministère des Finances

treat [tri:t] n petit cadeau, petite surprise
▷ vt traiter; **to ~ sb to sth** offrir qch à qn;
treatment n traitement m

treaty ['tri:tɪ] n traité m

treble ['trɛbl] adj triple ▷ vt, vi tripler

tree [tri:] n arbre m

trek [trɛk] n (long walk) randonnée f; (tiring
walk) longue marche, trotte f

tremble ['trɛmbl] vi trembler

tremendous [trɪ'mɛndəs] adj (enormous)
énorme; (excellent) formidable, fantastique

trench [trɛntʃ] n tranchée f

trend [trɛnd] n (tendency) tendance f; (of
events) cours m; (fashion) mode f; **trendy** adj
(idea, person) dans le vent; (clothes) dernier
cri inv

trespass ['trɛspəs] vi: **to ~ on** s'introduire sans
permission dans; **"no ~ing"** "propriété privée",
"défense d'entrer"

trial ['traɪəl] n (Law) procès m, jugement
m; (test: of machine etc) essai m; **trials** npl
(unpleasant experiences) épreuves fpl; **trial
period** n période f d'essai

triangle ['traɪæŋgl] n (Math, Mus) triangle m

triangular [traɪ'æŋgjuləʳ] adj triangulaire

tribe [traɪb] n tribu f

tribunal [traɪ'bju:nl] n tribunal m

tribute ['trɪbju:t] n tribut m, hommage m; **to
pay ~ to** rendre hommage à

trick [trɪk] n (magic) tour m; (joke, prank) tour,
farce f; (skill, knack) astuce f; (Cards) levée f
▷ vt attraper, rouler; **to play a ~ on sb** jouer
un tour à qn; **that should do the ~** (fam) ça
devrait faire l'affaire

trickle ['trɪkl] n (of water etc) filet m ▷ vi couler
en un filet or goutte à goutte

tricky ['trɪkɪ] adj difficile, délicat(e)

tricycle ['traɪsɪkl] n tricycle m

trifle ['traɪfl] n bagatelle f; (Culin) ≈ diplomate
m ▷ adv: **a ~ long** un peu long

trigger ['trɪgəʳ] n (of gun) gâchette f

trim [trɪm] adj (house, garden) bien tenu(e);
(figure) svelte ▷ n (haircut etc) légère coupe;
(on car) garnitures fpl ▷ vt (cut) couper
légèrement; (decorate): **to ~ (with)** décorer
(de); (Naut: a sail) gréer

trio ['tri:əu] n trio m

trip [trɪp] n voyage m; (excursion) excursion
f; (stumble) faux pas ▷ vi faire un faux pas,
trébucher; **trip up** vi trébucher ▷ vt faire un
croc-en-jambe à

triple ['trɪpl] adj triple

triplets ['trɪplɪts] npl triplés(-ées)

tripod ['traɪpɔd] n trépied m

triumph ['traɪʌmf] n triomphe m ▷ vi: **to ~
(over)** triompher (de); **triumphant** [traɪ'ʌmfə
nt] adj triomphant(e)

trivial ['trɪvɪəl] adj insignifiant(e);
(commonplace) banal(e)

trod [trɔd] pt of **tread**

trodden ['trɔdn] pp of **tread**

trolley ['trɔlɪ] n chariot m

trombone [trɔm'bəun] n trombone m

troop [tru:p] n bande f, groupe m; **troops**
npl (Mil) troupes fpl; (: men) hommes mpl,
soldats mpl

trophy ['trəufɪ] n trophée m

tropical ['trɔpɪkl] adj tropical(e)

trot [trɔt] n trot m ▷ vi trotter; **on the ~** (BRIT:
fig) d'affilée

trouble ['trʌbl] n difficulté(s) f(pl), problème(s)
m(pl); (worry) ennuis mpl, soucis mpl; (bother,
effort) peine f; (Pol) conflit(s) m(pl), troubles
mpl; (Med): **stomach** etc **~** troubles gastriques
etc ▷ vt (disturb) déranger, gêner; (worry)
inquiéter ▷ vi: **to ~ to do** prendre la peine de
faire; **troubles** npl (Pol etc) troubles; (personal)
ennuis, soucis; **to be in ~** avoir des ennuis;
(ship, climber etc) être en difficulté; **to have ~
doing sth** avoir du mal à faire qch; **it's no ~!**
je vous en prie!; **the ~ is ...** le problème, c'est
que ...; **what's the ~?** qu'est-ce qui ne va
pas?; **troubled** adj (person) inquiet(-ète);
(times, life) agité(e); **troublemaker** n
élément perturbateur, fauteur m de troubles;
troublesome adj (child) fatigant(e), difficile;
(cough) gênant(e)

trough [trɔf] n (also: **drinking ~**) abreuvoir m;
(also: **feeding ~**) auge f; (depression) creux m

trousers ['trauzəz] npl pantalon m; **short ~**
(BRIT) culottes courtes

trout [traut] n (pl inv) truite f

trowel ['trauəl] n truelle f; (garden tool)
déplantoir m

truant ['truənt] n: **to play ~** (BRIT) faire l'école
buissonnière

truce [tru:s] n trêve f

truck [trʌk] n camion m; (Rail) wagon m à
plate-forme; **truck driver** n camionneur m

true [tru:] adj vrai(e); (accurate) exact(e);
(genuine) vrai, véritable; (faithful) fidèle; **to
come ~** se réaliser

truly ['tru:lɪ] adv vraiment, réellement;
(truthfully) sans mentir; **yours ~** (in letter) je
vous prie d'agréer, Monsieur (or Madame etc),
l'expression de mes sentiments respectueux

trumpet ['trʌmpɪt] n trompette f

trunk [trʌŋk] n (of tree, person) tronc m; (of
elephant) trompe f; (case) malle f; (us Aut) coffre
m; **trunks** npl (also: **swimming ~s**) maillot m
or slip m de bain

trust [trʌst] n confiance f; (responsibility): **to
place sth in sb's ~** confier la responsabilité
de qch à qn; (Law) fidéicommis m ▷ vt (rely on)
avoir confiance en; (entrust): **to ~ sth to sb**
confier qch à qn; (hope): **to ~ (that)** espérer
(que); **to take sth on ~** accepter qch les yeux
fermés; **trusted** adj en qui l'on a confiance;

trustworthy adj digne de confiance

truth [tru:θ, (pl) tru:ðz] n vérité f; **truthful** adj (person) qui dit la vérité; (answer) sincère

try [traɪ] n essai m, tentative f; (Rugby) essai ▷ vt (attempt) essayer, tenter; (test: sth new: also: ~ **out**) essayer, tester; (Law: person) juger; (strain) éprouver ▷ vi essayer; **to ~ to do** essayer de faire; (seek) chercher à faire; **try on** vt (clothes) essayer; **trying** adj pénible

T-shirt ['tiːʃəːt] n tee-shirt m

tub [tʌb] n cuve f; (for washing clothes) baquet m; (bath) baignoire f

tube [tjuːb] n tube m; (BRIT: underground) métro m; (for tyre) chambre f à air

tuberculosis [tjubə:kjuˈləusɪs] n tuberculose f

tube station n (BRIT) station f de métro

tuck [tʌk] vt (put) mettre; **tuck away** vt cacher, ranger; (money) mettre de côté; (building): **to be ~ed away** être caché(e); **tuck in** vt rentrer; (child) border ▷ vi (eat) manger de bon appétit; attaquer le repas; **tuck shop** n (BRIT Scol) boutique f à provisions

Tue(s) abbr (= Tuesday) ma

Tuesday ['tjuːzdɪ] n mardi m

tug [tʌg] n (ship) remorqueur m ▷ vt tirer (sur)

tuition [tjuːˈɪʃən] n (BRIT: lessons) leçons fpl; (: private) cours particuliers; (US: fees) frais mpl de scolarité

tulip ['tjuːlɪp] n tulipe f

tumble ['tʌmbl] n (fall) chute f, culbute f ▷ vi tomber, dégringoler; **to ~ to sth** (inf) réaliser qch; **tumble dryer** n (BRIT) séchoir m (à linge) à air chaud

tumbler ['tʌmbləʳ] n verre (droit), gobelet m

tummy ['tʌmɪ] n (inf) ventre m

tumour (US **tumor**) ['tjuːməʳ] n tumeur f

tuna ['tjuːnə] n (pl inv: also: ~ **fish**) thon m

tune [tjuːn] n (melody) air m ▷ vt (Mus) accorder; (Radio, TV, Aut) régler, mettre au point; **to be in/out of ~** (instrument) être accordé/désaccordé; (singer) chanter juste/faux; **tune in** vi (Radio, TV): **to ~ in (to)** se mettre à l'écoute (de); **tune up** vi (musician) accorder son instrument

tunic ['tjuːnɪk] n tunique f

Tunis ['tjuːnɪs] n Tunis

Tunisia [tjuːˈnɪzɪə] n Tunisie f

Tunisian [tjuːˈnɪzɪən] adj tunisien(ne) ▷ n Tunisien(ne)

tunnel ['tʌnl] n tunnel m; (in mine) galerie f ▷ vi creuser un tunnel (or une galerie)

turbulence ['təːbjuləns] n (Aviat) turbulence f

turf [təːf] n gazon m; (clod) motte f (de gazon) ▷ vt gazonner

Turk [təːk] n Turc (Turque)

Turkey ['təːkɪ] n Turquie f

turkey ['təːkɪ] n dindon m, dinde f

Turkish ['təːkɪʃ] adj turc (turque) ▷ n (Ling)

turc m

turmoil ['təːmɔɪl] n trouble m, bouleversement m

turn [təːn] n tour m; (in road) tournant m; (tendency: of mind, events) tournure f; (performance) numéro m; (Med) crise f, attaque f ▷ vt tourner; (collar, steak) retourner; (change): **to ~ sth into** changer qch en; (age) atteindre ▷ vi (object, wind, milk) tourner; (person: look back) se (re)tourner; (reverse direction) faire demi-tour; (become) devenir; **to ~ into** se changer en, se transformer en; **a good ~** un service; **it gave me quite a ~** ça m'a fait un coup; **"no left ~"** (Aut) "défense de tourner à gauche"; **~ left/right at the next junction** tournez à gauche/droite au prochain carrefour; **it's your ~** c'est (à) votre tour; **in ~** à son tour; à tour de rôle; **to take ~s** se relayer; **turn around** vi (person) se retourner ▷ vt (object) tourner; **turn away** vi se détourner, tourner la tête ▷ vt (reject: person) renvoyer; (: business) refuser; **turn back** vi revenir, faire demi-tour; **turn down** vt (refuse) rejeter, refuser; (reduce) baisser; (fold) rabattre; **turn in** vi (inf: go to bed) aller se coucher ▷ vt (fold) rentrer; **turn off** vi (from road) tourner ▷ vt (light, radio etc) éteindre; (tap) fermer; (engine) arrêter; **I can't ~ the heating off** je n'arrive pas à éteindre le chauffage; **turn on** vt (light, radio etc) allumer; (tap) ouvrir; (engine) mettre en marche; **I can't ~ the heating on** je n'arrive pas à allumer le chauffage; **turn out** vt (light, gas) éteindre; (produce) produire ▷ vi (voters, troops) se présenter; **to ~ out to be ...** s'avérer ..., se révéler ...; **turn over** vi (person) se retourner ▷ vt (object) retourner; (page) tourner; **turn round** vi faire demi-tour; (rotate) tourner; **turn to** vt fus: **to ~ to sb** s'adresser à qn; **turn up** vi (person) arriver, se pointer (inf); (lost object) être retrouvé(e) ▷ vt (collar) remonter; (radio, heater) mettre plus fort; **turning** n (in road) tournant m; **turning point** n (fig) tournant m, moment décisif

turnip ['təːnɪp] n navet m

turn: **turnout** n (of voters) taux m de participation; **turnover** n (Comm: amount of money) chiffre m d'affaires; (: of goods) roulement m; (of staff) renouvellement m, changement m; **turnstile** n tourniquet m (d'entrée); **turn-up** n (BRIT: on trousers) revers m

turquoise ['təːkwɔɪz] n (stone) turquoise f ▷ adj turquoise inv

turtle ['təːtl] n tortue marine; **turtleneck (sweater)** n pullover m à col montant

tusk [tʌsk] n défense f (d'éléphant)

tutor ['tjuːtəʳ] n (BRIT Scol: in college) directeur(-trice) d'études; (private teacher) précepteur(-trice); **tutorial** [tjuːˈtɔːrɪəl] n (Scol) (séance f de) travaux mpl pratiques

tuxedo [tʌkˈsiːdəu] n (US) smoking m
TV [tiːˈviː] n abbr (= television) télé f, TV f
tweed [twiːd] n tweed m
tweezers [ˈtwiːzəz] npl pince f à épiler
twelfth [twɛlfθ] num douzième
twelve [twɛlv] num douze; **at ~ (o'clock)** à midi; (midnight) à minuit
twentieth [ˈtwɛntɪɪθ] num vingtième
twenty [ˈtwɛntɪ] num vingt
twice [twaɪs] adv deux fois; **~ as much** deux fois plus
twig [twɪg] n brindille f ▷ vt, vi (inf) piger
twilight [ˈtwaɪlaɪt] n crépuscule m
twin [twɪn] adj, n jumeau(-elle) ▷ vt jumeler; **twin(-bedded) room** n chambre f à deux lits; **twin beds** npl lits mpl jumeaux
twinkle [ˈtwɪŋkl] vi scintiller; (eyes) pétiller
twist [twɪst] n torsion f, tour m; (in wire, flex) tortillon m; (bend: in road) tournant m; (in story) coup m de théâtre ▷ vt tordre; (weave) entortiller; (roll around) enrouler; (fig) déformer ▷ vi (road, river) serpenter; **to ~ one's ankle/wrist** (Med) se tordre la cheville/le poignet
twit [twɪt] n (inf) crétin(e)
twitch [twɪtʃ] n (pull) coup sec, saccade f; (nervous) tic m ▷ vi se convulser; avoir un tic
two [tuː] num deux; **to put ~ and ~ together** (fig) faire le rapprochement
type [taɪp] n (category) genre m, espèce f; (model) modèle m; (example) type m; (Typ) type, caractère m ▷ vt (letter etc) taper (à la machine); **typewriter** n machine f à écrire
typhoid [ˈtaɪfɔɪd] n typhoïde f
typhoon [taɪˈfuːn] n typhon m
typical [ˈtɪpɪkl] adj typique, caractéristique; **typically** adv (as usual) comme d'habitude; (characteristically) typiquement
typing [ˈtaɪpɪŋ] n dactylo(graphie) f
typist [ˈtaɪpɪst] n dactylo m/f
tyre (US **tire**) [ˈtaɪəʳ] n pneu m; **I've got a flat ~** j'ai un pneu crevé; **tyre pressure** n (BRIT) pression f (de gonflage)

UFO [ˈjuːfəu] n abbr (= unidentified flying object) ovni m
Uganda [juːˈgændə] n Ouganda m
ugly [ˈʌglɪ] adj laid(e), vilain(e); (fig) répugnant(e)
UHT adj abbr = **ultra-heat treated**; **~ milk** lait m UHT or longue conservation
UK n abbr = **United Kingdom**
ulcer [ˈʌlsəʳ] n ulcère m; **mouth ~** aphte f
ultimate [ˈʌltɪmət] adj ultime, final(e); (authority) suprême; **ultimately** adv (at last) en fin de compte; (fundamentally) finalement; (eventually) par la suite
ultimatum (pl **~s** or **ultimata**) [ʌltɪˈmeɪtəm, -tə] n ultimatum m
ultrasound [ˈʌltrəsaund] n (Med) ultrason m
ultraviolet [ˈʌltrəˈvaɪəlɪt] adj ultraviolet(te)
umbrella [ʌmˈbrɛlə] n parapluie m; (for sun) parasol m
umpire [ˈʌmpaɪəʳ] n arbitre m; (Tennis) juge m de chaise
UN n abbr = **United Nations**
unable [ʌnˈeɪbl] adj: **to be ~ to** ne (pas) pouvoir, être dans l'impossibilité de; (not capable) être incapable de
unacceptable [ʌnəkˈsɛptəbl] adj (behaviour) inadmissible; (price, proposal) inacceptable
unanimous [juːˈnænɪməs] adj unanime
unarmed [ʌnˈɑːmd] adj (person) non armé(e); (combat) sans armes

u

unattended [ʌnə'tɛndɪd] adj (car, child, luggage) sans surveillance

unattractive [ʌnə'træktɪv] adj peu attrayant(e); (character) peu sympathique

unavailable [ʌnə'veɪləbl] adj (article, room, book) (qui n'est) pas disponible; (person) (qui n'est) pas libre

unavoidable [ʌnə'vɔɪdəbl] adj inévitable

unaware [ʌnə'wɛəʳ] adj: **to be ~ of** ignorer, ne pas savoir, être inconscient(e) de; **unawares** adv à l'improviste, au dépourvu

unbearable [ʌn'bɛərəbl] adj insupportable

unbeatable [ʌn'biːtəbl] adj imbattable

unbelievable [ʌnbɪ'liːvəbl] adj incroyable

unborn [ʌn'bɔːn] adj à naître

unbutton [ʌn'bʌtn] vt déboutonner

uncalled-for [ʌn'kɔːldfɔːʳ] adj déplacé(e), injustifié(e)

uncanny [ʌn'kænɪ] adj étrange, troublant(e)

uncertain [ʌn'səːtn] adj incertain(e); (hesitant) hésitant(e); **uncertainty** n incertitude f, doutes mpl

unchanged [ʌn'tʃeɪndʒd] adj inchangé(e)

uncle ['ʌŋkl] n oncle m

unclear [ʌn'klɪəʳ] adj (qui n'est) pas clair(e) or évident(e); **I'm still ~ about what I'm supposed to do** je ne sais pas encore exactement ce que je dois faire

uncomfortable [ʌn'kʌmfətəbl] adj inconfortable, peu confortable; (uneasy) mal à l'aise, gêné(e); (situation) désagréable

uncommon [ʌn'kɔmən] adj rare, singulier(-ière), peu commun(e)

unconditional [ʌnkən'dɪʃənl] adj sans conditions

unconscious [ʌn'kɔnʃəs] adj sans connaissance, évanoui(e); (unaware): **~ (of)** inconscient(e) (de) ▷ n: **the ~** l'inconscient m

uncontrollable [ʌnkən'trəuləbl] adj (child, dog) indiscipliné(e); (temper, laughter) irrépressible

unconventional [ʌnkən'vɛnʃənl] adj peu conventionnel(le)

uncover [ʌn'kʌvəʳ] vt découvrir

undecided [ʌndɪ'saɪdɪd] adj indécis(e), irrésolu(e)

undeniable [ʌndɪ'naɪəbl] adj indéniable, incontestable

under ['ʌndəʳ] prep sous; (less than) (de) moins de; au-dessous de; (according to) selon, en vertu de ▷ adv au-dessous; en dessous; **~ there** là-dessous; **~ the circumstances** étant donné les circonstances; **~ repair** en (cours de) réparation; **undercover** adj secret(-ète), clandestin(e); **underdone** adj (Culin) saignant(e); (: pej) pas assez cuit(e); **underestimate** vt sous-estimer, mésestimer; **undergo** vt (irreg: like **go**) subir; (treatment) suivre; **undergraduate** n étudiant(e)

(qui prépare la licence); **underground** adj souterrain(e); (fig) clandestin(e) ▷ n (BRIT: railway) métro m; (Pol) clandestinité f;

undergrowth n broussailles fpl, sous-bois m;

underline vt souligner; **undermine** vt saper, miner; **underneath** [ʌndə'niːθ] adv (en) dessous ▷ prep sous, au-dessous de;

underpants npl caleçon m, slip m; **underpass** n (BRIT: for pedestrians) passage souterrain; (: for cars) passage inférieur; **underprivileged** adj défavorisé(e); **underscore** vt souligner;

undershirt n (US) tricot m de corps;

underskirt n (BRIT) jupon m

understand [ʌndə'stænd] vt, vi (irreg: like **stand**) comprendre; **I don't ~** je ne comprends pas; **understandable** adj compréhensible; **understanding** adj compréhensif(-ive) ▷ n compréhension f; (agreement) accord m

understatement ['ʌndəsteɪtmənt] n: **that's an ~** c'est (bien) peu dire, le terme est faible

understood [ʌndə'stud] pt, pp of **understand** ▷ adj entendu(e); (implied) sous-entendu(e)

undertake [ʌndə'teɪk] vt (irreg: like **take**) (job, task) entreprendre; (duty) se charger de; **to ~ to do sth** s'engager à faire qch

undertaker ['ʌndəteɪkəʳ] n (BRIT) entrepreneur m des pompes funèbres, croque-mort m

undertaking ['ʌndəteɪkɪŋ] n entreprise f; (promise) promesse f

under: **underwater** adv sous l'eau ▷ adj sous-marin(e); **underway** adj: **to be underway** (meeting, investigation) être en cours; **underwear** n sous-vêtements mpl; (women's only) dessous mpl; **underwent** pt of **undergo**; **underworld** n (of crime) milieu m, pègre f

undesirable [ʌndɪ'zaɪərəbl] adj peu souhaitable; (person, effect) indésirable

undisputed ['ʌndɪs'pjuːtɪd] adj incontesté(e)

undo [ʌn'duː] vt (irreg: like **do**) défaire

undone [ʌn'dʌn] pp of **undo** ▷ adj: **to come ~** se défaire

undoubtedly [ʌn'dautɪdlɪ] adv sans aucun doute

undress [ʌn'drɛs] vi se déshabiller

unearth [ʌn'əːθ] vt déterrer; (fig) dénicher

uneasy [ʌn'iːzɪ] adj mal à l'aise, gêné(e); (worried) inquiet(-ète); (feeling) désagréable; (peace, truce) fragile

unemployed [ʌnɪm'plɔɪd] adj sans travail, au chômage ▷ n: **the ~** les chômeurs mpl

unemployment [ʌnɪm'plɔɪmənt] n chômage m; **unemployment benefit** (US **unemployment compensation**) n allocation f de chômage

unequal [ʌn'iːkwəl] adj inégal(e)

uneven [ʌn'iːvn] adj inégal(e); (quality, work)

irrégulier(-ière)

unexpected [ʌnɪk'spɛktɪd] *adj* inattendu(e), imprévu(e); **unexpectedly** *adv* (*succeed*) contre toute attente; (*arrive*) à l'improviste

unfair [ʌn'fɛəʳ] *adj*: **~ (to)** injuste (envers)

unfaithful [ʌn'feɪθful] *adj* infidèle

unfamiliar [ʌnfə'mɪlɪəʳ] *adj* étrange, inconnu(e); **to be ~ with sth** mal connaître qch

unfashionable [ʌn'fæʃnəbl] *adj* (*clothes*) démodé(e); (*place*) peu chic *inv*

unfasten [ʌn'fɑːsn] *vt* défaire; (*belt, necklace*) détacher; (*open*) ouvrir

unfavourable (*us* **unfavorable**) [ʌn'feɪvrəbl] *adj* défavorable

unfinished [ʌn'fɪnɪʃt] *adj* inachevé(e)

unfit [ʌn'fɪt] *adj* (*physically*: *ill*) en mauvaise santé; (: *out of condition*) pas en forme; (*incompetent*): **~ (for)** impropre (à); (*work, service*) inapte (à)

unfold [ʌn'fəʊld] *vt* déplier ▷ *vi* se dérouler

unforgettable [ʌnfə'gɛtəbl] *adj* inoubliable

unfortunate [ʌn'fɔːtʃnət] *adj* malheureux(-euse); (*event, remark*) malencontreux(-euse); **unfortunately** *adv* malheureusement

unfriendly [ʌn'frɛndlɪ] *adj* peu aimable, froid(e)

unfurnished [ʌn'fə:nɪʃt] *adj* non meublé(e)

unhappiness [ʌn'hæpɪnɪs] *n* tristesse *f*, peine *f*

unhappy [ʌn'hæpɪ] *adj* triste, malheureux(-euse); (*unfortunate*: *remark etc*) malheureux(-euse); (*not pleased*): **~ with** mécontent(e) de, peu satisfait(e) de

unhealthy [ʌn'hɛlθɪ] *adj* (*gen*) malsain(e); (*person*) maladif(-ive)

unheard-of [ʌn'hə:dɔv] *adj* inouï(e), sans précédent

unhelpful [ʌn'hɛlpful] *adj* (*person*) peu serviable; (*advice*) peu utile

unhurt [ʌn'hə:t] *adj* indemne, sain(e) et sauf (sauve)

unidentified [ʌnaɪ'dɛntɪfaɪd] *adj* non identifié(e); *see also* **UFO**

uniform ['ju:nɪfɔ:m] *n* uniforme *m* ▷ *adj* uniforme

unify ['ju:nɪfaɪ] *vt* unifier

unimportant [ʌnɪm'pɔ:tənt] *adj* sans importance

uninhabited [ʌnɪn'hæbɪtɪd] *adj* inhabité(e)

unintentional [ʌnɪn'tɛnʃənəl] *adj* involontaire

union ['ju:njən] *n* union *f*; (*also*: **trade ~**) syndicat *m* ▷ *cpd* du syndicat, syndical(e); **Union Jack** *n* drapeau du Royaume-Uni

unique [ju:'ni:k] *adj* unique

unisex ['ju:nɪsɛks] *adj* unisexe

unit ['ju:nɪt] *n* unité *f*; (*section*: *of furniture etc*)

élément *m*, bloc *m*; (*team, squad*) groupe *m*, service *m*; **kitchen ~** élément de cuisine

unite [ju:'naɪt] *vt* unir ▷ *vi* s'unir; **united** *adj* uni(e); (*country, party*) unifié(e); (*efforts*) conjugué(e); **United Kingdom** *n* Royaume-Uni *m* (R.U.); **United Nations (Organization)** *n* (Organisation *f* des) Nations unies (ONU); **United States (of America)** *n* États-Unis *mpl*

unity ['ju:nɪtɪ] *n* unité *f*

universal [ju:nɪ'və:sl] *adj* universel(le)

universe ['ju:nɪvə:s] *n* univers *m*

university [ju:nɪ'və:sɪtɪ] *n* université *f* ▷ *cpd* (*student, professor*) d'université; (*education, year, degree*) universitaire

unjust [ʌn'dʒʌst] *adj* injuste

unkind [ʌn'kaɪnd] *adj* peu gentil(le), méchant(e)

unknown [ʌn'nəun] *adj* inconnu(e)

unlawful [ʌn'lɔ:ful] *adj* illégal(e)

unleaded [ʌn'lɛdɪd] *n* (*also*: **~ petrol**) essence *f* sans plomb

unleash [ʌn'li:ʃ] *vt* (*fig*) déchaîner, déclencher

unless [ʌn'lɛs] *conj*: **~ he leaves** à moins qu'il (ne) parte; **~ otherwise stated** sauf indication contraire

unlike [ʌn'laɪk] *adj* dissemblable, différent(e) ▷ *prep* à la différence de, contrairement à

unlikely [ʌn'laɪklɪ] *adj* (*result, event*) improbable; (*explanation*) invraisemblable

unlimited [ʌn'lɪmɪtɪd] *adj* illimité(e)

unlisted ['ʌn'lɪstɪd] *adj* (*us Tel*) sur la liste rouge

unload [ʌn'ləud] *vt* décharger

unlock [ʌn'lɔk] *vt* ouvrir

unlucky [ʌn'lʌkɪ] *adj* (*person*) malchanceux(-euse); (*object, number*) qui porte malheur; **to be ~** (*person*) ne pas avoir de chance

unmarried [ʌn'mærɪd] *adj* célibataire

unmistak(e)able [ʌnmɪs'teɪkəbl] *adj* indubitable; qu'on ne peut pas ne pas reconnaître

unnatural [ʌn'nætʃrəl] *adj* non naturel(le); (*perversion*) contre nature

unnecessary [ʌn'nɛsəsərɪ] *adj* inutile, superflu(e)

UNO ['ju:nəu] *n abbr* = **United Nations Organization**

unofficial [ʌnə'fɪʃl] *adj* (*news*) officieux(-euse), non officiel(le); (*strike*) ≈ sauvage

unpack [ʌn'pæk] *vi* défaire sa valise ▷ *vt* (*suitcase*) défaire; (*belongings*) déballer

unpaid [ʌn'peɪd] *adj* (*bill*) impayé(e); (*holiday*) non-payé(e), sans salaire; (*work*) non rétribué(e)

unpleasant [ʌn'plɛznt] *adj* déplaisant(e), désagréable

unplug [ʌn'plʌg] *vt* débrancher

unpopular [ʌn'pɔpjuləʳ] *adj* impopulaire

u

unprecedented [ʌn'prɛsɪdɛntɪd] adj sans précédent

unpredictable [ʌnprɪ'dɪktəbl] adj imprévisible

unprotected ['ʌnprə'tɛktɪd] adj (sex) non protégé(e)

unqualified [ʌn'kwɔlɪfaɪd] adj (teacher) non diplômé(e), sans titres; (success) sans réserve, total(e); (disaster) total(e)

unravel [ʌn'rævl] vt démêler

unreal [ʌn'rɪəl] adj irréel(le); (extraordinary) incroyable

unrealistic ['ʌnrɪə'lɪstɪk] adj (idea) irréaliste; (estimate) peu réaliste

unreasonable [ʌn'riːznəbl] adj qui n'est pas raisonnable

unrelated [ʌnrɪ'leɪtɪd] adj sans rapport; (people) sans lien de parenté

unreliable [ʌnrɪ'laɪəbl] adj sur qui (or quoi) on ne peut pas compter, peu fiable

unrest [ʌn'rɛst] n agitation f, troubles mpl

unroll [ʌn'rəʊl] vt dérouler

unruly [ʌn'ruːlɪ] adj indiscipliné(e)

unsafe [ʌn'seɪf] adj (in danger) en danger; (journey, car) dangereux(-euse)

unsatisfactory ['ʌnsætɪs'fæktərɪ] adj peu satisfaisant(e)

unscrew [ʌn'skruː] vt dévisser

unsettled [ʌn'sɛtld] adj (restless) perturbé(e); (unpredictable) instable; incertain(e); (not finalized) non résolu(e)

unsettling [ʌn'sɛtlɪŋ] adj qui a un effet perturbateur

unsightly [ʌn'saɪtlɪ] adj disgracieux(-euse), laid(e)

unskilled [ʌn'skɪld] adj: ~ worker manœuvre m

unspoiled ['ʌn'spɔɪld], **unspoilt** ['ʌn'spɔɪlt] adj (place) non dégradé(e)

unstable [ʌn'steɪbl] adj instable

unsteady [ʌn'stɛdɪ] adj mal assuré(e), chancelant(e), instable

unsuccessful [ʌnsək'sɛsful] adj (attempt) infructueux(-euse); (writer, proposal) qui n'a pas de succès; **to be ~** (in attempting sth) ne pas réussir; ne pas avoir de succès; (application) ne pas être retenu(e)

unsuitable [ʌn'suːtəbl] adj qui ne convient pas, peu approprié(e); (time) inopportun(e)

unsure [ʌn'fʊəʳ] adj pas sûr(e); **to be ~ of o.s.** ne pas être sûr de soi, manquer de confiance en soi

untidy [ʌn'taɪdɪ] adj (room) en désordre; (appearance, person) débraillé(e); (person: in character) sans ordre, désordonné(e); (work) peu soigné(e)

untie [ʌn'taɪ] vt (knot, parcel) défaire; (prisoner, dog) détacher

until [ən'tɪl] prep jusqu'à; (after negative) avant ▷ conj jusqu'à ce que + sub; (in past, after negative) avant que + sub; **~ he comes** jusqu'à ce qu'il vienne, jusqu'à son arrivée; **~ now** jusqu'à présent, jusqu'ici; **~ then** jusque-là

untrue [ʌn'truː] adj (statement) faux (fausse)

unused¹ [ʌn'juːzd] adj (new) neuf (neuve)

unused² [ʌn'juːst] adj: **to be ~ to sth/to doing sth** ne pas avoir l'habitude de qch/de faire qch

unusual [ʌn'juːʒuəl] adj insolite, exceptionnel(le), rare; **unusually** adv exceptionnellement, particulièrement

unveil [ʌn'veɪl] vt dévoiler

unwanted [ʌn'wɔntɪd] adj (child, pregnancy) non désiré(e); (clothes etc) à donner

unwell [ʌn'wɛl] adj souffrant(e); **to feel ~** ne pas se sentir bien

unwilling [ʌn'wɪlɪŋ] adj: **to be ~ to do** ne pas vouloir faire

unwind [ʌn'waɪnd] vb (irreg: like **wind**) ▷ vt dérouler ▷ vi (relax) se détendre

unwise [ʌn'waɪz] adj imprudent(e), peu judicieux(-euse)

unwittingly [ʌn'wɪtɪŋlɪ] adv involontairement

unwrap [ʌn'ræp] vt défaire; ouvrir

unzip [ʌn'zɪp] vt ouvrir (la fermeture éclair de); (Comput) dézipper

○ **KEYWORD**

up [ʌp] prep: **he went up the stairs/the hill** il a monté l'escalier/la colline; **the cat was up a tree** le chat était dans un arbre; **they live further up the street** ils habitent plus haut dans la rue; **go up that road and turn left** remontez la rue et tournez à gauche
▷ adv 1 en haut; en l'air; (upwards, higher): **up in the sky/the mountains** (là-haut) dans le ciel/les montagnes; **put it a bit higher up** mettez-le un peu plus haut; **to stand up** (get up) se lever, se mettre debout; (be standing) être debout; **up there** là-haut; **up above** au-dessus
2: **to be up** (out of bed) être levé(e); (prices) avoir augmenté or monté; (finished): **when the year was up** à la fin de l'année
3: **up to** (as far as) jusqu'à; **up to now** jusqu'à présent
4: **to be up to** (depending on): **it's up to you** c'est à vous de décider; (equal to): **he's not up to it** (job, task etc) il n'en est pas capable; (inf: be doing): **what is he up to?** qu'est-ce qu'il peut bien faire?
▷ n: **ups and downs** hauts et bas mpl

up-and-coming [ʌpənd'kʌmɪŋ] adj plein(e) d'avenir or de promesses

upbringing ['ʌpbrɪŋɪŋ] n éducation f

update [ʌpˈdeɪt] vt mettre à jour

upfront [ʌpˈfrʌnt] adj (open) franc (franche)
▷ adv (pay) d'avance; **to be ~ about sth** ne rien
cacher de qch

upgrade [ʌpˈɡreɪd] vt (person) promouvoir;
(job) revaloriser; (property, equipment)
moderniser

upheaval [ʌpˈhiːvl] n bouleversement m; (in
room) branle-bas m; (event) crise f

uphill [ʌpˈhɪl] adj qui monte; (fig: task) difficile,
pénible ▷ adv (face, look) en amont, vers
l'amont; **to go ~** monter

upholstery [ʌpˈhəʊlstərɪ] n rembourrage
m; (cover) tissu m d'ameublement; (of car)
garniture f

upmarket [ʌpˈmɑːkɪt] adj (product) haut de
gamme inv; (area) chic inv

upon [əˈpɒn] prep sur

upper [ˈʌpəʳ] adj supérieur(e); du dessus ▷ n (of
shoe) empeigne f; **upper-class** adj de la haute
société, aristocratique; (district) élégant(e),
huppé(e); (accent, attitude) caractéristique des
classes supérieures

upright [ˈʌpraɪt] adj droit(e); (fig) droit,
honnête

uprising [ˈʌpraɪzɪŋ] n soulèvement m,
insurrection f

uproar [ˈʌprɔːʳ] n tumulte m, vacarme m;
(protests) protestations fpl

upset n [ˈʌpsɛt] dérangement m ▷ vt (irreg:
like **set** [ʌpˈsɛt]) (glass etc) renverser; (plan)
déranger; (person: offend) contrarier; (: grieve)
faire de la peine à; bouleverser ▷ adj [ʌpˈsɛt]
contrarié(e); peiné(e); **to have a stomach ~**
(BRIT) avoir une indigestion

upside down [ˈʌpsaɪd-] adv à l'envers; **to
turn sth ~** (fig: place) mettre sens dessus
dessous

upstairs [ʌpˈstɛəz] adv en haut ▷ adj (room) du
dessus, d'en haut ▷ n: **the ~** l'étage m

up-to-date [ˈʌptəˈdeɪt] adj moderne;
(information) très récent(e)

uptown [ˈʌptaʊn] (US) adv (live) dans les
quartiers chics; (go) vers les quartiers chics
▷ adj des quartiers chics

upward [ˈʌpwəd] adj ascendant(e); vers le
haut; **upward(s)** adv vers le haut; (more than):
upward(s) of plus de

uranium [juəˈreɪnɪəm] n uranium m

Uranus [juəˈreɪnəs] n Uranus f

urban [ˈəːbən] adj urbain(e)

urge [əːdʒ] n besoin (impératif), envie
(pressante) ▷ vt (person): **to ~ sb to do**
exhorter qn à faire, pousser qn à faire,
recommander vivement à qn de faire

urgency [ˈəːdʒənsɪ] n urgence f; (of tone)
insistance f

urgent [ˈəːdʒənt] adj urgent(e); (plea, tone)
pressant(e)

urinal [ˈjuərɪnl] n (BRIT: place) urinoir m

urinate [ˈjuərɪneɪt] vi uriner

urine [ˈjuərɪn] n urine f

URL abbr (= uniform resource locator) URL f

US n abbr = **United States**

us [ʌs] pron nous; see also **me**

USA n abbr = **United States of America**

use n [juːs] emploi m, utilisation f; (usefulness)
utilité f ▷ vt [juːz] se servir de, utiliser,
employer; **in ~** en usage; **out of ~** hors d'usage;
to be of ~ servir, être utile; **it's no ~** ça ne
sert à rien; **to have the ~ of** avoir l'usage de;
she ~d to do it elle le faisait (autrefois), elle
avait coutume de le faire; **to be ~d to** avoir
l'habitude de, être habitué(e) à; **use up** vt
finir, épuiser; (food) consommer; **used** [juːzd] adj (car) d'occasion; **useful** adj utile;
useless adj inutile; (inf: person) nul(le); **user** n
utilisateur(-trice), usager m; **user-friendly** adj
convivial(e), facile d'emploi

usual [ˈjuːʒuəl] adj habituel(le); **as ~** comme
d'habitude; **usually** adv d'habitude,
d'ordinaire

utensil [juːˈtɛnsl] n ustensile m; **kitchen ~s**
batterie f de cuisine

utility [juːˈtɪlɪtɪ] n utilité f; (also: **public ~**)
service public

utilize [ˈjuːtɪlaɪz] vt utiliser; (make good use of)
exploiter

utmost [ˈʌtməʊst] adj extrême, le (la) plus
grand(e) ▷ n: **to do one's ~** faire tout son
possible

utter [ˈʌtəʳ] adj total(e), complet(-ète) ▷ vt
prononcer, proférer; (sounds) émettre; **utterly**
adv complètement, totalement

U-turn [ˈjuːˈtəːn] n demi-tour m; (fig) volte-
face f inv

V

v. *abbr* = **verse** (= *vide*) v.; (= *versus*) c.; (= *volt*) V

vacancy ['veɪkənsɪ] *n* (BRIT: *job*) poste vacant; (*room*) chambre *f* disponible; **"no vacancies"** "complet"

vacant ['veɪkənt] *adj* (*post*) vacant(e); (*seat etc*) libre, disponible; (*expression*) distrait(e)

vacate [və'keɪt] *vt* quitter

vacation [və'keɪʃən] *n* (*esp us*) vacances *fpl*; **on ~** en vacances; **vacationer** (*us* **vacationist**) *n* vacancier(-ière)

vaccination [væksɪ'neɪʃən] *n* vaccination *f*

vaccine ['væksi:n] *n* vaccin *m*

vacuum ['vækjum] *n* vide *m*; **vacuum cleaner** *n* aspirateur *m*

vagina [və'dʒaɪnə] *n* vagin *m*

vague [veɪg] *adj* vague, imprécis(e); (*blurred: photo, memory*) flou(e)

vain [veɪn] *adj* (*useless*) vain(e); (*conceited*) vaniteux(-euse); **in ~** en vain

Valentine's Day ['væləntaɪnz-] *n* Saint-Valentin *f*

valid ['vælɪd] *adj* (*document*) valide, valable; (*excuse*) valable

valley ['vælɪ] *n* vallée *f*

valuable ['væljuəbl] *adj* (*jewel*) de grande valeur; (*time, help*) précieux(-euse); **valuables** *npl* objets *mpl* de valeur

value ['vælju:] *n* valeur *f* ▷ *vt* (*fix price*) évaluer, expertiser; (*appreciate*) apprécier; **values** *npl* (*principles*) valeurs *fpl*

valve [vælv] *n* (*in machine*) soupape *f*; (*on tyre*) valve *f*; (*Med*) valve, valvule *f*

vampire ['væmpaɪər] *n* vampire *m*

van [væn] *n* (*Aut*) camionnette *f*

vandal ['vændl] *n* vandale *m/f*; **vandalism** *n* vandalisme *m*; **vandalize** *vt* saccager

vanilla [və'nɪlə] *n* vanille *f*

vanish ['vænɪʃ] *vi* disparaître

vanity ['vænɪtɪ] *n* vanité *f*

vapour (*us* **vapor**) ['veɪpər] *n* vapeur *f*; (*on window*) buée *f*

variable ['vɛərɪəbl] *adj* variable; (*mood*) changeant(e)

variant ['vɛərɪənt] *n* variante *f*

variation [vɛərɪ'eɪʃən] *n* variation *f*; (*in opinion*) changement *m*

varied ['vɛərɪd] *adj* varié(e), divers(e)

variety [və'raɪətɪ] *n* variété *f*; (*quantity*) nombre *m*, quantité *f*

various ['vɛərɪəs] *adj* divers(e), différent(e); (*several*) divers, plusieurs

varnish ['vɑːnɪʃ] *n* vernis *m* ▷ *vt* vernir

vary ['vɛərɪ] *vt*, *vi* varier, changer

vase [vɑːz] *n* vase *m*

Vaseline® ['væsɪli:n] *n* vaseline *f*

vast [vɑːst] *adj* vaste, immense; (*amount, success*) énorme

VAT [væt] *n abbr* (BRIT: = *value added tax*) TVA *f*

vault [vɔːlt] *n* (*of roof*) voûte *f*; (*tomb*) caveau *m*; (*in bank*) salle *f* des coffres; chambre forte ▷ *vt* (*also:* **~ over**) sauter (d'un bond)

VCR *n abbr* = **video cassette recorder**

VDU *n abbr* = **visual display unit**

veal [vi:l] *n* veau *m*

veer [vɪər] *vi* tourner; (*car, ship*) virer

vegan ['vi:gən] *n* végétalien(ne)

vegetable ['vɛdʒtəbl] *n* légume *m* ▷ *adj* végétal(e)

vegetarian [vɛdʒɪ'tɛərɪən] *adj*, *n* végétarien(ne); **do you have any ~ dishes?** avez-vous des plats végétariens?

vegetation [vɛdʒɪ'teɪʃən] *n* végétation *f*

vehicle ['vi:ɪkl] *n* véhicule *m*

veil [veɪl] *n* voile *m*

vein [veɪn] *n* veine *f*; (*on leaf*) nervure *f*

Velcro® ['vɛlkrəu] *n* velcro® *m*

velvet ['vɛlvɪt] *n* velours *m*

vending machine ['vɛndɪŋ-] *n* distributeur *m* automatique

vendor ['vɛndər] *n* vendeur(-euse); **street ~** marchand ambulant

Venetian blind [vɪ'ni:ʃən-] *n* store vénitien

vengeance ['vɛndʒəns] *n* vengeance *f*; **with a ~** (*fig*) vraiment, pour de bon

venison ['vɛnɪsn] *n* venaison *f*

venom ['vɛnəm] *n* venin *m*

vent [vɛnt] *n* conduit *m* d'aération; (*in dress, jacket*) fente *f* ▷ *vt* (*fig: one's feelings*) donner libre cours à

ventilation [vɛntɪ'leɪʃən] n ventilation f, aération f
venture ['vɛntʃəʳ] n entreprise f ▷ vt risquer, hasarder ▷ vi s'aventurer, se risquer; **a business ~** une entreprise commerciale
venue ['vɛnjuː] n lieu m
Venus ['viːnəs] n (planet) Vénus f
verb [vəːb] n verbe m; **verbal** adj verbal(e)
verdict ['vəːdɪkt] n verdict m
verge [vəːdʒ] n bord m; **"soft ~s"** (BRIT) "accotements non stabilisés"; **on the ~ of doing** sur le point de faire
verify ['vɛrɪfaɪ] vt vérifier
versatile ['vəːsətaɪl] adj polyvalent(e)
verse [vəːs] n vers mpl; (stanza) strophe f; (in Bible) verset m
version ['vəːʃən] n version f
versus ['vəːsəs] prep contre
vertical ['vəːtɪkl] adj vertical(e)
very ['vɛrɪ] adv très ▷ adj: **the ~ book which** le livre même que; **the ~ last** le tout dernier; **at the ~ least** au moins; **~ much** beaucoup
vessel ['vɛsl] n (Anat, Naut) vaisseau m; (container) récipient m; see also **blood**
vest [vɛst] n (BRIT: underwear) tricot m de corps; (US: waistcoat) gilet m
vet [vɛt] n abbr (BRIT: = veterinary surgeon) vétérinaire m/f; (US: = veteran) ancien(ne) combattant(e) ▷ vt examiner minutieusement
veteran ['vɛtərn] n vétéran m; (also: **war ~**) ancien combattant
veterinary surgeon ['vɛtrɪnərɪ-] (BRIT) (US **veterinarian** [vɛtrɪ'nɛərɪən]) n vétérinaire m/f
veto ['viːtəu] n (pl **~es**) veto m ▷ vt opposer son veto à
via ['vaɪə] prep par, via
viable ['vaɪəbl] adj viable
vibrate [vaɪ'breɪt] vi: **to ~ (with)** vibrer (de)
vibration [vaɪ'breɪʃən] n vibration f
vicar ['vɪkəʳ] n pasteur m (de l'Église anglicane)
vice [vaɪs] n (evil) vice m; (Tech) étau m; **vice-chairman** n vice-président(e)
vice versa ['vaɪsɪ'vəːsə] adv vice versa
vicinity [vɪ'sɪnɪtɪ] n environs mpl, alentours mpl
vicious ['vɪʃəs] adj (remark) cruel(le), méchant(e); (blow) brutal(e); (dog) méchant(e), dangereux(-euse); **a ~ circle** un cercle vicieux
victim ['vɪktɪm] n victime f
victor ['vɪktəʳ] n vainqueur m
Victorian [vɪk'tɔːrɪən] adj victorien(ne)
victorious [vɪk'tɔːrɪəs] adj victorieux(-euse)
victory ['vɪktərɪ] n victoire f
video ['vɪdɪəu] n (video film) vidéo f; (also: ~ **cassette**) vidéocassette f; (also: ~ **cassette recorder**) magnétoscope m ▷ vt (with recorder) enregistrer; (with camera) filmer;

video camera n caméra f vidéo inv; **video (cassette) recorder** n magnétoscope m; **video game** n jeu m vidéo inv; **video shop** n vidéoclub m; **video tape** n bande f vidéo inv; (cassette) vidéocassette f
vie [vaɪ] vi: **to ~ with** lutter avec, rivaliser avec
Vienna [vɪ'ɛnə] n Vienne
Vietnam, Viet Nam ['vjɛt'næm] n Viêt-nam or Vietnam m; **Vietnamese** [vjɛtnə'miːz] adj vietnamien(ne) ▷ n (pl inv) Vietnamien(ne)
view [vjuː] n vue f; (opinion) avis m, vue ▷ vt voir, regarder; (situation) considérer; (house) visiter; **on ~** (in museum etc) exposé(e); **in full ~ of sb** sous les yeux de qn; **in my ~** à mon avis; **in ~ of the fact that** étant donné que; **viewer** n (TV) téléspectateur(-trice); **viewpoint** n point m de vue
vigilant ['vɪdʒɪlənt] adj vigilant(e)
vigorous ['vɪgərəs] adj vigoureux(-euse)
vile [vaɪl] adj (action) vil(e); (smell, food) abominable; (temper) massacrant(e)
villa ['vɪlə] n villa f
village ['vɪlɪdʒ] n village m; **villager** n villageois(e)
villain ['vɪlən] n (scoundrel) scélérat m; (BRIT: criminal) bandit m; (in novel etc) traître m
vinaigrette [vɪneɪ'grɛt] n vinaigrette f
vine [vaɪn] n vigne f
vinegar ['vɪnɪgəʳ] n vinaigre m
vineyard ['vɪnjɑːd] n vignoble m
vintage ['vɪntɪdʒ] n (year) année f, millésime m ▷ cpd (car) d'époque; (wine) de grand cru
vinyl ['vaɪnl] n vinyle m
viola [vɪ'əulə] n alto m
violate ['vaɪəleɪt] vt violer
violation [vaɪə'leɪʃən] n violation f; **in ~ of** (rule, law) en infraction à, en violation de
violence ['vaɪələns] n violence f
violent ['vaɪələnt] adj violent(e)
violet ['vaɪələt] adj (colour) violet(te) ▷ n (plant) violette f
violin [vaɪə'lɪn] n violon m
VIP n abbr (= very important person) VIP m
virgin ['vəːdʒɪn] n vierge f
Virgo ['vəːgəu] n la Vierge
virtual ['vəːtjuəl] adj (Comput, Physics) virtuel(le); (in effect): **it's a ~ impossibility** c'est quasiment impossible; **virtually** adv (almost) pratiquement; **virtual reality** n (Comput) réalité virtuelle
virtue ['vəːtjuː] n vertu f; (advantage) mérite m, avantage m; **by ~ of** en vertu or raison de
virus ['vaɪərəs] n (Med, Comput) virus m
visa ['viːzə] n visa m
vise [vaɪs] n (US Tech) = **vice**
visibility [vɪzɪ'bɪlɪtɪ] n visibilité f
visible ['vɪzəbl] adj visible
vision ['vɪʒən] n (sight) vue f, vision f; (foresight, in dream) vision

visit ['vɪzɪt] n visite f; (stay) séjour m ▷ vt (person: us: also: ~ **with**) rendre visite à; (place) visiter; **visiting hours** npl heures fpl de visite; **visitor** n visiteur(-euse); (to one's house) invité(e); **visitor centre** (US **visitor center**) n hall m or centre m d'accueil

visual ['vɪzjuəl] adj visuel(le); **visualize** vt se représenter

vital ['vaɪtl] adj vital(e); **of ~ importance (to sb/sth)** d'une importance capitale (pour qn/qch)

vitality [vaɪ'tælɪtɪ] n vitalité f

vitamin ['vɪtəmɪn] n vitamine f

vivid ['vɪvɪd] adj (account) frappant(e), vivant(e); (light, imagination) vif (vive)

V-neck ['viːnɛk] n décolleté m en V

vocabulary [vəu'kæbjulərɪ] n vocabulaire m

vocal ['vəukl] adj vocal(e); (articulate) qui n'hésite pas à s'exprimer, qui sait faire entendre ses opinions

vocational [vəu'keɪʃənl] adj professionnel(le)

vodka ['vɔdkə] n vodka f

vogue [vəug] n: **to be in ~** être en vogue or à la mode

voice [vɔɪs] n voix f ▷ vt (opinion) exprimer, formuler; **voice mail** n (system) messagerie f vocale; (device) boîte f vocale

void [vɔɪd] n vide m ▷ adj (invalid) nul(le); (empty): **~ of** vide de, dépourvu(e) de

volatile ['vɔlətaɪl] adj volatil(e); (fig: person) versatile; (: situation) explosif(-ive)

volcano (pl ~es) [vɔl'keɪnəu] n volcan m

volleyball ['vɔlɪbɔːl] n volley(-ball) m

volt [vəult] n volt m; **voltage** n tension f, voltage m

volume ['vɔljuːm] n volume m; (of tank) capacité f

voluntarily ['vɔləntrɪlɪ] adv volontairement

voluntary ['vɔləntərɪ] adj volontaire; (unpaid) bénévole

volunteer [vɔlən'tɪər] n volontaire m/f ▷ vt (information) donner spontanément ▷ vi (Mil) s'engager comme volontaire; **to ~ to do** se proposer pour faire

vomit ['vɔmɪt] n vomissure f ▷ vt, vi vomir

vote [vəut] n vote m, suffrage m; (votes cast) voix f, vote; (franchise) droit m de vote ▷ vt (chairman) élire; (propose): **to ~ that** proposer que + sub ▷ vi voter; **~ of thanks** discours m de remerciement; **voter** n électeur(-trice); **voting** n scrutin m, vote m

voucher ['vautʃər] n (for meal, petrol, gift) bon m

vow [vau] n vœu m, serment m ▷ vi jurer

vowel ['vauəl] n voyelle f

voyage ['vɔɪɪdʒ] n voyage m par mer, traversée f

vulgar ['vʌlgər] adj vulgaire

vulnerable ['vʌlnərəbl] adj vulnérable

vulture ['vʌltʃər] n vautour m

waddle ['wɔdl] vi se dandiner

wade [weɪd] vi: **to ~ through** marcher dans, patauger dans; (fig: book) venir à bout de

wafer ['weɪfər] n (Culin) gaufrette f

waffle ['wɔfl] n (Culin) gaufre f ▷ vi parler pour ne rien dire; faire du remplissage

wag [wæg] vt agiter, remuer ▷ vi remuer

wage [weɪdʒ] n (also: ~s) salaire m, paye f ▷ vt: **to ~ war** faire la guerre

wag(g)on ['wægən] n (horse-drawn) chariot m; (BRIT Rail) wagon m (de marchandises)

wail [weɪl] n gémissement m; (of siren) hurlement m ▷ vi gémir; (siren) hurler

waist [weɪst] n taille f, ceinture f; **waistcoat** n (BRIT) gilet m

wait [weɪt] n attente f ▷ vi attendre; **to ~ for sb/sth** attendre qn/qch; **to keep sb ~ing** faire attendre qn; **~ for me, please** attendez-moi, s'il vous plaît; **I can't ~ to ...** (fig) je meurs d'envie de ...; **to lie in ~ for** guetter; **wait on** vt fus servir; **waiter** n garçon m (de café), serveur m; **waiting list** n liste f d'attente; **waiting room** n salle f d'attente; **waitress** ['weɪtrɪs] n serveuse f

waive [weɪv] vt renoncer à, abandonner

wake [weɪk] vb (pt **woke** or ~**d**, pp **woken** or ~**d**) ▷ vt (also: ~ **up**) réveiller ▷ vi (also: ~ **up**) se réveiller ▷ n (for dead person) veillée f mortuaire; (Naut) sillage m

Wales [weɪlz] n pays m de Galles; **the Prince**

of ~ le prince de Galles

walk [wɔːk] n promenade f; (short) petit tour; (gait) démarche f; (path) chemin m; (in park etc) allée f ▷ vi marcher; (for pleasure, exercise) se promener ▷ vt (distance) faire à pied; (dog) promener; **10 minutes' ~ from** à 10 minutes de marche de; **to go for a ~** se promener; faire un tour; **from all ~s of life** de toutes conditions sociales; **walk out** vi (go out) sortir; (as protest) partir (en signe de protestation); (strike) se mettre en grève; **to ~ out on sb** quitter qn; **walker** n (person) marcheur(-euse); **walkie-talkie** ['wɔːkɪ'tɔːkɪ] n talkie-walkie m; **walking** n marche f à pied; **walking shoes** npl chaussures fpl de marche; **walking stick** n canne f; **Walkman®** n Walkman® m; **walkway** n promenade f, cheminement piéton

wall [wɔːl] n mur m; (of tunnel, cave) paroi f

wallet ['wɔlɪt] n portefeuille m; **I can't find my ~** je ne retrouve plus mon portefeuille

wallpaper ['wɔːlpeɪpəʳ] n papier peint ▷ vt tapisser

walnut ['wɔːlnʌt] n noix f; (tree, wood) noyer m

walrus (pl ~ or **-es**) ['wɔːlrəs] n morse m

waltz [wɔːlts] n valse f ▷ vi valser

wand [wɔnd] n (also: **magic ~**) baguette f (magique)

wander ['wɔndəʳ] vi (person) errer, aller sans but; (thoughts) vagabonder ▷ vt errer dans

want [wɔnt] vt vouloir; (need) avoir besoin de ▷ n: **for ~ of** par manque de, faute de; **to ~ to do** vouloir faire; **to ~ sb to do** vouloir que qn fasse; **wanted** adj (criminal) recherché(e) par la police; **"cook wanted"** "on recherche un cuisinier"

war [wɔːʳ] n guerre f; **to make ~ (on)** faire la guerre (à)

ward [wɔːd] n (in hospital) salle f; (Pol) section électorale; (Law: child: also: **~ of court**) pupille m/f

warden ['wɔːdn] n (BRIT: of institution) directeur(-trice); (of park, game reserve) gardien(ne); (BRIT: also: **traffic ~**) contractuel(le)

wardrobe ['wɔːdrəub] n (cupboard) armoire f; (clothes) garde-robe f

warehouse ['wɛəhaus] n entrepôt m

warfare ['wɔːfɛəʳ] n guerre f

warhead ['wɔːhɛd] n (Mil) ogive f

warm [wɔːm] adj chaud(e); (person, thanks, welcome, applause) chaleureux(-euse); **it's ~** il fait chaud; **I'm ~** j'ai chaud; **warm up** vi (person, room) se réchauffer; (athlete, discussion) s'échauffer ▷ vt (food) (faire) réchauffer; (water) faire chauffer; (engine) faire chauffer; **warmly** adv (dress) chaudement; (thank, welcome) chaleureusement; **warmth** n chaleur f

warn [wɔːn] vt avertir, prévenir; **to ~ sb (not) to do** conseiller à qn de (ne pas) faire; **warning** n avertissement m; (notice) avis m; **warning light** n avertisseur lumineux

warrant ['wɔrnt] n (guarantee) garantie f; (Law: to arrest) mandat m d'arrêt; (: to search) mandat de perquisition ▷ vt (justify, merit) justifier

warranty ['wɔrənti] n garantie f

warrior ['wɔriəʳ] n guerrier(-ière)

Warsaw ['wɔːsɔː] n Varsovie

warship ['wɔːʃɪp] n navire m de guerre

wart [wɔːt] n verrue f

wartime ['wɔːtaɪm] n: **in ~** en temps de guerre

wary ['wɛəri] adj prudent(e)

was [wɔz] pt of **be**

wash [wɔʃ] vt laver ▷ vi se laver; (sea): **to ~ over/against sth** inonder/baigner qch ▷ n (clothes) lessive f; (washing programme) lavage m; (of ship) sillage m; **to have a ~** se laver, faire sa toilette; **wash up** vi (BRIT) faire la vaisselle; (us: have a wash) se débarbouiller; **washbasin** n lavabo m; **wash cloth** n (us) gant m de toilette; **washer** n (Tech) rondelle f, joint m; **washing** n (BRIT: linen etc: dirty) linge m; (: clean) lessive f; **washing line** n (BRIT) corde f à linge; **washing machine** n machine f à laver; **washing powder** n (BRIT) lessive f (en poudre)

Washington ['wɔʃɪŋtən] n Washington m

wash: **washing-up** n (BRIT) vaisselle f; **washing-up liquid** n (BRIT) produit m pour la vaisselle; **washroom** n (us) toilettes fpl

wasn't ['wɔznt] = **was not**

wasp [wɔsp] n guêpe f

waste [weɪst] n gaspillage m; (of time) perte f; (rubbish) déchets mpl; (also: **household ~**) ordures fpl ▷ adj (land, ground: in city) à l'abandon; (leftover): **~ material** déchets ▷ vt gaspiller; (time, opportunity) perdre; **waste ground** n (BRIT) terrain m vague; **wastepaper basket** n corbeille f à papier

watch [wɔtʃ] n montre f; (act of watching) surveillance f; (guard: Mil) sentinelle f; (: Naut) homme m de quart; (Naut: spell of duty) quart m ▷ vt (look at) observer; (: match, programme) regarder; (spy on, guard) surveiller; (be careful of) faire attention à ▷ vi regarder; (keep guard) monter la garde; **to keep ~** faire le guet; **watch out** vi faire attention; **watchdog** n chien m de garde; (fig) gardien(ne); **watch strap** n bracelet m de montre

water ['wɔːtəʳ] n eau f ▷ vt (plant, garden) arroser ▷ vi (eyes) larmoyer; **in British ~s** dans les eaux territoriales Britanniques; **to make sb's mouth ~** mettre l'eau à la bouche de qn; **water down** vt (milk etc) couper avec de l'eau; (fig: story) édulcorer; **watercolour** (us **watercolor**) n aquarelle f; **watercress** n cresson m (de fontaine); **waterfall** n

chute f d'eau; **watering can** n arrosoir m;
watermelon n pastèque f; **waterproof** adj
imperméable; **water-skiing** n ski m nautique

watt [wɔt] n watt m

wave [weɪv] n vague f; (of hand) geste m, signe
m; (Radio) onde f; (in hair) ondulation f; (fig: of
enthusiasm, strikes etc) vague ▷ vi faire signe de
la main; (flag) flotter au vent; (grass) ondoyer
▷ vt (handkerchief) agiter; (stick) brandir;
wavelength n longueur f d'ondes

waver ['weɪvəʳ] vi vaciller; (voice) trembler;
(person) hésiter

wavy ['weɪvɪ] adj (hair, surface) ondulé(e); (line)
onduleux(-euse)

wax [wæks] n cire f; (for skis) fart m ▷ vt cirer;
(car) lustrer; (skis) farter ▷ vi (moon) croître

way [weɪ] n chemin m, voie f; (distance)
distance f; (direction) direction f;
(manner) façon f, manière f; (habit) habitude
f, façon; **which ~? — this ~/that ~** par où or
de quel côté? — par ici/par là; **to lose one's
~** perdre son chemin; **on the ~ (to)** en route
(pour); **to be on one's ~** être en route; **to be
in the ~** bloquer le passage; (fig) gêner; **it's a
long ~ a~** c'est loin d'ici; **to go out of one's
~ to do** (fig) se donner beaucoup de mal pour
faire; **to be under ~** (work, project) être en
cours; **in a ~** dans un sens; **by the ~** à propos;
"~ in" (BRIT) "entrée"; **"~ out"** (BRIT) "sortie";
the ~ back le chemin du retour; **"give ~"** (BRIT
Aut) "cédez la priorité"; **no ~!** (inf) pas question!

W.C. n abbr (BRIT: = water closet) w.-c. mpl,
waters mpl

we [wi:] pl pron nous

weak [wi:k] adj faible; (health) fragile; (beam
etc) peu solide; (tea, coffee) léger(-ère); **weaken**
vi faiblir ▷ vt affaiblir; **weakness** n faiblesse f;
(fault) point m faible

wealth [wɛlθ] n (money, resources) richesse(s)
f(pl); (of details) profusion f; **wealthy** adj riche

weapon ['wɛpən] n arme f; **~s of mass
destruction** armes fpl de destruction massive

wear [wɛəʳ] n (use) usage m; (deterioration
through use) usure f ▷ vb (pt **wore**, pp **worn**)
▷ vt (clothes) porter; (put on) mettre; (damage:
through use) user ▷ vi (last) faire de l'usage; (rub
etc through) s'user; **sports/baby~** vêtements
mpl de sport/pour bébés; **evening ~** tenue f de
soirée; **wear off** vi disparaître; **wear out** vt
user; (person, strength) épuiser

weary ['wɪərɪ] adj (tired) épuisé(e); (dispirited)
las (lasse), abattu(e) ▷ vi: **to ~ of** se lasser de

weasel ['wi:zl] n (Zool) belette f

weather ['wɛðəʳ] n temps m ▷ vt (storm:
lit, fig) essuyer; (crisis) survivre à; **under the
~** (fig: ill) mal fichu(e); **weather forecast** n
prévisions fpl météorologiques, météo f

weave (pt **wove**, pp **woven**) [wi:v, wəuv, 'wə
uvn] vt (cloth) tisser; (basket) tresser

web [wɛb] n (of spider) toile f; (on duck's foot)
palmure f; (fig) tissu m; (Comput): **the (World-
Wide) W~** le Web; **web page** n (Comput) page
f Web; **website** n (Comput) site m web

wed [wɛd] (pt, pp **~ded**) vt épouser ▷ vi se
marier

Wed abbr (= Wednesday) me

we'd [wi:d] = **we had**; **we would**

wedding ['wɛdɪŋ] n mariage m; **wedding
anniversary** n anniversaire m de mariage;
silver/golden wedding anniversary noces
fpl d'argent/d'or; **wedding day** n jour m du
mariage; **wedding dress** n robe f de mariée;
wedding ring n alliance f

wedge [wɛdʒ] n (of wood etc) coin m; (under door
etc) cale f; (of cake) part f ▷ vt (fix) caler; (push)
enfoncer, coincer

Wednesday ['wɛnzdɪ] n mercredi m

wee [wi:] adj (SCOTTISH) petit(e); tout(e)
petit(e)

weed [wi:d] n mauvaise herbe ▷ vt désherber;
weedkiller n désherbant m

week [wi:k] n semaine f; **a ~ today/on
Tuesday** aujourd'hui/mardi en huit; **weekday**
n jour m de semaine; (Comm) jour ouvrable;
weekend n week-end m; **weekly** adv une
fois par semaine, chaque semaine ▷ adj, n
hebdomadaire (m)

weep [wi:p] (pt, pp **wept**) vi (person) pleurer

weigh [weɪ] vt, vi peser; **to ~ anchor** lever
l'ancre; **weigh up** vt examiner

weight [weɪt] n poids m; **to put on/
lose ~** grossir/maigrir; **weightlifting** n
haltérophilie f

weir [wɪəʳ] n barrage m

weird [wɪəd] adj bizarre; (eerie) surnaturel(le)

welcome ['wɛlkəm] adj bienvenu(e) ▷ n
accueil m ▷ vt accueillir; (also: **bid ~**) souhaiter
la bienvenue à; (be glad of) se réjouir de; **you're
~!** (after thanks) de rien, il n'y a pas de quoi

weld [wɛld] vt souder

welfare ['wɛlfɛəʳ] n (wellbeing) bien-être m;
(social aid) assistance sociale; **welfare state** n
État-providence m

well [wɛl] n puits m ▷ adv bien ▷ adj: **to be
~** aller bien ▷ excl eh bien!; (relief also) bon!;
(resignation) enfin!; **~ done!** bravo!; **get ~
soon!** remets-toi vite!; **to do ~** bien réussir;
(business) prospérer; **as ~** (in addition) aussi,
également; **as ~ as** aussi bien que or de; en
plus de

we'll [wi:l] = **we will**; **we shall**

well: **well-behaved** adj sage, obéissant(e);
well-built adj (person) bien bâti(e); **well-
dressed** adj bien habillé(e), bien vêtu(e)

well-groomed [-'gru:md] adj très soigné(e)

wellies ['wɛlɪz] (inf) npl (BRIT) = **wellingtons**

wellingtons ['wɛlɪŋtənz] npl (also:
wellington boots) bottes fpl en caoutchouc

well: **well-known** adj (person) bien connu(e); **well-off** adj aisé(e), assez riche; **well-paid** [wel'peɪd] adj bien payé(e)

Welsh [welʃ] adj gallois(e) ▷ n (Ling) gallois m; **the Welsh** npl (people) les Gallois; **Welshman** (irreg) n Gallois m; **Welshwoman** (irreg) n Galloise f

went [went] pt of **go**

wept [wept] pt, pp of **weep**

were [wə:ʳ] pt of **be**

we're [wɪəʳ] = **we are**

weren't [wə:nt] = **were not**

west [west] n ouest m ▷ adj (wind) d'ouest; (side) ouest inv ▷ adv à or vers l'ouest; **the W~** l'Occident m, l'Ouest; **westbound** ['westbaund] adj en direction de l'ouest; (carriageway) ouest inv; **western** adj occidental(e), de or à l'ouest ▷ n (Cine) western m; **West Indian** adj antillais(e) ▷ n Antillais(e)

West Indies [-'ɪndɪz] npl Antilles fpl

wet [wet] adj mouillé(e); (damp) humide; (soaked: also: **~ through**) trempé(e); (rainy) pluvieux(-euse); **to get ~** se mouiller; **"~ paint"** "attention peinture fraîche"; **wetsuit** n combinaison f de plongée

we've [wi:v] = **we have**

whack [wæk] vt donner un grand coup à

whale [weɪl] n (Zool) baleine f

wharf (pl **wharves**) [wɔ:f, wɔ:vz] n quai m

⊙ **KEYWORD**

what [wɔt] adj 1 (in questions) quel(le); **what size is he?** quelle taille fait-il?; **what colour is it?** de quelle couleur est-ce?; **what books do you need?** quels livres vous faut-il?
2 (in exclamations): **what a mess!** quel désordre!; **what a fool I am!** que je suis bête!
▷ pron 1 (interrogative) que; de/à/en etc quoi; **what are you doing?** que faites-vous?, qu'est-ce que vous faites?; **what is happening?** qu'est-ce qui se passe?, que se passe-t-il?; **what are you talking about?** de quoi parlez-vous?; **what are you thinking about?** à quoi pensez-vous?; **what is it called?** comment est-ce que ça s'appelle?; **what about me?** et moi?; **what about doing …?** et si on faisait …?
2 (relative: subject) ce qui; (: direct object) ce que; (: indirect object) ce à quoi, ce dont; **I saw what you did/was on the table** j'ai vu ce que vous avez fait/ce qui était sur la table; **tell me what you remember** dites-moi ce dont vous vous souvenez; **what I want is a cup of tea** ce que je veux, c'est une tasse de thé
▷ excl (disbelieving) quoi!, comment!

whatever [wɔt'ɛvəʳ] adj: **take ~ book you prefer** prenez le livre que vous préférez, peu importe lequel; **~ book you take** quel que soit le livre que vous preniez ▷ pron: **do ~ is necessary** faites (tout) ce qui est nécessaire; **~ happens** quoi qu'il arrive; **no reason ~ or whatsoever** pas la moindre raison; **nothing ~ or whatsoever** rien du tout

whatsoever [wɔtsəu'ɛvəʳ] adj see **whatever**

wheat [wi:t] n blé m, froment m

wheel [wi:l] n roue f; (Aut: also: **steering ~**) volant m; (Naut) gouvernail m ▷ vt (pram etc) pousser, rouler ▷ vi (birds) tournoyer; (also: **~ round**: person) se retourner, faire volte-face; **wheelbarrow** n brouette f; **wheelchair** n fauteuil roulant; **wheel clamp** n (Aut) sabot m (de Denver)

wheeze [wi:z] vi respirer bruyamment

⊙ **KEYWORD**

when [wen] adv quand; **when did he go?** quand est-ce qu'il est parti?
▷ conj 1 (at, during, after the time that) quand, lorsque; **she was reading when I came in** elle lisait quand or lorsque je suis entré
2 (on, at which): **on the day when I met him** le jour où je l'ai rencontré
3 (whereas) alors que; **I thought I was wrong when in fact I was right** j'ai cru que j'avais tort alors qu'en fait j'avais raison

whenever [wen'ɛvəʳ] adv quand donc ▷ conj quand; (every time that) chaque fois que

where [weəʳ] adv, conj où; **this is ~** c'est là que; **whereabouts** adv où donc ▷ n: **nobody knows his whereabouts** personne ne sait où il se trouve; **whereas** conj alors que; **whereby** adv (formal) par lequel (or laquelle etc); **wherever** adv où donc ▷ conj où que + sub; **sit wherever you like** asseyez-vous (là) où vous voulez

whether ['weðəʳ] conj si; **I don't know ~ to accept or not** je ne sais pas si je dois accepter ou non; **it's doubtful ~** il est peu probable que + sub; **~ you go or not** que vous y alliez ou non

---

⊙ **KEYWORD**

which [wɪtʃ] adj 1 (interrogative: direct, indirect) quel(le); **which picture do you want?** quel tableau voulez-vous?; **which one?** lequel (laquelle)?
2: **in which case** auquel cas; **we got there at 8pm, by which time the cinema was full** quand nous sommes arrivés à 20h, le cinéma était complet
▷ pron 1 (interrogative) lequel (laquelle), lesquels (lesquelles) pl; **I don't mind which** peu importe lequel; **which (of these) are yours?** lesquels sont à vous?; **tell me which**

w

you want dites-moi lesquels or ceux que vous voulez

2 (*relative: subject*) qui; (: *object*) que; sur/vers *etc* lequel (laquelle) (*NB: à + lequel* = **auquel**; *de + lequel* = **duquel**); **the apple which you ate/ which is on the table** la pomme que vous avez mangée/qui est sur la table; **the chair on which you are sitting** la chaise sur laquelle vous êtes assis; **the book of which you spoke** le livre dont vous avez parlé; **he said he knew, which is true/I was afraid of** il a dit qu'il le savait, ce qui est vrai/ce que je craignais; **after which** après quoi

whichever [wɪtʃˈɛvəʳ] *adj*: **take ~ book you prefer** prenez le livre que vous préférez, peu importe lequel; **~ book you take** quel que soit le livre que vous preniez

while [waɪl] *n* moment *m* ▷ *conj* pendant que; (*as long as*) tant que; (*as, whereas*) alors que; (*though*) bien que + *sub*, quoique + *sub*; **for a ~** pendant quelque temps; **in a ~** dans un moment

whilst [waɪlst] *conj* = **while**

whim [wɪm] *n* caprice *m*

whine [waɪn] *n* gémissement *m*; (*of engine, siren*) plainte stridente ▷ *vi* gémir, geindre, pleurnicher; (*dog, engine, siren*) gémir

whip [wɪp] *n* fouet *m*; (*for riding*) cravache *f*; (Pol: *person*) chef *m* de file (*assurant la discipline dans son groupe parlementaire*) ▷ *vt* fouetter; (*snatch*) enlever (or sortir) brusquement; **whipped cream** *n* crème fouettée

whirl [wə:l] *vi* tourbillonner; (*dancers*) tournoyer ▷ *vt* faire tourbillonner; faire tournoyer

whisk [wɪsk] *n* (Culin) fouet *m* ▷ *vt* (*eggs*) fouetter, battre; **to ~ sb away** or **off** emmener qn rapidement

whiskers ['wɪskəz] *npl* (*of animal*) moustaches *fpl*; (*of man*) favoris *mpl*

whisky (IRISH, US **whiskey**) ['wɪskɪ] *n* whisky *m*

whisper ['wɪspəʳ] *n* chuchotement *m* ▷ *vt, vi* chuchoter

whistle ['wɪsl] *n* (*sound*) sifflement *m*; (*object*) sifflet *m* ▷ *vi* siffler ▷ *vt* siffler, siffloter

white [waɪt] *adj* blanc (blanche); (*with fear*) blême ▷ *n* blanc *m*; (*person*) blanc (blanche); **White House** *n* (US): **the White House** la Maison-Blanche; **whitewash** *n* (*paint*) lait *m* de chaux ▷ *vt* blanchir à la chaux; (*fig*) blanchir

whiting ['waɪtɪŋ] *n* (*pl inv: fish*) merlan *m*

Whitsun ['wɪtsn] *n* la Pentecôte

whittle ['wɪtl] *vt*: **to ~ away**, **to ~ down** (*costs*) réduire, rogner

whizz [wɪz] *vi* aller (or passer) à toute vitesse

who [hu:] *pron* qui

whoever [hu:ˈɛvəʳ] *pron*: **~ finds it** celui (celle) qui le trouve (, qui que ce soit), quiconque le trouve; **ask ~ you like** demandez à qui vous voulez; **~ he marries** qui que ce soit or quelle que soit la personne qu'il épouse; **~ told you that?** qui a bien pu vous dire ça?, qui donc vous a dit ça?

whole [həʊl] *adj* (*complete*) entier(-ière), tout(e); (*not broken*) intact(e), complet(-ète) ▷ *n* (*all*): **the ~ of** la totalité de, tout(e) le (la); (*entire unit*) tout *m*; **the ~ of the town** la ville tout entière; **on the ~**, **as a ~** dans l'ensemble; **wholefood(s)** *n(pl)* aliments complets; **wholeheartedly** [həʊlˈhɑːtɪdlɪ] *adv* sans réserve; **to agree wholeheartedly** être entièrement d'accord; **wholemeal** *adj* (BRIT: *flour, bread*) complet(-ète); **wholesale** *n* (vente *f* en) gros *m* ▷ *adj* (*price*) de gros; (*destruction*) systématique; **wholewheat** *adj* = **wholemeal**; **wholly** *adv* entièrement, tout à fait

🔵 **KEYWORD**

whom [hu:m] *pron* **1** (*interrogative*) qui; **whom did you see?** qui avez-vous vu?; **to whom did you give it?** à qui l'avez-vous donné?

2 (*relative*) que; à/de *etc* qui; **the man whom I saw/to whom I spoke** l'homme que j'ai vu/à qui j'ai parlé

whore [hɔ:ʳ] *n* (*inf: pej*) putain *f*

🔵 **KEYWORD**

whose [hu:z] *adj* **1** (*possessive: interrogative*): **whose book is this?**, **whose is this book?** à qui est ce livre?; **whose pencil have you taken?** à qui est le crayon que vous avez pris?, c'est le crayon de qui que vous avez pris?; **whose daughter are you?** de qui êtes-vous la fille?

2 (*possessive: relative*): **the man whose son you rescued** l'homme dont or de qui vous avez sauvé le fils; **the girl whose sister you were speaking to** la fille à la sœur de qui or de laquelle vous parliez; **the woman whose car was stolen** la femme dont la voiture a été volée

▷ *pron* à qui; **whose is this?** à qui est ceci?; **I know whose it is** je sais à qui c'est

🔵 **KEYWORD**

why [waɪ] *adv* pourquoi; **why not?** pourquoi pas?

▷ *conj*: **I wonder why he said that** je me demande pourquoi il a dit ça; **that's not why**

I'm here ce n'est pas pour ça que je suis là; **the reason why** la raison pour laquelle
▷ *excl* eh bien!, tiens!; **why, it's you!** tiens, c'est vous!; **why, that's impossible!** voyons, c'est impossible!

wicked ['wɪkɪd] *adj* méchant(e); (*mischievous: grin, look*) espiègle, malicieux(-euse); (*crime*) pervers(e); (*inf: very good*) génial(e) (*inf*)

wicket ['wɪkɪt] *n* (*Cricket: stumps*) guichet *m*; (*: grass area*) espace compris entre les deux guichets

wide [waɪd] *adj* large; (*area, knowledge*) vaste, très étendu(e); (*choice*) grand(e) ▷ *adv*: **to open ~** ouvrir tout grand; **to shoot ~** tirer à côté; **it is 3 metres ~** cela fait 3 mètres de large; **widely** *adv* (*different*) radicalement; (*spaced*) sur une grande étendue; (*believed*) généralement; (*travel*) beaucoup; **widen** *vt* élargir ▷ *vi* s'élargir; **wide open** *adj* grand(e) ouvert(e); **widespread** *adj* (*belief etc*) très répandu(e)

widow ['wɪdəu] *n* veuve *f*; **widower** *n* veuf *m*

width [wɪdθ] *n* largeur *f*

wield [wi:ld] *vt* (*sword*) manier; (*power*) exercer

wife (*pl* **wives**) [waɪf, waɪvz] *n* femme *f*, épouse *f*

wig [wɪg] *n* perruque *f*

wild [waɪld] *adj* sauvage; (*sea*) déchaîné(e); (*idea, life*) fou (folle); (*behaviour*) déchaîné(e), extravagant(e); (*inf: angry*) hors de soi, furieux(-euse) ▷ *n*: **the ~** la nature; **wilderness** ['wɪldənɪs] *n* désert *m*, région *f* sauvage; **wildlife** *n* faune *f* (et flore *f*); **wildly** *adv* (*behave*) de manière déchaînée; (*applaud*) frénétiquement; (*hit, guess*) au hasard; (*happy*) follement

 KEYWORD

will [wɪl] *aux vb* **1** (*forming future tense*): **I will finish it tomorrow** je le finirai demain; **I will have finished it by tomorrow** je l'aurai fini d'ici demain; **will you do it? - yes I will/no I won't** le ferez-vous? - oui/non

2 (*in conjectures, predictions*): **he will** *or* **he'll be there by now** il doit être arrivé à l'heure qu'il est; **that will be the postman** ça doit être le facteur

3 (*in commands, requests, offers*): **will you be quiet!** voulez-vous bien vous taire!; **will you help me?** est-ce que vous pouvez m'aider?; **will you have a cup of tea?** voulez-vous une tasse de thé?; **I won't put up with it!** je ne le tolérerai pas!

▷ *vt* (*pt, pp* **willed**): **to will sb to do** souhaiter ardemment que qn fasse; **he willed himself to go on** par un suprême effort de volonté, il continua
▷ *n* volonté *f*; (*document*) testament *m*; **against one's will** à contre-cœur

willing ['wɪlɪŋ] *adj* de bonne volonté, serviable; **he's ~ to do it** il est disposé à le faire, il veut bien le faire; **willingly** *adv* volontiers

willow ['wɪləu] *n* saule *m*

willpower ['wɪl'pauə'] *n* volonté *f*

wilt [wɪlt] *vi* dépérir

win [wɪn] *n* (*in sports etc*) victoire *f* ▷ *vb* (*pt, pp* **won**) ▷ *vt* (*battle, money*) gagner; (*prize, contract*) remporter; (*popularity*) acquérir ▷ *vi* gagner; **win over** *vt* convaincre

wince [wɪns] *vi* tressaillir

wind¹ [wɪnd] *n* (*also Med*) vent *m*; (*breath*) souffle *m* ▷ *vt* (*take breath away*) couper le souffle à; **the ~(s)** (*Mus*) les instruments *mpl* à vent

wind² (*pt, pp* **wound**) [waɪnd, waund] *vt* enrouler; (*wrap*) envelopper; (*clock, toy*) remonter ▷ *vi* (*road, river*) serpenter; **wind down** *vt* (*car window*) baisser; (*fig: production, business*) réduire progressivement; **wind up** *vt* (*clock*) remonter; (*debate*) terminer, clôturer

windfall ['wɪndfɔ:l] *n* coup *m* de chance

winding ['waɪndɪŋ] *adj* (*road*) sinueux(-euse); (*staircase*) tournant(e)

windmill ['wɪndmɪl] *n* moulin *m* à vent

window ['wɪndəu] *n* fenêtre *f*; (*in car, train: also:* **~pane**) vitre *f*; (*in shop etc*) vitrine *f*; **window box** *n* jardinière *f*; **window cleaner** *n* (*person*) laveur(-euse) de vitres; **window pane** *n* vitre *f*, carreau *m*; **window seat** *n* (*in vehicle*) place *f* côté fenêtre; **windowsill** *n* (*inside*) appui *m* de la fenêtre; (*outside*) rebord *m* de la fenêtre

windscreen ['wɪndskri:n] *n* pare-brise *m inv*; **windscreen wiper** *n* essuie-glace *m inv*

windshield ['wɪndʃi:ld] (*us*) *n* = **windscreen**

windsurfing ['wɪndsə:fɪŋ] *n* planche *f* à voile

windy ['wɪndɪ] *adj* (*day*) de vent, venteux(-euse); (*place, weather*) venteux; **it's ~** il y a du vent

wine [waɪn] *n* vin *m*; **wine bar** *n* bar *m* à vin; **wine glass** *n* verre *m* à vin; **wine list** *n* carte *f* des vins; **wine tasting** *n* dégustation *f* (de vins)

wing [wɪŋ] *n* aile *f*; **wings** *npl* (*Theat*) coulisses *fpl*; **wing mirror** *n* (*BRIT*) rétroviseur latéral

wink [wɪŋk] *n* clin *m* d'œil ▷ *vi* faire un clin d'œil; (*blink*) cligner des yeux

winner ['wɪnə'] *n* gagnant(e)

winning ['wɪnɪŋ] *adj* (*team*) gagnant(e); (*goal*) décisif(-ive); (*charming*) charmeur(-euse)

winter ['wɪntə'] *n* hiver *m* ▷ *vi* hiverner; **in ~** en hiver; **winter sports** *npl* sports *mpl* d'hiver; **wintertime** *n* hiver *m*

W

wipe [waɪp] *n*: **to give sth a ~** donner un coup de torchon/de chiffon/d'éponge à qch ▷ *vt* essuyer; (*erase: tape*) effacer; **to ~ one's nose** se moucher; **wipe out** *vt* (*debt*) éteindre, amortir; (*memory*) effacer; (*destroy*) anéantir; **wipe up** *vt* essuyer

wire ['waɪə^r] *n* fil *m* (de fer); (*Elec*) fil électrique; (*Tel*) télégramme *m* ▷ *vt* (*house*) faire l'installation électrique de; (*also: ~ up*) brancher; (*person: send telegram to*) télégraphier à

wiring ['waɪərɪŋ] *n* (*Elec*) installation *f* électrique

wisdom ['wɪzdəm] *n* sagesse *f*; (*of action*) prudence *f*; **wisdom tooth** *n* dent *f* de sagesse

wise [waɪz] *adj* sage, prudent(e); (*remark*) judicieux(-euse)

wish [wɪʃ] *n* (*desire*) désir *m*; (*specific desire*) souhait *m*, vœu *m* ▷ *vt* souhaiter, désirer, vouloir; **best ~es** (*on birthday etc*) meilleurs vœux; **with best ~es** (*in letter*) bien amicalement; **to ~ sb goodbye** dire au revoir à qn; **he ~ed me well** il m'a souhaité bonne chance; **to ~ to do/sb to do** désirer *or* vouloir faire/que qn fasse; **to ~ for** souhaiter

wistful ['wɪstful] *adj* mélancolique

wit [wɪt] *n* (*also: ~s: intelligence*) intelligence *f*, esprit *m*; (*presence of mind*) présence *f* d'esprit; (*wittiness*) esprit; (*person*) homme/femme d'esprit

witch [wɪtʃ] *n* sorcière *f*

KEYWORD

with [wɪð, wɪθ] *prep* **1** (*in the company of*) avec; (*at the home of*) chez; **we stayed with friends** nous avons logé chez des amis; **I'll be with you in a minute** je suis à vous dans un instant **2** (*descriptive*): **a room with a view** une chambre avec vue; **the man with the grey hat/blue eyes** l'homme au chapeau gris/aux yeux bleus **3** (*indicating manner, means, cause*): **with tears in her eyes** les larmes aux yeux; **to walk with a stick** marcher avec une canne; **red with anger** rouge de colère; **to shake with fear** trembler de peur; **to fill sth with water** remplir qch d'eau **4** (*in phrases*): **I'm with you** (*I understand*) je vous suis; **to be with it** (*inf: up-to-date*) être dans le vent

withdraw [wɪθ'drɔː] *vt* (*irreg: like* **draw**) retirer ▷ *vi* se retirer; **withdrawal** *n* retrait *m*; (*Med*) état *m* de manque; **withdrawn** *pp of* **withdraw** ▷ *adj* (*person*) renfermé(e)

withdrew [wɪθ'druː] *pt of* **withdraw**

wither ['wɪðə^r] *vi* se faner

withhold [wɪθ'həuld] *vt* (*irreg: like* **hold**) (*money*) retenir; (*decision*) remettre; (*permission*): **to ~ (from)** (*permission*) refuser (à); (*information*): **to ~ (from)** cacher (à)

within [wɪð'ɪn] *prep* à l'intérieur de ▷ *adv* à l'intérieur; **~ his reach** à sa portée; **~ sight of** en vue de; **~ a mile of** à moins d'un mille de; **~ the week** avant la fin de la semaine

without [wɪð'aut] *prep* sans; **~ a coat** sans manteau; **~ speaking** sans parler; **to go** *or* **do ~ sth** se passer de qch

withstand [wɪθ'stænd] *vt* (*irreg: like* **stand**) résister à

witness ['wɪtnɪs] *n* (*person*) témoin *m* ▷ *vt* (*event*) être témoin de; (*document*) attester l'authenticité de; **to bear ~ to sth** témoigner de qch

witty ['wɪtɪ] *adj* spirituel(le), plein(e) d'esprit

wives [waɪvz] *npl of* **wife**

wizard ['wɪzəd] *n* magicien *m*

wk *abbr* = **week**

wobble ['wɔbl] *vi* trembler; (*chair*) branler

woe [wəu] *n* malheur *m*

woke [wəuk] *pt of* **wake**

woken ['wəukn] *pp of* **wake**

wolf (*pl* **wolves**) [wulf, wulvz] *n* loup *m*

woman (*pl* **women**) ['wumən, 'wɪmɪn] *n* femme *f* ▷ *cpd*: **~ doctor** femme *f* médecin; **~ teacher** professeur *m* femme

womb [wuːm] *n* (*Anat*) utérus *m*

women ['wɪmɪn] *npl of* **woman**

won [wʌn] *pt, pp of* **win**

wonder ['wʌndə^r] *n* merveille *f*, miracle *m*; (*feeling*) émerveillement *m* ▷ *vi*: **to ~ whether/why** se demander si/pourquoi; **to ~ at** (*surprise*) s'étonner de; (*admiration*) s'émerveiller de; **to ~ about** songer à; **it's no ~ that** il n'est pas étonnant que + *sub*; **wonderful** *adj* merveilleux(-euse)

won't [wəunt] = **will not**

wood [wud] *n* (*timber, forest*) bois *m*; **wooden** *adj* en bois; (*fig: actor*) raide; (*: performance*) qui manque de naturel; **woodwind** *n*: **the woodwind** (*Mus*) les bois *mpl*; **woodwork** *n* menuiserie *f*

wool [wul] *n* laine *f*; **to pull the ~ over sb's eyes** (*fig*) en faire accroire à qn; **woollen** (*us* **woolen**) *adj* de *or* en laine; **woolly** (*us* **wooly**) *adj* laineux(-euse); (*fig: ideas*) confus(e)

word [wəːd] *n* mot *m*; (*spoken*) mot, parole *f*; (*promise*) parole; (*news*) nouvelles *fpl* ▷ *vt* rédiger, formuler; **in other ~s** en d'autres termes; **to have a ~ with sb** toucher un mot à qn; **to break/keep one's ~** manquer à sa parole/tenir (sa) parole; **wording** *n* termes *mpl*, langage *m*; (*of document*) libellé *m*; **word processing** *n* traitement *m* de texte; **word processor** *n* machine *f* de traitement de texte

wore [wɔː^r] *pt of* **wear**

work [wəːk] *n* travail *m*; (*Art, Literature*)

œuvre f ▷ vi travailler; (*mechanism*) marcher, fonctionner; (*plan etc*) marcher; (*medicine*) agir ▷ vt (*clay, wood etc*) travailler; (*mine etc*) exploiter; (*machine*) faire marcher or fonctionner; (*miracles etc*) faire; **works** n (BRIT: *factory*) usine f; **how does this ~?** comment est-ce que ça marche?; **the TV isn't ~ing** la télévision est en panne or ne marche pas; **to be out of ~** être au chômage or sans emploi; **to ~ loose** se défaire, se desserrer; **work out** vi (*plans etc*) marcher; (*Sport*) s'entraîner ▷ vt (*problem*) résoudre; (*plan*) élaborer; **it ~s out at £100** ça fait 100 livres; **worker** n travailleur(-euse), ouvrier(-ière); **work experience** n stage m; **workforce** n main-d'œuvre f; **working class** n classe ouvrière ▷ adj; **working-class** ouvrier(-ière), de la classe ouvrière; **working week** n semaine f de travail; **workman** (*irreg*) n ouvrier m; **work of art** n œuvre f d'art; **workout** n (*Sport*) séance f d'entraînement; **work permit** n permis m de travail; **workplace** n lieu m de travail; **worksheet** n (*Scol*) feuille f d'exercices; **workshop** n atelier m; **work station** n poste m de travail; **work surface** n plan m de travail; **worktop** n plan m de travail

world [wə:ld] n monde m ▷ cpd (*champion*) du monde; (*power, war*) mondial(e); **to think the ~ of sb** (*fig*) ne jurer que par qn; **World Cup** n: **the World Cup** (*Football*) la Coupe du monde; **world-wide** adj universel(le); **World-Wide Web** n: **the World-Wide Web** le Web

worm [wə:m] n (*also*: **earth~**) ver m

worn [wɔ:n] pp of **wear** ▷ adj usé(e); **worn-out** adj (*object*) complètement usé(e); (*person*) épuisé(e)

worried ['wʌrɪd] adj inquiet(-ète); **to be ~ about sth** être inquiet au sujet de qch

worry ['wʌrɪ] n souci m ▷ vt inquiéter ▷ vi s'inquiéter, se faire du souci; **worrying** adj inquiétant(e)

worse [wə:s] adj pire, plus mauvais(e) ▷ adv plus mal ▷ n pire m; **to get ~** (*condition, situation*) empirer, se dégrader; **a change for the ~** une détérioration; **worsen** vt, vi empirer; **worse off** adj moins à l'aise financièrement; (*fig*): **you'll be worse off this way** ça ira moins bien de cette façon

worship ['wə:ʃɪp] n culte m ▷ vt (*God*) rendre un culte à; (*person*) adorer

worst [wə:st] adj le (la) pire, le (la) plus mauvais(e) ▷ adv le plus mal ▷ n pire m; **at ~** au pis aller

worth [wə:θ] n valeur f ▷ adj: **to be ~** valoir; **it's ~ it** cela en vaut la peine, ça vaut la peine; **it is ~ one's while (to do)** ça vaut le coup (*inf*) (de faire); **worthless** adj qui ne vaut rien; **worthwhile** adj (*activity*) qui en vaut la peine; (*cause*) louable

worthy ['wə:ðɪ] adj (*person*) digne; (*motive*) louable; **~ of** digne de

 KEYWORD

would [wʊd] aux vb **1** (*conditional tense*): **if you asked him he would do it** si vous le lui demandiez, il le ferait; **if you had asked him he would have done it** si vous le lui aviez demandé, il l'aurait fait

2 (*in offers, invitations, requests*): **would you like a biscuit?** voulez-vous un biscuit?; **would you close the door please?** voulez-vous fermer la porte, s'il vous plaît?

3 (*in indirect speech*): **I said I would do it** j'ai dit que je le ferais

4 (*emphatic*): **it WOULD have to snow today!** naturellement il neige aujourd'hui! or il fallait qu'il neige aujourd'hui!

5 (*insistence*): **she wouldn't do it** elle n'a pas voulu or elle a refusé de le faire

6 (*conjecture*): **it would have been midnight** il devait être minuit; **it would seem so** on dirait bien

7 (*indicating habit*): **he would go there on Mondays** il y allait le lundi

wouldn't ['wʊdnt] = **would not**

wound[1] [wu:nd] n blessure f ▷ vt blesser

wound[2] [waʊnd] pt, pp of **wind**

wove [wəʊv] pt of **weave**

woven ['wəʊvn] pp of **weave**

wrap [ræp] vt (*also*: **~ up**) envelopper; (*parcel*) emballer; (*wind*) enrouler; **wrapper** n (*on chocolate etc*) papier m; (BRIT: *of book*) couverture f; **wrapping** n (*of sweet, chocolate*) papier m; (*of parcel*) emballage m; **wrapping paper** n papier m d'emballage; (*for gift*) papier cadeau

wreath [ri:θ, pl ri:ðz] n couronne f

wreck [rɛk] n (*sea disaster*) naufrage m; (*ship*) épave f; (*vehicle*) véhicule accidenté; (*pej: person*) loque (humaine) ▷ vt démolir; (*fig*) briser, ruiner; **wreckage** n débris mpl; (*of building*) décombres mpl; (*of ship*) naufrage m

wren [rɛn] n (*Zool*) troglodyte m

wrench [rɛntʃ] n (*Tech*) clé f (à écrous); (*tug*) violent mouvement de torsion; (*fig*) déchirement m ▷ vt tirer violemment sur, tordre; **to ~ sth from** arracher qch (violemment) à or de

wrestle ['rɛsl] vi: **to ~ (with sb)** lutter (avec qn); **wrestler** n lutteur(-euse); **wrestling** n lutte f; (*also*: **all-in wrestling**: BRIT) catch m

wretched ['rɛtʃɪd] adj misérable

wriggle ['rɪgl] vi (*also*: **~ about**) se tortiller

wring (*pt, pp* **wrung**) [rɪŋ, rʌŋ] vt tordre; (*wet clothes*) essorer; (*fig*): **to ~ sth out of** arracher qch à

w

wrinkle ['rɪŋkl] n (on skin) ride f; (on paper etc)
pli m ▷ vt rider, plisser ▷ vi se plisser
wrist [rɪst] n poignet m
write (pt **wrote**, pp **written**) [raɪt, rəut, 'rɪtn]
vt, vi écrire; (prescription) rédiger; **write down**
vt noter; (put in writing) mettre par écrit; **write
off** vt (debt) passer aux profits et pertes;
(project) mettre une croix sur; (smash up: car etc)
démolir complètement; **write out** vt écrire;
(copy) recopier; **write-off** n perte totale; **the
car is a write-off** la voiture est bonne pour la
casse; **writer** n auteur m, écrivain m
writing ['raɪtɪŋ] n écriture f; (of author) œuvres
fpl; **in ~** par écrit; **writing paper** n papier m
à lettres
written ['rɪtn] pp of **write**
wrong [rɒŋ] adj (incorrect) faux (fausse);
(incorrectly chosen: number, road etc) mauvais(e);
(not suitable) qui ne convient pas; (wicked) mal;
(unfair) injuste ▷ adv mal ▷ n tort m ▷ vt faire
du tort à, léser; **you are ~ to do it** tu as tort de
le faire; **you are ~ about that**, **you've got it
~** tu te trompes; **what's ~?** qu'est-ce qui ne va
pas?; **what's ~ with the car?** qu'est-ce qu'elle
a, la voiture?; **to go ~** (person) se tromper;
(plan) mal tourner; (machine) se détraquer; **I
took a ~ turning** je me suis trompé de route;
wrongly adv à tort; (answer, do, count) mal,
incorrectement; **wrong number** n (Tel): **you
have the wrong number** vous vous êtes
trompé de numéro
wrote [rəut] pt of **write**
wrung [rʌŋ] pt, pp of **wring**
WWW n abbr = **World-Wide Web**; **the ~** le Web

XL abbr (= extra large) XL
Xmas ['ɛksməs] n abbr = **Christmas**
X-ray ['ɛksreɪ] n (ray) rayon m X; (photograph)
radio(graphie) f ▷ vt radiographier
xylophone ['zaɪləfəun] n xylophone m

you eaten ~? vous avez déjà mangé?; **the best ~** le meilleur jusqu'ici or jusque-là; **as ~** jusqu'ici, encore

yew [ju:] *n* if *m*

Yiddish ['jɪdɪʃ] *n* yiddish *m*

yield [ji:ld] *n* production *f*, rendement *m*; (*Finance*) rapport *m* ▷ *vt* produire, rendre, rapporter; (*surrender*) céder ▷ *vi* céder; (*us Aut*) céder la priorité

yob(bo) ['jɔb(əʊ)] *n* (*BRIT inf*) loubar(d) *m*

yoga ['jəʊgə] *n* yoga *m*

yog(h)ourt *n* = **yog(h)urt**

yog(h)urt ['jɔgət] *n* yaourt *m*

yolk [jəʊk] *n* jaune *m* (d'œuf)

 KEYWORD

you [ju:] *pron* **1** (*subject*) tu; (*polite form*) vous; (*plural*) vous; **you are very kind** vous êtes très gentil; **you French enjoy your food** vous autres Français, vous aimez bien manger; **you and I will go** toi et moi or vous et moi, nous irons; **there you are!** vous voilà!
2 (*object: direct, indirect*) te, t' + *vowel*; vous; **I know you** je te or vous connais; **I gave it to you** je te l'ai donné, je vous l'ai donné
3 (*stressed*) toi; vous; **I told YOU to do it** c'est à toi or vous que j'ai dit de le faire
4 (*after prep, in comparisons*) toi; vous; **it's for you** c'est pour toi or vous; **she's younger than you** elle est plus jeune que toi or vous
5 (*impersonal: one*) on; **fresh air does you good** l'air frais fait du bien; **you never know** on ne sait jamais; **you can't do that!** ça ne se fait pas!

you'd [ju:d] = **you had; you would**

you'll [ju:l] = **you will; you shall**

young [jʌŋ] *adj* jeune ▷ *npl* (*of animal*) petits *mpl*; (*people*): **the ~** les jeunes, la jeunesse; **my ~er brother** mon frère cadet; **youngster** *n* jeune *m/f*; (*child*) enfant *m/f*

your [jɔː'] *adj* ton (ta), tes *pl*; (*polite form, pl*) votre, vos *pl*; *see also* **my**

you're [juə'] = **you are**

yours [jɔːz] *pron* le (la) tien(ne), les tiens (tiennes); (*polite form, pl*) le (la) vôtre, les vôtres; **is it ~?** c'est à toi (or à vous)?; **a friend of ~** un(e) de tes (or de vos) amis; *see also* **faithfully; mine'; sincerely**

yourself [jɔː'sɛlf] *pron* (*reflexive*) te; (: *polite form*) vous; (*after prep*) toi; vous; (*emphatic*) toi-même; vous-même; *see also* **oneself**; **yourselves** *pl pron* vous; (*emphatic*) vous-mêmes; *see also* **oneself**

youth [ju:θ] *n* jeunesse *f*; (*young man*) (*pl* ~**s**) jeune homme *m*; **youth club** *n* centre *m* de jeunes; **youthful** *adj* jeune; (*enthusiasm etc*) juvénile; **youth hostel** *n* auberge *f* de

---

y

yacht [jɔt] *n* voilier *m*; (*motor, luxury yacht*) yacht *m*; **yachting** *n* yachting *m*, navigation *f* de plaisance

yard [jɑːd] *n* (*of house etc*) cour *f*; (*us: garden*) jardin *m*; (*measure*) yard *m* (= 914 *mm*; 3 *feet*); **yard sale** *n* (*us*) brocante *f* (dans son propre jardin)

yarn [jɑːn] *n* fil *m*; (*tale*) longue histoire

yawn [jɔːn] *n* bâillement *m* ▷ *vi* bâiller

yd. *abbr* = **yard(s)**

yeah [jɛə] *adv* (*inf*) ouais

year [jɪə'] *n* an *m*, année *f*; (*Scol etc*) année; **to be 8 ~s old** avoir 8 ans; **an eight-~-old child** un enfant de huit ans; **yearly** *adj* annuel(le) ▷ *adv* annuellement; **twice yearly** deux fois par an

yearn [jə:n] *vi*: **to ~ for sth/to do** aspirer à qch/à faire

yeast [ji:st] *n* levure *f*

yell [jɛl] *n* hurlement *m*, cri *m* ▷ *vi* hurler

yellow ['jɛləʊ] *adj, n* jaune (*m*); **Yellow Pages®** *npl* (*Tel*) pages *fpl* jaunes

yes [jɛs] *adv* oui; (*answering negative question*) si ▷ *n* oui *m*; **to say ~ (to)** dire oui (à)

yesterday ['jɛstədɪ] *adv, n* hier (*m*); **~ morning/evening** hier matin/soir; **all day ~** toute la journée d'hier

yet [jɛt] *adv* encore; (*in questions*) déjà ▷ *conj* pourtant, néanmoins; **it is not finished ~** ce n'est pas encore fini or toujours pas fini; **have**

jeunesse

you've [ju:v] = **you have**

Yugoslav ['ju:gəuslɑːv] *adj* yougoslave ▷ *n*
Yougoslave *m/f*

Yugoslavia [ju:gəu'slɑːvɪə] *n* (*Hist*)
Yougoslavie *f*

zeal [ziːl] *n* (*revolutionary etc*) ferveur *f*;
(*keenness*) ardeur *f*, zèle *m*

zebra ['ziːbrə] *n* zèbre *m*; **zebra crossing** *n*
(BRIT) passage clouté *or* pour piétons

zero ['zɪərəu] *n* zéro *m*

zest [zɛst] *n* entrain *m*, élan *m*; (*of lemon etc*)
zeste *m*

zigzag ['zɪgzæg] *n* zigzag *m* ▷ *vi* zigzaguer,
faire des zigzags

Zimbabwe [zɪm'bɑːbwɪ] *n* Zimbabwe *m*

zinc [zɪŋk] *n* zinc *m*

zip [zɪp] *n* (*also:* **~ fastener**) fermeture *f* éclair®
or à glissière ▷ *vt* (*file*) zipper; (*also:* **~ up**)
fermer (avec une fermeture éclair®); **zip code**
n (US) code postal; **zip file** *n* (*Comput*) fichier *m*
zip *inv*; **zipper** *n* (US) = **zip**

zit [zɪt] (*inf*) *n* bouton *m*

zodiac ['zəudɪæk] *n* zodiaque *m*

zone [zəun] *n* zone *f*

zoo [zuː] *n* zoo *m*

zoology [zuː'ɔlədʒɪ] *n* zoologie *f*

zoom [zuːm] *vi*: **to ~ past** passer en trombe;
zoom lens *n* zoom *m*

zucchini [zuː'kiːnɪ] *n(pl)* (US) courgette(s) *f(pl)*